The World Atlas *of* Wine

Hugh Johnson   *Jancis* Robinson

Hugh Johnson Jancis Robinson

The World Atlas of Wine

FIFTH EDITION

Mitchell Beazley

Hugh Johnson, Jancis Robinson
THE WORLD ATLAS OF WINE

First published in Great Britain in 1971 by Mitchell Beazley, an imprint of Octopus Publishing Group Ltd, 2–4 Heron Quays, London E14 4JP

First published in this edition in 2005

Copyright © Octopus Publishing Group Ltd 1971, 1977, 1985, 1994, 2001, 2005

Text copyright © Hugh Johnson 1971, 1977, 1985, 1994; Hugh Johnson, Jancis Robinson 2001

Reprinted 2001 (twice), 2002 (twice), 2003, 2004

A CIP catalogue record for this book is available from the British Library.

ISBN 1 84000 332 4

Managing Editor Gill Pitts

Commissioning Editor Rebecca Spry
Research and Gazetteer Nathan Burley

Executive Art Editor Phil Ormerod
Designers Peter Gerrish, Colin Goody

Cartographic Editor Zoë Goodwin

Cartographic Proofreader Julia Harding
Editorial Research Lucy Bridgers
Proofreader Diane Pengelly
Index John Noble
Picture Research Rosie Garai
Production Director Julie Young

Revisions and new cartography for the fifth edition:
Cosmographics, Map Creation Ltd
Original cartography: Clyde Surveys Ltd

Printed and bound in China

How the maps work

The maps in this Atlas vary considerably in scale, the level of detail depending on the complexity of the area mapped. There is a scale bar with each map. Contour intervals vary from map to map and are shown in each map key. Serif type (eg MEURSAULT) on the maps indicates names and places connected with wine; sans serif type (eg Meursault) mainly shows other information.

Each map page has a grid with letters down the side and numbers across the bottom. To locate a château, winery, etc, look up the name in the Gazetteer (pages 338–351) which gives the page number followed by the grid reference.

Every effort has been made to make the maps in this Atlas as complete and up to date as possible. In order that future editions may be kept up to this standard, the publishers will be grateful for information about changes of boundaries or names that should be recorded.

Contents

Foreword

This fifth edition of *The World Atlas of Wine* appears exactly 30 years after the first. They have been the most eventful and fruitful years in the whole history of wine. In many countries the culture of wine drinking has progressed from being a minority interest to an accepted part of normal life. In some it has acquired the attributes of high fashion. The market has expanded exponentially, and that for wine information likewise.

The first *World Atlas of Wine* came into a wine world that was largely unmapped. Only the most revered classic regions of France and Germany had attracted the attention of serious cartographers. Indeed publication of the Atlas stimulated countries and regions around the world to get mapping themselves. As they surveyed and took stock they became more self-aware. Producers found more visitors knocking on their doors, too, as the routes to their vineyards were precisely revealed for the first time. What had been almost a concealed world, accessible only to professionals, began to learn the advantages (the disadvantages, too) of more public scrutiny.

This Atlas was inspired by the fact that, as its first Introduction said, "wine is the unique agricultural product whose price depends entirely on where it comes from." (I could really have left out the world "agricultural".) "The better the wine, the more exactly it defines its origin – down, eventually, to one diminutive field...."

Why one field? Because in the slowly evolved world of traditional agriculture the value of every individual field has been learned, generation after generation, by those who farmed it and whose prosperity, even subsistence, depended on gauging what crops to plant and how to tend them. Vines were given the stony slopes where annual crops struggled or failed. Vines struggled too, at first; but it did not take long to discover that once established in stony ground their grapes were riper and their wine stronger than the produce of more fertile fields.

Vineyards took their shapes, their names, and their value from their soils, their slopes, and their shelter from bad weather; all the factors that go to make up their individual terroir. Terroir is the voice of experience in agriculture.

The great debate

Over the 30-year existence of this Atlas this terroir-based view has been repeatedly challenged. New thinking, more relevant to new plantations than old, has made valuable contributions. Much the most significant shift in wine philosophy was the new emphasis on grape varieties as the traceable origins of the style, if not the character, of most wines. The book that brought enlightenment to this movement, cataloguing for the first time for the non-botanist the qualities and possibilities (not to mention the aliases) of many hundreds of varieties was Jancis Robinson's *Vines, Grapes and Wines*, in 1986. It was a turning point in our understanding of wine.

Up to that point the stress on "varietal", as opposed to geographical, distinctions, identities, and labelling had come mainly from the "New World". (It was I, I confess, who coined this now much-maligned wine world split. Times have changed. Much of the "Old World" has become "New"; a little of the "New" is deemed to be "Old".)

As an example of the radical differences that existed, the University of California at Davis in its advice to growers on what vines to plant used one yardstick only: local temperature. The complex valley-pattern of the California coast was studied in minute detail for cool spots to grow the varieties that flourish in France. In 1980 the 100th anniversary issue of *California Agriculture*, an issue devoted entirely to viticulture, not a single reference was made to soil; the environment of the greater part of the vine – its roots.

Terroir was held by modernists to be French hocus-pocus, essentially meaning old French vineyards. Some still hold that view – which is understandable in, say, the monotonous flats of the Riverina and Murray Darling areas. The vast majority today, though, have realized that if their land has peculiarities, beyond how much water you give it, they will have their effect in giving more or less character to the wine they make, and determining what that character is. They may be peculiarities of situation, altitude, exposure, soil structure, and drainage, or all of these and more. France adds the peculiarities of its hidebound (but ever-so-canny) legislation to the mix.

In a world of hot competition – and the wine world today is certainly that – these peculiarities matter. The producer's choice becomes stark. Is he (or she) selling a brand, or is he selling the identity of a vineyard? In a world awash with the juice of too few grape varieties this is the one real distinction. No surprise, then, that we see more vineyard names on labels all the time. When all the clones have been tested, the yeasts selected, the coopers and forests taken into account, the maceration and the malo done, the juice in the grapes is the wine in the bottle. And the juice comes from the ground. A new wine is both an invention and a discovery. The grower proposes; the terroir disposes.

When I set out in 1969 to make the maps in this book, or their forebears, bustling about in my Mini Minor, clipboard and blue pencil on the seat beside me, I knew I was dealing with something real and specific. In writing you can hide what you don't know. In making maps there is nowhere to hide. Maps bring hazy notions into sharp focus.

When I faced the reality of a fifth edition, though, I realized that I needed (or at least wanted) help. Writing the same book for a fifth time is not only much less fun than writing something new; it is almost impossible to stand back from the familiar words in a critical and focused way. In a wine world changing faster than ever I ran the risk of being swamped. So I turned to the world's most remarkable encyclopedist of wine, who also happens to be a great friend: Jancis.

Though she and I disagree on exactly when and where we first met, that seems to be the only thing. I have admired her mind, her style, her single-mindedness since whenever it was.

Jancis brings the same intellectual rigour to tasting wine as she does to questioning producers and professors. Her unbelievable energy has already given us *Vines, Grapes and Wines*, *The Oxford Companion to Wine* (twice), her memoirs (already), the charm of her television persona and a continuing no-nonsense commentary on the wine world in the press. She and I taste wine together often enough to know each other's tastes. I could not be passing on the baton to anyone who will carry it further, faster, or more gracefully.

Introduction

Like any wine professional and a high propor- tion of wine enthusiasts, I have found *The World Atlas of Wine* invaluable from the moment I became interested in wine. Of all the things we buy, wine is more geographically traceable than almost anything else. It is one of the very few things we can pluck off a shelf or wine list and tell from one glance who made it, when, and exactly where it comes from.

One of wine's special qualities is its proven ability to reflect accurately the environment in which it was grown. Man can do his utmost to take control, but nature is ultimately in charge. Of course some wines are made in such quan- tity that they incorporate the produce of dozens of different vineyards, blurring distinctions. Such wines are often named simply after a grape variety and a large geographical unit such as the Languedoc, Southeastern Australia or California. But all of the world's more interesting wines are labelled much more specifically than this. And the signs are that ambitious winemakers the world over are keen for their wines to express smaller and smaller spots on the globe. Single- vineyard bottlings are increasingly common everywhere. What any curious taster needs is a means of relating appellations and addresses to geography, a way of pinpointing the place behind the label, and setting it in the context of its neighbours and natural environment. Which is what makes *The World Atlas of Wine* such an invaluable friend.

I have always written with the Atlas by my side as, I suspect, do most of my peers. Its maps are the best yet produced, Hugh's prose match- less. But as I made these comments in print, and saw them reproduced on the back cover of the last, fourth edition, I never dreamt that Hugh would ask me to collaborate with him on the fifth edition.

Hugh made me a (very fair) proposal in December 1998. It took me five months to accept because although I was of course extremely flattered, I had an inkling of just how much work would be involved. I was not wrong. (In fact I found out only later that Hugh's wife and children had made him swear never to undertake such a major reference book alone again. Len Evans, Australia's Mr Wine, thinks it hilarious that Hugh has so cunningly taken advantage of my advanced workaholism.)

Hugh of course has been closely involved with this fifth edition, scrutinizing every image and map, reading every word, and writing quite a few of them too – particularly those about his great loves Tokaj and the history of wine.

This new edition

My job has been to bring this monumental fifth edition of the Atlas completely up to date, something I knew from my experience editing both first and second editions of *The Oxford Companion to Wine* would be no small task. The world of wine has changed almost unrec- ognizably since 1994, in some regions much more than others. This edition is very, very dif- ferent from its predecessors.

The most immediately obvious change is that for the first time all the maps, the mainstay of this book, have been completely redrawn, with the aim of making them even clearer and more useful. See below for more detail.

The changes in the introductory pages are also apparent at a glance with new illustrations and new texts on virtually every page. We have made few alterations to the historical sections of course, but elsewhere I have to confess to giv- ing in to my urge to educate. Most of the non-historical subjects have been completely overhauled, just as the sciences and techniques of vine-growing and winemaking have been in recent years. Today's wine-lovers are infinitely more sophisticated and better informed than their equivalents 30 years ago. They tend to know their malolactics from their *mis en bouteille* (although we have added a glossary at the back for those who do not). With this in mind, readers of the Atlas are treated to consid- erable detail on growing, making, and enjoying wine (and much more is known today even about this apparently intuitive activity).

The meat of the book, however, is still the maps and descriptions of individual wine regions. This was where I had the most difficult decisions about the extent to which I should rewrite what Hugh had so beautifully written in previous editions. Only a fool would tamper with his words unless absolutely necessary.

In the classic wine regions – most notably Burgundy, Bordeaux, and Germany – I have made only such changes as events have made unavoidable. The pace of change is indeed slower in these classic regions than elsewhere – although St-Emilion, for example, now occupies a very different place in the hierarchy of Bordeaux and its map has been enlarged and the accom- panying text amended accordingly. Similarly, increasing interest in the better-performing châteaux of the Entre-Deux-Mers and Premières Côtes de Bordeaux prompted a complete revision of this area's coverage, both map and text.

The most obvious change in Burgundy has been the emergence of serious wines from the southern Mâconnais, resulting in a brand new map of Pouilly-Fuissé. The maps I always searched for in the German section – a user- friendly overview, one showing how the various parts of the Mosel fit together, and another of Hochheim – have been added, but Hugh's orig- inal text remains relatively intact.

Almost everywhere else, it seems, has been in a state of perpetual evolution and, often, rev- olution – including parts of France, the cradle of modern wine. As a result, the whole of the south of France has been fully revised, with new maps for the southern Rhône, Languedoc, Roussillon, Provence, and Bandol and with a major revision of text everywhere south of a line drawn from Buzet to Geneva. New producers, new tech- niques, new wines, and even completely new areas are emerging not just from the fashionable Rhône Valley but all over the south of France.

France, however, is the most heavily regu- lated wine-producing country in the world. It is

extremely difficult for any wine made outside the carefully drawn boundaries and rules of its Appellations Contrôlées to make much of an impact (although there are signs of some revolt at the restrictions imposed by this state of affairs). In Spain and Italy, on the other hand, the wine authorities can give the impression of desperately chasing rather than leading individ- ual innovation.

Many of the more interesting new Spanish wines to emerge over the next few years will doubtless be made from vineyards outside the regions mapped in detail on pages 188-199, for the country is explosive with both potential and the will to realize it. In an attempt to keep up with the Spanish wine revolution as closely as possible however, coverage of Spain has been extended perhaps more dramatically than any- where else apart from Italy. Priorato, Navarra, Somontano, and Rías Baixas all feature in detail for the first time, with their own maps, while Ribera del Duero's map and text spread them- selves over a much larger area.

We have become used to the anarchic nature of the Italian winescape, but some clear pinna- cles have emerged and with this new edition receive the detailed attention they deserve. Barolo, Barbaresco, Montalcino, Montepulciano, and that cauldron of innovation the Tuscan Coast, all have their own maps and detailed descriptions, as does Puglia, suddenly a source of wines exported in bottle all over the world. Sicily, happily, is also making an increasing impact on the world's wine drinkers.

In most of the rest of Europe, excellent maps were already in place and all that has been needed has been to refine and update them. But so much has happened in many of these countries that I had to steel myself for a considerable rewrite in many cases. And developments in Portugal have been so considerable that they have demanded three new maps and many new words.

In some ways, the pace of change has been greatest around the eastern and southern Mediterranean. Not that countries such as Morocco, Tunisia, Israel, Lebanon, and Greece are set to deluge the world with serious challenges to France's first growths, but Morocco and Tunisia now have something seriously interesting to offer the world. And the Eastern Mediterranean is the source of a considerable amount of good to fine wine (not to mention something approaching wine mania in certain quarters) – which would all have been unthinkable in 1994.

Much of what is perhaps patronizingly, possibly inaccurately, called the New World, was already well-mapped in the fourth edition, progress here having been impossible to ignore. But all maps have been refined and in some cases reorganized with new ones added for North America, California, Sierra Foothills and the Delta, New York State, Casablanca and Aconcagua in Chile, and Hawkes Bay in New Zealand. It will surprise no-one to learn that it is the words towards the back of this book that have had to be changed most, so great have been the changes in countries such as the United States, Australia, and South Africa.

In the fourth edition Hugh wrote "There is no modern precedent for the revolution of manners and methods that has transformed New Zealand in the past 15 years from a footnote in the world's wine catalogue to a handsome chapter." Today, however, the number of such examples is overwhelming.

The wine industries of Argentina and Canada are those which have most obviously graduated from footnote to handsome chapter status between the fourth and this edition, with Argentina now an ambitious and potentially prolific wine exporter and Canada the world's most important source of a unique wine style.

Breathing hard down their necks, however, are countries such as Uruguay, Brazil, Mexico, China, India, and Georgia, all clamouring for individual attention as wine producers of note, but unthinkably exotic when the first edition of this Atlas appeared 30 years ago.

The expanding world of wine

The world of wine is now a much, much bigger place than it was in 1971. The first wave of expansion had been away from the equator to cooler regions, thanks to special, early ripening grape varieties. Newer wine regions are more likely to be in places that were for long considered impossibly hot or dry. Something as mundane as the widespread installation of refrigeration equipment has extended the world's wine regions towards the equator – often coupled with the installation of irrigation systems of various sorts. Temperature control is essential in warmer regions not just for cooling grapes and must but for extending the fermentation process so that enough colour and flavour can be leached out of them – and also for storing the result, both before and after bottling.

Left The top-quality Goldtröpfchen vineyards of Piesport alone are justification for this book. The map on page 221 shows just how vastly different they are from the flatland that fills the millions of dreary bottles labelled Piesporter Michelsberg.

Advances in tropical viticulture, sometimes resulting in several crops a year, tricking the vine into dormancy and budding by respectively pruning and administering special hormones, have also played their part in extending the wine map to places such as Thailand and northern Brazil.

What is interesting, however, is that within the warmer wine-producing countries the unavoidable trend is towards cooler regions. Throughout Australia for example, vine-growers are colonizing higher altitudes and higher latitudes; the introductory map of Southeastern Australia, which features the new Geographic Indications, is almost unrecognizably different from its equivalent in previous editions. California growers are moving out towards the coast and up into the hills. New Zealand's wine map has had to be extended south, while Chile needed a new map of the Casablanca Valley and Aconcagua north of Santiago.

Almost every wine-producing country in the world (with the possible exception of Algeria) is in a ferment of qualitative upgrade, and this is thanks to the extraordinarily privileged place that wine occupies in today's society.

Wine – an international passion

The 1990s saw a great surge of interest in wine across the globe. In western countries wine now enjoys the same sort of respectability and passion as, say, opera and fine art as a leisure interest. Hundreds of thousands of new recruits to the pleasures of fermented grape juice have emerged. Some of them have bulging wallets, which have sent the prices of a tiny minority of trophy wines spiralling apparently out of control. Others are more amateurish in the best and most literal sense of the word and seem to spend hours happily seeking out their own special loves and bargains.

In the east, whole countries have fallen for wine's charms since the appearance of the last edition, some of them fielding collectors with such determination and liquidity that they have in their time upturned the entire fine wine market.

Interest in wine is so widespread and so widely admired that the field has attracted thousands of outside investors in wine production as well as its consumption. They are typically those who have made a fortune elsewhere and seem determined to lose it in the most agreeable way they can imagine. But there are also signs that wine is now attracting the interest of the global corporations once more, whose interest may not be quite so benign in the medium and long term.

Certainly if there is one clear trend apparent in this Atlas it is that the world of wine's national boundaries have been well and truly smudged.

Winemakers now routinely travel between countries and hemispheres. Joint ventures between wine producers in two different continents abound. The winemaker who has never travelled and never absorbed a foreign influence is now the exception rather than the rule.

The danger here of course is a sacrifice of individuality, of local character – which is why the Atlas is needed to spell out loud and clear just how much geography matters.

How this Atlas works

The maps have been put together with the consumer, not the wine bureaucrat, in mind. If an appellation – AC, DOC, DO, AVA, GI or ward – exists but is of no practical interest to the wine drinker, our policy is to omit it. We have marked those wineries we think are of interest to the world's wine lovers, although doubtless scores if not hundreds more will emerge before the next, sixth edition of the Atlas does. (The exception here is the Côte d'Or, whose exceptionally detailed maps concentrate on vineyards rather than cellars – which tend to be huddled in the same village backstreets anyway.)

One of the most important changes to the maps in this edition has been to make the choice of type more rational: all wine names, whether appellations or wineries, are in type with serifs (eg the appellation of MEURSAULT) whereas geographical names are in sans serif type (eg the village of **Meursault**).

In deciding the order of different regions within countries, we have tried very roughly to go from west to east and from north to south, although like all rules this has its exceptions. Within France (a notable exception to the above rule), the Vins de Pays and VDQS wines have their own sections but their labels tend to appear on the geographically relevant page.

The policy in choosing which labels to feature on these pages (a wine publishing innovation when it was introduced in the first edition) is stricter than before. I have tried as far as possible to make the labels shown reflect my personal choice of the best wines made in that particular country, region or district. The vintage shown on the label has no particular relevance; my choices should have a track record over many vintages. The number of labels shown on each page is often determined far more by page design than qualitative considerations. (I don't really think, for example, that Bulgaria makes three times as many good wines as New York State.) Nor should anything be read into the order in which the labels are shown on the page.

A further innovation in this edition is the appearance of factfiles, compact tables of basic information on a particular region for those in a hurry. For more details, see page 21.

Abbreviations

The following abbreviations are some of the most common used in the factfiles and throughout the text:

ft	feet	**AC**	Appellation Contrôlée
g	grams	**AVA**	American
ha	hectares		Viticultural Area
hl	hectolitres	**EU**	European Union
in	inches	**GI**	Geographic Indication
kg	kilograms	**INAO**	Institut National des
km	kilometres		Appellations d'Origine
l	litres	**OIV**	Office International de
m	metres		la Vigne et du Vin
mm	millimetres		

Personal thanks

First of all I must thank Hugh Johnson, who could not have been a more generous, supportive, good-humoured, not to mention talented, collaborator. Commissioning editor Rebecca Spry has been unfailingly, indeed incomprehensibly, cheerful and accommodating. Lucy Bridgers got the project off to an elegant start before handing over to a human dynamo called Gill Pitts in whom are combined, most unusually, extreme efficiency, diligence, and a sense of humour. Cartographic editor Zoë Goodwin was also admirably chirpy while capably going about her arcane business, as was the ever-willing researcher Nathan Burley. Make no mistake, this was a dream team, by no means excluding the design and production team of Phil Ormerod, Peter Gerrish, Colin Goody, Rosie Garai, and Julie Young, and all others specified on page 4. For me, having any sort of editorial back-up, let alone such an amenable crew, was an unaccustomed luxury.

Other hard-working *éminences grises* in the cartographic field were Alan Grimwade and his team at Cosmographics, and Colin McCarthy and colleagues at Map Creation.

Enormous thanks are also due to everyone cited in and inadvertently missed off the list of Acknowledgements on page 352. We have prevailed upon the goodwill of a vast array of informants all over the world and can only bless them and the way improved technology has allowed us to communicate with such satisfying, almost dangerous (in terms of meeting deadlines) speed. Any faults in this book are much more likely to be mine than theirs, and they certainly cannot be held responsible for the many opinions expressed in this book, nor for such tendentious issues as choices of labels.

As ever, however, I owe most to Nick, Julia, Will, and Rose who have so good-humouredly indulged me one more time.

The World of Wine

Just under 8 million hectares of the world's surface were planted with vines in 1998, according to the official records of the Office International de la Vigne et du Vin (OIV) in Paris – which almost certainly means that in reality there were many more. By no means all vine-growers co-operate with statisticians.

Despite huge increases in vine planting in new wine-producing countries such as the United States, Australia, Chile, China, and India, the old guard, the world's most important wine producers at the top of the first column on the opposite page, have been pulling out their workhorse vines at such a rate that the world's total vineyard area is declining – by 13% since 1988. Global wine production meanwhile has declined much more slowly – by just 6% over the same period – suggesting that the world's vineyards are increasingly productive. Some of this may be explained by greater efficiency, but fertilizers and other agrochemicals designed to combat vine disease will have played their part.

The variation in average yields shown on this page is both instructive and misleading. (Like all other measurements here, they are given in metric units because metric Europe is still the most important wine-producing continent by far. See right for equivalents in acres and gallons. Divide by 17.5 to convert a yield in hl/ha to tonnes/acre.

Germany's vineyards have always been some of the most heavily milked. Uruguay's are exceptionally fertile. The Luxembourg figure has probably been misleadingly swollen and the UK one shrunk by their small statistical base.

Other countries, marked † in the Yield column, grow a substantial proportion of their vines for purposes other than winemaking (fresh grapes and raisins mainly), which reduces their apparent average wine yields. There is a similar effect in some Eastern European countries where many vineyards have been so badly neglected that they are not producing anything like their full potential. Average yields are naturally low in countries with a dry climate and shortage of irrigation water such as Spain, North Africa, and parts of Portugal.

Collecting global wine statistics has become an ever lengthier process now that so many countries have become vine-growers and wine producers (1998 was the most recent year for which figures were available even quite late in 2001). Pure curiosity has extended the boundaries of the world of wine enormously, and the effects of climate change may expand them further in the years to come.

The columns on the opposite page are slightly misleading in that those countries marked † devote much of their vineyard to products other than wine. The world's 24th, 25th, and 34th most important growers of vines, Iraq, Afghanistan, and Yemen respectively, have been omitted from the list because they do not officially produce wine at all.

The world still produces much more wine than it drinks, which has done nothing to deter the planting of new vineyards, stocked largely with the international grape varieties described on pages 24 and 25. Pull those corks!

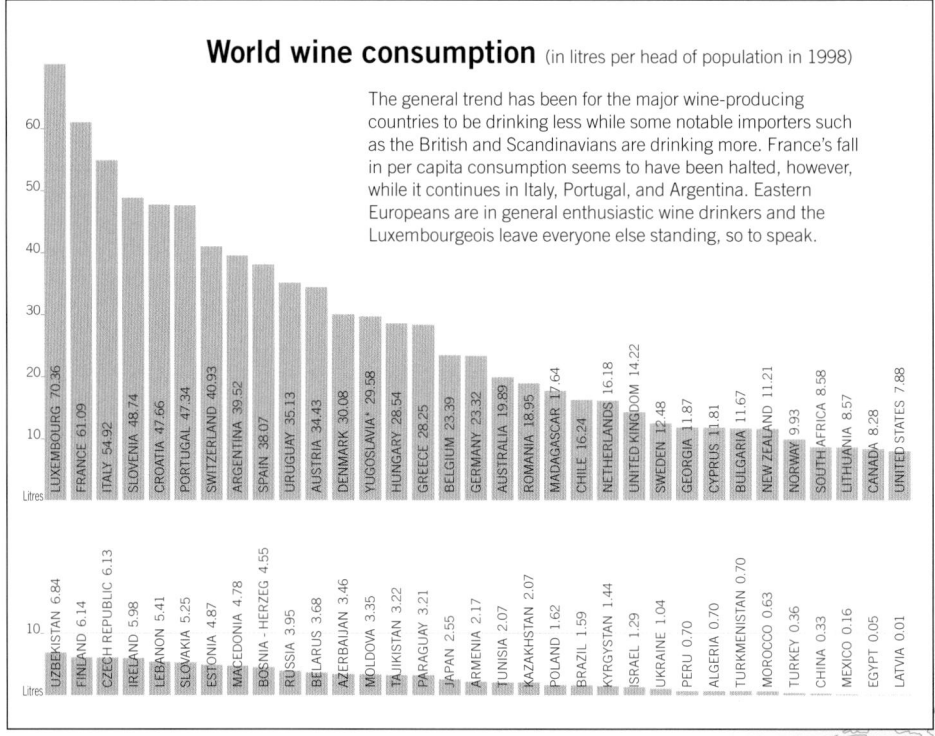

World wine consumption (in litres per head of population in 1998)

The general trend has been for the major wine-producing countries to be drinking less while some notable importers such as the British and Scandinavians are drinking more. France's fall in per capita consumption seems to have been halted, however, while it continues in Italy, Portugal, and Argentina. Eastern Europeans are in general enthusiastic wine drinkers and the Luxembourgeois leave everyone else standing, so to speak.

LUXEMBOURG 70.36, FRANCE 61.09, ITALY 54.92, SLOVENIA 48.74, CROATIA 47.66, PORTUGAL 47.34, SWITZERLAND 40.93, ARGENTINA 39.52, SPAIN 38.07, URUGUAY 35.13, AUSTRIA 34.43, DENMARK 30.08, YUGOSLAVIA* 29.58, HUNGARY 28.54, GREECE 28.25, BELGIUM 23.39, GERMANY 23.32, AUSTRALIA 19.89, ROMANIA 18.95, MADAGASCAR 17.64, CHILE 16.24, NETHERLANDS 16.18, UNITED KINGDOM 14.22, SWEDEN 12.48, GEORGIA 11.87, CYPRUS 11.81, BULGARIA 11.67, NEW ZEALAND 11.21, NORWAY 9.93, SOUTH AFRICA 8.58, LITHUANIA 8.57, CANADA 8.28, UNITED STATES 7.88

UZBEKISTAN 6.84, FINLAND 6.14, CZECH REPUBLIC 6.13, IRELAND 5.98, LEBANON 5.41, SLOVAKIA 5.25, ESTONIA 4.87, MACEDONIA 4.78, BOSNIA - HERZEG 4.55, RUSSIA 3.95, BELARUS 3.68, AZERBAIJAN 3.46, MOLDOVA 3.35, TAJIKISTAN 3.22, PARAGUAY 3.21, JAPAN 2.55, ARMENIA 2.17, TUNISIA 2.07, KAZAKHSTAN 2.07, POLAND 1.62, BRAZIL 1.59, KYRGYSTAN 1.44, ISRAEL 1.29, UKRAINE 1.04, PERU 0.70, ALGERIA 0.70, TURKMENISTAN 0.70, MOROCCO 0.63, TURKEY 0.36, CHINA 0.33, MEXICO 0.16, EGYPT 0.05, LATVIA 0.01

Wine production
(in 1,000's hectolitres)

Country	1998	1988	Yield '98 Hl/Ha
North America			
USA	20,450	18,237	56
Canada	343	560	49
Latin America			
Argentina	12,673	20,629	60
Brazil	2,782	3,762	46 †
Chile	5,475	4,227	38 †
Uruguay	1,132	740	103
Mexico	1,112	147	27 †
Peru	120	100	11 †
Bolivia	20	16	5 †
Europe			
Italy	54,188	61,863	60
France	52,671	57,530	58
Spain	30,320	21,565	26
USSR*	15,093	28,128	19
Germany*	10,834	9,708	102
Portugal	3,621	3,826	14
Yugoslavia*	4,025	5,762	38
Hungary	4,180	4,707	32
Romania	5,002	10,000	20
Greece	3,826	4,500	30
Austria	2,703	2,867	55
Bulgaria	3,308	3,399	30
Czech & Slovak Rep*	940	1,607	28
Switzerland	1,172	1,113	78
Albania	105	250	21
Luxembourg	160	143	160
Malta	32	19	32
United Kingdom	12	6	12
Belgium	1	2	–
Africa			
South Africa	8,156	8,465	73
Algeria	360	1,000	6 †
Tunisia	352	204	13 †
Morocco	298	280	6 †

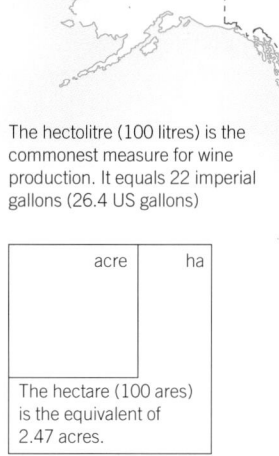

The hectolitre (100 litres) is the commonest measure for wine production. It equals 22 imperial gallons (26.4 US gallons)

	acre	ha

The hectare (100 ares) is the equivalent of 2.47 acres.

Country	1998	1988	Yield '98 Hl/Ha
Asia/Middle East			
Cyprus	710	630	36 †
Turkey	278	390	0.5†
Israel	90	140	11 †
Lebanon	186	50	7 †
Far East			
China	3,550	–	18 †
Japan	1,301	527	59
Australasia			
Australia	7,415	4,030	76
New Zealand	606	480	67
World total	258,776	274,417	33

6

29

Distribution of the world's vineyards (in 1,000s hectares)

Rank	Country	1998	1988	%Change
1	Spain	1,180	1,525	-29
2	France	914	1,018	-11
3	Italy	899	1,074	-19
4	USSR*	788	1,124	-43
5	Turkey†	602	600	0.5
6	United States	364	319	12
7	Iran†	270	193	29
8	Portugal	260	385	-48
9	Romania	253	268	-6
10	Argentina	210	268	-28
11	China†	194	143	26
12	Chile†	144	118	18
13	Hungary	131	142	-8
14	Greece	129	171	-33
15	South Africa	111	102	8
16	Bulgaria	109	139	-28
17	Germany*	106	100	6
18	Yugoslavia*	106	227	-114
19	Australia	98	57	42
20	Syria†	86	114	-33
21	Brazil†	60	61	-2
22	Algeria†	56	139	-148
23	Egypt†	56	47	16
26	Morocco†	50	58	-16

Rank	Country	1998	1988	%Change
27	Austria	49	58	-18
28	India†	43	13	70
29	Mexico†	41	64	-56
30	Czech & Slov Rep*	33	47	-42
31	South Korea	30	–	–
32	Tunisia†	27	31	-15
33	Lebanon†	26	22	15
35	Japan	22	28	-27

Rank	Country	1998	1988	%Change
36	Cyprus†	20	31	-55
37	Jordan†	15	6	60
38	Switzerland	15	14	7
39	Peru†	11	9	18
40	Uruguay	11	19	-73
	World total	7,799	8,989	-13

* 1988 figures are for production and vineyards within previous rather than current political boundaries.

† Country in which a significant proportion of vineyards are devoted to products other than wine.

— · — · International boundary

▓ Vineyards

The Ancient World

Wine is far older than recorded history. It emerges with civilization itself from the East. The evidence from tablets and papyri and Egyptian tombs fills volumes. Mankind, as we recognize ourselves, working, quarrelling, loving, and worrying, comes on the scene with the support of a jug of wine.

Pharaonic wine, however vividly painted for us to see, is too remote to have any meaning. Our age of wine, with still-traceable roots, begins with the Phoenicians and Greeks who colonized the Mediterranean, starting about 1100 BC in the case of the Phoenicians, about 350 years later in the case of the Greeks. It was then that wine began to arrive where it was to make its real home: Italy, France and Spain (although the Etruscans between the 8th and 4th centuries BC cultivated the vines that had been growing wild in Italy). The Greeks called Italy the Land of Staked Vines (see page 153), just as the Vikings called America Vínland for the profusion of native vines they found circa AD1000. North Africa, southern Spain, Provence, Sicily, the Italian mainland, and the Black Sea had their first vineyards in the time of the Greek and Phoenician Empires.

The wines of Greece herself, no great matter for much of modern times, were lavishly praised and documented by her poets. There was even a fashionable after-dinner game in Athens that consisted of throwing the last few mouthfuls of wine in your cup into the air, to hit a delicately balanced dish on a pole. Smart young things took coaching in the finer points of *kottabos*. But such treatment of the wine, and the knowledge that it was almost invariably drunk as what we would call "a wine cup", flavoured with herbs, spices, and honey and diluted with water (sometimes even seawater) seems to question its innate quality. That the wines of different islands of the Aegean were highly prized for their distinct characters is indisputable. Chios in particular was a supplier in constant demand. Whether the wines would appeal to us today we have no way of knowing.

Greeks industrialized winegrowing in southern Italy, Etruscans in Tuscany and further north, and Romans followed. So much was written about wine and winemaking in ancient Rome that it is possible to make a rough map

(below) of the wines of the early Roman Empire. The greatest writers, even Virgil, wrote instructions to winegrowers. One sentence of his – "Vines love an open hill" – is perhaps the best single piece of advice that can be given to a European winegrower.

Others were much more calculating, discussing how much work a slave could do for how little food and sleep without losing condition. Roman winegrowing was on a very large scale, and business calculation was at the heart of it. It spread right across the Empire, so that Rome was eventually importing countless shiploads of amphoras from her colonies in Spain, North Africa – the entire Mediterranean. Since Pompeii was a tourist resort and considerable *entrepôt* for the wine trade its remarkable survival gives us a great deal of detailed evidence.

How good was Roman wine? Some of it apparently had extraordinary powers of keeping, which in itself suggests that it was well made. The must was frequently concentrated by heating, and wine was stored over hearths to be exposed to smoke to achieve what must have been a madeira-like effect.

Rome's great vintages were discussed and even drunk for longer than seems possible; the famous Opimian – from the year of the consulship in Opimius, 121 BC – was being drunk when it was 125 years old.

The Romans had all that is necessary for ageing wine, although they did not use the materials as we do. Glass, for example, was not used for wine storage. Wooden barrels were used only in Gaul (which included Germany). Like the Greeks, the Romans used earthenware amphoras. They hold about 35 litres.

Most Italians of 2,000 years ago probably drank wine very like their descendants today; young, rather roughly made, sharp or strong according to the vintage. Even the Roman method of cultivation of the vine on trees, the festoons which became the friezes on classical buildings, is still practised to a decreasing extent in parts of the south of Italy and (especially) northern Portugal.

The Greeks took wine north to southern Gaul. The Romans domesticated it there. By the time they withdrew from what is now France in the fifth century AD the Romans had laid the

Above It would appear that their gods enjoyed drinking wine as much as the Ancient Egyptians themselves. Pharaoh Tuthmosis III of the 18th dynasty (1479-1425 BC) is shown making an offering of Nu jars filled with wine.

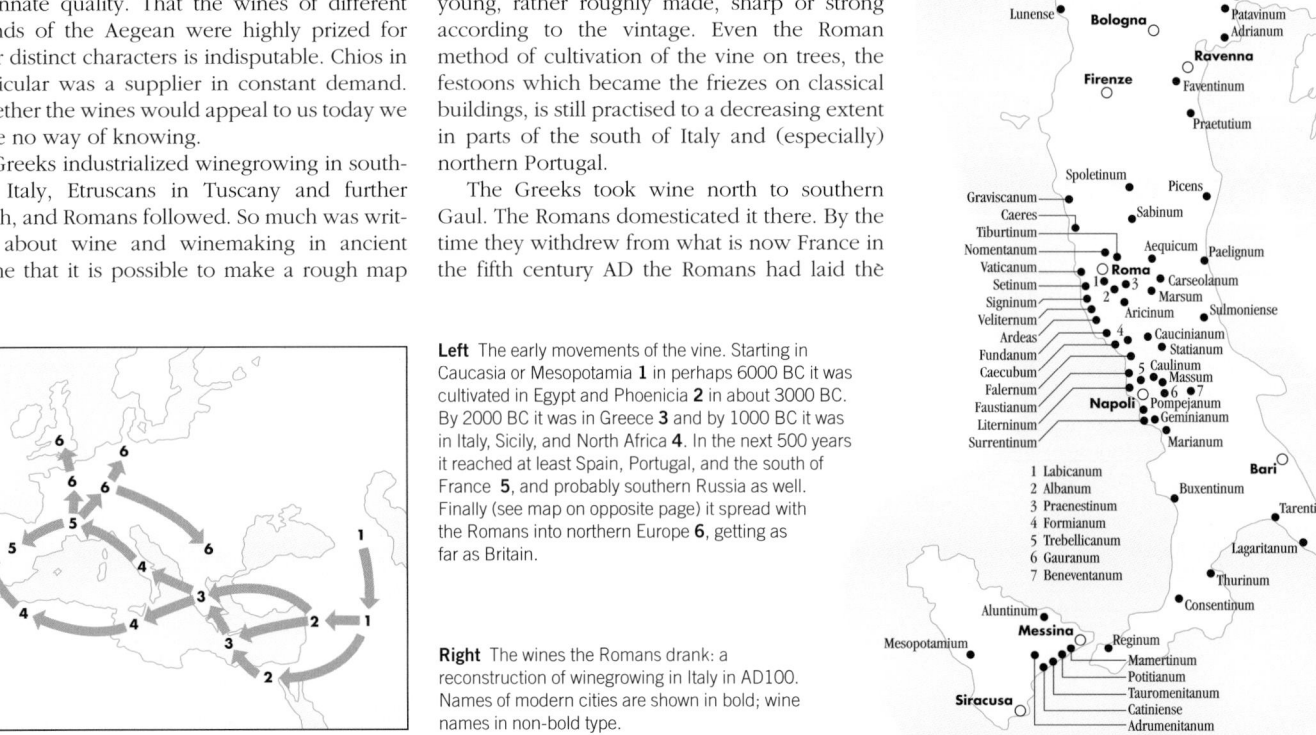

Left The early movements of the vine. Starting in Caucasia or Mesopotamia **1** in perhaps 6000 BC it was cultivated in Egypt and Phoenicia **2** in about 3000 BC. By 2000 BC it was in Greece **3** and by 1000 BC it was in Italy, Sicily, and North Africa **4**. In the next 500 years it reached at least Spain, Portugal, and the south of France **5**, and probably southern Russia as well. Finally (see map on opposite page) it spread with the Romans into northern Europe **6**, getting as far as Britain.

Right The wines the Romans drank: a reconstruction of winegrowing in Italy in AD100. Names of modern cities are shown in bold; wine names in non-bold type.

1 Labicanum
2 Albanum
3 Praenestinum
4 Formianum
5 Trebellicanum
6 Gauranum
7 Beneventanum

foundations for almost all of the most famous vineyards of modern Europe.

Starting in Provence, which had had Greek-planted vineyards already for centuries, they moved up the Rhône Valley and into the Languedoc, the Provincia Narbonensis. At the beginning of the 21st century, we still have no clear evidence of exactly when viticulture started in Bordeaux. The earliest mention is in the works of the poet Ausonius in the 4th century AD (Ausonius lived in St-Emilion, perhaps even at Château Ausone), but it probably began long before this.

All the early developments were in the river valleys, the natural lines of communication, which the Romans cleared of forest and cultivated, at first as a precaution against ambushes. Besides, boats were the best way of moving anything so heavy as wine. Bordeaux, Burgundy, Trier on the Mosel (where the museum preserves a fully laden and manned Roman wine-boat in stone) probably all started as merchant-centres for imported Italian or Greek wine, and then planted their own vines which eventually surpassed the imported product.

By the first century there were vines on the Loire and the Rhine; by the second in Burgundy, and by the fourth in Paris (not such a good idea), in Champagne, and on the Mosel. Burgundy's Côte d'Or remains the least easy vineyard to account for, having no convenient navigable river. It lay where the main road north (to Trier on the Mosel, the northern Rome) skirted the rich province of Autun. Presumably the Autunois saw the commercial opportunity, then found they had chosen a golden slope. The foundations had been dug for the French wine industry we still know.

Above Pompeii and Herculaneum, the Roman coastal resorts buried by the eruption of Vesuvius in AD79, are still not entirely explored. But in their houses (this is the Pompeii house of Lucius Caius Secundus), their streets, cellars, and bars we can get a very clear picture of what and how the Romans drank.

Below This map shows the approximate distribution of the grapevine *Vitis vinifera* throughout the Roman Empire in AD100. It displays a remarkably close correspondence with the vineyards of the 21st century; although there is much less in Spain and Portugal, and less in France but vastly more in Eastern Europe (and also apparently in Britain).

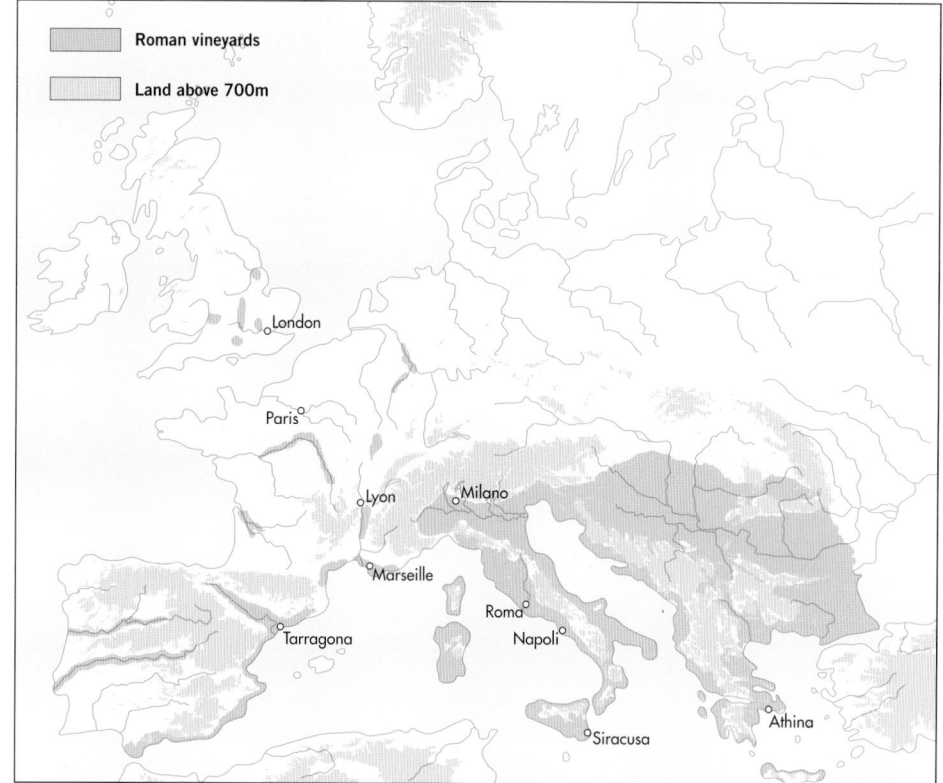

Roman vineyards

Land above 700m

London

Paris

Lyon
Milano

Marseille

Roma
Napoli

Tarragona

Siracusa

Athina

The Middle Ages

Out of the Dark Ages which followed the fall of the Roman Empire we gradually emerge into the illumination of the medieval period, to see in its lovely painted pages an entirely familiar scene: people enjoying drinking wine. Winemaking methods were not to change in their essentials until the 20th century. The Church was the repository of the skills of civilization in the Dark Ages – indeed the continuation of Rome's Imperial administration under a new guise. The Emperor Charlemagne recreated an Imperial system – and took great and famous pains to legislate in favour of better wine.

As expansionist monasteries cleared hillsides and built walls around fields of cuttings, and as dying winegrowers and departing crusaders bequeathed it their land, the Church came to be identified with wine – not only as the Blood of Christ, but as luxury and comfort in this world. Cathedrals and churches, but above all the multiplying monasteries, owned or created most of the greatest vineyards of Europe.

The Benedictines, from their great mother-houses of Monte Cassino in Italy and Cluny in Burgundy, went out and cultivated the finest vineyards, until their way of life became notorious: "Rising from the table with their veins swollen with wine and their heads on fire." Their great monasteries included Fulda near Frankfurt, Lorsch near Mainz, and major establishments in Alsace, Switzerland, Bavaria, and Austria.

Reaction came in 1112, when the young Saint Bernard split from the Benedictines and founded the ascetic order of the Cistercians, named for their new abbey of Cîteaux, within walking distance of the Côte d'Or. The Cistercian order was explosively successful, founding not only the great walled vineyards of the Clos de Vougeot in Burgundy and the Steinberg in the Rheingau, beside their abbey of Kloster Eberbach, but eventually magnificent monasteries all over Europe – and eventually, of course, becoming as notorious for their gluttony as the Benedictines. Alcobaça in Portugal seems to have been their Michelin 3-star establishment.

The one important exception to domination by the Church was the thriving vineyard of Bordeaux, where development was simply commercial with a single market in view. From 1152 to 1453 the great Duchy of Aquitaine, most of western France, was united by marriage to the crown of England and bent its efforts to filling great annual wine fleets with hogsheads of light claret, the *vin nouveau* the English loved.

But it was within the stable framework of the Church and the monasteries, in which tools and terms and techniques seemed to stand still, that the styles of wine and even some of the grape varieties now familiar to us slowly came into being. Few things in the medieval world were so strictly regulated. Wine and wool were the two great luxuries of northern Europe in the Middle Ages. Trade in cloth and wine made fortunes – most notably in Flanders and the great annual fairs that took place in Champagne, attracting merchants even over the Alps. No region became more obsessed with wine than

Germany, where vast barrels known as "tuns" were built for great vintages. The Heidelberg tun held the equivalent of 19,000 dozen bottles. Connoisseurship may have been rudimentary, but in 1224 the King of France held an international tasting. "The Battle of Wines" included 70 entries, from Spain, Germany, and Cyprus as well as all over France. The judge was an English priest. Cyprus won.

Above Remarkably little is unfamiliar in this 14th-century Italian manuscript, the *Tractatum de Septem Vitiis*. Though after all the trouble the cellarmaster is taking to examine the wine for clarity in the cellar it is surprising to see a guest apparently drinking it from the bottle.

The Evolution of Modern Wine

Up to the start of the 17th century wine was in the unique position of being the one and only wholesome and – up to a point – storable beverage. It had no challengers. Water was normally unsafe to drink, at least in cities. Ale without hops very quickly went bad. There were no spirits, nor any of the caffeine-containing drinks that appear essential to life today.

Europe drank wine on a scale it is difficult to conceive of; our ancestors must have been in a perpetual fuddle. It is hard to have confidence in the descriptions of wine that survive from before about 1700. With the exception of Shakespeare's graphic tasting notes, "a marvellous searching wine, and it perfumes the blood ere one can say 'What's this?'," they tend to refer to royal recommendations or miraculous cures rather than to taste and style.

In the 17th century all this changed, starting with chocolate from Central America, then coffee from Arabia and finally tea from China. At the same time the Dutch developed the art and commerce of distilling, turning huge tracts of western France into suppliers of cheap white wine for their stills; hops turned ale into more stable beer and great cities began to pipe the clean water they had lacked since Roman times. The wine industry was threatened with catastrophe unless it developed new ideas.

It is no coincidence that we date the creation of most of the wines we consider classics today from the second half of the 17th century. But these developments would never have succeeded without the timely invention of the glass wine bottle. Since Roman times wine had spent all its life in a barrel. Bottles, or rather jugs, usually of pottery or leather, were used simply for bringing it to table. The early 17th century saw changes in glassmaking technology that made bottles stronger and cheaper to blow. At about the same time some unknown thinker brought together the bottle, the cork, and the corkscrew.

Bit by bit it became clear that wine kept in a tightly corked bottle lasted far longer than wine in a barrel, which was likely to go off rapidly after the barrel was broached. It also aged differently, acquiring a "bouquet". The *vin de garde* was created and with it the chance to double and treble the price of wines capable of ageing.

It was the owner of Château Haut-Brion who first hit on the idea of what we might call "reserve" wines: selected, later-picked, stronger, carefully made, and matured. In the 1660s he opened London's first restaurant, under his own name, Pontac's Head, to publicize his produce.

In Champagne the oenologist monk Dom Pérignon went further, perfecting by blending a drink so luxurious that the aristocracy would beg for it. By accident, or rather by the inherent nature of the wine of the region, once bottled it started to sparkle. The oenologist disapproved; the clientele did not.

In the early 18th century burgundy changed its nature too. The most delicate wines, Volnay and Savigny, were once the most fashionable. Now

Right Bordeaux's vineyard area and wine production in relation to wars, pests, diseases, slumps, booms, and the weather, plotted up until 1988 by Philippe Roudié of Bordeaux University. Two great chemical aids, sulphur (against oidium mould) and Bordeaux mixture (copper sulphate and lime) against mildew had immediate effect. The 1990s were dominated by arguments over prices.

Below It is fascinating to compare A Jullien's 1866 classification of the world's great wines with our modern ideas. In his *Topographie de Tous les Vignobles Connus* his complete list named the vineyards shown on this map (in their original spelling).

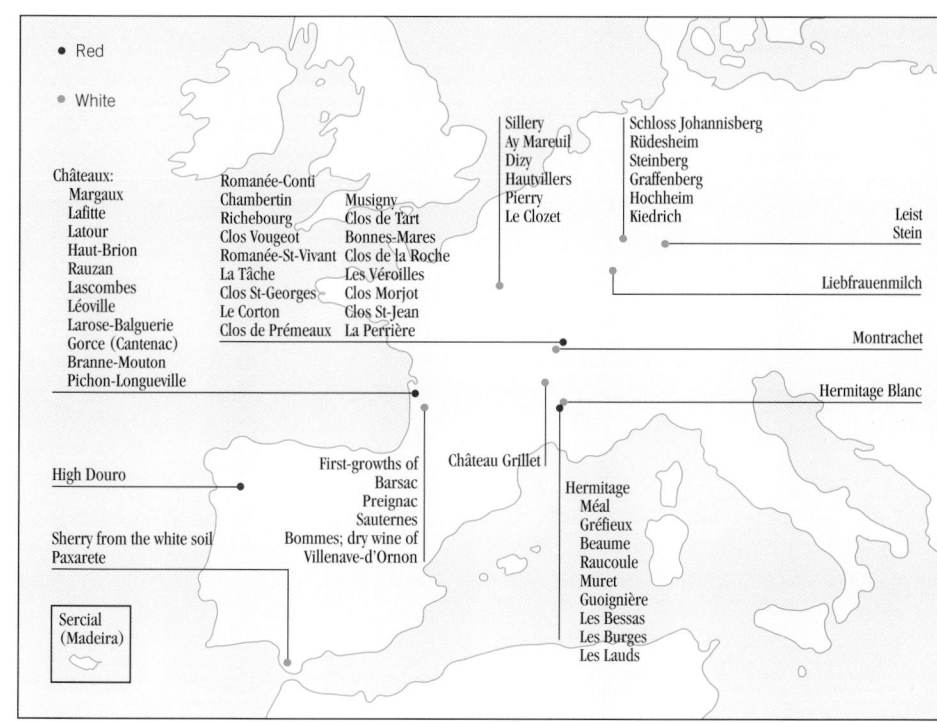

- ● Red
- ● White

Châteaux:
Margaux
Lafitte
Latour
Haut-Brion
Rauzan
Lascombes
Léoville
Larose-Balguerie
Gorce (Cantenac)
Branne-Mouton
Pichon-Longueville

Romanée-Conti
Chambertin
Richebourg
Clos Vougeot
Romanée-St-Vivant
La Tâche
Clos St-Georges
Le Corton
Clos de Prémeaux

Musigny
Clos de Tart
Bonnes-Mares
Clos de la Roche
Les Véroilles
Clos Morjot
Clos St-Jean
La Perrière

Sillery
Ay Mareuil
Dizy
Hautvillers
Pierry
Le Clozet

Schloss Johannisberg
Rüdesheim
Steinberg
Graffenberg
Hochheim
Kiedrich

Leist
Stein

Liebfrauenmilch

Montrachet

Hermitage Blanc

High Douro

First-growths of
Barsac
Preignac
Sauternes
Bommes; dry wine of
Villenave-d'Ornon

Château Grillet

Hermitage
Méal
Gréfieux
Beaume
Raucoule
Muret
Guoignière
Les Bessas
Les Burges
Les Lauds

Sherry from the white soil
Paxarete

Sercial
(Madeira)

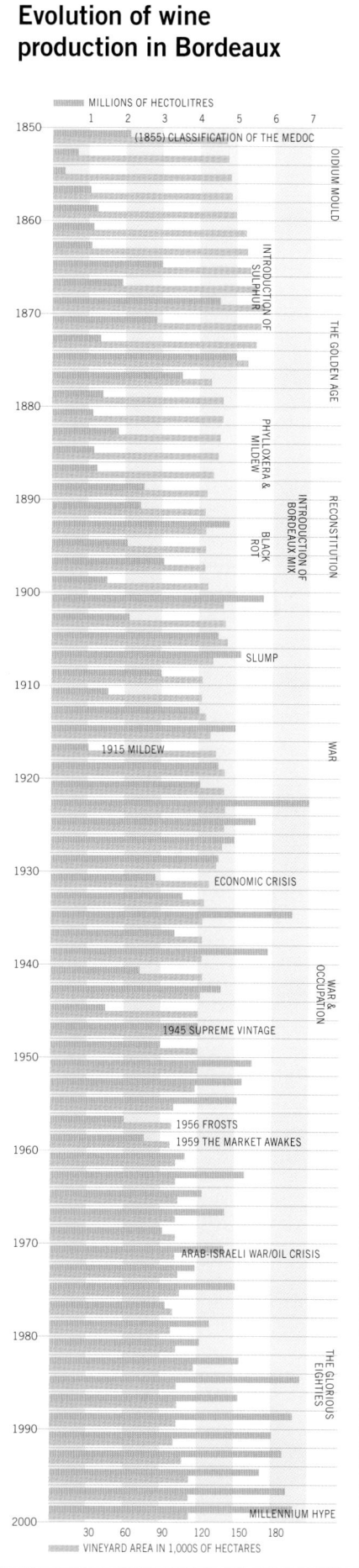

Evolution of wine production in Bordeaux

MILLIONS OF HECTOLITRES
1 2 3 4 5 6 7

1850 — (1855) CLASSIFICATION OF THE MEDOC — OIDIUM MOULD

1860 — INTRODUCTION OF SULPHUR

1870 — THE GOLDEN AGE

1880 — PHYLLOXERA & MILDEW

1890 — RECONSTITUTION / INTRODUCTION OF BORDEAUX MIX / BLACK ROT

1900 — SLUMP

1910

1915 MILDEW — WAR

1920

1930 — ECONOMIC CRISIS

1940 — WAR & OCCUPATION

1945 SUPREME VINTAGE

1950

1956 FROSTS
1959 THE MARKET AWAKES

1960

1970 — ARAB-ISRAELI WAR/OIL CRISIS

1980 — THE GLORIOUS EIGHTIES

1990

2000 — MILLENNIUM HYPE

30 60 90 120 150 180
VINEYARD AREA IN 1,000S OF HECTARES

these *vins de primeur* began to give way to the demand for long-fermented, dark-coloured *vins de garde*, especially from the Côte de Nuits. In Burgundy at least, though, the master-grape, the Pinot Noir, had been identified and made mandatory. Champagne, too, adopted Pinot Noir in emulation. Germany's best vineyards were being replanted to Riesling. But most other regions were still experimenting

The wine that benefited most from the development of the bottle was the fiery port the English had started to drink in the late 17th century – not out of choice, but because the duty on their preferred French wine was raised to prohibitive levels by an almost uninterrupted state of war. They had doubts about it at first, but as the century, and their bottles, grew older, their opinion of it rose sharply. The trend is graphically illustrated by the way the port bottle changed shape within a century (see below).

In 1866 André Jullien published the figures for the alcoholic strengths of recent vintages. By today's standards the burgundies are formidable: Corton 1858, 15.6%; Montrachet 1858, 14.3%; Volnay 1859, 14.9%; Richebourg 1859, 14.3%. In contrast Bordeaux wines of the same two years ranged from 11.3% (St-Emilion Supérieur) to 8.9% (Château Lafite).

The low natural strength of the Bordeaux wines explains what seems today a curious habit of the old wine trade. Up to the mid-19th century the wines for England – which was most of the best of Bordeaux – were subjected to what was known as *le travail à l'anglaise*. One recipe called for 30 litres of Spanish wine (Alicante or Benicarlo), two litres of unfermented white must and a bottle of brandy to each barrel of claret. The summer after the vintage the wine was set to ferment again with these additives, then treated as other wines and kept for several years in wood before shipping. The result was strong wine with a good flavour, but "heady and not suitable for all stomachs". It fetched more than natural wine.

Today's preoccupation with authenticity, even at the expense of quality, makes these practices seem abusive. But it is as if someone revealed as a shocking practice the addition of brandy to port. We like Douro wine with brandy in it; our ancestors liked Lafite laced with Alicante.

German wines of the last century would be scarcely more familiar to us. It is doubtful if any of today's pale, intensely perfumed, delicately or profoundly sweet wines were made. Grapes picked earlier gave more acid wine, which needed to mature longer in cask. "Old brown hock" was a recommendation.

Champagne was sweeter and fuller in colour and flavour – although otherwise very like it is today. Port and sherry had both been perfected. There was more stronger sweet wine: Málaga and Marsala were in their heydays. Madeira, Constantia, and Tokay (as it was then called) were as highly regarded as modern Trockenbeerenauslesen.

The wine trade was booming. In the winegrowing countries an unhealthy amount of the economy rested on wine: in Italy in 1880 it was calculated that no less than 80% of the population more or less relied on wine for a living. Both Italy (in Tuscany and Piemonte) and Spain (in Rioja) were creating their first modern export wines. California was in the midst of its first

Above The machine harvester is a vital part of the modern wine revolution. Most grapes are now picked by this method, rather than by hand. The savings are evident; but it can also work at night, bringing in cool grapes in hot regions.

wine-rush. This was the world phylloxera struck (see page 18). At the time, when it caused the pulling up of almost every vine in Europe and the New World, it seemed like the end of the world of wine.

In retrospect the rationalization of planting, the introduction of grafting, and the enforced selection of the most desirable grape varieties together made a chance for a great new beginning. But it was a slow and tortuous start, with every sort of setback in glut, fraud, Prohibition, Depression, World War – and bad weather. In 40 years (to take Bordeaux as the sample) only 11 could be described as generally good. It was against this depressing background that the French government made the first moves towards regulation and control in the fledgling

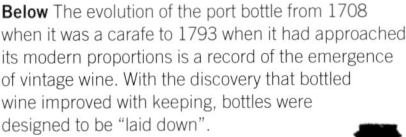

Below The evolution of the port bottle from 1708 when it was a carafe to 1793 when it had approached its modern proportions is a record of the emergence of vintage wine. With the discovery that bottled wine improved with keeping, bottles were designed to be "laid down".

1708   1719   1739   1741   1753   1780   1793

regime of Appellations Contrôlées. The notion of terroir was crystallized for the first time.

The 20th century saw two revolutions in the world of wine: the first scientific, the second industrial. As it began, the practical significance of Pasteur's science was just sinking in; fermentation was no longer a mystery but a process that could be controlled. Bordeaux had opened the first university department dedicated to oenology, at the same time as Montpellier, Geisenheim, Davis in California, and Roseworthy in Australia opened departments for the study of viticulture. The established wine world had enough problems to solve; the emerging one had every decision to take, starting with which varieties to plant.

But it was not until the 1950s, as America struggled out of the chaotic legacy of Prohibition, and Europe began to recover from World War II, that anything like prosperity returned to châteaux, wineries, and domaines.

For the warm countries of the New World the true revolution came with refrigeration and the ability to cool the fermenting must. California had a few rock-cut cellars, Australia nothing at all to restrain tumultuous fermentation and the loss of aromatic character. Almost the only aromatic, balanced, and profitably ageable table wines therefore came from northern Europe.

Once that nut was cracked, California took to varietal wines like a religion. Not many varieties: Zinfandel was California's own grape, but Chardonnay was "the sole source of the great French white burgundies", Cabernet "the premier red grape of the Bordeaux area of France". Their names became incantations, their wines categories that no winery could be without. Australia, whose founding winegrowers planted Shiraz, Semillon, and Riesling, had to hurry to introduce what the whole world started to want.

The modern world of wine started in the 1960s, with the almost simultaneous appearance of new wineries with high ambitions in California and Australia, and perhaps more significantly the launch by E & J Gallo of cheap palatable table wines (even if they were labelled "Chablis" and "Hearty Burgundy") to cater to a completely new public. The Australian equivalent was sweet "Moselle".

Armed with the science to improve quality, and with technology that accelerated with demand, ambitious winemakers felt there were no heights they could not scale. The great discovery of the 1960s was that French oak barrels, used judiciously, could give wines from very different terroirs more than a passing resemblance to the "classics" of France. No single factor did more to close the gap between French wine and its imitators.

Sadly it was a trick that soon got out of control as novices confused the taste of oak with the taste of good wine. Over-use of oak as flavouring, making wines that refresh no-one, is still a widespread problem, not only in the New World, but among French, Italian, and Spanish producers who have lost confidence in their own taste and bend to the wind of fashion.

The 21st century starts with the greatest supplies (indeed a looming glut) of good wine from more sources than the world has ever known. Added to all the scientific and technological advances the great leap at the end of the 20th century was in communication, hence in worldwide competition.

There are few, if any, secrets today in a world which used to play its cards close to the chest. The "Flying Winemaker" was an invention of the 1980s; a high-tech professional, usually Australian, originally commissioned to make wine in Europe in Australia's winter, now often making many wines at the same time all over the world. Winemakers, flying or earthbound, sometimes seem to be in constant confessional, spewing out every detail of their doings on back-labels and through their public relations people. The ever-present danger of a global village, of course, is that marketing takes over from the people with wine-stained hands. Marketeers play safe. Their advice will flood the market with last year's idea – in all probability Chardonnay.

The danger of sameness, of every producer aiming at the same global market with a "me-too" wine, has been well aired. To the majority of consumers, it must be said, it is not a danger at all. Base-level wine drinkers make up the majority, and what they want is continuity. Variety equals confusion and loss of confidence. To Anglo-Saxons the reassurance of labels in English has been another big factor in the rush to New World wines.

On the other hand the world's wine drinkers are slowly but measurably trading-up and taking more interest in what they are drinking. Quality wine is gaining at the expense of table wine – a trend that a future surplus at all levels will only accelerate.

The days are passing when, for example, branded Chardonnays can slug it out in the marketplace on the basis of low price and lots of advertising. As consumers learn more about wine, and about their own tastes, they are prepared to spend more (even if it means drinking less). It became clear in the last decades of the 20th century that the days of the nondescript are numbered. The vineyards of the Midi that once produced *vin ordinaire* are now the home of Vins de Pays. Few grudge the premium, and success spurs the producers.

There are many reasons to believe in the survival of variety. Indeed in its revival, as ambitious New World growers replace Cabernet and Merlot with Sangiovese or Syrah or even Nebbiolo or Tempranillo. Twenty years ago merchants' blends dominated Burgundy. Today it is individual growers, with all the complications they, their little vineyards, and their extended families bring, who are in the driving seat – and they have encouraged a new generation of small ambitious négociants/merchants, many of whom are trying to produce wines every bit as interesting as the growers'. Wine is complex, and all the better for it.

Below There is little romance in a big modern winery. Temperature control means that operations can take place even under the heat of the Australian sun. These fermenting tanks or "vinomatics" rotate to maximize colour extraction from the grape skins at the ideal temperature.

The Vine

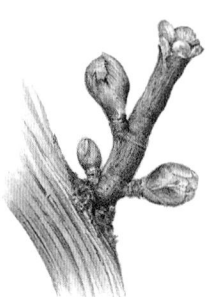

Stage 1 As early as March in northern Europe and September in the southern hemisphere, the buds left after winter pruning start to swell and the first signs of green can be seen emerging from the gnarled wood. This happens roughly when temperatures reach about 50°F (10°C) although different grape varieties vary.

Stage 2 Within ten days of budbreak, leaves start to separate from the bud and embryonic tendrils begin to be visible, and are all too vulnerable to frost which can strike as late as mid-May or mid-November in cooler districts of northern and southern hemispheres respectively. Late pruning can delay budbreak.

Stage 3 Between six and 13 weeks after budbreak the crucial flowering of the vine begins with the emergence of tiny caps of fused petals. These look very like miniature versions of the grapes that will be formed here once the caps fall, exposing stamens to be fertilized by pollen to create the berries.

Stage 4 The size of the eventual crop depends on the success of pollination. Poor weather during the ten- to 14-day flowering can result in *coulure*, whereby the stalks of an excessive number of very small berries shrivel, causing them to drop off, and also *millerandage*: different-sized berries on the same bunch.

Stage 5 The place of such buds as escape frost and rain is taken by hard, green baby grapes in June/December. These grapes swell during the summer and in August/February undergo *veraison*, whereby they soften and turn reddish or yellow. The ripening process begins and sugars start to build rapidly inside the grape.

It is an extraordinary fact that this wonderfully varied and evocative drink we call wine is the fermented juice of a single fruit, the grape. Every drop of wine we drink is made from rain (and in hotter regions irrigation water) recovered from the ground by the mechanism of the plant that bears grapes, the vine, and in the presence of sunlight converted by photosynthesis into fermentable sugar.

For the first two or three years of its life a young vine is too busy creating a root system and building a strong woody stalk to bear more than a few grapes. Thereafter, left to nature, it would rampage away, bearing some fruit but spending much more of its energy on making new shoots and putting out long, wandering branches of leafy wood, ideally seeking out a tree to climb, until it covered as much as an acre (nearly half a hectare) of ground, with new root systems forming wherever the branches touched the soil.

This natural form of reproduction, known in French as *provignage*, was used to make a vineyard in ancient times. To prevent the grapes rotting or the mice getting them, since they lay on the ground, little props were pushed under the stems to support each bunch. If the vine grew near trees, it used its tendrils to climb them to dizzy heights. The Romans planted elms especially for the purpose. Freelance labour was hired for the vintage; it was too dangerous to risk your own slaves.

Modern vines, of course, are not allowed to waste their precious energy on being "vigorous" – making long, leafy branches – however much they may try (see page 29). Better-quality grapes grow on a vine that is pruned in winter and regularly cut back to a very limited number of buds.

Like most other plants, vines will reproduce from seed but the seeds rarely turn out like their parents. Viticulturists propagate vines asexually instead so that they can be sure that the offspring are the same as the mother vine. Pips are only used for experimenting with new crosses between different varieties.

For planting a new vineyard every vine originates as a cutting – either planted to take root on its own or grafted onto a rootstock, a rooted cutting of another species specially selected for the soil type or resistance to drought or nematodes (tiny worms) for instance.

Nurserymen should try to take cuttings only from plants that are healthy and free of virus. The little "slips" are planted out for a season until they form roots. If there is any danger of virus infection, tissue-cultured vines, using only the virus-free growing-tip, have to be nurtured in a laboratory to become a rooted plant.

As a vine grows older its principal roots penetrate deeper into the ground. In very general terms, the younger the vine, the lighter and less subtle the wine – although vines can produce delicious fruit in their first year or two when yields are naturally low and the available flavour is concentrated into relatively few grapes. Somewhere between three and six years after being planted, the vine stabilizes, filling the space allotted to it above ground, and produces increasingly

The spread of phylloxera in Europe's vineyards

The phylloxera louse was first spotted in southern England in 1863 and three years later was already wreaking damage on vineyards in the southern Rhône Valley and the Languedoc. By 1869 it had reached Bordeaux and it reduced total French wine production by almost three-quarters between 1875 and 1889. Grafting onto resistant American rootstocks began in France in the late 1870s by which time phylloxera had already spread to Italy, Spain, Portugal, Austria, Switzerland, and Turkey. The first positive confirmation of the aphid in vineyards in the new German empire was in 1881.

Pests, diseases, and their effects on the vine

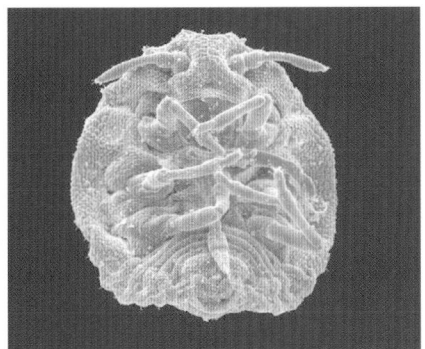

The phylloxera louse is shown in all its sinister detail by this electron micrograph. Native to North America, it reached Europe on steamships able to cross the Atlantic fast enough for it to survive on the botanical specimens collected by Victorians. American vines are resistant to it, and grafting European vines onto American roots is the only effective defence.

A phylloxera-affected vine is first ravaged at its roots which are destroyed within a few years of being attacked by the louse. Shoots then become stunted and lose their healthy green sheen. On fertile soils vines may continue to produce commercial quantities of grapes for some years after infection, and some particularly sandy soils seem to confer immunity.

Flavescence dorée is the most common form of grapevine yellows, a phytoplasma disease spread by leaf hoppers and currently prevalent in much of Europe, America, and Australia. Some varieties are much more sensitive to it than others and young vines may be killed whereas older vines will simply suffer a dramatically reduced yield. There is no known cure.

Pierce's disease is spread by this leaf hopper, the glassy-winged sharpshooter whose ability to fly long distances has put a wide range of northern California vineyards at risk. Vines die within five years of first succumbing to this bacterial disease, showing first dead spots on the leaves which eventually fall off. No varieties are resistant and there is no known cure.

concentrated wine, presumably thanks to an increasingly complex root system which regulates the water supply and, possibly, nutrients.

Yields typically start to decline after 25 or 30 years (or, more likely in many instances, the vine succumbs to disease or is of an unfashionable grape variety) so that it will be pulled out as uneconomic. Wine from vines older than this generally command a premium and may be labelled the produce of old vines, or *vieilles vignes* in French.

The best soils (see pages 22-23) drain quickly and deeply, drawing the roots down to great depths to find a stable but not too generous water supply. At the same time the vine constantly grows new feeder roots near the surface. Where irrigation is needed the best method is slow dripping beside the stem to encourage deep rooting within a restricted area.

The European vine family, called vinifera, or "wine-bearing", has countless enemies, the worst of them diseases and pests introduced far too recently (mostly from America) for it to have developed any natural resistance. In the 19th century first powdery mildew (oidium) and then downy mildew attacked Europe's vines – and vinifera vines planted in the New World. Laborious remedies were discovered for these two fungal diseases, though both still need treatment by spraying. Another common reason for the persistent drone of tractors spraying vineyards in the growing season is rot, specifically the malign form of botrytis fungus (as opposed to the benevolent form, which can produce such exceptional sweet wines as those described on page 102). This botrytis bunch rot, also called grey rot, can impart a fatally mouldy taste to grapes, and is increasingly resistant to anti-rot

chemicals (see pages 28-29 for alternative strategies). Fungal diseases are a particular problem in damp climates.

Towards the end of the 19th century, soon after a cure for the two mildews had been developed, a far more dangerous scourge was observed and, eventually, identified. The phylloxera louse feasts on the roots of the vine and eventually kills it. It almost destroyed the entire European vineyard, until it was discovered that native American vines (phylloxera came from America) are immune. Virtually every vine in Europe had to be replaced with a vinifera cutting grafted onto a rooted cutting from an American vine, a phylloxera-resistant rootstock.

Many of the world's newer wine regions (Chile and parts of Australia being the most obvious examples) have yet to experience this predatory aphid, and so happily plant their vinifera vines directly as ungrafted cuttings. In Oregon and New Zealand, however, this has proved a short-term stratagem, and in the 1980s vine-growers in northern California learnt to their cost that rootstocks have to be very carefully chosen if they are to offer reliable resistance to phylloxera. Hundreds of thousands of acres there had to be replanted with more suitable, truly phylloxera-resistant rootstocks.

The upper works of the vine are on the menu for a whole menagerie, too. Red spiders, the grubs of the cochylis and eudemis moths, various sorts of beetles, bugs, and mites find it nutritious. Most of them can be controlled by the various chemical sprays to which so many vines are subjected throughout the summer (or, by the world's swelling ranks of organic vine-growers, by more natural methods). There are two extremely dangerous exceptions, however.

At the beginning of the 21st century the leaf hoppers known as glassy-winged sharpshooters were spreading Pierce's disease, the fatal vine malady endemic to the southern United States (see page 268), at a terrifying rate to vineyards in northern California. Although there have been many and various responses to this devastating threat, including attempts to baffle it with Mexican wasps, there is still no known cure for vines other than the resistant southern native American vine varieties such as the Muscadines.

Parts of Europe and Australia have been suffering their own fatal scourge, grapevine yellows, of which France's *flavescence dorée* is the most common. Vines (and other plants) affected by the disease simply fail to grow properly, their leaves turn yellow, their shoots droop and bunches fall off. Infected plants begin the spread, and those little leaf hoppers are implicated here too.

Meanwhile, some viticulturists are perturbed by an increasingly common phenomenon they call black goo, a substance produced by fungi which seeps from mysteriously unhealthy young vines.

Today more and more of us may be enjoying wine, but winegrowers are beset by more and more challenges while producing it.

Wine and Weather

After the vine, the weather: the second most important ingredient in wine and the great variable. Every other major influence, including the climate – the expected, or long-term averaged, regional weather – is more or less constant and known in advance. But in the end it is the vagaries of a single year's weather that make or break a vintage.

Without sufficient rainfall or warmth, grapes will not ripen properly. An excess of either may well prejudice the quality of wine made from those grapes. A single phenomenon such as hail or frost can also affect quantity rather than quality, sometimes decimating the size of a crop. Frost in late spring when the season's buds are vulnerable is a grower's nightmare – as is hail at any time, although fortunately it tends to be localized. A bad storm can not only wreck a vintage, but may bruise the buds and wood of the vine so as to affect the following year's wine.

The climate of a wine region crucially affects the sort of wine it can produce. Cool-climate wines tend to be lower in alcohol and higher in acidity than those made in hot climates, whose flavours may be less refined but more emphatic.

Many factors influence climate, of which temperature and rainfall are undoubtedly the most important (sunlight is, of course, vital for photosynthesis, but temperature is more critical, especially in cool climates). Mean temperatures (the average of daily maximum and minimum temperatures) in the final month of ripening need normally to fall between 60 and 70°F (15 and 21°C) to produce fine table wines (hotter climates can make good table wines, and extremely good fortified wines). Winters need to be sufficiently cool to allow the vine its revitalizing winter sleep. But if temperatures regularly fall below about 5°F (-15°C) in winter (see Washington State, page 290, and Russia,

page 260, for example), then the risk of even dormant vines fatally freezing may be unecomomically high and some winter protection may be needed.

The difference between winter and summer temperatures is important. In continental climates such as those of the Finger Lakes, Ontario, and eastern Germany, where this difference is great and where the climate is affected principally by a large landmass, temperatures fall so rapidly in autumn that there is a risk that grapes will simply not ripen fully. In maritime climates, moderated by nearby sea or ocean, there is a much less marked difference between summer and winter temperatures. In warmer maritime climates such as Margaret River in Western Australia, winters may not always be cold enough for the vines to fall dormant (the Chardonnay vine in particular values its hibernation), and organic viticulture may be difficult because pests and diseases are not always killed off in the winter. In cooler maritime climates such as Bordeaux in France and Long Island in New York, the weather during flowering, the crucial, quantity-determining vine event in early summer, can often be unsettled or cool, which can prejudice both how much fruit is set and how even is the setting. This may lead to a substantial reduction in the eventual crop, or one in which grapes even on the same bunch ripen inconveniently at different times.

Temperatures also vary throughout the day. Air temperature is usually highest in early afternoon and lowest at dawn. Some regions have a much more marked contrast between day and night temperatures than others and are said to have a large diurnal temperature variation.

The vine needs water as well as warmth. An average annual rainfall of at least 20in (500mm) is generally required (and 30in/750mm or more in hotter climates where evaporation is much greater) to promote sufficient photosynthesis to ripen grapes. Many wine regions have much less rainfall than this, but growers with access to irrigation water – generally from rivers, aquifers, dams, and wells – make up for the shortage. Some varieties such as La Mancha's Airén grown as bushvines are particularly tolerant of near-drought conditions.

If a vine runs short of water, it is said to suffer water stress and tends to produce smaller grapes with thicker skins. Although this tends to reduce total yields, it can up to a certain point result in wines with real concentration of flavour and colour. Severe drought, however, stops the ripening process completely and results in unbalanced wines.

Availability of irrigation water rather than any climatic aspect is what limits the spread of the vine in many regions with hot summers, notably in the southern hemisphere and California.

Left Water deliberately sprayed onto vulnerable young vines in Margaux when the temperature drops below 32°F (0°C) forms a protective layer of ice which saves the embryonic leaves and all-important buds from late spring frost damage.

In theory there is no upper limit on annual rainfall. Even flooded vineyards can recover quickly, especially in winter, and parts of Galicia in northern Spain and the Minho in northern Portugal, for example, can receive an average of more than 60in (1,500mm) of rain a year. It is the timing of rain that is critical. If there is very heavy rainfall just before harvest, especially after a period of relatively dry weather, grapes can swell quickly and sugar, acids, and such flavours as have been built up may rapidly become diluted (see page 34 for details of how winemakers can try to compensate). Prolonged wet weather during the second half of the growing season also tends to encourage the fungal diseases to which vines are prone, and rotten grapes can be the distasteful result (although modern vine farmers wage war with an array of sprays and vine training techniques, see page 28, and are much less likely than their predecessors to be forced into picking grapes before they are fully ripe).

Wind can play an important part too. Winds can be beneficial by cooling hot vineyards and drying out damp ones, but constant wind stress, as in the Salinas Valley of Monterey in California, can stop photosynthesis and delay the ripening process. Vine-growers in more exposed parts of the southern Rhône Valley have to install windbreaks to minimize the effects of the notorious mistral, and the hot, dry *zonda* of Argentina is feared rather than welcomed by wine producers.

Above Another even more common use for water in the vineyard: drip irrigation of young vines at Richmond Grove's Coonawarra estate in South Australia. Some growers deliberately apply water to only one side of the vine, controlling vigour without reducing yield or quality.

Factfiles

One new feature of this edition is the inclusion of "factfiles" that accompany many of the maps. Compare these very different sets of statistics for the hot, dry climate of Mendoza and the much cooler, wetter one of Bordeaux.

On the accompanying graphs, curves are shown for the mean, or average, maximum and minimum temperatures plotted for each month. The average rainfall for each month is also represented. The Mendoza data runs from July through to June, that for Bordeaux from January to December. Studies in Australia by Richard Smart and Peter Dry have shown that the temperature experienced throughout the vines' growing period can be simply but accurately described by comparing the mean temperature for what is normally the warmest month: July in the northern hemisphere and January in the southern.

The factfiles distil the patterns shown by these diagrams into a set of easily assimilable numbers (supplied by Smart and John Gwalter), but they necessarily rely on the location of weather stations with records over many years. In many cases weather stations, denoted by an inverted red triangle on the maps, are located on the edge of towns rather than in vineyards themselves, which means that because of urban development and different elevations, they may experience slightly different, often warmer, temperatures.

Latitude / Altitude (ft/m)
In general, the lower the latitude, or nearer the equator, the warmer the climate. But this can be offset by altitude, an important factor also determining likely diurnal temperature variability: the higher the vineyard, the greater the difference between day (maximum) and night (minimum) temperatures.

Mean July/January temperature (°F/C)
Average temperature in what is usually the warmest month, a reliable guide to the likely temperature throughout the growing season.

Annual rainfall (in/mm)
Average total precipitation indicating the likely availability of water.

Harvest month rainfall (in/mm)
Average rainfall during the month when most of the grapes are most likely to be picked (although this can vary according to variety and individual year); the higher the rainfall, the greater the risk of rot.

Bordeaux

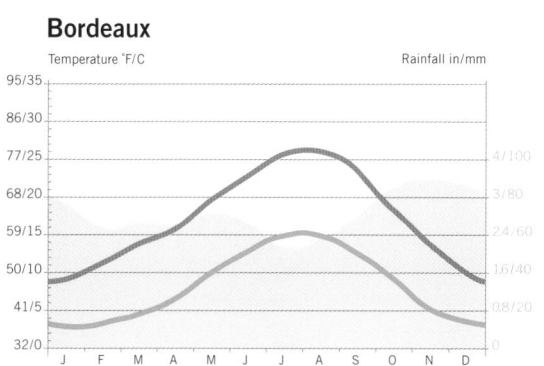

Bordeaux: Mérignac

Latitude / Altitude of WS **44.50° / 197ft (60m)**
Mean July temp at WS **68.5°F (20.3°C)**
Annual rainfall at WS **34in (850mm)**
Harvest month rainfall at WS **September: 2.8in (70mm)**
Chief viticultural hazards **Autumn rain, fungal diseases**
Principal grapes **Merlot, Cabernet Sauvignon, Cabernet Franc, Sémillon, Sauvignon Blanc, Muscadelle**

Mendoza

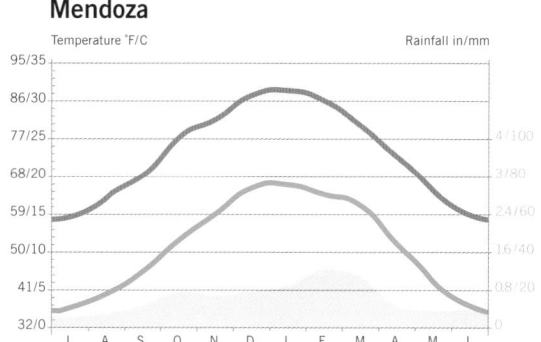

Argentina: Mendoza

Latitude / Altitude of WS **32.5° / 2,493ft (760m)**
Mean January temp at WS **75°F (23.9°C)**
Annual rainfall at WS **8in (200mm)**
Harvest month rainfall at WS **March 1.2in (30mm)**
Chief viticultural hazard **Summer hail**
Principal grapes **Bonarda, Malbec, Criolla Grande, Cereza, Cabernet Sauvignon, Barbera, Sangiovese**

Principal viticultural hazards
These are generalizations and may include climate-related challenges such as spring frost or autumn rain as well as endemic pests or vine diseases. See glossary for explanations.

Principal grapes
By no means exhaustive list of the varieties most commonly grown for wine in the region.

Terroir

There is no precise translation for the French word terroir. Terrain comes nearest, but has a less specific, less emotive connotation. Perhaps this is why many Anglo-Saxons long mistrusted it as a Gallic fancy: a conveniently mystical way of asserting the superiority of French soil and landscape and the unknowable peculiarities that give French wines special qualities.

Yet there is no mystery about terroir. Everyone – or at least every place – has one. Your garden and mine have terroirs; probably several. The front and back of a house almost certainly offer different growing conditions for plants. Growing environment is all that terroir means.

At its most restrictive the word means soil. By extension, and in common use, it means much more. It embraces the dirt itself, the subsoil and rocks beneath it, its physical properties and how they relate to the local climate, the macroclimate of the region, to determine both the mesoclimate of a particular vineyard and the microclimate of a particular vine (although this professional distinction is ignored by many who persist in using the word microclimate for the climate of a vineyard rather than of a vine). This includes for example how quickly a patch of land drains, whether it reflects sunlight or absorbs the heat, its elevation, its degree of slope, its orientation to the sun, and whether it is close to a cooling forest or warming lake or river.

Thus if the foot of a slope is frost-prone, it will have a different terroir to the hillside down which the cold air drains, even if the soil is the same (which is why, for instance, vines are not planted in the Willamette Valley in Oregon at altitudes below 200ft/60m). In general, the higher the altitude, the cooler the average temperature, especially at night (which explains why viticulture is possible at all as close to the equator as Zacatecas in Mexico or Salta and Mendoza in Argentina), but some hillside vineyards in northern California can be warmer than the valley floor because they lie above the fog line.

Above Coonawarra was the first Australian wine region to claim its own terroir, largely thanks to its famous and much fought over terra rossa. The key to the efficacy of this highly prized soil profile is the layer of well-drained limestone below the ruddy clay-loam. Terra rossa is also found in Spain's La Mancha and in North Africa.

Left Like most steep-sided valleys planted with vines, the port country in northern Portugal's Douro region offers some of the more obvious illustrations of how terroir can vary even within very short distances – particularly in terms of how long a plot of land is exposed to sunshine.

Similarly, an east slope that catches the morning sun may have identical soil to a west slope that warms up later and holds the evening rays, but its terroir is different and the wine it produces will be subtly different too – or even, in the case of the meandering Mosel in Germany at the northern limit of vine cultivation, the precise orientation of a slope can determine whether great wine or no wine can be produced from it.

The single most important aspect of terroir, however, given that vines have been planted somewhere with summers that are warm and dry enough for them to stand a chance of ripening, is the extent to which water and nutrients are available. If a vine is planted on fertile soils with a high water table such as some of the least favoured sites on the floor of the Napa Valley in California or the Wairau Valley in Marlborough, New Zealand, vines will have almost constant access to water and may indeed be waterlogged for part of the growing season. The vine's natural instinct will be to become "vigorous", growing shoots and leaves at such a rate that there is danger they will shade any fruit. Over-vigorous vines produce unripe grapes and wines that actually taste leafy and green.

If, on the other hand, a vine is planted in very infertile soil with access to barely any water, such as in many of the traditional vineyards of southern Spain, southern Italy, and northern Africa, photosynthesis virtually stops for a significant part of the summer. The vine suffers such water stress it "shuts down". The only reason sugars build up in the grapes is from the gradual evaporation of water from the berries. No interesting flavour compounds are formed, tannins don't ripen and the result can be extremely unbalanced wines that are high in alcohol but have harsh, unripe tannins and dangerously unstable colours.

There are all sorts of viticultural tricks that can compensate for these natural disadvantages (canopy management and controlled irrigation

are respectively the most obvious for the extreme environments described above) and the result can be some extremely good wine. But what sort of terroir naturally produces great wine?

Not surprisingly, it is the French who have studied this in greatest depth. Gérard Seguin of Bordeaux, whose soil profile is reproduced opposite, has shown that the very best soils are not particularly fertile ("medium potential", soil scientists call them) and drain quickly and deeply, drawing the roots down to great depths to find a stable water supply. Drainage, rather than precise chemical composition, seems to be the key to the perfect soil for great wine. Taking Bordeaux as the model, the best wines come from both the well-drained gravels of the Médoc and the clays of Pomerol, provided the latter have enough organic matter to allow water to move freely. In both these cases, water is available to the plant most of the time, but in no great quantity. In Burgundy, the vineyards that have over time proved to produce the finest wines tend to be those in the middle of the famous Côte d'Or where the combination of marl, silt, and limestone that has ended up there (see page 57) seems most propitious for water supply and therefore wine quality.

It should be said, however, that superior terroirs have a way of perpetuating themselves that is not entirely natural. The owner of Grand Cru land can afford to maintain it to perfection with drainage ditches, the precise amount and quality of fertilizer and ideal cultivation techniques, while such cosseting is uneconomic for a less glorified plot. Terroirs depend on man and his money for their expression, as witness the dip in Château Margaux's performance between 1966 and 1978 when the owner could no longer afford to maintain his first-growth in the style it merited.

An extension of this aspect of terroir is the view held by some organic winegrowers that the term should also apply to all the flora and fauna of the land, visible or microscopic. Some even hold that because terroir is inevitably changed by chemical fertilizers, they should be outlawed for any producers who wish to use such terroir classifications as France's AC and Italy's DOC system. And you could also argue that centuries of monoculture and such wholesome practices as ploughing and planting cover crops have almost certainly altered the land that was originally classified. But the interesting thing is just how much different, even adjacent, plots of land can vary in their effect on the resultant wine.

The special qualities of terra rossa soil in Australia's Coonawarra and the distinctive taste of Cabernet grown in Martha's Vineyard in the Napa Valley were always too obvious to ignore, but in general this phenomenon was ignored, even derided, by the majority of vine-growers outside Europe. But by the end of the 20th century the exciting if often practically inconvenient fact of terroir (causing grapes to ripen at different times within the same vineyard, for example) was acknowledged by enlightened growers in virtually every wine region.

Of all the elements that go to make up a grape growing environment, or terroir, the easiest to manipulate is soil. The result is that soil mapping has become an exact and exacting science. Many of the thousands who plant new vineyards each year now use sophisticated images (see page 28) to decide which plot of land to buy, how to modify various parts of it, and exactly which variety to plant where.

More and more wines made in the New World are now labelled not just with their region of origin but with the name of a vineyard – partly from increased awareness of the different potentials of each vineyard, and also perhaps from increased competition. It is now obvious that AN Other Chardonnay, however beautifully dressed and painfully expounded on its back label, has to draw credibility – and, more important, character – from more than just varietal flavour and nicely judged oak maturation.

St-Julien soil profile

The Médoc can claim to be the source of more fine wine than anywhere else in the world. This cross-section of a vineyard in St-Julien shows what makes the terroir here so special. While the climate in the Médoc has no claim to be unique, the soils and all-important subsoils are. The Médoc is basically a series of well-drained gravel mounds. Below them are these remarkably numerous and varied layers of different deposits, swept down the swollen River Garonne and Gironde Estuary in various phases of Ice Age floods. So long as the water table is deep enough, the roots will determinedly burrow through these layers for several feet in search of water and nutrients, as shown here in this example of a mature, 20 year-old vine.

Gravel and sand make the ground permeable and allow the rain to drain to a certain extent, but not entirely. The vine is thus fed a steady but meagre supply of water (except for periods of severe drought) throughout the growing season.

Below the topsoil, the soil that is cultivated and sometimes fertilized, is a layer of sand too compacted by years of work by man, horse, and machinery to offer the roots any nourishment or water. The roots penetrate this in search of more nutrients and water retained by the next layer of relatively recently deposited clays and gravels which has encouraged the development of rootlets. Below here is just-permeable hardpan which, along with the next layer of compact sand which has nothing to offer, the dogged, thirsty vine has managed to penetrate before sprouting more rootlets in the layer of rich clay beneath. Within the unpromising layer of hard, dry, compact sand below this, the vine has sought out small deposits, or lenses, of damp, nutritious clay and established rootlets there, as it has in the layer of clayey gravel below. The roots of this mature vine have even managed to burrow through the bottom layer of compact sand to establish rootlets in the clay bed immediately above the water table.

In areas with a much higher water table than this (there are some even in the Médoc and lots elsewhere) the root system would be much shallower and simpler, giving the vine much readier access to water and, of possible but unproven significance, a much more limited range of soil types and nutrients, such as nitrogen, phosphorus, and potassium.

For more information on terroir, and in particular the soils and subsoils of different wine regions, see James E Wilson's book *Terroir*.

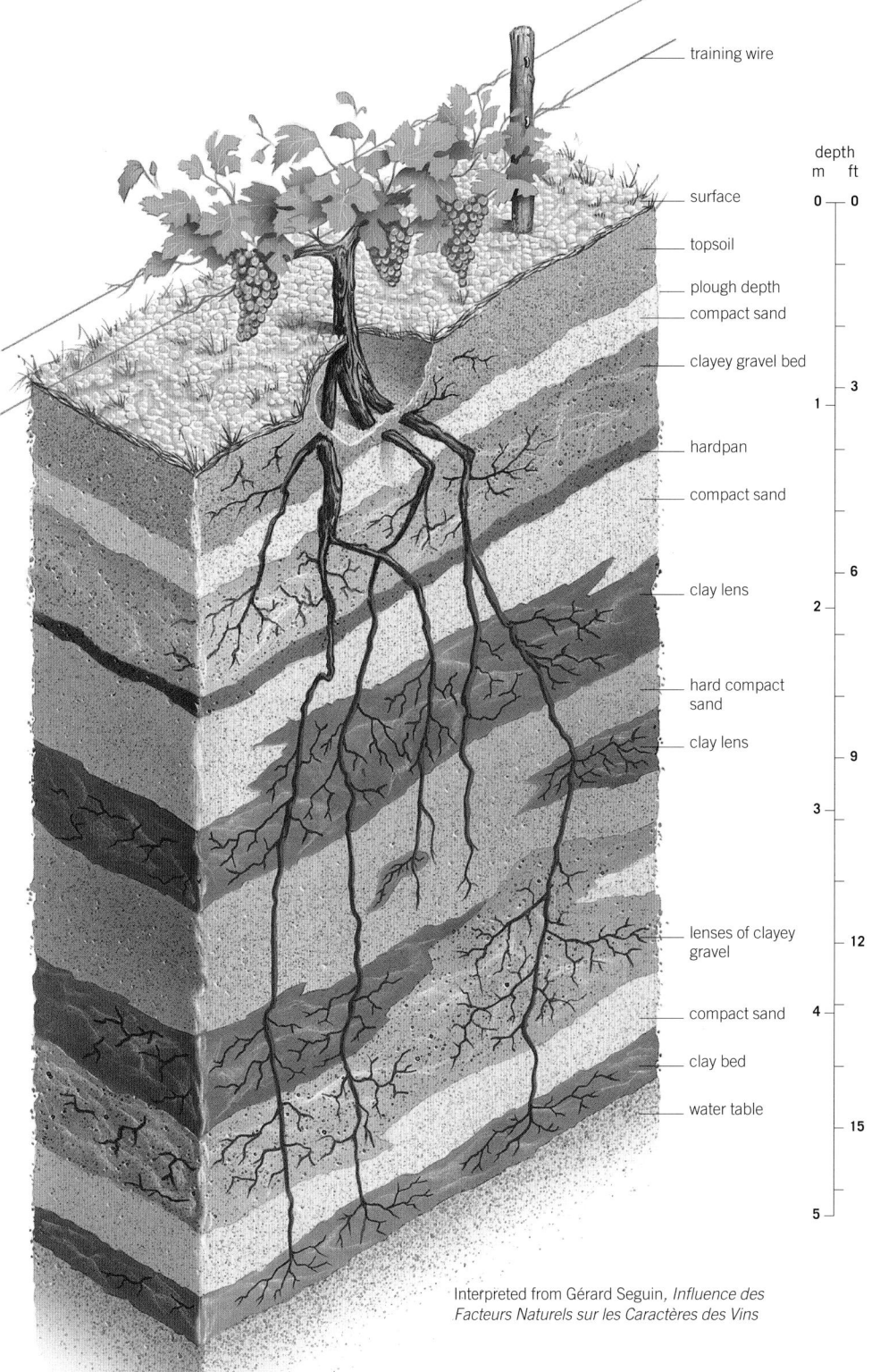

training wire

depth
m   ft

surface   0 — 0

topsoil

plough depth

compact sand

clayey gravel bed

1   3

hardpan

compact sand

6

clay lens

2

hard compact
sand

clay lens

9

3

lenses of clayey
gravel   12

compact sand   4

clay bed

water table

15

5

Interpreted from Gérard Seguin, *Influence des Facteurs Naturels sur les Caractères des Vins*

International Grapes

If geography determines the nuances of how a wine tastes, the raw material is the grape variety or varieties that go into the wine. Since the mid-20th century varieties have played an increasingly important role in the language of wine. Today far fewer wine drinkers know the name Chablis, for instance, than know the name of the grape from which wines in this northern French appellation are made: Chardonnay.

A passing acquaintance with the nine "international varieties" described on these pages would provide a good start to anyone's wine education. The most obvious characteristics outlined in italics below each grape name could be more or less guaranteed in any "varietally labelled" bottle – which includes the great majority of wine produced outside Europe and an increasing proportion of European, even French, wine.

But to progress in terms of wine knowledge, to get to grips with most of the good and great wines of Europe and to understand the subtleties of wines made elsewhere, you need to satisfy some geographical curiosity. A book like this can help to explain more than any other why Hermitage tastes different from the same grape, Syrah, grown 30 miles (48km) upstream on the differently angled slopes of Côte Rôtie.

Wine consumers have been so (understandably) grateful for the simplicity of varietal language that the last decade of the 20th century saw frenzied planting of the best-known grape varieties wherever in the world they would grow. Chardonnay fever took hold of growers

Brush What remains attached to the stem when grapes are destemmed at the winery, or knocked off the bunch during mechanical harvesting.

Pulp (or flesh) This is wine's main ingredient by volume, containing grape sugars, acids, and, mainly, water. The flesh of almost all wine grapes is this grey colour.

Pip (or seed) The number, size, and shape of pips is different for different grape varieties. All pips release bitter tannins if crushed.

Skin The most important ingredient in red wines, containing a high concentration of tannins, colouring matter, and compounds which determine the eventual wine's flavour.

Stem (or stalk) As grapes reach full physiological ripeness, stems turn from green and fleshy to brown and woody. Stems can make a wine taste tart and astringent.

Above Cross-section of a Pinot Noir grape towards the end of the ripening process.

just as consumers turned perversely from white to red wine. Tens of thousands of acres of young Chardonnay, Merlot, Cabernet Sauvignon, and Syrah/Shiraz have been the result.

But consumers, and growers, have also begun to feel the pull of another current, one summed up by the phrase ABC ("Anything But Chardonnay/Cabernet"). Indigenous grapes that have demonstrated over the years that they are particularly well-adapted locally are being re-evaluated. The grape varieties detailed on pages 26 and 27 are some of the more obvious beneficiaries.

Cabernet Sauvignon
Blackcurrant, cedar, high tannin

Synonymous with serious red wine capable of ageing into subtle splendour. For this reason Cabernet Sauvignon is also the best-travelled red wine variety, but since it is a relatively late-ripener it is viable only in warmish climates. It will not necessarily ripen fully every year even in its homeland the Médoc/Graves. But when it does ripen, the colour, flavour, and tannins packed into the thick skins of its tiny, dark blue berries can be remarkable. With careful winemaking and barrel ageing it can produce some of the longest-living and most intriguing reds of all. In Bordeaux and increasingly elsewhere it is blended with Merlot and Cabernet Franc, although it can make delicious unblended wine if grown somewhere as warm as Chile or the northern coastal districts of California, its second home.

Chardonnay
Broad, inoffensive – unless over-oaked

The white burgundy grape, but so much more versatile than Pinot Noir. Chardonnay can be grown and ripened without difficulty almost everywhere except at the extremes of the wine world (its early budding can put it at risk of spring frost damage). It has become the world's most popular white wine grape, perhaps because (unlike Riesling, for example) it does not have a particularly strong flavour of its own. But it routinely takes on whatever character the winemaker desires by submitting happily to the champagne process; to cool fermentation and fruit preservation to make something like Chablis; or to the fashionable recipe of malolactic fermentation, lees stirring, and barrel maturation (that can result in a certain sameness); and even to sweet wine production.

Merlot
Plump and plummy

Cabernet Sauvignon's traditional slightly paler, fleshier blending partner, especially in Bordeaux where its earlier ripening makes Merlot so much easier to grow that it is the most planted grape there. Wherever it is planted it is easier to ripen than Cabernet Sauvignon in cooler vintages and more alcoholic in warmer ones. Its bigger berries and thinner skins mean generally less tannic, more opulent wines that can be enjoyed sooner. Merlot also has an independent existence as a varietal, particularly in the US where it is regarded as easier to drink than Cabernet, and in northeast Italy where it is easier to ripen. It reaches its apogee in Pomerol where it can result in voluptuous, velvety essences. It is common in Chile where it has been confused with the old Bordeaux variety Carmenère.

Pinot Noir
Cherry, raspberry, violets, game, mid-ruby hue

This is the most elusive grape. It is relatively early ripening and extremely sensitive to terroir. Planted somewhere hot Pinot Noir will ripen too fast and fail to develop any of the many fascinating flavour compounds its relatively thin skins can harbour. Its perfect place on earth is the Côte d'Or in Burgundy where, if the clones, vine-growing, and winemaking techniques are right, it can convey intricate differences of terroir like no other variety. So haunting are great red burgundy's charms that growers everywhere try to emulate them, but so far only New Zealand, Oregon, and cooler corners of California have had much luck. It is rarely blended for still wine, but with Chardonnay and its cousin Pinot Meunier it is part of the standard recipe for champagne and other top-quality sparkling wine.

Riesling
Aromatic, delicate, racy, expressive

Riesling is to white wine what Cabernet Sauvignon is to red: it can make entirely different wines in different places and can age magnificently. Mispronounced (it's "Reessling"), underrated, and underpriced for most of the late 20th century, Riesling was long confused with other, lesser grapes which incorporated the word in their name, such as Welschriesling/Laski Rizling. The wine tends to be powerfully scented, reflecting minerals, flowers, lime, and honey depending on its provenance and sweetness (it makes great botrytized wines in its homeland Germany). With age it can take on kerosene-like compounds. Riesling is still the noblest grape of Germany and Alsace and is increasingly admired in Australia, despite the fact that its wines are unfashionably low in alcohol and devoid of oak.

Syrah/Shiraz
Black pepper, dark chocolate, notable colour and tannin

This grape has taken on a new lease of life as growers experiment with it in the relatively narrow bands of climate that will ripen it but not too fast. The northern Rhône Valley is its home, where it most famously makes great, dark, long-lived Hermitage and Côte Rôtie (where it was traditionally perfumed with a little Viognier). Syrah is now planted all over southern France where it is commonly used in blends. It tastes quite different in Australia where, called Shiraz, it is the country's most planted red grape, making dense, potent wines in places as warm as Barossa, though it can still have a hint of black pepper in the cooler reaches of Victoria. Today growers all over the world are experimenting with this easy-to-love grape, whose wines, however ripe, always have a savoury kick at the end.

Sauvignon Blanc
Grass, green fruits, razor-sharp, rarely oaked

Piercingly aromatic, extremely refreshing and, unlike most of the grapes on this page, best drunk relatively young. Sauvignon Blanc's original home in France is the Loire, particularly in and around Sancerre and Pouilly-Fumé, where it can vary considerably according to vintage. Grown in too warm a climate it can lose its characteristic aroma and acidity and can be too heavy in much of California and Australia. Once the vine's tendency to excessive vigour was tamed by canopy management, it has done particularly well in New Zealand, notably in Marlborough, as well as cooler parts of South Africa where it is sometimes blended with Chardonnay. In Bordeaux it is traditionally blended with Sémillon for both dry whites (often oaked, a style known as Fumé Blanc in the New World) and sweet.

Gewürztraminer
Lychees, roses, heady, high alcohol, deep-coloured

Gewürztraminer is a devil to spell – and often loses its Umlaut – but a dream to recognize. Its distinctive aroma, so strong that it earned the grape the prefix *gewürz*, or "spiced", in German, can easily be tiring, especially if combined with high residual sugar in the wine. But the best examples of Gewurztraminer from Alsace, where it is most revered, have an undertow of body and nerve, as well as a savoury finish, which stops them from cloying. Sufficient acidity is the key. Some fine examples have also emerged from New Zealand, cooler parts of Australia, Chile, British Columbia, and Oregon. This is the Musqué (ie perfumed), red-skinned mutation of Traminer, first noted in the northern Alto Adige near Tramin (Terlano) 1,000 years ago, and probably the Jura's Savagnin.

Sémillon
Figs, citrus, full-bodied, rich

Sémillon is included here on the strength of the exceptional quality of the sweet wine produced from it, particularly in Sauternes and Barsac where it is traditionally blended 4:1 with Sauvignon Blanc, together with a little Muscadelle. Its relatively thin skins make Sémillon (Semillon outside France) highly susceptible to the botrytis mould that can in the right conditions concentrate the grapes miraculously. It is the most planted white grape in Bordeaux where it is also responsible for some fine, oaked dry wines, especially in Graves. Australia's Hunter Valley also has a special affinity with it, making long-lived, complex, mineral-scented dry wines from early picked grapes. It can also do well in Washington State, and has been widely planted in South America and South Africa.

Regional Grapes

The grape varieties featured here and on the previous page are some of the best-known varieties of the European *vinifera* species of the *Vitis* genus, which also includes American and Asian vine species, and Virginia creeper.

In parts of the US, wine is made from American vines, but species such as *labrusca* have a particularly strong "foxy" flavour (characteristic of Concord grape jelly) which non-locals find off-putting. American and Asian vines can be extremely useful for breeding new varieties for particular conditions, however. Hundreds of hybrids have been bred by crossing them with European vinifera varieties, notably so that they will ripen in regions with short growing seasons.

Because many (though by no means all) hybrids produce inferior wine they are scorned, and in Europe outlawed. Many European vine breeders have concentrated on crossing various vinifera varieties to respond to a need or environment. Müller-Thurgau was an early crossing developed specifically to ripen in sites where Riesling wouldn't, for example.

Growers need to decide more than which variety and rootstock to plant. The life of a vine is usually about 30 years (although in fashion-conscious regions the variety is sometimes changed by simply lopping off the plant above ground and grafting on a new, more desirable variety). Just as important can be the choice of clone(s) of the favoured variety. Nurserymen have long observed, selected, and propagated particular plants with special characteristics: high yield, good resistance, early ripening, and so on. Today a grower can choose either a single or, usually better, several clones of whichever variety is to be planted.

Not all vines come with labels attached of course. The science of vine identification by observation of precise variations in grape and leaf shape, colour, and so on, is known as ampelography. It has revealed various fascinating relationships between varieties, but none quite so radical as the recent discoveries enabled by DNA analysis. This exact science has shown that Cabernet Franc and Sauvignon Blanc are the parents of Cabernet Sauvignon, and that Chardonnay, Aligoté, the Beaujolais grape Gamay, the Muscadet grape Melon de Bourgogne, Auxerrois, and a dozen others are all the progeny of Pinot Noir and the obscure but historic grape, Gouais Blanc. Further revelations are expected.

Analyzing grape juice

A portable spectrometer (right) analyzes the sugar content of a drop of grape juice in the vineyard. During the ripening process the levels of acidity (mainly tartaric and malic acids) fall while the fermentable sugars (mainly fructose and glucose) rise. As harvest approaches vine-growers constantly monitor the build-up of grape sugars, as well as the weather forecasts, in order to decide when to pick.

With dark-skinned grapes in particular many winemakers nowadays prefer to wait for a state known as "physiological ripeness". At this point the skins start to shrivel slightly, the stalks turn from green to brown and the grape is ripe enough to be pulled easily off the stalk, even if spectrometer analysis suggested a sufficient sugar level was reached some days before.

Measurements of sugar content

Specific gravity	1.060	1.065	1.070	1.075	1.080	1.085	1.090	1.095	1.100	1.105	1.110	1.115	1.120	1.125
°Oechsle	60	65	70	75	80	85	90	95	100	105	110	115	120	125
Baumé	8.2	8.8	9.4	10.1	10.7	11.3	11.9	12.5	13.1	13.7	14.3	14.9	15.5	16.0
Brix	14.7	15.8	17.0	18.1	19.3	20.4	21.5	22.5	23.7	24.8	25.8	26.9	28.0	29.0
% Potential alcohol V/V	7.5	8.1	8.8	9.4	10.0	10.6	11.3	11.9	12.5	13.1	13.8	14.4	15.0	15.6

Constituents of grape juice

Water	70–85%
Sugars	12–27%
Acids, total	0.3–1.5%
Tannins	0.0–0.2%
Nitrogen	0.01–0.2%

Cabernet Franc
Leafily aromatic

The less intense, softer progenitor of Cabernet Sauvignon. Because it ripens earlier, it is widely planted in the Loire and on the cooler, damper soils of St-Emilion, where it is often blended with Merlot. In the Médoc/Graves it is planted as an insurance against Cabernet Sauvignon's failure to ripen. Much more resistant to cold winters than Merlot, it can make appetizing wines in New Zealand, Long Island, and Washington. In northeast Italy it can taste positively grassy, and reaches its silky apogee in Chinon, Bourgueil, Saumur-Champigny, and Anjou-Villages.

Nebbiolo
Tar, roses, violets, orange with black tints

Piemonte's answer to Pinot Noir. In Barolo and Barbaresco it responds to every nuance of aspect and elevation. It will ripen only on the most favoured of sites. When fully ripe it is exceptionally high in tannins, acids, and pigments, but long cask and bottle ageing can result in hauntingly seductive wines. Nebbiolo makes a wide range of other, usually lesser, wines in northwest Italy (in Valtellina and Gattinara for example), but like Pinot Noir it has shown a reluctance to travel. Some Americans and Australians keep trying to prove otherwise.

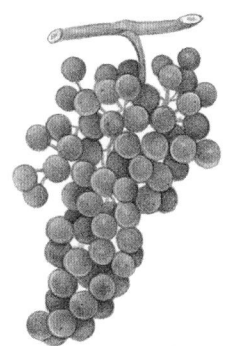

Tempranillo
Tobacco leaves, spice, leather

Spain's most famous grape. As Tinto Fino or Tinto del País it provides the backbone of Ribera del Duero's lively, deep-flavoured reds. In Rioja it is blended with Garnacha. In Catalunya it is known as Ull de Llebre, in Valdepeñas Cencibel. In Navarra it is often blended with Bordeaux grapes. As Tinta Roriz it has long been used for port and is increasingly respected as a table wine grape in Portugal, where in the Alentejo it is known as Aragonês. Its early budding makes it vulnerable to spring frosts; its thin skins to rot, but it is increasingly valued internationally for fine wine.

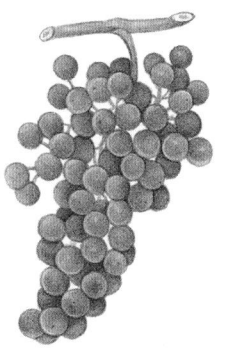

Touriga Nacional
Tannic, fireworks, occasionally porty

Portugal's greatest treasure, although just one of a wide range of distinctive and interesting grapes grown in the Douro Valley to make port, such as the unrelated Touriga Francesa, Tinta Barroca, and Tinto Cão. It is increasingly bottled as a varietal wine throughout Portugal, and is an increasingly important ingredient in Dão. It is also likely to be planted much more widely throughout the wine world for it is by no means short of class and personality. Touriga Nacional is always extremely high in tannin, alcohol, and colour, not least because it is naturally unproductive.

Grenache Noir
Pale, sweet, ripe, useful for rosé

Grenache is widely planted round the Mediterranean and is the most planted grape of the southern Rhône, where it is often blended with Mourvèdre, Syrah, and Cinsault. It is also widely grown in Roussillon where, with Grenache Blanc and Grenache Gris, its high alcohol levels are useful for the region's famous Vins Doux Naturels (see page 142). As Garnacha it is the most planted red grape in Spain. As Cannonau in Corsica, and as Grenache in California or Australia, it is not revered unless the vines are very old.

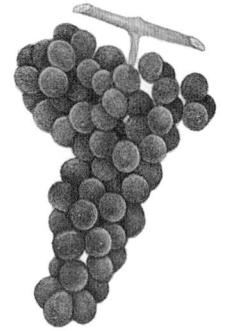

Mourvèdre
Animal, blackberries, alcoholic, tannic

This is a grape that needs considerable sunshine to ripen and is by far the most important grape in Bandol, Provence's most noble wine, although it is prone to oxidation. Throughout southern France it adds flesh to Grenache and Syrah blends in particular. In Spain, as Monastrell, it is the country's second most planted red grape and associated more with heft than quality. It was known, and somewhat overlooked, as Mataro in both California and Australia until being renamed Mourvèdre and enjoying a new lease of life with glamorously Gallic associations.

Zinfandel
Warm berry flavours, alcohol, sweetness

Zinfandel was regarded as California's own grape for a century, until it was established that, as Primitivo, it was known on the heel of Italy at least as early as the 18th century. The vine ripens unevenly but some berries build almost unparalleled sugars so that Zin, as it is known in the US, can be as strong as 16 or even 17% alcohol. It is more commonly grown to produce enormous crops of much less intense wine in California's Central Valley, much of it stripped of colour, flavoured with aromatic Muscat or Riesling, and sold as (pale pink) White Zinfandel.

Sangiovese
Savoury, lively, variable: from prunes to farmyard

Italy's most planted grape, in its many forms, and particularly common in Central Italy, most gloriously in Chianti Classico, Brunello di Montalcino, and Vino Nobile di Montepulciano. The least noble clones, overproduced, make light, tart red wine – oceans of it in Emilia-Romagna. The traditional Chianti recipe diminished it with the white grape Trebbiano as well as the local Canaiolo and a bit of deep Colorino. Today Tuscany's many ambitious producers coax maximum colour and flavour from it. It is increasingly planted elsewhere.

Malbec
Spicy and rich in Argentina, gamey in Cahors

Malbec is a conundrum. It has long been a blending grape all over southwest France, including Bordeaux, but the dominant grape only in Cahors where, known as Auxerrois or Cot, it has typically made rustic, sometimes rather animal wines suitable for only medium-term ageing. Emigrés took it to Argentina, where in Mendoza it was so clearly at home that it became the country's most planted red grape and makes gloriously velvety, concentrated, lively wines, high in alcohol and extract. It thrives particularly in Mendoza's Lujan de Cuyo district.

Muscat Blanc
Grapey, relatively simple, often sweet

This is the finest sort of Muscat and has small berries (*petits grains* in French) which are round rather than oval like those of the less noble Muscat of Alexandria (Gordo Blanco or Lexia in Australia where it is grown for the table). As Moscato Bianco in Italy, the finer Muscat is responsible for Asti and many fine, light fizzes. It also makes great sweet wines in southern France and Greece. Spain's Moscatel is usually Muscat of Alexandria. Australia's strong, sweet, sticky Muscats are made from a dark-skinned version, Brown Muscat. Muscat Ottonel is different and lighter.

Viognier
Heady, full-bodied, hawthorn blossom, apricots

Fashionable, distinctive variety that has now travelled from its home in Condrieu, northern Rhône, to virtually all corners of the wine world. Unless fully ripe its distinctively seductive aroma does not develop, which means that most memorable examples are relatively alcoholic; the trick is to keep the acidity too. California has managed in numerous examples. Best drunk young, it is increasingly blended with the other Rhône white grapes: nervy but aromatic Roussanne and big, almondy Marsanne – especially in southern France.

Chenin Blanc
Extremely versatile; honey and damp straw

Chenin Blanc is the grape of the middle Loire, sandwiched between the Melon de Bourgogne of Muscadet and the Sauvignon Blanc of the Upper Loire. Much misunderstood, it makes very ordinary off-dry wine in both California and South Africa where it is widely planted, but in the Loire it can make nervy, age-worthy, characterful wines of all stages of sweetness. Botrytized Vouvray is one of the great, long-lived, sweet white wines of the world. Chenin Blanc also makes lightly honeyed, dry still wines and some characterful sparkling Saumur and Vouvray.

Pinot Gris
Full, golden, smoky, pungent

This increasingly fashionable grape has its power base in Alsace where, with Riesling, Gewurztraminer, and Muscat, it is regarded as a noble grape variety, responsible for some of the region's most powerful, if quite soft, wines. This pink-skinned mutation of Pinot Noir is a cousin of Chardonnay. In Italy it is known as Pinot Grigio and can now produce some equally characterful dry whites, even if the majority is still tart and vapid. Growers elsewhere dither between calling it Gris or Grigio without much significance for style. It is Oregon's white wine speciality.

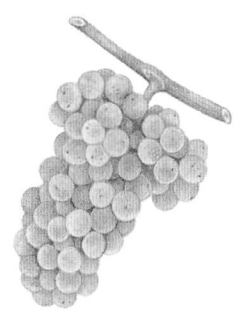

Pinot Blanc
Lively, light, Chardonnay-like

Lighter-skinned mutation of Pinot Noir which has often been confused with its cousin Chardonnay in the vineyard, especially in Italy where it is called Pinot Bianco. It is the everyday, inoffensive grape of Alsace, related to Auxerrois and sometimes called Clevner. It can make substantial wines, including wonderfully rich Trockenbeerenauslesen, in Austria as Weissburgunder. It is also popular in southern Germany for its full body. The grape is relatively low in acidity and flavour compounds so Pinot Blanc is generally drunk young.

In the Vineyard

We now know something about which grape variety to plant and the likely effect of weather and local environment on the vine. But how about choosing exactly where and how to plant vines? Vineyard site selection, while virtually unknown in the traditional wine regions of Europe where inheritance and appellation laws tend to dictate vineyard location, is becoming an increasingly important and exact science.

Whether in Spain or Australia (to choose two examples of countries whose wine map is currently most obviously under revision) a vineyard investor needs to know that a commercially viable quantity of healthy grapes is likely to be ripened on that site every year. Acting on a hunch is one possible tactic but close analysis of topography, climate, and soil data is safer.

Crude statistics on temperature, rainfall, and sunshine hours can help, but need careful interpretation. High average summer temperatures may look good on paper for instance, but photosynthesis effectively stops above a certain temperature (between about 85 and 95˚F, or 30 and 35˚C) depending on the location, so ripening could be adversely affected if there are too many very hot days. (Wind, excluded from many sets of meteorological statistics, can also stop photosynthesis by closing the stomata, the tiny openings on leaves and berries that regulate the process.)

In cooler areas, the critical aspect of temperature evaluation is whether grapes will ripen reliably. If average summer and autumn temperatures are relatively low for viticulture (such as those for England or Luxembourg), or if autumn usually arrives early with either predictable rains (as in Oregon) or a substantial drop in temperature (as in British Columbia), then relatively early ripening varieties may have to be planted. Chardonnay and Pinot Noir are fine for the Pacific Northwest but ripen too late for cooler northern Germany. Riesling will ripen in the Mosel (with the right terroir) but would be marginal for England and Luxembourg, where much earlier-ripening varieties such as Müller-Thurgau and Auxerrois are a safer choice.

The average summer rainfall and its likely timing would give a useful indication of the likelihood of fungal diseases such as those described on page 19. Monthly rainfall totals, with measurements of likely evaporation should give any would-be vigneron an idea of whether any irrigation is needed. If the site is in an area where supplementing natural rainfall is allowed, then comes the big question of whether there is a suitable source and quantity of water nearby. This is likely to be the most significant brake on vineyard expansion in both California and, especially, Australia where water is often unavailable or too saline.

Water may be needed for other purposes too. At the coolest limits of viticulture, the length of frost-free season and likelihood of spring frosts are crucial factors. In Ontario and the northeastern states of the US for example, the total number of frost-free days governs the length of the growing season and therefore which grape varieties are likely to ripen. In Chablis and the cool Casablanca Valley of Chile water is needed for sprinkler systems to protect young vines from frost by covering them with a layer of ice, but in Casablanca there is a distinct shortage of available water – frost having proved an unforeseen hazard.

The soil, or more likely soils, of any prospective vineyard site needs careful analysis. A series of soil samples taken at regular intervals, together with measurements of elevation and water availability, can be transformed into maps such as those on the left.

The fertility of the soil is a key ingredient in the likely quality of wine produced there. The soil should be neither too acid nor too alkaline and have a suitable degree of organic matter (the remains of other plants, animals, and insects) and minerals such as phosphorus, potassium, and nitrogen. Phosphorus is vital for photosynthesis. Too much potassium can result in wines dangerously high in pH and low in acidity. Too much nitrogen (a common ingredient in fertilizers) can result in excessively vigorous vines that put all their energy into growing leaves rather than ripening grapes. This is a vicious circle which leaves grapes dangerously shaded by an increasingly dark heavy canopy of leaves and shoots. The phenomenon is particularly common on very fertile soils, typically relatively young soils such as those in New Zealand and the floor of the Napa Valley. Vigour also varies with vine variety. Vigorous vines need special treatment, as outlined below.

But first a potential vine-grower must design the vineyard. The orientation of the rows, the ideal distance between the vines, how best to train them, the height of the posts (and, later, wires), and the number of buds to keep when pruning must all be taken into consideration. Whether to cultivate between the rows or leave grass or other cover crops to grow, and whether to ignore the sprawling shoots of summer or to trim them off are also important questions. The

Designing a vineyard

Sophisticated graphics such as these from the Australian Centre for Precision Agriculture can help identify which grape varieties and rootstocks should be planted where, which parts of the potential vineyard site are unsuitable for viticulture, and which may need chemical additions. (Lime may need to be added to very acid soils, for example.)

In this example of a digitized analysis of a New South Wales vineyard, soil samples were taken at regular intervals on a grid to plot both the depth and texture of the soil (eg subsoil clay) and the amount of readily available water. Elevation came from a local survey.

These aspects were then analyzed to identify specific zones with similar characteristics, as in the map on the right. These zones roughly correspond to a recommended grape variety that would be particularly suited to these "digitized terroirs" – although in practice varieties are usually planted in neater blocks.

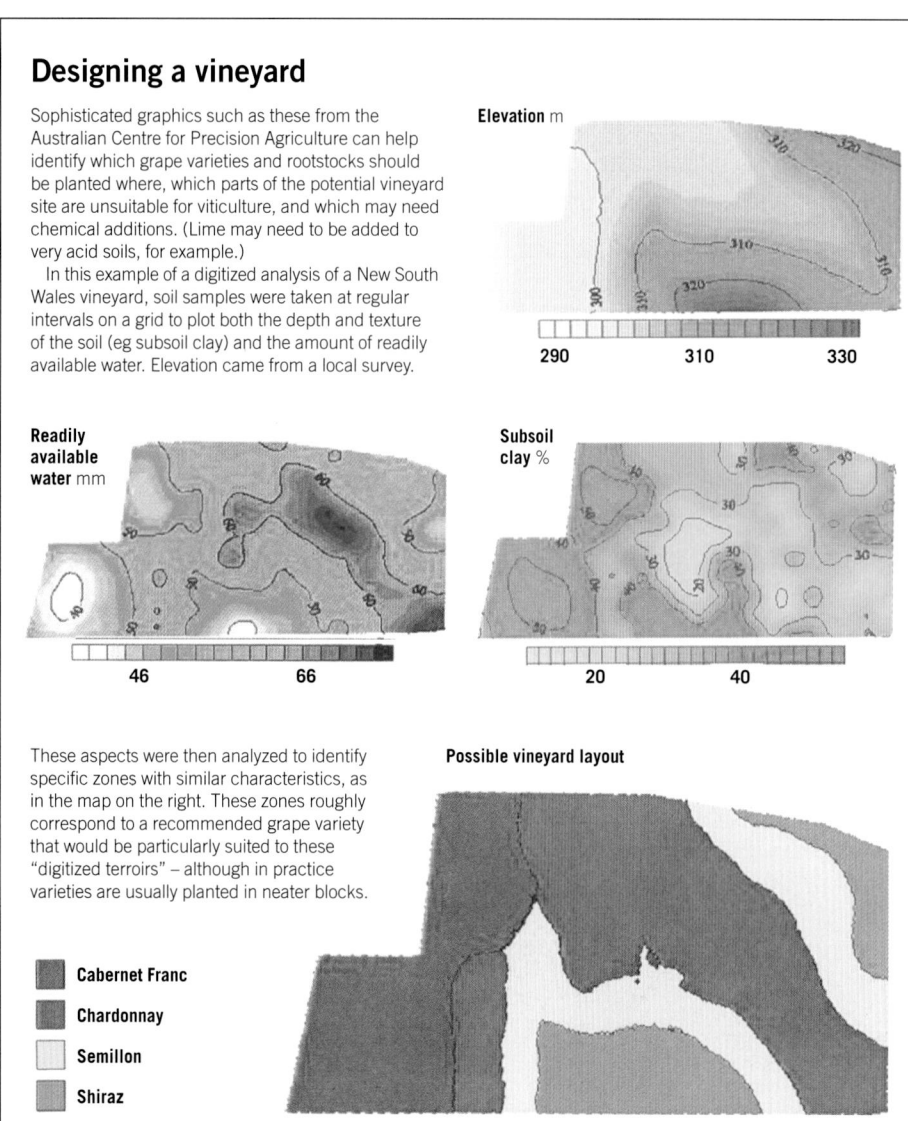

Elevation m

290   310   330

Readily available water mm

46   66

Subsoil clay %

20   40

Possible vineyard layout

- Cabernet Franc
- Chardonnay
- Semillon
- Shiraz

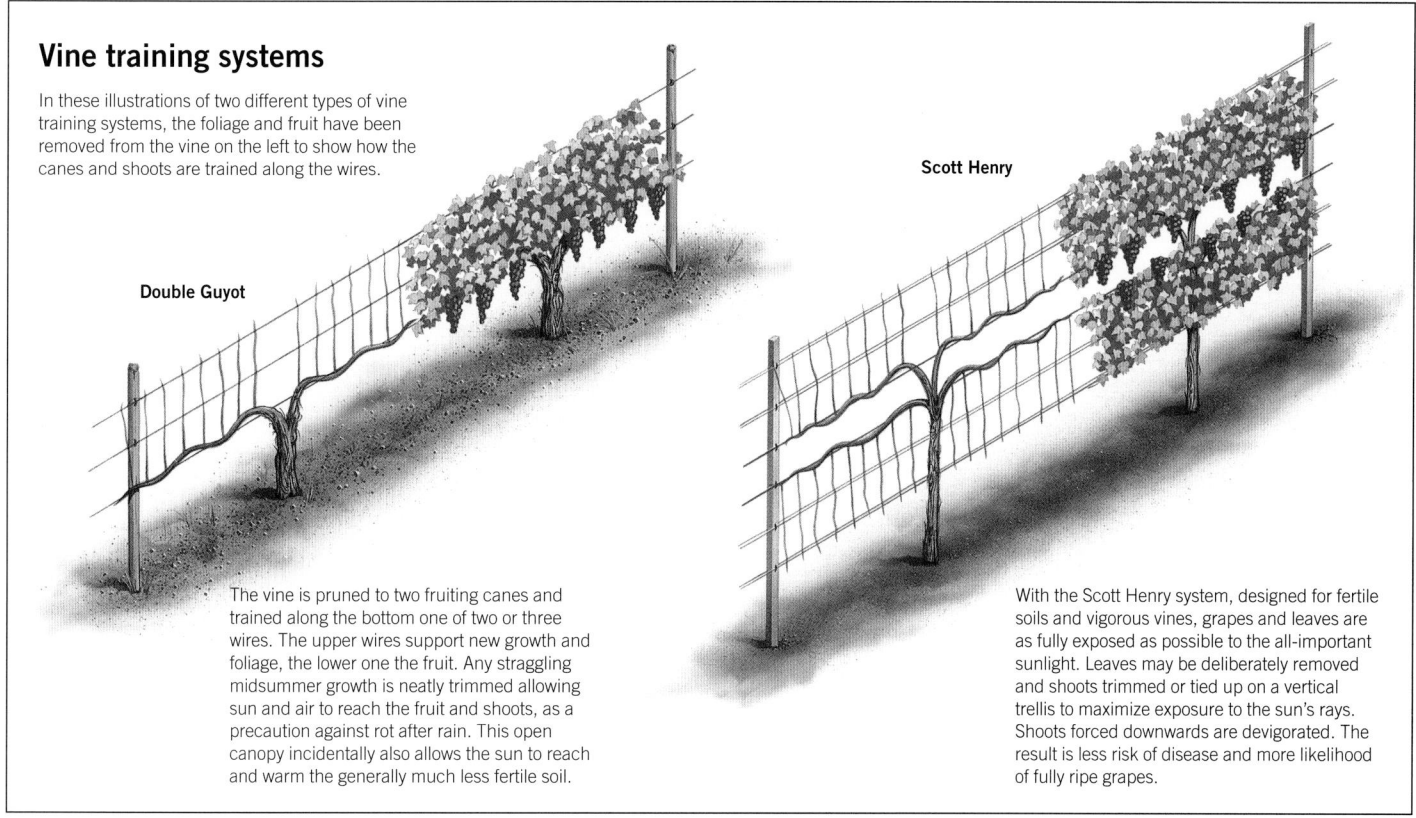

Vine training systems

In these illustrations of two different types of vine training systems, the foliage and fruit have been removed from the vine on the left to show how the canes and shoots are trained along the wires.

Double Guyot

Scott Henry

The vine is pruned to two fruiting canes and trained along the bottom one of two or three wires. The upper wires support new growth and foliage, the lower one the fruit. Any straggling midsummer growth is neatly trimmed allowing sun and air to reach the fruit and shoots, as a precaution against rot after rain. This open canopy incidentally also allows the sun to reach and warm the generally much less fertile soil.

With the Scott Henry system, designed for fertile soils and vigorous vines, grapes and leaves are as fully exposed as possible to the all-important sunlight. Leaves may be deliberately removed and shoots trimmed or tied up on a vertical trellis to maximize exposure to the sun's rays. Shoots forced downwards are devigorated. The result is less risk of disease and more likelihood of fully ripe grapes.

solutions to all these puzzles, which may not have been consciously thought about, have over centuries of experimentation in Europe resulted in the world's most precious vineyards and most universally admired wines.

Should the vine rows run north–south so as to allow the leaves the maximum chance to absorb sunshine? On a hillside site – more expensive to design and maintain – rows of vines are sometimes run along horizontal terraces built to follow contour lines so that tractors and people can easily move along them.

Then comes one of the most important decisions of all: how close to plant the vines, both between and within rows, and with it the sort of yields the vine-grower is aiming for (see page 84 for more on yields). In Mediterranean climates, where it is frequently too hot and dry, the answer is simple, and determined by the water supply: hence the widely spaced traditional bushes in low-latitude vineyards with a vine density of less than 1,000 vines per hectare. Yields per hectare are naturally low, curbed by the water supply.

Until recently, New World vineyards were typically planted in warm or hot regions, often on fertile virgin soil which threatened to oversupply the vine with nutrients. Growers left spaces as wide as 12ft (3.7m) for vineyard machinery between the rows, and often left 8ft (2.4m) between vines, a vine density of just over 1,000 vines per hectare. This economized on plants, posts, and wires – and the labour involved in installing them – and made cultivation and

mechanical harvesting easy. But all too often the price paid was excessive vigour, sprawling canopies burying their own fruit and most of the leaves needed for photosynthesis in deep shade. Not only do such grapes not ripen properly, resulting in wines that belie the climate with unattractively high acidity and unripe tannins, but the wood destined to carry the next year's crop does not ripen either. The embryo buds on the cane need exposure to the sun to make them fruitful. Too many layers of leaves thus start a vicious spiral of smaller crops and more foliage year by year. Liberal irrigation could result in economically viable yields per hectare, but each vine would be required somehow to ripen too heavy a charge of grapes.

This stereotype, now much modified (see below), contrasts markedly with the traditional vineyards of Bordeaux and Burgundy where yields per hectare are generally much lower, and yields per vine lower still. Here vines are planted as densely as 10,000 vines per hectare at intervals of 3ft (1m) along rows just 3ft (1m) apart (worked by *tracteurs-enjambeurs* that straddle the vines). Each vine is kept deliberately small, typically trained according to the single or double Guyot system (illustrated above). Planting and labour costs are much higher, but the grapes are given the maximum chance to ripen with beneficial effects on the quality of the wine.

Perhaps the greatest revolution in the world's vineyards in the last decade or two has been the application of so-called canopy management

techniques. Ingenious vine training systems have been devised to spread out and control the canopy of even the most vigorous vines. Several training systems deliberately divide the canopy into two, such as the Scott Henry system illustrated above and the lyre system shown on page 274. But the right training system depends on local conditions, particularly the fertility of the soil, and the way the vine variety grows. Riesling droops. The peculiar heart-shaped loop-training used on the Mosel, for example, (see page 222) has evolved to keep the grape bunches from trailing, while each independent plant (they are not wired together) benefits from all the sunlight available. Perhaps even more important on these steep slopes, it allows the poor mountaineering vineyard worker to move across the slope as well as up and down it.

Another important tool used today to modify wine quality and yield wherever possible is irrigation. By controlling the exact amount of water the vines receive and when it is administered, sometimes deliberately stressing the vines by withholding water, especially late in the season, growers can have a beneficial effect on both the quality and quantity of wine produced (so long as a massive rain- or hailstorm doesn't come along and ruin everything).

Vine-growing is, however, like all farming, utterly dependent on nature and local practicalities. Of all aspects of wine production it is at long last recognized as the single most important, and demanding, factor determining exactly how wine tastes.

The Winegrower's Year

For someone who grows grapes and makes wine, every act in vineyard and cellar is centred on the most important time of the year, the harvest and the winemaking weeks immediately after it. There is much variation between regions and producers, but the following is a rough outline of each month's key operations, the northern hemisphere being specified first, vineyard task above cellar work.

January / July

Pruning This chilly operation is usually done by hand in the middle of winter. The dry shoots, or *sarments* as the French call them, are increasingly popular for barbecues. Early budding vine varieties may be pruned deliberately late so as to delay budbreak and minimize frost risk.

Malolactic fermentation should be well under way in the cellar, either in tanks or barrels. Constant supervision and analysis is needed to check the progress of the lactic bacteria which encourage it and acid levels.

February / August

Pruning continues in the vineyard. The fully exposed wires, posts, and stakes are mended if necessary.

Topping up Wine contracts in cold weather so topping up reduces the risk of harmful oxidation by making sure that the "ullage" space between the barrel and the wine's surface is minimal. Bungs, usually plastic, must also be airtight. If the bung is kept at the top of the barrel rather than at an angle where it is kept fully moist, topping up has to be more frequent – perhaps once or twice a week.

March / September

Planting new vines is a spring operation. This usually means planting out grafted cuttings and nowadays increasingly installing vine guards to protect juicy young vines from predators such as rabbits, and effectively create a small greenhouse around them – provided they are strong enough to withstand the higher temperatures that result.

Bottling of wines that are designed to be drunk young. In smaller wineries this means booking a mobile bottler and ensuring all wines to be bottled are finished and stable.

July / January

Spraying against pests and disease gets into full swing. Rain and humid weather promote the fungal diseases that plague so many vines. Spraying techniques vary from one man with a tank on his back, to a machine such as the above, to aerial spraying by helicopter.

Bottling of fine wines in their second year before summer kicks in. The precise timing of bottling can vary according to the state of the wine, the efficiency of the bottle factory, and the cellar staff's sporting preoccupations.

August / February

Veraison Red wine grapes soften and turn from green to red. Increasingly growers also perform a summer or green harvest, whereby less ripe or excess bunches are removed. The aim is to concentrate the remaining sunshine and nutrients into fewer berries, making more concentrated wine. This can backfire if severe drought follows, giving dry berries and unbalanced wine.

In warm regions the winery must be prepared for vintage, which may even have already started in the hottest regions.

September / March

Harvesting is the most common and vital operation this month, although possibly even more important is deciding exactly when to pick (see pages 26 and 34). Pickers must be hired, organized, and in some cases fed and housed. Alternatively, picking machines and drivers must be ready.

In the winery this is the most exhausting period of the year when the truly dedicated may work around the clock. All the necessary winemaking equipment and additions such as yeast, sugar, acid, and so on, must be in place.

April / October

Desuckering Cutting off vine suckers neatens up the vine and concentrates energy into the young shoots that have emerged.

Racking, moving wine from one container to another with the aim of leaving potentially harmful sediment such as the lees of fermentation behind. This is usually done immediately after the alcoholic fermentation – a bit of aeration does no harm to most very young wine. A wine may be racked up to three or four times during its first year in barrel.

May / November

Spraying against frost (provided enough water is available) is the modern way of protecting the crop against catastrophe if the temperature falls below freezing point (see page 20 for how the young growth is protected by a coating of ice). Other methods of protecting the young buds include wind machines and small portable heaters. Temperature-operated alarms are needed in all cases.

Start to prepare and assemble wine orders so that they can be despatched before the heat of summer.

June / December

Shoot positioning is particularly important in damp climates where vines tend to be vigorous. Young shoots are tied onto wires so that the vine is in a good position to turn sunlight into a decent crop of good-quality grapes. A stable period of fine weather is needed while the vines flower (see page 18) to produce a large crop; unsettled weather may eliminate the need for a green harvest in August/February.

Fine wines may well be racked again over the next few weeks, certainly before the real heat of summer.

October / April

Even after the grapes have been picked, sunny weather can continue to build up carbohydrate reserves in the vine, helping it withstand winter and produce shoots in spring.

Punching down the cap of skins that have floated to the surface of the fermentation vat to keep it moist, aerate the wine, and encourage the extraction of colour and flavour from the skins. This has to be done every day and requires considerable force – those boots won't stay white for long. Various mechanical alternatives have been devised.

November / May

Vine leaves turn yellow, gold, and then, especially if the leaves are infected with a virus, a beautiful red. After the first frost they drop off. Any cover crops may be sown now.

Fining, or clarification, for serious red wines in their second year with whisked egg whites which attract tiny particles of solids remaining in the wine before falling to the bottom of the barrel. Other fining agents include special forms of clay and gelatin. First year wines may be transferred from fermentation vat to barrel about now.

December / June

In the vineyard cuttings may be taken for propagating young vines. The vines are now dormant and will withstand winter cold so long as the temperature does not fall below about -4°F (-20°C). Pruning may start.

Early tastings of the new wines begin. Some decisions may be taken about how different lots of wine will be used. Malolactic fermentation should be under way by now, whether in barrel or tank, encouraged by the introduction of special lactic bacteria and the warming of the cellar.

How Wine is Made

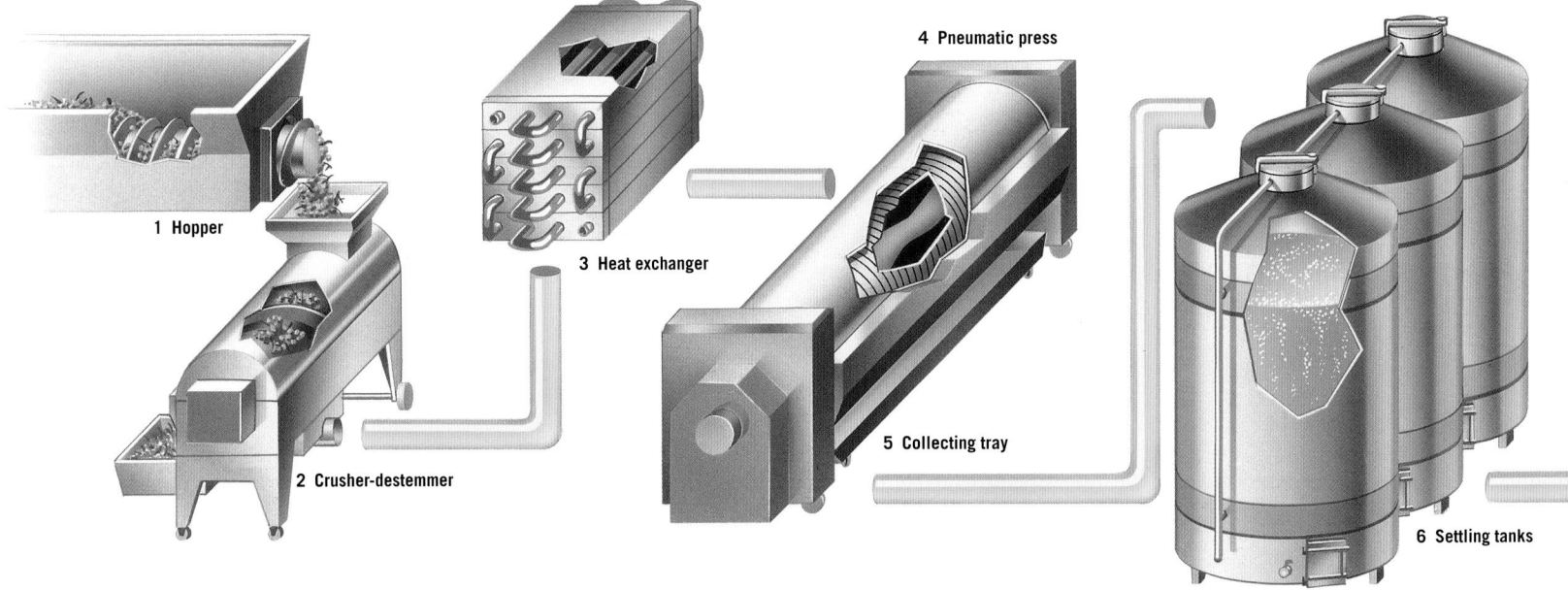

1 Hopper

2 Crusher-destemmer

3 Heat exchanger

4 Pneumatic press

5 Collecting tray

6 Settling tanks

How mass-produced white wine is made

In this example of an inexpensive white wine made
protectively in a well-equipped winery in a warm region,
the grapes will have been picked by machine. A truck
backs up to the winery and fills the hopper **1** with bunches
of grapes, and usually some "MOG" (material other than
grapes, such as leaves) as well. The screw feeds the
grapes into the crusher-destemmer **2**. Grapes are crushed
by rollers in the hopper. A rotating cylinder perforated with
holes big enough to allow grapes but not large, potentially
astringent stem fragments or leaves then destems the
grapes. The resulting mixture of grapes and pulp may well
then be pumped through a heat exchanger **3** to cool it
down. This slows down the oxidation process, helping to
prevent the loss of flavour and too early a start to the
fermentation. Sulphur dioxide is often added for the same
reason. The pulp is pumped into the pneumatic press **4**
and the rubber membrane is slowly inflated, pressing the
grape pulp against the perforated stainless steel cylinder
but keeping the pips whole so as not to release their bitter
oils. The juice is collected in the lower tray **5** from which it
is pumped to the stainless steel settling tanks enclosed in
cooling jackets **6**. Here the juice may be covered with a
blanket of inert gas such as carbon dioxide to prevent
oxidation. Special enzymes may be added to encourage

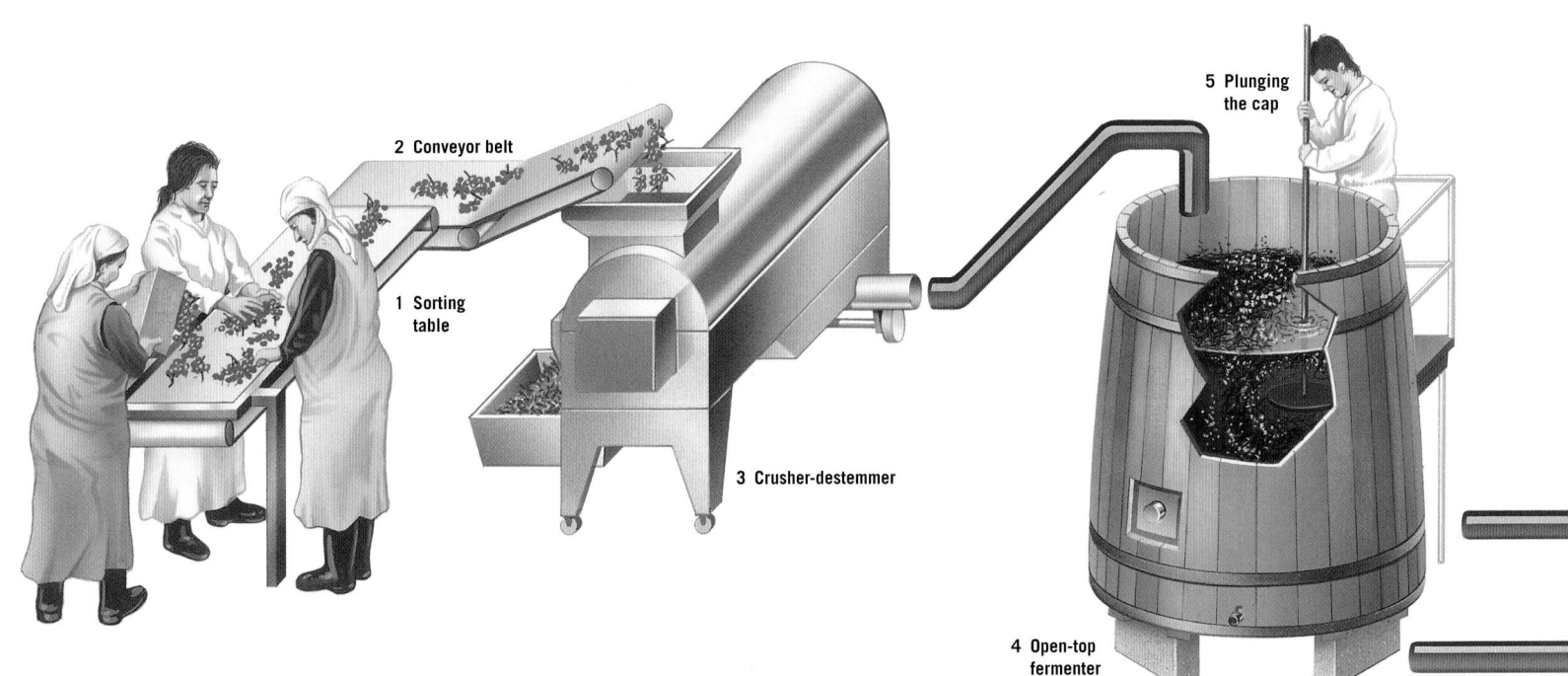

5 Plunging the cap

2 Conveyor belt

1 Sorting table

3 Crusher-destemmer

4 Open-top fermenter

How top-quality red wine is made

This diagram shows how a typical fine red wine is made in
the most traditional way possible. Hand-cut bunches of
grapes are gently transferred from small containers designed
to prevent the grapes being crushed in transit from vine to
winery onto a sorting table **1**. Any unripe, damaged or
mouldy grapes are cut out and any other matter removed
by hand. The conveyor belt **2** carries the bunches to the
crusher-destemmer **3** (see **2** above) where the stalks are
removed and most of the grape skins are crushed. The
settings can be adjusted according to how many stems
and whole grapes are required. For less tannic grapes
such as Pinot Noir some or all of the stems may be retained
at this stage to give the wine structure. The grape must,
including the all-important skins for colour, flavour, and
tannin, is then pumped into an open-top fermenter **4**, which
these days is often made of stainless steel, but traditionally
was made of oak, concrete or even slate. Here yeasts
naturally present in the atmosphere will slowly set in motion
the alcoholic fermentation. Some winemakers cool the must
before fermentation to give some extra skin contact time,
others heat the must immediately to encourage the
alcoholic fermentation. Sugar levels start to fall as the level
of alcohol rises and the carbon dioxide given off pushes up
the grape skins and pulp to form a cap, which protects the

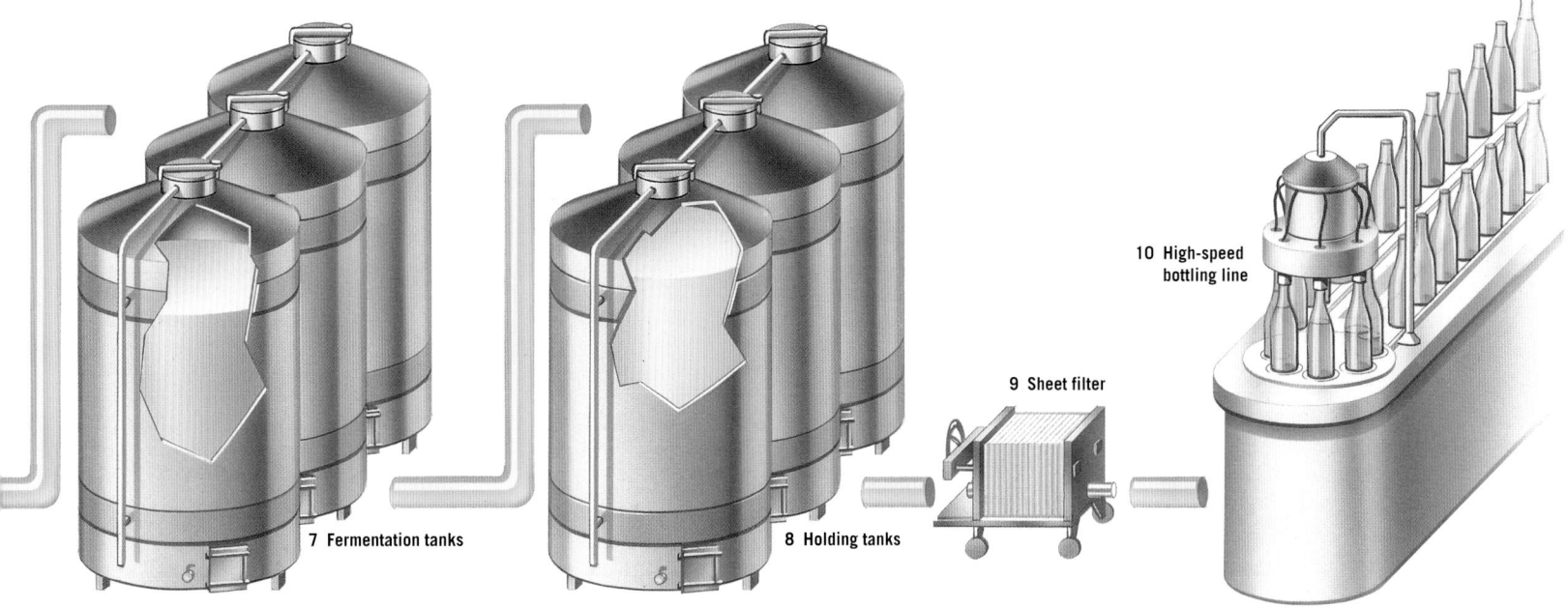

7 Fermentation tanks

8 Holding tanks

9 Sheet filter

10 High-speed bottling line

some of the suspended solids to settle out of the liquid after about 24 hours in the settling tanks. The now much cleaner grape juice is pumped into temperature-controlled stainless steel fermentation tanks **7**. The juice is inoculated with a strain of specially selected cultured yeast. The temperature is kept low for inexpensive white wines, usually between 54 and 63°F (12 and 17°C) to preserve fresh, fruity aromas. The higher the temperature, the faster

the fermentation and the sooner the fermentation tank can be used for another batch of grapes, however. The length of the fermentation can vary from a few days to a month, the carbon dioxide escaping through a valve not shown here. The wine is racked off the lees, becoming even cleaner, and put into holding tanks **8** protected from oxygen. The wine is then stored at a low temperature until required to fill an order so as to keep it as fresh as possible.

It may have to be blended and is then cold-stabilized, chilled to almost 32°F (0°C) to precipitate tartrate crystals, and probably fined. All commercial wines are then filtered to remove any potentially harmful bacteria. It may be pumped through a sheet filter **9**, or a membrane filter, to remove any particles held in suspension. The star-bright wine is then bottled by means of a high-speed bottling line **10** just before being shipped, keeping storage costs low.

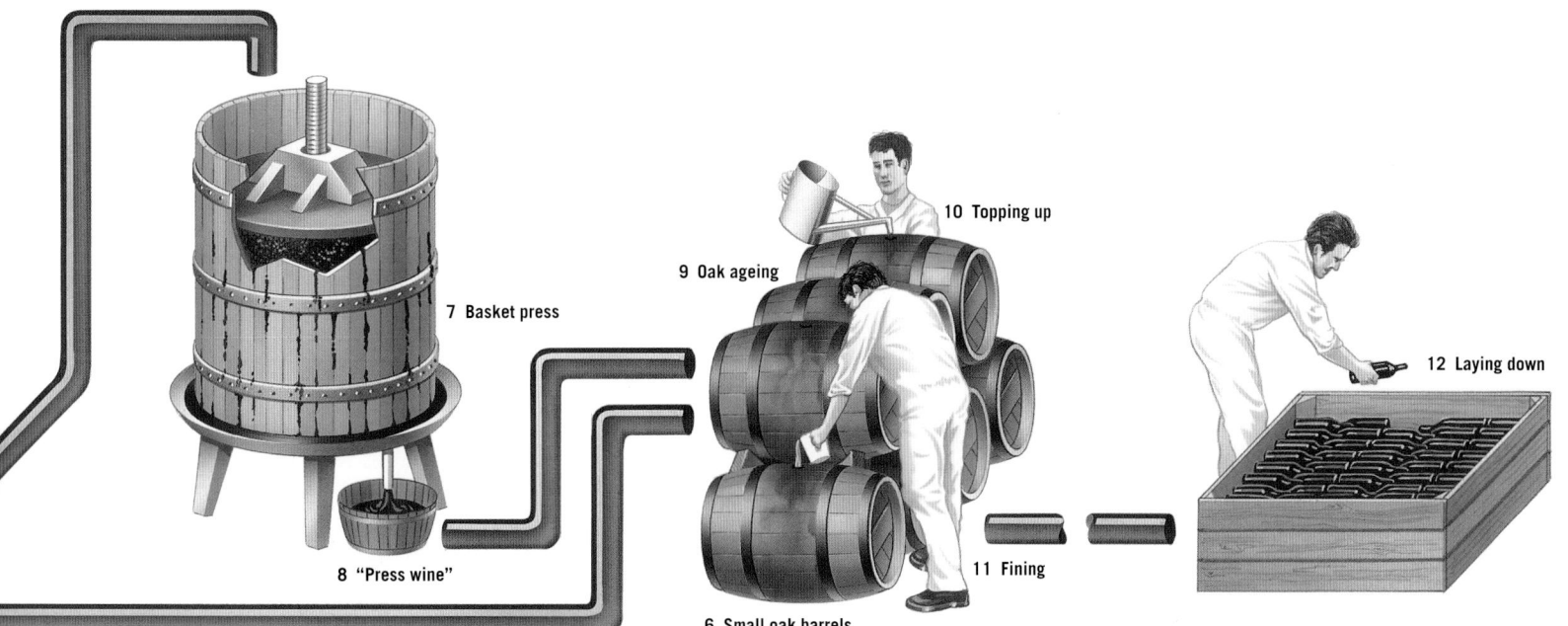

7 Basket press

8 "Press wine"

9 Oak ageing

10 Topping up

6 Small oak barrels

11 Fining

12 Laying down

must against oxidation. The cap is regularly plunged down **5** or broken up by pumping the must over it to prevent its drying out. After the alcoholic fermentation is over some winemakers allow an extended period of maceration to extract even more phenolics from the skins, while others transfer the wine into small oak barrels **6** before all the sugar has been fermented into alcohol. In either case, the second, malolactic fermentation takes place. The solids left

at the bottom of the fermentation vat are then transferred to a press, in this case a traditional basket press **7**, where the "press wine" is squeezed out and collected below **8**. This "press wine" is much more tannic and in cooler regions usually kept separate, in warmer ones blended immediately to add valuable structure. The wine is then aged in oak barrels **9** for up to 18 months. Evaporation means that these barrels will have to be topped up **10**, and the wine will

occasionally be "racked" off its sediment into a new barrel to aerate it and prevent the build-up of harmful compounds. The wine will also probably be fined **11**, clarified by adding a fining agent that attracts any suspended solids, and lightly filtered to ensure that it is microbiologically stable. Before bottling a final blend may be made. After careful bottling the wine is laid down in bins **12** and stored for bottle ageing, being labelled and capsuled just before despatch.

The Art of the Winemaker

If in the vineyard nature is ultimately in charge, man takes over in the winery, *chai, cantina, bodega* or *Keller*.

Winemaking basically consists of a series of decisions dictated by the grapes and their condition and by the style of wine the winemaker has set his or her heart on (occasionally these two aspects conflict). The diagrams on the previous pages show the steps involved in making two very different sorts of wine: a relatively inexpensive unoaked white and a high-quality, traditionally made, barrel-aged red wine.

Harvesting the grapes

The winemaker's first and possibly most important decision is when to pick. He should have been monitoring the sugar and acid levels in the grapes and their general health in the weeks leading up to the usual harvest date.

Decisions on harvest date need to be taken in conjunction with the weather forecast. If, for example, the grapes are not quite ripe enough for the wine he wants to make but rain is predicted, he will have to calculate whether to leave the grapes on the vine and then hope that there will be sufficient warm, dry weather afterwards for them to ripen fully. Some varieties are much more sensitive than others to the exact date of harvest. Syrah and Merlot, for example,

can easily lose quality – a certain liveliness in the wine – if kept too long on the vine, whereas Cabernet Sauvignon is much more tolerant of a few extra days. If they are already suffering from fungal disease, the rain will exacerbate this so the best, regretful decision may be to pick the grapes just slightly less ripe than ideal. White wine is much more forgiving of a few rotten grapes than red in which the colour is rapidly lost and the wine tainted by a mouldy taste.

The winemaker, in conjunction with whomever is in charge of labour, also has to decide at what time of day to pick. In hot climates grapes are generally picked either at night (easier by machine with big spotlights) or very early in the morning in order to deliver the grapes to the winery as cool as possible. In the old days grapes would be thrown into the back of trucks and sit in the sun, often squashed and increasingly oxidized, so that they arrived at the winery having lost a substantial proportion of their primary fruit flavour. Nowadays any winemaker with pretensions to quality will insist that grapes arrive as cool as possible in small stable units, typically little plastic, stackable boxes which keep the bunches whole (although whole bunches are an impossibility if the grapes are picked by machine since they operate by literally shaking the grapes off the vine).

Machines are used increasingly in the vineyard, not just for picking but for pruning and lifting wires and therefore the canopy during the growing season. But the greatest wines in the world are still picked by hand, no matter how expensive and elusive the pickers, because they can not only snip whole bunches off the vine but also make intelligent decisions about which fruit to pick.

Preparing grapes for fermentation

Once the grapes arrive at the winery they may be deliberately chilled – some hot climate wineries even have cold rooms where grapes may be kept for hours or days until a fermentation vat is available. Even more likely at a top-quality winery in any climate is that the grapes are subject to further selection. One of the most obvious winery innovations in the 1990s was the installation of sorting tables, typically a slow-moving belt, onto which grapes are tipped to be minutely examined before arriving at the crusher or crusher-destemmer. (Mechanical crushing releases the all-important juice and replaces the human foot – still used for some high-quality port.)

Most white grapes are destemmed before going to be pressed because stems can be astringent and would spoil a light, aromatic wine. For some full-bodied white wines, however, and most top-quality sparkling and sweet white wine, the winemaker may choose to put whole bunches into the press. This is because

the stems can act as useful conduits of the juice – and in any case only the first portion of it, the so-called "free-run" juice, may be used.

For white wines a winemaker must decide whether he is going to make it protected as much as possible from oxygen, preserving every ounce of fresh fruit flavour (preventing oxidation and stunning yeasts right at the start with added sulphur dioxide, complete destemming, low temperatures throughout, and so on) or to adopt deliberately oxidative techniques, exposing the grapes to oxygen and aiming for secondary, more complex flavours from the fruit rather than the pure, unadorned hit of primary aromas. Riesling, Sauvignon Blanc, and other aromatic grape varieties tend to be vinified protectively while most top-quality white burgundy is made oxidatively. Oxidative handling may include a period of deliberate "skin contact", not as exciting as it sounds but a few hours either in the press before it is turned on or in a special holding tank during which further flavour will be leeched into the must from the skins. If the skins are allowed contact with juice for white wine for too long, however, they impart far too much astringence – which is why grapes for white wine, unlike red wine grapes whose skins are needed for colour and tannin, are pressed before fermentation.

The harsher the pressing process, the tougher the resultant white wine, however. Over the years presses have been designed with increasing ingenuity to squeeze out the juice as gently as possible, without breaking the pips or extracting astringence from the grape skins. Pneumatic presses, which operate by filling a horizontal cylinder with grapes and an inflatable rubber bag, are now most common, some of them being completely insulated from oxygen for protective juice handling. Winemakers are increasingly careful to separate different portions of what flows from the press, the earlier juice being the finer and least astringent.

Now the winemaker has his white juice, he may well decide to clarify it, to clear it of all the little grapey fragments still in suspension in it, particularly for protectively made wines. Centrifuges were once used for this but they can easily spin out too many solids. More usual today is to let solids settle to the bottom of a holding tank and then run off the clear juice into the fermentation tank. It is important at this stage that fermentation still hasn't started, which is why low temperatures and sulphur additions are important.

Red wine grapes meanwhile are usually crushed and destemmed, although a few handfuls of stems may be deliberately thrown into the fermentation vat to increase the tannin level, and some particularly traditional winemakers, especially in Burgundy, like to ferment whole bunches. This works only in climates with growing seasons long enough to ripen the stems fully as well as the fruit, otherwise the stems would make the wine taste horribly tough (most Australian red grapes, for example, would have unacceptably low acid levels if not picked until the stems were ripe).

Left Dr Bailey Carrodus of Yarra Yering in the Australian state of Victoria punches down a cap of Pinot Noir grape skins in an effort to extract maximum colour and flavour without allowing the cap to dry out. The French call this exhausting process *pigeage*.

Above Winemakers regularly use hydrometers to check the specific gravity and therefore sugar and alcohol levels of fermenting must in the winery.

(A very particular exception to the destemming rule for reds is a fermentation technique called carbonic maceration, characteristic of Beaujolais, some Côtes du Rhône, and naturally tough Carignan in the Languedoc-Roussillon, where the aim is to produce fruity wines without much tannin. Here whole bunches are put into a sealed fermentation vat, the bottom layer of grapes is crushed by the weight of grapes above and starts fermenting naturally, giving off carbon dioxide. The whole vat becomes saturated in carbon dioxide under whose influence the whole grapes in the upper part of the vat undergo a special sort of internal fermentation whose products have a characteristic soft, almost rubbery smell.)

The fermentation process

Now, and only now, can the winemaker consider conventional fermentation, the miraculous transformation of sweet grape juice into much drier, more complex-flavoured wine. If yeast is put into contact with grape sugars, it converts them into alcohol, heat, and carbon dioxide. The riper the grapes, the stronger the wine they are capable of making. Fermentation vats naturally warm up as the process gets under way, so in warmer climates they may well need cooling jackets to keep the "must", as the pulpy mixture between grape juice and wine is known, below the temperature at which precious flavour compounds may be boiled off. The gas that is generated can make a winery a heady place at harvest time where the smell is an intoxicating mixture of carbon dioxide, grapes, and alcohol – especially if the fermentation vats are open-topped, as for some traditional red wines.

White wines are made in sealed vats so as to protect the must from damaging oxidation and avoid any browning. A vat full of red must has its own protection, the thick "cap" of skins that float on the surface – which is why open-topped red wine fermenting vats are even a possibility.

Right An alternative to Bailey Carrodus's punching down method of keeping the cap submerged: a header board fitted snugly into a fermentation tank.

Many aspects of winemaking have been subjected to detailed scrutiny and improvement over the last few decades, but yeast still presents some mystery and controversy. We will doubtless learn more about the exact effect of different species of yeast on different sorts of must. But for now the winemaker's initial choice is whether or not to use specially selected and prepared yeast, so-called cultured yeast, as opposed to relying on the strains of yeast that are naturally in the atmosphere, called wild or ambient yeast.

In new wine regions there is no choice; wine yeasts need time to build up a population and the only ambient strains available are more likely to be harmful than benevolent. With a small but increasing number of exceptions, most New World wines are therefore made by adding specially cultured yeast to the must, which may, if it has been chilled, need warming before fermentation can be persuaded to start. (Once one vat has started, the addition of fermenting must from it will kick-start a second, but some winemakers believe in a deliberate few days' maceration of red grapes before fermentation as they warm up.)

Cultured yeast, typically selections from yeast naturally present in other, more established wine regions, behaves predictably. Particularly powerful yeast can be chosen for high-alcohol wines, those which encourage coagulation of sediment may be useful for sparkling wines. Traditionalists, however, prefer to leave everything to the ambient yeast in the belief that, while their behaviour may not be quite as predictable, they add more interest to the wine's flavour (and are certainly less likely to result in the homogenization of wine that we have witnessed over the past decade or so).

The winemaker's nightmare is a "stuck fermentation", when fermentation stops before all the sugar has been converted into alcohol and the winemaker is left with a dangerously vulnerable mixture, which can all too easily fall prey to oxidation and nasty bacteria. The level of alcohol in a finished wine is an effective weapon against many bacteria.

The exact pace – time and temperature – of a red wine fermentation is critical to the sort of wine that results. The warmer the fermentation (up to the dangerous flavour-evaporation limit), the more flavour and colour will be extracted. Long, cool fermentations tend to result in light, fruity wines, but if a fermentation is too short and hot, the wine will also be low in body and flavour. The temperature rises as fermentation gets under way but is generally between about 72 and 86°F (22 and 30°C) even for full-bodied red wines, and cooler for aromatic white wines.

To extract tannins, flavour, and colour from the grape skins, the cap and the must need to be encouraged to commune with each other. This is generally done by either pumping the must over the cap or by physically punching it down into the liquid, although there is an increasing array of mechanical ways of submerging

Above Lees of fermentation of white wines in barrel may be stirred with all sorts of instruments. *Bâtonnage*, as it is known in French, wards off the smelly odours associated with reduction as well as making the wine paler and gentler by buffering the amount of extraction from the oak.

the cap. The science of this process, and any post-fermentation maceration designed to extract and soften tannins, has become extremely exact, and a key factor in how much more palatable many young red wines are today. Vinomatics, sealed fermentation vats that mechanically churn the skins and the must, may be useful for paler varieties such as Pinot Noir, or less ripe vintages.

Improving on nature

It is at the fermentation stage, red or white, that the winemaker decides whether or not to add acid or sugar. To many wine drinkers this may sound like cheating. Many winemakers, on the other hand, maintain it is essential to achieving a well-balanced wine. French winemakers, apart from those in the far south, have been adding sugar to fermentation vats to increase the alcohol content (not sweetness) of the final wine for 200 years ever since this process, now called chaptalization, was proposed by the agriculture minister Jean-Antoine Chaptal.

The AC laws incorporate detailed limits to the amount of sugar that may be added, generally the equivalent of no more than an additional 2% of alcohol, although even more can be added in cool climates such as England and Luxembourg. In practice, thanks to warmer summers and anti-rot strategies, growers have recently been able to pick grapes riper and riper – less and less additional sugar is needed. It is rare to taste an obviously chaptalized wine, but some Beaujolais made in the 1990s seemed oddly alcoholic for its charge of flavour and extract.

In less ripe vintages in cooler climates, winemakers may also decide to exclude a portion of juice from the red wine fermentation vat so as to improve the all-important ratio of flavour-filled

skins to juice (a practice called *saignée* in France). This traditional practice is increasingly being replaced by more mechanical manipulation. During the 1990s, for example, equipment for concentrating the must and removing a certain amount of water became much more common in Bordeaux's top estates (these machines would be too expensive for basic wine). Used only to rescue inferior vintages, they cannot add harmony to an unbalanced must and may eventually go the frequently mothballed way of winery centrifuges. Their counterpart for sweet white wine production is cryoextraction, a technique whereby water is frozen out of white grapes that have failed to reach an ideal sugar level, a sort of artificial Icewine production.

Winemakers in warm climates on the other hand routinely add ("adjust" is the word they prefer) acidity to musts from grapes that have ripened to sugar levels that are only dreamt of in Beaujolais but whose natural acidity has dropped to an unappetizingly low level on the way. Tartaric acid, grapes' natural acid, is the acid of choice, but in some hot regions such as parts of California's Central Valley and Australia's Riverland, grapes can ripen so fast that there is just not enough body to support the necessary added acidity and the wines taste tart and hollow.

There is another, arguably more natural, way in which winemakers can accentuate the acidity of a wine. Alcoholic fermentation of any wine may be followed by a second sort of fermentation, the "malolactic", in which the grapes' harsher malic (appley) acids are converted into softer, lactic (milky) acids. Understanding and mastery of this second fermentation, by warming the wine and possibly adding special lactic bacteria, was the key factor in the mid-20th century in making red wines drinkable younger by lowering the overall acidity and adding some extra flavours as well.

But those extra flavours may not be necessary in an aromatic, probably protectively made white wine, and if the malolactic fermentation is deliberately suppressed (by filtering or fining the necessary yeasts and proteins out of the wine), the effect is to make the wine taste crisper. In practice malolactic fermentation is encouraged in most good quality Chardonnay to add texture and flavour, and in warmer climates it is compensated for by added acidity.

Malolactic fermentation is invariably good for red wine and in recent years a fashion has emerged for conducting it not in large tanks as was the rule, but in individual barrels. This needs much more labour and supervision so is warranted only for high-quality wines, but the result is a perceptibly smoother, more seductive texture when the wine is released – a characteristic that some wine tasters have come to associate with quality. Increasingly, therefore, winemakers are running red wine out of the fermentation vat just before the end of fermentation into barrels where the wine will finish its alcoholic and then its malolactic fermentation.

Oak and clarification

Full alcoholic fermentation in barrel, on the other hand, has become *de rigueur* for any full-bodied white wine with aspirations to a high price. Indeed by the end of the 20th century oak had become The Other Ingredient in wine, such a high proportion of good to great wine both red and white being matured if not fermented in small oak barrels. Indeed practically all serious red wine undergoes the smoothing process of maturation in oak, and all but the most aromatic, lean, and lively whites are both fermented and matured in small (225l) oak barrels.

Oak has been used for storing wine for centuries because it is both watertight and easy to work. Its more recently appreciated attributes, however, are that oak flavours have a natural affinity for those of wine, adding more complex compounds, and, perhaps more importantly, its physical properties are unparalleled for gently clarifying and stabilizing wine while deepening the colour of a red and softening the texture of any well-made wine.

Fermenting a white wine in barrel, provided it has not been stripped of all of its solids and left defenceless against the assault of all the tannins and pigments in the oak, makes the wine much smoother in texture yet deeper in flavour. Another fashionable white winemaking ploy to add more flavour, whether the wine was fermented in barrel or tank, is regularly to stir the lees of the fermentations so as to impart some of their often rather milky flavour to the wine.

White wines may be barrel-aged for as few as three months to take up just a little oak flavour (the older the barrel, the less flavour and oak tannins). Serious red wines are usually matured for longer, up to 18 months or possibly more, in older or larger oak casks. To separate the new wine from the larger particles of the lees, the

Above Just some of the many options for giving a wine oak flavour without the expense of a barrel: oak chips in different sizes, of different provenances, and different levels of toast. Perforated containers holding these, or even whole staves, are commonly inserted in fermentation tanks.

Above Traditional German *Fuder* or upright oak casks at von Buhl in Pfalz. Oak flavour is the last thing required of these old containers, treasured instead for their permeability to oxygen and their ability to stabilize a wine in the slowest, most natural way.

Above Giovanni Manetti gives some scale to Fontodi's *botte*, the traditional wine vat of Chianti Classico and much of Italy. Like *Fuder*, these casks, generally made of Slavonian oak, are lined with tartrates from the wines previously made in them and impart no oak flavour.

Above Armand Rousseau's cellar in Gevrey-Chambertin is lined with traditional Burgundian barrels, known as *pièces*. The proportion of new barrels used for each appellation is extremely carefully judged. No self-respecting Burgundy producer wants his or her wine to taste of oak.

so-called gross lees, the wine is generally racked (see page 31) into a clean barrel quite soon after fermentation and several times thereafter, generally more often in Europe than the New World. This aerates the wine, softening its tannins and minimizing the risk of nasty odours building up in the barrel. Some wine is always lost by evaporation, however, and the barrels need regular topping up, another process that beneficially exposes the wine to a little air and softens its rough edges. The winemaker's job during barrel maturation is regularly to taste the contents of each barrel, and to judge not just when the wine should be racked but also when it is ready for bottling.

However a wine is matured after fermentation it will have to be bottled. Before a wine is subjected to this often rather brutal process, the winemaker has to be sure it is stable: that it does not contain any potentially dangerous bacteria and will not do anything inconvenient if subjected to extreme cold. It must be clarified, for the wine is still likely to be cloudier than the consumer has come to expect. Inexpensive white wines are often therefore put into a tank and fiercely chilled so that any tartaric acid that remains in solution is precipitated before bottling and won't reappear as (completely harmless but worrying-looking) crystals in the bottle later on. The great majority of wine of either colour is filtered in some way so as to remove any danger of refermentation, and fined (see page 31) so that any remaining particles drop out of the wine. Filtration is a heavily political subject among wine folk, however. Overdone, it can remove flavour and the potential for ageing; underdone, it can leave the wine prey to harmful bacteria and refermentation, particularly if the bottle gets too warm.

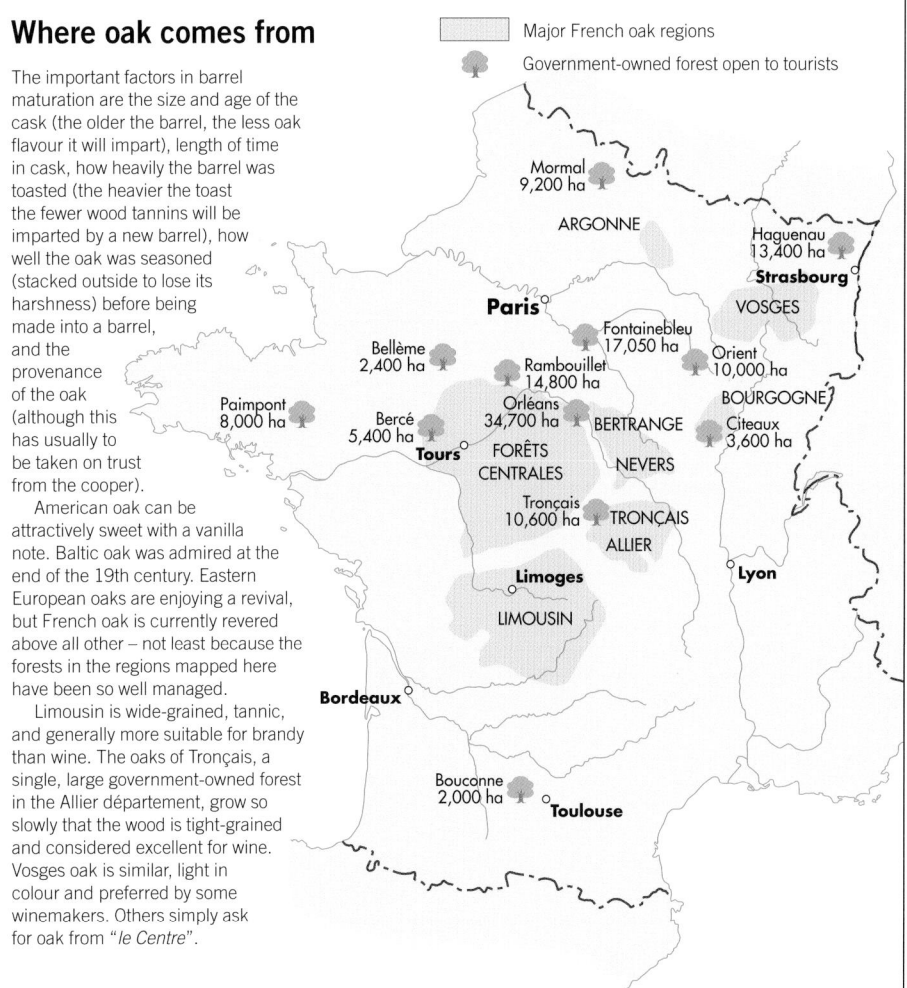

Where oak comes from

☐ Major French oak regions

🌳 Government-owned forest open to tourists

The important factors in barrel maturation are the size and age of the cask (the older the barrel, the less oak flavour it will impart), length of time in cask, how heavily the barrel was toasted (the heavier the toast the fewer wood tannins will be imparted by a new barrel), how well the oak was seasoned (stacked outside to lose its harshness) before being made into a barrel, and the provenance of the oak (although this has usually to be taken on trust from the cooper).

American oak can be attractively sweet with a vanilla note. Baltic oak was admired at the end of the 19th century. Eastern European oaks are enjoying a revival, but French oak is currently revered above all other – not least because the forests in the regions mapped here have been so well managed.

Limousin is wide-grained, tannic, and generally more suitable for brandy than wine. The oaks of Tronçais, a single, large government-owned forest in the Allier département, grow so slowly that the wood is tight-grained and considered excellent for wine. Vosges oak is similar, light in colour and preferred by some winemakers. Others simply ask for oak from "*le Centre*".

Mormal 9,200 ha
ARGONNE
Haguenau 13,400 ha
Strasbourg
VOSGES
Paris
Bellème 2,400 ha
Fontainebleu 17,050 ha
Orient 10,000 ha
Rambouillet 14,800 ha
BOURGOGNE
Paimpont 8,000 ha
Bercé 5,400 ha
Orléans 34,700 ha
BERTRANGE
Citeaux 3,600 ha
Tours
FORÊTS CENTRALES
NEVERS
Tronçais 10,600 ha
TRONÇAIS
ALLIER
Limoges
Lyon
LIMOUSIN
Bordeaux
Bouconne 2,000 ha
Toulouse

Anatomy of a Winery

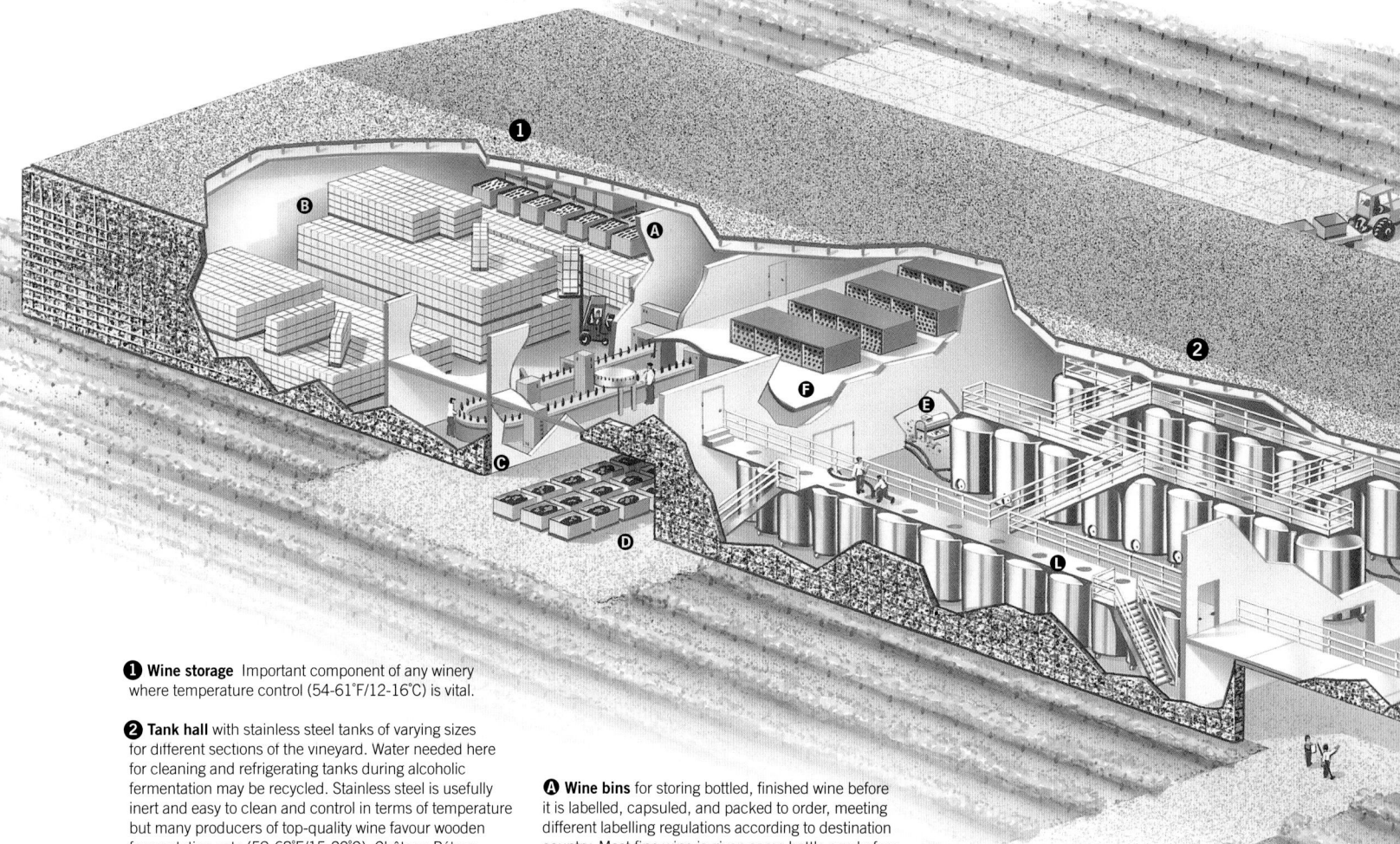

1 Wine storage Important component of any winery where temperature control (54-61°F/12-16°C) is vital.

2 Tank hall with stainless steel tanks of varying sizes for different sections of the vineyard. Water needed here for cleaning and refrigerating tanks during alcoholic fermentation may be recycled. Stainless steel is usefully inert and easy to clean and control in terms of temperature but many producers of top-quality wine favour wooden fermentation vats (59-68°F/15-20°C). Château Pétrus proves that concrete works well too.

3 Barrel cellar Usually underground, the floor of this one is only slightly lower than ground level but is still quite cool enough (54°F/12°C in winter, 64°F/18°C in summer). After alcoholic fermentation the wine is transferred into barrel for maturation and clarification for up to two years. The second, malolactic fermentation takes place in tank here.

A Wine bins for storing bottled, finished wine before it is labelled, capsuled, and packed to order, meeting different labelling regulations according to destination country. Most fine wine is given some bottle age before being despatched as the process of bottling can disturb the wine's equilibrium.

B Wine ready for shipment Producers choose either cardboard cartons or, more durable and much smarter-looking, wooden cases (usually pine). Stencilled case ends can be wine trophies, and are useful for identification during storage.

C Modern bottling line Hygiene and accuracy of fill are the chief requirements for fine wine. For minimal effects of oxygen there should be a gap of less than 0.4in (10mm) between the bottom of the cork and the surface of the wine in the bottleneck when it is young, although this will increase during ageing as the cork absorbs wine.

This is a somewhat stylized drawing of an extremely stylish winery, Dominus in the Napa Valley. It has been chosen for several reasons to illustrate the sort of ingredients and design features deemed necessary in a modern winery.

Firstly because most winemaking operations evolve organically: a small cellar there, with a larger one grafted on later; then bottle storage space; to which a bottling hall is added, and so on. This winery was designed for a working, full-size operation from scratch.

Secondly, this winery is unusual in that it is slap bang in the heart of the New World, but the principles behind it were born in the Old World for it is owned and operated by Christian Moueix of Libourne, Château Pétrus et al.

Thirdly, its design credentials are impeccable. The Swiss architects behind the new Tate Modern art gallery in London, Herzog & de Meuron, were responsible for the project.

And a fourth good reason for choosing to represent Dominus winery on these pages is that it is probably the only way you will ever see it for, unlike almost all other Napa Valley wineries, Dominus is closed to the public.

Its most striking design feature is entirely specific to this particular winery but is a response to one of any wine producer's major concerns: temperature. The climate in the Napa Valley is extreme. It is often very hot during the day, but can be very cool at night. The usual response to these conditions is to install air conditioning, a *sine qua non* in all but the world's coolest wine regions.

An increasing number of wineries and particularly wine stores in northern California are now being constructed in caves expressly bored into the hillsides. This can be much more economical than the ongoing energy costs of maintaining artificially low temperatures and

has the added advantage of relatively high natural humidity. The architects came up with a novel approach for this winery, however: walls that would themselves provide natural temperature control.

The winery walls are effectively gabions, stacked wire cages filled with stones, forming an inert mass that insulates the rooms against extreme temperatures. The gabions are filled more or less densely depending on the requirements of each section of the winery. The result is that parts of the walls are impenetrable while others allow in dramatic pinpricks of light: natural Napa Valley brilliance during the day, and artificial light at night. A local basalt ranging from dark green to black was chosen to blend with the landscape, although of course the building, up-and-running for the 1997 crush, still looks quite shockingly different from any other winery in the world.

Right The winery is difficult to ignore in early spring, but being surrounded by vines which in California grow to a height of well over six feet (two metres), the building has been designed to be fully integrated in high summer.

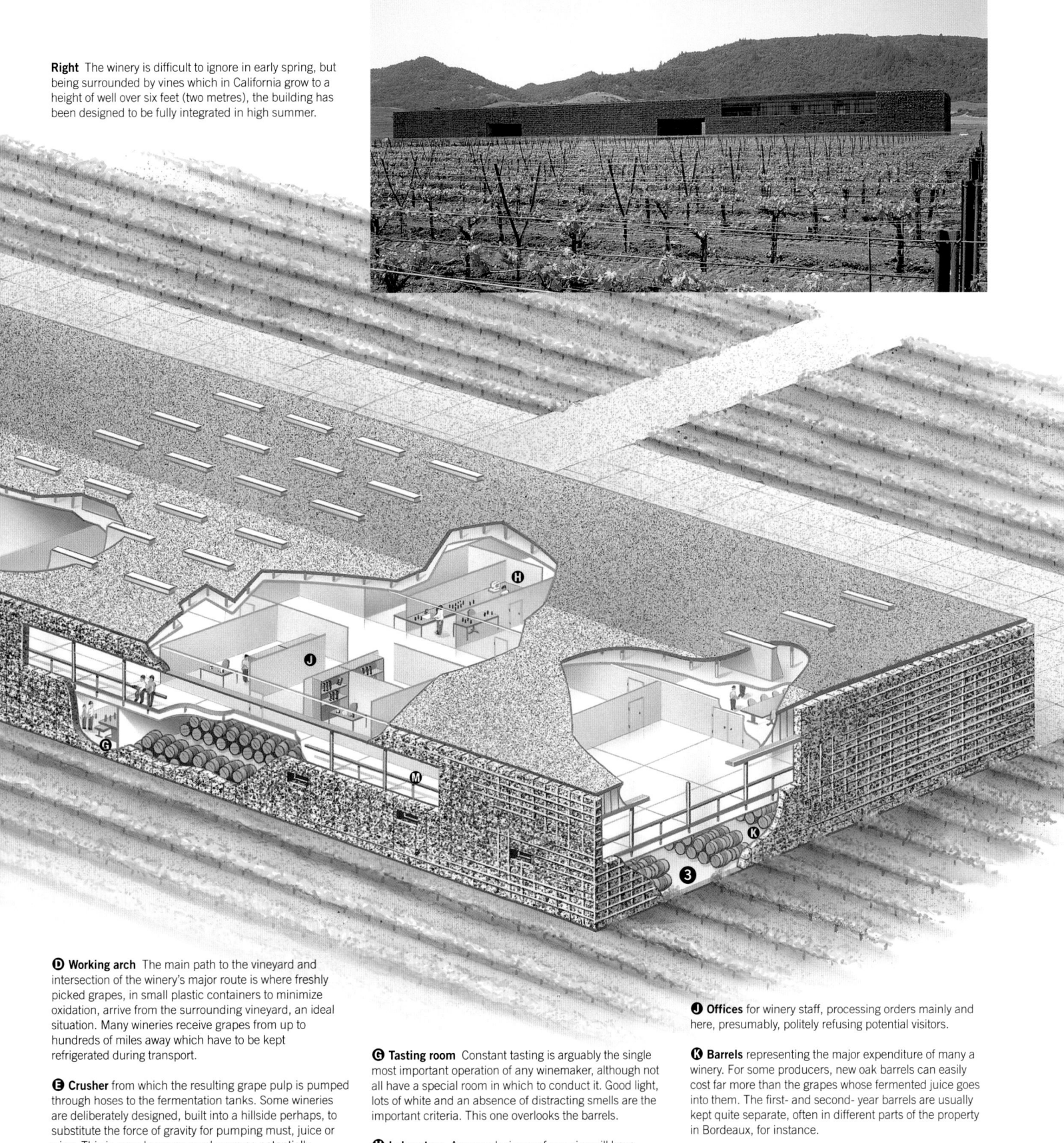

D Working arch The main path to the vineyard and intersection of the winery's major route is where freshly picked grapes, in small plastic containers to minimize oxidation, arrive from the surrounding vineyard, an ideal situation. Many wineries receive grapes from up to hundreds of miles away which have to be kept refrigerated during transport.

E Crusher from which the resulting grape pulp is pumped through hoses to the fermentation tanks. Some wineries are deliberately designed, built into a hillside perhaps, to substitute the force of gravity for pumping must, juice or wine. This is seen by some producers as potentially harmful to quality. The jury is out.

F Wine library Older vintages are stored here as controls and for the purposes of research and entertainment. In the Napa Valley producers are expected to donate special bottles, often big formats, to America's popular charity wine auctions.

G Tasting room Constant tasting is arguably the single most important operation of any winemaker, although not all have a special room in which to conduct it. Good light, lots of white and an absence of distracting smells are the important criteria. This one overlooks the barrels.

H Laboratory Any good winery of any size will have some equipment for wine analysis, and others should use external specialist labs. Quality control involves a full chemical analysis of wine throughout its various stages, particularly malolactic fermentation. Different importing countries set limits on some of wine's components such as residual sugar, volatile acidity, sulphur, even some specific chemicals associated with pesticide residues.

J Offices for winery staff, processing orders mainly and here, presumably, politely refusing potential visitors.

K Barrels representing the major expenditure of many a winery. For some producers, new oak barrels can easily cost far more than the grapes whose fermented juice goes into them. The first- and second- year barrels are usually kept quite separate, often in different parts of the property in Bordeaux, for instance.

L Catwalks Necessary so that winery staff can safely fill tanks with hoses, supervise pumping the must over the cap of skins, and generally monitor progress. Ladders would be the less stable alternative.

M Covered passageways link the various parts of the winery and afford views over the vineyards.

Wine and Time

There is a myth about wine that refuses to wither, let alone die, which is that all wine improves with age. One of wine's most magical properties is that some of it is capable of evolving and improving for decades, and very occasionally centuries, thus providing us with a particularly stimulating direct link to past generations. The great majority of wine made today, however, is ready to drink within a year or so of being bottled, and some wines are best drunk straight off the bottling line.

Almost any inexpensive wine, especially whites and rosés, as well as such light-bodied, low-tannin reds as those made from Dornfelder, Gamay (Beaujolais for example), Grignolino, Jaen, Lambrusco, Lagrein, Bulgaria's Pamid, Portugieser, and the Australian crossing Tarrango are at their best young. The pleasure in them is a matter of freshness and youthful fruitiness before it starts to fade. As a general rule, the more expensive a wine, even when quite young, the more it is designed to be aged. One of the very few white grapes that makes high-quality, often highly priced wine which can be at its most appealing in youth is Viognier, whose seductive perfume, usually accompanied by relatively low acidity, tends to fade after two or three years in bottle. Champagne and other top-quality sparkling wines are the only other highly priced unfortified wines that are ready to drink straight off the shelf.

Most of the great white wines and practically all the best reds, however, are sold long before they are ready to drink. Such wines are grown to be aged. When young they contain an unresolved complex of acids and sugars, minerals and pigments, tannins and all sorts of flavour compounds. Good wines have more of these things than ordinary wines, and great wines more than good wines. Which is why, in the end, they have more flavour and character. But it takes time for these elements, the primary grape-derived aromas and the secondary ones of fermentation and in many cases oak, to resolve themselves into a harmonious whole and for the distinct scent of maturity, called (by analogy with flowers) the bouquet, to form. Time, and oxygen.

It was not until Louis Pasteur was asked by Napoleon III in 1863 to find out why so much wine went bad on its way to the consumer, to the great detriment of the French wine trade, that the role of oxygen was discovered. Pasteur established that too much contact with air allows the growth of harmful bacteria that turn the wine into vinegar. On the other hand he found that it was very slight amounts of oxygen acting gradually that make wine mature. There is enough oxygen in the headspace between the liquid and the cork and dissolved in a bottle of wine to account for an ageing process lasting for years. Pasteur showed, by sealing wine in test tubes, alternately full and half-full, that the oxygen in a half-full tube caused the same deposit in a few weeks as is found in very old bottles, and that it affected colour in exactly the same way as extreme old age.

In fact he immensely speeded up the process that happens in a bottle: the oxygen in the wine

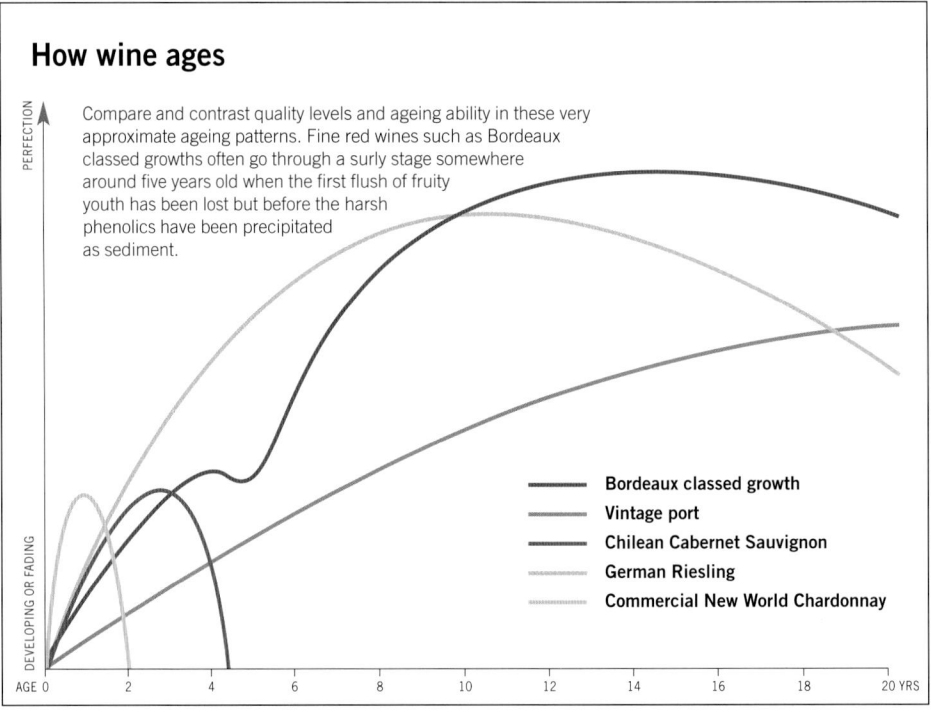

How wine ages

PERFECTION

DEVELOPING OR FADING

Compare and contrast quality levels and ageing ability in these very approximate ageing patterns. Fine red wines such as Bordeaux classed growths often go through a surly stage somewhere around five years old when the first flush of fruity youth has been lost but before the harsh phenolics have been precipitated as sediment.

——— Bordeaux classed growth
——— Vintage port
——— Chilean Cabernet Sauvignon
——— German Riesling
——— Commercial New World Chardonnay

AGE 0   2   4   6   8   10   12   14   16   18   20 YRS

acts on its constituents to mature them, but beyond the period of maturity it continues to act and from then on the wine deteriorates.

Pasteur found that barrel-aged wine has several opportunities to absorb oxygen: first of all through the staves (so that their thickness, whether or not they are encrusted with tartrate crystals, the size of the barrel, and whether it stands in a draught, all become relevant); then when it is being racked from one barrel to another and being topped up.

The ageing that takes place in bottle is a totally different process – almost the opposite in fact. Rather than absorbing oxygen the wine gradually loses it. The life of all its constituents is dependent on the very small amount in solution, and between the wine and the cork. As the oxygen supply diminishes the possibilities for further change are being reduced – so the process of ageing wine in bottle is "reductive" as opposed to oxidative.

A youthful fine red wine goes into bottle from barrel containing a mix of tannins, pigments, flavour compounds (these three known collectively as phenolics), and some more complex compounds formed by them. In the bottle tannins continue to interact with pigments and acids to form new compounds and larger molecules which are eventually precipitated. This means that as it ages, it loses colour and astringency but gains complexity, and sediment. In fact, holding a bottle of fine wine up to the light to examine how much sediment there is gives a good clue as to how mature it is – although the more heavily a wine has been filtered before bottling, the less sediment will form. Flavour compounds interact and react with other phenolics. At the same time acids and alcohol react together and with oxygen to form

compounds called esters and aldehydes. The overall effect is to produce a much more subtle and many-layered liquid.

The equivalent process in white wines, which have a much lower charge of phenolics, is less well understood, but gradual oxidation turns the phenolics gold and eventually brown as primary and secondary fruity and "winey" aromas and crisp acids mellow into honeyed, nutty or savoury complexities. If the main preservative of red wine is tannin, of white it is acidity. White wines with sufficient acidity (and sufficient substance to balance it) will mature as long as reds – or in the case of some botrytized sweet whites, German Rieslings, Tokajis, and Loire Chenin Blancs (all particularly high in acidity), even longer.

The most frequently asked question about any specific wine is "When will it be at its best?" The inconvenient truth is that even a wine's maker can only guess, and often the answer is clear only after a wine has started to decline, to lose fruit and flavour at such a rate that the acidity starts to dominate. All that is predictable about fine wine is its unpredictability.

Those who buy wine by the case of a dozen bottles and monitor the wine's progress bottle by bottle frequently find that a wine seems wonderfully opulent in youth, then goes through a sullen, dumb stage (when many of the complex compounds are formed) before emerging as an even more magnificent wine afterwards.

Bottle variation, even of different bottles from the same case, is a common phenomenon. The case may have been filled with bottles from different lots (many bottles nowadays have lot numbers marked on the glass) but often there is no rational explanation, just further proof that wine is a living, capricious entity.

It is certainly true that different vintages of the same wine vary enormously in their ageing ability. Generally speaking, the more tannins in a red wine and the more acidity in a white, the longer the wines will age. So red grapes with thick skins, typically the product of a dry year, are likely to age longer than those from wet years whose skin to pulp ratio is much lower. Similarly, white wines made from grapes grown in a cool year are likely to need longer before their acidity mellows to an acceptable level. This is a common phenomenon in Burgundy (and the correlation between acidity and ageability explains why white wines that have undergone the second softening malolactic fermentation often age faster than good white wines that have not).

Another factor – quite apart from storage conditions, which are discussed on page 42 – is the size of bottle in which a wine is stored. The amount of headspace is more or less constant no matter what the size of the bottle, which means that there is twice as much oxygen per volume of wine in a half-bottle as in a bottle, and only half as much in a magnum (two bottles in one). The ageing effect of that oxygen is therefore much faster in a half-bottle and much slower in larger bottles. This is why halves seem to deteriorate so rapidly and why collectors will pay a premium for the large bottle sizes. Stately ageing is deemed the best.

But, in very general terms, it is possible to say which sorts of wine are most worthy of ageing, or "laying down" as English parlance has it. In approximately descending order of potential life in bottle for red wines, to take some obvious candidates for the cellar, are well-made examples of vintage port, Barolo, Barbaresco, Brunello di Montalcino, Hermitage, classed-growth claret, Bairrada, Aglianico, Madiran, Côte Rôtie, fine red

Old and new

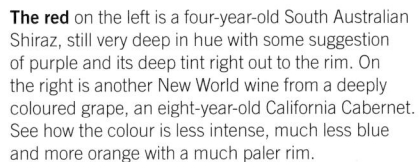

The red on the left is a four-year-old South Australian Shiraz, still very deep in hue with some suggestion of purple and its deep tint right out to the rim. On the right is another New World wine from a deeply coloured grape, an eight-year-old California Cabernet. See how the colour is less intense, much less blue and more orange with a much paler rim.

The white on the left is a two-year-old California Chardonnay but it could be almost any young white wine. A Riesling would be greener, a Muscadet almost water-white. The wine on the right is a 15-year-old Grand Cru white burgundy. Notice how white wines also acquire a brown tinge with age but gain rather than lose colour.

burgundy, Châteauneuf-du-Pape, Chianti Classico Riserva, Georgian Saperavi, Ribera del Duero, Dão, Australian Cabernet, California Cabernet, Rioja, Argentine Malbec, Zinfandel, New World Merlot, and New World Pinot Noir.

By far the most important body of wines that positively demand to be kept are the Crus Classés of Bordeaux. A generation ago such wines were made to endure, on the assumption that they would be kept a minimum of seven or eight years, and more likely 15 or more. Today's wine drinker is less patient. Modern taste looks for softer tannins (the all-important flattering "mouthfeel") and riper flavours that mean the wine can be drunk after a mere five years or so. California can manage this style virtually every year, but Bordeaux still depends on nature: the 1986 Bordeaux vintage, for example, is determinedly old-fashioned; many are still obdurate.

Red burgundy poses fewer problems because its tannins are rarely obtrusive enough to make patience essential, although some Grands Crus are so obviously stuffed with substance in youth that it would be a shame, and a great waste of money, to drink them at less than ten years old. All but the very finest white burgundies mature even faster, and Chardonnay is not usually a particularly long-lived grape variety.

In general terms the white wines that most obviously benefit from bottle age, in declining order of longevity, are fine examples of Tokaji, Sauternes, Loire Chenin Blanc, German Riesling, Chablis, Hunter Valley Semillon, sweet Jurançon, white burgundy from the Côte d'Or, and dry white Bordeaux. Most sherry, madeira, and sparkling wine is ready to drink as soon as it is bottled, although vintage and de luxe champagne should have enough guts to withstand and benefit from further ageing in bottle.

When to drink a wine is of course partly a matter of personal, even national, taste. The British have notoriously had a penchant for old wine, while the French and Americans frequently drink their fine wines a decade before the British.

What is sure is that almost all wine is now being made so that early drinking is at least possible, if not always desirable.

Left The temperature at which bottles are stored has a perceptible impact on how rapidly they age (see overleaf). It is wise to keep champagne at the bottom of a wine rack where temperatures are lowest, and the bottles are least likely to be damaged by light.

Storing Wine

If good wine is worth paying extra for (which in the majority of cases it is) it is worth keeping and serving (see overleaf), in good condition.

There is nothing mysterious or difficult about handling wine. But doing it well can add vastly to the pleasure of drinking it – and doing it badly can turn nectar into sludge. Wine asks only to be kept lying quietly in a dark, cool, ideally slightly damp place. Strong light can harm wine, particularly sparkling wine (which is why bottles of champagne are so often wrapped in paper) over an extended period. Warmth speeds up reactions so the warmer any wine is kept, the faster and less subtly it will mature. And if a bottle of wine is kept in a very dry place, air may start to penetrate the cork.

Wine storage is a problem for almost everyone. Few houses today come with underground cellars like the one opposite, the perfect place for keeping a collection. One option is to pay someone else to store your wine for you in ideal conditions. This has the obvious disadvantages of continuous expense and loss of spontaneity (some particularly impetuous hosts or their partners may not see this as a disadvantage) but it does shift the responsibility onto a professional's shoulders. Many fine wine merchants offer this service. The best truly monitor your wine collection and advise you when to drink what. The

Stoppers

Synthetic corks

Old champagne cork

Young champagne cork

Long cork

Screw cap

Agglomerate cork

Wine can be stored only if there is an effective stopper. These corks of varying quality and age (the old champagne cork shows the effect of years of compression; the long cork has been in a bottle of Bordeaux for several decades) are all susceptible to cork taint – even the cheap agglo versions made of cork chips glued together. A cork that has come into contact with mould will develop the thoroughly off-putting mustiness associated with trichloroanisole, or TCA which, when transmitted to the liquid, results in unpleasantly "corked" or "corky" wine. Cork producers are trying to upgrade their production techniques but

many wine producers have become so exasperated by the incidence of cork taint that they have adopted alternative stoppers. Synthetic corks, usually made of plastic, are the most popular, particularly with New World producers. They allow wine drinkers to continue the cork-pulling ritual beloved by many without any risk of cork taint. Some producers have adopted screw caps instead, particularly for aromatic wines such as Riesling for which no oxygen ingress is thought necessary for ageing. There are concerns that in the long term wine will age differently and very possibly less gracefully under stoppers other than natural cork.

worst have been known to abscond with their clients' wine. Most are delighted to act as brokers in a fine wine market owned by their clients. Any professional wine warehouse should be able to guarantee ideal temperature and humidity, and a sound tracking and retrieval system.

Wine collectors without their own cellars, who are determined to keep their bottles about them, have to improvise. Some go so far as to build their own extensive cellars from scratch, either excavating or heavily insulating. The United States in particular has several specialists in cellar design and construction. In Europe, a more common installation is not a many-roomed wine mansion with en suite tasting and viewing facilities but a utilitarian concrete cylinder, basically a spiral staircase encircled by horizontal wine storage spaces (see picture, left), which can be sunk into the ground. This is hardly practical in, for example, an often-torrid apartment block. For these circumstances, and for very hot climates, special wine storage units like many-shelved refrigerators (see picture opposite) are available, but they are hardly economical in terms of either investment or space.

In cooler climates it may be easier to find a corner of a house or flat that can be converted into a small private wine "cellar" (and remember that every cellar begins with a single bottle). Many older townhouses in Britain were built with coal holes, often under the pavement. With good insulation from excessive damp, which may cover labels with so much mould they are illegible, these can provide excellent wine storage.

Spaces under stairs are also favourites for wine storage. They tend to be naturally dark but can also easily be converted into a cupboard. Wine can also be stored in disused fireplaces, or in any room that is used so little that it is relatively cool. Some enthusiasts even dedicate a whole room to wine by insulating it thoroughly.

Wine is not over-fussy about temperature: anything from 45-64°F (7-18°C) will do, although 50°F (10°C) would be ideal. What matters more is that it varies as little as possible (next to an uninsulated boiler or water heater will not do). No wine will stand alternate boiling and freezing. In high temperatures it will not only age faster, there is the danger of the cork's expanding and contracting so rapidly that it stops being a perfect seal and the wine starts seeping around it. If there is any sign of this, drink the wine as soon as possible. But if coolness is impracticable, steady moderate warmth will do. Just beware very high temperatures, above 95°F (35°C), which could rob the wine of its subtlety.

Left Those with access to a ground floor can have a spiral cellar such as this excavated. They may not be the most beautiful wine cellars in the world, but they are very efficient in terms of space, so long as there is somewhere suitable for the trapdoor entrance.

This is why fine wine today is generally shipped either in temperature-controlled containers or only at cool times of year. Temperature also explains why bottles stored in the coldest cellars of the Scandinavian state monopolies have always tasted different from the same wines matured somewhere warmer.

No special equipment is needed in a cellar, coal hole or cupboard. Traditionally bottles have always been kept lying horizontally so as to prevent the cork from drying, shrinking, and letting in air, whether they are stored in a case or individually. (Stacking bottles upside down achieves the same end, but labels and capsules are more difficult to read.) Bottles can be stacked in a pile if they are all the same, but as they are more likely to vary it is better to keep them in a rack for easy identification and retrieval of each one.

Recent research has suggested that wines age even more gracefully if stored at an angle so that the cork is kept in contact with both liquid and the air bubble, although designers of wine racks are yet to catch up with this development. Champagne researchers have established that champagne corks are kept suitably moist and swollen by the carbon dioxide-saturated headspace so that it is safe to avoid any contamination from a possibly tainted cork by storing a champagne bottle upright, a position madeira producers have always favoured.

There are several good arguments for buying certain wines young, at their opening price, and "laying them down" in cellar or cupboard until they reach perfect maturity. Many fine wines simply never come on the market again after they are first offered – or if they do, as in the case of the Bordeaux microchâteaux or California cult Cabernets, for example, it will be at several times the release price. Do not think that all fine wine will appreciate in value, however; it all depends on the vagaries of the market, and

Left Temperature-controlled storage for wine bottles, ideal for smaller quantities in environments that tend to be too warm – or too dry, for humidity is controlled too. Up to three compartments at different temperatures are offered. Capacity can vary from 3 to 20 dozen bottles.

even currency movements. With more modest wines the only object of cellaring the wine is to be able to drink them in good condition when they have matured to suit your taste.

The wines on page 41 are particularly good candidates for any modest cellar. Many French and Italian, and an increasing proportion of Australian, reds benefit from additional ageing after they are released. Wine producers in Spain and to a certain extent Portugal have traditionally released wines only when they are ready to drink, although this benevolent habit is being eroded.

One of the under-sung pleasures associated with owning even a modest wine collection is

Above This wine cellar has obviously been grown organically. Unopened wooden cases of young wines are stored elsewhere. This is the collection of ready-to-open bottles arranged for ease of access in horizontal wine racks inserted into traditional bins in which bottles of the same type would have been stacked on top of each other.

that of handling, sorting, cataloguing (if you are that way inclined), rearranging, and choosing from such a varied selection of packages of potential delight.

For some wine collectors, keeping records is a substantial part of the fun. Specially designed cellar books are available and are the most traditional method of recording what was bought, from whom, and at what price, as well as when individual bottles were opened and how they tasted. Some people also record who shared these bottles and what food was served. Modern cellar records are more likely to be electronic.

Serving Wine: 1

Wine is not a solitary drink. It is essentially sociable, and one of the greatest pleasures it has to offer is the sharing of it. The more thought that goes in to the process of sharing, the more pleasure it can give.

One option is to lurch to the nearest wine store at the last minute and pull the cork just before serving a chilly, cloudy red or lukewarm white, but wine is as sensitive as most wine drinkers and rewards those prepared to undertake a little basic planning. This means some realistic advance calculation of the likely number of bottles and types of wines you will need.

Some of the attentions paid to wine are frivolous, some of the rituals absurd. Others can make all the difference between mere satisfaction and real delight. It is no affectation, but simply making the most of a good thing, to serve more than one wine at anything other than the most casual meal. A young wine served first tends to show off the qualities of an older one; a white wine is usually good at ushering in a red one; a light wine a massive one; a dry wine a sweet one. But most of these combinations played the other way round would be a disaster for the second wine. In the same way a really

good wine puts in the shade a lesser wine served after it, and the same thing happens to a dry white wine served after a red.

The question of how much to serve is more difficult. There are six good glasses of wine (which means generous glasses filled one-third full, not small ones filled to the brim) in a normal bottle. At a light lunch one glass a person might be enough, whereas at a long dinner, five or six might not be too much. A total of half a bottle a person (perhaps one glass of white wine and two of red) is a reasonable average for most people and occasions – but the circumstances and mood of the meal, and above all how long it goes on, are the deciding factors. There is a golden rule for hosts: be generous but never pressing, and be sure to pour copious quantities of water too.

If the number of wine drinkers at the table calls for more than one bottle with each course, consider serving two slightly different wines together – perhaps different vintages of the same wine/producer or the same grape but of different provenance. (To avoid confusion, try to serve different wines in glasses of different shapes and/or sizes.)

Once likely quantities have been decided, bottles containing sediment can be stood up in time for it to fall to the bottom of the bottle – which can take anything from a few minutes to a few hours, depending on the structure and quantity of the sediment. Even more importantly, this preparation allows time for all bottles to be brought to their ideal temperature.

Nothing makes more difference to enjoying wine than its temperature. It is possible both to flatter and deceive by manipulating the serving temperature, and all too easy to make a fine wine taste coarse by getting it wrong. Stone-cold claret and lukewarm Riesling wines are abominations – not because they offend any rule of etiquette, but simply because the wines taste so far from their best. And there are several good reasons why this should be so.

Our sense of smell (and hence the greater part of our sense of taste) is susceptible only to vapours. Red wine generally has a higher molecular weight – and is thus less volatile, or smelly, than white. The object of serving red wine *"chambré"*, at what is known as room temperature, is to warm it to the point where its aromatic elements begin to vaporize – which is

Left Cut the foil, possibly taking it off completely if you want to see all of the bottleneck. Take the cork out gently, keeping the bottle (and sediment) as still as possible.

Top Having wiped the lip of the bottle (with particular care if the foil was so old it may have contained lead), hold the bottle in one hand and the decanter in the other. Pour steadily, ideally with the bottleneck against a strong source of light such as a naked light bulb or a candle.

Above Continue to pour until you see the sediment (if any) moving into the lower neck of the bottle. Then stop when the dregs start to move dangerously close to the rim. If there is much more sediment than this, stand the wine for longer, stopper the decanter and try again later.

at a progressively higher temperature for more solid and substantial wines. An aromatic light red such as Beaujolais or Chinon can be treated as a white wine; even cold, its volatility is almost overwhelming. On the other hand, a full-scale red wine may need the warmth of the room, of the cupped hand around the glass, and possibly of the mouth itself to volatilize its complex constituents.

Tannins are much more obvious at low temperatures. Thus, the warmer a tannic young red wine is served, the softer, more generous, and more evolved it will taste. The illusion of maturity can be created for a young Cabernet or red Bordeaux, for example, by judiciously serving it on the warm side, which will increase the apparent flavour and decrease its astringency. Pinot Noir or red burgundy, however, tends to be lower in tannin and more naturally aromatic. This explains the long tradition of serving red burgundy cooler than red Bordeaux, almost straight out of the cellar.

Cold is also necessary to counterbalance the richness of very sweet wines, even if doing so may mask some of their flavours. On the chart below, most of the sweetest white wines are entered at the coldest point. It is a good idea to pour them very cold and let them warm up slightly while you sip them: the process seems to release all their aroma and bouquet. This balancing act is explained by the fact that, like tannin, acidity tastes more pronounced at lower temperatures, so white wines whose acidity needs to be emphasized, whether because they are high in sugar, over-aged or from particularly hot climates, can be given apparent zip by serving them particularly cool.

The chart sets out in some detail the wide range of temperatures that brings out the best in different wines. It is based on personal experience, often modified in discussions (not to mention arguments) with other wine-lovers. Personal taste and habits vary widely from individual to individual; and, indeed, from country to country. In very general terms, fuller bodied wines are best served warmer than wines low in alcohol (which is why so much white burgundy and Chardonnay is served too cold); hard wines need warming more than soft; and dry wines are usually happier at room temperature than sweet.

But it is worth remembering that when the term *chambré* was invented the prevailing temperature in French dining rooms was unlikely to have been above 60˚F (15 or 16˚C). A wine served too hot lacks refreshment value and is practically very difficult to cool down, whereas a wine served too cool will naturally approach room temperature and can easily be warmed by cupping the glass in a hand.

It is easier to serve white wine at the right temperature than red as it can be put in a refrigerator. But the fastest way to cool a bottle is to put it in a bucket of ice and water (not ice alone, which will not touch much of the bottle), or a special cooling jacket. In a very warm room (and especially a hot garden) it is a good idea between pourings to keep the bottle in the bucket – or, if it is already chilled, in a vacuum bottle cooler which does not entail water and drips. This may mean pouring the wine initially a bit too cold but it will warm up all too quickly in the glass. A useful tip for large quantities (several bottles in a big bucket) is to make a monster block of ice by putting a polythene bag of water in the deep-freeze: the bigger the block the slower it thaws. Tall Germanic bottles should be put in the water upside-down for a few minutes first to cool the wine in the neck.

Persuading a red wine to reach the right temperature is harder. If it starts at cellar temperature it can take several hours in a normal room to raise it 10 or 12 degrees. The kitchen is the logical place – but many kitchens are well over 68˚F (20˚C), especially while dinner is cooking. At this sort of temperature red wines may be thrown out of balance; the alcohol starts to vaporize and produces a heady smell, which masks its character. Some of its flavour may even be lost forever.

One practical way of warming red wine in a hurry is first to decant it, then to stand the decanter in water at about 70˚F (21˚C). It does no harm to heat the decanter (within reason) first. Microwave ovens also come into their own for heating wine bottles in a hurry, although if the wine has a sediment the oven has to be tall enough to stand the bottle or decanter in. The danger, however, is being too impatient and heating the wine beyond the point of no return. A little experimentation with a bottle of water would be prudent.

It may be difficult to get a red wine to the optimum temperature, but there are times when it is necessary to make an effort to keep it there. Vacuum bottle coolers, or even ice buckets, may be needed when serving red wine in hot climates or high temperatures. In a restaurant do not hesitate to ask for an ice bucket if your red wine has been served too warm. You will be continuing a long and noble tradition of connoisseurship.

Serving wine out of doors presents its own demands, quite apart from getting the temperature right. A subtle bouquet, particularly of a red wine, is much more likely to be stolen by a passing breeze than if the same wine were served indoors. Bold, assertive wines generally show better outside than cellar treasures which are best reserved for the dining room.

Wine and temperature

This chart suggests the ideal temperature for serving a wide range of wines. "Room temperature" is low by modern standards: all the better for fine wine. White and pink wines are in yellow; reds and fortifieds in purple. The top coloured line gives the most general guidance on ideal serving temperatures.

Scale markers: ▼ DOMESTIC FRIDGE TEMP · ▼ IDEAL CELLAR TEMPERATURE · ▶ ROOM TEMPERATURE

Category band: SWEET WINES | DRY WHITES | LIGHT REDS | FULL-SCALE REDS

°C: 4 5 6 7 8 9 10 11 12 13 14 15 16 17 18
°F: 39 41 43 45 46 48 50 52 54 55 57 59 61 63 64

Wine entries (approximate serving-temperature positions, cool → warm):

- MUSCADET; CHABLIS; GRAND CRU CHABLIS
- MACON; CHINON; BEST WHITE BURGUNDIES & GRAVES; RED BURGUNDY
- GEWURZTRAMINER & PINOT GRIS; BORDEAUX BLANC
- BEAUJOLAIS NOUVEAU; BEAUJOLAIS CRUS
- SANCERRE/POUILLY; SAUTERNES; COTES DU RHONE (RED); TOP RED RHONE
- GROS PLANT; ALSACE RIESLING; VINTAGE PORT
- JURANÇON; WHITE RHONE; LANGUEDOC-ROUSSILLON REDS
- SYLVANER; FINO & MANZANILLA; ORDINARY RED BORDEAUX
- ALIGOTE; TAWNY PORT; CREAM SHERRY
- TOKAJI; NON-VINTAGE CHAMPAGNE; AMONTILLADO; MADEIRA; CAHORS; FINE RED BORDEAUX
- MONTILLA; MADIRAN
- VIN JAUNE; BANDOL
- SPARKLING WINE (eg SEKT, CAVA); BEST CHAMPAGNE
- EISWEIN; GOOD GERMAN & AUSTRIAN WINE; BEST DRY GERMAN WINE; BEST SWEET GERMAN WINE
- LIEBFRAUMILCH ETC
- SWEET LOIRE/CHENIN BLANC; CHIANTI CLASSICO RISERVAS; BEST PORTUGUESE REDS
- FRASCATI; VALPOLICELLA; CHIANTI
- ASTI; ORVIETO; SICILIAN REDS; SUPERTUSCANS
- SOAVE; BARBERA/DOLCETTO; BAROLO
- VINHO VERDE & RIAS BAIXAS; VERDICCHIO; HUNGARIAN WHITES; PUGLIAN REDS; RIBERA DEL DUERO & PRIORATO
- NAVARRA & PENEDES
- TOKAJI ASZU; RIOJA RESERVAS
- MOSCATO & MOSCATEL; FENDANT; VALDEPENAS; CHILEAN REDS
- LAMBRUSCO; DOLE; LIGHT ZINFANDELS; ARGENTINE REDS
- RETSINA; PINOTAGE
- SA CHENIN BLANC; CALIFORNIA/AUSTRALIAN/OREGON PINOT NOIR
- CHARDONNAY; TOP CALIFORNIA/AUSTRALIAN CHARDONNAYS
- MOST MUSCATS; NZ PINOT NOIR; BEST CALIFORNIA CABERNETS & ZINFANDELS
- NZ SAUVIGNON; CALIFORNIA SAUVIGNON BLANC
- RIESLING; OLD HUNTER VALLEY SEMILLON
- BAROSSA RIESLING; LIQUEUR MUSCAT; TOP AUSTRALIAN CABERNET/SHIRAZ
- PINK & BLUSH WINES; URUGUAYAN TANNAT

Serving Wine: 2

The next, rather obvious, step is to open the bottle(s). In most cases this means removing the foil, or capsule, and pulling the cork. Foils are usually cut neatly just below the brim of the bottle so as to keep the look of the bottle intact but this is just convention. Special foil cutters are a strictly optional boon.

Corkscrews are surprisingly varied; corkscrew collectors can be even more obsessive than wine collectors. Below are some of the better designs. The only essentials in a corkscrew that does actually incorporate a screw is that it is a hollow helix rather than a solid shaft which could pierce the cork straight through and give no leverage, and that it ends in a good, sharp point.

Opening bottles of sparkling wine requires a special technique. Well-chilled bottles that have not recently been agitated make the least fuss when opened (warm, shaken fizz can spume alarmingly, and wastefully). It's worth remembering that the pressure inside a champagne bottle is not dissimilar to that inside the tyre of a truck, so an unguarded cork pushed out of a bottle can do a great deal of damage. After taking off the foil and untwisting the wire muzzle, hold the cork down into the bottleneck while gently twisting the bottle off it, ideally at an angle. The cork should pop out discreetly with minimum loss of liquid. Seriously recalcitrant champagne corks can be persuaded to turn by a "champagne star" that fits into the four grooves in the top of the cork to give more torque.

Very old corks can pose problems. They can easily disintegrate under the pressure of a corkscrew, particularly one of the more powerful modern designs. The two-pronged sort, the so-called butler's friend (because it theoretically enabled him to replace the contents of a bottle with inferior wine without having pierced the cork), can be useful for such bottles. Vintage port is one of the longest-living wines and gave rise to the traditional port tongs, tongs of metal specially designed to make a clean incision through a bottleneck under a very old cork after being heated in an open flame.

Vintage port is also necessarily associated with one of wine's most controversial rituals: decanting, or pouring wine from its original bottle into another container, typically a glass carafe, before serving it. The most obvious reason for doing this is to leave behind any crunchy and often bitter sediment that has formed in the bottle (and there will be a great deal in a bottle of mature vintage port). The other, more contentious, reason is to aerate the wine, exposing it to the oxygen which Pasteur found so powerful a tool in ageing a wine (see page 40).

Decanting is much discussed but little understood, largely because its effect on a given wine is unpredictable. There is a mistaken idea that it is something you only do to ancient bottles with lots of sediment – a mere precautionary measure to get a clean glass of wine. But experience shows that it is usually young wines that benefit most. The oxygen they contain has had little chance to take effect. But the air in the decanter works rapidly and effectively. In a matter of a few hours it can often induce the opening of what was a closed bud. This can mean literally twice as much of the scent and flavour that you paid for. Some strong young wines – Barolo springs to mind – can benefit by even as much

Corkscrews
The most common foil cutter **1** can rapidly become addictive. **2** is a classic old corkscrew suitable for use on even the most ancient cork while **3** is the design most commonly used by wine waiters because it incorporates a knife for cutting the foil. **4** is the notorious butler's friend model while **5** is the relatively expensive Leverpull which extracts corks with just two easy movements, twisting the cork off the screw with a further two. **6** is the champagne star for twisting the most obdurate champagne corks.

Decanters
Virtually any neutral-tasting container can be used as a decanter but glass is perfect in that it shows off the wine's colour – and the ideal decanter has a stopper so that delicate wines are not exposed to more oxygen than necessary. **7** is a typically shaped bottle-sized decanter, although magnum sizes are useful for maximum aeration of particularly tight, closed wines. **8** is a traditional port decanter but can be used for any wine.

Glasses
All of the glasses (**9-12**) conform to the basic requirements of a good wine glass, having a stem and a bowl that allows swirling without any loss of wine. Glass **10** is the standard shape and size of tasting glass agreed by an international panel for official standards organizations many years ago, but some tasters, particularly non-professionals, may find it a little constricting.

as 24 hours in a decanter. An hour makes all the difference to others. A good rule of thumb is that young, tannic, alcoholic wines need, and can withstand, much earlier decanting than old lighter-bodied wines. But full white wines such as white burgundies can benefit from decanting too – and will look even more beguiling than reds.

Those who feel most passionately opposed to decanting argue that there is a danger of losing some fruit and flavour while the wine is poured into and evolves in the decanter. Better, they feel, to pour straight from the bottle, taste and evaluate the wine's state of maturity and aerate in the glass if necessary by swirling the wine around. It is certainly true that some very old wines can lose such charm as remains extremely rapidly after decanting, yet these are the wines most likely to have a heavy deposit. Trial and individual taste are the surest guides.

The technique of decanting is illustrated on page 44. The only essential equipment is a carafe and a corkscrew. If the wine is very young and unevolved, it will do no harm at all to swirl it about a bit in the decanter, exposing it

to even more oxygen, and if the surface area of the wine in the decanter is extensive, it may even help to leave the decanter unstoppered.

It was once widely believed that pulling the cork from a bottle of wine and leaving it unstoppered to "breathe" would have a marked effect on the wine. In reality the area of wine in a bottle-neck is too small to make much difference.

The amount of oxygen in a half-empty bottle of wine on the other hand can have an enormous, usually harmful, effect on the wine. This is especially marked on leftovers in an unfinished bottle. For this reason, leftover wine is generally best kept in a smaller bottle of about the same capacity as the leftovers so that it is exposed to very little oxygen. And the process of deterioration can be slowed by keeping the leftovers in a refrigerator, low temperatures having the effect of slowing chemical reactions.

The wine drinker requires one more vital piece of equipment: a glass. Wonderfully complicated experiments and blind tastings have shown that a slight modification to the basic shape can accentuate what certain types of wine

have to offer. But there is no absolute need to have different glasses for different wines. White wines have traditionally been served in smaller glasses than red – perhaps because some are more naturally aromatic and need less headspace – but this is mere convention.

Strong and sweet wines are usually served in smaller quantities than dry table wines, so there is logic to using a small glass, and sparkling wines appreciate a nice long trajectory for each bubble, which means a tall, narrow glass.

It may seem too obvious to mention, but wine glasses should be clean, that is polished and untainted with smells of detergents or cupboards. Although some can withstand modern dishwashers, many are best rinsed with hot water and polished by hand with a linen cloth, ideally when still hot. Cupboard or cardboard smells usually come from keeping glasses upside down, on a shelf or in a box. This may be necessary on open shelves, but it is better to keep them right way up in a clean dry, airy cupboard. Sniff them before putting them on the table. It is good practice for the nose.

Special glasses
Generally speaking the basic wine shape will suit almost any wine, but champagne and sparkling wines tend to taste best, and keep their fizz longest, if served in particularly tall glasses such as **14**, some of which go in towards the rim too. Glass **15** is quite big enough for port while the traditional sherry copita **16** is almost a pastiche of the standard wine glass. Some people like their red burgundy served in goldfish bowls such as **13**.

Wine coolers
The traditional way of cooling a bottle of wine is to leave it in an ice bucket such as **17** filled with a fast-cooling mixture of water and ice cubes. A sleeve or cooling jacket **18** filled with coolant kept in the freezer can be just as effective (and is a lot more portable) while a vacuum bottle cooler **19** will efficiently keep bottles cool, or warm, no matter what the ambient temperature.

13 15 17 19 14 16 18

Tasting and Talking about Wine

A great deal of wine, even good or great wine, flows over tongues and down throats of people who drink it but don't actually taste it. They are not attuned to it; not receptive to what it has to offer. They are preoccupied or deep in conversation; they have just drunk whisky or gin which numb the senses; they have a cold; or they have simply never been told about how to get the most out of every mouthful.

Nothing the winemaker can do dispenses with the need for a sensitive and interested drinker. If the sense of taste were located in the mouth (where our impulses tell us it is), anyone swallowing a mouthful of wine would get all the sensations it has to offer. But in fact the nerves that receive anything more distinctive than the basic sensations of sweet, sour, salt, and bitter, such as the complex flavours of wine, are located higher in the head and deeper in the brain, at the top of our noses.

The most sensitive bit of what we call our sense of taste is actually our sense of smell. The real organ of discrimination is in the upper nasal cavity, where in normal breathing the air never goes. And the only sensations that can reach it are the vapours of volatile substances. To reach the brain the vapours of wine need to be inhaled (either through the nose or the back of the mouth) into the upper part of the nasal cavity, where they are dissolved in moisture. From the moisture long, thin nerve processes (vacilli) take the sensations to the olfactory bulb, above the nasal cavity and right in the brain. It is often remarked how smells stir memories far more rapidly and vividly than the other sensations. From the position of the olfactory bulb, nearest neighbour to the temporal lobe where memories are stored, it seems that smell, the most primitive of our senses, has a privileged position of instant access to the memory bank.

Experienced tasters often rely on the immediate reaction of their memory to the first sniff of a wine. If they cannot relate it straight away to wines they have tasted in the past they must fall back on their powers of analysis, located in the parietal lobe. In the frontal lobe their judgement of the wine is formed (to be stored in turn in the temporal lobe for future reference). The range of reference available is the great difference between an experienced taster and a beginner. There is little meaning in an isolated sensation though it may be very pleasant. Where the real pleasures of wine tasting lie are in the cross-references, the stirring of memories, the comparisons between similar and yet subtly different products of the same or neighbouring ground. Wines differ from one another in terms of colour, texture, strength, structure, body, and length, as well as their complex of flavours. A taster takes all these into account.

Tastings come in many different forms, from the simple act of enjoyment round a friendly table to the professional blind tasting tests involved in qualifying as a Master of Wine. One which puzzles many wine neophytes is the tasting ritual acted out in so many restaurants whereby the wine waiter pours a small sample of the chosen wine for you to taste. The purpose of this is for you to check that the wine is firstly

How to taste and appreciate wine

Eyes
Pour a tasting sample into the glass so that it is no more than a quarter full. First check the wine is clear (cloudiness or fizziness indicate a fault) and look straight down on to it to see how intense the colour is (the deeper a red, the younger the wine and/or thicker-skinned the grapes, a valuable clue if tasting a mystery wine "blind"). Red wines become paler with age, white wines deeper. Tilt the glass away from you against a white background and observe the colour in the middle of the liquid and at the rim. All wines turn slowly brown with age and the rim is the first place where any brick colour is noticeable in a red. Young reds are more purplish-blue than brick. Old reds lose colour completely at the rim. The glossier the colour and the more subtly shaded its different colour gradations, the better the wine.

Nose
Take one sniff with all your concentration, then swirl the wine around and sniff once more. The stronger the impression, the more intense the aroma or bouquet. A subtle, maturing wine may need the swirl before it gives off much smell. If you are tasting blind, this is the moment when you are hoping for a massive intuitive clue, some relationship to something from your tasting memory bank. If you are tasting to assess the wine, note whether it smells clean (most wines do nowadays), intense, and what the smell reminds you of. It is much easier to remember a smell if you can attach words to it. As you taste or drink the wine (and these two activities can feel very different) notice how the smell changes. Good wines tend to become more interesting, inexpensive commercial wines often less so, with time. A very small percentage of the population is anosmic, unable to use the sense of smell to the full.

Mouth
This stage involves taking a good mouthful of wine and exposing all of the taste buds distributed over the tongue and insides of the cheeks to it. If the nose is best at sensing the subtle flavours in a wine, the mouth is best at measuring its constituents: tip of the tongue usually for sweetness, upper edges for the all-important acidity, back of the tongue for bitterness, insides of the cheeks for drying tannins, and the entrance to the throat for any hot excess of alcohol. Once a mouthful has been swallowed or, by professionals, spat out, a judgement can be made as to whether all these elements are in balance (young reds are often deliberately high in tannins) and how persistent the wine is on the palate – a good indicator of quality. At this stage the wine can be judged, possibly even identified, in its entirety.

at the right temperature and secondly that it is not obviously faulty, most usually corked (see page 42). You cannot send it back just because you don't like it.

What is much harder than appreciating wine is communicating its sensations. There is no notation of taste, as there is of sound or colour; apart from the words sweet, salt, sour, and bitter, every word in the language of taste is borrowed from the other senses. And yet words, by giving an identity to sensations, help to clarify them. Some of the most helpful of the great many words used by tasters are listed in the glossary at the back of this book.

From talking about wine to writing about it is but a step – which few wine drinkers ever take. Yet there is a strong case for keeping notes on what you drink or taste in a more or less organized way. In the first place, having to commit something to paper makes you concentrate; the prime requirement for being able to taste wine properly at all. In the second it makes you analyze and pin labels on the sensations passing across your palate. In the third it is an *aide-mémoire*: when somebody asks you what a wine is like you can look it up and say something definite. In the fourth it allows you to extend comparison between wines over time –

either the same wine a year later, or different but related wines on different occasions.

In short, keeping tasting notes is like keeping a diary: obviously a good idea, but hard to get off the ground. A little guidance may help. Professional tasting sheets are often divided into three, to remind tasters to make a note of the appearance of the wine, how it smells, and the impact of the wine on the palate. There may even be a fourth space for overall impressions. Different tasters evolve their own tasting language and shorthand and there is no point in being too prescriptive. The single most important note to be made is the full name of every wine tasted. A date can be useful on tasting notes too in case you ever have the chance to monitor the same wine later in its life and make comparisons. And a note of the place and/or fellow tasters may help to jog your memory when you come to read these (usually increasingly illegible) notes again.

Are scores appropriate for judging wine? Under some professional circumstances, such as competitions or judging panels, they are unavoidable – either as symbols, or the numbers that have become such a powerful weapon in wine retailing today. The habit of applying points out of 100 to wines has been seized on

Above Tasting in Burgundy cellars such as these of the famous Hospices de Beaune can be a nerve-racking experience. The wine is generally much cooler than the usual serving temperature and spittoons are thin on the ground. Before gushing over the first sample, remember that the usual tasting sequence is from lesser to greater wines

with delight by a new generation of wine buyers around the world, for it offers an international scoreboard (reflected often by a similarly calibrated international marketplace), and can be understood no matter what your native language. But, despite the apparent accuracy and precision of a score out of 100, let no-one forget that wine tasting is an essentially subjective process. A score that is the average of a panel can be deeply suspect, an average which tends to exclude any wine with real individuality (which is bound to displease someone). And even the pronouncements of a single palate can be misleading. We all have our own likes and dislikes among wine flavours and styles. We all begin with one set of preferences and then our taste evolves and continues to change throughout our wine-drinking lives. The best judge of the right styles of wine for your palate is you. There are no absolutes of right and wrong in wine appreciation.

Wine, Food, and Travel

Do the above three words have a certain magic about them? Of course they do. Because where there is a glass of wine, a plate of food cannot be very far away. Where there are wine producers anxious to share their precious liquid with you, chances are that if they don't actually drag you to their own table, they will point you firmly in the direction of a nearby restaurant or picnic counter, increasingly often their very own. Wine tourism is becoming a delightfully common reality.

Wine is made for food. Almost all food tastes better with wine (chocolate cake just might be an exception) and almost all wine tastes better with food. It makes medical sense to take some solid matter with this delicious liquid too; any harmful effects of alcohol can be substantially buffered by eating as well as drinking.

For some reason the ordinary wine-drinking public has been terrorized into feeling that food and wine matching is a critical and abstract science they will never understand. But despite the social wine terrorists, there are no hard rules about which foods go with which wines. And if you drink what you feel like drinking and eat what you feel like eating, the chances are the wine and food will taste somewhere between fine and fantastic together.

There are, however, some explanations for how some of the supposed "rules" came about. Red wine tends to be higher in chewy tannins than white. Chewy food such as meat goes best with, or at least best disguises, chewiness in wine. Ergo the red wine with meat rule. Similarly, fish tends to need acidity with it (as witness the slice of lemon, the caper, the mayonnaise). More white wines are high in acidity than red. Therefore we have inherited "white wine with fish" as another rule.

But, like all rules, these are made to be broken. There is no disaster or shame in drinking white wine with red meat – indeed a full-bodied Chardonnay, Pinot Gris or Sémillon can be a very delicious accompaniment. Likewise, light reds such as Beaujolais or Pinot Noir can be divine with fish, particularly but by no means exclusively, with fuller-flavoured and textured fish such as salmon and tuna. (Bordeaux wine producers firmly drink claret with practically everything, including delicate white fish.)

It is a demonstrable fact that you can drink any wine with any food. If you do seek a perfect match, the best place to do so is in one of those grand restaurants in which the menu hardly changes from week to week. Such an establishment should have a knowledgeable wine waiter, or sommelier, whose very purpose is to suggest two or three perfect matches in different price brackets for each dish.

For the rest of us, life can be too short to find the perfect wine for everything we eat. But a useful shorthand is to match overall weight of the dish (how strong the flavour and texture is) with the weight, or alcohol in the wine. Thus a powerful daube might inspire a Châteauneuf-du-Pape; a tangy young goat's cheese a Sancerre; Dungeness crab a rich California Chardonnay.

Note how each of these combinations, which sprung quite naturally to mind, have a geographical logic to them. It is to be expected that the cuisine in long-established wine regions should evolve so as to suit the wines of that region – and it seems as though the pattern is much the same in newer wine regions.

The bold, outdoor flavours of California wines have inspired a bold, outdoor cuisine. (It may be an insult to an anglophone nation to use a French word, but the word "cooking" is not entirely appropriate to describe the bright, breezy assemblage of top-quality ingredients that typifies modern California menus.)

Australia's new-found adaptation of Asian flavours and their influence on superlative local seafood has resulted in a re-evaluation of the more delicate white wines produced there, the Rieslings in particular.

As Austrian wines have slimmed down and become some of the most elegantly modern of all, so has the food served by Austria's most admired chefs, without any loss of national identity or pride in truly local produce.

Travelling in wine regions is some of the most stimulating in every way. Wine is almost by definition made in beautiful settings (no industrial estates or financial districts are mapped in this book). Sceptics may urge us to take off our rosé-tinted spectacles, but wine producers really do tend to be more interesting, idiosyncratic, and varied than most commercial practitioners. (Most have to be driven by something other than sheer profit.) And if they share a characteristic it is generosity, a desire to share their product and their knowledge.

The clever wine tourist avoids mealtimes (between 12 to 2pm or even 3pm in much of Europe) for winery visits; remembers that they are likely be given the simplest wine first so should not wax lyrical too soon; spits, but only where indicated; is appreciative when they can be; and tries to buy something, even if it is only the increasingly prevalent winery T-shirt.

Left One of the treats for any wine tourist is a picnic, furnished by a store as appealing as this one in Sarlat, deep in the Dordogne in Bergerac country where the local pâtés, terrines, and rillettes are cut appetizingly by the crunch of the region's Cabernets.

The World of Wine

France

Wine producers in the rest of the world love to hate the French. They have so many indisputable advantages in France and can regard them with an infuriating mixture of arrogance and insouciance. But what makes France the undisputed mistress of the vine; the originator and producer of more, and more varied, great wines than all the rest of the world?

It is not just the national character and its preoccupation with matters of the heart, palate and liver. It is also a matter of geography. France, washed by the Atlantic and lapped by the Mediterranean, is uniquely well-situated. Her climate is more Mediterranean than continental but she has no shortage of wine regions at the limit of grape-ripening potential where growing seasons are at their longest and most interestingly variable.

But France not only has good vineyards; she defines, classifies and controls them. The listing, in order, of the best sites has been going on for 200 years. In the last 80 or so it has been codified in ever-increasing detail as the law of the land in every sense.

It started with the Appellation d'Origine Contrôlée which restricted the use of the name Roquefort to cheese made and matured in a certain area, by a certain method, from ewe's milk. The same principle applies to each wine appellation: restriction of area, of method, and of grape varieties. The law also stipulates the maximum crop per hectare (yield) and minimum natural alcohol level. AOCs (or ACs for short) are administered by the Institut National des Appellations d'Origine (INAO).

Just below the AC category is a small collection of wines known as VDQS (see page 152 for more details), which may eventually be promoted to AC status. The second biggest category of French wine is made up of Vins de Pays, the "country wines" described in detail on pages 150-152. At the bottom of the ladder of quality is basic Vin de Table. And a further substantial proportion of every French harvest, up to 20%, is sold for distillation, either grapes of the Gers département for armagnac and Charente for cognac, or as EU surplus production to be distilled into industrial alcohol.

Language of the Label

Quality designations

Appellation (d'Origine) Contrôlée (AC) wines whose geographical origins, varietal make-up and production methods are precisely regulated – generally the best and certainly the most traditional

VDQS AC-in-waiting (see page 152)

Vin de Pays "country wine", often from areas larger than AC zones, in which non-traditional varieties and higher yields are allowed (see page 150)

Vin de Table basic wine for which no geographical origin, grape variety or vintage may be claimed

Other common expressions

Blanc white

Cave (coopérative) co-operative winery

Château wine estate or even farm, typically in Bordeaux

Coteaux de, Côtes de typically hillsides

Cru literally a "growth", a specified superior plot of land

Cru classé cru that has been selected by an important classification such as the 1855 in Bordeaux (discussed on page 84)

Domaine vineyard holding, Burgundy's generally smaller-scale answer to château

Grand Cru literally "great growth": in Burgundy, the finest vineyards; in St-Emilion, nothing special

Méthode classique, méthode traditionnelle sparkling wine made using the same method as for champagne

Mis (en bouteille) au château/domaine/la propriété estate-bottled wine made by the same enterprise as grew the grapes

Négociant merchant bottler, an enterprise that buys in wine or grapes (cf domaine)

Premier Cru literally "first growth": in Burgundy a notch down from Grand Cru; in the Médoc, one of the top four châteaux

Proprietaire-récoltant owner-vinegrower

Récoltant vinegrower

Récolte vintage

Rosé pink

Rouge red

Supérieur usually just slightly higher in alcohol

Vielles vignes old vines and therefore in theory denser wine, though the "old" is unregulated

Vigneron vinegrower

Villages suffix denoting selected communes, or parishes, within an appellation

Vin wine

Viticulteur vinegrower

— · — · —	International boundary
— · — · —	Département boundary
○	Chief town of département
Côtes de Millau	VDQS
●	Centre of VDQS
Marcillac	AC not mapped elsewhere
●	Centre of AC area
	Champagne *(page 78-81)*
	Loire Valley *(page 116-123)*
	Burgundy *(page 54-77)*
	Savoie and Jura *(page 148-149)*
	Rhône *(page 129-137)*
	Southwest *(page 112-114)*
	Dordogne *(page 115)*
	Bordeaux *(page 82-111)*
	Languedoc-Roussillon *(page 138-143)*
	Provence *(page 144-146)*
	Alsace *(page 124-127)*
	Other traditional vine-growing areas

Proportional symbols

40 Area of vineyard per département in thousands of hectares (no figure given if area <1000 hectares)

Left Lavender, one of southern France's most evocative crops, next to vines in full flower in Provence. Baron Le Roy, the father of France's famous wine appellation system, originally proposed that suitable vineyard land for Châteauneuf-du-Pape be defined by being dry enough to support lavender and thyme.

BELGIQUE

LUXEMBOURG

DEUTSCHLAND

SCHWEIZ

ITALIA

ESPAÑA

Calais

Lille

PAS-DE-CALAIS

NORD

Arras

SOMME

Amiens

Somme

AISNE

Charleville-Mézières

Meuse

ARDENNES

Laon

Reims

MARNE

Châlons-en-Champagne

22

Moselle

Vins de Moselle

Metz

MOSELLE

MEUSE

Bar-le-Duc

Toul

Côtes de Toul

MEURTHE-ET-MOSELLE

Nancy

Strasbourg

BAS-RHIN

6

SEINE-MARITIME

le Havre

Rouen

EURE

Seine

VAL-D'OISE

Pontoise

SEINE-ST-DENIS

SEINE-ET-MARNE

HAUTE-DE-SEINE

PARIS

Versailles

YVELINES

VAL-DE-MARNE

Evry

ESSONNE

Melun

Aisne

Oise

Marne

Aube

Troyes

AUBE

5

HAUTE-MARNE

Chaumont

VOSGES

Épinal

Rhin

Colmar

9

HAUT-RHIN

BELFORT

Belfort

Vesoul

HAUTE-SAÔNE

St-Lô

CALVADOS

Caen

ORNE

Alençon

EURE-ET-LOIR

Chartres

Evreux

Beauvais

OISE

MAYENNE

Laval

SARTHE

le Mans

LOIR-ET-CHER

Blois

Montoire-sur-le-Loir

Coteaux du Vendômois

LOIRET

Orléans

Vins de l'Orléanais

8

YONNE

Auxerre

Chablis

6

St-Bris-le-Vineux

Sauvignon de St-Bris

CÔTE-D'OR

Dijon

Beaune

9

Doubs

DOUBS

Besançon

MAINE-ET-LOIRE

Angers

Coteaux d'Ancenis

22

INDRE-ET-LOIRE

Tours

10

Valençay

8

CHER

Bourges

NIÈVRE

Nevers

Loire

1

3

le Creusot

SAÔNE-ET-LOIRE

Mâcon

13

JURA

Lons-le-Saunier

2

L. Léman

HAUTE-SAVOIE

Annecy

Thouars

Vins du Thouarsais

3

DEUX-SÈVRES

le Roche-sur-Yon

Vendéens

8

VENDÉE

2

Niort

VIENNE

Poitiers

Haut-Poitou

2

INDRE

Châteauroux

Châteaumeillant

Châteaumeillant

ALLIER

Moulins

St-Pourçain-sur-Sioule

St-Pourçain

Allier

AIN

Bourg-en-Bresse

Roanne

Côte Roannaise

1

Lyon

RHÔNE

22

Belley

Vins du Bugey

2

Chambéry

SAVOIE

Isère

la Rochelle

CHARENTE-MARITIME

39

40

Angoulême

CHARENTE

HAUTE-VIENNE

Limoges

CREUSE

Guéret

PUY-DE-DÔME

Clermont-Ferrand

Côtes d'Auvergne

Boën-sur-Lignon

LOIRE

Côtes du Forez

St-Étienne

ISÈRE

Grenoble

117

Bordeaux

GIRONDE

Libourne

15

CORRÈZE

Tulle

DORDOGNE

Périgueux

CANTAL

Aurillac

HAUTE-LOIRE

le Puy

Tournon

18

Valence

13

ARDÈCHE

Privas

Côtes du Vivarais

DRÔME

Die

Clairette de Die

HAUTES-ALPES

Gap

HAUTE-PROVENCE

Digne

Coteaux de Pierrevert

Pierrevert

ALPES-DE-HAUTE-PROVENCE

ALPES-MARITIMES

Nice

LOT-ET-GARONNE

Buzet

Côtes du Brulhois

8

Agen

la Villedieu-du-Temple

Vins de Lavilledieu

LOT

Cahors

6

Marcillac-Vallon

Marcillac

Estaing

Vins d'Estaing

Entraygues

Vins d'Entraygues et du Fel

Rodez

AVEYRON

Côtes de Millau

LOZÈRE

Mende

GARD

68

Nîmes

108

VAUCLUSE

54

Avignon

10

BOUCHES-DU-RHÔNE

Marseille

VAR

32

Draguignan

Toulon

LANDES

Mont-de-Marsan

Adour

GERS

Côtes de St-Mont

20

Auch

TARN-ET-GARONNE

Montauban

Gaillac

Albi

9

TARN

3

Tarn

3

HÉRAULT

Montpellier

PYRÉNÉES-ATLANTIQUES

2

Pau

HAUTES-PYRÉNÉES

Tarbes

Tursan

Geaune

St-Mont

HAUTE-GARONNE

Toulouse

Côtes de la Malepère

Carcassonne

87

AUDE

Narbonne

ARIÈGE

Foix

PYRÉNÉES-ORIENTALES

Perpignan

36

Garonne

Lot

Coteaux du Quercy

Rhône

1:3,625,000

Km 0   50   100   150 Km

Miles 0   50   100 Miles

Burgundy

The very name of Burgundy has a sonorous ring. Is it the chapel- or the dinner-bell? Let Paris be France's head, Champagne her soul; Burgundy is her stomach. It is a land of long meals, well-supplied with the best materials (Charolais beef to the west, Bresse chickens to the east, fish in the rivers and snails on the vines). It was the richest of the ancient duchies of France. But even before France became Christian it was famous for its wine.

Burgundy is not one big vineyard, but the name of a province that contains at least three of France's best. By far the richest and most important of its regions is the Côte d'Or, Burgundy's heart, composed of the Côte de Beaune in the south and the Côte de Nuits in the north. But Chablis and the Mâconnais have reputations which owe nothing to their richer brother's. And immediately south of the Mâconnais is Beaujolais, quite different from Burgundy in scale, style, soil and grape (see pages 72-74).

And yet for all the ancient fame and riches, Burgundy still feels simple and rustic. There is hardly a grand house from one end to the other of the Côte d'Or – none of the elegant country estates which stamp the Médoc as a creation of

leisure and wealth in the 18th and 19th centuries, for example. Most of the few big holdings of land, those of the Church, were broken up by Napoleon. Burgundy is still one of the most fragmented of France's important winegrowing districts. The average holding may be bigger than it used to be, but is still a mere 15 acres (6ha).

The fragmentation of Burgundy is the cause of the single great drawback of its wine: its unpredictability. From the geographer's point of view the human factor is unmappable, and in Burgundy, more than in most places, it needs to be given the limelight. For even having pinned down a wine to one particular *climat* (plot of vines) in one particular commune in one particular year, it could still, in many cases, have been made by any one of six or seven people owning small parcels of the land, and reared in any one of six or seven cellars. *Monopoles*, or whole vineyards in the hands of one grower, are rare exceptions. Even the smallest grower has parcels in two or three vineyards. Bigger ones may own a total of 50-100 acres (20-40ha) spread in small lots in a score of vineyards throughout the Côte. Clos de Vougeot's 125 acres (50ha) are divided among 80 growers.

For this very reason about 65% of burgundy is still bought in barrel from the grower when it is new by négociants (or shippers), who blend it with other wines from the same appellation to achieve marketable quantities of a standard wine. This is offered to the world not as the product of a specific grower, whose production of that particular wine may be only a cask or two, but as the wine of a given district (be it as specific as a vineyard or as vague as a village) *élevé* – literally, raised – by the shipper.

In the 1980s a few greedy, careless *négociants-éleveurs* earned a certain notoriety for these large-scale blenders. Reputations still vary enormously but of the larger shippers the revitalized Bouchard Père et Fils, Joseph Drouhin, Faiveley, Louis Jadot, and Louis Latour (for its best whites) are reliable, and significant vineyard owners themselves.

The profession took on a new respectability towards the end of the century with the emergence of a number of ambitious young négociants making some of Burgundy's best wines. Dominique Laurent and Verget led the field in red and white wine-rearing respectively. The map opposite shows the whole of winegrowing

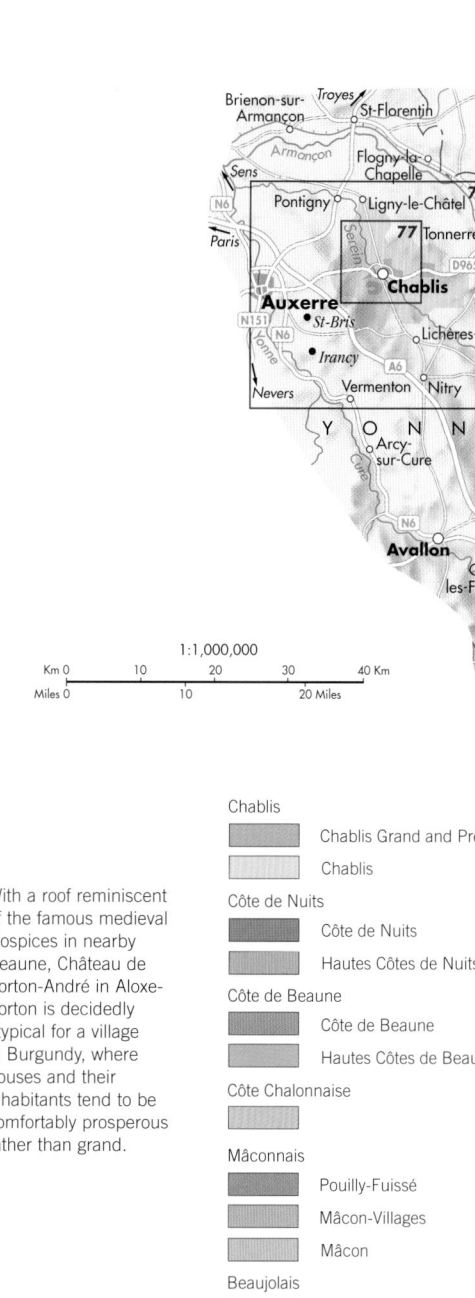

With a roof reminiscent of the famous medieval Hospices in nearby Beaune, Château de Corton-André in Aloxe-Corton is decidedly atypical for a village in Burgundy, where houses and their inhabitants tend to be comfortably prosperous rather than grand.

1:1,000,000

Chablis

Chablis Grand and Premier Cru

Chablis

Côte de Nuits

Côte de Nuits

Hautes Côtes de Nuits

Côte de Beaune

Côte de Beaune

Hautes Côtes de Beaune

Côte Chalonnaise

Mâconnais

Pouilly-Fuissé

Mâcon-Villages

Mâcon

Beaujolais

Beaujolais-Villages

Beaujolais

Morgon •   Principal wine commune

57   Area mapped at larger scale on page shown

▼   Weather station (WS)

Burgundy: the relative sizes and positions of the big southern areas of Beaujolais and the Mâconnais, the northern region of Chablis, the much smaller Côte Chalonnaise, and the narrow strip of the Côte d'Or and its little-known hinterland, the Hautes Côtes de Beaune and the Hautes Côtes de Nuits. These regions are all mapped in detail on pages 57–77.

There is a total of nearly 100 Appellation Contrôlées in Burgundy. Most refer to geographical areas and appear on the following pages. Built into these geographical appellations is a quality classification which is practically a work of art in itself (it is explained in detail on page 58). However, the following appellations can be applied to wine made from grapes grown in any part of Burgundy, including vineyards within famous communes whose soil and situation are below par: Bourgogne (for Pinot Noir or Chardonnay), Bourgogne Grand Ordinaire (for a mixture of local Burgundian grapes), and Burgundy's house red and white, respectively, Bourgogne Passetoutgrains (for a mixture of Gamay with at least a third Pinot Noir), and Bourgogne Aligoté (for white wine made from Burgundy's other white grape).

Burgundy: Dijon

Latitude / Altitude of WS **47.15° / 722ft (220m)**
Mean July temperature at WS **67.5°F (19.72°C)**
Average annual rainfall at WS **27in (690mm)**
Harvest month rainfall at WS **September: 2.2in (55mm)**
Principal viticultural hazards **Frost, disease (especially mildew) and autumn rain**
Principal grape varieties at WS **Pinot Noir, Chardonnay, Gamay, Aligoté**

Côte d'Or: the Quality Factor

A Burgundian understandably feels a certain reverence towards the rather commonplace-looking ridge of the Côte d'Or – like the Athenians towards an unknown god. One is bound to wonder at the fact that a few small parcels of land on this hill give superlative wines, each with its own positive personality, and that others do not. Surely one can discover the factors that distinguish one parcel from another – giving to some grapes more sugar, thicker skins, and a pulp richer in minerals?

One can. And one cannot. Soil and subsoil have been analyzed time and again. Temperature and humidity and wind direction have been recorded; wines have been analyzed by gas chromatography... yet the central mystery remains. One can only put down certain physical facts, and place beside them the reputations of the great wines. No one has yet proved conclusively how the two are connected (even if wine-loving geologists are attracted to the Côte d'Or like moths to a flame).

The Côte lies along an important geological fault line where the seabed deposits of several different geological epochs, each rich in calcium from defunct shellfish, are exposed like a sliced layer-cake. Exposure has weathered their rocks into soils of different ages and textures; the varying degrees of slope have mixed them in different proportions. Minor local fault lines which lie at right angles to the Côte add variations to the mix.

The altitude of the mid-slope is roughly constant at about 820ft (250m). Higher, on the thinly soiled hard rock cap of the hill, the climate is harsher; grapes ripen later. Lower down, where the soil is more alluvial, valley mists and unseasonal frosts are more common.

The Côte faces east with a bias to the south, locally skewed (especially in the Côte de Beaune) to full south and even west exposure. Along its lower part, generally about a third of the way up, runs a narrow outcrop of marlstone, making limy clay soil. Marl by itself would be too rich a soil for the highest quality wine, but in combination with the stones and scree washed down from the hard limestone higher up it is perfect. Erosion continues the blending below the actual outcrop, the distance depending on the angle of incline.

In the Côte de Beaune the marly outcrop, or Argovien, is wider and higher on the hill; instead of a narrow strip of vineyard under a beetling brow of limestone there is a broad and gentle slope vineyards can climb. The vines almost reach the scrubby peak in places.

On the dramatic isolated hill of Corton the soil formed from the marlstone is the best part of the vineyard, having only a little wood-covered cap of hard limestone above it.

In Meursault the limestone reappearing below the marl on the slope forms a second and lower shoulder to the hill, limy and very stony; excellent for white wine.

Such illustrations are only random examples of the varied structure of the Côte. And with each change of soil comes a change in drainage and aspect, in the soil's temperature – in any one of a hundred factors which affect the vine and therefore the wine.

Burgundy is the northernmost area in Europe to produce great red wine. It is vital that the Pinot Noir vines are ripened before the cold and damp of autumn sets in. The climate peculiar to

--- · --- Département boundary

Wine-producing areas

59 Area mapped at larger scale on page shown

A———A Cross-section (see opposite page)

1:220,000

Km 0 1 2 3 4 5 Km
Miles 0   1   2   3 Miles

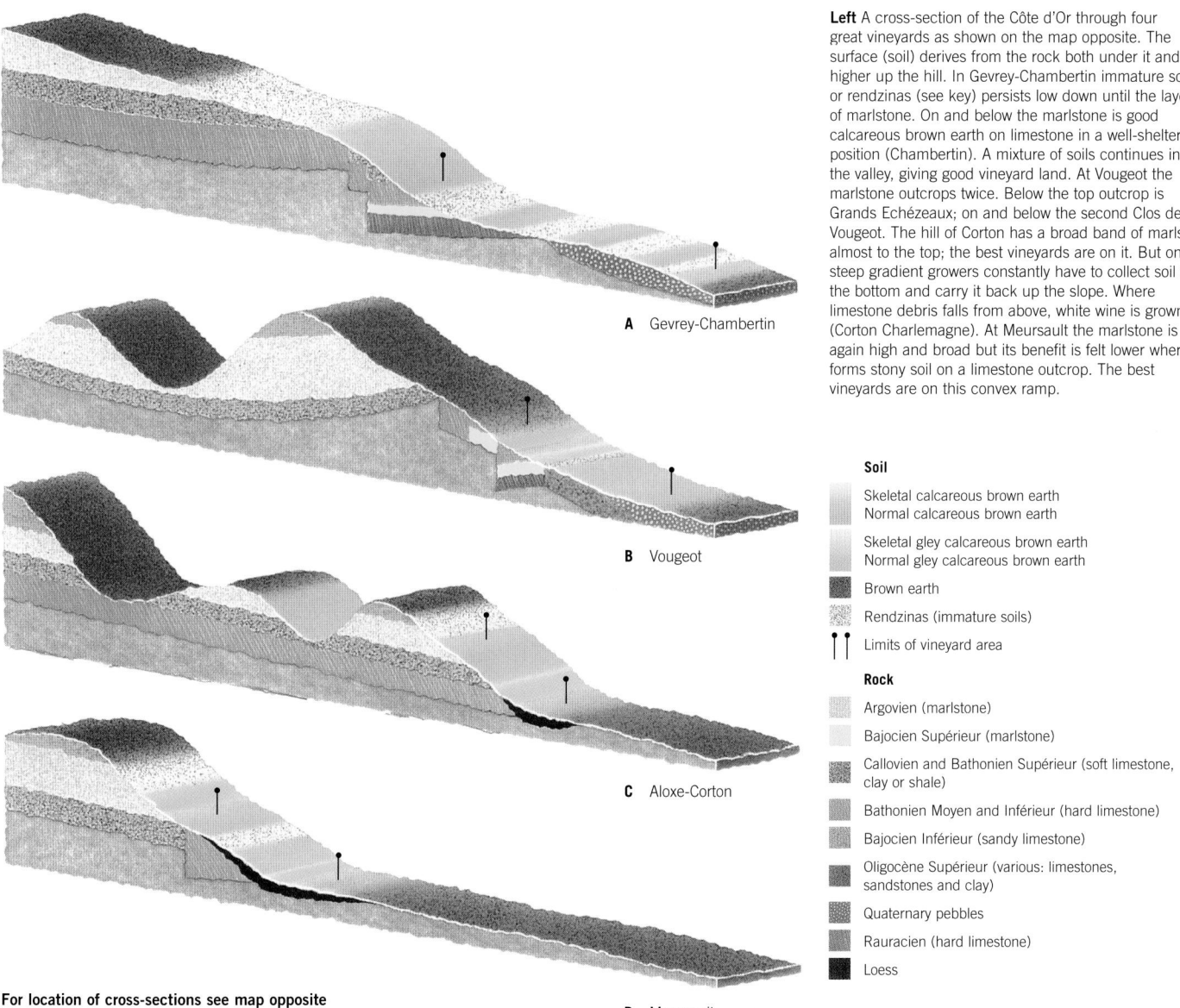

Left A cross-section of the Côte d'Or through four great vineyards as shown on the map opposite. The surface (soil) derives from the rock both under it and higher up the hill. In Gevrey-Chambertin immature soil or rendzinas (see key) persists low down until the layer of marlstone. On and below the marlstone is good calcareous brown earth on limestone in a well-sheltered position (Chambertin). A mixture of soils continues into the valley, giving good vineyard land. At Vougeot the marlstone outcrops twice. Below the top outcrop is Grands Echézeaux; on and below the second Clos de Vougeot. The hill of Corton has a broad band of marlstone almost to the top; the best vineyards are on it. But on this steep gradient growers constantly have to collect soil from the bottom and carry it back up the slope. Where limestone debris falls from above, white wine is grown (Corton Charlemagne). At Meursault the marlstone is again high and broad but its benefit is felt lower where it forms stony soil on a limestone outcrop. The best vineyards are on this convex ramp.

A Gevrey-Chambertin

B Vougeot

C Aloxe-Corton

D Meursault

For location of cross-sections see map opposite

Soil

Skeletal calcareous brown earth
Normal calcareous brown earth

Skeletal gley calcareous brown earth
Normal gley calcareous brown earth

Brown earth

Rendzinas (immature soils)

Limits of vineyard area

Rock

Argovien (marlstone)

Bajocien Supérieur (marlstone)

Callovien and Bathonien Supérieur (soft limestone, clay or shale)

Bathonien Moyen and Inférieur (hard limestone)

Bajocien Inférieur (sandy limestone)

Oligocène Supérieur (various: limestones, sandstones and clay)

Quaternary pebbles

Rauracien (hard limestone)

Loess

each vineyard, the so-called mesoclimate (see page 22), in combination with the physical structure, undoubtedly has the most decisive effect. The best vineyards of the Côte face due east; it is the morning sun they want, to warm the ground gradually and retain the heat all day. They are sheltered from the southwest, from the most rain-bearing wind – but not so sheltered as to be frost pockets on still nights.

The other, unmappable, quality factor is the grower's choice of vines and the way they are pruned and fertilized. There are more or less vigorous clones of the classic varieties, and a grower who chooses the most productive, prunes inadequately or overfeeds the soil, inevitably compromises quality. A lot of disappointing short-lived wine was made this way in the 1970s, but now the pursuit of quality seems to have the upper hand over greed.

The reasons why the Côte d'Or needs mapping in more detail than any other wine region arise both from its singular pattern of soils and mesoclimates and from its unique history.

Of all regions this is the one where wine quality has been studied the longest – certainly since the 12th century when Cistercian and Benedictine monks got to work in earnest. It is said that they "tasted the soil" – so eager were they to explore its potential and distinguish one *cru* from another. The word *cru* means both the land and the wine, defined as an entity distinct from the next *cru* on the hill. Where to draw the lines was the entire aim of the monks' passionate enquiry.

The great Dukes of Burgundy of the house of Valois in the 14th and 15th centuries did everything possible to encourage and profit by the region's wines. Every generation since has added to the sum of local knowledge that is expressed in the *climats* and *crus* of the hills from Dijon to Chagny.

The map opposite gives the essential overview. At the top of the not-very-impressive hills is a broken plateau with abrupt scarps (steep hills) where geological fault-lines protrude. This is the Hautes Côtes, divided into those of Beaune and those of Nuits, rising to over 1,300ft (400m) and subject to cold and exposure that puts their crop a week behind the pampered Côtes below.

This is not to say that in their more sheltered east- and south-facing combes the Pinot Noir and Chardonnay cannot produce generally lightish but sometimes fine wines of true Côte d'Or character. The best communes in the Hautes Côtes de Beaune include Nantoux, Echevronne, La Rochepot, and Meloisey; in the Hautes Côtes de Nuits, where red wines dominate, Marey-lès-Fussey, Magny-lès-Villers, Villers-Fontaine and Bévy.

At the southern tip of the Côte de Beaune is a recent appellation, Maranges, responsible for delicate reds from the three communes just west of Santenay bearing the suffix -lès-Maranges.

The sheltered vineyards of the two Côtes are densely concentrated in the north, where they face east on a more or less consistent and unbroken slope. South of Nuits the communes of Comblanchien and Corgoloin slice marble from the hills; an abrupt change from the ranks of vines. Just south of Ladoix-Serrigny, the northernmost village of the Côte de Beaune, vines spread out south and west from the oval hill of Corton in a more sprawling landscape with more southern slopes. The Côte de Beaune produces more than twice as much wine as the Côte de Nuits, almost half of it white. The Côte de Nuits concentrates on one thing only: the Pinot Noir.

Côte d'Or

The Côte d'Or – the Côte de Beaune and the Côte de Nuits, separated only by a few miles where vines give way to marble quarries – is an irregular escarpment some 30 miles (50km) long. Its top is a wooded plateau; its bottom the beginning of the plain-like valley of the River Saône. The width of the slope varies from a mile and a half to a few hundred yards – but all the good vineyards lie in this narrow strip.

The classification of the qualities of the land in this strip is the most elaborate on earth, further complicated by slight differences in nomenclature and spelling between different producers. It is the work of the Institut National des Appellations d'Origine (INAO), based on classifications going back more than 100 years. This divides the vineyards into four classes and stipulates the precise labelling of each wine accordingly.

Below The Hospices de Beaune is the city of Beaune's most famous landmark and site of a world-famous wine auction each November. Built in the mid-15th century the distinctive building housed Beaune's wine-funded (free) hospital, or Hôtel-Dieu, until the late 20th century. It was founded by the Duke of Burgundy's Chancellor Nicolas Rollin and his third wife Guigone de Salin and endowed with vineyards in the surrounding countryside. Since then growers have continued to bequeath vineyards throughout the Côte de Beaune to the Hospices and its wine auction. They are marked with a cross on the maps that follow.

Grands Crus are the first class, of which 30 are effectively in operation today. Each has its own appellation. The single, simple vineyard name – Musigny, Corton, Montrachet or Chambertin (sometimes prefixed by "Le") – is the patent of Burgundy's highest nobility.

Premiers Crus, the next rank, use the name of their commune, followed by the name of the vineyard (or, if the wine comes from more than one Premier Cru vineyard, the commune name plus the words Premier Cru). Examples would be, respectively, "Chambolle-Musigny, (Les) Charmes" or, if the wine were a blend between Amoureuses and another Premier Cru vineyard or two, then "Chambolle-Musigny Premier Cru".

Some Premiers Crus are better than others, which is hardly surprising since there are 561 in all, and in only five communes of the Côte de Beaune are there any Grands Crus at all. Premiers Crus such as Perrières in Meursault and Rugiens in Pommard, as well as Les Amoureuses in Chambolle-Musigny and Clos St-Jacques in Gevrey-Chambertin, consistently yield wine that is markedly superior to that of most others.

Appellation Communale is the third rank; that is, with the right to use the commune name. Such wines are often referred to as "village" wines as in, for example, "village Meursault". The name of a specific vineyard, or *lieu-dit*, is

permitted, and increasingly used, on the label of these wines but must be printed in smaller type than the commune name. A few such vineyards, while not officially Premiers Crus, can be considered in the same class.

Fourth, there are less propitiously sited vineyards even within some famous communes (typically, east of the main road, the N74), which have only the right to call their wine Bourgogne. Their produce may be clearly inferior but, in the hands of an able winemaker, can be one of the Côte d'Or's rare bargains.

The INAO also lays down the regulations which control quality, demanding that only the classic grapes be used (Pinot Noir for red wine, Chardonnay for white); that only so much wine (from 35hl/ha for the best, to 60 or so for the more ordinary) be made; that it achieve a certain minimum strength (from 12% alcohol for the best white and 11.5% for the best red, down to 10% for the most ordinary red).

The consumer must remember to distinguish the name of a vineyard from that of a commune. Many villages (Vosne, Chassagne, Gevrey, etc) have affixed their name to that of their best vineyard. The difference between Chevalier Montrachet (from one famous vineyard) and a Chassagne-Montrachet (from anywhere in a big commune) is not obvious, but it is vital.

The wine merchants of Beaune

1 Chanson Père & Fils
2 Bouchard Aîné & Fils
3 Patriarche Père & Fils
4 Caves de la Reine Pédauque
5 Joseph Drouhin
6 Louis Latour
7 Remoissenet Père & Fils
8 Bouchard Père & Fils
9 Louis Jadot
10 Champy

Côte de Beaune: Santenay

The maps on this and the following eight pages represent the conclusion of the first complete official survey and classification of the vineyards of the Côte d'Or by the INAO. They trace the vineyards of the Côte from south to north. The orientation of the maps has been turned through between 45 and 90 degrees so that in each section the intricacies of the Côte lie along the bottom of the page.

The Côte de Beaune starts without a great explosion of famous names. It leads in gradually, from the relatively obscure villages of Sampigny, Dézize, and Cheilly, which share the one well-known *cru* of Maranges (all beyond the limits of this map; see page 56), into the commune of Santenay. After the hamlet of Haut-Santenay and the little town of Bas-Santenay (a spa frequented by local gamblers and bons viveurs) the Côte half-turns to take up its characteristic slope to the east.

This southern end of the Côte de Beaune is the most confused geologically and in many ways is atypical of the Côte as a whole. Complex faults in the structure of the hills make radical changes of soil and subsoil in Santenay. Part of the commune is analogous to parts of the Côte de Nuits, giving deep, if not exquisitely fine, red wine with a long life. Other parts give light wine more typical of the Côte de Beaune.

Some of the highest vineyards have proved too stony to pay their way. Les Gravières (the name draws attention to the stony ground, as the name Graves does in Bordeaux) and La Comme are the best *climats* of Santenay.

As we move into Chassagne-Montrachet the quality of these excellent red-wine vineyards is confirmed. The name of Montrachet is so firmly associated with white wine that few people expect to find red here at all. But almost all the vineyards from the village of Chassagne south grow at least some red wine: Morgeot, La Boudriotte, and (overleaf) Clos St-Jean are the most famous. Their wines are solid, long-lived and deep-coloured, coming closer in character to Gevrey-Chambertin than to, say, Volnay.

Visiting at around the time of the French Revolution, Thomas Jefferson reported that white-winegrowers here had to eat hard rye bread while red-wine men could afford it soft and white. But Le Montrachet had been famous for white wine since the 16th century, and at least part of the village's soil is much better suited to Chardonnay than to Pinot Noir. White winegrowing really took over in the second half of the 20th century as the world fell in love with Chardonnay. Nowadays Chassagne-Montrachet is known to the world chiefly for its dry but succulent, golden, flower-scented white wine.

Some of the growers of *Chassagne-Montrachet also have holdings in the Grands Crus of Montrachet and its neighbours, which are discussed overleaf. Similarly, the name Chassagne-Montrachet is found on labels of many a producer based outside the village. These labels are from some of Chassagne and Santenay's best growers.*

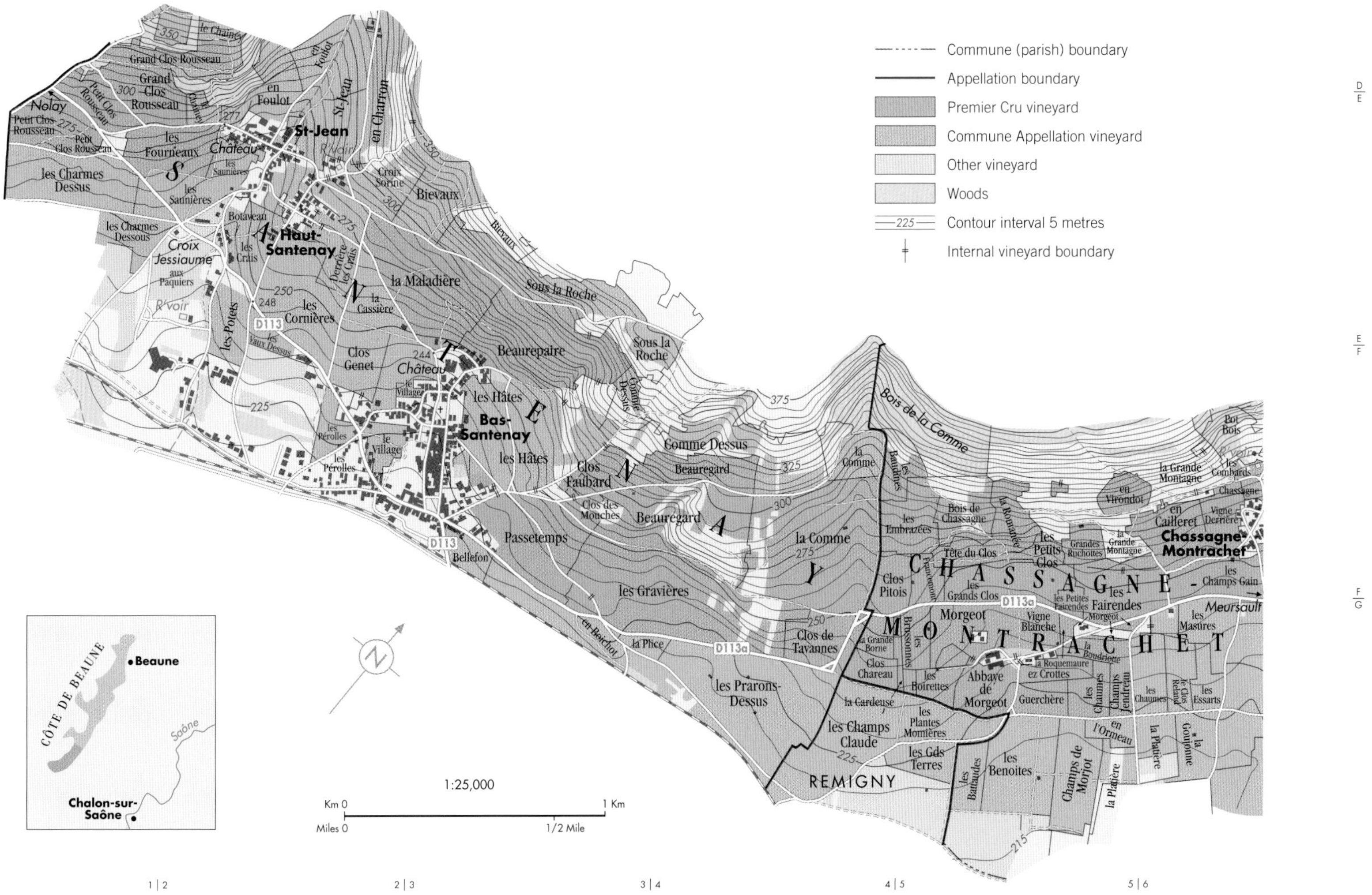

Côte de Beaune: Meursault

A side valley in the hills just north of Chassagne leading up to the hamlet of St-Aubin, home of well-priced, slightly earthy wines, divides the vineyards of the commune in two. South of it there is excellent white wine but the emphasis is on red. North, on the border of Puligny, there is the best white wine in Burgundy, if not the whole world.

The Grand Cru Montrachet earns its fame by an almost unbelievable concentration of the qualities of white burgundy. At its incomparable best it has (given ten years) more scent, a brighter gold, a longer flavour, more succulence and yet more definition; everything about it is intensified – the mark of truly great wine. Perfect exposure to the east, yet an angle which means the sun is still flooding down the rows at nine on a summer evening, and a sudden streak of limestone soil (see page 57) are factors giving it an edge over its neighbours. So much greater is demand for than supply of this illustrious wine, however, that expensive disappointments are by no means unknown.

The other Grands Crus grouped about it are less famous, not quite so perfectly situated, but the wines can sometimes be more carefully made.

Chevalier Montrachet tends to have less depth (its soil is stonier; the best has been used for renewing Le Montrachet). Bâtard-Montrachet lies on heavier ground and often fails to achieve quite the same finesse, though it can take as long to age. Les Criots (in Chassagne) and Bienvenues belong in the same class – as at their best do the Puligny Premiers Crus Les Pucelles, Les Combettes, Les Folatières, and Le Cailleret (and the best of Meursault's Les Perrières).

There is a real distinction between Puligny-Montrachet and Meursault even though the vineyards of the one flow without a break into the other's. In fact the hamlet of Blagny – which makes excellent wine high up on stony soil – is in both, and boasts a classically complicated appellation: Premier Cru in Meursault, Blagny Premier Cru in Puligny-Montrachet, and AC Blagny when (which is rare) the wine is red.

Meursault is a slightly softer, richer but less vividly fine, lively and fruity wine than Puligny-Montrachet. The words "buttery" and "mealy" are used of it, whereas Puligny, with higher, more nervous acidity, is more a matter of apples and peaches. Overall, Meursault has less brilliant distinction (and no Grand Cru) but a very

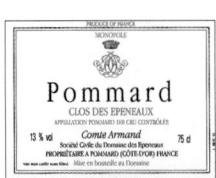

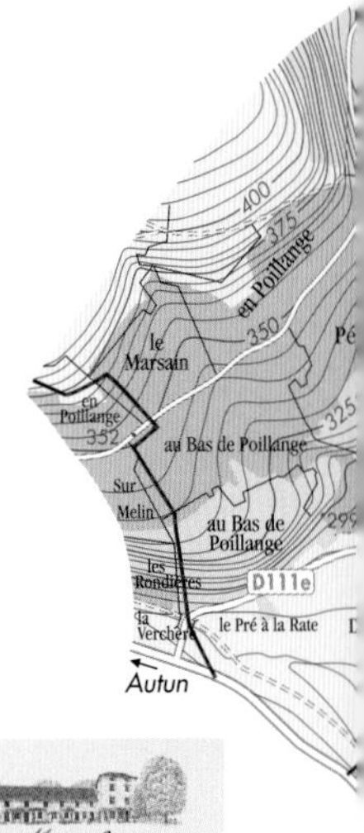

No other spot on the globe can boast this concentration of great dry white winemakers and vineyards. Lafon and Coche-Dury are the indisputable current stars of Meursault; those of Puligny-Montrachet are more contentious. On the northern limit of the Côte d'Or's prime white wine country the red wines of Volnay and Pommard (the latter discussed overleaf) have their own distinctive charm. De Montille makes some of the finest Volnays, but does not have holdings in its two most famous vineyards.

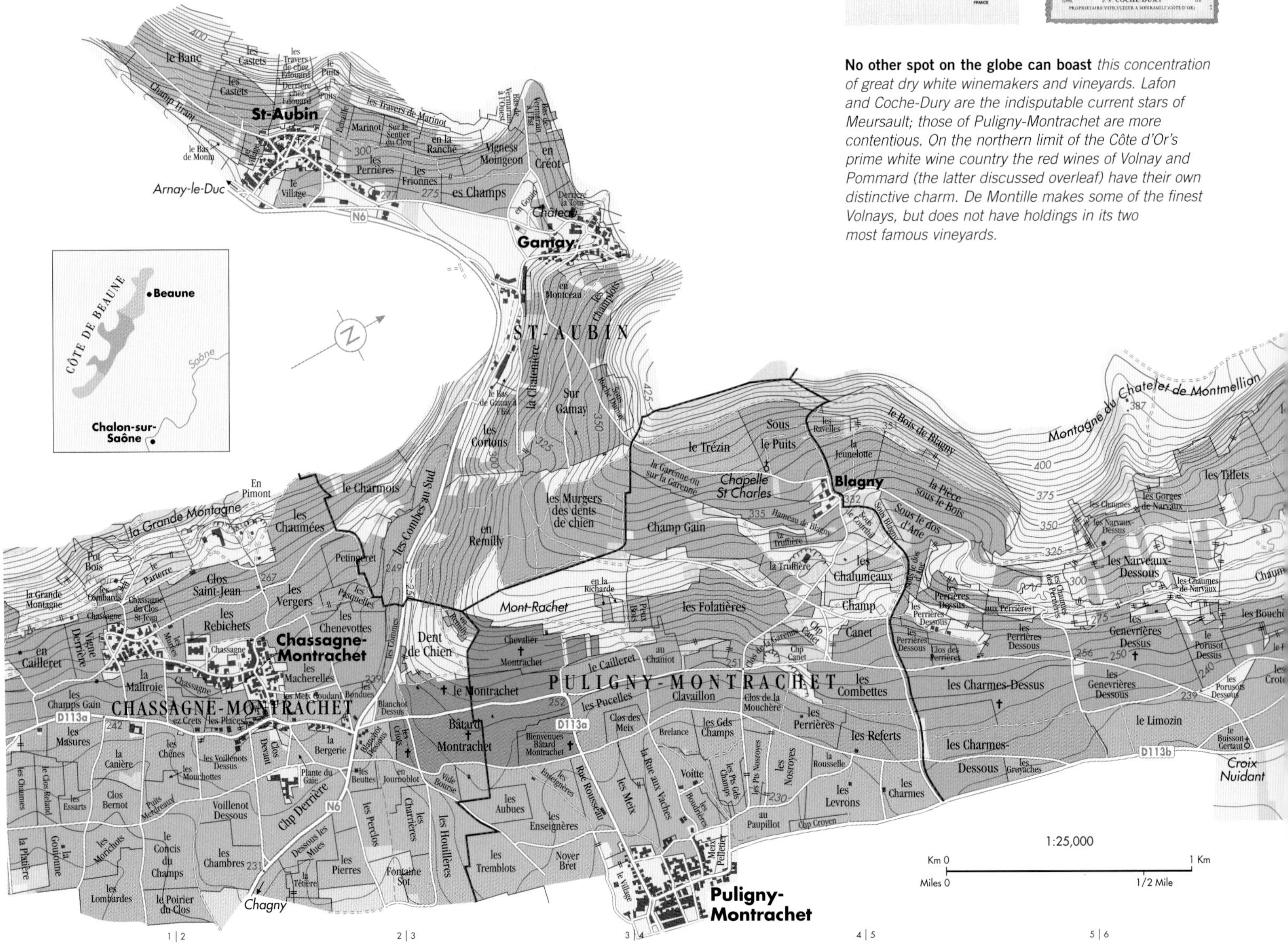

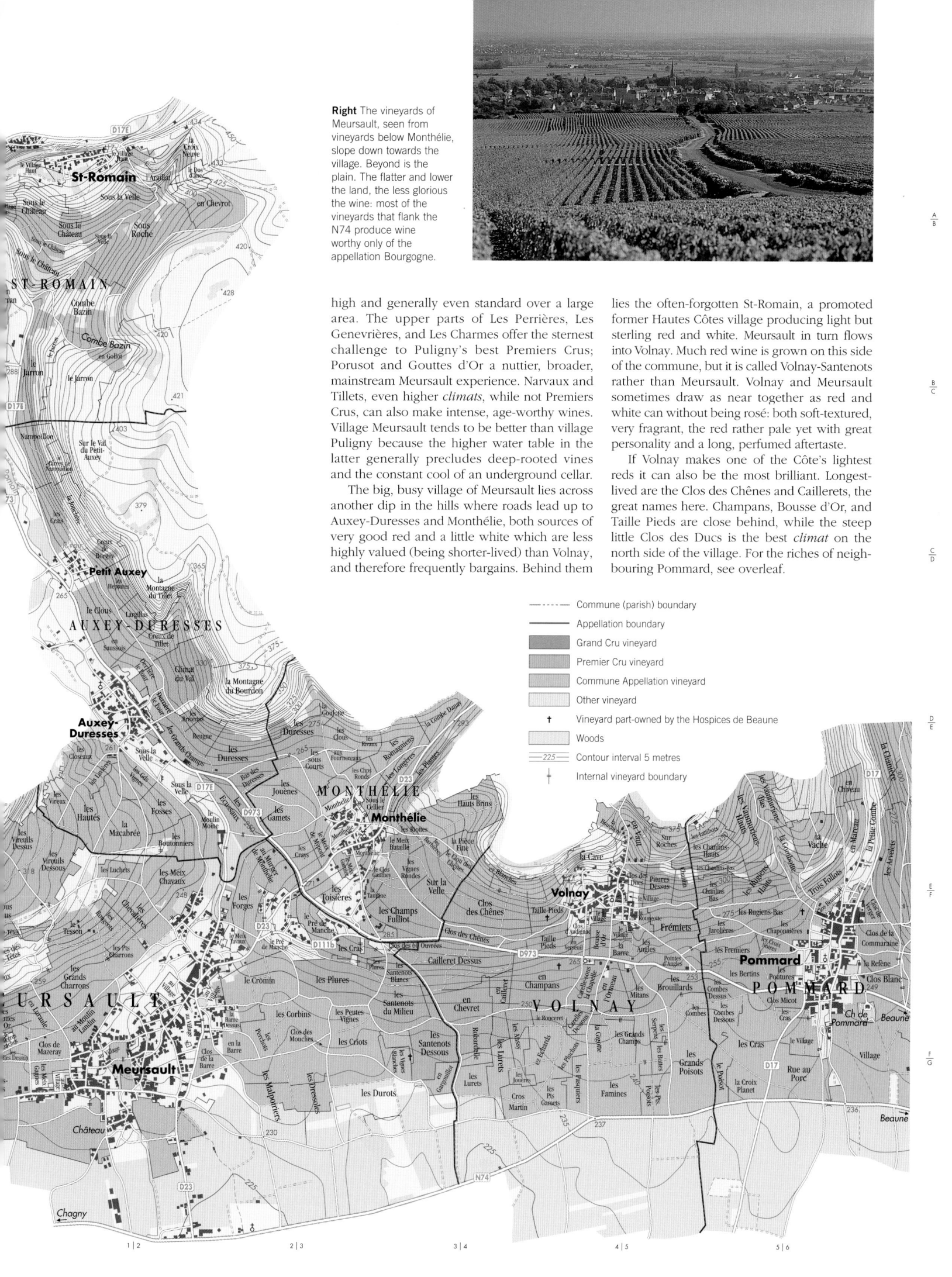

Right The vineyards of Meursault, seen from vineyards below Monthélie, slope down towards the village. Beyond is the plain. The flatter and lower the land, the less glorious the wine: most of the vineyards that flank the N74 produce wine worthy only of the appellation Bourgogne.

high and generally even standard over a large area. The upper parts of Les Perrières, Les Genevrières, and Les Charmes offer the sternest challenge to Puligny's best Premiers Crus; Porusot and Gouttes d'Or a nuttier, broader, mainstream Meursault experience. Narvaux and Tillets, even higher *climats*, while not Premiers Crus, can also make intense, age-worthy wines. Village Meursault tends to be better than village Puligny because the higher water table in the latter generally precludes deep-rooted vines and the constant cool of an underground cellar.

The big, busy village of Meursault lies across another dip in the hills where roads lead up to Auxey-Duresses and Monthélie, both sources of very good red and a little white which are less highly valued (being shorter-lived) than Volnay, and therefore frequently bargains. Behind them

lies the often-forgotten St-Romain, a promoted former Hautes Côtes village producing light but sterling red and white. Meursault in turn flows into Volnay. Much red wine is grown on this side of the commune, but it is called Volnay-Santenots rather than Meursault. Volnay and Meursault sometimes draw as near together as red and white can without being rosé: both soft-textured, very fragrant, the red rather pale yet with great personality and a long, perfumed aftertaste.

If Volnay makes one of the Côte's lightest reds it can also be the most brilliant. Longest-lived are the Clos des Chênes and Caillerets, the great names here. Champans, Bousse d'Or, and Taille Pieds are close behind, while the steep little Clos des Ducs is the best *climat* on the north side of the village. For the riches of neighbouring Pommard, see overleaf.

---------- Commune (parish) boundary

———— Appellation boundary

◾ Grand Cru vineyard

◾ Premier Cru vineyard

◾ Commune Appellation vineyard

◾ Other vineyard

† Vineyard part-owned by the Hospices de Beaune

◾ Woods

══225══ Contour interval 5 metres

✝ Internal vineyard boundary

Côte de Beaune: Beaune

Logically you would expect the Pommard vineyards bordering Volnay (mapped on the previous page) to give the most Volnay-like, fragrant and ethereal wines. But far from it. The commune boundary marks a soil change that makes Les Rugiens (ruddy, as its name suggests, with iron-rich earth) Pommard's standard-bearer for a different style entirely: dark, heady and tannic. Many vineyards entitled to the simple village Pommard appellation, which make up 80% of the commune, produce wines in this style which lack grace and distinction. But there are two or three exceptional Premiers Crus – above all Rugiens and Epenots – and four or five fine growers. It is worth remembering that in Burgundy the grower counts as much as the vineyard, and the saying goes "there are no great wines; only great bottles of wine".

Pommard's most prestigious vineyard is the lower part of Les Rugiens (Les Rugiens-Bas on the map on page 61), above the village. One of the best *cuvées* of the Hospices de Beaune, Dames de la Charité, is made from Rugiens and Epenots combined. The Clos de la Commaraine and the wines of the growers Courcel, Armand, Gaunoux, and de Montille are Pommard's finest; sturdy wines that need ten years to develop the lovely savoury character of the best burgundy.

In the line of famous vineyards that occupy what the Burgundians call "the kidney of the slope", at about the 800ft (250m) line above Beaune, a large proportion belongs to the city's négociants: Drouhin, Jadot, Bouchard Père et Fils, Chanson, and Patriarche among them. The late Maurice Drouhin was one of the more recent entries on the centuries-old list of donors to the Hospices de Beaune. His firm's part of the Clos des Mouches is celebrated; it makes a succulent white Beaune as well as a superb red one. A part of Les Grèves belonging to Bouchard Père et Fils is known as the Vigne de l'Enfant Jésus, and makes another marvellous wine. No Beaune is a Grand Cru; the best is usually gentle wine, lasting well but not demanding to be kept the ten years or more that a Romanée or Chambertin would.

Travelling north from Beaune the road crosses a plain, and the hills and vineyards retreat. Ahead looms the prow of Corton, the one isolated hill of the whole Côte d'Or, with a dark cap of woods. Corton breaks the spell that prevents the Côte de Beaune from having a red Grand Cru. Its massive smooth slide of hill, vineyard to the top, presents faces to the east, south and west; all excellent. Indeed, it has not one but two Grand Cru appellations: for white wine and red, covering most of the hill. The white, Corton-Charlemagne, is grown on the upper slopes to the south and west, where debris from the limestone top is washed down, whitening the brown marly soil. What is truly strange is that only in the last 100 years or so has Charlemagne been planted with Chardonnay. This massive, often superlative white wine, at best a rival to Montrachet, is a recent conversion.

The big tannic red is grown in a broad band all round – too broad on the east-facing slopes, where some of the lower Grand Cru land is frankly inferior. Top red Cortons come only from Le Corton itself, Les Bressandes, Le Clos du Roi, and Les Renardes. Confusingly, the part marked Corton Charlemagne on the map grows both white wine (above) and red Corton (below). There is an Alice in Wonderland air about the legalities, but none whatsoever about the wine.

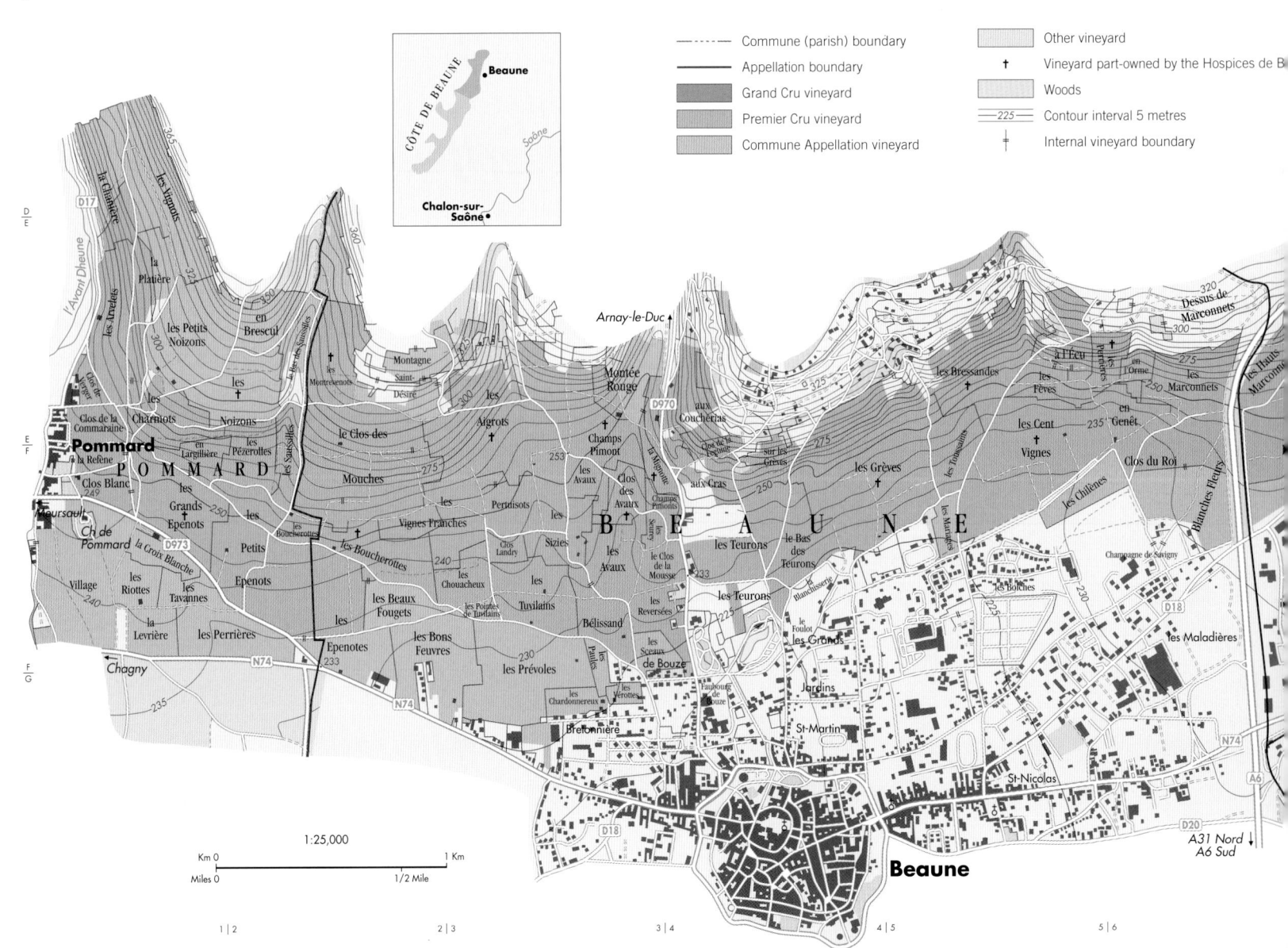

The most famous grower of Corton is Louis Latour, whose grand press house, known as Château Grancey and pictured on page 54, stands in an old quarry in Les Perrières. Aloxe-Corton is the appellation of the lesser wines (red and white) grown below the hill to the south, while Pernand-Vergelesses round the back of the hill has some Premier Cru vineyards which face east and the hill of Corton, as well as some of its west-facing Grand Cru slopes.

If Savigny and Pernand are slightly in the background it is only because the foreground is so imposing. The best growers of both make wines up to the highest Beaune standard, now fully reflected in their price. Up a side valley, Savigny, producing wines that are *"Nourrissants, Théologiques et Morbifuges"* according to local publicity, can be a marvel of finesse.

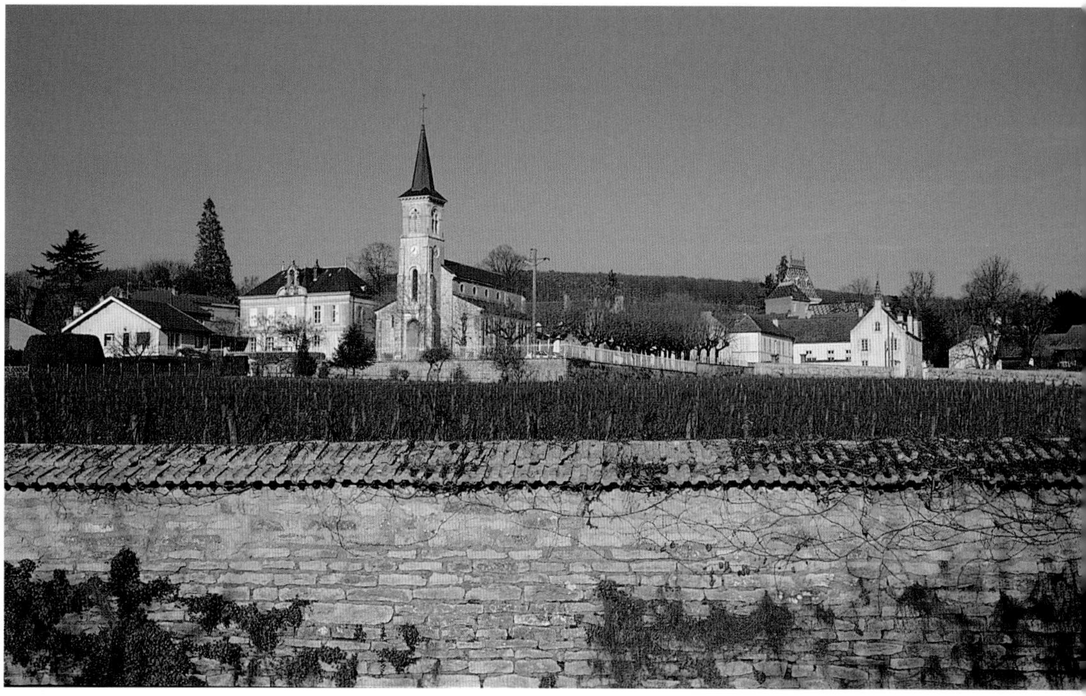

Above Winter in the village of Aloxe-Corton when these precious Pinot Noir vines have a chance to rest and build up the strength to ripen another vintage in this relatively cool climate.

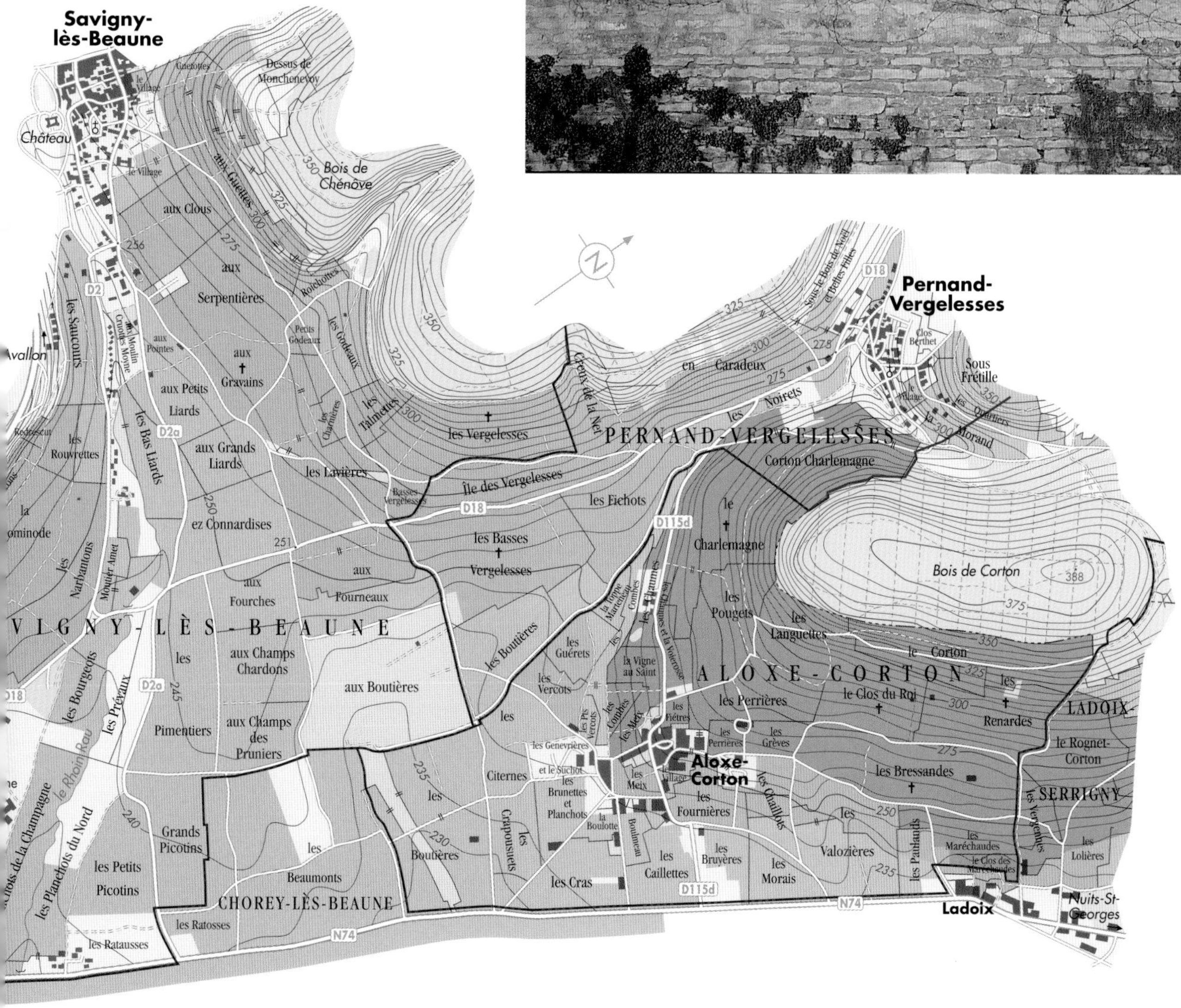

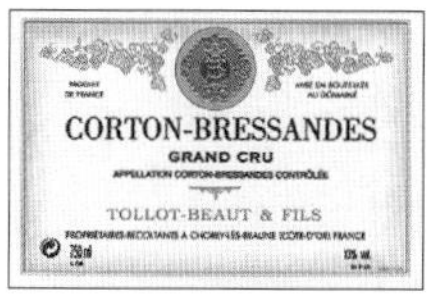
CORTON-BRESSANDES
GRAND CRU
TOLLOT-BEAUT & FILS

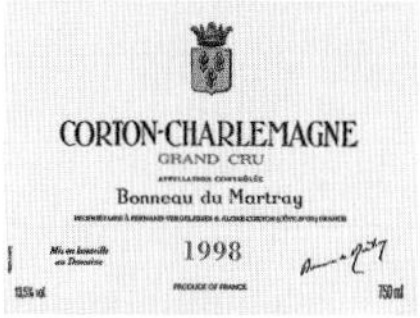
CORTON-CHARLEMAGNE
GRAND CRU
Bonneau du Martray
1998

The Hospices de Beaune *vinifies and bottles the produce of its own vineyards. Beaune is also home to the great majority of Burgundy's négociants or merchants, of which the two shown (Louis Jadot and Bouchard Père et Fils) own many a fine vineyard. Most of the growers on the famous hill of Corton live in either Aloxe-Corton or Pernand-Vergelesses.*

Hospices de Beaune
BEAUNE
Appellation Beaune Contrôlée
Cuvée Nicolas-Rolin

BEAUNE BRESSANDES
LOUIS JADOT
Domaine des Héritiers Louis Jadot

GRAND VIN DE BEAUNE GRÈVES
VIGNE DE L'ENFANT JÉSUS
1990
BOUCHARD PÈRE & FILS

CORTON
GRAND CRU
CLOS DU ROI
DOMAINE CHANDON DE BRIAILLES

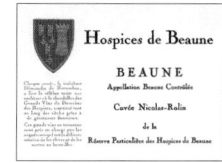

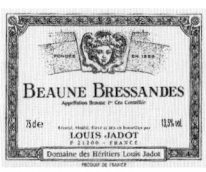

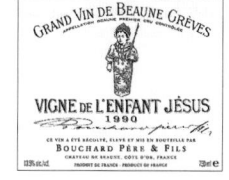

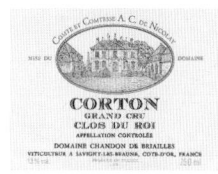

Left The angle of the vineyards sloping down towards the medieval Clos de Vougeot (site of much Burgundian bacchanalia and marked "Château" on the map) shows just how gentle is much of the golden slope, or Côte d'Or.

Côte de Nuits: Nuits-St-Georges

More "stuffing", longer life and deeper colour are the signs of a Côte de Nuits wine compared with a Volnay or Beaune. This is red wine country: white is a rarity.

The line of Premiers Crus, wriggling its way along the hills of the Côte de Nuits, is threaded with clutches of Grands Crus. These are the wines that express with most intensity the inimitable sappy richness of the Pinot Noir. The line follows the outcrop of marlstone below the hard limestone hilltop, but it is where the soil has a mixture of silt and scree over the marl that the quality really peaks. Happily, this corresponds time and again with areas that enjoy the best shelter and most sun.

The wines of Prémeaux go to market under the name of Nuits-St-Georges. The quality is very high and consistent: big strong wines which almost approach the style of Chambertin at their best. Clos de la Maréchale is a *monopole* currently farmed out by its owners to the excellent house of Faiveley, Clos Arlot is another *monopole*: both are impeccable. Equally fine are Les St-Georges and Vaucrains just over the commune boundary, with tense, positive flavours that demand long bottle age – something that cannot be said of most Côte de Nuits-Villages, a junior appellation for the extreme northern and southern ends of this Côte.

Unlike bustling Beaune, Nuits is a one-restaurant town, but it is the home of a number of négociants. The town is divided by the little River Meuzin. North of its valley the Premiers Crus leading into Vosne-Romanée are a worthy introduction to that extraordinary parish.

Vosne-Romanée is a modest little village. There is nothing here – other than an uncommon concentration of famous names on the backstreet nameplates – to suggest that the world's most expensive wine lies beneath your feet. The village stands below a long incline of reddish earth, looking up severely trimmed rows of vines, each ending with a stout post and a taut guy.

Nearest the village is the Romanée-St-Vivant vineyard. The soil is deep, rich in clay and lime. Mid-slope is La Romanée-Conti with poorer, shallower soil. Higher up, La Romanée tilts steeper; it seems drier and less clayey. On the right the big vineyard of Le Richebourg curves around to face east-northeast. Up the left flank runs the narrow strip of La Grande Rue, and beside it the long slope of La Tâche. These are among the most highly prized of all burgundies. Romanée-Conti and La Tâche are both *monopoles* of the Domaine de la Romanée-Conti, which also has substantial holdings in both Richebourg and Romanée-St-Vivant (and Echézeaux and Grands Echézeaux for good measure). For the finesse, the velvety warmth combined with a suggestion of spice, and the almost oriental opulence of their wines, the market will seemingly stand any price. Romanée-Conti is the most perfect of all, but the entire group has a family likeness: the result of small crops, old vines, late picking, and great care.

Clearly one can look among their neighbours for wines of similar character at less stupendous prices (though frighteningly similar prices in the case of Domaine Leroy). All the other named vineyards of Vosne-Romanée are splendid. Indeed, one of the old textbooks on Burgundy remarks drily: "There are no common wines in Vosne."

The big, some would say too big, 75-acre (30-ha) Echézeaux Grand Cru – which includes most of the dark pink *climats* around that marked Echézeaux du Dessus on the map – and the

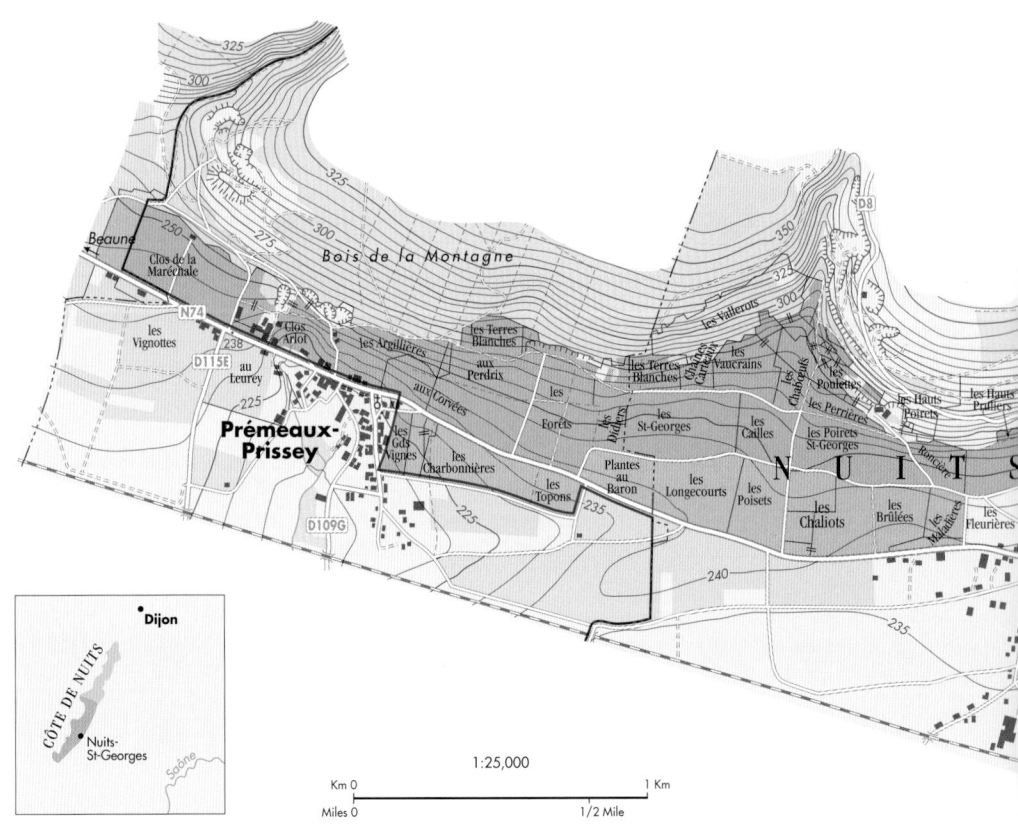

This selection includes some of Burgundy's most expensive and most famous wine as well as an unusual white from Henri Gouges and a fine representative from the hills above the Côte d'Or, the so-called Hautes Côtes.

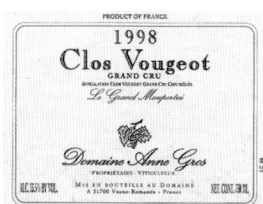

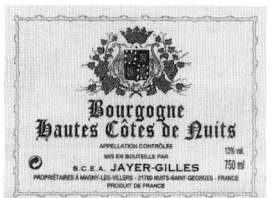
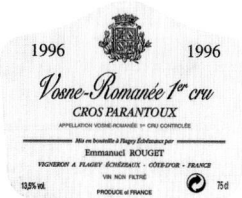
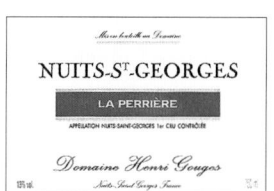
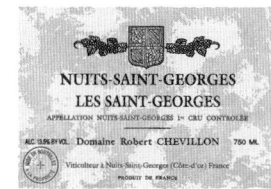

smaller Grands Echézeaux are really in the commune of Flagey, a village over the railway to the east which has been absorbed (at least oenologically) into Vosne. Some very fine growers have property here, and make beautiful, delicate, so-called "lacy" wines. They are often a bargain – because the name looks hard to pronounce? Grands Echézeaux has more regularity, more of the lingering intensity which marks the very great burgundies, and certainly higher prices.

One high stone wall surrounds the 125 acres (50ha) of the Clos de Vougeot; the sure sign of a monastic vineyard. Today it is so subdivided that it is anything but a reliable label on a bottle.

But it is the *climat* as a whole that is a Grand Cru. The Cistercians used to blend wine of the top, middle, and sometimes bottom slopes to make what we must believe was one of the best burgundies of all... and one of the most consistent, since in dry years the wine from lower down would have an advantage, in wet years the top slopes. It is generally accepted, however, that the middle and especially top of the slope tend to produce the best wine today. There are wines from near the top in particular (just outside the Clos) that can be almost as great as Musigny. The name of the grower, as ever, must be your guide.

`------`	Commune (parish) boundary
`——`	Appellation boundary
▨	Grand Cru vineyard
▨	Premier Cru vineyard
▨	Commune Appellation vineyard
▨	Other vineyard
▨	Woods
`—250—`	Contour interval 5 metres
✝	Internal vineyard boundary

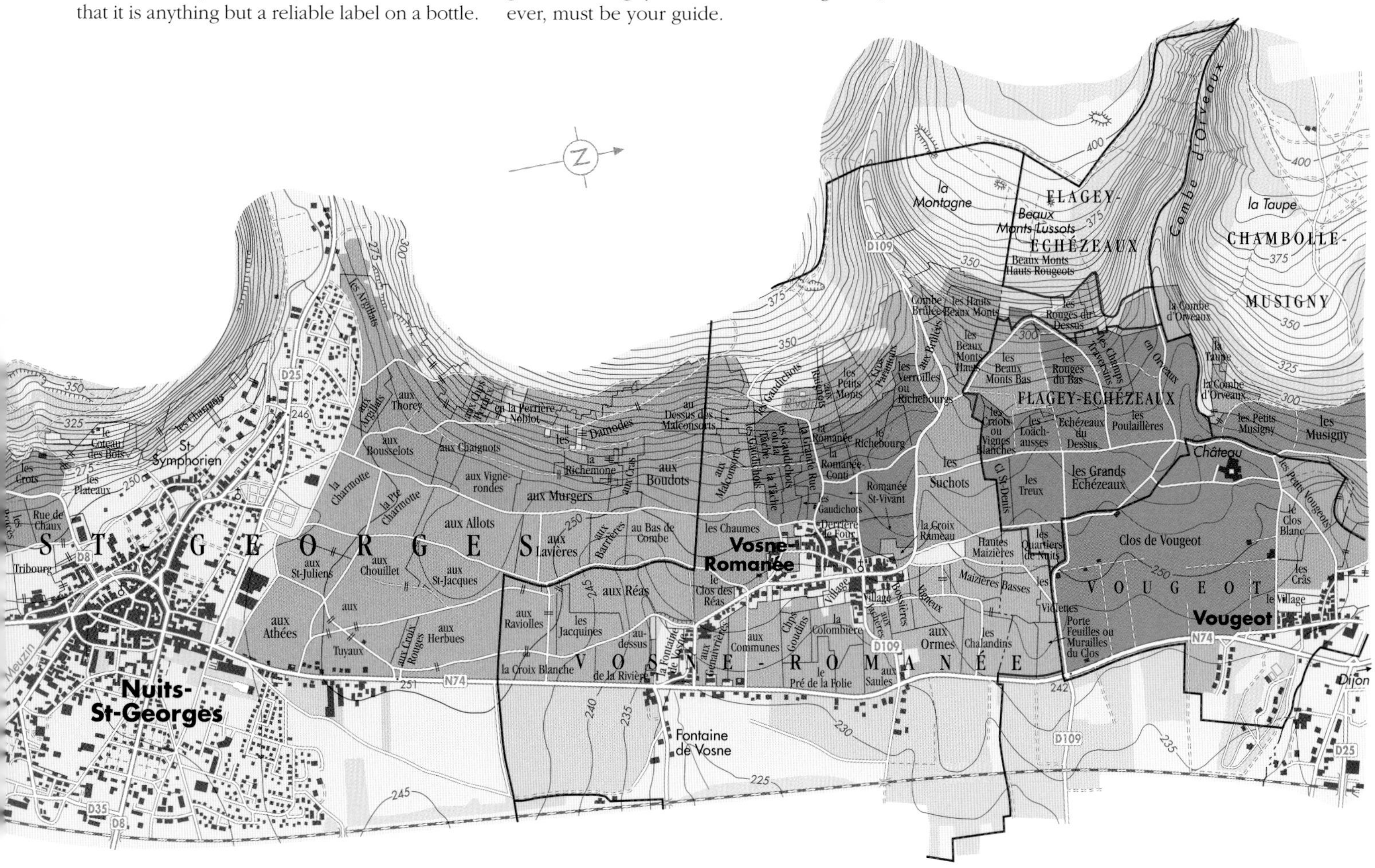

Côte de Nuits: Gevrey-Chambertin

Here, at the northern end of the Côte d'Or, the finest, longest-living, eventually most velvety red burgundies are made. Nature adds rich soil to the perfect combination of shelter and exposure provided by the hills. The narrow marlstone outcrop, overlaid with silt and scree, follows the lower slopes. From it Chambertin and the Grands Crus of Morey and Chambolle draw their power: wines of weight and muscle, unyielding when young, but the best will offer unmatched complexity and depth of flavour.

The Grand Cru Les Musigny stands apart, squeezed in under the barren limestone crest, obviously related to the top of the Clos de Vougeot. The slope is steep enough to oblige the vignerons to carry the brown limy clay, heavy with pebbles, back up the hill after prolonged rainy weather. This and the permeable limestone subsoil allow excellent drainage. Conditions are right for a wine with plenty of "stuffing".

The glory of Musigny is that it covers its undoubted power with a lovely, haunting delicacy of perfume; a uniquely sensuous savour. A great Musigny makes what is so well described as a "peacock's tail" in your mouth, opening to reveal ever more ravishing patterns of flavour. It is not as strong as Chambertin, not as spicy as Romanée-Conti – but whoever called it "feminine" must have been a great respecter of women. It needs ten to 15 years' ageing. Bonnes Mares is the other Grand Cru of Chambolle. It starts as a tougher wine than Musigny, and ages perhaps a little slower, never quite achieving the tender grace of its neighbour.

Les Amoureuses and Les Charmes – their names perfectly expressive of their wine – are among the best Premiers Crus of Burgundy. But any Chambolle-Musigny is likely to be very good.

The commune of Morey is overshadowed in renown by its five Grands Crus. Clos de la Roche, with little Clos St-Denis (which gave its name to the village), like Chambertin, are wines of great staying power, strength and depth, fed by soil rich in limestone. The Clos des Lambrays is a *monopole* promoted to Grand Cru rank in 1981; a wine to wait for. Clos de Tart, the *monopole* of the house of Mommessin, is consistently fine, intense but not weighty.

Morey has more than 20 tiny Premiers Crus, few of whose names are well-known but whose general standard is very high. The vineyards climb the hill, finding soil higher up than anywhere else in the area. The lofty, stony Monts-Luisants is even used for white wine.

Gevrey-Chambertin has a vast amount of good land. Suitable vineyard soil stretches further from the hill here than elsewhere; some east of the main road is still appellation Gevrey-Chambertin rather than plain Bourgogne. Its two greatest vineyards, Chambertin and Clos de

Commune (parish) boundary
Appellation boundary
Grand Cru vineyard
Premier Cru vineyard
Commune Appellation vineyard
Other vineyard
Woods
275 Contour interval 5 metres
† Internal vineyard boundary

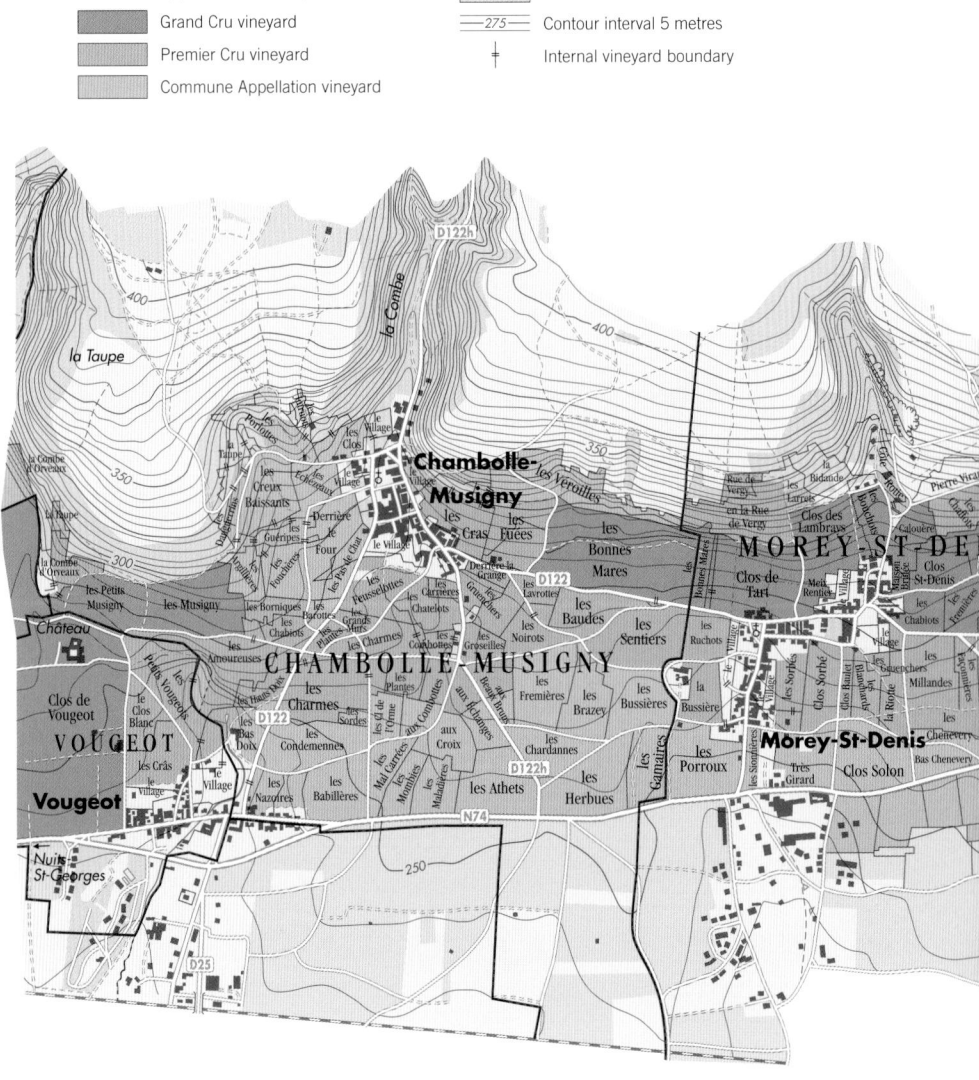

The northern end of the Côte d'Or is home to reputations of all ages, from that of the long-established Domaine Comte Georges de Vogüé, via the more recently glorious Domaine Dujac to the virtual arriviste Dominique Laurent, a relatively small new-wave négociant who makes wine from vineyards all over the Côte d'Or.

Above Chambolle-Musigny, whose fragrant yet muscular wines are capable, after years in bottle, of turning heads and capturing hearts. Its Premiers Crus Les Amoureuses and Les Charmes, just north of the well-drained slopes of Le Musigny, can be finer than many a Grand Cru bottling.

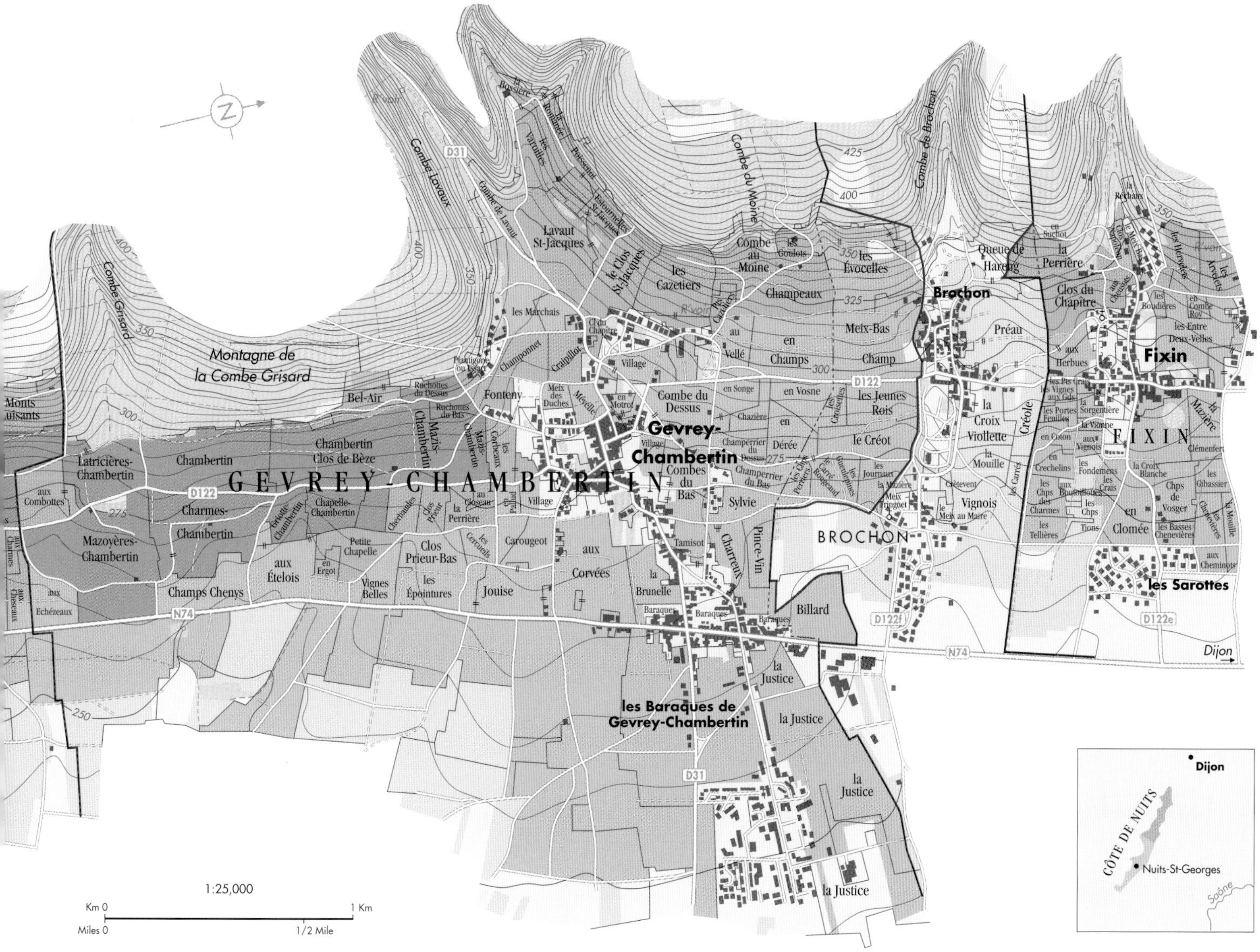

Bèze, lie under the woods on a gentle slope. They were acknowledged Grands Crus at a time when the citizens of Gevrey were quarrelling with the worthies of Beaune who were handing out the honours. Otherwise their constellation of vineyards – Mazis, Latricières, and the rest – would likely have been Grands Crus in their own right, too. They have the right to add Chambertin after their names, but not (like Clos de Bèze) before. French wine law can be more subtle than theology.

The commune also has a higher slope with a superb southeast exposure. Its Premiers Crus – Cazetiers, Lavaut St-Jacques, Varoilles and especially Clos St-Jacques – are arguably peers of the Grands Crus.

There are more famous individual vineyards in this village than in any other in Burgundy. To some, the forceful red wine they make *is* burgundy. Hilaire Belloc once told a story about his youth, and ended dreamily: "I forget the name of the place; I forget the name of the girl; but the wine... was Chambertin."

The slopes to the north, once called the Côte de Dijon, were until the 18th century considered to be among the best. But growers were tempted to grow bulk wine for the city and planted the "disloyal" Gamay. Brochon became known as a "well of wine". Today its southern edge is included in Gevrey-Chambertin; the rest of its vineyards have only the right to the appellation Côte de Nuits-Villages.

Fixin, however, has some tradition of quality with the Premiers Crus La Perrière, Les Hervelets, and Clos du Chapître potentially up to the standards of Gevrey-Chambertin. Marsannay, which is situated just off the map to the right, specializes in delicious Pinot Noir rosé. The appellation also produces some flirtatious red wine, but its white is distinctly ordinary.

Côte Chalonnaise

The Côte Chalonnaise may not produce any of Burgundy's most famous wines, but it can boast its most famous three-star landmark in the form of the restaurant Lameloise in the small town of Chagny, which lies just across the N74 from Chassagne-Montrachet.

Indeed so close is the north of the Côte Chalonnaise to the southern tip of the Côte d'Or that it is surprising that its wines taste so perceptibly different, like slightly undernourished country cousins. The rolling, pastoral hills south of Chagny are in many ways a continuation of the Côte de Beaune, although the regular ridge is replaced here by a jumble of limestone slopes on which vineyards appear among orchards and pasture. These vineyards rise to a markedly higher altitude than those of the Côte de Beaune, resulting in a slightly later vintage and a more precarious ripening process. The "Côte Chalonnaise", once called the "Région de Mercurey", was named for its proximity to Chalon-sur-Saône to the east.

The map shows only the most celebrated, central strip of the Côte, specifically the five major communes which give their names to the appellations Rully, Mercurey, Givry, Montagny, and Bouzeron, and some of their better-known vineyards on mainly east- and south-facing slopes. The more successful producers are also marked. See the locator map opposite for the total extent of the Côte Chalonnaise.

In the far north Rully makes more white than red. The white is brisk, high in acid, in poor vintages ideal material for sparkling Crémant de Bourgogne and in good vintages lively, apple-fresh, lean white burgundy that can be exceptional value. Rully reds also tend to leanness – but are not without class.

Mercurey is much the biggest producer, accounting for two in every three bottles of wine from the Côte Chalonnaise, and 90% of its wine is red. Pinot Noir here is on a par with a minor Côte de Beaune: firm, solid, almost rough when young, but ageing well, and it is steadily being improved. The négociants Rodet and Faiveley are among the important producers.

There has been rampant Premier Cru inflation here, the total number in Mercurey alone doubling during the 1990s to 30 on more than 250 acres (100ha) of vineyard. This significantly higher proportion of Premiers Crus than in the Côte d'Or to the north is characteristic of the Côte Chalonnaise, which is why they command a much lower premium.

Mercurey's neighbour Givry is the smallest of the four major appellations and is almost as dedicated to red wine. It is often lighter, easier, and more enjoyable young than Mercurey, although the Clos de Jus, recovered from scrubland in the late 1980s, is producing solidly powerful wine that is well worth ageing. Of all the Côte Chalonnaise appellations this one is currently the most dynamic, boasting a number of small, ambitious domaines.

Montagny to the south is the one all-white appellation and includes neighbouring Buxy, whose co-operative is probably the most successful in southern Burgundy. At one time any Montagny reaching 11.5 degrees' natural alcohol was automatically awarded Premier Cru status, but the Premiers Crus have now, quite properly, been geographically delineated. The whites

Left Evening sunlight on the Château de la Saule and Chardonnay vineyards just west of Montagny which, with neighbouring Buxy, is the source of some of Burgundy's best-value white wine. The farmers of the Côte Chalonnaise produce much more than just wine in this gentle, pastoral landscape.

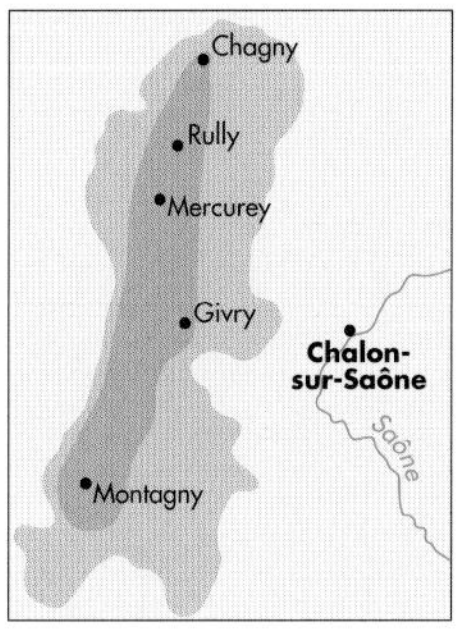

"Premier Cru" means much less on *a Côte Chalonnaise label than on one from the Côte d'Or to the north for there has been a proliferation of them in villages such as Mercurey and Givry. Aligoté reaches singular heights in the northern village of Bouzeron.*

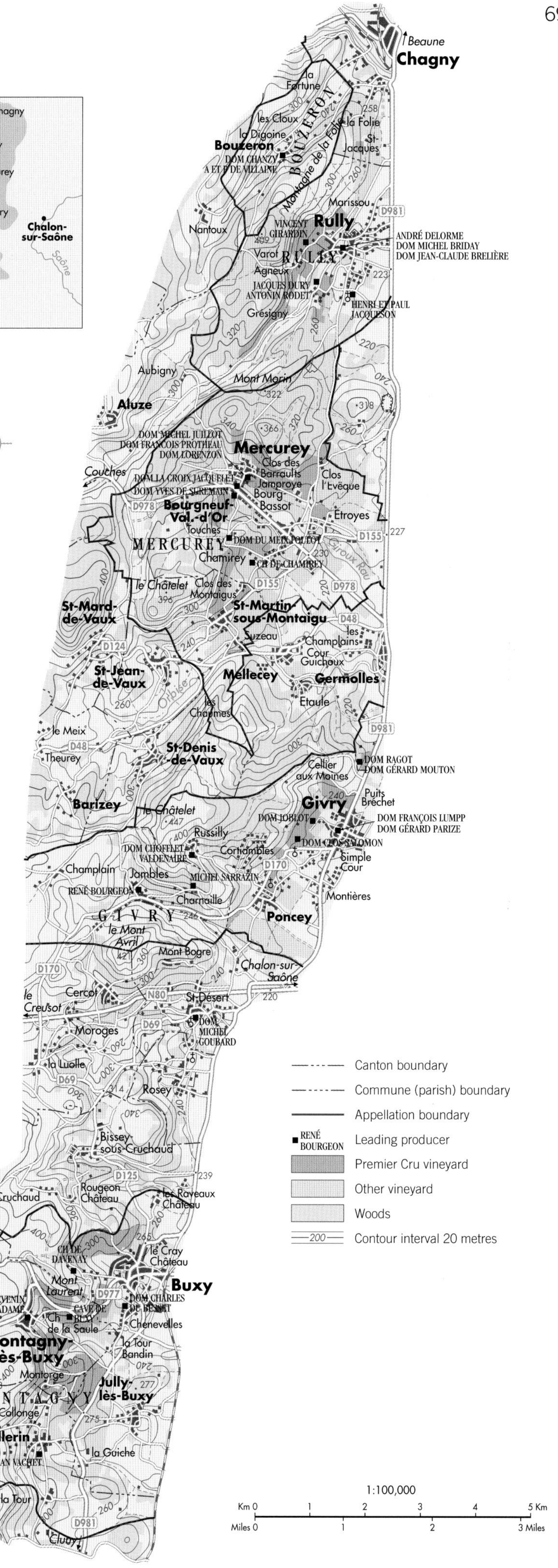

here are fuller and can be more like minor Côte de Beaune wines than the leaner Rullys. Some, on the other hand, can be rather heavy and obvious like many Mâcon-Villages. The firm of Louis Latour long ago discovered what good value they can be and is responsible for a significant proportion of total production.

Bouzeron, the village just north of Rully, has its own appellation exclusively for the wines of one grape. Indeed it is the only appellation for a single-village Aligoté white in Burgundy; a reward for perfectionist winemaking by, among others, Aubert de Villaine, the co-owner of the Domaine de la Romanée-Conti.

The whole area, Bouzeron included, is a good source of generic red and white burgundy, which is now delimited as Bourgogne Côte Chalonnaise but is often declassified to the less specific Bourgogne appellation. At two or three years the reds can offer marvellous drinking. But perhaps the region's most distinctive offering is its sparkling Crémant de Bourgogne which can provide a usefully inexpensive alternative to champagne.

Canton boundary
Commune (parish) boundary
Appellation boundary
RENÉ BOURGEON Leading producer
Premier Cru vineyard
Other vineyard
Woods
200 Contour interval 20 metres

1:100,000
Km 0   1   2   3   4   5 Km
Miles 0   1   2   3 Miles

Mâconnais

The town of Mâcon on the Saône, 35 miles (55km) south of Chalon, gives its name to a wide, hilly and profoundly rural area whose wines vary in quality but have been improving rapidly. Mâcon red (mainly Gamay) is just recognizably burgundian in character; the white much more definitely burgundy.

With its characteristic limestone subsoil, overlaid either with clay or alluvial topsoil, this is primarily white wine country – in fact the Mâconnais produces three times more white wine than the rest of Burgundy. The slightly warmer climate than that of the Côte d'Or suits the Chardonnay grape, which seems at home in the Mâconnais. Often plumped out with some Pinot Blanc, Chardonnay accounts for about two-thirds of all Mâconnais wine.

A further 25% of vines are Gamay, the mainstay of Mâcon Rouge, but an increasing proportion of land is devoted to Pinot Noir and is therefore sold as Bourgogne Rouge. Mâcon Rouge is rarely thrilling, for the Gamay grape, when grown on limestone as opposed to the granite of Beaujolais to the south, can take on a hard, rustic edge.

The locator map shows which section of the greater Mâconnais region is mapped in detail here. The unshaded area to the north and west of this section is responsible for the most basic Mâcon Blanc, Rouge, and a little Rosé. Mâcon-Villages should in theory guarantee superior quality from the region's best villages, but in practice applies to virtually all white Mâcon. A surer guide to white wine quality is to seek out wines sold under the name of one of the 43 villages allowed on wine labels, some of which are marked on the map. Of these, some also have the right to the red Beaujolais-Villages appellation which extends into the southern end of the Mâconnais at the bottom of the map.

In this buffer zone, the villages of Chasselas, Leynes, St-Vérand, and Chânes also qualify for the strange St-Véran appellation of convenience for Chardonnay grown on the southern and northern fringes of the Pouilly-Fuissé appellation mapped in detail opposite. Soils in this southern part of the St-Véran appellation tend to be red, acidic, and sandy, producing very different and generally much simpler, leaner wines than those made on the limestone of Prissé and Davayé to the north of Pouilly-Fuissé.

Pouilly-Vinzelles and Pouilly-Loché made just to the east of the central Pouilly-Fuissé zone are theoretical alternatives to the real thing, but are in very short supply.

Mâcon-Prissé, also grown on limestone, can be good value and Lugny, Uchizy, and Loché all have their fans as providers of keenly priced, plump burgundian Chardonnay. Two of the best villages however are Viré and Clessé, both on the strip of limestone which threads its way north through the region vaguely parallel to the main north-south A6 autoroute from the Pouilly-Fuissé cluster of excellence and then up to form the backbone of the Côte d'Or. A special AC, Viré-Clessé, was created in 1999 for the wines of these villages and many more (see map).

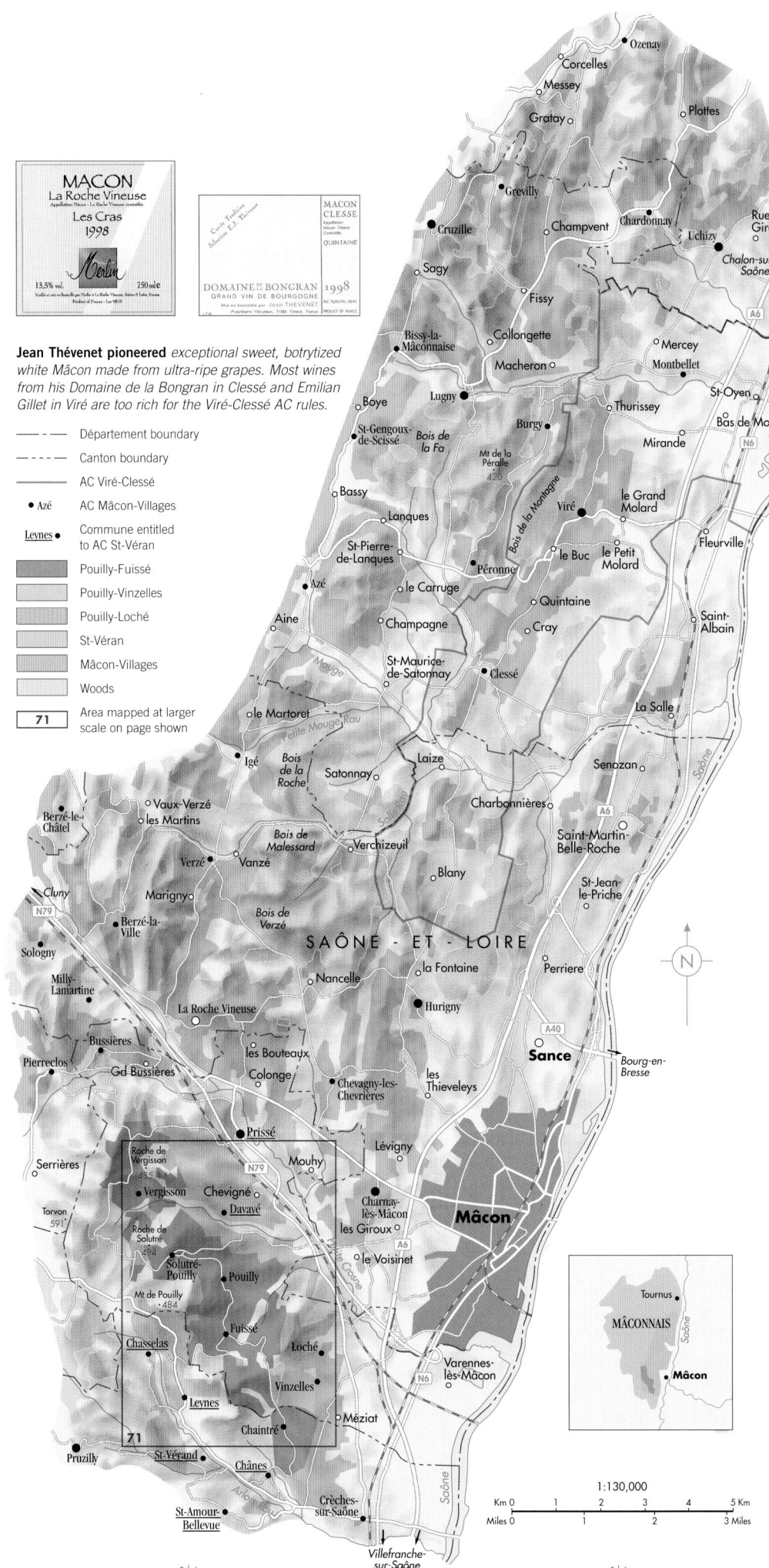

Jean Thévenet pioneered *exceptional sweet, botrytized white Mâcon made from ultra-ripe grapes. Most wines from his Domaine de la Bongran in Clessé and Emilian Gillet in Viré are too rich for the Viré-Clessé AC rules.*

- – – – Département boundary
- - - - - Canton boundary
- ――― AC Viré-Clessé
- • Azé   AC Mâcon-Villages
- Leynes•   Commune entitled to AC St-Véran
- Pouilly-Fuissé
- Pouilly-Vinzelles
- Pouilly-Loché
- St-Véran
- Mâcon-Villages
- Woods
- 71   Area mapped at larger scale on page shown

1:130,000

Km 0   1   2   3   4   5 Km
Miles 0   1   2   3 Miles

Pouilly-Fuissé

Most Mâconnais wines have been associated with simplicity rather than excellence but close to the Beaujolais border is a pocket of white-winegrowing with distinction of a different order. The Pouilly-Fuissé district is a sudden tempest of wave-shaped limestone hills, rich in the alkaline clay the Chardonnay vine loves.

The map shows how the five very different Pouilly-Fuissé villages (Vergisson, Solutré-Pouilly, Fuissé, Chaintré, and Pouilly) shelter on the lower slopes; the contour lines alone are enough to suggest just how irregular the topography is, and how varied the vineyards. Above the corn grown on the lower land, tree-rimmed combes twist and turn, pushing their neat vines towards every compass point.

Vines on the south-facing, open slopes of Chaintré may ripen a full two weeks before those on the north-facing slopes of Vergisson, whose wines can be some of the most full-bodied in a long, late vintage. The village of Solutré-Pouilly shelters under the pale pink rock of Solutré which rears above it, while the twin villages of Pouilly and Fuissé are relatively low-lying and peaceful, but for the constant prowl of wine-loving tourists.

The best Pouilly-Fuissé is full to the point of richness and capable of sumptuous succulence with time. Perhaps a dozen small growers make wines that frequently reach these heights, applying wildly varying policies on oak, lees-stirring, and the occasional addition of second-crop berries to add acidity to what can be a rather fat wine. Unfortunately many others are bland in comparison, virtually indistinguishable from Mâcon-Villages, and their producers have tended to lean heavily on Pouilly-Fuissé's international reputation.

After a period of stagnation in the 1980s, the appellation is now in flux, and flowing quite noticeably in the right direction. The most obvious catalyst was the miniature Domaine Guffens-Heynen of Vergisson, run by the outspoken winemaking firebrand Jean-Marie Guffens and his talented vine-grower wife. The previous leader of Pouilly-Fuissé, Château de Fuissé, has had to raise its game, but now this area can boast a host of over-achievers such as Domaines J-A Ferret and Robert-Denogent, Daniel Barraud, and Olivier Merlin (based just to the north of this zone on excellent land on the west-facing slopes of La Roche Vineuse – see label on page 70).

This area is currently more obviously *mouvementé* than the white wine country of the Côte de Beaune to the north. Guffens has based his négociant business Verget, one of the most recent success stories in all of Burgundy, in Sologny northwest of the Pouilly-Fuissé zone, while Dominique Lafon, of one of Meursault's very finest domaines, has chosen to invest in nearby Milly-Lamartine. Co-ops are important all over the Mâconnais and that at Chaintré is much the biggest producer of Pouilly-Fuissé.

Three top quality domaine-bottled examples plus one from the leading white wine négociant house of Verget, whose fame has spread from its base in the Mâconnais throughout the Côte d'Or and as far north as Chablis.

Key to map:

- - - - - - Commune (parish) boundary

■ **DANIEL BARRAUD** Leading producer

En Servy Noted vineyard

Vineyards

Woods

=200= Contour interval 10 metres

1:35,714

Km 0   1 Km

Miles 0   1 Mile

Below A typical Burgundian village scene at harvest-time, with stacked grape hods on their way to encumber the pickers' backs and the geraniums so characteristic of much-visited villages such as Fuissé.

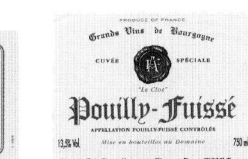

Beaujolais

In one of the marriages of grape and ground the French regard as mystical, in Beaujolais' sandy clay over granite the Gamay grape, undistinguished virtually everywhere else, gives uniquely fresh, vivid, fruity, light but infinitely swallowable wine.

Lightness is not a fashionable virtue, and even committed wine drinkers may overlook Beaujolais for much of the year. But each November we are reminded of it for a few weeks as the newborn vintage is announced. So popular was Beaujolais Nouveau in the late 1970s and 1980s that it seemed to be the world's favourite drink; a sort of worldwide vintage festival, as though folk-memory were reviving the ancient Bacchanalia. Such rapid cashflow is something all winemakers would like, yet only Beaujolais could generate.

But there has been a price to pay. The precocious version of Beaujolais has been so popular – at its peak in 1992 almost half of all wine sold as straight Beaujolais was released as a Nouveau – that there has been little incentive to produce more serious wine. Perceptions – and in some cases the reality – of quality have suffered as a result.

The Beaujolais region covers a 34-mile (55-km) stretch from granite-based hills immediately south of Mâcon, the southern end of Burgundy, to the much flatter land northwest of Lyon. Beaujolais in total produces twice as much wine as Burgundy proper and, as one would expect, the region is far from homogeneous. Its soil divides it sharply, around the valley of the little River Nizerand, just north of Villefranche, the region's capital. South of here in "Bas" Beaujolais, coloured green on the map, the soil is clay, the wine plain Beaujolais. Its villages remain obscure: the highest their wine can aspire to is the extra degree of alcohol that enables them to qualify as Beaujolais Supérieur. From this deep well nearly 70 million litres of wine a year are drawn – and rapidly drunk.

Very fresh and new (and natural), it can be the ultimate bistro wine, served by the *pôt* in Lyon's famously authentic *bouchons* (small brasseries). Far more often its alcohol is exaggerated by added sugar, sacrificing its racy, almost stinging fragrance and easy-flowing lightness to become merely raw and heavy. Plain "Bas" Beaujolais rarely keeps well, even in a good vintage: its clay soil is too cold to ripen full flavours in the Gamay.

The northern part of the region, "Haut" Beaujolais, is granite-based, with a variously sandy topsoil that drains, warms and ripens the Gamay, often to perfection. Thirty-nine of its villages or communes, marked in the areas coloured blue and mauve on the map, have the right to the appellation Beaujolais-Villages. These vineyards climb the wooded mountains to the west to heights above 1,480ft (450m).

It is almost always worth paying more for a -Villages wine, even as a Nouveau, for its extra concentration. On the other hand -Villages wines are scarcely ever at their best by late November. They demand and deserve at least three months in bottle. Only individual growers who bottle (very much the minority) often use the names of the Beaujolais-Villages communes. Most Beaujolais is sold by merchants, who blend a generalized "-Villages" to their clients' tastes.

Ten of these communes, marked in magenta within the mauve area on the map, have the right to use their own names on labels and are expected to show distinct characteristics of their own. These are the Beaujolais Crus, mapped in detail overleaf and lying just south of the Mâconnais, close to Pouilly-Fuissé. In this northern region a small amount of Beaujolais Blanc is also made – indeed some villages can sell their red wine as Beaujolais-Villages and their white as Mâcon-Villages.

The Gamay is in its element here. Each Gamay vine in Beaujolais is staked individually, without trellising. Its plants are almost like people, leading independent lives: after ten years they are no longer trained, but merely tied up in summer with an osier to stand free. A Gamay vine will live as long as a human.

Beaujolais is traditionally made by carbonic maceration, in which whole bunches go into the vat uncrushed and the grapes, at least at the top of the vat, begin fermenting internally – a high-speed fermentation that emphasizes the characteristic smell and flavour of the fruit and minimizes tannins and malic acid. After three or four days of maceration the grapes are pressed and the fermentation finished in a vat without skins – again minimizing any astringency. Within a month of harvest the wine is made, ready to be filtered, bottled, labelled, shipped, and drunk.

Well off the map to the west, over a mountain ridge and in the Upper Loire basin in fact, are three much smaller regions similarly devoted to the Gamay grape (see the map of France on page 53). The Côte Roannaise, on south- and southeast-facing slopes of the Loire near Roanne, also enjoys a granite base and several individual domaines here can produce wines that have the same refreshing integrity as Beaujolais in its purest form. Further south, growing Gamay on similar soils, the Côtes du Forez is dominated by a single, superior co-op. Côtes d'Auvergne is even more extensive, almost plum in the centre of France near Clermont-Ferrand, and makes light reds and rosés from Gamay and a little light white.

Left Bent backs in a vineyard near the village of Fleurie. Beaujolais is one of the very few French wine regions not to have been invaded by machine harvesters since the vinification process depends on whole bunches rather than individual grapes shaken off the vine.

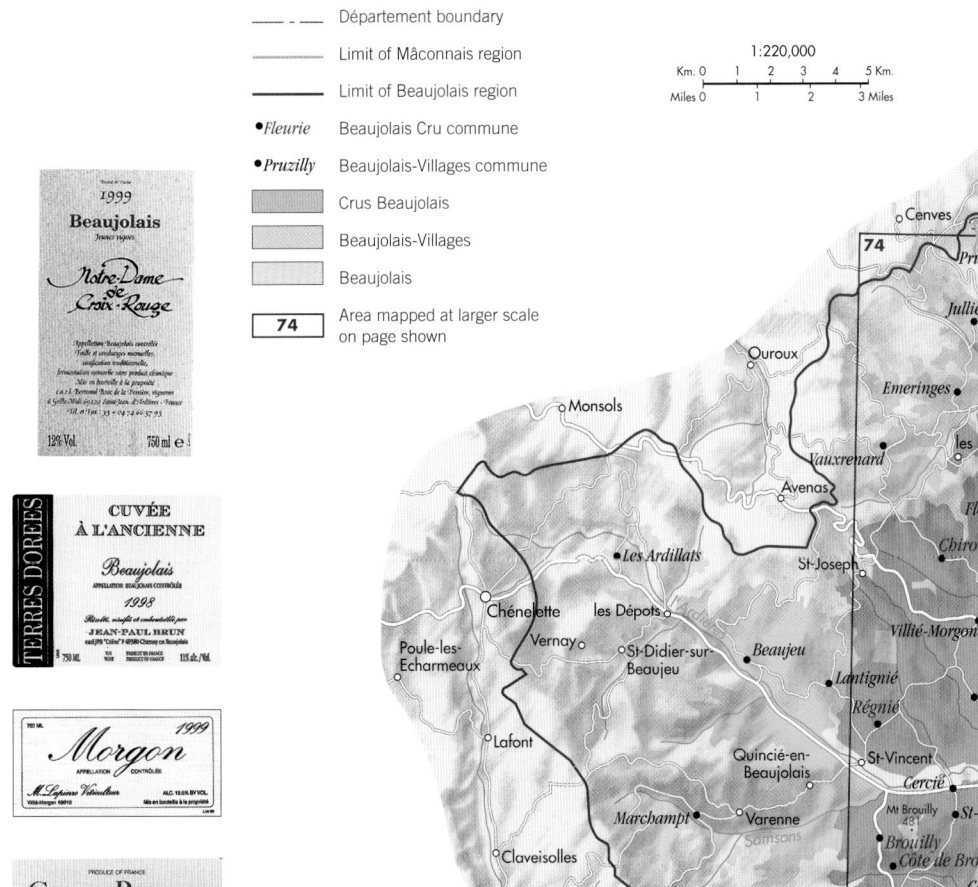

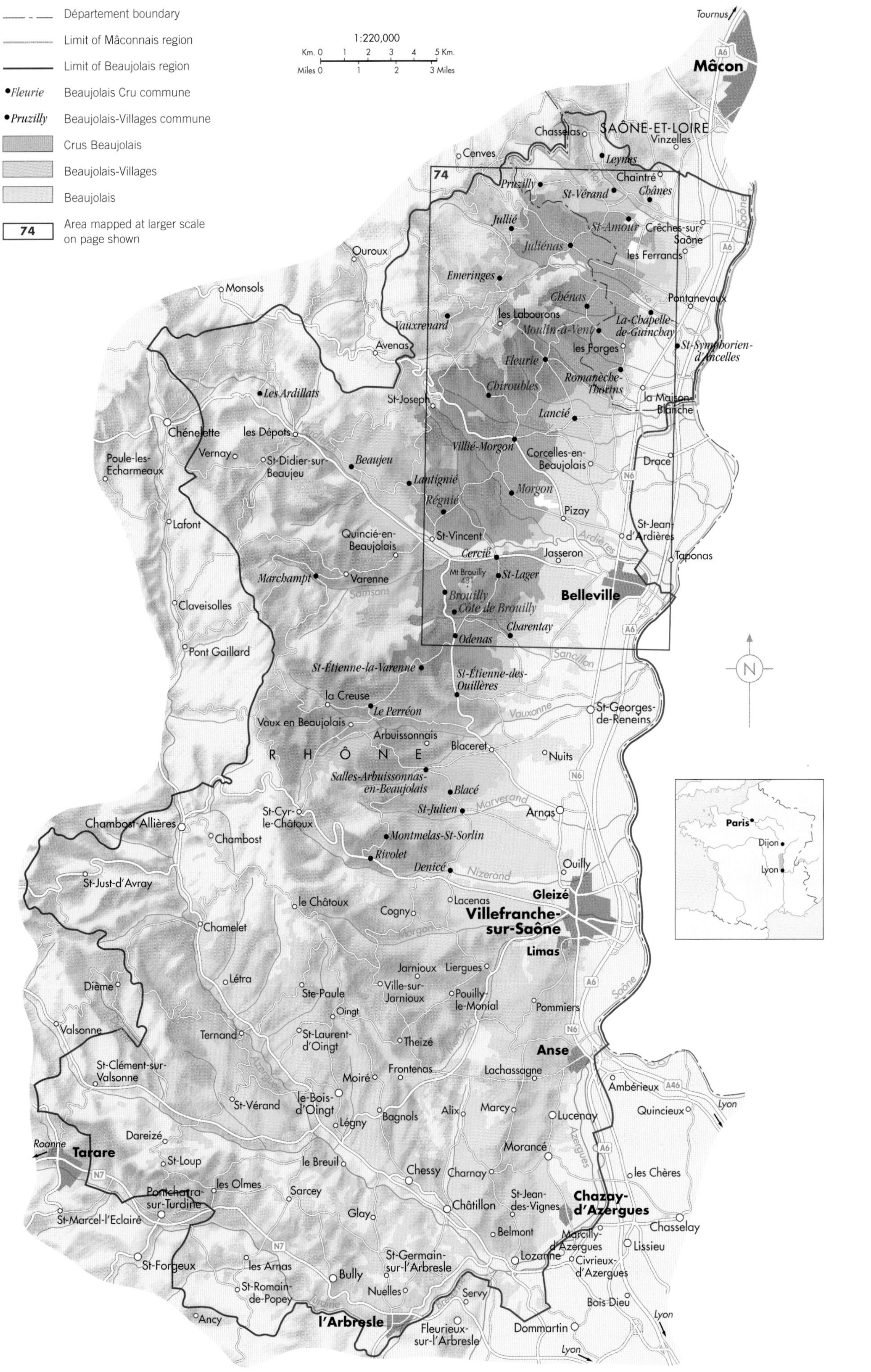

Département boundary
Limit of Mâconnais region
Limit of Beaujolais region
Fleurie   Beaujolais Cru commune
Pruzilly   Beaujolais-Villages commune
Crus Beaujolais
Beaujolais-Villages
Beaujolais
74   Area mapped at larger scale on page shown

1:220,000
Km. 0 1 2 3 4 5 Km.
Miles 0   1   2   3 Miles

Scores of independent, *traditional winemakers hide out in the rolling hills of Beaujolais in the north of the region, detailed overleaf. The so-called crus of Beaujolais rarely use the B word on their labels, so it is worth memorizing the names in magenta on the map.*

The Crus of Beaujolais

The ten Crus of Beaujolais are all contained within this zone of steep hills, wooded on their heights, and almost continuous vines. Its whole extent is 15 miles (24km) by half as much. And yet the wines at their best display to perfection the effects of terroir on a single grape, the Gamay. Each Cru has a personality which good growers explore and express with as much vigour as the vintage allows. They range from crisply fragrant wines to drink young to rich brooding bottles that need several years for their heady pungency to evolve.

The Cru villages lie on spurs, outlying volcanic knolls, and on the Beaujolais mountains themselves. This is much more seriously hilly country than the Côte d'Or.

All the Cru vineyards are sited sufficiently high for frost damage to be relatively rare; the best on east and south slopes, sheltered from the lively westerlies. Soils range from decomposing slate (in Morgon) to limestone (in parts of St-Amour). Underlying it all is the granite of ancient volcanoes – obviously so in the stump of Mont Brouilly, with its acid, sandy soils.

Brouilly is the largest of the Beaujolais Crus, its 3,000 acres (1,200ha) of vines filling most of the southern quarter of the map. With a production at times approaching one million cases, it can best be described as variable. Côte de Brouilly on the slopes of Mont Brouilly can reach appropriately greater heights; especially wines from the southeastern slopes (Château Thivin, for example).

Morgon, the second largest of the Crus, is one of the most distinctive in terms of soil and savour. It centres on the Mont du Py, on a rock formation of crumbling slate that gives more rigour than any other Cru, and almost as much breadth and substance as Moulin-à-Vent. There is also less exciting low-ground Morgon.

Régnié to the west has only had Cru status since 1988. Its soils are relatively sandy and so the wines tend to be soft and forward. To the north Chiroubles is Beaujolais at its prettiest, both as wine and village.

Fleurie is central in every way. Good young Fleurie epitomizes the spirit of the region: the scent is strong, the wine fruity and silky, limpid; a joy to swallow. The transition to the severity of Moulin-à-Vent is a tale of terroir writ large. Here the soil is rich in iron and manganese, probably but unprovably implicated in the concentration, dumbness even, of its young wines and their ability to age for ten years into something Burgundian in character.

Chénas, the smallest Cru, has lost most of its best land to Moulin-à-Vent. Juliénas is Fleurie-like in youth but at best fatter, fleshier and spicier with the backbone to keep it going for five years. Juliénas is steep, ideally sheltered and drained. No Cru has a higher overall standard. St-Amour provides a final stage from Beaujolais to St-Véran and the Mâconnais.

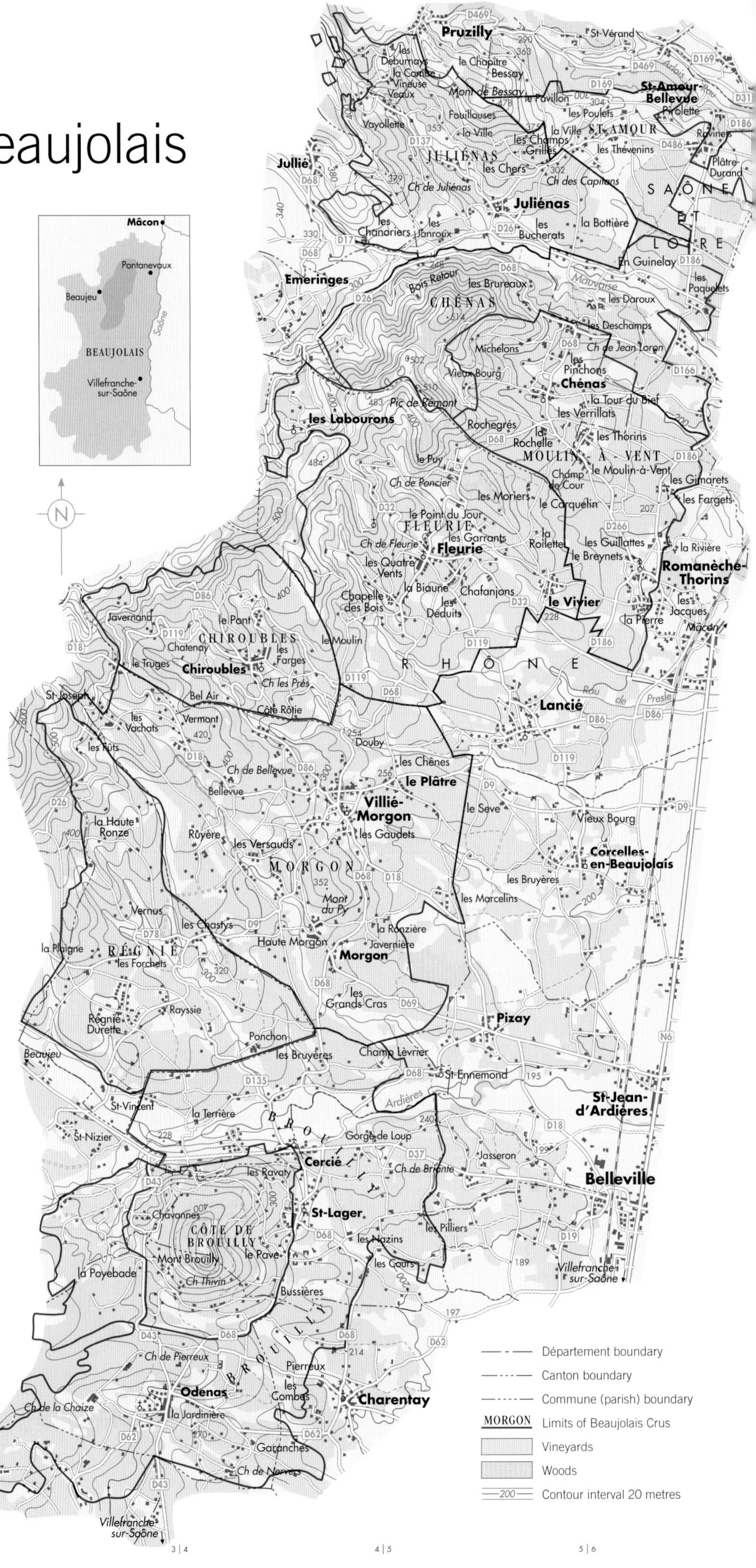

1:75,000

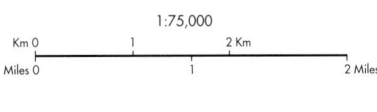

Km 0   1   2 Km

Miles 0   1   2 Miles

Département boundary

Canton boundary

Commune (parish) boundary

MORGON Limits of Beaujolais Crus

Vineyards

Woods

200 Contour interval 20 metres

Chablis

Chablis is almost the sole survivor of what was once a vast winegrowing region; the main supplier to Paris, only 110 miles (180km) away to the northwest. A century ago the département of the Yonne had 100,000 acres (40,000ha) of vines – many of them red – and filled what was to become the role of the Midi. Before this Chablis' waterways flowing into the River Seine were thronged with wine-barges, except in spring when they were cleared for the massive *flottage* of firewood to the capital from every upstream forest.

First phylloxera crushed, then the railways bypassed the winegrowers of the Yonne, leaving it one of France's poorest agricultural regions. By 1945 Chablis had a mere 1,000 or so acres (400ha) of vines left. Its trickle of wine was dwarfed by the flood from Spain, California, Australia, and other countries that kept its fame alive by abusing its name. "Chablis" became shorthand for any white wine, even while the region itself appeared to be dying.

The second half of the 20th century saw a great renaissance and a new justification for its renown. For Chablis is one of the great inimitable originals. Chardonnay responds to its cold terroir of limestone clay with flavours no-one can reproduce in easier (or any other) wine-growing conditions – quite different even from those of the rest of Burgundy to the south.

Chablis sends one rummaging for descriptive phrases even more desperately than most wines. There is something there one can so nearly put a finger on. It is hard but not harsh, reminiscent of stones and minerals, but at the same time of green hay; when it is young it actually looks green, which many wines are supposed to. Grand Cru Chablis, and even some of the best Premier Cru Chablis, tastes important, strong, almost immortal. And indeed it does last a remarkably long time; a strange and delicious sort of sour taste enters into it when it reaches about ten years of age, and its golden-green eye flashes meaningfully (although it can go through an awkward middle-age off-puttingly reminiscent of wet wool, which may help to explain why Chablis fanatics are less numerous than they should be).

Cool-climate vineyards need exceptional conditions to succeed. Chablis lies 100 miles (160km) north of Beaune – and is therefore nearer to Champagne than to the rest of Burgundy. Geology is its secret: the outcrop of the rim of a great submerged basin of limestone. The far rim, across the English Channel in Dorset, gives its name, Kimmeridge, to this unique pudding of prehistoric oyster-shells. Oysters and Chablis, it seems, have been related since creation.

There are two other regions, one in France and one in Germany, where similar soils give wine of unique quality. They are quite unrelated, and yet their wines are each the world's best of their different grape varieties, despite (or perhaps because of) their cold growing conditions. Sancerre is one, where Sauvignon Blanc can reach aromatic perfection on chalky clay. The other is the region of Franken (Franconia in

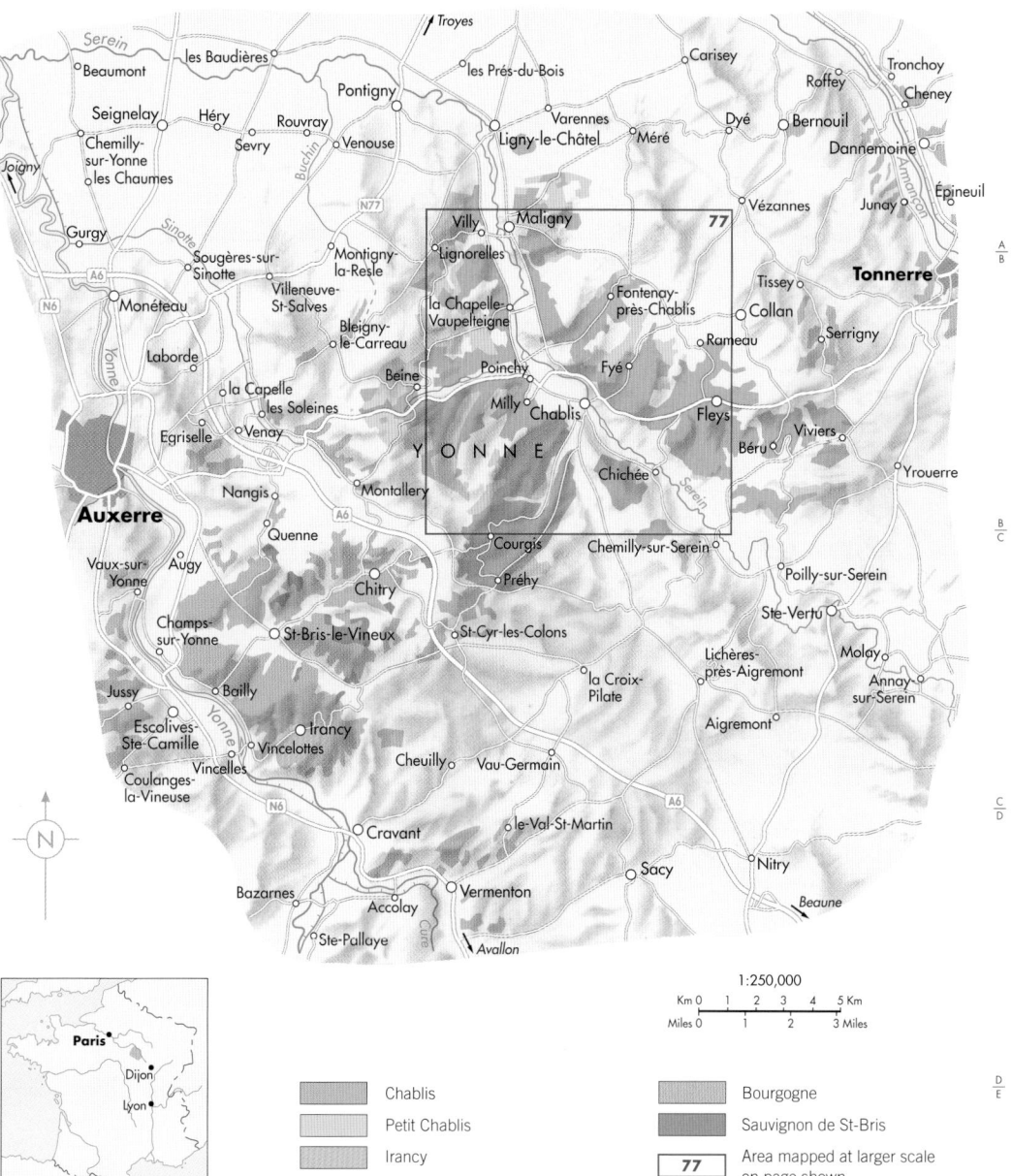

English) where Silvaner, on Muschelkalk, achieves a quality and longevity unknown elsewhere.

The hardy Chardonnay (known here as the Beaunois – the vine from Beaune) is Chablis' only vine. Where the slopes of Kimmeridgian clay face the sun it ripens excellently.

But Chablis and Petit Chablis, the much-expanded outlying area, are by no means the only appellations of the Yonne. There remains a rump of the once-huge Auxerre vineyard in reasonable heart at Irancy where virtually all vines are Pinot Noir, as they are at Coulanges-la-Vineuse to the west whose wines are sold as Bourgogne Coulanges. The Sauvignon Blanc of St-Bris-le-Vineux, unusual for this part of France, has its own VDQS: Sauvignon de St-Bris (see page 152), while the village's Pinot Noir and Chardonnay are included in the Côtes d'Auxerre appellation. The vineyards around Tonnerre, sold as Bourgogne Epineuil, expanded dramatically in the 1990s. The small amount of wine that is made in Joigny (off the map to the northwest) is sold, in a publicity masterstroke for local restaurateur-turned-vigneron Michel Lorain, as Bourgogne Côte St-Jacques.

Above The Premier Cru vineyard Les Fourneaux above the village of Fleys in the far east of the enlarged section mapped in detail overleaf. Grapes that fail to ripen fully in the northern region of Chablis are transformed into sparkling Crémant de Bourgogne.

Map legend:

Chablis
Petit Chablis
Irancy
Bourgogne
Sauvignon de St-Bris
77 Area mapped at larger scale on page shown

1:250,000
Km 0 1 2 3 4 5 Km
Miles 0 1 2 3 Miles

Heart of Chablis

The classification of Chablis into four grades is one of the clearest demonstrations anywhere in the northern hemisphere of the importance of southern slopes: Grand Cru wines always taste richer than Premiers Crus, Premiers Crus than plain Chablis, and Chablis than Petit Chablis.

All the Grands Crus lie in a single block (see above) looking south and west over the village and the river, their total 259 acres (105ha) representing less than 3% of the total Chablis vineyard area. Each of the seven has its own style. Many regard Les Clos and Vaudésir as best of all. Certainly they tend to be the biggest in flavour. But more important is what all have in common: intense, highly charged flavour on the scale of the best whites of the Côte de Beaune but with more of a nervy edge – which, with age, leads to noble complexity. Grand Cru Chablis must be aged, ideally for ten years, and many examples are still majestic at 20, 30 or even 40.

Les Clos is the biggest, with 61 acres (24ha), and best-known; many would also say the first in flavour, strength and lasting-power. Fine vintages of Les Clos can develop almost a Sauternes-like perfume in time. Les Preuses should be very ripe, round and perhaps the least stony in character, while Blanchot and Grenouilles should be highly aromatic. Valmur is some critics' ideal: rich and fragrant; others prefer the definition and finesse of Vaudésir. La Moutonne is not officially classified as a Grand Cru but should be, and the name can be found on labels. Bougros comes last in most accounts – but the hallmark of the producer is often more distinctive than that of the precise corner of this relatively homogeneous slope.

There used to be many more named Premiers Crus, but the lesser-known ones have long since been permitted to go to market under the names of the dozen best-known. The map opposite shows both the old names and the new ones that are now in common use. The Premiers Crus vary considerably in exposure and gradient; certainly those on the north bank of the River Serein, flanking the Grands Crus to the northwest (La Fourchaume, for example) and east (Montée de Tonnerre and Mont de Milieu), have the advantage.

A Premier Cru Chablis will have at least half a degree of alcohol less than a Grand Cru, and be correspondingly less impressive and intense in scent and flavour. Nonetheless, it should still be a highly stylish wine and can last at least as long as a Premier Cru white from the Côte d'Or. Its principal fault, these days, is likely to be dilution as a result of over-production.

The 1970s and 1980s saw a very substantial increase in the vineyard area in Chablis – the cause of continuing controversy among growers. The issue that divides them is the soil. Conservatives credit the Kimmeridgian limestone with unique properties; their opponents claim the same properties for the closely related Portlandian that crops up much more widely in the area. The INAO has favoured the latter, thus allowing expansion, to a total of more than 9,880 acres (4,000ha) by 1998. In 1960 there was more land dedicated to Premier Cru Chablis than straight Chablis. Today, although Premier Cru land has expanded considerably, nearly four times as much vineyard is allowed to produce Chablis.

Above The great, sun-soaking slope of Grand Cru vineyards above the village of Chablis, with their noticeably white soil. The main slope is Valmur and Les Clos, with the excellent Premier Cru Vaillons in the foreground.

Some say that quality has suffered as a result of this expansion. It remains, as it always will this far from the equator, very uneven from year to year as well as variable (particularly in style) from grower to grower. Most growers today favour tank-fermented fresh wines with no barrels. A few producers show that oak (but rarely new oak) has special properties to offer. The introduction of malolactic fermentation has softened the acidity; tending to age the wines more quickly. But on balance good Chablis is as good as ever – and maybe better, for winemaking skills have improved here as everywhere.

Far more unpredictable is the quantity of each harvest – still perilously subject to frost damage, although since the dramatic expansion of vineyards prices are much more stable than they used to be.

Grand Cru Chablis, largely ignored by the world's fine wine traders, remains even now half the price of Corton-Charlemagne. Parity would be closer to justice.

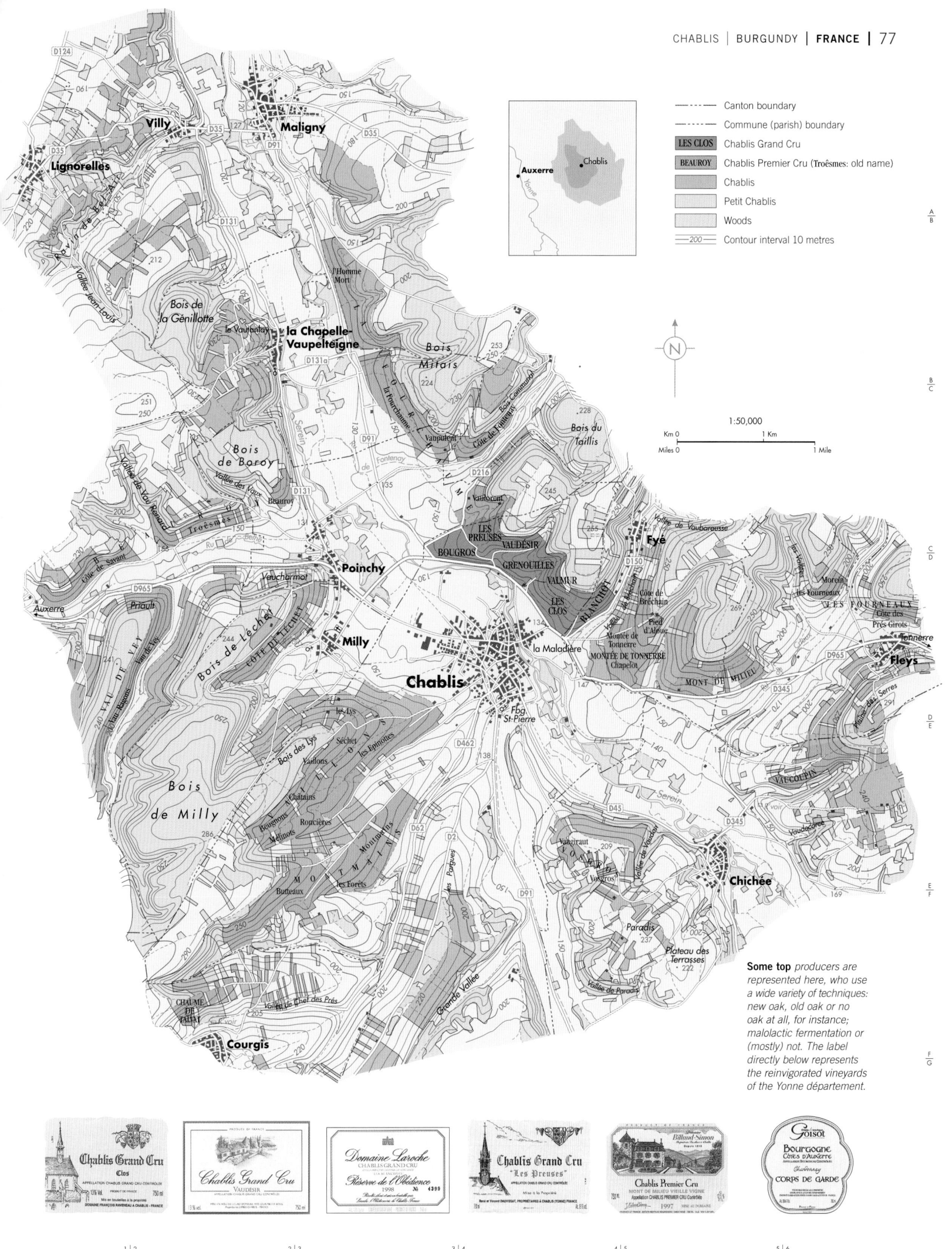

Villy

Maligny

Lignorelles

Legend:
- ─·─·─ Canton boundary
- ─··─··─ Commune (parish) boundary
- LES CLOS — Chablis Grand Cru
- BEAUROY — Chablis Premier Cru (Troêsmes: old name)
- Chablis
- Petit Chablis
- Woods
- ═200═ Contour interval 10 metres

Auxerre · Chablis

Bois de la Génillotte

la Chapelle-Vaupelteigne

Bois Mitais

Bois du Taillis

1:50,000

Km 0   1 Km
Miles 0   1 Mile

Bois de Baroy

Vaupulent

Côte de Fontenay

Beauroy

Vaucoupin

LES PREUSES

VAUDÉSIR

BOUGROS

GRENOUILLES

Fyé

Poinchy

VALMUR

Veucharmot

LES CLOS

BLANCHOT

Côte de Bréchain

Pied d'Aloue

Milly

Priault

Bois de Léchet

la Maladière

Montée de Tonnerre

MONTÉE DE TONNERRE
Chapelot

Morein
les Fourneaux

VES FOURNEAUX
Côte des Prés Girois

Tonnerre

Auxerre

Fleys

Chablis

les Lys

Bois des Lys

Séchet
les Epinottes

Vaillons

Châtains

Roncières

Mélinots

Bougros
les Forêts

Butteaux

Bois de Milly

Fbg
St-Pierre

MONT DE MILIEU

MONTMAINS

Vaugiraut

Vosgros

Chichée

Paradis

Plateau des
Terrasses

CHAUME
DE TALVAT

Vallée de Chef des Prés

Courgis

Grande Vallée

Vallée de Paradis

Some top *producers are represented here, who use a wide variety of techniques: new oak, old oak or no oak at all, for instance; malolactic fermentation or (mostly) not. The label directly below represents the reinvigorated vineyards of the Yonne département.*

Chablis Grand Cru — Clos

Chablis Grand Cru — VAUDÉSIR

Domaine Laroche — Chablis Grand Cru — Réserve de l'Obédience — 1998

Chablis Grand Cru — "Les Preuses"

Billaud-Simon — Chablis Premier Cru — MONT DE MILIEU VIEILLE VIGNE — 1997

GOISOT — Bourgogne Côtes d'Auxerre — CORPS DE GARDE

Champagne

To be champagne, a wine must do more than sparkle. It must come from the Champagne region in northeast France. This is the basic tenet of wine law in France, throughout Europe and now, thanks to tenacious negotiation, in much of the rest of the world. It would be claiming too much to say that all champagne is better than any other sparkling wine. But the best champagne has a combination of freshness, richness, delicacy, and raciness, and a gently stimulating strength that no sparkling wine from anywhere else has yet achieved.

Part of Champagne's secret lies in its combination of latitude and precise position. The latitude in the factfile opposite is higher than for any other wine region in this Atlas (except for England – whose best sparkling wines are fair copies of champagne). Normally, it would be impossible to ripen grapes so far from the equator, but the climate here is moderated by its proximity to the sea. Ripening month (July in the northern hemisphere) temperatures, for example, are higher than in Germany's Franken, California's Santa Maria, and New Zealand's Marlborough. This means that the relatively early-ripening varieties grown in Champagne more or less reliably reach just the right levels of sugar and acidity before autumn sets in. Any warmer, and the acidity would fall too low to yield interesting sparkling wines. Any cooler and the risk of unripe grapes would be too high.

Champagne, whose soil and climate have so much to offer, is only 90 miles (145km) northeast of Paris, centred on a small range of hills rising from a plain of chalk and carved in two by the River Marne. And yet this region whose location is clearly so vital for wine quality is arguably the one for which detailed mapping is least necessary. The names of the wine villages, for example, need hardly concern the wine drinker, for the essence of champagne is that it is a blended wine, known in all but a handful of cases by the name of the maker, not the vineyard.

The map overleaf shows Champagne's heart, but the whole region is much more extensive. Almost three-quarters of the vineyards are in the Marne département, but there are vineyards in the Aube to the south that specialize in vigorous if slightly rustic Pinot Noir (about 19% of the total), and the mainly Pinot Meunier vineyards on the banks of the River Marne extend westwards well into the Aisne département (about 7%).

Demand for champagne is higher than ever and so by 2004 the total possible champagne-producing area of 80,275 acres (32,500ha) (delimited in 1927) is expected to be planted, and the Champenois are already arguing about how it might be extended. Only 10% of this precious vineyard belongs to the large exporting houses responsible for the worldwide reputation of champagne. The rest is owned not by great landowners but by more than 19,000 growers, many of whom are part-time.

More and more of these growers are making and selling their own wine rather than selling grapes to the *maisons*, and their champagnes now account for almost a quarter of all sales. About a twelfth of all champagne is put on the market by one of the co-ops established in Champagne's dog days in the early 20th century. But the champagne market is still dominated by the famous names, the big houses of Reims and Epernay shown left – together with a few, such as Bollinger of Aÿ, based outside the two Champagne towns.

Because it is obviously so successful here, the champagne recipe has been much copied. Take Pinot Noir, Pinot Meunier, and Chardonnay grapes and apply a kid-glove process now called the "traditional method" (the Champenois having objected even to the world's admiring use of the old term "champagne method").

The grapes are pressed, in four-ton lots, so gently that the juice, even from the dark-skinned Pinots Noir and Meunier, is pale and only a precisely prescribed amount of juice from each lot may be used for champagne.

The juice ferments lustily at first, but as it slows down the doors are thrown open to let in the autumnal chill. In the cold (today, of course, air-conditioned), fermentation stops. The wine spends a chilly winter, still with the potential of more fermentation latent in it.

So it used to be shipped. England in the 17th century was an eager customer for barrels of this delicate, rather sharp wine. The English bottled it on arrival, in bottles that were stronger than any known in France. It re-fermented in spring: the corks went pop and the beau monde found that they had created a sparkling wine.

Whether or not it was the English who did it first (and the inhabitants of Limoux claim to have made the first Brut sparkling wine, in the 16th century), premature bottling is vital to the process which changed Paris's favourite local wine into the prima donna of the world.

For the wine continued to ferment in the bottle and the gas given off by the fermentation dissolved in the wine. If the natural effect was encouraged by a little more sugar, a little more yeast, what had been a pretty but very light wine was found to improve immeasurably, gaining strength and character over a period of two years or more. Above all, the inexhaustible bubbles gave it a miraculous liveliness.

The chief difference between champagne brands lies in this making of the *cuvée*, as the blend is called. Everything depends on experience in assembling the young wines – which are sometimes deepened by a dose of older, reserve wine – and on how much the house is prepared

The major champagne houses of Reims

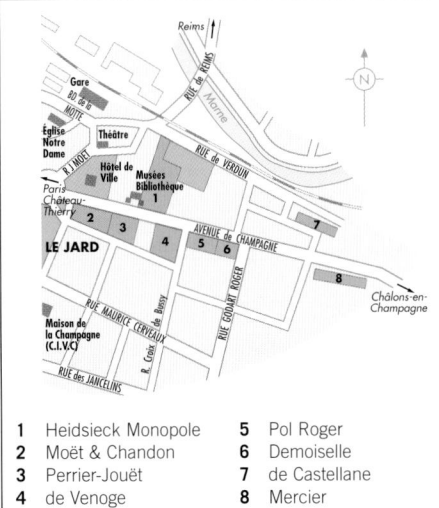

1	Heidsieck Monopole	8	Piper-Heidsieck
2	G H Mumm	9	Charles Heidsieck
3	Palmer	10	Taittinger
4	Krug	11	Ruinart
5	Lanson	12	Pommery
6	Veuve Clicquot Ponsardin	13	Henriot
		14	Abel Lepitre
7	Louis Roederer	15	Jacquesson

The major champagne houses of Epernay

1	Heidsieck Monopole	5	Pol Roger
2	Moët & Chandon	6	Demoiselle
3	Perrier-Jouët	7	de Castellane
4	de Venoge	8	Mercier

Language of the Label

Blanc de blancs all-Chardonnay champagne
Blanc de noirs champagne made exclusively from dark-skinned grapes
Cuvée a blend, which all champagne is
Non-vintage champagne containing wines from more than one year
Réserve much used but meaningless term
Vintage wine from a single year

Sweetness levels

Brut dry
Sec dryish
Demi-sec medium dry
Doux medium sweet

Bottler codes

NM *négociant-manipulant*, champagne-maker who buys in grapes
RM *récoltant-manipulant*, grower who makes his or her own wine
CM *coopérative de manipulation*, a co-op
RC *récoltant-coopérateur*, grower selling wine made by a co-op
MA *marque d'acheteur*, buyer's own brand

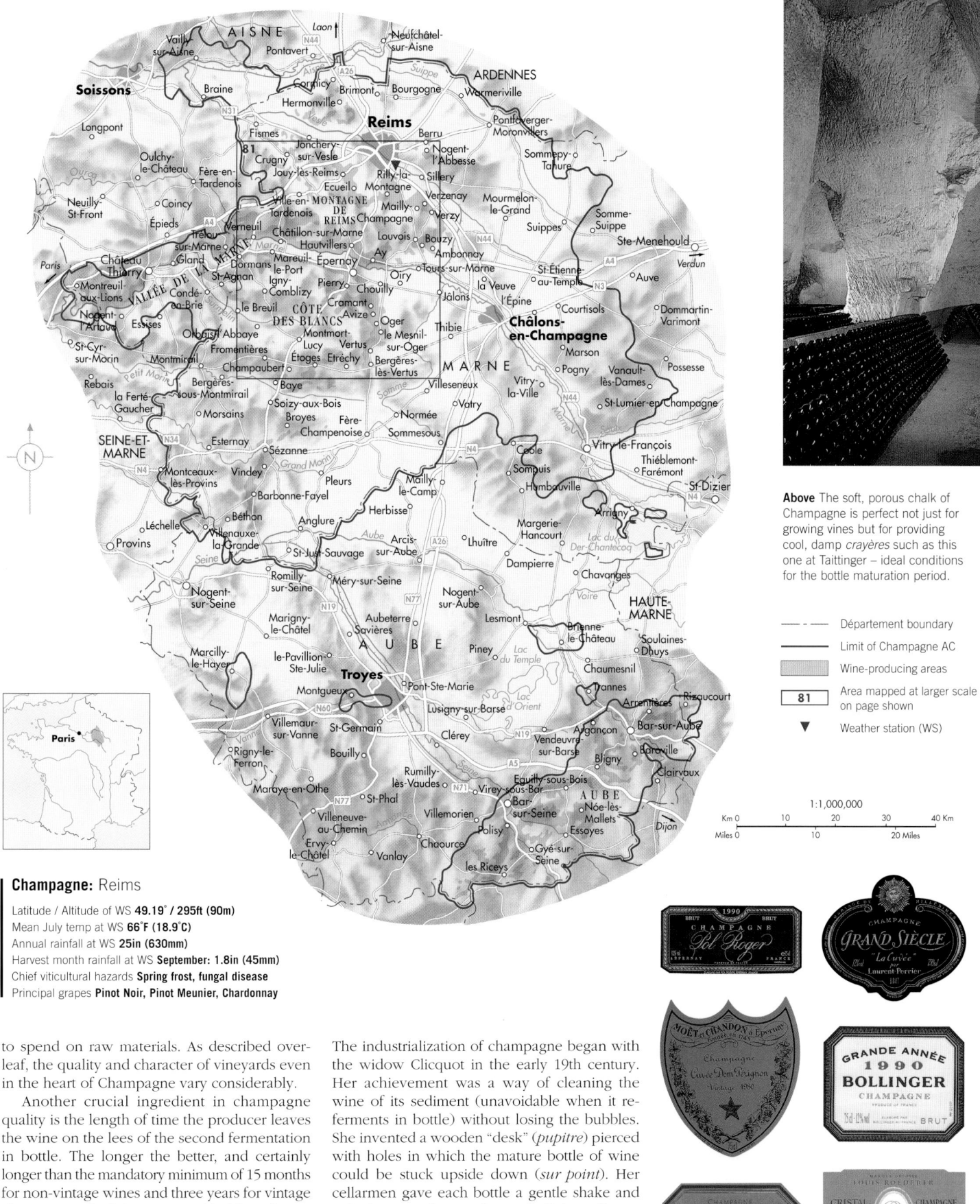

- - - - Département boundary
───── Limit of Champagne AC
▨ Wine-producing areas
81 Area mapped at larger scale on page shown
▼ Weather station (WS)

1:1,000,000
Km 0   10   20   30   40 Km
Miles 0   10   20 Miles

Champagne: Reims

Latitude / Altitude of WS **49.19° / 295ft (90m)**
Mean July temp at WS **66°F (18.9°C)**
Annual rainfall at WS **25in (630mm)**
Harvest month rainfall at WS **September: 1.8in (45mm)**
Chief viticultural hazards **Spring frost, fungal disease**
Principal grapes **Pinot Noir, Pinot Meunier, Chardonnay**

to spend on raw materials. As described overleaf, the quality and character of vineyards even in the heart of Champagne vary considerably.

Another crucial ingredient in champagne quality is the length of time the producer leaves the wine on the lees of the second fermentation in bottle. The longer the better, and certainly longer than the mandatory minimum of 15 months for non-vintage wines and three years for vintage champagne, for it is contact with this sediment as much as anything that gives champagne its subtle flavour.

The reputation of an established house is based on its non-vintage wines, blended so that no difference is noticeable from year to year. Styles vary from the challenging concentration of a Krug or Bollinger to the seductive delicacy of a Taittinger, with Pol Roger, Clicquot, and Roederer as models of classical balance.

The industrialization of champagne began with the widow Clicquot in the early 19th century. Her achievement was a way of cleaning the wine of its sediment (unavoidable when it re-ferments in bottle) without losing the bubbles. She invented a wooden "desk" (*pupitre*) pierced with holes in which the mature bottle of wine could be stuck upside down (*sur point*). Her cellarmen gave each bottle a gentle shake and twist (*remuage*) every day until all the sediment had been dislodged from the glass and settled on the cork. Then they released the cork, let the egg-cupful of wine containing the sediment escape (*dégorgement*), topped up the bottle with sweetened wine, and put in a new cork. To make disgorging easier today, the neck of the bottle is frozen first: a plug of murky ice shoots out when the bottle is opened, leaving perfectly clear wine behind.

Choosing one's favourite *non-vintage champagne is a quasi-political act but this selection of luxury cuvées constitutes the acknowledged aristocracy of Champagne. Most are specially selected vintage wines but Krug and Laurent-Perrier's Grand Siècle are equally admired (and expensive) multi-vintage blends.*

Left Snow is a regular feature in vineyards as far north as Champagne's such as these above Le Mesnil-sur-Oger. Seen in the distance here is an exception for a wine region otherwise dedicated to blending: the walled Clos du Mesnil sold by the house of Krug as a single-vineyard champagne.

Heart of Champagne

Long before the wines of Champagne were made to sparkle they were highly prized in Paris under the names of "*vins de la rivière*" and "*vins de la montagne*". The river was the Marne, the "mountain" the wooded eminence, at best rising to less than 1,000ft (300m), that separates it from the sacred city of Reims where France's kings were crowned. Most prized of all were the wines of Ay, with its propitious south-facing slope down to the river opposite Epernay.

Chalk – the proper soft, white stuff – is Champagne's trump card. Not only can cool, damp cellars be easily hewn from it, but chalk retains moisture and acts as a perfectly regulated vine humidifier which actually warms the soil and produces grapes rich in nitrogen – particularly useful for making yeast work effectively.

Today three grapes dominate. Until recently the most widely grown was Pinot Meunier, a sort of country cousin of Pinot Noir: easier to grow and ripen, obviously fruity but not so fine. This still provides the base wine for all but the very finest champagnes, but Pinot Noir has overtaken Pinot Meunier to become the region's most planted grape, with just under 40% of the total vineyard. Chardonnay is planted on just over a quarter.

The master plan for great champagne is to combine the qualities of the best grapes from the distinct parts of the region – of which, broadly speaking, there are three. In this marginal climate full ripeness is the exception, and slight variations of slope and aspect are crucial.

The Montagne de Reims is planted with Pinot Noir and to a lesser extent Pinot Meunier. Pinot planted on such north-facing slopes as those of Verzenay and Verzy produce base wines notably more acid and less powerful than those grown on the southern flanks of the Montagne de Reims at Ay but they can bring a particularly refined, laser-etched delicacy to a blend. Montagne wines contribute to the bouquet, the headiness and, with their firm acidity, to what the French call the "carpentry" – the backbone of the blend. The village of Bouzy, whose lower slopes can be too productive for top quality champagne, is famous with English-speakers for obvious reasons, but also because it makes a small quantity of still red wine. The invariably tart still wines of the Champagne region – both white and occasionally light red – are sold under the Coteaux Champenois appellation.

The Vallée de la Marne in the west has a succession of south-facing slopes which trap the sun and make these the fullest, roundest and ripest wines, with plenty of aroma. These too are predominantly black-grape vineyards, famous for Pinot Noir in the best-exposed sites but with Pinot Meunier and, increasingly, Chardonnay planted elsewhere.

The east-facing slope south of Epernay (topographically not unlike the Côte de Beaune) is the Côte des Blancs, planted with Chardonnay that gives freshness and finesse to the blend. Wine from here may be sold as Blanc de Blancs, without the traditional proportion of dark-skinned Pinot. Cramant, Avize, and Le Mesnil are three villages with long-respected names for their (unblended) wine. The first (and still the best) brand of Blanc de Blancs was Salon, from Le Mesnil. (The Côte de Sézanne is effectively a slightly less distinguished extension of the Côte des Blancs.)

These (and all Champagne-appellation) vineyards have what you might call a concealed classification – concealed because it is never mentioned on the labels. The *échelle* (ladder) *des crus* gives the grapes of every commune a percentage rating. Up until the turn of the last century an indicative grape price was agreed for the harvest as a whole. A grower in one of the Grand Cru communes would be paid 100% of the price. Premiers Crus would receive between 99% and 90%, according to their place on the ladder, and so on down to 80% for some of the outlying areas. Now the grape price is agreed on an individual basis between the grower and the Champagne house, although the vineyard ratings may still apply.

The map indicates the Grand Cru and Premier Cru areas in the heart of the Champagne region, where almost all the finer wines are grown. Such super-luxury "prestige" brands as Dom Pérignon, Krug, Pol Roger's Sir Winston Churchill, Roederer Cristal, Perrier-Jouët's Belle Epoque, Veuve Clicquot's La Grande Dame or Taittinger's Comtes de Champagne naturally have the highest average *échelle* rating in their constituent wines.

Such wines should never be served very cold: too icy and their flavour is unfathomable. Nor should they be served too young. Great champagnes can mature for 20 years or more, gaining unsuspected depths of flavour. Most vintage wines are at their best between eight and 15 years old. Even a non-vintage from a good house, especially those such as Bollinger with a high proportion of powerful Pinot Noir in the blend, may improve for four or five years. Cheap champagnes, their excess of acidity all too ineffectively disguised by an excess of *dosage*, have little to offer at any stage.

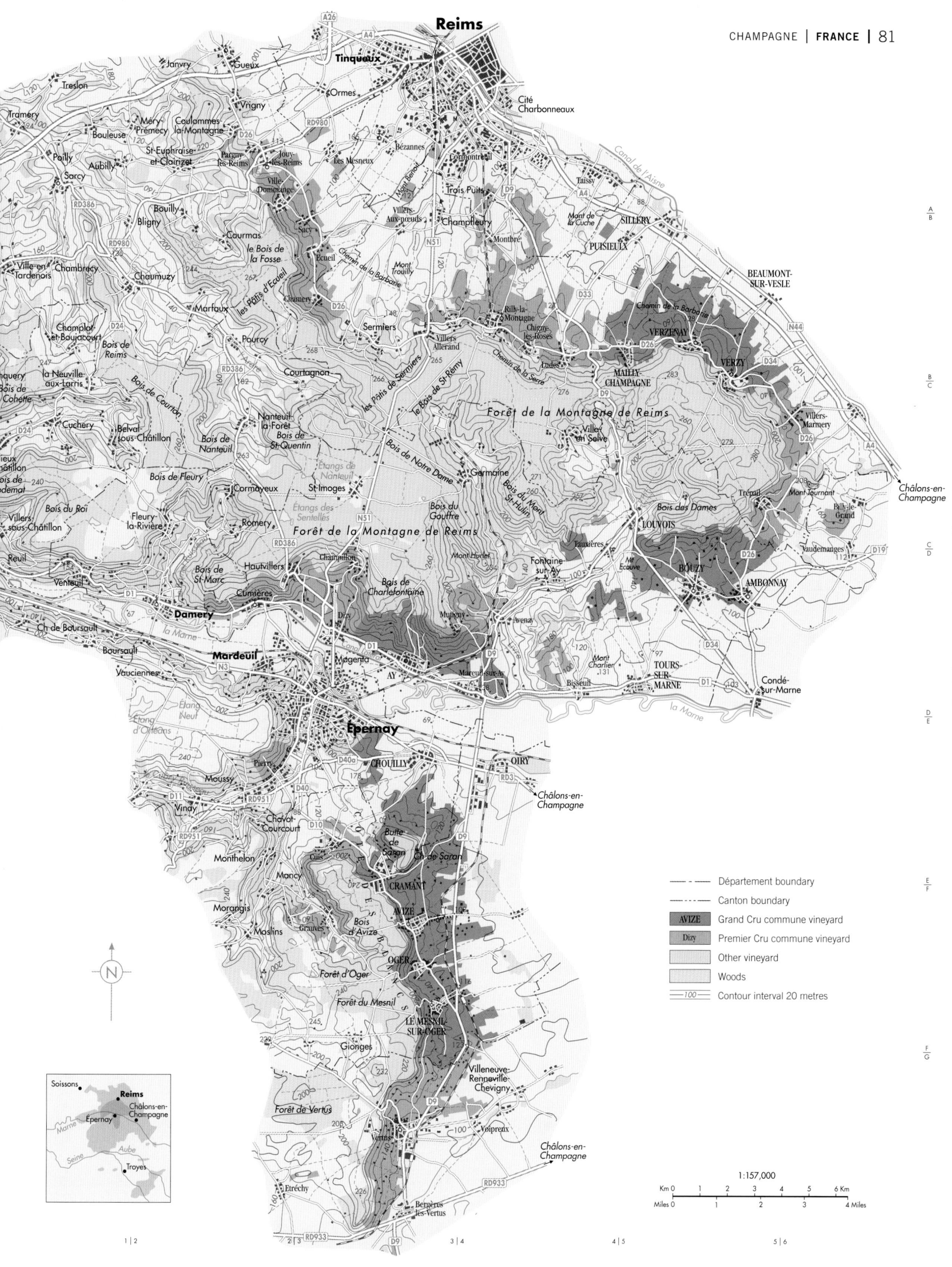

Reims

Tinqueux

A26
A4
A26

Janvry
Gueux
Treslon
Tramery
Bouleuse
Poilly
Sarcy
Aubilly
Méry-
Prémecy
Coulommes-
la-Montagne
St-Euphraise-
et-Clairizet
Pargny-
les-Reims
Jouy-
les-Reims
Vrigny
Ormes
Les Mesneux
Bézannes
Cormontreuil
Cité
Charbonneaux
RD980
RD980
RD386
RD386
Ville-en-
Tardenois
Chambrecy
Chaumuzy
Courmas
Sacy
Écueil
le Bois de
la Fosse
les Pâtis d'Écueil
Chamery
Sermiers
Villers-
Aux-nœuds
Champfleury
Mont Berol
Trois Puits
Taissy
Montbré
Rilly-la-
Montagne
Chigny-
les-Roses
Villers-
Allerand
Ludes
Mailly-
Champagne
Sillery
Puisieulx
Beaumont-
sur-Vesle
Verzenay
Verzy
Chemin de la Barbarie
Canal de l'Aisne
A4
N51
N44
D33
D26
D34
Mont de
la Cuche
Champlat-
et-Boujacourt
Bois de
Reims
la Neuville-
aux-Larris
Bois de
Cohette
Cuchery
Belval-
sous-Châtillon
Marfaux
Pourcy
Courtagnon
Nanteuil-
la-Forêt
Bois de
Nanteuil
Bois de
St-Quentin
les Pâtis de Sermiers
le Bois de St-Rémy
Bois de St-Rémy
Forêt de la Montagne de Reims
Ville-
en-Selve
Villers-
Marmery
Bois de
Fleury
Cormayeux
St-Imoges
Bois de Notre Dame
Germaine
Bois du Mont
St-Hulin
Trépail
Mont Tournant
Châlons-en-
Champagne
Bois du
Roi
Villers-
sous-Châtillon
Fleury-
la-Rivière
Romery
Étangs de
Nanteuil
Étang des
Sentelles
Bois du
Gouffre
Bois des Dames
Billy-le-
Grand
Louvois
Vaudemanges
Reuil
Venteuil
Damery
Ch de Boursault
Boursault
Vauciennes
Mardeuil
Bois de
St-Marc
Hautvillers
Champillon
Cumières
Dizy
Mutigny
Avenay
Bois de
Charlefontaine
Mont Hurlet
Magenta
Ay
Mareuil-sur-Ay
Fontaine-
sur-Ay
Bouzy
Ambonnay
Mt Écouve
Tauxières
Bisseuil
Mont
Charlier
Tours-
sur-
Marne
Condé-
sur-Marne
la Marne
N3
D1
D1
D9
D9
D34
D26
D19
Épernay
Pierry
Moussy
Vinay
Chavot-
Courcourt
Chouilly
Oiry
Châlons-en-
Champagne
Cuis
Guis
Cramant
Avize
Oger
Forêt d'Oger
Forêt du Mesnil
Le Mesnil-
sur-Oger
Gionges
Villeneuve-
Renneville-
Chevigny
Monthelon
Mancy
Morangis
Maslins
Bois
d'Avize
Butte
de
Saran
Ch de Saran
Forêt de Vertus
Vertus
Voipreux
Bergères-
les-Vertus
Étréchy
Étang
Neuf
Étang
d'Orléans
RD951
RD951
RD933
RD933
D40a
D40
D10
D11
D9
D9

N
N (compass)

— · — · —	Département boundary	
— ·· — ·· —	Canton boundary	
AVIZE	Grand Cru commune vineyard	
Dizy	Premier Cru commune vineyard	
	Other vineyard	
	Woods	
—100—	Contour interval 20 metres	

Soissons
Reims
Épernay
Châlons-en-
Champagne
Marne
Seine
Aube
Troyes

1:157,000

Km 0   1   2   3   4   5   6 Km
Miles 0   1   2   3   4 Miles

1 | 2   3 | 4   4 | 5   5 | 6

A/B
B/C
C/D
D/E
E/F
F/G

Bordeaux

If the name of Burgundy suggests richness and plenty, Bordeaux has more than a hint of elegance about it. In place of the plump prelate who seems to symbolize Burgundy, Bordeaux calls to mind a distinguished figure in a frock coat. Picture him tasting pale red wine from a crystal glass. He has one thumb tucked into his waistcoat, while through the open door beyond him there is a glimpse of a turreted house, insubstantial in the pearly seaside light. He enters his moderate enthusiasms in a leather pocket book, observing the progress of beauty across his palate like moves in a game of chess.

Aspects of Bordeaux appeal to the aesthete, as Burgundy appeals to the sensualist. One is the nature of the wine: at its best indescribably subtle in nuance and complexity. Another is the sheer intellectual challenge of so many estates in so many regions and subregions that no-one has mastered them all.

Bordeaux is the largest fine-wine district on earth. The whole département of the Gironde is dedicated to winegrowing. All of its wine is Bordeaux. Its production, 6.5 million hectolitres in 1998, dwarfs that of Burgundy (see page 53).

Red wines now outnumber white by six to one. The great red-wine areas are the Médoc; the best of the Graves, Pessac-Léognan immediately south of the city of Bordeaux on the south bank of the Garonne; and St-Emilion and Pomerol along the north bank of the Dordogne. The country between the two rivers is called Entre-Deux-Mers, a name found only on bottles of its dry white wines, although this region also makes three-quarters of all the red wine sold as AC Bordeaux and Bordeaux Supérieur. A fringe of villages facing Bordeaux and the Graves across the Garonne comprise the Premières Côtes de Bordeaux where some of Bordeaux's best-value wines lurk. In the far south of the map lies Bordeaux's centre of sweet white wine production. Some of the fringe appellations mapped here are rarely seen on bottles outside the region.

Bordeaux's great glories are its finest red wines (the world's archetypes for blends of Cabernet and Merlot), the tiny production of very sweet, golden Sauternes which can live every bit as long, and some unique dry whites made in the Graves.

But not all Bordeaux is glorious and the region's big problem is geographical. The most favoured areas, for the reasons outlined on pages 84 and 85, may be capable of producing some of the world's greatest wines and can command some of the world's highest prices. In less glamorous areas, however, are literally thousands of vine-growers without the incentive, will or, in some cases, the physical ability to produce interesting wine. The marginality of Bordeaux's climate means that in some years, basic red Bordeaux looks a very puny thing alongside the Cabernets so reliably ripened in much of the New World. The straight Bordeaux appellation, which is applied to more red wine than the total South African or German vintage each year, too rarely upholds the glory of this world-famous region.

Compared with Burgundy the system of appellations in Bordeaux is simple. The map opposite shows them all. Within them it is the wine châteaux (sometimes grand estates, sometimes no more than a smallholding with cellar attached) that look after their own identification problem. On the other hand there is a form of classification by quality built into the system in Burgundy that is missing in Bordeaux. Here, in its place, is a variety of local classifications, unfortunately without a common standard.

By far the most famous of these is the classification of the châteaux of the Médoc – and Château Haut-Brion of the Graves – which was finalized in 1855, based on the prices the wines had fetched over the previous 100 years or more. Its first-, second-, third-, fourth-, and fifth-"growths", or *crus*, to which were later added Crus Exceptionnels, Crus Bourgeois Supérieurs, Crus Bourgeois, Crus Artisans, and Crus Paysans, represent the most ambitious grading of the products of the soil ever attempted.

The overriding importance of situation in deciding quality is proved by the classified growths, or Crus Classés – which tend to occupy the best soils. Where present standards depart from it there is usually an explanation (an industrious proprietor in 1855 and a lazy one now, or, more likely nowadays, vice versa). Even more to the point, in many cases land has been added, or exchanged; the vineyard is not precisely the same. In fact, more weight is placed today on the old classification than the system really justifies. The super-luxury first-growths generally fetch about twice the price of the second-growths, but thereafter a fifth-growth may fetch more, for example, than a second if it is better run. The relative qualities of different châteaux really need expressing in a more subtle way

Above Bordeaux is not just a wine but a thoroughly mercantile city with its own once-flourishing port based on the River Garonne. The merchants who ran the Bordeaux wine trade were situated along the quayside, before moving out to modern warehouses in the suburbs.

than by suggesting that one is always "better" than another. The system adopted on the maps that follow is simply to distinguish between classed-growths (in areas where they exist) and the more significant others.

The most notable development in recent years has been the emergence of so-called microchâteaux, defined by us on the maps as producing fewer than 1,000 cases a year, particularly in St-Emilion, for which collectors will pay even more than for a Médoc first-growth (rarity can equal quality in the mind of a collector).

The vineyards of a château sometimes surround it in a neat plot. More often they are scattered and intermingled with those of their neighbours. They can produce annually anything from ten to 1,000 barrels of wine, each holding 300 bottles, or 25 cases. The best vineyards make a maximum of 5,000 litres from each hectare of vines, the less good ones considerably more.

The *maître de chai* is an important figure at the château. Until recently a senior local expected to have learnt his craft from his father and grandfather, he is nowadays more likely to be a highly qualified, well-travelled young scientist. At little properties it is the owner himself, at big ones sometimes an old retainer. It is he who welcomes visitors and lets them taste the new wine, cold and dark and unpalatable, from the casks in his care. Be knowing rather than enthusiastic; the wine will not be ready to drink for two years after it has been bottled at the very least – and maybe not for 20.

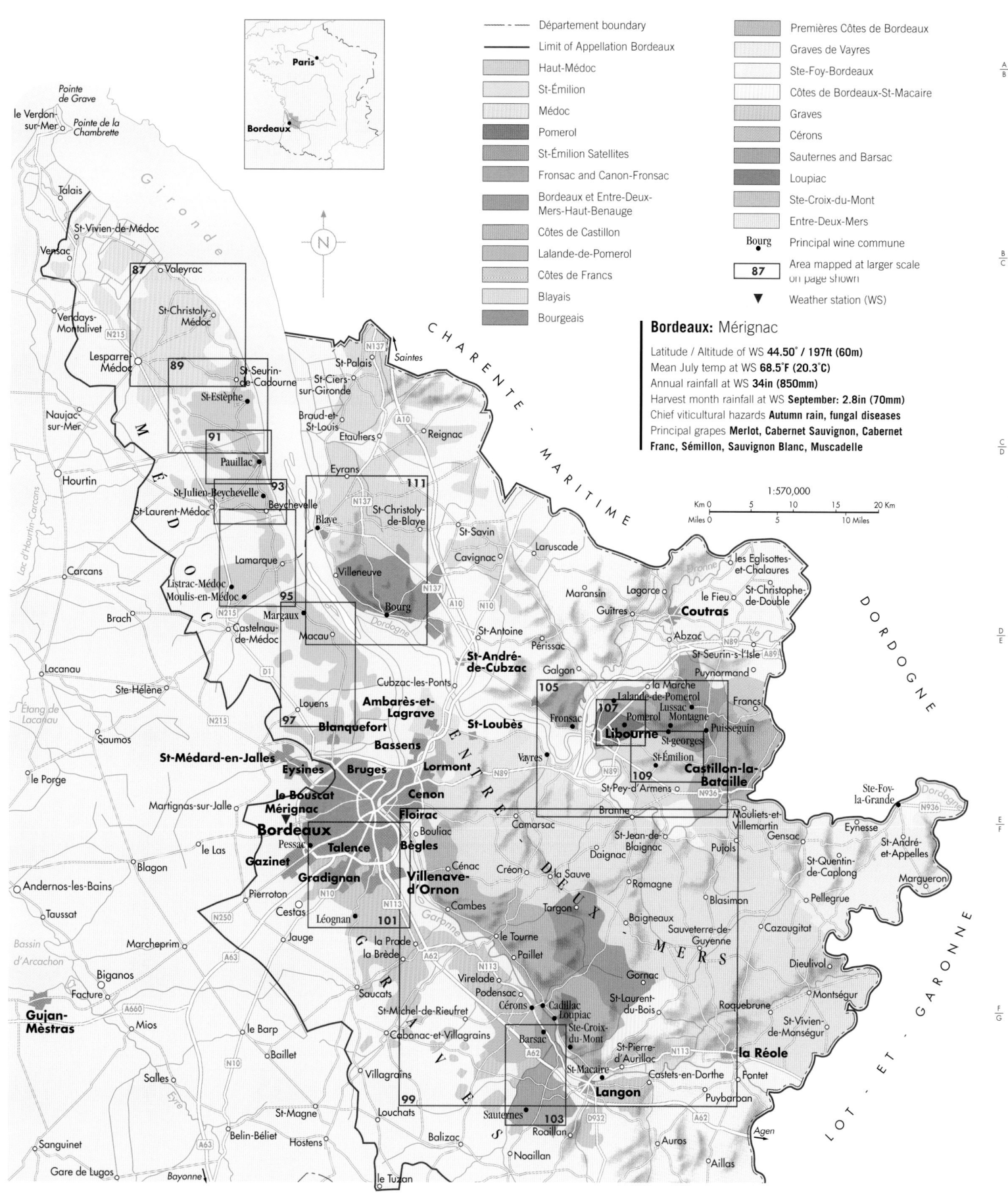

Bordeaux: the Quality Factor

Although the quality and quantity of wine it produces each year can vary quite markedly, the Bordeaux region, the world's biggest resource of fine wine, clearly has some advantages. Its position near the sea and threaded with rivers gives it a moderate and stable climate with relatively few frosts severe enough to kill vines in winter or harm buds in spring. Europe's biggest forest, on the ocean side and in the Landes département to the south, protects it from strong salt winds and moderates rainfall. The weather during flowering in June is variable, which is why the crop size varies too, but summers and, particularly, autumns are usually reliably warm and sunny. Both average temperature and rainfall are slightly higher than in Burgundy – compare the factfiles for Bordeaux (page 83) and Dijon (page 55) – which means that Bordeaux can successfully grow later-ripening grape varieties.

Merlot, Cabernet Sauvignon, Cabernet Franc, and Petit Verdot are the main grapes grown for red wines, in that order of declining importance, with some Malbec still grown north of the Gironde.

Sémillon and an increasing proportion of Sauvignon Blanc are the main white wine grapes (supplemented by Muscadelle in sweet wine districts and some Ugni Blanc and Colombard in lesser appellations). Because these grapes all flower at slightly different times, growing a mix of them can provide the château owner with some insurance against a few days of bad weather at the critical time in June, and against a particularly cool autumn which may fail to coax Cabernet Sauvignon to its full ripeness. Practically all Bordeaux wine estates therefore are planted with a mixture of grape varieties, the proportions varying according to local conditions, tradition and, increasingly, fashion. (The fleshy Merlot makes a natural filler for Bordeaux

Cabernet's more angular frame in any case. The fact that its wines mature earlier than Cabernet Sauvignon is making it even more popular in our fast forward age.) Cabernet Franc, which flowers and ripens a little sooner than Cabernet Sauvignon offers additional insurance cover and, often, an attractive aroma. Petit Verdot ripens latest of all but when it does ripen fully, which it does increasingly thanks to global warming, it can add quite sumptuously spicy top notes to a Médoc blend.

This difference in varietal mix, unknown in Burgundy for example, is just one (important) factor in explaining the huge differences that can be found between the wines of one property and another.

Another factor is the status of the vineyard. Success breeds success, meaning more money to spend on costly care of the land (see table) – or on buying more. Differences that were originally

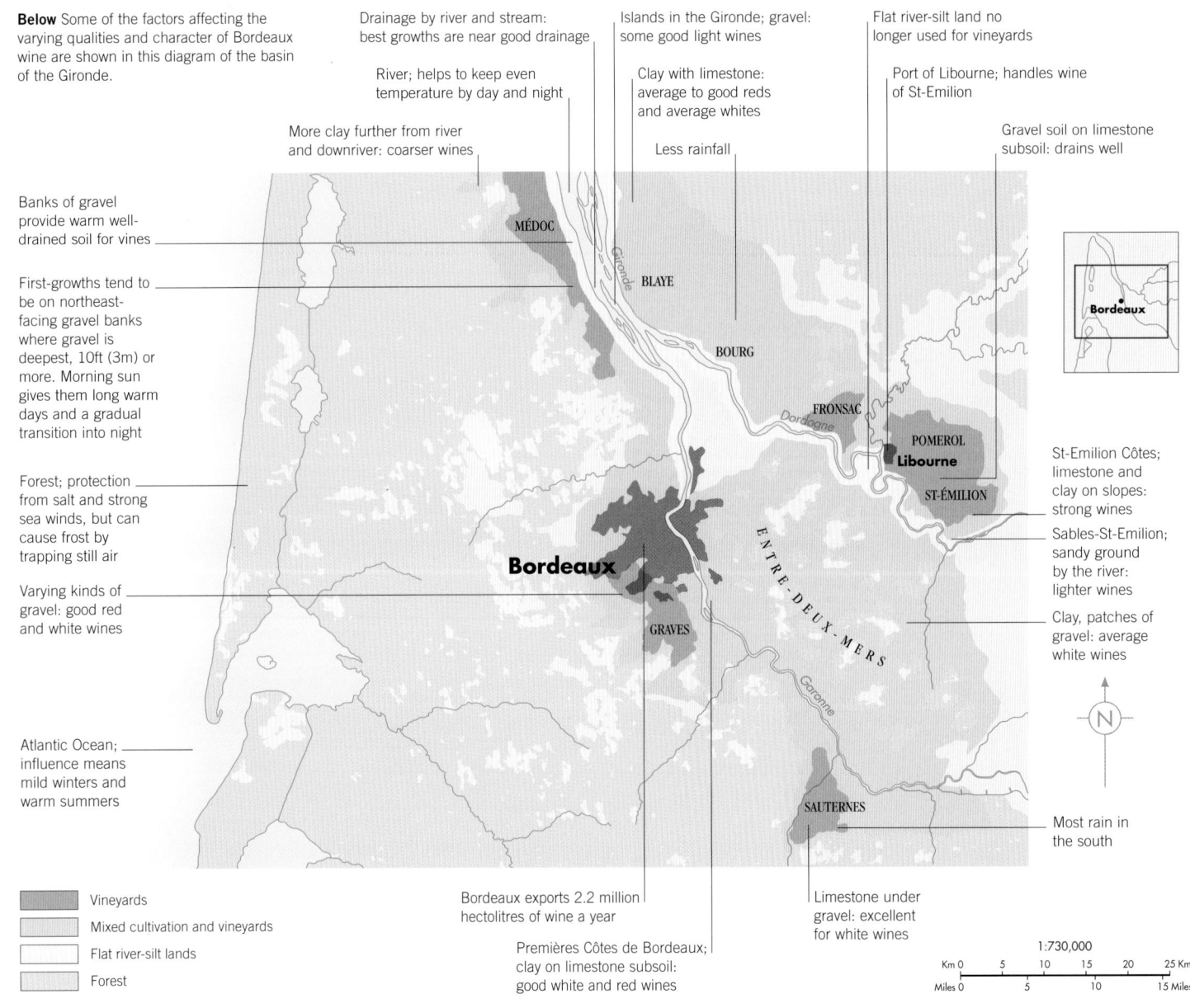

Below Some of the factors affecting the varying qualities and character of Bordeaux wine are shown in this diagram of the basin of the Gironde.

Drainage by river and stream: best growths are near good drainage

River; helps to keep even temperature by day and night

More clay further from river and downriver: coarser wines

Islands in the Gironde; gravel: some good light wines

Clay with limestone: average to good reds and average whites

Less rainfall

Flat river-silt land no longer used for vineyards

Port of Libourne; handles wine of St-Emilion

Gravel soil on limestone subsoil: drains well

Banks of gravel provide warm well-drained soil for vines

First-growths tend to be on northeast-facing gravel banks where gravel is deepest, 10ft (3m) or more. Morning sun gives them long warm days and a gradual transition into night

Forest; protection from salt and strong sea winds, but can cause frost by trapping still air

Varying kinds of gravel: good red and white wines

Atlantic Ocean; influence means mild winters and warm summers

St-Emilion Côtes; limestone and clay on slopes: strong wines

Sables-St-Emilion; sandy ground by the river: lighter wines

Clay, patches of gravel: average white wines

Most rain in the south

MÉDOC

Gironde

BLAYE

BOURG

FRONSAC

Dordogne

POMEROL

Libourne

ST-ÉMILION

Bordeaux

ENTRE-DEUX-MERS

GRAVES

Garonne

SAUTERNES

Bordeaux

N

Vineyards

Mixed cultivation and vineyards

Flat river-silt lands

Forest

Bordeaux exports 2.2 million hectolitres of wine a year

Premières Côtes de Bordeaux; clay on limestone subsoil: good white and red wines

Limestone under gravel: excellent for white wines

1:730,000

Km 0   5   10   15   20   25 Km

Miles 0   5   10   15 Miles

marginal can thus increase over the years, and this certainly goes some way to explaining the vast difference in quality between, say, a classified growth and its unclassified neighbour.

But there are clearly marked differences in soil structure and soil type all over the Bordeaux region – however difficult it can be to identify a precise soil type with, say, first growth quality. Even within one part of Bordeaux, the Médoc being perhaps the most intriguing example, the soil is said to "change at every step". And a look at the map shows how one stretch of it, between St-Julien and Margaux, is an exception to the streak of superlative wine quality that otherwise exists going north from Margaux. It also suggests that there is something very special about the plateau of Pomerol and St-Emilion.

In very general terms Bordeaux is made up of alluvial sandy gravels, deposited in gentle mounds by melted glaciers from the mountains of the centre and the Pyrenees millions of years ago. These gravels, still fully exposed unlike the other gravels deposited in most of the rest of southwest France, are most marked in the Graves (hence the name), Sauternes, which is effectively a continuation of it, and the Médoc.

Dr Gérard Séguin of the University of Bordeaux has done the most significant work on identifying what it takes to produce great wine here. As illustrated on page 23, it seems that (contrary to traditional belief) geology, that is the exact chemical composition of the soil, is scarcely a factor at all in deciding quality, at least not in Bordeaux. A vine will find all the nourishment it needs almost anywhere; but the poorer the soil the deeper and wider the vine will root. Hence the paradox that poor soil makes good wine. Give a vine rich soil, such as in some of the more fertile areas of the Entre-Deux-Mers, or spread generous additions of fertilizer or manure around it, and its roots will stay near the surface.

But plant it in stony ground as in the best sites of the Médoc, give it only the bare necessities, and it will plunge metres deep to reach a distinctly submerged water table which will allow the vine a regular but very sparing supply of water. Drainage is all-important so it is soil structure, helped in many cases by a slight slope and a system of carefully man-made drains, that holds the key to wine quality.

Enlarging on this idea, Dr Séguin has suggested that the nearer a vineyard is to an effective drain, the drier the subsoil will be and the deeper the roots will go; that the first-growths are vineyards nearest the drainage channels, the second-growths slightly further from them, and so on. There is an ancient Bordeaux saying that "the vines should look at the river". This theory explains it. It also explains why old vines tend to give the best wine: their roots are deepest. The theory can be examined by studying the streams, or *jalles*, on the following maps in relation to the classed- and other growths. Add to this the way stones store heat on the surface, and prevent rapid evaporation of moisture from under them, and it is easy to see that they offer wonderfully stable conditions of both

Above The grandest Bordeaux château of all, Château Margaux in the village of Margaux. Wine labelled simply Margaux will come from anywhere in the commune and be much more basic than one labelled Château Margaux.

temperature and humidity which allows even the late-ripening Cabernet Sauvignon a good chance of ripening every year.

In St-Emilion and Pomerol conditions are very different. Being further inland they suffer a slightly harsher climate. Cabernet Sauvignon can be difficult to ripen in many sites not least because the soils tend to be damper and cooler. There are gravels on the plateau on the St-Emilion-Pomerol border around Châteaux Cheval Blanc and Figeac producing gentler, more Médocain wines, but St-Emilion lies on a limestone base, as the picture on page 108 shows, which tends to accentuate the body and structure of wines made here. Sand dominates the plain below the limestone Côtes and results in palpably lighter wines. As St-Emilion slides into Pomerol on the plateau the soil gets progressively heavier with more clay in places. Heavy clay or sand which drains badly are normally the least propitious components for wine – the bigger particles of gravel are best – but Château Pétrus of Pomerol flourishes on its almost pure special clay thanks to drainage channels and its position on a slight mound of hard, iron-rich subsoil.

On this cooler side of the Gironde, the so-called right bank, few growers risk Cabernet Sauvignon so Merlot and Cabernet Franc predominate, with the proportion of sumptuous Merlot being especially high in Pomerol. Given all these variations in the Bordeaux recipe, it is perhaps remarkable that we blind tasters ever confuse a left with a right bank wine.

The cost of growing vines and making wine varies considerably according to both appellation and ambition in Bordeaux. The grander the AC, the lower will be the permitted yield and, on any decent property, the greater the care taken in both vineyard and cellar.

The table below gives the most recent (1998) estimates of production costs in French francs for a typical AC Bordeaux (**A**), a typical AC Médoc (**B**), and a typical well-run classed-growth (**C**).

	A	B	C
Number of vines per ha	3,333	6,666	10,000
Harvest costs per ha	2,181	5,192	10,125
Total viticultural costs per ha	35,963	51,533	116,910
Yield (hl) per ha	62	55	45
Total viticultural costs per hl	580	937	2,598
Vinification cost per hl	47	55	195
Barrel ageing (6 months)		316	
Barrel ageing (18 months)			988
Total costs per hl	627	1,308	3,781
Total costs per bottle	5	10	28

Source: Centre de Gestion et de Compatabilité Agricole de la Gironde (CGCAG)

The new microchâteaux put even more labour and care into cosseting their vines and barrels than a first growth, but according to the (unsalaried) owners of Le Pin which inspired them, their total costs were about 50 francs a bottle in 1999. Of course the costs in the table leave the wine unbottled, unsold, and untransported, but to the wine drinker they look incredibly low compared with the selling price. Packaging and marketing costs can't be that high, can they?

Left The tower of Château La Tour de By, almost on the banks of the Gironde and one of the northern Médoc's many reliable Crus Bourgeois. These wines represent some of Bordeaux's best value.

Northern Médoc

Geographically, the Médoc is a great tongue of flat or barely undulating land isolated from the body of Aquitaine by the broad brown estuary of the Gironde.

In common usage its name is given to more fine wine than any other name in the world: Margaux, St-Julien, Pauillac, St-Estèphe, and their surrounding villages are all "Médoc" in location and in style. But the appellation Médoc is both more limited and less prestigious. It is more clearly understood under its former name of Bas- (meaning lower) Médoc. The term Bas was dropped for reasons of – shall we say? – delicacy. But the fact remains. The lower Médoc, the tip of the tongue, the farthest reaches of the region, has none of the high points, either physically or gastronomically, of the Haut-Médoc to its south.

The well-drained dunes of gravel give way to lower and heavier land north of St-Estèphe, with St-Seurin, the last commune of the Haut-Médoc, riding a characteristic hump between areas of channelled marsh. North and west of here is fertile, long-settled land, with the bustling market town of Lesparre as its capital since the days of English rule six centuries ago.

Until recently, vineyards took their place here with pasture and orchard and woodland. Now they have spread to cover almost all the higher ground where gravel lightens the clay, centring on the villages of St-Yzans, St-Christoly, Couquèques, By and Valeyrac along the banks of the Gironde Estuary, and covering much of the interior in St-Germain-d'Esteuil, Ordonnac, Blaignan, and (the biggest) Bégadan.

There are no classed-growths but there is an impressive number of worthy Crus Bourgeois. Twenty-five years ago the names of only three or four were known to the wider world. Much replanting and upgrading has happened since, and the lower Médoc now has an important place as a supplier of sound, solid reds. A dozen châteaux have built good reputations, using the expensive methods of the Haut-Médoc, and ageing their wines in new (or newish) barrels. These higher standards will be more clearly signalled when a new official classification into Crus Bourgeois, Crus Bourgeois Supérieurs and, the best, Crus Bourgeois Exceptionnels makes its way onto the labels.

Clay suits Merlot better than Cabernet, giving the wine here a softer edge, even a passing resemblance to St-Emilion. The clearest way to see the difference between Médocs Haut and Bas is to compare one of the best of these wines with a Cru Bourgeois from St-Estèphe. Young, there may be little to distinguish them: both are vigorous (like the vines on the rich soils of the Bas-Médoc), tannic, dry, and *très* Bordeaux". At five years, though, the Haut-Médoc wine is finding that fine-etched personality, that clean transparency of flavour, that will go on developing. The Bas-Médoc has begun to soften, but remains a sturdy, rather rustic wine, often deep-coloured, satisfying, and savoury rather than enlightening and inspiring. At ten years of age there has been more softening, but usually at the expense of "structure"; not the refining of character that we find further south.

One of most ambitious châteaux is Château Potensac (which can also use the name Château Lassalle), with the same perfectionist owners as Château Léoville-Las-Cases in St-Julien, and situated on the same slight plateau as Château La Cardonne and the well-run Château Tour Haut-Caussan. Châteaux Livran at St-Germain, Greysac at By, and Laujac, west of Bégadan, all have well-established names, although today the wine tends to have more substance, fruit, and character at Châteaux La Tour de By, La Clare, Rollan de By, and Vieux Château Landon in Bégadan, and Châteaux La Tour St-Bonnet and Les Ormes Sorbet in St-Christoly and Couquèques. Bégadan is the most important commune of the area as a producer, thanks largely to the prodigious output of its growers' co-operative.

Some of the most obvious *candidates for elevation to Cru Bourgeois Exceptionnel status in the reclassification. Note how similar many of these labels are.*

Canton boundary
Commune (parish) boundary
CH GREYSAC   Leading Cru Bourgeois
Ch Sipian   Cru Bourgeois
Vineyards
Woods
20   Contour interval 10 metres

1:65,000

Km 0   1   2   3   4 Km
Miles 0   1   2 Miles

Lesparre-Médoc
Blaye
Bordeaux

St-Vivien-de-Médoc
Janton
Ch Bellegrave   Ch Bellerive
Cantelaude
le Pointon
la Matte de Valeyrac
Valeyrac
Sipian
l'Ardiley   Ch Sipian   Ch Lartigue   Villeneuve   la Rivière
VALEYRAC
la Verdasse
le Moulin de la Verdasse   Ch le Bourdieu   Troussas
l'Oustau Neuf   Ch le Temple   Bois de Troussas   la Lagune
la Clède   CH MONTHIL   Lassus   CH GREYSAC   CH LA TOUR DE BY   la Tour de By
Courbian   le Peyrat   CH LA CLARE   Condissas   Port de By
St-Vivien-de-Médoc   les Bertins   Ch de By   CH ROLLAN DE BY
la Caussade   **By**   Ch la Tour Seran
CH LAUJAC   CH VIEUX ROBIN   Grande Palu de By
Laujac   Canissac   Bégadanet   la Banche
Meillan   BÉGADAN   St-Jean Cave Co-op   les Cabans   Petite Palu de By
Matroutat   Ch St-Saurnin   CH PATACHE D'AUX   CH LA TOUR ST-BONNET
la Lande   CH ST-BONNET
le Sablona   le Bourdieu   **Bégadan**   le Breuil   Ch le Bosca
St-Vivien-de-Médoc   Nouret   Ch la Barrail   le Fourneau   St-Christoly-Médoc
Cazot   Trembleaux   CH PLAGNAC   Bois de Gombeau   Ch la Croix-Landon   CH LES GRANDS CHÊNES
Bassin Terre   Ch de Panigon   Biars   les Bernèdes   ST-CHRISTOLY
Escurac   VIEUX CHÂTEAU LANDON   Ch Tour Blanche   le Sablonat   Castillon   Ch Moulin-de-Castillon
la Pouyade   Déguenon   la Tour   CH LES ORMES SORBET   Mazails
CIVRAC   la Métairie   la Lande   **Couquèques**
Andron   Ch Bournac   Cantérane   COUQUÈQUES   Lamena
Montignac   **Civrac-en-Médoc**   les Petites Granges   Queyzans
le Fourneau   Ch les Granges d'Or   CH SIGOGNAC
Bâdet   Co-op Agricole   Ch la Gorce   Ch Canteloup   ST-YZANS
Prignac-en-Médoc   la Pigotte   St-Brice Cave Vinic   le Moulin
Bessan   la Landette   la Colonne   Taillanet
Uch   Ch la Tour-Prignac   BLAIGNAN   Cantemerle   la Hourqueyre   le Plantey   CH LOUDENNE
Gelade   le Moulin d'Uch   CH TOUR HAUT-CAUSSAN   **Caussan**   **St-Yzans-de-Médoc**
St-Vivien-de-Médoc   Ch Grivière   Moulin de Courrian   Ch Blaignan   Peyressan
PRIGNAC   Co-op Vinic   Ch la France   Hontané   ORDONNAC   St-Seurin-de-Cadourne
Centre Comm.   la Gravette   CH CHANTELYS   Romefort   Ch Hontemieux   l'Abbaye de l'Île
Coulon   Ch Lafon   Ch POTENSAC
Lesparre-Médoc   Gautheys   CH LA CARDONNE   Potensac   Chenal de la Maréchale
Ch Hombanoh   CH PREUILLAC   Plautignan   **Ordonnac**   Palus de Lussac
Gare   **St-Trélody**   Cave Co-op Vinic. Bellevue   Lussan
Hosp.   Ch Vernous   le Gay   Barbehère   Ch Pabeau   Ch Grand Moulin
Hourtin Petit Bosc   Fongrouse   l'Hôpital   Marque   Hourbit   St-Seurin-de-Cadourne
Raynaud   les Marceaux   Boyenfran   Senillac   Loquey
Ste-Marie   Ch d'Escot   CH CASTÉRA   Barbannes   ST-SEURIN
Couloumey   Canquillac   Garraméy   **St-Germain-d'Esteuil**   Cassan   Doyac
Planque   Roque   Brion
Caillou   Lagoneaussan   CH LIVRAN   Barbannes   le Trale
Bénet   Palus de Doyac
Bayron   **ST-GERMAIN-D'ESTEUIL**   Miqueu   Brie   Estey d'Un
Plassan   Lucbeil   Ch Hauterive   Chenal de la Calupeyre
Conneau   Pillet   Lagunas   Peyres
Liard   St-Laurent-Médoc   **Artiguillon**   **VERTHEUIL**

LESPARRE

JAU-DIGNAC-ET-LOIRAC

Gironde

MÉDOC

N

St-Estèphe

The gravel banks which give the Haut-Médoc and its wines their character and quality, stretching along the shore of the Gironde, sheltered from the ocean to the west by forest, begin to peter out at St-Estèphe. It is the northernmost of the four famous communes that are the heart of the Médoc. A *jalle* – the Médoc word for a stream – divides it from Pauillac, draining on the one hand the vineyards of Château Lafite, on the other three of the five classed-growths of St-Estèphe: Châteaux Cos d'Estournel, Cos Labory, and Lafon-Rochet.

There is a distinction between the soils of Pauillac and St-Estèphe: as the gravel washed down the Gironde diminishes there is a stronger

St Estèphe has only *five classed-growths but no shortage of outstanding Crus Bourgeois, some of which are shown here. Indeed Château Sociando-Mallet, like Château Charmail, is in St-Seurin-de-Cadourne rather than St-Estèphe and has been known to outshine first-growths on occasion.*

mixture of clay found in it. Higher up in Margaux, there is very little. In St-Estèphe it is heavier soil, which drains more slowly. This is why vines grown in St-Estèphe seem to withstand particularly dry summers, such as that of 1990, better than those in the well-drained gravels to the south. Even in less extreme weather the wines tend to have more acidity, are fuller and more solid, and often have less perfume – but they fairly fill your mouth with flavour. They have traditionally been sturdy clarets which can become venerable without losing vigour. In recent years, however, the tendency to make red Bordeaux to the same bigger, bolder model has had the effect of blurring some of the differences between St-Estèphe and wines from other communes.

Cos d'Estournel is the most spectacular of the classed-growths. It has an eccentric Chinese-pagoda'd edifice, impressively crowning the steep slope up from the Pauillac boundary, overlooking the meadows of Château Lafite. Together with Château Montrose, overlooking the river, it makes the biggest and best of the St-Estèphes; strong wines with a dark colour and a long life. "Cos", as it is nearly always called (with the S pronounced), has been the leader in the commune in recent years, having a succulence and persistence of flavour (partly perhaps because of a high proportion of Merlot in the vineyard but also because of marked determination at its helm) which can be more seductive than that of its rival second-growth. The situation of Montrose on its gravel mound overlooking the Gironde anticipates that of Latour in Pauillac just to the south. Some find a similar echo in its intense, tannic, deeply flavoured wine. Classic Montrose vintages take 20 years to mature.

The other two classed-growths near Cos d'Estournel, Châteaux Lafon-Rochet and Cos Labory, languished for many years. Cos Labory is content to be full of fruity flavour at a fairly young age. Lafon-Rochet was bought and rebuilt by Guy Tesseron, a cognac merchant, in the 1960s – the first Médoc château to be rebuilt in the 20th century. The wine was famously tough, but recent vintages have been softened by much more Merlot in the blend. Calon-Ségur, north of the village of St-Estèphe and the northernmost classed-growth of the Médoc, comes somewhere between Cos d'Estournel and Montrose in style: firm and long-lived, but not too aggressive. Some 250 years ago the Marquis de Ségur, owner of both Lafite and Latour, reputedly said his heart was at Calon. It still is, on the label.

Above all, St-Estèphe is known for its Crus Bourgeois. There is an explosion of them on the plateau south and west of the village. Châteaux Phélan Ségur and de Pez are both outstanding producers of very fine wine. Pez has an extraordinary historical record: as the property of the Pontacs of Haut-Brion its wine was sold as Pontac in London in the 17th century – possibly before any other growth of the Médoc. Today it belongs to the champagne house of Roederer.

Among the many worthy burgesses of the commune, Château Meyney is unusual in the Médoc for having monastic origins. Its situation

by the river, neighbour to Montrose, might make one look for finer wine with more potential for development. In practice it is sturdy and reliable without notable finesse. More dashing wines, still in the hearty St-Estèphe style, are made at Château Les Ormes de Pez by the owner of Château Lynch-Bages in Pauillac. Châteaux Tronquoy-Lalande, Capbern Gasqueton, and Beau-Site, south, east and west of the village, are all deserving of their good reputations. Château de Marbuzet is under the same ownership as Cos, while Châteaux Haut-Marbuzet, Chambert-Marbuzet, and MacCarthy are all the property of an outstanding winemaker, Henri Duboscq, whose style is distinctly oaky, richly tasty and one of the surest things in the district. Andron Blanquet, Le Crock, and Lavillotte continue the list of St-Estèphes that express the terroir with vigour and style, while Lilian Ladouys is a newcomer that burst on the scene in the late 1980s with glamorous early vintages. The growers' co-operative, the "Marquis de St-Estèphe", is also an important source of typical wine.

To the north of St-Estèphe the gravel bank diminishes to a promontory sticking out of the *palus* – the flat river-silted land beside the estuary on which no wine of quality grows. On top of the promontory the little village of St-Seurin-de-Cadourne has a dozen Crus Bourgeois. The gentle Château Coufran, the more tannic Château Verdignan, the full-blooded Château Sociando-Mallet, and the admirable Château Bel Orme Tronquoy de Lalande are the leaders here, along with a big co-operative whose wine is sold as "Canterayne".

Where St-Seurin ends is the end of the Haut-Médoc: any wine grown beyond that point is

Below Château Lilian Ladouys, one of the many properties throughout the Médoc that were substantially refitted and renovated in the 1990s, thanks to the perceived glamour and often real profit attached to wine.

only entitled to the appellation Médoc, plain and simple (see pages 84-85). The beautiful Château Loudenne, overlooking the Gironde and which for over a century, until 1999, flew the British flag, occupies its first gravel knoll.

The country behind St-Estèphe, further from the river, has a scattering of Crus Bourgeois, few of them well known. Cissac and Vertheuil lie on stronger and less gravelly soil at the forest's edge. Château Cissac is the outstanding growth: for long vigorous enough to be a Pauillac, although softening in the 1990s. At Cissac, Châteaux du Breuil, and Hanteillan, and at Vertheuil, Châteaux Le Bourdieu, and Le Meynieu are worth at least occasional investigation.

—·—·—	Canton boundary
—··—··—	Commune (parish) boundary
CH COS LABORY	Cru Classé
Ch de Pez	Cru Bourgeois
	Premier Cru Classé vineyard
	Cru Classé vineyard
	Other vineyard
	Woods
—20—	Contour interval 10 metres

1:42,000

Km 0 — 1 — 2 Km
Miles 0 — 1 Mile

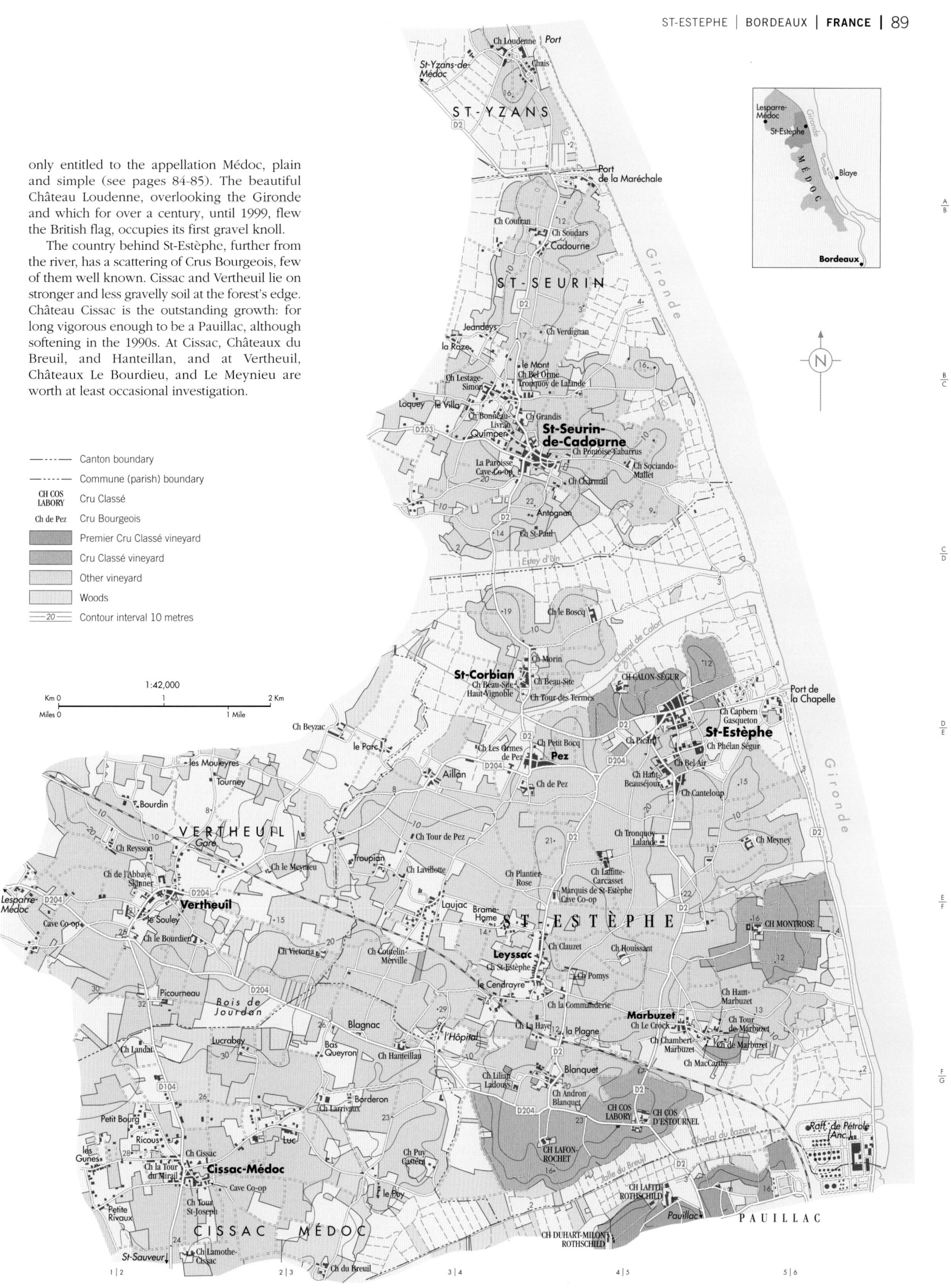

Pauillac

If one had to single out one Bordeaux commune to head the list, there would be no argument. It would be Pauillac. Châteaux Lafite, Latour, and Mouton Rothschild, three out of the first five of the Médoc and Graves, are its obvious claim. But many claret-lovers would tell you that the wines of Pauillac have the quintessential flavour they look for in Bordeaux – a combination of fresh soft-fruit, oak, dryness, subtlety combined with substance, a touch of cigar-box, a suggestion of sweetness and, above all, vigour. Even the lesser growths approach their ideal claret.

At Pauillac the gravel mounds, or *croupes*, of the Médoc get as near as they ever do to being hills. The highest part, with Châteaux Mouton Rothschild and Pontet-Canet on its summit, reaches 100ft (30m) – quite an achievement in this coastal area, where a mere swelling of the ground provides a lookout point.

The town of Pauillac is the biggest of the Médoc. Happily, its long-established oil refinery has ceased operation and become a mere (though colossal) depot. Its old quay has become a marina; a few restaurants have opened (that of Château Cordeillan-Bages under Lynch-Bages auspices even notching up two Michelin stars) – yet the town could scarcely be called animated.

The vineyards of the châteaux of Pauillac are on the whole less subdivided than in most of the Médoc. Whereas in Margaux (for example) the châteaux are bunched together in the town, and their holdings in the surrounding countryside are inextricably mixed up – a row here, a couple of rows there – in Pauillac whole slopes, mounds and plateaux belong to a single proprietor. One would therefore expect greater variations in style derived from terroir. One is not disappointed.

The three great wines of Pauillac are all dramatically different. Châteaux Lafite Rothschild

Below Château Lynch-Moussas, well inland and surrounded by forest, is in a very different situation from fellow fifth-growth Château Lynch-Bages whose wine is generally more bumptious, concentrated, and sought after.

and Latour stand at opposite ends of the parish; the first almost in St-Estèphe, the second almost in St-Julien. Oddly enough, though, their characters tend in quite the opposite direction: Lafite more towards the smoothness and finesse of a St-Julien, Latour more towards the emphatic firmness of a St-Estèphe.

Lafite, with 250 acres (100ha) one of the biggest vineyards in the Médoc, makes about 1,000 barrels of its fabulously expensive wine; a perfumed, polished, and quintessentially gentlemanly production in a unique circular subterranean *chai*. Its second label is Carruades. The firmer and more solid Latour seems to spurn elegance, expressing its supremely privileged situation on the hill nearest the river in robust depths that take decades to reveal their complexity. Latour has the great merit of evenness over uneven vintages. Even the château's second wine, Les Forts de Latour, from separate parcels of land shaded as for a Premier Cru Classé west of the main road (the D2), is considered and priced as a second-growth. A junior selection, still often richly savoury, is sold simply as Pauillac. Mouton Rothschild is a third kind of Pauillac: strong, dark, and full of the savour of ripe blackcurrants. Given the ten or often even 20 years they need to mature (depending on the quality of the vintage), these wines reach into realms of perfection where they are rarely followed. But millionaires tend to be impatient: too much is drunk far too young.

Smelling the richness and feeling the force of Cabernet Sauvignon in these wines it is strange to think that it is a mere 200 years since it was recognized as the best vine for the Médoc. Up to that time even the first-growths had established the superiority of their terroirs with a mixture of inferior grape varieties – above all Malbec.

No visitor to Pauillac should miss the little museum of works of art connected with wine – old glass, paintings, tapestries – as well as the very fine *chais*, which make Château Mouton Rothschild the showplace of the whole Médoc.

The southern approach to Pauillac saw dramatic developments in the early 1990s. Ancient rivalry between the two halves of the historic Pichon estate, whose respective second-growth châteaux face each other across the road, took on a new dimension. For years Pichon-Lalande (as it is known for short) had the better name for its singularly rich and sensuous wine. Then the insurance group AXA bought Pichon-Longueville (as well as much else) and started what can best be described as an aggressive building programme, restoring the glamorous château itself and erecting a dramatic visitors' centre and one of the few buildings in the Médoc which would naturally be called a winery (in Bordeaux *cuviers* are generally full of fermentation tanks and *chais* are stacked with barrels). It must be said that the wine improved just as dramatically, orchestrated by the owner of Château Lynch-Bages, Jean-Michel Cazes.

Lynch-Bages, though "only" a fifth-growth, has long been loved, particularly in Britain, for its richly fragrant wine – a sort of Mouton for

Pauillac is a hotbed *of competition, whether among its three first-growths or between the two Pichons, Lalande and Longueville. There is no shortage of great wine here.*

not-quite-millionaires. With the AXA-owned Cru Bourgeois Château Pibran and Château Haut-Bages Averous, the second wine of Lynch-Bages, M. Cazes directed a cast of model modern Pauillacs until retiring in 2000. The mystery château meanwhile is Pontet-Canet, the biggest Cru Classé of all. Superbly sited as a neighbour to Mouton, it is however utterly different: tannic and reserved where Mouton is opulent.

Château Duhart-Milon belongs to the Rothschilds of Lafite, and Château d'Armailhac (formerly Mouton-Baronne) to Mouton. Both clearly benefit from the wealth and technical knowledge of their proprietors and managers. The neighbouring classed-growth Clerc Milon also belongs to the extensive (Mouton) Rothschild stable. Châteaux Batailley and Haut-Batailley lie back from the river in the fringe of the woods. (Haut-Batailley is related in ownership to the great Château Ducru-Beaucaillou in St-Julien.) La Couronne does duty both as château and *chai*. One does not expect from them quite the same finesse as from the great wines made nearer the river, but both are consistently well-made and good value. Haut-Batailley has the more finesse of the two.

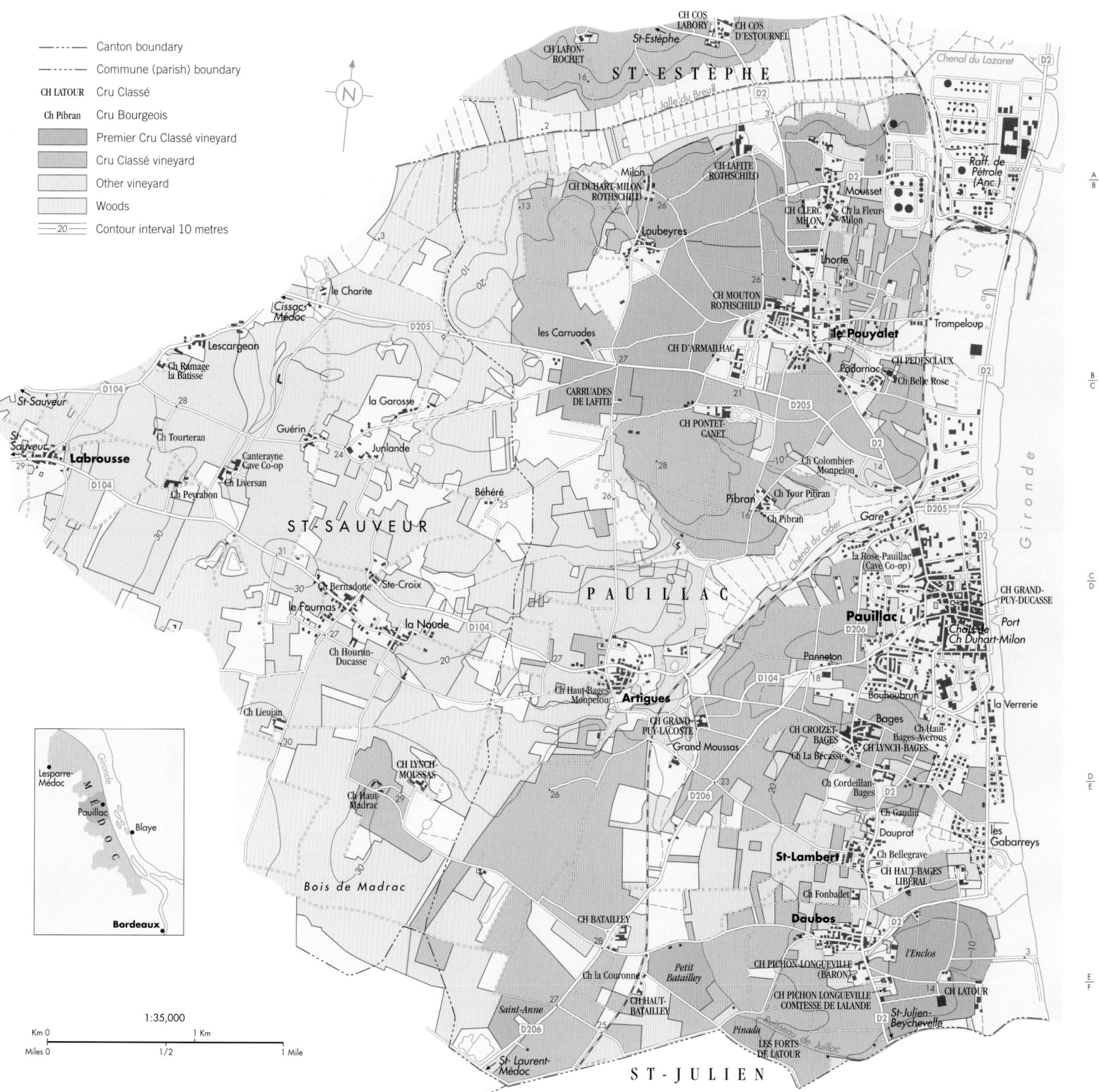

The two châteaux called Grand-Puy, Lacoste and Ducasse, both have high reputations, although the former is better known, consistently producing some of Pauillac's most vital and delicious wines. Lacoste is one fine continuous vineyard on high ground, surrounding its château, while the Ducasse property is scattered in three separate parcels to the north and west of Pauillac and its old château is on the quay in the town itself.

Haut-Bages Libéral, its vineyards superbly sited in St-Lambert, has acquired new premises and a new lease of life. Lynch-Moussas, run in conjunction with Batailley, sells consistently good wine at modest prices. Both Croizet-Bages and Pedesclaux are staunchly conservative – and, in the opinion of many, none the worse for it.

Pauillac, having so many large estates, is not, like St-Estèphe, a warren of small-to-middling growers. Its one small Cru Exceptionnel, La Couronne, has already been mentioned. Of the Crus Bourgeois, Châteaux Pibran and Haut-Bages-Averous are in more than capable hands; Fonbadet, screened from the road in St-Lambert by trees, has old vines and serious wine; and Haut-Bages Monpelou is co-owned with Château

Batailley. The local co-operative, under the name of La Rose-Pauillac, is also making creditable wine, though in diminishing quantities.

The map includes part of the next parish to the west, St-Sauveur. There are no wines of outstanding quality here; the Crus Bourgeois marked, however, are respectable and useful. Château Liversan (which includes Fonpiqueyre) belongs to the Polignac family; Château Peyrabon is a big, well-run vineyard; Château Bernadotte was acquired by Pichon-Lalande's owner in 1993; and the wine of Ramage la Batisse is fragrant and serviceable.

St-Julien

No other commune in Bordeaux has so high a proportion of classed-growths as St-Julien. It is a small commune, with the smallest production of the famous four of the Médoc. Yet almost all of it is superlative winegrowing land: typical mounds of gravel, not as deep as in Pauillac (a cross-section of a St-Julien vine and its soil is shown on page 23), but all are either close to the river or sloping south to the considerable valley (considerable by Médoc standards, that is) drained by the Jalle du Nord and the Chenal du Milieu.

Thus the great châteaux divide into two groups: the riverside estates epitomized by the Léovilles around the village of St-Julien itself, and the southern group centred on the village of Beychevelle, led by Château Beychevelle and its neighbours and reaching back inland with Gruaud-Larose and Lagrange. Further inland in the next commune, St-Laurent, lie three more classed-growths whose appellation is Haut-Médoc and whose style is altogether less finely tuned. The few Crus Bourgeois St-Julien can find room for are grouped round Beychevelle – and led by the redoubtable Château Gloria.

If Pauillac makes the most striking and brilliant wine of the Médoc, and Margaux the most refined and exquisite, St-Julien forms the transition between the two. With comparatively few

exceptions its châteaux make rather round and gentle wine – gentle, that is, when it is mature: it starts as tough and tannic in a good year as any.

The principal glory of the commune is the vast estate of Léoville, once the biggest in the Médoc, now divided into three. It lies on the Pauillac boundary, and it would be a brave man who would say that he could distinguish a Léoville from a Longueville every time he tasted one (although he certainly should be able to distinguish a Château Latour, which lies equally close).

Château Léoville-Las-Cases has the most extensive vineyards of the three, with 225 acres (some 90ha). Its restrained, almost austere, long-lived wine is so obviously "classic", and Delon family who run it so astute, that Léoville-Las-Cases has been known to command higher prices than the first-growths.

Château Léoville-Barton runs it close. It belongs, together with the neighbouring Château Langoa Barton, to the old Irish family of Barton, who moved to Bordeaux as merchants early in the 18th century. Anthony Barton lives in the beautiful 18th-century Château Langoa, and makes his two wines side by side in the same *chai*. Langoa is usually reckoned the slightly lesser wine of the two, being fuller and more tannic, but both are among the finest of

clarets in a traditional manner and are never less than good value, even in tricky years.

Léoville-Poyferré has had a much more patchy past, but in the 1980s and 1990s it justified its great name with excellent forceful wines.

What was the united Léoville like? It is hard to know how much of today's contrasts are due to diverging traditions and how much to the slightly varied terroirs. A different balance of Cabernet and Merlot will produce different barrels from the same vineyard. On the other hand, people who taste the wines of several grape varieties from one vineyard before they have been "assembled" in one barrel have often said that even while they tasted of the different grapes, each had the characteristic style of the estate.

To the south of the Léovilles, Château Ducru-Beaucaillou with its Italianate mansion has established a style of its own, distinct in emphasizing finesse at a very high level, while its neighbour Branaire (once Branaire-Ducru) is somehow more four-square. On the other hand Château Beychevelle and its neighbour St-Pierre convey finesse and elegance with an easy plumpness that is intensely seductive.

Château Gruaud-Larose begins the "inland" section of St-Julien with wines whose richness and drive puts them in the very top rank. There

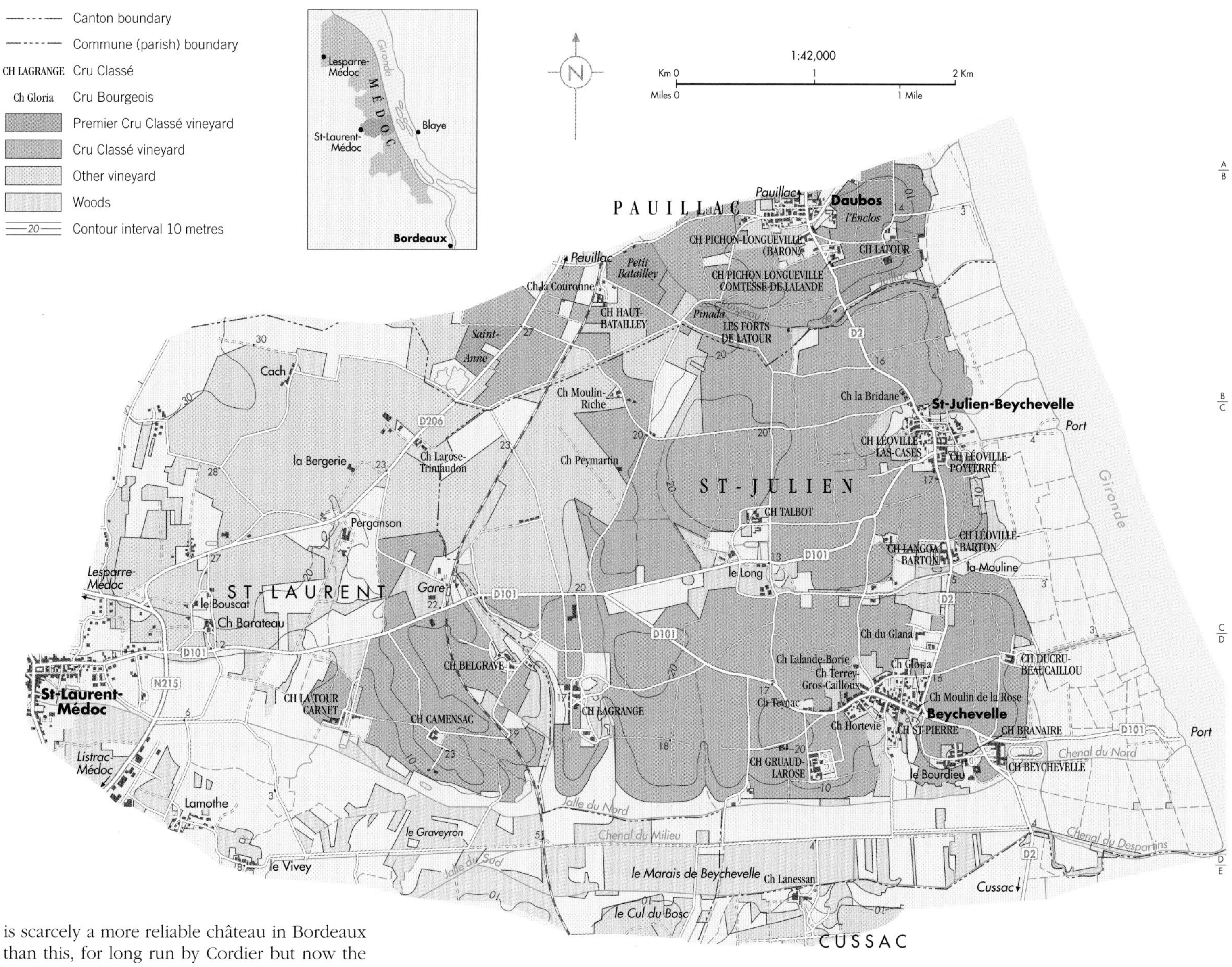

Canton boundary
Commune (parish) boundary
CH LAGRANGE Cru Classé
Ch Gloria Cru Bourgeois
Premier Cru Classé vineyard
Cru Classé vineyard
Other vineyard
Woods
20 Contour interval 10 metres
Lesparre-Médoc
MÉDOC
Gironde
Blaye
St-Laurent-Médoc
Bordeaux
1:42,000
Km 0
1
2 Km
Miles 0
1 Mile
PAUILLAC
Pauillac
Daubos
l'Enclos
CH PICHON-LONGUEVILLE (BARON)
CH LATOUR
Petit Batailley
CH PICHON LONGUEVILLE COMTESSE DE LALANDE
Ch la Couronne
CH HAUT-BATAILLEY
Pinada
LES FORTS DE LATOUR
Saint-Anne
Cach
Ch Moulin-Riche
Ch la Bridane
St-Julien-Beychevelle
Port
CH LÉOVILLE-LAS-CASES
CH LÉOVILLE-POYFERRÉ
la Bergerie
Ch Larose-Trintaudon
Ch Peymartin
ST-JULIEN
CH TALBOT
Perganson
CH LÉOVILLE-BARTON
CH LANGOA-BARTON
la Mouline
le Long
Lesparre-Médoc
ST-LAURENT
Gare
le Bouscat
Ch Barateau
Ch du Glana
St-Laurent-Médoc
CH BELGRAVE
Ch Lalande-Borie
Ch Terrey-Gros-Cailloux
Ch Gloria
CH DUCRU-BEAUCAILLOU
CH LA TOUR CARNET
CH LAGRANGE
Ch Teynac
Ch Moulin de la Rose
CH CAMENSAC
Beychevelle
Ch Hortevie
CH ST-PIERRE
CH BRANAIRE
Port
Listrac-Médoc
CH GRUAUD-LAROSE
le Bourdieu
Chenal du Nord
CH BEYCHEVELLE
Lamothe
Jalle du Nord
le Graveyron
Chenal du Milieu
Chenal du Despartins
le Vivey
Jalle du Sud
le Marais de Beychevelle
Ch Lanessan
Cussac
le Cul du Bosc
CUSSAC
Gironde
D2
D101
D206
N215

is scarcely a more reliable château in Bordeaux than this, for long run by Cordier but now the jewel in the Merlaut family's crown. Château Talbot, which occupies the central high ground of the commune, is still owned by part of the Cordier family. It may be a shade less fine, but is consistently dense, smooth, and savoury, perhaps owing almost as much to the skill of the winemaking as to its site.

Château du Glana, the large Cru Bourgeois next door, has not been as favoured recently as Hortevie, Moulin de la Rose, Terrey-Gros-Cailloux, and Lalande-Borie, the last created by the owner of Ducru-Beaucaillou.

The last of the classed-growths, Château Lagrange, used to be very highly regarded for its rich, substantial wine. A new (Japanese) régime since 1984 brought it back into focus. It lies far back in the country in the sleepy hinterland on the border of St-Laurent (whose appellation is Haut-Médoc) and in a group with three other classed-growths, all in different stages of resurrection. La Tour Carnet is most advanced; recently very attractive. Camensac was replanted a few years later by the owner of the huge and popular Cru Bourgeois Larose-Trintaudon. Its wine is gaining substance and recognition. Château Belgrave has also, like so much in the Médoc since the early 1980s, been restored.

CHATEAU LÉOVILLE BARTON 1990
SAINT-JULIEN
RÉCOLTE 1996
Grand Vin de Léoville du Marquis de Las Cases
SAINT-JULIEN
CORDIER
GRAND CRU CLASSÉ
1993
Château Gruaud Larose
SAINT-JULIEN
GRAND CRU CLASSÉ
CHATEAU TALBOT
SAINT-JULIEN
1996
CHÂTEAU BEYCHEVELLE
GRAND VIN 1995
SAINT-JULIEN
1996
1995
CHATEAU LAGRANGE
SAINT-JULIEN
Château Léoville Poyferré
Saint-Julien
1990
Grand Cru Classé en 1855
2000
Château Branaire
(DULUC-DUCRU)
Saint-Julien
Mis en Bouteille au Château

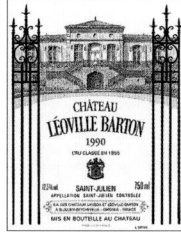

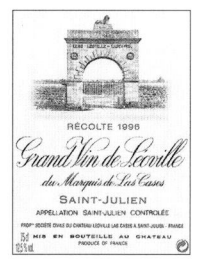

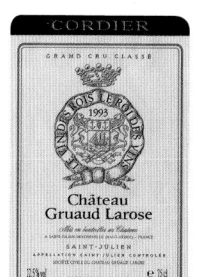

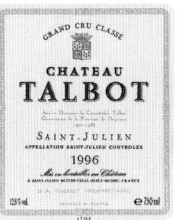

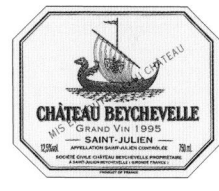

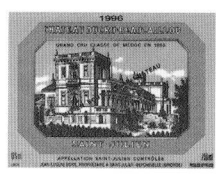

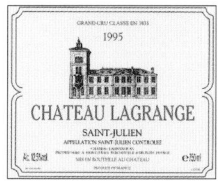

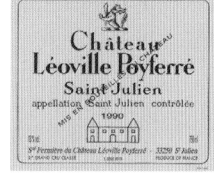

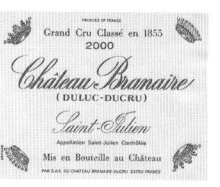

St Julien *is the epitome of claret: harmonious, digestible, and exceptionally well mannered. Château Léoville-Las-Cases however sets its sights on being considered an honorary top-flight Pauillac, as far as both tannin levels and price are concerned.*

Central Médoc

This is the bridge passage of the Médoc, the mezzo forte between the andante of St-Julien and the allegro of Margaux. Four villages pass without a single classed-growth; their appellation simply Haut-Médoc. Here the gravel mounds rise less proudly above the river and the water table is higher, leaving vine root systems shallower and the wines they produce less complex. The commune of Cussac maintains some of the momentum of St-Julien with the outstanding Cru Bourgeois Château Lanessan, facing St-Julien across the canal that separates the parishes. Lanessan and its neighbour Caronne Ste-Gemme (largely in neighbouring St-Laurent) are well-run estates whose owners can afford high standards.

Otherwise Cussac has little of the all-important gravel. The forest here comes close to the river. Château Beaumont occupies its best outcrop. Its wine is easy, fragrant, quick to mature. Oddly Château Tour du Haut-Moulin in Vieux Cussac is just the opposite: dark, old-fashioned, needing years – but worth the wait.

The riverside here is worth a visit to see the handsome 17th-century battlements of the Fort-Médoc – an anti-English precaution now turned to peaceful uses. At Lamarque an earlier fortress, the splendid Château de Lamarque, has established a name for carefully made, satisfyingly full-bodied wine with the true stamp of the Médoc on it. Lamarque is the Médoc's link with Blaye on the other side of the Gironde: a regular car-ferry service runs from the pier.

A good deal of replanting has given the area a purposeful look which was lacking 15 years ago. Château Malescasse was one of the first to be restored. And in the next commune south, Arcins, the big old properties of Château Barreyres and Château d'Arcins have been hugely replanted by the Castels, whose Castelvin is a staple of the French diet. They, their well-managed neighbour Château Arnauld, and the co-op "Chevalier d'Ars" are steadily making Arcins better known. The food in the little Lion d'Or, the Médoc's wine trade canteen, also helps.

It is not by the river, though, but west of Arcins that the gravel ridges rise and fan out inland, culminating at Grand Poujeaux (in the commune of Moulis) and at Listrac. These two communes are dignified with appellations of their own instead of the portmanteau "Haut-Médoc". In recent years Listrac and Moulis have risen steadily in estimation.

Quality rises with the gravel. Immediately over the parish boundary, Château Chasse-Spleen is one of the "Exceptionnel" Bourgeois growths that can be considered as honorarily classified, almost as an honorary St-Julien, for its smoothness, its accessibility, and yet its firm, oak-aged structure. Château Poujeaux can be just as impressive. Between these two properties, the village of Grand Poujeaux is surrounded by a knot of excellent Crus Bourgeois with "Grand Poujeaux" in their names: Gressier, Dutruch, and La Closerie, all reliable for stout-hearted, long-lived reds with the flavour that makes the Médoc unique. Just north of here, Château Maucaillou has stood out in flavour and value in recent years.

Listrac has a higher plateau, limestone beneath its gravel, and a name for tough, tannic wines that need time. The name here is Fourcas: of the three châteaux that bear it, Hosten and Dupré have long been outstanding. Much replanting and infilling has recently enlarged the vineyard considerably. Since 1973 Baron Edmond de Rothschild has created Château Clarke, with 137 acres (55ha) of vines. The twin châteaux Fonréaud and Lestage have 192 acres (77ha) between them. These redeveloped estates temper the Listrac austerity and make rounder wines, which can only help to make the appellation better known.

Beyond the Jalle de Tiquetorte, in the southeast corner of the area, we enter the sphere of Margaux. The extensive Château Citran is now owned by the Merlaut family. It and the smaller Villegeorge (off this map to the south, but a Cru Bourgeois Exceptionnel to watch) lie in the commune of Avensan. Both are well known, and approach Margaux in style.

Soussans is among the communes whose AC is not merely Haut-Médoc but Margaux. Its Château La Tour de Mons has made such fine wines in the past that critics have mooted promotion to classed-growth. Tayac is another important Cru Bourgeois. Paveil de Luze was for a century the stylish country resort of one of the great merchant families of Bordeaux, making the kind of easy, elegant wines the family liked.

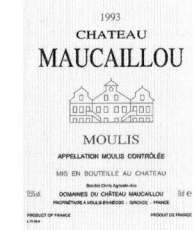

Sturdy wines and dependable value *is represented in this selection rather than real excitement, although Château Chasse-Spleen can in certain vintages reach great heights.*

Right This view of Château Lanessan almost on the border with the commune of St Julien shows how great, well-drained soils are much rarer in this central stretch of the Médoc and vineyards are interspersed with woodland.

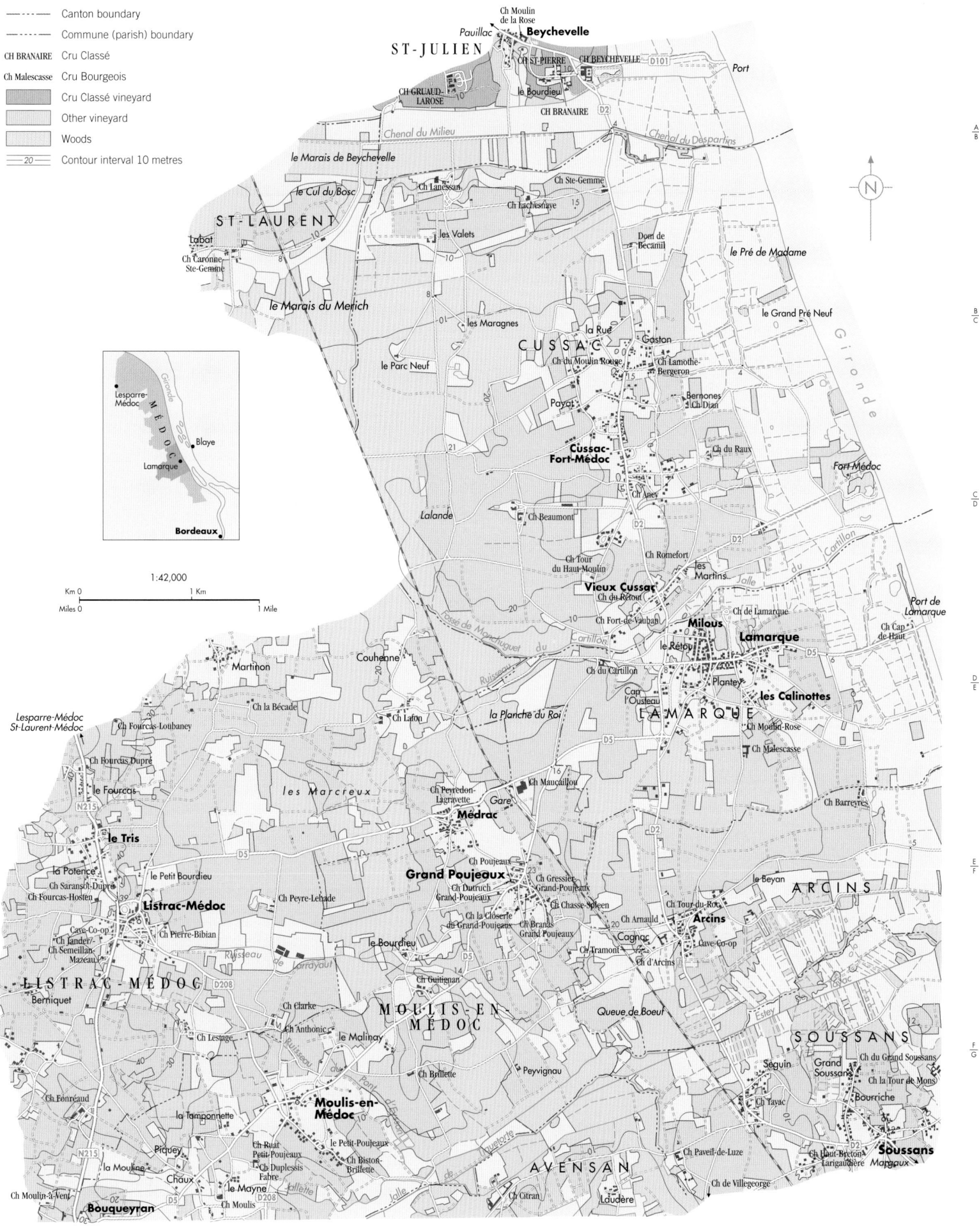

Canton boundary
Commune (parish) boundary
CH BRANAIRE Cru Classé
Ch Malescasse Cru Bourgeois
Cru Classé vineyard
Other vineyard
Woods
20 Contour interval 10 metres

1:42,000

Km 0   1 Km
Miles 0   1 Mile

Lesparre-Médoc
Blaye
Lamarque
Bordeaux

Ch Moulin de la Rose
Pauillac
Beychevelle
ST-JULIEN
CH ST-PIERRE
CH BEYCHEVELLE
D101
Port
CH GRUAUD-LAROSE
le Bourdieu
CH BRANAIRE
D2
Chenal du Milieu
Chenal du Despartins
le Marais de Beychevelle
le Cul du Bosc
Ch Lanessan
Ch Ste-Gemme
ST-LAURENT
Ch Lachesnaye
1.5
Tabot
les Valets
Dom de Becamil
le Pré de Madame
Ch Caronne Ste-Gemme
8
10
le Marais du Merich
8
10
les Maragnes
le Grand Pré Neuf
la Rue
Gaston
CUSSAC
Ch du Moulin Rouge
Ch Lamothe-Bergeron
le Parc Neuf
Payat
Bernones
Ch Dian
4
Cussac-Fort-Médoc
Ch du Raux
Fort Médoc
Lalande
Ch Arcy
Ch Beaumont
D2
D2
Ch Tour du Haut-Moulin
Ch Romefort
les Martins
Port de Lamarque
Vieux Cussac
Ch du Rétou
Ch de Lamarque
Ch Cap de Haut
20
Ch Fort-de-Vauban
Milous
Lamarque
10
le Rétou
Fossé de Montruget
Cartillon
Cap l'Ousteau
Plantey
les Calinottes
Couhenne
Martinon
la Planche du Roi
LAMARQUE
Ch Moulin-Rose
Ch la Bécade
Ch Lafon
D5
Ch Malescasse
Lesparre-Médoc
St-Laurent-Médoc
Ch Fourcas-Loubaney
16
les Marcreux
Ch Peyredon-Lagravette
Ch Maucaillou
Ch Barreyres
Ch Fourcas Dupré
le Fourcas
N215
Gare
Médrac
D2
5
le Tris
Ch Poujeaux
Grand Poujeaux
Ch Gressier-Grand-Poujeaux
le Beyan
ARCINS
la Potence
le Petit Bourdieu
Ch Dutruch Grand-Poujeaux
Ch Chasse-Spleen
Ch Tour-du-Roc
Ch Saransot-Dupré
Ch Peyre-Lehade
Ch Arnauld
Arcins
Ch Fourcas-Hosten
Listrac-Médoc
Ch la Closerie du Grand-Poujeaux
Ch Brands Grand Poujeaux
20
Cagnac
Cave-Co-op
Cave-Co-op
Ch Jandet
Ch Semeillan-Mazeau
Ch Pierre-Bibian
le Bourdieu
Ch Tramont
Ch d'Arcins
D5
Ruisseau
de Larrayaut
LISTRAC-MÉDOC
Ch Guitignan
14
D208
Berniquet
Ch Clarke
MOULIS-EN-MÉDOC
Queue de Boeuf
SOUSSANS
Ch Lestage
Ch Anthonic
le Malinay
Séguin
Grand Soussans
Ch du Grand Soussans
Ch Brillette
Peyvignau
Ch la Tour de Mons
Bourriche
Ch Fonréaud
la Tamponnette
Ch Tayac
Moulis-en-Médoc
Ch Paveil-de-Luze
Ch Haut-Breton Larigaudière
Soussans
Piquey
Ch Ruat Petit-Poujeaux
le Petit-Poujeaux
Margaux
Chaux
Ch Duplessis Fabre
Ch Biston-Brillette
AVENSAN
Ch de Villegeorge
Ch Moulin-à-Vent
le Mayne
N215
la Mouline
Ch Moulis
Ch Citran
Laudère
Bouqueyran
D208

Margaux and the Southern Médoc

Margaux and its "satellites" are considered to make the Médoc's most polished and fragrant wine. Their historical record says so; and at long last contemporary reality is catching up. There are more second- and third-growths here than anywhere, and although there are still too many under-performers, a new broom has been sweeping through the southern Médoc.

The map shows a rather different picture from Pauillac or St-Julien. Instead of the châteaux being spread out evenly over the land, they are huddled together in the village. An examination of the almost unliftable volumes of commune maps in the *mairie* shows a degree of intermingling of one estate with another which is far greater than in, say, Pauillac. One would therefore look to differences in grape varieties, technique and tradition more than changes of soil to try to explain the differences between the châteaux.

In fact the soil of Margaux is the thinnest in the Médoc, with the highest proportion of rough gravel. It has the least to offer the vine in the way of nourishment but it drains well even in rainy years. The result is wines that start life comparatively supple, although in poor years they can turn out thin. In good and great years, however, all the stories about the virtues of gravel are justified: there is a delicacy about good Margaux, and a sweet haunting perfume, that can make it the most exquisite claret of all.

The wines of Châteaux Margaux and Palmer are the ones that most often reach such heights. Château Margaux is not only a first-growth of the Médoc, it is the one that most looks the part: a pediment at the end of an avenue; the air of a palace with *chais* to match. After underinvestment from the late 1950s, the Mentzelopoulos family acquired it and has been making superlative wine here again from 1978, as well as a seminal oaked white Pavillon Blanc de Château Margaux grown on the western limit of the map opposite which, being white, qualifies only as a humble AC Bordeaux. The third-growth Château Palmer, however, keeps up a formidable challenge and, unlike so many red Bordeaux today, acutely expresses its origins.

Château Lascombes (which was restored and greatly enlarged by Alexis Lichine before being sold to English brewers Bass) is a case where buying more land diluted second-growth quality in the 1970s and early 1980s. With more than 200 acres (80ha) of vineyard, this is one of the Médoc's largest wine estates. Things have been slowly improving, however – not least since a clear distinction was made, in 1982, between the Lascombes vines and those producing its second wine Château Segonnes.

Of the famous pair which used to be the big Rauzan estate, as famous in the 18th century as Léoville was in St-Julien, Rauzan-Ségla (once Rausan-Ségla) is today much the better, having been reformed in the 1980s and taken firmly in hand by the family behind the fashion house Chanel from 1994. The smaller Rauzan-Gassies still lags far behind second-growth standards and shows little inclination to narrow the gap.

There are several distinguished pairs of châteaux in Margaux. The two second-growths Brane-Cantenac and Durfort-Vivens are owned by different members of the ubiquitous Lurton family, yet make distinctly different wine: the Brane fragrant and almost melting, the Durfort much less generous. A tiny vestige of the third-growth Desmirail has been resurrected to join them as a third bowstring.

Fourth-growth Pouget is the often forceful brother of third-growth Boyd-Cantenac. Malescot St-Exupéry (which can be miraculously scented and one of the best of Margaux) and the small third-growth Château Marquis d'Alesme-Becker belong to the Zuger brothers Roger and Jean-Claude respectively.

Still in Margaux proper, fourth-growth Château Marquis de Terme, although rarely seen abroad, now makes rather good wine. Château d'Issan is perhaps the most beautiful house in the Médoc: a 17th-century manor within the complete moat of an old château-fort by the river. The admirable gentle slope of its vineyard toward the river is one of the best situations in Margaux.

Above Margaux's other great property, Château Palmer, signals its multinational owners, chiefly the négociants Mähler-Besse and Sichel, by flying French, Dutch, and British flags.

The Crus Bourgeois include a couple on the theme of Labégorce: their names stick in the mind like a nursery rhyme. Of the two, the Belgian-owned Labégorce-Zédé is currently the best known, though Château Labégorce is giving it a hard run. Closer to the village of Margaux, Château La Gurgue is under the same, superior management as the recently revived third-growth Château Ferrière.

Our rather erratic path to and fro in Margaux becomes a little simpler as the châteaux thin out in Cantenac and farther south. Most of the land in the communes of Cantenac, Labarde, and Arsac, as well as Soussans to the north, has been granted the appellation Margaux, making wines of very similar style and quality.

In Cantenac itself, the château of Prieuré-Lichine was deservedly famous for making some of Margaux's most consistent claret when it was owned by Alexis Lichine – and also for being the first to admit passers-by in a way which has, remarkably, only just become accepted practice. Château Kirwan was once in eclipse but has been restored and began to shine again in the 1990s.

Yet another tale of restoration and renewed quality has been the lonely Château du Tertre, isolated on high ground in Arsac, saved in the 1960s by the owner of Château Calon-Ségur and now under new ownership. Recent vintages have been excellent, as have those of du Tertre's Cru Bourgeois neighbour Château Monbrison, a thoroughly modern Margaux.

Château Cantenac-Brown, which competes for the prize of ugliest Médoc château (it looks like a Victorian English school), flanks Brane-Cantenac and, like Pichon-Longueville in Pauillac, is run by AXA, the insurance company, both as a wine producer and a company retreat.

There are three more important classed-growths before the Haut-Médoc vineyards come to an end: Giscours, whose half-timbered farm buildings in the overblown style of Le Touquet

Of these exceptionally high achievers the once glorious Château Rauzan-Ségla has been recently revived. Châteaux La Lagune and Cantemerle lie south of the boundary of the Margaux appellation and are therefore sold as Haut-Médoc.

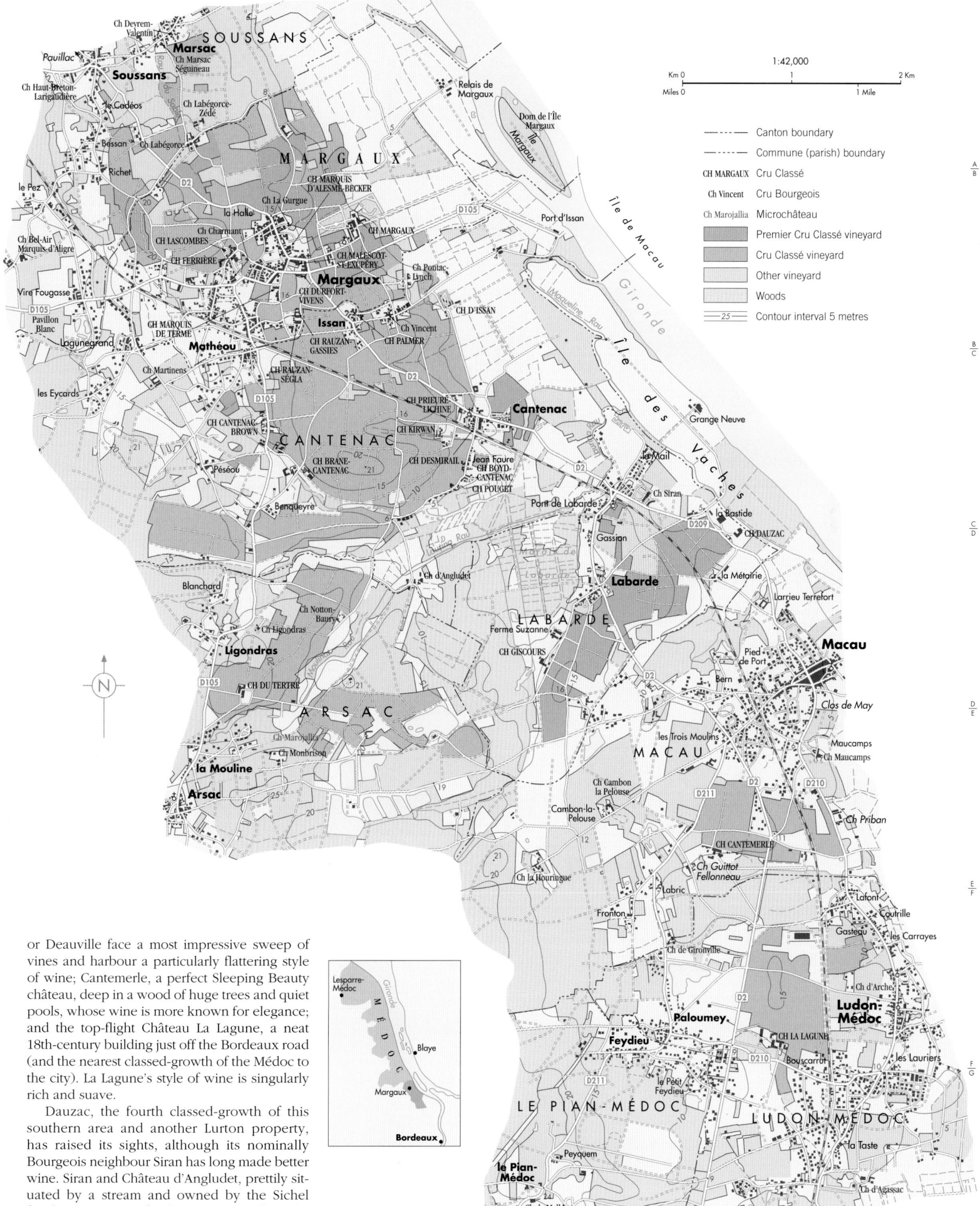

or Deauville face a most impressive sweep of vines and harbour a particularly flattering style of wine; Cantemerle, a perfect Sleeping Beauty château, deep in a wood of huge trees and quiet pools, whose wine is more known for elegance; and the top-flight Château La Lagune, a neat 18th-century building just off the Bordeaux road (and the nearest classed-growth of the Médoc to the city). La Lagune's style of wine is singularly rich and suave.

Dauzac, the fourth classed-growth of this southern area and another Lurton property, has raised its sights, although its nominally Bourgeois neighbour Siran has long made better wine. Siran and Château d'Angludet, prettily situated by a stream and owned by the Sichel family, co-owners of Palmer, consistently make wine of classed-growth quality.

Graves and Entre-Deux-Mers

This detailed map, new to this fifth edition, is testament to the efforts being made in some of Bordeaux's less glamorous wine areas. Most of the wine sold as lowly AC Bordeaux is made in the Entre-Deux-Mers, the lozenge of pretty farmland between the Garonne and Dordogne rivers, even if the name Entre-Deux-Mers itself is reserved on wine labels for the harmless dry white produced there, in much smaller quantity.

Much of this basic red is all too basic and not quite red enough. Indeed there have been discussions about the possibility of demoting the least impressive red Bordeaux from Appellation Contrôlée status to some local Vin de Pays – de la Gironde, perhaps (a glance at the map on page 151 shows the Bordeaux département as a curious exclusion zone from this useful device).

But there are some producers of red wines that qualify for no grander an appellation than Bordeaux or the slightly stronger Bordeaux Supérieur who are trying much harder than others. Many of them are marked on this map of the most interesting part of Entre-Deux-Mers.

A number of substantial châteaux, and the odd exceptional co-operative, have changed the aspect of the region, especially of the parishes in the north of this map towards the Dordogne and St-Emilion, from one of mixed farm and orchard to vinous monoculture. Some of the most successful are the Lurton family's excellent Château Bonnet south of Grézillac, Château Tour de Mirambeau south of Branne, Château Thieuley near Créon, and Château Toutigeac in the little-used sub-appellation Haut-Benauge. Many of these make even more successful dry whites (from Sémillon and Sauvignon grapes) than reds. Château de Sours of St-Quentin-de-Baron has even managed to sell its deep pink Bordeaux rosé *en primeur*.

Even more exciting are the Premières Côtes de Bordeaux, a 37-mile (60-km) strip stretching from north of the city of Bordeaux as far as the rarely-seen Bordeaux Ste-Macaire appellation. Rising up from a narrow alluvial right riverbank worthy only of the straight Bordeaux AC are south- and southwest-facing gravel and limestone hills leading to a plateau richer in clay, both of which can produce red wines of real concentration and personality. Some of the greater Bordeaux region's most ambitious newcomers have bought somewhere along this strip. The Danish owners of Château de Haux have made thoroughly convincing modern red and white wines, while at Château Carsin the perfectionist owners are Finns, the (female) winemaker an Australian.

Since the Premières Côtes encircle the sweet white appellations of Cadillac, Loupiac and Ste-Croix-du-Mont, it is hardly surprising that good sweet wines can also be produced here. Those made in the south of the zone are sold as Cadillac while the dry whites are sold as straightforward Bordeaux. Château Reynon at Béguey near Cadillac has succeeded with fresh Sauvignon white and a particularly fulsome red. Château Fayau at Cadillac is keeping up the local tradition of sweet, fruity white.

It is too much to claim that the liquorous Ste-Croix-du-Mont has become a moneymaking proposition, as it once was, but three châteaux, Loubens, du Mont, and La Rame, make great efforts, and in neighbouring Loupiac Châteaux Loupiac-Gaudiet and de Ricaud are ready to run the risks inherent in making truly sweet, rather than just semi-sweet, wine (see page 102).

Just across the River Garonne, to the north of Barsac in the Graves lies Cérons, a separate appellation long forgotten (it includes Illats and Podensac), which has found new prosperity (at Château d'Archambeau, for example) by making mainstream white and red under the Graves appellation, largely abandoning its tradition of a style midway between Graves Supérieures (the sweetish white of Graves) and Barsac: softly rather than stickily sweet.

There is much more to the Graves region than the most famous Pessac-Léognan sector of it (mapped separately overleaf). The southern end of the Graves has been coming to life.

Map Legend

■ VILLA BEL AIR Leading producer

- Barsac
- Cadillac and Premières Côtes de Bordeaux
- Cérons
- Côtes de Bordeaux-St-Macaire
- Entre-Deux-Mers
- Entre-Deux-Mers-Haut-Benauge
- Graves
- Loupiac
- Pessac-Léognan
- Premières Côtes de Bordeaux
- Ste-Croix-du-Mont
- Sauternes

101 Area mapped at larger scale on page shown

Paris
Bordeaux

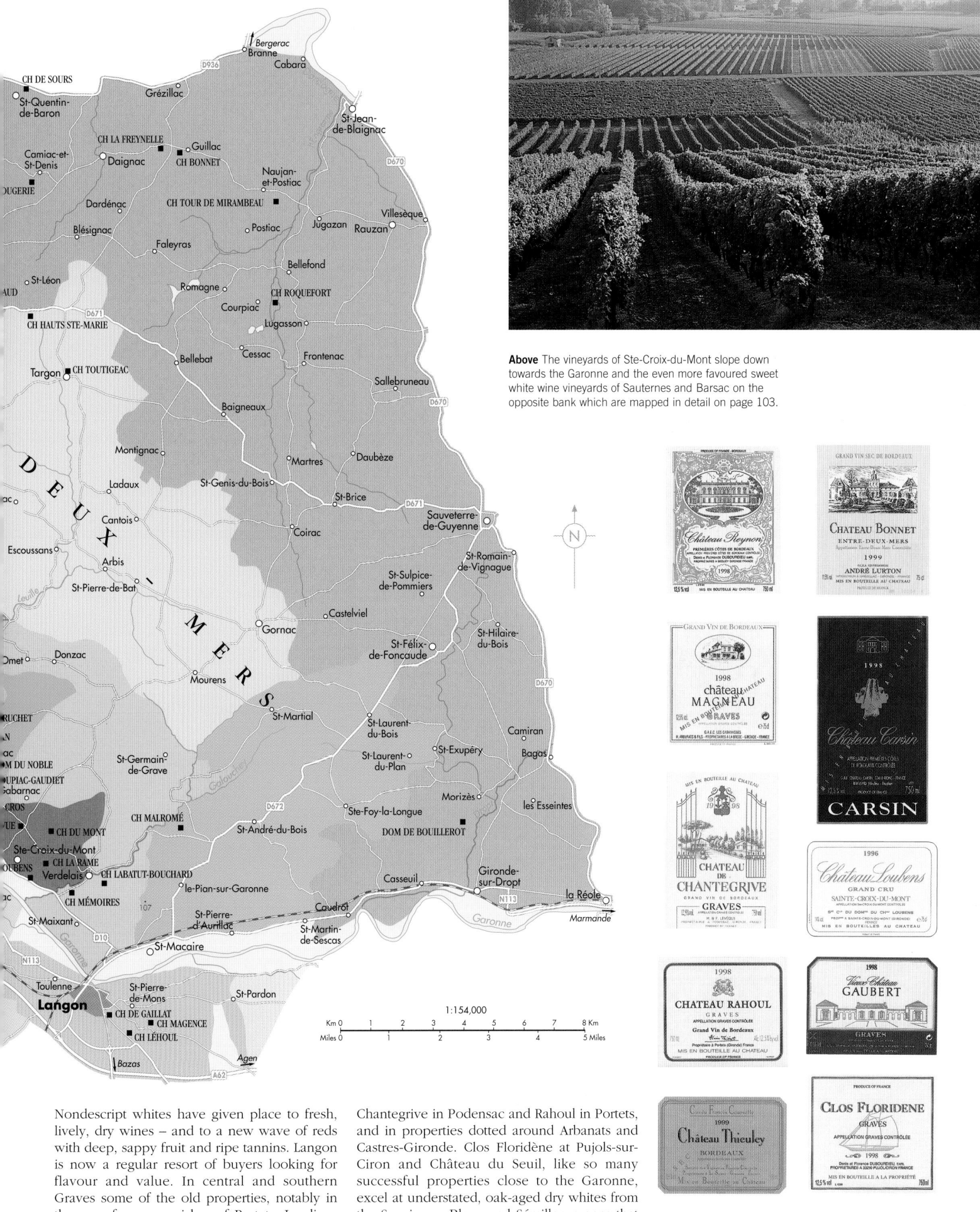

Above The vineyards of Ste-Croix-du-Mont slope down towards the Garonne and the even more favoured sweet white wine vineyards of Sauternes and Barsac on the opposite bank which are mapped in detail on page 103.

(opposite bank which are mapped in detail on page 103.)

1:154,000

Km 0   1   2   3   4   5   6   7   8 Km
Miles 0   1   2   3   4   5 Miles

Nondescript whites have given place to fresh, lively, dry wines – and to a new wave of reds with deep, sappy fruit and ripe tannins. Langon is now a regular resort of buyers looking for flavour and value. In central and southern Graves some of the old properties, notably in the once-famous parishes of Portets, Landiras, and St-Pierre-de-Mons, have new owners and new philosophies.

The ability of Graves soil to make red and white wine equally well is seen at Châteaux de Chantegrive in Podensac and Rahoul in Portets, and in properties dotted around Arbanats and Castres-Gironde. Clos Floridène at Pujols-sur-Ciron and Château du Seuil, like so many successful properties close to the Garonne, excel at understated, oak-aged dry whites from the Sauvignon Blanc and Sémillon grapes that seem so at home in this quiet southern corner of the Gironde, even if the proportion of white wine produced in the Graves appellation is hardly more than a quarter and continues to fall.

Producers in the area mapped above left tend to be either leaders or laggards. These leading labels represent a wide range of styles, from the deliciously straightforward dry white Château Bonnet to luscious Ste-Croix-du-Mont and a host of oaked dry whites and reds.

Pessac-Léognan

It was here, in the southern outskirts of the city of Bordeaux, that the whole concept of great red Bordeaux was launched, in the 1660s, by the owner of Château Haut-Brion. Its arid sand and gravel had already supplied the region and its export market with its best red wine since at least 1300, when the archbishop who became Pope Clement V (of Avignon) planted what is now Château Pape Clément.

Pine trees have always been the main crop of the Graves, as this and the woodlands that stretch south of it are still called collectively. The vineyards are clearings, often isolated from one another in heavily forested country crossed by shallow river valleys. The map opposite shows how the city and its oldest vineyards reach out into the forest, which continues (as the Landes) south and west from here to the Basque foothills of the Pyrenees.

Right The respectable but not classified Léognan Château de France showing with its intensely gravelly soil under autumn foliage just why the Graves was so named. Like most properties here it produces both white and red wines.

Now the city has swallowed all the vineyards in its path except the superlative group on the deep gravel soils of Pessac: Haut-Brion and its neighbour and old rival, La Mission Haut-Brion, the little Les Carmes Haut-Brion (north of Haut-Brion and off this map) and, further out of town, the archi-episcopal Pape Clément.

Châteaux Haut-Brion and La Mission are found with difficulty, deep in the suburbs, on opposite sides of the old Arcachon road which runs through Pessac. Haut-Brion is every inch a first-growth, a suave equilibrium of force and finesse with the singularity of great Graves: hints of earth and fern, tobacco and caramel; a flavour not so high-toned but frequently more intriguing than even a Lafite or a Margaux. La Mission tastes denser, riper, more savage – and often just as splendid. In 1983 the American owners of Haut-Brion bought its old rival, including Château La Tour Haut-Brion also made within the old La Mission estate – not to unite the vineyards but to continue the match. The game is played out each year, not just between the two famous reds, but between their incomparably rich white sisters too, Châteaux Haut-Brion Blanc and Laville Haut-Brion. There are few more vivid examples of what terroir, the uniqueness of each piece of ground, means on this Bordeaux soil.

The map shows what was once termed "Hautes Graves", but which in 1987 was given its own appellation: Pessac-Léognan. Most of the wine is red, with much the same grape recipe as in the Médoc. Pessac-Léognan differs in producing a little white of sometimes superlative quality within the same appellation, in most cases from châteaux also classified for their red wine. A very simple "yes or no" classification, last reviewed in 1959, includes 16 châteaux, six for both red and white and three for white wine only. A revision has been expected for many a year: it will certainly include châteaux beyond this map, in the wider Graves to the south which is busily upgrading and converting from the predominant white wine production of old times to a healthy mix, with red dominant (see pages 98 and 99).

The commune of Léognan, well into the forest, is the hub of this map. Domaine de Chevalier is its outstanding property, despite its modest appearance. The domaine has never had a château. Although its *chai* and *cuvier* have been impeccably rebuilt and its vineyard expanded recently, it retains the air of a farm in a clearing in the pines. There is something almost Californian about the winery with its two flavours... both of which can turn out to be brilliant. Only about 1,500 cases of a magnificently long-lived barrel-fermented Sauvignon/ Sémillon white are made each year.

Château Haut-Bailly is the other leading classed-growth of Léognan; unusual in these parts for making only red wine, but deeply and persuasively. Château de Fieuzal's red has provided a serious challenge since the 1980s, however – and its white is also very fine, if in decidedly limited quantities, as is the way with the top Graves properties. Malartic-Lagravière is similar, and has been thoroughly modernized by its new Belgian owner.

Château Carbonnieux is different. This old Benedictine establishment was for long much more famous for its fine, reliable white than for its light red, although the red has gained weight recently. Château Olivier, producing both colours, has also been taken in hand.

No-one has been more active in the Graves of late than André Lurton, president of the local growers' organization, owner of Châteaux La Louvière, de Rochemorin, de Cruzeau, and Couhins-Lurton, and driving force behind much of the recent renewal. (Château Bouscaut, classified, if by no means the best, is owned by his niece Sophie Lurton).

The commune of Martillac marks the southern limit of Pessac-Léognan. Its largest classed-growth Château Smith Haut Lafitte, has been lavishly transformed of late – both the wines, into a red and white of some class, and the property, into a wine- and grape-based hotel-cum-health hydro (although hydro would strike classicists as hardly the right word). Château Latour-Martillac can produce fine, ageworthy whites and its reds have been slowly improving – reflecting the prevailing tendency.

One wonders what the hosts of the Médoc's grandest salons would do without the dry whites of Pessac-Léognan to serve before their own reds. Acknowledge that other great wine region in eastern France, perhaps?

Some of the most *successful properties of Pessac-Léognan are represented below. All except La Louvière were included in the 1959 classification, La Mission Haut-Brion for white wine only and all the rest for red wine only, even though Smith Haut Lafitte, de Fieuzal, Pape Clément, and Haut-Brion also produce white wine.*

Legend:

- – – – Canton boundary
- – · – · Commune (parish) boundary
- CH HAUT-BRION — Cru Classé
- Ch Bardins — Unclassified château
- Premier Cru Classé vineyard
- Other vineyard
- Woods
- — 25 — Contour interval 5 metres

Map labels:

Verthamon, CH HAUT-BRION, CH LA MISSION HAUT-BRION, la Médoquine, Petit Bois, **Bordeaux**, les Echoppes, Bellegrave, CH LA TOUR HAUT-BRION, Suzon, Baraillot, le Poujau, CH LAVILLE HAUT-BRION, **TALENCE**, CH PAPE CLÉMENT, Arcachon, **Pessac**, le Breuil, **Talence**, le Béquet, Chiquet, **PESSAC**, N10, Dunoyer-Marly, **Plume la Poule**, Sardine, Pacaris, la Paillère, Maucamp, Cité Ladonne, Providence, D651, St-Bris, Aéroport, St Agron, A63, Cestas, le Pont de la Maye, Brannes, Cité Prairie, le Pailley, Bénédigues, Bourdillat, Madère, Bordeaux centre, Beaudon, Cité Jardin, Gazaillan, Chouiney, la Mignonne, Sarcignan, Martinon, Monjoux, **Gradignan**, Ch Baret, Pontac, le Brucat, Rosiers, Bellevue, **GRADIGNAN**, Plumat, Villenave-d'Ornon, Ch Pontac-Monplaisir, Ch Poumey, **Chambéry**, la Taille, la Générale, la Honfan, les Sables, Branlac, Peycamin, Ch Brown, **VILLENAVE**, Couhins, **Canteloup**, Belin-Béliet, Caloy, le Barbut, les Graves, CH COUHINS-LURTON, CH COUHINS, Gr Bardins, Chaut, les Platanes, le Bicon, Veyres, **le Bouscaut**, les Brousteys, les Palomières, CH OLIVIER, Ch la Tour Léognan, Ch le Hannetot, CH BOUSCAUT, **CADAUJAC**, Dussole, le Gascon, la Rivière, Dom de Grandmaison, CH CARBONNIEUX, Broustey Conilh, Pireques, la Bouhume, Ch Concheroy, l'Oustalade, Tibouet, Ch La Louvière, Ch le Thil Comte Clary, **LÉOGNAN**, Lapeyre, Clairbois, les Sables, CH HAUT BAILLY, Ch le Pape, CH SMITH HAUT-LAFITTE, Frigères, Rataboul, Ch Larrivet Haut-Brion, D111, Luxeau, l'Hermiton, les Pédocs, la Morelle, Ch Gazin Rocquencourt, Rambaud, les Peyreyres, la Salle, Lignac, **Léognan**, le Livran, Paté, Ch Haut-Bergey, le Brulat, Ch Haut-Lagrange, Ch Malleprat, CH MALARTIC-LAGRAVIÈRE, Marquet, Ch de Rochemorin, Toulouse, DOM DE CHEVALIER, **MARTILLAC**, Bois de Bernin, Mignoy, Ch de France, le Breyra, Mondet, **Martillac**, Langon, les Bouges, CH DE FIEUZAL, Ch Haut-Gardère, Tartavisat, Ch Ferran, Bongis, Saucats, CH LATOUR-MARTILLAC, Ch la Garde, Saucats, Dom de la Solitude, la Brède, Ch Haut-Nouchet

1:47,500

Km 0 — 1 — 2 Km
Miles 0 — 1 Mile

Inset map: Dordogne, Libourne, **Bordeaux**, Garonne, GRAVES, Sauternes

Sauternes and Barsac

All the other districts of Bordeaux mapped in this Atlas make wines that can be compared with, and preferred to, one another (and are frequently compared with similarly styled wines made all over the globe). Sauternes is different: under-appreciated but incomparable, it is a speciality which finds few real rivals. Potentially one of the world's longest-living wines, it depends on local conditions and on a very unusual fungus and winemaking technique. In great vintages the results can be sublime: a very sweet, rich-textured, flower-scented, glittering golden liquid. In other years it can frankly fail to be Sauternes (properly so-called) at all.

Above all it is only the best-situated and best-run châteaux of Sauternes – and in this we include Barsac – that make such nectar. Ordinary Sauternes is just sweet white wine.

The local conditions in this warm and fertile corner of Aquitaine include the mists which form along the little River Ciron on autumn evenings, lasting till after dawn. The special technique which only the considerable châteaux can afford to employ is to pick over the vineyard as many as eight or nine times, usually beginning in September and sometimes going on until November. This is to take full advantage of the peculiar form of mould (known as *Botrytis cinerea* to the scientist, or *pourriture noble* – "noble rot" – to the poet) which forms on the Sémillon, Sauvignon Blanc, and Muscadelle grapes during the mild, misty nights, then multiplies in the heat of the day to reduce the grape skins to brown pulp. Instead of affecting the blighted grapes with a flavour of rot, this botrytis engineers the escape of a proportion of the water in them, leaving the sugar, acids, and the flavouring elements in the juice

more concentrated than ever. The result of painstaking fermentation and ageing in small barrels is wine with an intensity of taste and scent and a smooth, unctuous texture which can be made no other way.

But it does mean picking the grapes as they shrivel, sometimes berry by berry – and the proprietors of little-known châteaux can afford only to pick the entire crop at once, and hope for as much botrytis as possible.

Production is absurdly low, since evaporation is actually encouraged. From each one of its 250-odd acres (roughly 100ha) Château d'Yquem, the most famous of the Sauternes producers, makes only about 7hl (933 bottles) of wine. A first-class Médoc vineyard would make five or six times as much.

The risk element is appalling, since humid weather in October can turn the mould into the noxious fungus known as grey rot and rob the grower of all chance of making sweet wine, and sometimes of any wine at all. Costs are correspondingly high, and the price of even the finest Sauternes (with the exception of Yquem), makes it one of the least profitable wines to the grower. Prices have been rising gradually but few wine drinkers realize just how underpriced great sweet white Bordeaux is compared with its red counterpart.

Sauternes was the only area outside the Médoc to be classed in 1855. Château d'Yquem was made a First Great Growth – a rank created for it alone in all Bordeaux. Strangely, for its dominant hilltop position, it has a "perched", therefore unusually high, water-table that keeps its vines growing well even in drought. Eleven other châteaux were made first-growths and 12 more were classed seconds.

Five communes, including Sauternes itself, are entitled to use the name. Barsac, the biggest of them, has the alternative of calling its wine either Sauternes or Barsac, although its wine tends less to lusciousness, more to clean sweetness and finesse. Styles of Sauternes vary almost as much as standards, even if most of the finest properties cluster around Yquem. Château Lafaurie-Peyraguey can taste as floral as it sounds; Château Suduiraut in Preignac (when on form) is lush and sumptuous; Château Rieussec (bought by the Rothschilds of Lafite in 1985) is often deep-coloured and rich. Other current top performers include Clos Haut Peyraguey and Châteaux Sigalas-Rabaud, Guiraud, de Fargues (under the same management as Yquem), and, since its recent upgrade, La Tour Blanche which doubles as a winemaking school. A quite different, but long-living style of unoaked wine is made at Château Gilette. In Barsac Châteaux Climens, Coutet, and Doisy-Daëne currently lead the field.

The economics of Sauternes have always been knife-edge. For decades it could not be produced profitably at all: poor vintages persisted; demand dwindled. Vineyards were pulled up, or planted instead with red grapes, or used to make dry white wine – which cannot even be sold as Graves; its appellation is bare Bordeaux. Happily the last two decades have seen a revival. The 1980s and 1990s saw a run of good vintages, idealistic new owners have appeared, and Sauternes is back in fashion – in certain quarters. In France it is highly appreciated as a partner for *foie gras*. The Anglo-Saxon world drinks it as the richest of endings to a rich meal (although it can easily be swamped by too sweet a dessert). It deserves a far more appreciative following.

At Château d'Yquem, where production costs are higher than at any other property in the world (and many times higher than any red wine château), pickers have to bend almost double (left) to pick only those grapes most affected by the curious botrytis fungus, or noble rot, that first dessicates the grapes (above) and then covers them in what looks like ash, concentrating sugars and acids, and in the best vintages endows the wines with near immortality. The grapes look so disgusting when picked it is hard to imagine what delicious nectars they will yield.

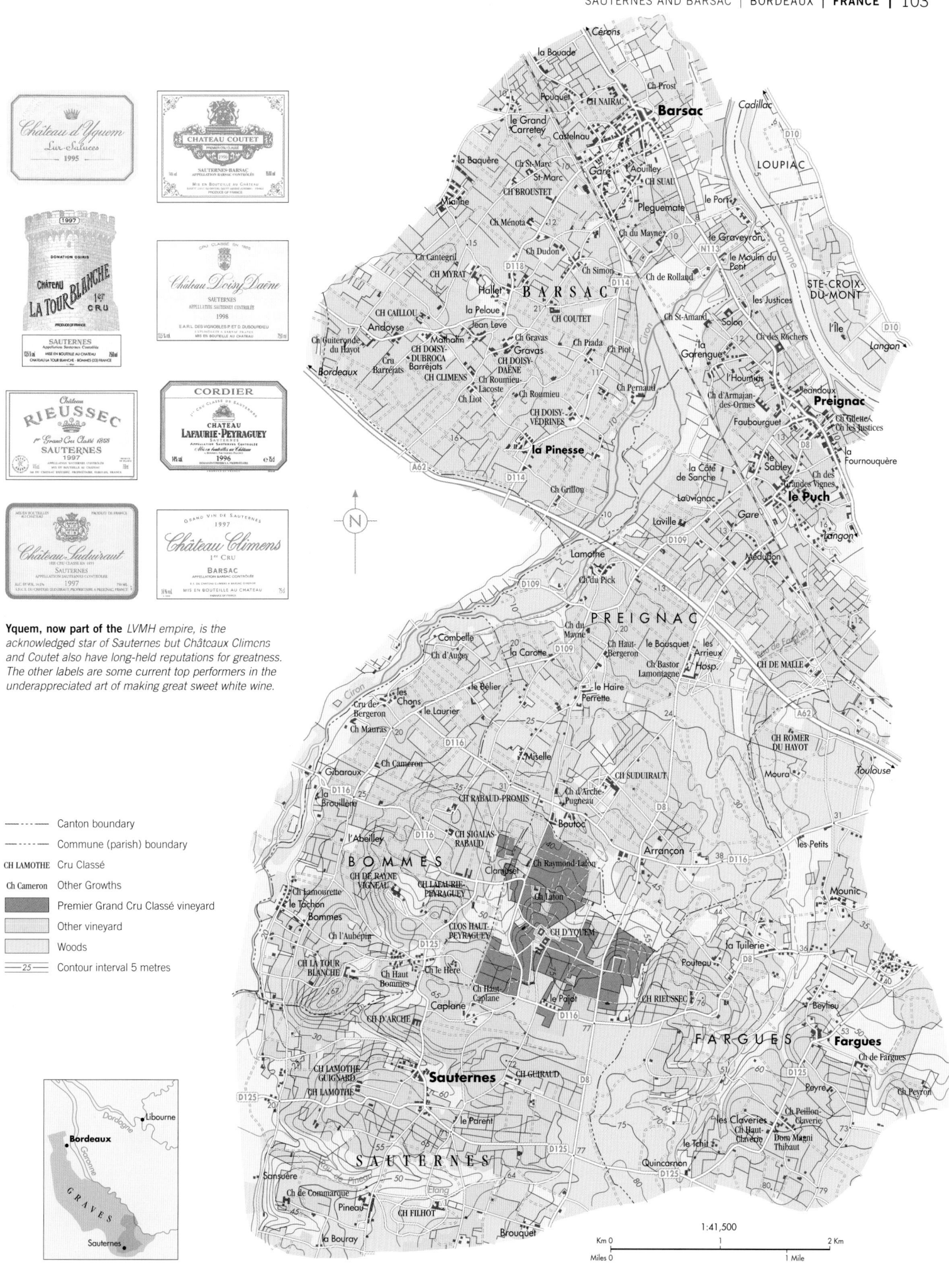

Yquem, now part of the *LVMH empire, is the
acknowledged star of Sauternes but Châteaux Climens
and Coutet also have long-held reputations for greatness.
The other labels are some current top performers in the
underappreciated art of making great sweet white wine.*

Canton boundary

Commune (parish) boundary

CH LAMOTHE Cru Classé

Ch Cameron Other Growths

Premier Grand Cru Classé vineyard

Other vineyard

Woods

25 Contour interval 5 metres

1:41,500

Km 0   1   2 Km

Miles 0   1 Mile

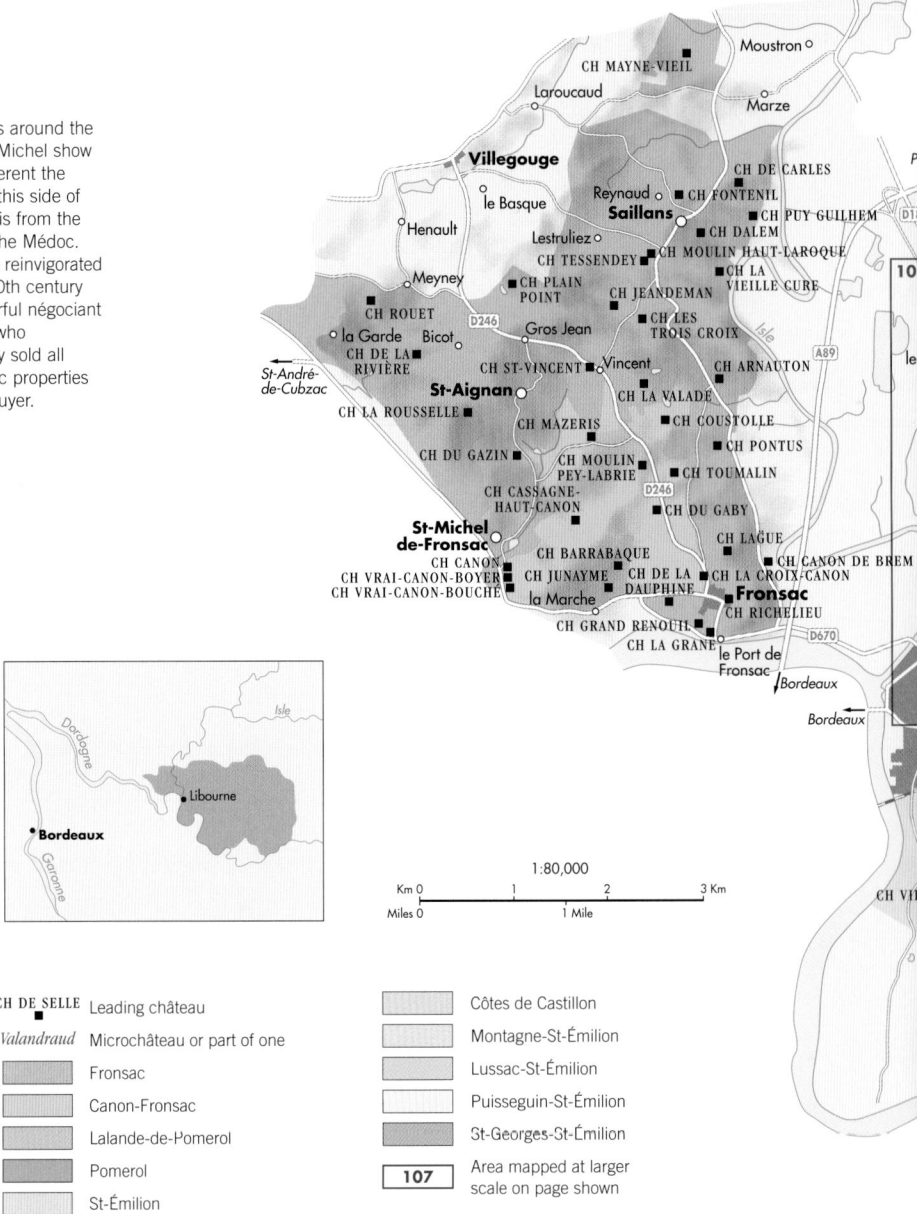

CH DE SELLE ■ Leading château

Valandraud Microchâteau or part of one

Fronsac

Canon-Fronsac

Lalande-de-Pomerol

Pomerol

St-Émilion

Côtes de Castillon

Montagne-St-Émilion

Lussac-St-Émilion

Puisseguin-St-Émilion

St-Georges-St-Émilion

107 Area mapped at larger scale on page shown

1:80,000

Libournais

The French name for this, Bordeaux's most dynamic region derives from its ancient capital, Libourne. Anglo-Saxons with Bordeaux in their blood call it "the right bank" – of the river-system of the Garonne and the Dordogne, that is (just as the Médoc is, less frequently, known as the left bank).

The region's most illustrious parishes are fashionable St-Emilion and Pomerol. But they are the heart of a much larger and more diffuse wine district. To the south and east seven small villages share the name of St-Emilion, and a further four to the northeast can add the name to their own. Pomerol adjoins the communes Néac and Lalande with Fronsac to the west.

With their mixture of vines, woods, and pastures and their little hills and valleys, the villages to the east, north, and west are more attractive than the celebrated but somewhat monotonous Pomerol and St-Emilion vineyards of the plateau in the centre (mapped in detail on pages 107 and 109 respectively).

Even today, despite the glamour that attaches to many Pomerol and St-Emilion properties, these outlying areas can still seem remote and little-visited. It is hard even to identify the modest châteaux. Formerly, a network of private contacts all over France, Belgium, and the

Low Countries was the principal market for their sound and solid red wine. Recently, though, they have considerably raised their profile (and their standards).

The châteaux shown on this map include most of the best- and better-known of the hinterland and of Fronsac, which holds a special position as a historic region in its own right. Fronsac wines are splendidly fruity and full of character, tannic when young, a touch rustic in style compared with the high gloss of, say, Pomerol, but improving year by year with investment in modernization. The limestone slopes along the river are known as Canon-Fronsac, although even locals can be at a loss to describe what differentiates the two appellations.

North of Pomerol, Néac shares the appellation of Lalande-de-Pomerol: both are like unpolished Pomerol. Châteaux de Chambrun, La Croix St-André, and Bertineau St-Vincent can provide polish, however.

The equivalent back-country châteaux to the north of St-Emilion are led in reputation by the splendid Château St-Georges, which overlooks the whole district from its hill. But many make excellent wine.

The vine is still dominant in this pretty, hilly landscape, even if there are no names to conjure

with. Montagne makes excellent "satellite" St-Emilion. So do Lussac and Puisseguin, often making up in satisfying solidity what they lack in finesse. Still further east, the Côtes de Castillon and Côtes de Francs (the latter is not shown), on the boundary with Bergerac and Montravel, keep up the family resemblance. Château Puygueraud is the outstanding property of the Côte de Francs, but the whole district is in benevolent turmoil, often thanks to the investment of money earned from grander properties in St-Emilion.

The cluster of villages south and east of St-Emilion qualify for the appellation of St-Emilion itself, a few of them producing some of the right bank's more sought-after wines. The map shows the location of two of four plots which make up the heavily hyped Château de Valandraud (the other two are to be found on the more detailed map of St-Emilion on page 109). The new owner of Château Monbousquet has also proved that these sandier flatlands can make head-turning wines, while those of Châteaux Teyssier and Faugères are in hot pursuit. Château Bellefont-Belcier (see map, page 109) now enjoys a high reputation. To the north in St-Christophe, Château Haut-Sarpe is a Grand Cru Classé, and nearby Château Fombrauge is also of note.

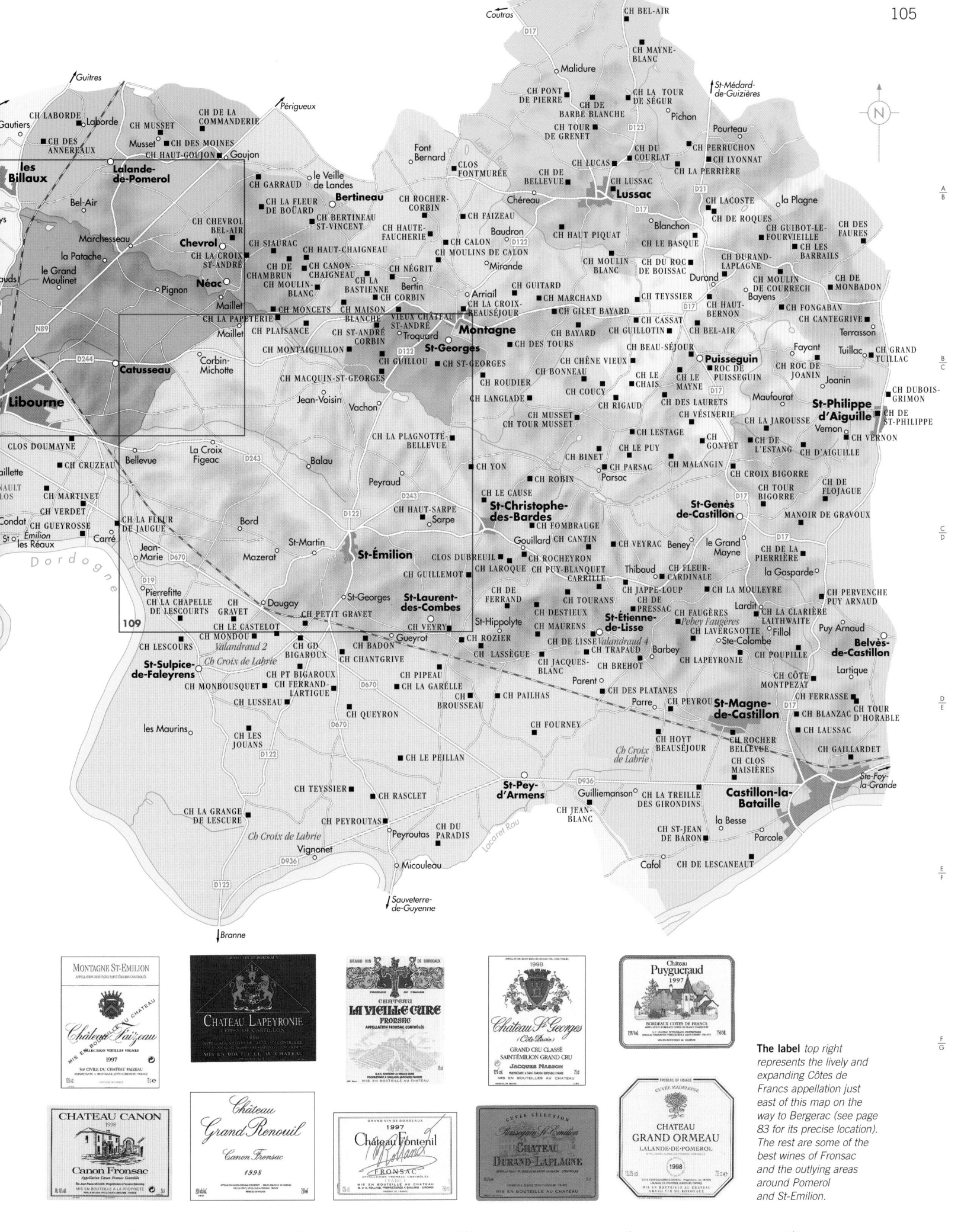

The label *top right represents the lively and expanding Côtes de Francs appellation just east of this map on the way to Bergerac (see page 83 for its precise location). The rest are some of the best wines of Fronsac and the outlying areas around Pomerol and St-Emilion.*

Pomerol

Pomerol is, relatively speaking, the new star in the firmament of Bordeaux. You would think it had all been known for centuries. Yet although the Romans had vineyards in Pomerol, 100 years ago the region was known only for "good common wine" – much of it, surprisingly, white. Even 50 years ago it was not considered in the top flight. But today Pomerol's most sought-after châteaux fetch a higher price than the much larger first-growths of the Médoc, and an astonishing number of small properties, for an area no bigger than St-Julien, are generally agreed to be among the best in the whole of Bordeaux.

Pomerol is such a curious corner of the world that it is hard to get your bearings. There is no real village centre. Almost identical small roads criss-cross the plateau apparently at random. Every family makes wine, and every house stands apart among its vines. The landscape is evenly dotted with modest houses – each rejoicing in the name of château. The church stands oddly isolated too, like yet another little wine estate. And that is Pomerol; there is nothing more to see.

Pomerol is another big gravel bank, slightly rising and falling but remarkably flat overall. In the western and southern parts the soil tends to be sandy; to the east and north, where it meets St-Emilion, it is usually enriched with clay. Pomerol is entirely planted with vines, to the exclusion of all lesser plants. In the eastern part

are the best growths, lying so cheek by jowl with St-Emilion that it is surprising to find that they really do seem to be reliably different.

Nonetheless the consensus is that Pomerols are the gentlest, richest, and the more instantly appealing clarets. They have deep colour without the acidity and tannin that often go with it, a ripe-plummy, even creamy smell, and sometimes great concentration of all their qualities: the striking essence of a great wine.

Pomerol is a democracy. It has no classification, and indeed it would be very hard to devise one. There is no long tradition of steady selling to build on. Châteaux are small family affairs and subject to change as individuals come and go. Nor is the complexity of the soil, as it switches from gravel to gravelly clay to clay with gravel, or from sandy gravel to gravelly sand, exactly reflected in vineyard boundaries.

There is a good deal of agreement, however, about which are the outstanding vineyards of Pomerol. Château Pétrus was for years allowed by all to come first, with perhaps Trotanoy as runner-up – though Vieux Château Certan would contest this. Then along came Le Pin, microscopic even by Pomerol standards (hardly five acres, or 3ha), the creation of Jacques Thienpont, a member of the Belgian family which also owns "VCC". Wine made in such tiny quantity can be hand-reared with, exceptionally, the softening malolactic fermentation taking place in the remarkably few new oak

casks used every year. The result is an ultra-wine, with an excess of everything, including charm. This has been reflected in quite extraordinary demand, and prices even higher than those of Pétrus – and could be said to have inspired the rash of "microchâteaux" in St-Emilion eastwards along the plateau. (See the heart of St-Emilion map on page 109 for their location, and page 110 for a more detailed explanation.)

The map opposite distinguishes in larger type the growths whose wines currently fetch the highest prices. Clos l'Eglise and Châteaux Clinet, L'Eglise-Clinet (how confusing these names are), and La Fleur de Gay are relatively recent jewels in the Pomerol crown. Châteaux La Fleur-Pétrus, La Conseillante, Lafleur, L'Evangile, Latour à Pomerol, Petit Village, and Certan de May all have long track records of excellence.

The tight grouping of these châteaux on the clay soil is an indication of their character as well as quality. These properties generally make the densest, fleshiest, and most opulent wines. Before being overwhelmed by the complications of Pomerol it is worth knowing that the average standard here is very high. The village has a name for reliability. Bargains, on the other hand, are not often found.

The most potent influence in the district is the *négoce*, the merchant-houses, of Libourne, led with authority and style by the family firm of Jean-Pierre Moueix. They either own or manage a high proportion of the finest properties.

One advantage that has certainly helped the popularity of this little region is the fact that its wines are ready remarkably soon for Bordeaux. The chief grape here is not the tough-skinned Cabernet Sauvignon, whose wine has to live through a tannic youth; in Pomerol it is Merlot, secondary in the Médoc, that is the leading vine. Great growths have about 70-80% Merlot, with perhaps 20% Cabernet Franc, known here as Bouchet. The greatest Pomerol, Pétrus, is almost pure Merlot, growing in almost pure clay – with astonishing results.

Even the best Pomerol has produced all its perfume and achieved its dazzling finesse within a dozen years or so, and most are already attractive at five years old.

Left The many wine tourists attracted to Pomerol can find driving around this small plain criss-crossed with narrow lanes a frustrating experience. The tiny "châteaux" can look confusingly similar and the church spire provides a rare navigation aid.

Some of Bordeaux's most voluptuous *and most expensive wines are represented here, the peaks reached by the long-established Château Pétrus and the relative newcomer Le Pin.*

Legend:
- Canton boundary
- Commune (parish) boundary
- CH PÉTRUS — Leading château
- Ch Bel-Air — Other good château
- La Fleur-de-Gay — Microchâteau or part of one
- First-growth vineyard
- Other vineyard
- Woods
- 50 — Contour interval 5 metres

1:25,000
Km 0 _____ 1 Km
Miles 0 _____ 1/2 Mile

St-Emilion

The ancient and beautiful town of St-Emilion, epicentre of what is currently Bordeaux's most seismic wine region, is propped in the corner of an escarpment above the Dordogne. Behind it on the gravelly plateau vines flow steadily on into Pomerol. Beside it along the ridge they swoop down steep limestone slopes (the Côtes) into the plain. It is the little but much-visited rural gem of the Bordeaux region – inland and upland in spirit, Roman in origin, hollow with cellars and heady with wine. Even the church at St-Emilion is a cellar: cut, like them all, out of solid rock. The hotel restaurant in the town square is actually on the church roof, and you sit beside the belfry to eat your lampreys stewed in red wine *à la bordelaise*.

St-Emilion makes rich red wine. Before many people can really come to terms with the dryness and slight asperity of Médoc wines, they love the solid tastiness of St-Emilion. The best made in ripe and sunny seasons grow almost sweet as they mature.

The grapes of St-Emilion are the plump Merlot and the Cabernet Franc. Cabernet Sauvignon, which ripens later, has problems ripening in this climate, slightly less tempered by the ocean, and in its damper, cooler soils. On the whole the wines here take less time to reach perfection than Médoc wines, if a little longer than Pomerols: say four years for the wine of a poor vintage; eight and upwards for a good one. Yet the best can live as long.

The classification of St-Emilion is more rigorously topical than that of the Médoc. It regularly divides its châteaux (most recently in 1996) into Premiers Grands Crus Classés and Grands Crus Classés. Other St-Emilions may be described as Grand Cru, and apply for classification, by passing two tasting panels (careful label inspection

is needed). There are currently 13 of the first, headed by Cheval Blanc and Ausone in a separate, super-category of two, and 55 of the second. The plain Grands Crus run into hundreds. The most recent promotion to Premier Grand Cru Classé was Angélus, and even quite famous properties may be demoted.

But there is an increasing number of wines, some of them highly sought-after, which operate outside the classification system. In the early

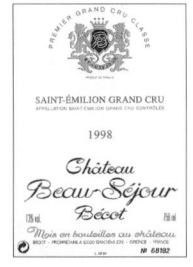

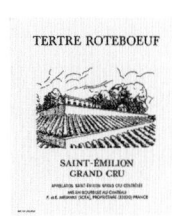

Reputations have *been won and lost at amazing speed in St-Emilion. Cheval Blanc and Figeac have been two of the steadiest properties in the last half-century, whereas the Beauséjours have found and lost favour in both official and unofficial classifications.*

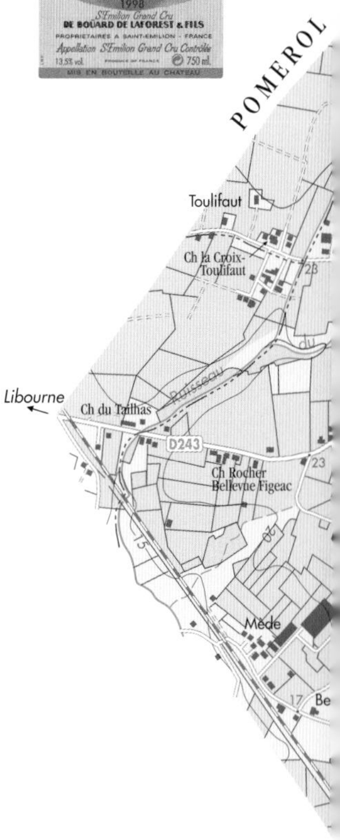

POMEROL

Toulifaut
Libourne
Ch la Croix-Toulifaut
Ch du Tailhas
Ch Rocher Bellevue Figeac
D243
Méde
Be

Left Wine is the life-blood of St-Emilion, its pretty, narrow streets housing far more wine shops and tourist restaurants than butchers or bakers. The vineyards of the Côtes can be seen in the distance, as well as the 13th-century tower pictured in more detail overleaf.

Canton boundary
Commune (parish) boundary
CH AUSONE   Premier Grand Cru Classé (1996)
Ch Laroze   Grand Cru Classé
Ch Gracia   Other

Ch de Valandraud   Microchâteau or part of one
Premier Grand Cru Classé vineyard
Other vineyard
Woods
Contour interval 5 metres

1:26,400
Km 0 — 1 Km
Miles 0 — 1/2 Mile

1980s Château Le Tertre Roteboeuf was one of the first properties to be taken under new, fanatical management and pushed to the limits of quality and desirability without seeking official rank. Since then, dozens if not hundreds of the 830 châteaux to be found within this appellation have been modernized, and their wines made generally smoother and more concentrated.

Another new, arguably less benevolent, wave began in the early 1990s with the emergence of Château de Valandraud, a fiercely unfiltered, concentrated wine conjured up by a local négociant from a few tiny parcels of vines (two of which are marked on the map on the previous page, two on the Libournais map on page 105). This, the first of the so-called "microchâteaux" of St-Emilion, has been followed by an army of them, appearing as if from nowhere. Those which had emerged by 2001 are marked in magenta on the map but more are expected, so great are the financial rewards of producing extremely obvious wines in quantities minute enough (generally less than 1,000 cases) to create demand.

There are two distinct districts of St-Emilion, not counting the lesser vineyards of the river plain and the parishes to the east and northeast which are allowed to use the name (described and mapped on pages 104-105).

One group of the finest châteaux lies on the border of Pomerol, on the sandy and gravelly plateau. The most famous of this group, and the whole of St-Emilion, is Cheval Blanc, a trim,

cream-painted house in a grove of trees which is far from suggesting the splendid red wine, some of the world's most beautifully balanced, which its predominantly Cabernet Franc vines produce. Of Cheval Blanc's neighbours, it is the big Château Figeac which comes nearest to its level, but in lighter, very fragrant style, from even more gravelly soil and with a proportion of Cabernet Sauvignon.

The other, larger, group, the Côtes St-Emilion, occupies the escarpment around the town. The plateau ends so abruptly that it is easy to see just how thin a layer of soil covers the soft but solid limestone in which the cellars are cut. At the recently revitalized Château Ausone, the jewel of the Côtes, in one of the finest situations in all Bordeaux overlooking the Dordogne Valley, you can walk into a cellar with vines, as it were, on the ground floor above you.

The Côtes wines may not be quite so fruity as the "Graves" wines from the plateau (the name Graves is confusingly applied to them because of their gravel soil), but at their best they are some of the most perfumed and "generous" wines of Bordeaux. They usually have 1% more alcohol than wine from the Médoc. The Côtes provide shelter from the north and west, an incline towards the sun, and relative immunity to frost. On the plateau around Château Cheval Blanc a slight dip in the ground acts as a sump in which freezing air can collect on cloudless winter nights.

In a remarkably short time St-Emilion has been transformed from a sleepy backwater into a hotbed of ambition and hotly contested allocations, but the comfort of St-Emilion to the ordinary wine-lover is the number of other châteaux of moderate fame and consistently high standards which can provide utterly enjoyable and relatively affordable wine.

Bourg and Blaye

Other fine labels come from Châteaux Bel-Air La Royère, Haut-Bertinerie (off the map), Les Jonqueyres, and Tayac. Falfas is one of Bordeaux's most successful organic wine producers.

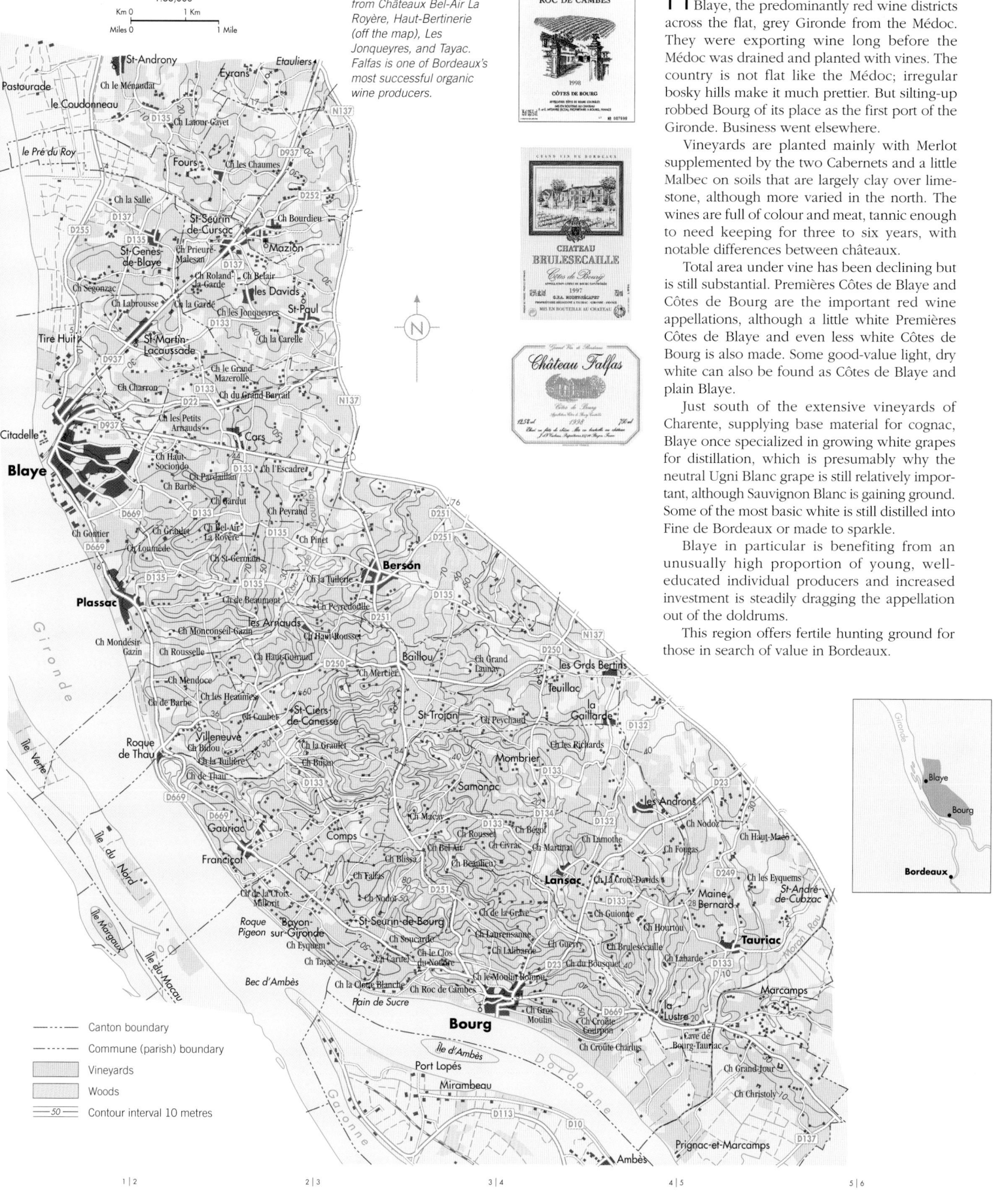

History has not been kind to Bourg and Blaye, the predominantly red wine districts across the flat, grey Gironde from the Médoc. They were exporting wine long before the Médoc was drained and planted with vines. The country is not flat like the Médoc; irregular bosky hills make it much prettier. But silting-up robbed Bourg of its place as the first port of the Gironde. Business went elsewhere.

Vineyards are planted mainly with Merlot supplemented by the two Cabernets and a little Malbec on soils that are largely clay over limestone, although more varied in the north. The wines are full of colour and meat, tannic enough to need keeping for three to six years, with notable differences between châteaux.

Total area under vine has been declining but is still substantial. Premières Côtes de Blaye and Côtes de Bourg are the important red wine appellations, although a little white Premières Côtes de Blaye and even less white Côtes de Bourg is also made. Some good-value light, dry white can also be found as Côtes de Blaye and plain Blaye.

Just south of the extensive vineyards of Charente, supplying base material for cognac, Blaye once specialized in growing white grapes for distillation, which is presumably why the neutral Ugni Blanc grape is still relatively important, although Sauvignon Blanc is gaining ground. Some of the most basic white is still distilled into Fine de Bordeaux or made to sparkle.

Blaye in particular is benefiting from an unusually high proportion of young, well-educated individual producers and increased investment is steadily dragging the appellation out of the doldrums.

This region offers fertile hunting ground for those in search of value in Bordeaux.

Wines of the Southwest

South of the great vineyard of Bordeaux, west of the Midi, and sheltered from the Atlantic by the forests of the Landes, the vine flourishes in scattered areas which still have strong local gastronomic traditions, each by a river – the vine's old link to distant markets. This was the "High Country" that the jealous merchants of Bordeaux excluded from the port until their own wine (sometimes, to compound the injury, beefed up with sturdier stuff made upstream) was sold. The Bordeaux grape varieties may dominate the areas on the fringes of the Gironde département where Bordeaux wine is made (including Bergerac discussed overleaf), but elsewhere in this southwestern corner is France's most varied collection of indigenous wine grapes, many peculiar to their own small appellation.

Cahors, famous for the depth and body of its wines since the Middle Ages, is typical. Although it is usually softened by some Merlot, it eschews both Cabernet Sauvignon and Cabernet Franc and depends for its soul and flavour on a grape known elsewhere in France as Côt, in Argentina and Bordeaux as Malbec, and here as Auxerrois. Thanks to this grape, and to summers that are generally warmer than Bordeaux's, Cahors tends to be fuller and more vigorous, if a little more rustic, than typical red Bordeaux. But phylloxera literally decimated the region's vineyards, railways from the Languedoc severely reduced demand for their produce and the fierce winter of 1956 ravaged such vineyards as remained.

Nowadays the busy town of Cahors finds itself upstream of most vineyards, which no longer dominate the sandy gravels down by the River Lot (see picture overleaf). Today maize and sunflowers are more common crops on these alluvial flatlands than vines and many of the

Below The vines of Irouléguy, such as these near St-Etienne-de-Baïgorry, lie in the dramatic landscapes of the western Pyrenees and grow a rich mix of fiercely local grape varieties. All three colours of wine are made, sharing a lively bite and proudly individual flavours.

newer vineyards, reminiscent of English gardens with their neat grass and vine hedges, have been planted up on the rocky *causses*. At these cooler elevations grapes take longer to ripen and the resulting wines are firmer than the precocious riverside Cahors. Some of the best producers believe a blend of both styles is best. Few would demand that their wines were kept for longer than four or five years. Fancy winemaking techniques and new oak barrels are still a relative rarity in Cahors, although this has been changing rapidly as the region has attracted more than what seems its fair share of inward investment from well-heeled outsiders, whether from Paris or New York. The style of Cahors is expected to continue to evolve, although is unlikely to resemble the "black wine" of legend (and fact: several generations ago its colour and tannin content well-earned the epithet).

As far again upstream from Cahors as Cahors is from the Gironde département boundary (and therefore marked on the map of France on page 53 rather than here) are the vineyards of the Aveyron département. Up in wild country are the last vestiges of the Massif Central's once-flourishing vignoble. Marcillac is the most important wine, a peppery red made from Fer Servadou. Its multi-hued VDQS neighbours, Vins d'Entraygues et du Fel and Vins d'Estaing, are rare and becoming rarer, in contrast to the Côtes de Millau to the south whose mountain reds, made from a thorough southwestern cocktail of grapes, were recognized as a VDQS as recently as 1994.

The hill country around the River Tarn west of Albi, and downstream of the magnificent gorge cut by the river into the Cévennes, seems tame by comparison. Its rolling green pastureland is gentle in both aspect and climate, studded with beautiful towns and villages of which 73 are contained within the appellation Gaillac. Wine was probably made here long before vines were cultivated downstream in Bordeaux but, as in Cahors, the phylloxera louse crippled the wine trade which has been revived with real enthusiasm only in the last decade or so. Much of this is because of increased sophistication in matching the varied terroirs of Gaillac to its extremely various vine varieties. The most characteristic red wine ingredients are the peppery local Braucol (Fer Servadou) and much lighter Duras. Syrah is a welcome intruder, Gamay less so but useful for early drinking Gaillac Primeur, and Bordeaux red grapes are tolerated. Darker-skinned grapes now predominate and work best on the gravelly clay soils south of the Tarn and around Cunac (off the map to the east of Albi). The southeast-facing Premières Côtes that rise on the river's right bank are particularly well-suited to the sweet and sweetish wines for which Gaillac with its long, dry autumns was once famous. They are made from such local specialities as Mauzac (whose apple peel flavours are also common in Limoux), Len de l'El and the relatively rare Ondenc supplemented by the three Sauternes grapes (see page 102). Modern white wines are typically off-dry and made with

varying degrees of sparkle including the gently fizzing Perlé, and are a speciality of the limestone vineyards to the north, notably around the hill town of Cordes. Outsiders can find this proliferation of grapes and wine styles confusing but for innovators such as Robert Plageoles – whose standard range of still reds, pinks, and whites is supplemented not only by a sweet, cloudy, low-alcohol fizz made by the traditional *méthode gaillacoise* but also by a Gaillac variant on a dry sherry – it serves only as inspiration.

Immediately to the west between the Tarn and Garonne, Côtes du Frontonnais is the local red and rosé wine of Toulouse. Nowadays Château Bellevue La Forêt is by no means the only producer to make of the native Négrette grapes, mixed with sundry others of the southwest (and sometimes Syrah or Gamay) a notable red: limpid and fruity. Fronton and Villaudric

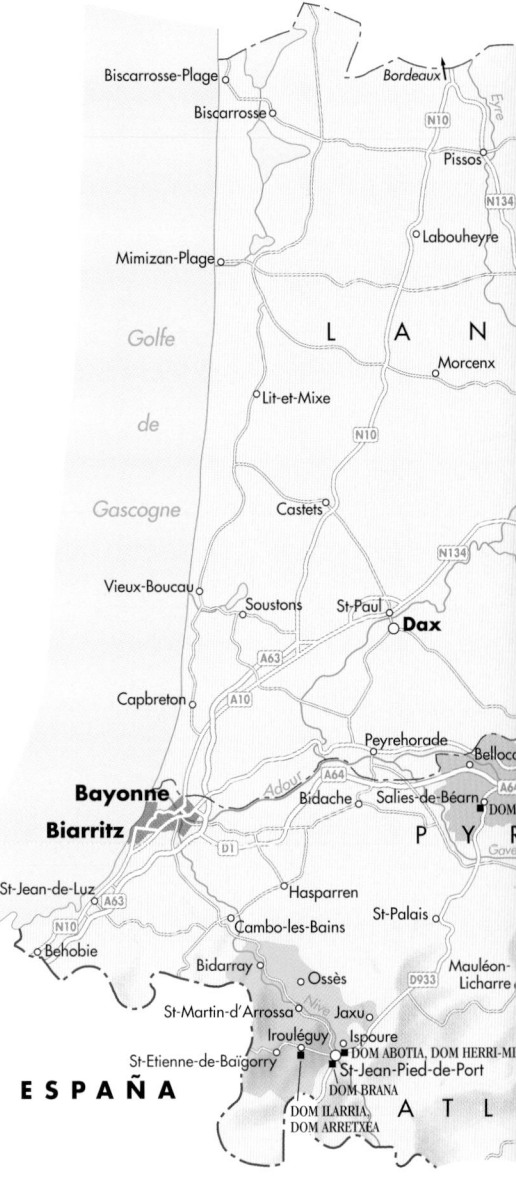

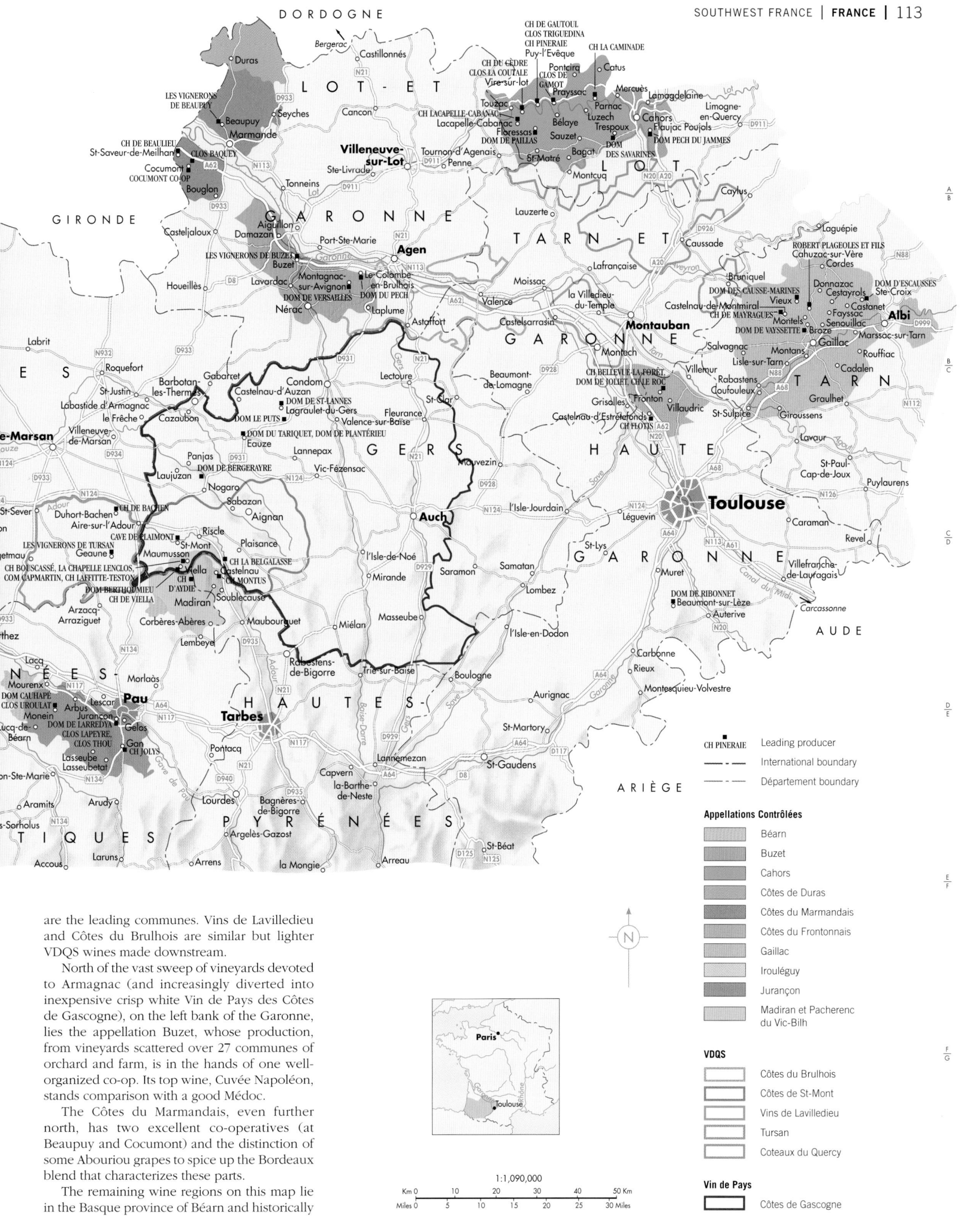

are the leading communes. Vins de Lavilledieu and Côtes du Brulhois are similar but lighter VDQS wines made downstream.

North of the vast sweep of vineyards devoted to Armagnac (and increasingly diverted into inexpensive crisp white Vin de Pays des Côtes de Gascogne), on the left bank of the Garonne, lies the appellation Buzet, whose production, from vineyards scattered over 27 communes of orchard and farm, is in the hands of one well-organized co-op. Its top wine, Cuvée Napoléon, stands comparison with a good Médoc.

The Côtes du Marmandais, even further north, has two excellent co-operatives (at Beaupuy and Cocumont) and the distinction of some Abouriou grapes to spice up the Bordeaux blend that characterizes these parts.

The remaining wine regions on this map lie in the Basque province of Béarn and historically

CH PINERAIE ■   Leading producer
— · —   International boundary
— · —   Département boundary

Appellations Contrôlées

Béarn
Buzet
Cahors
Côtes de Duras
Côtes du Marmandais
Côtes du Frontonnais
Gaillac
Irouléguy
Jurançon
Madiran et Pacherenc du Vic-Bilh

VDQS

Côtes du Brulhois
Côtes de St-Mont
Vins de Lavilledieu
Tursan
Coteaux du Quercy

Vin de Pays

Côtes de Gascogne

1:1,090,000

Km 0   10   20   30   40   50 Km
Miles 0   5   10   15   20   25   30 Miles

depended on the port of Bayonne rather than Bordeaux. The general Béarn and Béarn-Bellocq appellations encompass the red, white, and rosé wines made outside the celebrated wine zones of Madiran and Jurançon, the two true jewels of the southwest.

Madiran is Gascony's great red wine, grown on clay and limestone hills along the left bank of the River Adour. The local red grape, Tannat, is well-named for its dark and tannic, tough and vigorous wines, often blended with some Cabernet and Pinenc (Fer Servadou). The region's dynamic winemakers differ on whether and how to tame these monsters, using varying degrees of new oak and even deliberate oxygenation. Some of these wines can be drunk earlier but after seven or eight years fine Madiran is truly admirable: aromatic, full of flavour, fluid, and lively, well able to withstand both comparison with classed-growth Bordeaux and an accompanying *confit de canard*.

The winemaking talent of this region has been turning its attention to the local white too, not least the energetic Plaimont co-operative union which dominates production of the VDQS Côtes de St-Mont and has done much to rescue local vine varieties from extinction. Sweet and dry white Pacherenc du Vic-Bilh is made within the Madiran zone from Arrufiac, Courbu, and Petit Manseng grapes, and is more

exciting every year, but is still overshadowed by its counterpart south of Pau, Jurançon.

Jurançon is one of France's most distinctive white wines, a tangy, green-tinged essence made on the steep Pyrenean foothills in a wide range of sweetness levels. Gros Manseng grapes are responsible for the dry, earlier-picked versions while the smaller, thicker-skinned Petit Manseng berries are much more suitable for leaving on the vine into November and sometimes even December, to shrivel and concentrate both sugars and acidity. These sweet, *moelleux* wines are lively enough to drink, as the French do, at the beginning of a meal, with the local *foie gras* for instance, and are perhaps closer to Vouvray in style than to the weight of a good Sauternes.

The VDQS Tursan, downstream of Madiran, is being revitalized, although red wines far outnumber the interesting whites made from Baroque grapes.

The tiny appellation of Irouléguy is the final Basque bastion, doggedly making firm, refreshing rosé, red, and white wines of the local grapes, including Tannat, Courbu, and the Mansengs, grown on south-facing terraces as high as 1,300ft (400m) above the Atlantic. The rosé label carries what might well be a Basque rallying cry: *Hotx Hotxa Edan*. Alas, it means only "chill before serving".

Above The valley of the sinuous River Lot defines the Cahors wine appellation, but there is a huge difference between the wines produced on the flat river banks and the higher ground. As can be seen here, viticulture no longer has a monopoly on riverside land.

A wide variety of appellations, wine styles, and label designs from all over this extensive, heterogeneous French wine region. It is distinguished by a particularly rich heritage of indigenous grape varieties.

Dordogne

B ordeaux's beautiful hinterland, the *bastide* country of the Dordogne leading back into the maze of green valleys cut into the stony upland of Périgueux, is an understandable favourite with tourists. For them, the new dedication in the region's vineyards and cellars is a bonus.

Even the small Côtes de Duras appellation, effectively a bridge between Entre-Deux-Mers and Bergerac, produces a number of thoroughly respectable wines from Bordeaux grapes. Some reds, some sweet whites, but in particular zesty, dry Sauvignon Blanc.

Traditionally the wines of Bergerac were seen as country bumpkins beside the sophisticates of Bordeaux. The most ordinary red and dry white wines of the Dordogne département's catch-all appellation still resemble the most basic AC Bordeaux, with the same shortcomings, but there is now a critical mass of producers determined to prove that Bergerac can produce far more serious wines – of all three hues and, in whites, all sweetness levels. Luc de Conti of Château Tour des Gendres deserves considerable, although not exclusive, credit. Thanks to a combination of lower yields and mastery of cellar hygiene and oak ageing, the new wave of ambitious wine producers (not all of them French) is producing deep-flavoured, well-structured wines to rival some of Bordeaux's smartest appellations.

The grapes are very similar to the Bordeaux varieties. The climate is a little more extreme than that of the Atlantic-influenced Gironde, and there is limestone on higher ground. The range of whites is wide, if confusing, and worth exploring. Bergerac Sec can be a forceful dry white made from any combination of Sémillon (still the most widely grown vine variety in the département) and Sauvignon Blanc although some quite sumptuous sweet white is also produced. Côtes de Bergerac distinguishes superior red wines made within the Bergerac zone.

Within the greater Bergerac region are many individual appellations – so many that some are virtually ignored. Rosette, for example, occupies a rather magnificent amphitheatre of vines north of the town of Bergerac, but only a handful of growers choose to sell their delicate, slightly sweet whites under this name. In the same area the appellation Pécharmant is celebrated locally for its oaked reds in the image of claret.

Just over the departmental boundary from Côtes de Castillon is the complex Montravel white wine zone in which Côtes de Montravel and Haut-Montravel are sweeter wines coming from respectively the north and east of the zone. Straight Montravel made all over the zone is a dry wine, made with increasing confidence, often using both Sauvignon Blanc and oak, while Sémillon is king of the sweet wines, which are remarkably like the best sweet whites made over the border in Côtes de Francs. Muscadelle is allowed here too.

The most distinctive, most glamorous wines of this part of France are sumptuously sweet, white and made in distinctly small quantities in two zones southwest of the town of Bergerac.

Indeed, the total production of Saussignac, Monbazillac's western neighbour and home to some extraordinarily determined producers, is only a few thousand cases.

The total output of Bergerac's most famous wine, Monbazillac, is 30 times greater and average quality has improved considerably since 1993 when machine picking was abandoned in favour of several selective harvests by hand (and much lighter doses of sulphur dioxide have become the norm). Like the Sauternes region, Monbazillac lies just east of where a tributary flows into the left bank of a major river (in this case the Gardonette and the Dordogne). The grapes are also the same, but the wines are not, one reason perhaps being Muscadelle's particular aptitude in Monbazillac. Botrytis may sweep through the vineyards of Monbazillac when there is none in Sauternes. The best young Monbazillacs, such as those of Château Tirecul La Gravière, are more exuberant, more sprightly than the best young Sauternes, whereas mature Monbazillac takes on an amber nuttiness that is decidedly uncharacteristic of Bordeaux's most famous sweet white wine.

In short, Bergerac may have decided to use as its slogan "the other great vineyard of Aquitaine", but it is not Bordeaux, and nowadays certainly not "poor man's Bordeaux".

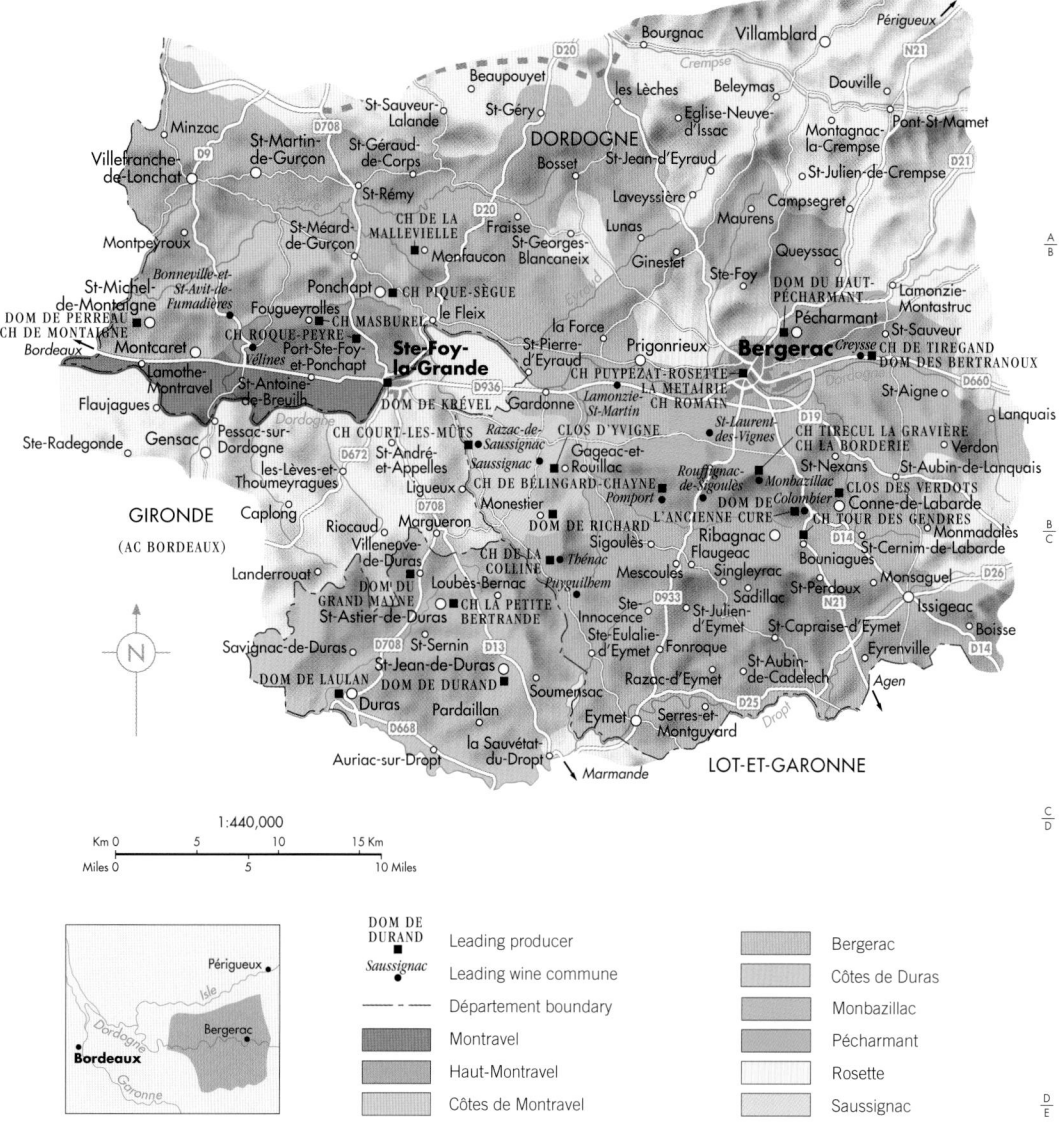

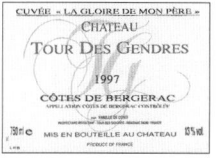

These, some of the *best wines of greater Bergerac, are not internationally known names but deserve greater recognition and acclaim. The Dordogne can provide fine answers to the reds, and dry and sweet whites, of Bordeaux.*

Loire Valley and Muscadet

1:1,000,000

Km 0   10   20   30   40 Km
Miles 0   10   20 Miles

Pays Nantais

Appellations Contrôlées:

Muscadet (and VDQS Gros Plant du Pays Nantais)

Muscadet de Sèvre-et-Maine

Muscadet des Coteaux de la Loire

Muscadet Côtes de Grand Lieu

VDQS:

Coteaux d'Ancenis

Fiefs Vendéens

Anjou-Saumur

Appellations Contrôlées:

1 ■ Quarts-de-Chaume

2 ■ Bonnezeaux

Savennières (with La-Roche-aux-Moines, Coulée-de-Serrant)

Coteaux de l'Aubance and Anjou-Villages-Brissac

Anjou Coteaux de la Loire

Coteaux du Layon

Saumur

Saumur-Champigny

Coteaux de Saumur

Complex as it is, the River Loire is worth mapping as a whole, for although its wine districts are so far-flung (see the map of France on page 53 for the outlying ones), with wide variations of climate, soil, and tradition, and four or five important grape varieties, the wines do have a family likeness. They are light and invigorating, with palpable acidity. The classic word for them is charming; the classic mystery that they are not more widely appreciated outside northern France. These wines are unwarranted casualties of the modern wine drinker's obsession with sheer mass.

Part of the problem may be that the majority are white. They divide clearly between the dry wines to the east (Sancerre and Pouilly) and west (Muscadet), with the sweeter wines of Touraine and Anjou in the middle, made from the Loire's own grape, the much-traduced Chenin Blanc. The best reds of Touraine and Anjou, however, have all of the fragrance and charm of Cabernet Franc – deepened with increasing proportions of Cabernet Sauvignon. New(ish) oak is used more than ever; sulphur noticeably less. The best-known wines of the Loire are described and mapped on these and the next six pages.

Brittany's wine country – one might almost say Neptune's vineyard – is the Pays Nantais,

the home of Muscadet. Muscadet was the first modern success story for the Loire. In the mid-20th century it was a little-known country wine. Today it is the accepted drink with the glorious seafood of northern France. In the last 35 years the vineyard area has more than doubled in size. Muscadet is not expensive, and yet is perfect in context – very dry, slightly salty, but firm rather than acid: in fact in hot years it can lack acidity. "It casts its pale golden glow," as one French critic has said, "over the purple of lobsters and the pearl of oysters, the pink of shrimps and the red of mullet."

Muscadet is the name of the wine, not of a place or a grape (which in Muscadet's case is a cousin of Chardonnay, Melon de Bourgogne). The Sèvre-et-Maine region (mapped opposite in detail) has 85% of Muscadet's vineyards, densely planted on low sandy hills. The heart of the district lies around Vertou, Vallet, St-Fiacre, and La Chapelle-Heulin; the area where the wines are ripest, liveliest, and most scented. They are traditionally bottled *sur lie* – straight from the fermentation vat, unracked – the lees deepening both flavour and texture (as, in a different way, they do in champagne). The best producers are, happily, determined to throw off Muscadet's reputation as a simple wine, experimenting with

extended lees ageing, distinguishing between different vineyards and sometimes releasing almost Burgundian four or five year-old wines.

Muscadet des Coteaux de la Loire made well inland tends to be a little leaner, while the newish (1994) Côtes de Grand Lieu has the most maritime influence. Straight Muscadet can be made anywhere within the green Pay Nantais boundary, as can the second wine of the region, the VDQS Gros Plant du Pays Nantais.

Outside the areas mapped in detail Jasnières produces some fine, usually dry, Chenin Blanc and necessarily light reds and rosés from local Pineau d'Aunis grapes within the confusingly named Coteaux du Loir zone.

Cheverny meanwhile flourishes in myriad forms, of which some quite piercing Sauvignon Blanc is probably best; sharp, dry whites made from Romorantin are labelled Cour-Cheverny.

Irregular quality dogs growers this far north. Ripeness in many Loire vineyards can vary so widely from one year to another that they seem hardly to produce the same wine. A fine autumn ripens grapes almost to raisins, but a wet one means a very acid product. Hence the importance of the sparkling wine industry here.

For a description of the Loire Valley's Vins de Pays and VDQS wines, see pages 150-152.

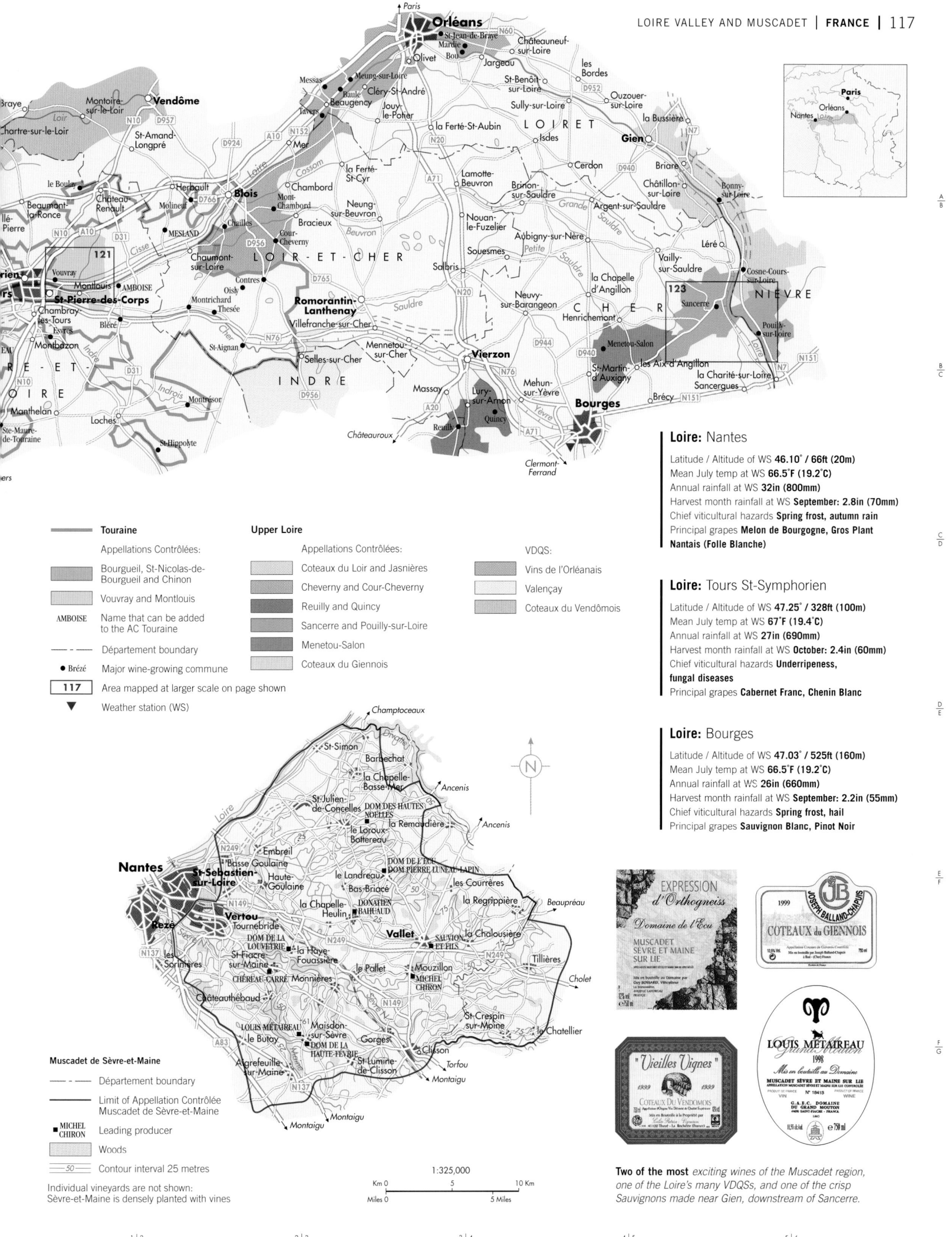

Touraine

Appellations Contrôlées:

Bourgueil, St-Nicolas-de-Bourgueil and Chinon

Vouvray and Montlouis

AMBOISE Name that can be added to the AC Touraine

— - — - — Département boundary

● Brézé Major wine-growing commune

117 Area mapped at larger scale on page shown

▼ Weather station (WS)

Upper Loire

Appellations Contrôlées:

Coteaux du Loir and Jasnières

Cheverny and Cour-Cheverny

Reuilly and Quincy

Sancerre and Pouilly-sur-Loire

Menetou-Salon

Coteaux du Giennois

VDQS:

Vins de l'Orléanais

Valençay

Coteaux du Vendômois

Loire: Nantes

Latitude / Altitude of WS **46.10˚ / 66ft (20m)**
Mean July temp at WS **66.5˚F (19.2˚C)**
Annual rainfall at WS **32in (800mm)**
Harvest month rainfall at WS **September: 2.8in (70mm)**
Chief viticultural hazards **Spring frost, autumn rain**
Principal grapes **Melon de Bourgogne, Gros Plant Nantais (Folle Blanche)**

Loire: Tours St-Symphorien

Latitude / Altitude of WS **47.25˚ / 328ft (100m)**
Mean July temp at WS **67˚F (19.4˚C)**
Annual rainfall at WS **27in (690mm)**
Harvest month rainfall at WS **October: 2.4in (60mm)**
Chief viticultural hazards **Underripeness, fungal diseases**
Principal grapes **Cabernet Franc, Chenin Blanc**

Loire: Bourges

Latitude / Altitude of WS **47.03˚ / 525ft (160m)**
Mean July temp at WS **66.5˚F (19.2˚C)**
Annual rainfall at WS **26in (660mm)**
Harvest month rainfall at WS **September: 2.2in (55mm)**
Chief viticultural hazards **Spring frost, hail**
Principal grapes **Sauvignon Blanc, Pinot Noir**

Muscadet de Sèvre-et-Maine

— - — - — Département boundary

—— Limit of Appellation Contrôlée Muscadet de Sèvre-et-Maine

■ MICHEL CHIRON Leading producer

Woods

50 Contour interval 25 metres

Individual vineyards are not shown: Sèvre-et-Maine is densely planted with vines

1:325,000

Km 0   5   10 Km
Miles 0   5 Miles

Two of the most exciting wines of the Muscadet region, one of the Loire's many VDQSs, and one of the crisp Sauvignons made near Gien, downstream of Sancerre.

Anjou

The white wines of Anjou and Touraine have this in common with those of Germany: in their best vintages they achieve resplendent sweetness and go on improving for many years, or decades when noble rot really takes hold.

The grape that gives us all this is the Chenin Blanc, called locally Pineau de la Loire. The area mapped here is where it reaches its ripest state, where several geographical circumstances combine to give it the dry, open, schistous slopes, sheltered from north to east, which it needs. The River Layon, heading northwest to join the Loire, has cut a gully deep enough for its right bank to provide perfectly exposed, but sheltered, corners of hill. A large part of its course has the appellation Coteaux du Layon, providing sweet (*moelleux*) wines notably above the general Anjou standard. But the particularly well-protected Quarts de Chaume with only 120 acres

(under 50ha) and Bonnezeaux (about double) are outstanding enough to have appellations of their own, like Grands Crus in Burgundy.

The elusive River Aubance, parallel with the Layon to the north, sees similar sweet white wines made with similarly increasing skill. The Coteaux de l'Aubance has been invaded by what can seem like an army of talented wine producers such as Christophe Daviau, the Lebretons, Christian Papin, and Didier Richou.

Just south of Angers and – exceptionally for an Angevin wine district – north of the Loire, is Savennières. Again it is the Chenin Blanc, although here the wine is dry, fearsomely so in youth. The law demands a savagely restricted crop – only 20hl/ha – and this combination of concentration and acidity requires time to shine. Three or four years is the minimum age to drink it, and 20 sees it in full cry. Within Savennières

two Grands Crus have their own sub-appellations: La Roche aux Moines with less than 70 acres (just under 30ha) and La Coulée de Serrant with a mere 12 fiercely biodynamic acres (5ha).

These are historically the most distinguished wines of Anjou, but the region's basic Anjou appellation has also been in a state of benevolent transformation. Anjou Blanc can nowadays be a fine example of firm, characterful Chenin Blanc. The sometimes sickly Rosé d'Anjou has been overtaken by the delicately scented, off-dry rosé Cabernet d'Anjou.

Light Anjou-Gamay is still widely drunk in the region but perhaps the most remarkable change has been the speed with which Angevin winemakers have mastered their vines and new oak barrels to become accomplished producers of reds. The best of these, typically pioneered by the Aubance young turks and stiffened by Cabernet Sauvignon, earn the appellation Anjou-Villages which, in riper vintages, can provide the subtle thrill of a great Touraine red at half the price.

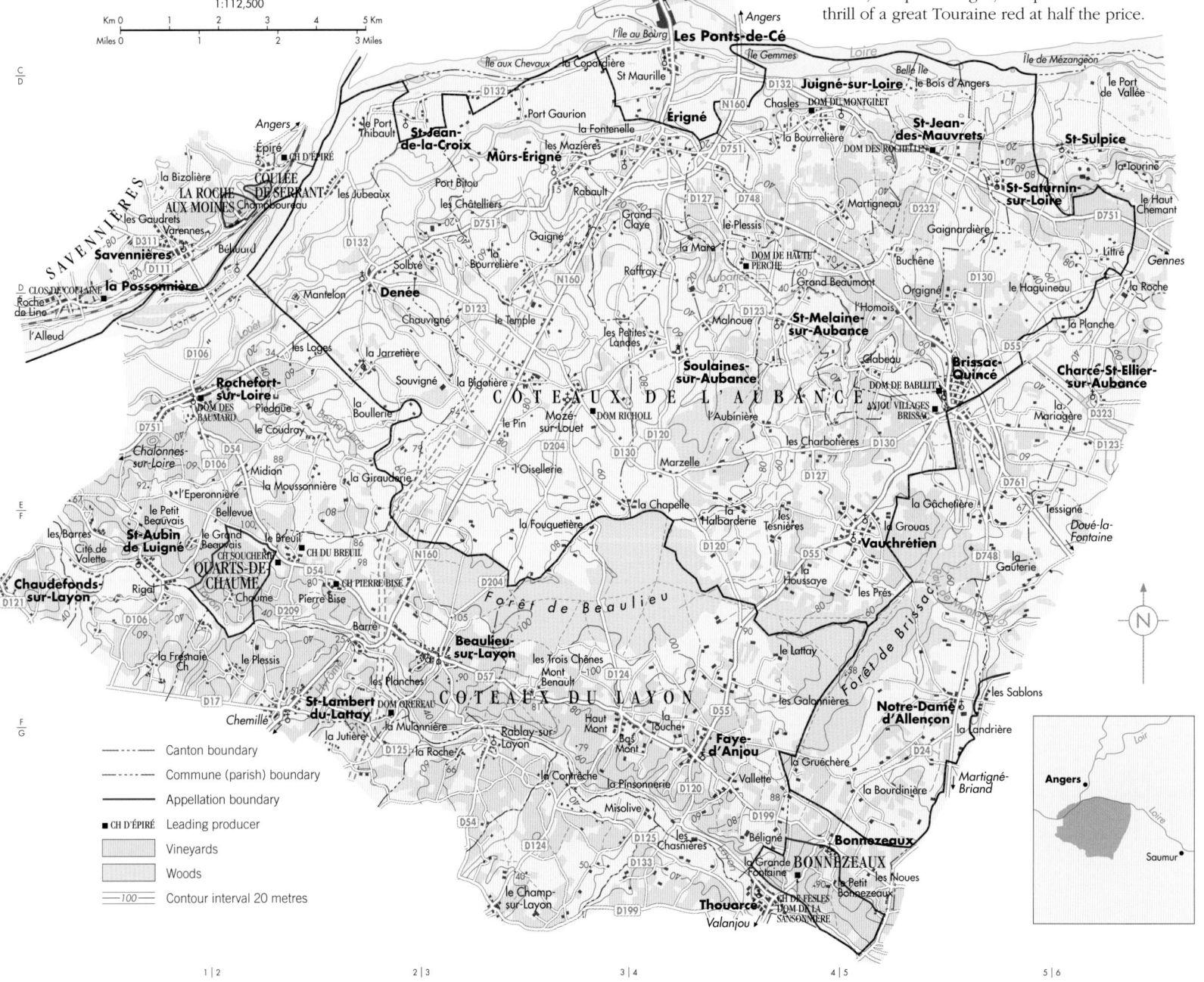

1:112,500

Km 0 1 2 3 4 5 Km
Miles 0   1   2   3 Miles

- - - - -   Canton boundary
- - - - -   Commune (parish) boundary
———   Appellation boundary
■ CH D'ÉPIRÉ   Leading producer
▨   Vineyards
▨   Woods
═100═   Contour interval 20 metres

Saumur

Carbon dioxide has long been vital to the wine economics of the Saumur region. Saumur Mousseux mops up the Chenin Blanc (and up to 10% Chardonnay) grown all over Saumur, and even parts of Anjou's Coteaux du Layon and Coteaux de l'Aubance, that might be considered too tart to enjoy as a still wine.

The town of Saumur, lying 30 miles (48km) upstream of Angers, is the Loire's Reims and Epernay rolled into one. It even has its own natural underground cellars carved in this case out of the soft local *tuffeau*. Substantial enterprises produce substantial quantities of often quite insubstantial sparkling wine, but the best sparkling Saumurs may have a component that was fermented in oak and another that has benefited from considerable age. It is in the nature of Chenin Blanc to make more flirtatious fizz than the grapes used for champagne, however. Crémant de Loire may contain grapes grown virtually anywhere in this long eastward stretch of the Loire but rules governing its production are stricter and the wines, generally, finer.

Still Saumur is light and comes in all three hues, but today the single most important wine made in the greater Saumur region comes from

Some of Anjou's best wines *are sweet, long-living nectars based on the Chenin Blanc grape as well as appetizing reds made mainly from Cabernet Franc. The three bottom labels represent some of the non-sparkling stars of Saumur.*

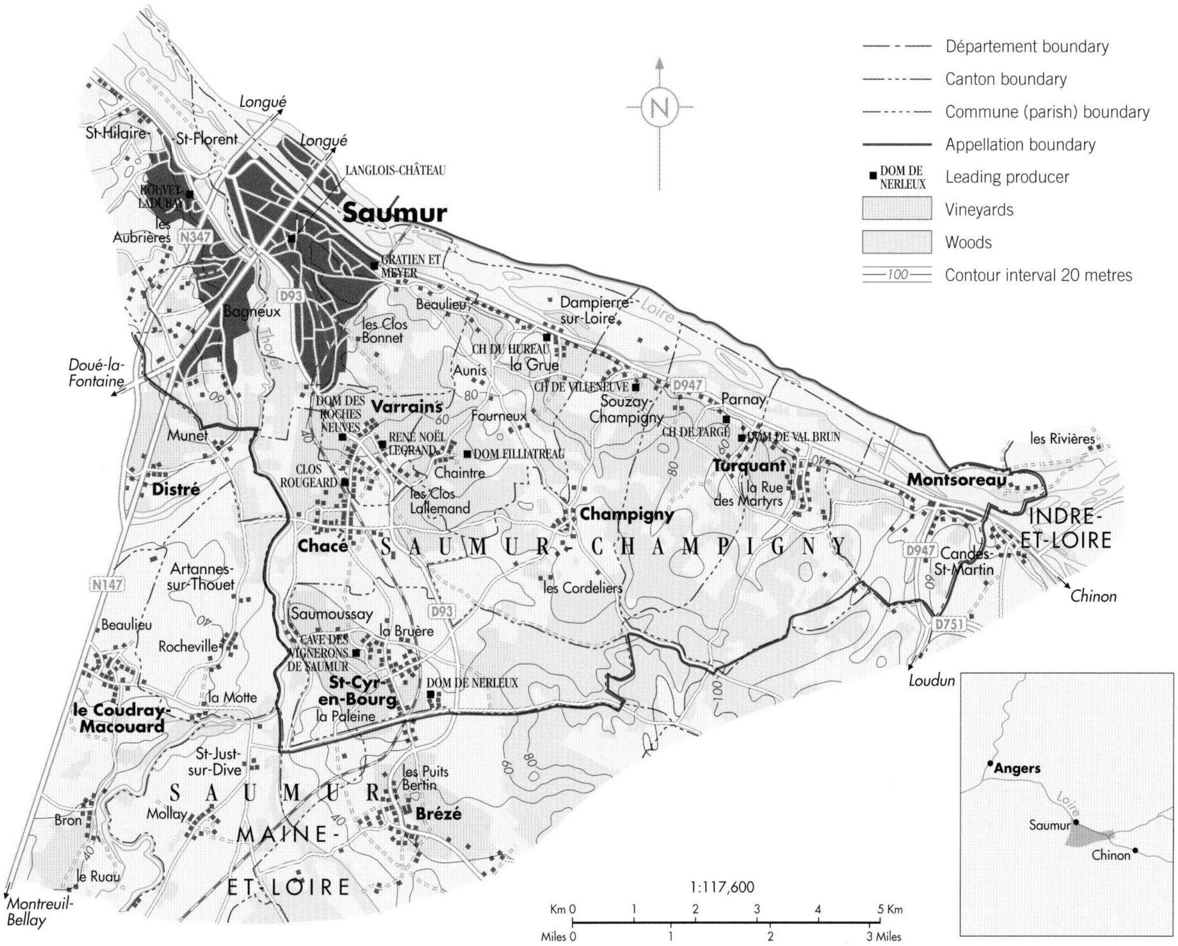

a small enclave of vineyards on the left bank of the River Loire. The fashionable red Saumur-Champigny is named for two of the more important settlements within the region – although St-Cyr-en-Bourg is now a very much more important wine centre than the little village of Champigny. Vineyards are densely planted along the white cliffs by the river while inland, around St-Cyr-en-Bourg with its reliable co-op, the local *tuffeau* becomes yellower and sandier and tends to produce slightly lighter wines.

Not that weight, happily, is considered a virtue in Saumur-Champigny. This is one of Cabernet Franc's most delicate expressions, from land that is effectively an extension of the best red wine country of Touraine just over the

Above Domaine Filliatreau of Saumur-Champigny is just one of many middle Loire producers whose premises have been carved out of the local *tuffeau* which, like the chalk of Champagne, offers ideal maturation conditions for Saumur's substantial sparkling wine industry.

département boundary. Saumur-Champigny's popularity in the bistros of Paris, which some would describe as extreme, has done little to encourage the sort of manic obsession with quality now evident in parts of Anjou, but producers as gifted as the Foucault brothers at Clos Rougeard – and others whose labels feature on this page – can still fashion serious wines, some of them worth ageing, from this particular bend in the River Loire.

– ⋅ – ⋅ –	Département boundary
– – – –	Canton boundary
⋅⋅⋅⋅⋅⋅	Commune (parish) boundary
——	Appellation boundary
■ DOM DE NERLEUX	Leading producer
	Vineyards
	Woods
=100=	Contour interval 20 metres

1:117,600

Km 0 1 2 3 4 5 Km
Miles 0 1 2 3 Miles

Chinon and Bourgueil

St-Nicolas-de-Bourgueil, Bourgueil, and Chinon make Touraine's and the Loire's most celebrated red wines. Saumur-Champigny is the only one that – only rarely – comes close. At this Atlantic-influenced western end of the Touraine, Cabernet Franc – known here as Breton – makes a wine with the raspberry fruitiness of an exceptional Beaujolais and the rasping savour of a freshly sharpened pencil. In an average year the purple wine is excellent, drunk cool, within a few months of the vintage. In outstandingly ripe years such as 1990, 1996, and 1997 it has the substance and structure to mature for a decade, a phenomenon that is likely to intensify now that up to 25% Cabernet Sauvignon is allowed into these extremely individual wines. For their quality they are absurdly undervalued.

Chinon makes the silkiest, most tender wine of the district from a patchwork of varied soils – whose produce is increasingly bottled separately. Vineyards on riverside sand and gravel make lighter, earlier-drinking styles of Chinon. *Tuffeau*, particularly the south-facing slopes of Cravant-les-Coteaux east of Chinon and the plateau above Beaumont to the west, tends to produce wines with the structure of a good Bourgueil, whose steeper slopes and higher limestone content makes wine which can improve for up to ten years in bottle. The wine of St-Nicolas-de-Bourgueil from lighter soils to the west can be a little leaner but is often similar; more depends on the grower than the commune (see the map and, especially, labels below for specific recommendations).

A hundred years ago Chinon's wine was rated the equal of Margaux. In charm, if not in force or structure, it can come surprisingly close today and production is expanding accordingly. Very little white wine is made in the region.

The greater Touraine region produces a host of other, usually less serious, reds, rosés, and whites, all called Touraine but sometimes with the geographical suffixes Amboise, Azay-le-Rideau or Mesland. (Noble Joué, an unusually dry, characterful *vin gris* made on the southern outskirts of Tours between Esvres and Joué-lès-Tours from Pinots Meunier, Noir, and Gris would also like official recognition.) A dizzying range of grapes is allowed but light Gamay is characteristic for reds and Sauvignon, sometimes extremely good value, for sharp whites.

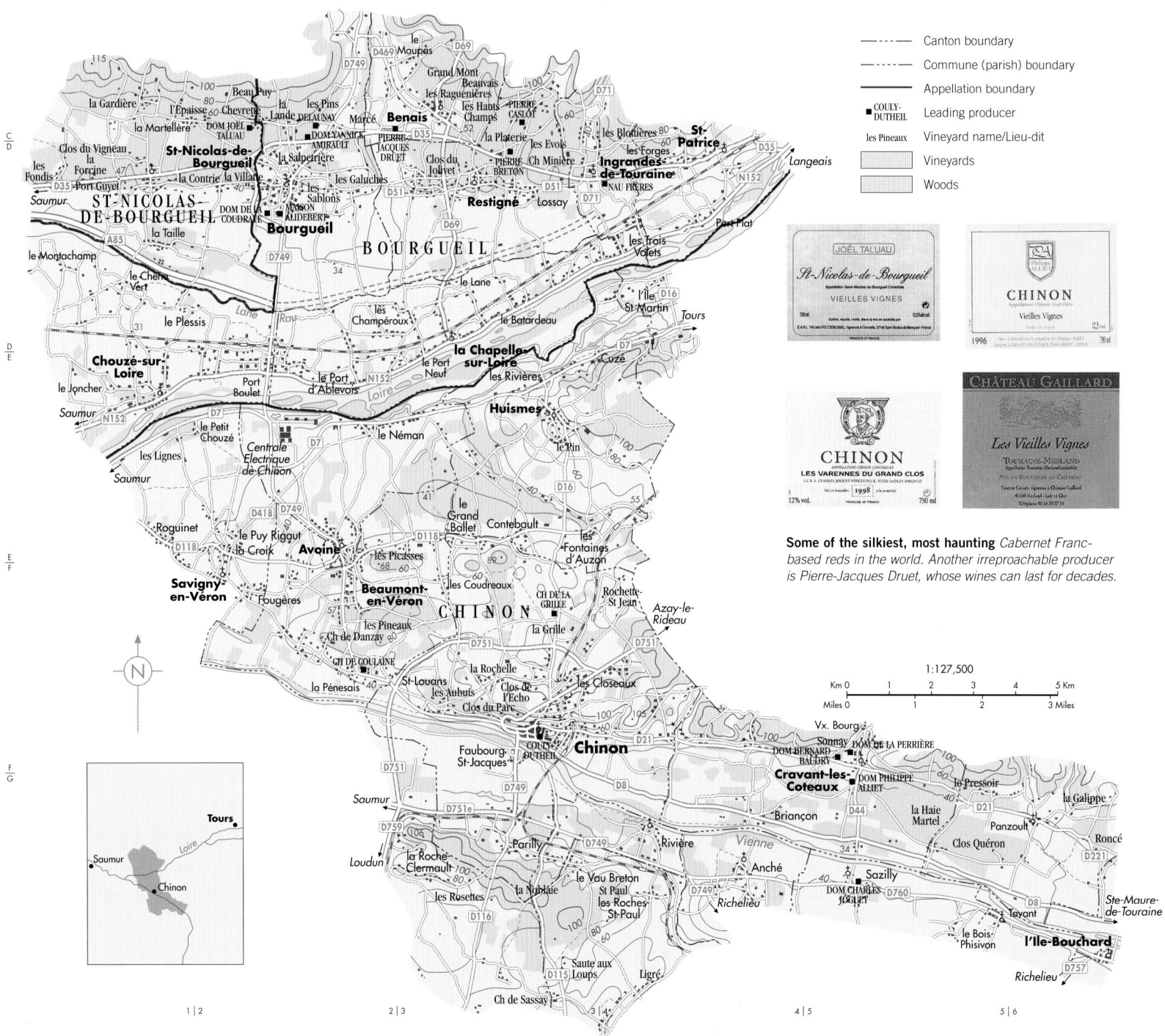

–––––––	Canton boundary
–·–·–·–	Commune (parish) boundary
–––––––	Appellation boundary
■ COULY-DUTHEIL	Leading producer
les Pineaux	Vineyard name/Lieu-dit
	Vineyards
	Woods

Some of the silkiest, most haunting *Cabernet Franc-based reds in the world. Another irreproachable producer is Pierre-Jacques Druet, whose wines can last for decades.*

1:127,500

Km 0   1   2   3   4   5 Km
Miles 0   1   2   3 Miles

Vouvray and Montlouis

Just as Savennières stands almost at the gates of Angers, Vouvray and Montlouis lie just outside Tours on the way to Amboise. Everything royal and romantic about France is summed up in this land of renaissance châteaux and ancient towns along the immense but gentle river.

Low hills of soft local *tuffeau* flank the Cisse along the reach from Noizay to Rochecorbon. For centuries they have provided both cellars and cave-dwellings to the winegrowers of the district. The Chenin Blanc here, although often drier than in Anjou, at its best is honey-like and sweet. What distinguishes it more than anything, however, is its long life. For a comparatively light wine its longevity is astonishing. You may expect port to live for half a century, but in a pale, firm, rather delicate wine

 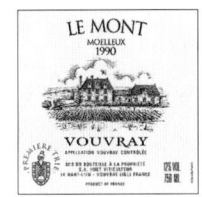

Vouvray reflects each vintage's extremely varied character more vividly than any other appellation. A cool, rainy year means that Vouvray Sec will predominate with perhaps a little Demi-Sec; a warm autumn may result in great Moelleux wines like these.

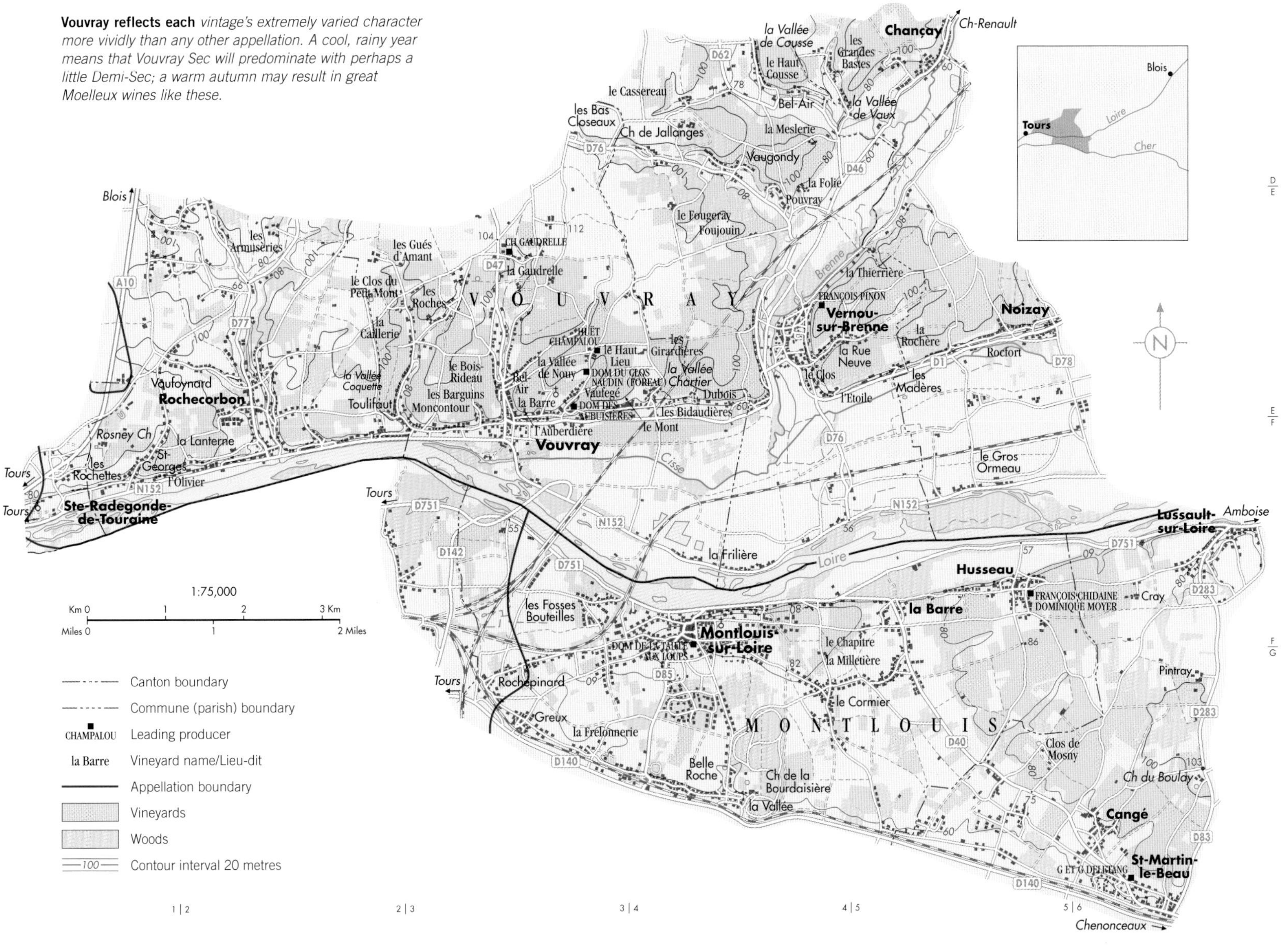

the ability to improve and go on improving for so long in bottle is matched only occasionally in Germany. Acidity is the key.

The first distinction in Vouvray is whether any given bottle is dry (*sec*), off-dry (*sec-tendre*, an unofficial but increasingly popular style), medium dry (*demi-sec*), sweet (*moelleux*) or for that matter *pétillant* or fully sparkling. This far from the equator, the weather varies enormously from year to year, as does the ripeness and health of the grapes. Vouvray therefore alters character radically from vintage to vintage: some years dry and austere, requiring many years' softening in the bottle, but every now and then a gloriously rich expression of noble rot, requiring several different harvests through each vineyard. Less successful vintages may be converted into very good sparkling wines, which have a honeyed character and ageing potential that sets them apart from sparkling Saumur.

Normally only the richer vintages carry the name of one of the handful of famous Clos on the best slopes, on the clay and gravel above the riverside *tuffeau*. The best-known producer, Huët, owns three: Le Haut Lieu above the cellars,

Le Mont which can show real concentration, and the Clos de Bourg, favourite of winemaker Noël Pinguet and the first of his conversions to biodynamic viticulture in the late 1980s. Prince Poniatowski owns Le Clos Baudoin, the Domaine Freslier the Quarts de Moncontour, and the Allias family Le Clos du Petit Mont at the top of the Vallée Coquette. The biggest company in Vouvray, Marc Brédif, which is now owned by the Ladoucettes of Château du Nozet in Pouilly-sur-Loire, is a négociant with high standards.

As everywhere else throughout the Loire Valley, certain producers have been infected with the virus that demands they experiment with small, new oak barrels, and stirring the lees of fermentation too, but for the moment the essence of Vouvray winemaking is, as in Germany, to capture in the bottle the fermented fruit juice in as pure a form as possible.

Montlouis has very similar conditions to Vouvray, without the perfect sheltered, south-facing situation of the first rank of Vouvray's vineyards along the Loire. Soils tend to be slightly sandier and so Montlouis is typically a little lighter, earthier and slightly softer, and more Montlouis is destined for sparkling Mousseux.

1:75,000

Km 0   1   2   3 Km

Miles 0   1   2 Miles

- – – – – Canton boundary
- – – – – Commune (parish) boundary
- CHAMPALOU   Leading producer
- la Barre   Vineyard name/Lieu-dit
- ───── Appellation boundary
- Vineyards
- Woods
- ═100═ Contour interval 20 metres

Pouilly and Sancerre

The wines of Pouilly and Sancerre on the Upper Loire are perhaps the easiest to recognize in France. On these limestone hills bisected by the river, in a near-continental climate, the Sauvignon Blanc can make better, certainly finer and more complex, wine than anywhere else in the world. But it does so all too rarely. The popularity of Sancerre, and Pouilly-Fumé made across the lazy River Loire, has allowed average yields to rise at a far greater rate than quality so that too many of the wines produced are simply crisp and vaguely fruity. Sauvignon de Touraine in a good year can be a safer bet than Sancerre or Pouilly-Fumé from an unreliable source.

Pouilly-sur-Loire is the town; its wine is only called Pouilly-Fumé when it is made from the Sauvignon Blanc grape, often known here as the Blanc Fumé. Without the word Fumé, Pouilly-sur-Loire is a light, inconsequential wine made from the mild Chasselas. (Neither has anything to do with Pouilly-Fuissé, the white wine of Mâcon described on page 71.)

It would be a brave taster who maintained he or she could always distinguish between a Pouilly-Fumé and a Sancerre. The best of each are on the same level; the Sancerre perhaps slightly fuller and more obvious, the Pouilly-Fumé more perfumed. Many Pouilly vineyards are lower than those of Sancerre which tend to lie at altitudes of between 650 and 1,150ft (200

and 350m), but most of the best are north of Pouilly and just across the river from the hilltop town of Sancerre.

Whenever the local limestone soils have high proportion of flint (*silex*) there is potential for ageworthy, almost acrid wines described as having a gunflint (*pierre à fusil*) character. This is common in vineyards close to Sancerre itself, while those in the west of the appellation tend to have a higher proportion of clay and make rather sturdier wines. In between the two zones, the limestone is often mixed with gravel and the wines rather lighter.

The village of Bué, its best vineyard the Clos du Chêne Marchand, makes the roundest, most solid wine of Sancerre. Chavignol (especially Les Monts Damnés) can be finer. Ménétréol gives steelier wine – provided the winemaker is committed to quality. The total area of Sancerre vineyard more than trebled in the last quarter of the 20th century to 5,900 acres (2,400ha), almost two and a half times the extent of the Pouilly-Fumé vignoble.

In the more homogeneous Pouilly, de Ladoucette's Disneyland-original Château du Nozet may be the biggest and best-known estate, but Didier Dagueneau has pioneered seriously low yields and experimentation with oak (echoed by Vincent Pinard and others in Sancerre).

Such ambitious producers are understandably interested in proving that their wines are

worth ageing, but – in stark contrast to the great white wines of Vouvray, for example – the great majority of Sancerre and Pouilly-Fumé reaches its appetizing, flirtatious peak within a year or two of bottling.

Sancerre's other passion is its pale Pinot Noir which in less ripe vintages can be disconcertingly light but can also be a pretty, country version of red burgundy. It may represent only about a sixth of total production (and none at all within the Pouilly-Fumé appellation), but some of the more ambitious producers have proved recently that in good years it can provide just as much pleasure as many a wine from the Côte de Beaune at a similar price.

Well inside the great bend of the river are the other so-called Vignobles du Centre (see map of the Loire Valley on page 117). The historic vineyards of Quincy and Reuilly, and a rapidly expanding fragment at Menetou-Salon, also make fruity Sauvignon Blancs and pale Pinot Noir to rival Sancerre, often at keener prices and without the nonchalance engendered by a famous name.

Quincy is perhaps the most rustic of these three appellations and applies only to white wine. Reuilly makes an increasing amount of all three colours, as does Menetou-Salon which, thanks to a high proportion of limestone soil, is fast establishing a reputation as a more reliable name than its neighbour to the east, Sancerre.

Left Neither Sancerre nor Pouilly-sur-Loire but vineyards in Menetou-Salon which, with Quincy and Reuilly, produces similarly bracing, nervy, occasionally reticent wines from Sauvignon Blanc grapes grown in the Upper Loire Valley.

—·—·— Département boundary

—···—···— Canton boundary

—··—··— Commune (parish) boundary

■ COTAT Leading producer

le Paradis Vineyard name/Lieu-dit

———— Appellation boundary

▨ Vineyards

▨ Woods

—200— Contour interval 20 metres

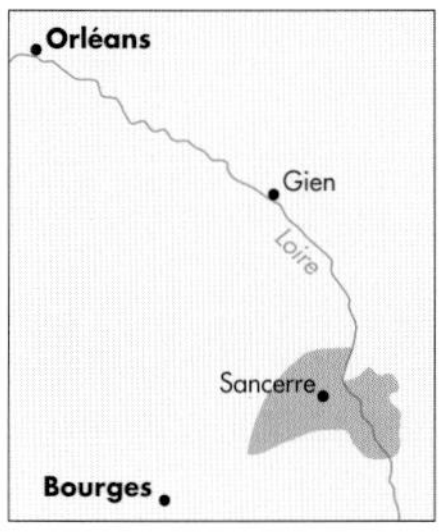

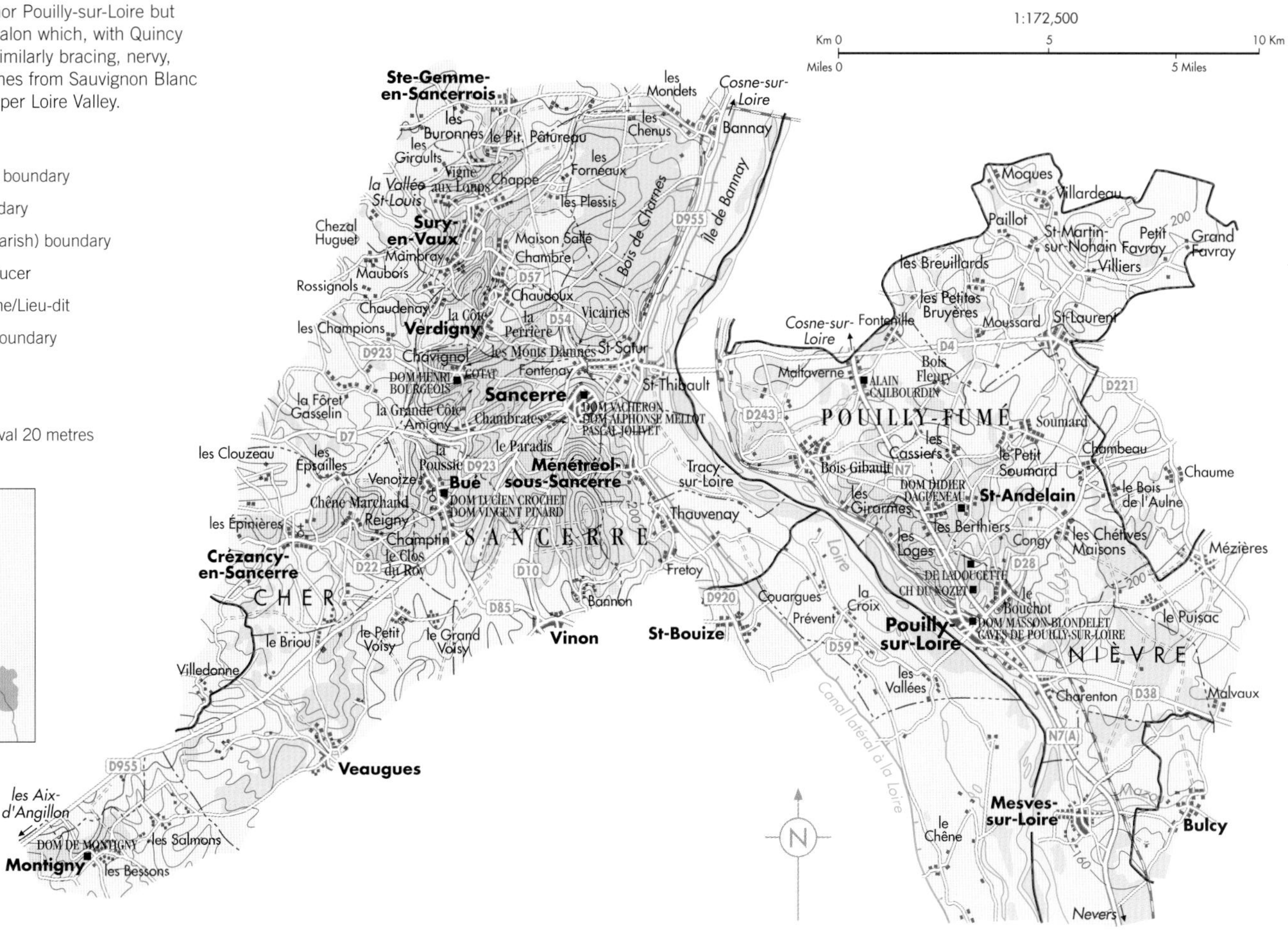

1:172,500

Km 0 ———— 5 ———— 10 Km

Miles 0 ———— 5 Miles

Below The meandering River Loire and a vineyard view over the town of Pouilly-sur-Loire which gives its name to the wine Pouilly-Fumé.

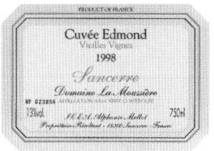

Didier Dagueneau's label *(top right) is just one of a series of mould-breaking designs and styles of Pouilly-Fumé. A restless innovator, he has experimented with oak, sweet wines, ungrafted vines, Riesling, and much else besides.*

Alsace

The wine of Alsace reflects the ambivalent situation of a border province. There are two possible physical boundaries between France and Germany: the Rhine and the crest of the Vosges which run parallel 15 miles (25km) west of the river. The Rhine has been the political frontier through most of history, but the mountains have always been the line that makes the great climatic, stylistic, even linguistic difference. Alsace wine was historically classed as "Rhenish", or of the Rhine. Its markets were in Germany, Switzerland, and in the parts of northern Europe reached by the Rhine and the North Sea.

Yet Alsace has never been German, except in periods of military occupation. Its language and its market may be, but its soul is entirely French. Alsace makes Germanic wine in the French way. The tone is set by the climate, the soil, and the choice of grape varieties: all comparable with German wine regions, the nearest of which is Baden just across the Rhine. What does differ is the interpretation put on these things – because German and Alsatian winegrowers have held such differing views of what they want their wine to do and be.

The Germans prize natural balance above all. Their best wines, whether sweet or dry, are fine balancing acts between grape sugar and acidity, with alcohol almost incidental and certainly not boosted by chaptalization (adding sugar before fermentation). German wine at its finest is not necessarily for the table but for the drawing-room or the garden. Alsace wine is the great adjunct to one of France's richest cuisines. Alsace gives the flowery scented grapes of

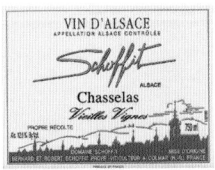

Some particularly *successful examples of the many lesser grape specialities of Alsace – Chasselas, Sylvaner, and Klevener de Heiligenstein – as well as, on the right, wines from three of the noble grapes made outside the Haut-Rhin considered in detail overleaf.*

Germany the body and authority of such table wines as white burgundy – proper accompaniments to strong and savoury food.

Traditionally, Alsace winemakers sought bone dry, firm, strong wines, fermenting every ounce of the sugar produced by the long dry summers of Alsace and, often, adding even more to make the wine even stronger. This contrasted with the German model of featherlight wines with natural grape sugar lingering delicately therein. But of late these two stereotypes have been moving towards each other. The average residual sugar level of Alsace wine has been increasing while German wines are becoming drier and stronger (increasingly aided by chaptalization). The best producers on both sides of the Rhine are proud that all of this is a result of lowering yields and concentrating what each grape has to offer. But consumers complain that Alsace wine is becoming more difficult to match with food, and that labels give them so few clues as to how sweet the wine is likely to be.

The major clues on Alsace labels, most unusually for France, are varietal. The grapes that give their names and special qualities to the wines of Alsace are the Riesling of the Rhine – responsible here and in Germany for the best wine of all – Sylvaner, Muscat, Pinots Blanc and Gris, and the uniquely perfumed Gewurztraminer.

Gewurztraminer is the perfect introduction to the province. You would not think that so fruity a scent could come from a wine that can be so clean and dry. *Würze* means spice in German – although a more accurate description would make mention of rose petals, grapefruit, and, sometimes, lychees.

To the initiated, a wine with so marked a character can become dull after a while. It has its place with some of the richest of the very rich Alsatian dishes: goose or pork. But most Alsatians consider the Riesling their true *grand vin*. It offers something much more elusive: a balance of hard and gentle, flowery and strong, which leads you on and never surfeits.

There is renewed interest today in the Pinot Gris (once called Tokay d'Alsace), which makes the fullest-bodied but least perfumed wine of the region; it has an obvious place at table as an alternative to a white burgundy.

Alsace Muscat is usually a blend of Muscat Ottonel and Muscat Blanc grapes. At its best it keeps all of Muscat's characteristic grapey scent, but makes a dry wine as clean as a whistle: a very good apéritif.

Klevener de Heiligenstein is a grape speciality of the area round the village of Heiligenstein just north of Barr, in a limestone-dominated area which extends as far north as Ottrott. The lightly spicy, sometimes slightly buttery wine is relatively light in alcohol, and in good vintages it can age well.

Much more important is Pinot Blanc – a name used both for Pinot Blanc itself, the everyday grape of Alsace which usually manages to transmit some of the characteristic smokiness of the region's whites, and for the softer Pinot Auxerrois (the two are frequently blended). To keep matters complicated the Auxerrois is sometimes labelled Klevner, or even Clevner. It is also the most common base wine for sparkling Crémant d'Alsace made by the traditional method, which at its best can rival the Crémants of Burgundy and the Loire.

In a class above the commonest wines of the region comes Sylvaner. Alsace Sylvaner is light and sometimes attractively tart. Without the tartness it can be a little dull and coarse in flavour. It is often the first wine at an Alsatian dinner, to build up to the main wine, the Riesling.

The lesser grapes, Chasselas and Knipperlé (there are others), are not usually identified on the label. They are often the open wines of cafés. Very young, particularly in the summer after a good vintage, they are so good that visitors should not miss them by insisting on a smarter one with a name. The term Edelzwicker (noble mixture) is usually applied to a mixture of grape varieties but rarely noble ones.

Of these grapes, only Riesling, Pinot Gris, Gewurztraminer, and Muscat – the Alsace grape nobility – are generally allowed the controversial Alsace Grand Cru appellation discussed on pages 126-128. In 1983, 25 of the region's best-located vineyards were designated and a further 25 added in 1993. Those sites so far approved as Grands Crus which are not within the areas mapped in more detail overleaf are numbered on the map opposite, many of them clustered on a patch of particularly well-favoured clay-limestone due west of Strasbourg on some of the lowest-lying vineyard land of the Bas-Rhin département. Steinklotz is particularly well-

Left Vineyards near Niedermorschwihr below the Vosges just west of Colmar, the spiritual heart of the Alsace wine region. Vines in Alsace are some of France's most productive, and the only ones officially allowed to emblazon their names on wine labels.

known for Pinot Gris and Pinot Noir, Altenberg de Bergbieten for Riesling. In the bottom left-hand corner of the map, 12 miles (20km) south of the main concentration of Haut-Rhin Grands Crus is the historic Rangen vineyard which rises steeply above the village of Thann. Schoffit and Zind-Humbrecht make superbly rich wines, especially Riesling and Pinot Gris, from these warm volcanic soils.

One of the attractions of Alsace for wine-makers and more intellectual connoisseurs is the mosaic of soil types within the region and the challenge of matching grapes to them. But what distinguishes Alsace from other French wine regions is its low rainfall (see factfile over-leaf). A quick comparison with other pages shows that only Perpignan is drier than Colmar, and even Toulon in Provence is wetter than Strasbourg. Drought may sometimes plague vine-yards here but ripeness is usually guaranteed.

Like its counterparts from the Loire and from Germany, Alsace wine is essentially about fruit rather than oak which, if used at all, is used almost exclusively in the form of old oval casks whose contribution is slow stabilization rather than oak flavour. Similarly, most Alsace wine-makers have deliberately suppressed the second malolactic fermentation for their whites, but it is generally necessary to soften the 6% or so of Alsace wine that is red and made from Pinot Noir grapes. Colours and styles vary enor-mously from the traditional tart, dark rosé to some deep crimson, oaky wines made from barrel-aged, low-yield fruit. As in Germany, the holy grail of perfect red Pinot is hard for wine-makers to ignore.

Another challenge for the region's wine-makers is to make the most of its finest autumns when seriously ripe grapes can be picked to make either Vendange Tardive wines or, even sweeter, rarer, and generally botrytized, Sélection des Grains Nobles made from several different pickings. A late-picked Gewurztraminer has perhaps the most exotic smell of any wine in the world, and can at the same time keep a remark-able cleanness and finesse of flavour. Even in these rarefied categories, however, it can be dif-ficult to predict how rich a wine will be; some are intense rather than sweet. Some are miracu-lous; others merely expand their category by volume rather than real quality.

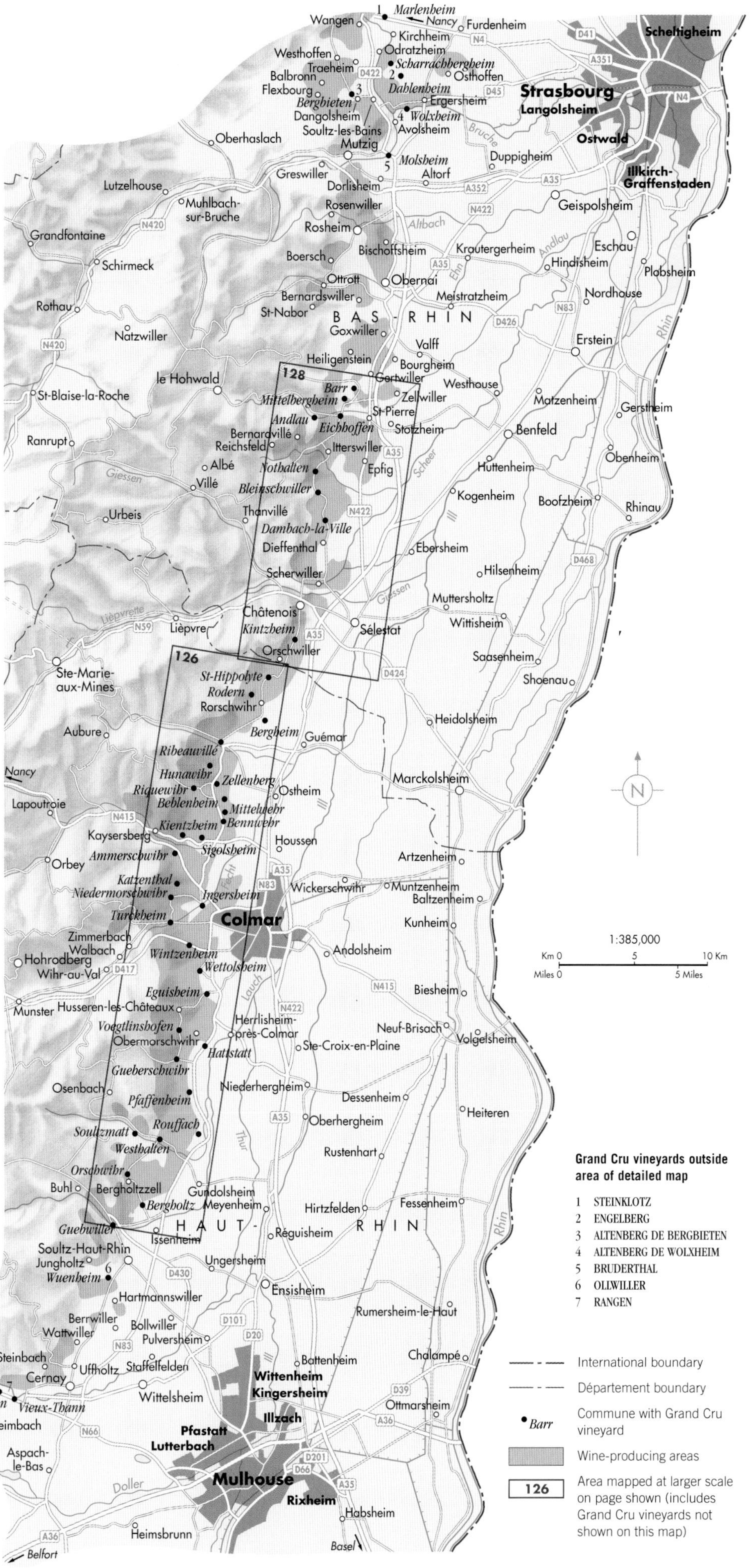

Grand Cru vineyards outside area of detailed map

1 STEINKLOTZ
2 ENGELBERG
3 ALTENBERG DE BERGBIETEN
4 ALTENBERG DE WOLXHEIM
5 BRUDERTHAL
6 OLLWILLER
7 RANGEN

International boundary

Département boundary

• Barr   Commune with Grand Cru vineyard

Wine-producing areas

126   Area mapped at larger scale on page shown (includes Grand Cru vineyards not shown on this map)

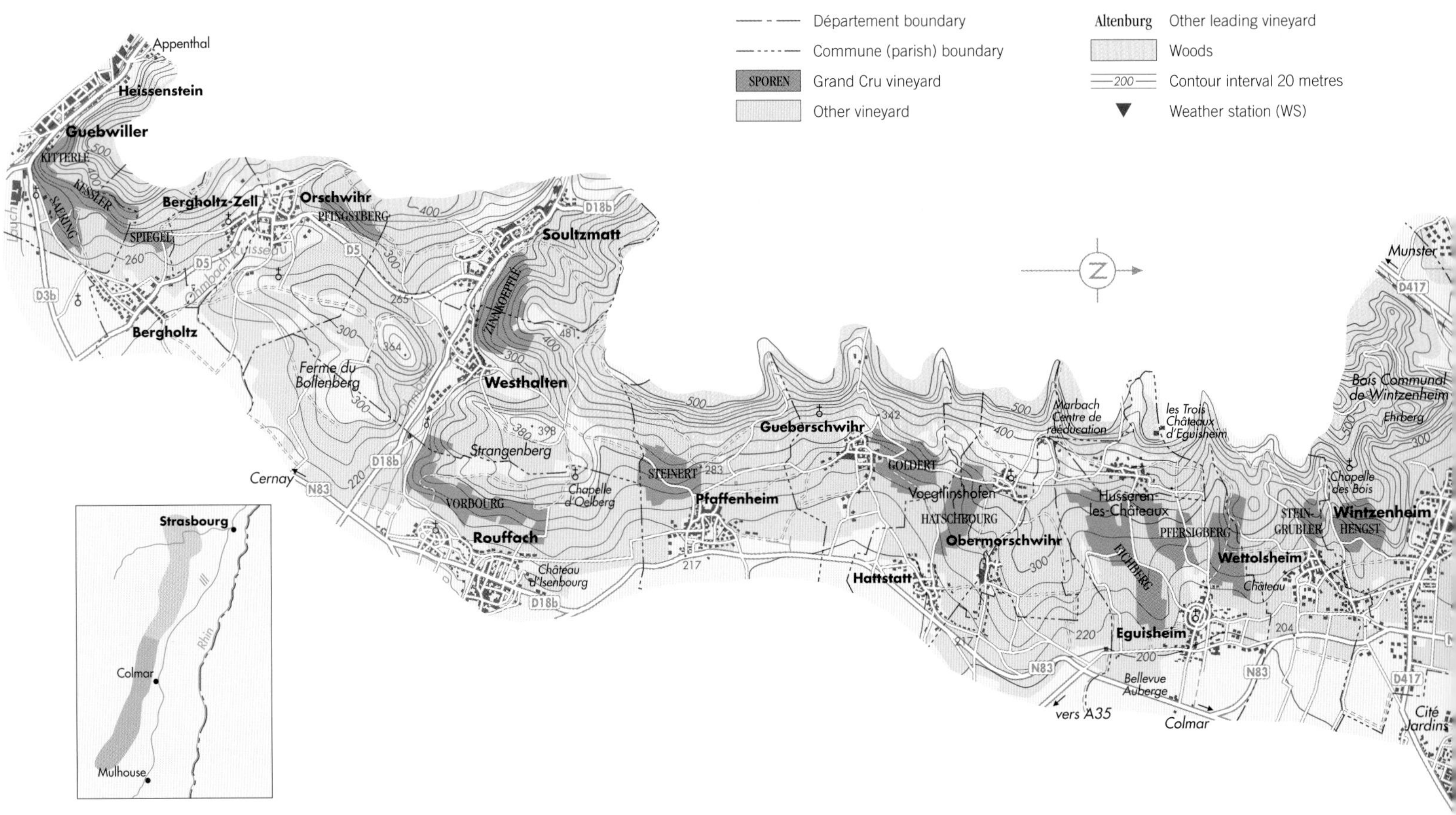

Map legend:
- ───·─── Département boundary
- ───·····─── Commune (parish) boundary
- SPOREN Grand Cru vineyard
- Other vineyard
- Altenburg Other leading vineyard
- Woods
- ──200── Contour interval 20 metres
- ▼ Weather station (WS)

Map labels include: Appenthal, Heissenstein, Guebwiller, KITTERLE, KESSLER, SAERING, SPIEGEL, Bergholtz-Zell, PFINGSTBERG, Orschwihr, Bergholtz, Ferme du Bollenberg, ZINNKOEPFLE, Soultzmatt, Westhalten, Strangenberg, Cernay, Chapelle d'Oelberg, VORBOURG, Rouffach, Château d'Isenbourg, STEINERT, Pfaffenheim, Gueberschwihr, GOLDERT, Voegtlinshofen, HATSCHBOURG, Obermorschwihr, Hattstatt, Marbach Centre de rééducation, Husseren-les-Châteaux, les Trois Châteaux d'Eguisheim, PFERSIGBERG, FICHBERG, Eguisheim, Bellevue Auberge, vers A35, Colmar, Munster, Bois Communal de Wintzenheim, Ehrberg, Chapelle des Bois, STEIN-GRUBLER, HENGST, Wintzenheim, Wettolsheim, Cité Jardins

Inset map: Strasbourg, Colmar, Mulhouse, Rhin, Ill

Heart of Alsace

The map on these pages lays the heart of the Alsace vineyard on its side, making it directly comparable to the maps of the Côte d'Or. The north lies to the right. As in so many of the great wine regions of Europe, a range of east-facing foothills provides an ideal environment for the vine. Spurs and re-entrants offer extra shelter and a privileged sunwards tilt in places where the vines face east, southeast or south. A dense pine forest nearby can lower the average temperature of a vineyard by a full degree centigrade compared with one next to a planting of young oaks. Every nuance of the unfolding landscape is echoed in the alignment of the vine rows to catch each minute of sunlight.

And Alsace is sunny. The high Vosges to the west are the secret of these vineyards, which lie along the mountain flank at an altitude of between 600 and 1,200ft (180 and 360m), in a green ribbon that is rarely more than a mile wide. The lorry drivers grinding their way up through Kaysersberg towards St-Dié invariably encounter a thick bank of clouds as they reach the crest of the Vosges, with clouds banking up to the west. The higher the mountains are, the drier the land they shelter from moist west winds. The map shows the central stretch of the Haut-Rhin vineyards, clustered under the wooded slopes to the north and south of the city of Colmar – where the mountains can keep the sky clear of clouds for weeks on end. In this protected climate classic firm Riesling thrives.

Ironically, the winegrowing conditions are so ideal that Alsace has been seen during long periods of its troubled history as a source of *vin ordinaire* or reliable blending material – rather as France once regarded Algeria. Hence the lack of a long-hatched hierarchy of the better and the best vineyards in the manner of the Côte d'Or.

Instead the modern wine industry developed through the enterprise of farmers (many of them working land that has been in the family since the 17th century) turning merchant and branding their own and their neighbours' wines, distinguishing them only by their grapes. Such famous names as Hugel, Dopff, Trimbach, Humbrecht, Becker, Kuehn, or Muré are the result. Alsace also had France's first co-operative cellar, in 1895, and such co-operatives as Eguisheim, Kientzheim, Beblenheim, and Westhalten rank high among some of the better producers today.

The newish Grand Cru appellation (see page 124), an attempt to designate the best vineyards, is a change in emphasis which is not without its problems. The Grands Crus, marked on the map in violet, are slowly changing the way Alsace wines are perceived. Their restricted yields and increased levels of ripeness offer at least theoretically a higher quality level. They should promote the wines from being a mere varietal (an expression of a grape) to enjoying appellation status in the fullest sense: the specific linkage of terroir and grape variety based on soil, situation and – up to a point – tradition.

But the Alsace wine trade has until recently been organized to sell individual combinations of brands and varieties rather than shared vineyards, whose exact boundaries are the subject of much dispute anyway. The most famous names outside the region such as Hugel and

Some of Alsace's finest *producers are represented here, from the large merchant houses of Trimbach and Hugel to such a passionate individualist as Deiss. The wines vary enormously in sweetness with Sélection des Grains Nobles being even richer and more sumptuous than a Vendange Tardive.*

Latitude / Altitude of WS **47.55° / 689ft (210m)**
Mean July temp at WS **66.4°F (19.1°C)**
Annual rainfall at WS **23in (590mm)**
Harvest month rainfall at WS **September: 2.4in (60mm)**
Chief viticultural hazards **Soil erosion,
occasional drought**
Principal grapes **Riesling, Gewurztraminer,
Pinot Gris, Pinot Noir**

Right The walled medieval
village of Riquewihr is one
of the region's prettiest
and a Mecca for tourists.
The Schoenenbourg
vineyards in the
foreground are much
better for the aromatic
Riesling than the lower
Sporen vineyards on
the far left.

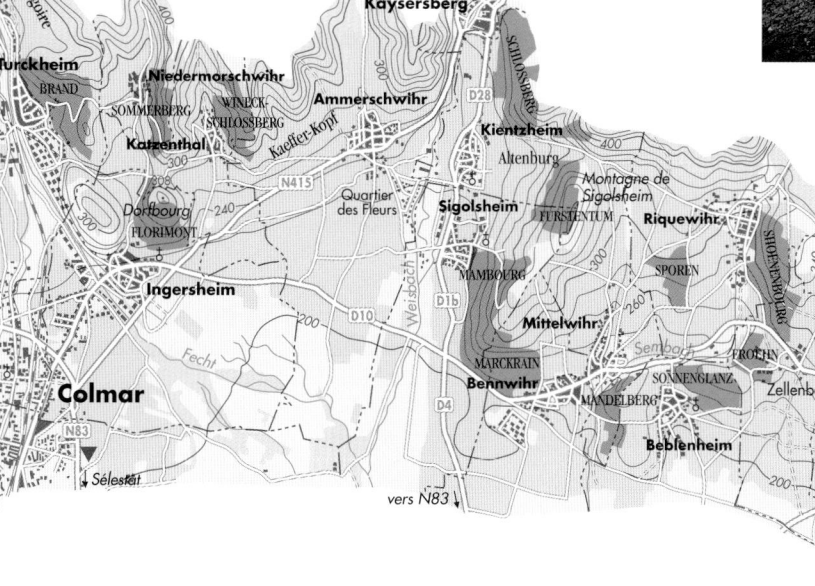

Trimbach are merchants first and growers second. This emphasis on individual vineyards has the effect of transferring power from the merchants to the growers and has not, therefore, been universally welcomed.

The decrees will eventually stipulate which of the noble grapes may be grown in each Grand Cru (and only one may appear on each label). Some sites are deemed best for Riesling, others for Gewurztraminer, Pinot Gris or occasionally Muscat, but blends, even magnificent blends such as Marcel Deiss's from the Altenberg vineyard, are (so far) officially outlawed, as are Sylvaner and Pinot Noir (although special cases such as Zotzenberg, see overleaf, can be pleaded). Eventually many growers will have to switch varieties to conform.

Some site/variety associations are already well in place, usually on the basis of growing and tasting experience, which often turns out to have some geological link.

At Guebwiller at the southern end of this stretch of vineyards, for example, the sandstone of Kitterlé is famous for its luscious wines from a range of grape varieties, particularly those grown by Schlumberger. Just north of here at Westhalten the more limestone slope of Zinnkoepflé faces due south and concentrates Gewurztraminer and Riesling to new heights, whereas the marls and sandstone of the southeast-facing Vorbourg at Rouffach have a particular affinity for Muscat.

Hatschbourg at Voegtlingshofen is a splendid vineyard of marl and limestone ripening dense-textured Pinot Gris and Gewurztraminer, like Goldert next door. Eichberg at Eguisheim grows fine Gewurztraminer and Riesling on marl and sandstone while Hengst at Wintzenheim is famous for the same varieties.

The granite underpinnings of the Vosges produce Rieslings with extra richness when they influence vineyards such as Turckheim's Brand and Kientzheim's Schlossberg. At Riquewihr the clay marls of Schoenenbourg also produce glorious Riesling, although the clays of the Sporen south of the village are more suitable for Gewurztraminer. At Bergheim the mixed-soil Altenberg (the name of no fewer than three different Grands Crus) is a superb all-rounder.

But some producers, especially those with a certain reputation, eschew the Grand Cru system. The finest Riesling in Alsace, some would say the world, is grown in Trimbach's Clos Ste-Hune within the Rosacker Grand Cru above Hunawihr. The word Rosacker is never mentioned on the label because the Trimbachs do not believe that the rest of this mainly limestone vineyard matches Clos Ste-Hune in quality.

Indeed, the word Clos, signifying a self-contained vineyard often within another, can be shorthand for quality, as in Domaine Weinbach's Clos des Capucins just in front of the Fallers' house in Kientzheim; Muré's Clos St-Landelin within the Vorbourg vineyard; and Zind-Humbrecht's Clos Hauserer near the Hengst Grand Cru; Clos Jebsal near Turckheim; Clos St-Urbain in Thann's Grand Cru Rangen (on the map on page 125); and Clos Windsbuhl near Hunawihr.

But while the concepts of the Grand Cru and Clos appeal to many winemakers, others may produce equally fine selections simply as *cuvées* of their best grapes. Alsace, it seems, will always be in dispute.

Not that the casual tourist will feel anything but pampered. A signposted Route des Vins takes a meandering course the whole length of the Alsace wine country, calling at some of the prettiest wine towns in the world. The richest possible operatic Gothick is the standard architecture here: overhanging gables, flower-filled courtyards, well-heads and cobbles, leaded lights and carved beams survive en masse in many of the villages. Riquewihr and Kaysersberg are the most beautiful. The city of Colmar, the capital of Alsace, has a magnificent collection of timber-framed houses which date from the 15th century.

Between the settlements the high-trained vines block out the view along the narrow lanes, until you reach a ridge and suddenly see the gleaming green sea rolling against the mountains before and behind, disappearing in a haze in the distance.

Bas-Rhin

The villages mapped on the previous two pages are all in the Haut-Rhin, but north of Orschwiller is the Alsace's other, less famous département, Bas-Rhin. "Bas" has no connotation of being lower in quality here – it refers only to the area's location lower down the Rhine. Indeed the growers of the Bas-Rhin claim that their wines, while being less obvious and rich than those of the Haut-Rhin, are no less fragrant and can be decidedly more elegant.

Here the peaks of the Vosges are not so high and their climatic protection from the rain less marked. The proportion of Vendange Tardive and Sélection des Grains Nobles wines is markedly lower in the Bas-Rhin than the Haut-Rhin, but there is no shortage of fine sites in this northern half of Alsace. Only the southern half of Bas-Rhin's wine country is mapped below; for the northern half see the map on page 125. The Grands Crus are marked on this map in violet.

The most southerly Grand Cru mapped below is Praelatenberg between Orschwiller and Kintzheim, its granitic soils being particularly suitable for Riesling – just like the Schlossberg vineyard in the confusingly similarly named Kientzheim on the previous page.

Similarly, the granite of the Vosges Mountains which hug the western edge of the village influences the vineyards around Dambach-la-Ville, Bas-Rhin's most important wine centre. Wines made here are noticeably dry and firm and Riesling can age magnificently in Alsace's uniquely steely fashion. Frankstein is Dambach's extensive, possibly too extensive, Grand Cru.

Muenchberg is the next notable Grand Cru to the north. Overlooking Nothalten, its volcanic sandstone base makes it a Bas-Rhin counterpart to the Grand Cru Rangen in Thann at the southern end of the map of Alsace on page 125. Riesling and Pinot Gris can have an explosive intensity here too, especially in the hands of such a passionate winemaker as André Ostertag.

Zotzenberg north of Mittelbergheim has long been famous for the splendid quality of age-worthy wine produced by its old Sylvaner vines. It may prove the first official exception to the four varieties officially embraced by the Grand Cru regulations, although some Zotzenberg Sylvaner has already been replaced by the approved Riesling and Gewurztraminer.

At the northern limit of this map is Barr's Kirchberg Grand Cru in which Klipfel in particular grows exceptionally good Gewurztraminer.

Bas-Rhin is clearly good hunting ground for those seeking less famous but reliable producers and vineyards of Alsace.

Well to the west of Alsace lies the Côtes de Toul appellation, which makes exceptionally light white and pink, or *gris*, wines from Pinot Noir, Gamay, and Auxerrois.

Some of the Bas-Rhin's *best producers include the two iconoclasts Marc Kreydenweiss and André Ostertag, some of whose wines are so atypical of the Alsace region they have had difficulty being accepted by the Appellation Contrôlée authorities.*

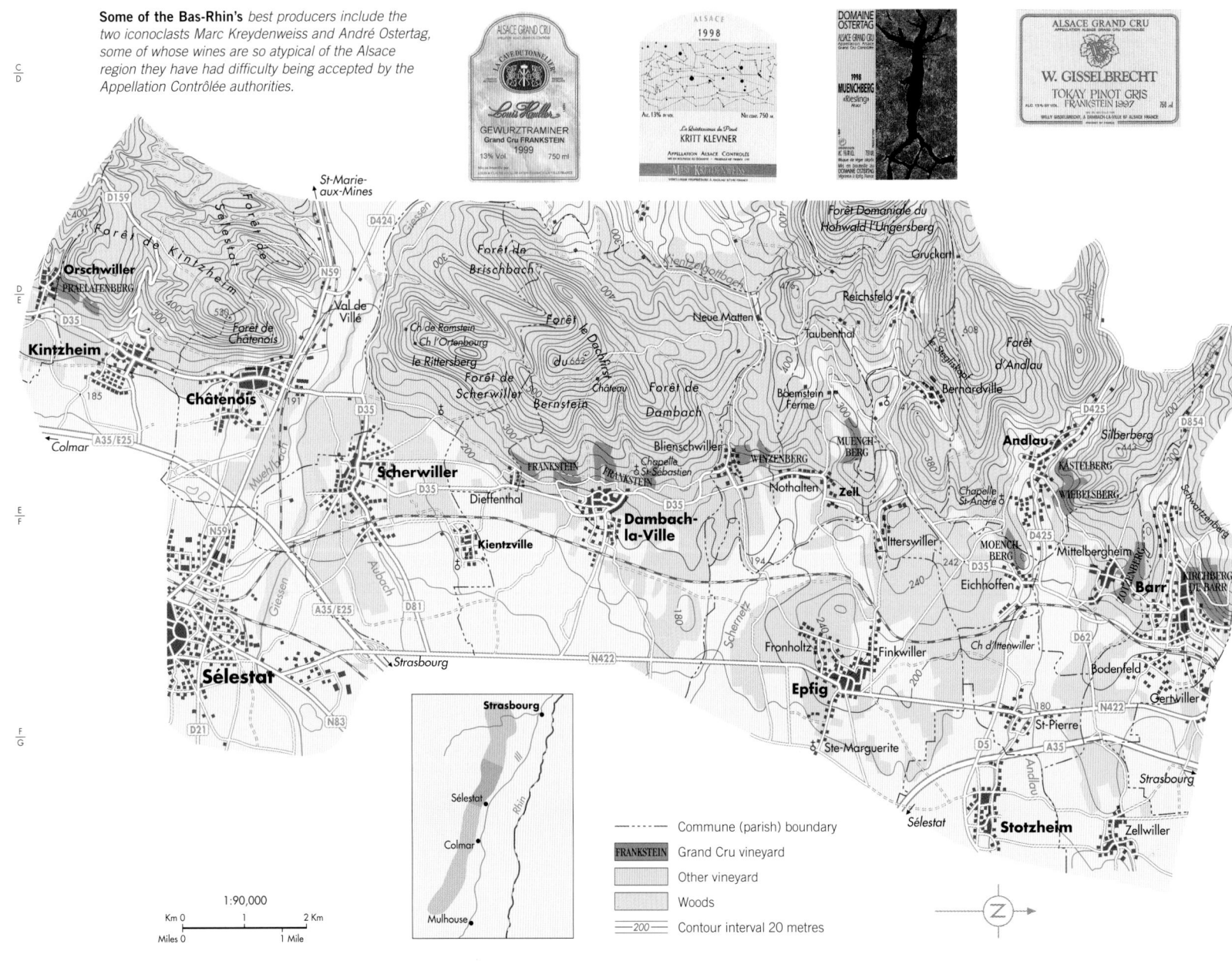

Northern Rhône

The valley of the Loire and the valley of the Rhône are two sides of the same coin. They contain respectively the best of northern and the best of southern French viticulture. Most Loire wine is white, most Rhône red. In each case there is a wide variety of wine styles but they all have something in common; in the case of the Rhône, substance.

Rhône red wines vary from the intensely concentrated and tannic, ruby-black or purple-black in youth, to relatively simple but solid alcoholic fruit juice. The best have depth, length, and mature to lingering harmony comparable to the greatest wines of Bordeaux. White wines are in the minority and tend to headiness, but thanks to much-improved winemaking can now be as notable as all but the best of the red.

The vineyards around the Rhône Valley fall naturally into two groups: the north (*septentrionale*, as the French call it), with less than a tenth of total production, almost all fine wine, and the much more diverse south (*méridionale*), where the landscape is quite different. In the course of the Rhône as it flows from Switzerland through France, the country changes from oak forest, where the vine shares the fields with peach trees and nut trees, to the herbal scrub and olive groves of Provence. A quick comparison of the rainfall (see factfiles on pages 130 and 135) in the two regions is enough to explain why the northern Rhône is so much greener and less Mediterranean than the south. The break comes at about Montélimar where for a short stretch the vine is absent from the broad valley.

In the north the vine perches on terraced cliffs of crumbling granite wherever the best

exposure to the sun can be found. The grape of the northern Rhône is Syrah, alias Shiraz. But the northern Rhône can also boast three highly distinctive and increasingly fashionable white wine grapes – Marsanne, Roussanne, and Viognier – even if they make relatively little wine in total.

On the following pages the best areas of the northern and southern Rhône are mapped in detail. Côte Rôtie, Condrieu, and Hermitage, the most majestic Rhône wines, all belong in the northern sector. Around them lie several others of strong local character, long traditions and evolving reputations.

Cornas, for example, is the stubborn country cousin to the noble Hermitage, made of the same Syrah grapes grown on granite and with just as much authority and power, if less finesse. The appellation today is reduced to a mere 225 acres (90ha) of steep terraces, the problem being a lack of young, enthusiastic vine-growers – unusual for France (especially the Rhône) these days. Jean-Luc Colombo and his experiments with heavy oaking, and the venerable Auguste Clape are perhaps the most famous Cornas producers, but Thierry Allemand and Paul Jaboulet Aîné also produce some fine bottlings, the latter having acquired some prime vineyard land on the retirement of a small-holder, a common modern phenomenon.

The temptation to stretch a good name to bursting point has overtaken St-Joseph, the west-bank appellation to the north of Cornas which now stretches almost 25 miles (40km) from Glun to the village of Condrieu (with considerable land to the north allowed to produce both St-Joseph and Condrieu). Until 1969 it was

a group of six communes, of which Mauves, which has very similar granitic soils to the hill of Hermitage across the river, was arguably the best. Since 1969 St-Joseph has been allowed to expand into a total of 45 communes, and to grow from 240 to over 2,100 acres (850ha). A St-Joseph should be the sappiest, fastest-maturing North Rhône red without losing its Syrah nerve, but too much St-Joseph today is grown not on the steep granite banks of the river but on the much cooler plateau. Such wines are difficult to distinguish from a northern Côtes du Rhône, the catch-all appellation of the Rhône Valley which applies to 50 communes north of Montélimar (and 113 in the south). The names of the original six communes, Glun, Mauves, Tournon, St-Jean-de-Muzols, Lemps, and Vion, together with Chavanay in Condrieu country to the north, remain pointers to the best wines. From these two enclaves come fine, sometimes vineyard-designated, wines made by the likes of Jean-Louis Chave, Stephan Montez, Chapoutier, and Jean-Louis Grippat. St-Joseph also produces one of the Rhône's least-known but most persuasive and food-friendly whites, often better than its red, from the Hermitage grapes Marsanne and Roussanne.

Champagne method wines seem somehow out of place in this rustic, southern environment. But St-Péray, south of Cornas, has an old name for its heavyweight, golden sparkling (and sometimes still) wine made from Roussanne and Marsanne grapes. On the River Drôme, off the map to the east, totally different grapes (Clairette and Muscat) respectively make two different styles of sparkling wine: substantial Crémant de Die and featherlight, grapey Clairette de Die Tradition (so called even though Clairette may not account for more than 30% of the blend with Muscat). Light, still wines are sold locally as Châtillon-en-Diois.

The narrowness of the northern Rhône Valley has limited any expansion of the most venerable appellations here, but some growers are experimenting with areas not blessed with AC status. Some of the more energetic producers of Côte Rôtie and Condrieu (see opposite) have sought out specially favoured spots on the opposite bank of the river for recent plantings. The produce of these vineyards outside the approved areas must be sold as Vins de Pays, in this case often des Collines Rhodaniennes (see the map on page 151). Similarly, well-financed producers from further north such as Louis Latour of Beaune and Georges Duboeuf of Beaujolais are capitalizing, with keenly priced Vins de Pays, on the potential and low land prices of the Coteaux de l'Ardèche.

Rhône: Valence

Latitude / Altitude of WS **44.55˚ / 525ft (160m)**
Mean July temp at WS **72.5˚F (22.5˚C)**
Annual rainfall at WS **33in (840mm)**
Harvest month rainfall at WS **September: 5in (130mm)**
Chief viticultural hazards **Poor weather at flowering, fungal diseases**
Principal grapes **Syrah, Viognier**

– – – Département boundary

▨ Côte Rôtie

▨ Château Grillet

▨ Condrieu

▨ Condrieu/St-Joseph

▨ St-Joseph

▨ Hermitage

▨ Crozes-Hermitage

▨ Cornas

▨ St-Péray

▨ Côtes du Rhône

▨ Coteaux du Tricastin

131 Area mapped at larger scale on page shown

▼ Weather station (WS)

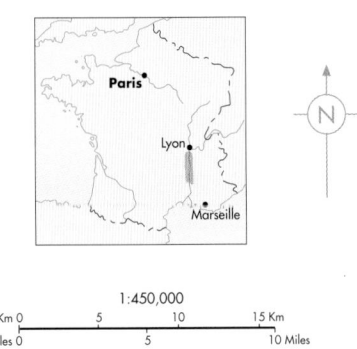

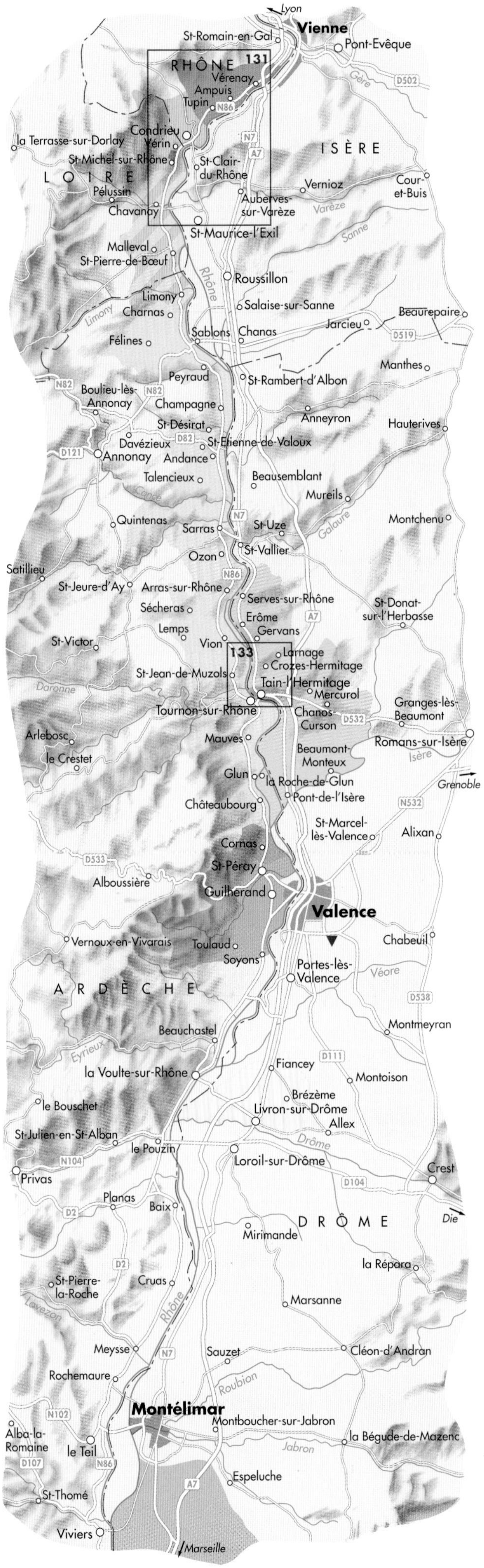

1:450,000

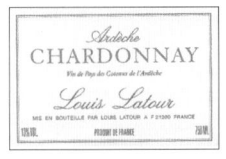

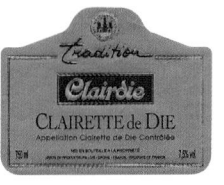

Some of the best wines made in the northern Rhône outside the classic appellations detailed on the next three pages. The Louis Latour Chardonnay is made southwest of Valence in the Ardèche département while Clairette de Die is made southeast of the town well off the map. (See map on page 53.)

Côte Rôtie and Condrieu

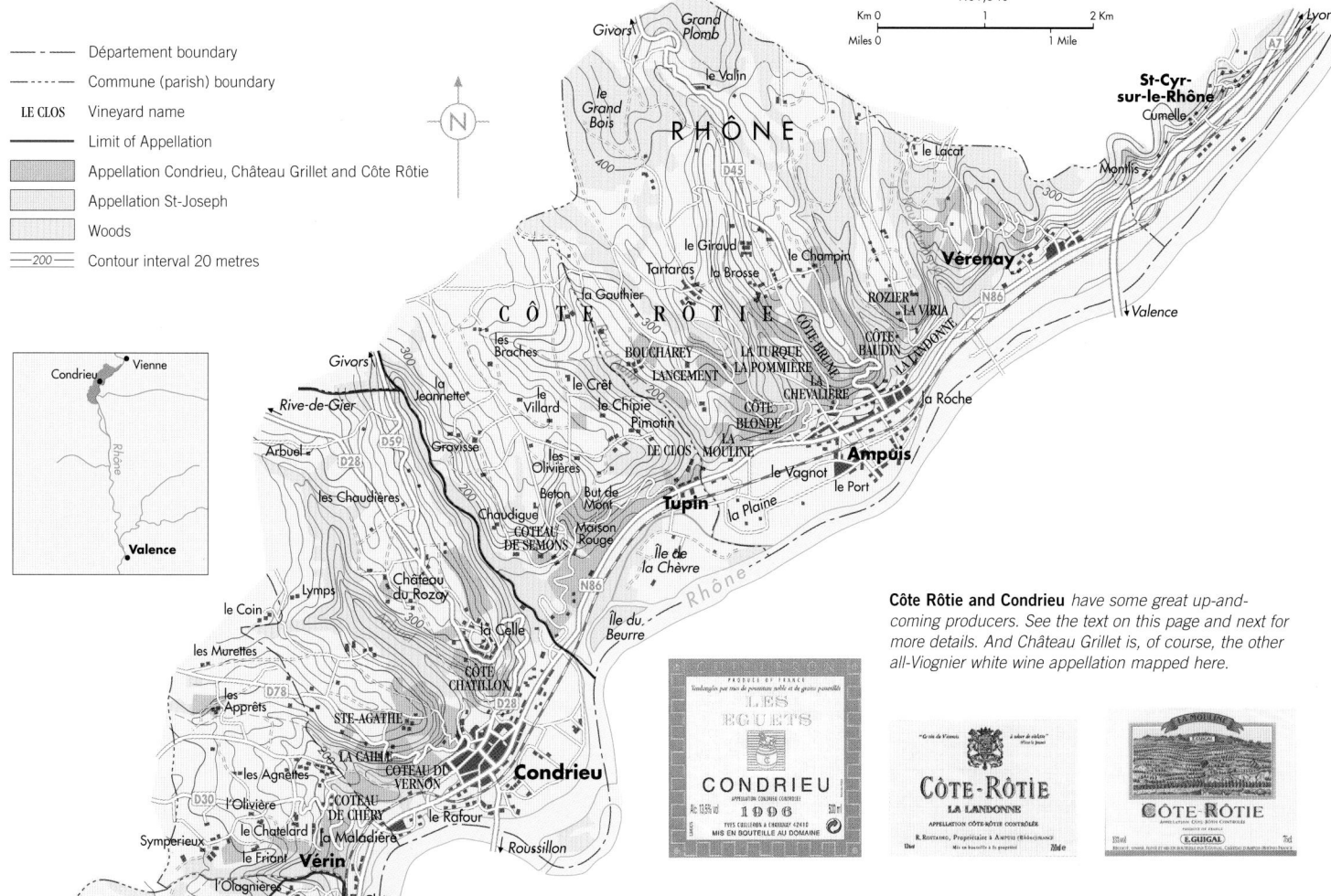

Côte Rôtie and Condrieu *have some great up-and-coming producers. See the text on this page and next for more details. And Château Grillet is, of course, the other all-Viognier white wine appellation mapped here.*

C ôte Rôtie's ribbon of vineyards, hugging the granite western walls of the valley at Ampuis in perilous terraces, have only recently known worldwide fame. Until the spotlight picked out the single-minded Marcel Guigal and his exceptional wines in the 1980s, Côte Rôtie was an insider's wine, astonishing all who discovered it with its magical soft-fruity finesse, southern in warmth but closer to a great red burgundy in the way firm tannin supported delicate flavours.

Côte Rôtie is certainly Roman or earlier in origin. Up to the 19th century its wine was sold by the *vase* of 76 litres, the measure of a double amphora. It long maintained its almost secret niche as one of France's greatest wines. When this Atlas was first published, in 1971, its total was only 173 acres (70ha) and dwindling. Its price barely justified the hard work. The world has since "discovered" it, prices have risen steeply, and in 30 years the vineyards have more than tripled to 495 acres (200ha), definitively overtaking Hermitage, supposedly the most famous Rhône wine.

As the name implies, this southeast-facing slope (so steep that gradients can reach 60% in places) is indeed roasted (*rôtie*) in summer. Many parts of this strip of vineyards barely 1,640ft (500m) wide are exposed to the sun all day. The stony schist from which these riverside plots are hewn retains every degree of heat (which is why newer plantings on the plateau above rarely ripen anything like as fully).

Just how far north and south true Côte Rôtie extends has been disputed for centuries, but all are agreed that the original vineyards are centred on the two most obvious slopes above Ampuis, the Côte Blonde, comprising many different plots of sandy/slaty soil with a pale limestone element, and the equally extensive Côte Brune to the north, whose heavier clay is darkened by iron and whose wines are traditionally harder. Being equal in quality but not in style, their wines were in the past blended by merchants to produce a unified Côte Rôtie. But today the fashion is for vineyard-designated bottlings, a trend accelerated by the dominant figure in the appellation, the perfectionist Marcel Guigal. By bottling separately wines labelled La Mouline (Côte Blonde), La Landonne and La Turque (Côte Brune), after ageing them in new oak for up to 42 months, he has come as close as any grower to creating a new Romanée-Conti. These are wines for millionaires, impressed by power and pungency, but not always for lovers of the classic gentle Côte Rôtie, matured in barrels that are themselves mature. They might be more satisfied by the likes of Gangloff, Ogier, and Rostaing's Côte Blonde bottling.

The picture is further complicated by the divergence between the names on Guigal labels, the most famous names of Côte Rôtie,

Hermitage

and those on local maps. The toughest of all Guigal's wines La Landonne, also bottled by René Rostaing, is the only one that is an officially recognised plot. La Mouline is a sumptuous, velvety monster produced from some of the southernmost vineyards of Ampuis just north of the commune of Tupin. La Turque is high above the centre of Ampuis, while the bottling under Guigal's more recently acquired Château d'Ampuis label is a blend from six quite different vineyards, all of them around Ampuis but well south of La Landonne.

If the traditional description of the style of Côte Rôtie differs quite markedly from current reality, so do the grapes that go into it. Practically every textbook refers to the fact that Côte Rôtie producers may add up to 20% of white Viognier grapes to the Syrah on which the wine depends. In practice, most Côte Rôtie produced today is made exclusively from Syrah.

The extraordinarily heady, recognizably perfumed Viognier grape is the speciality of the even smaller appellation of Condrieu into which the Côte Rôtie vineyards merge, where schist and mica give way to granite. Many of the local growers make both of these sought-after white and red wines, much as the bigger merchants would like to acquire their wines or, preferably, their vineyards.

Among the top producers of classical, fragrant, almost exclusively dry Condrieu are Georges Vernay with his Coteau du Vernon, Pierre Dumazet, André Perret, and Guigal who now produces a de luxe bottling, La Doriane, from grapes grown on the Côte Chatillon and Colombier vineyards. Younger, equally ambitious producers who have been experimenting with late-picked and oaked versions include Yves Cuilleron, Yves Gangloff, Robert Niéro, and François Villard.

All this creative energy demands vineyards and Condrieu, too, has been growing, from barely 30 acres (12ha) in the 1960s to over 240 (98ha) at the turn of the century. New sites are not always in the awkward inaccessible spots where the finicky Viognier vine flourishes – not least because, in order to produce an economic crop level, it should be sheltered from the cool, north wind at flowering time. The most favoured vineyards in Condrieu tend to have a powdery, mica-rich topsoil called locally *arzelle* and they include Coteau de Chéry, Chanson, Côte Bonnette, and Les Eguets.

The best Viognier of all, theoretically, is Chateau Grillet: 9.4 acres (3.8ha) in a privileged amphitheatre of vines with its own appellation – reflected more in its price than its current quality. These wines combine alcoholic power with a haunting but surprisingly fragile aroma and are some of the very few luxury-priced whites that should be drunk young.

Yes, the renowned hill of Hermitage really is as tiny as the map below right suggests! And, unlike appellations to the north, expansion is limited by long-standing decree. France's main north-south artery the Rhône, and its accompanying roads and railway, snakes under its narrow terraces, making the vineyard's magnificent stance looking south down the river above Tain (as shown below) familiar to millions.

The slopes of Hermitage, which was an extension of the Massif Central until the river burrowed a course round its western rather than eastern flank, amount to just 331 acres (134ha) of terraced granite. The slopes, which face due south, are not quite as steep as those of Côte Rôtie but still steep enough to outlaw mechanization, and make repairing the ravages of erosion a back-breaking annual task. The topsoil that slides down the hill after heavy storms is made up largely of decomposed flint and limestone, especially in the central and eastern parts away from the river.

A hundred years ago this imposing hill's *climats* were named beside Château Lafite and Romanée-Conti as among the best red wines of the world. Writing in the 19th century, the wine merchant A Jullien listed them in order of merit: Méal, Gréfieux, Beaume, Raucoule, Muret, Guoignière, Bessas, Burges, and Lauds. Spellings have changed but the *climats* remain and, although Hermitage is typically, and possibly ideally, a blend from several different *climats*, their names are seen on an increasing proportion of wine labels as the urge to get to grips with individual vineyard characteristics takes hold of both producers and consumers.

In general the lightest, most aromatic red wines, all from Syrah, come from Beaumes, Les Diognières, and L'Hermite, beside the chapel on top of the hill after which Jaboulet's famous Hermitage is named. Within L'Hermite is a parcel of ancient and deceptively straggly vines from which Chapoutier makes its exceptionally concentrated Pavillon Ermitage (using the old spelling). Firmer and more complex wines come from Péléat and Les Rocoules. Les Gréffieux, in which Chapoutier has the largest holding, Le Méal, and both Les Bessards tend to produce the most tannic and longest-lived wines.

The adjective "manly" has stuck to Hermitage ever since it was first applied to it (even if in recent years the supposedly feminine Côte Rôtie seems to have taken a dose of testosterone). Hermitage, once used extensively to strengthen fine red Bordeaux, has almost the qualities of port without the added brandy. Like vintage port Hermitage throws a heavy sediment in, often onto, the bottle (it needs decanting) and improves for many years until its scent and flavour are almost overwhelming.

Young Hermitage of a good vintage is as closed and tannic as any young great red, but nothing can restrain its abounding perfume and the fistfuls of fruit that seem crammed into the glass. As it ages the immediacy of its impact does not diminish, but its youthful assault gives way to the sheer splendour of its mature presence. You could not drink it and fail to be impressed.

Right The famous chapel on the hill of Hermitage has been renovated. It looks down on some of the granite hill's most favoured vines and the River Rhône flanked by no shortage of industry around Tain l'Hermitage and Tournon, its twin town across the river.

Unlike the appellations of Condrieu and Côte Rôtie to the north, Hermitage has long been fashionable. Most of the available land is therefore planted and there has been little opportunity to extend the vineyard area. The appellation is dominated by just four producers: Chave, based across the river in Mauves, and the large merchant houses Chapoutier, Jaboulet, and the smaller Delas whose names, aimed at all that traffic below, adorn the walls that prop up their terraces.

But there has been another opportunity for enthusiastic newcomers to this wine area, joined by an increasing number of local producers keen to bottle the fruit of their own labours rather than sell it to the co-operative. Like most great wines Hermitage has its shadow. Crozes-Hermitage is to the Grand Cru what a village Gevrey-Chambertin is to Le Chambertin. Crozes, the village round the back of the hill, gives its name to an appellation that extends almost ten miles (16km) both north and south of Tain and Hermitage itself, including about 250 acres (100ha) of vineyard, only a fraction of them mapped here (see the map on page 130).

Until quite recently only one Crozes wine, Paul Jaboulet's Domaine de Thalabert made in one of Crozes' most successful areas just north of Beaumont Monteux, was regularly comparable to a Hermitage and much of the rest was pallid stuff. Today, however, we can choose from two basic styles – one full of youthful blackcurrant fruit for early drinking and the other, more serious bottlings that mimic the mass of Hermitage and can be kept for up to ten years.

Growers such as Alain Graillot, Albert Belle, Domain Pochon, and Domaine du Colombier led the way but new merchants such as Tardieu Laurent and the Tain co-operative are also responsible for some admirable bottlings.

Some of the best Crozes-Hermitage is white, and the Hermitage hill was historically almost as famous for its white wine, from Roussanne and, particularly, Marsanne grapes which even today account for about a quarter of the Hermitage vines. Jullien named "Raucoule" as the best vineyard for white Hermitage and it is still known for the aroma of its whites. Today Chante-Alouette is the best-known name. Besides being a vineyard (though not one that is named on the traditional maps of Hermitage), it is a trademark of Chapoutier and a thoroughly remarkable, often misunderstood wine. Golden, dry, and full with a remarkably delicate, eventually nutty flavour, it has to mature, like red Hermitage, for a decade at least.

Another white wine has been resurrected here recently. The extraordinary sweet *vin de paille* of Hermitage is made in tiny quantities in very ripe years by the likes of Chave and Chapoutier, from grapes that are traditionally shrivelled on straw (*paille*) mats.

Hermitage is a small appellation but its wines can be red, sweet white vin de paille and dry white as long-lived as Chapoutier's Chante-Alouette. The red label is for Chave's Ermitage Cuvée Cathelin, which is made only in exceptional vintages.

- - - Département boundary

le Méal   Noted vineyard

Appellation Hermitage Contrôlée

Appellation Crozes-Hermitage Contrôlée

Woods

—200— Contour interval 10 metres

1:35,000

Km 0   1   2 Km

Miles 0   1 Mile

Southern Rhône

The funnel end of the Rhône Valley, where it releases its traffic to the Mediterranean, has a place in every traveller's affections. History and natural history combine to make it one of the richest regions of France for interests of every kind. Who cannot picture the vast engineering of the Romans, lizards alert on its slumbering stones, plots of early vegetables screened from the mistral, the pines and almonds yielding to olive groves in the far south – and always, on hillside or plain, sand or clay, the cross-stitch of vines?

These vines lie baking on broad terraces of smooth, round stones warmed by the sun, almost invariably a rich mix of varieties. In the south the dominant grape for red wines is the versatile Grenache, increasingly supplemented by Syrah and Mourvèdre. The heart of the region, the vineyard that sums up all its qualities, is Châteauneuf-du-Pape in which a grand total of 13 grapes are allowed, in theory at least (see overleaf). Around it is a cluster of villages with their own sweet, spicy story to tell, related by a swelling band of ambitious producers. The southern Rhône is also a region well picked over by the large merchant bottlers, whose produce varies just as widely as that of smaller domaines.

The most common appellation is Côtes du Rhône, a general one for the red, white or rosé of the Rhône Valley, encompassing more than 100,000 acres (40,000ha). Its annual crop can be three times as much as that of Beaujolais, and not very much less than all of Bordeaux.

Within this there is, of course, wide variation of quality and style, lighter soils and cooler climes

making lighter wines. Some Côtes du Rhône is extremely ordinary, but even this portmanteau appellation has its treasures, typically either the produce of one of the better merchants or the lesser wines of producers in grander appellations. The archetype was Château de Fonsalette from the same stable as Château Rayas, the great Châteauneuf-du-Pape. Coudoulet de Beaucastel is Château de Beaucastel's riposte. But there are achievers in outlying areas too, such as Domaine Gramenon near Grignan in the far north, or Domaine La Réméjeanne west of Bagnols-sur-Céze, Domaine Rouge Garance at St-Hilaire-d'Ozilhan, and the Estézargues co-operative, all in the Gard département.

Grenache must now account for at least 40% of all red Côtes du Rhône; its most usual but by no means only blending partners being Syrah and Mourvèdre. White and rosé wines account for just 2% of production apiece.

The Côtes du Rhône-Villages appellation is a very distinct step up, and one that can offer some of France's best value. Of the 95 communes eligible for the -Villages suffix, all of them in the south, the 16 best have the right to append their names to the already cumbersome moniker Côtes du Rhône-Villages. These favoured villages are marked in italics on this map and some of the best-known are mapped in detail overleaf. Others which have established some degree of fame outside their own region include Valréas, Vinsobres, Visan, and, on the right bank of the Rhône, Chusclan which, with nearby Laudun, has a reputation for fine rosés as well as reds. The two northernmost of

the Côtes du Rhône-Villages, Rousset-les-Vignes, and St-Pantaléon-les-Vignes, used to sell their wines as Haut-Comtat, a name little seen today.

Between these northern villages and the Rhône lies the up-and-coming appellation Coteaux du Tricastin in a parched mistral-swept landscape better known in the past for its truffles than its wine. Mourvèdre will not ripen so far from the Mediterranean so it is Cinsault that bolsters fruity Grenache and stiffening Syrah here. Even the best Coteaux du Tricastins need no more than two or three years' ageing.

Also promoted to AC status in 1973 and battling against higher altitudes and cooler conditions than most Côtes du Rhône is Côtes du Ventoux. The tradition here was for reds and rosés that were light in every way and lively when very young, but an increasing number of individual producers are now aiming for more substantial wines, and succeeding. The best-known label is La Vieille Ferme, an outpost of the renowned Château de Beaucastel of Châteauneuf-du-Pape.

On the right bank of the Rhône in the south of the Ardèche département is the Côtes du Vivarais, promoted to AC in 1999 (see the map of France on page 53). It makes wines rather like featherweight Côtes du Rhône from scattered, predominantly limestone, vineyards in conditions that are exceptionally cool for this torrid part of France.

The vineyards of the Costières de Nîmes, discussed and mapped with the Eastern Languedoc on pages 138-139, are in many ways a westward extension of southern Rhône.

  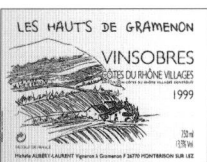  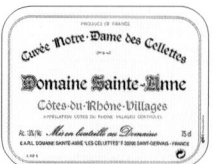 

Some of the many exciting wines *made in the southern Rhône outside the area shown in detail on the map overleaf. Côtes du Ventoux is a transitional area between Rhône and Provence.*

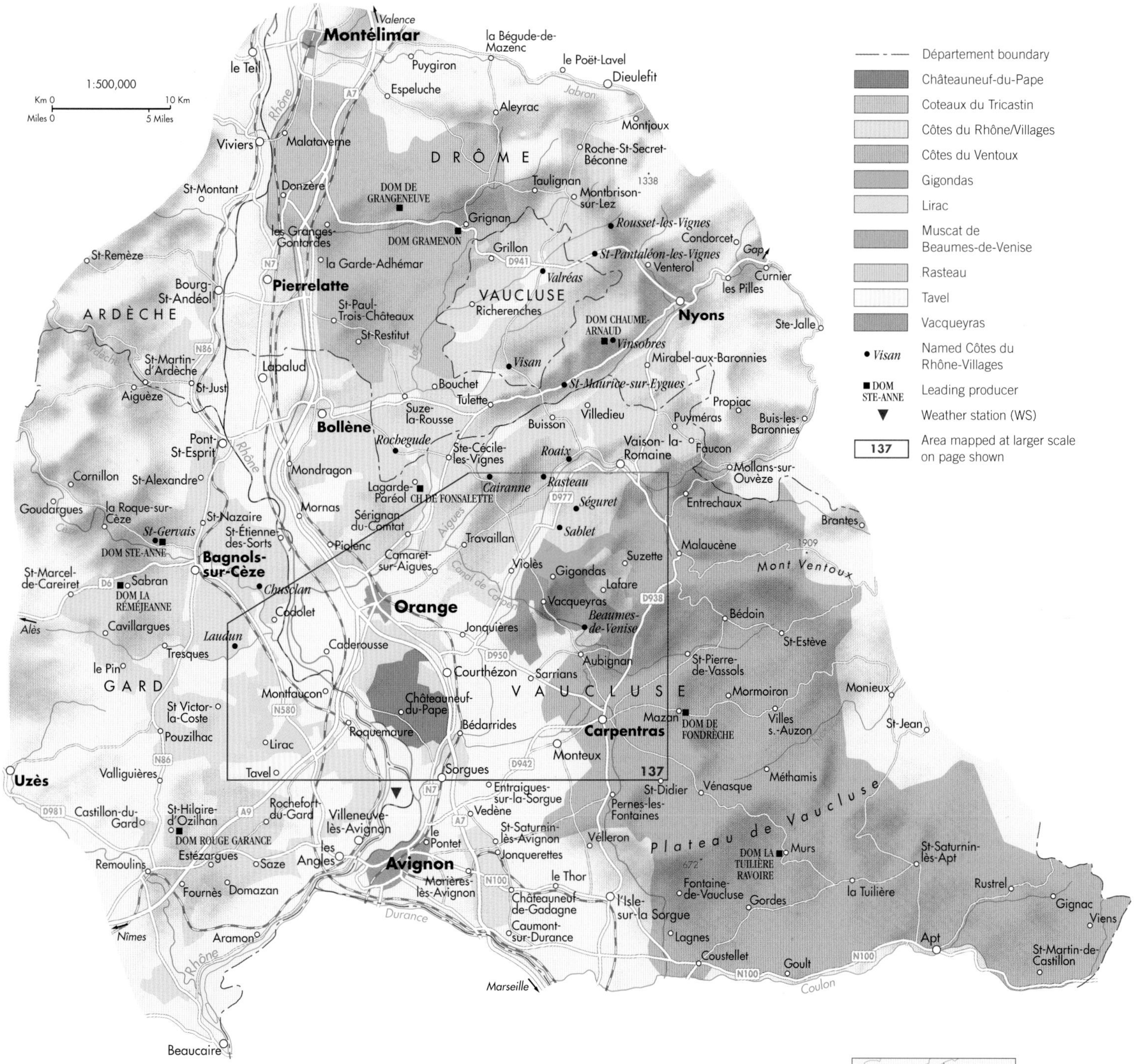

A/B

1:500,000

Km 0 ——— 10 Km
Miles 0 ——— 5 Miles

- - - Département boundary

Châteauneuf-du-Pape

Coteaux du Tricastin

Côtes du Rhône/Villages

Côtes du Ventoux

Gigondas

Lirac

Muscat de Beaumes-de-Venise

Rasteau

Tavel

Vacqueyras

• *Visan*   Named Côtes du Rhône-Villages

■ DOM STE-ANNE   Leading producer

▼   Weather station (WS)

137   Area mapped at larger scale on page shown

Valence
Montélimar
le Tell
Puygiron
la Bégude-de-Mazenc
le Poët-Laval
Dieulefit
Espeluche
Aleyrac
Montjoux
Roche-St-Secret-Béconne
Viviers
Malataverne
DRÔME
1338
St-Montant
Donzère
DOM DE GRANGENEUVE
Taulignan
Montbrison-sur-Lez
Grignan
Gap
les Granges-Gontardes
DOM GRAMENON
Grillon
• *Rousset-les-Vignes*
Condorcet
la Garde-Adhémar
• *St-Pantaléon-les-Vignes*
Curnier
ARDÈCHE
St-Remèze
Bourg-St-Andéol
N7
Pierrelatte
St-Paul-Trois-Châteaux
VAUCLUSE
Richerenches
Valréas
Venterol
les Pilles
Nyons
St-Martin-d'Ardèche
N86
St-Restitut
DOM CHAUME-ARNAUD
Ste-Jalle
Aiguèze
St-Just
Visan
Vinsobres
Mirabel-aux-Baronnies
Lapalud
Bouchet
Tulette
• *St-Maurice-sur-Eygues*
Pont-St-Esprit
Bollène
Suze-la-Rousse
Villedieu
Propiac
Puyméras
Buis-les-Baronnies
Cornillon
Rochegude
Buisson
St-Alexandre
Mondragon
Ste-Cécile-les-Vignes
Vaison-la-Romaine
Faucon
Goudargues
la Roque-sur-Cèze
Lagarde-Paréol CH. DE FONSALETTE
Roaix
Mollans-sur-Ouvèze
St-Gervais
St-Nazaire
Sérignan-du-Comtat
Cairanne
Rasteau
D977
Entrechaux
Brantes
DOM STE-ANNE
St-Étienne-des-Sorts
Travaillan
Séguret
Bagnols-sur-Cèze
Mornas
Piolenc
Sablet
Suzette
Malaucène
1909
St-Marcel-de-Careiret
Sabran
Chusclan
Camaret-sur-Aigues
Violès
Gigondas
Lafare
Mont Ventoux
Alès
DOM LA RÉMÉJEANNE
Codolet
Jonquières
Vacqueyras
D938
Bédoin
Cavillargues
Laudun
Orange
Beaumes-de-Venise
St-Estève
le Pin
Caderousse
D950
Aubignan
St-Pierre-de-Vassols
Mormoiron
Monieux
GARD
Montfaucon
Courthézon
Sarrians
VAUCLUSE
St-Jean
St-Victor-la-Coste
Pouzilhac
Châteauneuf-du-Pape
Bédarrides
Carpentras
Mazan
DOM DE FONDRÈCHE
Villes s.-Auzon
Valliguières
Lirac
Roquemaure
Monteux
137
Méthamis
Uzès
Tavel
Sorgues
D942
St-Didier
Vénasque
Castillon-du-Gard
St-Hilaire-d'Ozilhan
N7
Entraigues-sur-la-Sorgue
Pernes-les-Fontaines
D981
Rochefort-du-Gard
Villeneuve-lès-Avignon
Vedène
St-Saturnin-lès-Avignon
Velleron
Plateau de Vaucluse
St-Saturnin-lès-Apt
Remoulins
DOM ROUGE GARANCE
Estézargues
les Angles
le Pontet
Jonquerettes
672
Rustrel
Saze
Avignon
le Thor
l'Isle-sur-la-Sorgue
DOM LA TUILIÈRE RAVOIRE
Murs
Fournès
Domazan
Morières-lès-Avignon
N100
Fontaine-de-Vaucluse
Gordes
la Tuilière
Gignac
Aramon
Châteauneuf-de-Gadagne
Apt
Viens
Nîmes
Caumont-sur-Durance
Lagnes
Coustellet
St-Martin-de-Castillon
Durance
Goult
N100
Beaucaire
Marseille
Coulon

F/G

Rhône: Avignon

Latitude / Altitude of WS **44˚ / 164ft (50m)**
Mean July temp at WS **74˚F (23.3˚C)**
Annual rainfall at WS **24in (610mm)**
Harvest month rainfall at WS **September: 2.6in (65mm)**
Chief viticultural hazard **Drought**
Principal grapes **Grenache Noir, Syrah, Carignan, Cinsault, Mourvèdre**

Paris
Orange

Châteauneuf-du-Pape and environs

Châteauneuf-du-Pape, mapped here with its most famous neighbouring villages, is the renowned centrepiece of the southern Rhône, just north of Avignon on hills dominated by a ruined papal summer palace. The deep red wine of Châteauneuf has the distinction not only of having the highest minimum strength of any French wine (12.5% alcohol, which often in practice surpasses 14%) but of being the first to be so regulated. Its most famous grower, the late Baron Le Roy of Château Fortia, initiated here what has become the national system of Appellations Contrôlées. Part of his original proposal, made in 1923, was that suitable land for fine Châteauneuf vines would be that arid enough to support both lavender and thyme. In addition, grape varieties, pruning, quantity, and strength were to be strictly controlled and, unusually, unsatisfactory grapes eliminated before fermentation. The Baron's foresight was rewarded by Châteauneuf-du-Pape's emerging from obscurity to become world famous.

Some 110,000hl of wine a year are made here, 97% of it red but hugely variable in quality. Most is good to average; lightened in colour (not alcohol) by increasing the proportion of Grenache grapes so that it can be drunk after a mere year or two. A number of big estates, however, like Bordeaux châteaux, are the producers of the classic dark and deep Châteauneuf, each using its own cocktail of the 13 permitted grape varieties to make more or less spicy, more or less tannic or smooth, shorter- or longer-lived wine. Grenache is the backbone of the AC, often blended with Mourvèdre which needs a warm climate to ripen, and Syrah together with some Cinsault, Counoise (a local speciality), and small amounts of Vaccarèse, Picpoul Noir, Terret Noir, and the light-skinned Grenache Blanc, Clairette, Bourboulenc, Roussanne (which is much easier to grow in the southern than the northern Rhône), and the neutral Picardan. Only Château de Beaucastel persists with all of these.

Modern winemaking methods have given new interest to what had become a somewhat disillusioned appellation. Today, such estates as the Châteaux de Beaucastel and Rayas, Domaine du Vieux Télégraphe, Clos des Papes, and Château La Nerthe, which have standards as high as the best in France, have been joined by a host of sometimes idiosyncratic individuals such as Henri Bonneau, André Brunel at Les Cailloux, and the Férauds at Domaine du Pegau, whose limited edition bottlings appeal so much to the fine wine collector. Their reds, always rich and spicy but often tough in youth, can age to sumptuous, sometimes gamey, depths of flavour and their rare whites, succulent from an early age, develop exotic scents, occasionally reminiscent of orange peel, after seven or eight years. Many of the principal estates use heavy embossed bottles of dark glass which help to identify their wines.

The Châteauneuf-du-Pape cliché is the *galet*, the rounded, heat-absorbing stone found almost exclusively in some of its vineyards, but in reality soils within this relatively small area are much more varied than most wine drinkers realize. The famous vineyards of Rayas, for instance, have hardly any *galets* and quite a high proportion of clay. Wine produced on the predominantly north-facing vineyards between Mont-Redon and Orange tends to be lighter and more elegant with much softer tannins than those of hotter sites. The use of new wood and a proportion of Mourvèdre are other factors responsible for the extraordinary variation in style among Châteauneufs made today.

Châteauneuf-du-Pape is surrounded by more than 100 communities that produce Côtes du Rhône; those allowed to produce Côtes du Rhône-Villages are marked in magenta on the map. Some, however, have achieved even more glorified status, that of being awarded their own appellation. Gigondas, producing a tight-knit powerhouse of a red needing six or seven years' ageing from a hot bowl of vineyards beneath the much-painted Dentelles de Montmirail, rivals Châteauneuf-du-Pape itself. Ambitious producers such as Domaine de Santa Duc and Château de St-Cosme have successfully experimented with new oak (by no means the norm in the southern Rhône) while traditionalists such as Domaine de Cayron still make sumptuously heady wines.

Vacqueyras earned its own appellation in 1990 and, although generally more restrained than Gigondas, it can also offer the spice and herbs of the southern Rhône at a fair price. North of here, Cairanne and Rasteau have also proved themselves worthy of AC status, although all they can currently muster is Rasteau's appellation exclusively for its rather rustic Vins Doux Naturels (see page 142). Beaumes-de-Venise also produces such a wine, its own strong, sweet, golden Muscat.

The Côtes du Rhône-Villages wines are all characters worthy of closer study. Sablet, Valréas, St-Gervais, and Rochegude tend to be milder and ready to drink younger.

Rosé is the historic speciality of Tavel and Lirac, the two southernmost of the true Rhône appellations. The potent dry Grenache rosé of Tavel, orange-tinted after a year or two, has its fervent admirers – though it is best drunk before the orange tint appears. Tavel demonstrates that fame is no friend of progress. Lirac, formerly also best known for rosé, can be better value. With lower permitted yields, it inclines more today to softly fruity reds less dominated by Grenache than Tavel. Its whites are laden with a minimum of one third Clairette grapes.

Left The vineyards of Château Rayas, arguably the greatest Châteauneuf-du-Pape of all, look as unprepossessing as its idiosyncratically low-tech cellar, yet the wines can be superbly rich and satisfying.

The spread of appellations here reflects the extent of this map, way beyond the strict borders of the Châteauneuf-du-Pape appellation. Increasingly fine white wines, such as Château de Beaucastel's pioneering oaked Vieilles Vignes Roussanne, are also made.

Eastern Languedoc

The Languedoc is France's open back door, its melting pot, its link with the outside world. The boundary between the southern Rhône Valley and the eastern limit of the Languedoc is a disputed one, with increasingly good reason as the quality of wine made in the Languedoc's most easterly appellation Costières de Nîmes has improved so startlingly that many of its glossy Syrah- and Grenache-based wines bear a remarkable resemblance to the most luscious Côtes du Rhônes.

This, happily, is typical of the entire Languedoc-Roussillon region today. Up to 1994, this Atlas crammed all of the 120-mile (190km) sweep of Mediterranean coast and its hinterland onto one map. And until very recently the story of this area, France's Midi producing more than a third of all French wine, was a dismal one of subsidies and surplus production of mainly thin red *vin ordinaire* together with some strong, sweet Vins Doux Naturels (see page 142) that were of little interest outside France. The hill vignerons had been crushed by phylloxera. The arid plains of the Hérault département from Narbonne to Montpellier were comprehensively milked on an industrial scale to produce red wine so light and pale that it had to be blended with Algerian imports. An apparently permanent crisis of over-production began. But by the end of the 1990s, the Languedoc-Roussillon had established itself as France's best-value and most exciting wine region by far.

Despite financial incentives to pull up vines in some of the least propitious sites – generally flat and too fertile to grow interesting grape flavours – this is still the biggest wine region in the world with over 736,000 acres (298,000ha) of vines (Bordeaux has 284,000 acres or 115,000ha). The majority of its 30,000 growers take their grapes to no less than 357 co-operatives, clustered in vast groupings, including Val d'Orbieu, one of the world's biggest wine companies. Two-thirds of the region's wine is made in these cellars, which vary from down-at-heel to startlingly modern, just as the co-operatives' wines vary from dull to worthy.

But the most exciting wines tend to be made by passionate individuals, often first-generation wine producers who would, in another age, have signed up for more conventional professions. They typically operate where the Romans grew vines (some of the first in Gaul) on hillsides with such shallow soils that nothing else would flourish.

The appellations of the Coteaux du Languedoc with their sub-appellations (see the arc of names in magenta around Montpellier) encompass most, but not all, of the likely spots for top quality viticulture in the eastern Languedoc – as the distribution of leading producers clearly shows. St-Chinian (mapped overleaf) and Faugères, which have already come out from under the Coteaux du Languedoc umbrella to establish their own appellations, are typical. Altitude is all, with much of Faugères and the northern sector of St-Chinian around Berlou (famous for its co-op) well above 600ft (200m) in spectacularly

mountainous country dominated by the dramatic peaks of the Cévennes (see picture overleaf). Vines grown on schist here can produce sharply etched wines while those grown lower down on the bizarre purple clay and limestone soils around the village of St-Chinian itself are softer and more supple.

The wines produced on the flanks of the rocky finger that is Pic St-Loup north of Montpellier from the likes of Château de Cazeneuve, Domaine de l'Hortus, and Chateaux de Lancyre and Lascaux are so consistently, so herbily dramatic that this may be the next *cru* to emerge as a separate appellation from the Coteaux du Languedoc. But Montpeyroux north of Clermont l'Hérault is even higher and puts an eloquent case for similar treatment. Producers such as Domaines l'Aiguelière, d'Aupilhac, and Font Caude, like their counterparts in Pic St-Loup, may be located within the boundaries of one of the Languedoc's relatively few controlled appellations, but they certainly don't limit themselves to producing AC wines.

Not for nothing is the Languedoc known as France's New World. Its wine producers have always been more anarchic than those closer to

Paris and Brussels, and the straitjacket of AC regulations seems a particularly tight fit here. Most producers make a range of Vins de Pays (considered in detail on pages 150-152) as well as AC wines. And many, particularly but not exclusively those outside the official appellation zones, make nothing but Vins de Pays – whether carrying some local geographical name or the more internationally recognizable Vin de Pays d'Oc with a grape name. The reliably hot summers can ripen a usefully wide range of grape varieties and here at least French prejudice against *vins de cépage* – those that Anglo-Saxons call varietal wines – is much less marked.

Map legend:
- Département boundary
- St-Christol: Coteaux du Languedoc sub-appellation
- DOM CLAVEL: Leading producer
- Clairette de Bellegarde
- Clairette de Languedoc
- Coteaux du Languedoc
- Costières de Nîmes
- Faugères
- Muscat de Frontignan
- Muscat de Lunel
- Muscat de Mireval

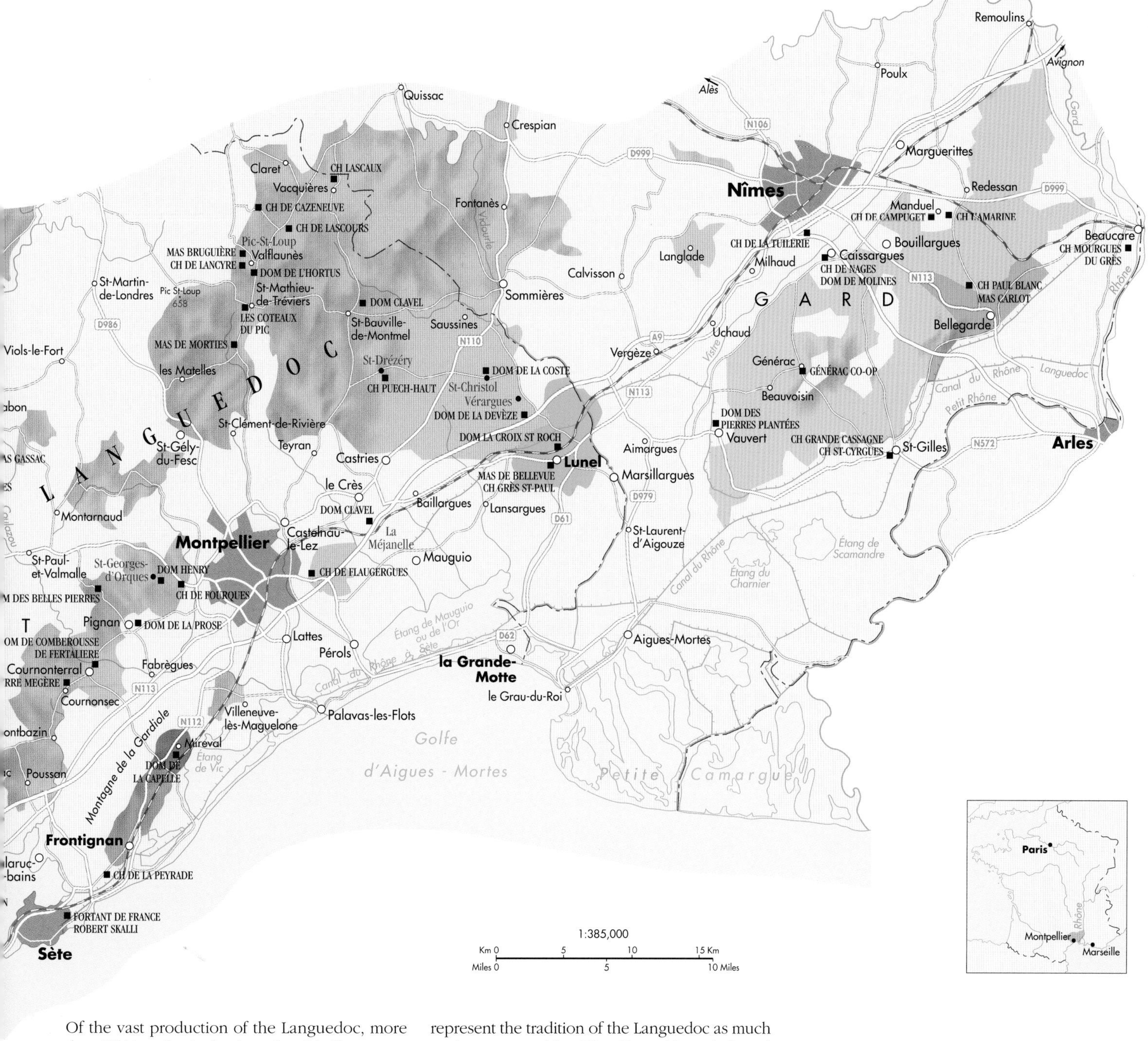

Remoulins
Poulx
Avignon
Alès
Quissac
Crespian
Marguerittes
Claret
CH LASCAUX
Nîmes
Redessan
Vacquières
Fontanès
Manduel
CH DE CAMPUGET
CH L'AMARINE
CH DE CAZENEUVE
Beaucare
CH DE LASCOURS
Langlade
CH DE LA TUILERIE
Bouillargues
CH MOURGÈS DU GRÈS
Pic-St-Loup
MAS BRUGUIÈRE
CH DE LANCYRE
Valflaunès
Milhaud
CH DE NAGES
DOM DE MOLINES
St-Martin-de-Londres
DOM DE L'HORTUS
St-Mathieu-de-Tréviers
Calvisson
Caissargues
CH PAUL BLANC
MAS CARLOT
Pic St-Loup 658
LES COTEAUX DU PIC
DOM CLAVEL
GARD
Sommières
St-Bauville-de-Montmel
Bellegarde
MAS DE MORTIES
Saussines
Viols-le-Fort
les Matelles
St-Drézéry
DOM DE LA COSTE
Générac
GÉNÉRAC CO-OP
L A N G U E D O C
CH PUECH-HAUT
St-Christol
Vérargues
Beauvoisin
St-Clément-de-Rivière
DOM DE LA DEVÈZE
St-Gély-du-Fesc
Teyran
DOM LA CROIX ST ROCH
DOM DES PIERRES PLANTÉES
Vauvert
CH GRANDE CASSAGNE
CH ST-CYRGUES
St-Gilles
Arles
Castries
Aimargues
Montarnaud
Lunel
St-Paul-et-Valmalle
le Crès
Marsillargues
St-Georges-d'Orques
DOM HENRY
DOM CLAVEL
MAS DE BELLEVUE
CH GRÈS ST-PAUL
CH DE FOURQUES
Castelnau-le-Lez
Baillargues
Lansargues
St-Laurent-d'Aigouze
Pignan
DOM DE LA PROSE
CH DE FLAUGERGUES
La Méjanelle
Étang de Scamandre
Montpellier
Lattes
Mauguio
Étang du Charnier
Fabrègues
Pérols
Cournonterral
Étang de Mauguio ou de l'Or
Cournonsec
Aigues-Mortes
Villeneuve-lès-Maguelone
Palavas-les-Flots
la Grande-Motte
Montbazin
Poussan
Mireval
DOM DE LA CAPELLE
Golfe d'Aigues-Mortes
le Grau-du-Roi
Petite Camargue
Étang de Vic
Frontignan
Balaruc-les-bains
CH DE LA PEYRADE
FORTANT DE FRANCE ROBERT SKALLI
Sète

1:385,000
Km 0 ... 5 ... 10 ... 15 Km
Miles 0 ... 5 ... 10 Miles

Paris
Montpellier
Marseille

Of the vast production of the Languedoc, more than 80% is red, whether based on Mediterranean grape varieties such as Mourvèdre, Grenache, Syrah, or Cinsault with a decreasing proportion of tough Carignan (which has traditionally been vinified by carbonic maceration in an effort to tame it), or on international favourites such as Merlot and, to a lesser extent, Cabernet Sauvignon. White winemaking has become increasingly sophisticated, however, as evinced by a sea of inexpensive Chardonnay and a dizzying range of blends of such fashionable grape varieties as Viognier, Roussanne, Marsanne, and Rolle (Vermentino), but oak can be more popular with the makers than the drinkers of these wines. Even red grapes may reflect so obviously their *garrigue*- or mineral-scented origins that oak seems an unnecessary shroud.

Clairette du Languedoc and Picpoul de Pinet are white wines embraced by the AC system. The first is often impossibly flabby, although the co-op at Adissan has led a return towards the sweet version perhaps known in Roman times, while the second, most unusually for France, is a varietal AC, in this case dependent on the quirky, lemon-scented Picpoul grape. These

represent the tradition of the Languedoc as much as the sweet golden Vins Doux Naturels based on Muscat, of which Muscat de Frontignan was once world famous. Muscats de Mireval and Lunel south of Nîmes rarely show the zest of a Frontignan wine, and few of them have as much individuality as the only high-altitude Muscat, that of St-Jean de Minervois which lies in the Cévennes foothills between St-Chinian and Minervois (see overleaf).

Sète, just along the coast from the sands of Frontignan, has had a reputation since Roman times as a port where wine was "trafficked" on an enormous scale. Béziers (mapped overleaf) was synonymous with *gros rouge*. Both may still be surrounded by substantial estates, the châteaux of the south, but their huge all-purpose farm buildings are filled with stainless steel fermenters now that the new *vins de cépages* have turned the market on its head.

The Languedoc has proved that it can play a decent game on that horribly level playing field which is home to the most basic producers of the New World. Fortunately for us all, it has also proved that it can produce serious, terroir-driven essences of southern France too.

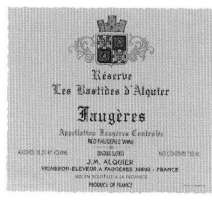

The best wines of the eastern Languedoc tend to come from the hills, but by no means necessarily from those parts blessed with Appellation Contrôlée status, as Mas de Daumas Gassac was the first to prove. Domaine de la Grange des Pères is a more recent star, also near Aniane in the foothills of the dramatic Cévennes.

Western Languedoc

In the west, the Languedoc *vignoble* is wilder, more mountainous, more traditional, tougher, and more varied in its soils and climates. It is typically higher and cooler than the eastern Languedoc, and the build of the wines more closely resembles that of a Bordeaux than a southern Rhône. There is no broad plain here, just a narrow alluvial corridor between the Corbières mountains and the Minervois terraces through which are funnelled the River Aude, the Canal du Midi, and the road and rail links between the Mediterranean and Atlantic that have superseded this 17th-century miracle of engineering.

Of the two main appellations of the western Languedoc, Minervois is slightly more civilized, more polished. The terrain is not quite so rugged as that of Corbières, although at its northern limit where vineyards push up into the foothills of the dominating Montagne Noire, their hold on the rocky, *garrigue*-covered foothills of the Cévennes looks every bit as precarious as that of the gnarled Corbières vines on what are effectively the foothills of the Pyrenees. The village of Minerve is overlooked by some of the appellation's highest, latest-ripening vineyards.

Just downhill in a wide sweep west, the Petite Causse is a belt of clay-limestone in the best circle seats of the south-facing amphitheatre that is the Minervois appellation. The vineyards around La Livinière produce so many wines which seem to combine the rugged scents of the high vineyards with the suave, suppleness of lower altitude wines that they have earned their own sub-appellation.

In the southwest is Clamoux where Atlantic influence starts to make its presence felt in the form of higher acid levels and a slightly leaner style. The Argent Double, the hotter, drier land sloping down towards the Aude and the Serres subregion closest to the Mediterranean provide much of the dreary blended Minervois that can be found at come-hither prices in every French supermarket although, as the map shows, there are some truly ambitious producers, both individuals and co-operatives, here too.

Below Early spring, when the vines are still stump-like, in vineyards below Vieussan, one of the highest villages in the St-Chinian AC huddled against the steep Cévennes.

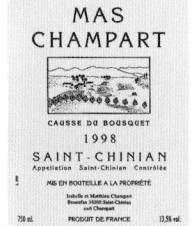

Just a few of the dozens of producers of great-value, handcrafted wines from appellations such as Minervois and Corbières as well as an exceptional answer to champagne made at the Domaine de l'Aigle near Limoux.

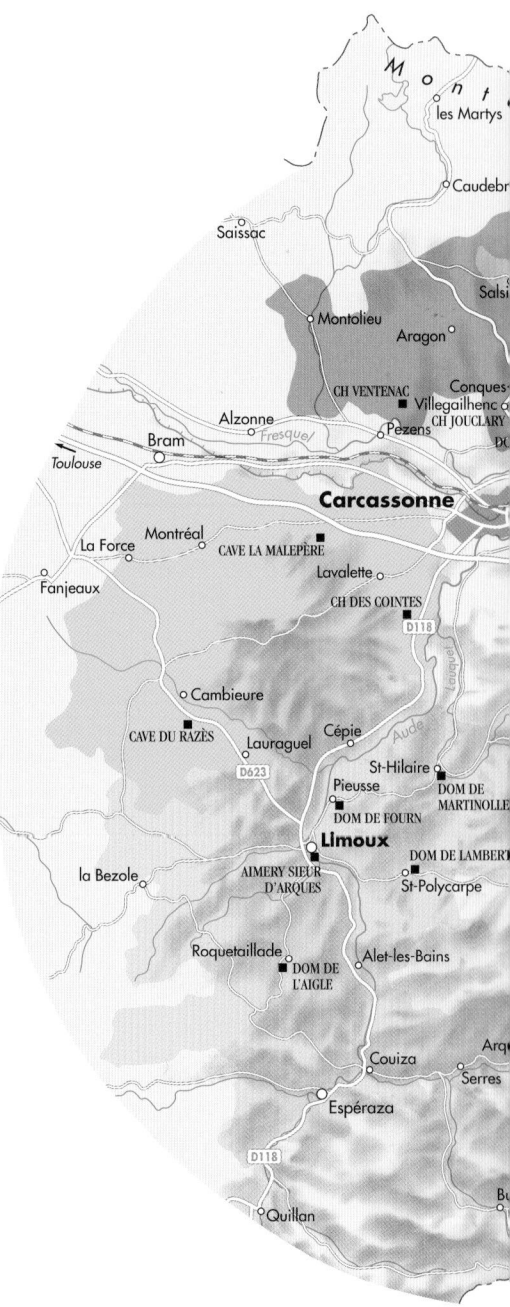

Although more than 98% of all Minervois is red or occasionally rosé, the ancient Bourboulenc grape underpins some increasingly fine white blends, with Maccabéo, Grenache Blanc, and the white Rhône varieties, in which oak is often now a well-integrated component. Bourboulenc, commonly called Malvoisie, comes into its own on a strange outcrop of the Coteaux du Languedoc appellation called La Clape, an eccentric detached limestone massif that in Roman times was an island south of the port of Narbo (today's Narbonne). These whites really are marine-, not to say iodine-, scented. A sweet Minervois Noble is also made by some.

The Corbières landscape is even more dramatic: a geological chaos of mountain and valley reaching from the sea 40 miles (60km) back into the Aude département. Limestone alternates with schist, volcanic rock and sand; the influence of the Mediterranean with intermittent influence from the Atlantic, blowing down the Aude Valley and over its western hills.

Red Corbières, other than at its most mundane, tastes wilder and more concentrated, often rather tougher, than Minervois whose vineyards benefit from a little more summer rain. Indeed drought and summer fires are constant threats in many parts of the varied Corbières appellation, which has always been a hotbed of local politics. The most recent reshuffle, in 1991, divided Corbières into no fewer than 11 zones, but locals are already arguing over how to reduce this to a more manageable seven or eight.

One thing is sure, there is a considerable difference between wines made close to the lagoons of the Mediterranean coast and the produce of the high, dry terraces of schist in the southwest. The low, barren hills around Boutenac were some of the first to earn a reputation for truly fine red Corbières with real ageing potential.

But if the local geography of the Corbières appellation is complex, that of Fitou seems plain barmy. Fitou consists of two distinct enclaves within Corbières: a clay-limestone band around the saltwater lagoons on the coast and a patch of mountainous schist 15 or so miles (24km) inland, separated by a great wedge of Corbières. When Fitou was granted the Languedoc's first

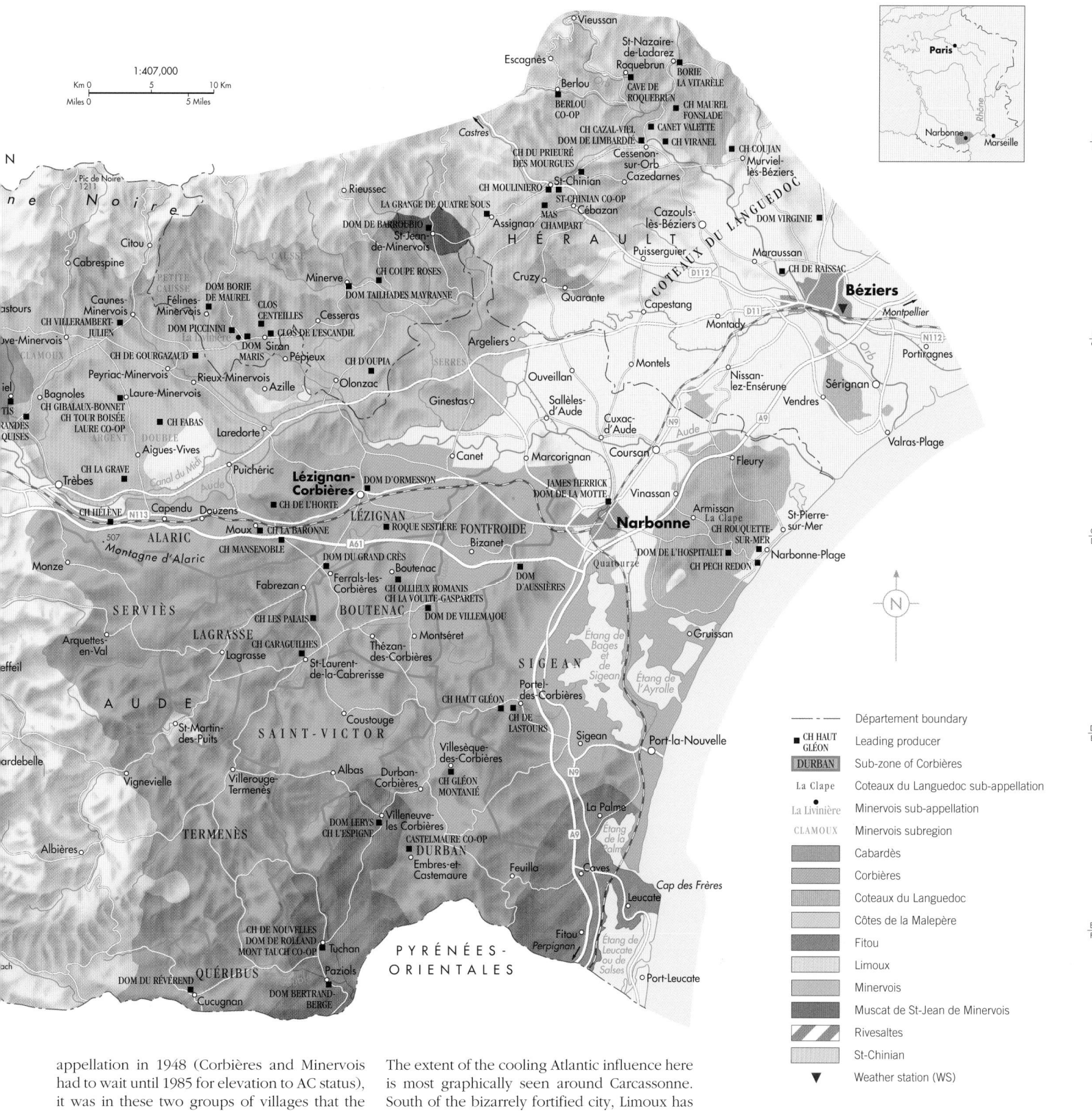

appellation in 1948 (Corbières and Minervois had to wait until 1985 for elevation to AC status), it was in these two groups of villages that the lobbyists shouted loudest.

The irony is that for much of the 1980s and 1990s, Fitou lagged behind its northern neighbours. And still, although there are one or two ambitious co-ops, there are not enough landmark producers. As the proportion of Grenache is increased at the expense of Carignan in Fitou Montagneux, and Syrah and Mourvèdre gain ground in Fitou Maritime over the next few years just as the appellation regulations decree, we can hope for better.

The extent of the cooling Atlantic influence here is most graphically seen around Carcassonne. South of the bizarrely fortified city, Limoux has established at least a national reputation for its fine traditional method fizz, whether Blanquette, based on the original Mauzac grape or, increasingly embellished with Chardonnay, Crémant de Limoux. And oak-fermented Limoux Chardonnay without bubbles adorns many a three-star restaurant's wine list.

To the north of Limoux the Côtes de la Malepère and Cabardès appellations grow both Mediterranean grapes and the Cabernet family blowing in from the west.

Legend:

- — — · — Département boundary
- ■ CH HAUT GLÉON — Leading producer
- DURBAN — Sub-zone of Corbières
- La Clape — Coteaux du Languedoc sub-appellation
- La Livinière — Minervois sub-appellation
- CLAMOUX — Minervois subregion
- Cabardès
- Corbières
- Coteaux du Languedoc
- Côtes de la Malepère
- Fitou
- Limoux
- Minervois
- Muscat de St-Jean de Minervois
- Rivesaltes
- St-Chinian
- ▼ Weather station (WS)

Languedoc: Béziers

Latitude / Altitude of WS **43° / 262ft (80m)**
Mean July temp at WS **73.4°F (23°C)**
Annual rainfall at WS **28in (710mm)**
Harvest month rainfall at WS **September: 2½in (65mm)**
Chief viticultural hazards **Drought**
Principal grapes **Carignan, Grenache Noir, Cinsault, Syrah, Merlot, Cabernet Sauvignon**

Roussillon

Roussillon is so much more than a suffix, being very different both physically and culturally from the Languedoc. Its inhabitants consider themselves Catalans who happen to find themselves in France, but only since 1659. Their yellow and red striped banners are everywhere, their local dialect with its double Ls more closely resembles Spanish than French.

The landscape here may be more dramatic – at the eastern end of the Pyrenees the peaks of the Canigou Range, snow-covered most of the year, swoop more than 7,500ft (2,500m) down to the Mediterranean – but the region is softer, less wild than the rocky lower contours of the Corbières hills to the north. Sunshine (an average of 325 days a year) helps, and explains the fields and groves (and vineyards) of fruit and vegetables to which the Perpignan plain and Agly, Têt, and Tech valley floors are devoted. The effects of that sunshine are concentrated by the east-facing amphitheatre created by the Corbières, Canigou, and the Albarès mountains which separate modern France from Spain.

This means that France's first fruits of season regularly come from here, and the vineyards on the plain are some of the driest and hottest in France, their low bushes yielding fully ripe Grenache grapes of all hues as early as mid-August. They tend to be used for the most basic of Roussillon's famous Vins Doux Naturels (VDN). These once-popular apéritifs are not in fact naturally sweet wines, as the name implies, but part-fermented grape juice stopped from becoming wine by adding alcohol, at a slightly earlier point than in the port-making process.

Even though all of the Languedoc's Muscats are VDNs, Roussillon makes more Vin Doux Naturel than anywhere else in France – more than 90% of the French total – and Rivesaltes, made in a vast area of Roussillon mainly from Grenache Noir, Blanc, and Gris, is France's most popular VDN by far. From the most fertile sites and aged for the statutory minimum of 16 months it can be a very ordinary sweet wine, but examples aged for years in wood in the region's relatively warm climate and carrying declarations of age, or even the much-favoured *"Hors d'Age"* are much more ambitious, and of varying hue. The reds may beguile with cherry-chocolate flavours punctuated by a dry, tannic finish. The looser, more oxidative whites are more obviously raisined. There are rosés too.

Muscat de Rivesaltes comes from the same generous zone incorporating all but the highest vineyard land of the Pyrénées Orientales département together with the two enclaves of Fitou in the Aude mapped on the previous page. Permitted yields are lower for the Muscat and the wine, made from Muscat of Alexandria with some Muscat Blanc grapes, is generally finer, although most are best drunk young.

The curious inland region of Maury in the far northern uplands of Roussillon has its own appellation for VDN, mostly red or rosé, and – especially now that the legal minimum of Grenache Noir has been increased to 75% – can be as noble and certainly as slow-developing as a good Banyuls. It is grown on similar soils.

Banyuls is France's finest VDN, grown at yields that sometimes average less than 20hl/ha on France's southernmost vineyards, steep windswept terraces of dark brown schist sloping to the sea just north of a rather sleepy Spanish frontier post. Grapes vary considerably but come predominantly from ancient Grenache Noir bushes ripened to very high degrees, often shrivelling to raisins on the vine. For Grand Cru, made only in particularly good years, 30 months of barrel-ageing and 75% of Grenache Noir is mandatory. Ageing techniques and therefore hues and wine styles vary just as widely as for port (see pages 210-211), and sometimes for similar reasons. Pale wines heady with rancio flavour may result from long ageing in old wooden barrels in relatively warm conditions, while *rimage* wines are aged, like vintage port, at a much more stately pace in bottle.

Less potent wines made from the vineyards devoted to Banyuls are called after the pretty port of Collioure, famously home to artists and anchovy packers. These deep crimson essences, more Spanish than French, also testify to the robust alcohol levels achieved by the vines, mainly Grenache but increasingly supplemented by Syrah and Mourvèdre.

The table wines of Roussillon are certainly easier for outsiders to understand than its VDNs, even if they are evolving in style and composition every year. Côtes du Roussillon is the base level, still made largely from Carignan although this tough old Midi grape is now limited to 60% of the blend, and Grenache, Cinsault, and, particularly, Syrah and Mourvèdre are playing an increasingly important role. But for the moment, this is an appellation in search of a personality other than being vaguely warm and welcoming. More interesting have been Roussillon's white table wines, even if many of the best have been sold as simple Vin de Pays, and sometimes Vin de Table, rather than under the Côtes du Roussillon appellation. Roussillon can boast an exotic palette of pale-skinned grape varieties which can be transformed into heady, perfumed, dry table wines (see factfile).

Côtes du Roussillon-Villages are bolder, more positive wines (reds only) thanks to lower yields and higher strength. This superior appellation is restricted to the northern third of the area and allows the villages of Latour-de-France and Caramany their own sub-appellations. Caramany's were the first Midi reds to aspire to higher things in the 1960s by introducing carbonic maceration to tame the ubiquitous Carignan grape. Côtes du Roussillon-Villages can still offer good value for firm, solid, age-worthy wines whose aromas come from the soil and their sheer vinosity, rather than from following international fashion.

Left The patchiness of this vineyard above Banyuls shows clearly that growers here are not motivated by maximum profit. Ancient vines, minuscule yields, and wines that may need many years in the cellar comprise the old-fashioned Banyuls recipe.

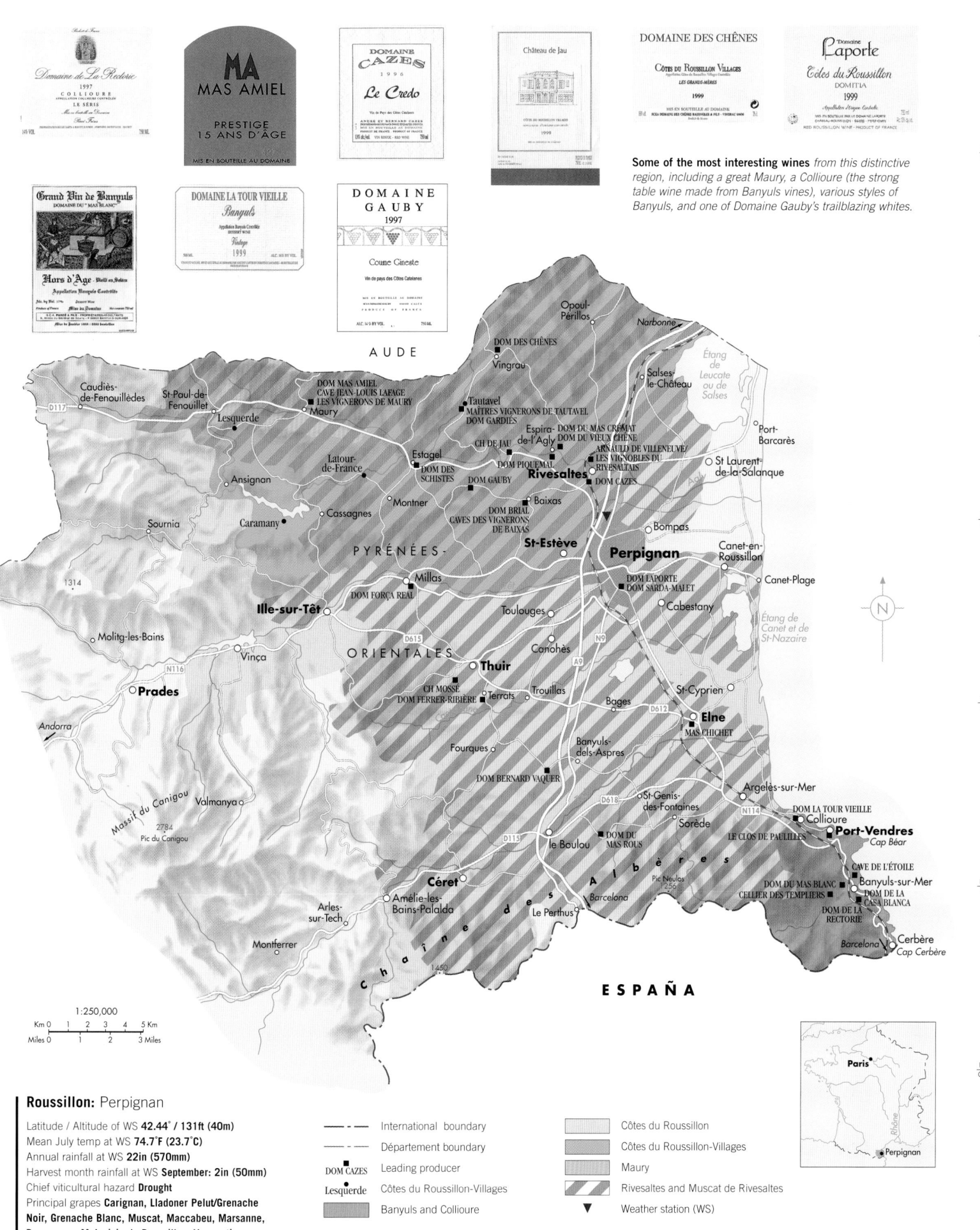

Some of the most interesting wines *from this distinctive region, including a great Maury, a Collioure (the strong table wine made from Banyuls vines), various styles of Banyuls, and one of Domaine Gauby's trailblazing whites.*

Roussillon: Perpignan

Latitude / Altitude of WS **42.44° / 131ft (40m)**
Mean July temp at WS **74.7°F (23.7°C)**
Annual rainfall at WS **22in (570mm)**
Harvest month rainfall at WS **September: 2in (50mm)**
Chief viticultural hazard **Drought**
Principal grapes **Carignan, Lladoner Pelut/Grenache Noir, Grenache Blanc, Muscat, Maccabeu, Marsanne, Roussanne, Malvoisie du Roussillon, Vermentino**

Legend:
— International boundary
— Département boundary
■ DOM CAZES — Leading producer
Lesquerde — Côtes du Roussillon-Villages
Banyuls and Collioure
Côtes du Roussillon
Côtes du Roussillon-Villages
Maury
Rivesaltes and Muscat de Rivesaltes
▼ Weather station (WS)

Scale 1:250,000
Km 0 1 2 3 4 5 Km
Miles 0 1 2 3 Miles

Provence

Provence! The name alone has such resonance, let alone the place, that visiting wine drinkers have been prepared to forgive a region whose most distinctive offering was for long an excess of over-strong and under-flavoured rosé.

Happily this quintessentially Mediterranean region has been invaded by the same sort of individuals hellbent on upgrading quality as have been making their mark elsewhere so that now, although 80% of Provençal wine is still pink, and far too much of it is still intensely boring (if garlic-friendly), an increasing proportion is gently made and intriguingly perfumed. And, most exciting of all, seriously interesting reds are being made all over the region.

A glance at the map explains why these reds may vary considerably in character. The classic appellation Côtes de Provence alone, France's most extensive, encompasses the northern outskirts of Marseille, the southern flanks of the Montagne Ste-Victoire, Mediterranean islands, the warm coastal hinterland of resorts such as Le Lavandou and St-Tropez, cooler, subalpine retreats north of Draguignan, and even a pocket of vines around Villars well north of Nice.

The generally cooler, limestone enclave of Coteaux Varois, a much more recent recruit to AC status, is sheltered from softening maritime influence by the Massif de la Ste-Baume so that some vineyards in the wooded hills north of Brignoles may not be picked until early November, while vintage time on the coast is early September. (The Burgundy négociant Louis Latour has had notable success with Pinot Noir grapes grown even further north near Aups, suggesting just how cool it is here.)

In the west, the landscape of Coteaux d'Aix-en-Provence (of which the university town itself is in fact on the southeastern border) is less dramatic, as the wines tend to be – although Counoise grapes add interest to some rosés. The hillside vineyards of the Côtes du Lubéron on the other side of the River Durance enjoy cooler nights and a more Rhône-like environment. Coteaux de Pierrevert (see map of France, page 53) makes noticeably lighter wines.

Between Coteaux d'Aix-en-Provence and the River Rhône itself is the splinter appellation created in 1995 and named after the extraordinary hilltop tourist trap Les Baux-de-Provence. Warmed by the sea and buffeted by Provence's famous mistral, this area is even better suited to organic viticulture than most of the rest of Provence. It also provides a notable illustration of the current tensions between the Provençal wine fraternity and the INAO, the headquarters of the French AC system in Paris. The point at issue concerns grape varieties: whether to encourage "tradition" or sheer quality.

Having been ruled by successive waves of invaders from the east, north, west, and south (Sardinians for much of the 19th century), Provence boasts a fine and varied legacy of grape varieties, some of them such as Tibouren and Calitor (Pécoui Touar) apparently unknown elsewhere. The INAO's current preoccupation seems to be to reduce and eventually eliminate

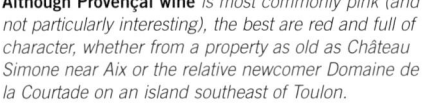

Although Provençal wine *is most commonly pink (and not particularly interesting), the best are red and full of character, whether from a property as old as Château Simone near Aix or the relative newcomer Domaine de la Courtade on an island southeast of Toulon.*

the Carignan that was planted here, as in the Languedoc, to supply cheap, light reds for northern France in the early 20th century, while encouraging the Grenache and Cinsault (so useful for rosés), and the sturdier Mourvèdre and Syrah which preceded it. Cabernet Sauvignon is officially viewed as a somewhat sinister intruder, whose influence should be strictly controlled.

Many fine Provençal reds (and some whites) are therefore sold today as Vin de Pays, including all of those from Les Baux's Domaine de Trévallon, arguably the region's finest producer of all. Trailblazer of the Cabernet/Syrah blend for Provence was Georges Brunet, who arrived at a dilapidated Château Vignelaure northeast of

Aix-en-Provence from Château La Lagune in Bordeaux. (Vignelaure is now in the hands of an Irish racehorse trainer.)

As might be expected of a region with a history of winegrowing which dates back to Roman times, Provence harbours some well-established individual wine zones. Arguably the most historic is Palette on the north-facing, limestone-influenced bank of the River Arc just east of Aix, where the Rougier family has been making extraordinarily dense wine of all three colours from a palette (hence the name?) of local grapes at Château Simone for 200 years.

Cassis, centred on the small port to the east of Marseille, also makes a serious effort with its

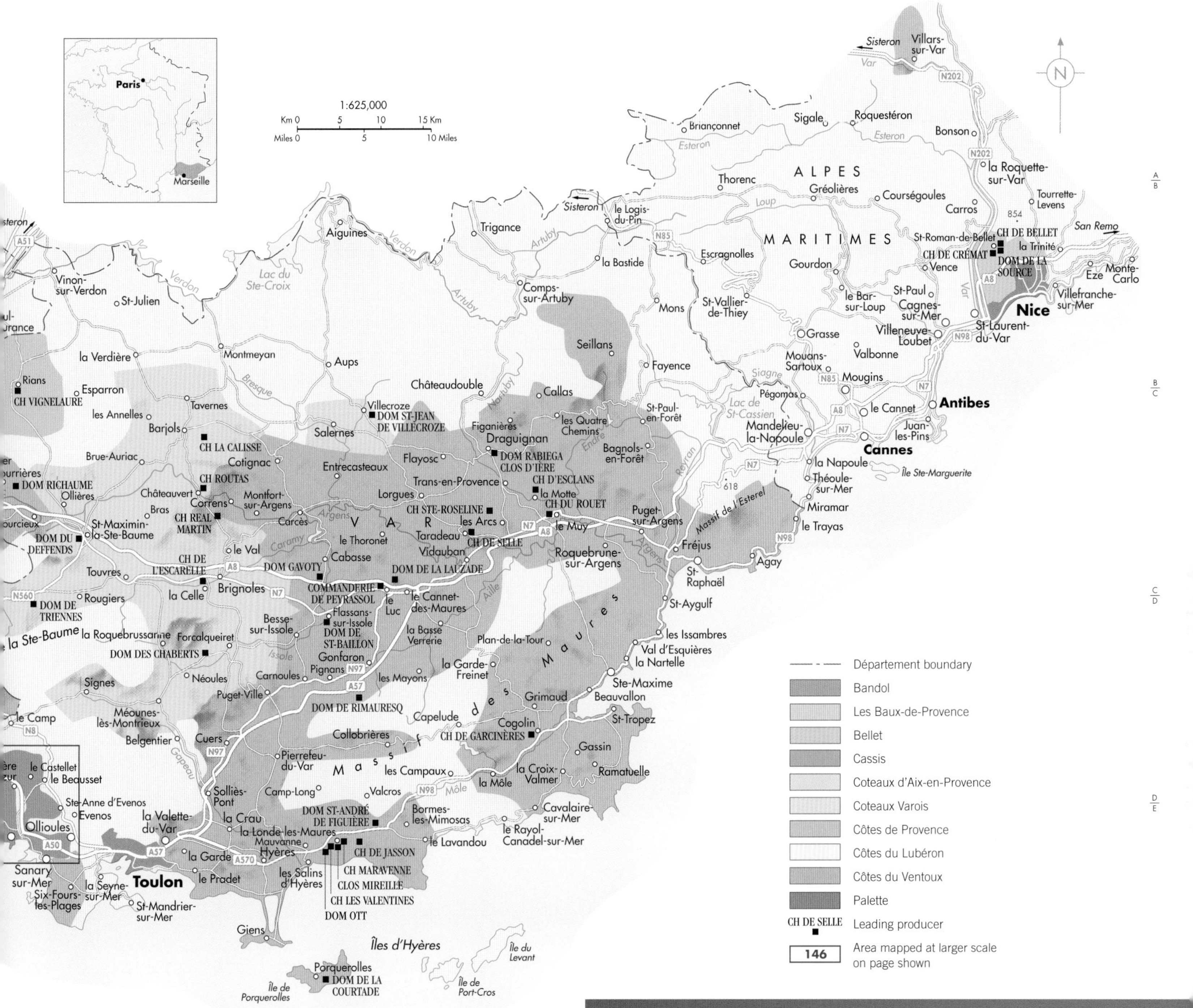

Paris•

Marseille•

1:625,000

Km 0   5   10   15 Km

Miles 0   5   10 Miles

ALPES

MARITIMES

VAR

Massif des Maures

Massif de l'Esterel

Nice

Antibes

Cannes

Toulon

Îles d'Hyères

Île du Levant

Île de Port-Cros

Île de Porquerolles

- - - · Département boundary

Bandol

Les Baux-de-Provence

Bellet

Cassis

Coteaux d'Aix-en-Provence

Coteaux Varois

Côtes de Provence

Côtes du Lubéron

Côtes du Ventoux

Palette

CH DE SELLE ■ Leading producer

146 Area mapped at larger scale on page shown

white, particularly herby in this case and *de rigueur* with *bouillabaisse*. In the far east of Provence, a handful of vignerons continue to resist the encroachment of Nice on the vineyards of Bellet, cooled by winds from the sea and the Alps and enriched by such Italianate grapes as Braquet (Brachetto), Folle Noire (Fuella), and Rolle (Vermentino). Wines made close to tourist centres are rarely underpriced.

One can therefore readily imagine inflation affecting the wines of the Côtes du Lubéron. This fashionable ridge marks the northern boundary of Provence, and produces red wines comparable to the Côtes du Ventoux and some surprisingly fresh whites.

Right Domaine Richeaume, on the lower flanks of the Montagne Ste-Victoire, is just one of many organically run domaines in Provence where the relatively low rainfall reduces the need for fungicides.

1|2   2|3   3|4

Bandol

On south-tilted terraces among the pines well inland of the touristy port itself, the appellation Bandol feels both its isolation and its unique status keenly. In size it is dwarfed by the oceans of Côtes de Provence that make up the bulk of wine produced in this exceptionally sunny corner of southeast France. But in stature it is Provence's most important wine and one, moreover, that fulfils many modern wine drinkers' criteria for pleasure.

The wine is mainly red, made substantially from the fashionable Mourvèdre grape (the only such French appellation), and with its full-blooded almost feral herbiness is extremely easy to appreciate. Thanks to a climate benign enough to ripen a vine variety with one of the longest growing cycles of all, most red Bandol is voluptuously ripe and can easily be enjoyed at only six or seven years. (A substantial, often Cinsault-dominated rosé is much drunk in the region and small quantities of full white Bandol are also made from, according to the rule-book, Clairette, Bourboulenc, Ugni Blanc, and, inexplicably, Sauvignon Blanc.)

Terroirs in this relatively small appellation vary enormously. On the red clay soils that predominate, the tannins of Mourvèdre can be quite marked so the wine is usually blended with some of the Grenache and Cinsault that are also grown. Grenache can easily reach such high alcohol levels here that it is a common choice for any north-facing vineyard. Soils in the northwest corner are particularly pebbly; the young soils that stretch from St-Cyr to Le Brûlat tend to produce finer, more supple wines, while the oldest soils of the appellation lie south of Le Beausset. Those at higher altitudes such as those at 1,000ft (300m) or so around Château de Pibarnon tend to be noticeably less fertile than most and here the vintage may extend to mid-October.

If Bandol is struggling to adapt to changes in the outside world (the new oak barrique represents a highly contentious issue; larger, old oak casks are still the norm in this region), it can boast a heartening overall standard of quality. Yields are some of the lowest in France, and the Mourvèdre vines must be fully mature before they are allowed to produce red wine. Fortunately, any rain tends to be followed by a sharp mistral that blows away the risk of rot. The low-acid Mourvèdre may not be the easiest grape to vinify but the winemaking techniques in this beautiful corner of France are becoming increasingly sophisticated.

Most of the bigger domaines manage vineyards all over the appellation but recent newcomers such as Luc Sorin from Burgundy and Guillaume Tari from Bordeaux are more likely to concentrate on a single estate, Domaines Sorin and de la Bégude respectively.

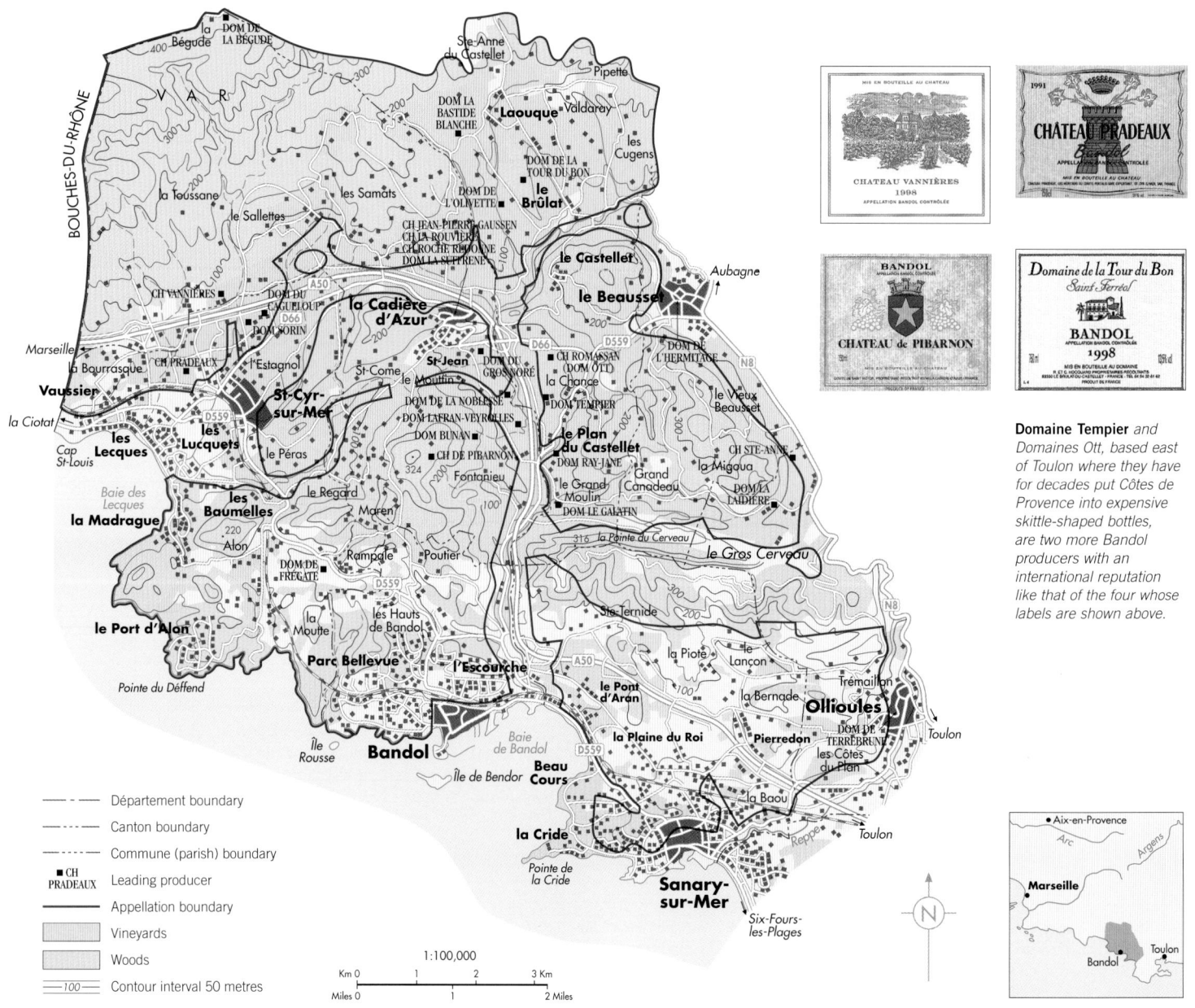

Domaine Tempier *and Domaines Ott, based east of Toulon where they have for decades put Côtes de Provence into expensive skittle-shaped bottles, are two more Bandol producers with an international reputation like that of the four whose labels are shown above.*

— · — Département boundary

— · · — Canton boundary

— · · · — Commune (parish) boundary

■ CH PRADEAUX Leading producer

——— Appellation boundary

▓ Vineyards

▒ Woods

═100═ Contour interval 50 metres

1:100,000

Km 0   1   2   3 Km
Miles 0   1   2 Miles

Corsica

Corsica is sunnier and drier than anywhere in mainland France but, being the most mountainous island in the Mediterranean, it is made up of a patchwork of different terroirs with only an unusually dry July and August in common. It is closer to Italy than France in many respects, including the straightforward one of distance, but France has been the major influence on its modern wine history. When France lost Algeria in the 1960s, an army of skilled growers, encouraged by de Gaulle, migrated to the then-malarial east coast. By 1976 Corsica's vineyard area had quadrupled, covered almost entirely with bulk-producing vines.

Corsica's contribution to the European wine lake has since been stemmed and, thanks to vast subsidies from Brussels and Paris, the island's cellars are now relatively well-equipped, its winemakers trained at one of the mainland's oenological institutes, and its vineyards much reduced and planted only with vine varieties that at least have the potential to produce wines that modern consumers might actually want to drink.

Even so, the great majority of all wine produced on the island is also consumed there with no more reverence than it deserves. The wine most commonly exported is basic Vin de Pays blessed only by Corsica's seductive *nom de verre*, L'Île de Beauté, under which almost half of all wine made on the island now travels.

An increasing proportion of Corsican wine, however, is serious stuff that has rediscovered its birthright in the hardy traditional grape varieties and the rocky hills where they grow best.

Research continues into Corsica's own heritage of grapevines, of which the only one grown to any great extent today is Sciacarello. This grape is associated principally with the island's oldest wine region on the granitic west coast around Ajaccio, the capital (and the birthplace of Napoleon), at Calvi, and in the Sartène region round Propriano. It makes highly drinkable, soft yet spicy red and a rosé that remains lively despite its high alcohol content.

The Niellucio, often cited as the other native Corsican grape, is in fact Tuscany's Sangiovese, which may have been imported by the Genoese who ruled the island until the late-18th century. This much tougher grape dominates the northern appellation of Patrimonio, inland from the port of Bastia. Patrimonio was the first full appellation to be created in Corsica, in 1968, and remains one of the best. The only area on the majestically craggy island to have limestone soil, it produces firm Rhônish reds, well-balanced whites and rich Muscat Vins Doux Naturels (see page 142) of high quality.

Sweet wines, of Muscat or Vermentino ("Malvoisie de Corse", known as Rolle elsewhere), are also the speciality of Cap Corse, the long northward point of the island (which is also home to the Corsican white wine grape Codivarta). Rappu, a strong, sweet red made here, around Rogliano, from Aleatico grapes, also has a strong following, and not just on the island. The local Vermentino also produces a heady, soft, golden dry white. Wines made on this northern tip of Corsica are labelled Coteaux du Cap Corse.

The appellation of Calvi in the northwest uses Sciacarello, Niellucio, and Vermentino, as well as some of the more international grapes, to produce full-bodied table wines; Figari and Porto-Vecchio do the same in the south. It is thirsty country with wines that could scarcely be called thirst-quenching, although Porto-Vecchio seems to have come furthest in making wines, particularly whites, with a degree of modern, fruity crispness.

In comparison with these concentrated wines of traditional character, the regular Vins de Corse with no further geographical suffix but typically made around Aléria and Ghisonaccia on the eastern coastal plain are of no special interest.

In some ways Corsican wine can be compared with Provençal. The rosé in both cases is commonly the best, or certainly the most appropriate, drink there. Each has found a new generation of growers eager to make the most of their terroir, and a local, some would say captive, market eager to find in their wines the elusive scents of the hot herbs of the *maquis*.

Right Nowhere on the island is far from the sea. From Domaine de Torraccia's vineyards near Porto-Vecchio you can see Elba on a clear day.

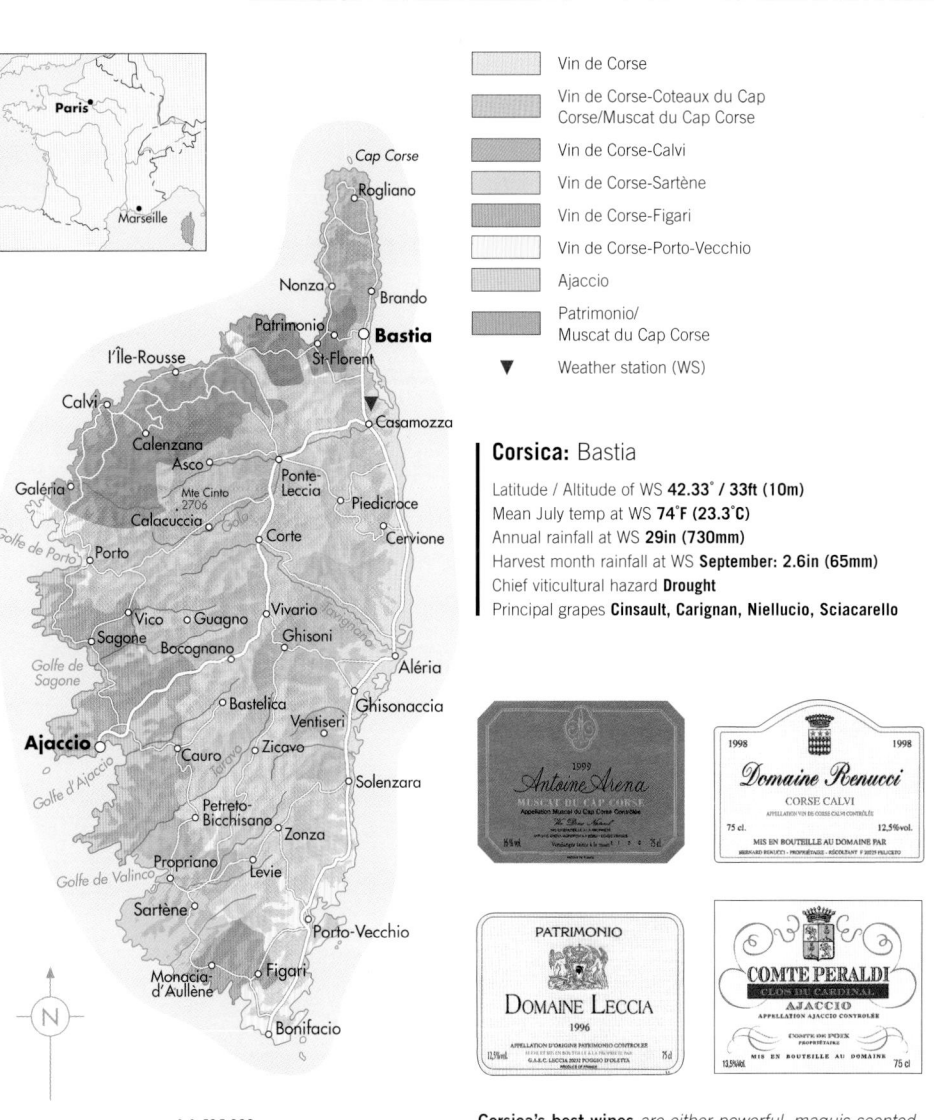

Vin de Corse

Vin de Corse-Coteaux du Cap Corse/Muscat du Cap Corse

Vin de Corse-Calvi

Vin de Corse-Sartène

Vin de Corse-Figari

Vin de Corse-Porto-Vecchio

Ajaccio

Patrimonio/ Muscat du Cap Corse

▼ Weather station (WS)

Corsica: Bastia

Latitude / Altitude of WS **42.33° / 33ft (10m)**
Mean July temp at WS **74°F (23.3°C)**
Annual rainfall at WS **29in (730mm)**
Harvest month rainfall at WS **September: 2.6in (65mm)**
Chief viticultural hazard **Drought**
Principal grapes **Cinsault, Carignan, Niellucio, Sciacarello**

Corsica's best wines are either powerful, maquis-scented reds or full-bodied Muscats made on the Cap Corse in the far north of the island.

Jura

A little enclave of vines scattered among woodland and meadow in what seem like France's remotest hills, the Jura *vignoble* may have shrivelled since the phylloxera louse invaded at the end of the 19th century, yet its wines are varied and wholly original. Its appellations Arbois, Château-Chalon, L'Etoile, and Côtes du Jura are all highly individual and hold particular fascination for students of food and wine pairing.

This is a verdant land of trenchermen, heavily influenced by the gastronomic excesses and indeed soils and weather of Burgundy to the immediate west, except that here winters can be even more severe. As in the Côte d'Or, the best vineyards slope, sometimes steeply, south and southeast to catch the sun. Jurassic limestone is, not surprisingly, characteristic of Jura as well as Burgundy (L'Etoile takes its name from tiny, star-shaped fossils in the soil).

Jura is increasingly growing the grapes of Burgundy: Chardonnay to a considerable and not always inspiring extent; Pinot Noir in a more limited way. The best wines, however, are made from local vine varieties, particularly the late-ripening Savagnin, also known as Naturé. Savagnin, often fleshed out with Chardonnay, brings rigour and a hazelnut note to white table wines, which can be both delightful and distinctive if made carefully.

This noble grape is also wholly responsible for Jura's famous strong yellow wine, *vin jaune*. To make France's answer to sherry, Savagnin grapes are picked as ripe as possible, fermented and then left in old Burgundian barrels for just over six years during which the wine evaporates and oxidizes, but on its surface grows a film of yeast, similar but by no means identical to the famous flor of the Jerez region (see page 199). The firm, intensely nutty wine is put into its signature *clavelin* 62cl bottle, supposedly the volume left of an original litre put into cask. Not for neophytes, this is a wine that can last for decades and is often best opened well in advance of sipping, preferably with a local *poulet de Bresse*. The AC Château-Chalon is limited to this odd but potentially excellent wine, but *vin jaune*, of distinctly varying quality, is made throughout the region.

The most common dark-skinned Jura grape is the perfumed Poulsard, often called Ploussard, especially around Pupillin (a sub-appellation of Arbois) where it is most popular. The reds produced are rarely very deep-coloured but can be interesting: soft, smooth and satisfying with the local game. A considerable proportion of silky rosé, effectively a light red often described as *corail* or coral, is made. Trousseau is a deeper-coloured but rarer Jura grape. It can be found in the north in Arbois, and is increasingly sold in varietal form. Pinot Noir tends to do best around Arlay due west of Château-Chalon.

What this map of the Jura does not show is the full extent of the region's second most important appellation after Arbois, the Côtes du Jura. Its vineyards line the Bourg-en-Bresse road southwest from Lons-le-Saunier as far as St-Amour and produce mainly white wines, including *vin jaune*.

Jura has always produced fine sparkling wine and the relatively new appellation for traditional method fizz is Crémant du Jura. But this is much less distinctive than Jura's liquorous *vin de paille*, also made throughout the region from Chardonnay, Savagnin and/or Poulsard grapes, generally picked early and dried in carefully ventilated conditions until January when these raisins are fermented to more than 15% alcohol and then aged in old barrels for two or three years. Like *vin jaune*, these wines are for very long keeping. One final speciality is Macvin du Jura, which now has its own appellation, a fragrant mixture of grape juice and grape spirit.

Above In the Jura even the buildings, like these overlooking Château-Chalon vineyards, look halfway between Burgundian and Swiss. The grapes, however, are a mixture of Burgundian and local varieties.

Three of these labels represent long-standing traditional styles but Rijckaert has invaded the region from the Mâconnais and imported a new, livelier style of winemaking with more intense fruit and acidity.

AC Arbois
AC Château-Chalon
AC l'Etoile
Vineyards
Woods
Contour interval 50 metres

1:310,000
Km 0   5   10 Km
Miles 0   5   10 Miles

Savoie

The map on this page covers an area almost as large as the whole of the Bordeaux wine region on page 83, and yet Savoie produces less than a fiftieth as much wine as Bordeaux – because its wine areas, and even individual vineyards, are so widely dispersed. Mountains so often get in the way. Cultivable land is at a premium. This is alpine France, complete with all the demands of tourism: winters cold enough to attract hordes of skiers and lakes which warm the nearby vineyards in summer.

A small but growing area of Savoie is now devoted to the vine but it yields wines that are so varied, from such a rich mix of local vine specialities, that it seems extraordinary to the outsider that almost all of them go under the same basic appellation, Vin de Savoie.

A Vin de Savoie is more than twice as likely to be white as red or rosé. It is also about ten times more likely to be light, clean, and fresh – at one with Savoyard mountain air, lakes and streams – than it is to be deep and heady, although some producers have been experimenting with extracting more from the region's most valuable dark-skinned grape, the peppery Mondeuse. The great majority of wine sold as straight Vin de Savoie is made from the Jacquère grape: dry and mild like ethereal Muscadet.

But within the greater Savoie region, no fewer than 17 individual *crus* are allowed to add their name to the label, provided certain conditions, different for each *cru* but stricter than for basic Vins de Savoie, are met. On the southern shores of Lac Léman (Lake Geneva), for example, only the Chasselas grape so beloved by neighbouring Switzerland, is allowed for wines labelled with the *crus* Ripaille (which can be quite a rich, golden wine), Marin, and Marignan. (Crépy, a similar wine made in this area, has its own small appellation.)

South of here in the Arve Valley is the *cru* of Ayze which produces still and sparkling whites from its own grape speciality the Gringet, probably related to Savagnin.

Savoie's third individual appellation is Seyssel, best-known for its sparkling wines made from Altesse with some local Molette grapes. Still wines are made mainly from Altesse. Both have a certain historic reputation.

Just north of Seyssel is Frangy, an isolated *cru* specializing in this case in the local, characterful Altesse. The superiority of the Altesse, or Roussette, grape is recognized by a special appellation for any Savoie wine made from it, within certain conditions: Roussette de Savoie. (Those *crus* authorized only for the production of Roussette de Savoie are marked in magenta on the map above.)

South of Seyssel are the extensive vineyards of Chautagne, a *cru* best known for its reds, particularly its grainy Gamay. To the west of the Lac du Bourget is Jongieux. A wine labelled simply Jongieux is made exclusively from Jacquère but some Altesse is grown here too.

Lying to the south of the town of Chambéry, whose herby vermouth is now all too difficult to find, is Savoie's most extensive vineyard area

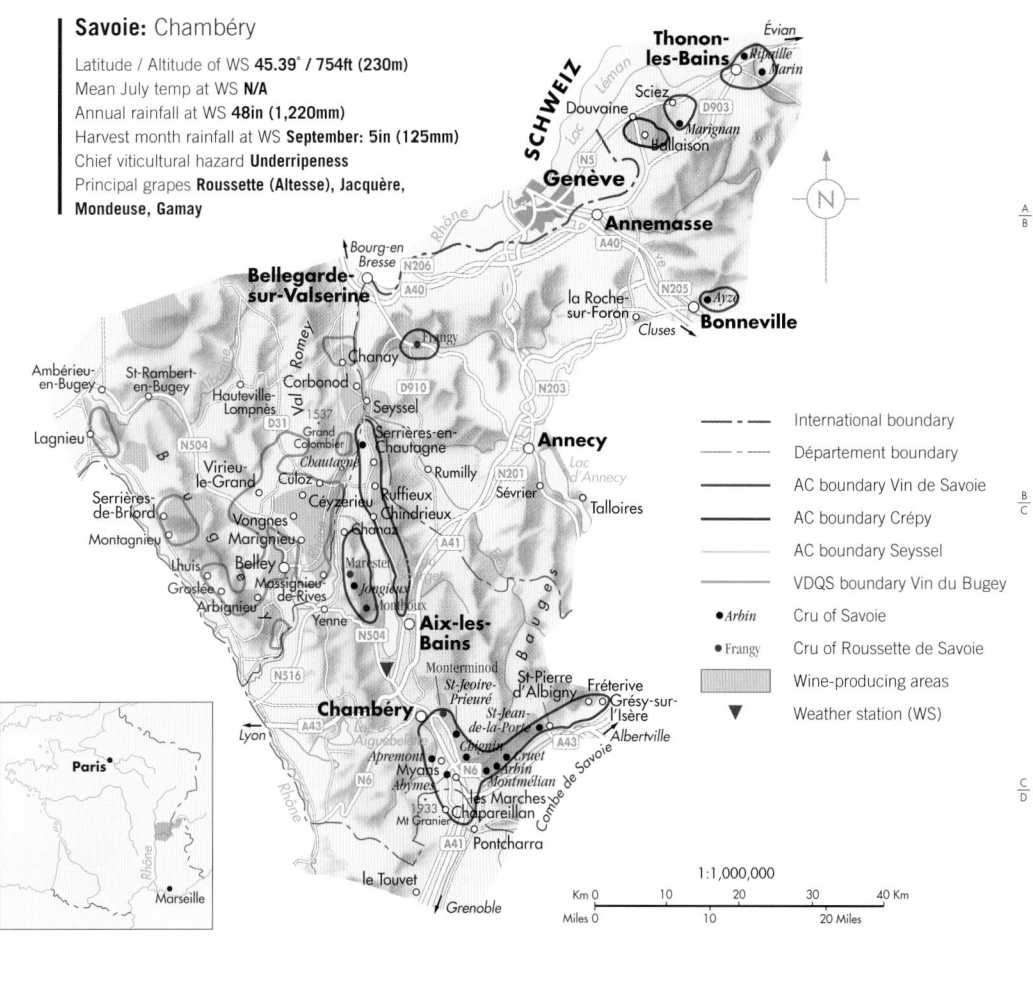

Savoie: Chambéry
Latitude / Altitude of WS **45.39˚ / 754ft (230m)**
Mean July temp at WS **N/A**
Annual rainfall at WS **48in (1,220mm)**
Harvest month rainfall at WS **September: 5in (125mm)**
Chief viticultural hazard **Underripeness**
Principal grapes **Roussette (Altesse), Jacquère, Mondeuse, Gamay**

International boundary
Département boundary
AC boundary Vin de Savoie
AC boundary Crépy
AC boundary Seyssel
VDQS boundary Vin du Bugey
● *Arbin* Cru of Savoie
● *Frangy* Cru of Roussette de Savoie
Wine-producing areas
▼ Weather station (WS)

1:1,000,000
Km 0   10   20   30   40 Km
Miles 0   10   20 Miles

The Chignin-Bergeron from Quenard is one of the few Savoie wines to travel extensively outside the region. Most of the winemakers expect us to visit them.

facing south and southeast on the lower slopes of Mont Granier. This area includes the popular *crus* of Apremont and Abymes where, arguably, most flavour is extracted from the reticent Jacquère grape.

Following the Isère river up the Combe de Savoie is a cluster of *crus* where all of Savoie's varieties are grown, but especially Jacquère and some Altesse. Of these, Chignin is responsible for one of the best-known ambassadors of fine Savoie wine. Its speciality Chignin-Bergeron, made exclusively from the Roussanne grape of the Rhône, is one of Savoie's most powerful and powerfully scented whites. Chignin and Arbin can also ripen Mondeuse well (in fact the valley floor here is warm enough in spring and summer to accommodate nurseries, some of them famous throughout France for their vine cuttings).

Delicate sparkling wines made outside Seyssel and Ayze but also by the traditional method are sold simply as Vin de Savoie but may eventually be granted their own appellation Crémant de Savoie.

Right Chasselas vines near Crépy are overlooked, like virtually all Savoie vineyards, by mountains, many of them snow-covered for much of the winter and spring.

Due west of the Lac du Bourget the VDQS vineyards of Bugey, growing much the same grapes as Savoie together with some particularly successful Chardonnay (though not Chasselas), are delineated with equal precision and complexity. Bugey's three individual *crus* are Manicle, Montagnieu, which is best known for its smooth-scented Roussette, and Cerdon, known particularly for its sparkling rosé.

Vins de Pays

Vin de Pays d'Oc

—··—··— International boundary

—·—·—· Département boundary

———— Boundary of Vin de Pays d'Oc

Côtes du Brian   Name of Vin de Pays

Vin de Pays areas are distinguished by colour

1:1,136,000

Km 0   10   20   30 Km

Miles 0   10   20 Miles

N

Map labels:

Bagnols-sur-Cèze · Coteaux de Cèze · Duché d'Uzès · Cèze · Alès · Uzès · Cévennes · G A R D · le Vigan · Gard · Coteaux du Pont du Gard · Duché d'Uzès · Côtes du Vidourle · La Vaunage · Nîmes · Coteaux Flaviens · Beau... · Lodève · Val de Montferrand · La Bénovie · La Vistrenque · Bérange · Vidourle · Coteaux du Salagou · Mont-Baudile · Gorges de l'Hérault · Hérault · Lunel · Bédarieux · H É R A U L T · Côtes du Céressou · La Vicomté d'Aumelas · Montpellier · Aigues-Mortes · Étang de Vaccarès · Arles · La Haute Vallée de l'Orb · Coteaux de Laurens · Orb · Collines de la Moure · Canal du · Sables du Golfe du Lion · Grand Rhône · St Pons · Jaur · Caux · Coteaux de Bessilles · Pézenas · Golfe-les-Flots-d'Aigues-Mortes · Petit Rhône · Coteaux de Murviel · Côtes de Thongue · Côtes de Thau · Canal du Midi · Monts de la Grage · Cessenon · Bessan · Étang de Thau · Sète · Golfe du Lion · Côtes du Brian · Coteaux de Fontcaude · Coteau du Libron · Béziers · Pointe du Sablon · Cesse · Val de Cesse · Coteaux d'Enserune · L'Ardailhou · Agde · Castelnaudary · Côtes de Lastours · Coteaux de Peyriac · Côtes de Pérignan · Cap d'Agde · Canal du Midi · La Cité de Carcassonne · Hauts-de-Badens · Val de Cesse · Aude · Carcassonne · Coteaux de Miramont · Lézignan-Corbières · Orbieu · Narbonne · Côtes de Prouille · Hauterive · Coteaux de Narbonne · Aude · Val de Dagne · Coteaux de la Cabrerisse · Limoux · La Haute Vallée de l'Aude · Hauterive · A U D E · La Vallée du Paradis · Coteaux du Littoral Audois · Cap Leucate · Quillan · Pays du Torgan · Vals d'Agly · Étang de Leucate · Cucugnan · Agly · Côtes Catalanes · Coteaux de Fenouillèdes · Vals d'Agly · P Y R É N É E S - O R I E N T A L E S · Perpignan · Têt · Prades · Catalan · Port Vendres · Cap Bear · Font-Romeu · Tech · Céret · La Côte Vermeille

and Roussillon (Vin de Pays d'Oc). The last is by far the most important single Vin de Pays, sub-divided into the dozens of local ones shown on the map above.

The regulations stipulate the precise production area, a generous maximum yield of 90hl/ha, minimum natural alcohol levels, and which grape varieties are officially permitted for that particular Vin de Pays – generally a wide range of local grapes plus an appropriate selection of the major international varieties.

It is frankly admitted that some Vins de Pays have more validity than others. Some names have scarcely been used while the annual production of Vin de Pays d'Oc approaches 300 million litres, or more than 5% of France's total annual harvest. (This explains why about 70% of all Vin de Pays is red; the south of France is red wine country.)

Vins de Pays give growers an escape route from the straitjacket of AC regulations. The range of permitted grape varieties is wider, yields are higher, there is no minimum age for vines and the geographical area is much less restricted. So a grower in the northern Rhône, for example, can sell the produce of a vine too young to produce Condrieu, or a Merlot planted on the opposite bank of the river, as a Vin de Pays des Collines Rhodaniennes. The excellent wines of Domaine de Trévallon in western Provence, disqualified from the appellation Les Baux-de-Provence because of an excess of Cabernet Sauvignon, can be sold as (particularly expensive) Vin de Pays des Bouches-du-Rhône. Shippers such as Louis Latour of Burgundy and Georges Duboeuf of Beaujolais have been able to expand southwards into

France's Vins de Pays are a relatively recent creation of French wine officialdom, but a hugely successful one. If the VDQS category, discussed overleaf and mapped on page 53, was created to distinguish ACs-in-waiting, the Vin de Pays category was created in 1973 (and formalized only in 1979) as a spur to the vast table wine, or Vin de Table, category. A Vin de Pays, or country wine, is seen by the French as a superior table wine, providing the humblest sort of French wine with the chance to earn the greatest French compliment: geographical context. By qualifying as a Vin de Pays, a table wine becomes a Vin de Pays de Somewhere Specific. Names have been deliberately chosen to exclude any possibility of confusion with proper ACs, with delightfully creative results.

The Vin de Pays names, shown on these two maps, read like poetry to anyone with a feeling for the French countryside: Vals, Coteaux and Monts, Gorges and Pays, Marches and Vicomtés, Balmes and Fiefs. Who could resist Vallée du Paradis (an area northeast of Corbières) or L'Île de Beauté (Corsica's Vin de Pays name)?

Vins de Pays operate at three levels: 95 small local districts or zones, 54 départements (but specifically not the "fine wine" départements of Alsace, Bordeaux, Champagne, Côte d'Or, and Beaujolais), and four big regions – the whole of the Loire Valley (Vin de Pays du Jardin de la France – another pretty name), most of South-west France (Vin de Pays du Comté Tolosan), a big slice of eastern France (Vin de Pays des Comtés Rhodaniens), and all of the Languedoc

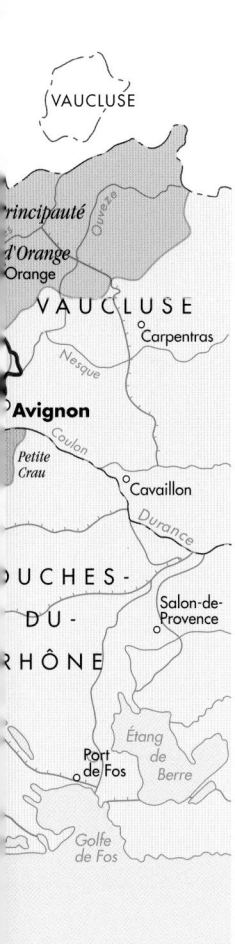

pastures new by, for instance, selling respectively Pinot Noir and Viognier as Vins de Pays des Coteaux de l'Ardèche. And, to give a final example, Muscadet producers who wish to profit from Chardonnay's liking for their region can sell the wine as Chardonnay, Vin de Pays du Jardin de la France.

The Vin de Pays category could also be said to have come to the rescue of hundreds if not thousands of vine-growers in Southwest France. Much of the embarrassing surplus of grapes originally intended for armagnac and cognac stills (see map, page 53) has been diverted into crisp white Vin de Pays des Côtes de Gascogne and Charentais respectively.

This relatively new category of French wine has been embraced warmly. By the end of the last century it accounted for more than a third of all wine made in France, mopping up much of the wine that would previously have been classified as lowly Vin de Table. And its success on export markets doubtless owes much to a very un-French aspect of these wines' appeal: a third of them are now sold not on the basis of their geography but as varietal wines, *vins de cépage*,

wines with such internationally recognizable words as Chardonnay and Merlot on their labels. The Vins de Pays provide French wine producers with a means of fighting the New World on its own ground. Most French drinkers might still regard Vins de Pays as inferior, but in many export markets, particularly Germany and the UK, the varietal versions at least are seen as hearteningly familiar, and so much easier to understand than the complexities of the AC system.

A high proportion of Vin de Pays is either of this welcome-to-wine basic commercial sort, or a slightly pallid version of the local AC style. But under the accommodating umbrella of these 150-odd names, some fascinating, serious and occasionally underpriced wines lurk.

Vins de Pays do not have to be inexpensive, however. The first Vin de Pays to reach serious heights – and prices – was Mas de Daumas Gassac, an estate near Aniane northwest of Montpellier (see page 138). Here a curious mix of white grapes make particularly intriguing white wine, and mainly Bordeaux grapes make red wine of formidable colour, concentration and depth on a very particular terroir: immensely

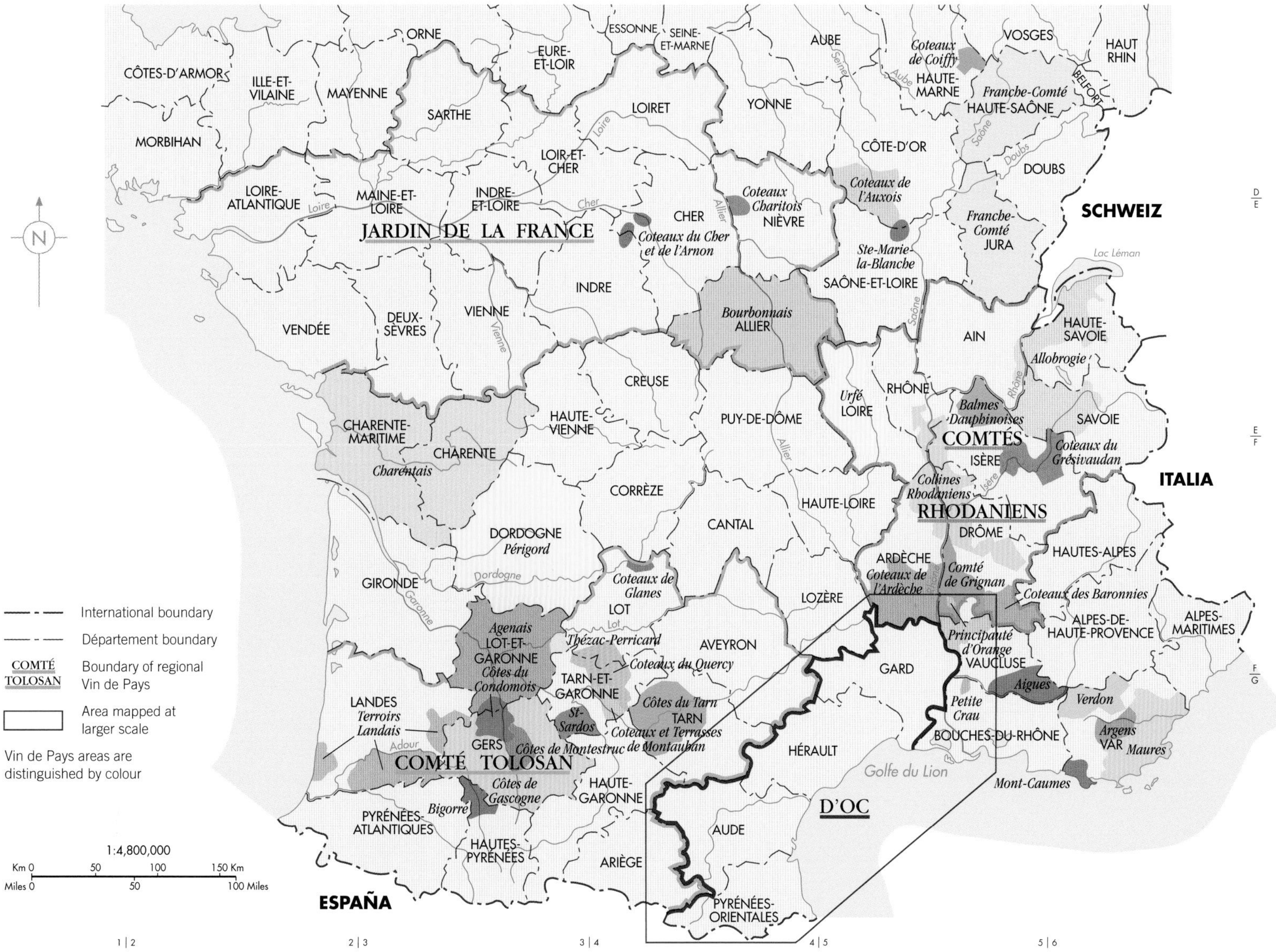

VDQS

deep and well-draining beds of volcanic debris. An appellation, one would think, in the making, but now just one of dozens of characterful Vins de Pays expressing terroirs unacknowledged by the AC system. Domaine Grange des Pères, for example, is another highly-regarded deep-flavoured red to have emerged from this region, and so obvious is the potential here that Robert Mondavi of California has tried to move in.

Foreigners – from other parts of France and elsewhere – have become increasingly important to the Languedoc economy, largely because of Vin de Pays production. Itinerant Australian winemakers have been upgrading winemaking techniques in French co-operatives for years, but Hardys of Australia was the first to take a direct stake when it bought Domaine de la Baume near Béziers. Australian rival Southcorp acquired James Herrick Wines near Narbonne much later, but inward investment has also come from the varied likes of the Rothschilds (both Mouton and Lafite); Laroche of Chablis, Boisset, Louis Latour, and Antonin Rodet of Burgundy; Duboeuf of Beaujolais, and a growing list of others. Land is cheap here relative to more famous wine regions, the climate more reliable and the Vin de Pays possibilities varied and particularly easy to sell internationally.

Indeed, so much does the Languedoc belong to the greater world of wine nowadays that in the mid-1990s, when California was desperately short of inexpensive varietal wine, American brand owners sourced it from the Languedoc's vast reserves of Vins de Pays. Their customers hardly noticed.

The Vins Délimités de Qualité Supérieure (VDQS; mapped on page 53) represent hardly 1% of French wine production but they can instil every bit as much local pride as any fully-fledged Appellation Contrôlée, which they all may eventually claim. Recent examples of promotion to AC status are the Côtes du Forez in the Loire, the Côtes du Vivarais in the southern Rhône, and Cabardès in western Languedoc, where the Côtes de la Malepère is working hard for similar elevation. (Sauvignon de) St-Bris southwest of Chablis is another candidate for promotion. There are also promotions from Vin de Pays status to VDQS, most recently Coteaux du Quercy, which makes Cabernet Franc-based red and rosé south of Cahors.

The other VDQSs of Southwest France – Côtes de Millau, Côtes de St-Mont, Côtes du Brulhois, Tursan, and the respective Vins de Lavilledieu, d'Entraygues et du Fel, and d'Estaing – are described on pages 112-114. Vin du Bugey in Savoie is mapped and described on page 149.

Such wines as are still made in the north-eastern corner of France are known by the French as Vins de l'Est. The pale, crisp VDQS Vins de Moselle are light red or pale pink Gamays (like the AC Côtes de Toul), and, mainly, whites from Auxerrois, Gewurztraminer, Müller-Thurgau, Pinots Blanc and Gris, and Riesling.

Of all the wine regions of France, the Loire has the greatest concentration of VDQSs, beginning almost on the mouth of the river with Gros Plant du Pays Nantais, one of France's few varietally labelled wines and made in the Muscadet zone. Gros Plant is an almost unbelievably tart

grape which positively demands shellfish, and is clearly a candidate for distilling into brandy (as it is, called Folle Blanche, into cognac).

The pale VDQS Fiefs-Vendéens is the produce of the Vendée département south of Nantes. Coteaux d'Ancenis, made north of Muscadet country in fair quantity, is mostly minor red and rosé from Gamay and Cabernet, but includes a little smoky-sweet white Malvoisie (Pinot Gris).

Well south of the River Loire itself, Vins du Thoursais and Haut Poitou are crisp, light, often varietal wines (the French authorities object less to grape names featuring on VDQS wines than on AC labels).

The Coteaux du Vendômois vineyards around Vendôme, like the AC Jasnières to the west, make necessarily light but sometimes characterful reds and rosés from local Pineau d'Aunis grapes.

Valençay on the Cher southern tributary is shrinking but still makes a wide range of crisp wines from at least six different grape varieties, whereas Gamay is the predominant grape in Châteaumeillant's pale reds and rosés made south of Touraine.

The Vins de l'Orléannais vineyards round Orléans were once extensive enough to have spawned a famous vinegar but are today in decline. Way upstream, on the Allier tributary almost in the centre of France, St-Pourçain seems on a sure footing with its pale Gamays, Pinots, Chardonnays, and Sauvignons, while the Côtes d'Auvergne continues a long tradition of growing Gamay in, for the Loire basin, relatively sultry conditions.

Left The walled and heavily restored Cité of Carcassonne lends its name to a specific Vin de Pays made nearby and is also midway between two of the Languedoc's most transitional wine zones. The VDQS Côtes de la Malepère to the south produces increasingly convincing reds from Bordeaux grape varieties, while Cabardès blends them with Grenache, Syrah, and even the Fer of Marcillac.

Italy

No longer playing second fiddle to France, Italy has established her own highly distinctive, if occasionally exasperating, wine personality. At the top end her wines have a vivacity and style all of their own. At the bottom end, like any major European wine producer, she still has too high a proportion of dull, over-productive vines, but these are steadily becoming a minority and it is the quality of what is produced in between that has improved so impressively over the last few years.

Some would say there is no excuse. Colonizing Greeks called Italy Oenotria – the land of wine (or, strictly, staked vines – a sure sign of viticultural ambition). The map overleaf reminds us that there is little of Italy that is not, at least marginally, wine country. Only France – and only in some years – makes more wine than Italy.

In terms of geography, Italy cannot fail to produce good wine in great variety, if slopes, sunshine, and a temperate climate are the essentials. Her peculiar physique, that of a long spine of mountains reaching south from the sheltering Alps almost to North Africa, means that there can hardly be a desirable combination of altitude with latitude and exposure that is absent. Many of her soils are volcanic; much is limestone or tufa; there is plenty of gravelly clay: Oenotria indeed.

Because Italy is so well suited to the vine and today produces such wonderful and wonderfully distinctive wines, it is easy to forget just how recent this phenomenon is. Hardly more than a generation ago, only a tiny proportion of Italian wine was even bottled by the producer. The great majority was shipped to the cities for domestic consumption, drunk with no more ceremony than a thirst-quenching gulp of water, and such wine as was exported was mostly blended by the big shippers.

It is hardly surprising therefore that wine labels strike the outsider as distinctly unevolved, their chief inconvenience being an almost impenetrable confusion of names. Because wine is omnipresent, so much a part of everyday life, made by so many proud and independent people, every conceivable sort of name is pressed into use to mark originality. Thus one bottle may carry on it not only the official (DOC) name and the name of the producer, but also the name of the property, a part of the property, or of anything else that takes the producer's fancy – and fantasy it often is. Helpful back labels are eschewed and regions rarely named on labels where the name of an obscure town is often the only geographical reference. Italy still needs a labelling system (which is not necessarily the same thing as a new wine law) which would set out clearly who made the wine, where it was made, and how it should be referred to.

From the 1960s on the Italian government undertook the monumental task of tidying up the multiplicity of Italian wines into defined identities – hundreds of them. The Italian DOC (Denominazione di Origine Controllata) system was an Italian answer to France's Appellation Contrôlée system, complete with boundaries (often too generous), maximum yields (ditto) and specified grape varieties and production methods.

A superior form of DOC, DOCG (for which the denomination was not just controlled, but guaranteed – a nice distinction) was also created, and eventually in the 1980s awarded to such obviously superior wines as Barolo, Barbaresco, Vino Nobile di Montepulciano, Brunello di Montalcino, and, as a spur to improvement, a much-revised Chianti. (See box overleaf for the complete DOCG roster today.)

Over the years, though, a serious drawback in the basic DOC system became clear. What it effectively did was fossilize the current practice of the majority of winemakers in each region, particularly over-generous yields, regardless of whether it led to the best results or not. Indeed, it penalized progressive winemakers who knew that certain changes in, for example, grape varieties or maturation techniques could greatly improve their products.

The result was the proliferation of Vini da Tavola in the 1970s and 1980s – that is unclassified and undemarcated wines of the lowest official standing – which frequently excelled the DOC wines in both quality and price; a number became Italy's benchmarks for vinous brilliance. Vini da Tavola became the test-benches of all new ideas, imported grape varieties, and techniques borrowed from around the world.

But by the end of the 1980s Vini da Tavola continued to multiply and the situation had

Right All likely and many unlikely parts of Italy are planted with vines. Here they cling to terraces on the stunning Ligurian coast in an area called Cinque Terre.

become absurd (and threatened to become untenable as European Union regulations would eventually outlaw all sorts of useful information such as vintage and grape variety on the labels of table wines).

In 1992 a new law was passed to restructure the whole system of classification with restrictions, including maximum permitted yields, decreasing steadily from the pinnacle of DOCG to DOC and then to a new category, IGT, created for the innovative Vini da Tavola (or at least the great majority for which DOCs were not created). This has spawned yet another long list of names (see the blue box opposite). The principle of this category, like France's Vins de Pays, is that they can use the geographical and varietal name, but strictly in that order.

In theory an IGT does not have the status of a DOC, but the market says otherwise about many of them – particularly many of those made from the non-traditional grape varieties that are now planted all over Italy. Cabernet Sauvignon (which had first been introduced in the early 19th century) and Chardonnay spearheaded this new invasion but Merlot, Syrah, and others are now almost commonplace. The IGTs are listed here although their boundaries are not drawn on the detailed maps that follow for fear of a confusing overlap with those of Italy's hundreds of DOCs. IGTs are appearing on an increasing

DOCG Wines

Albana di Romagna (Emilia Romagna)
Asti and Moscato d'Asti (Piemonte)
Barbaresco (Piemonte)
Barolo (Piemonte)
Brachetto d'Acqui or Acqui (Piemonte)
Brunello di Montalcino (Tuscany)
Carmignano (Tuscany)
Chianti (Tuscany)
Chianti Classico (Tuscany)
Franciacorta (Lombardy)
Gattinara (Piemonte)
Gavi or Cortese di Gavi (Piemonte)
Ghemme (Piemonte)
Sagrantino di Montefalco (Umbria)
Recioto di Soave (Veneto)
Taurasi (Campania)
Torgiano Rosso Riserva (Umbria)
Valtellina Superiore (Lombardy)
Vermentino di Gallura (Sardinia)
Vernaccia di San Gimignano (Tuscany)
Vino Nobile di Montepulciano (Tuscany)

International boundary
Regione boundary
Wine-producing area
Land above 600 metres
157 Regional map page number

1:6,000,000

Km 0   100   200 Km
Miles 0   50   100 Miles

Above Vineyards nestling high above Merano in the Alto Adige, where Italy meets the Austrian Tyrol and where German is more commonly spoken than Italian. The summers can be remarkably hot here in Italy's most northerly wine region.

proportion of labels, however – not least because many of the names (Umbria, Sicilia, for example) have more market resonance than those of individual DOCs.

The map on the opposite page is intended as a reminder of the whereabouts of the regions (Toscana or Campania, for example) and as a key to the subsequent more detailed maps. All the important current DOCs and DOCGs appear on the four pages (157, 165, 173, and 182) that carve up the country into northwest, northeast, centre, and south, except those in the complex centres of quality winegrowing which are given large-scale maps of their own.

And the wine? Are all Italy's best wines still red? Most, but by no means all. Italy learned to make "modern" (ie fresh and crisp) white wine in the 1960s. In the 1980s she began to add back the character that was lost in the process, and by the late 1990s had succeeded. Soave, Verdicchio, Pinot Grigio – all can now be found in deliciously fruity form, as well as in old paint-stripper mode.

Italy's red wines continue to get better and better. They range from the silky and fragile to the purple and potent, in every style and aroma from redoubtable natives to, inevitably, the international Cabernet standard. This quite extraordinarily rapid revolution in wine quality does not, unlike the improvements in French, California or Australian wine, reflect systematic investigation and experimentation at universities and research stations. It has been achieved largely by practical advice from a growing band of well-travelled consultants, initially specialists in winemaking but now taking an increasingly active role in the much-needed revitalization of Italy's vineyards. Much more of outdoor Oenotria, as well as its cellars, needs to be converted to concentrate on quality rather than quantity, with the heavily milked overhead *tendone* vine training system, more suitable for table grapes, a persistent culprit.

Yet to be true to the spirit of Italy the qualities of all her wine must be seen in the context of the incredibly varied, sensuous Italian table. The true genius of Italy lies in spreading a feast. In the great Italian feast, wine plays the chief supporting role.

Language of the Label

Quality designations

Denominazione di Origine Controllata e Garantita (DOCG) wines recognized as either Italy's best, or supported by the most skilful politicians

Denominazione di Origine Controllata (DOC) Italy's original answer to France's AC (see page 52)

Indicazione Geografica Tipica (IGT) Italy's relatively recent answer to France's Vin de Pays (see page 150)

Vino da Tavola table wine, Italy's most basic category

Other common expressions

Abboccato lightly sweet
Amabile semi-sweet
Annata vintage year
Azienda agricola wine estate which does not buy in grapes or wine, unlike an *azienda vinicola*
Bianco white
Cantina cellar or winery
Cantina sociale, cantina cooperativa co-operative winery
Casa vinicola wine firm
Chiaretto very pale red
Classico original, rather than expanded, zone
Consorzio growers' association
Dolce sweet
Fattoria literally farm
Frizzante semi-sparkling
Gradi (alcool) alcoholic strength as a percentage by volume
Imbottigliato (all'origine) bottled (at source)
Liquoroso strong, usually fortified
Metodo classico, metodo tradizionale bottle-fermented sparkling wine
Passito strong, usually sweet wine made from dried grapes
Podere very small agricultural property, smaller than a *fattoria*
Recioto wine made from half-dried grapes, a Veneto speciality
Riserva special, long-aged selection
Rosato rosé (rare in Italy)
Rosso red
Secco dry
Spumante sparkling
Superiore wine that has undergone more ageing than normal DOC and contains 0.5-1% more alcohol
Tenuta holding or estate
Vendemmia vintage
Vendemmia tardiva late harvest
Vigna, vigneto vineyard
Vignaiolo, viticoltore vine-grower
Vino wine

Indicazione Geografica Tipica Wines

Allerona (Umbria)
Alta Valle della Greve (Tuscany)
Alto Livenza (Veneto/Friuli-VG)
Alto Mincio (Lombardy)
Alto Tirino (Abruzzi)
Arghillà (Calabria)
Barbagia (Sardinia)
Basilicata (Basilicata)
Benaco Bresciano (Lombardy)
Beneventano (Campania)
Bergamasca (Lombardy)
Bettona (Umbria)
Bianco di Castelfranco Emilia (Emilia Romagna)
Calabria (Calabria)
Camarro (Sicily)
Cannara (Umbria)
Civitella d'Agliano (Latium)
Colli Aprutini (Abruzzi)
Colli Cimini (Latium)
Colli del Limbara (Sardinia)
Colli del Sangro (Abruzzi)
Colli della Toscana Centrale (Tuscany)
Colli di Salerno (Campania)
Colli Ericini (Sicily)
Colli Trevigiani (Veneto)
Collina del Milanese (Lombardy)
Colline Frentane (Abruzzi)
Colline Pescaresi (Abruzzi)
Colline Savonesi (Liguria)
Colline Teatine (Abruzzi)
Condoleo (Calabria)
Conselvano (Veneto)
Costa Viola (Calabria)
Daunia (Apulia)
Del Vastese or Histonium (Abruzzi)
Delle Venezie (Veneto/Trentino-AA/Friuli-VG)
Dugenta (Campania)
Emilia or dell'Emilia (Emilia Romagna)
Epomeo (Campania)

Esaro (Calabria)
Fontanarossa di Cerda (Sicily)
Forlì (Emilia Romagna)
Fortana del Taro (Emilia Romagna)
Frusinate or del Frusinate (Latium)
Irpinia (Campania)
Isola dei Nuraghi (Sardinia)
Lazio (Latium)
Lipuda (Calabria)
Locride (Calabria)
Marca Trevigiana (Veneto)
Marche (Marches)
Maremma Toscana (Tuscany)
Marmilla (Sardinia)
Mitterberg tra Cauria and Telor Mitterberg zwischen Gfrill und Tollor Mitterberg (Trentino-AA)
Montenetto di Brescia (Lombardy)
Murgia (Apulia)
Narni (Umbria)
Nettuno (Latium)
Nurra (Sardinia)
Ogliastra (Sardinia)
Orcia (Tuscany)
Osco or Terre degli Osci (Molise)
Paestum (Campania)
Palizzi (Calabria)
Parteolla (Sardinia)
Pellaro (Calabria)
Planargia (Sardinia)
Pompeiano (Campania)
Provincia de Mantova (Lombardy)
Provincia de Modena or Modena (Emilia Romagna)
Provincia di Nuoro (Sardinia)
Provincia di Pavia (Lombardy)
Provincia di Verona or Veronese (Veneto)
Puglia (Apulia)
Quistello (Lombardy)
Ravenna (Emilia Romagna)

Roccamonfina (Campania)
Romangia (Sardinia)
Ronchi di Brescia (Lombardy)
Rotae (Molise)
Rubicone (Emilia Romagna)
Sabbioneta (Lombardy)
Salemi (Sicily)
Salento (Apulia)
Salina (Sicily)
Scilla (Calabria)
Sebino (Lombardy)
Sibiola (Sardinia)
Sicilia (Sicily)
Sillaro or Bianco del Sillaro (Emilia Romagna)
Spello (Umbria)
Tarantino (Apulia)
Terrazze Retiche di Sondrio (Lombardy)
Terre del Volturno (Campania)
Terre di Chieti (Abruzzi)
Terre di Veleja (Emilia Romagna)
Tharros (Sardinia)
Toscana or Toscano (Tuscany)
Trexenta (Sardinia)
Umbria (Umbria)
Val di Magra (Tuscany)
Val di Neto (Calabria)
Val Tidone (Emilia Romagna)
Valdamato (Calabria)
Vallagarina (Veneto/Trentino-AA)
Valle d'Itria (Apulia)
Valle del Belice (Sicily)
Valle del Crati (Calabria)
Valle del Tirso (Sardinia)
Valle Peligna (Abruzzi)
Valli di Porto Pino (Veneto)
Veneto (Veneto)
Veneto Orientale (Veneto)
Venezia Giulia (Friuli)
Vigneti delle Dolomiti (Trentino-AA)

Northwest Italy

Northwest Italy means Piemonte (Piedmont in English) to any wine-lover. In its bitter-sweet vermouths, its grapey *spumantes*, its pungent purple wines for dishes of game and cheese, it epitomizes the sensuality of the Italian table at its best. On the next few pages its heart is shown in detail.

But the Langhe and Monferrato hills around Alba and Asti are not the only great vineyards of the northwest. Their noblest grape, Nebbiolo, gives excellent, if different, results in several corners of the region – most notably in the hills above Novara and Vercelli (famous for rice), where under the name of Spanna it rejoices in no fewer than six different DOCs – surely a case for rationalization. The newish Colline Novaresi DOC may be made from virtually all the local red or white grapes, and is used for declassified Boca, Fara, Ghemme, Sizzano, and Erbaluce, just as Colline Vercellesi wipes up wannabe Spanna made in the Vercelli and Biella provinces.

The DOCG Gattinara (above all from Le Colline Monsecco) is considered the king of these, with Ghemme and Lessona as consorts and Bramaterra not far behind. All benefit from a subalpine climate, a southern exposure and fast-draining glacial soil. In practice all depends on the grower and the amount of the permitted Bonarda or Vespolina grapes added. The weight and intensity of Barolo is not quite there, but perfume is not lacking. Spanna, which in the old days could become distinctly gamey in bottle, has benefited as much as any other wine from the new brooms that have been sweeping through Italy's cellars.

Nebbiolo also grows in the far northeast corner of the map opposite, where Lombardy meets Switzerland. In Valtellina, on south-facing sun-traps on the north bank of the River Adda, the grape, known here as Chiavennasca, makes sinewy, mountain-climbing reds. The heartland, Valtellina Superiore, which includes the Grumello, Inferno, Sassella, and Valgella sub-zones, makes infinitely better wine than that sold simply as Valtellina. It was elevated to DOCG status in 1998. Some dry Sfurzat is made from semi-dried grapes.

North of Turin on the road up to the Valle d'Aosta and the Mont Blanc tunnel to France there are two more Nebbiolos, of high reputation but low output, Carema and Donnaz. Carema is still in Piemonte (but nonetheless calls the Nebbiolo Picutener); Donnaz is made in Donnas over the provincial boundary in the Valle d'Aosta, Italy's smallest wine region. Alpine conditions may make these Nebbiolos less potent and deep-coloured but they have their own finesse.

Aosta's own red grape is Petit Rouge, which tastes not unlike the Mondeuse of Savoie: dark, fresh, berryish, and bracing. It forms the basis of Enfer d'Arvier and Torrette among other wines subsumed into the Valle d'Aosta DOC. Fumin grapes make longer-lived reds. The busy valley also makes some recherché whites from imported grapes: the very light Blancs de la Salle and de Morgex and some winter-weight Malvoisie and Petite Arvine from Switzerland.

Where the hilly turbulence of Piemonte merges with the Lombard plain to the east, conditions become less alpine and extreme. It is hard to offer a translation as musical as the name of the fulcrum of Lombardic viticulture that is Oltrepò Pavese, meaning the part of the province of Pavia that lies beyond the River Po. Far harder, though, is to convey in any orderly way the profusion of its wines, some with a DOC, some not, and much even sold without a geographical origin at all. Many of Italy's best Pinot Nero and some Pinot Bianco for the making of sparkling wines come from here without mentioning the fact.

The DOC Oltrepò Pavese Rosso calls for two-thirds Barbera mollified with a variety of local grapes, of which Bonarda (which in Oltrepò Pavese is the local alias for the Croatina grape) is the most prevalent and characterful, although Uva Rara can add spice to a blend. The zone's leading estate is Frecciarossa, "red arrow", from Castéggio. Buttafuoco and Sangue di Giuda are reds with bubbles more memorable for their names than for their flavours. Oltrepò white wines include "Pinot", which can be either Bianco or Nero (made white) or Grigio or all of these. Pinot Grigio is most common without bubbles: a dense and potentially delicious wine that suggests its relationship to a German Grauburgunder. Italian (in other words Welsch) Riesling is not unbearably dull in the Oltrepò Pavese (although Riesling Renano, "real" Riesling, is better); Moscatos are excellent and even Müller-Thurgau makes respectable wines. In such conditions one can reasonably expect almost any grape to thrive. All that is lacking in this productive but scarcely celebrated area is a name to conjure with. See page 164 for details of Lombardy's flourishing sparkling wine industry around Brescia. The Colli Piacentini around Piacenza is bidding for recognition with international varietal bottlings and an often *frizzante* red made from Barbera and Bonarda.

South from Piemonte over the final curling tail of the Alps, known as the Ligurian Apennines, we are on the Mediterranean, with scarcely enough room between the mountains and the sea to grow grapes. Liguria's production is tiny, but highly individual and worth investigating. Of its grapes only Vermentino (also known as Pigato here) and Malvasia are widely grown elsewhere: the white Albarola, Bosco, and Buzzetto are as esoteric as they sound. Cinque Terre is the white wine served with fish on the steep coast near La Spezia. Its liquorous version is called Sciacchetrà. Other less-known coastal whites should be tasted on a visit to Genoa: you will not find them elsewhere.

Potentially the most memorable Ligurian wine, however, is the red Rossese, whether of Dolceacqua near the French border or of Albenga, nearer Genoa. Unlike anything made west along the coast in the Alpes Maritimes, Rossese can be truly fresh, fruity in the soft-fruit or berry sense of Bordeaux, inviting to smell and refreshing to drink. And, unlike the most famous wines of northwest Italy, it does not need any ageing.

Right Ancient stone pillars support vines on subalpine terraces in the Valle d'Aosta, which leads up to the Mont Blanc Tunnel and French Switzerland. Some of the latter's more exotic indigenous vine varieties can be found in Aosta's high-maintenance vineyards.

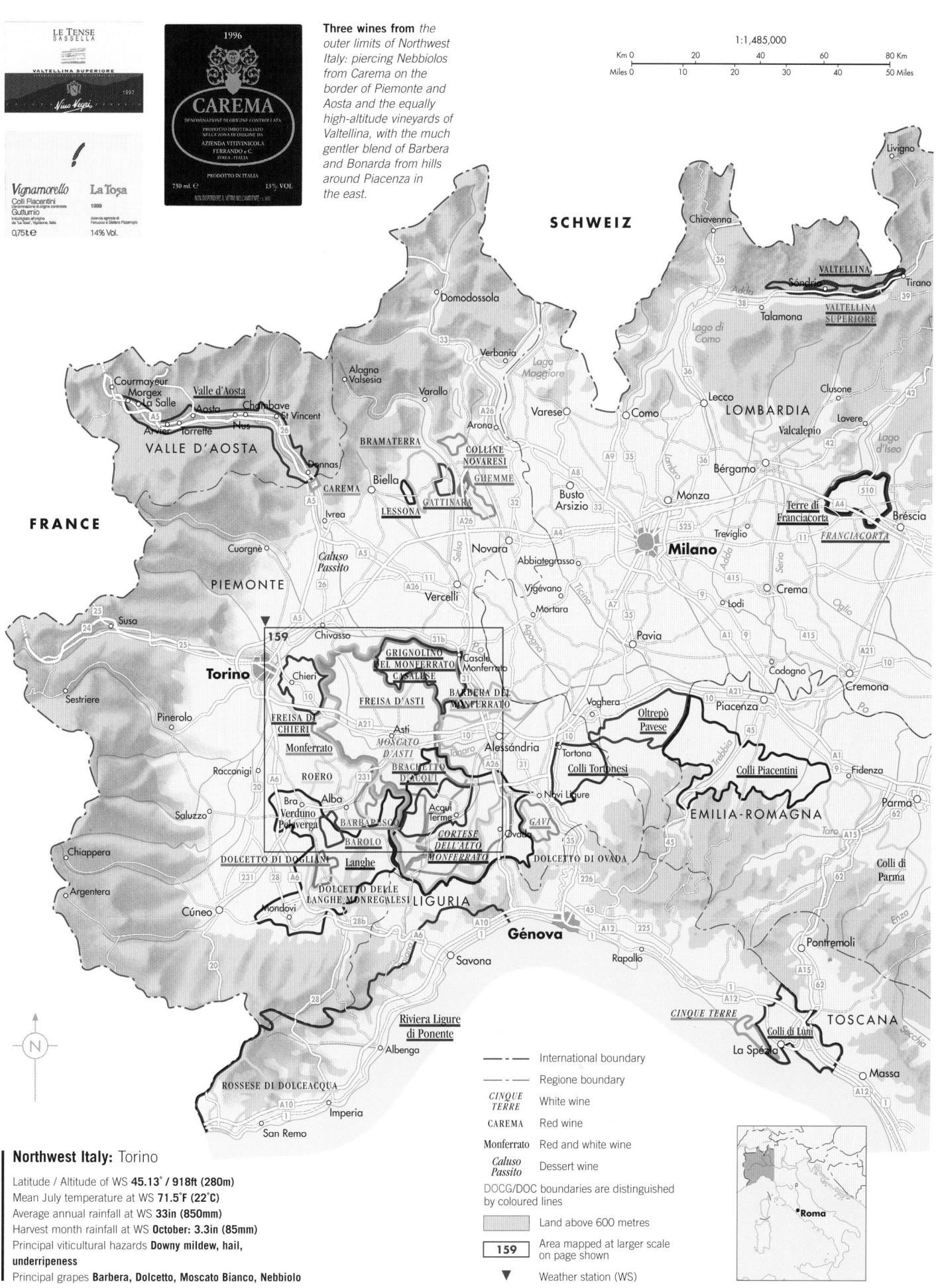

Three wines from *the outer limits of Northwest Italy: piercing Nebbiolos from Carema on the border of Piemonte and Aosta and the equally high-altitude vineyards of Valtellina, with the much gentler blend of Barbera and Bonarda from hills around Piacenza in the east.*

1:1,485,000

Km 0   20   40   60   80 Km
Miles 0   10   20   30   40   50 Miles

SCHWEIZ

FRANCE

VALLE D'AOSTA

PIEMONTE

LOMBARDIA

Milano

EMILIA-ROMAGNA

LIGURIA

TOSCANA

International boundary

Regione boundary

CINQUE TERRE — White wine

CAREMA — Red wine

Monferrato — Red and white wine

Caluso Passito — Dessert wine

DOCG/DOC boundaries are distinguished by coloured lines

Land above 600 metres

159 — Area mapped at larger scale on page shown

▼ — Weather station (WS)

Northwest Italy: Torino

Latitude / Altitude of WS **45.13° / 918ft (280m)**
Mean July temperature at WS **71.5°F (22°C)**
Average annual rainfall at WS **33in (850mm)**
Harvest month rainfall at WS **October: 3.3in (85mm)**
Principal viticultural hazards **Downy mildew, hail, underripeness**
Principal grapes **Barbera, Dolcetto, Moscato Bianco, Nebbiolo**

Piemonte

Piemontese food and wine are as inseparable as those of Burgundy. They are strong, rich, individual, mature, somehow autumnal. Truffles play an important part. One feels it must be more than coincidence that this is the Italian province nearest to France. Piemonte means at the foot of the mountains – the Alps. The Alps almost encircle the region, so that from its heart, the Monferrato hills around Asti, they form a continuous dark – or in winter and spring sparkling white – horizon. Piemonte has a climate of its own, with a very hot growing season followed by a misty autumn and a cold, often foggy, winter.

At vintage time in Barolo the hills are half hidden. Ramps of copper and gold vines, dotted with hazel and peach trees, lead down to the

Below All-important slopes in Serralunga d'Alba in the Barolo zone, for long best-known as the home of Fontanafredda, one of the very few large-scale producers in this region, which is characterized by small, family farms. The formerly royal estate of Fontanafredda is now owned by a bank.

valley of the Tanaro, lost in the fog. It is a magical experience to visit Serralunga or La Morra and see the dark grapes coming in.

The two best red wines of Piemonte, Barolo and Barbaresco, take their names from villages mapped in detail on the next pages. The rest have the names of their grapes – Barbera, Dolcetto, Grignolino, Freisa, Favorita. If to the grape they add a district name (for example Barbera d'Asti) it means they come from a limited and theoretically superior area. The map shows the most important zones of central Piemonte – including that of the famous Moscato d'Asti *frizzante*, the quintessence of sweet Muscat grapes in its most celebratory form. Asti (it dropped its Spumante suffix some years ago) is often scorned by wine snobs for the very cheerful simplicity that is its *raison d'être*. It also has the considerable merit of containing less alcohol than virtually any other wine.

Light-skinned Cortese grapes are grown south of Alessandria to the east to produce Gavi, one of Italy's more fashionable dry white wines

in the 1980s. Demand for whites then also led to the promotion of an old local grape, Arneis, from a mere Nebbiolo-stretcher to make soft, light but perfumed wines not unlike Pinot Blanc – especially in the Roero hills northwest of Alba on the sandy soils of the west bank of the Tanaro. More market-minded growers have successfully added Chardonnay (and Cabernet and Sauvignon Blanc) to their portfolios. Langhe Chardonnay is particularly popular.

The Nebbiolo has no rival as the finest red grape of northern Italy. It does not have to meet Barolo or Barbaresco specifications to make mellow fragrant wine – indeed some seriously worthwhile Nebbiolo d'Alba, Langhe Nebbiolo, and red Roero is made nowadays.

At the level just below noble, Barbera is the most important regional grape. Like Nebbiolo, Barbera is dark and naturally high in acidity, but it is often rather plummy and is approachable much earlier than Nebbiolo. The grapes have traditionally been picked earlier than Nebbiolo but they need relatively warm sites and later picking to bring the acidity down to palatable levels, as growers in Asti and Alba have shown. One of the most exciting and popular developments in Piemonte during the 1990s was the emergence of a host of Barberas aged in small oak casks, this grape apparently showing much more affinity for new oak than Nebbiolo.

Barbera's one possible rival is Dolcetto, which will still ripen in the coolest, highest sites: soft, where Barbera often bites, but capable of a marvellous balance between fleshy, dusty-dense, and dry with a touch of bitter. The best Dolcetto comes from Alba, Diano d'Alba, Dogliani, and Ovada (for its most potent style).

Grignolino is consistently a lightweight cherry red but can be a fine and piquant one; at its best (from Asti or Monferrato Casalese) extremely clean and stimulating. All these are wines to drink relatively young.

Other specialities of this prolific region, the spaghetti-junction of *denominazioni* as the map makes all too obvious, include another frothy sweet red wine, Brachetto d'Acqui; light red Verduno from Pelaverga grapes; sweet pink or red Malvasia di Casorzo d'Asti; the interesting yellow *passito* (made from semi-sweet grapes) with the DOC Erbaluce di Caluso; Loazzolo sweet white from dried Moscato grapes; and the agreeable blend of Barbera and Grignolino sold as Rubino di Cantavenna. One of the favourites of Turin itself is Freisa, often from Asti, a fizzy and frequently sweet red wine not unlike a tarter, less fruity form of Lambrusco. You either love it or loathe it.

A forgiving Piemonte DOC has been invented for Barbera, Bonarda, Brachetto, Chardonnay, Cortese, Grignolino, Moscato, and Spumante sourced anywhere within the region, to ensure that no IGTs sully Piemonte's reputation. Monferrato, between the River Po and the Apennines, encompasses grapes such as Cortese, Dolcetto, and Freisa. No-one has ever accused Piemonte of a paucity of grapes, flavours, and names.

Light red Grignolino and white Moscato each represent the flirtatious, aromatic side of Piemonte's wide range of wines, as do Freisa and Favorita. Dolcetto, like the widely planted Barbera, is increasingly being subjected to oak ageing, an essential component in most of Piemonte's successful Chardonnays.

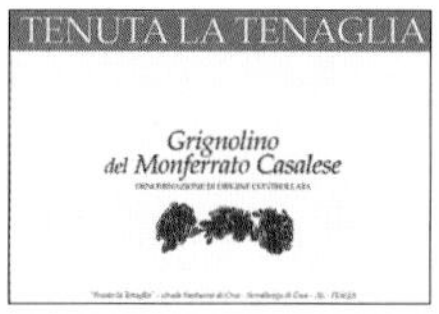

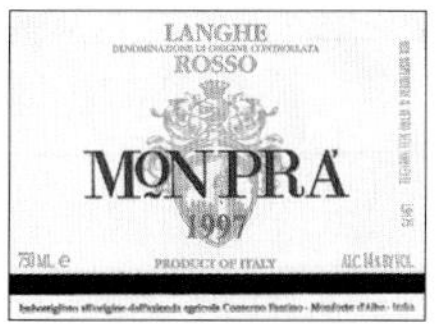

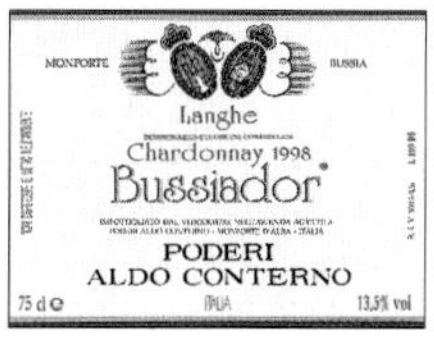

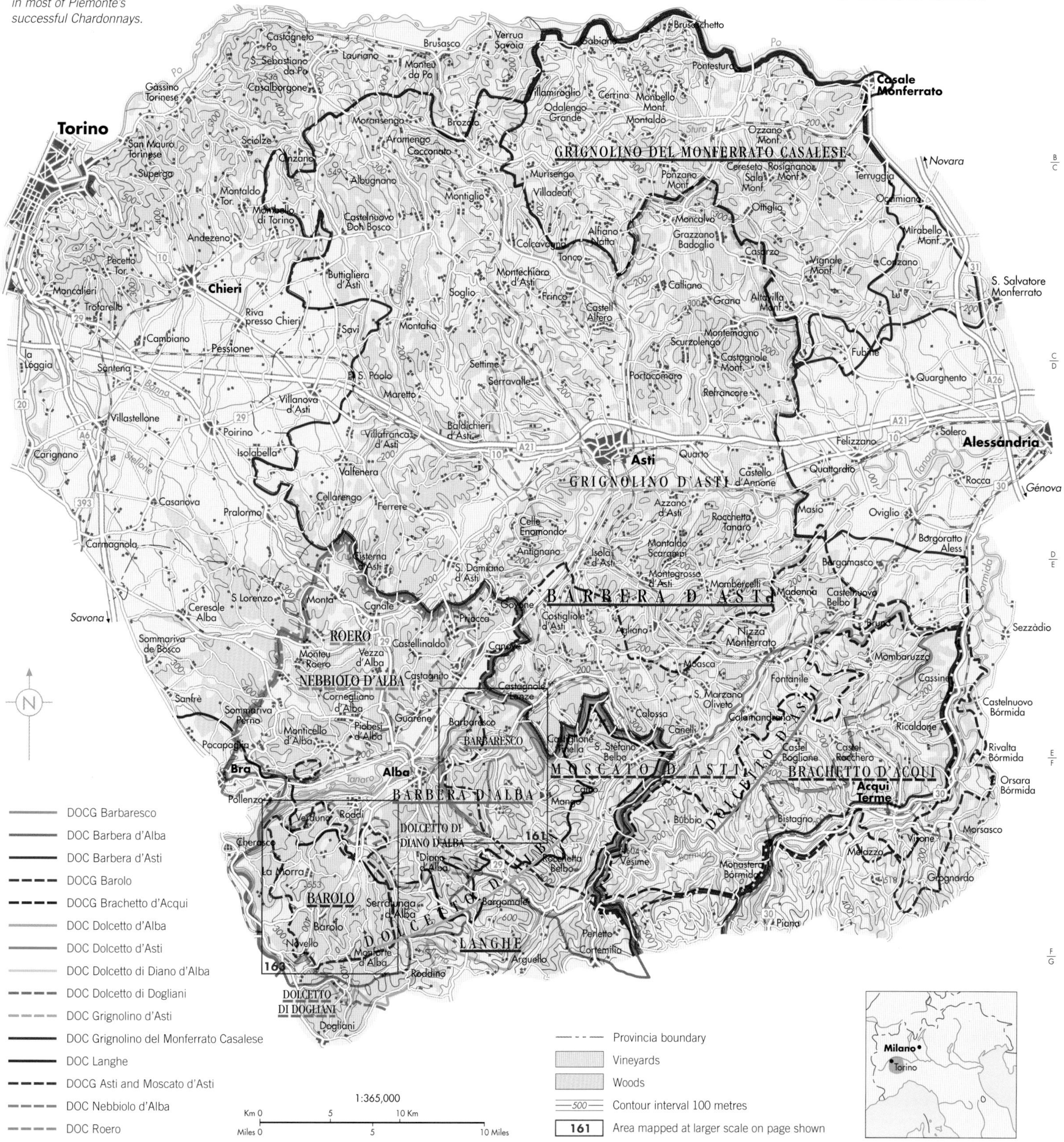

TENUTA LA TENAGLIA
Grignolino
del Monferrato Casalese

LANGHE
ROSSO
Mon PRA
1997

Langhe
Chardonnay 1998
Bussiador
PODERI
ALDO CONTERNO

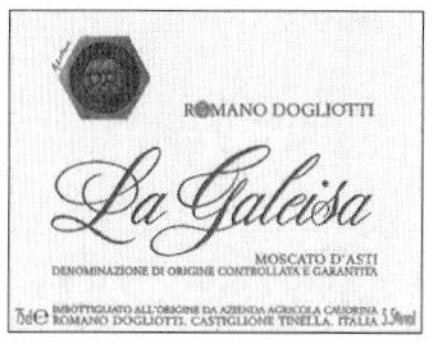

ROMANO DOGLIOTTI
La Galeisa
MOSCATO D'ASTI

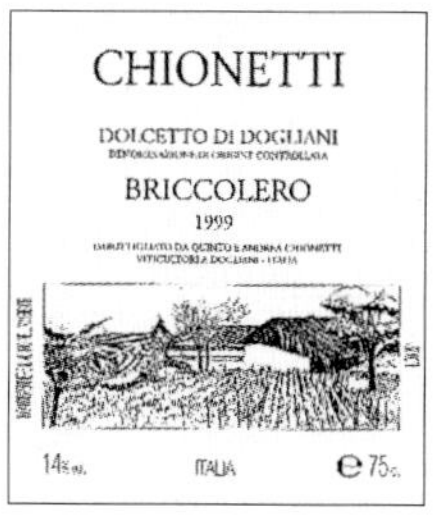

CHIONETTI
DOLCETTO DI DOGLIANI
BRICCOLERO
1999

Torino

Casale Monferrato

Chieri

GRIGNOLINO DEL MONFERRATO CASALESE

Asti

GRIGNOLINO D'ASTI

Alessándria

BARBERA D'ASTI

ROERO

NEBBIOLO D'ALBA

BARBARESCO

Bra

Alba

MOSCATO D'ASTI

BRACHETTO D'ACQUI

Acqui Terme

BARBERA D'ALBA

DOLCETTO DI DIANO D'ALBA

BAROLO

LANGHE

DOLCETTO DI DOGLIANI

Legend

— DOCG Barbaresco
— DOC Barbera d'Alba
— DOC Barbera d'Asti
- - - DOCG Barolo
- - - DOCG Brachetto d'Acqui
— DOC Dolcetto d'Alba
— DOC Dolcetto d'Asti
— DOC Dolcetto di Diano d'Alba
- - - DOC Dolcetto di Dogliani
- - - DOC Grignolino d'Asti
— DOC Grignolino del Monferrato Casalese
— DOC Langhe
- - - DOCG Asti and Moscato d'Asti
- - - DOC Nebbiolo d'Alba
- - - DOC Roero

- - - Provincia boundary

Vineyards

Woods

—500— Contour interval 100 metres

161 Area mapped at larger scale on page shown

1:365,000
Km 0   5   10 Km
Miles 0   5   10 Miles

Milano
Torino

Barbaresco

Nebbiolo finds its most dazzling expression in the Langhe hills, on the calcareous clay marls of the right bank of the River Tanaro, to the northeast of Alba in the Barbaresco zone, and to the southwest of the city around the village of Barolo (mapped and discussed overleaf). The Nebbiolo grape is a particularly late ripener so the finest wine tends to come from slopes with a southern tilt that are not too high, between about 490 and 1,150ft (150 and 350m) altitude.

Today the grower and his vineyard (the terms *sorì* and *bricco* recur continually for distinguished sites) hold the key to Barolo and Barbaresco. Tastings reveal consistent differences of quality, of aroma, of potency, and of finesse that in the Côte d'Or would justify the

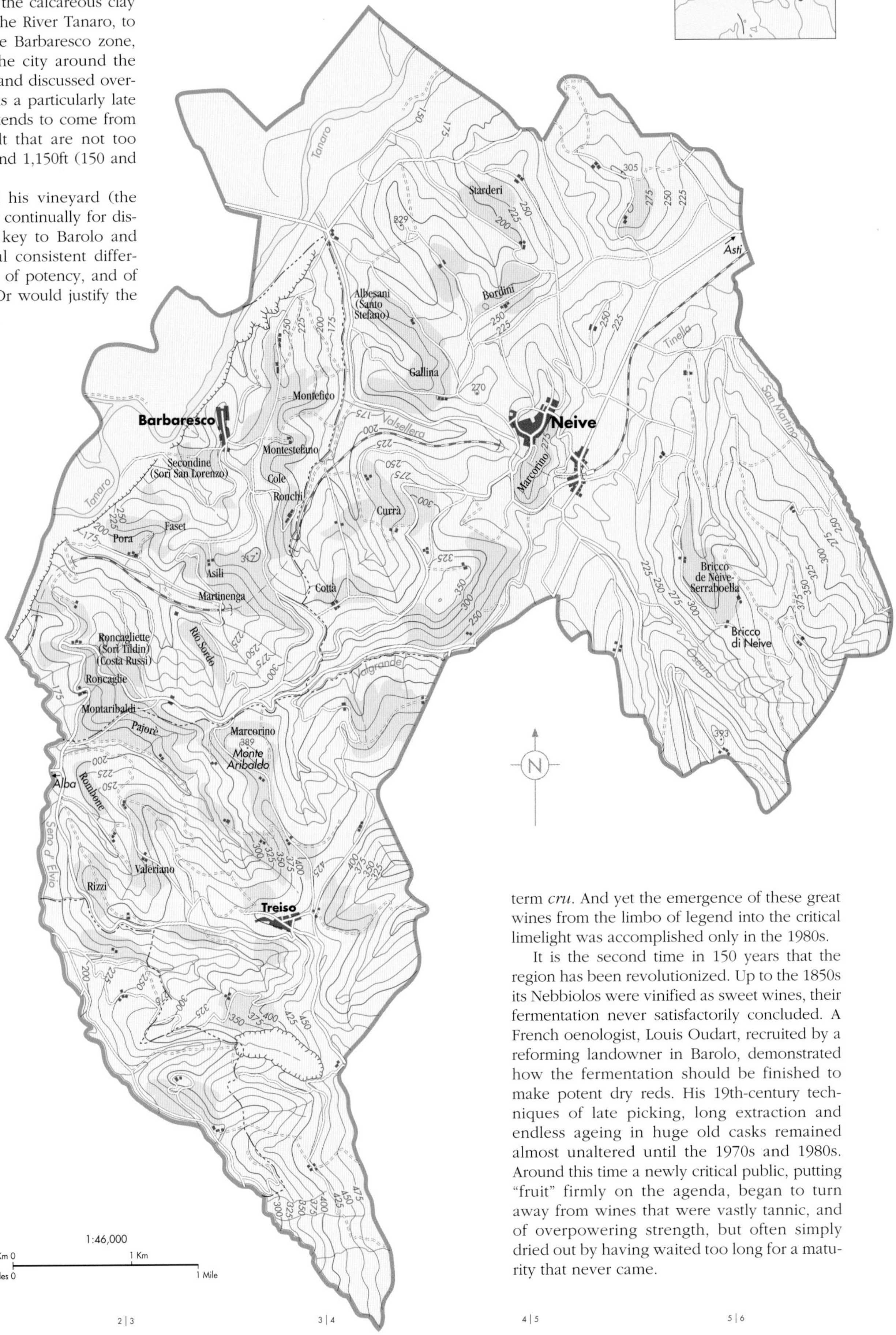

The number of *individual growers bottling their own Barbaresco has been growing substantially in recent years, thanks to international appreciation of heady, intensely charcterful wines like the ones above.*

Commune boundary
DOCG Barbaresco
Faset — Noted vineyard
Vineyards
200 — Contour interval 25 metres

1:46,000

Km 0 — 1 Km
Miles 0 — 1 Mile

term *cru*. And yet the emergence of these great wines from the limbo of legend into the critical limelight was accomplished only in the 1980s.

It is the second time in 150 years that the region has been revolutionized. Up to the 1850s its Nebbiolos were vinified as sweet wines, their fermentation never satisfactorily concluded. A French oenologist, Louis Oudart, recruited by a reforming landowner in Barolo, demonstrated how the fermentation should be finished to make potent dry reds. His 19th-century techniques of late picking, long extraction and endless ageing in huge old casks remained almost unaltered until the 1970s and 1980s. Around this time a newly critical public, putting "fruit" firmly on the agenda, began to turn away from wines that were vastly tannic, and of overpowering strength, but often simply dried out by having waited too long for a maturity that never came.

Modern vinification had no problem finding the solutions: choosing the right moment to pick (nowadays pushing phenolic ripeness to the limit); fermentation in stainless steel at controlled temperatures; shorter macerations; shorter ageing periods in large old oak or, more controversially, ageing in small, new or newish barrels; and, for those who invested in new-fangled rotary fermenters in the mid-1990s, maceration for days rather than the weeks or even months that were traditional.

The results are still tannic wines that need to age, but ones in which the tannin merely frames a stunning array of haunting flavours. Great Barolos and Barbarescos can overlay smoky woodland notes on deep sweetness, the flavour of raspberries on leather and spice, leafy light-ness on jam-like concentration. Older wines advance to animal or tarry flavours, sometimes suggesting wax or incense, sometimes mush-rooms or truffles. What unites them is the racy cut of their tannins, freshening rather than over-whelming the palate.

Barbaresco has less than half as much vine-yard as Barolo. It is a big village on a ridge that wobbles west towards Alba, flanked all the way by vineyards of renown. Asili, Martinenga, and Sorì Tildin are bywords for the finest reds: Roncagliette produces wines with the sort of balance so characteristic of those made around the village of Barbaresco itself to the north. A lit-tle lower to the east lies Neive, in whose castle Oudart experimented with Nebbiolo, and in

whose vineyards Barbera, Dolcetto, and, espe-cially, Moscato, are still more important than Nebbiolo, whose finest sites in Neive include Bricco di Neive and Santo Stefano. So thrilling were the powerful wines produced from some of Neive's best sites in the 1990s that attention has been increasingly focused on the area and a growing number of small growers are now bot-tling under their own labels.

South on higher slopes, some of which are more suitable for Dolcetto, lies the commune of Treiso, whose Nebbiolo tends to be particularly elegant and perfumed. Pajorè was the most important *cru* historically. The authorities have divided the entire Barbaresco zone into contigu-ous subzones, some of very much better quality than others. Only the best Barbaresco vineyards are marked on the map opposite, named as they are most likely to be found on a label (although again as in Burgundy, spellings vary – especially since Piemonte has its own dialect).

Barbaresco once played understudy to the much more famous Barolo, until Angelo Gaja, in a dazzling Missoni sweater, strode onto the world stage. Gaja has no inhibitions: his wines, whether classic Barbaresco (though no longer labelled as such now that this showman has

opted out of the DOCG's strictures), experimen-tal Cabernet, Chardonnay or Sauvignon Blanc, or Barbera treated like first-growth claret, state their case, and cost a fortune.

Bruno Giacosa had shown in the 1960s that Barbaresco could have the intensity if not always the sheer physical weight of Barolo, but it was Gaja who modernized the message, importing new barriques and new ideas without apparently a second thought in this most tradi-tional of regions. In 2000 Gaja announced that he was renouncing the name he had made so famous and selling all the wine previously sold as Barbaresco DOCG, including his fabulously expensive single-vineyard Sorì San Lorenzo, Sorì Tildin, and Costa Russi, as Langhe Nebbiolo, the catch-all appellation for declassified Barolo and Barbaresco and for wines containing up to 15% of "foreign" varieties such as Cabernet, Merlot, and Syrah.

With this notable exception, and that of out-standing producers such as Giacosa and Marchesi di Gresy, overall standards of winemaking are still less evolved in Barbaresco than in Barolo, and historically a much higher proportion of the grapes were sold to the region's large merchant bottlers and co-operatives.

The vineyards of Barbaresco are generally slightly lower and warmer than those of Barolo, so the harvest is often earlier but the wines in general lack quite the staying power of Barolo at its best – which can be an advantage for today's frenetic wine consumers.

Barolo

Barbaresco is a great example of Nebbiolo, but Barolo is the greatest. The Barolo zone starts just two miles southwest of Barbaresco, with the Dolcetto vineyards of Diano d'Alba lying between, and is subject to many of the same influences and characteristics already described on page 160. Two little tributaries of the Tanaro, the Tallòria dell'Annunziata and Tallòria di Castiglione, split Barolo into the three main though highly convoluted hill ranges mapped opposite, rising nearly 165ft (50m) higher than the Barbaresco zone.

There are more than 2,950 acres (1,200ha) of Barolo vineyards concentrated in this zone, just big enough for five villages in the relatively populous Langhe hills. Compare the map opposite with that of the much flatter Pessac-Léognan region on page 101, which is on more or less the same scale. So many different expositions, altitudes, and mesoclimates, and two main soil types, have provided endless fodder for the discussion of possible subzones.

To the west of the Alba road around La Morra, soils are very similar to those in Barbaresco, calcareous marls from the epoch geologists know as Tortonian. These western hills of the zone in the communes of Barolo and La Morra tend to offer slightly less tense, more openly fragrant wines. The great vineyards here include Brunate, Cerequio, Rocche di La Morra, and La Serra in La Morra, and Barolo's most famous site, Cannubi, on slightly lower ground.

To the east, however, in the vineyards of Castiglione Falletto, Serralunga d'Alba, and those to the north of Monforte d'Alba, soils are Helvetian, much less fertile, with more sandstone. They tend to produce even more concentrated wines, Barolo's beefiest, which demand extremely long ageing, and with the years acquire a distinctive orange rim to their inky black depths. Prime examples include Bussia and Ginestra in Monforte and, in Castiglione Falletto, Vietti's Villero and the wine Scavino calls in Piemontese dialect Bric dël Fiasc (Bricco Fiasco in Italian). Such examples of linguistic variation/flexibility abound. The only exception to the sternness of Castiglione Falletto's Barolos might be Bricco Rocche which, with its relatively sandy soils, can produce rather perfumed wines.

To the east lies Serralunga d'Alba with its enormous former royal estate of Fontanafredda, an association that helped develop Barolo's status as "the wine of kings, the king of wines". Serralunga d'Alba has some of Barolo's highest vineyards, but the warmth that builds up in the narrow valley that separates it from Monforte d'Alba to the west compensates for the altitude and even Nebbiolo can be ripened on the most suitable sites most years. It was in Serralunga that Gaja expanded from Barbaresco into the Barolo zone in the late 1980s, both wines having been awarded DOCG status in 1980.

Even before this, however, Barolo could boast dozens of dedicated grower-bottlers (domaines seems a better word than estates for this most Burgundian of Italy's wine regions). Traditions here are, as in Burgundy, that the same family who tends the vines makes the wine – even if there has been considerable evolution in the way that vivacious, expressive, almost burgundian wine is made over the last two or three decades. Barolo is arguably the world's most uncompromising wine, depending on decades of bottle age to show its true allure, its ethereal bouquet. A few traditionalists have such a faithful and knowledgeable following that they can afford to continue to make such a wine. Others have adapted Barolo to modern times to a greater or lesser degree, by reducing fermentation and barrel ageing times so that the wines can be broached earlier. No-one is right, and only those who decided to ignore the unique qualities of this grape and this place would be wrong.

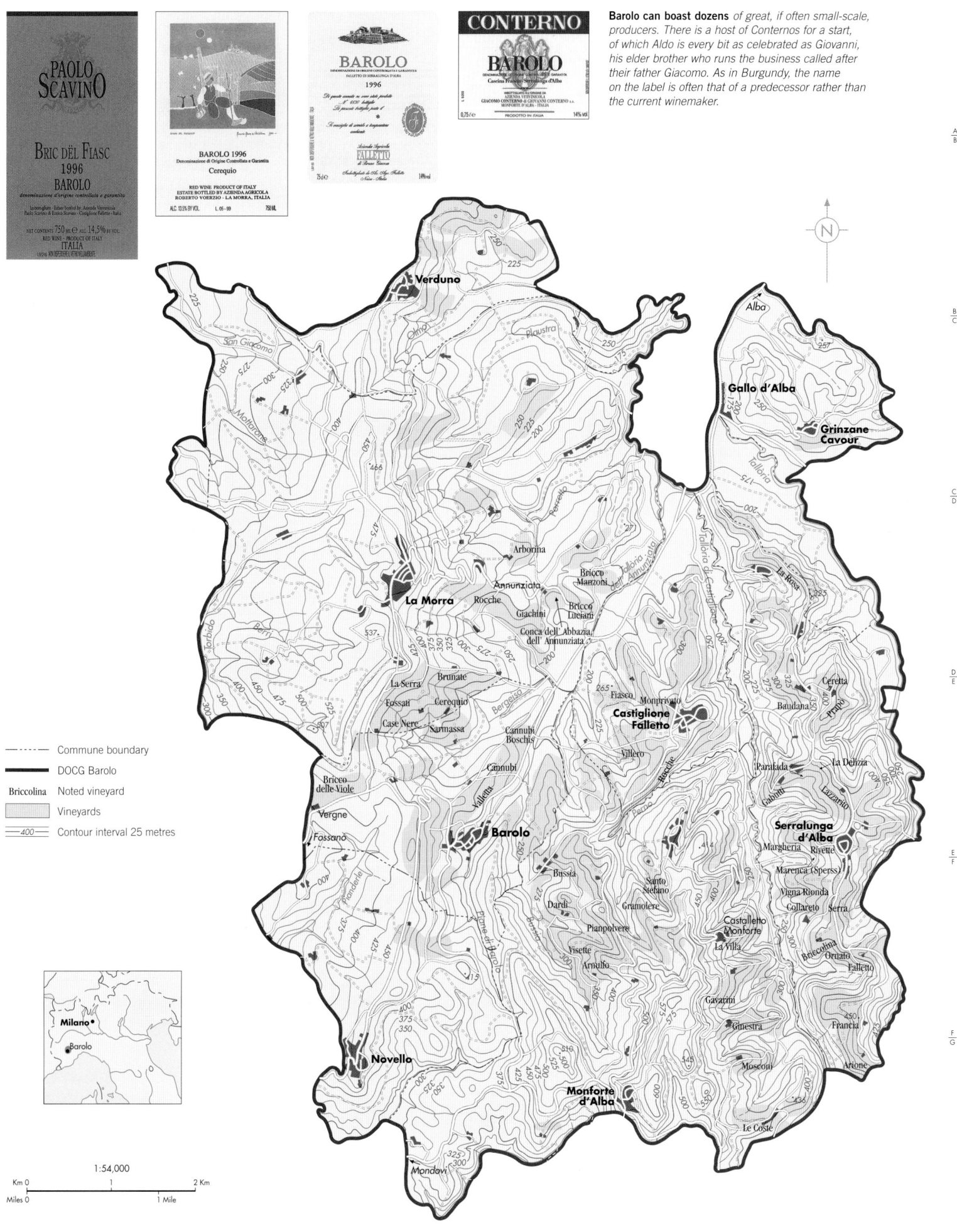

Commune boundary
DOCG Barolo
Briccolina Noted vineyard
Vineyards
400 Contour interval 25 metres

1:54,000

Northeast Italy

Northeast Italy owes less to tradition and more to modern ideas than the rest of the country. Whether it is the realism of the Venetians, the pressure of Austrian influence, the moderate climate, or all of these, more (bottled) wine is exported from the northeast than from anywhere else, more varieties of grapes are grown and investigated, and a more prosperous and professional air pervades the vineyards than in any but the most celebrated zones elsewhere.

Verona and its wines, Trentino and the Alto Adige, and Friuli-Venezia Giulia as shown here are mapped and discussed in detail on pages 166 to 171.

The wines of western Lombardy are discussed on page 156. Far across the Lombard plain from them, east of Milan and within sight of snowcapped Alps, the country between Brescia and Bergamo has built itself the reputation for making Italy's best *metodo classico* wine: Franciacorta, Italy's great sparkling success story, developed in the 1970s on the Berlucchi family estate in direct imitation of champagne, and since taken up by farm after farm in the region south of Lake Iseo. Chardonnay and Pinot Nero are perfectly suited to a climate without extremes. The finest wines, both sparkling and still (and including wines successfully modelled on both Bordeaux and burgundy) are from charismatic Maurizio Zanella of Ca' del Bosco, whose Cuvée Annamaria Clementi exhibits a finesse seen only in Champagne's greatest wines. Bellavista is another fine exponent of sparkling Franciacorta, Riserva Vittorio Moretti its finest *cuvée*. Varietal reds and whites are sold as Terre di Franciacorta.

Below So mountainous is the terrain that vineyards can be planted only on the slopes of the main valleys in Trentino-Alto Adige. The proportion of wine qualifying as DOC here is exceptionally high for an Italian wine region.

Of the other Lombardy wines on this map, the Garda-side wines are very close in character to those on the Verona side of Lake Garda. There is little to choose between Chiaretto from the Riviera del Garda (of which the best part is south of Salò, particularly around Moniga del Garda) and Bardolino. Both are reds so light as to be rosé, or rosés so dark as to be red, with a gentle flavour, soft-textured and faintly sweet, made all the more appetizing by a hint of bitterness, like almonds, in the taste which is common to all the best reds in this part of Italy. They should be drunk very young.

White Lugana, from the south end of Lake Garda, is a particularly appealing Trebbiano-based wine, offering a hint of lusciousness in a perfectly dry wine – and estates such as Ca' dei Frati have shown that other great still whites can be made from international varieties too. Garda is a recent catch-all DOC that allows blending between the standard-issue Veneto zones of Soave, Valpolicella, and Bianco di Custoza.

Only one name from the flat Po Valley is famous, for some less-educated wine drinkers infamous: the sparkling red Lambrusco from around Módena, above all from Sorbara. There is something decidedly appetizing about this vivid, grapey wine with its bizarre red foaming head. It cuts the richness of Bolognese food admirably. How its faint but unmistakable resemblance to Coca-Cola founded a great American fortune (in one year Riunite, the co-operative of Reggio nell' Emilia, shipped 11 million cases to the States) is one of the most extraordinary success stories in the history of wine.

The character of the wine changes in the Veneto and eastwards. On green volcanic islands in the plain are the increasingly successful Colli Berici and Euganei near Vicenza and Pádova. The red grapes are the Cabernets of Bordeaux and, above all, the early ripening Merlot, which plays an ever more dominant role all the way from the valley of the Adige north of Lake Garda to Slovenia, and again in Italian Switzerland. White grapes are a mixture of the traditional – Garganega of Soave, Prosecco, light and sharp Verdiso, and the more solid Tocai and Sylvaner, Riesling, Sauvignon Blanc, and Pinot Bianco.

The DOCs of the region are a series of defined areas that give their names to whole groups of red and white wines. Those known simply as (for example) Colli Euganei Rosso are standard wines made of an approved mixture of grapes. The better wines generally use a varietal name with the DOC name, as in Colli Euganei Pinot Bianco, although there are also DOCs, like Gambellara between Soave and the Colli Berici, that are limited to a traditional grape, in this particular case the Garganega.

Breganze, north of Vicenza, is a case of a DOC brought to prominence (like Franciacorta) by one fanatical winemaker. Fausto Maculan outstripped the traditional whites of Tocai and Vespaiolo (although he makes them) by proving that this is a good Cabernet region – and by resurrecting the old Venetian taste for sweet wines from dried grapes with his golden Torcolato.

The productive north of the Veneto and its eastern neighbour, Friuli-Venezia Giulia, where most of the serious wines are white, is mapped on page 170.

Emilia Romagna's reputation as a wine producer is steadily rising. The hills around Bologna, the Colli Bolognesi, now produce some very respectable Cabernet, Merlot, and Sauvignon Blanc. The country south of Bologna and Ravenna still produces oceans of varietal Romagna wine with Trebbiano di Romagna the least remarkable. Albana di Romagna was the first white wine to be elevated to DOCG status, to the amazement of virtually everyone but local politicians, in 1986. Like so many Italian whites, Albana comes in all levels of sweetness, although virtually the only interesting wines come from the hills to the east of Forlì. Fattoria Zerbina's sweet versions are probably best.

More reliable than Albana by far, if highly variable, is this extensive zone's red: Sangiovese di Romagna. It can be thin and overcropped, but it can also be gutsy and sophisticated enough to show why some of the Sangiovese clones most popular with discerning Tuscan producers come from Romagna. There is also promising evidence that such wine can blend well with Cabernet.

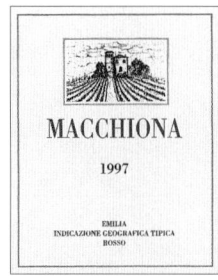

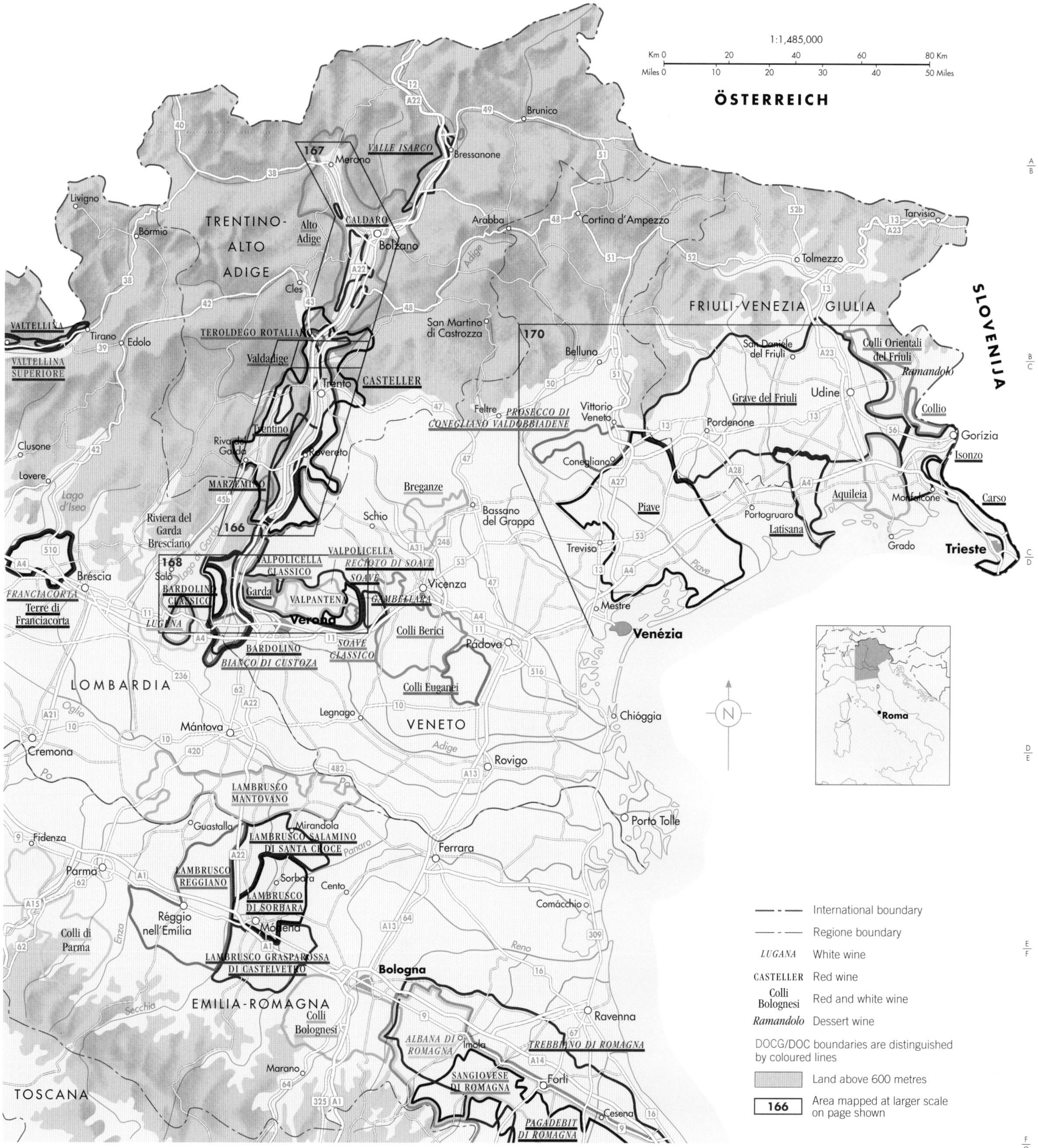
1:1,485,000
Km 0 20 40 60 80 Km
Miles 0 10 20 30 40 50 Miles
ÖSTERREICH
SLOVENIJA
TRENTINO-ALTO ADIGE
FRIULI-VENEZIA GIULIA
LOMBARDIA
VENETO
EMILIA-ROMAGNA
TOSCANA
VALLE ISARCO
CALDARO
Alto Adige
TEROLDEGO ROTALIANO
Valdadige
CASTELLER
Trentino
MARZEMINO
VALTELLINA
VALTELLINA SUPERIORE
Riviera del Garda Bresciano
FRANCIACORTA
Terre di Franciacorta
LUGANA
BARDOLINO CLASSICO
BARDOLINO
BIANCO DI CUSTOZA
VALPOLICELLA
VALPOLICELLA CLASSICO
VALPANTENA
Garda
RECIOTO DI SOAVE
SOAVE
SOAVE CLASSICO
GAMBELLARA
Breganze
Colli Berici
Colli Euganei
PROSECCO DI CONEGLIANO VALDOBBIADENE
Piave
Grave del Friuli
Colli Orientali del Friuli
Ramandolo
Collio
Isonzo
Carso
Aquileia
Latisana
LAMBRUSCO MANTOVANO
LAMBRUSCO SALAMINO DI SANTA CROCE
LAMBRUSCO REGGIANO
LAMBRUSCO DI SORBARA
LAMBRUSCO GRASPAROSSA DI CASTELVETRO
Colli di Parma
Colli Bolognesi
ALBANA DI ROMAGNA
TREBBIANO DI ROMAGNA
SANGIOVESE DI ROMAGNA
PAGADEBIT DI ROMAGNA
Brunico
Bressanone
Merano
Bolzano
Livigno
Bórmio
Cles
Arabba
Cortina d'Ampezzo
Tarvisio
Tolmezzo
San Martino di Castrozza
Tirano
Edolo
Belluno
San Daniele del Friuli
Udine
Trento
Feltre
Vittorio Veneto
Pordenone
Gorízia
Clusone
Riva del Garda
Rovereto
Conegliano
Lovere
Lago d'Iseo
Bassano del Grappa
Schio
Monfalcone
Portogruaro
Grado
Trieste
Treviso
Lago di Garda
Salò
Bréscia
Vicenza
Mestre
Verona
Venézia
Pádova
Legnago
Chióggia
Mántova
Cremona
Rovigo
Porto Tolle
Mirandola
Guastalla
Fidenza
Ferrara
Parma
Sorbara
Cento
Réggio nell'Emília
Módena
Comácchio
Bologna
Ravenna
Ímola
Forlì
Marano
Cesena
Oglio
Po
Adige
Piave
Panaro
Enza
Secchia
Reno
Roma
167
166
168
170
International boundary
Regione boundary
LUGANA White wine
CASTELLER Red wine
Colli Bolognesi Red and white wine
Ramandolo Dessert wine
DOCG/DOC boundaries are distinguished by coloured lines
Land above 600 metres
166 Area mapped at larger scale on page shown

CA'DEL BOSCO
CUVÉE ANNAMARIA CLEMENTI

MACULAN
1998
TORCOLATO

Francesco Bellei
Lambrusco di Sorbara
denominazione di origine controllata
fermentazione naturale in bottiglia
750 ml. e ITALIA 12% vol.
NON DISPERDERE IL VETRO NELL'AMBIENTE

ROCCA DI BONACCIARA
MERLOT
TENUTA BONZARA

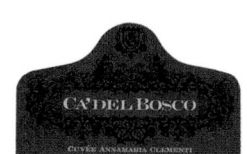

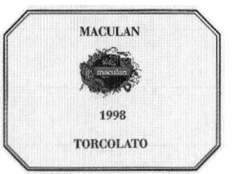

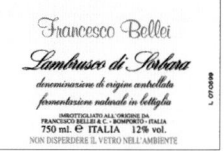

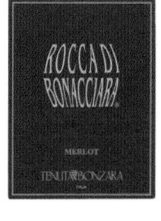

Outside the principal wine zones *discussed in detail on the next six pages northeast Italy produces a vast array of wine styles. Three still red wines flank a truly great sparkling white (third from left), a unique sweet white (third from right), and an exceptional fizzy red, Lambrusco, whose name has been devalued by commercial blends.*

Trentino

The valley of the Adige forms the dramatic corridor into the Alps that links Italy with Austria over the Brenner Pass. It is a rock-walled trench, widening in places to give views of distant peaks but, like the Rhône Valley, an inevitably thronging north-south link with all the excesses of traffic and industry that go with it.

Its vineyards form a lovely contrast to the traffic at its heart. They pile up every available slope from river to rock-walls in a pattern of pergolas which look from above like deeply leafy steps.

The catch-all DOC for the whole valley is Valdadige (in German, Etschtaler). But each part of the valley has its own specialities, indeed its own indigenous grapes. Growing conditions are fine for almost any white grape, and the usual candidates have been widely planted. Picked early they have every quality needed for good sparkling wine, the speciality of the town of Trento. But the native red grapes are too well-loved (as well as being too productive) to be deposed by a tide of imported varieties.

On the way north to Trento the snaking gorge is known as the Vallagarina, the home of Marzemino, a dark-hued, light-bodied red whose fame comes almost entirely from the last act of *Don Giovanni*. The northern end of Trentino is the unique home of the full-blooded red Teroldego, from the grape of the same name grown on the cliff-hemmed, pergola-carpeted, gravelly valley floor known as the Campo Rotaliano, which lies between Mezzolombardo and Mezzocorona. Teroldego Rotaliano is one of Italy's great characters, a dense purple wine of high extract and good ageing qualities, smooth and even softly berry-flavoured in the mouth but too often marked, at least when young, with the penetrating bitterness that is the telltale sign of overcropped Teroldego vines. Elisabetta Foradori is the queen of fine, ripe Teroldego Rotaliano.

The Schiava or Vernatsch, from the Tyrol (also known in Germany as Trollinger), needs a similar champion. Another red grape, which often displays some of the same bitterness, it is made here in the Trentino in two DOCs, the light Casteller and the more substantial Sorni (which also contains Teroldego and the Lagrein of Bolzano). Schiava is perhaps best appreciated as a *rosato* produced in the village of Faedo at the northern end of this map.

The eastern Adige slopes round San Michele are particularly successful for white grapes and, in recent years, for the international red varieties too. Leaders here are Pojer & Sandri, based at Faedo and producer of one of the world's very rare interesting Müller-Thurgau, the Istituto Agrario Provinciale, Maso Cantanghel, Cesconi, and the Lavis co-op. Some of the better wines are marketed as IGTs rather than within the embrace of the DOC system.

The western arm of the valley near Trento, linking it with three small lakes, grows the same wide range of grapes (all these zones grow good base wine for *spumante*) but specializes in sweet Vino Santo of high quality from yet another indigenous variety, the Nosiola.

1:257,000

	Km 0	2 4 6 Km
	Miles 0	2 4 Miles

DOC Valdadige (Etschtaler)
DOC Trentino
DOC Sorni
DOC Alto Adige (Südtiroler)
DOC Teroldego Rotaliano
DOC Caldaro (Kalterer)
DOC Casteller
DOC Vino Santo
Provincia boundary
■ ZENI   Leading producer
Vineyards
Woods
—1000— Contour interval 200 metres

Alto Adige

The Alto Adige, alias the Südtirol, the southern tip of Austria's Tyrol, is Italy's most northerly wine region and one of its most vigorous and exciting. Its Alpine peaks proclaim both a cultural and a viticultural melting pot. German is a more common language than Italian, yet French grape varieties are more widespread than Teutonic ones. Its vineyards traditionally supplied inexpensive, soft, light red wines to Germany, but are systematically being replanted with more ambitious grapes – both the racy varietal whites on which Alto Adige's modern reputation has so far been based and varieties that will produce serious red wines in warmer areas.

Production is centred on the benchland of the Adige Valley. Vineyard altitudes varying from 650 to almost 3,300ft (200 to 1,000m) allow for infinite permutations of mesoclimate and grape variety. Most wines are sold under the blanket DOC Alto Adige (Südtiroler) plus the name of the grape.

Higher vineyards, often steep and terraced as in the Isarco (Eisack) Valley, which stretches for 15 or 20 miles (24 or 32km) northeast of Bolzano (off the map), are home to German varieties – Müller-Thurgau, Riesling, Sylvaner, and even (so close is Austria) Grüner Veltliner, whose aromas benefit from the wide fluctuations between day and night temperatures.

On slightly lower slopes Chardonnay, Pinot Bianco, and Pinot Grigio are fruity and lively, while the village of Terlano, on the way north to Merano, is highly rated for Sauvignon Blanc. The Gewürztraminer grape owes its name to its presumed origin, the village of Tramin (Termeno in Italian) 12 miles (19km) south of Bolzano. The renowned producer Hofstätter shows why.

The workhorse red grape is the Schiava (alias Vernatsch). Its wines are pale, soft, and rather simple, often with a bitter herbal twist. The best and most famous is Santa Maddalena (Sankt Magdalener). Lago di Caldaro (Kalterersee), a zone that extends far from the lake itself, Colli di Bolzano (Bozner Leiten), and Meranese di Collina (Meraner Hügel) are all Schiava DOC, often made semi-sweet for the German market. The Lagrein, also a local grape, produces much more serious

stuff, including the deeply fruity rosé Lagrein Kretzer and darker Lagrein Dunkel, both of which have ageing potential.

Red varieties imported in the 19th century – Pinot Noir, Merlot, and Cabernet – can be very good, especially from growers who have abandoned the traditional pergolas for low wires. All of these, together with Lagrein, are replacing Schiava in the region's warmest sites east of Lake Caldaro and on the slopes above Bolzano.

Most wine is made in co-ops, and the better private producers such as Lageder, Hofstätter, Widmann, and Niedrist have now been joined by such ambitious co-operative wineries as those of Colterenzio, San Michele Appiano, Terlano, Termeno, Caldaro, and Cortaccia.

Map legend

— DOC Meranese di Collina (Meraner Hügel)
— DOC Santa Maddalena (Sankt Magdalener)
— DOC Caldaro (Kalterer)
— DOC Teroldego Rotaliano
— DOC Trentino
— DOC Terlano (Terlaner)
— DOC Colli di Bolzano (Bozner Leiten)
— DOC Sorni
- - - Provincia boundary
■ FRANZ HAAS Leading producer
Vineyards
Woods
—1000— Contour interval 200 metres
▼ Weather station (WS)

Alto Adige: Bolzano

Latitude / Altitude of WS **46.28° / 754ft (230m)**
Mean July temperature at WS **71°F (21.7°C)**
Average annual rainfall at WS **26in (650mm)**
Harvest month rainfall at WS **October: 2in (50mm)**
Principal viticultural hazard **Spring frosts**
Principal grapes **Schiava, Chardonnay, Pinot Bianco, Pinot Grigio, Lambrusco, Teroldego, Lagrein**

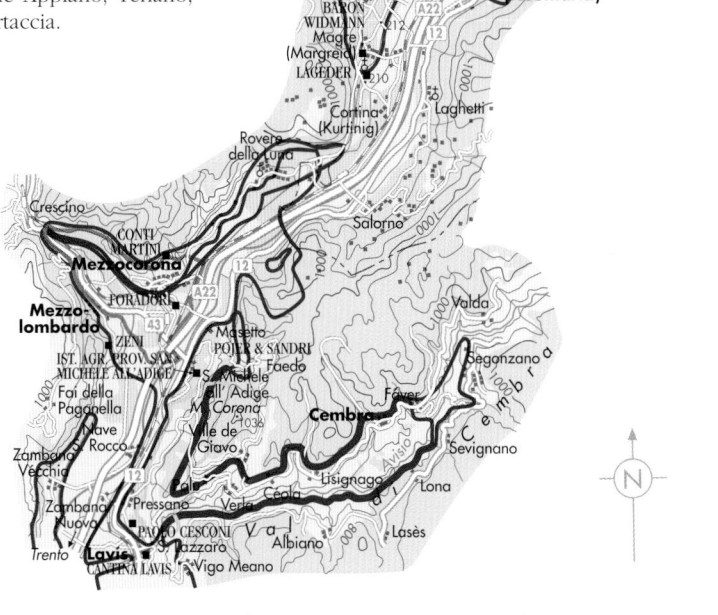

Left In vineyards such as these in the narrow valley between Bolzano and Merano, pergolas are being replaced by vines trained on wires, resulting in lower yields and more concentrated wines.

Verona

The lovingly gardened hills of Verona, stretching from Soave, east of the city, westwards to Lake Garda, have such fertile volcanic soil that vegetation grows uncontrollably; the vine runs riot on every terrace and pergola, among villas and cypresses that are the image of Italian grace.

Their Soave is Italy's most famous white wine and comes in two almost unrecognizably different forms. The most common is the bland mouthwash spewed forth by the powerful Cantina Sociale and the big négociant firms. They are supplied by hundreds of growers with regrettably few incentives to do anything other than maximize yields.

Real Soave, with its insistent combination of almonds and lemons, does exist, thanks to the persistence of small estates such as Pieropan and Anselmi (which, in 1999, after a series of disputes with local authorities, decided to operate outside the DOC system). These stalwarts have been joined by a new band of such conscientious producers as La Cappuccina, Fattori & Graney, Gini, Inama, Pra, and Tamellini.

They operate in the original, classical area of Soave centred on the eastern end of the Lessini Hills northeast of the village of Soave. This is the Classico zone, now surrounded by much flatter, more fertile land also allowed to call its wines Soave, a picture that is all too common in the modern Italian winescape.

The important grapes are Garganega and a local (rather than the Tuscan or pan-Italian) form of Trebbiano which make wines of an intensity and mouth-filling texture that bring the meaning of Soave (suave) into focus. Chardonnay and Pinot Blanc are also allowed, so long as Garganega makes up at least 70% of the wine.

The best producers typically make a range of single-vineyard or *cru* bottlings, expressing such characterful local sites as Vigneto La Rocca and Capitel Foscarino, as well as experimenting with oak ageing and a wonderfully lively sweet version made from dried grapes, Recioto di Soave.

Soave cohabits with Valpolicella, whose DOC zone has been extended far beyond the original Classico zone until it reaches the boundaries of Soave, with the improving Valpantena a permitted subzone dominated by the house of Bertani. Plain Valpolicella should have a beautiful cherry colour and flavour, a gentle sweet smell, and a trace of bitterness as you swallow. The mass-produced article can often disappoint but there are now many more producers who recognize the need to make truly distinctive as opposed to commercially viable wine in Soave – just as the last decade of the 20th century saw a return to some of the more difficult-to-work but higher-quality hillside sites.

Valpolicella Classico, from four fingers of higher-altitude vineyard sheltering San Ambrogio,

Fumane, and Negrar, has the same qualities as wine made outside this heartland but in an intensified form (although there are exceptional operators such as Dal Forno and Trabucchi outside the Classico zone). The leading estates are extremely ambitious for Valpolicella Classico, seeing it, with justice, as one of Italy's most promotable products in every sense.

Vines are being planted on white-pebbled terraces at much higher densities and Guyot-trained to extract more flavour from every grape, above all late-ripening Corvina, the best of the region. Indeed some producers have even preferred to operate outside the DOC law, which imposed a maximum of 70% on the Corvina component and demanded the inclusion of tart and obviously inferior Molinara grapes as well as the traditional but neutral Rondinella. There is also some experimentation with rarer indigenous grapes such as Oseleta.

The most potent form of Valpolicella is as Recioto or Amarone, respectively the sweet (sometimes fizzy) and dry (also bitter) results of loft-drying selected grapes to make highly concentrated and potent wines, the climax of every Veronese feast. Such wines are the direct descendants of the Greek wines shipped by the Venetians in the Middle Ages, adapted to the Venetian hinterland. And there is evidence that sweet Veneto wines were admired as early as

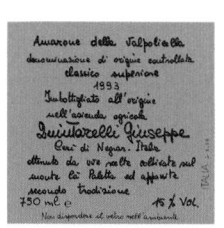

The three wines in the left column *are made from dried grapes, a speciality of the Veneto. On the right are some of the finest wines made in the Soave and Valpolicella zones, although those words no longer appear on the label (see above).*

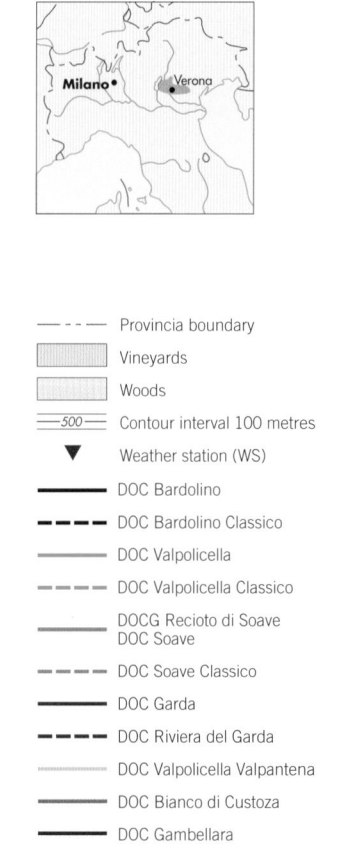

– – – – –	Provincia boundary
	Vineyards
	Woods
—500—	Contour interval 100 metres
▼	Weather station (WS)
———	DOC Bardolino
– – – –	DOC Bardolino Classico
———	DOC Valpolicella
– – – –	DOC Valpolicella Classico
———	DOCG Recioto di Soave DOC Soave
– – – –	DOC Soave Classico
———	DOC Garda
– – – –	DOC Riviera del Garda
———	DOC Valpolicella Valpantena
———	DOC Bianco di Custoza
———	DOC Gambellara
———	DOC Lugana

the 6th century when Cassiodorus mentions
Acinatico, revered for its sweetness by the court
of the Gothic kings of Italy.

The old practice of *ripasso* strengthens
Valpolicella from the main crop into Valpolicella
Superiore by refermenting it on the pressed
grape skins, preferably of Corvina, after an
Amarone has finished fermentation. The first wine
to be marketed as a *ripasso*, Masi's Campofiorin,
induced new respect for Valpolicella wine in
the 1980s.

Such estates as Dal Forno, Le Ragose,
Quintarelli, and Tedeschi, and such merchants
as Bertani, are also building up a constituency
for Valpolicella Classico and its variants as one
of Italy's surest things in wine.

Bardolino, from lower ground on the pretty
lakeside of Garda, is a paler, more insubstantial
wine – almost a rosé, or *chiaretto*, drinkable as
soon as fermented. Chiaretto del Garda, from
the further shore, is similar.

Bianco di Custoza made to the south can,
like Gambellara just east of Soave, be a surer bet
than everyday Soave.

Right Lake Garda lies behind the Valpolicella vineyards of
Allegrini, a producer which, like Anselmi of Soave, opted
out of the DOC system with its IGT wines La Poja and La
Grola. Allegrini's faith in the Molinara grape does not
match that enshrined in the DOC regulations.

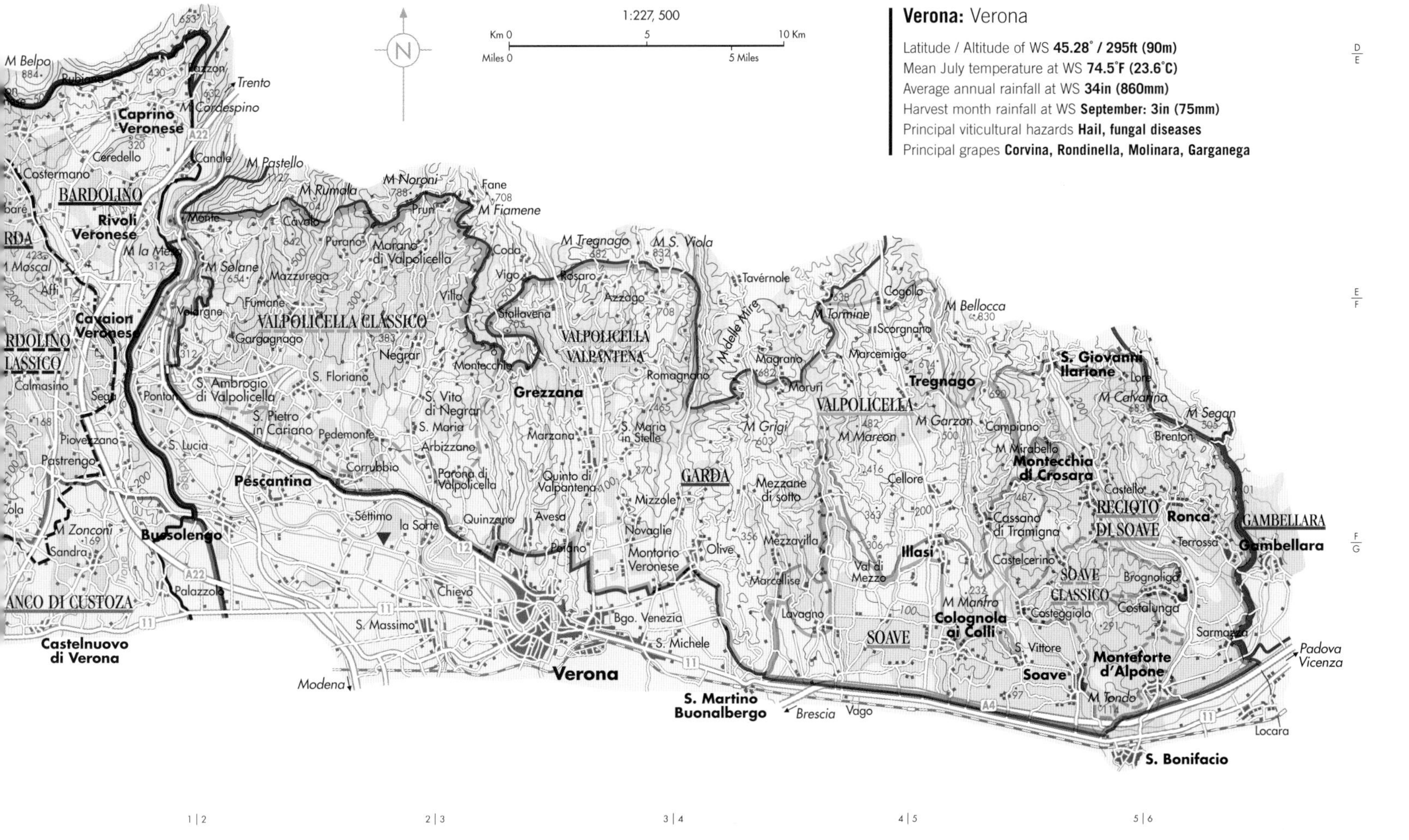

1:227, 500

Km 0   5   10 Km
Miles 0   5 Miles

Verona: Verona

Latitude / Altitude of WS **45.28° / 295ft (90m)**
Mean July temperature at WS **74.5°F (23.6°C)**
Average annual rainfall at WS **34in (860mm)**
Harvest month rainfall at WS **September: 3in (75mm)**
Principal viticultural hazards **Hail, fungal diseases**
Principal grapes **Corvina, Rondinella, Molinara, Garganega**

Eastern Veneto and Friuli-Venezia Giulia

Italy's northeast corner is the country's one region where aromatic, sharply etched white wines dominate both image and production. The map on this page embraces the vine-growing part of Friuli-Venezia Giulia, and a small part of its western neighbour the Veneto. The Veneto has two great wine centres, Verona (see page 168) and Conegliano, 40 miles (65km) north of Venice, site of Italy's principal viticultural research station. Northern Veneto runs into the Dolomites, and the region of Conegliano-Valdobbiadene already has a faintly Alpine aspect. Its local speciality, the white Prosecco grape, is rather charmless as a still wine, but is very good base material for the much-admired *spumante* of the region. Prosecco is thus the local fizz of Venice, and its Superiore form, Cartizze from Valdobbiadene, is

one of Italy's best in the brisk, light-bodied manner, its slight sweetness providing perfect cover for Prosecco's inherent bitterness.

Still within the Veneto, the wide plain of the Piave, heavily planted with vines, produces some fresh dry white Verduzzo (an important grape of the northeast) and is a useful source of Cabernet and Merlot of fair to substantial quality. Eastwards from Venice, the great Bordeaux grapes make the running for red wine. Mass-produced, as they usually are, they can taste very green; on such estates as Venegazzù and Ornella Molon, in the province of Treviso, they have been married into truly claret-like blends. An indigenous red grape, Raboso, helps to define Venetian taste in red wine, which, as in white, is definitely for the austere and dry.

Most of the Cabernet planted in Friuli was long thought to be Cabernet Franc (sometimes spelt Frank) but some has more recently been discovered to be the old Bordeaux variety Carmenère (misidentified as Merlot in Chile). When over-cropped, as it still is routinely, Carmenère can take on a distinctly animal note.

On the whole the "Cabernet" is heartiest to the west of the region, especially in Lison-Pramaggiore (where the Merlot can be a little dry and heartless for the grape that makes Pomerol). Going east, early ripening Merlot seems better suited to the large crops and coolish climate of this part of Italy. Merlot dominates the DOCs Grave del Friuli and Isonzo. The coastal areas with their flat vineyards tend to make less concentrated wines from these grapes

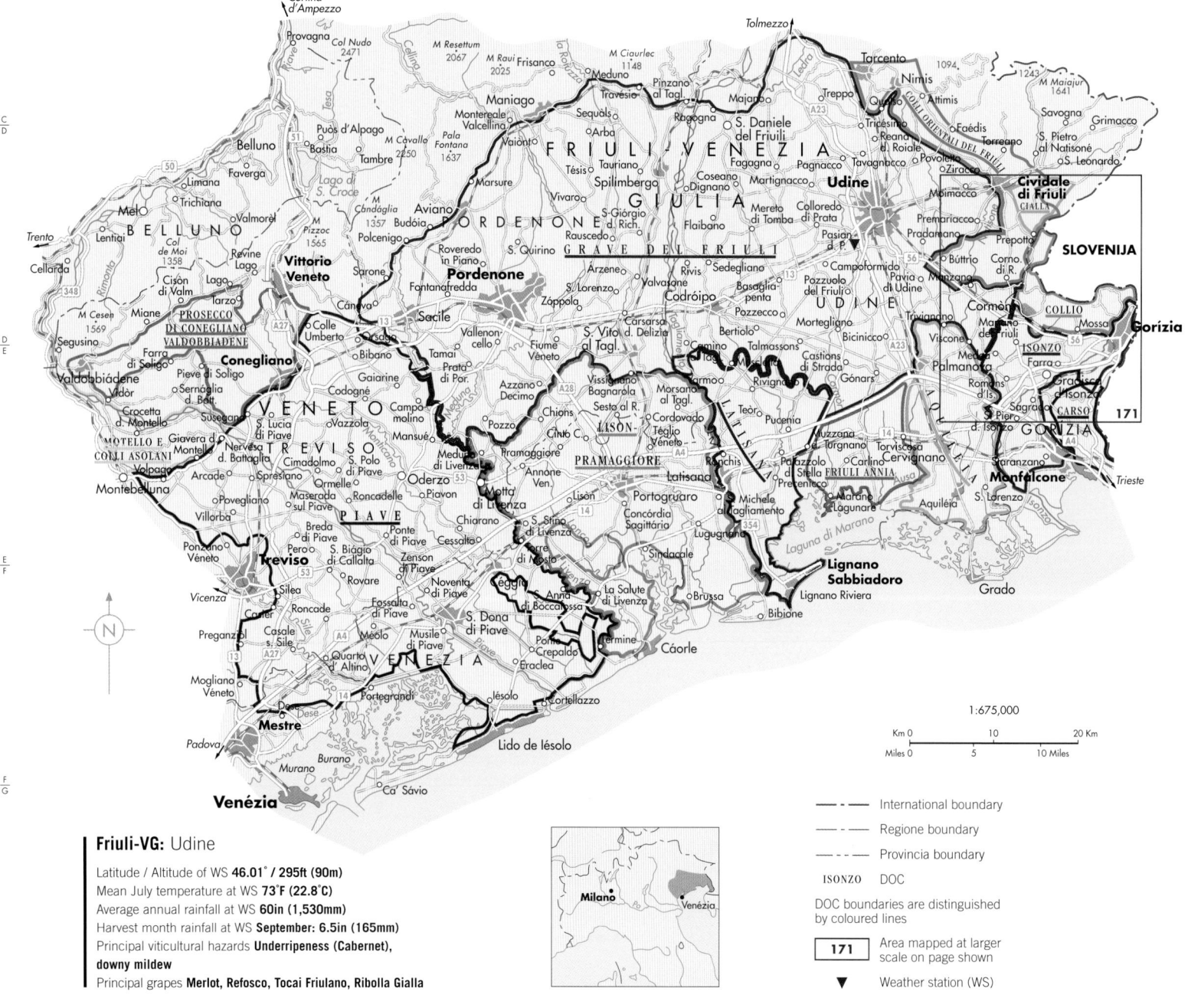

Friuli-VG: Udine

Latitude / Altitude of WS **46.01˚ / 295ft (90m)**
Mean July temperature at WS **73˚F (22.8˚C)**
Average annual rainfall at WS **60in (1,530mm)**
Harvest month rainfall at WS **September: 6.5in (165mm)**
Principal viticultural hazards **Underripeness (Cabernet), downy mildew**
Principal grapes **Merlot, Refosco, Tocai Friulano, Ribolla Gialla**

1:675,000

Km 0 — 10 — 20 Km
Miles 0 — 5 — 10 Miles

— · — · — International boundary
— — — Regione boundary
— — — Provincia boundary
ISONZO   DOC
DOC boundaries are distinguished by coloured lines
| 171 | Area mapped at larger scale on page shown
▼   Weather station (WS)

than is made from more limited hillside plantations in the Colli Orientali del Friuli, although
some Isonzo producers on particularly well-
drained vineyards are now managing to make
wines every bit as good as their counterparts in
the better known hillside zones of Friuli.

Within the united DOC of Lison-Pramaggiore,
Pramaggiore is noted for reds (Cabernet, Merlot,
and Refosco) and Lison for Tocai and other
whites. Tocai di Lison (which has a Classico
heartland around the town of Lison) begins to
promise the silky satisfaction this grape will give
further east.

Grave del Friuli is much the biggest DOC of
Friuli-Venezia Giulia, encompassing all the gravelly lowlands in the region's centre. Half its
harvest is Merlot, with some Cabernet and also
the often underrated, bracing Refosco. Grave
whites are chiefly the lean, dry Verduzzo (best
in sweet form in the Ramandolo zone north of
Udine) and the much more substantial Tocai
Friulano, but a good quantity of Pinot Bianco is
also grown.

Certain producers' names stand out in this
big and by no means homogeneous area: di
Lenardo, Pighin, Pittaro, and Vistorta are among
them. They are all in the province of Udine,
towards the Colli Orientali del Friuli, the southern part of which is mapped in detail on this
page with the very similar Collio Goriziano in
the province of Gorizia. Gorizia's hills, the natural boundary between Italy and Slovenia (see
page 253), enjoy a mellow climate modified by
the Adriatic.

Collio (as Collio Goriziano is more usually
known) built its reputation on the freshness of
its cool-fermented, unoaked varietals such as
the green-scented Tocai Friulano, Pinot Bianco,
Pinot Grigio, and Sauvignon Blanc in the 1970s
when such a high-tech style of winemaking was
rare in Italy. Today it is the norm, and the
region's winemakers are now trying to make
their whites, including Ribolla Gialla, Traminer,
Malvasia, and Riesling Italico (Welschriesling)
with more extract and personality.

The hills inland produce similar, if slightly
less vividly consistent wines. Parts of the Colli
Orientali del Friuli feel more alpine than maritime, but the southwestern end between
Búttrio and Manzano is warm enough to ripen
even Cabernet Sauvignon. Red grapes play a
more important part than in Collio, including
such local specialities as the characterful
Refosco (Terrano), Schioppettino, and Pignolo
alongside the red Bordeaux varieties.

A great deal of local pride is tied up in Picolit,
a strong white dessert wine which could be
described as the Italian Jurançon: a wine more
hay-like and flowery, while less pungently honeyed, than Sauternes.

For years Friuli's best wines *were all labelled varietally
but as individual producers such as the ones shown
here earn reputations for themselves, they are trying to
establish their own special wine names – a decidedly
Italian habit.*

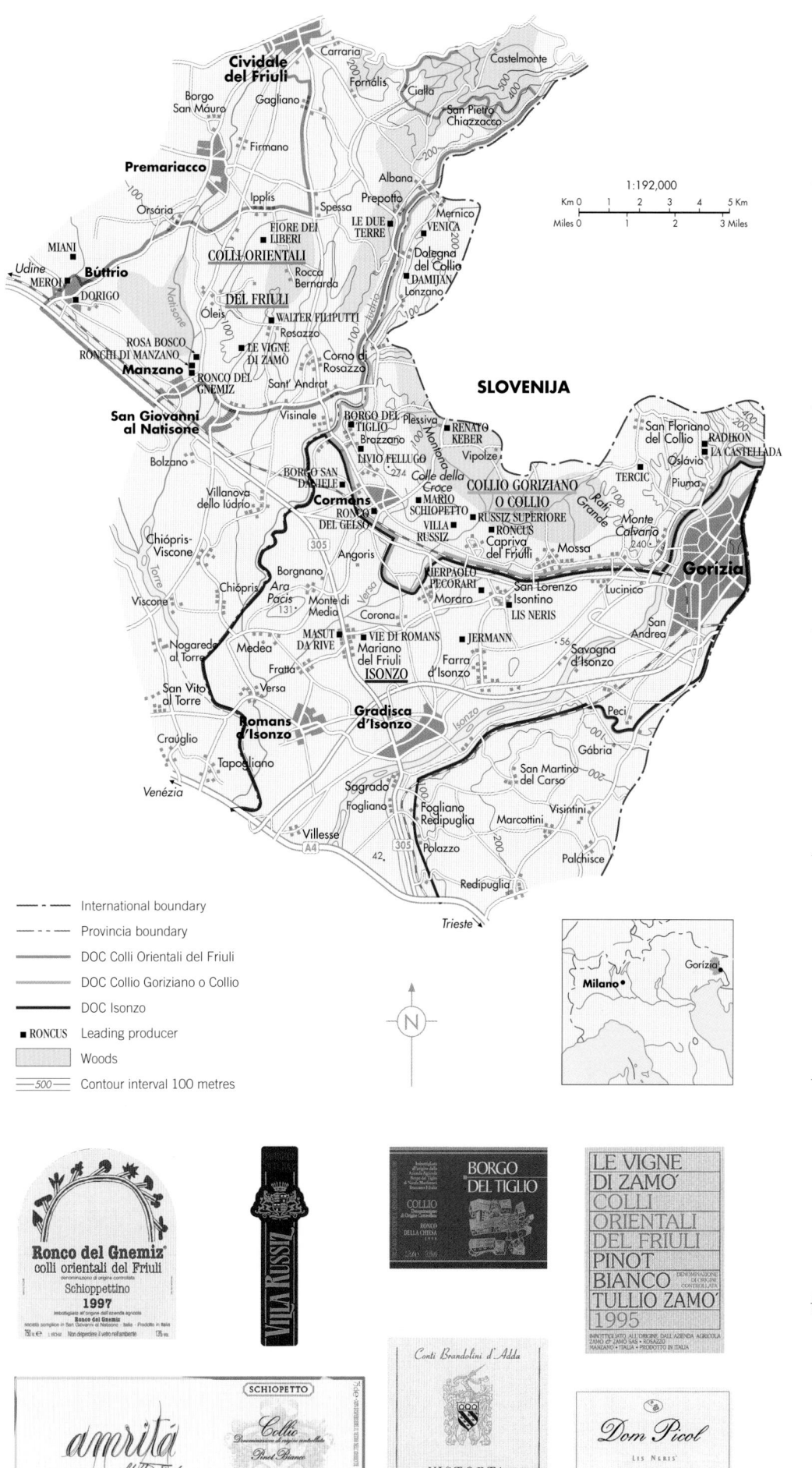

Central Italy

If Chianti Classico is the heart of Tuscany (Toscana in Italian, mapped on page 177), the map opposite shows the dynamic heart of Italy: the incomparable cities of Florence and Rome and the wines that revive their citizens and thousands of visitors.

The wines made here vary enormously, not just because latitudes do but because the terrain and particularly the altitude do. Italy's Apennine spine imposes strict upper limits on vine-ripening territory (compare factfile data for Florence and Perugia, for example, on pages 177 and 181 respectively), while the seas on either side wash maritime wine regions of wildly differing characters.

Until quite recently Florence's red Chianti and Rome's white Frascati were practically the only wines made here that were known outside Italy. (No wine is more identified with a city than Frascati; Rome would seize up without it.) By the 1980s Brunello di Montalcino and, to a lesser extent, its neighbour Vino Nobile di Montepulciano (see pages 179 and 180) had firmly imprinted themselves in the minds of those who could afford them, as had the host of

Below The unique profile of San Gimignano, west of Chianti Classico. Once it had 70 fortified towers; today there are 13. White Vernaccia has been its speciality since the Middle Ages, but today more of its vineyards are being planted with red varieties.

Supertuscans, often glorious bottlings outside the scope of any DOC, made all over Tuscany.

Today, however, they are being joined, apparently on an almost weekly basis, by more and more exciting wines – conjured up without historical precedent, or even in some cases geographical inspiration – made all over the area mapped opposite. Some examples are more obvious than others. The burgeoning vineyards of the Tuscan Coast, the Upper (Alta) Maremma, are mapped overleaf. The rapidly evolving winescape of Umbria is discussed on page 181. But between these two fast-emerging wine regions are other areas undergoing radical vinous development.

The most obvious is Morellino di Scansano, a hilly, relatively well-established wine zone in the far southwest of Tuscany which seems particularly suitable for Sangiovese (called Morellino here). Moris Farms and Le Pupille led the way in the 1980s, but investment has been flooding in to this southern part of the Maremma from wine producers already established in other parts of Italy, particularly since vineyard land here is so much less expensive than further inland, and the grapes can be considerably easier to ripen on these unusually acid soils.

Sangiovese – indeed all red wine – made here is much rounder and fuller than in Chianti Classico. Montecucco is a new DOC between Scansano and Montalcino.

The Sovana DOC zone to the southeast of Morellino di Scansano, once known for the inconsequential Bianco di Pitigliano, is being planted with Cabernet as well as Sangiovese and the juicy Ciliegiolo ("cherry-like") grape. Ciliegiolo is the speciality of the land closer to the coast in the hotter, drier climate around Orbetello and is sold generally as a Maremma Toscana IGT. La Parrina estate in the Parrina DOC leads the coastal reds here.

Another hotbed of wine ambition is just over the border in Latium (Lazio to Italians) in Montefiascone, the centre of production of what is more usually the dullest white wine with the strangest name in the world: Est! Est!! Est!!!. The Cotarella brothers, one of whom directs the Florentine wine house of Antinori, have shown through their Falesco négociant business that this area can produce sumptuously modern Merlot, even if it has to be sold simply as IGT Lazio.

Chianti and its blood-brothers (the blood being the juice of the highly variable Sangiovese grape) are the dominant red wines of the northern part of the map. In the east their influence stretches from Sangiovese di Romagna (discussed on page 164) to the Marches' Adriatic coast, where Rosso Piceno is a transitional blend of Sangiovese and the extremely worthwhile Montepulciano grape. Just south of Ancona, full-bodied Rosso Conero is currently the finest expression of Montepulciano. Much further south in its true homeland, Montepulciano d'Abruzzo can vary from powerfully fruity bargain to stretched, rustic disappointment, with its *rosato* version Cerasuolo.

The Abruzzi was long regarded as a vinous wilderness with one exception: the extraordinary wines made here for decades by Eduardo Valentini of Loreto Aprutino. His Montepulciano d'Abruzzo is like an essence of this combination of grape and place, while his fastidiously selected, magnificently age-worthy, full-bodied white Trebbiano d'Abruzzo (made from grapes also known as Bombino) had no peer, until Gianni Masciarelli arrived on the scene. (His reds are still better than his Trebbiano though.) See page 183 for details of the wines of Molise.

West of the Apennines, Sangiovese dominates Tuscan and Umbrian vineyards south from the outlying reaches of the Chianti zone. Count Bonacossi at Carmignano, just east of Florence was one of the first to recognize the virtues of flavouring it with some Cabernet Sauvignon. Over the border of Latium, the Cesanese family of vines is remarkable chiefly for its unpredictability; these wines can be still or sparkling, sweet or dry. Aleaticos, from wherever you may find them, are a more curious proposition: Moscato-scented sweet reds.

The white grapes that put their stamp on most Central Italian wine are the rather dreary Trebbiano of Tuscany (the same tart, neutral grape known as Ugni Blanc in France) and the much more characterful, often full-bodied Malvasia Bianco. Trebbiano, which is known as Procanico on the Tuscan coast and the island of Elba, is decidedly surplus to requirements in

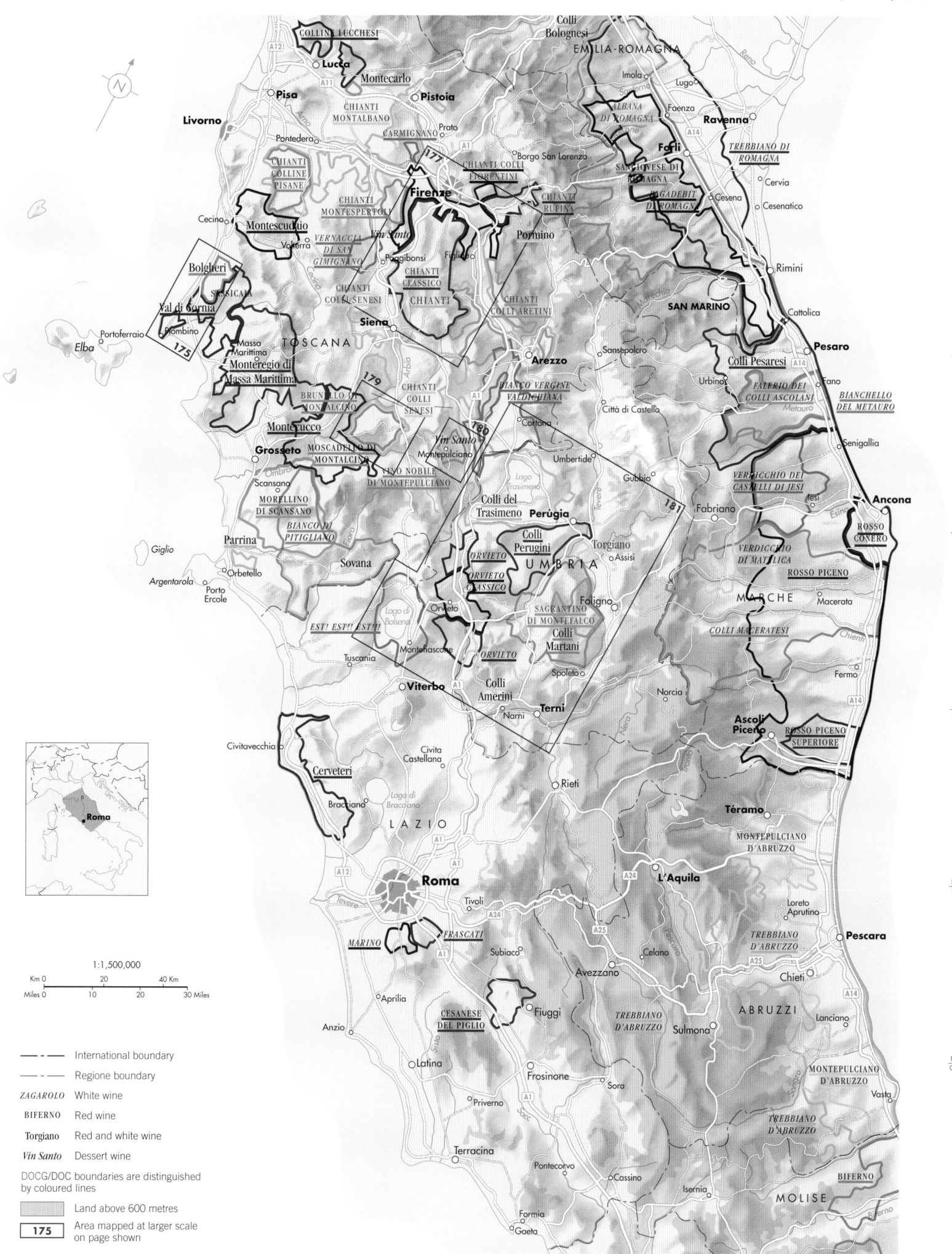

COLLINE LUCCHESI
Lucca
Montecarlo
Pisa
Pistoia
Livorno
CHIANTI MONTALBANO
CARMIGNANO
Pontedera
Prato
CHIANTI COLLINE PISANE
Cecina
Montescudaio
Volterra
Vin Santo
Firenze
Borgo San Lorenzo
CHIANTI COLLI FIORENTINI
CHIANTI MONTESPERTOLI
VERNACCIA DI SAN GIMIGNANO
Poggibonsi
Figline
Pontino
CHIANTI RUFINA
Bolgheri
SASSICAIA
Val di Cornia
Piombino
CHIANTI COLLI SENESI
CHIANTI CLASSICO
CHIANTI
Siena
CHIANTI COLLI ARETINI
Massa Marittima
TOSCANA
Monteregio di Massa Marittima
BRUNELLO DI MONTALCINO
CHIANTI COLLI SENESI
Montecucco
BIANCO VERGINE VALDICHIANA
Arezzo
Sansepolcro
Città di Castello
Cortona
Vin Santo
Montepulciano
Umbertide
Lago Trasimeno
Gubbio
Grosseto
MOSCADELLO DI MONTALCINO
Scansano
VINO NOBILE DI MONTEPULCIANO
MORELLINO DI SCANSANO
Colli del Trasimeno
Perúgia
Fabriano
Parrina
BIANCO DI PITIGLIANO
Colli Perugini
Torgiano
Assisi
Sovana
ORVIETO
UMBRIA
Foligno
SAGRANTINO DI MONTEFALCO
Colli Martani
Spoleto
ORVIETO CLASSICO
Orvieto
EST! EST!! EST!!!
Lago di Bolsena
Montefiascone
ORVIETO
Tuscania
Colli Amerini
Narni
Terni
Norcia
Viterbo
Civitavecchia
Civita Castellana
Rieti
Cerveteri
Bracciano
Lago di Bracciano
LAZIO
Roma
Tivoli
MARINO
FRASCATI
Subiaco
Aprilia
Anzio
CESANESE DEL PIGLIO
Fiuggi
Latina
Avezzano
Celano
Frosinone
Sora
Priverno
Terracina
Pontecorvo
Formia
Gaeta
Cassino
Isernia
Vasto

Pisa

EMILIA-ROMAGNA
Imola
Lugo
Faenza
ALBANA DI ROMAGNA
Ravenna
Forlì
TREBBIANO DI ROMAGNA
Cervia
Cesenatico
SANGIOVESE DI ROMAGNA
Cesena
PAGADEBIT DI ROMAGNA
Rimini
SAN MARINO
Cattolica
Colli Pesaresi
Pesaro
Fano
Urbino
FALERIO DEI COLLI ASCOLANI
BIANCHELLO DEL METAURO
Senigallia
VERDICCHIO DEI CASTELLI DI JESI
Ancona
ROSSO CONERO
VERDICCHIO DI MATELICA
ROSSO PICENO
Macerata
MARCHE
COLLI MACERATESI
Fermo
ROSSO PICENO SUPERIORE
Ascoli Piceno
Téramo
MONTEPULCIANO D'ABRUZZO
L'Aquila
TREBBIANO D'ABRUZZO
Pescara
Loreto Aprutino
Chieti
ABRUZZI
TREBBIANO D'ABRUZZO
Sulmona
Lanciano
MONTEPULCIANO D'ABRUZZO
TREBBIANO D'ABRUZZO
BIFERNO
MOLISE

Roma

International boundary
Regione boundary
ZAGAROLO White wine
BIFERNO Red wine
Torgiano Red and white wine
Vin Santo Dessert wine

DOCG/DOC boundaries are distinguished by coloured lines

Land above 600 metres

175 Area mapped at larger scale on page shown

1:1,500,000
Km 0   20   40 Km
Miles 0   10   20   30 Miles

The two far left *labels together with Umani Ronchi's Cabernet-based IGT Pelago and Bisci's Verdicchio di Matelica represent the best of the Marches, while Valentini makes the most famous Montepulciano d'Abruzzo.*

Central Italy today, although there have been fruitless attempts to add nominal excitement by selling it under consortium trademarks such as Galestro and Bianco della Lega.

Neither Trebbiano nor Malvasia, unfortunately, has any marked aroma. Hence there is a certain blandness and sameness in Central Italian whites avoided only by the very best examples even of such famous names as Frascati and Marino made in the volcanic Alban hills south of Rome. (Orvieto is discussed with other Umbrian wines.)

Where other white grapes contribute to the mix it is all to the good. Montecarlo from near Lucca, often called the best Tuscan (DOC) white, contains Sémillon, Sauvignon Blanc, and Pinot Bianco. On the Adriatic coast, Verdicchio takes its inspiration from the lively grape of the same name and can be a dry white wine with considerable personality and, unusually for a Central Italian white, some ageing potential.

In the far south of Tuscany, where reds will presumably eventually dominate, Bianco di Pitigliano can contain Grechetto, a minority grape with crispness and fragrance that also plays a satisfying part in Umbria. Altogether more significantly, the DOC Pomino, devised by the Frescobaldi family of Chianti, abandons the Tuscan varieties but manages to make an original Florentine wine of Sauvignon, Pinot Bianco, and Chardonnay.

One of the more characterful Central Italian white grapes is Vernaccia, at its apogee in San Gimignano where an increasing number of producers are restraining yields and managing to produce wines that taste of history not bitterness. Vermentino is also improving, especially close to the coast. Marchesi Antinori's Tenuta Belvedere from Bolgheri points the way.

At the time of writing, the most distinctive wine produced on the island of Elba (which generally follows a Sangiovese and Trebbiano path) is sweet red Aleatico, the result of drying these heavily perfumed grapes. Central Italy is the home of such vinous creativity, however, that this could change in a single vintage.

Even more than in other parts of Italy, this region's wines are, alas, too various and idiosyncratic to be mapped individually.

Below The Abruzzi region east of Rome between the Appenines and the Adriatic is one of Italy's least visited. Its red and white varieties both have high potential, though their names cause confusion: Montepulciano is the red grape and Trebbiano d'Abruzzo (alias Bombino) the white.

Tuscan Coast

It is debatable whether any winegrower since "Chianti" Ricasoli has made such an impact on Italian wine as the founder of Sassicaia, the little vineyard near the Tuscan coast that upset the whole DOC system. Sassicaia was totally non-traditional, unmistakably superb – and at the time classed as a lowly Vino da Tavola, quite simply because there were no other other vineyards here and therefore no DOC regulations.

The Marchese Incisa della Rochetta chose a stony hectare of the big San Guido estate in the 1940s to plant Cabernet. He hankered after the Médoc. The nearest vineyards were miles away. Bolgheri was neglected peach orchards and abandoned strawberry fields.

The estate lies six miles (10km) from the sea on the first slopes of the graphically named Colline Metallifere, a range rich in minerals that forms an amphitheatre with a marvellously benign climate. Vines flower in May and grapes ripen in late September, before autumn rains end the long, dry spring and summer. When the Marchese's early wines started to lose their tannin they revealed flavours not seen in Italy before.

His nephews, Piero and Lodovico Antinori, tasted the wines. Piero talked to Professor Peynaud in Bordeaux. Antinori started to bottle and market Sassicaia with the 1968 vintage. By the mid-1970s it was world famous. Then, in the 1980s, Lodovico Antinori began planting a selection of plots with varied soils on his property, Ornellaia, with Cabernet Sauvignon, Merlot, and, less successfully, Sauvignon Blanc. The best plots have turned out to be the higher, stonier plantings, together with a patch of clay whose Merlot goes into his Masseto.

Meanwhile his brother Piero upgraded the *rosato* from his Belvedere estate and in 1990 produced a Cabernet/Merlot blend called Guado al Tasso from a plot on higher ground. The soil turns sandier here; the wine lighter. This may well be the westernmost site for great reds.

New wine estates have proliferated, as the map shows; many have yet to establish their reputations. (Tenuta del Terriccio to the north of the area mapped with its minty Lupicaia Bordeaux blend was an early hit.) Gaja of Barbaresco established Ca' Marcanda. Ruffino of Chianti is here too. Cabernet and some Merlot are the usual choices.

The DOC Bolgheri is evolving fast. (Sassicaia has its own DOC within it.) All other wines must be blends (of Cabernet, Merlot or Sangiovese for reds) which means, for example, that the all-Sangiovese Cavaliere and all-Merlot Masseto are sold as IGTs.

If Bolgheri has shown itself perfect Cabernet territory, Merlot may be the grape for the wine zone in the southern half of this map, the recent Val di Cornia DOC around Suvereto. The soils are certainly notably higher in clay than those of Bolgheri. The owner of Bellavista of Franciacorta has Merlot as the focus of his Petra estate. Lodovico Antinori has bought land here. So has the San Luigi estate in Piombino right on what might today be called Tuscany's gold coast. The Monteregio di Massa Marittima DOC just south of the dynamic Suvereto subzone is probably next.

‑ ‑ ‑ ‑	Provincia boundary
‑ ‑ ‑ ‑	Comune boundary
————	DOC Bolgheri
————	DOC Bolgheri Sassicaia
————	DOC Val di Cornia

Val di Cornia subregion

————	Suvereto
■ ORNELLAIA	Leading producer
Aia Nuova	Noted vineyard

1:154,000

Km 0   1   2   3   4   5 Km
Miles 0   1   2   3 Miles

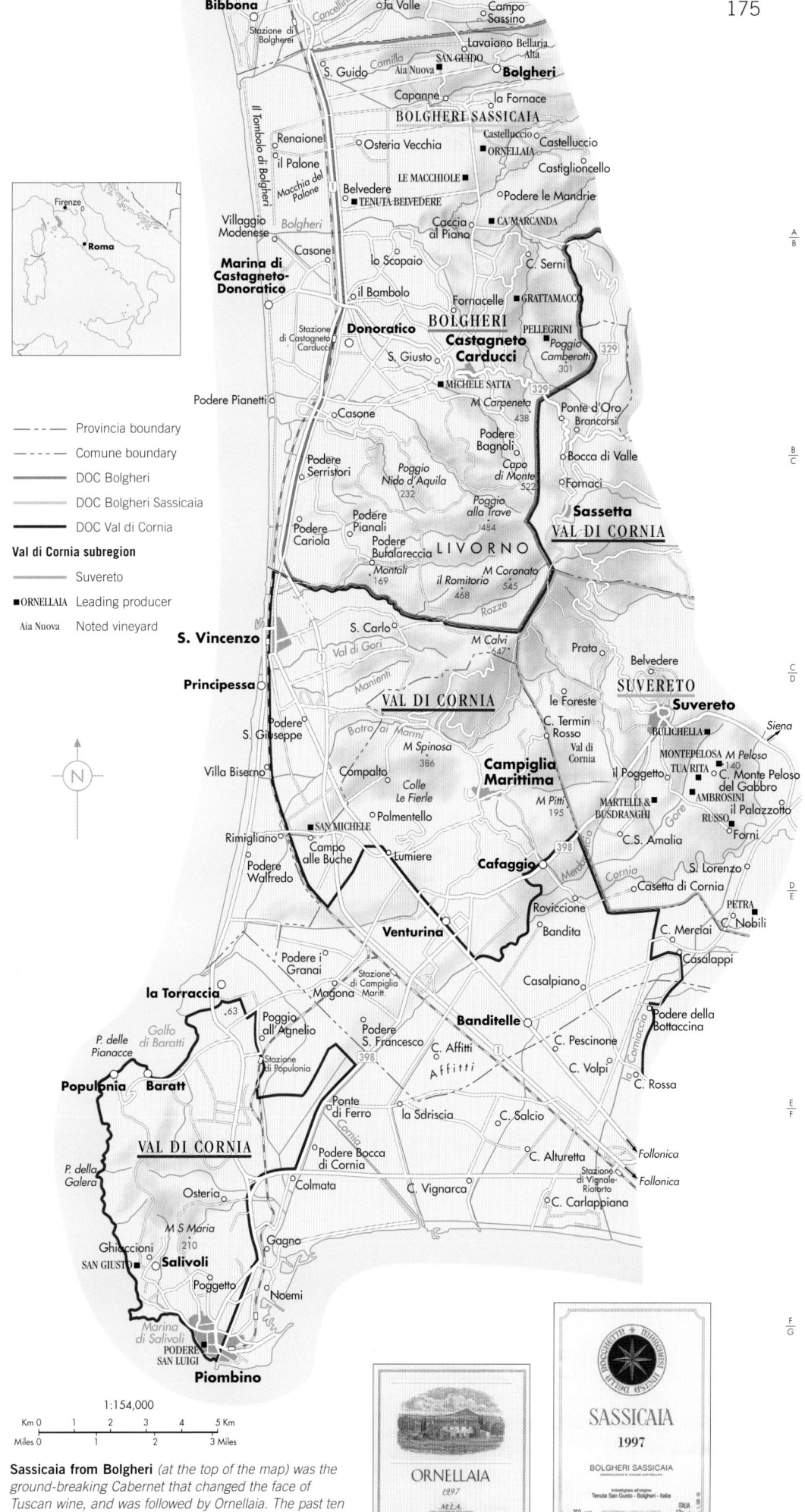

Sassicaia from Bolgheri (at the top of the map) was the ground-breaking Cabernet that changed the face of Tuscan wine, and was followed by Ornellaia. The past ten years have seen the number of Tuscan IGTs multiply.

Heart of Chianti

The hills between Florence and Siena can come as near to the Roman poet's idea of gentlemanly country life as anywhere on earth. The blending of landscape, architecture, and agriculture is ancient and profound. The villas, cypresses, olives, vines, rocks, and woods compose pictures that could be Roman, Renaissance, Risorgimento – there is no way of telling (provided all the tourists park their cars discreetly).

In this timeless scene, once a promiscuous tangle of the crops deemed necessary to Tuscan peasant life, vineyards now march up hill and down dale, typically owned and regimented by well-heeled outsiders.

The original Chianti zone, one of the first anywhere to be delimited, in 1716, was limited to the land around the villages of Radda, Gaiole, Castellina, and Greve. The red line on the map opposite shows that Chianti Classico has since been expanded, but it is still unquestionably the best of Chianti's eight subzones and, today, one of Italy's greatest concentrations of fine winemaking.

Of the other subzones, Chianti Rufina, east of Florence and partly mapped here, is the most distinctive, making some particularly elegant wines for long ageing. Some highly successful estates around San Gimignano in the Chianti Colli Senesi subzone, the hills above Siena, are also emerging. Chianti made in the hills above Florence, Pisa, and Arezzo (the Chianti Colli Fiorentini, Colline Pisane, and Colli Aretini subzones) tends to be less distinguished, as are the wines of the Chianti Montalbano subzone northwest of Florence. As to the exact boundaries of the subzones, even the Consorzio is vague.

The map on page 173 shows just how large an area – almost 100 miles (160km) from north to south and more extensive than the Bordeaux wine region – is allowed to produce wine labelled simply Chianti, a much less ambitious drink than any labelled Chianti Classico.

The general Chianti formula was, famously, established more than a century ago by the illustrious Baron Ricasoli, sometime Prime Minister of Italy, at his castle of Brolio. As long ago as 1872 he distinguished between two forms of Chianti: a simple one for drinking young and a more ambitious version aimed at the cellar. He allowed some of the then prevalent white grape, Malvasia, into the blend for early drinking Chianti with the red grapes then grown, Sangiovese and Canaiolo. Unfortunately the proportion of usefully productive white wine vines grew and Trebbiano crept in. When the DOC laws defined Chianti in 1963 they insisted on 10% and allowed up to 30% – far too much – white grapes into Chianti of any style. Pallid Chianti (too often beefed up with red imported from the south of Italy) became the rule, and it became clear, to such as the ancient Antinori family of Florence, that either the rules must change, or it must make its best wine in its own way and give the wine a new name.

The Antinoris' excellent Tignanello was their rebel flag, made since 1975, like Carmignano, from Sangiovese with a small proportion of Cabernet. To underline the point they rapidly added Solaia, with the proportions of Cabernet and Sangiovese reversed. Within a few years there seemed scarcely a castello or villa in Chianti that

had not followed them with a "Supertuscan" (sold initially as a defiant Vino da Tavola, nowadays corralled into the IGT category) of their own construction, many of them excellent and some original.

But as the character of many of these rebel wines became increasingly distant from anything obviously Tuscan, and as new, much higher quality clones of Sangiovese as well as better ways of growing them were identified, the concept of Chianti Classico Riserva as a truly fine wine emerged.

Ironically, but in typical Italian fashion, this was some time after the entire Chianti production zone was awarded DOCG status in 1984

Chianti subzones:

———	Classico
———	Colli Aretini
———	Colli Fiorentini
———	Colli Senesi
———	Montespertoli
———	Rufina
———	DOC Pomino
– – – –	Provincia boundary
■ FONTODI	Leading producer
▦	Vineyards
▦	Woods
═250═	Contour interval 50 metres
▼	Weather station (WS)

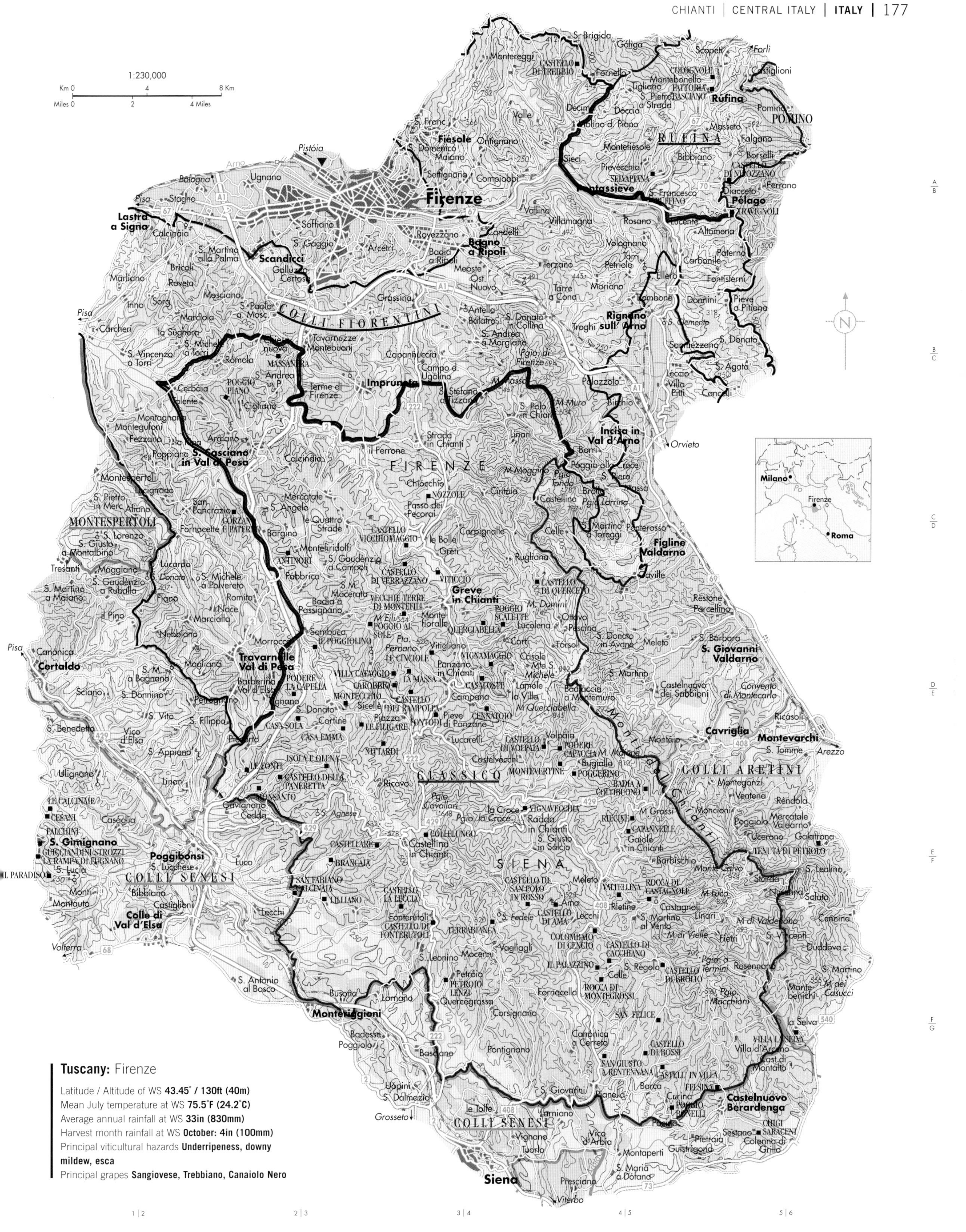

1:230,000

Km 0   4   8 Km
Miles 0   2   4 Miles

N

Milano

Firenze

Roma

Tuscany: Firenze

Latitude / Altitude of WS **43.45° / 130ft (40m)**
Mean July temperature at WS **75.5°F (24.2°C)**
Average annual rainfall at WS **33in (830mm)**
Harvest month rainfall at WS **October: 4in (100mm)**
Principal viticultural hazards **Underripeness, downy mildew, esca**
Principal grapes **Sangiovese, Trebbiano, Canaiolo Nero**

(one of the worst vintages ever). Today there is marked distinction between the two styles of wine coming from the Chianti region. A wine labelled Chianti is normally a tangy, ultra-digestible mouthful of fruit ready for drinking a year or two after it was made. Chianti Classico Riserva on the other hand is nowadays an extremely serious wine made substantially (75 to 100% of the blend) from low-cropped, top-quality Sangiovese vines, aged in wood – large and/or small oak – with a life expectancy of ten years or even more.

Soils here vary between calcareous marls (including the characteristic marl known as *galestro*), rocks and warmer, sandier soils such as those around San Gimignano in the far west of the map which can coax dense, mineral-laden whites from the local Vernaccia grape (see page 174), or indeed from others.

The vineyards of Chianti Classico are at altitudes of between 820 and 1,640ft (250 and 500m) or even higher. At these altitudes, and in a climate with quite wet autumns, the challenge in all but the hottest, driest years is to ripen not just

Below Late evening sun lights the hamlet of Volpaia, looking south over Radda. At 2,100ft (650m) this is one of Chianti's highest vineyards, too cold for Sangiovese and planted with Chardonnay, Sauvignon, and Müller-Thurgau.

the sugars but the tannins of the relatively late-ripening Sangiovese. An increasing number of producers achieve this, with Italian brio, fashioning wines that are complex, firm, and savoury rather than voluptuous. The rest of their output may include olive oil, a non-Riserva Chianti Classico to drink earlier (often good value), a fairly inconsequential local dry white (see page 174), perhaps a Vin Santo (Tuscany's famous dried-grape, long-aged sweet white, or rather tawny; see page 180) and a Supertuscan IGT or two.

These wines are typically fastidiously made (almost invariably with top-quality barriques), fantastically named (the wine-lover is expected to know by heart which fantasy name identifies which grape variety or varieties) and ambitiously priced. So fashionable were these bottlings of such non-traditional grape varieties as Cabernet, Merlot, Syrah, and Chardonnay in the 1980s and early 1990s that they invariably commanded a substantial premium over any wine with the word Chianti on the label. Today some producers would argue that it is Chianti Classico Riserva that is every estate's truest expression.

At Siena a unique institution, the Enoteca or Wine Library of Italy, housed in an old Medici fortress, provides an opportunity to taste not only every possible Chianti but most other Italian wines of note in fitting splendour.

The map on the previous page shows, besides the chaotic hilliness of the Chianti countryside, and the scattering of vines (and olives) among woods, the cellars of most of the leading producers of Chianti Classico. Many, but by no means all of them, are members of the Chianti Classico Consorzio, nowadays more a marketing organization than a group of definitively superior producers.

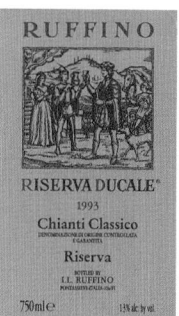

The Classico Riservas of Chianti *now share top billing with blends of Sangiovese and Cabernet or Merlot. Carmignano was the original Sangiovese/Cabernet blend; Tignanello its great successor, while Castello di Ama l'Apparita is an excellent Merlot. Rufina is the zone just east of Florence, Ruffino a long-established brand.*

Montalcino

The largest of the outlying areas of the vast Chianti region is the Colli Senesi, the Siena Hills. Forty miles (65km) south of Siena they roll in stately waves, woodland-topped, with here and there as a landmark a village, a rough stone castle or bare tufa cliff.

Until the 1970s little was heard of this part of Tuscany. It was purely local knowledge that the climate here was more equable than farther north – the sea is only 30 miles (50km) away, via Grosseto – and that summers are regularly warmer and extremely dry. Monte Amiata, rising to 5,600ft (1,700m) just to the south, collects the summer storms that come from that direction.

At the same time as Ricasoli was devising an ideal formula for Chianti, in an enclave in the Colli Senesi around the little town of Montalcino, Clemente Santi and his kin (now called Biondi-Santi) were establishing at their estate, Il Greppo, a model for what they labelled Brunello di Montalcino. This dense, muscular wine was made only from the Sangiovese grape, known locally as Brunello, without the blending customary in Chianti. Odd bottles of ancient vintages of this wine were so impressive that eventually other producers emerged and from the 1980s Montalcino has been engulfed in a tidal wave of international interest in what was clearly Tuscany's answer to Barolo.

Montalcino has the double advantage of the warm, dry climate of the Tuscan coast (see page 175) with, in the best vineyards south of the town, the rockier, less fertile soils of the best Chianti sites, This can result in the most concentrated, long-lived forms of Sangiovese on the planet for ripening is not the perennial problem it can be in Chianti Classico.

The old method was to ferment this strong, dark wine long and slowly on its skins to extract the maximum colour and flavour. It was then aged for years in large old Slavonian oak casks and decades in bottle. The result was a wine for heroes, or rather heroic millionaires, supercharged with flavour, extract, and impact.

Even in Montalcino, however, wine laws have been adapted to modern tastes. The mandatory minimum four years in oak have been reduced to two (the wine not to be released until four years old) so that today's Brunello is much more likely to have been bottled while there was still sufficient fruit to counterbalance its power. And Montalcino was the first DOCG to be graced with a "junior DOC", Rosso di Montalcino, a (relatively) lighter wine which can be released at only a year old. This has swept up the less concentrated fruit and allowed Brunello to retain an average quality level that is in general admirably high.

This is all the more remarkable because the zone has been expanded so enormously, from just over 150 acres (60ha) in 1960 to more than 3,700 (1,500ha) today. Altitudes vary from 490ft (150m) above sea level in the Val d'Orcia in the south where the most potent wines tend to be made to 1,640ft (500m) just south of the town where wines are more elegant and aromatic. Some areas are definitely better than most but it is too soon for the politically sensitive business of individual site classification.

The only question mark over Brunello di Montalcino's future is the invasion of the new oak barrique which has had the effect of smudging this very particular zone's highly distinctive character – more obvious in its Sangiovese than in the international grapes now widely planted in Montalcino. The resulting wines may be sold under the Sant' Antimo DOC – same boundaries as Brunello, different name.

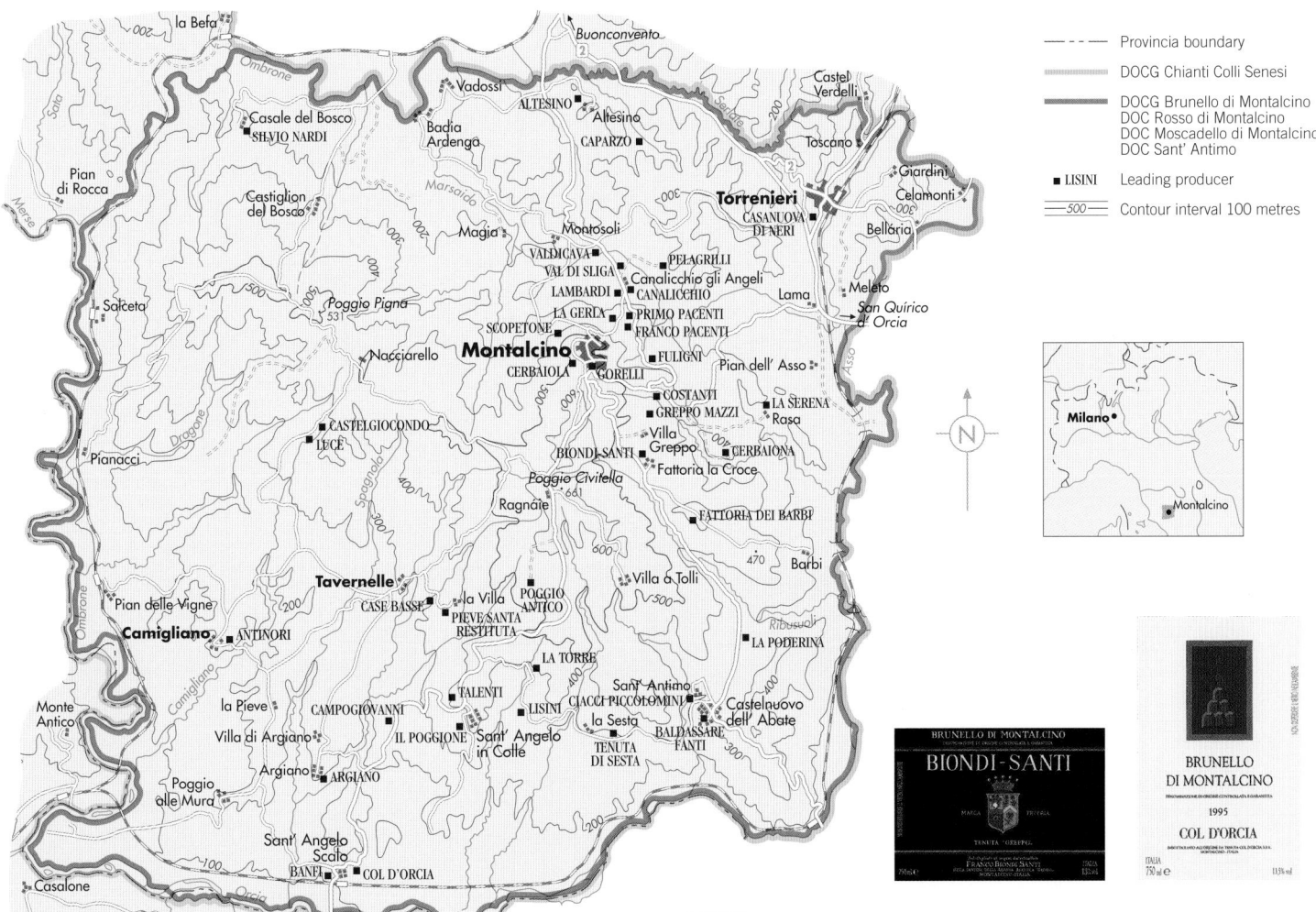

Biondi-Santi was the original sole producer of Brunello di Montalcino. Now there are scores of them, most maintaining a remarkably high standard.

---- Provincia boundary

DOCG Chianti Colli Senesi

DOCG Brunello di Montalcino
DOC Rosso di Montalcino
DOC Moscadello di Montalcino
DOC Sant' Antimo

■ LISINI   Leading producer

═500═ Contour interval 100 metres

1:135,000

Km 0   1   2   3   4   5 Km
Miles 0   1   2   3 Miles

Montepulciano

Montalcino's neighbours to the east, across an intervening enclave of "mere" Chianti, have ancient pretensions of their own embodied in their DOC, Vino Nobile di Montepulciano. Montepulciano is a hill town of great charm surrounded by vineyards planted with a mixture of Sangiovese, called here Prugnolo Gentile, with the other standard Chianti ingredients. Some producers admit to ignoring the legal requirement to blend grapes other than Sangiovese in their best wines. Others value the colour and structure of Colorino grapes in the blend. This "noble wine", elevated with Barolo, Barbaresco, and Brunello di Montalcino to DOCG status in 1980, tends to taste like a sort of halfway house between Chianti Classico and Brunello, with the fragrance of the former and the body of the latter.

Until quite recently winemaking skills have been more uneven here than in Montalcino, and the wines, still weighed down by a heavy charge of tannins, can lack the sheer dramatic intensity of the best Brunello.

As in Montalcino, minimum ageing periods have been reduced (to just one year in wood for both normal and Riserva versions), and Rosso di Montepulciano can be surprisingly soft. The barrique invasion continues here too, smoothing the wine's hard edges, which in some cases is no bad thing.

Vineyard altitudes here tend to vary less than in Montalcino and most of the best sites are at between 820 and 1,475ft (250 and 450m). Soils are generally sandier and the wines more accessible, although the pervading warmth of south Tuscany leaves no shortage of ripeness.

Led by the stylish house of Avignonesi, wine producers here have dallied with various Supertuscan formulae, including the vibrantly oaked white Marzocco. The Sangiovese, and Merlot, grapes grown on Antinori's substantial holdings around Montepulciano are used for blending rather than selling as Vino Nobile.

Yet perhaps Montepulciano's greatest triumph is its Vin Santo, the forgotten luxury of many parts of Italy, Tuscany above all. It is orange coloured, smoky scented, extraordinarily sweet, intense, and persistent, aged four years in tiny flat *caratelli* (barrels), traditionally (but no longer) under the roof tiles of a Renaissance *palazzo*.

— · — · —	Regione boundary
— - — - —	Provincia boundary
▨▨▨▨▨	DOCG Chianti Colli Senesi
━━━━━	DOCG Vino Nobile di Montepulciano DOC Rosso di Montepulciano
━━━━━	DOC Bianco Vergine Valdichiana
▪ FASSATI	Leading producer
—500—	Contour interval 100 metres

1:138,460

Km 0   1   2   3   4   5 Km
Miles 0   1   2   3 Miles

Below The town of Montepulciano hugging the skyline of a ridge dotted with olives and cypresses, clearly visible from its rival Montalcino 20 miles (32km) to the west. Its vineyards lie to the east towards and across the Chiana.

The Vino Nobile that *made the name of Montepulciano now shares the limelight with a growing range of varietals – white and red – and blends.*

Umbria

At last Umbria, like the Tuscan Coast (see page 175), is seething with winemaking ambition. Its isolation and the absence of any large cities or useful ports kept the region and its wines in obscurity for generations, even though its wine traditions are as ancient as any.

Orvieto was an important Etruscan city. The magnificent cellars cut in the volcanic rock of its dramatic hilltop 3,000 years ago are unique examples of prehistoric technology, specifically designed for long, cool fermentation, the object being sweet wine. Classic Orvieto was *amabile*, as sweet as possible, depending on the season and the amount of botrytis conjured by autumn mists in the vineyards. Alas for Orvieto, the 1960s and 1970s fashion for dry white wines turned it into yet another Central Italian blend of Trebbiano (at times called Procanico here) and Malvasia, and the fortunes of this supposed leader of Umbrian wine foundered.

Enter Dr Giorgio Lungarotti who, on his estate at Torgiano near Perugia, was the first in modern times to prove that Umbria could make great red wine. His Rubesco Riserva 1975, 1979, and 1983 broke new ground for the reputation of Central Italy's only landlocked region. His daughter continues to keep Torgiano on the map.

Umbria's climate varies enormously, from cooler-than-Chianti-highland weather in the north around Lake Trasimeno, to a Mediterranean climate at Montefalco and Terni in the south.

It was in the southwest at Antinori's Castello della Sala estate that the next significant development in Umbrian wine history was to take place. The estate was initially designed to make Orvieto, but from the mid-1980s on winemaker Renzo Cotarella continued to produce a stunning range of non-traditional white wines. A barrel-fermented Chardonnay was perhaps only to be expected, but Cervaro della Sala has almost from the start had a purity and singularity to

establish it as one of Italy's greatest white wines. A botrytized Muffato from a range of international varieties plus Grechetto showed other possibilities, while an unusually refined, if highly variable, Pinot Nero (Noir) indicated others.

The next breakthrough established an entirely new DOCG, Sagrantino di Montefalco, inspired by the thrilling 1991 and 1993 reds made from the local, dazzlingly fruity (and also mightily tannic) Sagrantino grape around the town of Montefalco by Arnaldo Caprai. Colpetrone was soon to follow.

Umbria was well on its way and today makes a truly Italian farrago of reds and whites from grapes both local and imported, including Orvieto of some real interest once more. No patterns matching grapes and places have yet emerged, but the role of consultant oenologists, the demigods of the modern Italian wine scene, will continue to be vital. The Cotarella brothers have been making particularly successful raids into Umbria from their Falesco winemaking base at Montefiascone over the border in Latium and, like other producers, are more likely to label their wines IGT Umbria than with a local DOC such as Colli Perugini, Colli del Trasimeno, Colli Martani (especially good for Grechetto), or Colli Amerini. Umbria has arrived.

Sweet Orvieto was once the only Umbrian *wine of note. Today the region is better known for ground-breaking reds such as Sagrantino di Montefalco and the complex white Cervaro della Salla.*

1:695,000

Km 0   5   10   15   20   25 Km
Miles 0   5   10   15 Miles

— · — Regione boundary

— - — Provincia boundary

MONTEFALCO DOCG

ORVIETO DOC

■ LA FIORITA Leading producer

DOCG/DOC boundaries are distinguished by coloured lines

▼ Weather station (WS)

Umbria: Perugia

Latitude / Altitude of WS **43.07˚ / 1,673ft (510m)**
Mean July temperature at WS **73.5˚F (23.1˚C)**
Average annual rainfall at WS **36in (910mm)**
Harvest month rainfall at WS **September: 2.75in (70mm)**
Principal viticultural hazard **Some esca in older vineyards**
Principal grapes **Sangiovese, Ciliegiolo, Sagrantino, Trebbiano, Grechetto**

Southern Italy

In the old days the strong, deep crimson wines of the south (Puglia, and the islands described overleaf in particular) helped producers of smarter wines to the north through their crisis of the 1960s and early 1970s before they discovered how to ripen grapes reliably themselves. Nowadays a small but increasing proportion of wine from the far south finds its way into bottle. Since Puglia (Apulia in English) makes more wine than the whole of Australia, this is having

a certain impact – not just because wines made somewhere this hot are inevitably potent, but also in terms of sheer quantity.

But southern does not necessarily mean sun-baked. Indeed there are many vineyards on the map below that are routinely harvested long after all the grapes of Tuscany have been transformed into wine.

Historically it was near Naples in the inland parts of Campania, particularly the province of

Avellino, which set the pace for the region's truly distinctive wines. The Aglianico (a corruption of Ellenico, or Greek, like civilization itself down here) is southern Italy's greatest dark-skinned grape, making wines with a powerful, obviously noble, brooding character. The vine ripens so late that it could not practically be grown much further north. In the hills of Taurasi, where it finds its finest expression, it is often picked in the snow, and is naturally so high in acidity that the malolactic fermentation is no routine achievement. As everywhere in Italy, however, Aglianico is being tamed, and to a certain extent smothered, by the application of modern, super-soft winemaking techniques.

The name of Greco di Tufo, a substantial white from inland Campania of remarkably original flavour – apple peel fragrance and mineral depths – shares the credit between its assumed Greek origins and the tufa rock on which it

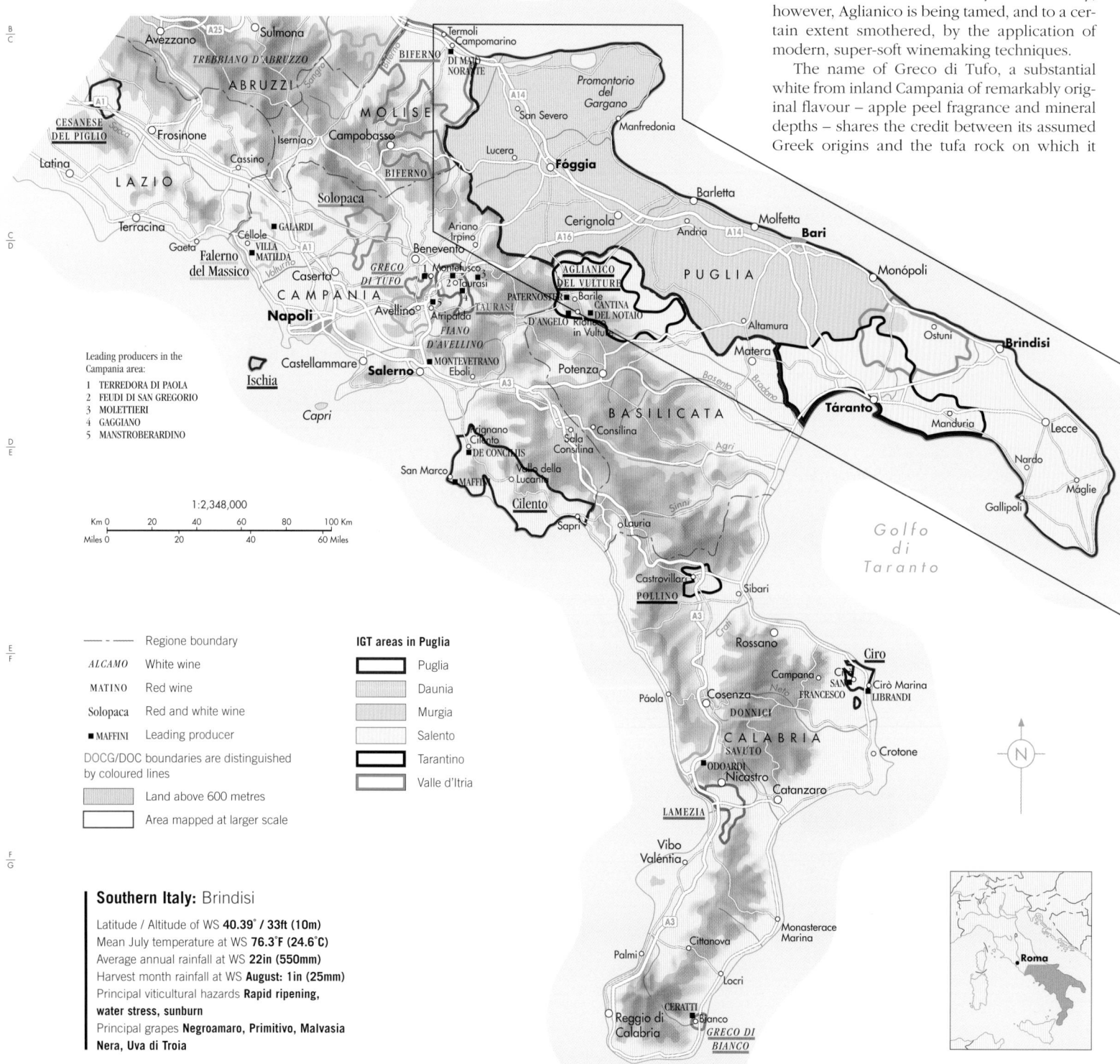

Leading producers in the Campania area:
1. TERREDORA DI PAOLA
2. FEUDI DI SAN GREGORIO
3. MOLETTIERI
4. GAGGIANO
5. MANSTROBERARDINO

1:2,348,000

Km 0   20   40   60   80   100 Km
Miles 0   20   40   60 Miles

– – – Regione boundary

ALCAMO   White wine

MATINO   Red wine

Solopaca   Red and white wine

■ MAFFINI   Leading producer

DOCG/DOC boundaries are distinguished by coloured lines

Land above 600 metres

Area mapped at larger scale

IGT areas in Puglia

Puglia

Daunia

Murgia

Salento

Tarantino

Valle d'Itria

Southern Italy: Brindisi

Latitude / Altitude of WS **40.39° / 33ft (10m)**
Mean July temperature at WS **76.3°F (24.6°C)**
Average annual rainfall at WS **22in (550mm)**
Harvest month rainfall at WS August: **1in (25mm)**
Principal viticultural hazards **Rapid ripening, water stress, sunburn**
Principal grapes **Negroamaro, Primitivo, Malvasia Nera, Uva di Troia**

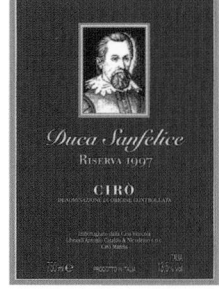

Map legend:

— - — Regione boundary

SAN SEVERO DOC

■ FELLINE Leading producer

DOC boundaries are distinguished by coloured lines

▼ Weather station (WS)

1:2,000,000

Km 0   20   40   60 Km
Miles 0   20   40 Miles

Above *Trulli*, small stone houses such as these near Alberobello, are the most distinctive feature of the Puglian landscape, which is very much flatter than in the rest of southern Italy. They offer some shelter from the region's sweltering summers.

Labels on wines from this part of Italy *were for long a rarity but nowadays an increasing proportion of the vast amount of wine made here is sold in bottle, bearing the labels of established producers such as those shown above or importers' own labels.*

grows. In the same hilly province, Avellino, the Fiano grape makes a more delicate, subtle white, a wine that combines lightness with firmness and a hauntingly floral scent.

These are the established names of modern Campanian wine but some surprisingly good wines are emerging from less obvious areas such as the coastal vineyards around the temples of Paestum, where producers such as Montevetrano, De Conciliis, and Maffini are making wines of world class, almost exclusively from Campania's rich heritage of indigenous grape varieties. Villa Matilde on the other hand, to the north in the Falerno del Massico zone named after the most celebrated wine of the ancient world Falernum (see page 12), makes the most of them, with fine reds based on Aglianico and Piedirosso and improving whites made from Falanghina grapes. Fontana Galardi's Terra di Lavoro is an impressive, highly distinctive red made in this northern corner of Campania.

In Basilicata to the south, Aglianico del Vulture is the region's sole DOC, grown (with unusual skill for this part of the world) from a different selection of Aglianico from that grown in Taurasi on the slopes of an extinct volcano up to 2,500ft (760m). Less famous than Taurasi, it can often

offer better value, although winemaking standards vary wildly. Leading producers are Paternoster and D'Angelo which has had some success adding a softening dose of Merlot to Aglianico.

Aglianico is also grown on the Adriatic coast of southern Italy in the little-known region of Molise. The region's leading producer, Luigi Di Majo of Campomarino, can coax a more broachable varietal version from his vines on the Di Majo Norante estate, even though they may be picked as late as November. Ramitello is his even more approachable blend of Montepulciano d'Abruzzo with Aglianico made to the specifications of the local Biferno DOC, while Falanghina makes flavour-packed whites. Borgo di Colloredo is another Molise estate with ambition.

Calabria has just one strong red of reputation, Cirò on the eastern coast, but DOCs for several other zones, including Donnici, Lamezia, Pollino, and Savuto, of which the last hints at the potential for the local Gaglioppo grape. Calabria's most original wine is the strong, tangy and sweetly perfumed Greco di Bianco made, unexpectedly, around a village called Bianco near the very tip of the Italian toe.

If the wine producers of Calabria and Basilicata could do with the kick that their coastline inevitably suggests, Puglia's wine scene is in a state of revolution – albeit many leagues behind that which has revitalized French wine's workaday underbelly, the Languedoc, but working in the same, positive direction. No longer is this region dismissed as fit only for the blending vat or European wine lake. It is now abuzz with lauded Italian oenologists, flying foreign winemakers cooking up blends for the supermarket buyers of northern Europe, and some of the smarter companies in Italian wine on the lookout for good investments. Antinori, for example,

bought two estates in the late 1990s: one, on higher ground towards Basilicata, previously owned by Gancia from even further north, and another near Brindisi. Initially at least the company used the international varieties it inherited rather than indigenous ones for its Tormaresca IGT Puglia label.

At the end of the 1990s, the proportion of DOC wine made in Puglia was well under 5% of the total. Many buyers are more interested in an IGT Chardonnay or Primitivo (California's Zinfandel) del Salento than, say, a DOC called Gravina or Ostuni.

Not that there is a shortage of interesting local grapes. Negroamaro is the cautionary name of the principal red grape in the south of Puglia. It can make almost port-like roasted reds in Salice Salentino, Squinzano, Leverano and Copertino. Uva di Troia, more likely to be grown in the centre and north with Abruzzo's Montepulciano, may prove superior. Malvasia Nera, with different strains identified respectively with Lecce and Brindisi, is Negroamaro's more usual blending partner however and can add a certain velvet to the texture. These wines, when not reined in by imported technology, are extremely high in alcohol.

Virtually all of Puglia's most interesting wines are red and made south of the Taranto-Brindisi road in the southern part of the area designated IGT Salento. Land here is relatively flat and unremittingly hot, so there is no great variation in exposition and mesoclimate. Indeed one of the few material vinous distinctions of the heel of Italy is that Primitivo is the traditional speciality of Manduria on the southern coast.

As local growers continue to focus more and more on the bottle rather than the tanker, interest in this region can only increase.

Sicily

Right Vines on the black, fertile volcanic soils below the slopes of Mount Etna which threatens in the distance. Etna DOC wines come in all three colours but progress here has been slower than in many other parts of Sicily.

The Italian wine establishment (if that is not a contradiction in terms) has at last woken up to the enormous potential of the beautiful, climatically favoured, Mediterranean island of Sicily. It produces even more wine than the staggering volume made in Puglia, but enjoys a much more varied landscape as well as cultural heritage. The southeastern tip is south of Tunis; the distant island of Pantelleria, whose Muscats are justly famous, is on the same latitude as this North African city and closer to it than it is to Palermo. Sicily can be very hot, and the sea of white Catarratto vines planted in Trapani province in the west is regularly warmed to boiling point by winds from Africa. Irrigation is a necessity for a good half of Sicilian vineyards, but inland the landscape can be quite green and lush, and the mountains in the northeast are usually snow-capped for several winter months.

The great majority of Sicilian wine is white, made in vast quantities by a co-op and still either embarrassingly surplus to anyone's requirements or shipped in bulk to the mainland for transformation into something else. But an increasing proportion, red and white, is now bottled, having been made with some skill (and modern equipment bought with the EU subsidies that have been poured into this once poverty-stricken island).

The grape that may make Sicily's vinous reputation is Nero d'Avola, whose other name, Calabrese, suggests its roots are Calabrian but which produces its most exciting wine in the southeast corner of Sicily around the baroque town of Noto. Here, notably in wines labelled Eloro Pachino made around the town of Eloro, it reaches full, glorious expression of mulberry-scented fruit but with quite enough structure to age well. This sort of red was once fermented hot and fast and sold off for blending but early

peaks on the Sicilian wine-landscape such as Regeleali's Rosso del Conte showed just how magnificent it could be if handled more considerately. Nero d'Avola can have difficulty ripening in the island's higher vineyards but skilful producers such as Abbazia Sant'Anastasia have successfully transplanted it to the north coast where they blend it with both Syrah and Merlot.

Sicily has not, of course, escaped experimentation with international grape varieties – indeed Planeta's barrel-fermented Chardonnay has been regarded by Italians as one of their finest examples – but there are signs of a gradual re-evaluation of Sicily's own grapes, even if many of the best producers blend them with foreign imports. Other interesting red grapes are Frappato, which can make good lively wines to be drunk young, including the light red Cerasuolo for which Vittória is famous, and Nerello Cappuccio, distinct from Etna's Nerello Mascalese.

Light-skinned grapes grown for the fortified wine Marsala, or for Alcamo table wine or the European wine lake, dominate the hot, dusty west of the island, making Catarratto Italy's second most planted variety after Trebbiano. Some of the flying winemakers parachuted in to the island have made convincing, lightly oaked bottlings of this grape but interesting wines are more likely made from Grecanico and Inzolia.

Many of Sicily's most exciting modern wines are sold as IGTs for, with the recently renovated red Faro, the rest of Sicily's DOCs are reserved for her particular speciality: dessert wine. The Moscatos of Noto and Pantelleria, and the Malvasia of the volcanic islands of Lipari are outstanding examples of one of Italy's oldest vinous traditions.

Marsala, like a very distant cousin of sherry crossed with madeira, has been famous since Nelson's day, when he fortified the Royal Navy with it. In the 1980s it seemed as though it might come back into fashion, but has now sunk into the deepest of doldrums. The historic houses of this overplanted zone, Pellegrino and Donnafugata, have put their eggs in the table wine basket, and even Marco De Bartoli, who virtually alone carries on Marsala's winemaking traditions, labels his two best wines, Vecchio Samperi Riserva 30 Anni and Vigna La Miccia, as Vini da Tavola.

1:2,143,000

Km 0   20   40   60 Km
Miles 0   10   20   30   40 Miles

---- - - ----   Provincia boundary

ALCAMO   White wine

ELORO   Red wine

Etna   Red and white wine

Marsala   Dessert wine

■PLANETA   Leading producer

DOC boundaries are distinguished by coloured lines

   Land above 500 metres

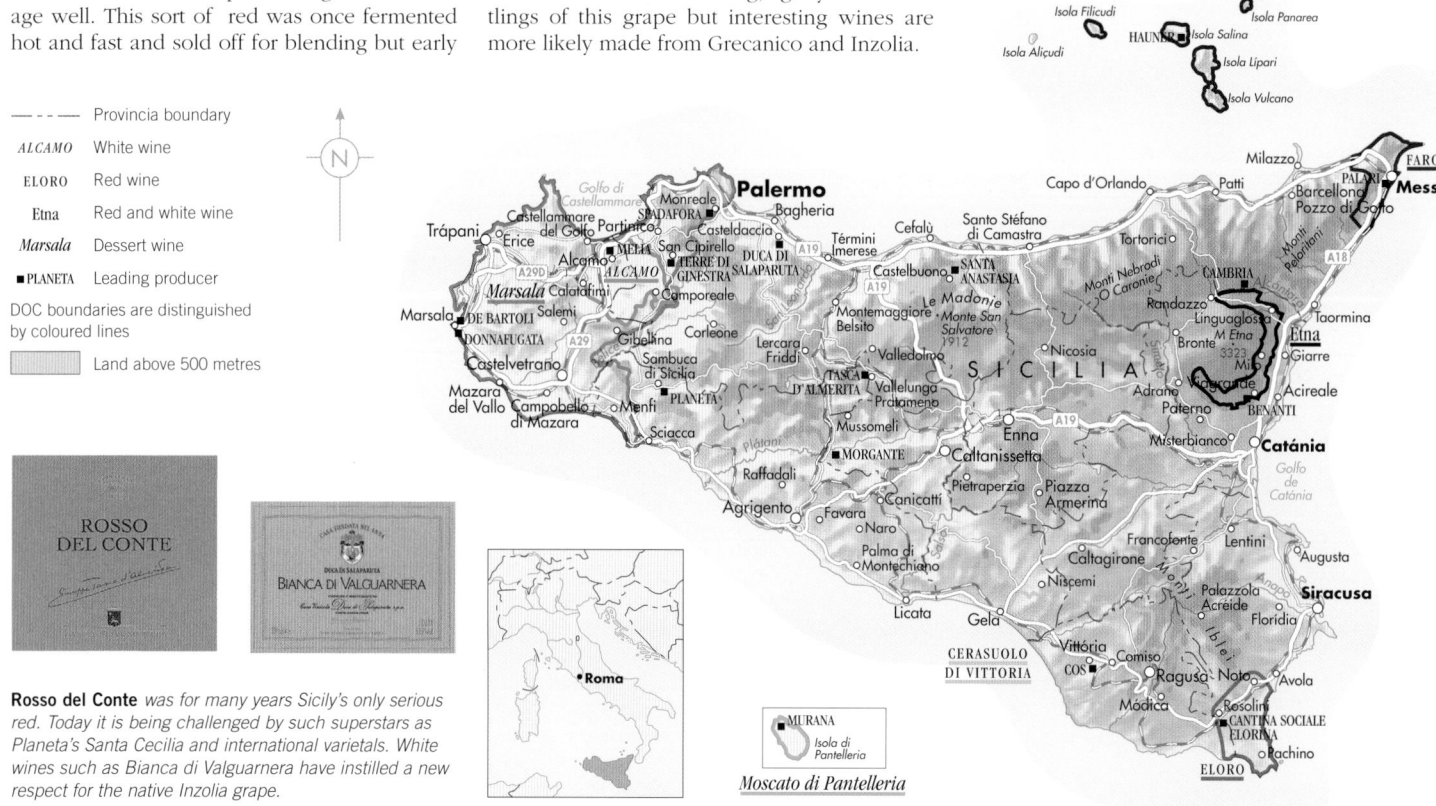

Rosso del Conte *was for many years Sicily's only serious red. Today it is being challenged by such superstars as Planeta's Santa Cecilia and international varietals. White wines such as Bianca di Valguarnera have instilled a new respect for the native Inzolia grape.*

Sardinia

Italy's northern major Mediterranean island, Sardegna in Italian, has over the centuries seen many of the same influences as Sicily but, with some very isolated exceptions, has been noticeably slower to join the international modern winemaking party.

Wine has never played an important part in either Sardinian culture or agriculture, although there was a flurry of heavily subsidized planting in the mid-20th century to provide reds, so alcoholic they almost tasted sweet, for blending on the mainland. (Sardinian reds were once fermented with the express purpose of leaving some residual sugar in the wine and sweet reds such as Anghelu Ruju continue this tradition.)

During the 1980s, however, the subsidies subsided and the island's total vineyard shrank by almost three quarters to less than a third of the Sicilian total, and today there is all too little about Sardinia's DOC system to encourage or nurture quality.

The great majority of Sardinia's grapes are either Spanish in origin, dating from the four centuries to 1708 when the island was governed by Aragón, or introduced by the subsequent Savoy regime. Cannonau, the local form of Spanish Garnacha (Grenache), a chameleon of potentially high quality, sweet or dry, accounts for 20% of production. Its DOC production zone has generously been increased to encompass the whole of the island, as has that of Vermentino di Sardegna, which may be produced at yields as high as 130 hl/ha and still qualify for a DOC status. The light, lemony Vermentino is Sardinia's most characteristic white grape and may be found on the Ligurian coast as Pigato and all over southern France now as Rollo or Rolle.

Carignano del Sulcis is a better-designed, more specific DOC to accommodate some senior Carignan (Spain's Cariñena) bushvines in the southwest of the island, but even here yields of 105 hl/ha are considered quite acceptable. Bovale, both Bovale Sardo and Bovale Grande (Sardinian and big Bovale respectively), makes full-bodied red wines and is thought to be the Spanish Bobal's Sardinian cousin.

Red Monica and Girò and white Nuragus and Nasco are typically Sardinian grapes of more obscure origin, though doubtless DNA analysis will eventually reveal all.

Vermentino di Gallura, made in the north, is one of Italy's more surprising DOCGs, although Gallura's combination of heat and marine winds concentrate Vermentino grapes to a unique extent. Capichera is the leading producer of what has claim to be southern Italy's finest white, with an oaked Vendemmia Tardiva (late-harvest) version as well. Many of Sardinia's complicated DOCs, like Sicily's, are for sweet wines, but sweet wine production has been declining, and anyway the DOC system is of even less significance here than elsewhere.

Sardinia's wines of real distinction operate outside the DOC system. The most obvious of these is Turriga, a combustively concentrated barrique-aged blend of old-vine Cannonau and Carignano made under the auspices of producer

Argiolas by Antinori's winemaker emeritus Giacomo Tachis, who has long been fascinated by Sardinia and Sicily. This wine has enjoyed such international success that a handful of similar wines such as Argiolas' own Costera and Korem, the Santadi co-op's Terre Brune and Rocca Rubia, and Sella e Mosca's somewhat unSardinian Marchese di Villamarina Cabernet have also made some impact.

Wine-lovers can only regret that this island with so many ancient bushvines of fashionable and potentially interesting local varieties and an ideal Mediterranean grape-growing climate produces such a tiny proportion of exciting wine.

Malta, on the other hand, is in a ferment of reinvention. For long a substantial importer of wine from mainland Italy or the islands for blending, bottling, and selling as vaguely Maltese produce, this island republic 60 miles (100km) south of Sicily has been quietly revolutionizing wine production. Meridiana has co-operated with Antinori to produce some extremely convincing fine wines from Bordeaux varieties, while old-timers Delicato and Marsovin have been modernizing their fleshy reds from Gellewza grapes and full-bodied whites from local Gennarua and Ghirghentina (possibly Sicily's Inzolia) grapes.

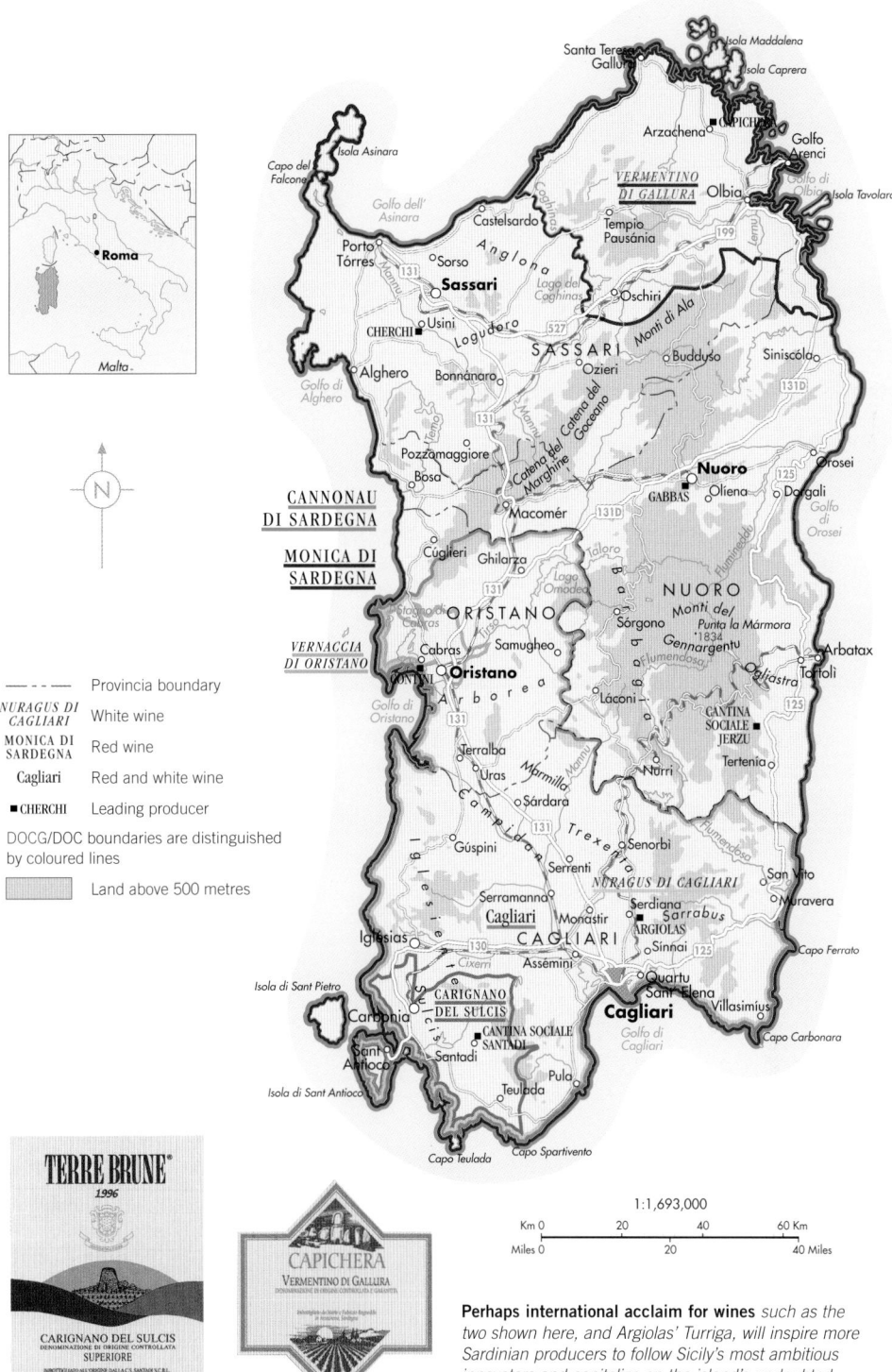

Perhaps international acclaim for wines *such as the two shown here, and Argiolas' Turriga, will inspire more Sardinian producers to follow Sicily's most ambitious innovators and capitalize on the island's undoubted potential both in terms of climate and grape varieties.*

Spain

The entire wine world is quite clearly in a state of perpetual evolution and reinvention, but of all the wine-producing countries Spain may have changed most comprehensively since the last edition of this Atlas was published. The officially designated wine regions mapped below are not only considerably more numerous, they are now connected, thanks to EU membership, by an impressive network of *autopistas* making wine producers who until recently felt as though they were operating in a quaint, rustic vacuum, part of a vibrant, remarkably cohesive, modern community. Spain now has a number of consultants known locally not as flying but driving winemakers who are spreading sophistication in the most unlikely places.

The final years of the 20th century saw an extraordinary level of investment in both new and reclaimed vineyards and spanking new

bodegas (cellars). And many of the most exciting current developments are taking place outside the official *denominaciónes*: 55 DOs plus one DOCa, Rioja, at the time of writing but doubtless there are more to come.

As a glance at the map shows, much of Spain is in all but one way ideal vine country. Her majestically uncivilized mountains may be too inhospitable, and parts of the north just too exposed, but the rest is perfectly suited to the vine with its combination of low 40s latitude and high altitude. Much of Spain is plateau: most of Old Castile – Castilla y León and Castilla-La Mancha – for a start. A good 90% of all Spanish vineyards lie at altitudes higher than any major French wine region.

The result in much of Spain is cold winters and very hot summers, with sunshine often so relentless that the vines shut down and the

grapes stop ripening for much of the summer, leaving the early autumn an unseemly scramble to accumulate sugar and aroma before temperatures drop. The really big problem in the south, east, and some of the north of the country however is summer drought. Dry soils cannot support many vines, so in most Spanish wine regions they are planted unusually far apart and trained (if that is the right word) in bushes only just above ground level. Being officially allowed to irrigate, from 1996, was a major breakthrough for Spanish vine-growers, although only the well-funded can afford to bore for water and install the systems to distribute it. (So fashionable is irrigation nowadays, however, that it has even been installed in some of the wetter parts of Atlantic Galicia.) This low vine density, less than a sixth of that of a typical Bordeaux or Burgundy vineyard, explains why Spain has the

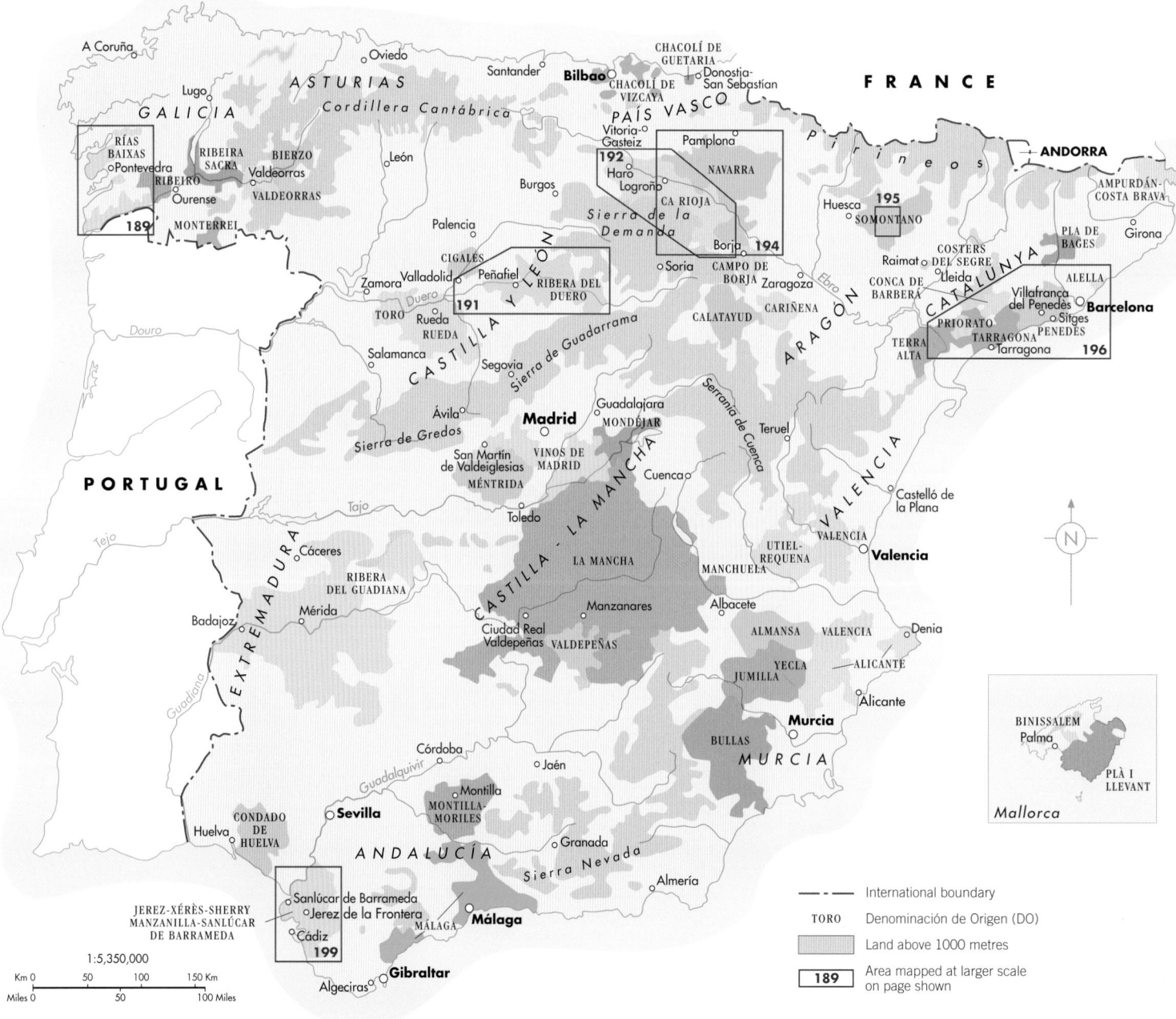

International boundary

TORO   Denominación de Origen (DO)

Land above 1000 metres

189   Area mapped at larger scale on page shown

most land devoted to the vine in the world, yet produces substantially less wine than either France or Italy – although average yields, thanks to irrigation and an increased propensity to train vines on wires, are rising dramatically.

The DO system is very much more embryonic than France's AC hierarchy: most DOs are so large that they include all sorts of different terrains and conditions. There is more than a streak of Latin anarchy (see Italy) in Spaniards' attitudes to these regulations too so that, particularly in the matter of grape varieties, there can be some disparity between what is permitted and what is planted. In most cases this is all to the good, as so many wine producers are anxious only to improve quality. A defining characteristic, however, is that buying in grapes, and often wine, is still far more common in Spain than the estate bottling phenomenon.

Spanish bodegas were traditionally places where wine was aged, often for much longer than is customary or, in some cases, advisable. Nevertheless the Spanish habit of releasing wine when it is ready to drink rather than ready to sell is appealing to say the least.

Things are changing in the bodegas. For centuries American oak was the wood of choice for barrels, thanks to the country's transatlantic seafaring. From the 1980s, however, French coopers have found Spanish new wave winemakers some of their most avid customers. Not just source of oak but also time in barrel is becoming more French. The Reserva and Gran Reserva categories were devised implicitly to honour extended oak ageing, but an increasing number of producers now value intensity over antiquity and are abandoning or devaluing their Gran Reservas.

The smallest of Spain's several and very different zones in terms of wine production is Galicia in the green northwest. Traditions here are Celtic (as the Gallic name suggests) and Christian with almost no Moorish influence. The Atlantic, the hills, the wind, and a good deal of rain (see the small blue map) are the chief physical factors. Wines are mainly light, dry, and refreshing, although too many are still dominated by the Palomino and red-fleshed Alicante

Right Typically widely spaced bushvines in Toro, one of Spain's many once-obscure wine regions currently being revitalized. The blue map below shows just how little rainwater is available to these vines.

Bouschet vines pressed into service here after phylloxera. Those which leave the region are a relatively small proportion and invariably white but locals also seem to relish Galicia's tart reds. Almost all Spanish whites need added acidity to give them zip, but not here. Rías Baixas is described in detail on page 189, but whites from nearby Ribeiro's handful of serious producers, blended from the naturally crisp Albariño, Treixadura, and Loureira, deserve more attention. The near-abandoned Ribeiro region shipped wine to England long before the Douro Valley to the south. Ribeira Sacra further inland still makes Galicia's potentially most interesting red wine, in archaic conditions on apparently impossibly steep terraces. Ribeira Sacra's fruitily scented local Mencía grape is also grown in the small but revitalized Monterrei region (which is warm enough to ripen Tempranillo) and in Valdeorras, whose great asset is the firm, white Godello grape.

Mencía makes Bierzo's best reds. Interest from some of Spain's most talented winemakers will soon make this region, technically part of Castilla-León, much more famous. The majority of Castilla-León's vineyards lie in the high, landlocked Duero Valley. Ribera del Duero, Tempranillo country and now Rioja's main rival for red wine fame, is mapped in detail on page 191 but growing even faster is Toro to the west. In 1998 Toro had eight bodegas; there were 25 two years later. Toro has its own strain of Tempranillo, Tinta de Toro, which produces such strapping, deep crimson, exuberant wines that it is being planted in other regions too.

Castilla-León's most famous white wines come from Rueda, between Toro and Ribera del Duero. In the early 1970s the old wine centres of Rueda and Nava del Rey, traditional producers of sherry-like whites, came under the prospecting eye of the famous Rioja bodega Marqués de Riscal which was looking for a new source for white wines of fashionable fruity freshness. The

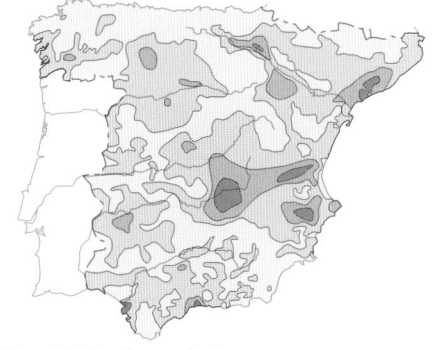

Wine production litres per hectare

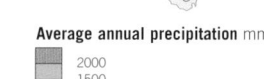

1000
500

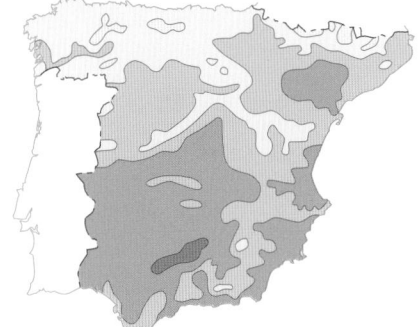

Average annual precipitation mm

2000
1500
1000
500

Average daily July temperature °C

28
24
20
16

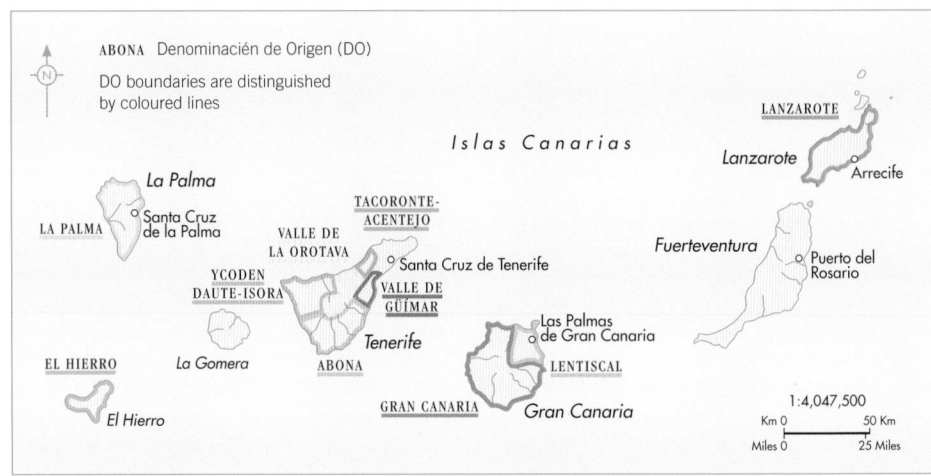

Left Stone windbreaks protect low-trained vines cowering in the black volcanic soil of Lanzarote which, like much of the Canary Islands (above), has its own DO.

attraction was not the landscape, flat and bare, nor the Palomino that had been widely planted post-phylloxera here too. It was the local white grape, Verdejo – and also the ancient network of deep cellars which once supplied the court at Valladolid – that encouraged Riscal to build a modern white wine bodega.

Carefully vinified, Verdejo has good fruity acidity, an attractively green spine, and the ability to age well in cask. Sauvignon Blanc does unusually well here too. Red wines made in the area are for the moment sold as Vinos de la Tierra under the name Medina del Campo.

Cigales to the north is currently devoted to producing light *clarete* reds for the inhabitants of Valladolid, but Bodega Frutos Villar has shown there are other possibilities.

Way up on the Atlantic coast round the cities of Bilbao and Santander are the piercingly refreshing Basque whites of, respectively, Chacolí de Vizcaya/Bizkaiako Txakolina and Chacolí de Guetaria/Getariako Txakolina (political correctness in Spain embraces four languages: Gallego, Basque, Catalan, and mainstream Castilian). Remarkably like Basque wines on the other side of the French border, they are served locally in delicate glass tumblers.

The River Ebro flows southeast from the Cantabrian Cordillera on the north coast to the Mediterranean in Catalunya. The Upper Ebro embraces Rioja and Navarra (see pages 192-194), where Tempranillo and Garnacha meet, but also Campo de Borja, which already produces some extremely juicy, young inexpensive Garnacha, and the co-operative-dominated Calatayud and Cariñena.

Somontano (page 195) is one of Spain's most cohesive DOs, while Catalunya (pages 196-197) is one of its most varied regions.

South down the east coast the vineyards inland from Valencia and Alicante have for the moment only modest traditions and no singularity of style – except strength. Valencia, Utiel-Requena, Almansa, Yecla, Jumilla, Alicante, and Bullas constitute the Levante, long accustomed to providing potent bulk blending wine for a dwindling export market. Its salvation lies in diversification and as much lightening of style as it can manage in such a hot climate and with grapes as heavy as Monastrell (Mourvèdre) and Bobal (Sardinia's Bovale). Some interesting wines are deliberately strong and sweet and Agapito Rico has shown that serious Syrah can be grown here, but the most successful exports are such combinations as carefully vinified Monastrell leavened by Merlot, Tempranillo or Syrah. Air-conditioned cellars are still a novelty, so most wines have to be shipped out young.

Most central of all to Spanish life is the *meseta*, the high plateaus south of Madrid whose endless flat vineyards weary the eye. The extent of La Mancha, its chief DO, is clear from the map and just its DO-classified vineyards, less than half of the total, cover twice as much ground as all of Australia's vineyards put together. The town of Valdepeñas traditionally gave its name to a large part of this production: strong but pale red wine made largely from Airén (Spain's most-planted white grape on which Brandy de Jerez depends) tinted with some red. Red grapes are Garnacha and, increasingly, Cencibel, the local name for Tempranillo. Technology in this region has rushed straight from the antique (huge clay, amphora-like *tinajas*) to stainless steel and oak.

Between here and Madrid are the DOs of Méntrida, Vinos de Madrid, and Mondéjar, but the most innovative vineyards are those of Marqués de Griñon near Toledo with their palette of imported grape varieties (including fashionable Syrah and Petit Verdot) and new ways of growing and watering vines.

Due west of La Mancha in Extremadura near the Portuguese frontier is the extensive and relatively recent DO Ribera del Guadiana. As in La Mancha, much of the wine produced goes into Brandy de Jerez, but there is considerable

potential for robust, ripe table wines, as Alentejo over the Portuguese border suggests.

Andalucía in the far south of Spain is dominated by fortified wines and brandy, and is covered in more detail on pages 199-200.

Despite their distance from Brussels (they are over 700 miles/1,150km from mainland Spain), the Canary Islands have joined in the controlled appellation game with zest. The islands of La Palma, El Hierro, Lanzarote, and Gran Canaria each have one DO, while the proud island of Tenerife has no fewer than five (see above).

Nor are the Spanish Balearic islands in the Mediterranean to be left out. Mallorcan pride in its wines and its native Manto Negro is being revived in the form of the Binissalem and Plà i Llevant *denominaciónes*.

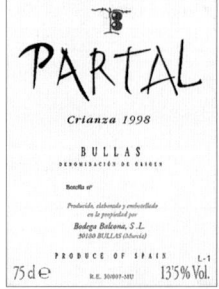

These are just a few of the more distinctive wines made outside Spain's best-known wine regions which are mapped in detail on the following pages.

Rías Baixas

The wines of Rías Baixas (pronounced something like "ree-ass by-shuss") are as far from the Spanish stereotype as it is possible to imagine: delicate, lively, aromatic whites that go perfectly with the shellfish that is the Galician standard diet.

Everything about Galician wine is small scale. Some of the best producers make only a few hundred cases of wine a year; most growers have only a few hectares of vines. This damp green corner of Spain (compare the annual rainfall of Vigo with that of any other Spanish weather station) was until recently extremely poor and virtually ignored by the rest of the country. Any Gallego with any gumption emigrated, but tended to cling fiercely to ownership of minuscule parcels of inherited land.

This, and Galicia's physical isolation, put a brake on development of Rías Baixas and neighbouring wine regions. It was not until the 1990s that these singular wines found a ready and rapturous market outside Galicia.

Like the wines, the landscape is exceptional for Spain: irregular Atlantic inlets called *rías*, effectively shallow fjords, lined with hills densely forested with local pine and rapacious eucalyptus imported in the 1950s. Even the vines look quite different.

As in Portugal's very similar Vinho Verde country across the River Miño, vines have traditionally been trained on pergolas, horizontal trellises well above light-dappled shoulder height. The widely spaced, spindly trunks are often trained up posts of granite, so common is it in this part of the world. For the thousands of small farmers who grow vines simply to make wine for themselves, this high canopy allows them to use every square foot of precious earth, but it can also help ventilate the grapes, an important consideration here where sea mists regularly invade the vineyards even in summer.

Grapes grow all over the area mapped here but the Rías Baixas *denominación* is made up of a lengthening roster of subregions as they meet the DO regulations. Val do Salnés is the most important, and the coolest and dampest being both northerly and right on the coast. The thick-skinned Albariño grape dominates here as it can best resist the mildew that persistently threatens. In O Rosal to the south, the best vineyards are carved out of clearings on the south-facing hillsides and produce wines notably lower in acidity than those of Val do Salnés. Condado do Tea (Tea, pronounced "tay-er", is a small tributary of the Miño) is the warmest of the subzones, being furthest from the coast, and its wines tend to be more powerful and less refined. Soutomaior, south of Pontevedra, and Ribeira do Ulla, just south of Santiago de Compostela, are two smaller, more recently accredited subzones.

In the two southern subzones Albariño grapes have traditionally been blended with the equally perfumed but less structured Treixadura and the laurel-scented Loureira. Blends may make the best wine, but varietal Albariño is easiest to sell as it now has such a faithful following in Madrid and even across the Atlantic.

Rías Baixas: Vigo

Latitude / Altitude of WS **41.13˚ / 820ft (250m)**
Mean July temperature at WS **66.7˚F (19.3˚C)**
Average annual rainfall at WS **60in (1,520mm)**
Harvest month rainfall at WS **September: 3.5in (90mm)**
Principal viticultural hazard **Fungal diseases**
Principal grapes **Albariño, Treixadura, Loureira Blanca**

Scale 1:567,000

- · - · - International boundary
- - - - Provincial boundary
──── Boundary of Rías Baixas DO

Rías Baixas subzones
Condado do Tea
O Rosal
Ribeira do Ulla
Soutomaior
Val do Salnés
VALMIÑOR ■ Leading producer
──400── Contour interval 200 metres
▼ Weather station (WS)

Most of these, *some of Rías Baixas' finest, are at their best drunk at about two years old. DO Ferreiro is based in Val do Salnés, where partial malolactic fermentation can mitigate the subzone's naturally high acidity.*

Ribera del Duero

For many years, before the late 1970s, Spain's most prestigious and expensive red wine appeared a complete oddball. Few had tasted Vega Sicilia, and fewer still knew where, in the vast dustbowl of central Spain, such a remarkable vineyard was to be found.

The plain of Old Castile, stretching in tawny leagues north from Segovia and Avila to the old kingdom of León, is traversed by the adolescent Duero, the river that in Portugal becomes the Douro and the home of port (see page 207). It is the broad valley of the Duero and its tributaries, from Valladolid upstream to Aranda de Duero, that has an ancient winemaking tradition – more, one would think, because of the thirsty population (Valladolid, as the capital of 17th-century Spain, formulated strict wine laws) than because the fierce continental climate favoured the vine. At 2,624ft (800m) the nights are remarkably cool – in late August it can be 95°F (35°C) at noon and 43°F (6°C) at night. Spring frosts are all too common. Grapes are routinely picked in November. The light and air here have a high-altitude dryness and brightness about them, as do the wines. They are concentrated reds of remarkably intense colour, fruit, and savour – quite different in style from those of Rioja, less than 60 miles (100km) away to the northeast.

Vega Sicilia, the one perfectionist property at Valbuena de Duero, proved that very fine red wine could be made. The estate was planted in

imitation of Bordeaux in the 1860s, at the same time as the first such steps were being taken in Rioja. But here the Bordeaux grapes were used, adding cosmopolitan glamour to the native Tempranillo (known here as Tinto Fino or Tinto del País). Vega Sicilia's Unico, made only in good vintages, aged longer in oak than virtually any other table wine, and sold at ten years (after some years in bottle nowadays), is a wine of astonishing, penetrating personality. Its younger brother, the five-year-old Valbuena from the same estate, displays its charms considerably earlier.

Rather than plant Cabernet, Merlot, and Malbec (still used at Vega Sicilia but only as a complement to Tinto Fino) the region has now won its spurs with the the local grape almost single-handed. In the mid-1960s the co-operative at Peñafiel, just to the east, its cellars under the Moorish castle atop a splendidly isolated hill, had greatly refined its winemaking, using the Tinto Fino and ageing its Reservas, notably the tasty Protos, in oak.

Next to follow was Alejandro Fernández at Pesquera de Duero. Fernández has been fanatically pursuing perfection for his 100% Tinto Fino since the early 1980s. Concentrated fruit and high alcohol sound merely aggressive, but Pesquera has a luscious quality which promises many years of staying power – and has been joined by more recent adventures for Fernández, including a new Ribera in Condado de Haza.

From two bodegas in the 1950s to 24 when the DO was created in 1982, to more than 110 today (many of them unencumbered by vineyards), this wide, high plateau has seen a quite remarkable transformation of land previously given over to cereals and sugar beet. Many of the new plantings depend not on Ribera's own strain of Tempranillo, but on cuttings imported from other regions, which may affect quality. Viticulturists can easily be foxed by Ribera's extremely varied soils, even within a single vineyard, where grapes may ripen at infuriatingly different paces. Limestone outcrops, more common north of the river, help to retain rainfall that is far from generous.

The tradition of buying in grapes is just as strong here as in Rioja (even Vega Sicilia with more than 500 acres (200ha) has contracts with other growers), and many of these new bodegas vie with each other for fruit. Some of the best comes from round La Horra, but top winemakers such as Teófilo Reyes and Peter Sisseck, the Dane who made Dominio de Pingus Spain's rare and most expensive wine, are cagey about their sources – invariably the oldest and truest of gnarled, low Tinto Fino bushes.

Two of the most successful producers in the region are not even within the DO boundaries. Abadía Retuerta, a vast new property funded by the Swiss pharmaceutical company Novartis, is at Sardón de Duero just west of the official boundary. (In 1982 when the DO regulations

Left Condado de Haza, the second estate of Alejandro Fernández, the owner of Pesquera and the man who initiated Ribera del Duero's current frenetic round of expansion. This south-facing slope leads down to the River Duero.

were being drawn up there were no vines here, but there had been almost continuously from the 17th century when the abbey was one of Valladolid's chief suppliers of wine until the early 1970s.) Vines may be relatively young here but there is no shortage of technology and talent (including Pascal Delbeck of St-Emilion) dedicated to producing various combinations of Tempranillo and red French varieties – including some particularly successful Petit Verdot – from different parts of this extensive vineyard.

Mauro is an older bodega founded in 1980 and now established in a handsome old stone building even further west in Tudela by Vega Sicilia's longtime winemaker Mariano García. Here the grapes are Tempranillo, Garnacha, and Syrah, grown in cereal country around Santibáñez de Valcorba, which is slightly lower and warmer than Ribera del Duero. At eight o'clock on a spring evening, the temperature and crickets suggest mid-afternoon. The richness of the wines reflect this warmth.

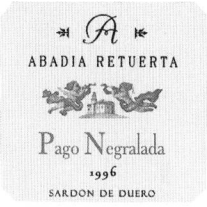

All of these wines *are some of the most ambitious, carefully selected, and vinified expressions of Tempranillo. The top two are made just west of the official Ribera del Duero DO boundary.*

1:671,000

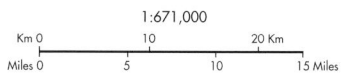

Key to producers

1 DOMINIO DE PINGUS
2 ARZUAGA NAVARRO
3 VEGA SICILIA
4 HERMANOS CUADRADO C.B
5 DEHESA DE LOS CANÓNIGOS
6 HACIENDA MONASTERIO

Ribera del Duero: Valladolid

Latitude/Altitude of WS **41.43° / 2,755ft (840m)**
Mean July temperature at WS **70.5°F (21.4°C)**
Average annual rainfall at WS **16in (410mm)**
Harvest month rainfall at WS **October: 1.8in (45mm)**
Principal viticultural hazards **Spring frost, autumn rain**
Principal grapes **Tinto Fino/Tinto del País (Tempranillo)**

– · – · – Provincial boundary
━━━ Boundary of Ribera del Duero DO
La Horra Wine centre
MAURO ■ Leading Producer
══1000══ Contour interval 100 metres
▼ Weather station (WS)

Left The River Ebro forms much of the physical boundary between the DOs of Rioja Alavesa on the right in this picture and Rioja Alta around San Vicente (which produces some particularly fine wine).

Rioja

Rioja is a transitional region in all senses of the word. Not only is it currently undergoing an identity crisis about the style of its wines, but it can also suffer both the fiercely hot, dry summers of southern wine regions and the mildews, rain, and frost of northern climes.

Without the massive wall of the rocky Sierra de Cantabria it would be too buffeted by Atlantic winds for vines to survive. In the far northwest of the region some of the highest vineyards above Labastida can struggle to ripen at all. In the east, on the other hand, vines ripen fully as high as 2,600ft (800m) thanks to the warming influence of the Mediterranean, which reaches as far west as Elciego. Growers in Alfaro in the east may harvest four to six weeks before those around Haro, where the last grapes may not be picked until the end of October.

The region is divided into three zones. Rioja Alta is the western, higher part south of the broad, poplar-lined River Ebro, as well as the non-Basque land around San Vicente de la Sonsierra north of the river. Rioja Alavesa, that part of Rioja in Alava province, is Basque and, quite literally nowadays, is another country, with its own language, its own police force, and its own substantial grants which have encouraged a rash of new bodegas on this northern bank of the Ebro. Rioja Baja, the extensive hotter, eastern section, has its own anomalous enclave just east of the industrial capital of the region, Logroño. The historic Marqués de Murrieta Castillo Ygay bodega could not be allowed to belong to Rioja Baja, which is considered, not always accurately, to be generally inferior. The soils of Rioja Baja are even more varied than those of Rioja Alta and its vines much more sparsely cultivated.

Vines are virtually the only crop in the two western subzones though, where the landscape is a spotted patchwork of small plots of low bushvines on soils variously soft clay-red and limestone white, tinted with yellow alluvial deposits. These terraces, at different levels of erosion by the river (the higher the better), are more likely to be dominated by clay in Rioja Alta and limestone in Rioja Alavesa. The red soils around Fuenmayor are some of Rioja's most productive, and clay is so important there as to have spawned a huge ceramic factory. This was the area of Rioja invaded briefly in the 1970s by some of the bigger sherry companies, vainly hopeful of making a quick killing.

Tempranillo is by far the most important grape of Rioja but it blends well with plumper Garnacha, best in Rioja Alta upstream of Nájera and in Rioja Baja in the high vineyards of Tudelilla. Graciano (Morrastel of the Languedoc) is a fine but finicky Rioja speciality that now seems safe from extinction, Mazuelo (Carignan) is allowed, and experimentation with Cabernet Sauvignon uneasily tolerated.

Oddly enough, Spain's most famous, most important wine began the century with a search for its true character. The reputation of the region was made in the late 19th century when Bordeaux négociants came here to fill the embarrassing voids in their blending tanks left by the incursions of phylloxera north of the Pyrenees. They had their proof of Rioja's potential in the wines of the two Marquéses, de Riscal and Murrieta, who had established their own estates, in 1860 in Elciego and in 1872 just east of Logroño respectively.

Haro with its rail links to the Atlantic coast was the ideal centre for blending wine brought in by cart from as far away as Rioja Baja. The Bordeaux merchants showed how to age it in small barrels, and thus were born many of Haro's most important bodegas, all founded around 1890 and clustered about the railway station – some even with their own platforms.

Until the 1970s most Rioja was juicy stuff made in homespun conditions by small-scale farmers. (In villages like San Vicente you can still see stone *lagares*, or troughs, behind half-open doors hung with the handwritten claim "Se Vende Rioja".) Blending and élevage, not even

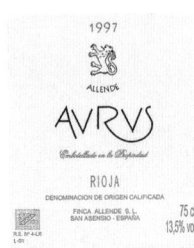

Rioja is in flux. *Seen here are labels from a few of the exciting new bodegas with global ambitions, some of whose wines have been attacked for being atypical. Castillo Ygay, on the other hand, spends five years in oak.*

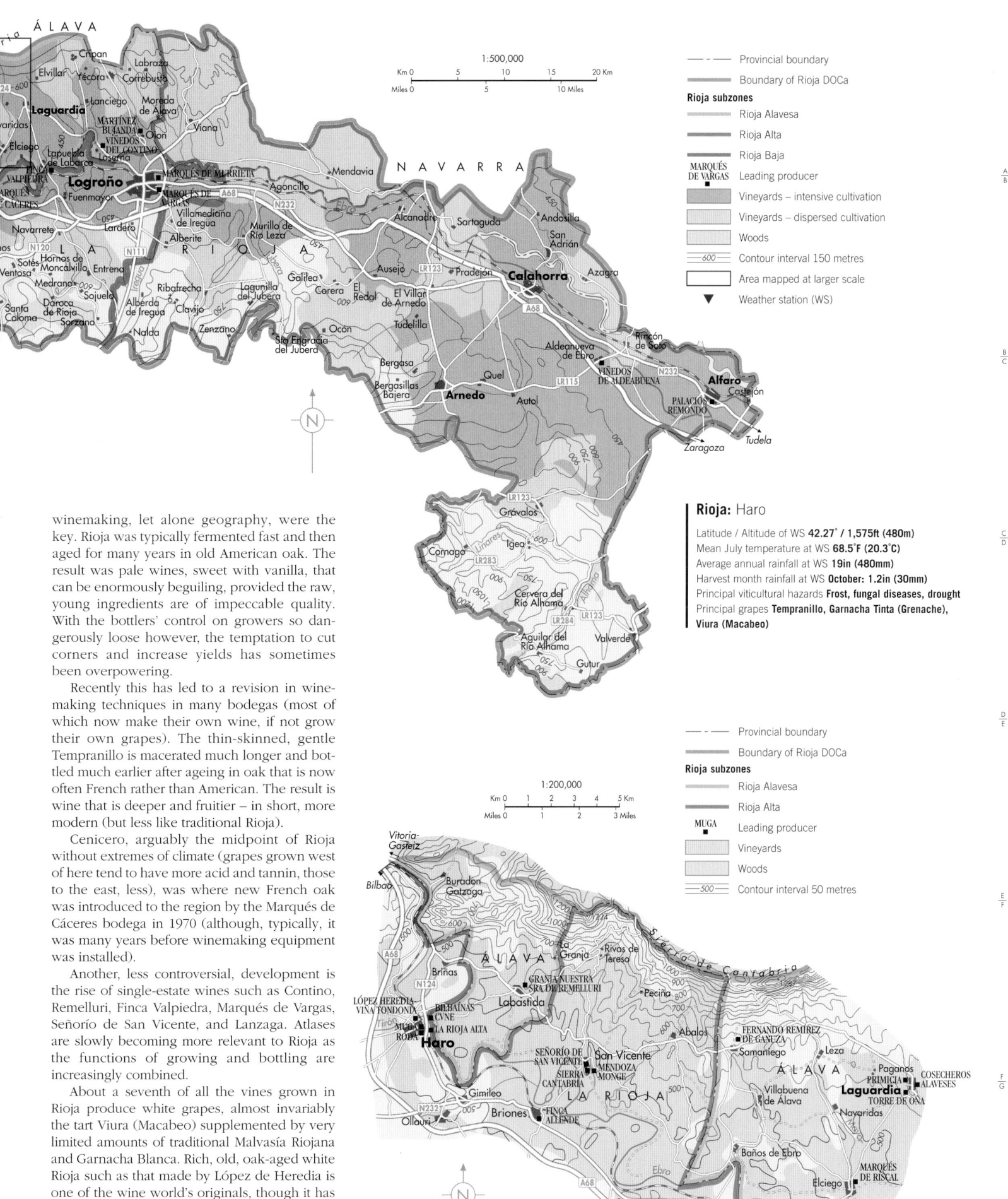

Rioja: Haro

Latitude / Altitude of WS **42.27˚ / 1,575ft (480m)**
Mean July temperature at WS **68.5˚F (20.3˚C)**
Average annual rainfall at WS **19in (480mm)**
Harvest month rainfall at WS **October: 1.2in (30mm)**
Principal viticultural hazards **Frost, fungal diseases, drought**
Principal grapes **Tempranillo, Garnacha Tinta (Grenache), Viura (Macabeo)**

winemaking, let alone geography, were the key. Rioja was typically fermented fast and then aged for many years in old American oak. The result was pale wines, sweet with vanilla, that can be enormously beguiling, provided the raw, young ingredients are of impeccable quality. With the bottlers' control on growers so dangerously loose however, the temptation to cut corners and increase yields has sometimes been overpowering.

Recently this has led to a revision in winemaking techniques in many bodegas (most of which now make their own wine, if not grow their own grapes). The thin-skinned, gentle Tempranillo is macerated much longer and bottled much earlier after ageing in oak that is now often French rather than American. The result is wine that is deeper and fruitier – in short, more modern (but less like traditional Rioja).

Cenicero, arguably the midpoint of Rioja without extremes of climate (grapes grown west of here tend to have more acid and tannin, those to the east, less), was where new French oak was introduced to the region by the Marqués de Cáceres bodega in 1970 (although, typically, it was many years before winemaking equipment was installed).

Another, less controversial, development is the rise of single-estate wines such as Contino, Remelluri, Finca Valpiedra, Marqués de Vargas, Señorío de San Vicente, and Lanzaga. Atlases are slowly becoming more relevant to Rioja as the functions of growing and bottling are increasingly combined.

About a seventh of all the vines grown in Rioja produce white grapes, almost invariably the tart Viura (Macabeo) supplemented by very limited amounts of traditional Malvasía Riojana and Garnacha Blanca. Rich, old, oak-aged white Rioja such as that made by López de Heredia is one of the wine world's originals, though it has all but disappeared in favour of cool-fermented, rather neutral white wines whose provenance is apparent on the label but rarely in the glass.

Navarra

Camped round the northeastern boundary of Rioja, the wine region of Navarra was for long in competition with it, until the Bordeaux merchants chose to place their post-phylloxera trade not with this green land of asparagus and nurseries but with Rioja and its ready rail link from Haro.

For most of the 20th century Navarra's relatively sparse vineyards were dedicated chiefly to Garnacha and the useful *rosadas* and strong, deep, bulk reds that it produced. But then came a revolution in the form of Cabernet Sauvignon, Merlot, Chardonnay, and the grape of western Rioja, Tempranillo. Garnacha seemed very old hat and by the 1980s Navarra was spewing forth a host of bottlings of Tempranillo with Cabernet, Cabernet with Merlot, and some pretty competent Chardonnay as well as the inexpensive pink wine that had looked like the region's destiny. The all-important co-operatives still soak up much of the region's Garnacha but, by the late 1990s, the produce of old vines was increasingly recognized as rich, intense red wine, a valuable ingredient in a blend such as Chivite's Gran Feudo Viñas Viejas and Lautus from Guelbenzu of Cascante.

In a way, the most exported wines of Navarra are like a cross between Rioja and Somontano: obviously oaked wines but using a full palette of both Spanish and international varieties. French oak is used much more commonly than in Rioja, perhaps because oak ageing came so much later to Navarra, but also because there is so very much more acreage devoted to French vines. The resultant wines also tend to be deeper coloured (than traditional Rioja anyway), perhaps because the skins tend to be left in the fermentation vat longer.

Navarra is no more homogenous than Rioja, however. There is a world of difference between the hot, dry, flat Ribera Baja and Ribera Alta subzones on the banks of the River Ebro in the south which have to be irrigated (with a system of canals initiated by the Romans) and the less-planted, cooler climes, and more varied soils of the north. The persistence of the westerlies here has spawned virtual forests of wind-powered generators on mesas above the vineyards. Ribera Alta is a bit warmer and more exposed to the influence of the Mediterranean than Ribera Baja, which is protected by Mont Moncayo. Fitero in Ribera Baja can produce particularly good Garnacha because its poor, Châteauneuf-like soils are well exposed, and Corella has earned a reputation for excellent botrytized Moscatel de Grano Menudo (Muscat Blanc).

Wines produced towards the north of Ribera Alta tend to be paler and less alcoholic than

Above Vines are still grown by the Monasterio de la Oliva at Carcastillo. Medieval monks and other pilgrims traversed Navarra en route to Santiago de Compostela and particularly appreciated the region's wines.

further south. Northern Navarra is much more mountainous and, thanks to its altitude and Atlantic influence, can be quite cool on a day that is positively torrid in the south. As in Rioja, northern Navarra's altitude means that the Bordeaux grape varieties are picked considerably later than in Bordeaux itself – sometimes as late as December in some particularly high altitude vineyards.

Clay with some limestone, older than the soils in the south, is the norm here but soils, aspects and elevations can be so varied in the northern Tierra de Estella and Valdizarbe subzones that those trying to pick suitable sites in their many viticulturally undeveloped areas have to select with extreme care to avoid spring frost and failure to ripen in the autumn.

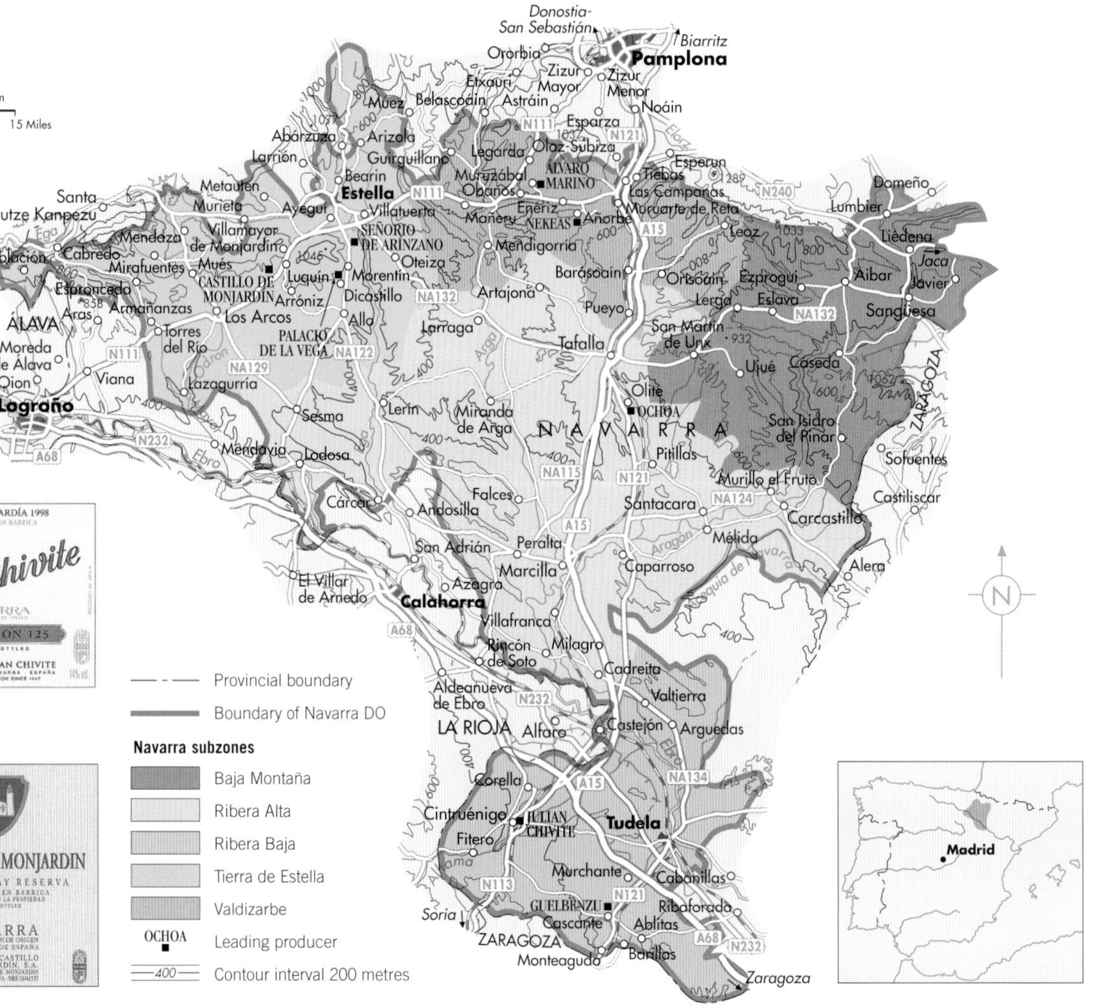

1:800,000

Km 0 — 10 — 20 Km
Miles 0 — 5 — 10 — 15 Miles

While most of Navarra's output is either fruity rosé or, increasingly, oaked red blends of various combinations of Spanish and Bordeaux grape varieties, the regions's most stunning wine is Chivite's late-harvest sweet white.

Navarra subzones

- Baja Montaña
- Ribera Alta
- Ribera Baja
- Tierra de Estella
- Valdizarbe

OCHOA — Leading producer

--- 400 --- Contour interval 200 metres

--- - --- Provincial boundary

——— Boundary of Navarra DO

Somontano

On a clear day the snow-covered Pyrenees can be seen in the distance from Somontano, whose name means "at the foot of the mountains". It is not the Pyrenees, however, which make viticulture possible in this well-tended, unusually cohesive wine region, but the Sierra de Guara and Sierra de Salinas. These mountains protect Somontano from cold northern influence and provide an amphitheatre, a gentle south-facing bowl of suitable vineyard land concentrated on the villages of Salas Bajas and Salas Altas, and scattered along the banks of the Vero and Cinca rivers.

This is a small, adolescent DO whose existence was initiated not by nature nor by a particularly ambitious individual but by the local government which, in the late 1980s, encouraged Viñas del Vero to plant Tempranillo and international varieties to add cosmopolitan glamour to the local Moristel and Parraleta vines.

Despite its glorious history, Aragón is something of a wasteland, lagging far behind its neighbours Catalunya and Navarra in terms of viticultural development. Much of it to the west is too extreme and unprotected for vines to flourish; to the south there is desert. But the Somontano region offered the potential of a mild climate and considerably more rain than most of the rest of the central Spanish plateau, a perfectly respectable total of between 20 and 24 inches (500 and 600mm) a year on average.

Today, Somontano may not have reached the heights of the best that Ribera del Duero, Rioja, and Priorat can produce, but its wines are among the most reliable and best value in Spain, as the great majority of production from about 4,950 acres (2,000ha) is in the hands of the top three companies – Viñas del Vero, the privately owned Enate, and the model co-op Bodegas Pirineos – each of which continues to invest in upgrading quality, both in terms of equipment and technique.

Wines are attractively plump though never massive, thanks to predominantly sandy soils (although there is a bit of gravel in the lower reaches of the River Vero and some limestone south of Barbastro, the main town). Naturally crisp acidity is a distinguishing mark, not least because soils here are low in potassium which keeps pH levels usefully low too. There are mouthfilling Bordeaux-variety reds, some savoury Tempranillo, much more convincing Chardonnay than most of Spain can manage, and some of Spain's rare but refreshingly dry Gewürztraminer. Bodega Pirineos works hardest at maintaining the region's indigenous varieties, squeezing every ounce of flavour out

of the light, loganberry-scented Moristel by encouraging the malolactic fermentation in barrel. Pirineos also perseveres with low-yielding but more structured and mineral-scented Parraleta. A serious dry wine from late-picked, old-vine Macabeo is essayed too. (Garnacha was the other traditional vine variety of the region where locals still make their own barrel-aged, rancio version of it.)

The region is remarkably homogenous and, perhaps surprisingly, is yet to be invaded by an ambitious loner. Recent developments in the early 21st century included Blecua, an ambitious new estate winery in a thoroughly Napa Valley idiom built by Viñas del Vero, and some short-term consultancy at Lalanne by itinerant Telmo Rodriguez of Remelluri in Rioja. The area is ripe for invasion by a small dynamo.

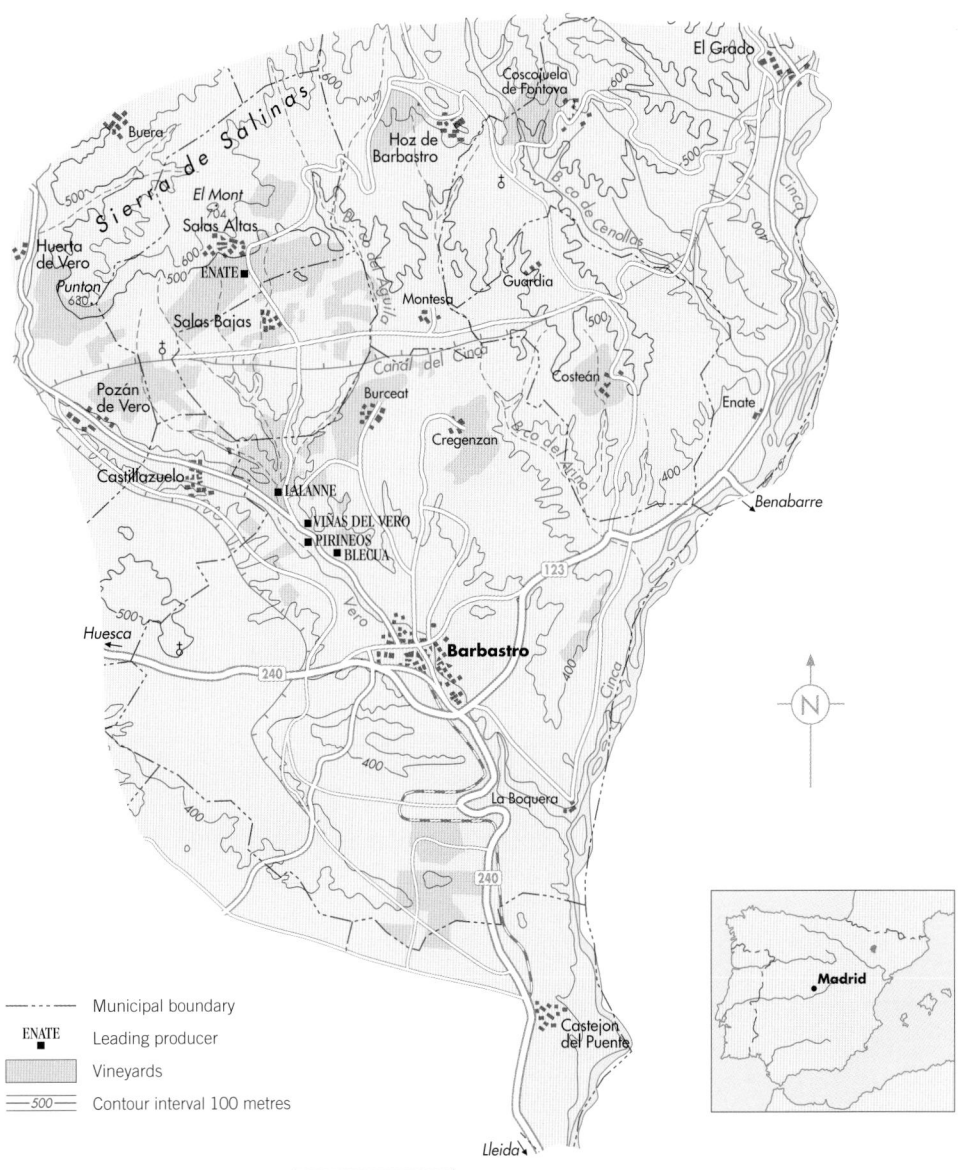

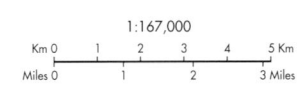

For such a relatively small region, *Somontano can offer proficiency in a surprisingly wide array of grape varieties, including some natives and one of Spain's few convincing Gewürztraminers.*

Catalunya

Catalans claim to work harder than other Spaniards and arguably have more in common culturally with Roussillon just across the French border. The wine producers of Catalunya (traditionally known as Catalonia by English speakers), inspired by a ready market in Barcelona, produce more varied wine, and from more varied terrain, than those of any other Spanish region. For a start, most obviously on hypermarket shelves and wine lists throughout Spain, there is Cava, Spain's answer to champagne, of which 95% is produced in Catalunya, mainly from the vineyards on the fertile plateau in and around the Penedès wine capital of Sant Sadurní d'Anoia.

The industry, for that is what it is, is dominated by Codorníu and Freixenet, whose acrimonious rivalry has at times acted as a brake on Cava's progress rather than a spur to greater quality. The winemaking method may be that of Champagne; the grapes nowadays are very different. Neutral Macabeo dominates most Cava blends, its late budding promising good insurance against spring frost in Penedès' relatively cool vineyards. Flavour, sometimes too much, comes from the local Xarel-lo, best planted at lower altitudes.

Parellada is regarded as the finest Cava ingredient, yielding appley wine of real crispness in the northern Penedès if not allowed to overproduce. Chardonnay is an increasingly familiar ingredient and Pinot Noir is now also permitted. These last two are helping make Cava less of a shock to non-Spanish palates, if arguably less Catalan. Lower yields and longer bottle ageing periods are also imbuing Cava with a seriously creamy rather than aggressively frothy quality – at a price. The great Catalan gift to the world's producers of sparkling wine – apart from its indigenous cork – was the gyropallet (see below), a giant crate which substitutes computer-controlled riddling for painstaking and variable *remuage* by hand.

The market for fizz in Spain has not grown as expected and the big (and not so big) Cava houses have been putting increasing energy into still varietal wines. International vine varieties imported from France are more widespread in Penedès than anywhere else in Spain, partly as a result of the pioneers of such wines in the 1960s – Miguel Torres and, on a much smaller scale, Jean León, now owned by Torres, the Catalan giant of still wine producers.

The current Miguel Torres is famous for his early experiments with Cabernet Sauvignon and Chardonnay (the former of which won him international fame at the Gault Millau "wine olympics" of 1979 by "beating" some of the most famous names in Bordeaux). Since then, Torres has grown in size rather than stature, producing a wide range of dependable if unexciting combinations of local and imported varieties that were hugely successful on the Spanish market. Viña Sol (Parellada) was one of Spain's first modern, cool-fermented white wines; Coronas the best-distributed Catalan Tempranillo (known locally as Ull de Llebre). Investment in Chile has provided a diversion, as have experiments with imports such as Riesling, Gewürztraminer, and Pinot Noir in higher vineyards, but since the late 1990s most of Torres' most successful wines have come from fruit grown in the quite distinct inland Conca de Barberá region, still mainly a Cava supplier, in limestone hills to the north of Tarragona. Grans Muralles, informed by low-yielding Catalan varieties, showed the way from the 1996 vintage towards a much more concentrated style of Torres red.

The Penedès appellation has proved too constricting for a producer of the size of Torres, the prime mover behind the recent controversial Catalunya DO which encompasses all Catalan regions and sanctions blending between them. But there is a number of conscientious growers, mainly from vineyards on higher land carved out of the mediterranean scrub and pines, who are doing their best to squeeze serious local character out of relatively low-yielding vines – more often than not imported varieties. The hottest, lowest vineyards of the Baix-Penedès by the coast traditionally supplied super-ripe Moscatel and Malvasía grapes for dessert wines and have more recently poured forth Monastrell, Garnacha, and Cariñena for blended dry(ish) reds which do not have the same trouble ripening here as they do in Penedès' highest but most interesting vineyards.

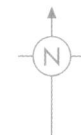

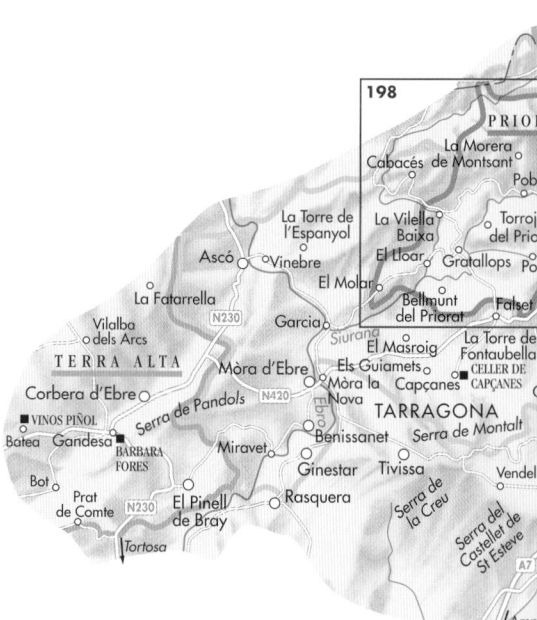

Left The gyropallet, a Catalan invention that scores low on romance but high in efficiency, particularly since the art of hand-riddling bottles of traditional method sparkling wine is dying out. These robots work in the cellars of Segura Viudas at Sant Sadurní d'Anoia.

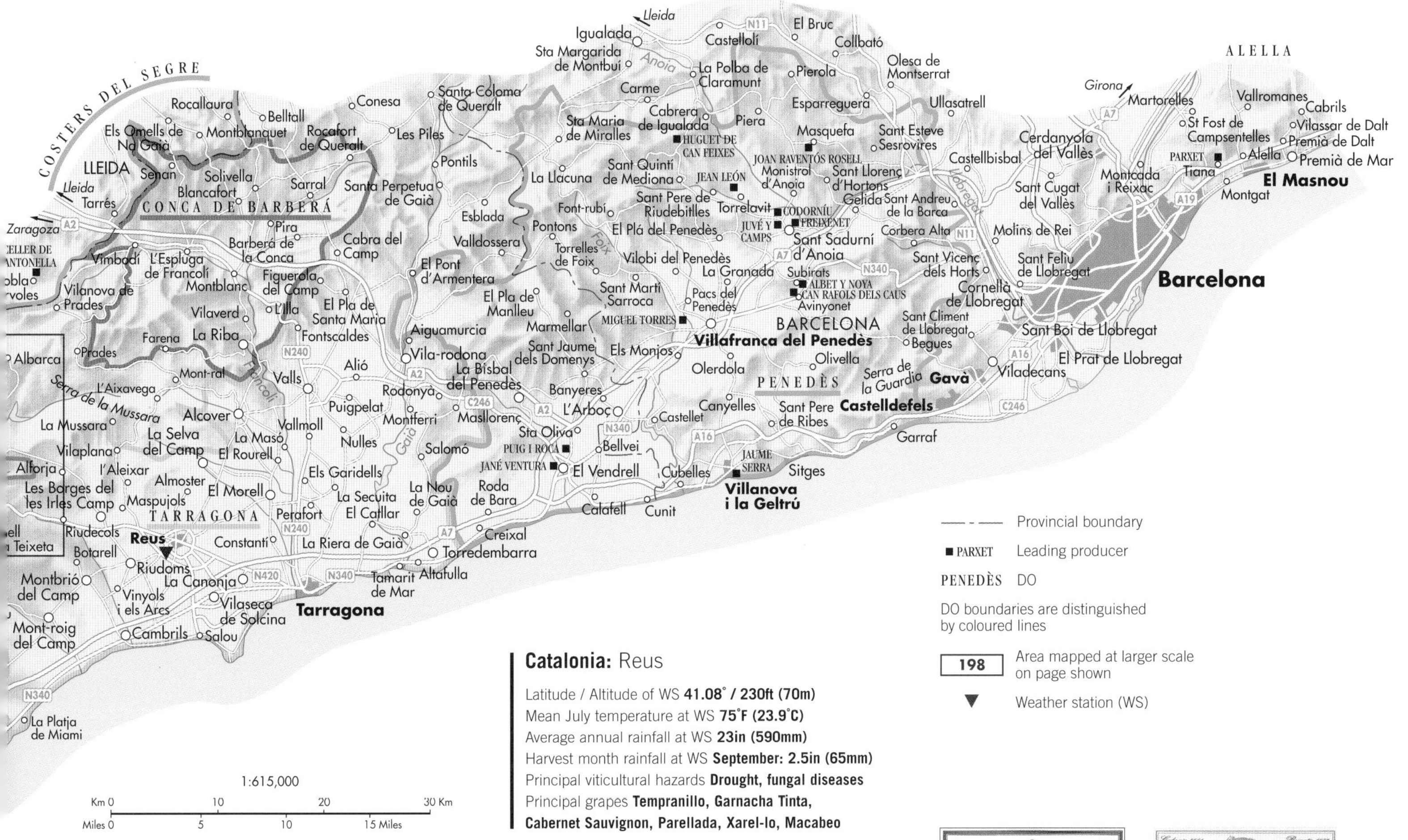

Catalonia: Reus

Latitude / Altitude of WS **41.08˚ / 230ft (70m)**
Mean July temperature at WS **75˚F (23.9˚C)**
Average annual rainfall at WS **23in (590mm)**
Harvest month rainfall at WS **September: 2.5in (65mm)**
Principal viticultural hazards **Drought, fungal diseases**
Principal grapes **Tempranillo, Garnacha Tinta, Cabernet Sauvignon, Parellada, Xarel-lo, Macabeo**

--- - --- Provincial boundary

■ PARXET Leading producer

PENEDÈS DO

DO boundaries are distinguished by coloured lines

198 Area mapped at larger scale on page shown

▼ Weather station (WS)

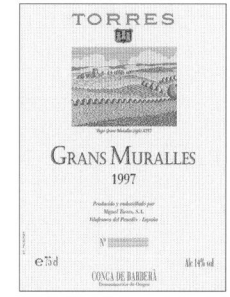

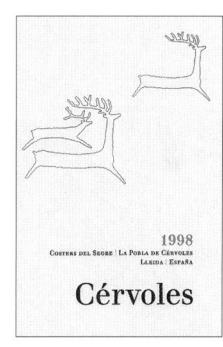

Tarragona, immediately west of Penedès around the city of that name and reaching high up into the Catalan coastal ridge, is even more varied. Many of the vineyards supply grapes for Cava. The eastern coastal plain El Camp de Tarragona still produces vast quantities of sweet, heavy red wine, sometimes long aged in barrel to take on a rancio character. But in the west, on higher vineyards, growers are increasingly inspired by what has happened to the Priorat enclave described overleaf. Around Falset, a high-altitude, one-horse town that is gateway to the Priorat zone but lies just outside it, seriously concentrated dry red wines can be produced, although they lack the benefit of Priorat's distinguishing soil type.

The Falset zone, brought to international attention in the 1990s by the Capçanes co-op, is campaigning for its own DO to elevate it nominally as well as geographically above El Camp de Tarragona and the third subzone Ribera d'Ebre further south and up into the hills on the banks of the River Ebre (the Ebro of Rioja).

In the high country of the hot, sunny Terra Alta DO west of Tarragona, imported red varieties are fast taking over from the Catalan whites traditionally grown for the Cava industry.

If Tarragona is effectively three contiguous regions travelling under one name and Penedès is four, Costers del Segre is even more extraordinary: at least four widely scattered subzones (see map of Spain on page 186). Les Garrigues is just over the Montsant range from fashionable

Priorat and has similar, though slightly more civilized countryside. At altitudes of up to 2,460ft (750m) are old Garnacha and Macabeo bush-vines with considerable potential, as well as Tempranillo and new international varieties going up on trellises at high speed among the almonds and olives. Breezes from the Mediterranean minimize the risk of frost.

Lightish but spicy international varietals are made on lower ground to the northeast in the Segre and Vall de Riu Corb zone, while Artesa way to the north has more in common with Somontano in Aragón (see page 195). And then there is Raimat, quite literally an oasis in the semi-desert northwest of Lleida, thanks to an irrigation system developed by the Raventós family of Codorníu on this vast agricultural estate. The wines produced here are more New World than Catalan.

On the coast immediately north of Barcelona Alella's vine-growers do battle with its real estate developers and have also leapt aboard the international varietal bandwagon.

Off this detailed map, but on the introductory map of Spain, is the relatively new Pla de Bages DO centred on the town of Manresa due north of Barcelona. Although it has some interesting old Picapoll (Languedoc's Picpoul), it too is being planted with Cabernet and Chardonnay while Ampurdàn-Costa Brava is the northernmost of Catalunya's DOs and has recently progressed from making mainly tourist rosé from its substantially Cariñena vines.

Catalunya now produces some seriously *interesting still wine as well as oceans of Cava. Cérvoles, for example, is made in red and white versions from ancient vines in the hinterland of Conca de Barberá rediscovered by the owners of Castell de Remei of Costers del Segre.*

Priorat

As recently as 1990 the Catalan government published a substantial tome on 1,000 years of Catalan wine in which Priorat (known as Priorato in Castilian) was not even mentioned. By the late 1990s this tiny wine region was producing some of Spain's most exciting, and most expensive, wine.

Extraordinarily, this rapid transformation was the work of one man – and not the one who today is most readily associated with Priorat. René Barbier's eponymous family firm now belongs to Cava giant Freixenet and produces table wines in Sant Sadurní d'Anoia. The man himself lost his heart to an almost abandoned wine region in the wilds of the hills northwest of Tarragona.

Before the arrival of the phylloxera louse there were 12,350 acres (5,000ha) of vineyards in this dizzying landscape of crinkle-folded hills (this is not country for the faint-hearted driver). By 1979 when René Barbier first saw the potential of this historic wine region there were just 1,500 acres (600ha) of mainly Cariñena (Carignan) vines. By 1989 he had formed a gang of five who would launch five "Clos", new producers initially sharing premises and grapes in Gratallops but soon launched as separate, technically adept but locally inspired makers of wine quite distinct from the rustic, raisiny ferments that were then the norm for Priorat – wines indeed very different from the oaky Spanish norm.

Such was the international acclaim for these concentrated wines (their scarcity helped too) that the region has now been invaded and quite literally reshaped by incomers from Penedès and far beyond. By the turn of the century there were 2,500 acres (1,000ha) either under vine or being bulldozed into tractor-friendly terraces prior to planting, with another 2,500 acres earmarked by planting rights. And all this activity has been superimposed on a region where shepherds and donkey carts are still commonplace, and the best-known wine village of Gratallops has fewer than 200 permanent residents.

So why are the wines so special? This enclave is surrounded by equally high, vertiginous terrain. Priorat is admittedly protected from the northwest by Montsant, a long ridge of craggy outcrops. But it is its particularly unusual soil, llicorella, a dark brown slate whose jagged rockfaces sparkle in the sun with their sprinkling of quartzite, that makes the best Priorat the mineral-laden essence that it is.

Annual rainfall is often under 16 inches (400mm) a year, which in most wine regions would make irrigation a necessity. Priorat's soils are unusually cool and damp, however, so that the vine roots tunnel Douro-style through faults in the llicorella to find surprisingly fresh water. The result in the best sites is almost ridiculously low yields of arrestingly concentrated wine.

Cariñena is still the most widely planted vine by far but only the oldest vines produce wine of real quality. Ancient Garnacha planted in cooler, slower-ripening sites provides the backbone of most serious Priorat, fleshed out with some of the more recently planted Cabernet Sauvignon, Syrah, and Merlot.

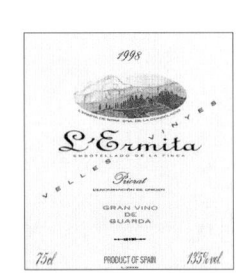

Clos Mogador is run by the original *begetter of modern Priorat and its Clos, René Barbier, one of the few wine producers to live in the region full-time. Alvaro Palacios is based near his family's Rioja Baja bodega.*

Below The 50-degree schistous slope of L'Ermita near Gratallops, made famous – and expensive – by Priorat's superstar Alvaro Palacios, is planted mainly with low-yielding Garnacha vines, supplemented by Cabernet Sauvignon and some ancient Cariñena.

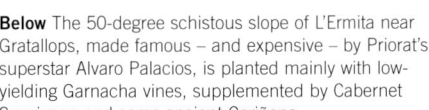

- - - Municipal boundary
— Boundary of Priorat DO
MAS MARTINET ■ Leading producer
Gran Clos Named vineyard
Vineyards
—500— Contour interval 100 metres

1:146,000

Sherry Country and the South

The Levante on the Mediterranean coast is already hot enough. South of the Levante the vine needs very special conditions to produce some very special wine. Andalucía is fortified wine and brandy country, although those making table wines in Condado de Huelva (see map of Spain, page 186) to the east of the town of the same name, do their best to make the wine as refreshing as they possibly can in these temperatures (see factfile below).

For true refreshment, the locals are more likely to choose a wine with more finesse, even if a combination of strength and delicacy is not one of the qualities you normally find in scorched-earth wines. Where the sun fairly grills the ground, and the grapes ripen as warm as fruit in a pie, wine sometimes develops wonderful sinews, power, and depth. But finesse?

This is sherry's great distinction. It is a question of chalk, of the breed of the Palomino Fino grape, of huge investment and long-inherited skill. Not every bottle of sherry, by a very long way, has this quality – in fact the sherry aristocracy could be said to have been ruined by the high proportion of poor wine shipped from Jerez. But a real fino, the unstrengthened produce of the bare white chalk dunes of Macharnudo or Sanlúcar de Barrameda, is an expression of wine and wood as vivid and beautiful as any in the world.

The sherry country, between the romantic-sounding cities of Cádiz and Seville, is almost a caricature of grandee Spain. Here are the bull ranches, the castles on the skyline, the patios, the guitars, the flamenco dancers, the night-turned-into-day. Jerez de la Frontera, the town that gives its name to sherry, lives and breathes sherry as Beaune does burgundy and Epernay champagne.

The comparison of sherry with champagne can be carried a long way. Both are white wines with a distinction given them by chalk soil, both needing long traditional treatment to achieve their special characters. Both are revivifying apéritifs, of which you can drink an astonishing amount in their home countries and only feel more alive than you have ever felt before. They are the far-northern and the far-southern interpretation of the same equation, or the same poem: the white grape from the white ground.

Not all the ground is white. The chalk areas (*albarizas*) are best; the *pagos* (districts) of Carrascal, Macharnudo, Añina, and Balbaina the most famous. Some vineyards are on sand and produce second-rank wines for blending.

The shippers' headquarters and bodegas are in the sherry towns of Sanlúcar, El Puerto de Santa María, and, especially, Jerez. There are little bars in each of these towns where the tapas, the morsels of food without which no Andalucían puts glass to mouth, constitute a banquet.

Your copita, a glass no more imposing than an opening tulip, fills and empties with a paler wine, a cooler wine, a more druggingly delicious wine than you have ever tasted.

But the most celebrated sights of Jerez are the bodegas of the shipping houses. Their towering whitewashed aisles, dim-roofed and crisscrossed with sunbeams, are irresistibly cathedral-like. In them, in ranks of butts (barrels) sometimes five tiers high, the new wine is put to mature. It will not leave until it has gone through an elaborate blending process which is known as the solera system. Only the occasional wine of notable distinction is sold unblended as a single vintage wine or one straight from an *almacenista*, or stockholder.

The first job when the new wine has got over its fermentation is to sort it into categories: better or worse, lighter or more full-bodied. Each wine is put into the *criadera* (nursery) appropriate to its character. Each character or category of wine has a traditional name.

From the *criaderas* the shipper tops up a number of soleras, consisting of perhaps 20, perhaps several hundred butts; each wine going into the solera nearest to its character. As new wine goes into butts at one end of the solera, mature wine for blending is drawn from the other. The solera system is simply a progressive topping-up of older barrels from younger of the same style, so that wine is continuously being blended, and hence always emerges tasting the same.

The solera wines are the shipper's paintbox for blending the house brand. Mass-market sherry

Above Palomino Fino grapes are now harvested in small plastic boxes to minimize damage and oxidation in quality-conscious vineyards such as this one run by González Byass.

- —·— Provincial boundary
- Boundary of Jerez DO
- Tehigo   Vineyard area
- Chalk soil
- Clay and sandy soil
- —200—   Contour interval 100 metres
- ▼   Weather station (WS)

1:661,000

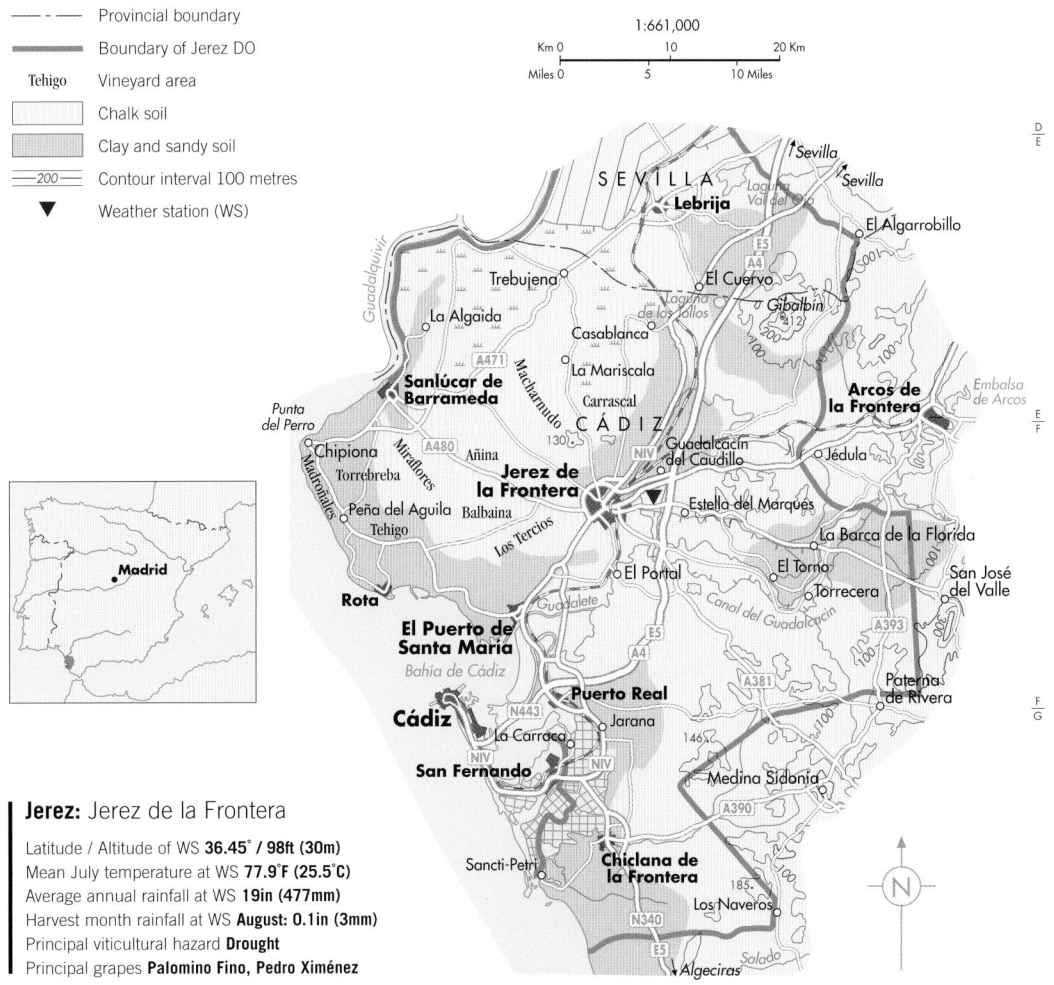

Jerez: Jerez de la Frontera

Latitude / Altitude of WS **36.45° / 98ft (30m)**
Mean July temperature at WS **77.9°F (25.5°C)**
Average annual rainfall at WS **19in (477mm)**
Harvest month rainfall at WS **August: 0.1in (3mm)**
Principal viticultural hazard **Drought**
Principal grapes **Palomino Fino, Pedro Ximénez**

when it is sold is a sweetened, strengthened blend, but sherries sold straight from the solera are dry wines for the connoisseur. All young sherry is originally classified as either a wine light and delicate enough to be a fino, which will mature under a protective, bread-like layer of a strange Jerez yeast called flor, or a fuller wine that is classified as an oloroso. Olorosos are matured in contact with air and deliberately fortified to more than 15.5% alcohol, closer to 18% in fact, which will kill off any incipient flor.

Sherries sold as finos are the finest, palest sherries; distinctive, bone dry wines which need a minimum of blending. They will age excellently in wood, but also have qualities that make them perfect young – and fast-faders; an open bottle should ideally be drained within hours rather than days or weeks. Even lighter and drier are the manzanillas of Sanlúcar de Barrameda, made just like a fino and blessed with a faintly salty tang which is held to come from the sea.

Amontillado – a softer, darker wine – comes next. The best amontillados are old finos, finos which did not quite have the right freshness to be drunk young, although the name is more often found on labels of commercial blends that are medium in every sense of the word. (A fino is turned into a classical amontillado either by allowing the flor to die, or by killing it off by adding alcohol; the sherry is then matured in contact with air, as olorosos are.) The great amontillado soleras (for only from the solera can you taste the real individuality of the wine) are dry and almost stingingly powerful in flavour, with a dark, fat, rich tang. A big brand amontillado will be merely a sweetened blend of the most ordinary olorosos, called *rayas*.

True classical oloroso, dry and dark, is rare but a great favourite with Jerezanos themselves. Such wines have great possibilities for ageing but are too heavy for a fino solera. Olorosos

Below It seems extraordinary that a drink as quintessentially refreshing as fino sherry should come from soleras of wines matured for years in dusty barrels such as these in Pedro Domecq's bodega La Mezquita.

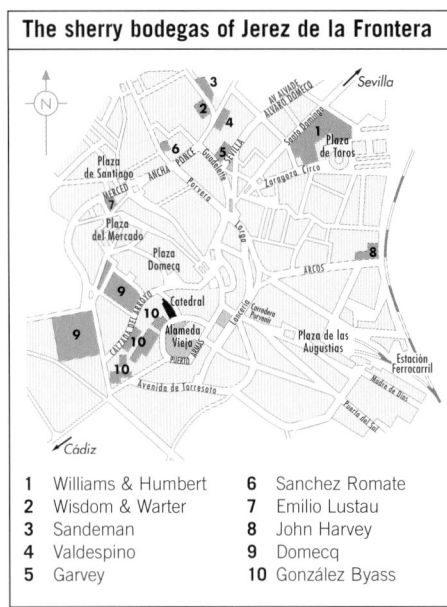

The sherry bodegas of Jerez de la Frontera

1	Williams & Humbert	6	Sanchez Romate
2	Wisdom & Warter	7	Emilio Lustau
3	Sandeman	8	John Harvey
4	Valdespino	9	Domecq
5	Garvey	10	González Byass

are also the basis for many of the best sweet sherries, some of the most intriguing made exclusively from Pedro Ximénez grapes (often simply called PX), which are traditionally dried to make sweetening wines for sherry. Commercial brands labelled oloroso or cream are blended *rayas* plus sweetening wines; pale cream is typically the same with its natural colour taken out. Palo cortado, on the other hand, is a true, classical, rich-yet-dry rarity, something between fino and oloroso.

No blend, medium-sweet or sweet as most blends are, can compare with these astonishing natural sherries. They are as much collectors' pieces as great domaine-bottled burgundies.

Sherry is by far the most famous of Andalucía's *vinos generosos*, but the mountainous coast to the east, the Costa del Sol, and the hot, dry hills behind it also have their specialities, related to sherry but stylistically distinct (see map, page 186). Sherry even takes the name of one of its main styles, amontillado, from its resemblance to the wines of Montilla.

Montilla-Moriles, to give the full name, is a shrinking wine region just south of Córdoba, but still has 25,000 acres (10,000ha) of vineyard, partly on the same chalk that gives rise to the finos and olorosos of Jerez. Until 50 years ago its produce was blended at Jerez as though the two regions were one. But Montilla is different. Its special attraction lies in its very high natural strength, which has always allowed it to be shipped without fortification, in contrast to sherry, which may be lightly fortified.

The Montilla grape is not Palomino but Pedro Ximénez, the one that in Jerez is kept for the sweetest wine. The hotter climate of Montilla gives an even higher sugar content to the grapes, which ferment rapidly in open earthenware *tinajas*. The flor yeast also forms quickly. Within a year or two the wine is ready, with more softness than sherry, slipping down like

table wine despite its high strength. People claim to find in them the scent of black olives (which are of course their perfect partners).

Although Montilla is usually at its best young, pale and dry, the bodegas use the same methods as the bodegas of Jerez to make wines ranging from apéritif to dessert. Fino styles are a bit heavier than in Jerez.

No gulf separates Montilla from Málaga, once world famous for its splendidly raisiny dessert wines. Málaga is in reality a wide range of *vinos generosos* with one common factor: the bodegas must, by law, be in the capital city of the Costa del Sol. The vineyards are widely dispersed with Pedro Ximénez grown inland and Moscatel mainly on the coast. Crops are very small and the concentrated wines capable of indefinite ageing, the better qualities in soleras. *Arrope* (boiled-down must), a technique used by the Romans, concentrates the flavour further. Today's market, alas, has been so indifferent to superlative Málagas that the best producer, Scholtz Hermanos, shut up shop in 1996. There are slight stirrings of renewal however in the encouraging form of López Hermanos and the golden sweet Molino Real.

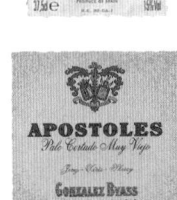

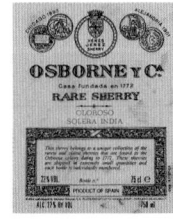

Sherry comes in far more different styles *than the average wine drinker realizes. This collection runs from tangy pale through exceptionally ancient to tooth-rottingly dark sweet essences like the PX from Sánchez Romate (bottom left). The Alvear PX is a Montilla.*

Portugal

Portuguese wine would make a fascinating case study for modern business managers. It was precisely Portugal's prolonged isolation from fashionable trends and nostrums which preserved its rich heritage of indigenous grape varieties and now gives it real distinction in a Europe so comprehensively invaded by a handful of international grapes.

Touriga Nacional, for example, unquestionably produces great red table wine as well as port and is increasingly to be found on wine labels in Portugal and beyond. Touriga Francesa and Tinto Cão are other port grapes clearly capable of making the transition from fortified to less potent wine, while Trincadeira Preta (the Tinta Amarela of port) has great richness and Jaen (Mencía in Spain's Galicia) can make distinguished, juicy young wine. And these are not the only Portuguese red grapes of great character. The grape known as Tempranillo in Spain is also extremely successful in Portugal, called Tinta Roriz in the north and Aragonês in the south. Arinto is probably Portugal's most aristocratic white grape but Bical can also age well and Dão's Encruzado has great potential for full-bodied whites. All this without taking into account the great white grapes of Portugal's wine island, Madeira (see page 212).

All these flavours are now more accessible to outsiders because Portugal has started to make much more gentle, voluptuous wines, even if acidity and tannins are still pronounced compared to the wines of Spain. Portugal has retained her individuality but she has at long last joined the greater world of wine, as the following pages demonstrate.

For years Portugal was known to the world's wine drinkers only for her great sweet fortified wine, port (examined in detail on pages 207-211), and the country's other wine style conceived specifically for export – wines neither red nor white, sweet nor dry, still nor sparkling – of which Mateus and Lancers were the leading ambassadors in the mid-20th century.

The Portuguese have always been prodigious drinkers of their own wine and, knowing no other, were quite accustomed to local styles made, as they had been for centuries, often searingly high in acidity in the north and distinctly rustic in the south. The country is not vast but different regions are subject to the very different influences of Atlantic, Mediterranean, and even continental climates. Soils too vary enormously, from granite, slate, and schist in the far north to clay and sand in the south. Portugal's wine industry clearly deserved more detailed attention.

This is coming at last. From the early 1990s Portugal's table wines, particularly her highly individual reds, have been catching up fast with the evolution in modern winemaking. Temperature control, destemmers, new oak barrels – all have played their part in capturing the fruit of Portugal's distinctive grape varieties in the bottle, and in producing wines that do not require ageing for a decade before they are drinkable. Although Portugal now has a host of talented native oenologists, some of whom are accorded

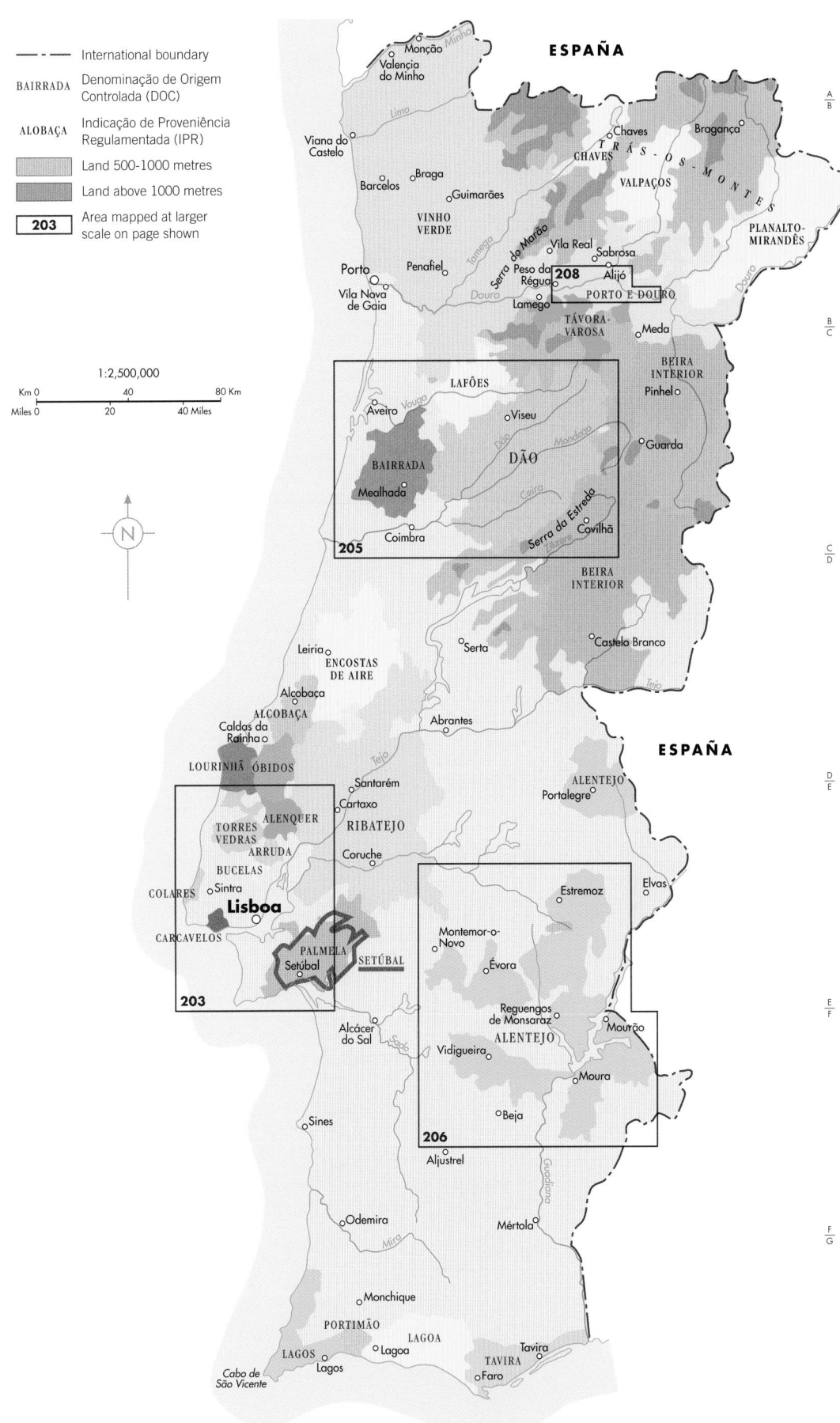

Key:

— ·· — International boundary

BAIRRADA — Denominação de Origem Controlada (DOC)

ALOBAÇA — Indicação de Proveniência Regulamentada (IPR)

Land 500-1000 metres

Land above 1000 metres

203 — Area mapped at larger scale on page shown

1:2,500,000

Km 0   40   80 Km
Miles 0   20   40 Miles

the sort of cult consultant status enjoyed by their counterparts in Italy, Australian-trained outsiders such as David Baverstock and Peter Bright can also claim some of the credit for this in their pioneering work at Esporào and JP Vinhos respectively.

Not that Portuguese wine has been without laws and regulations. The Douro lays claim to be the world's first demarcated wine region (in 1756), and long before Portugal's entry into the EU in 1986 many other districts had been demarcated and every aspect of their wines controlled. This was not always to the benefit of their quality, or to the liking of merchants and their local clients, who routinely ignored what the law prescribed to blend the kinds of wines they preferred.

With entry into the EU Portugal's wine map, like that of Spain, has sprouted a rash of demarcated regions. The regulations of Portugal's DOCs, emulating those of France's Appellations Contrôlées, prescribe the permitted local grape varieties. Increasingly important however is the Vinho Regional category of wines from much larger regions but with more flexible regulations. In 2000 there were fewer than ten IPRs (Indicações de Proveniência Regulamentada), DOCs-in-waiting, a category which is expected to disappear eventually. The map on page 261 shows the approved wine names; the key is the guide to their status. While some of the newly hatched regions have authentic character and important potential, others are likely to be mere straws in the wind. Time will tell.

A previously neglected region whose life may be changed by its Vinho Regional status is Trás-os-Montes, "behind the mountains", at the

Language of the Label

Quality designations
Denominação de Origem Controlada (DOC) Portugal's answer to France's AC (see page 52)
Indicação de Proveniência Regulamentada (IPR) DOCs-in-waiting, like France's VDQS
Vinho Regional Portugal's answer to France's Vin de Pays (see page 150)
Vinho de Mesa basic table wine

Other common expressions
Adega cellar
Amarzém cellar
Branco white
Colheita vintage
Doce sweet
Garrafado (na origem) bottled (estate bottled)
Garrafeira merchant's special reserve
Maduro old or mature
Quinta farm or estate
Rosado rosé, pink
Séco dry
Tinto red
Verde young
Vinha vineyard

northern rim of the Douro Valley, remote granite uplands most beautiful at their golden harvest time. Its IPRs, Chaves, Valpaços, and Planalto-Mirandês, offer quantities of strong co-op wines, and are also a major source of rosé long tapped by the Sogrape company for Mateus.

Beiras, virtually all of the northern half of the country south of the Douro Valley, is a name used for wines that do not qualify as either Dão or Bairrada. Most wines labelled Vinho Regional Beiras seem like very pale, if extremely varied, shadows of Dão and Bairrada at best, but there is no reason why some well-made reds should not emerge from those shadows, as Boas Quintas, Caves Primavera, and Quinta de Foz de Arouce have shown.

The vinous future of the south of Portugal seems much more assured. Estremadura and the Setúbal Peninsula are discussed opposite, while the fashionable Alentejo, "beyond the Tagus", is mapped on page 206.

The productive Ribatejo region is named after the banks of the River Tagus (Tejo) which flows southwest from the Spanish border to Lisbon. The fertile river banks used to produce vast quantities of decidedly light wine, but in the late 1980s EU subsidies persuaded hundreds of growers here to uproot their vines. Total production has shrunk and the focus of Ribatejo wine production has now moved away from the river bank and, in some cases, towards imported grape varieties such as Cabernet Sauvignon and more recently Syrah (which seems to have a promising future in Portugal). The multi-named Periquita/Castelão Francês/João de Santarém and Trincadeira Preta are the most important local red wine grapes while whites are typically based on the arrestingly perfumed Fernào Pires.

Ribatejo nomenclature can be confusing to outsiders. The region produces wines from exclusively Portuguese grapes labelled DOC Ribatejo, with or without one of its seven sub-regions such as Cartaxo or Almeirim, as well as Vinho Regional Ribatejano from international as well as Portuguese grapes.

The Algarve's four DOCs are perhaps the country's most questionable. Portugal's southern holiday coast may have attracted the odd celebrated investor, but as a wine region the Algarve is still particularly good at tourism.

Of Portugal's many wildly differing styles of wine, the most singular remains Vinho Verde, the youthful "green" (as opposed to *maduro*, or aged) wine of the northernmost province, the Minho, which accounts for almost a fifth of Portugal's wine harvest. The name green describes its fresh, often underripe style, not its colour, which is red (much of it sold in Portugal) or almost water-white.

In this damp climate, vines are extremely vigorous, malic acid unusually high, and natural grape sugars relatively low, resulting in reds and whites with a low alcohol content and definite tartness, a decidedly local taste. Although most white Vinho Verde is made from a blend of grapes, typically including Azal, Loureiro, Trajadura, Avesso, and some Pedernão (Arinto), some of the best is made from the white Alvarinho grape (Albariño in Spain) grown around Monção.

The grapevine is not the only plant in Portugal of interest to wine drinkers. The southern half of the country has the world's greatest concentration of cork oaks, so that Portugal is the principal supplier of wine corks.

Below Because land is so short in the densely populated Minho, vines are often trained up fencing posts or grown on overhead trellises or pergolas. Grapes tend be picked before fungal diseases threaten in this damp climate.

All four of these wines were made in Vinho Verde country but the Covela is decidedly untraditional, a blend of the local Avesso grape with some imported Chardonnay given some very unPortuguese new oak.

Estremadura and Setúbal Peninsula

Estremadura, once called simply Oeste or "the west", is Portugal's most productive wine region, even if the average holding of its more than 55,000 grape growers is not much more than a hectare. This ultra-maritime region makes very inexpensive wine, some of it good value, from sand and clay soils.

This is a region of co-ops, whose best produce tends to be made by one of the country's more celebrated consultant oenologists and bought by one of the larger Portuguese merchants, or direct by a foreign importer. As everywhere however, the number of ambitious small estates in this large coastal region west of Lisbon is increasing – even if the temptation to grow international rather than Portuguese grapes seems stronger here than in much of the rest of Portugal.

For long this part of Portugal was famous for three historic wines. Bucelas, occasionally spelt Bucellas, is least threatened by extinction as other investors have followed Quinta da Romeira's commitment to the region. The naturally crisp, lemony Arinto grape is grown in a particularly windy, warm area 15 miles (25km) north of Lisbon, which benefits from more clay and even more warmth than the rest of Estremadura. The resultant wines have a certain tangy refreshment but are probably best drunk young and unoaked.

Colares, right on the Atlantic coast, is one of the world's stranger wine zones. Ramisco vines are literally grown on the windswept beach, hugging the phylloxera-immune sand, their old limbs like driftwood, bearing small bunches of intensely blue grapes. The wine, all initially made by the local co-op, is typically black and tannic and needs as long to mature as the claret of 100 years ago. Colares' distinction is its ungrafted vines, and its struggle to resist coastal property developers. Carcavelos, whose luscious amber wine became famous during the Peninsula war, has lost that particular battle to the estate agents of Estoril.

Much more important today than these once-famous names are the vineyards of the Setúbal Peninsula between the Tagus (Tejo) and Sado estuaries southeast of Lisbon, divided into the very different clay-limestone hills of Serra da Arrábida, whose slopes are cooled by Atlantic winds, and the much hotter, more fertile inland sandy plain of the River Sado east of Palmela.

The region's most traditional wine is the rudely robust Moscatel de Setúbal, a rich, pale orange Muscat that is lightly fortified and perfumed by long maceration with the headily aromatic Muscat of Alexandria skins.

Setúbal's most important producers, JP Vinhos and José Maria da Fonseca, were also pioneers of Portugal's new wave of modern table wines. JP Vinhos could claim to be Portugal's most experienced producer of modern white wines, whether from Chardonnay or the local Fernão Pires, while both companies have for many years made extremely accessible, medium-weight reds from the dominant local red grapes Periquita and, more recently, from Tinta Miúda (Spain's Graciano), which is also grown in Estremadura.

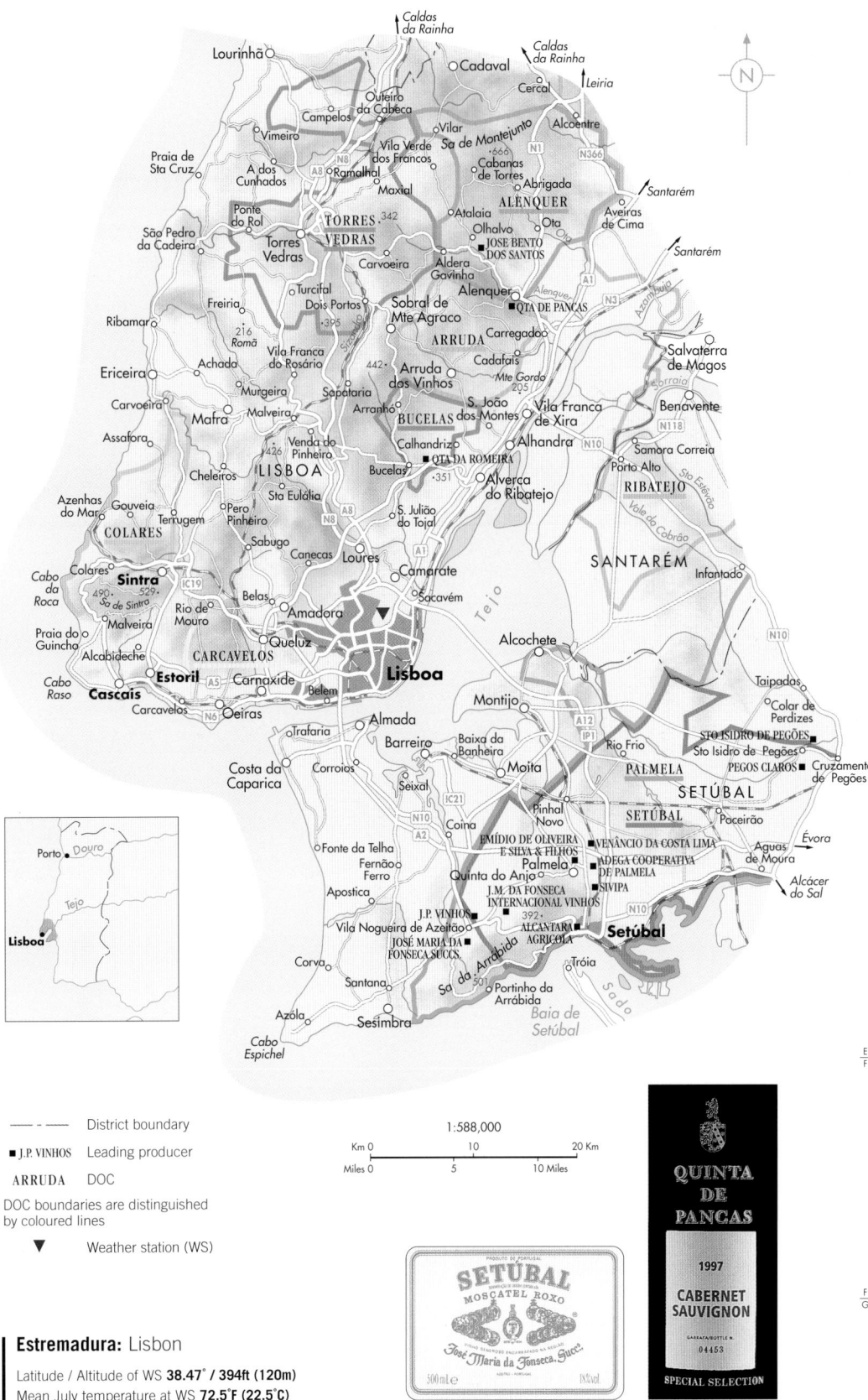

--- - --- District boundary

■ J.P. VINHOS Leading producer

ARRUDA DOC

DOC boundaries are distinguished by coloured lines

▼ Weather station (WS)

1:588,000
Km 0 — 10 — 20 Km
Miles 0 — 5 — 10 Miles

Estremadura: Lisbon

Latitude / Altitude of WS **38.47˚ / 394ft (120m)**
Mean July temperature at WS **72.5˚F (22.5˚C)**
Average annual rainfall at WS **26in (670mm)**
Harvest month rainfall at WS **September: 1.4in (35mm)**
Principal viticultural hazards **Rain during fruit set, autumn rain**
Principal grapes **Periquita, Camarate, Trincadeira, Fernão Pires, Arinto**

Moscatel Roxo is a rare *Setúbal speciality; Quinta da Pancas of Estremadura one of the first Portuguese producers to have mastered Cabernet Sauvignon. Imported grape varieties are still very much a minority in the country's vineyards. Long may this last.*

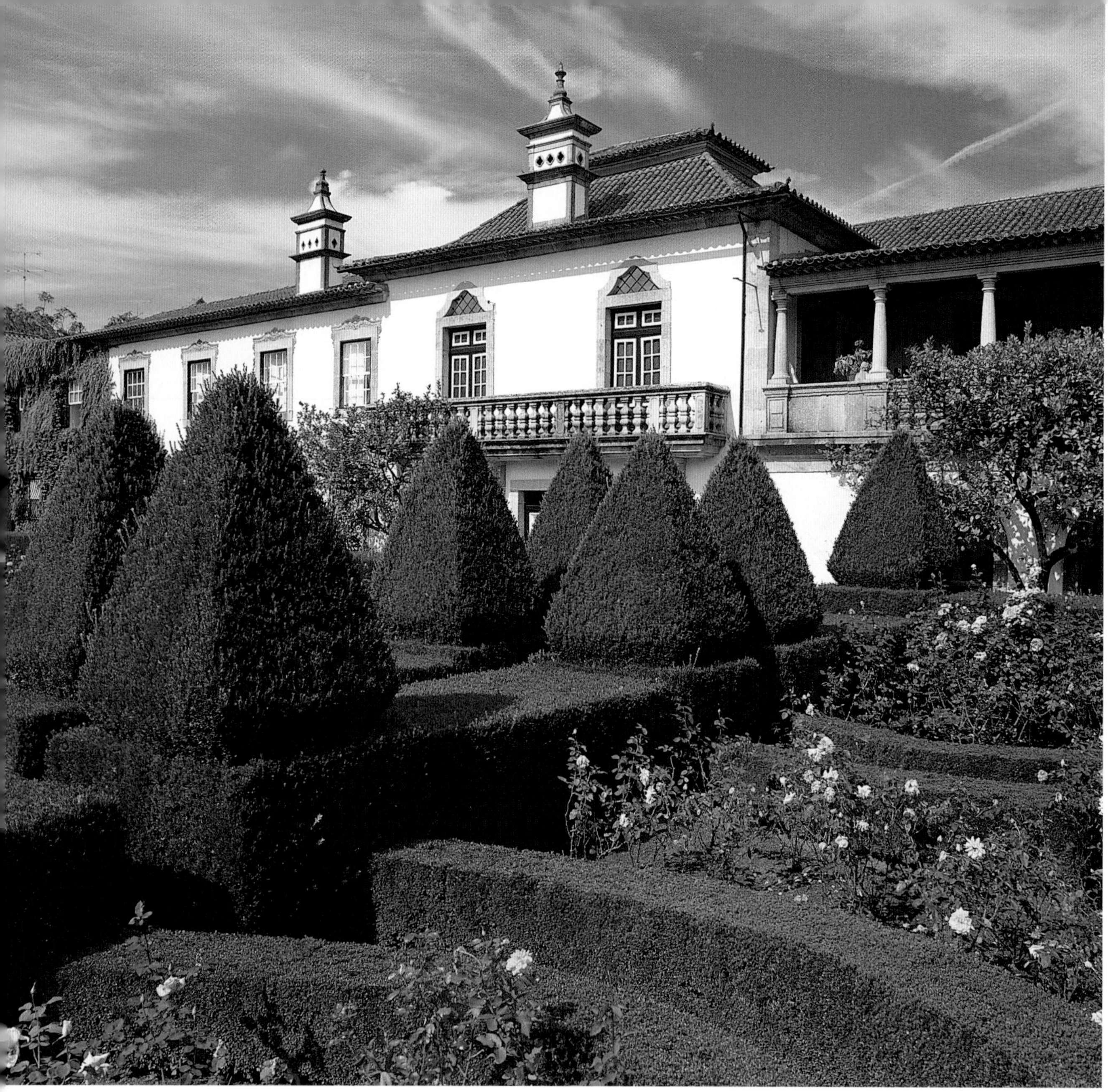

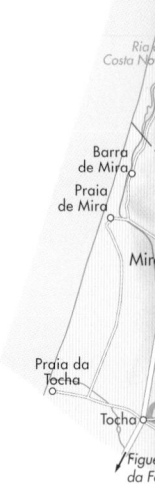

Ria de
Costa Nov

Barra
de Mira
Praia
de Mira

Mira

Praia da
Tocha

Tocha

Figue
da Fo

Bairrada and Dão

Bairrada and Dão, two of Portugal's longest-established wine regions, are currently in the throes of (entirely beneficial) transition. Bairrada is a thoroughly rural district lying astride the highway that links Lisbon and Oporto, filling most of the area between the granite hills of Dão and the Atlantic coast. This proximity to the Atlantic makes it one of the country's rainier wine regions and growers here have the same problems ripening grapes and keeping them free of fungal diseases as their counterparts in Bordeaux.

Bairrada's low hills encompass some extremely varied and expressive terroirs, but heavy, lime-rich clay predominates and gives body and typical Portuguese bite to its overwhelmingly (85%) red wine. The defining ingredient though is Bairrada's indigenous Baga grape. Passionate local winemakers such as Luis Pato liken Baga to Piemonte's Nebbiolo in its uncompromisingly heavy charge of acids and tannins. Baga produces wines of considerable

character that demand patience (some of the traditional bottlings need 20 years' cellaring) and sympathy – not qualities that mark out the typical modern wine drinker. Some producers have a policy of ageing their better wines themselves and it is possible to find venerable, delicious red Bairrada from the likes of Casa de Saima and Quinta de Baixo. All red Bairrada benefits from aeration.

Many of the region's 7,000 growers belong to the co-operatives which, along with Sogrape's vinification centre, comprise the biggest wineries. But the most ambitious smaller producers are admirably cohesive and well-organized, and a serious research programme is well under way to help fashion Bairrada for the 21st century. Destemming has become more common and some producers are carefully thinning crops and trimming vegetation to push the grape to the limits of ripeness.

Increasingly interesting whites are made from Maria Gomes (Fernão Pires) grapes and

the local Bical which, like Baga, is notable for its acidity. Bical makes eminently respectable sparkling wines as well as increasingly full-bodied still ones.

The name of Dão was until the 1990s associated with aggressively tannic, dull reds, the result of a ridiculous statute that sent all its grapes to heavy-handed co-operatives. Happily the European Union disallowed this monopoly and the result is far juicier, friendlier wines, including some of Portugal's finest. Red Dão has changed more, and for the better, than any other Portuguese wine since the 1980s.

Dão, named after the river that runs through it, is effectively a granite plateau, where bare rocks show through the sandy soil. Vineyards are only a subplot in the landscape, cropping up here and there in clearings in the sweet-scented pine forests. Its capital, Viseu, is one of Portugal's prettiest towns. The Serra do Caramulo protects the region from the Atlantic and the Serra da Estrela and Serra da Nave mountains from the

1:588,000

Km 0   10   20 Km
Miles 0   5   10 Miles

— - — District boundary

■ LUIS PATO   Leading producer

BAIRRADA   DOC

DOC boundaries are distinguished
by coloured lines

south and east. This means that in winter Dão is cold and wet; in summer mild and dry – much drier than Bairrada.

As is usual in Portugal (indeed Bairrada is unusual in this respect) a dizzying range of grapes is grown in the Dão region, to produce increasingly fruity reds – though still with a certain granitic substance – and potentially firm, fragrant whites suitable for ageing. This affinity for the cellar, in whites as well as reds, was already obvious from traditional Dãos, bottled by merchants who would buy, blend, and age wines from the co-ops before selling them as their own Reservas or Garrafeiras.

The finest individual estates such as Quinta dos Roques/Quinta das Maias and Quinta da Pellada/Quinta de Saes have been producing single varietals as well as blends as they experiment with individual grapes, of which Touriga Nacional for long ageing, Jaen (Galicia's Mencía) for fruity early drinking, and Tinto Cão for perfume have shown great promise. Full-bodied Encruzado has already proved itself one of Portugal's finest white grapes. Sogrape, pioneer of varietal wines in the region, has invested heavily in its Quinta dos Carvalhais range. Fruit has been rediscovered in Dão.

The potential of this part of the world for truly remarkable table wines was always clear, thanks to one eccentric, mysterious, and highly idiosyncratic example. Right on Barraida's eastern boundary the Buçaco Palace Hotel has selected and matured its own red and white wines in a wholly traditional way. The reds would usually come from north of the handsome university town of Coimbra while whites were handpicked from both Bairrada and Dão, blended and aged for years in barrel in the Palace cellars. Both reds and whites on the hotel wine list still go back for decades, and the "current" vintages for both colours at the turn of the century were from the 1970s and 1960s. They look and taste like relics of another age, in the most fascinating sense.

Luis Pato is the most dynamic producer *in Bairrada, bottling the produce of young and in this case old vines separately. Destalking is a relative novelty for wines such as these, some of northern Portugal's best.*

Alentejo

In comparison with the tapestry of vines that seems to smother northern Portugal, the Alentejo, the southern third of the country, is relatively vine-free. Its wide, sun-browned spaces are dotted with silver olives and dark cork oaks, browsed bare by sheep, but only occasionally green with vines. Smallholdings are rare. Ranch-like estates, unknown in the densely populated north, are the norm.

Even in midwinter, this is a land of sun and open vistas. The visitor is aware that arid Spain is just over the border; winemakers do their shopping there. Rainfall is low and temperatures so routinely high that picking starts in the third week of August. Rich loamy soils are interspersed with granite and schist.

Six of the Alentejo's eight subregions are based on an important co-op, none more important than that of Reguengos which, in Terras D'el Rei, produces a best-seller within Portugal. A significant proportion of the region's wines is sold as varietal and/or Vinho Regional Alentejano. Evora can boast a particularly long history of bottling wine, notably the Cartuxa and floridly labelled Pêra Manca of Eugénio de Almeida.

But it has been newcomers who have tended to bring Alentejo wines to international attention. When José Roquette, owner of one of Lisbon's rival football teams, blessed his Reguengos estate Herdade do Esporão with an Australian winemaker and almost Napa-like dream winery in the late 1980s, the Portuguese took note. When the Lafite Rothschilds invested in Quinta do Carmo in Borba in 1992, the world took note (even if the wines have been slow to shine). Oenologist João Portugal Ramos has energized the entire region, providing it with a popular and easily exportable brand, Marquês de Borba.

Historically various port shippers would buy a cask or two of strapping Alentejo red for their dinner tables, the most remarkable of all being Mouchão, made by the Anglo-Portuguese Reynolds family and now deservedly famous. There are few wine traditions here and this is excellent pioneer country with the added advantage, until the recent arrival of the spotlight of fashion, of relatively low prices.

Red grapes are now more popular than the floral white Roupeiro. Aragonês (Tempranillo), local speciality Trincadeira Preta, and Periquita have all risen to the fore, as has the red-fleshed Alicante Bouschet, which seems to take on a certain nobility in Alentejo. Touriga Nacional, Cabernet Sauvignon, and Syrah have inevitably been imported.

Right Trincadeira grapes being harvested by hand at Herdade do Esporão in Reguengos – although machine harvesters are becoming increasingly common in this sparsely populated region.

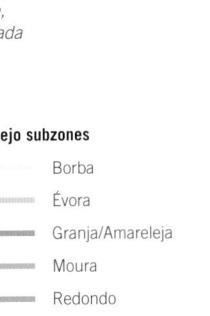

Mouchão was one of the first wines to be exported from the Alentejo region. Incógnito is one of the most recent, an experimental Syrah bottled anonymously by a Dane, Hans Kristian Jørgensen. There is Cabernet in the Tapada de Coelheiros, blended with Aragonês (Tempranillo).

— · — International boundary

— · — District boundary

▬▬ DOC Alentejo

■ CORTES DE CIMA Leading producer

══400══ Contour interval 200 metres

▼ Weather station (WS)

Alentejo subzones

Borba

Évora

Granja/Amareleja

Moura

Redondo

Reguengos

Vidigueira

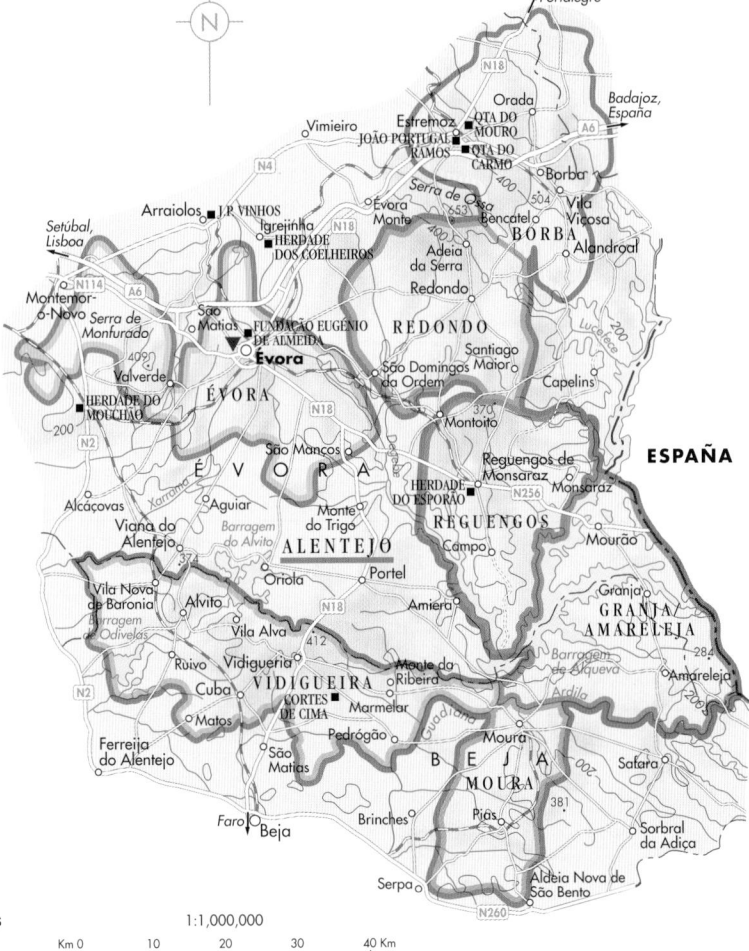

Alentejo: Evora

Latitude / Altitude of WS **38.34° / 1,050ft (320m)**
Mean July temperature at WS **73.5°F (23.1°C)**
Average annual rainfall at WS **24in (620mm)**
Harvest month rainfall at WS **August: 0.2in (5mm)**
Principal viticultural hazards **Drought, isolated spring frosts**
Principal grapes **Aragonês (Tempranillo), Trincadeira, Periquita, Alicante Bouschet, Roupeiro, Antão Vaz**

1:1,000,000

Km 0 — 10 — 20 — 30 — 40 Km
Miles 0 — 10 — 20 Miles

Douro – Port Country

Of all the places where men have planted vineyards, the Upper Douro is the most improbable. To begin with there was hardly any soil: only 60-degree slopes of schist and slate, flaking and unstable, baked in a 100°F (38°C) summer sun. It was a land of utter desolation.

The vine, however, is one of the few plants not quite deterred by these conditions. The Mediterranean-type climate suits it. What was needed was simply the engineering feat of building walls along the mountainsides, thousands of them, like contour lines, to hold up the patches of ground (one could hardly call it soil) where vines could be planted.

Once the ground was stabilized and rainwater no longer ran straight off, an enterprise undertaken as early as the 17th century, olives, oranges, oaks, chestnut trees, and vines flourished, like those shown below.

After phylloxera had laid waste the region's vineyards, in the efficient 1970s, the old stone-walled terraces were gradually replaced by bulldozed, wider terraces (*patamares*) supported by banks of schist rather than walls. Their great advantage is that they are wide enough for tractors and mechanization. Their disadvantage is the reduction in vine density (and the vast quantities of herbicide used to keep them free of weeds that would otherwise compete for the Douro's pitifully low water supply). Along the *patamares*, and wherever the angle of elevation allows, growers are now increasingly planting vine rows up rather than across the slope, which also allows mechanization but encourages much denser planting.

Many of the original terraces dating from the 17th century survive in the mountains above Régua, in the original port-wine zone which then extended as far as the Tua tributary and which in 1756 was given its first official limits (the first such limits ever given to any wine). Today this area remains the biggest port producer, but the search for quality has led further and further upstream, and since the blasting of the Cachão da Valeira, the upper reaches of the valley have been accessible by river.

The Douro reaches Portugal from Spain in a wilderness which has been accessible by road only since the late 1980s when EU funds started to flood into Portugal. It has carved a titanic canyon through the layered rock uplands, the so-called Upper Douro, or Douro Superior, the driest, flattest, least developed part of the Douro (off to the east of the main map) which can, nevertheless, produce some very fine grapes.

To the west, the 4,600ft (1,400m) Serra do Marão stops the Atlantic rain clouds of summer from refreshing the schists of the heart of port country, Cima Corgo, mapped in detail overleaf. Often there is no summer rain at all, although the Baixo Corgo downstream of the Corgo tributary and off the main map to the west is wetter

than either Cima Corgo or, especially, Douro Superior, the driest area of all. To make great port the vines have to insinuate their roots as far down into the schist as possible in their search for water; the Baixo Corgo is reckoned too damp for top-quality port.

The best port vineyards of all today are those around and above Pinhão, including the valleys of the Tedo, Távora, Torto, Pinhão, and Tua tributaries. Because orientations and altitudes vary so dramatically, the character of wine produced even in neighbouring vineyards can be quite different. In the Tedo Valley, for instance, wine

tends to be particularly tannic, while that made just across the river around Quinta do Crasto is relatively light and fruity.

Each port vineyard is classified, from A down to F, according to its natural advantages and the vines that are planted on it. The higher the classification, the more money will be paid for the grapes in the highly regulated market that governs relations between the grape growers and port producers.

Vintage time anywhere is the climax of the year, but on the Douro, perhaps because of the hardship of life, it is almost Dionysiac. There is

Right Cacti growing by the Douro near Quinta do Crasto, producer of some fine Douro table wine, hint at just how low rainfall can be in this part of the world. Vine terraces hug the contours on the opposite bank.

an antique frenzy about the ritual, the songs, the music of drum and pipe (or, more likely nowadays, loud portable stereo), and the long nights of treading by the light of hurricane lamps while the women dance together.

The famous shipping firms have their own quintas, or wine farms, up in the hills where they go to supervise the vintage. They are rambling white houses, vine-arboured, tile-floored, and cool in a world of dust and glare. Most of the famous port quintas are shown on the map on these pages, names that have become much more familiar since the late 1980s with the rise in single quinta ports. AXA-renovated Quinta do Noval above Pinhão has been world-famous for years, but there are now scores more whose names appear on labels. These will be either a major shipper's quinta whose name is used for vintages not quite fine enough to be generally declared (as Taylor for instance sells Quinta de

Vargellas, and Graham Quinta dos Malvedos) or, more like a Bordeaux château, year in and year out and not just for off years (as for Quinta do Vesúvio and Quinta do Passadouro, for example). The main source of grapes and wine for port, however, is not the big estates but still a multitude of small farmers, even if more and more of them are being tempted to sell under the name of their own quintas.

This is particularly true for the table wines – most red, all labelled Douro – that have been emerging from the Douro since EU funds have been transformed into winemaking niceties such as temperature control. Traditionally, Douro table wines were made from grapes not ripe enough or from a site not warm enough for port, but light wines have become so important for producers such as Sogrape (Ferreira and Quinta da Leda, the latter situated off the detailed map to the east), Ramos Pinto, Quinta

de la Rosa, Quinta do Crasto, Quinta do Fojo, and Quinta da Gaivosa (in the Baixo Corgo), that they have been planting vineyards specifically for table wines.

Ferreira's Barca Velha was the prototype Douro table wine but there are now dozens of pretenders to that particular throne, some of them, Quinta do Crasto for example, making positively fruity, modern wines. Styles of red Douro vary enormously and too many seem to have been picked too early to have anything of port's fireworks or the Douro's exceptionally distinctive *goût de terroir*, but Quinta do Côtto (off the detailed map to the west), like Quinta de la Rosa and Quinta da Gaivosa, shares a distinctive Priorat-like schistous minerality, while Niepoort's bottlings of Redoma (in all three colours) have a confidence all of their own.

Until pioneering work in the 1970s by José Ramos Pinto Rosas and João Nicolau de

Douro: Vila Real

Latitude / Altitude of WS **41.19° / 1574ft (480m)**
Mean July temperature at WS **70.3°F (21.3°C)**
Average annual rainfall at WS **44in (1,130mm)**
Harvest month rainfall at WS **September: 2.2in (55mm)**
Principal viticultural hazards **Rain during fruit set, drought, erosion**
Principal grapes **Touriga Nacional, Touriga Francesa, Tinto Cão, Tinta Roriz (Tempranillo), Tinta Barroca**

District boundary
Parish boundary
QTA DA FOZ Quinta
Vineyards
Woods
500 Contour interval 100 metres
▼ Weather station (WS)

1:122,500

Km 0   2   4   6 Km
Miles 0   1   2   3   4 Miles

Right One of the many cruise ships from Régua that ply the River Douro, just about to pass the gates to Quinta do Seixo, downstream from Pinhão.

Almeida, little was known about the vines that grew in the Douro, typically a tangled jumble of different bushvines. These two researchers worked out which varieties regularly made the finest port: Touriga Nacional, Tinta Roriz (Spain's Tempranillo), Tinta Barroca, Touriga Francesa, and Tinto Cão. These occupy an increasing proportion of the Douro's now much more disciplined vineyards, but Sousão is also grown in Baixo Corgo, and Tinta Amarela in Cima Corgo.

To make white port – a local favourite – Viozinho, Gouveio, Malvasia, and Rabigato are some of the best light-skinned grapes that yearly do battle with the Douro's baking hot summers and freezing cold winters.

Four of the most interesting table wines *now emerging from the Douro. Redoma is a distinctive wine made by Dirk Niepoort in all three colours. Fojo is a relative newcomer, the top wine of Quinta do Fojo in the Pinhão Valley. Gaivosa and Côtto have slightly longer reputations.*

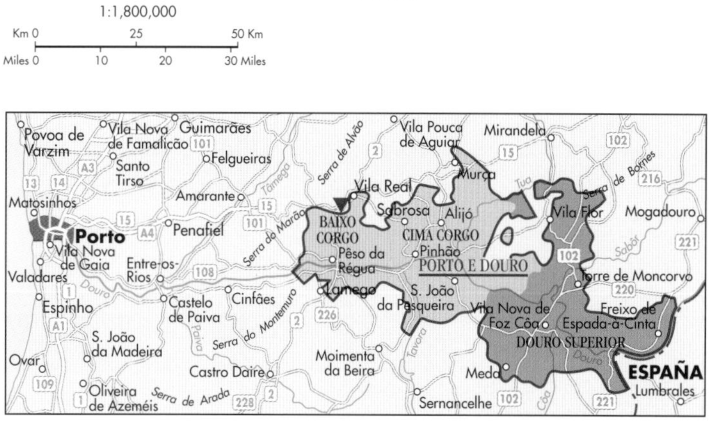

1:1,800,000

Km 0   25   50 Km

Miles 0   10   20   30 Miles

The Port Lodges

If the grapes for port are grown in the savage wilderness of the Douro Valley, most of the wine is still aged in the huddles of shippers' lodges pictured below in Vila Nova de Gaia near the mouth of the river. But before it can be shipped downstream – in the old days by boat and nowadays by rumbling tanker – those grapes must be transformed into the uniquely strong sweet wine that is port (a name protected within Europe).

Port is made by running off partially fermented red wine, while it still contains at least half its grape sugar, into a vessel a quarter full of (often chilled) brandy. The brandy stops the fermentation so that the resulting mixture is both strong and sweet. But the wine also needs the pigmentation of the grape skins to colour it, and their tannin to preserve it. In normal wines these are extracted during the course of fermentation,

but since with port the fermentation is unnaturally short, pigmentation and tannin have to be procured some other way – which traditionally in the Douro means by treading.

Treading is a means of macerating the grape skins in their juice so as to extract all their essences. The naked foot is the perfect tool for this, being warm and doing no damage to the pips, which would make the juice bitter if they were crushed. Rhythmically stamping thigh-deep in the mixture of juice and skins in a broad stone trough (*lagar*) is the traditional treatment for giving port its colour, its grapiness, and its ability to last and improve for many years.

Most port producers, or shippers, have introduced some sort of mechanical substitute for treading, either computer-controlled mechanical paddles or an autovinifier, a specially adapted closed fermenting vat which automatically pumps new wine over the skins. But there are still shippers who feel that the much more expensive old-fashioned treading is best, and still many quintas where it goes on, particularly in the best area, the Cima Corgo (the area mapped on the previous two pages).

After the harsh Douro winter but before the sweltering summer can imbue the port with a character known as "Douro bake", most young port is still shipped downstream, although as the narrow cobbled streets of Vila Nova de Gaia become increasingly choked with traffic, and a reliable electricity supply and therefore air conditioning becomes more of a reality in the Douro, more and more port is being matured upstream.

The city of Oporto and Vila Nova de Gaia across the river are still rich in English influence, with the port trade dominated by English and Anglo-Portuguese families. Oporto's handsome Georgian Factory House has been the meeting place for British port shippers (still, technically, on British soil) for centuries. They meet for lunch here every Wednesday to discuss matters of mutual interest, including the likely vintage of the port served according to strict rules such as being passed only from right to left.

Across the river the port lodges with their dusty stacks of ancient, blackened barrels have much in common with the sherry bodegas. Superior port is matured in barrels called pipes containing 550 to 600 litres (although a pipe as

Below Hoardings on the roofs of the port shippers' lodges in Vila Nova de Gaia face Portugal's second city across the Douro. Oporto (Porto in Portuguese) gave its name to port when the wine was first shipped from here by English merchants in the late 17th century.

a notional unit of commercial measurement is 534 litres), for anything from two to 50 years. The most basic sort of port is matured, briefly, in much bigger vats.

Perhaps three years out of ten conditions are near perfect for port-making. The best wine of these years needs no blending; nothing can improve it except time. It is bottled at two years like red Bordeaux, labelled simply with its shipper's name and the date. This is vintage port, and it is made in tiny quantities; there is never enough of it. Eventually, perhaps after 20 years, it will have a fatness and fragrance, richness and delicacy, which is incomparable.

A great vintage port is incontestably among the world's very best wines. Most other port, from near-vintage standard to merely moderate, goes through a blending process to emerge as a branded wine of a given character. This wine, aged in wood, matures in a different way, more rapidly to something much mellower. A very old wood port is comparatively pale ("tawny" is the term) but particularly smooth. The best aged tawnies, usually labelled 20 years (although other permitted age claims are 10, 30 and Over 40 years), can cost as much as vintage ports; many people prefer their gentleness to the full, fat fieriness which vintage port can keep for decades. Chilled tawny is the standard drink of port shippers.

Ports labelled Colheita (Portuguese for "harvest") are wood-aged ports from a single year, expressive tawnies which are usually drunk as soon as possible after the bottling date, which should appear on the label.

Run-of-the-mill "wood" ports labelled simply Ruby are not kept for nearly so long, nor would such age find any great qualities in them to reveal. (Inexpensive wines labelled Tawny with no indication of age are usually a blend of such young ruby ports with some white port, port made in exactly the same way but from white grapes.) They taste best while they are still fruity with youth, and often fiery, too, with just two or three years as the average age of a blend. France

is the great market for these wines, although port at its roughest and readiest is the big seller wherever port is sold.

Vintage port has disadvantages. It needs keeping for a very long time. And it needs handling with great care. As the making of the wine does not reach its end until after bottling, the sediment forms a "crust" on the side of the bottle: a thin, delicate, dirty-looking veil. If the bottle is moved, other than very gingerly, the crust will break and mix with the wine, so that it has to be filtered out again. In any case the wine must be decanted from its bottle before it is served. A port sold as a crusted or crusting port is a blend of different years bottled early enough to be sure of throwing a heavy sediment in bottle. It is the other port style that demands a decanter.

The more common compromise between vintage and wood port is the extremely varied Late Bottled Vintage (LBV) category – port kept in barrel for four to six years, and bottled once it has rid itself of its crust. This is the modern man's vintage port, being accelerated and cleaned in this way. The most commercial LBVs have nothing like the character of vintage port but the increasing number of more traditional bottlings can deliver some of the exuberant concentration of true vintage port. They are meant to be drunk long before it.

The majority of these labels appear *on vintage port bottles (once stencilled rather than labelled) containing wines that throw a heavy sediment and need decanting, but tawny ports such as Sandeman's and Ferreira's Duque de Bragança can be served straight from the bottle.*

The port lodges of Vila Nova de Gaia

1 Fonseca
2 Graham
3 Smith Woodhouse
4 Churchill
5 Ferreira
6 Niepoort
7 Martinez
8 Cockburn
9 Warre
10 Burmester
11 Quarles Harris
12 Taylor
13 Silva & Cosens (Dow)
14 Delaforce
15 Borges
16 Ramos-Pinto
17 Sandeman
18 Croft
19 Offley Forrester
20 Noval
21 Cálem
22 Osborne
23 Barros
24 Rozès
25 Kopke
26 Wiese & Krohn

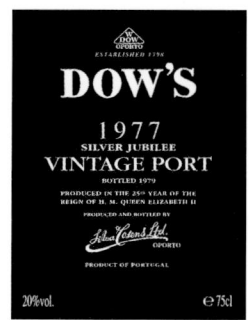
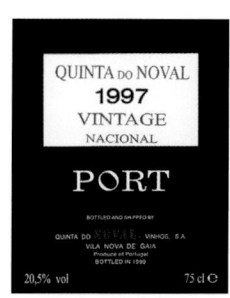
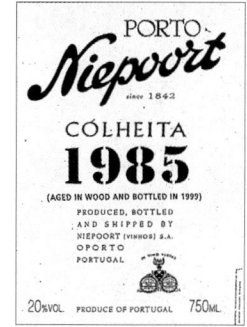
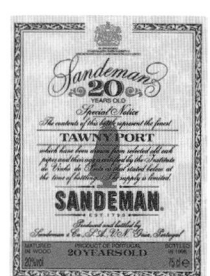

Madeira

The cluster of volcanic islands 400 miles (640km) off the coast of Morocco, which the ancients knew as the Enchanted Isles, are known to us as Madeira, Porto Santo, and the Desertas. Madeira (the only one mapped here) is the largest of the little archipelago and one of the prettiest in the world, as steep as an iceberg and as green as a glade.

The story goes that when the Portuguese landed on the island (in 1420, at Machico in the east) they set fire to the dense woods that gave the island its name. The fire burned for years, leaving the already fertile soil enriched with the ashes of an entire forest.

Certainly it is fertile today. From the water's edge to over halfway up the 6,000ft (1,800m) peak it is steadily terraced to make room for patches of vine, sugarcane, corn, beans, potatoes, bananas, and little flower gardens. As in northern Portugal the vines are grown above head height in arbours, making room for yet more cultivation beneath. Hundreds of miles of *levadas*, little irrigation canals, distribute water from the peaks to the crops.

Wine has been the principal product of the islands for 400 years. Madeira, though, was not the first of the islands the Portuguese planted. From the outset the settlers saw them as an extension of the sweet-wine vineyards of the Mediterranean. The Ottoman Empire was then enveloping the sources of Malmsey: Crete and the Aegean Islands. Porto Santo, low, sandy, and with a North African climate, looked much more promising than tall, green, rainy Madeira.

The settlers planted Porto Santo with the Malvasia grape (which is named after the southern Greek port of Monemvasia), concentrated its sugar in the sun, and found a ready market for the sweet wine that resulted – even at the court of François I of France.

The planting of Madeira itself – with both vines and sugarcane – came later. Settlement of the American colonies meant increased traffic and trade and the bigger island, with its port of Funchal, became the victualling place for westbound ships. Conditions here are very different from those on Porto Santo; rain is rarely far off, especially on the north coast unprotected from the winds off the Atlantic; Malvasia, Verdelho, and the other vines they introduced often struggled to ripen. The marriage of sugar with acid and astringent wines was an obvious expedient.

The sweet-and-sour result was more than adequate as ballast on sailing ships, and an effective anti-scurvy protection into the bargain. It was travelling as ballast that made madeira. A bucket or two of brandy (or cane spirit) fortified it for its long sea voyages. One crossing of the equator would finish off any normal wine, but it was found to mellow madeira wonderfully – and a double equator crossing even more so. In the 18th century it became the favourite wine of the American colonies. Savannah, Georgia, was famous for its madeira merchants and connoisseurs. Bottles of 18th-century madeira, labelled with the name of the ship that brought them, are still kept there, not in cellars but in sunlit rooms – and the wine survives.

Madeira: Funchal

Latitude / Altitude of WS **32.41˚C / 164ft (50m)**
Mean July temperature at WS **70.9˚F (21.6˚C)**
Average annual rainfall at WS **25in (640mm)**
Harvest month rainfall at WS **September: 1.2in (30mm)**
Principal viticultural hazard **Fungal diseases**
Principal grapes **Tinta Negra Mole, Verdelho, Sercial, Malvasia, Bual**

Instead of long hot sea voyages, madeira today is subjected to ordeal by fire. An effect similar to the tropical heat is produced by warming the wine in hot stores (*estufas*) for at least three months to 120°F (45°C). (More moderate temperatures for longer periods are better; best is no artificial heat at all, but many years in a sun-baked loft.) When it comes out it has the faintly caramel tang by which all madeiras can be recognized. Too much of a burnt sugar taste means that the *estufa* was too hot.

Today Madeira shippers blend their wine into consistent brands. The old practice was a solera system like that used for sherry, now disallowed by the EU for wines older than ten years. Some older bottled solera wines are very fine, if you can find them, but the very highest quality of madeira, as of port, has traditionally been the reserve wine of a single vintage – and, in the case of madeira, of a single grape variety.

The double disaster of oidium in the 1850s and phylloxera in the 1870s, then the Russian Revolution and American Prohibition, almost put an end to madeira, caused the closure or amalgamation of many merchant firms, and for

Left Almost all of Madeira's vineyards are in the hands of smallholders quite content to grow Tinta Negra Mole rather than the noble grape varieties. Henriques & Henriques, which has 25 acres (10ha), is one of the very few shippers to own vineyards.

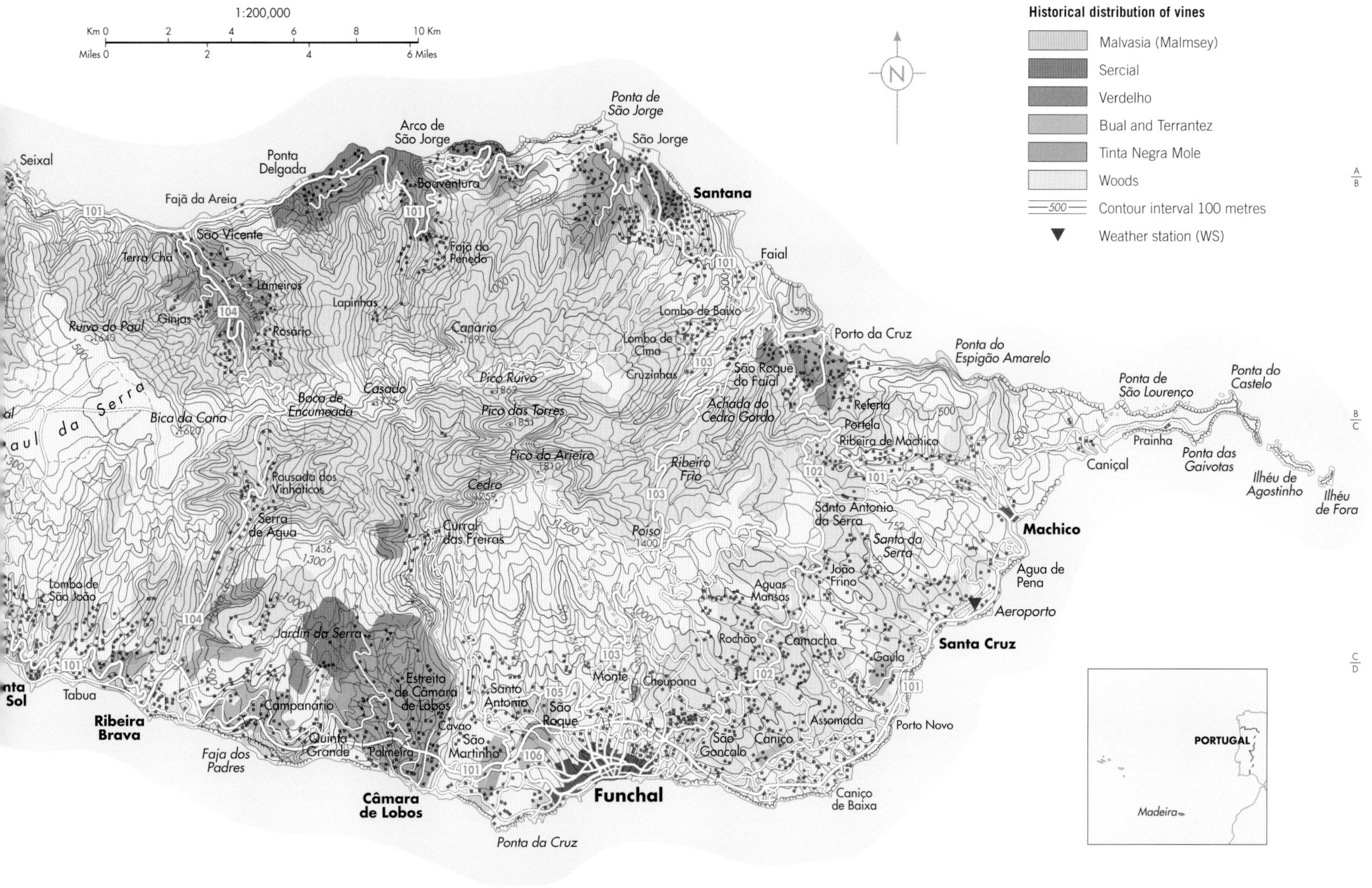

Historical distribution of vines

Malvasia (Malmsey)

Sercial

Verdelho

Bual and Terrantez

Tinta Negra Mole

Woods

—500— Contour interval 100 metres

▼ Weather station (WS)

a long while interrupted the flow of good quality wine. The vineyards were largely turned over to American hybrids (Black Spanish, the chief one, is known in Madeira as Jacquet), while the classic varieties became rarities. The most planted vinifera vine was the Tinta Negra Mole, at best a fair substitute for the vines that made the island's reputation, which today accounts for about 90% of all grapes grown on the island.

The practice until Portugal joined the EU in 1986 was to cite the classic vine varieties of Madeira on labels whether the wine was really made from them or (more likely) not. Today, unless made from one of the traditional varieties, they must be labelled simply according to age (3, 5, 10, and 15 years) and sweetness, controlled by the addition of *vinho surdo* or "deaf wine": grape juice prevented from fermenting at all by the addition of brandy. Today's madeiras are mainly made port-style by stopping the fermentation with spirit.

The traditional grape varieties are associated with a particular level of sweetness. The sweetest of the four, and the earliest-maturing, is Malmsey or Malvasia: dark brown wine, very fragrant and rich, soft textured and almost fatty, but with the sharp tang that all madeiras have. It is the perfect wine to end a rich dinner on an uplifting note (and since madeira is aged in wood rather than bottle, it tends to contain fewer hangover-inducing elements than vintage port).

Bual madeira is lighter and slightly less sweet than Malmsey – but still definitely a dessert wine. A smoky note steals in to modify its richness. Alas the Bual is a rare vine today.

Verdelho (the most planted white grape on the island) is made less sweet and softer than Bual. The faint honey and distinct smoke of its flavour make it good before or after meals.

The tiny plantings of the Sercial (Cerceal on the mainland) vine, which makes the driest wine of Madeira, are in the island's highest vineyards and are harvested late. Sercial wine, the slowest-developing of them all, is light, fragrant, distinctly sharp – unpleasantly astringent young, in fact – but marvellously appetizing old. It is more substantial than a fino sherry, but still a perfect apéritif.

These four varietal names are permitted only if the wine is made from 85% of the variety in question (even the *vinho surdo* is included).

To be labelled Vintage, a madeira must be from a single year, of a single variety, and aged in cask for at least 20 years. In practice the very finest wines may spend a century in the barrel, or decanted into glass demijohns, before being bottled. In bottle they develop at a snail's pace.

Vintage madeira is a wine that age seems unable to exhaust or diminish. The older it is the better it is – and an opened bottle of virtually any good madeira seems to retain its freshness for months.

After Prohibition killed the American market, *shippers had to pool their resources to survive. The top two labels and Blandy's (generally sweeter wines than Cossart Gordon) all belong to the Madeira Wine Company, and hence port shippers Symingtons.*

Germany

Germany's wines are the most misunderstood in the world. Her best vineyards lie as far north as grapes can be persuaded to ripen. Many are on land unfit for normal agriculture: if there were no vines there would be forest and bare mountain. All in all their chances of giving the world's best white wine look slim. And yet on occasion they do, and stamp it with a racy elegance that no-one, anywhere, can imitate.

Their secret is the balance of two decidedly unfashionable ingredients: sugar and acidity. Sugar without acid would be flat; acid without sugar would be sharp. But in good years the two are so finely counterpoised that they have the inevitability of great art. They provide the stage for a stirring fusion of essences from the grape and the ground that is more apparent in German wines than any others because they are far lower in alcohol (another unfashionable trait) and therefore more brilliantly transparent. Thanks to all that acidity, the best also age magnificently – far better than most other white wines.

Germany's sweeter wines are best enjoyed, unlike most wines, alone in all their glory rather than with food. But rather than being seen as a merit, today this is a commercial handicap that has resulted in far drier German wines and has led growers to make many, sometimes all, of their wines completely or almost completely dry and offer them as wines for the table like any others.

Since the vogue for *trocken* (dry) wines began in the early 1980s the genre has advanced from thin productions (a fully dry Mosel Kabinett can be painfully tart) to wines of firm and convincing elegance; principally dry Spätlesen. Yet so far the world at large has not learned to love them. It is a challenge that a new generation of growers is facing vigorously with wines of thrilling vitality. The tragedy is that they are being undercut and demoralized by the ethos of bulk production which is, sadly, sanctioned by their government. A country whose chief ambassador is Liebfraumilch rather than an eloquent exponent of serious wine quality has no place in the competitive international wine marketplace.

But since 1971 German wine law seems almost to have set out deliberately to confuse and even mislead the consumer. The laws were apparently framed for the short-term advantage of growers who overproduce to sell at unsustainably low prices. The result, too much totally undistinguished wine, has been a critical and commercial disaster for German wine as a whole – but especially for the perfectionists (and there are many) who have dazzlingly good wines to offer.

The German wine label (see box), one of the most explicit yet confusing on earth, is both cause and instrument of much of the industry's problems. The most regrettable deception is the existence of Grosslagen, commercially useful, large geographical units whose names are indistinguishable to most wine drinkers from those of Einzellagen, individual vineyards. Take the Rheinhessen village of Nierstein, mapped in detail on page 233. It is blessed with many fine vineyards whose wines are full of fire and character

labelled, for example, Niersteiner Hipping or Niersteiner Pettenthal. But there is a vast Grosslage which includes the much less distinguished produce of 15 villages in the flat hinterland of Nierstein called Niersteiner Gutes Domtal. Oceans of blended semi-sweet blandness are so labelled

Language of the Label

Quality designations

Qualitätswein mit Prädikat (QmP) wines made from the naturally ripest grapes. Germany's best sweet wines are QmP although, depending on the character of the vintage, this category can comprise anything from 7% (1984) to 83% (1976) of the crop. No chaptalization is allowed. The additional Prädikat, or classifications, are in ascending order of ripeness:

Kabinett light, refreshing wines, ideal apéritifs

Spätlese literally "late harvest", meaning riper than Kabinett. Wines can vary from dry and fairly full to sweet and lighter. Can age well

Auslese made from riper grapes, sometimes botrytized, than Spätlese with, usually, some residual sugar. Need ageing

Beerenauslese (BA) rare, sweet wines, made from botrytized grapes (*beeren*)

Eiswein wines from grapes high in sugar and acidity concentrated by being frozen on the vine; less rare than a TBA

Trockenbeerenauslese (TBA) very rare, very sweet, very expensive wines made from hand-picked grapes fully "dried" (*trocken*) on the vine by botrytis

Qualitätswein bestimmter Anbaugebiete (QbA) literally a "quality wine from a designated wine region" but the criteria are ludicrously low in terms of natural ripeness and the wines also routinely chaptalized

Classic new category of dry wines for good everyday drinking made from a single grape variety

Selection top-quality dry wines from a single variety

Landwein Germany's half-hearted answer to Vins de Pays; not a popular designation when QbA is so widely available

Deutscher Tafelwein very small category of the most basic, lightest wine

Other common expressions

Amtliche Prüfungsnummer (AP Nr) every lot of wine has to be officially "tested" and gets this test number; the first digit signifies the test station, last two the year of the test

Erzeugerabfüllung or Gutsabfüllung estate bottled

Halbtrocken medium dry

Trocken dry

Weingut wine estate

Weinkellerei wine cellar or winery

Winzergenossenschaft/Winzerverein wine growers' co-op

every year. The only way the consumer can tell the difference between such a heavily blended bulk product and the painstaking produce of a difficult-to-work single vineyard is by memorizing the names of all Germany's Grosslagen. Our maps clearly distinguish between Grosslagen and Einzellagen.

The Riesling (see page 25) is the great grape of Germany. The great majority of Germany's best wines are made from it, and it is planted to the exclusion of almost everything else in the best sites of the Mosel-Saar-Ruwer, Rheingau, Nahe, and Pfalz (the Palatinate). In a lesser site in a lesser year it stands no chance of ripening.

For larger and less risky production, Germany turned during the mid-20th century to the Müller-Thurgau, a much earlier-ripening, more productive crossing bred in 1882. The wines are bland and lack the lovely backbone of fruity acidity of the Riesling, and in 1996 lovers of fine German wine had the satisfaction of seeing Riesling regain its rightful place as Germany's most planted vine. Nevertheless standard cheap German wines with no mention of the grape on the label can be assumed to be made (at least mainly) from the Müller-Thurgau, which still covers about a fifth of all German vineyard.

Plantings of Silvaner are far behind these two varieties, although it thrives on the best sites in Franken (Franconia), where it makes better wine than Riesling, and can also make some excellent wine in Rheinhessen and Baden.

New crossings, bred especially for ripeness, enjoyed a great vogue in the early 1980s, particularly in Rheinhessen and the Pfalz (which makes some good Scheurebe in ripe years). Two factors have dampened the early enthusiasm for them: their strident, over-obvious flavours, and experience of very cold winters, when they have proved less hardy than the Riesling. This has encouraged Germany's indefatigable vine breeders to incorporate genes from cold-hardy Mongolian vines.

Spätburgunder (Pinot Noir), the commoner Portugieser, the newish crossing Dornfelder, and, in Württemberg, the Trollinger grape, are Germany's increasingly important sources of red wine, although only the valley of the Ahr nearly as far north as Bonn cultivates more red, mainly Spätburgunder, than white.

Until recently German wine law made no attempt to limit yields (which are some of the highest in the world) or to classify vineyards as the French do. Any vineyard in Germany can, in official theory, produce top-class wine. The law

Left Mosel vines (all the best are Riesling) are trained as individuals, each on its own stake, with no wire trellis. They look down on one of the vine's loveliest landscapes: forest on the heights, vineyard on the steep slopes, and the tortuous river winding below.

DANMARK

POLSKA

ČESKÁ REPUBLIKA

NEDERLAND

BELGIQUE

LUX

FRANCE

SCHWEIZ

ÖSTERREICH

SCHLESWIG-HOLSTEIN

MECKLENBURG · VORPOMMERN

NIEDERSACHSEN

NORDRHEIN-WESTFALEN

SACHSEN-ANHALT

BRANDENBURG

HESSEN

THÜRINGEN

SACHSEN

RHEINLAND-PFALZ

SAARLAND

BADEN-WÜRTTEMBERG

BAYERN

Kiel · Hamburg · Schwerin · Bremerhaven · Bremen · Hannover · Berlin · Potsdam · Magdeburg · Halle · Leipzig · Naumburg · Meissen · Dresden · Erfurt · Düsseldorf · Köln · Bonn · Bad Neuenahr · Koblenz · Bad Ems · Cochem · Boppard · Bacharach · Bernkastel-Kues · Bingen · Wiesbaden · Frankfurt · Aschaffenburg · Schweinfurt · Bamberg · Würzburg · Mainz · Alzey · Bad Kreuznach · Worms · Bensheim · Wertheim · Trier · Ludwigshafen · Mannheim · Bad Mergentheim · Neustadt · Heidelberg · Saarbrücken · Landau · Heilbronn · Karlsruhe · Baden-Baden · Stuttgart · Offenburg · Tübingen · Breisach · Freiburg · München · Lorrach · Meersburg · Friedrichshafen

1:3,600,000

Km 0 40 80 120 160 Km
Miles 0 20 40 60 80 100 Miles

— · — · — International boundary
— · · — Landesgrenze (state boundary)
○ Landeshauptstadt (state capital)

Legend:
- Ahr
- Baden
- Franken
- Hessische Bergstrasse
- Mittelrhein
- Mosel-Saar-Ruwer
- Nahe
- Pfalz
- Rheingau
- Rheinhessen
- Saale-Unstrut/Sachsen
- Württemberg

concerns itself instead only with ripeness, or "must weight", the measure of sugar in the grapes at harvest time, outlined on page 26, which crucially decides what will appear on the label (see box).

But nobody truly pretends that all German vineyards are equally well sited, with equally perfect soil. On our detailed maps that small proportion of vineyards we consider consistently superior are clearly indicated in lilac and (best of all) purple. This bold vineyard classification, made in collaboration with Germany's consortium of top-quality growers, the VDP (Verband Deutsches Prädikatsweingüter), local wine organizations and experts, was first published in the previous (1994) edition of this Atlas. As was hoped, it seemed to encourage German officialdom along a tortuous path beset by politics of all sorts towards its own vineyard classifications, although yet again (see page 226) the will to distinguish clearly between the great and the merely serviceable seems to be lacking.

The German government has steadily backed away from what it chooses to call "elitism". The French are not afraid to call it quality.

Mosel

The River Mosel is acquainted with the reflections of vines all the way from its rising in the Vosges Mountains to its union with the Rhine at Koblenz. In France and then Luxembourg it is known as the Moselle. Within Germany the collective name for the wine region made up of all of the very varied vineyards which drain into this most important tributary of the Rhine is Mosel-Saar-Ruwer, in recognition of the Mosel's own two great vinous side-valleys (see opposite and overleaf).

In the Mosel are, cheek by jowl, slope by the flat, the best and worst aspects of German wine. Giant bottling plants devoted to churning out the pap that has earned German wine such a bad name nestle by vineyards whose slope makes them both a source of some of the finest wine in the world and near impossible to work. For only on well-exposed sites will Riesling ripen this far north, so with every twist and turn of this snakelike river comes a dramatic change in vineyard potential. In general all the best sites face south and slope steeply down towards the reflective river. Their harvest-time reflections of golden leaves in the peaceful stream inspired the Roman poet Ausonius in the fourth century AD. He would recognize the vineyards today, if not the dammed and domesticated river.

Although all the great Mosels are made from Riesling, about 40% of the valley's output is blended and sold under a Grosslage name and almost half of all vineyard, the flattest, least promising land, is devoted to other varieties: dreary Müller-Thurgau, tart Elbling or Kerner, one of the better recent crossings. The Mosel-Saar-Ruwer is underpopulated and difficult to work so vineyard area is declining, but it is still Germany's fourth biggest wine region (after Rheinhessen, Pfalz, and Baden).

Most of the great wine is made between Zell and Serrig on those sections mapped in detail on the pages that follow. See pages 222-223 for a description of some of the potentially fine vine-growing sites between Zell and Cochem. Downstream of Cochem a particularly high proportion of Riesling is grown. The same is true of its virtual continuation, the much more patchily planted Mittelrhein region along the banks of the Rhine centred on Koblenz.

Upstream of Trier the rolling farmland is regularly under threat from spring frosts and is almost completely devoted to the hardy, historic, if rustic, Elbling vine. Elbling makes extremely thin, acid wine, both still and (often lightly) sparkling, both in the Obermosel and in Luxembourg across the river. Luxembourg's growers, routine chaptalizers, are even more reliant on Rivaner (Müller-Thurgau) and are increasingly planting such inherently low-acid grapes as Auxerrois.

Right There are no great vineyards on the Mosel without precipitous slopes. The Karthäuserhof is the remains of a Carthusian monastery, today one of the finest estates of the Mosel-Saar-Ruwer. Napoleon confiscated all church lands and sold them to the highest bidders.

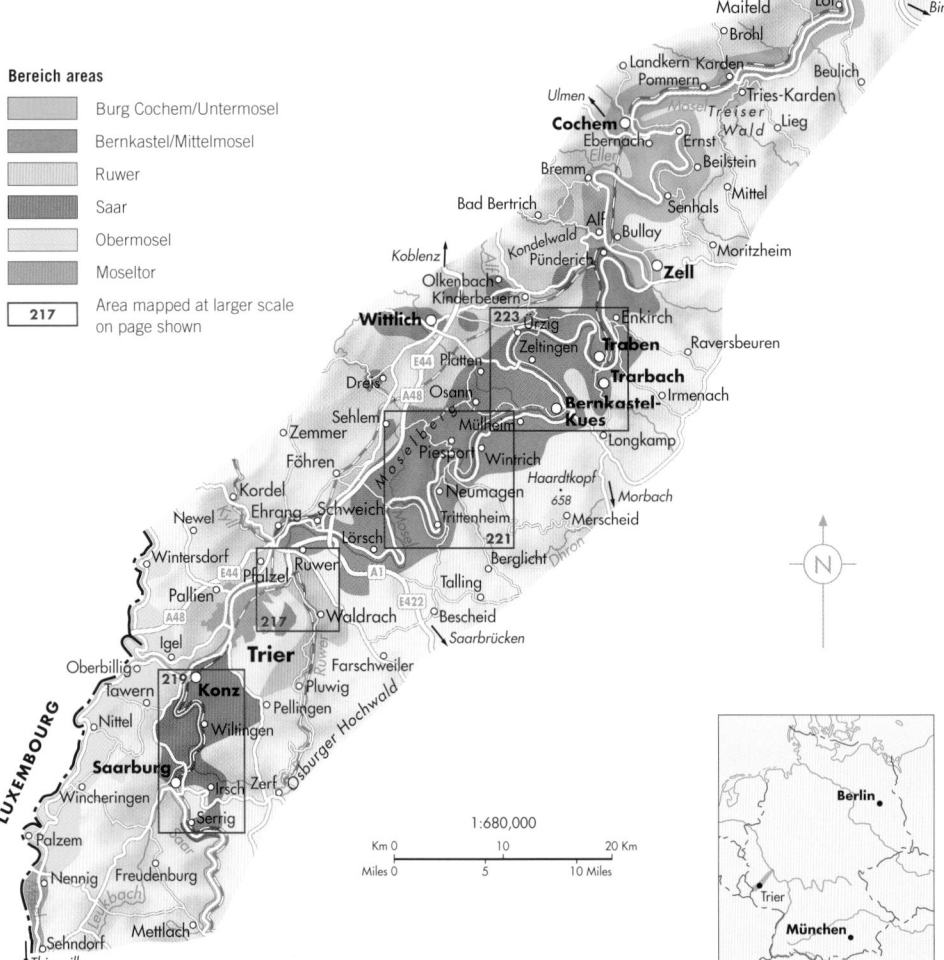

Bereich areas

- Burg Cochem/Untermosel
- Bernkastel/Mittelmosel
- Ruwer
- Saar
- Obermosel
- Moseltor
- 217 Area mapped at larger scale on page shown

1:680,000

Km 0   10   20 Km
Miles 0   5   10 Miles

Ruwer

The Ruwer is a mere stream. Its vineyards add up to about half those of one Côte d'Or commune. There are years when most of its wine is unsatisfactory: faint and sharp. Yet like the Saar, when conditions are right it performs a miracle: its wines are Germany's most delicate; gentle yet infinitely fine and full of subtlety.

Waldrach, the first wine village, makes good light wine but rarely more. Kasel is far more important. The von Kesselstatt estate and the Bischöfliches Weingut of Trier have holdings here. There are great Kaselers in hot years. Unlike so many German wine producers, the great Ruwer estates tend to have a monopoly on the top sites. Karlsmühle of Mertesdorf, for example, are the sole owners of the Lorenzhöfer and can make wines of inspiring precision.

Mertesdorf and Eitelsbach could not be called famous names, but each has one supreme vineyard, owned by one of the world's best winegrowers. In Eitelsbach the Karthäuserhofberg vineyard extends proudly above an old monastic manor of the same name.

Across the stream Mertesdorf's Maximin Grünhaus echoes that situation, set obliquely to the left bank of the river with the manor house, also formerly monastic property, at its foot. The greater part of its hill of vines is called Herrenberg; the top-quality part Abtsberg (for the abbot) and the less-well-sited part Bruderberg (for the brothers). A subterranean aqueduct, still passable by foot, connects the Grünhaus property with Trier, an important wine city with Roman origins, 5 miles (8km) up the Mosel.

Included in the city limits of Trier is the isolated clearing of Avelsbach, belonging to the State Domain and Trier Cathedral, and the famous old Thiergarten. Avelsbach wine is similar to that of the Ruwer: supremely delicate – sometimes even more perfumed and forthcoming.

The city of Trier was the northern *capital of the Roman empire and powerbase of the Emperor Constantine. Several of its great wine estates are charities, some still making use of Roman rock-cut cellars. Karthäuserhofberg (top left) is unique in having only a neck label on its bottle.*

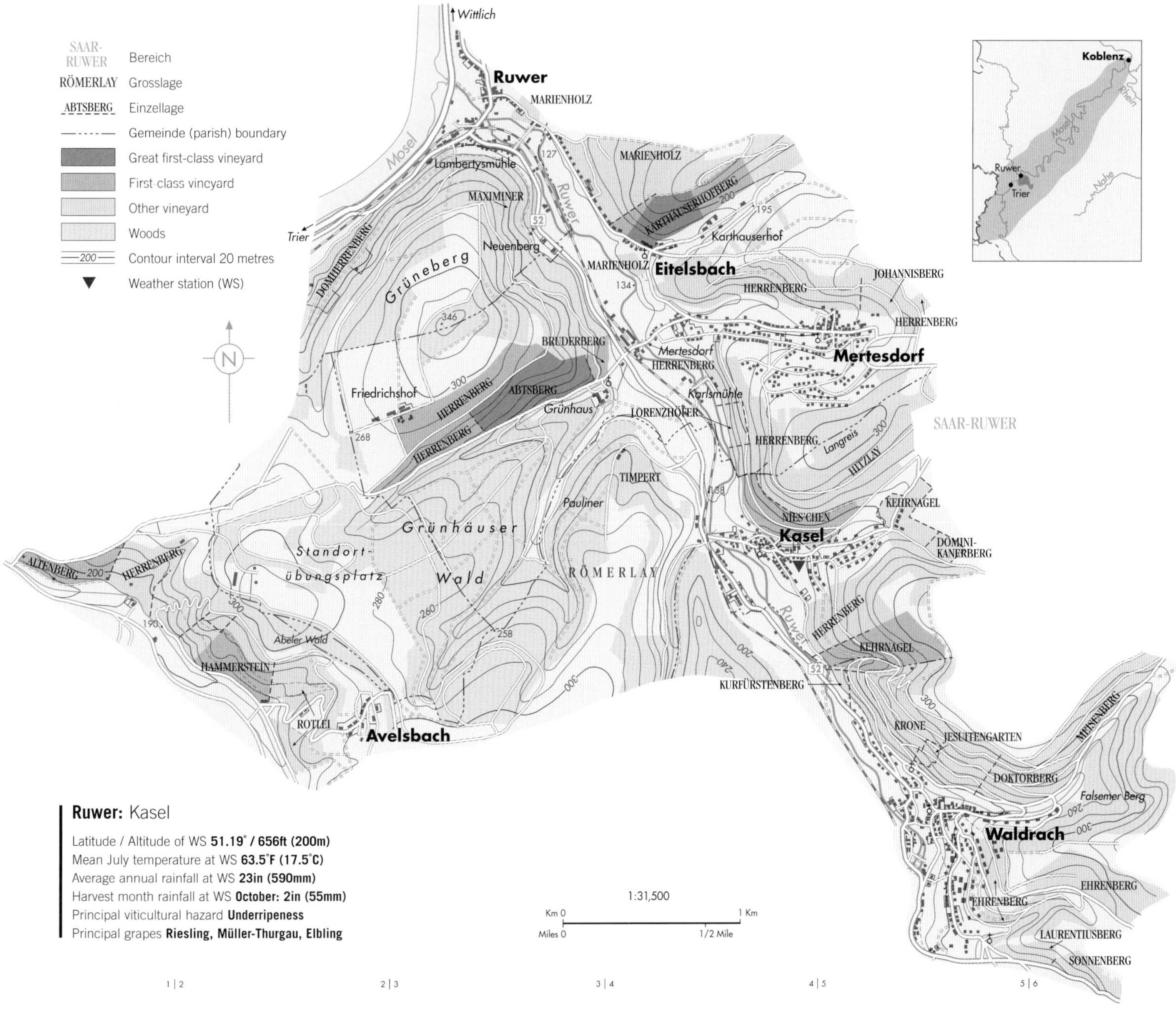

SAAR-RUWER	Bereich
RÖMERLAY	Grosslage
ABTSBERG	Einzellage
---------	Gemeinde (parish) boundary
	Great first-class vineyard
	First-class vineyard
	Other vineyard
	Woods
—200—	Contour interval 20 metres
▼	Weather station (WS)

Ruwer: Kasel

Latitude / Altitude of WS **51.19° / 656ft (200m)**
Mean July temperature at WS **63.5°F (17.5°C)**
Average annual rainfall at WS **23in (590mm)**
Harvest month rainfall at WS **October: 2in (55mm)**
Principal viticultural hazard **Underripeness**
Principal grapes **Riesling, Müller-Thurgau, Elbling**

1:31,500

Km 0   1 Km

Miles 0   1/2 Mile

Saar

German wine, its problems and its triumphs, is epitomized nowhere better than in the valley of the Mosel's tributary, the Saar. The battle for sugar in the grapes rages most fiercely in this cold corner of the country. It is won only perhaps three or four years in ten (the sequence of the 1993, '94, '95, and '97 vintages was exceptional). Yet those years gave one of the world's superlative and inimitable white wines; every mouthful a cause for rejoicing and wonder.

A mere 1,500 acres (600ha) of vines share the valley with orchard and pasture. It is calm, open agricultural country; impossible to believe that only just upstream the blast furnaces of the industrial Saar are at work.

The map opposite shows more clearly than any other the way the south-facing slopes – here nearly all on steep hills sidling up to the river – offer winegrowers the greatest chance of enough winegrowing to reach full ripeness.

As in the best parts of the Mosel, the soil is primarily slate and the grape Riesling. The qualities of Mosel wine – apple-like freshness and bite, a marvellous mingling of honey in the scent and steel in the finish – can find their apogee in Saar wine. If anything, the emphasis here is more on the steel than the honey.

Unsuccessful vintages make wine so sharp that even the best growers can sell their produce only to the makers of sparkling Sekt, who need high acidity in their raw material. But when the sun shines and the Riesling ripens and goes on ripening far into October, even November, the great waft of flowers and honey which it generates would be almost too lush were it not for the rapier-like acidity. Then the Saar comes into its own. It makes sweet wine that you can never tire of: the balance and depth make you sniff and sip and sniff again.

Superlative sites are few. Most are in the hands of rich and ancient estates that can afford to wait for good years and make the most of them. The labels of the principal ones – austere compared with the flowery creations of some parts of Germany – appear opposite. One of the first State Domains was based here, its headquarters in the nearby Roman city of Trier, but it has been broken up.

The most famous estate of the Saar is that of Egon Müller, whose house appears on the map as Scharzhof at the foot of the Scharzhofberg in Wiltingen. Müller's finest are among the world's most expensive white wines. Among the other owners of parts of the Scharzhofberg are von Kesselstatt and Trier Cathedral (Hohe Domkirche), which adds the word Dom before the names of its vineyards. Egon Müller also manages the Le Gallais estate, with the famous Braune Kupp vineyard at the other end of Wiltingen. The top vineyards such as (travelling upstream) Kanzemer Altenberg, Ockfener Bockstein, Ayler Kupp, and Saarburger Rausch are renowned – for their good vintages. The Grosslage name for the whole of the Saar is Scharzberg – almost suspiciously easy to confuse with the great Scharzhofberg.

Many of the Mosel's vineyards, particularly in the Saar, belong to a group of religious and charitable bodies in Trier. The Friedrich-Wilhelm-Gymnasium (Karl Marx's old school), the Bischöfliches Konvikt (a Catholic boarding school), the Bischöfliches Priesterseminar (a college for priests), the Vereinigte Hospitien (an almshouse), and the cathedral are all important winegrowers. The two Bischöfliches and the cathedral operate their total of 260 acres (105ha) of vineyards, here and in the Middle Mosel, together as the Vereinigte Bischöfliches Weingut. In their deep, damp Roman cellars in the city one has the feeling that wine is itself an act of charity rather than mere vulgar trade.

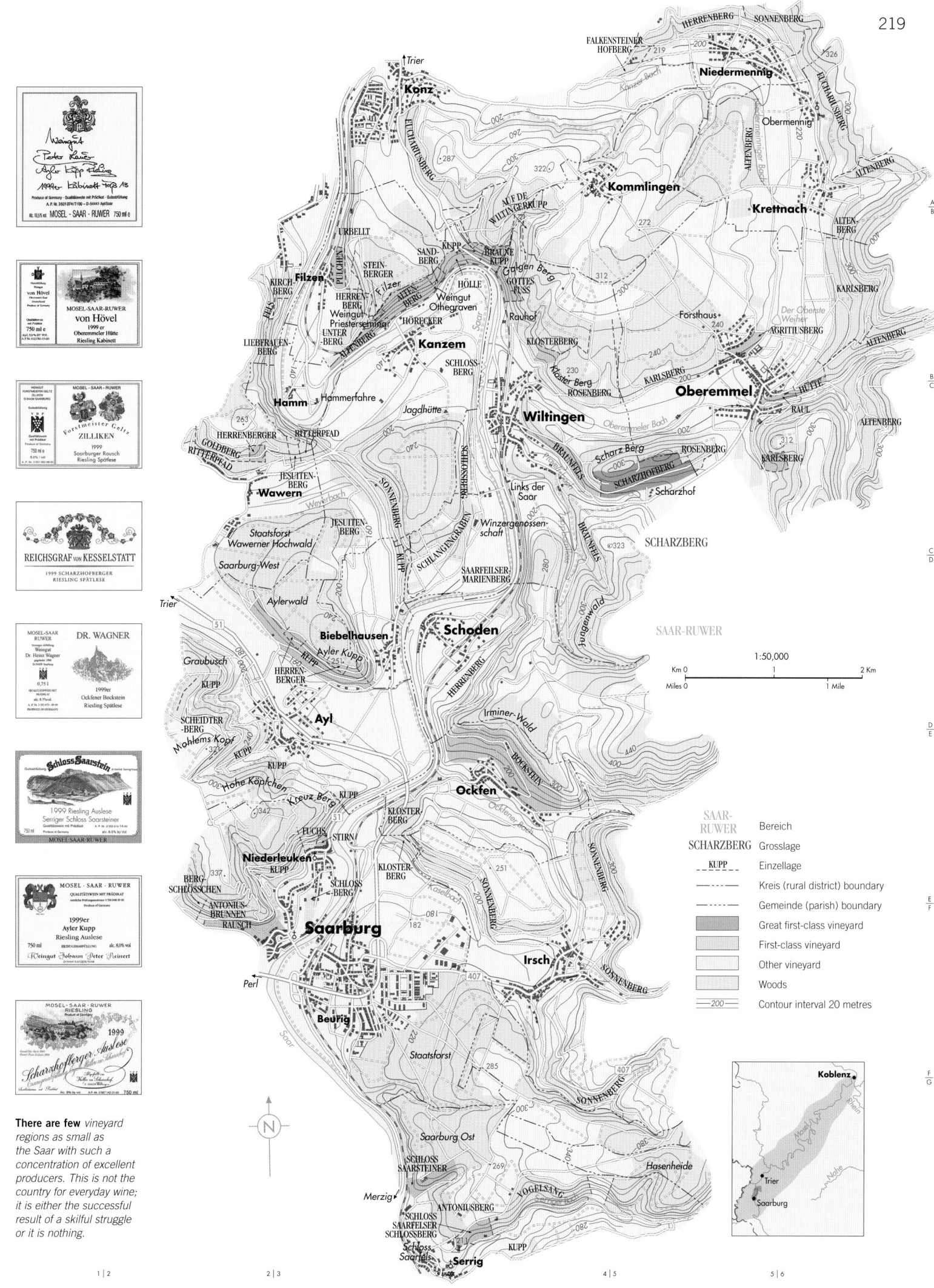

There are few vineyard regions as small as the Saar with such a concentration of excellent producers. This is not the country for everyday wine; it is either the successful result of a skilful struggle or it is nothing.

SAAR-RUWER

SCHARZBERG Grosslage

KUPP Einzellage

SAAR-RUWER Bereich

— — — Kreis (rural district) boundary

— · — · Gemeinde (parish) boundary

Great first-class vineyard

First-class vineyard

Other vineyard

Woods

—200— Contour interval 20 metres

1:50,000

Middle Mosel: Piesport

Only in the central 40 miles (65km) of the Mosel's sinuous meanderings – which take it only half that distance as the crow flies – is the river's greatest wine made, on sites established by the Romans in the 4th century. The spectacular river walls of slate, rising over 700ft (200m) in places, provide perfect conditions for the Riesling vine, introduced here in the 15th century and firmly rooted in the best sites during the 18th.

The wines of the river vary along its banks even more than, say, the wines of Burgundy vary along the Côte d'Or. Given south, southeast or southwest exposure, the steeper the bank the better the wine. It is only because the thin soil here is pure slate, through which rain runs as if through a sieve, that any of it stays in place on near-precipices. The coincidence of fast-drying, stable soil in vineyards that are held up to the sun like toast to a fire is the Mosel's secret.

There is no formal agreement on what constitutes the Mittel (Middle) Mosel. In the maps on these pages we have where possible (for reasons of space) extended it beyond the central and most famous villages to include several whose wine is often underrated.

One obvious candidate is Thörnich, whose Ritsch vineyard has been brought to glorious life by Carl Loewen. Another in this category is Klüsserath just downstream. The Bruderschaft vineyard is immediately typical of a fine Mosel site: a steep bank curving from south to southwest. Then the long tongue of land which ends in Trittenheim is almost a cliff where the village of Leiwen jumps the river to claim the vineyard of Laurentiuslay – of which fine examples abound, thanks to a concentration of ambitious young vintners here. This steep site flattens to only a gentle slope before the bend, the end of the local Grosslage whose name is St Michael.

The best-exposed sites of Trittenheim are Milz's monopolies Felsenkopf and Leiterchen (over the bridge) and the finest section of the Apotheke vineyard. These are the first vineyards of the Mosel, travelling downstream, that have for long made wine of indisputable breed: always delicate but not faint.

The town of Neumagen, a Roman fort and landing place, keeps in its little leafy square a remarkable Roman carving of a Mosel wine ship, laden with barrels and weary galley slaves. The wines of Dhron, its partner, are slightly better known, particularly Dhroner Hofberger on some of the village's steepest slopes.

Piesport has a standing far above its neighbours. It contains the ideal site: a steep amphitheatre facing due south. The name of the slopes flanking the village, Goldtröpfchen, is famous for honeyed wines with magical fragrance and breed, which can, thanks to the particularly deep clay-like slate here, exude almost baroque aromas. Half of the slopes are classified as a great growth, half as a first-class growth. The vast plantation across the river (see

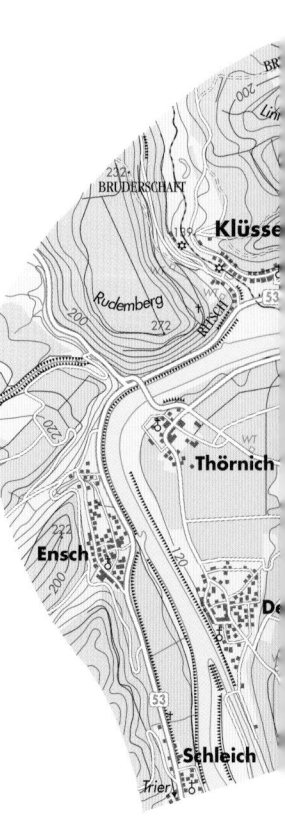

Left The village of Piesport lies at the foot of its glorious crescent of steep vineyards facing the sun. Across the river lies Niederemmel on flat land with slim chance of ripening Riesling grapes. Compare this view with the one on page 8.

photograph) known as Piesporter Treppchen is not close to the same class. By rights, it should go by the village name of Niederemmel.

Michelsberg is the Grosslage name for this part of the river, from Trittenheim to Minheim. "Piesporter Michelsberg", therefore, is not normally Piesporter at all – a typical and all too common example of how German wine law with its Grosslagen misleads the consumer.

Wintrich and Kesten can all make fine wines. But there are no perfectly aligned slopes in this stretch, except for the beginning of the great ramp that rises to its full height opposite the village of Brauneberg. In Kesten it is called Paulinshofberger. In Brauneberg it is the Juffer and Juffer Sonnenuhr, 100 years ago reckoned to be the greatest wine of the Mosel, perfectly satisfying the taste for wine that was full-bodied and golden.

BERNKASTEL	Bereich
ST MICHAEL	Grosslage
HELD	Einzellage
	Kreis (rural district) boundary
	Gemeinde (parish) boundary
	Great first-class vineyard
	First-class vineyard
	Other vineyard
	Woods
200	Contour interval 20 metres

1:50,000

Km 0   1   2 Km
Miles 0   1 Mile

The Kabinett wines of the Mosel (such as that of Fritz Haag) are the lightest high-quality wines on earth. With a mere 7 or 8% alcohol they allow the palate to explore the tension between tartness and the sweetness of golden Riesling. Apples often spring to mind, but no apple has such penetrating length of flavour.

Left Mosel vines, each on its own stake, are pruned to two long canes tied down to make a distinctive heart shape from which the upper buds will break. Each vine needs regular attention, tying-in, and training right through the growing season.

Middle Mosel: Bernkastel

The view from the bridge at Bernkastel is of a green wall of vines 700ft (200m) high and 5 miles (8km) long. Only the Douro, in the whole gazetteer of rivers to which the vine is wedded, has anything approaching a comparable sight.

From Brauneberg to the Bernkastel suburb of Kues many of the hills are relatively gentle. One of the more notable wines produced in this stretch is the Eiswein regularly gathered by Max Ferd. Richter from the Helenenkloster vineyard above Mülheim. The top sites are exceptionally steep, however, in Lieser, a village perhaps best known for the grim mansion formerly owned by the von Schorlemer estate at the foot of the Rosenlay. In the Niederberg-Helden it has a perfect full south slope.

The greatest vineyard of the Mosel starts abruptly, rising almost sheer above the gables of Bernkastel; dark slate frowning at slate. The butt of the hill, its one straight south elevation, is the Doctor – perhaps the most famous vineyard in Germany. From its flank the proudest names of the Mosel follow one another. Comparison of the first-growths of Bernkastel with those of Graach and Wehlen, often with wines from the same growers in each place, is a fascinating game. The trademark of Bernkastel is a touch of flint. Wehleners, grown on shallow stony slate, are rich and filigree while those grown on the deeper, heavier slate of Graach have a more earthy, mineral distinction.

The least of these wines should be something of very obvious personality: pale with a gleam of green and dozens of little bubbles in the bottom of the glass, smelling almost aggressively of grapes, filling and seeming to coat the mouth with sharpness, sweetness, and scent.

The greatest of them, long-lived, pale gold, piquant, profound yet frivolous, are wines that beg to be compared with music and poetry.

But the name of Bernkastel is used for very much more wine than her slopes can grow. The law allows it without shame; Bereich Bernkastel is a possible name for any QbA wine from the Middle Mosel. And Bernkastel has two Grosslage names: Badstube (exclusive to its five best sites) and Kurfürstlay, available to vineyards as far off as Brauneberg and Wintrich. The law pretends to believe that such niceties are likely to be remembered.

Zeltingen brings the Great Wall to an end. It is the Mosel's biggest wine commune, and among its best. At Urzig, across the river, red slate, in rocky pockets instead of a smooth bank, gives the Würzgarten (spice garden) wines a different flavour, more penetrating and racy than Zeltingers. Erden's finest vineyard, the Prälat, is probably the warmest in the entire Mosel Valley, sandwiched between massive and precipitous red slate cliffs and the river. Wines from the Treppchen vineyard are usually more austere. Lösnich and Kinheim begin a decline.

In Lösnich and Kinheim the contour lines are wider apart; though this is all heavily planted, largely with Riesling, the high drama is at an end. This is not to say that highly enjoyable, fresh and fragrant wines are not found in the many growers' cellars and on their flowery summer terraces. For relaxed wine tourism few places on earth beat the Mosel Valley, from Trier right down to Koblenz where it meets the Rhine.

Traben-Trarbach is one community. The wines of Trarbach are well-known. Enkirch, particularly those of its Batterieberg, deserve to be.

The Middle Mosel ends just downstream from here at Zell, famous for the undistinguished wines of its Grosslage Schwarze Katz (the eminently illustratable black cat). At this point the landscape changes dramatically, with most of the vineyards planted on narrow terraces, inspiring this lower section of the Mosel Valley's relatively

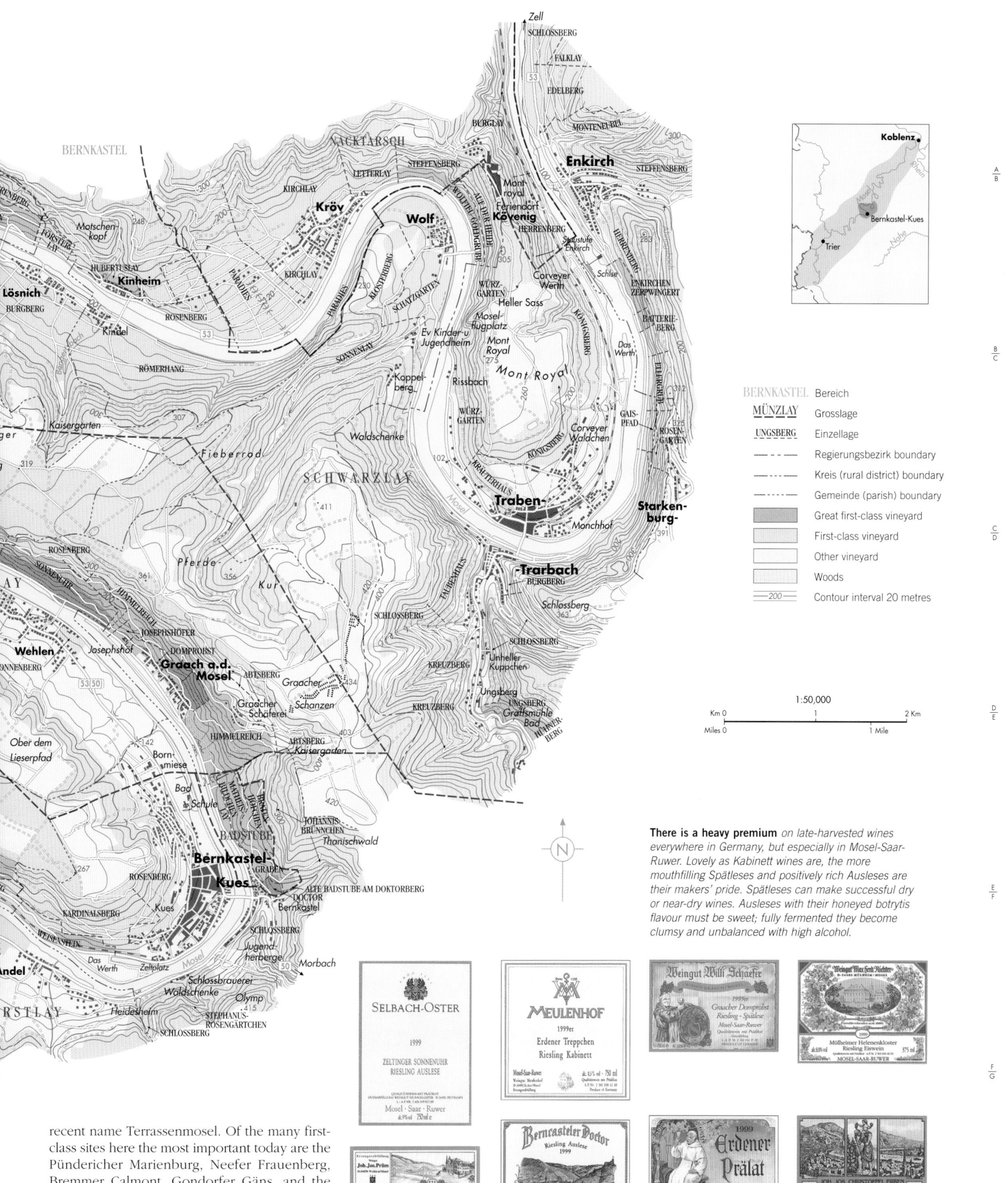

Koblenz

Bernkastel-Kues

Trier

BERNKASTEL Bereich
MÜNZLAY Grosslage
UNGSBERG Einzellage
– – – – Regierungsbezirk boundary
——— Kreis (rural district) boundary
– – – Gemeinde (parish) boundary
▓▓ Great first-class vineyard
▒▒ First-class vineyard
░░ Other vineyard
▒▒ Woods
—200— Contour interval 20 metres

1:50,000

Km 0   1   2 Km
Miles 0   1 Mile

There is a heavy premium *on late-harvested wines everywhere in Germany, but especially in Mosel-Saar-Ruwer. Lovely as Kabinett wines are, the more mouthfilling Spätleses and positively rich Ausleses are their makers' pride. Spätleses can make successful dry or near-dry wines. Ausleses with their honeyed botrytis flavour must be sweet; fully fermented they become clumsy and unbalanced with high alcohol.*

recent name Terrassenmosel. Of the many first-class sites here the most important today are the Pündericher Marienburg, Neefer Frauenberg, Bremmer Calmont, Gondorfer Gäns, and the Uhlen (a great site) and Röttgen of Winningen. Heymann-Löwenstein makes superb dry versions of the fuller, earlier-maturing wines made here.

1 | 2   2 | 3   3 | 4   4 | 5   5 | 6

Nahe

Nahe wine seems to capture all the qualities best loved in German wine. It is very clean and grapey, with all the intensity and life expectancy of the Riesling, like a good Mosel or Saar wine. At the same time it has some of the full flavour that in the Rheingau at its best evokes the alchemist's shop, as though rare minerals were dissolved in it, possibly gold itself.

The River Nahe, flowing north out of the Hunsrück hills to join the Rhine at Bingen, is surrounded by scattered outbreaks of wine-growing where either its own banks or its tributaries' face south. But at the Rotenfels cliffs, immediately above the Traiser Bastei vineyard, a range of hills rears up along the north bank, and there are all the makings of a great vineyard.

Bad Kreuznach is the wine capital of the Nahe. It is a pleasant spa, with a casino and rows of strange brushwood erections down which salt water is poured to produce ozone for the benefit of convalescents.

Bad Kreuznach itself has some of the Nahe's best vineyards: the Kahlenberg, Krötenpfuhl, and Brückes sites, facing south over the town, can make exceptional wine. The whole Bereich, or region, right down to the Rhine at Bingen, is known simply as Nahetal. In the Upper Nahe the commune of Schlossböckelheim includes the Grosslage Burgweg while the Kronenberg Grosslage is north of Bad Kreuznach.

Upstream of the Bad Münster bend the red precipice of the Rotenfels, said to be the highest

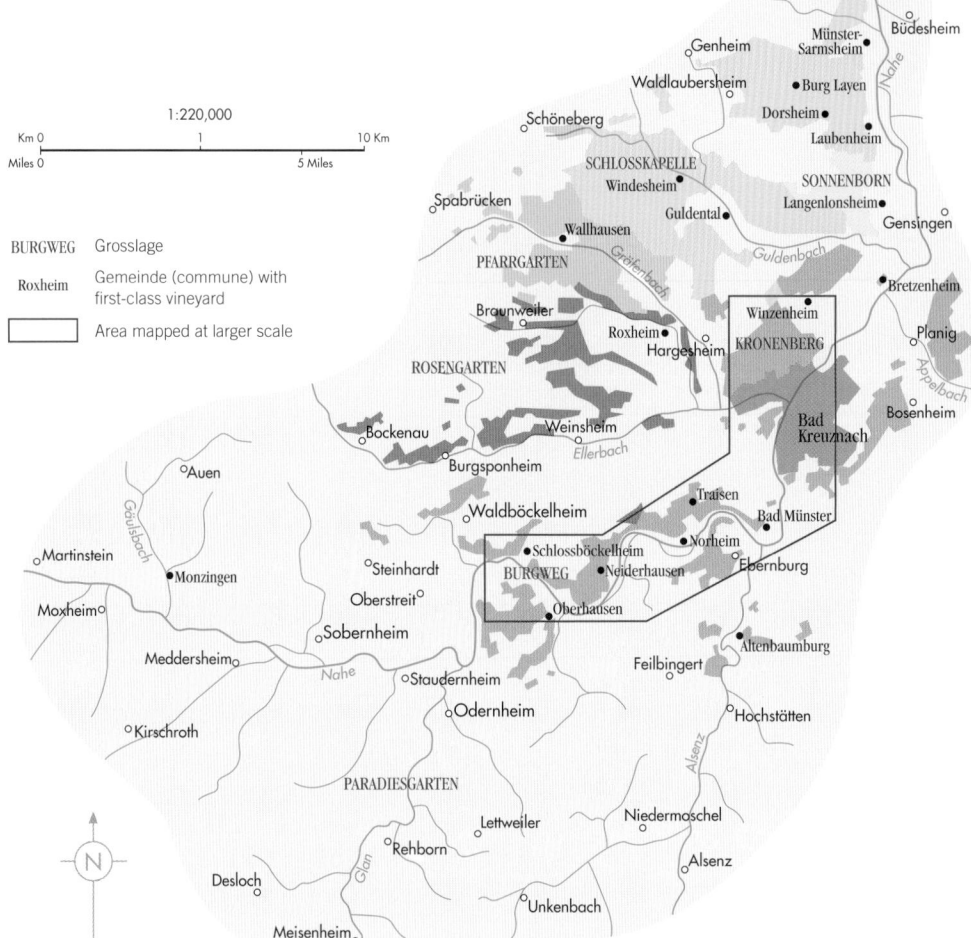

1:220,000

Km 0   1   10 Km
Miles 0   5 Miles

BURGWEG	Grosslage
Roxheim	Gemeinde (commune) with first-class vineyard
▢	Area mapped at larger scale

Left Looking west from Bad Münster to the next bend of the Nahe, where the river has carved out a cliff 650ft (200m) high. The crumbled rock at its foot is the Bastei vineyard, famous for ripe, deeply mineral-charactered wine.

cliff in Europe north of the Alps, blocks the river's path. At the cliff-foot there is a bare 100ft (30m) of fallen rubble, a short ramp of red earth. The vines are planted thick in the cramped space, enjoying ideal soil, and a virtual suntrap. This is the Traiser Bastei. The degree of spice and fire in a Bastei of a good year is exceptional for such a northerly vineyard. It can be reminiscent of great Pfalz wine, with the freshness and finesse of the Saar thrown in.

From this bend on upstream is a succession of fine slopes, through the villages of Norheim and Niederhausen, to the Nahe's most illustrious vineyard, the Niederhäuser Hermannshöhle. It

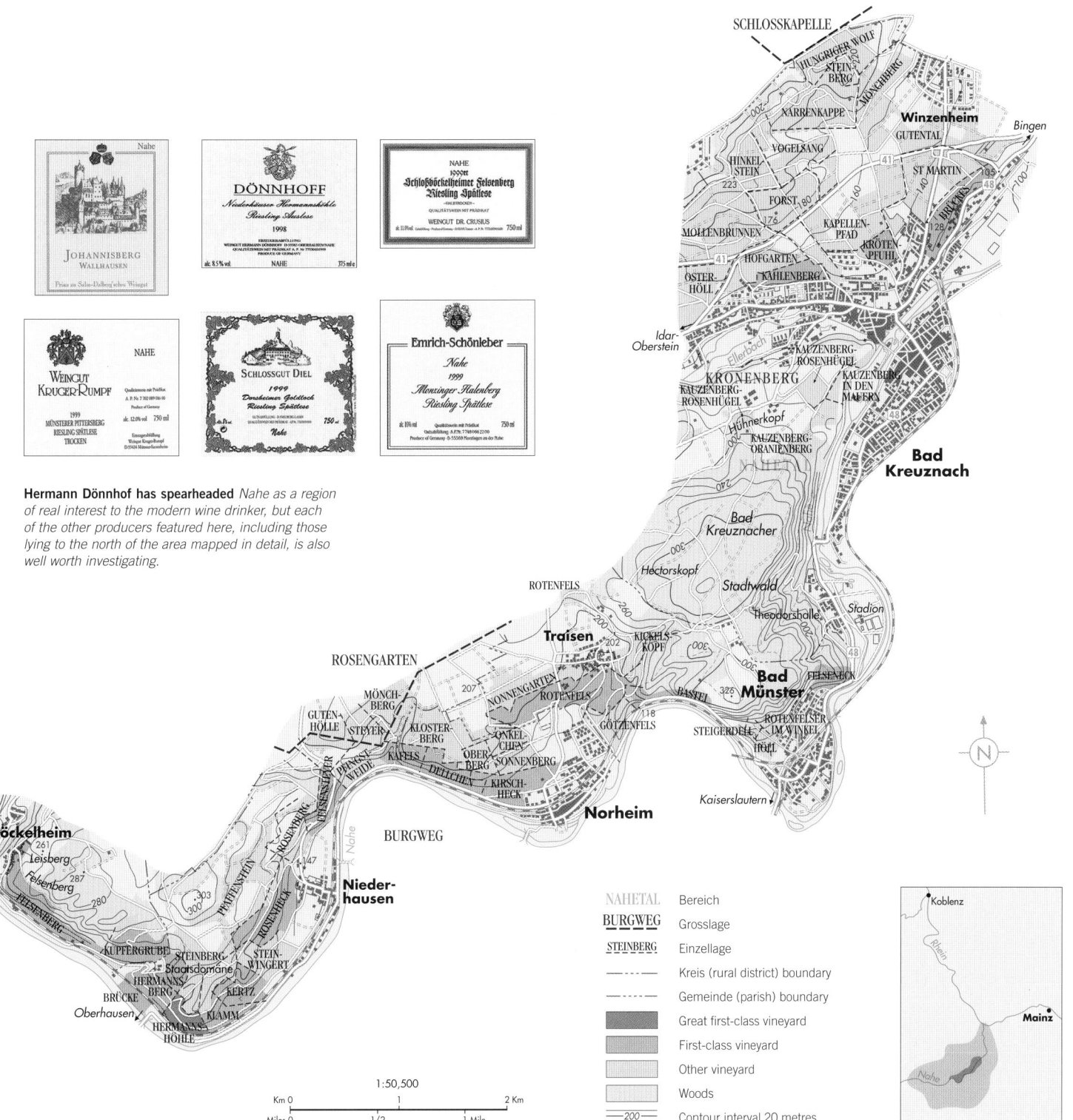

Hermann Dönnhof has spearheaded *Nahe as a region of real interest to the modern wine drinker, but each of the other producers featured here, including those lying to the north of the area mapped in detail, is also well worth investigating.*

NAHETAL — Bereich
BURGWEG — Grosslage
STEINBERG — Einzellage
------- Kreis (rural district) boundary
------- Gemeinde (parish) boundary
Great first-class vineyard
First-class vineyard
Other vineyard
Woods
200 Contour interval 20 metres

1:50,500

Km 0 — 1 — 2 Km
Miles 0 — 1/2 — 1 Mile

was rated first in the Royal Prussian Surveyor's classification of the Nahe's vineyards published in map form in 1901. This was a decisive development for the region's wine industry, encouraging the Prussian government to establish a new Domain here the following year. Scrub-covered arid hillsides and old copper mines were cleared using convict labour to create several new vineyard sites, including the towering walls and terraced vineyards of the Schlossböckelheimer Kupfergrube (copper mine). Since then its wines have challenged those of the long-established Felsenberg for Schlossböckelheim supremacy.

From the 1920s the Nahe State Domain and several large estates based in Bad Kreuznach but with vineyards here produced wines of a brilliance and pungent minerality as spectacular as the rocky landscape. At last, in 1930, the Nahe was recognized as an independent wine-growing region, but the fame of the top growers was always greater than that of the region itself. From the late 1980s the State Domain failed to play the leading role for which it was established and is now, as Gutsverwaltung Niederhausen-Schlossböckelheim, in private hands. The once-great estates of Bad Kreuznach have also fallen by the wayside, selling many of

their vineyard possessions here. The major beneficiary of this turmoil has been the exceptional Hermann Dönnhof estate of Oberhausen which has assumed the dominant role.

Upstream of the area mapped in detail is Monzingen, with two first-class vineyards in Halenberg and Frühlingsplätzchen. The broad valley here yields comparatively gentle Rieslings. Downstream towards the Rhine a series of side-valleys from the west give fine south-facing slopes to the wine villages marked on the map opposite. Armin Diel of Schlossgut Diel and Prinz Salm of Schloss Wallhausen are two of the leading growers of an increasingly vibrant district.

Rheingau

If the Rhine is one of the world's great wine rivers, it was historically the Rheingau that represented it most majestically. Alas, the crown of great wine achievement seems to have been ceded to the Pfalz, even though, or perhaps because, the potential of the Rheingau is so startlingly obvious. For almost all its length the Rhine flows steadily northwest, except for the point just below Mainz where the high forested Taunus Mountains stand in its way. It turns southwest for only 20 miles (32km) until it reaches the Rüdesheimer Berg. There, with a flurry of rocks and rapids, it forces a passage northwards again, leaving behind a perfectly tilted, south-facing bank of vineyards.

This western end of the Rheingau is mapped below, where the Rüdesheimer Berg Schlossberg, by far the Rheingau's steepest slope, drops almost sheer to the river. The eastern end is mapped on the opposite page and the classical central section overleaf.

A new vineyard classification of the Rheingau was essayed in 2000, although the fact that it rated 35% of all the vineyards as superior (as compared with just 3% Grands Crus and 11% Premiers Crus in the Côte d'Or) left it as limp and flabby as the wines that have so damaged Germany's vinous reputation abroad.

Unlike other Rhine wine regions, the Rheingau depends almost exclusively on Riesling, as the Middle Mosel does. The climate is comparatively dry and sunny. The river's presence makes for equable temperatures and, they say, gives extra sunlight by reflection off its surface. The river is more than half a mile (800m) wide here, a throbbing highway for slow strings of enormous black barges.

The Rheingau style of wine should be the noblest in Germany, uniting the flowery scent of

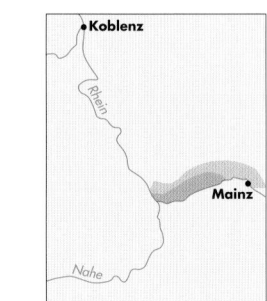

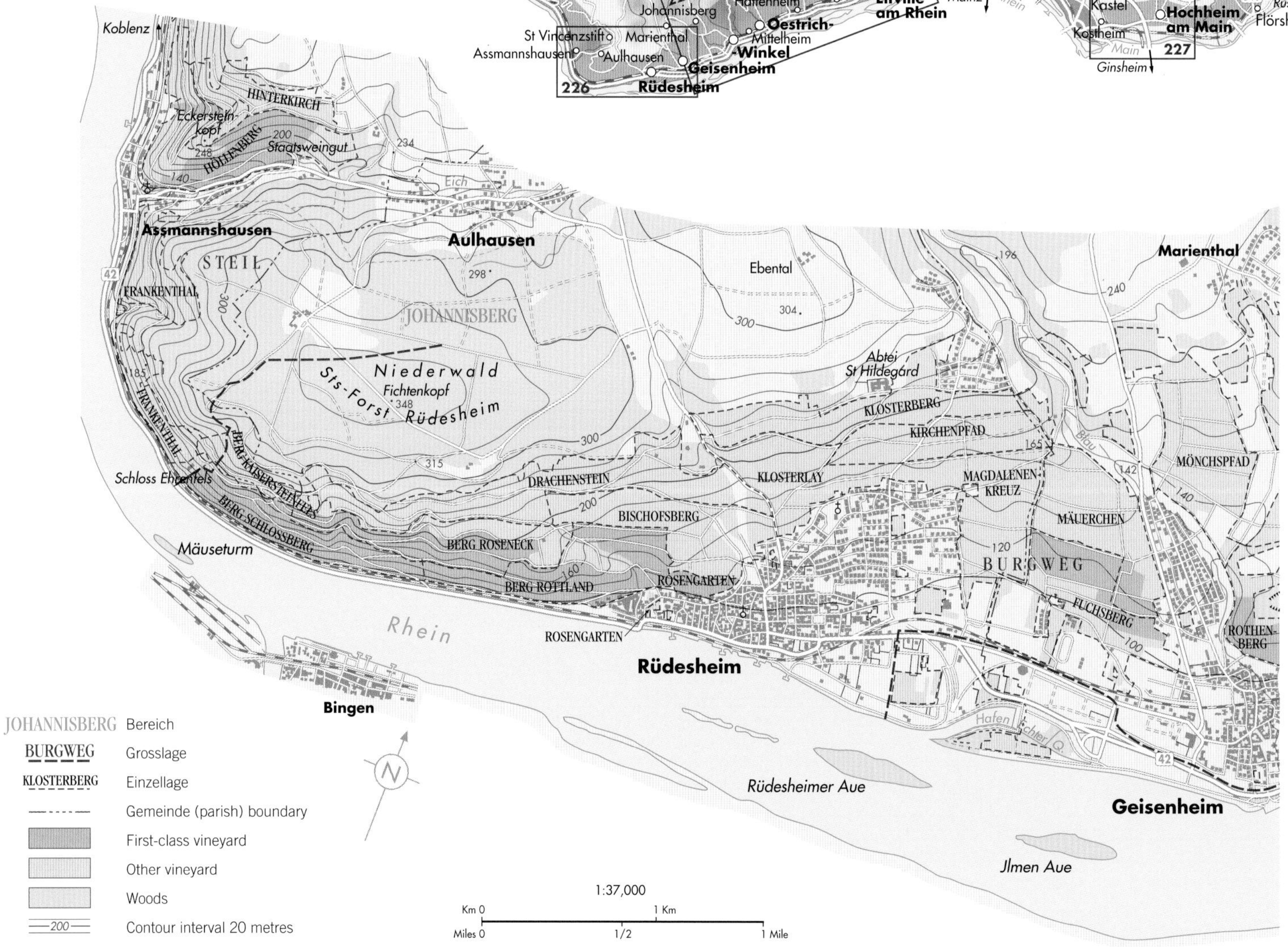

▨	Bereich Johannisberg
226	Area mapped at larger scale on page shown
▼	Weather station (WS) *See overleaf for factfile*

1:377,000

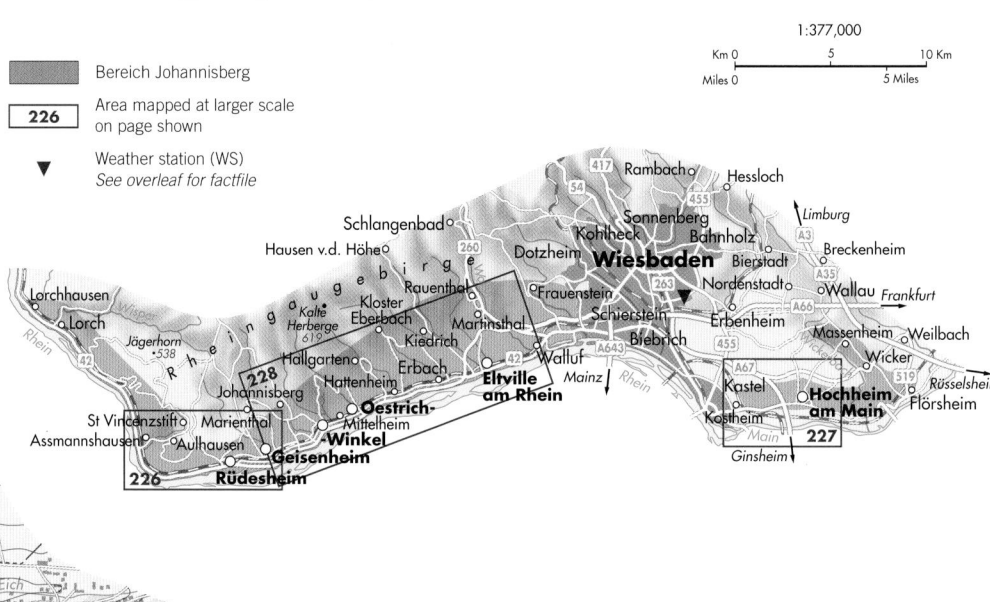

JOHANNISBERG Bereich
BURGWEG Grosslage
KLOSTERBERG Einzellage
------ Gemeinde (parish) boundary
▨ First-class vineyard
▨ Other vineyard
▨ Woods
—200— Contour interval 20 metres

1:37,000

the Riesling with a greater and more golden depth of flavour than the Mosel. Its character is bolder, more mineral. Soft and charming are words you should never hear in the Rheingau.

Assmannshausen is the westernmost town mapped. It lies around the corner from the main Rheingau and is an exception to all the region's rules, being famous only for its fashionable red wine made from Spätburgunder (Pinot Noir) grapes. Ambitious, cosmopolitan growers such as August Kesseler have revolutionized the colour and structure of such wines, from pale and suspiciously smoky to deep and sturdy. Dry red Assmannshäuser is the country's most famous red wine. Its pink Trockenbeerenauslesen, made only rarely, cost fortunes.

The Rüdesheimer Berg is distinguished from the rest of the parish by having the word Berg before each separate vineyard name. At their best (which is not always in the hottest years, since the drainage is too good at times) these are superlative wines, full of fruit and strength and yet delicate in nuance. In hotter years the vineyards behind the town come into their own.

The wine school of Geisenheim, just east of Rüdesheim, is one of the most famous centres of wine learning, especially cool climate viticultural research, in the world.

Nearly 18.5 miles (30km) east of Rüdesheim, the other side of sprawling Wiesbaden from the vineyards mapped overleaf, the Rheingau has an unexpected outpost: Hochheim. Hochheim vineyards (which gave us the word hock) lie on gently sloping land just north of the warming River Main, isolated in country that has no other vines. Good Hochheimers match the quality of the best Rheingauers, and style of those of Nackenheim-Nierstein in Rheinhessen, with their own thrilling full-bodied earthiness, thanks to deep soils and an unusually warm mesoclimate. Growers such as Franz Künstler and Domdechant Werner have injected new life into a region previously most readily associated with Queen Victoria, whose visit to the source of wines notably popular with her subjects is commemorated by the Königin Victoriaberg vineyard and label. Kirchenstück grows the most elegant wines while Hölle and Domdechaney produce wines so rich they are distinctly atypical of the Rheingau's elegant signature.

Above The Höllenberg vineyard at Assmannshausen looks down on the lively town and the Rhine, Germany's great commercial highway. The slopes opposite, not so blessed by sunshine, are abandoned to dense woodland.

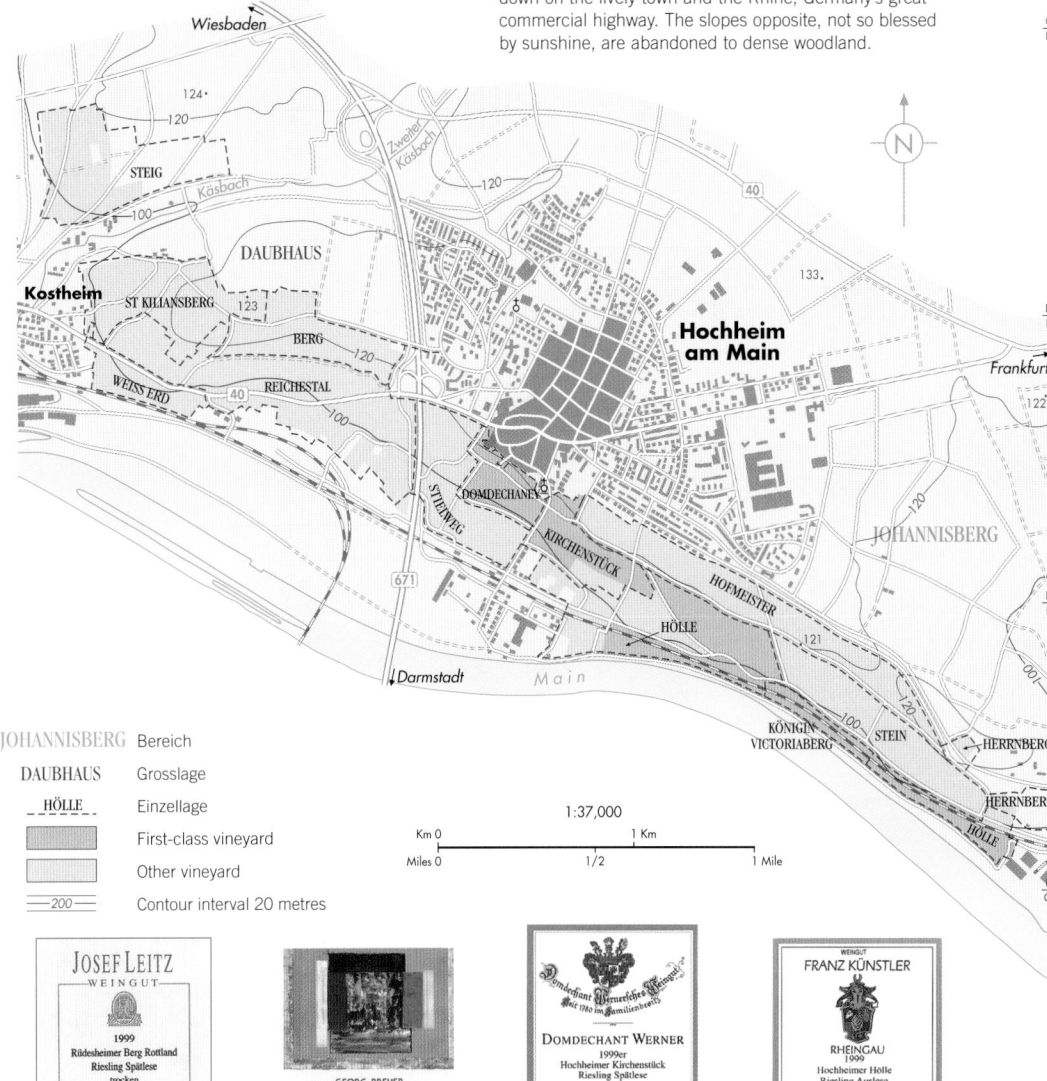

The three labels starting *second from the left are top examples of the full-bodied wines of the Rüdesheim Berg, an area to watch in vintages of high acidity, when its wines can have the structure of immortality. The two far right labels represent the best of Hochheim, and the far left is a notable example of Germany's most famous red wine.*

JOHANNISBERG Bereich

DAUBHAUS Grosslage

HÖLLE Einzellage

First-class vineyard

Other vineyard

200 Contour interval 20 metres

1:37,000

Km 0 ... 1 Km
Miles 0 ... 1/2 ... 1 Mile

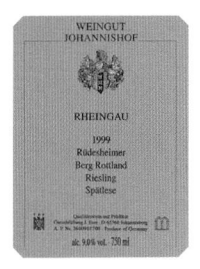

JOHANNISBERG Bereich
GOTTESTHAL Grosslage
KLOSTERBERG Einzellage
– – – – – Gemeinde (parish) boundary
First-class vineyard
Other vineyard
Woods
200 Contour interval 20 metres

For location map see page 226

Rheingau: Wiesbaden (see page 226)
Latitude/Altitude of WS **50.02° / 459ft (140m)**
Mean July temperature at WS **66°F (18.9°C)**
Average annual rainfall at WS **19in (490mm)**
Harvest month rainfall at WS **October: 1.4in (35mm)**
Principal viticultural hazards **Underripeness, fungal diseases**
Principal grapes **Riesling, Spätburgunder**

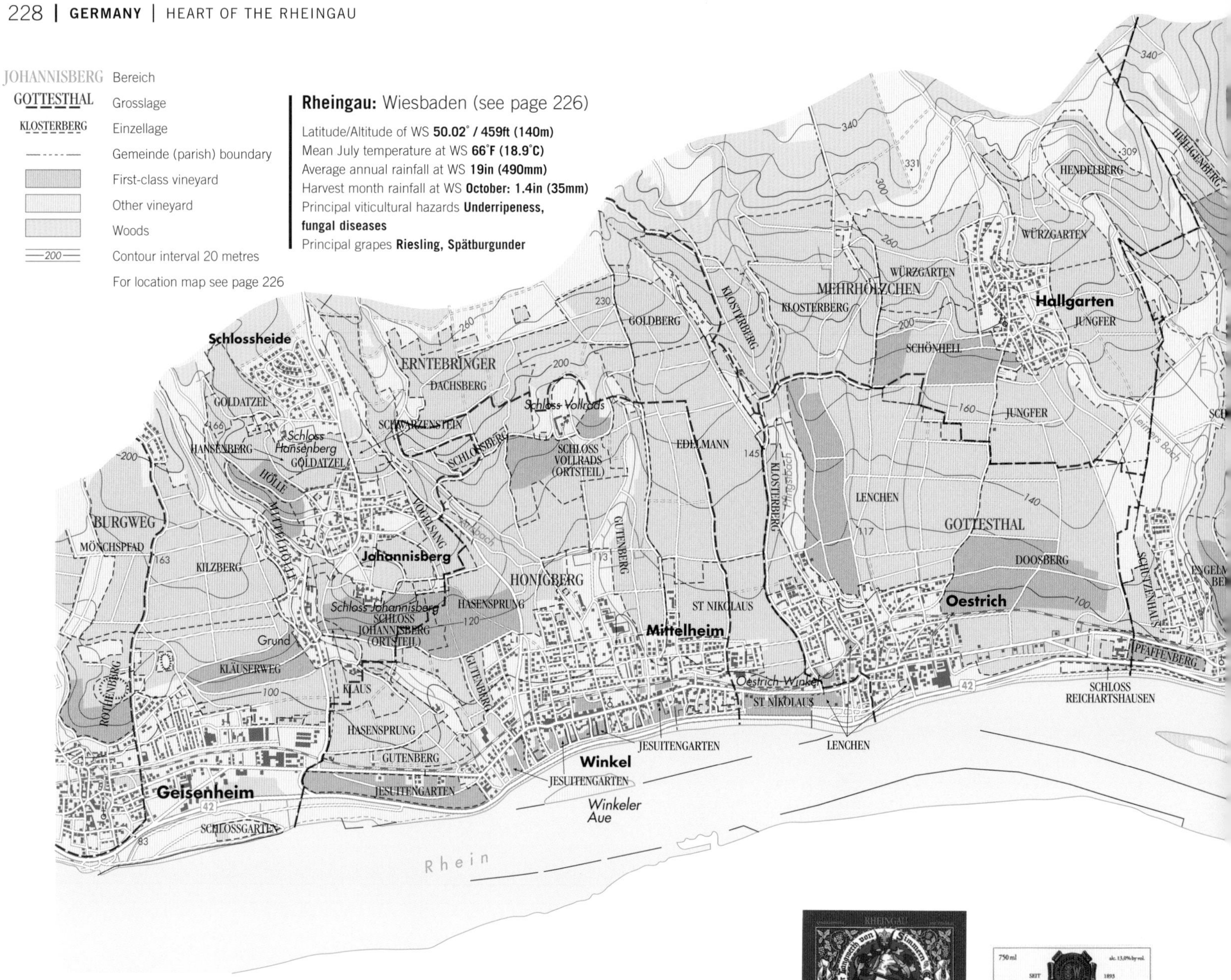

Heart of the Rheingau

This broad stretch of south-facing vineyards, sheltered to the north by hills of the Taunus and warmed to the south by reflection from the broad River Rhine, is the classical focus of fine German wine production. The river promotes the mists that encourage botrytis as the grapes ripen. Decidedly mixed soils include various forms of slate and quartzite as well as marls, which make the Rheingau rather more Burgundian than Germany's other Riesling areas.

The entire Rheingau region was given the Bereich name of Johannisberg, its most famous single parish, in 1971. Thus might all the Médoc be allowed to use the name Margaux. But in the west of this section Schloss Johannisberg, standing above a great apron of vines, dominates the landscape between Geisenheim and Winkel. It is credited with the introduction in the 18th century of nobly rotten, sweet rarities to Germany, even if its wines no longer overshadow neighbours such as the Johannishof estate.

Schloss Vollrads is another magnificent and historic property whose wines have recently failed to reach their full potential. The estate stands more than a mile (2km) back from Winkel and leaves the name of the town off its label – unfortunately for Winkel, whose name would otherwise be better known than it is. Even its second-best site, Hasensprung (hare's leap), is capable of richly nuanced, aromatic wine.

Mittelheim has little identity as distinct from the more important Winkel and Oestrich. Its name does not appear on any wine of special note. There are those who say the same about Oestrich. Oestrichers have been criticized for lack of breed, but character and lusciousness they certainly have. Doosberg and Lenchen are not names to be dismissed.

In Hallgarten the Rheingau vineyards reach their highest point. In the Würzgarten and Schönhell there is marly soil that gives strong, long-lived wines; but no single vineyard makes the village name world famous.

The boundaries of Hattenheim stretch straight back into the hills to include the high ridge of the Steinberg, enclosed like the Clos de Vougeot by a Cistercian wall. Below in a wooded hollow stands the old monastery which might fairly be called the headquarters of German wine, Kloster Eberbach. The place and the implications of continuous industry and devotion to one idea of beauty going back 600 years make any comment seem trivial. Today Kloster Eberbach is the base of the German Wine Academy, which tries to educate the world about German wine.

Like Hallgarten, Hattenheim has marl in the soil. On its border with Erbach is the only site that makes great wine right down by the river, in a situation that looks as though the drainage would be far from perfect. In Hattenheim this is called Mannberg; in Erbach Marcobrunn. Wine from either side of the parish boundary is very full flavoured, and often rich, fruity, and spicy. Marcobrunn, heavily influenced by marl, is every inch the great growth in the right hands, and Nussbrunnen and Wisselbrunnen are capable of producing wines just as good. The principal owner of Mannberg is Baron Langwerth von

The map shows the Heart of the Rheingau region with the following labelled places and vineyards:

Bad Schwalbach, Kloster Eberbach, Honig Berg, KLOSTER BERG, Am Hahnwald, Kloster Tiefenthal, **Rauenthal**, LANGENSTÜCK, Bübenhauser Höhe, Hagelplatz, WASSEROS, GRÄFEN BERG, **Kiedrich**, LANGENSTÜCK, *Rauenthaler Berg*, NONNEN BERG, **Martinsthal**, **Eichberg**, KLOSTERBERG, GEHRN, WÜLFEN, ROTHENBERG, LANGENBERG, Wachholderhof, WASSEROS, Staatsweingut, WILDSAU, EINZELLAGEFREI, TAUBENBERG, RÖDCHEN, OBERBERG, HONIGBERG, **HEILIGENSTOCK**, SANDGRUB, TAUBENBERG, STEINMÄCHER, BERG-BILDSTOCK, HEILIGENBERG, KALBSPELICHT, LANGEN-STÜCK, **Oberwalluf**, *Wiesbaden*, HASSEL, MICHELMARK, SANDGRUB, GÖTTESACKER, NUSSBRUNNEN, HOHENRAIN, TAUBEN-BERG, SONNENBERG, WALKENBERG, WISSEL-BRUNNEN, MICHELMARK, STEINMORGEN, VITUSBERG, Steinheimer Hof, VITUSBERG, **Walluf**, MANNBERG, SIEGELSBERG, **Erbach**, SONNENBERG, MARCOBRUNN, RHEINGARTEN, SCHLOSSBERG, STEINMORGEN, Hof Drais, RHEIN-BERG, **JOHANNISBERG**, Schloss Rheinhartshausen, **Eltville am Rhein**, Weinbauschule, RHEINGARTEN, RHEINHELL, RHEINHELL, Marianenaue, *Rhein*

1:37,000 — Km 0 ... 1 ... 2 Km / Miles 0 ... 1 Mile

Many Rheingau labels *have the nostalgic charm of designs unaltered for a century or more; a mark of the confidence and self-esteem of the region. Burgundy's Côte d'Or is the nearest parallel. But Burgundy has found its feet in the modern wine world, while the Rheingau has drifted below its magnificent potential. The six producers here are currently among the leaders.*

Simmern; of Marcobrunn Schloss Schönborn, Schloss Rheinhartshausen, the State Domain, and the Knyphausen estate.

Erbacher Siegelsberg, which lies parallel with Marcobrunn, is next in quality. In Erbach the town's land goes back into the hills in a long narrow strip: good vineyards, but not the best.

Kiedrich's beautiful Gothic church is the next landmark. The vineyards of the village make exceptionally well-balanced and delicately spicy wine. Robert Weil (now Japanese-owned) is the biggest Kiedrich-based estate and today makes the Rheingau's most sumptuous wines. Gräfenberg is reckoned the best part of the vineyard, although Wasseros is almost its equal.

The wines that fetch the high prices, and by which the vineyards are ultimately judged, have traditionally been the late-picked, sweet and intense botrytized Beerenauslesen and Trockenbeerenauslesen which demand to be drunk with conscious attention, and on their own rather than with food. The leaders of the modern Rheingau, however, have deliberately moved away from this tradition: about two-thirds of their wine is now made dry. The Charta organization of top growers leads the way with dry wines of Spätlese quality and low yields.

Rauenthal, the last of the hill villages and the furthest from the river, can make a different kind of superlative wine. The complex Rauenthalers of Bernhard Breuer are some of the most sought-after in Germany. The Auslesen of the State Domain and of two lordly growers, Baron Langwerth von Simmern and Count Schönborn, as well as those of several smaller growers on the Rauenthaler Berg, are prized for the combination of power and delicacy in their flowery scent and in their spicy aftertaste.

Eltville makes larger quantities of wine but without the supreme cachet. The town is the headquarters of the State Domain, whose wines (especially Steinbergers) have in the past been and should be among the best.

Without the fame of their neighbours, Walluf and Martinsthal share much of their quality. At Walluf the stars are JB Becker and Toni Jost.

Above Schloss Johannisberg is the symbol of the Rheingau, visible for miles across the river above its spreading apron of vines. This is where late-picked Spätlese was first officially recorded in Germany in 1775.

Pfalz

The Pfalz (once called Palatinate in English) is Germany's biggest and today perhaps most exciting vineyard; a 50-mile (80-km) stretch north of Alsace, under the lee of the German continuation of the Vosges Mountains – the Haardt.

Like Alsace, it is the sunniest and driest part of its country, and has the never-failing charm of half-timbered villages among orchards, seeming part of a better, sunlit, half-fairytale world. A labyrinthine road, the Deutsche Weinstrasse, like the Route du Vin of Alsace, starts at the gates of Germany (literally: there is a massive gateway on the border at Schweigen) and winds northwards through vines and villages. A great part of the wine of the area (Südliche Weinstrasse is its Bereich name) is made by efficient co-operatives which have revolutionized casual old country methods and made the district famous as a source of good-value wine.

Riesling is the most planted vine here, with Müller-Thurgau in second place, but a rich mix of other varieties make up 60% of the region's vines. The Pfalz is Germany's workshop for a range of whites and reds of every complexion, including the whole Pinot family, with the emphasis on dry wines for the table, even using small barrels for ageing in the modern style. Pinot in all three colours (Weissburgunder, Grauburgunder, and Spätburgunder), with and without oak influence, are increasingly popular.

Neustadt an der Weinstrasse used to mark a sharp dividing line between country wines of little pretension to the south and a very different world: the Mittelhaardt, where some of Germany's biggest and most famous estates were well-established in the luxury and export markets. In the Mittelhaardt, the name given to the short string of little townships mapped in detail opposite, Riesling is particularly important. Historically three famous producers have dominated this, the kernel of the Pfalz: Bürklin-Wolf, von Bassermann-Jordan, and von Buhl. But any monopoly of quality they ever had has disappeared in a surge of ambitious and original winemaking on all sides. Today truly exciting wines throbbing with fruit come from producers such as Rebholz as far south as Siebeldingen and Müller-Catoir of Neustadt-Haardt.

Mittelhaardt wine's special quality is succulent richness balanced with thrilling acidity – even when, as often today, it is finished *trocken* or *halbtrocken*. It is far removed from the steely nerve of, say, Saar wine, and has more alcohol.

The Einzellagen on the hilly west side of the villages are the ones that most often attain the

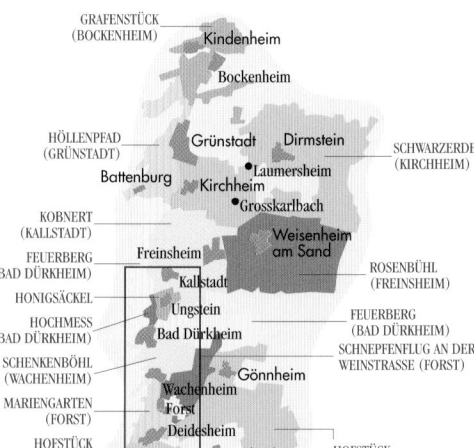

Above The Haardt mountains stretching south of Neustadt an der Weinstrasse are less of a sheltering wall than in the Mittelhaardt. Here, near Siebeldingen, the vineyards climb the lower slopes in conditions favourable to a wide range of grape varieties, stimulating profitable experiments.

The traditional Pfalz label was much given to stately coats of arms. The trend here today is to emphasize the site-name ("Gaisböhl", "Hohenmorgen") before that of the commune ("Ruppertsberg", "Deidesheim"). It is logical: the vineyard, not the political entity, is what distinguishes the quality.

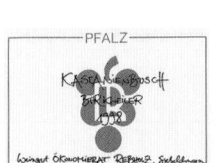

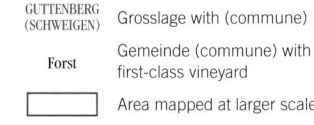

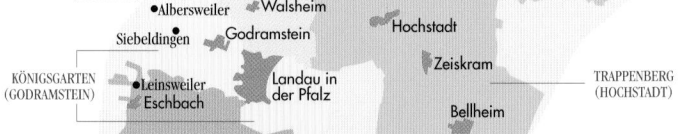
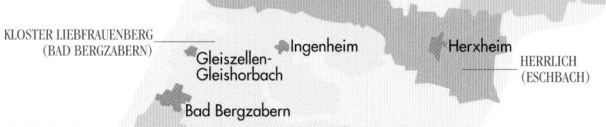

summits of succulence. In the south, Ruppertsberg is one of the first villages of the Mittelhaardt; its best sites (Linsenbusch, Hoheburg, Reiterpfad, Nussbien, Spiess) are all on moderate slopes, well exposed, and largely Riesling.

Forst has a reputation as the source of the country's most succulent wine (not in mere sugar – it is frequently made as a dry Spätlese – but in style and character). A black basalt outcrop above the village provides dark warm soil, rich in potassium, which is quarried and spread on other vineyards, notably in Deidesheim. The Jesuitengarten, Forst's most famous vineyard, and the equally fine Kirchenstück lie just behind the church. Freundstück (largely Reichsrat von Buhl's) and, above it, part of Ungeheuer are in the same class.

Historically Forst was respected as the finest wine village of the Pfalz, with its top sites – Kirchenstück, then Jesuitengarten – most highly rated in the classification of 1828. More recently the larger village of Deidesheim to the south has been rated by many the best village of the whole area, besides being one of the prettiest in Germany. (This is unrivalled geranium and window box country.) Von Bassermann-Jordan and von Buhl have their cellars here. Hohenmorgen, Langenmorgen, Leinhöhle, Kalkofen, Kieselberg, and Grainhübel are the top vineyards.

The village of Wachenheim, where Bürklin-Wolf is based, marks the end of the historic kernel of the Mittelhaardt with a cluster of famous small vineyards. Belz, Rechbächel, Goldbächel, Pechstein, and Gerümpel are the first growths. Richness is not a marked characteristic of Wachenheim; its great quality is finely poised sweetness and purity of flavour.

Bad Dürkheim is the biggest wine commune in Germany, with 2,000 vineyard acres (800ha). A Wurstmarkt (fair) is held here before the vintage. There is red Dürkheimer (often made from the popular, relatively new Dornfelder grape) to drink with the sausages as well as white. Riesling is in the minority except in the best sites of Herrenberg and Spielberg.

From here north we are in the Unterhaardt, whose most celebrated parishes are Kallstadt and Ungstein. Kobnert and Honigsäckel are the respective Grosslage names for their best sites. Their first growths are Saumagen, planted in what was a Roman chalkpit, and Annaberg, famous for rich Scheurebe. But the outstanding wines are now found well north of what was once considered this firm line. In short, fine, often fiery wine is now made all over this dynamic region.

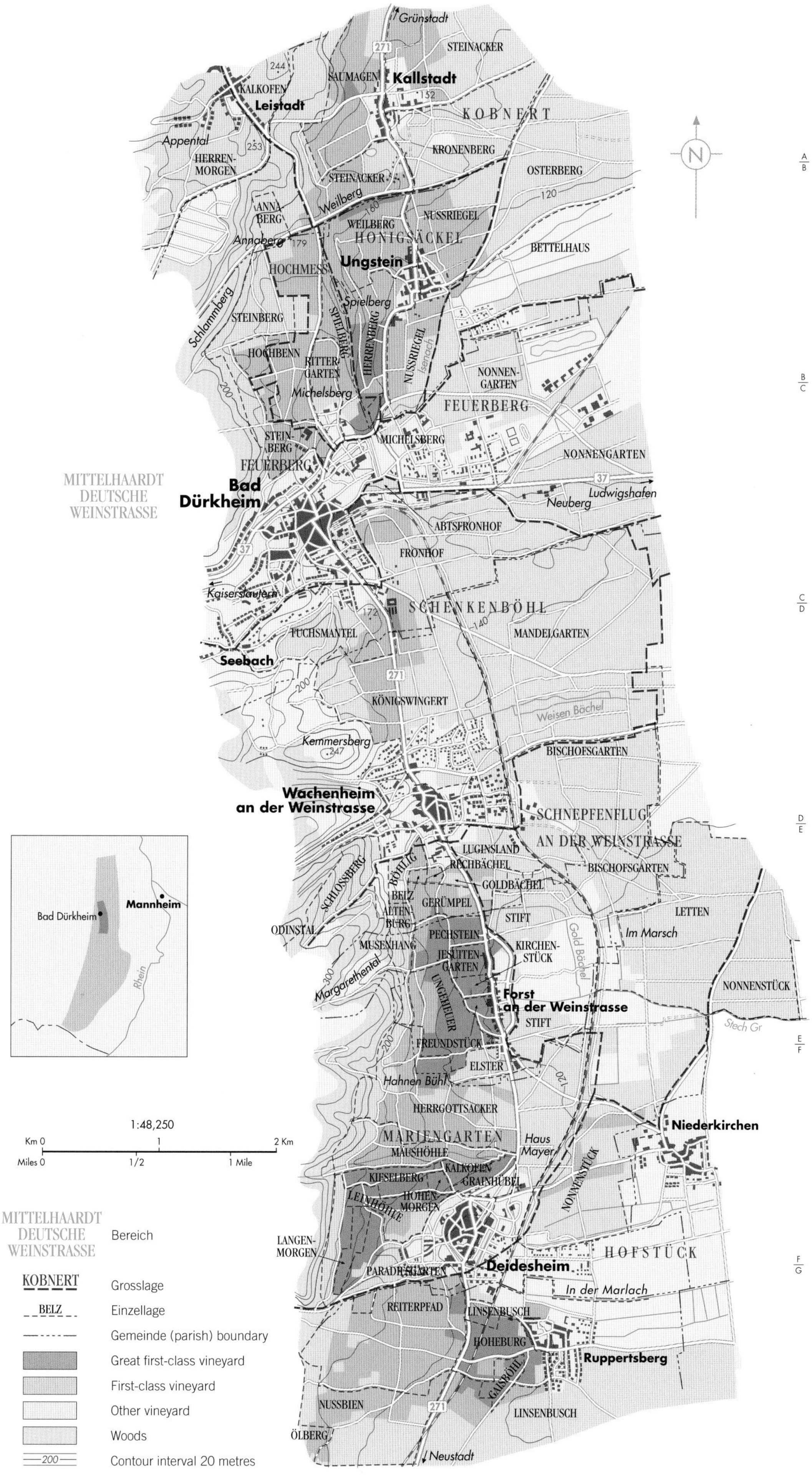

1:48,250

Km 0 ———— 1 ———— 2 Km

Miles 0 ———— 1/2 ———— 1 Mile

MITTELHAARDT
DEUTSCHE
WEINSTRASSE

MITTELHAARDT DEUTSCHE WEINSTRASSE	Bereich
KOBNERT	Grosslage
BELZ	Einzellage
– – – –	Gemeinde (parish) boundary
▓	Great first-class vineyard
▒	First-class vineyard
░	Other vineyard
▒	Woods
—200—	Contour interval 20 metres

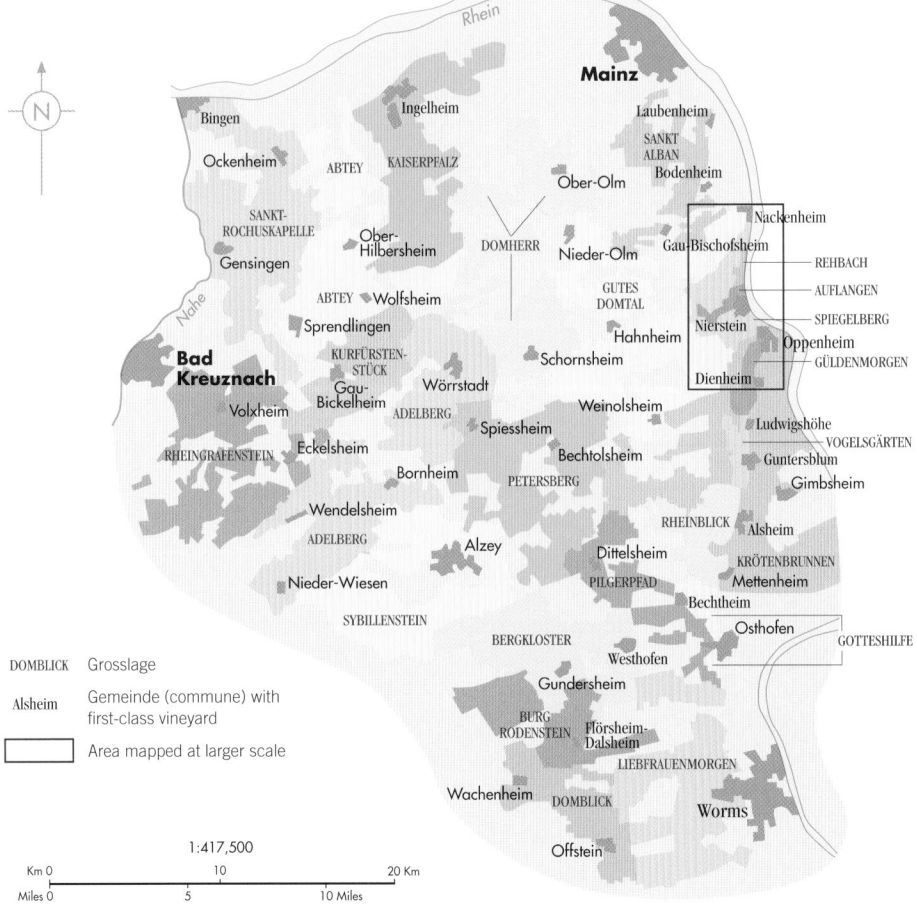

Rheinhessen

Germany's most extensive wine region, Rheinhessen, lies in the crook of the Rhine hemmed in by the river on the east and north, the Nahe on the west and the Pfalz to the south. The city of Mainz, which hosts a great annual wine fair, is its main centre of activity. The 150-odd Rheinhessen villages, spaced out over an area 20 by 30 miles (30 by 50km) and all apparently some sort of "heim", grow wine along with other crops. It is dull, undulating, fertile, mixed-farming country, without exceptional character except where the Rhine flows by, carving steep slopes for terraced vineyards.

The bulk of Rheinhessen wine, made from Müller-Thurgau or Silvaner, is equally unexceptional; light, soft, usually sweetish but sometimes dry, earthy and vigorous enough to claim attention.

Much of the blander stuff finds its outlet as Liebfraumilch. This is now legally defined as a Qualitätswein (QbA) from Rheinhessen, Pfalz, Nahe or Rheingau; it contains at least 70% Riesling, Silvaner, Kerner or, most usually, Müller-Thurgau and has a minimum of 18g/l of residual sugar (the maximum for a *halbtrocken* wine). Liebfraumilch can be expected to be mild and semi-sweet and is made strictly for export. The locals are far more interested in dry wines, increasingly in dry Silvaners, which can be very satisfying, and a wide range of finely etched flavours from some of the most fastidious wine-growers in Germany.

DOMBLICK — Grosslage

Alsheim — Gemeinde (commune) with first-class vineyard

☐ Area mapped at larger scale

1:417,500

Km 0   10   20 Km
Miles 0   5   10 Miles

Left Views are long and undramatic in the interior of Rheinhessen, here near Gau-Bischofsheim. The suffix "heim" or "home" crops up monotonously here in almost every village name. But few produce wines of any particular distinction.

Three Bereich names cover the whole region: Bingen the northwest, Nierstein the northeast, and Wonnegau the south, between the principal towns of Alzey and Worms. For centuries Worms was one of the great Rhineland cities, seat of the famous "Diet" of 1521 which excommunicated Martin Luther, translator of the Bible into German. Its Liebfrauenstift vineyard around the Liebfraukirche has the doubtful distinction of having christened Liebfraumilch, the rock on which quality German wine so nearly foundered. At the other extreme of Rheinhessen, the town of Bingen, facing Rüdesheim (see page 226) across the Rhine, has excellent vineyards on the steep slopes of its first-growth Scharlachberg.

Wonnegau produces some respectable wines, Silvaners especially, around Alzey and to its southeast on chalky soil. But by far the best and most important vineyards of Rheinhessen are concentrated in the short stretch of the Rheinfront mapped on this page.

The town of Nierstein has become as famous as Bernkastel. This is partly through its size and the number of its growers (about 300), and partly because its name is widely and shamelessly borrowed for Niersteiner Gutes Domtal, a Grosslage available to 15 villages, but to only one part of Nierstein, and that the least distinguished. These cheap blends are the bane of German wine. The irony is that Nierstein proper has some superb vineyards, as producers such as St Antony and Heyl zu Herrnsheim eloquently demonstrate.

The two towns that flank it, Oppenheim and Nackenheim, have vineyards as good as most of Nierstein, but none better than the sand-red roll of hill, the Roter Hang, going north with the river at its foot. Hipping, Brudersberg, Pettenthal, and Rothenberg (which is in Nackenheim) make wine as fragrant and full of character as the Rheingau, though they are a shade softer and more luxuriant. Gunderloch is the prime exponent of Nackenheim Rothenberg. Oppenheim's first growths are firmer and less elegant.

Any true Niersteiner will use one of the vineyard names marked on the detailed map. The best also tend to specify that they are made from Riesling, although some fine Weissburgunder and Grauburgunder have also been made here for many years. Rheinhessen grows Germany's most varied range of grape varieties, including many of the newer crossings, especially Kerner, Scheurebe, Bacchus, Faberrebe, and Dornfelder.

Outside the area of the detailed map (but see the Rheinhessen map opposite) the best villages are those just north and south – Bodenheim, Guntersblum, Alsheim, and Bechtheim – as well as Flörsheim-Dalsheim, in the rain shadow of Donnersberg, where Weingut Keller proves that great wine can also be made in the gentle hill country of Rheinhessen.

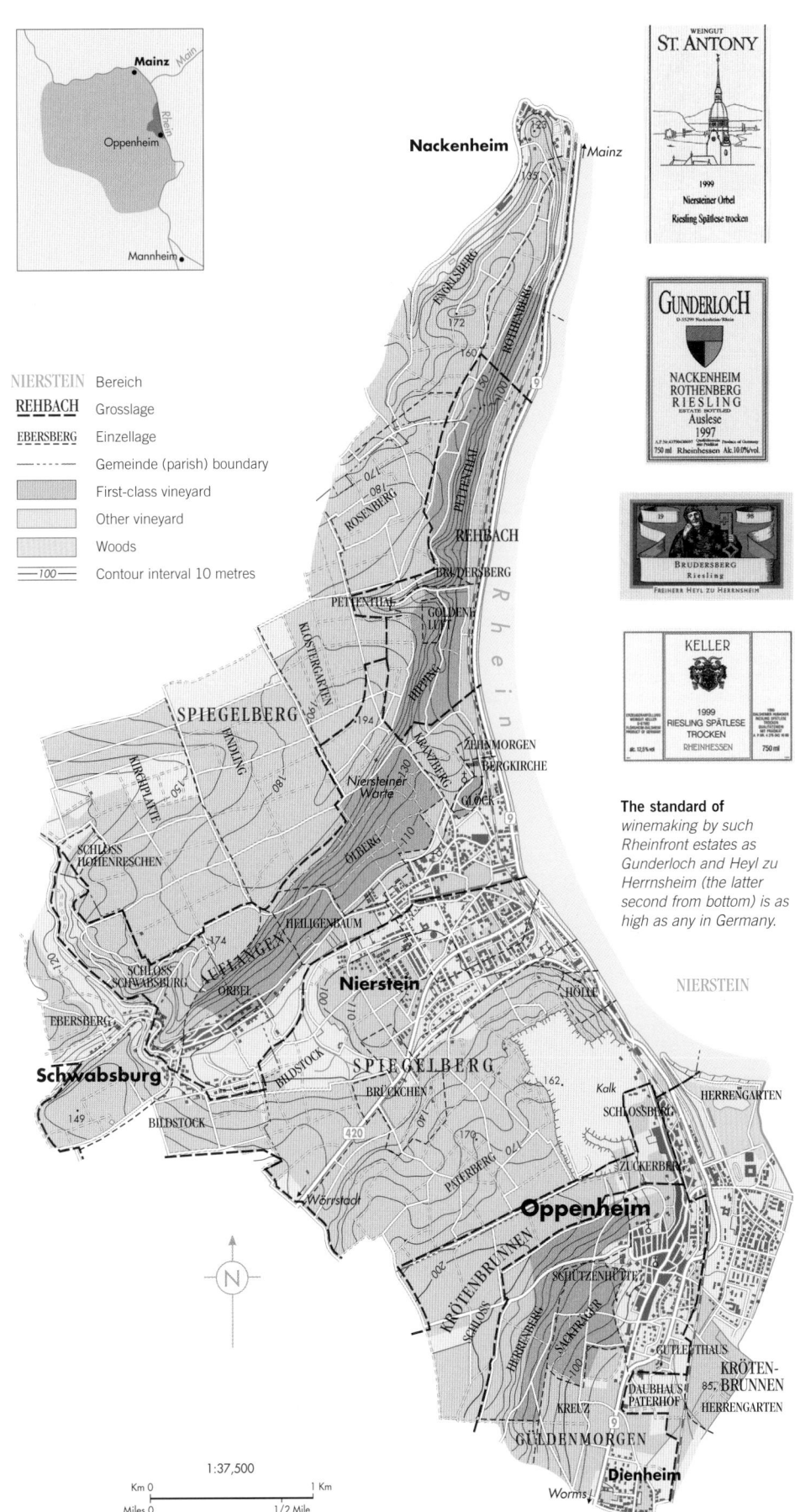

NIERSTEIN	Bereich
REHBACH	Grosslage
EBERSBERG	Einzellage
– – – – –	Gemeinde (parish) boundary
	First-class vineyard
	Other vineyard
	Woods
—100—	Contour interval 10 metres

The standard of *winemaking by such Rheinfront estates as Gunderloch and Heyl zu Herrnsheim (the latter second from bottom) is as high as any in Germany.*

1:37,500

Km 0 ——— 1 Km

Miles 0 ——— 1/2 Mile

Baden and Württemberg

The south of Germany, with its warmer climate, could be expected to be more of a wine region than parts further north. A hundred years ago it was. But the peculiar combinations of soil, climate, and social structure that make good quality winemaking possible and worthwhile in apparently unlikely spots on the Mosel and Rhine have only a few parallels in the huge state of Baden-Württemberg. The best of its wine is excellent, but it is so scattered and so keenly drunk in the region that the outside world rarely hears of it. Until recently, that is. Nowhere in Germany has the rationalization and modernization of the wine industry gone further and faster. Baden's vineyards have recently doubled in size and quadrupled in production. Only the Pfalz and Rheinhessen produce more.

The locomotive of this great surge forward has been the co-operatives. Ninety per cent of the crop is handled by more than 100 of these establishments, and more than half of all this wine is marketed by the mammoth Badischer Winzerkeller at Breisach, the frontier town on the Rhine between Freiburg and Alsace. At the other end of the scale, talented smaller producers such as Dr Heger in Kaiserstuhl have pioneered imported ideas to add some exciting novelties to the region's repertoire.

One way to define Baden's style is to say that it is the opposite of the Mosel's. Ethereal floweriness is not so much to the point as substantial wineyness. Baden is a trifle damper and cloudier than the Alsace vineyards just across the Rhine, umbrella'd by the Vosges. Its vineyards skirt the Black Forest, where mist and rain form part of some of Germany's loveliest pictures. The bulk of Baden's vineyards lie in a narrow 80-mile (130-km) strip between the forest and the Rhine Valley; the best of them either on privileged southern slopes in the forest massif or on the voicanic outcrop that forms the Kaiserstuhl, a distinct island of high ground in the Rhine Valley.

No one grape is dominant. Müller-Thurgau forms almost a third of the crop (the national average is closer to a fifth) but has recently been overtaken by Spätburgunder (Pinot Noir), used for increasingly weighty reds and pale Weissherbst. The third most planted variety, Pinot Gris, goes by two names: Ruländer when it is made unctuous, Grauburgunder when (more often now) it is bottled as a full, dry, rather French wine. Riesling makes classically elegant and long-lived wines, Weissburgunder (Pinot Blanc) smooth, soft wines, (Gewürz)traminer spicy ones, Silvaner (on the Kaiserstuhl) some wines almost as full of character as it makes in Franken. The highly aromatic new varieties are little used. Badeners regard wine primarily as accompaniment to food. Few German wines fill the role better.

The Kaiserstuhl and Tuniberg furnish one-third of all Baden's wine. Their dramatic outcrops have been remodelled by earth-moving on a heroic scale (called Flurbereinigung in German) to make modern vineyards out of old terraces and ledges. Red Spätburgunder is locally considered the best wine; Silvaner and Grauburgunder are sometimes splendid: stiff with flavour.

To the north, just south of the luxurious Black Forest spa of Baden-Baden, the Ortenau is a pocket of fine winegrowing with an emphasis on red wine. The lordly estates at Durbach, of the Margrave of Baden (Schloss Staufenberg) and of Count Wolff Metternich, make worthy Klingelberger (the local name for Riesling), Ruländer, Spätburgunder, and Traminer, although they have been overtaken in local reputation by Andreas Laible of Durbach. Much further north the Kraichgau and Badischer Bergstrasse form one Bereich, disparate as they are, with their best wines (at least in a visitor's opinion) made from the minority grapes, Riesling and Grauburgunder, grown in the best sites.

Far to the south, in the Markgräflerland, the corner of Germany between Freiburg and Basel, the favourite grape is the Gutedel, the local name for the Chasselas planted across the border in Switzerland. It makes very refreshing, if rather reticent, wine. Its cross with Silvaner, the Nobling, is tastier. Weissherbst is popular too. Trials indicate that Chardonnay is also very much at home here.

The Seewein (lake wine) of the southern-most area of all, around Meersburg on the Bodensee, is traditionally the off-dry pink-tinted Weissherbst of Spätburgunder. Müller-Thurgau is the principal white grape in the area. The Margrave of Baden has another splendid estate

Below The Kaiserstuhl boasts some of Germany's most spectacular modern terracing, the result of bulldozing whole hills of ancient patches and pockets of vineyard into ordered battlements of vines.

The Burgunders, or Pinots, *Spät- (Noir) and Grau- (Gris) play a lead role in Baden. Riesling is known locally as "Klingelberger"; that from Durbach is famous beyond the borders of Baden.*

here, Schloss Salem – even if it has no Riesling to match up to his noble Durbacher wine.

Württemberg, extensive though its vineyards are (almost four times the size of the Rheingau's vineyards, for example), remains better known to the world at large for its motorcars (at Stuttgart) than its wine. The region, which like Baden extends far beyond the limits of this map (see page 215), grows more red (or Weissherbst) wine than white, largely of its own varieties, the Trollinger, Lemberger, and Schwarzriesling (or Pinot Meunier) as well as the universal Spätburgunder. The climate is more continental and not always kind to the winegrowers in Württemberg, so sites are chosen with care, lining the River Neckar and its tributaries, but the region is now a producer of serious red wine. The Bereich to the north of the state capital Stuttgart, the Württembergisch Unterland, has three-quarters of the region's vineyards.

Stuttgart and Heilbronn, in fact, almost bracket the whole industry. Visitors flock to taste its products: pale Trollinger, Lemberger, Muskateller, Müller-Thurgau, and Silvaner. Although Traminer can be good, Riesling, as almost everywhere in Germany, makes by far the most exciting whites.

In the far north, north of Mannheim, is the tiny wine region Hessische Bergstrasse, which produces mainly dry Riesling and that mainly for locals.

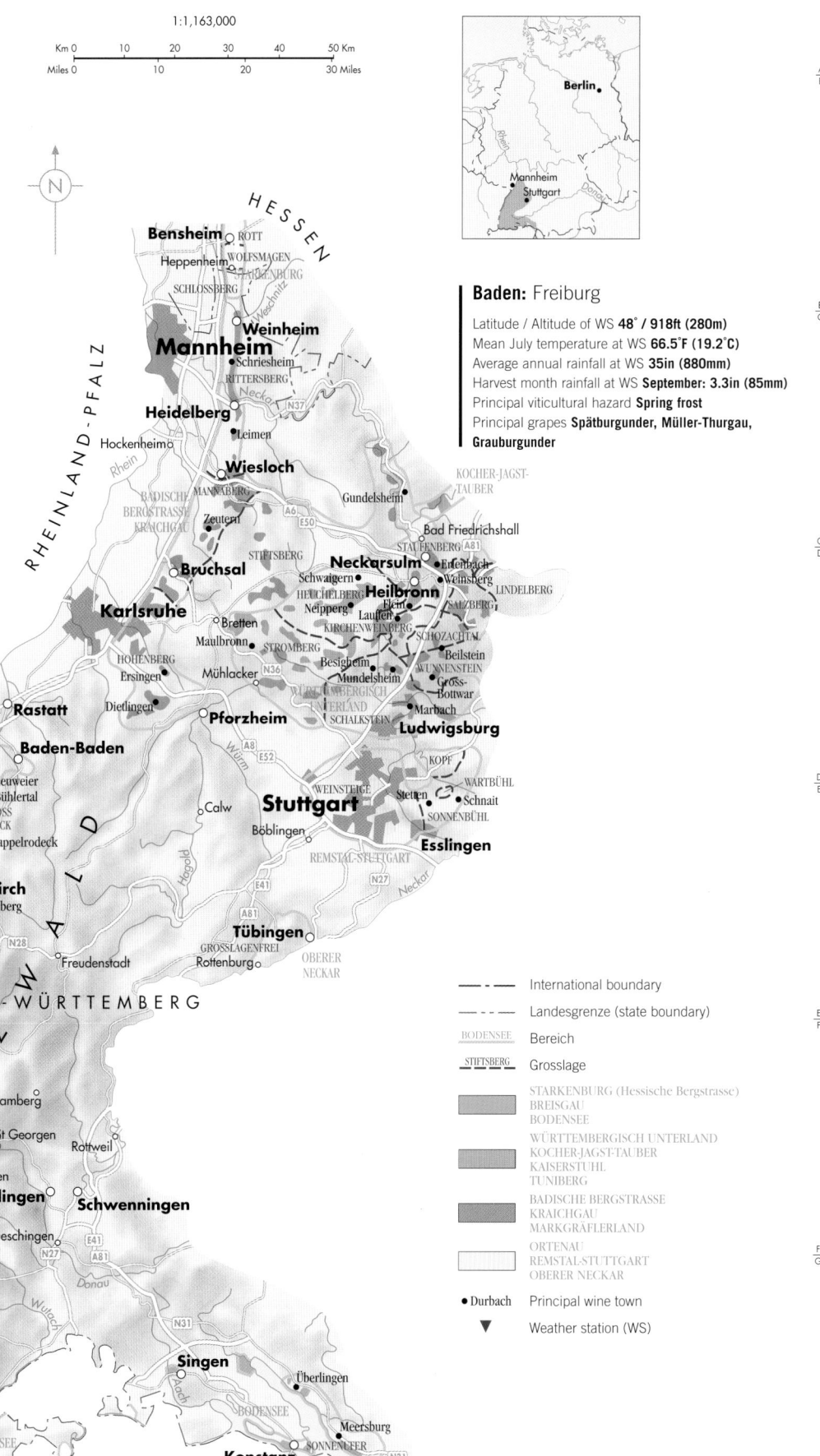

Baden: Freiburg

Latitude / Altitude of WS **48° / 918ft (280m)**
Mean July temperature at WS **66.5°F (19.2°C)**
Average annual rainfall at WS **35in (880mm)**
Harvest month rainfall at WS **September: 3.3in (85mm)**
Principal viticultural hazard **Spring frost**
Principal grapes **Spätburgunder, Müller-Thurgau, Grauburgunder**

— · — · —	International boundary
— — —	Landesgrenze (state boundary)
BODENSEE	Bereich
STIFTSBERG	Grosslage
	STARKENBURG (Hessische Bergstrasse) BREISGAU BODENSEE
	WÜRTTEMBERGISCH UNTERLAND KOCHER-JAGST-TAUBER KAISERSTUHL TUNIBERG
	BADISCHE BERGSTRASSE KRAICHGAU MARKGRÄFLERLAND
	ORTENAU REMSTAL-STUTTGART OBERER NECKAR
● Durbach	Principal wine town
▼	Weather station (WS)

Left Vineyards remain in the very heart of the baroque city of Würzburg, which straddles the River Main with its splendid bridges. The Marienburg Fortress looks out over the steeply sloping Schlossberg. The city's charitable foundations maintain splendid *weinstuben* where their own wines match local food.

Franken

Franken (Franconia in English) is out of the mainstream of German wine both geographically and by dint of its quite separate traditions. Politically it lies in the otherwise beer-centric former kingdom of Bavaria, which gives its State cellars a grandeur that is found nowhere else in Germany, and its consumers high expectations.

Franken is unusual in that it makes greater wines of Silvaner than of Riesling. And in savour and strength it draws away from the delicate sweetness of most German and nearer to some French wines, making its wines some of the best from Germany to drink with food. Franken wines were traditionally bottled in squat Bocksbeutel flasks rather than flutes, although dry wines are increasingly found in burgundy- and Bordeaux-like shapes.

The name Steinwein was once loosely used for all Franken wine. Stein is, in fact, the name of one of the two famous vineyards of the city of Würzburg on the Main, the capital of the district. The other is Leiste. Both distinguished themselves in the past by making wines that were incredibly long-lived. A Stein wine of the great vintage of 1540 was still just drinkable in the 1960s.

Such wines were Beerenauslesen at least: immensely sweet. Franken makes few such rarities today. Most Franken wine is relatively full-bodied and entirely dry having, in the case of Spätlese *trocken*, something like the size and strength of white burgundy.

Franken takes the grapevine into countryside whose climate is decidedly continental. In the Steigerwald, the easternmost of the three Franconian Bereichs, the vine looks almost a stranger in a setting of arable fields with forests of magnificent oaks crowning its sudden hills. Some of the finest wines come from the parishes of Iphofen (home of Hans Wirsching) and Rödelsee, as well as the dolls'-house princedom of Castell.

This is the one part of Germany where the growing season is regularly too short for the

The biggest estates in Franken are those of the ancient civic and ecclesiastical charities and the Bavarian State. The three labels shown here are from leading independent growers.

MAINDREIECK	Bereich
EWIG LABEN	Grosslage
Homburg	Gemeinde (commune) with first-class vineyard
	Grosslagenfrei

1:500,000

Km 0 — 10 — 20 Km
Miles 0 — 5 — 10 Miles

Sachsen and Saale-Unstrut

Riesling to prosper. The razor-sharp Silvaner is the answer. In Franken this normally second-division grape gains first-division status – not for pyrotechnics of fragrance but for a combination of the subtle and forceful that commands respect. Two to five years in bottle make all the difference. Making allowance for the flavours of quite different grapes, Premier or even Grand Cru Chablis are comparable wines.

But even in Franken, unfortunately, Müller-Thurgau seems to offer a better return, at least on less-than-ideal sites. It has gained the upper hand in nearly half the 6,000 acres (2,400ha) of vineyard in the region. (For comparison, the Nahe has about three-quarters as much vineyard, the Rheingau just over half, and the Pfalz almost four times.) A minority of Franken wines are made of the super-aromatic grape varieties Bacchus and Kerner. Scheurebe and Rieslaner, an even later-ripening Silvaner x Riesling crossing, can make particularly good dessert wines and substantial dry wines here, provided they reach full ripeness.

The heart of winegrowing Franken is all included in the Bereich Maindreieck, following the fuddled three-cornered meandering of the Main from Escherndorf (with its celebrated Einzellage Lump, and such talented producers as Horst Sauer) and Nordheim upstream of Würzburg, south to Frickenhausen, then north again through the capital to include all the next leg of the river and the outlying district around Hammelburg. What distinguishes all these scattered south-facing hillsides is the peculiar limestone known as Muschelkalk (whose origins are not so different from the Kimmeridgian clay of Chablis, or indeed of Sancerre). The much smaller Bereich Steigerwald, to the east of the Main, has heavier gypsum and marl soil. The third Bereich, further downstream to the west, has lighter loam based on sandstone. This is the Mainviereck where the total extent of the vineyard is limited but includes such stars as Rudolf Fürst and Fürst Löwenstein's Franken holdings.

The yellow areas marked on the map (which does not include the scattered vineyards on the Main as far east as Bamberg) are Grosslagenfrei, meaning that the wine villages are so scattered they have not been grouped in Grosslagen. Their wines are sold under individual site names or the name of the Bereich. Most Franken wine is made by co-operatives.

Würzburg is the essential visit: one of the great cities of the vine, with three magnificent estate cellars in its heart belonging respectively to the Bavarian State (Staatliche Hofkellerei), a church charity (the Juliusspital), and a civic charity (the Bürgerspital).

The Staatliche Hofkellerei lies under the gorgeous Residenz of the former prince-bishops, whose ceiling paintings by Tiepolo are reason enough to visit the city. There is also the noble Marienburg Castle on its hill of vines, the great baroque river bridge and the bustling *weinstuben* (wine bars) belonging to these ancient foundations, where all their wines can be enjoyed with suitably savoury food.

With the reunification of Germany, two small wine regions were added to the tight embrace of German wine bureaucracy. Sachsen (Saxony) is on the banks of the Elbe, in fine-china country between Dresden and Meissen, and Saale-Unstrut lies around the confluence of those two rivers southwest of Leipzig. Both of these regions are roughly on the same latitude as London, but their much more continental climate frequently blesses them with magnificent summers, even if the risk of devastating spring frosts is high. Substantial replanting in the 1990s increased the total vineyard area to about 1,500 acres (600ha) in Saale-Unstrut and nearly 1,000 acres (400ha) in Sachsen by the end of the decade and century.

By the late 1990s re-established estates such as Lützkendorf in Bad Kösen (Saale-Unstrut) and Schloss Proschwitz in Meissen (Sachsen), as well as new ones such as Günter Born in Höhnstedt, west of Halle (Saale-Unstrut) and Zimmerling in Pillnitz (Sachsen) had proved that both regions can produce dry wines with remarkable substance and character for their northerly location. Although the workhorse grape of both regions is the ubiquitous Müller-Thurgau, Weissburgunder, Grauburgunder, Riesling, and Traminer grapes dominate the many steep, south-facing sites with which each region is blessed. These wines are often compared with those of Franken, although they are more aromatic and less earthy.

An enclave of Saale-Unstrut vineyards close to the Süsser See near Halle lies northwest of the area mapped below.

Above The south-sloping Königslicher Weinberg at Pillnitz near Dresden, which has its own church, is one of the easternmost vineyards in Germany, with an inevitably extreme continental climate.

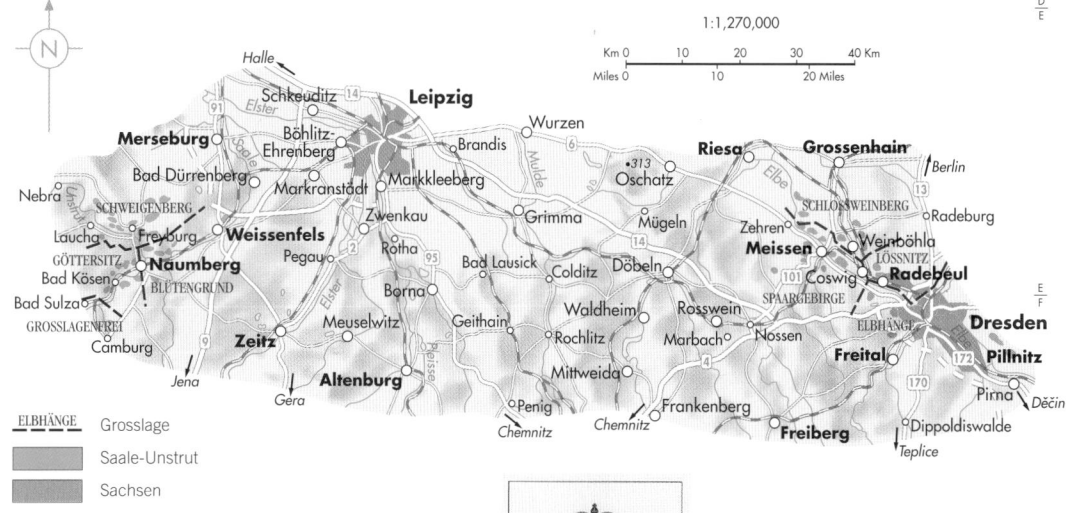

1:1,270,000

ELBHÄNGE	Grosslage
	Saale-Unstrut
	Sachsen

KARSDORFER HOHE GRÄTE SILVANER 1999 SAALE UNSTRUT
WEINGUT U. LÜTZKENDORF
11,5%vol · 0,5l

SKULPTUR: MAŁGORZATA CHODAKOWSKA

SCHLOSS PROSCHWITZ
GRAUBURGUNDER
Spätlese
Qualitätswein mit Prädikat
Trocken
Sachsen
1999
Weingut
Schloss Proschwitz
Prinz zur Lippe
Gutsabfüllung
D 01665
MEISSEN
13,0% vol L/A P.Nr. 10 11 00   750 ml

Schloss Proschwitz's
Prinz sur Lippe was pioneer of the Meissen region, wrestling back old family vineyards from the state ownership to make remarkable Pinots, Blanc and Gris. Saxony also has a sparkling wine tradition, and in the 19th century discreetly supplied Champagne.

Switzerland

Despite her proximity to some of the world's most enthusiastic wine importing countries, Switzerland has until recently kept her wines to herself. Even now that a reformed, less protectionist domestic wine market means that Switzerland must actively seek customers abroad, only about 2% of the country's wine is drunk outside of her borders.

This is not because the wine isn't any good, even though making fine wine in Switzerland is necessarily a challenge. It is largely a question of identifying which particular patches of land are best exposed to grape-ripening light and heat, whether directly from the sun, or reflected from lakes and rivers, or radiated from the often rocky ground.

Making any sort of wine in a country with Switzerland's cost structure is inevitably expensive, however. The land of milk and money will never be able to produce bargains for the mass

Below The eponymous château at Aigle, one of the Vaud's wine villages whose wines often have a mineral quality thanks to the local soil.

market, and Swiss wine producers are increasingly concentrating on making wine with real individuality. This should not be too difficult since every vineyard, almost every grape, is tended as and by an individual. The country's 37,000 acres (15,000ha) of vineyards are divided between thousands of full- and part-time growers who ensure that their impeccable and often spectacular plots of vines are attentively gardened rather than commercially farmed.

Not that Switzerland has remained immune to trends elsewhere. Her wine industry has, reluctantly, been forced to obey much stricter laws, specifically abandoning the practice of blending bulk imports into Swiss wine. Red wine production is on the increase, hybrids largely a distant memory, and an Appellation Contrôlée system is gradually instilling labelling rigour and curbing the scourge of overproduction.

By scrupulous care of their vines, making use of irrigation especially in the drier parts of the Valais, the Swiss have regularly achieved yields as high as Germany's. By managing to produce such big quantities, adding sugar when necessary, they make growing grapes pay in spite of

the difficult terrain and the costs of a high standard of living. And in the winery, routine malolactic fermentation (unlike in Germany or Austria) compensates for any natural excess tartness.

Switzerland has the highest vines in Europe and is home to the first vineyards on two of the world's great wine rivers, the Rhine and the Rhône, both of which rise, remarkably close to each other, in the Gotthard Massif.

Every Swiss canton grows some grapes for winemaking, In recent years more than four-fifths of the country's wine has come from the western cantons of French-speaking Switzerland: Suisse romande. Valais has replaced Vaud as the most productive wine canton and nowadays produces slightly more red than white. Geneva is the country's third most important grape-growing canton followed by Italian-speaking Ticino in the south (which produces around 5% of all Swiss wine) and then the German-speaking canton of Zürich.

Despite the rise of red wine, the most planted Swiss grape is still the pale Chasselas, which manages to achieve a personality in Switzerland's most favoured sites (see overleaf). The grape dominates wine production in Vaud and plays an important role in Valais, Geneva, and Neuchâtel. Pockets of Malvoisie (Pinot Gris), Pinot Blanc, Johannisberg (Sylvaner), Ermitage (Marsanne), and Chardonnay are found in Valais and elsewhere in Suisse romande. In the eastern, German-speaking part of Switzerland Müller-Thurgau, originally bred by the Swiss Dr Müller of Thurgau, is the most important white wine grape.

For Switzerland's fashionable and increasingly impressive red wines, Gamay and the vine known here variously as Blauburgunder, Clevener or Pinot Noir are grown all over Switzerland, with the exception of Ticino which concentrates on Merlot, introduced in 1907 from Bordeaux after phylloxera all but destroyed the region's wine industry. In recent years, Syrah and the light-skinned Viognier have made considerable inroads in Valais. Merlot and even Cabernet Sauvignon are increasingly planted in the vineyards of Geneva.

But Switzerland's most distinctive wines tend to be made from one of her long list of rare vine specialities: Petite Arvine, Amigne, Humagne Blanc, Heida, Rèze, Cornalin, and Humagne Rouge in the French-speaking areas, Completer and the old German vines Räuschling and Elbling in German-speaking Switzerland, and red Bondola in Ticino. Of these, Petite Arvine, Completer, and the red Cornalin and Humagne Rouge can make some very fine wine indeed.

Uniquely Swiss styles of wine include Dôle, a wildly variable blend of Pinot Noir and Gamay, pink Œil-de-Perdrix from Neuchâtel's Pinot Noir, and from German cantons both pink Süssdruck and Schillerwein from a mix of pale- and dark-skinned grapes.

Eastern Switzerland grows about 17% of Switzerland's wine grapes, typically in isolated sites able to ripen the Blauburgunder that was introduced here from France during the wars of

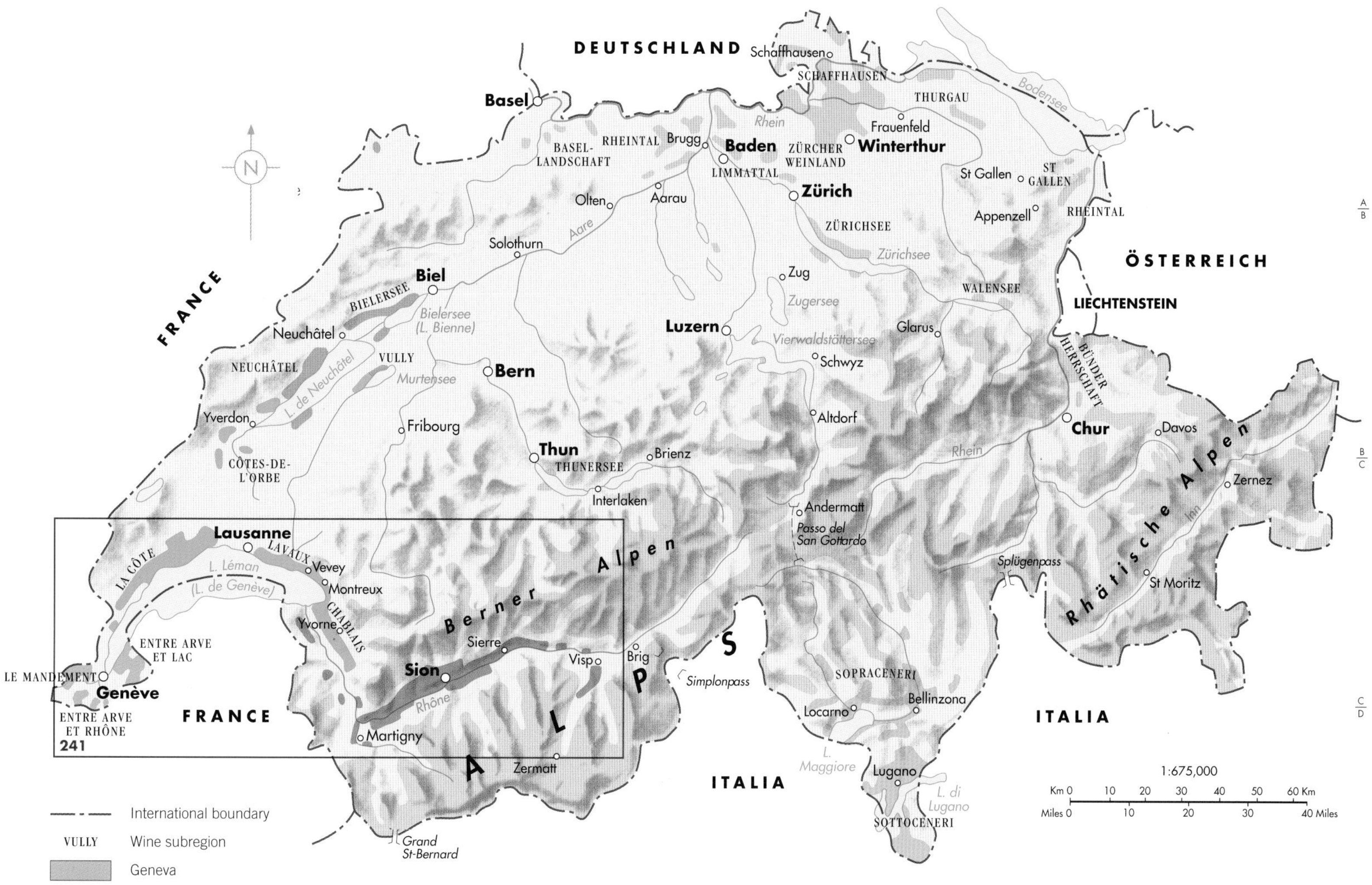

DEUTSCHLAND

Schaffhausen
SCHAFFHAUSEN
THURGAU
Rhein
Bodensee
Basel
BASEL-
LANDSCHAFT
RHEINTAL
Brugg
Baden
ZÜRCHER
WEINLAND
Frauenfeld
Winterthur
St Gallen
ST
GALLEN
RHEINTAL
Olten
Aarau
LIMMATTAL
Zürich
ZÜRICHSEE
Appenzell
ÖSTERREICH
Solothurn
Aare
Zug
Zürichsee
LIECHTENSTEIN
Biel
BIELERSEE
Bielersee
(L. Bienne)
VULLY
Bern
Zugersee
WALENSEE
Luzern
Vierwaldstättersee
Schwyz
Glarus
BÜNDNER
HERRSCHAFT
Neuchâtel
NEUCHÂTEL
L. de Neuchâtel
Murtensee
Fribourg
Yverdon
CÔTES-DE-
L'ORBE
Thun
THUNERSEE
Brienz
Interlaken
Altdorf
Andermatt
Passo del
San Gottardo
Rhein
Chur
Davos
Zernez
Inn
Rhätische Alpen
Berner
Alpen
Lausanne
LAVAUX
LA CÔTE
L. Léman
Vevey
Montreux
CHABLAIS
Yvorne
Sierre
Sion
Rhône
Visp
Brig
Simplonpass
Splügenpass
St Moritz
ENTRE ARVE
ET LAC
LE MANDEMENT
Genève
ENTRE ARVE
ET RHÔNE
241
FRANCE
Martigny
Zermatt
A
L
P
S
SOPRACENERI
Bellinzona
Locarno
ITALIA
ITALIA
L.
Maggiore
Lugano
L. di
Lugano
SOTTOCENERI
Grand
St-Bernard

FRANCE

1:675,000
Km 0   10   20   30   40   50   60 Km
Miles 0   10   20   30   40 Miles

A/B
B/C
C/D
D/E
F/G

— · — International boundary

VULLY   Wine subregion

Geneva

Vaud

Valais

Neuchâtel/Three Lakes

Ticino

Eastern Switzerland

Land above 2000 metres

241   Area mapped at larger scale
on page shown

The exceptional variety that Switzerland can offer is
apparent in these labels, with a total of three languages
and particularly eye-catching designs from some of the
top red wine producers in Italian-speaking Ticino and
German-speaking eastern Switzerland, where Completer
is the name of a local heady white wine grape.

the 17th century. Some of these reds are insipid
while Bündner Herrschaft's best are dear and can
be excellent, benefiting from the warm autumn
wind, the föhn. This favoured region's white speciality is the austere but ancient Completer.

The quality spectrum in Switzerland's other
red wine region, Ticino, is even wider, with
Merlot varying from the frankly cynical to some,
nurtured on the sunniest slopes, that stand comparison with Italy's finest Supertuscans.

Vineyards on the south-facing slopes above
Lake Neuchâtel are devoted to Pinot Noir and
Chasselas, for delicate wines of all three colours,
often enlivened by the light bubble left by prolonged lees contact. Producers around the
village of Auvernier make much of their unfiltered Chasselas, a welcome variation on the
usual recipe. Wines very similar to Neuchâtel's
are grown north of Bielersee to the immediate
northeast, with particularly fine Pinot Noir coming from small plots above the towns of Schafis,
Ligertz, and Twann.

See over for more detail on the Upper Rhône
Valley regions of Valais, Vaud, and Geneva.

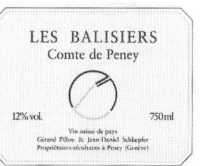

1|2   2|3   3|4   4|5   5|6

Valais, Vaud, and Geneva

The steep sides of the Valais, the valley which the young River Rhône carved through the Alps, are followed by gentler slopes in the Vaud, where the waters broaden into Lac Léman (Lake Geneva). An almost continuous, south-facing band of vines hugs the lake and river's sunny north bank all the way so that between them these three cantons produce almost three-quarters of all Swiss wine: Valais a hotbed (literally) of vinous experimentation; Vaud the traditional heart of Swiss wine, where Cistercian monks introduced viticulture from Burgundy more than 1,000 years ago; Geneva, trying hard to upgrade its wines.

In the high Valais peculiarly alpine conditions, brilliant sun and summer drought, can make concentrated, superripe wines. The average rainfall in Sion, a major wine centre, is less than two-thirds that of Bordeaux and many Valais growers have built special channels of mountain water to irrigate their vines.

The Rhône's first vines grow near Brig: historic varieties such as Lafnetscha, Himbertscha, Gwäss, Heida, and the almost extinct Hafnätscha, throwbacks to the age before the Simplon Tunnel and its railway transformed the Valaisian economy. Just southwest of here are Europe's highest vines at Visperterminen, at 3,600ft (1,100m) lying almost in the shadow of the Matterhorn.

Large-scale wine production begins just before Sierre (the driest place in Switzerland) and continues in a 30-mile (50-km) stretch as far downstream as Martigny where the Rhône executes a dramatic right turn towards Lac Léman. Here are the headquarters of many of the firms that turn out the Valais staples of white Fendant (as Chasselas is known here) and red Dôle (at least 85% of this wine is a Pinot-dominant blend of Pinot Noir and Gamay). Dôle requires a certain minimum ripeness: the seriously anodyne rejects have been sold off as Goron. Many of the best, containing only enough Gamay to add a certain fruitiness, come from the calcareous slopes round Sierre.

The great majority of Valais grapes are grown by smallholders and processed by the dominant co-operative. Provins has taken notable steps to encourage quality but it is innovative small-scale producers who have shown the way, particularly with red wines which by the turn of the century constituted nearly 60% of total Valais production. Traditional varieties such as the tannic Cornalin and rustic Humagne Rouge are now increasingly supplemented not just by Pinot Noir and Gamay but by Syrah which has travelled particularly well upstream from its home in the French Rhône Valley.

Of the 27 light-skinned grape varieties grown in Valais (its isolation helped), Petite Arvine is the most widely successful indigenous vine. Its combination of nervy acidity and considerable extract is particularly winning in the arid climate around Sion and Martigny. Valais whites are in general extremely potent, whether Johannisberg (Sylvaner), Ermitage (Marsanne), Malvoisie (Pinot Gris; sometimes *flétri*, strong and sweet, traditionally from raisined grapes), Chardonnay or the local Amigne, a speciality of the village of Vétroz, Humagne Blanc (not apparently related to Humagne Rouge), Heida, and Rèze grown high in the Alps to produce a rare, sherry-like Vin de Glacier in the Val d'Anniviers.

Vaud's vineyards, favoured by the mildness encouraged by Lac Léman's great body of water, are quite different, 80% of them devoted to a single grape, Chasselas. Yields are still too high – averaging more than 110hl/ha – to produce much thrilling wine, although there are pockets of vineyards from which the world's most characterful expressions of this grape are regularly coaxed.

—·—·—		International boundary
------		Canton boundary
CHABLAIS		Wine subregion
VINZEL		Leading wine commune
<u>CALAMIN</u>		Special Grand Cru
▓		Vineyards
░		Woods
═1000═		Contour interval 200 metres
▼		Weather station (WS)

Chablais is the easternmost of Vaud's wine regions and Chasselas can reach record ripeness levels around the villages of Aigle and Yvorne. The pretty vine-terraced north shore of the lake is divided into Lavaux (encompassing the area between Montreux in the east and Lausanne, where some of Switzerland's most famous and expensive white wines are grown), and La Côte, which stretches in an arc that is less glorious and spectacular from west of Lausanne to the city of Geneva.

Within Lavaux wine villages such as Chardonne, St-Saphorin, Rivaz, and Epesses luxuriate in a reputation that was established in the Middle Ages, but two specially designated *crus*, Calamin and Dézaley, enjoy even greater esteem, and even higher prices. Calamin, all 17 acres (7ha) of it, lies within the village of Epesses, while the 160 acres (65ha) designated Dézaley includes such estates as Clos des Abbayes and Clos des Moines, both now owned by the city of Lausanne. Within these two *crus*, Chasselas can be a nervy, smoky, flinty expression of different terroirs and expositions, all the best of which benefit from light reflected from the lake and heat radiated from the stony terraces initiated by the Cistercians.

The best wines of La Côte tend to come from such villages as Aubonne, Féchy, Bougy-Villars, Mont-sur-Rolle, and Morges. Vineyards within the subregion of Nyon are under increasing pressure from developers trying to extend the city of Geneva.

Geneva's own vineyards were plagued first by phylloxera and then by the poor quality hybrids that were planted in the early 20th century. Today Chasselas is planted on just under 50% of the Geneva vineyard while Gamay accounts for more than 30% and Pinot Noir is increasingly common. The powerful co-op dominates production and draws on three areas. The largest is Mandement (Satigny is the country's biggest wine commune), which has the ripest and tastiest Chasselas. The vineyards between the Arve and the Rhône are milder, and those between the Arve and the lake pretty dry and pallid: a far cry from the potent Fendant of Sion.

As in Valais, the pace is being set by a small group of ambitious individuals who have shown that innovation (planting Cabernet Sauvignon, for example) can be more rewarding than following local custom. The picture-book village of Dardagny, for instance, has earned itself a reputation for unusually invigorating Pinot Gris.

Above Precipitous south-facing vineyards at Chexbres in Lavaux benefit from reflection off Lac Léman, like those of the neighbouring, even more celebrated village of Dézaley.

Switzerland: Geneva

Latitude / Altitude of WS **46.15° / 1,345ft (410m)**
Mean July temperature at WS **66.9°F (19.4°C)**
Average annual rainfall at WS **35in (880mm)**
Harvest month rainfall at WS **September: 3.5in (90mm)**
Principal viticultural hazard **Spring frost**
Principal grape **Chasselas**

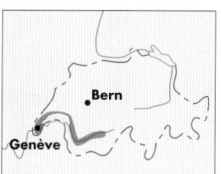

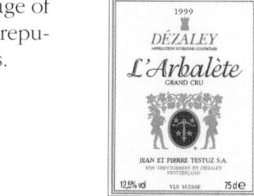

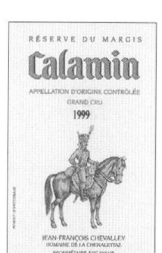

Chasselas is at its *most splendidly characterful in the top four labels, together with a Geneva Merlot and some more of Valais' grape specialities.*

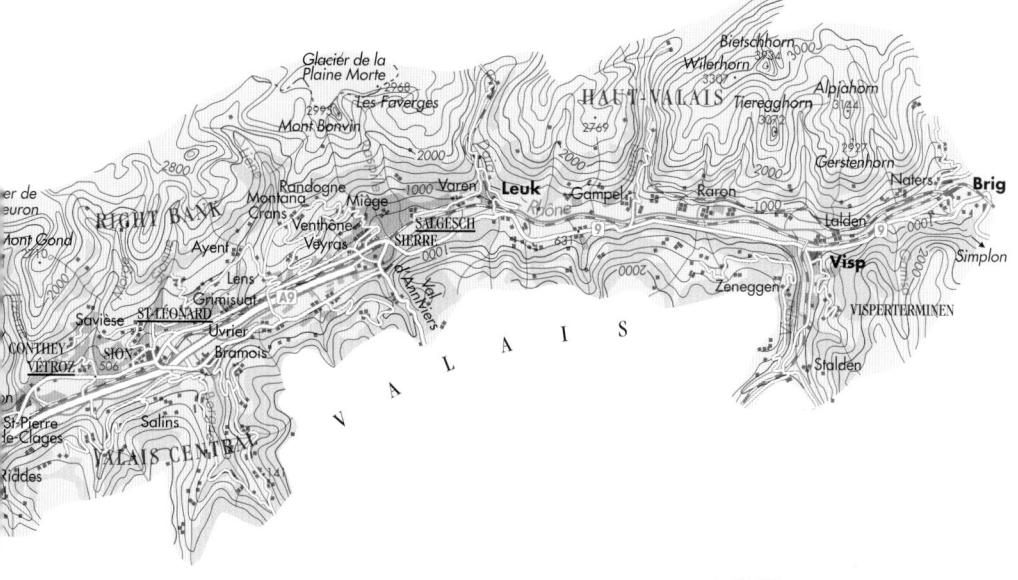

1:450,000

Km 0   5   10 Km
Miles 0   3   6 Miles

Austria

No country in Europe has changed its attitude and upgraded its standards of wine production so dramatically since the mid-1980s as Austria. And yet the great majority of the world's wine drinkers have no idea what Austrian wine tastes like, imagining only that it must be rather like German wine.

Those fortunate wine drinkers who have been exposed to Austria's new wave of intensely pure, dry (*trocken*) wines know that in many ways they have more in common with Alsace than Germany while having their own distinct, finely etched personality. There is something of the freshness of the Rhine in them but more of the fieriness and high flavour of the Danube.

Modern Austria is a mere fraction of what the name meant before the First World War. But its kernel, Niederösterreich or Lower Austria, surrounding the capital Vienna, where the Alps descend to the great Pannonian Plain that reaches across Hungary, is a region full of variety. It embraces slate, sand, clay, gneiss, loam, and fertile loess, parched fields and perpetually green ones, craggy precipices above the Donau (Danube), and the tranquil shallow mere of the Neusiedlersee. Except for a few tiny vineyards in the Tyrol, only eastern Austria, the part mapped here, makes wine.

Austrian vineyards are much closer to the equator than most of Germany's, and the climate is even more extreme – with colder winters but warmer, sunnier summers, as the factfile below suggests. The result is much higher natural alcohol levels, accentuated by Austria's decidedly lower average yields in the vineyard. Germany produces about 12 million hectolitres of wine from about 247,000 acres (100,000ha) of vineyard, while Austria, which has roughly half as much land devoted to the vine, produces less than a quarter as much wine, between 2 and 3 million hectolitres a year. In 1993 Austria tightened its wine laws by imposing a maximum yield of 9,000kg (roughly 60hl) per hectare for wines allowed to carry a geographical name. Chaptalization, once commonplace, is now forbidden for quality wines (as it is in Germany).

The catalyst for all of this worthy activity was the highly publicized Austrian wine scandal of 1985 in which a few dishonest (not to say criminal) merchants were caught adding diethylene glycol to their wines to give them more body and more appeal to the German blenders who then constituted Austrian wine's principal export market (and did not usually trouble to spell out the non-German provenance of such wines on their labels).

Austria: Vienna

Latitude / Altitude of WS **48.04° / 590ft (180m)**
Mean July temperature at WS **67.6°F (19.8°C)**
Average annual rainfall at WS **26in (660mm)**
Harvest month rainfall at WS **September: 1.5in (40mm)**
Principal viticultural hazard **Spring frost**
Principal grapes **Grüner Veltliner, Riesling, Welschriesling, Weissburgunder (Pinot Blanc)**

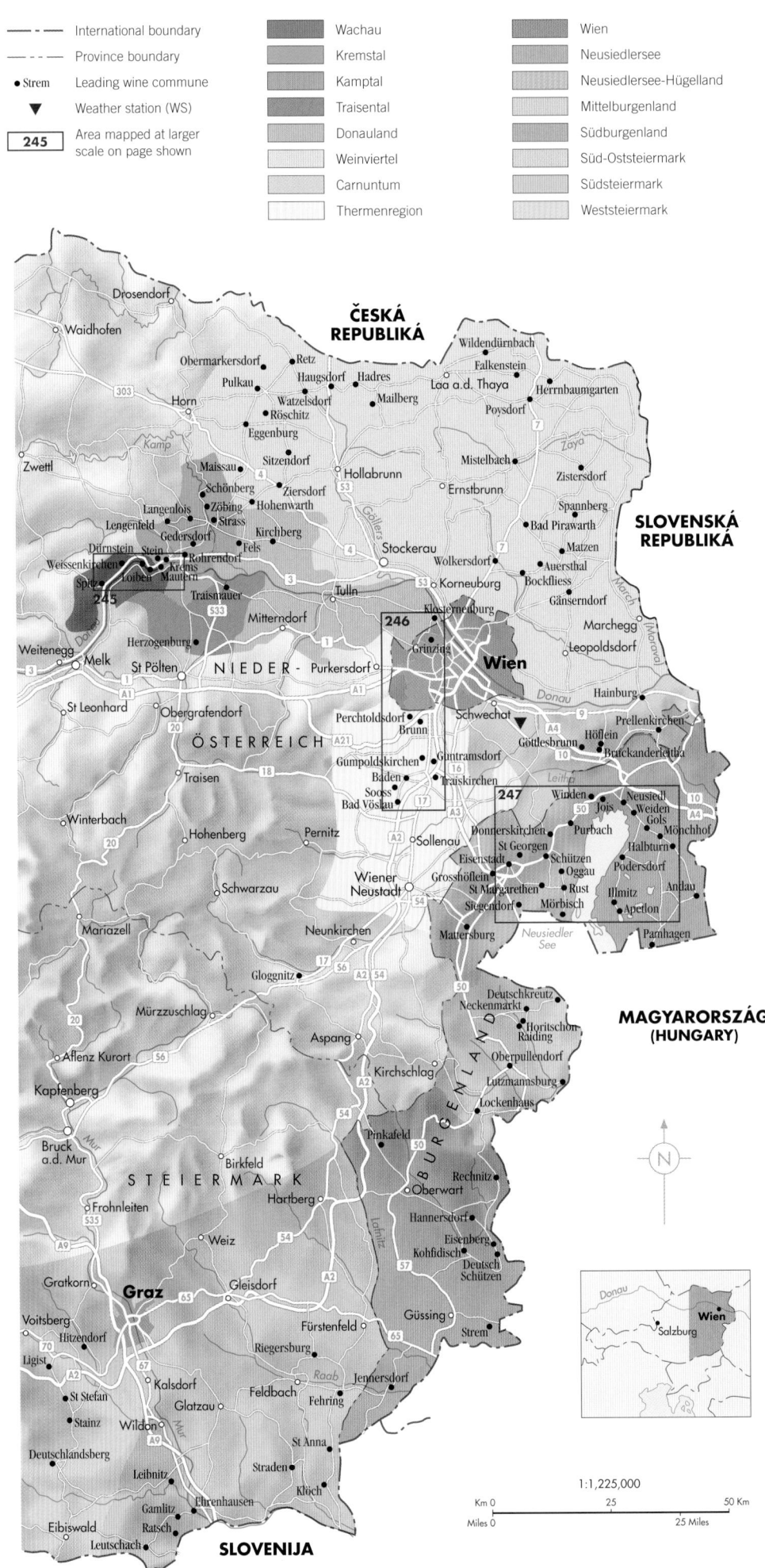

Legend:
International boundary
Province boundary
• Strem — Leading wine commune
▼ Weather station (WS)
245 — Area mapped at larger scale on page shown

Wachau
Kremstal
Kamptal
Traisental
Donauland
Weinviertel
Carnuntum
Thermenregion
Wien
Neusiedlersee
Neusiedlersee-Hügelland
Mittelburgenland
Südburgenland
Süd-Oststeiermark
Südsteiermark
Weststeiermark

1:1,225,000

This was a miserable period for Austria's wine industry but out of this misfortune has come forth fruit, in abundance – and none of the oily, unnatural sweetness of old. The most commonly encountered fruit flavours are those of Austria's own white grape Grüner Veltliner, which is grown on more than a third of the country's vineyard. This is not a grape with a long history in Austria but one that has proved over the last 50 years to be very much at home there.

Veltliner wine when it is well-made and drunk young is marvellously fresh and fruity, with plenty of acidity and a flavour that reverberates on a wavelength somewhere between grapefruit and dill. To compare it with Riesling is like comparing a wild flower with a finely bred garden variety.

Although there are circumstances in which the savage can outshine the aristocrat (see page 244), most Grüner Veltliner is made light, spicy and for early consumption, particularly in the country's most extensive wine region, Austria's Weinviertel (meaning "wine quarter"). This rolling, wooded countryside north of Vienna, with its baroque churches and pretty villages, is the very essence of Mitteleurop. Just over the border to the north, with a similar climate and equally varied soils, are the main winelands of the Czech Republic and Slovakia. The hills of Slovakia form a barrier between the Weinviertel and the warming influence of the Pannonian Plain to the southeast so that wines made here tend to be the freshest and lightest made in Austria. Mailberg with its warming combination of loess, sand, and a particularly well-sheltered valley has a reputation for growing some of the Weinviertel's most successful reds, from Zweigelt, one of Austria's red grape specialities, although the less interesting Blauer Portugieser vine is more common.

Almost 70% of Austria's grapes are white, although dark-skinned vine varieties are increasingly popular with ambitious growers, who may sell them as varietals but often blend them to produce a *cuvée*. Cabernet Sauvignon, Merlot, and Blauburgunder (Pinot Noir) are planted to a limited but growing extent and are typically blended with Zweigelt in Niederösterreich and with Blaufränkisch or St Laurent, a soft, fruity grape, in Burgenland.

The most famous wine regions of Niederösterreich, the Wachau and Kremstal, are considered in detail overleaf but Kamptal, the productive buffer zone between Kremstal and Weinviertel, also has some gifted winemakers. Its south-facing, often loess-dominated vineyards, protected by mountains from northern chill, benefit from much the same climate and aspect as Kremstal and Wachau to the west and produce similarly dense Riesling and Grüner Veltliner, as well as a slightly greater range of other, often lesser, varieties. Its main river influence is not the broad, east-flowing Danube but its south-flowing tributary, the Kamp. The most important wine centres are Langenlois, which has been a wine town for centuries; Zöbenstein, famous for its Heiligenstein vineyard (known as

Some of Austria's extremely varied wines, *including an experimental Viognier from the Weinviertel, and below that two Kamptal wines made by Willi Bründlmayer.*

a Ried in Austria); and Gobelsburg, where the grand Schloss Gobelsburg has been restored to glory by an association with the talented Willi Bründlmayer of Langenlois.

Austria's wine purge has extended to wine geography, with a flurry of redrawn boundaries and a renaming of the resultant wine regions. Mixed farming predominates in Traisental and Donauland-Carnuntum, which produces some quite ordinary Müller-Thurgau (it makes up a twelfth of all Austrian vines) as well as fine Grüner Veltliner and the related, red-skinned Roter Veltliner. In the far east of the region on the outskirts of Vienna are the monastic cellars and influential national wine school of Klosterneuburg.

The wines of Wien, as Vienna is known to Austrians, and the Thermenregion, which includes the village of Gumpoldskirchen, are considered on page 246. Carnuntum is the most southerly and hottest of Nierösterreich's wine regions. Sheltered to the north by mountains and the famous Vienna woods, it is wide open to Pannonian warmth and has since the mid-1990s established a reputation for its Zweigelt and Blaufränkisch reds. Göttlesbrunn and Höflein are the best-sited villages; elsewhere can be fatally cold for vines in winter or dangerously dry in summer.

Steiermark (Styria) in the south, just over the border from Slovenia's inland wine country, is Austria's most distinctive and far-flung wine region. Unlike the more northerly regions, it has produced exclusively dry wines, not unlike those of inland Slovenia, for decades. It may have only 7% of the country's vineyards, and those are widely dispersed, but its reputation for intense piercing Sauvignon Blanc, Chardonnay, and Welschriesling is unmatched within Austria. Chardonnay, travelling most unusually under a local alias, Morillon, is well entrenched here. Südsteiermark has the greatest concentration of revered producers. Traminer is a speciality of the volcanic soils of Klöch in Süd-Oststeiermark, while pink Schilcher made from the rare Blauer Wildbacher grape is that of Weststeiermark.

Below Autumnal vineyards in the gently rolling countryside of southern Styria, or Südsteiermark, a wine region much admired for the definition of its whites.

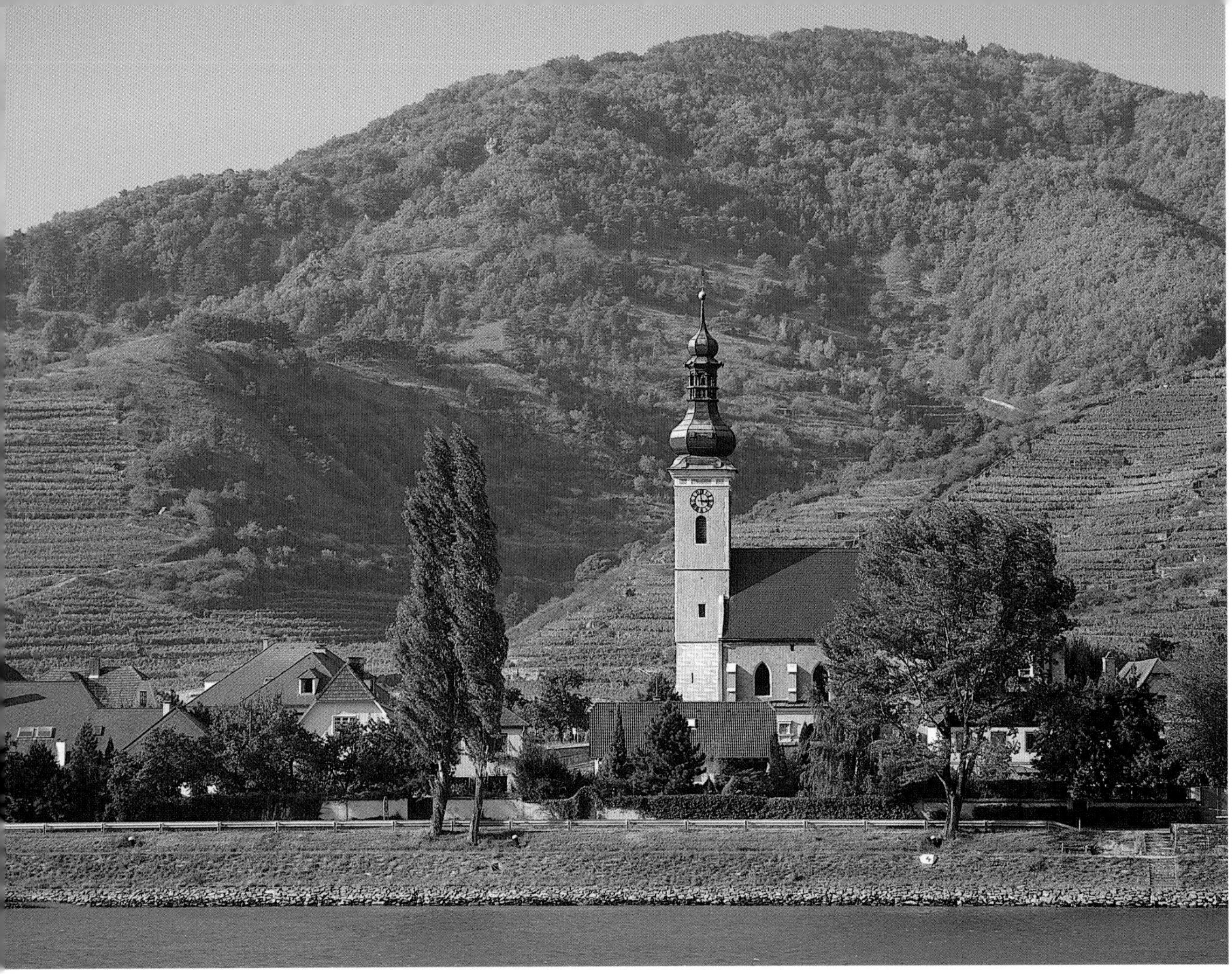

Left Unterloiben and its church lie between the Danube and steeply terraced vineyards protected by the hills from northern chill. The Wachau is one of the very few places where currents of moist northern air meet Pannonian warmth.

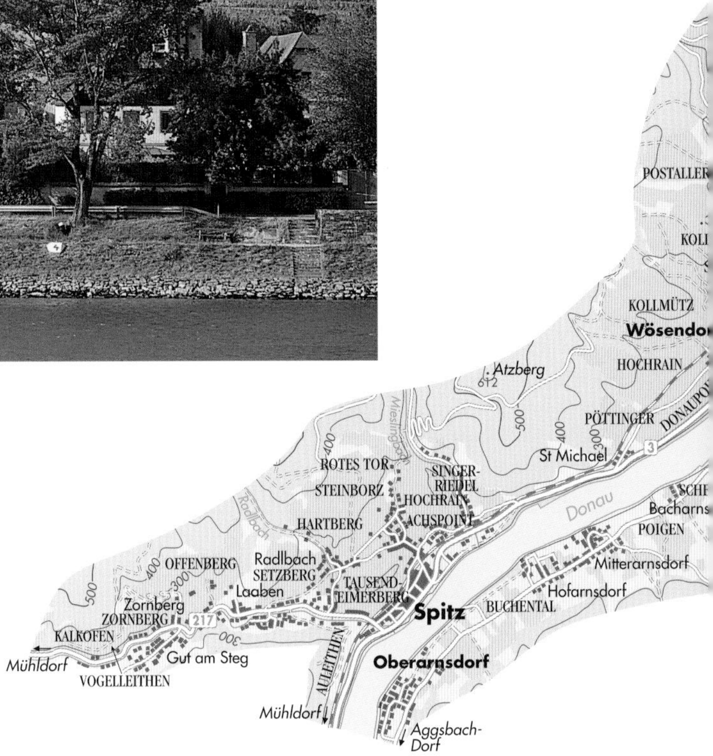

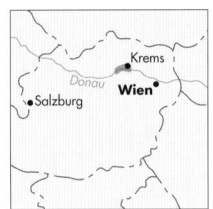

Wachau and Kremstal

If ever there were a region which justified a geographical approach to wine, and an atlas to communicate it, it would be the stunningly beautiful Wachau, a complex meeting point of northern and southern climates and a rich mosaic of different soils and rocks. Forty miles (65km) before it reaches Vienna the broad grey Danube broaches a range of 1,600ft (490m) hills. For a short stretch the craggy north bank of the river, as steep as the Mosel or Côte Rôtie, is patchworked with vines on ledges and outcrops, along narrow paths leading up from the river to the crowning woods.

There are plots of deep soil and others where a mere scratching finds rock, patches with daylong sunlight and others that always seem to be in shade. This is the Wachau, Austria's most famous wine region, even if, with 3,700 acres (1,500ha), it constitutes just 3% of the country's wine country.

What gives the (almost invariably dry white) wines of the Wachau their distinction is the geography. They are concentrated because the warm Pannonian climate reaches up the Danube Valley here to its westernmost point of influence; grapes in these low-yielding vineyards may reach potential alcohol levels of 15% or more. Yet the wines are far from flabby monsters (even if the super-ripe vintage of 1998 encouraged growers to push everything to the limit), because the vineyards are cooled at night by refreshing, northern air rich in oxygen from the woods above. These steeply terraced vineyards may need irrigation in high summer (rainfall often falls below the practical natural minimum of 20in/500mm a year) but the nights here are cool, and the Danube acts as a natural heat regulator.

Grüner Veltliner was the traditional Wachau grape and makes its most vividly persuasive wines here – at their best green-tinged, high-spirited and fiery, almost peppery performances which can age in a positively burgundian fashion. Grüner Veltliner can thrive on the lower banks in loess and sand, but growers have been dedicating their highest and steepest sites, on less fertile gneiss and granite at the top of the hill, to Riesling, and their clientele is enraptured.

Top Wachau Rieslings from such established growers as Hirtzberger at Spitz, Prager at Weissenkirchen, FX Pichler at Oberloiben, Emmerich Knoll at Unterloiben, and the famous Freie Weingärtner co-op at Dürnstein, can have the steely cut of the Saar in a mouth-filling structure which is every bit as full as an Alsace Riesling. New oak does not feature here, although there are some experiments with botrytized grapes.

The Wachau growers have their own system of designating wines; local taste codified in fact. Steinfeder is a light wine up to 10.7% alcohol for early drinking. Federspiel is made from slightly riper grapes, up to 11.9%, which can usually be enjoyed any time in its first five years, while wines labelled Smaragd after a local emerald green lizard, can be seriously full-bodied – usually dry, but with alcohol levels of 13 or 14% which may repay six or more years' ageing.

Cool northern influence is at its strongest west of Spitz while the Loibens (Unter- and Ober-) enjoy a noticeably softer climate than even Weissenkirchen. Dürnstein, in whose castle

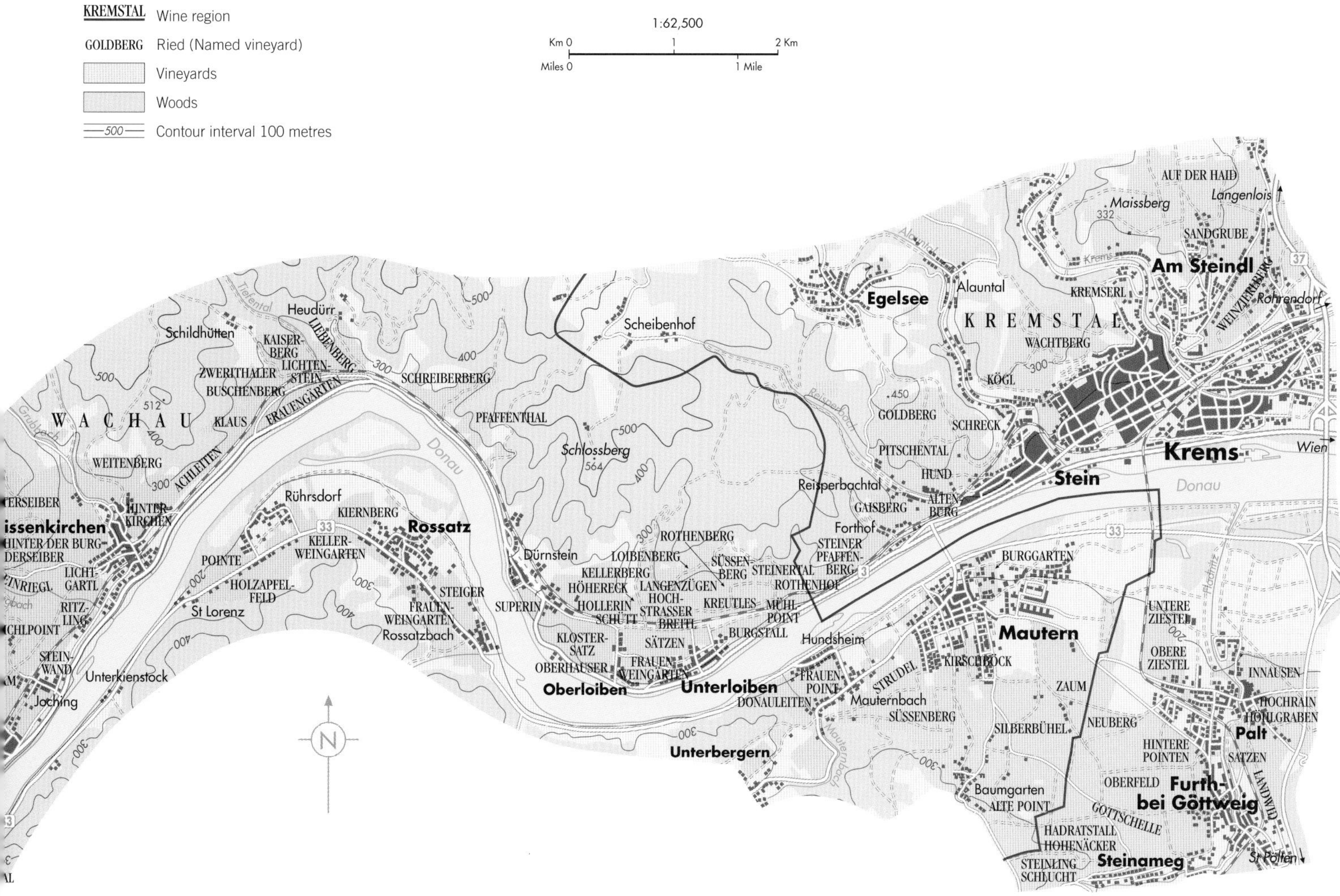

KREMSTAL Wine region

GOLDBERG Ried (Named vineyard)

Vineyards

Woods

━500━ Contour interval 100 metres

1:62,500

Km 0   1   2 Km

Miles 0   1 Mile

Richard the Lion-Heart was imprisoned, is the natural capital of the Wachau and the scenic climax of the valley. The baroque steeple, the ruined castle, and the village's tilting vineyards are irresistibly romantic.

Most of the Wachau's finest wines are grown on the south-facing north bank of the Danube but Nikolaihof makes some firm, organic wines (fungicides are rarely called for in this dry climate) around Mautern on the south bank.

It is somehow no surprise to learn that this 12-mile (20-km) strip of vineyards is home to no fewer than 900 different named sites, or Rieden (with boundaries still too debatable to map precisely here). There is no room to describe them individually but one site, Achleiten to the east of Weissenkirchen, is so distinctive it is worth mentioning. The slate and gneiss make the minerally wines a blind taster's dream.

The pretty twin towns of Stein and Krems mark the end of the Wachau and the start of the very similar but slightly less dramatic Kremstal region. The clay and limestone vineyards round here, including the famous Steiner Hund, can give particular density to both Riesling and Grüner Veltliner.

The crack corps of *the Wachau producers are represented here, although quality standards are also extraordinarily high among the cohesive group of producers known as Vinea Wachau Nobilis Districtus, or famous vineyard district of the Wachau region.*

The Krems Valley runs north up to Langenlois in the valley of the Kamp, on strangely soft loess – half soil, half rock – source of some famous Grüner Veltliners but also of full-bodied reds. Kremstal is an intermediate zone between the sharp focus of the Wachau and the greater variety of Kamptal (already discussed on page 243). Parts of the region are high and steep enough to need terracing as in the Wachau. The most talented wine producers include Malat, Nigl, and Undhof-Salomon who can make racy whites with every bit as much concentration as many Wachau wines.

The detailed map here includes only the southwestern sector of Kremstal. Further east lies Rohrendorf (see map on page 242), site of the extensive Lenz Moser winery, on lower hills of sandier soil.

Vienna and Thermenregion

No capital city is so intimate with wine as Vienna (or Wien). Prague was once a substantial vine-grower and Paris may still boast an isolated patch of vines within Montmartre, but in Vienna more than 1,700 acres (700ha) of vineyards still hold their ground right up to the tramlines within the heart of the residential districts and surge up the side of the surrounding hills into the Vienna woods. North, west, and south, where the line of hills circles and protects the city, there are vines. Vienna also has its own unusually elegant biennial wine fair VieVinum held in the grandeur of the imperial palace, with no shortage of the delicate stemware in which Austria, so close to Bohemia, specializes.

Most of Vienna's wine is drunk as *Heurige*, in *Heurigen* – for this untranslatable word means both the new wine and the tavern where it is drunk. Every vintner seems to be tavernkeeper too, and chalks up on a board the wines and their (modest) prices, by jug or litre bottle, labelless, to be drunk on the spot or carried away. Good *Heurige* is sensational; spirited, sprightly stuff which goes straight to your head. Most of it is Grüner Veltliner. Some is Weissburgunder (Pinot Blanc), Traminer, and Müller-Thurgau; some is Riesling, although this is the grape most likely to provide Vienna's wines for the cellar.

Viennese connoisseurs know every grower in Neustift, Grinzing, Sievering, Nussdorf, and Kahlenberg, the wine villages of Vienna. The atmosphere in their leafy taverns varies from formulaic tourist-trap to idyllic. In most of them Beethoven wrote at least a concerto.

Vineyards continue to the south of the city along the Südbahn (as the region bisected by the southbound railway was once known but is now called Thermenregion, for its hot springs) flanking the last crinkle of the alpine foothills facing the hot Hungarian plain. Unlike the vineyards of Vienna, those of Thermenregion are too far from the River Danube to benefit from its refreshing influence. The Thermenregion also has the *Heurigen* tradition, however, and without nearly so many tourists.

Only the historically most important northeastern corner of Thermenregion is mapped here. In the 1970s the fat, rich white wines of Gumpoldskirchen were some of Austria's best known: spicy, late-gathered wines made from the lively Zierfandler, the heavier Rotgipfler or the local hero Neuburger.

Thermenregion still has a distinctive varietal mix but the white wine trend today is for dry Riesling and Neuburger and oaked Chardonnay, as well as for both dry and deliberately sweet Beerenauslese and Trockenbeerenauslese from Zierfandler and Rotgipfler.

The region has an unusually high proportion of red grapes, however, including the insubstantial Blauer Portugieser but also the soft, Pinot-like St Laurent. The spas of Baden and Bad Vöslau and some of the Steinfeld southern part of the region have a reputation for their well-ripened reds: Zweigelts and St Laurents as well as Cabernet Sauvignon and Merlot treated to new French oak.

----- · · · · City boundary

NUSSBERG Grosslage

[ ] Vineyards

[ ] Woods

≈500≈ Contour interval 100 metres

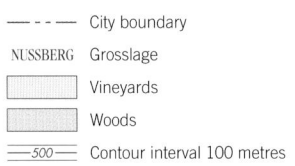

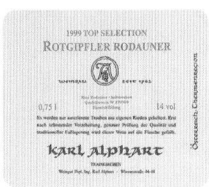

Chardonnay has *been invading the vineyards of Vienna, joining more traditional varieties such as Riesling, while the vineyards of the Thermenregion around Gumpoldskirchen are becoming increasingly famous for their full-bodied red wines as well as their rich, spicy whites.*

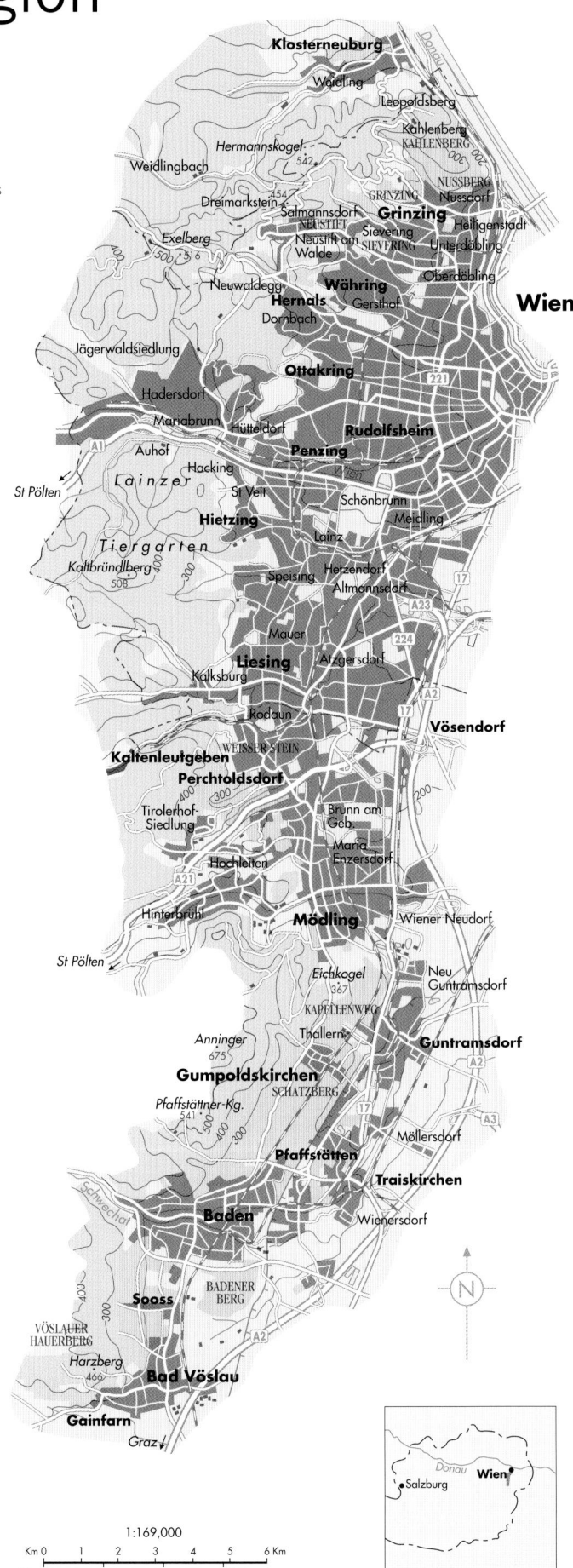

1:169,000

Km 0 1 2 3 4 5 6 Km

Miles 0 1 2 3 Miles

Burgenland

Burgenland lies on the Hungarian border – indeed the Hungarian red-wine district of Sopron is carved out of it. It grows a wider range of different grapes than any other Austrian wine region and the ubiquitous Grüner Veltliner covers barely a fifth of Burgenland's vineyards. Other popular grapes include Welschriesling, Blaufränkisch, Zweigelt, Müller-Thurgau, Weissburgunder (Pinot Blanc), Neuburger, Muskateller (Muscat Ottonel), St Laurent, Sämling 88 (Scheurebe), and the new-fangled Cabernet Sauvignon and Chardonnay. And like much of Hungary, its historic speciality is sweet wines made on the flat and often sandy shores of the Neusiedl lake, an extraordinary giant marshy pool, more than 20 miles (32km) long and only a metre deep. Of Burgenland's four areas, Neusiedlersee is today making Austria's greatest sweet white and red wines.

The rise of this unglamorous corner of the wine world to international fame has been extraordinarily rapid. After the Second World War fewer than 250 acres (100ha) of vines were grown between the marshy ponds on the east shore of the lake around villages such as Illmitz and Apetlon which then knew only dirt roads and no electricity. Wide village streets are still flanked by simple, single-storey cottages thatched with local reeds. Horse-drawn vehicles are no surprise. The Hungarian border is just a few kilometres away. The country is so flat here, and the lake so surrounded by waist-high reeds, that views of the lake are few and far between. One small 80ft (25m) rise is revered as a hill.

This may sound an unlikely description of great wine country. The secret is the lake, enveloped by mist through its long, warm autumns, encouraging so much botrytis, or noble rot, that bunch after bunch of grapes look as though they have been dipped in ash. This is Austria's hottest wine region (too hot for early ripening Riesling), wide open to Pannonian warmth, so red grapes (grown in a landscape not too dissimilar from the Médoc's) ripen reliably each year, yet the lake helps keep them reasonably crisp. And the final ingredient is some of the world's most thoughtful, curious, and well-travelled winemakers.

Alois Kracher, father and son, have done most to put Illmitz on the world wine map with an extraordinary range of sweet white wines (often carefully designed blends) created in vineyard and a simple winery-cum-laboratory, but they are by no means alone. These richly dramatic wines are made both traditionally in large old oak casks and in the more concentrated modern style that brings a smile to French coopers' faces.

The best Neusiedlersee red wines tend to come from (slightly) higher ground further away from the lake around the villages of Frauenkirchen, Mönchhof, and Gols. Here too the introduction of new French oak barrels has added rigour to the local grapes Zweigelt and St Laurent, neither of which are naturally high in tannin. Producers such as Achs, Heinrich, Nittnaus, Stiegelmar, and Umathum seem to make better red wines with every vintage.

Across the lake in Neusiedlersee-Hügelland there are real hills (which often encourage real rain), some much grander baroque architecture, and a serious history of fine winemaking. The most historically famous wine of Burgenland comes from Rust, and Ruster Ausbruch was regularly compared with Tokaji (see page 250). In sweetness Ausbruch is ranked between Beeren- and Trockenbeerenauslese. Vineyards slope east down to the villages of Purbach, Donnerskirchen, Rust, and Mörbisch and, being higher than those on the east of the lake, are slightly less prone to botrytis. Serious amounts of red wine are made here and in the vineyards that stretch west almost as far as Neustadt and south past Mattersburg.

In Mittelburgenland to the immediate south, one vine in every two is Blaufränkisch and the result is increasingly sophisticated versions of this invigorating red grape, using oak in a style pioneered by Hans Igler.

In favoured vintages *(which are not exceptional) Burgenland can boast one of the world's highest concentrations of botrytized grapes up to TBA quality, and fine reds such as those of Umathum and Triebaumer too.*

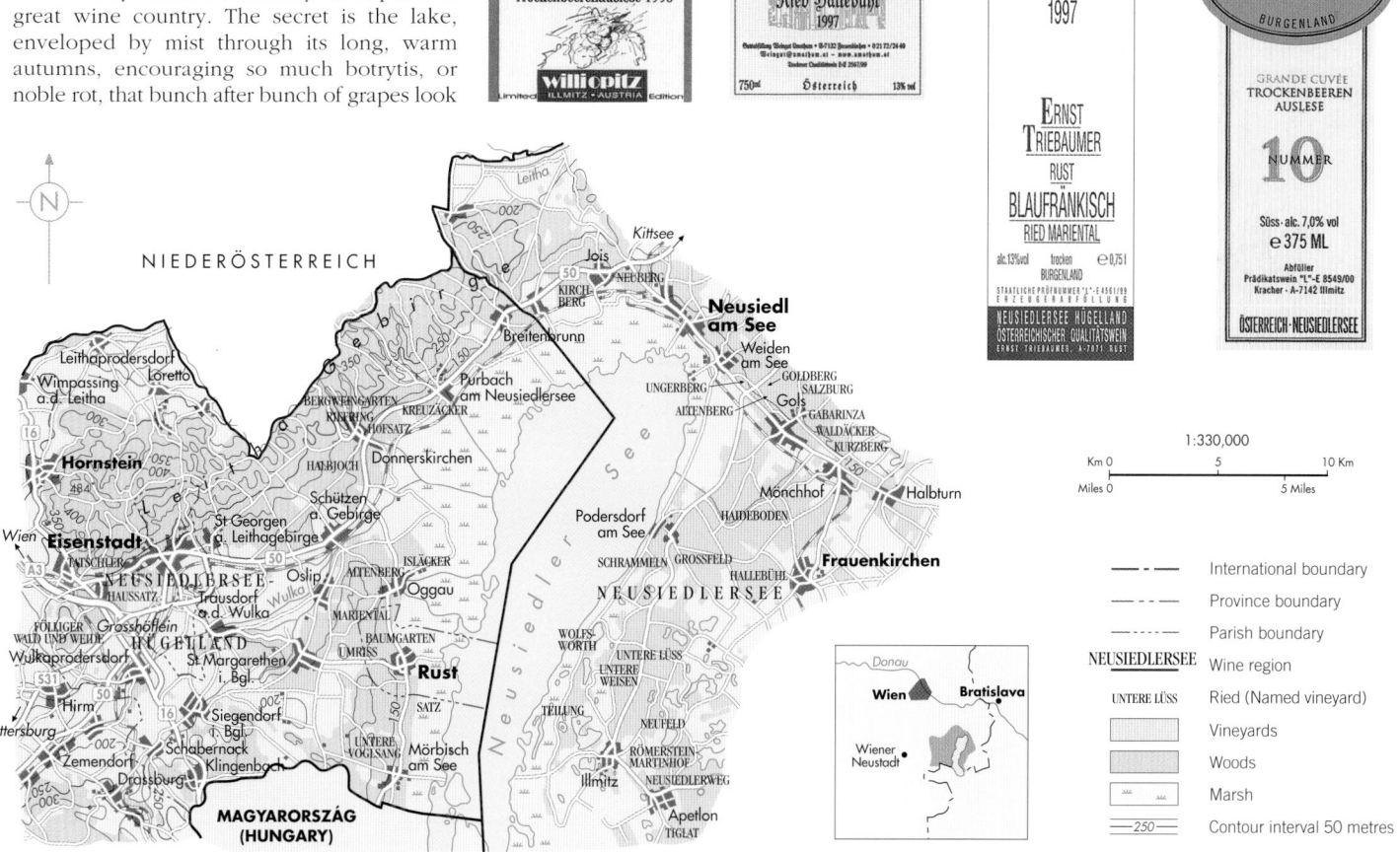

Hungary

Of all the wine-producing countries east of Vienna, Hungary has for centuries had the most distinctive food and wine culture, the most developed native grape varieties, and the most refined wine laws and customs. For this reason no country had more to lose by accommodating the taste of foreign buyers who looked on it as another cheap source of same-again wines.

From the 1960s, however, Hungary began to lose confidence in her traditions, her wines became less special – made to a price rather than a standard. The 1970s and 1980s saw planting of international grape varieties on a large scale – a trend that accelerated in the 1990s as formerly state-held land was privatized and many foreign investors sought easily exportable bargains. Modern winemaking technology and low-temperature, reductive winemaking invaded with a vengeance, resulting in distinctly fruitier but often duller wines than had been the norm. By the turn of the century, however, national pride was sufficient to sanction experimentation with Hungarian oak barrels and there was a glimmer of hope that Hungary's extraordinary palette of indigenous white grape varieties was beginning to be recognized as an asset rather than a liability.

The characteristic traditional Hungarian wine is white – or rather warmly gold – and spicy. It tastes, if it is a good one, distinctly rich, not necessarily downright sweet but full of fire and even a shade fierce. It is wine for meals cooked with more spice and pepper and fat than a light wine could stand. Like Germany, Hungary treasures her sweetest wines most. Tokaji (see overleaf) is her pride and joy. But most of the country makes wine, both traditional and international types.

The map opposite shows 22 wine regions defined by law in 1997, several of them with new names, cancelling familiar and historic ones.

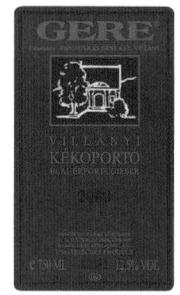

As a rule of thumb *northern and west-central Hungary is white wine country, the south the home of the best reds. The important exception is the red of Eger in the northeast. Hungarian wine (Tokaji apart) has always been labelled by place and grape variety. Prominent growers' names have only recently emerged as part of the picture.*

Hungary's great grape varieties begin with the strong, acidic Furmint and the softer perfumed Hárslevelű – the grapes of Tokaji, but not only Tokaj. They continue with the now all too rare Kéknyelű ("blue-stalk") of Lake Balaton (see opposite), capable of wonderful richness and attack, and the Szürkebarát, alias Pinot Gris, also lushest on Lake Balaton – although Nagyréde winery 50 miles (80km) northeast of Budapest claims the most extensive planting of this fashionable variety in Europe.

Quite different – lighter – are the aromatic, lively Leányka (the Fetească Albă of Romania); the even grapier Királyleányka (Fetească Regală); the fresh, even tart, Ezerjó of Mór; the Olasz Rizling (Welschriesling), tastier in Hungary than in many places; the Mézesfehér ("white honey"), rich and mouthfilling – and usually sweet; the rare, tart and fragrant Juhfark of Somló; and the popular new crossings Irsai Olivér, Cserszegi Fűszeres, Zenit, and Zefír; and all these before the Tramini, Sauvignon, Chardonnay, and Muskotály, or Muscat, are counted.

Hungarian red varieties are in the minority, although there are plans afoot to correct this imbalance. The soft, spicy Kadarka (called Gamza in Bulgaria) was once widely planted – a worker rather than a star and at its best as Szekszárd in

Left The extinct volcano of Mount Badacsony slopes south to Lake Balaton, Europe's biggest lake, offering ideal soils and exposures for the full-bodied and fiery white wines Hungarians love. Balaton is a busy holiday region with a potent thirst.

the south. Kékfrankos (alias Nagyburgundi) is Austria's Blaufränkisch, a relatively lightweight refresher here as elsewhere. In the north this and earlier ripening grapes such as Cabernet Franc and Merlot seem best suited; Kékoporto (Portugieser) is also planted. Hungary's most serious, ageworthy reds tend to be the rather unHungarian Merlot and Cabernet blends from the sunny far south.

Half of Hungary's vineyards are on the easily mechanized Great Plain, the Alföld, between the Duna (Danube) and the Tisza in the southern centre of the country, the regions now known as Kunság and Csongrád, on sandy soil which is little use for anything but vines. Great Plain wine, the red mainly Kadarka, the white Olasz Rizling or Ezerjó, is the day-to-day wine of Hungarian cities.

The other half of Hungary's vineyards is scattered among the hills that cross the country from southwest to northeast, culminating in the Tokajhegyalja, the Tokaji Hills.

In the south the districts of Szekszárd, Villány, Mecsekalja (incorporating Pécs), Tolna, and Hajós-Baja grow both red and white wines, but the emphasis today is on red. The climate here is Hungary's warmest. Kadarka is the historic grape, Kékfrankos well-entrenched, and Cabernet the rising star, making full-bodied, even sometimes big and wild, wines with firm tannins and acidity which need age, but are often over-oaked in pursuit of fashion.

Villány is the most favoured area, where such growers as József Bock, Attila, and Tamás Gere and the Tiffáns have substantial followings for Cabernet Sauvignon, Kékoporto and Merlot. On the slopes of Szekszárd the deep, reddish loess also gives tannic reds of Kadarka, Merlot, and the Cabernets. The names to look for are Vesztergombi, Tamás Duzsi, Heimann, and Péter Vida. In Tolna nearby, Antinori of Tuscany, known for his prescience, is also at work. Szekszárd also produces a Bikavér blend, an appellation otherwise limited to Eger.

Egri Bikavér was once Hungary's famous wine in the West, a rugged red sold as Bull's Blood. Eger, at the eastern end of the Mátra Hills in the northeast of the country, is one of Hungary's most important wine centres, a baroque city with huge cellars, magnificent caverns cut in the hills' soft, dark tufa. Hundreds of time-blackened oak casks, 10ft (3m) across and bound with bright red iron hoops, line 8 miles (13km) of tunnels. Their age and less-than-pristine condition played a part, along with the substitution of Kékfrankos for Kadarka, in an apparent thinning of the blood in this historic wine. New World winemaking help has been drafted in by the major producer, a common phenomenon in the modern winescape of Hungary. And at least two other producers are leading the way with serious wines. Vilmos Thummerer and Tibor Gál (trained in Tuscany, another Antinori connection), are the modern face of Eger, with Bikavér only part of much larger red and white portfolios. Of the whites the winner is the charming, fragrant Leányka.

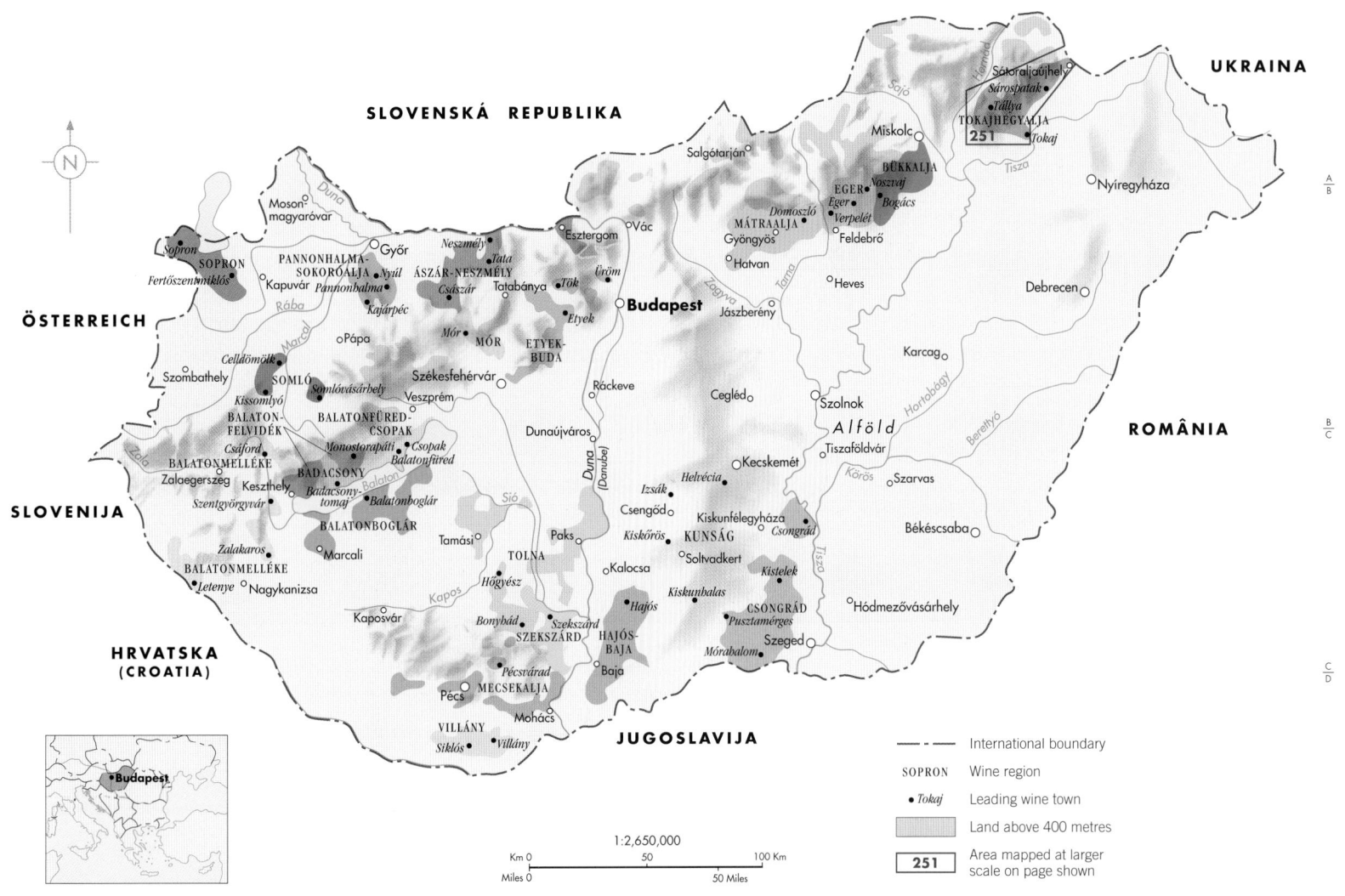

West of Eger along the south-facing slopes of the Mátra range is Hungary's second-biggest vineyard, Mátraalja, formed of the old districts of Gyöngyös-Visonta and Debrő. The sweet white Hárslevelű of Debrő was its great historic wine. Traditional Olasz Rizling and Kadarka are being supplanted by the international favourites. Racy Gyöngyös Chardonnay and Sauvignon are prime export wines.

In the far west, almost on the Austrian border, is Sopron, a red wine outpost growing Kékfrankos, a lively wine but hardly a great one.

To the east of here, Ászár-Neszmély was best-known for dry whites from traditional grapes but today produces a range of thoroughly international varietals from several new, ultra-modern wineries designed with exports in mind. Etyek-Buda, just west of Budapest, is another flourishing source of largely internationally styled whites, including sparkling, vast quantities of which are made in the cellars of Budafok, just south of the capital.

The small, isolated hill districts of Somló north of Lake Balaton, growing Furmint and Olasz Rizling on volcanic soil, and Mór to the north, growing Ezerjó on limestone, also have very distinct characters: Mór for tart, fresh, high-flavoured wine; Somló for more firm and mineral flavours, especially in its now-rare Juhfark – a water-pale wine so dry and tight in youth that its latent character can easily go unperceived. Both are among Hungary's "historical wine regions".

Lake Balaton, besides being the biggest lake in Europe, has a special significance for Hungarians. In a country with no coast, it is the sea and chief beauty spot. Balaton's shores are thick with summer villas and holiday resorts, fragrant with admirable cooking. It has good weather and a happy social life. The north shore of Lake Balaton has all the advantages of good southward exposure and shelter from cold winds, as well as the air-conditioning effect of a big body of water. It is inevitably a vineyard.

Its special qualities come from the climate, and from the combination of a sandy soil and extinct volcano stumps (Mount Badacsony is the most famous) which sprout from otherwise flat land. The steep slopes of basalt-rich sand drain well and absorb and hold the heat.

Olasz Rizling is the common white grape. Its wine can be very good when it is only a year old; dry but fresh and clean and not too strong. The real specialities, however, are the grapes that make powerful, honey-scented wine: Furmint, Szürkebarát, and Kéknyelű. Even at a year old, tasted from the barrel, a Szürkebarát can still be as white as milk and prickly and fierce with fermentation. In two or three years these wines – of which the Kéknyelű is reckoned the stiffest and best – have remarkable presence. They are aromatic, fiery, and quintessentially Hungarian; not exactly dessert wines but very much the wines for the pungent local food.

The Lake Balaton region has been divided into four appellations: the classic Badacsony and Balatonfüred-Csopak, with Balatonfelvidék are on the north shore. The south shore (formerly Dél-Balaton) is now Balatonboglár, best-known on export markets for Chapel Hill. The best grower is Ottó Légli. Various outlying vineyards to the west are grouped as Balatonmelléke.

Of all these subregions Balatonfüred-Csopak and Badacsony make the best wines. Normally the standard quality will carry the simple name Balatoni, with the grape name. The name Badacsonyi on a label implies a stronger, sweeter, and to the Hungarian way of thinking altogether better wine. The name to watch here is that of the Szt Orbán winery, whose owner, Huba Szeremley, will go to any lengths to restore and enhance the reputation of the region.

The singular flavour of Bálaton is not limited to its native vines. Whatever variety is planted picks up something of the dense and spicy style derived from deep volcanic soil and warm summers by the water. Here Sauvignon and Chardonnay become honorary Hungarians and Irsai Olivér adds body to its penetrating perfume. Little red wine is made, although the peninsula of Tihany can ripen excellent Kékfrankos.

Tokaj

Right Everything about Tokaji is original: grapes, soils, and winemaking are all unique. In the cold cellars, many miles of narrow tunnels deep in tufa rock, thick cellar mould contributes yeasts for long slow fermentation. Here wine is racked in the traditional way in the State Cellars at Tolcsva.

The word legend is more often used about Tokaji than any other wine. (Tokay is the old English spelling; the original is Tokaji; the town that inspired the name, at the bottom of the map opposite, Tokaj.) And with good reason. When Hungary became communist in 1949 the quality of what all agreed was the greatest wine of Eastern Europe was compromised. The famous vineyards and great estates of the Tokaji hill range, Tokajhegyalja, southernmost bastion of the Tatra, the western extension of the Carpathians lost their identity. They were confiscated and their wines were homogenized in the vast collective cellars that took control. Vines were moved from steep slopes to flat land, reduced from 10,000 to a lazy 2,500 plants per hectare, and forced to spew out absurd quantities. The wine was allowed to oxidize. It was as if all the châteaux of the Médoc sent their wines to be finished and bottled in one cellar – which then pasteurized them. After 50 years memories even of Lafite and Yquem would become dim.

Tokaji, though, has been legendary for 400 years. Only champagne has spawned as many anecdotes. History relates how the sumptuous Tokaji Aszú, made from botrytized grapes, was first produced – methodically, rather than by chance – by the chaplain of the Rákóczi family in their vineyard called Oremus (his name was Szepsy; the year 1650). How the Polish knights who raised the Turkish siege of Vienna in 1683 took home a passion for Tokaji. How in 1703 the great patriot Prince Rákóczi of Transylvania used it to woo Louis XIV and drum up support against his Hapsburg overlords. How Peter and Catherine the Great kept a detachment of Cossacks in Tokaj to escort their supplies – and how its miraculous restorative properties led potentates to keep Tokaji at their bedsides.

Tokaji was the first wine knowingly to be made from botrytized or "nobly rotten" grapes; over a century before Rhine wine, and perhaps two centuries before Sauternes. The conditions that cause the rot, the shrivelling of the grapes, and the intense concentration of their sugar, acid, and flavour are endemic to Tokaj.

The range is volcanic, rising in typically sudden cones from the north edge of the Great Plain. Two rivers, the Bodrog and the Tisza, converge at the southern tip of the range, where Mount Kopaszhegy, Bald Mountain, rises 1,700ft (530m) above the villages of Tokaj and Tarcal (just as the Garonne and the Ciron converge in Sauternes). From the plain come warm summer winds, from the mountains shelter and from the rivers the rising autumn mists that promote botrytis.

Of the three grape varieties in Tokaj today, some 70% of the vines are the late-ripening, sharp-tasting, thin-skinned Furmint, highly susceptible to botrytis infection. Another 20-25% is Hárslevelű ("lime-leaf"), less susceptible but rich in sugar and aromas. Between 5 and 10% is Muscat Blanc à Petits Grains – either used as a seasoning grape, as Muscadelle is in Sauternes, or as a sumptuous speciality on its own.

The vineyards of the Tokajhegyalja were first classified in 1700 by Prince Rákóczi. By 1737 they were divided into first, second, third, and unclassed growths, besides three great growths, one in Tokaj itself and two in Tarcal, which had an Yquem-like standing *hors concours*. The map opposite shows the principal villages of the region (there are 28 in all) whose slopes form a wide V, thus facing southeast, south or southwest. The northernmost make delicate and fine *aszús* from sandy soil. It was here that the original Oremus vineyard of the Rákóczis made the first of all Aszú wines. The new Oremus cellar, owned by Vega Sicilia of Spain, has moved south to Tolcsva.

In Sárospatak, with its splendid castle on the river, Megyer and Pajzos were two of the first vineyards to be privatized. Kincsem is the great vineyard of Tolcsva, named after Hungary's greatest racehorse by its former owners the Waldbott family, who are reclaiming it. The old Imperial Cellars in Tolcsva were still owned by the state co-op at the beginning of this century.

Olaszliszka ("Olasz" means Italian) is a 13th-century Italian settlement; more legend says the Italians introduced winemaking. Here the soil is clay with stones, producing more potent wines. Erdőbénye lies up by the oak forest, the source of barrels. Szegilong has a number of classed growths, and is seeing a revival. Bodrogkeresztúr and Tokaj itself, by the river, have the most regular botrytis: a number of small growers here, led by Dr Leskó, managed to produce and bottle their own wines under the communists.

From Tokaj, round the south side of Mount Kopaszhegy into Tarcal, the steep and sheltered vineyards are the Côte d'Or of the region; a succession of once-famous site names (the greatest is Szarvas) which continues through Tarcal onto the road to Mád with Terézia and the great growth Mézesmály. In Mezőzombor, Disznókő was one of the first vineyards to be privatized and spectacularly restored by AXA of France. Mád, the former centre of the wine trade, has the famous first growths Nyulászó, Szt Tamás, Király, and Betsek, as well as the steep, abandoned Kővágó, whose restoration is an important project. If the current renaissance of Tokaji has a figurehead it is István Szepsy, a descendant of the Rákóczi family chaplain and an excitingly innovative grower here. If it has a market leader it is Royal Tokaji, also in Mád, founded in 1989 by Hugh Johnson and others, and the first independent company of the new regime.

Tokaji is made by a unique two-stage process. In a good vineyard and vintage, shrivelled *aszú* grapes are picked progressively as they develop the mould, while grapes not shrivelled by botrytis are left on the vine, often until November. These are then pressed and fermented to make a base wine, which used to be held over for the following year but this is no longer permitted. The *aszú* grapes meanwhile are stored in an almost-dry heap, gently leaking the fabulous Eszencia – juice with up to 800g/l of sugar – to be reverently kept as the region's greatest treasure.

The vintner adds a paste of crushed *aszú* to a vat of the base wine (though some now use must) in the proportion of one kilo to one litre. A second fermentation starts, controlled by a combination of the sugar content and the cellar temperature (the higher the former and the lower the latter the slower the fermentation). The richest and finest wines maintain the highest degree of natural sugar; hence the lowest of alcohol.

The measure of sweetness is still theoretically the number of 20-kilo *puttonyos*, or vineyard hods, of *aszú* added to 137 litres (one *gönci* barrel) of base wine, although today sweetness is, more conventionally, measured in grams of residual sugar per litre. Wine sold as a 6-*puttonyos* Aszú must have more than 150g/l; Aszú Eszencia is 7-*puttonyos* wine, in which second fermentation is minimal, intensity phenomenal. Three *puttonyos* make it the rough equivalent of a German Auslese, four or five put it into the Beerenauslese class of sweetness and concentration. Nowadays, ageing periods are shorter than they were in the past. Aszú wines may be aged for no more than three years and Aszú Eszencia wines for just five years. Ageing normally takes place both in barrel and bottle; earlier bottling is now the norm. If no *aszú* has been added, the wine is Szamorodni (literally "as it comes") – developing a style rather like a light sherry and either Száraz (dry) or Edes (fairly sweet). Regrettably the unregulated term Late Harvest has recently appeared on labels to add to an already complicated picture.

Two more peculiarities of circumstance give Tokaji its unique character. Some producers leave the casks with a little headspace, and the pitch-black, small-bore tunnels are thickly veiled in a particular cellar mould, *Cladosporium cellare*. A rich store of yeasts and bacteria can therefore attack and feed on the oxygen in the wine, rather as flor does on fino sherry but much more slowly, weaving a complex web of flavours.

The most luxurious Tokaji of all is that made only from the juice that *aszú* berries naturally exude as they are waiting to be crushed. This Eszencia is so sweet it will hardly ferment at all. And of all the essences of the grape it is the most velvety, oily, peach-like, and penetrating. Its fragrance lingers in the mouth like incense. In the old days Eszencia was stabilized with brandy. Today it has the lowest degree of any wine – if you can call it wine at all. No age is too great for it (or indeed for any great Aszú wine). What it is like at 200 years (some of the great Polish cellars kept it that long) only the Tsars can tell.

What does the future hold? Since 1990 the state has been privatizing its land and cellars, restoring them to their rightful owners or selling them to newcomers. Six new ventures were begun by 1993, three of them by French insurance companies. Huge amounts of capital have been poured into upgrading vineyards, renewing equipment, and researching the finest qualities of the land. Estate-bottled Tokajis are again on the market and the names of the first growths are again becoming familiar. It is an exciting prospect, codified in ever-increasing detail as the law of the land in every sense.

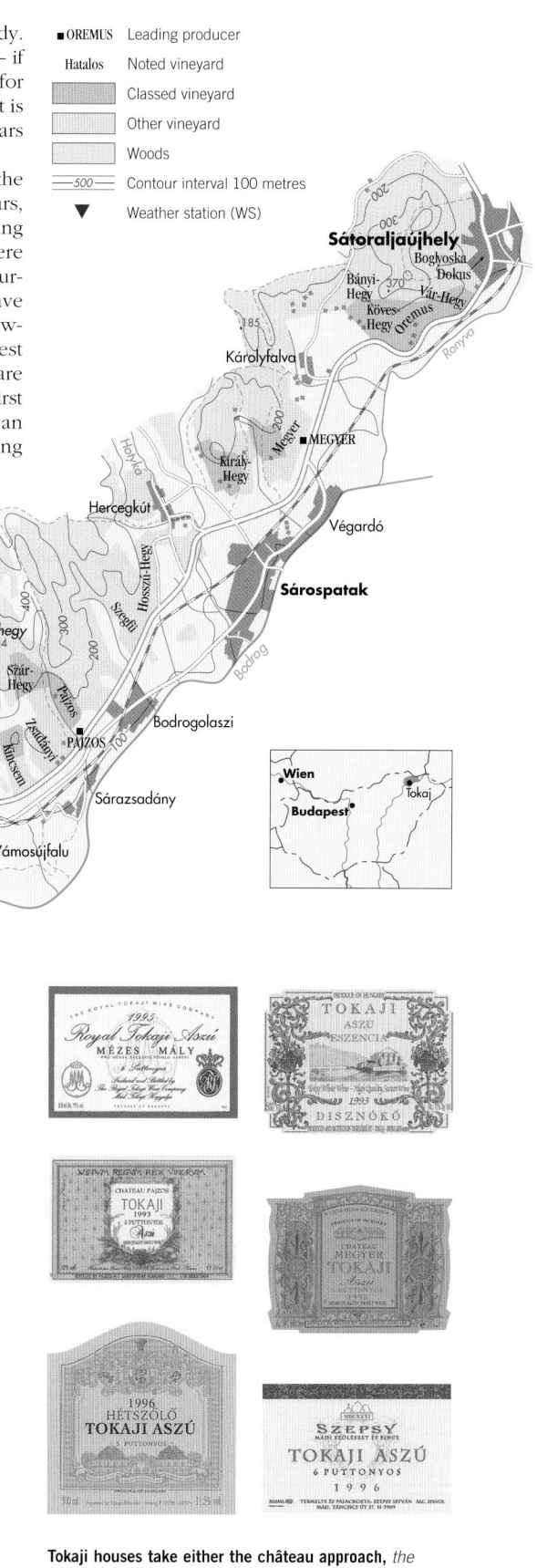

Tokajhegyalja: Tokaj

Latitude / Altitude of WS **47.30˚ / 426ft (130m)**
Mean July temperature at WS **70.4˚F (21.3˚C)**
Average annual rainfall at WS **23in (590mm)**
Harvest month rainfall at WS **October: 2in (50mm)**
Principal viticultural hazards **Autumn rain, grey rot**
Principal grapes **Furmint, Hárslevelű**

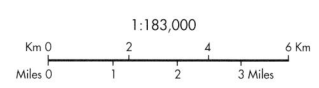

1:183,000

Tokaji houses take either the château approach, *the wines of the property blended in the house style; or the Burgundy approach, where individual vineyard wines are kept separate. Top left is a single-vineyard wine. Aszú Eszencia (top right) is the equivalent of a 7-puttonyos wine.*

The Czech Republic and Slovakia

It would be strange if the Czech and Slovak republics could not make good wine, lying as they do along the northern border of such incorrigibly vinous countries as Austria and Hungary. But for the moment potential is much more inspiring than the reality, all too often in the form of an undistinguished litre of lean Müller-Thurgau. The Czech wine market is dominated by a handful of German-owned blenders and packagers, with little interest in those few quality-orientated family concerns whose cult offerings can be run to earth only in the very best Czech wine shops.

The Protestant Czechs in the north and west of the new republic are themselves more likely to drink their delicious beer than the wine favoured by the Catholics of Moravia, now the eastern half of the Czech Republic, and the independent state of Slovakia to the east. Both of these areas are much more important wine producers than Bohemia, whose vineyards are closest to Prague.

Across Germany's eastern border from Sachsen, Bohemia has only about 1,000 acres (400ha) of vines, mainly along the right bank of the Elbe north of Prague, making light, Germanic-style wines, most notably at Mělník, Roudnice nad Labem, Most, and Velké Žernoseky, which is notable for its Rýnský Ryzlink (Riesling).

Moravia makes by far the majority of Czech wine from vineyards that are just over the border from Austria's Weinviertel, concentrated south of the capital Brno, from Znojmo spreading east across the peaceful Pálava Hills for some 70 miles (110km). In this region the most successful wines are Sauvignon Blancs (which have real zest without exaggerated aromas) from Znojmo's two well-equipped cellars at Šatov and Nový Šaldorf, also from Valtice, Pavlov, and Velké Pavlovice; Rulandské Šedé (Pinot Gris) from Pavlov, Mikulov, and Znojmo; Riesling from Valtice, Mikulov, Bzenec, and Nový Šaldorf; and the local and very tasty variety Pálava from Pavlov and Šatov. Muškát Moravský (Moravian Muscat) also has a certain following. The most planted white grapes are Müller-Thurgau, Veltlínské Zelené (Grüner Veltliner), and Ryzlink Vlašský (Welschriesling). The reds are not so interesting. Svatovavřinecké (St Laurent) and Frankovka (Blaufränkisch) are the most satisfactory grapes at present. Pinot Noir has performed better than Cabernet, although increased mastery of malolactic fermentation and oak ageing, as well as a new Moravian Cabernet crossing, may change this.

Slovakia has much the biggest wine region of the formerly united country, with about two-thirds of its acreage and production. Slovakia's vineyards cluster round Bratislava and scatter east along the Hungarian border, enjoying a marginally warmer climate and adding Ezerjó and Leányka to their repertoire.

Rača, just north of Bratislava, is known for hearty red Frankovka, St Laurent, and also Pinot Noir. Pezinok makes good Veltliners, and Rieslings in a wide range including a popular Silvaner blend. Modra has the best name for Riesling and Ruländer; Nitra perhaps ranks slighter lower for the same wines. Further south Sereď has produced Hubert sparkling wine since the early 19th century, while the Ruban cellars near Nové Zámky are respected for their spicy Ruländers, Veltliners, and Traminers and ripe red Limberger.

Slovakia has also inherited in its extreme east two villages that were once part of the Tokaj region in Hungary. The Tokaji and Yellow Muscat, as well as Traminer, from Nové Mesto, are nothing to be ashamed of.

A Bohemian label (top left) is flanked by a trend-setting Moravian vin de paille below which are a Moravian Chardonnay and a single-vineyard Riesling. The Slovakian pair includes a Frankovka (Austria's Blaufränkisch and Washington's Lemberger).

Slovenia

The relatively prosperous new nation of Slovenia (mapped in its entirety on page 255) just touches the Adriatic in Istria, then runs north up the Italian border to the Julian Alps and east through the dwindling Karavanke Alps to the Pannonian Plain. The southern slopes of the Alps and their rolling foothills provide some excellent grape-ripening sites that are grouped into three distinct wine regions: Primorska on the coast has a Mediterranean climate, while Posavje (along the Sava river) and, mapped below, Podravje (along the Drava river) are more continental.

Slovenia produces more white wine than red and can boast such indigenous grape varieties as Šipon, Ranina, Kraljevina, Pinela, Zelen, and Rebula. Various international grapes are also grown, often under a local name. Sauvignon Blanc is known as Muškatni Silvanec (inspired by the German synonym Muskat Silvaner). Pinot Blanc is Beli Pinot or Beli Burgundec, while Pinot Noir is Modri Pinot and Pinot Gris is Sivi Pinot. Traminec is Traminer, Renski Rizling is Riesling, Rizvanec is Müller-Thurgau, Laški Rizling is Welschriesling, and Modra Franinja is Blaufränkisch. Pikolit and Refošk are Italy's Picolit and Refosco respectively. Merlot, Cabernet, and Chardonnay, however, do not travel under aliases. Some grape blends can seem random but are increasingly assembled to express both terroir and the philosophy of the winemaker.

Podravje wines tend to have relatively low alcohol and crisp acidity, often masked by unfermented sugar. The most sought-after wines, however, are botrytized Trockenbeerenausleses, sweet rivals to the most famous wines of Austria's Burgenland to the north, made in vintages most favourably influenced by the radiator of the Pannonian Plain. Eisweins are sometimes produced and production of sparkling wines is also increasing, but Radgove is still the capital of such activity in Slovenia. Maturation in new, small oak barrels has been introduced and has resulted in some entirely new Slovene wine styles.

Wines from Posavje can be even lighter and tarter. The standard issue is pink Cviček, a popular local answer to the Austrian Schilcher. In Bela Krajina the climate is partly influenced by the Gulf of Kvarner (see map overleaf) so that wines grown here tend to be stronger and even red grapes will ripen. The climate is also particularly suitable for delicate botrytized wines. The fragrant Rumeni Muškat Eiswein has enjoyed particular success.

The westernmost Primorska region predictably favours the Italian style of dry whites and firm reds. Indeed in some cases, Slovene regions are simply a continuation of their neighbours across the border in Friuli: Brda continues Collio while Kras is eastern Carso. Around Koper on the coast, Refošk is particularly popular and when grown on the red, iron-rich soils of the harsh Kras (Karst) plateau it produces the famous Teran wine. Most of the vineyards in this area are influenced both by the sea and the Alps and tend to produce aromatic, powerful wines, although whites are still way ahead of reds in overall quality.

Slovenia sees its role clearly as a producer of better-quality wine. With its 50,000 acres (20,000ha) of vineyards, production is more or less in tune with local needs (Slovenia ranks fourth in the world in per capita wine consumption), although some producers are slowly beginning to build reputations on export markets.

Right The neat rigour of these vineyards following contour lines above the town of Ptuj in Podravje demonstrates the well-organized nature of viticulture and the wine business in modern Slovenia, however difficult the results may be to find outside the country.

This all-black line-up *may look rather sinister but it has a particularly fine example from each of Slovenia's three dynamic subregions. Slovenians are such enthusiastic wine drinkers that their wines are rarely seen abroad.*

Croatia and The Balkans

This section of the Atlas was once called the Former Yugoslavia, but the political turmoil of the 1990s demonstrated the irrelevance of such an inclusive term – for wine as much as for politics.

The winemaking traditions of the former Yugoslav republics are quite different, although there are similarities between the historic wine cultures of Croatia and Slovenia (which is discussed separately on the previous page).

The Balkans are rich in ancient grape varieties that persist, despite the inevitable invasion of French grapes, on the strength of their character and perfect adaptation to local conditions. Some 300 varieties are said to grow between the Pannonian Plain to the north, Greece to the south, the Adriatic to the west, and Bulgaria to the east.

Mountainous Bosnia-Herzegovina is the exception. Both its terrain and its Muslim inheritance make commercial winegrowing an unlikely occupation, except in the hinterland of the Dalmatian coastal strip and around the city of Mostar. Mostar's Žilavka is a white grape of memorable character: its wine full-flavoured and dry with a unique apricot smell. For the moment the local red Blatina grape pales beside it, although some of the area's emerging family operations may change this state of affairs.

Croatia (Hrvatska) is a complete contrast – a region full of original, if elusive, rewards with marked distinctions between the wines made along the Adriatic Dalmatian coast and those from the continental interior. Istria, closer in many ways to coastal Slovenia and northeast Italy, makes mainly Merlot and Teran (Refosco) reds and whites from Malvasia.

Žlahtina white is typical of the wines from the island of Krk and is used for sparkling wines on the nearby mainland. The sandy island of Susak (much of whose population is now to be found in New Jersey) has withstood the phylloxera louse but its indigenous pink-skinned Trojiščina grape is threatened with extinction because of its low yields.

From Rijeka south the great red grape is Plavac Mali, for a while thought to be an antecedent of Zinfandel. Among its most potent manifestations are dense and sweetish Dingač and pungent Postup from the steep, seaside terraces of the Pelješac peninsula north of Dubrovnik. It also turns up in formidable home-made Prošek – at best a fair substitute for port – from little rocky patches between fig and olive trees. A pale version is known as Opol, a traditional Dalmatian style of deep pink wine designed for simple summer drinking.

Since independence several small but ambitious wine businesses have emerged along the coast, joined most notably perhaps by Miljenko (Mike) Grgić, a Dalmatian famous for his Napa Valley winery Grgich Hills, who on the Pelješac peninsula produces a red from Plavac grapes and a white from Pošip, supposedly identical to Hungary's Furmint, and also grown on the nearby island of Korčula. Grk is a grape and white wine made in more limited quantities in

Above Low bushvines planted on the island of Hvar just off the Dalmatian coast. Such islands have a long tradition of viticulture which is increasingly recognized by outsiders, sometimes even to the point of financial investment.

Bili Žal on the eastern side of Korčula. Fine Plavac, including some experimental late-harvest wine, is made on the sunny island of Hvar but the speciality of the nearby island of Vis is the white Vugava grape.

Several more or less white wines of strong personality are made on these beautiful islands, where winemaking equipment is gradually being modernized. The pale, perfumed Bogdanuša and Parč of Hvar, and Maraština, delicate (as at Smokvica on Korčula) or potent in white Prošek, are all characters as different from a modern Sauvignon Blanc as you could hope to find. With Dalmatian food – tiny oysters, raw ham, grilled fish, smoky and oniony grilled meats, and mounds of sweet grapes and figs – the fire and flavour of such local wines can seem ambrosial.

Inland, continental Croatia produces rather less distinctive, mainly white wines which tend to follow the traditions of central Europe. Some notable, traditionally made sparkling wines are emerging, particularly from some of the new family operations in the Plešivica area west of Zagreb. Wines similar to those of inland Slovenia across the border are made north of the capital in Varaždin and Sveti Ivan Zelina. Most of Croatia's best Chardonnays come from here.

The Croatian region of Slavonia (Srednje Slavonija), more famous in the greater world of wine for the oak it provides for Italy's beloved *botte*, or larger casks, is slowly trying to re-establish its vinous traditions. Traminac (Traminer) and Riesling seem the best bets, although some

Silvaner and Austria's red Zweigelt are also grown. Kutjevo is an important grower of the local workhorse grape Graševina (Welschriesling).

Vojvodina shares the torrid characteristics of the Pannonian Plain with Hungary to the north and Romania to the east. Its grapes and wine styles show heavy Magyar influence in mainly full, sweetish whites plus some promising Pinot Noir. The vineyards with the best potential are on the Fruška Gora, the hills which relieve the flatness of Vojvodina along the River Danube north of Belgrade.

South of Belgrade in Serbia (Srbija) the town of Smederevo gives its name to the white Smederevka, a scarcely memorable grape that rapidly gives way to more invigorating red wines made from Prokupac in southern Serbia. But today, the bulk of Serbian wine production is semi-sweet white of no particular distinction.

Kosovo is different. Before the disintegration of Yugoslavia, its wine industry was heavily dependent on exports of Amselfelder, a sweet, red blend designed expressly for the German market. Albania's ancient wine industry, probably the origin of Hungary's Kadarka grape, is in equal turmoil but certainly has potential. Of the indigenous red wine grapes of this part of the world, the finest is Montenegro's Vranac, heady but with structure and even, with three or four years' ageing, class. The 13th July winery of Podgorica exports a fine example.

Even further south, on the border with Greece, the hot winelands of Macedonia are clearly best-suited to red wine production but are yet, in the modern age, to show just what they can achieve. The main producer, Tikveš of Kavadarci, sells a brand romantically known as T'ga Za Jug, or "longing for the south".

Four Croatian labels, including *Mike Grgić's Pošip and an accomplished Chardonnay from near Split. Top left is a solid representative of Montenegro's indigenous Vranac and bottom right a wine from Macedonia in the south.*

Bulgaria

Of all the wine countries of Eastern Europe Bulgaria has been the most single-minded in directing its wine industry towards exports and designing it to earn hard currency. Massive plantings of international grape varieties on fertile land in the 1950s were intended to pump out a river of everyday wine for the Soviet Union (and later for the West). For a time the plan succeeded beyond anyone's dreams.

By 1966 Bulgaria had become the sixth-largest wine exporter in the world. In 1978 Bulgaria began to make a serious impression on British claret-lovers in search of a bargain. Her wine exports reached a peak in the early 1980s, and to this day – in stark contrast to other Eastern European wine producers – constitute almost half of all wine produced.

But Gorbachev's 1980s anti-alcohol purge had a profound effect on Bulgaria. As the Bulgarian economy foundered and the market for their produce shrank, the country's vineyards were simply neglected or abandoned (although the minimal pesticide use has at least made parts of the country a birdwatcher's paradise). It is difficult to know exactly how much wine is today consumed or privately sold by those who grow it, but official figures suggest that by the late 1990s Bulgarian average yields had fallen to barely half the French average, although there are some signs that vineyards are now better tended.

During the 1990s the wineries and bottling plants that were once state-owned were privatized, some of the better wineries attracting investors from Japan, the United States, and Western Europe, sometimes to the tune of millions of dollars. There is serious ambition in these business plans (and a serious UK advertising budget in at least one case), but Bulgaria still needs to draw winemaking and grape-growing activities closer together to regain its old reputation for robust, fruity wines. Although Suhindol, Svishtov, and Haskovo wineries already own some vineyard, and Suhindol is aiming to be self-sufficient by 2009, only a tiny minority of Bulgarian vines are currently in the hands of the important wine producers (who succumbed to a passionate but injudicious affair with oak chips in the 1990s).

It was unadulterated, frank, unusually vigorous Cabernet Sauvignon that built Bulgaria's reputation for value in the late 1970s and early 1980s. Merlot has since joined the party and by the beginning of this century, thanks to long overdue investment in temperature control and an influx of Australian winemaking expertise, some Bulgarian producers had finally, and rather late in the day, mastered Chardonnay, and fresh, fruity reds. Bulgaria, if its figures are to be believed, still has considerably more Cabernet vineyard than California, despite the extraordinary recent expansion on the West Coast. Other minor imported grapes are Riesling and Sauvignon Blanc.

This is not to say that Bulgaria does not have some extremely respectable grape varieties of her own. Mavrud is a fine, late-ripening, characterful red grape that can produce strapping, spicy reds suitable for a long life, but this unique variety has been waning even in its homeland of Assenovgrad near Plovdiv, Bulgaria's second city after Sofia. Melnik is another, even rarer, southern speciality grown right on the Greek border (see below). It makes scented, powerful wines, some of them strangely sweet but impressive survivors of long ageing in old oak. Much more common than either of these though is Pamid, which gives pale, gulping wine, and Gamza, Hungary's lively Kadarka, but apparently more widely planted in Bulgaria today.

Most of the wines exported from *Bulgaria are based on Bordeaux red grapes but white winemaking has been improving and the two local red grapes featured here have real personality. The Melnik is grown in vineyards between the Bulgarian and Macedonian borders.*

Bulgaria: Plovdiv

Latitude / Altitude of WS **42.08˚ / 623ft (190m)**
Mean July temp at WS **74.5˚F (23.6˚C)**
Annual rainfall at WS **20in (520mm)**
Harvest month rainfall at WS **September: 1.2in (30mm)**
Chief viticultural hazard **Fungal diseases**
Principal grapes **Cabernet Sauvignon, Merlot, Rkatsiteli, Gamza, Misket, Welschrizling, Ugni Blanc**

— · — · —	International boundary
BLACK SEA	Wine region
VARNA	Appellation of origin (Controliran)
•Varna	Leading wine town
•Byala	Other town with winery
■ BLUERIDGE	Other named winery
▒	Wines of controlled appellation of origin (Controliran)
▒	Land above 1000 metres
▼	Weather station (WS)

Among whites, the dominant local varieties are Georgia's crisp Rkatsiteli and Dimiat (Serbia's everyday Smederevska). Red Misket (a local crossing of Dimiat and Riesling) and Muscat Ottonel are popular, as is Aligoté, surprisingly widely planted in Eastern Europe.

Bulgarian officials seem determined to dragoon the country's wine industry into a regime as strict as France's Appellation Contrôlée system. Controliran is the equivalent of an appellation, but with many limitations. Reserve wines must be matured in oak, often American, sometimes French or Bulgarian. Lawmakers have furthermore redrawn the country's wine map twice in the last 25 years, in 1978 and 2000, the latest wine regions being shown on this map.

The great majority of Bulgaria's Cabernet and Merlot grapes are grown in the Thracian Valley south of the Balkan Mountains, the Stara Planina,

and vinified at Blueridge (which was designed by Australians), Slaviantzi, Sliven, and Iambol wineries. Although this area has relatively hot summer days, it is cooled by mountain air from the Balkans, which run east-west across the centre of the country. Further south is the Haskovo winery, which has built up a reputation for reds, especially soft Merlots.

The ambitious Svishtov winery, one of the first to control its own grape supply, and Rousse winery to the east are on the Danube, which forms the border with Romania. Suhindol, a large co-operative further south, but well north of the Balkan Mountains, is even more ambitious in terms of vineyard ownership, and was the first Bulgarian winery to be privatized in the wake of the fall of communism.

Most of Bulgaria's best white wines come from around Shumen and Preslav in the coolest,

northeast part of the country, although Pomorie on the hot, southern Black Sea coast has white wine, and brandy, ambitions.

The Valley of the Roses between the Balkan and Sredna Gora mountains, famous for its damask roses grown for their essential oils, or attar, produces perfumed wines too: both Misket and Muscat as well as some Cabernet Sauvignon.

Over the Rhodope and Pirin mountains (Zapadri Rodopi and Pirin Planina) in the warm southwest of the country, close to the borders of Greece and Macedonia, the Struma Valley produces only a small amount of wine. The Damianitza winery in Melnik is synonymous with the Shiroka Melnishka Losa ("broadleafed vine of Melnik"), or Melnik, which makes what are surely Bulgaria's most original wines. And originality has unfortunately become an all too rare commodity in Bulgarian wine.

Romania

Romania will surely export some great wine one day. It is not only a matter of situation – although Romania lies on the same latitudes as France – but of temperament. Romania is a Latin country in a Slav sandwich. It has long enjoyed a natural affinity with the culture of France – and France a weakness for Romania. Its wine literature shares the sort of hard-headed lyricism of much of French gastronomic writing.

There is admittedly a great difference between the Atlantic influence which makes France moist and mild, and the continental influence which dominates Romania and its hot, dry summers. But there are local moderating influences: the Black Sea and the height of the Carpathian Mountains.

In this part of the world political history is inescapable. Romania today is far larger than it was a century ago. Before 1918 Transylvania and Banat were part of Hungary; Dobrogea of Bulgaria. On the other hand the ancient region of Bessarabia, now the recently coined republic of Moldova (described on page 260), was the northern half of Romanian Moldavia.

The Carpathians curl like a conch in the middle of Romania. They occupy almost half the country, rising from the surrounding plain to about 8,000ft (2,400m) at their peaks, and enclosing the high Transylvanian plateau. Across Wallachia, the south of the country, the Danube (Dunărea) flows through a sandy plain, turning north towards its delta and isolating the Black Sea province of Dobrogea.

In Romania, as in the old Soviet Union, a great planting programme in the 1960s turned huge tracts of arable land into vineyard, so that by the late 1990s Romania's 600,000-plus acres (250,000ha) of vines made it the fifth largest grower and producer of wine in Europe, and by far the most important in the old Soviet Bloc. Non-Romanians may well be surprised by this as, unlike Bulgaria and Hungary which export the majority of the wine they produce, Romania drinks most of her wine herself.

Three-quarters of the wine consumed in Romania is white, made mainly from local vine varieties. Fetească Albă (famous in Hungary as Leányka) and Fetească Regală (a 1930s crossing of the Grasă of Cotnari and Fetească Albă) are the most widely planted, but Welschriesling and Aligoté are also common, as is Merlot. Cabernet Sauvignon, Sauvignon Blanc, Gewürztraminer, Pinot Gris, and Muscat Ottonel are other international grape varieties with a track record in

---

- –·––·– International boundary
- BANAT   Wine region
- COTNARI   Wine subregion
- •Sadova   Leading wine town
- ▪ PANCIU   Winery
-    Wine-producing area
-    Land above 1000 metres
- ▼   Weather station (WS)

1:3,750,000

Km 0   50   100   150 Km
Miles 0   50   100 Miles

Romania: Bacău

Latitude / Altitude of WS **46.35° / 623ft (190m)**
Mean July temp at WS **67.8°F (19.9°C)**
Annual rainfall at WS **21in (540mm)**
Harvest month rainfall at WS **September: 1.8in (45mm)**
Chief viticultural hazards **Spring frost, drought**
Principal grapes **Fetească Albă, Fetească Regală, Welschriesling, Aligoté, Merlot, Cabernet Sauvignon**

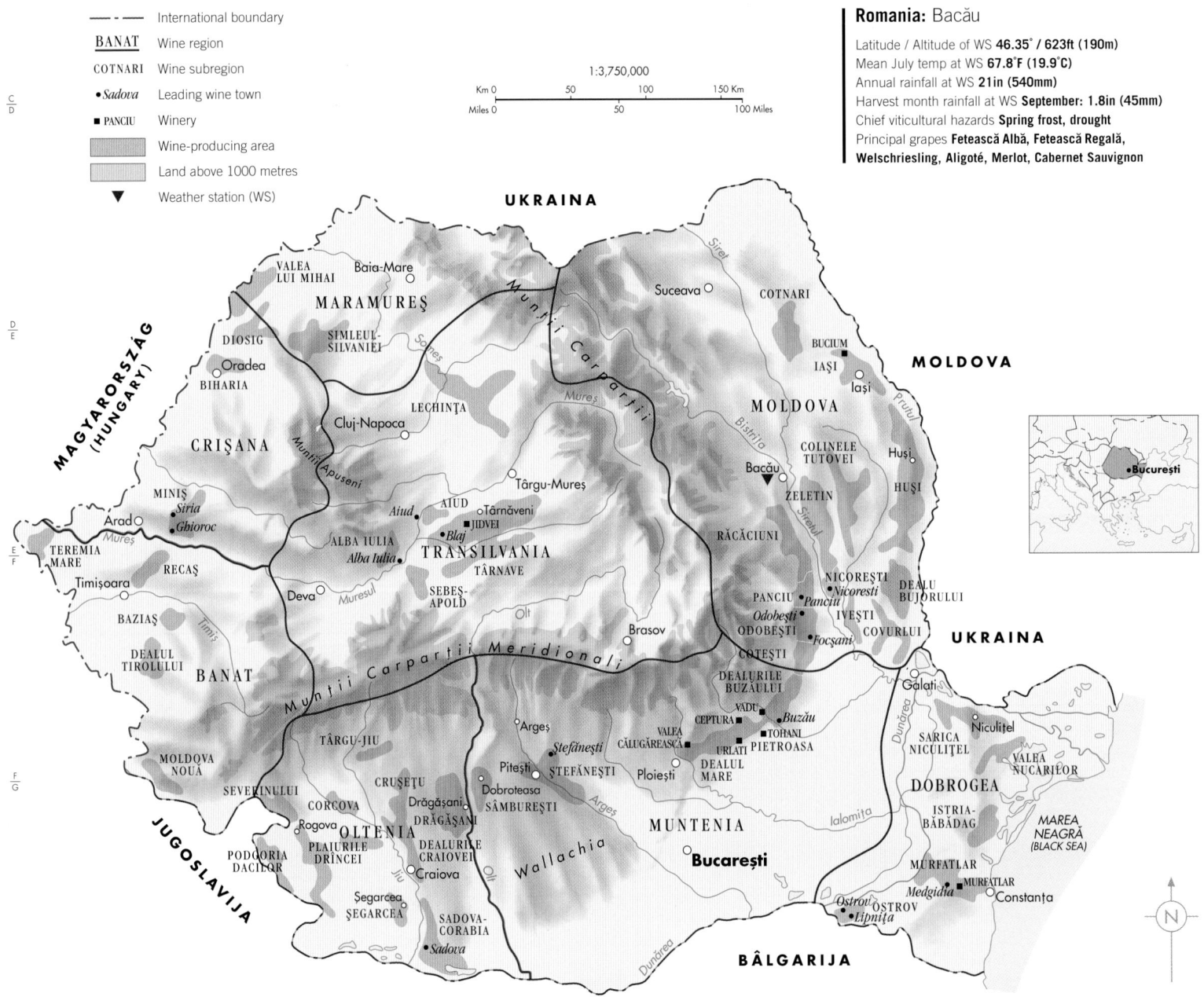

Romania. There is also a little Chardonnay and Pinot Noir. Of Romania's own red varieties, Băbească makes light, fruity wines, and Fetească Neagră more serious stuff.

Like Hungary, Romania has one wine whose name was once famous all over Europe. But while Tokaji struggled on through socialism to re-emerge in splendour, Cotnari, which was known in Paris as "Perle de la Moldavie", faded from sight. It is now being resurrected. Cotnari was traditionally a natural white dessert wine made in the northeast of the country. It is like Tokaji but without oxidation: pale, delicate, and aromatic; the result of botrytis attacking the indigenous "fat" Grasă and tart Frâncusa, scented with what is considered the indigenous and highly perfumed Tămîioasă (the frankincense grape) and Feteasca Albă. Barrel ageing is brief: complexity develops in the bottle. Cotnari comes from the part of Moldavia that was left to the Romanians after first the Tsars then the Soviets had annexed its northern half – annexation that led to intense planting further south.

The country today is divided into eight wine regions, of which Romanian Moldova, to the east of the Carpathians, is by far the biggest, with over a third of all Romania's vineyards. Wallachia, consisting of the Muntenia and Oltenia hills, the southern ramparts of Transylvania, comes next with more than a quarter.

Northern Moldova is white wine country, with Cotnari as its pearl. The great concentration of production, though, is further south in the central Moldavian Hills: Vrancea, with Focsani as its capital and 100,000 acres (40,500ha) under vine. Cotesti, Nicoresti, Panciu (known for sparkling wine) and Odobesti (a brandy centre) are the lilting names of its wine towns. The terrain varies but much of it is sand, as in the Great Plain of Hungary. The vines have to be planted in pockets dug deep enough for their roots to reach the subsoil, sometimes as much as 10ft (3m) below the surface. It seems a desperate expedient, especially as it takes the vine some time to grow up to ground level and come to bear fruit. But good light wines are being made where nothing would grow before.

Following the curve of the Carpathians Moldova gives way to Muntenia, better known by the name of its most famous vineyards at Dealul Mare. These hills, well-watered, south-sloping, and with the highest average temperatures in Romania, are largely dedicated to Cabernet, Merlot, and a grape thought to be Pinot Noir, as well as full-bodied Fetească Neagră, Burgund Mare (Austria's Blaufränkisch), and, more recently, some appetizing Sangiovese. In Soviet days red wines from here were generally made sweet for the demands of the Russian market. Exports to the West have helped to correct this although some of the (extremely well-made and even better-priced) Cabernets and Pinot Noirs are still on the sweet side. One white speciality stands out: unctuous and aromatic dessert Tămîioasă from Pietroasa.

Romania's short Black Sea coast gives Dobrogea, across the Danube to the east, the country's sunniest climate and lowest rainfall. Murfatlar has a reputation for soft red wines and luscious white ones, even sweet Chardonnays, from exceptionally ripe grapes grown on limestone soils, tempered by on-shore breezes.

The outcrops of Carpathian foothills scattered through Muntenia and Oltenia each have their own specialities. Pitesti is known for aromatic white wines (particularly from Stefănesti); Drăgăsani for Cabernet Sauvignon, Merlot, and Pinot Gris, especially from Sâmburesti. South of here on the Danube plain Segarcea has an established name for Cabernet, and a growing one for Pinot Noir.

In the western corner of Romania the Hungarian influence is plainly felt; many of the red wines of Banat are made from Pinot Noir and Hungary's Kadarka (here spelt Cadarca). The best come from Minis. The principal white grape is the Welschriesling.

Transylvania, meanwhile, remains like an island in the centre of the country: a plateau 1,500ft-plus (460m) above sea level, cool and relatively rainy, favouring much fresher and crisper whites than are produced in the rest of Romania. Târnave makes the best dry Fetească; Alba Iulia the most aromatic Muscat Ottonel and Gewürztraminer.

Below Sun-soaked vineyards near Buzău in the north of the Dealul Mare zone where mainly red grapes are made into increasingly dry wines. Romania has no shortage of grapes but urgently needs more investment in equipment.

A hotchpotch of languages, graphics, *and wine styles is at least truly representative of the current state of the Romanian wine industry, whose potential is frustratingly unrealized – so far. Fetească Neagră is a grape variety to watch.*

The Former Soviet Republics

One of the many extraordinary things about wine is that it provides an accurate reflection of social history. Nowhere has this been more obvious than in what, until the fall of communism, was the Soviet Union.

In the 1950s the Soviet Union officially decided in favour of wine, theoretically at the expense of vodka. In 1950 she had nearly a million acres (400,000ha) of vineyards. By 1985 she had almost 3.5 million (1.4 million) which made her second only to Spain in the world league table of area under vine, and third in production, behind Italy and France. This was certainly the biggest and fastest extension of the world's winegrowing capacity ever seen. Yet even this was not enough: the Union was an insatiable wine importer, buying in some 7 million hectolitres a year – about as much wine as the entire annual production of Portugal – much of it from other eastern bloc countries and from Cyprus.

In the mid-1980s, however, Gorbachev decided that even wine was a dangerous sap to Soviet morale and set about sobering up his citizens by shutting down hundreds of wineries and pulling up almost a third of all vineyards, so that by the late 1990s the former Soviet republics together produced an official total of just 3% of the world's wine.

The second Russian revolution of 1991 has not changed the system overnight, but it has opened the door to those enterprises in what is now the Commonwealth of Independent States (CIS) which produce interesting wine to bypass Moscow. There are numerous chronic difficulties: no bottling equipment or even bottles, for example, in many wineries, unreliable transport and a certain anarchy over exactly which and how much fruit goes into which wines. Serious wine producers are pressing for some sort of wine regulation to combat the fraud that is so widespread, but the spotlight is now back on the regions that gave Russia her best wines in the past. Without exception these lie in the broad sweep mapped opposite around the north coast of the Black Sea as far east as the Caspian Sea.

Moldova in the extreme west is the ex-Soviet republic with the most vines and the most obvious potential, for, thanks to the efforts of

French colonists at the end of the 19th century, the great majority are the most saleable varieties in the world: Cabernet Sauvignon and Merlot.

The Kremlin cellars of the Tsars looked for their finest table wines to what was then Moldavia (and anciently Bessarabia). Moldova's history has been a tug-of-war between Russia and Romania. Happily for its (largely Romanian) people, neither side prevailed and Moldova won the prize of independence in 1991. (See page 259 for details of wine production in Romanian Moldova.)

During the Soviet years Moldova's natural affinity for the vine was paid the backhanded compliment of a colossal, indiscriminate planting programme, reaching almost 600,000 acres (240,000ha) and furnishing one-fifth of the Soviet Union's wine drinking requirements in the early 1980s. A combination of particularly severe winters with Gorbachev's anti-alcohol campaign has since removed 140,000 acres (57,000ha). But for a country with a population of 4.3 million, 460,000 acres (183,000ha), or one tenth of the area of the country, is still a lot of vines.

The elements that combine to grow first-class grapes in Moldova are the latitude of Burgundy, relatively poor soils, the valley slopes of many rivers, and a climate tempered by the Black Sea. Winters are occasionally cold enough to kill unprotected vines, but long-established vineyards in the best sites have an almost model climate.

The great majority of vines are planted in southern and central Moldova around the capital

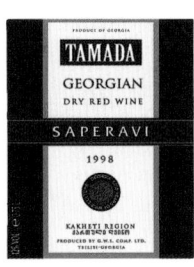

Ancient and modern: *bottles of this pre-revolutionary 1905 White Muscat still lie in the Massandra cellars. The Georgian Saperavi, the country's most famous grape, was made using Australian expertise and French capital.*

Chişinău in the Bugeac zone. Moldova's most famous vineyard today is at Purcari in the southeast, where Cabernet and Saperavi, the splendid red Georgian grape producing dark, plummy, acidic wines for long ageing, make a formidable claret-like blend. Only the country's lack of infrastructure and stable commercial environment has frustrated foreign attempts to capitalize on Moldova's most obvious asset.

The second most important vine-grower among the ex-Soviet republics is Moldova's eastern neighbour the Ukraine. While there are significant vineyards around the Black Sea ports of Odessa and Kherson, by far the most interesting wine region is the Crimea (Krym).

The Crimea became part of the Russian Empire under Catherine the Great at the end of the 18th century. The Mediterranean climate of its south coast soon made it the natural resort area for the more adventurous aristocracy. It was developed by the famously rich and cultured anglophile Count Mikhail Vorontzov in the 1820s. Vorontzov built a winery, and later his palace, at Alupka, southwest of Yalta, and founded a wine institute (wine being his passion) at Magaratch nearby, which continues to be the most important in the CIS.

In a precise parallel with what was going on in Australia at the same time (and California a generation later) Vorontzov began by imitating as closely as possible the great wines of France. His success was as limited as someone trying to make burgundy in Barossa. The south coast was too hot. Only six miles (10km) inland, on the other hand, it was too cold. Winter temperatures go down to –4°F (–20°C) and vinifera vines have to be completely buried to survive at all. Notwithstanding, there are vast inland plantings by the Soviets, mainly of Rkatsiteli, but also of special winter-hardy crossings bred at Magaratch.

A generation after Vorontzov, Prince Lev Golitzin was more scientific. After the Crimean war of 1853-56 the Tsar built a summer palace, Livadia, between Alupka and Yalta. Golitzin had remarkable success making Russia's second favourite drink, sparkling *"shampanskoye"*, 30 miles (50km) east along the south coast at his Novy Svet ("New World") estate – a tradition

Left Well-tended vineyards in Georgia, one of the few ex-Soviet republics to have a long history of making table wines. They have such a reputation that many times more "Georgian" wine is now sold in the CIS than could possibly have been made there.

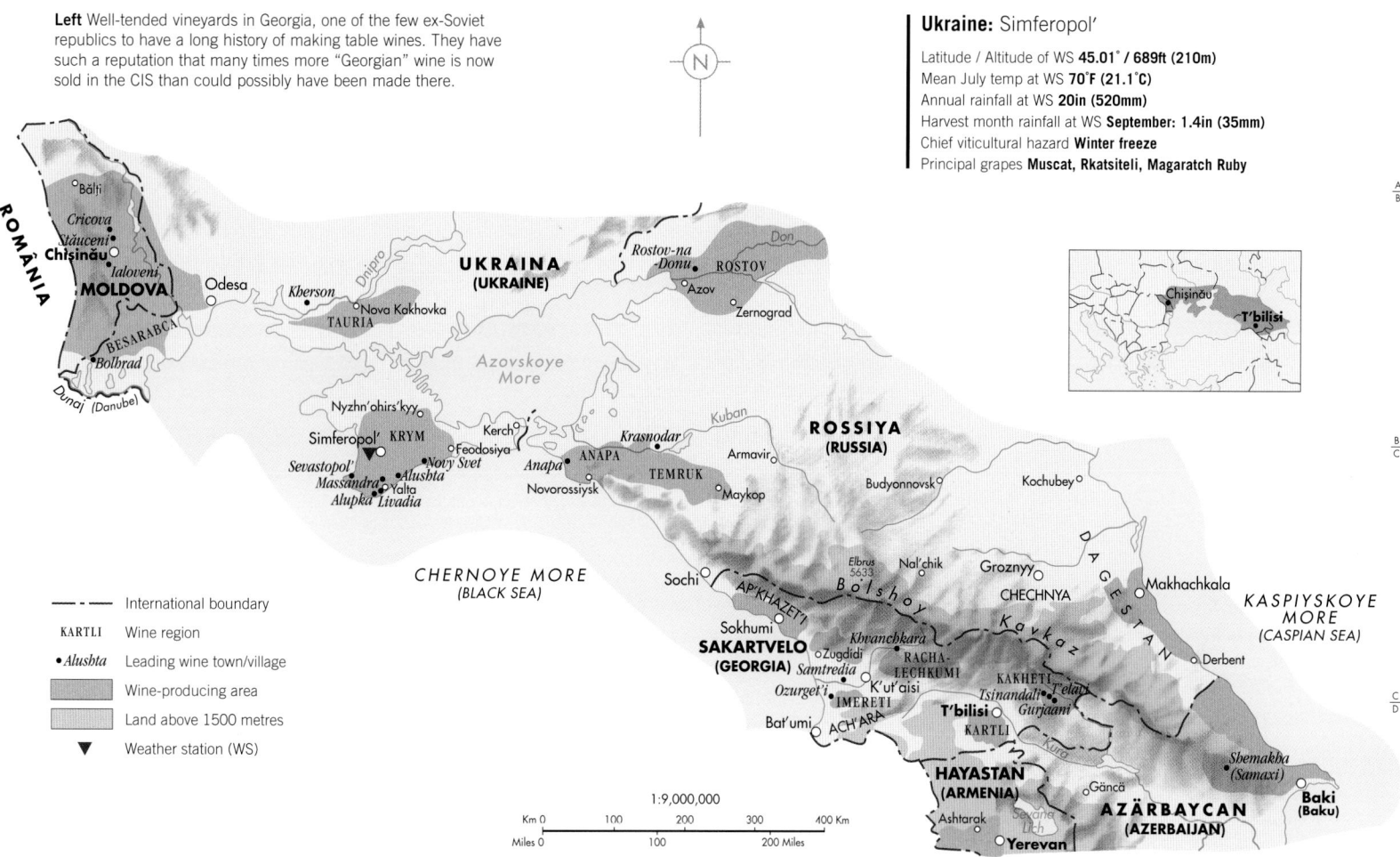

Ukraine: Simferopol'

Latitude / Altitude of WS **45.01˚ / 689ft (210m)**
Mean July temp at WS **70˚F (21.1˚C)**
Annual rainfall at WS **20in (520mm)**
Harvest month rainfall at WS **September: 1.4in (35mm)**
Chief viticultural hazard **Winter freeze**
Principal grapes **Muscat, Rkatsiteli, Magaratch Ruby**

— — — International boundary
KARTLI Wine region
• *Alushta* Leading wine town/village
Wine-producing area
Land above 1500 metres
▼ Weather station (WS)

1:9,000,000

Km 0   100   200   300   400 Km
Miles 0   100   200 Miles

that continues. But the destiny of the Crimea clearly lay in dessert wines. In 1894 the Tsar built "the world's finest winery" at Massandra, near Livadia, with Golitzin in charge, to develop the potential of the south coast, a narrow 80-mile (130-km) belt between mountains and sea, for strong, sweet wines of all sorts.

These wines established a fabulous reputation in pre-revolutionary Russia, and were not undervalued by Stalin who, during the Second World War, had the entire stock moved from the cellars of Massandra to the delightfully named Number One Winery in Georgia until it became clear that there was no danger of Hitler's troops getting their hands on them.

The names of Massandra, Livadia, Alupka, and Novy Svet, as well as those of Alushta, Ai-Danil, and Ayu-Dag, re-emerged in the West in 1990 at an extraordinary sale held in London by Sotheby's, when wines from the official collection at Massandra, started by Golitzin and dating back to 1880, were auctioned.

They were called "Port", "Madeira", "Sherry", "Tokay", "Cahors" (a wine with historic status within the Russian Orthodox church), or even "Yquem", as well as Muscats, White, Pink, and Black. Most of the wines were extremely fine, a large number superb, and the White and Pink Muscat of Livadia perhaps best of all.

The Massandra winery still houses nearly a million bottles of these wines, 1,200 different bottlings in all, dating from the late 19th century, in what must be the world's largest, and certainly most distinctive, collection of old wines.

Georgia is a very different case (although its vineyards were also shrunk dramatically by Gorbachev). Far from being a recent colony of the vine, it may be the oldest wine region of all. Archaeologists have found in this general area between the Black and Caspian seas pips from what were obviously cultivated vines dating from thousands of years BC. Its own grape varieties are said to number over 500, of which a few dozen are officially sanctioned, including Mtsvane, Matrassa, the sterling, red-fleshed Saperavi, and characterful, crisp Rkatsiteli. The varied climates of its five wine regions, in fertile valleys south of the densely wooded Caucasus, offer terroirs for them all. Georgians are notorious for their relish and capacity for wine, Georgian wine being, according to local lore, uniquely powerless to induce a hangover.

Kakheti, where more than two-thirds of all Georgian grapes are grown, spans the easternmost foothills of the Caucasus. Its famously long-living inhabitants see a natural connection with the potency and nutritional value of Saperavi. Here Georgians still use pre-classical methods, conducting fermentation and maceration for three or four months in huge jars called *kwevris* buried in the ground, with highly aromatic and marvellously varied, if primitive, results.

Kartli, on flatter land round the capital T'blisi, produces the wines most recognizable to European palates. In Imereti to the west wine is also made the old fashioned way, and then revved up with added raw spirit. North of here in Racha-Lechkumi the climate is much wetter and local Alexandreuili and Mudzuretuli grapes are grown to make largely sweet wines. Local varieties and sweet wines also predominate in the humid, subtropical zone around the Black Sea coast.

A joint venture with Pernod-Ricard, based on Australian winemaking techniques applied in a modern winery in the Kakhetian city of T'elavi, is Georgian wine's most energetic exporter.

Today the red Saperavi gives the best available wines (some of them sweet and all of them fiery), although Rkatsiteli has proved itself a useful and adaptable grape throughout much of this area. Georgia's incredibly cheap and popular *shampanskoye* is made by the special continuous rather than batch method designed to meet Soviet thirst for fizz – one of the old Union's more benign technological innovations.

Vineyards around Krasnodar and in Dagestan benefit from the respective gentle influences of the Black and Caspian seas but those around Rostov-on-Don, Sevastopol', and within Chechnya bear the brunt of a severely continental climate in winter. Vines have to be specially protected, usually by labour-intensive burying, to survive the winter.

Grapes are also an important crop in many of the ex-Soviet Central Asian republics. In fact, according to official figures, Uzbekistan produces more wine than either Ukraine or Georgia, but is yet to launch such ferments on the international wine market. Like Dagestan, Armenia, and Azerbaijan mapped here, the Central Asian republics tend to produce wines that are sweet, strong, and, for the moment, less than refined.

Greece

Of all the wine-producing countries that have been radically transformed since the last edition of this Atlas (and there are many), it is perhaps Greece that is the most exciting. This is partly because it holds out hope of going backwards as well as forwards in time. Modern Greek wine's reputation is built not on imported international grapes – although these are certainly grown – but on indigenous grapes which may well be able to trace their lineage back to Ancient Greece, the cradle of modern wine culture as we know it.

This new era for Greek wine began in 1985 with the return of a handful of agronomists and oenologists from formal training in France. An influx of funds from both the EU and ambitious individuals allowed them to upgrade technology in some of the larger négociants (notably Boutari and Kourtakis) and to establish new, much smaller wineries in cooler areas where land was relatively cheap. Their successors are just as likely to have learnt their skills at Adelaide in Australia, Davis in California or TEI in Athens. An increasingly affluent middle class has provided buyers for these new wines – aeons away from the oxidized ferments once typical of Greek wine.

Intuitively many outsiders may feel that Greece must be too hot and dry to make good quality wine, but altitude and (north-facing) exposure often play their part. In fact some wines made in cooler vintages on the Mantinia plateau in the Peloponnese interior have to be deacidified and in Naoussa in Macedonia in the north of Greece, some vintages have been critically plagued by rain and rot.

Greece now has a relatively sophisticated yet rational and useful appellation system, with 20 appellations for table wines and a further eight for various sweet wines made principally from dried white Muscat and red Mavrodaphne grapes, as well as a Greek answer to Vins de Pays (the Greeks have adopted French as their wine language).

Northern Greece is the area with perhaps the most unrealized potential – and where the Greek wine revolution was heralded most conspicuously in the 1960s at Château Carras.

Physically Macedonia relates more to the Balkan landmass than the Mediterranean limbs of Greece. This is red wine country, dominated by one variety, the Xinomavro, whose name ("acid black") denotes sourness but whose wines are some of the most impressive in Greece. Naoussa is the most important appellation and the country's first (1971). With age the best-made wines can acquire a bouquet as haunting as all but the finest Barolo – although many wineries here in the north are still poorly equipped. There is snow on the slopes of Mount Vermio in winter but summers are so dry that irrigation is essential. The land is sufficiently varied and extensive for individual *crus* to deserve identification.

Goumenissa, at slightly lower altitudes on the slopes of Mount Piakos, produces a rather lighter version of Naoussa. Investment has been pouring in to Amyntaio on the northwest-facing side of Mount Vermio, which is so cool that it can produce aromatic whites, a denominated Xinomavro rosé, and fine sparkling wine.

Zitsa is the only appellation in Epirus in the northwest, with Debina the most planted white grape for still and fizzy dry wines. Epirus has Greece's highest vines at Métsovo, at nearly 4,000ft (1,200m), and the oldest Cabernet Sauvignon planted at Katogi Averoff in 1963.

An increasing number of fine, more international Vins de Pays are made around Drama in Thrace in the far northeast of the country, just as, proving modern Greeks' confidence in their wine, there are isolated developments all over northern Greece. Gerovassiliou of Epanomi just south of Thessaloniki is experimenting for example with Petite Sirah and Viognier as well as the indigenous white Malagousia.

Négociants and co-ops dominate central Greece for the moment while Athens' backyard, Attica, the country's biggest single wine region with 27,000 acres (11,000ha) under vine, has been devoted to retsina, the curious, resinated ferment that for so long dogged Greece's vinous reputation. Savatiano and Roditis are the indigenous white grapes and can be made into exceptional unresinated wines by the likes of Château Matsa and Kokotos (producers of Château Semeli).

These white grapes are also grown on the Peloponnese, currently Greece's best-known wine region thanks to its beautiful coastline, accessibility from Athens, and the lure of its ancient sites. Nemea, near Mycenae, is the most important appellation, making rather luscious red wines exclusively from Aghiorghitiko (St George) grapes. Relatively ordinary wine is made on the flatland but some stunning wines are emerging from lower-yielding vineyards at altitudes up to 2,145ft (650m). Gaia is the leading producer but is being challenged by a number of new neighbours. There is pressure for some official distinction between the valley floor and such obviously superior hillside sites as Koutsi, Asprokambos, Gymno, ancient Nemea, and Psari.

Patras in the northern Peloponnese is predominantly a white wine region and source of the

Above The dark, volcanic island of Santorini is closely associated with Greece's modern wine revolution. Yannis and Konstantinos Boutaris have built an ultra-modern wine tourism centre near this traditional Cycladic chapel.

finest Roditis. The rediscovered mineral-scented white Lagorthi grape has also been making waves, thanks to Antonopoulos's Adoli Ghis (meaning "guileless earth") bottling. Oenoforos, buying in grapes from the cool, north-facing Aighialia plateau with its strange canyons, is another producer who is keeping up the pace of change in a region that was long associated only with richly sticky Muscat and Mavrodaphne.

Of the Greek islands, Crete is much the biggest wine producer, famous in Venetian times for its sweet Malmseys. These seem, alas, to be extinct but the island's moribund wine industry has recently attracted much-needed funds and enthusiasm.

Cephalonia (Keffallonia) and its Ionian neighbour Zákinthos (with its own lively red Avgoustiatis grape) come next in importance, especially for fresh white Robola and Tsaoussi, Moschofilero, and imported grapes. Corfu is not an island for wine tourists.

In the Aegean, several islands make sweet wines of Muscat. Lemnos makes both dry and sweet Muscats but Samos is the best and most famous, and the prime exporter, with utterly clean and tempting wines. Paros grows its own Malvasia as well as the tough red island grape Mandelaria which can also be found on Crete (where négociant Boutari makes reliable everyday wines) and Rhodes whose most common grape is the full-bodied but under-performing white Athiri.

But of all the islands, Santorini is the most original and compelling. Its potent and intense wines, white and (very) dry, are made from ancient Assyrtiko vines, trained in little nests crouching on the windswept heights of this dormant volcano. Gaia's Thalassitis is an inspiring example.

From left to right: *Two of the finest Greek reds plus a variety of the country's unexpected white wine treasures – Tselepos' fine Moschofilero from the cool Mantinia plateau, a passport to international recognition, evidence of Crete's vinous revival, and the rare Samos Nectar.*

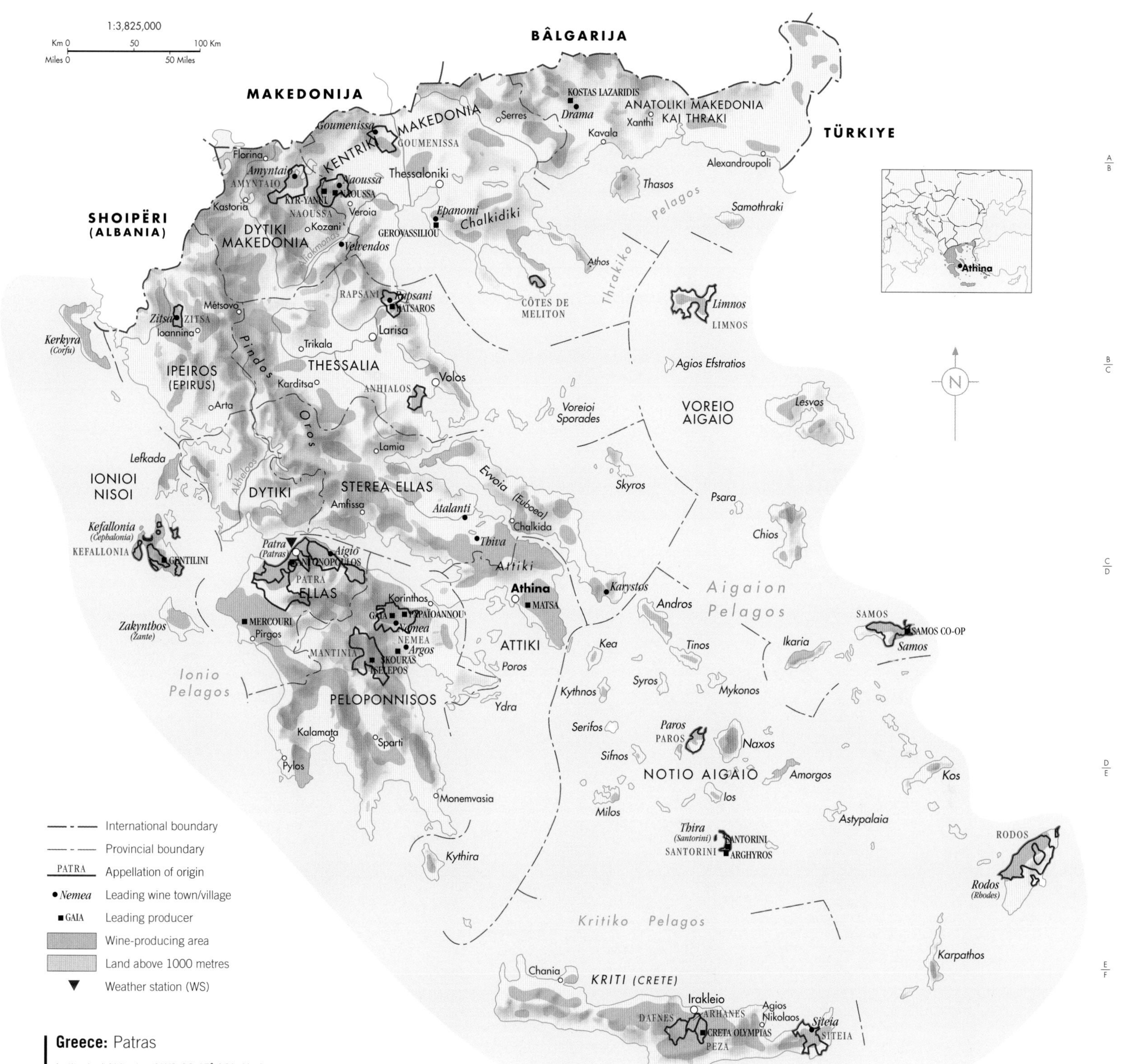

1:3,825,000
Km 0 50 100 Km
Miles 0 50 Miles
BÂLGARIJA
MAKEDONIJA
TÜRKIYE
SHOIPËRI (ALBANIA)
ANATOLIKI MAKEDONIA KAI THRAKI
KENTRIKI MAKEDONIA
DYTIKI MAKEDONIA
IPEIROS (EPIRUS)
THESSALIA
IONIOI NISOI
DYTIKI
STEREA ELLAS
ATTIKI
PELOPONNISOS
VOREIO AIGAIO
NOTIO AIGAIO
KRITI (CRETE)
KOSTAS LAZARIDIS
Drama
Serres
Xanthi
Kavala
Alexandroupoli
Goumenissa
GOUMENISSA
Florina
Amyntaio
AMYNTAIO
Naoussa
NAOUSSA
KYR-YANNI
Kastoria
Thessaloniki
Veroia
Kozani
Epanomi
GEROVASSILIOU
Chalkidiki
Velvendos
Aliakmonas
Thasos
Samothraki
Thrakiko Pelagos
Athos
CÔTES DE MELITON
Limnos
LIMNOS
Agios Efstratios
Lesvos
RAPSANI
Rapsani
TSATSAROS
Metsovo
Zitsa
ZITSA
Ioannina
Kerkyra (Corfu)
Larisa
Trikala
Pindos Oros
Karditsa
Volos
ANHIALOS
Arta
Voreioi Sporades
Lamia
Lefkada
Akheloos
Evvoia (Euboea)
Skyros
Psara
Chios
Amfissa
Atalanti
Chalkida
Thiva
Kefallonia (Cephalonia)
KEFALLONIA
GENTILINI
Patra (Patras)
Aigio
ANTONOPOULOS
PATRA
ELLAS
Attiki
Karystos
Athina
MATSA
Korinthos
GAIA
PAPAIOANNOU
Nemea
NEMEA
MERCOURI
Pirgos
Zakynthos (Zante)
MANTINIA
Argos
SKOURAS
TSELEPOS
Andros
Aigaion Pelagos
Kea
Tinos
Ikaria
SAMOS
SAMOS CO-OP
Samos
Poros
Ionio Pelagos
Syros
Mykonos
Kythnos
Ydra
Kalamata
Sparti
Serifos
Paros
PAROS
Naxos
Sifnos
Pylos
Amorgos
Kos
Ios
Monemvasia
Milos
Astypalaia
Thira (Santorini)
SANTORINI
ARGHYROS
RODOS
Rodos (Rhodes)
Kythira
Kritiko Pelagos
Karpathos
Chania
Irakleio
Agios Nikolaos
DAFNES
ARHANES
CRETA OLYMPIAS
PEZA
Siteia
SITEIA
Athina
International boundary
Provincial boundary
PATRA Appellation of origin
• Nemea Leading wine town/village
■ GAIA Leading producer
Wine-producing area
Land above 1000 metres
▼ Weather station (WS)

Greece: Patras

Latitude / Altitude of WS **38.15° / 3ft (1m)**
Mean July temp at WS **79.2°F (26.3°C)**
Annual rainfall at WS **28in (720mm)**
Harvest month rainfall at WS **August: 0.2in (5mm)**
Chief viticultural hazards **Drought, sudden storms**
Principal grapes **Roditis, Muscat, Mavrodaphne**

DRY RED WINE
NAOUSSA
BOUTARI
Net Cont. 750 ml
Alc. 11.5% by vol

AGIORGITIKO
GAIA ESTATE
APPELLATION OF ORIGIN NEMEA OF SUPERIOR QUALITY
1997
e 750 ml
13.5% vol

MANTINIA
TSELEPOS
1999
MOSCHOFILERO
750 ml • 12 % alc./vol.

ANTONOPOULOS VINEYARDS
CHARDONNAY
Aged in New Oak

DRY WHITE WINE
ξερολιθιά
Xerolithia
PEZA
CRETA OLYMPIAS
e750ml
11.5% Vol.

Samos
NECTAR

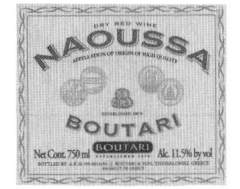

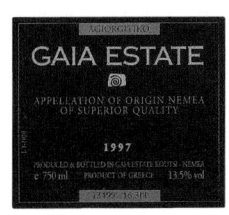

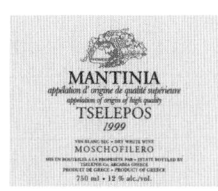

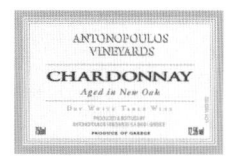

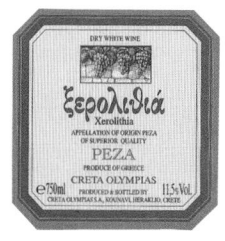

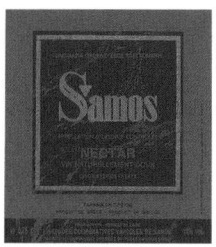

Eastern Mediterranean

It is a sobering thought that some spot on the map below, unfamiliar as it is to most modern wine-lovers, may be the very place where man first tasted wine (see page 12). Whether it was in Turkey or Armenia that the first wine was made, there is no doubt that the Middle East is wine's birthplace. The Eastern Mediterranean was the France and Italy of the ancient world – until the eighth century and the advent of Islam.

The Prophet forbade his followers to use wine – though how many of them obeyed is a moot point. Caliphs and Sultans were not all abstainers. Christians and Jews made the wine – no matter who drank it. But not until the end of the 19th century did wine begin to return to its homeland in earnest. As phylloxera destroyed Europe's vineyards, Asia stepped into the breach. In 1857 the Jesuits founded the substantial cellars of Ksara in what is now Lebanon. In the 1880s a Rothschild started winegrowing once more in Israel. The Ottoman Empire exported nearly 70 million litres in one year in the 1890s. In 1903 Nestor Gianaclis planted the first vines of a new Egyptian wine industry, near Alexandria, a city famous for its wine in Roman times.

The Cyprus wine industry was successfully revived for a long period (see overleaf for details), but in the late 20th century the world's wine drinkers were relatively ignorant of the wines of the Eastern Mediterranean, with two exceptions that were so notable they have inspired a wine revolution in their countries of origin.

Turkey is not (yet) one of them. Few wine enthusiasts, for example, know that Turkey is the most important grape-grower of the Levant. She has the fifth largest vineyard acreage in the world, but hardly 3% of her grapes are made into wine. The rest are eaten, fresh or dried. The wine industry is held back by lack of a domestic market, for 99% of the population remains Muslim. Kemal Atatürk, founder of the secular republic, built state wineries in the 1920s in the hope of persuading his people of the virtues of wine. He ensured the survival of indigenous Anatolian grape varieties, which may yield clues to the origins of viticulture itself. But Turks are hard to wean off raki, the country's aniseed-flavoured spirit, and about a quarter of the wine produced in any vintage leaves the country, mostly in bulk.

Turkey's climate varies enormously. Thrace and Marmara in the hinterland of Istanbul are in the most European part of the country in every way, including its wine-friendly soils and warm coastal climate which are similar to those of Bulgaria's Black Sea coast to the north and the north-eastern corner of Greece. About two-fifths of all Turkish wine is grown here, and the proportion of imported grape varieties grown is higher than elsewhere. Sarafin, inspired by the Napa Valley and the first Turkish producer to concentrate exclusively on international grapes, has vineyards on the Gallipoli Peninsula, for example.

About a fifth of all Turkish wine is made from productive vines grown around Izmir on the Aegean coast, rich in classical relics and remains. The Aegean's white wines tend to be better than its reds, especially those made from Misket (Muscat) and Sultaniye.

Some vines are grown in North Anatolia around Tokat, and in the southwest of the country around Denizli. Most of the rest of Turkey's wine is grown in the higher-altitude vineyards of continental Anatolia, where winters are very cold and summers extremely dry. Mid-Anatolia (also known as Cappadocia) lies between the capital, Ankara, and Nevsehir. Eastern Anatolia, around the town of Elâziğ, Malatya, and Diyarbakir (off the map), consists of the historic vineyards of the Euphrates Valley. Yields here are low and the grape varieties grown are strictly local specialities, some of which have considerable potential even if winemaking equipment is still relatively primitive.

The State Monopoly controls a score of wineries and accounts for most exports. High-strength blending wine is most in demand, although the names of Trakya and Buzbağ, its lighter and darker red wines (from Thrace and southeast Anatolia respectively) are familiar. Buzbağ is a noted bargain, a wine of powerful yet pleasing character from one of the nearest vineyards to Noah's. There is also a white (Semillon) Trakya.

Of the private firms, Doluca and Kavaklidere are the leaders in terms of size, Diren a pioneer of modern winemaking practices. Doluca operates in Thrace (its Villa Doluca brand is reliable). Kavaklidere operates near Ankara and concentrates on Anatolia's own varieties: Narince, Emir, and Sultaniye whites (including a very fresh Primeur) and Boğazkere, Kalecik Karasi, and Öküzgözü reds.

Iran is another country that, according to the OIV statistics on page 11, has more land under

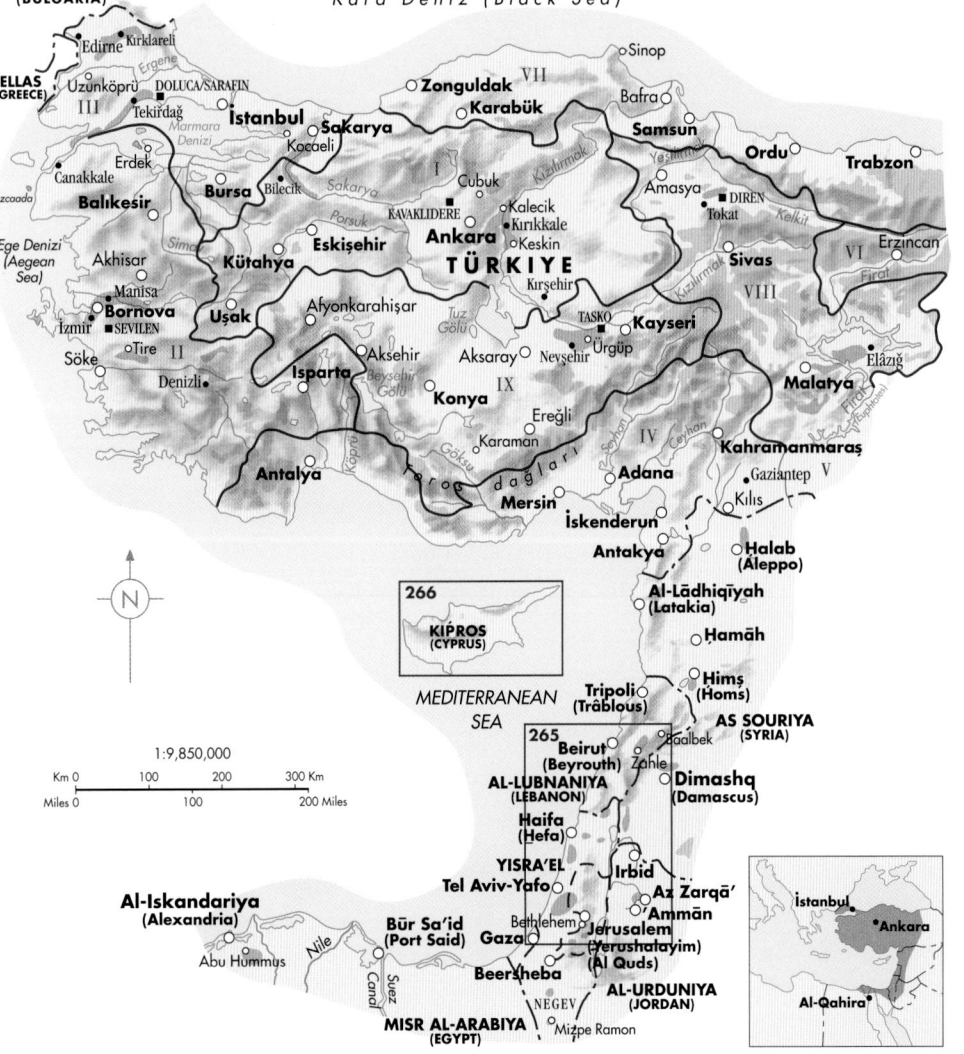
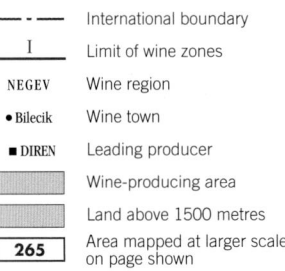

— · — · —	International boundary
I	Limit of wine zones
NEGEV	Wine region
• Bilecik	Wine town
■ DIREN	Leading producer
	Wine-producing area
	Land above 1500 metres
265	Area mapped at larger scale on page shown

1:9,850,000

Two of the Lebanon's increasingly exciting wines above a mould-breaker from Israel and one from Turkey's most modern winery. Both Israel and Lebanon have developed into serious wine-drinking nations. Turks prefer raki.

Above Minimal chemicals are needed for these high-altitude vines in Lebanon's Bekaa Valley, where there are promising new plantings of Merlot, Tempranillo, Chardonnay, and Sauvignon Blanc, as well as improved stock of Cabernet Sauvignon, Syrah, and Mourvèdre.

Until the 1980s Israeli wines were of sacramental interest only. But late-1970s planting on the volcanic soils of the Golan Heights, from the Sea of Galilee up to 4,000ft (1,200m) towards Mount Hermon, signalled a new direction for Israeli wine. California technology was shipped in, and the top Galilee red and white varietals, under the Yarden label, and Gamla and Golan second and third labels, have been consistently good and sometimes excellent. A wine culture is now well and truly established in Israel, complete with wine magazines, international wine lists in restaurants, recognized wine regions, and dozens of small but ambitious new wineries such as Castel near Jerusalem and Margalit in the Sharon Plain.

The wine region with the most obvious potential is Galilee, which includes the sub-regions of the Golan Heights and the already sought-after high-altitude Upper Galilee. The three leading wineries are all investing. Golan is building a new winery on the Lebanese border. Carmel has built its hi-tech winery in Ramat Arad while Barkan, the second biggest producer after Carmel, is developing a modern winery near Rehovot in the heavily planted Samson coastal region, as well as planting heavily in the extreme Negev Desert. Israeli farming prowess is increasingly good at coaxing wine from often unlikely environments that will stand international comparison.

The Gianaclis vineyards still operate in Egypt, northwest of the Nile Delta at Abu Hummus, but are now run by Egypt's biggest brewer, with advice from Bordeaux. Most Egyptian vines produce table grapes but the state, which controlled the wine industry until 1998, allowed out a trickle of wine of questionable quality for local tourists. Privatization may herald yet another wine renaissance.

vine than any in Europe bar France, Italy, and Spain. From Persia, and in particular the town of Shiraz (no connection with the grape of the same name has been established), came both diverse wines and beautiful verse inspired by wine and enriched with its imagery. But modern Iran is no wine producer, like Iraq, Jordan, and Syria, all of which have considerable vineyard acreage but no official wine industries.

Lebanon is a very different case. If pressed to name a wine of the Eastern Mediterranean, many wine drinkers would cite Chateau Musar, which one remarkable man, Serge Hochar, somehow continued to produce through the country's 20 years of civil war. Musar's winery is in the northern suburbs of Beirut but the vines are in the war-ravaged Bekaa Valley. At 3,000ft (900m) dry-farmed Cabernet Sauvignon and Cinsault produce extraordinarily aromatic wines, like rich and exotic Bordeaux, long-aged before sale and capable of ageing for decades after. Other wineries have begun to challenge Musar. Château Kefraya makes refreshing rosé of some character, as well as a serious Bordeaux/Rhône combination red. The senior and biggest operation, Ksara, is coming up on the inside lane, and by the turn of the century Massaya, Domaine Wardy, and Clos St Thomas were all serious new players.

Across the much-disputed border, Israel is the other seat of wine revolution in this part of the world. It has only about a quarter as much land planted with vines as Lebanon, but exports far more wine, largely to satisfy world demand for kosher wine. Sweet kiddush wines were for years the standard output of the original co-operative wineries of Carmel Mizrahi at Rishon le Zion and Zichron Yaacov that were a gift to Israel from Baron Edmond de Rothschild. They still control more than half of all grapes in the most traditional winegrowing areas in Israel, increasingly supplemented nowadays by the more modern vineyards of Ramat Arad in the northern Negev Desert.

1:2,380,000

Km 0   50   100 Km

Miles 0   50 Miles

- Bekaa Valley
- Galilee/Galil
- Samaria/Shomron
- Samson/Shimshon
- Judean Hills
- — · — · International boundary
- ■ CH MUSAR   Leading producer
- Land above 1000 metres

For location map see opposite page

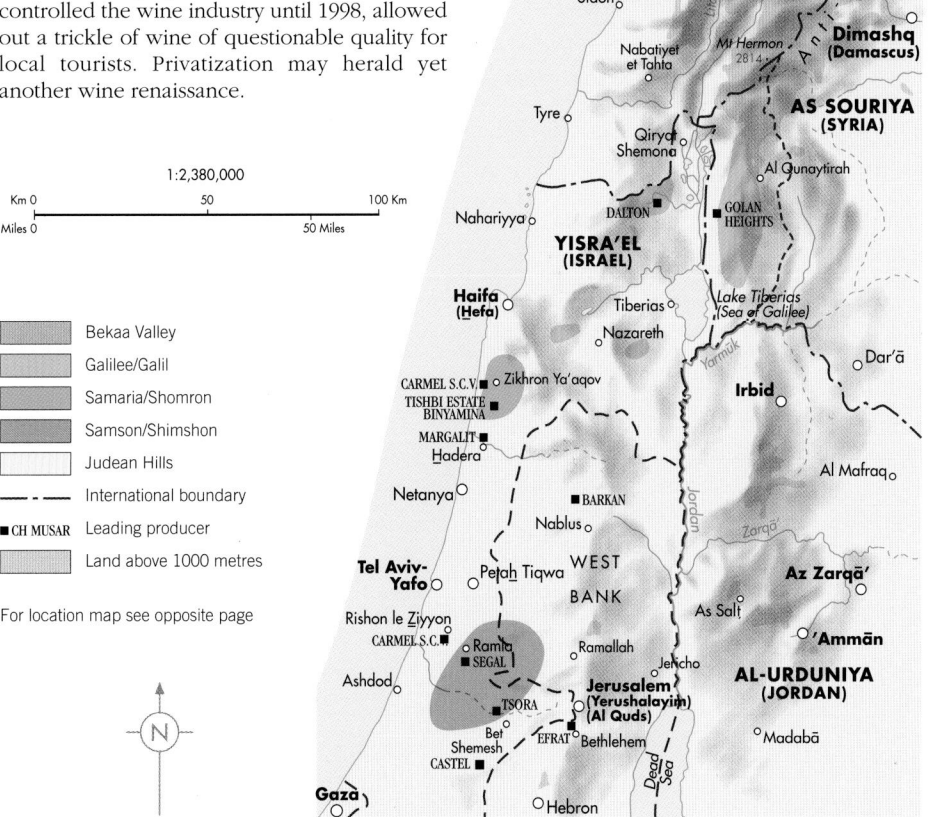

Cyprus

This beautiful Mediterranean island not only has one of the oldest winegrowing traditions in the world, it was for long the most developed and successful of the wine countries of the Eastern Mediterranean; the first (during its period of British rule, starting in 1878) to restore wine to the prime place in the economy it had before the Muslim invasion.

For three decades from the 1950s Cyprus exported huge volumes of wine: ersatz "sherry" to Britain and extremely basic unfortified wines to Eastern Europe. In the 1990s both of these once-lucrative markets shrivelled, the second as a result of the fall of communism. Cypriot wine authorities have had to try to drag the island's vineyards and cellars into the modern wine age. The industry is now benefiting from a scheme to uproot the least successful vineyards and is beginning to produce table wines that stand international comparison.

The whole south-facing side of the Troodos Mountains is potential wine-producing country; the mountains, attracting rain, make viticulture possible on what would otherwise be too dry an island. The vineyards lie where the rains fall, in idyllic green valleys at 1,980ft (600m) up to nearly 4,950ft (1,500m) in the hills.

During the era of basic bulk wines, the coastal towns of Limassol and, to a lesser extent, Paphos, although some way from the vineyards, evolved into wine production centres. Today an increasing number of small wineries are being established much closer to the vineyards, to the

Right Commandaria has been made from vineyards such as these near Agios Yeorgios since at least the late 12th century when crusading Knights Templar established their Grande Commanderie here.

benefit of wine quality – although the overwhelming majority of the island's grapes are still vinified by one of the four major companies.

The most individual of Cyprus wines is the liquorous Commandaria, made of raisined grapes, both red and white, in 14 villages - marked on the map - on the lower slopes of the Troodos.

Commandaria is now made both as a simple commercial dessert wine, popular for sacramental use, and in very small quantities as the quite alarmingly concentrated wine of legend (it can have four times as much sugar as port). The taste and texture of an old Commandaria are more than treacly; the best have a remarkable haunting fresh grapiness.

Cyprus has never been invaded by phylloxera and its strict quarantine has slowed its exposure to international grape varieties. Over 70% of the island's vineyards devoted to wine production (for Cyprus is also a considerable grower of grapes for the table) is planted with the indigenous grape Mavro, so common that its name simply means "black". The local Xynisteri and Muscat of Alexandria and now Palomino are used for both fortified and light white wines, while Grenache and Cabernet Sauvigon are the most significant incomers for red wine. Earlier picking is gradually making fruitier wines.

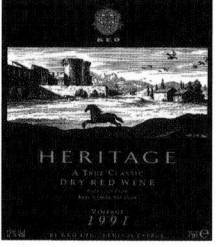

The island's oldest producer ETKO takes the Cabernet route (right) while its chief rival KEO bases Heritage on the finicky but perfumed indigenous Maratheftiko vine.

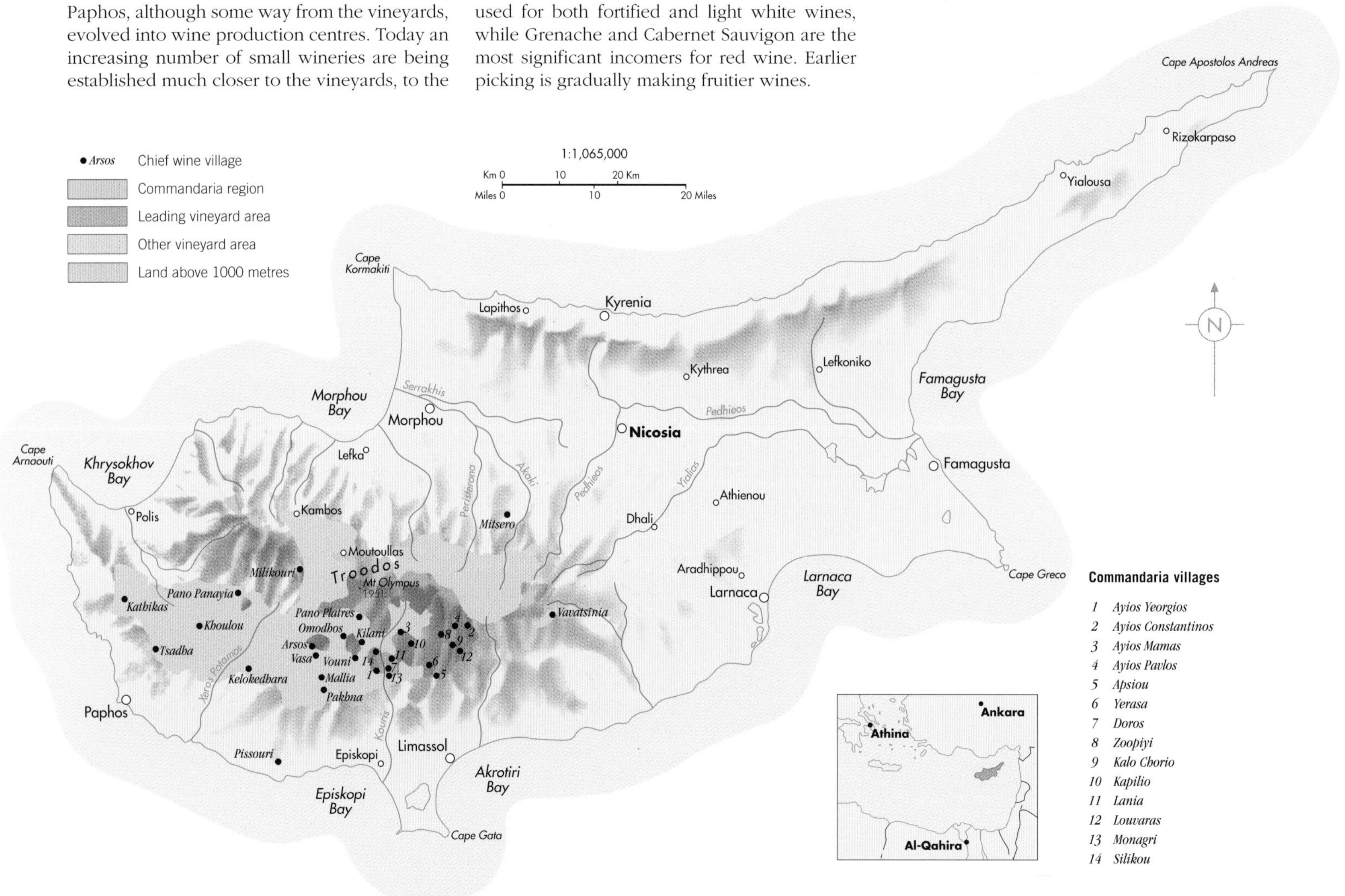

• Arsos   Chief wine village

Commandaria region

Leading vineyard area

Other vineyard area

Land above 1000 metres

1:1,065,000

Commandaria villages

1 Ayios Yeorgios
2 Ayios Constantinos
3 Ayios Mamas
4 Ayios Pavlos
5 Apsiou
6 Yerasa
7 Doros
8 Zoopiyi
9 Kalo Chorio
10 Kapilio
11 Lania
12 Louvaras
13 Monagri
14 Silikou

North Africa

North Africa is at long last recovering from a sleep that has lasted almost half a century, ever since the French withdrew. In the mid-20th century Algeria, Morocco, and Tunisia between them accounted for no less than two-thirds of the entire international wine trade. Almost all of this vast quantity of wine went to Europe (mainly to France) as usefully strong, deep red for blending. Algeria alone had one million acres (over 400,000ha) of vines. The lack of domestic demand in these substantially Muslim countries meant that after independence the decline was immediate. In each country (and in Egypt, see page 265), the state took over the shrivelling wine industry with the result that there was almost no investment.

The potentially interesting side-effect of this prolonged stasis is that the average age of vines in these countries is remarkably high, with a significant proportion at least 50 years old. If modern winemaking techniques could be harnessed to the fruit yielded by these ancient low-yielding vines – mainly bushvines of fashionable Rhône varieties – some fascinating wines might result, even if virus diseases have reduced yields to almost uneconomic levels.

Morocco is already en route for revival via a number of joint ventures – although the big money, from French bottler Castel, is being spent on planting new, mechanizable vineyards – and much-needed modern winemaking equipment. Common sense would in any case suggest that of North Africa's three most important wine producers, Morocco should have the best vineyards, benefiting from altitude (see factfile) and the influence of the Atlantic.

Morocco has had an appellation system in place for some time. Fourteen Appellations d'Origine Garantie (AOG), each with its own specified grape varieties, are shown on the map, running across the country from southwest to northeast over the northwest-facing foothills of the all-important Atlas Mountains. Carignan was once dominant, supplemented by Cinsault. But Bordeaux and Rhône grapes are now recognized as preferable for reds, while Clairette, Muscat, and a bit of Sauvignon and Chardonnay, struggle to produce refreshing whites when the average winery is still equipped as French co-operatives were in the 1930s. The vineyards around Meknès and Fès have the finest reputation, altitudes of around 2,000ft (600m) bringing a welcome night-time drop in temperature. Of the readily available brands the best is Médaillon.

Pale pink *vin gris* is Morocco's prototype "blush wine" made of short-macerated red grapes, often Cinsault. South of Casablanca, the fortified village of Boulaouane within the Doukkala AOG gives its name to one of the best-known *vins gris* in France, now being modernized by Castel. Gris de Boulaouane, well chilled, becomes a welcome and familiar friend to visitors in a land that lacks white grapes.

Tunisia, which in some years produces almost as much wine as Morocco, is also trying to improve quality to generate exports. The state has been so active in encouraging joint ventures whereby expertise and capital are imported from Europe that by the turn of the century at least seven were under way. The results include the introduction of much-needed temperature control in wineries and upgraded vineyards.

The coolest wine regions are those on the coast. Northern Bizerte's ocean breezes and unusually cool clay soils can result in reasonable white wines, well-balanced reds, and some fine sweet Muscat, Tunisia's speciality – probably since Carthaginian times. Dry Muscat, still too often oxidized, is the speciality of the sandy soils of Cap Bon, otherwise known as Keliba, on the east coast.

The westernmost vineyards of Jendouba south of Béja are Tunisia's hottest and wineries there are most prone to the faults associated with primitive equipment and non-existent cooling systems. There is real potential for powerful, deep-flavoured reds, however, from the better-equipped wineries of Grombalia, the terra rossa hills between here and Tunis, maritime Mornag just southwest of Tunis, and Tébourba west of Tunis, whose speciality is the very pale pink Gris de Tunis.

Algeria, once by far the world's biggest wine exporter, lags behind its neighbours. So many of her vineyards have been either neglected or pulled up that between 1966 and 1997, when 80% of her vines were more than 40 years old, her crop shrank from 16 million hectolitres of wine to less than half a million. This is not to say that Algerian wine is, or need be, of poor quality; the problem is infrastructure. The State Monopoly, which still controls production tightly, claims to have planted 24,700 acres (10,000ha) of international grape varieties in the mid-1990s, mainly in the traditional areas of Tlemcen, Medea, and Zaccar, and is now attempting to develop the wineries necessary to turn them in to exportable wine.

On the right is a red *from Tunisia, while the three Moroccan wines consist of the product of a small domaine between Casablanca and Rabat flanked by two from Meknès. The one on the left is from Castell's new trellised vineyards.*

International boundary
GHARB Wine region
Wine-producing area
Land above 1000 metres
▼ Weather station (WS)

Morocco: Meknès

Latitude / Altitude of WS **33.53˚ / 1,804ft (550m)**
Mean July temp at WS **77.5˚F (25.3˚C)**
Annual rainfall at WS **22in (570mm)**
Harvest month rainfall at WS **September: 0.6in (15mm)**
Chief viticultural hazards **Wind, drought**
Principal grapes **Cinsault, Carignan, Grenache Noir**

1:10,200,000

Km 0   100   200   300 Km
Miles 0   50   100   150   200 Miles

North America

The vine must be a tenacious plant to persist in its hold on a continent where it has been so prone to pests, disease, climatic extreme, and disaster as it has in North America.

Today the United States is the world's most important producer outside Europe, with only France, Spain, and Italy making more wine. Canada's wine industry is in dynamic transformation, and one of these days Mexico (mapped on page 286) may also catch up with wine's extraordinary recent leap in social status.

When the early colonists first landed they were particularly impressed by the rampant grapevines whose fruit festooned the forests. The grapes were sweet, if strange to taste. It was natural to assume that wine would be one of the good things of the New World.

Yet more than 300 years of American history are a saga of the shattered hopes of would-be winegrowers. Wine made from American vines tasted distinctly odd, while European vinifera vines planted in the new colonies withered and died. The colonists did not give up. Having no notion what was killing their vines, they assumed it was their fault and tried different varieties and methods.

As late as the Revolution, Washington tried, and Jefferson, a great amateur of wine who toured France for the purpose, made a determined attempt. Nothing came of it. The American soil was riddled with the European vine's deadliest enemy, phylloxera, while the hot, humid summers of the south and east encouraged diseases unknown in Europe, and in the north European vines were prey to the harsh winters. Native American vines had evolved resistance to all of these hazards.

We now know of well over a dozen vine species indigenous to North America, almost all of them and particularly *Vitis labrusca* producing wine so rank and feral it has long been described as "foxy" – a flavour familiar today in grape juice and jelly but unappealing to wine drinkers weaned on Europe's only vine species, *Vitis vinifera*.

Now that American and European vines coexisted on this continent new to wine, their genes commingled in random and spontaneous combinations from which various grape varieties with less obvious foxiness emerged. The Alexander grape, discovered in Pennsylvania and grown in Indiana, was the earliest of these accidental American hybrids; Catawba, Delaware, Isabella, and red Norton followed.

Almost wherever land was colonized, the European settlers would experiment with vine-growing and winemaking, especially in New York (where winters were bitterly cold), Virginia (where summers were inconveniently sultry), and New Jersey, which was somewhere in between. But it was at Cincinnati, Ohio that the first commercially successful American wine was born – Nicholas Longworth's famous Sparkling Catawba. By the mid-1850s the wine was celebrated on both sides of the Atlantic and, with 1,200 acres (485ha) of vineyard, he was making a fortune.

Success was short-lived. Black rot, the Civil War, and finally Longworth's death in 1863 ended Cincinnati's challenge to Reims. But the point was made. Longworth's "champagne" makers soon found new employers: the new Pleasant Valley Wine Co of Hammondsport on New York's Finger Lakes. This time American wine had found a permanent home – still important today (and described on page 294).

By the time of the Civil War, vine-breeding had become a deliberate activity, resulting in scores of new varieties especially adapted for American conditions, including the almost rudely hardy but extremely foxy Concord, introduced in 1854 and today the mainstay of the great grape belt along the southern shore of Lake Erie through northern Ohio, Pennsylvania, and New York, which supplies America's grape juice and jelly.

In the South the Carolinas and Georgia had their own native Muscadine vines, particularly Scuppernong, whose viscous juice made wine even further from the European model than these American hybrids, although they are at least resistant to the Pierce's disease that is ravaging vinifera vines (see page 19).

Winemaking reached the West Coast by a quite different route. The earliest Spanish settlers in Mexico had imported vinifera there in the 16th century with tolerable success. Their primitive vine, known as the Mission and identical to Argentina's Criolla Chica, flourished in Baja California. But not for 200 years did the Franciscan fathers move north up the coast of California. In 1769 the Franciscan Junípero Serra, founding the San Diego Mission, is said to have planted California's first vineyard.

There were none of the problems of the East Coast here. *Vitis vinifera* had found its Promised Land. The vine moved up the coast with the chain of missions, arriving at the northernmost, Sonoma, by 1805. The well-named Jean-Louis Vignes brought better vines than the Mission from Europe to Los Angeles. The Gold Rush brought massive immigration. By the 1850s northern California had been well and truly conquered by the vine.

Thus by the mid-19th century America had two wine industries, poles apart. All-vinifera California enjoyed an early golden age in the 1880s and 1890s, only to see its burgeoning wine industry besieged by the scourges of mildew and phylloxera – just like Europe.

But then came a blow greater than any of these: total Prohibition of alcohol throughout North America between 1918 and 1933. Both western and eastern vine-growers limped through, making supposedly sacramental wine and shipping huge quantities of grapes, juice, and concentrate to a nation which suddenly discovered home winemaking, with the warning "Caution – do not add yeast or the contents will ferment".

The lasting legacy of the culture that spawned this outright ban on all things alcoholic, long after Repeal in 1933, has been a wine industry thwarted by unnecessarily complex organization, obstructive legislation, and extreme suspicion on the part of the one-third of 21st-century Americans who are teetotal and the further third who drink only spirits or beer.

Left Strong sunshine and Mexican labour are crucial to wine production in North America's most important wine state by far, California. Washington State is the second most important grape grower, with less than a twentieth the area of vineyards. New York comes next.

Map legend:
- State boundary
- Phoenix · State capital
- Vineyards
- 410 ▽ Acres of vineyard (1999) per state
- 10 ◗ Number of wineries per state

1:21,750,000

Km 0   200   400   600   800 Km
Miles 0   200   400 Miles

Despite this, and despite phylloxera and Pierce's disease, wine is currently basking in the glow of fashion and enthusiasm bordering on obsession among that minority of Americans who do own a corkscrew. This has been translated into a flurry of activity and experiment on the part of would-be wine producers all over the continent, even New England and the Rocky Mountain states. Ever since the development of the railroads, grapes and wine have been shipped from viticulturally well-endowed states, particularly California, for blending and bottling in less fortunately situated wineries, some of which grow hardly a single vine. In all only North Dakota produces no wine commercially at all, four states have only one winery, but more than a dozen have over 1,000 acres (400ha) of vines and/or more than 25 wineries – a sign of considerable vinous activity.

The mushrooming wine industries of Canada, Mexico, Texas, New York, and all of the United States west of the Rockies are considered in detail on the following pages, but there are hundreds of wineries (some of them producing wines from fruits other than grapes too) and thousands of acres of vines elsewhere. They may produce juice or jelly or heavily flavoured drinks based on the produce of American vines or, increasingly, more subtle and sophisticated ferments from either vinifera or the so-called French hybrids. This new generation of varieties such as white Vidal, Seyval Blanc, and Vignoles, and red Baco Noir and Chambourcin was bred in post-phylloxera Europe from American and vinifera vines and introduced to North America (where they have enjoyed far more success than in Europe) by Philip Wagner of Boordy Vineyards, Maryland in the mid-20th century.

French hybrids dominate vine-growing in the Midwest, with Pierce's-resistant Norton making some particularly appealing soft reds. Missouri is the only state with a long history of vine-growing on any scale and was Ohio's only serious 19th century rival east of the Rockies. Augusta made this point when in 1980 it became America's first AVA, or American Viticultural Area. These 140-odd vine-growing areas (often delineated with more regard for political than natural boundaries, and producer rather than consumer sensitivities) represent a first, tentative step towards some sort of controlled appellation system for US wine.

Michigan, surrounded by the Great Lakes, is today the fourth most important vine-grower of all the states (after California, Washington, and New York). Most is Concord, but vinifera and French hybrids on the lake-girt Old Mission and Leelanau peninsulas are promising.

Pennsylvania has almost as much vineyard, and Ohio is also important. But the eastern state that, after New York, offers the most excitement today is unquestionably Virginia, home to more than 50 small, passionate wineries, with Merlot and Cabernets being particularly successful.

New Jersey's wine industry has almost as long a history but is much smaller; that of Maryland smaller still. Both hedge bets between vinifera and French hybrids.

The rest of the South, those states bordering on the Gulf of Mexico as far as Texas, has a small but growing wine industry of its own, expanding from the usefully loose-berried Muscadine vines native to its hot, damp woods to French hybrids, vinifera, and newer Muscadine hybrids which can produce quite mainstream flavours. Cooler, higher parts of the South can have conditions very similar to Virginia's.

All over this great and thrilling continent, a worthy trend is (just) discernible: to produce wines that will be appreciated outside their region while truly expressing their origins.

California

Above Santa Maria's Bien Nacido vineyard with the winery premises shared by Au Bon Climat and Qupé in the distance. Barbera grapes grow in the foreground while Nebbiolo is grown on the high ground top right.

California's importance in the world of wine is not to be underestimated. The Golden State is home to so many vines, virtually all vinifera, that it produces over 90% of the wine made in the US, the world's most important wine producer outside Europe.

Here at the vine's western limit there is a distinct shortage of geographical generalities and physical truisms. Few of the dozens of California cult wines that began in the 1990s to command three- and four-figure dollar sums per bottle existed in the 1980s, for example. Wine now basks in the glow of social approbation (in stark contrast to American society's official attitude to any form of alcohol in the 1920s and its view of wine as an unsophisticated drink fit only for immigrants and winos in the mid-20th century). But California's vine-growers seem to be beset by far more than their fair share of problems.

Phylloxera returned after a century to haunt vineyards in fashionable Napa and Sonoma in the early 1990s. And as the new century dawned, the even more deadly Pierce's disease threatened not only the vineyards of southern California but those to the north (see page 19). Meanwhile, wine production was inextricably bound up with disputes over land development and water, a precious commodity in the state.

California's wine geography presents a series of surprises, and much more variety than outsiders give it credit for. The potential of a vineyard site is linked hardly at all to latitude but is crucially determined by what lies between it and the Pacific. The more mountains there are between the site and the sea, the less chance there is of the sea air, often fog, reaching it to moderate the climate.

So cold is the inshore water of the Pacific here that it causes a perpetual fog bank all summer just off the coast. Each day that the summer temperatures approach 90°F (32°C) inland, the rising hot air draws the fog inland to fill its space. The Golden Gate Bridge straddles its most famous pathway, but everywhere up and down the coast that the Coast Range dips below about 1,500 feet (460m) the fog, or at any rate cold Pacific air, spills over and cools the land. Certain valleys that are end-on to the ocean act as funnels to allow sea air to invade 75 miles (120km) inland. San Francisco Bay even has an effect on the climate in the Sierra Foothills, nearly 150 miles (240km) to the east.

Since foggy San Francisco Bay is northern California's chief air conditioning unit, vineyards close to the waters of the Bay, such as those of Carneros skirting the south of Napa and Sonoma counties, can be rather cool too. Within the inland Napa Valley, sheltered by its unbroken ridge of western hills from Pacific influence, it is those most southerly vineyards just north of the town of Napa that are the coolest due to the breezes off the Bay, and those around Calistoga at the northern limit of the valley that are hottest.

For similar reasons, if the result of different topography, the vineyards of the Santa Maria Valley way down the coast in Santa Barbara County 140 miles (225km) northwest of Los Angeles, are some of the coolest in the state.

The Central (or San Joaquin) Valley on the other hand, the flat farmland that still makes agriculture California's most important economic activity (and grows three-quarters of the state's wine grapes), is too far inland to be directly influenced by the Pacific fog bank. It is one of the world's sunniest wine regions, but one that, like almost everywhere in California, requires increasingly expensive irrigation.

The small map on this page illustrates this phenomenon vividly, even if this particular classification of climate variation in California wine country is relatively crude. The Winkler system of degree days takes no account of rainfall, for instance, although California's Mediterranean climate means that summers are very much drier than those of most European wine regions (see factfiles). Total annual rainfall is not exceptionally low but it does tend to be concentrated in the first few months of the year, topping up dams used throughout the summer for irrigation. This being California however, an historical roughly decade-long cycle of damaging flood and drought results respectively in erosion of the hillsides that offer the most fashionable vineyard sites, then both a water shortage and particularly tough wines. And in the warmth that is typical of a California September, atypical rain can wreak havoc.

The most important of California's 80-plus AVAs are mapped opposite and on the following pages but even they should not be given too much significance. Some of the viticultural areas are so small that they affect only one winery. One of the most common, North Coast, for example, encompasses Lake, Mendocino, Napa, and Sonoma counties.

There are excellent winemakers who still ignore AVAs, preferring to use good grapes from wherever they can get them. Others are already specific about one vineyard. Hundreds of individual vineyard names are now in use on labels – powerful confirmation that California is moving on from the stage where it was only the grape variety and the brand name that counted. Geography has definitively entered the picture.

Fashion, however, has always been important in California. Wine producers and consumers tend to act more uniformly than would normally be expected of a geographical unit roughly half

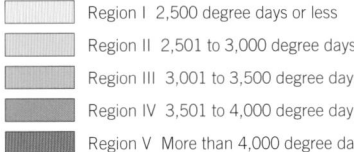

The Climate Regions of California Winegrowing

Winkler classified California's wine regions on a scale of "degree days" which measures the length of time the thermometer remains over 50°F (10°C) between 1 April and 31 October.

Thus if the mean temperature over a five-day period was 70°F (21°C), the "summation" of heat would be (70 - 50 = 20) x 5 = 100 degree days.

- Region I   2,500 degree days or less
- Region II 2,501 to 3,000 degree days
- Region III 3,001 to 3,500 degree days
- Region IV 3,501 to 4,000 degree days
- Region V   More than 4,000 degree days

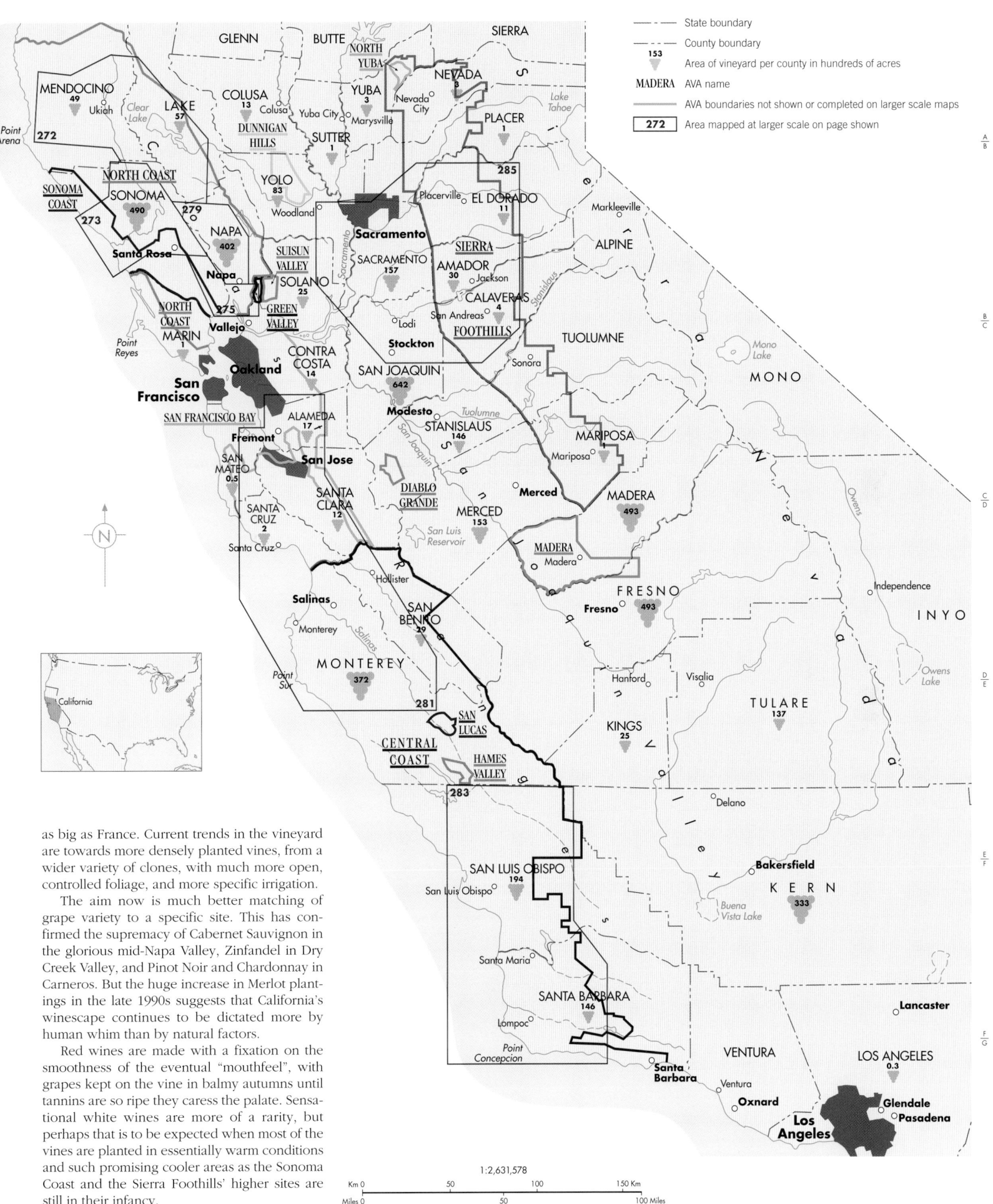

as big as France. Current trends in the vineyard are towards more densely planted vines, from a wider variety of clones, with much more open, controlled foliage, and more specific irrigation.

The aim now is much better matching of grape variety to a specific site. This has confirmed the supremacy of Cabernet Sauvignon in the glorious mid-Napa Valley, Zinfandel in Dry Creek Valley, and Pinot Noir and Chardonnay in Carneros. But the huge increase in Merlot plantings in the late 1990s suggests that California's winescape continues to be dictated more by human whim than by natural factors.

Red wines are made with a fixation on the smoothness of the eventual "mouthfeel", with grapes kept on the vine in balmy autumns until tannins are so ripe they caress the palate. Sensational white wines are more of a rarity, but perhaps that is to be expected when most of the vines are planted in essentially warm conditions and such promising cooler areas as the Sonoma Coast and the Sierra Foothills' higher sites are still in their infancy.

1:2,631,578

Mendocino

On the next 14 pages, the detailed maps of California's complex wine regions follow a wine-lover's notional state-wide journey very roughly northwest to southeast. Mendocino County, the state's northernmost outpost of the vine has two very different zones: east and west of the Coastal Range.

Most distinctive is the Anderson Valley in the east where ocean fogs can drift in easily to hang thick and low. The little Navarro River tumbles down the valley through resin-scented redwoods. Anderson Valley has a super-cool, sometimes too cool, ripening season, at least in its lower reaches below Philo. Higher, on the ridges above the fog, Zinfandel ripens splendidly – a fact that a few reclusive Italian families discovered long ago.

Edmeades (now part of Kendall-Jackson) and Navarro are two of the more recent pioneer wineries that first made these red treasures and highly aromatic, sharply etched white wines from grapes that would ripen in Germany. Riesling and Gewürztraminer are perfectly in tune with the climate if not the market. It took a French company to put Anderson Valley on the map, in the shape of Roederer of Champagne who in 1982 chose to set up shop here and not, like so many of its peers, in Carneros. The quality of Roederer Estate's sparkling wines suggests it was a good choice. Pommery followed soon afterwards by buying fizz pioneer Scharffenberger, which it renamed Pacific Echo in 1989.

East and well tucked in behind the coastal hills that rear up to 3,000ft (900m) north of Cloverdale and the Sonoma county line are the bulk of Mendocino's plantings, protected from Pacific influence and therefore in much warmer, drier conditions. The fogs do not reach Ukiah, nor very often the Redwood Valley, and these areas are warm enough to be rated Region III, or even IV in places, on the heat-summation scale

Two great white wines, *of a sort that are arguably not as fashionable as they deserve to be but are prime products of Mendocino's cooler reaches.*

described on the page 270. Their typical wines (from some deep alluvial soils) are full-bodied, often rather soft reds of Cabernet, Petite Sirah or, from particularly ancient vines above Ukiah, spicy Zinfandel. The distinctly cooler, under-appreciated Potter Valley can make very fine botrytized wines.

The oldest winery in this region is Parducci (founded in 1931, a date that proclaims a visionary: Prohibition was still in force). Fetzer was an important addition in 1968 and has become increasingly important as a source of dependable value and as one clear, confident voice in favour of organic wine production in a state so well suited to it. The winery is now owned by distillers Brown-Forman, while the Fetzer family grow their organic grapes under the (maternal) name Kohn.

A charming alcove of inland Mendocino, McDowell Valley is a tiny appellation established by eponymous early specialists in Rhône grape varieties.

Lake County, further east along the winding Route 175 from Hopland, is another warm region, comparable to the head of the Napa Valley. Today, its main claim to vinous fame is as the birthplace of the Kendall-Jackson empire.

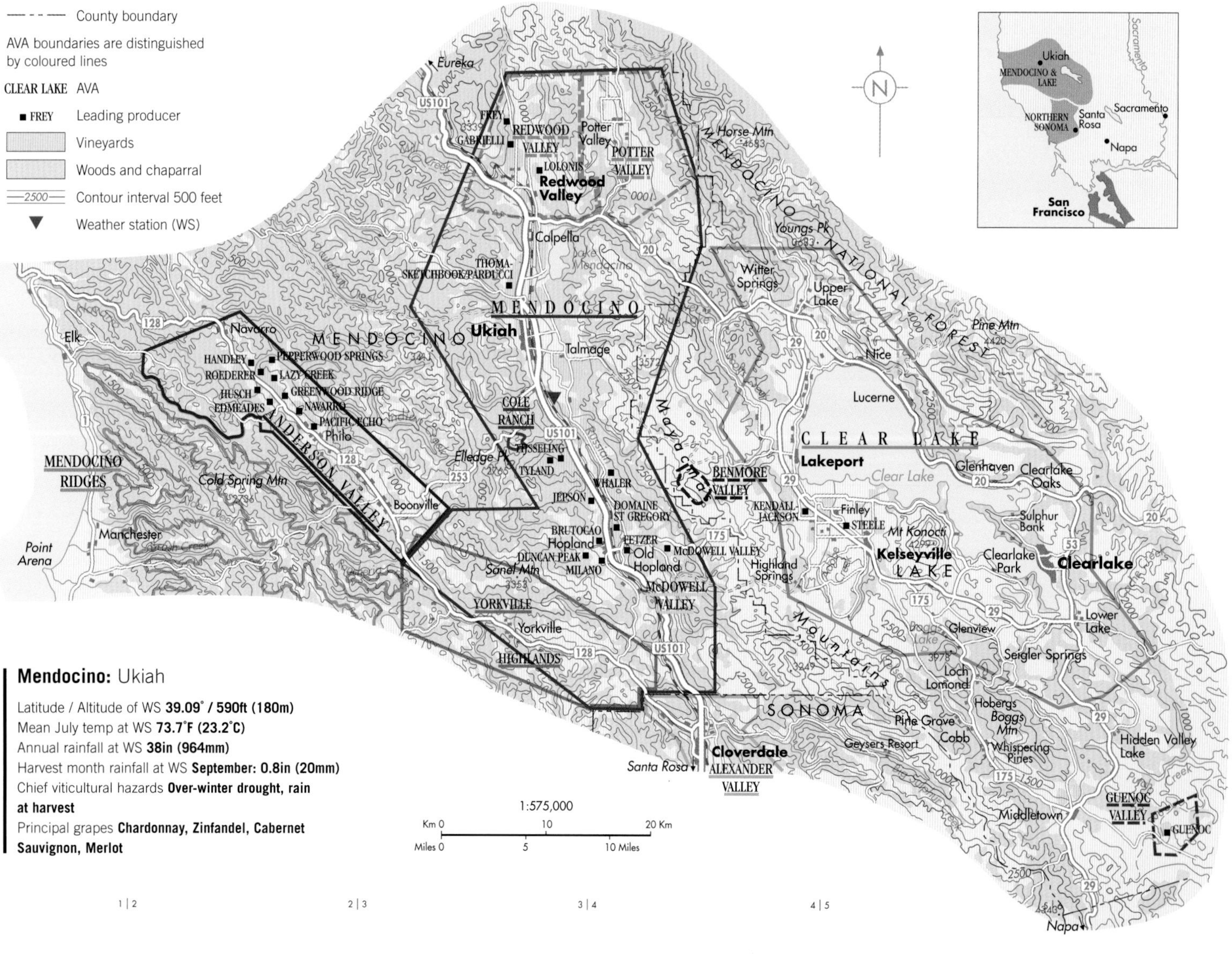

— – - – County boundary

AVA boundaries are distinguished by coloured lines

CLEAR LAKE AVA

■ FREY Leading producer

Vineyards

Woods and chaparral

2500 Contour interval 500 feet

▼ Weather station (WS)

Mendocino: Ukiah

Latitude / Altitude of WS **39.09° / 590ft (180m)**
Mean July temp at WS **73.7°F (23.2°C)**
Annual rainfall at WS **38in (964mm)**
Harvest month rainfall at WS **September: 0.8in (20mm)**
Chief viticultural hazards **Over-winter drought, rain at harvest**
Principal grapes **Chardonnay, Zinfandel, Cabernet Sauvignon, Merlot**

1:575,000

Km 0   10   20 Km

Miles 0   5   10 Miles

Sonoma

For location map see opposite page

Sonoma County grows far more grapes than Napa County and in more varied conditions. Sonoma is where fine wine production started in northern California and, although in the late 20th century Sonoma was eclipsed by Napa's seminal role in the state's wine renaissance, there are signs that it may reassume a dominant position in California wine lore.

One important sign: the development of Gallo Sonoma, the much-touted fine wine outpost of the world's biggest wine producer. Another: the potential for planting in cooler, unexplored territory is significantly greater in Sonoma than in Napa.

Gallo Sonoma provided the spur and lobbied for the regional AVA represented almost in its entirety on the main upper section of the map on this page. The existence of the generous Northern Sonoma AVA allows Gallo to blend the produce of its substantial holdings in Dry Creek Valley, Alexander Valley, Knights Valley, Chalk Hill, Russian River Valley, and Green Valley and label these blends with an appellation a little more specific than that of Sonoma County. The all-encompassing Sonoma County AVA runs north up the coast from the head of Tomales Bay and San Pablo Bay, the northern lobe of San Francisco Bay, between the Napa Valley and the ocean. Its northern half is drained by the Russian River (named after a Russian fur-trading post) and its tributary creeks. Most of the county's vineyards now lie in this region, mapped here.

Another winery, Chardonnay specialist Sonoma-Cutrer, pushed through the equally commodious Sonoma Coast AVA so that it could blend the produce of its several and various holdings, from Russian River down to Carneros, and still call the wines estate bottled. But this vast region, reaching as far west as the ocean but swooping south and east to take in much of

Any number of labels would have qualified here. Most obvious omissions include Kistler's superb vineyard designated bottlings. The Marcassin winery and estate vineyard are just off the map to the west almost on the coast in California's most fashionable new wine region, the western portion of the eccentric Sonoma Coast AVA.

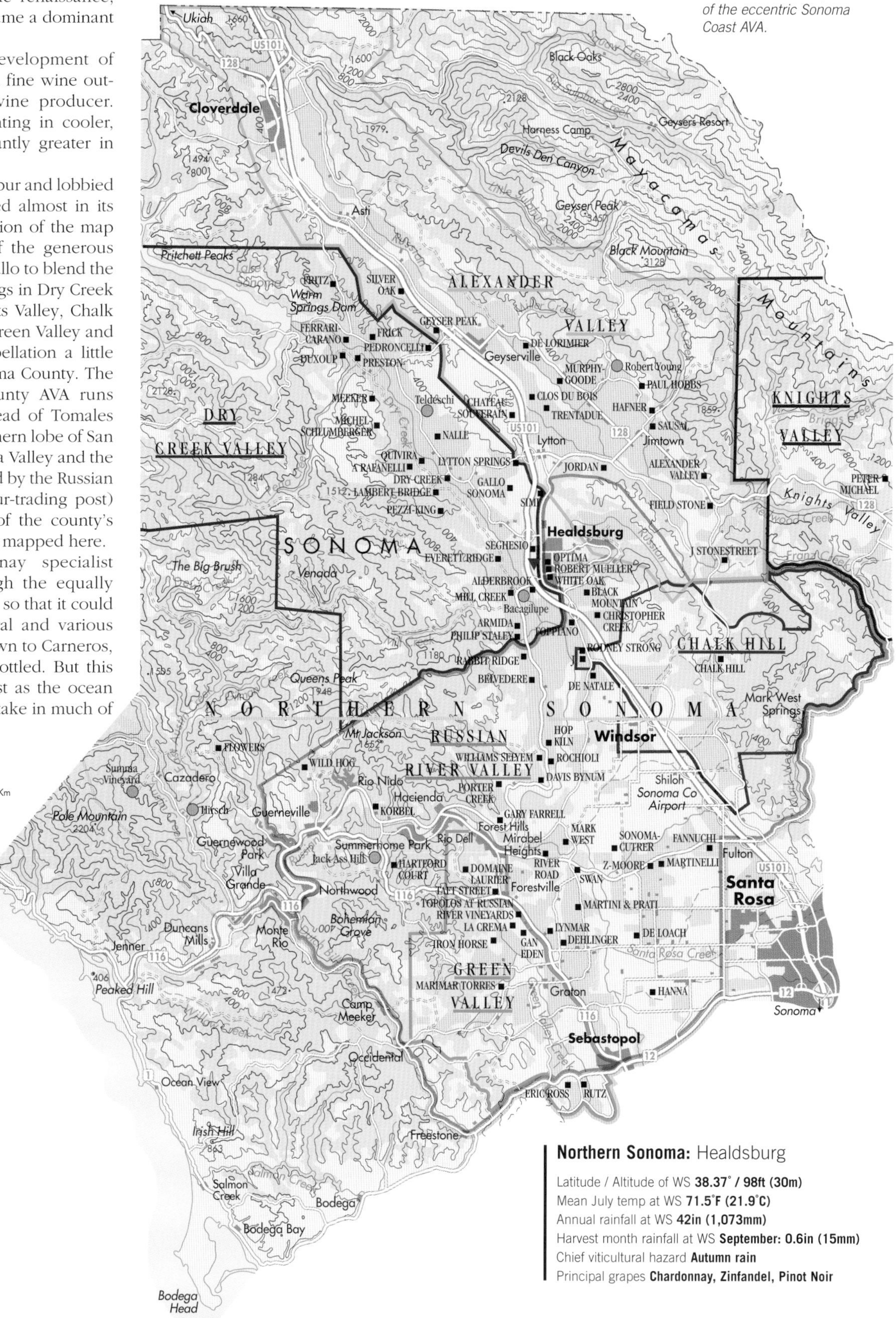

1:280,000

- – – County boundary

AVA boundaries are distinguished by coloured lines

CHALK HILL AVA
- KORBEL Leading producer
- Hirsh Noted vineyard
- Vineyards
- Woods and chaparral
- 800 Contour interval 400 feet
- ▼ Weather station (WS)

Northern Sonoma: Healdsburg

Latitude / Altitude of WS **38.37° / 98ft (30m)**
Mean July temp at WS **71.5°F (21.9°C)**
Annual rainfall at WS **42in (1,073mm)**
Harvest month rainfall at WS **September: 0.6in (15mm)**
Chief viticultural hazard **Autumn rain**
Principal grapes **Chardonnay, Zinfandel, Pinot Noir**

Left Early spring in Saintsbury's lyre-trained vineyard in Carneros. Saintsbury pioneered the admirable practice of releasing different bottlings of Pinot Noir for early and later drinking respectively.

Sonoma Valley as far as San Pablo Bay (of which only part is mapped here), long used mainly for blends, is increasingly associated with some of the state's finest estate-grown Chardonnay and Pinot Noir too.

Ambitious producers such as Helen Turley for her Marcassin label, Flowers, Littorai, Dehlinger, Merry Edwards, Lynmar, and Kendall-Jackson's Hartford Court are colonizing particularly cool territory out towards the coast where the marine influence creates some of the state's coolest vine-growing conditions.

As elsewhere in California, climate is a function of the accessibility of Pacific fogs and resultant cloud cover. Russian River is the coolest of the AVAs fully mapped on page 273, and those few who live in the narrow winding valley itself tend to wear sweatshirts more often than T-shirts, even in summer. The coolness is particularly marked between the river mouth and Guerneville; rather less so on the Santa Rosa Plain, and much less so as far inland as Healdsburg. This is one of California's serious Pinot Noir regions where the likes of Williams Selyem, Rochioli, and Gary Farrell have etched a Burgundian tradition of vineyard-designated bottlings, albeit in a distinctly unBurgundian style: open, jewel-like fruit, and charm rather than brooding structure.

Green Valley Sonoma (to distinguish it from Green Valley in the Sacramento Delta – see page 284) is an even cooler enclave mostly within Russian River which is carving out a reputation for particularly lively Chardonnay (Kistler with Dutton Ranch is an important grower here) and fine sparkling wines from Iron Horse.

Chalk Hill is another subsection of the greater Russian River AVA (Sonoma's AVAs tend to have even more layers than its finest wines). Only the lower stretches are fog-cooled, and then only intermittently. Higher up is Cabernet and Chardonnay country, although Chalk Hill winery has made some good Sauvignon Blanc.

Distinctly warmer are the densely planted AVAs to the north of here, even if, as in Chalk Hill, Dry Creek's valley floor is cooler than the hillsides, indeed positively damp at times,

particularly at the southern end. (Compare Healdsburg's annual rainfall with that of somewhere as close as the town of Sonoma.) This encouraged 19th-century Italian settlers to plant the rot-prone Zinfandel above the fog-line and farm it without irrigation, thus earning Dry Creek a reputation for some of the finest examples of this finicky variety. As throughout these northern California valleys, the east side tends to make fuller wines than the west, thanks to the warm caress of the setting sun. The best sites in the canyon enclosing Dry Creek with substantial benchland are distinguished by a very well-drained mixture of gravel and red clays known as Dry Creek conglomerate. Zins and Cabernet thrive here, while the valley floor is left to white varieties, particularly Sauvignon Blanc.

The broader, more open Alexander Valley is much warmer, thanks to the shelter from ocean influence afforded by some low hills just northeast of Healdsburg. On its alluvial soils Cabernet is consistently ripened to distinctive, almost chocolaty richness. Knights Valley, its Napa-wards offshoot and almost an extension of the head of the Napa Valley, is warmer than Dry Creek but cooler (because higher) than Alexander Valley.

The Sonoma Valley AVA mapped opposite is nowadays less important than the northern section mapped on the previous page, although the town of Sonoma could hardly be more important to California wine historians. It has all the atmosphere of a little wine capital – in fact of the capital of a very little republic: the original if short-lived Bear Flag Republic of California. Sonoma's tree-shaded square, with its old mission buildings and barracks, its stone-built City Hall and ornate Sebastiani Theatre is faintly romantic in style, and thickly layered with history.

The hills overlooking the town were the site of Agoston Haraszthy's famous estate of the 1850s and 1860s. Part of his Buena Vista cellars still stands in the side-valley to the east, although the winery has migrated to Carneros. Another famous 19th-century winery, Gundlach-Bundschu, was revived in the 1970s on the

same southern slopes. On the road to Santa Rosa is Jack London's Valley of the Moon.

Like the Napa Valley, but in a smaller compass, the Sonoma Valley is progressively warmer towards the north, in this case into the lee of Sonoma Mountain, which shelters the valley from western storms. The Mayacamas Mountains constitute the eastern edge. Kistler's own vineyard bottling, Landmark's local output and Sonoma-Cutrer's Les Pierres vineyard (just west of Sonoma town) are all evidence that this AVA can grow perfect Chardonnay.

Evidence of excellent Cabernet first came from Louis Martini's famous Monte Rosso vineyard about 1,100ft (335m) up in the eastern hills, and more recently from the outstanding Laurel Glen Cabernets from Sonoma Mountain, a significant sub-appellation in the west whose best wines seem to benefit from unusually thin, rocky soil, altitude, and long sunshine hours.

At Sonoma Valley's southern end is the part of the cool Carneros district that lies in Sonoma County. Politically, Carneros straddles the Napa/Sonoma county line. As a viticultural area, therefore, it has four appellations: Sonoma Valley, Sonoma Coast, Napa Valley, and Carneros.

Los Carneros (commonly known as Carneros), literally "the rams", is a district in which much hope and capital were invested in the late 1980s and early 1990s by sparkling wine producers, many of them from Champagne (notably Taittinger's Domaine Carneros) and Codorníu Napa and Gloria Ferrer (Freixenet) from Spain's Cava country. It encompasses the south of both Sonoma and Napa valleys on the north shore of San Pablo Bay: low, rolling hills of shallow soils that vary from clay to coarse and rocky. Strong winds rattle the vine-leaves more often than not and slow the ripening process to such an extent that Carneros produces some of California's most delicate wines. This makes them some of the state's better base wines for sparkling wine blends.

Following champagne traditions, Pinot Noir and, especially, Chardonnay are the dominant grape varieties here, in vineyards regularly plundered by wineries situated in warmer country to the north.

If the sparkling produce of these vineyards disappointed the incomers, it was more a result of consumers' unexpected infatuation with still red wine than because of any great inherent fault in the wines.

The best still wines from Carneros can be delicious, the Chardonnays having more ageing potential than the California norm for this variety. Fans of Russian River Pinot Noir may find a dimension missing from most Carneros Pinots, but they can certainly charm.

Some of the most celebrated vineyards, whose names can be found on a host of top producers' labels, are Hyde, Hudson, Sangiacomo, Truchard, Winery Lake (planted by pioneer Rene DiRosa), and Durell (whose Carneros Chardonnay is one of Kistler's finest). Syrah, Merlot, and Cabernet Franc can shine here and clearly have a future.

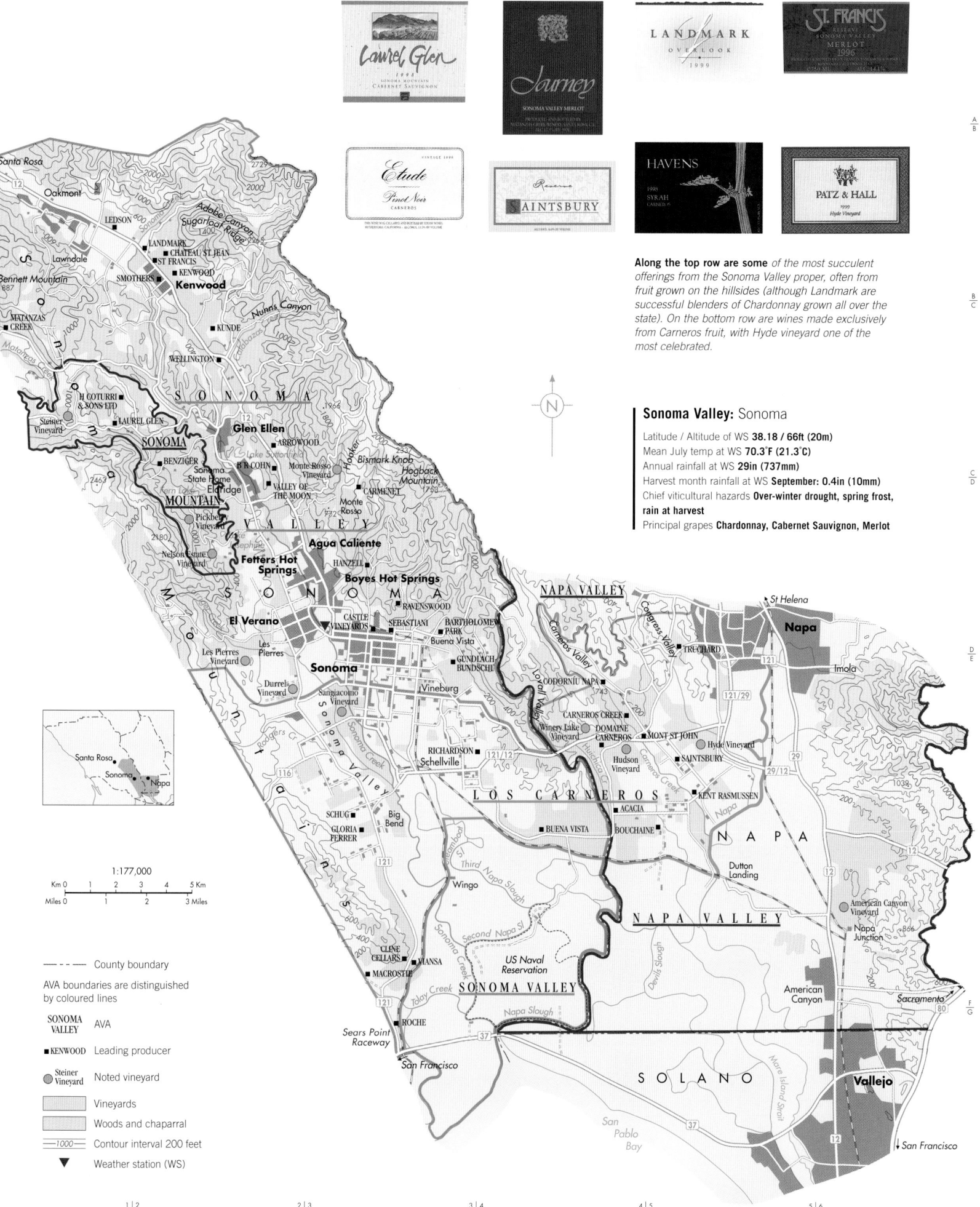

Along the top row are some *of the most succulent offerings from the Sonoma Valley proper, often from fruit grown on the hillsides (although Landmark are successful blenders of Chardonnay grown all over the state). On the bottom row are wines made exclusively from Carneros fruit, with Hyde vineyard one of the most celebrated.*

Sonoma Valley: Sonoma

Latitude / Altitude of WS **38.18 / 66ft (20m)**
Mean July temp at WS **70.3°F (21.3°C)**
Annual rainfall at WS **29in (737mm)**
Harvest month rainfall at WS **September: 0.4in (10mm)**
Chief viticultural hazards **Over-winter drought, spring frost, rain at harvest**
Principal grapes **Chardonnay, Cabernet Sauvignon, Merlot**

1:177,000

Km 0   1   2   3   4   5 Km
Miles 0   1   2   3 Miles

------- County boundary

AVA boundaries are distinguished by coloured lines

SONOMA VALLEY AVA

■ KENWOOD Leading producer

⬤ Steiner Vineyard Noted vineyard

▦ Vineyards

▦ Woods and chaparral

══1000══ Contour interval 200 feet

▼ Weather station (WS)

Napa Valley

Perhaps the most surprising thing about the surprising Napa Valley is that it produces less than 5% of all the wine made in California. Ever since Robert Mondavi opened his Oakville winery in 1966, the Napa Valley has been regarded as the epicentre of the new, golden era for California wine. The construction of Mondavi's famous adobe arch with its cunning Mission connotations signalled the start of the transformation of a sleepy farming community of walnut and prune orchards into the world's most glamorous, most cosseted, and most heavily capitalized wine region.

But its 35,000 acres (14,000ha) of vines would fit eight times into Bordeaux and twice into Burgundy or Champagne. For all the noise made about it, it is really quite small, and yet far more varied than most outsiders realize.

Take soils. A common complaint from Europeans about California wine lore is that it takes no account of different soil types. One explanation for this apparent insouciance is that things are just so darned complicated. In the Napa Valley alone nearly 150 different soil types have been identified, many of them interlaced and layered within a few yards. The appeal of a site classification system as simple as Winkler's degree day measurement (see page 270 and opposite) is obvious.

In very general terms the valley is the result of the Napa River, now a lazy trickle, tunnelling its way between the Mayacamas Mountains on the west and the Vaca Range on the east. Their respective peaks are the igneous outflows Mount Veeder and Atlas Peak, responsible at various times for a wide range of mineral deposits. (That volcanic activity continues is obvious at the head of the valley in Calistoga where visitors frolic in mud baths and hot springs.) Loosely speaking therefore, soils are thinnest, oldest, and least fertile on the sides of the valley while the valley floor is dominated by deep, fertile alluvial clays. There are some deep but well-drained soils on the piedmonts on both sides of the valley.

As for climate, as elsewhere in northern California, the open (in this case southern) end of this narrow (3 miles/5km at most) valley, about 30 miles (48km) long, is much cooler, by an average of at least 10˚F (6.3˚C), during the summer than the northern end. In fact Carneros (see previous page) is virtually at the coolest limit of fine wine production while Calistoga is as hot as any fine wine producer would care for. Much of the land in between is just right for a wide range of grape varieties. The long summer season of relatively high temperatures, thanks to Napa Valley's relatively low latitude, warms up air which rises, encouraging the influx of cooling draughts of ocean air, whether from Sonoma's Russian River via the Chalk Hill gap (see page 273) or, more persistently, from Carneros as far north as the eastern Stags Leap District. Eastern slopes in general benefit from sunshine during the warmer afternoon hours, resulting in softer wines than those made on the west side from grapes ripened by morning sun, which generally have more definition.

The two diagrams at the bottom of the opposite page, supplied by California viticultural consultants Terra Spase, show actual morning and afternoon temperatures on one particular day, illustrating the typical variance between the two sides of the valley. Note how the south of the valley is consistently cooler than the north, and the land above the fog line is much warmer than the valley floor in the early morning.

Moving north up the valley, wines tend to taste progressively richer with riper tannins, while those made on the less fertile, dry-farmed hillsides, which are increasingly colonized by the vine despite problems with erosion and land use disputes, have more structure and concentration than the valley floor counterparts they look directly down on. High altitude vineyards such as those of Mayacamas, Chateau Potelle, and Cain Cellars along the Mayacamas Ridge in the west and Oakville Vineyard, Chappellet, and Bancroft Ranch on the eastern side of the valley often benefit from strong morning sunshine above a valley floor shrouded in fog. Then cool breezes bathe the mountaintops in late afternoon while the valley floor radiates heat trapped below an inversion layer.

This is the theory. What gets in the way of matching geographical influence to bottle is less natural caprice – although vintages vary here far more than many wine drinkers realize – than how the Napa Valley is organized. To the literally millions of tourists attracted to "The Valley" each year, there seems an infinity of wineries flanking the overcrowded Highway 29 and the rather quieter Silverado Trail. But in fact there are fewer than 300, and more than 1,100 grape-growers. The symbiotic functions of selling wine and growing vines are more distinct here than in most fine wine districts. Some of the wineries have but a line of ornamental vines of their own. They will buy in fruit, sometimes wine, and very possibly blend different lots so that these expressive nuances are lost. Even if the wine is labelled with a more specific AVA than Napa Valley, unless the vineyard is named, it can be difficult to locate the precise grape source.

Cabernet Sauvignon is the Napa Valley's grape. In fact Napa's best Cabernets are incontrovertibly some of the world's most successful. They have unparalleled opulence and exuberance, yet the finest examples have rigour too. Some of the more austere hillside examples apart, these are Cabernet Sauvignons that can

Below Mustard blooms in springtime at one of Shafer's vineyards on the eastern side of "The Valley". Note the advanced age of the vines (unusual) and the drip irrigation system (*de rigueur*).

be drunk with pleasure when only three or four years old, a practical advantage which makes some Europeans suspect them of being facile. It is still too early to know how well and for how long many of the most expensive, so-called California cult wines will age (like their counterparts from the St-Emilion microchâteaux), but there is ample evidence of sensational ageing ability among the best Napa Cabernet with a history, whether it be the great early 20th century vintages from pioneers such as Beaulieu and Inglenook or later classics such as Chateau Montelena, Mayacamas, and Heitz Martha's Vineyard from the mid-1970s. These are great wines by any measure.

The cool Carneros and the southern end of the valley between Yountville and the town of Napa are generally too cool to ripen Cabernet and since the great post-phylloxera replantings of the 1990s have become a useful source of Chardonnay and Sauvignon Blanc. Some good Sauvignon Blanc is produced just north of Yountville but further north, Cabernet and Merlot now reign, even if a definitive style of Napa Merlot has yet to be discerned. Plantings of the other Bordeaux grapes Cabernet Franc and to a certain extent Petit Verdot and Malbec have increased a little, chiefly to make up blends called Meritage here to distinguish them from the 100% Cabernet Sauvignon wines that are still commonplace. While all-Cabernet wines produced in the more temperate climate of Bordeaux can be stern in the extreme, their Napa equivalents taste just fine thanks to the extra ripeness imbued in Napa Cabernet, particularly since "mouthfeel" and therefore "extended hang time" have been worshipped.

Cumulative Growing Degree Days
(see page 270)

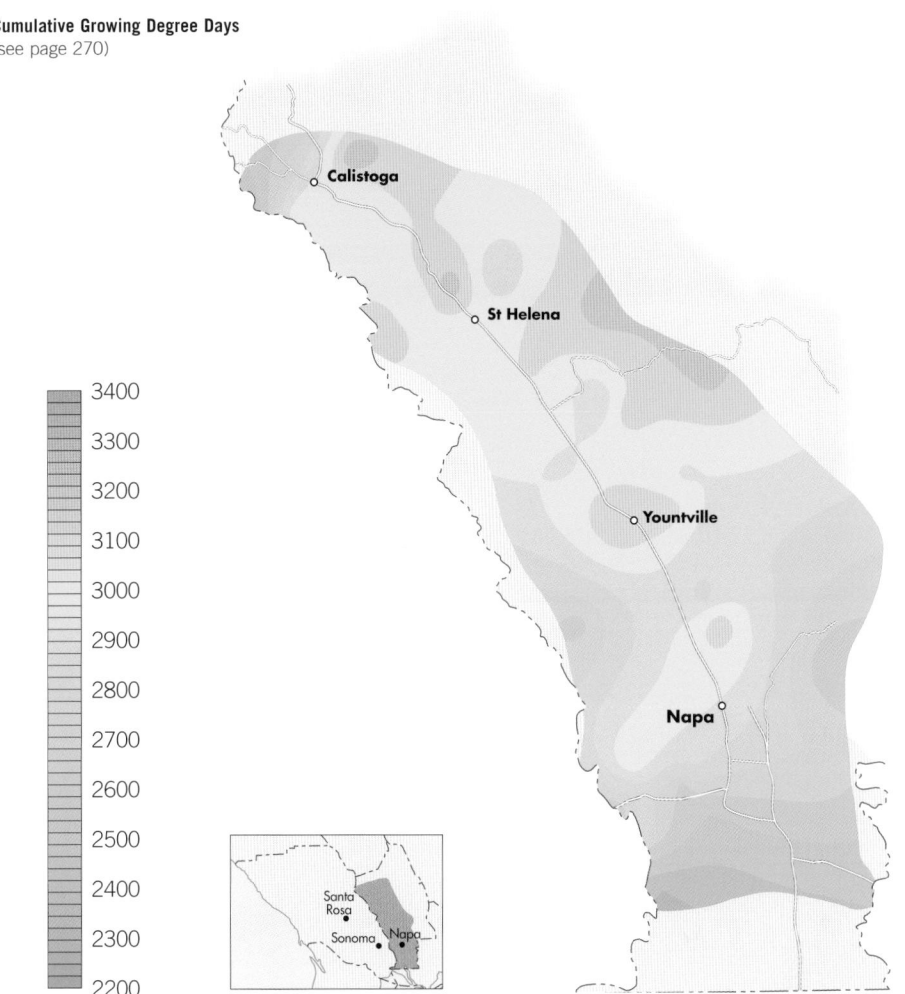

Early Morning Temperatures

Late Afternoon Temperatures

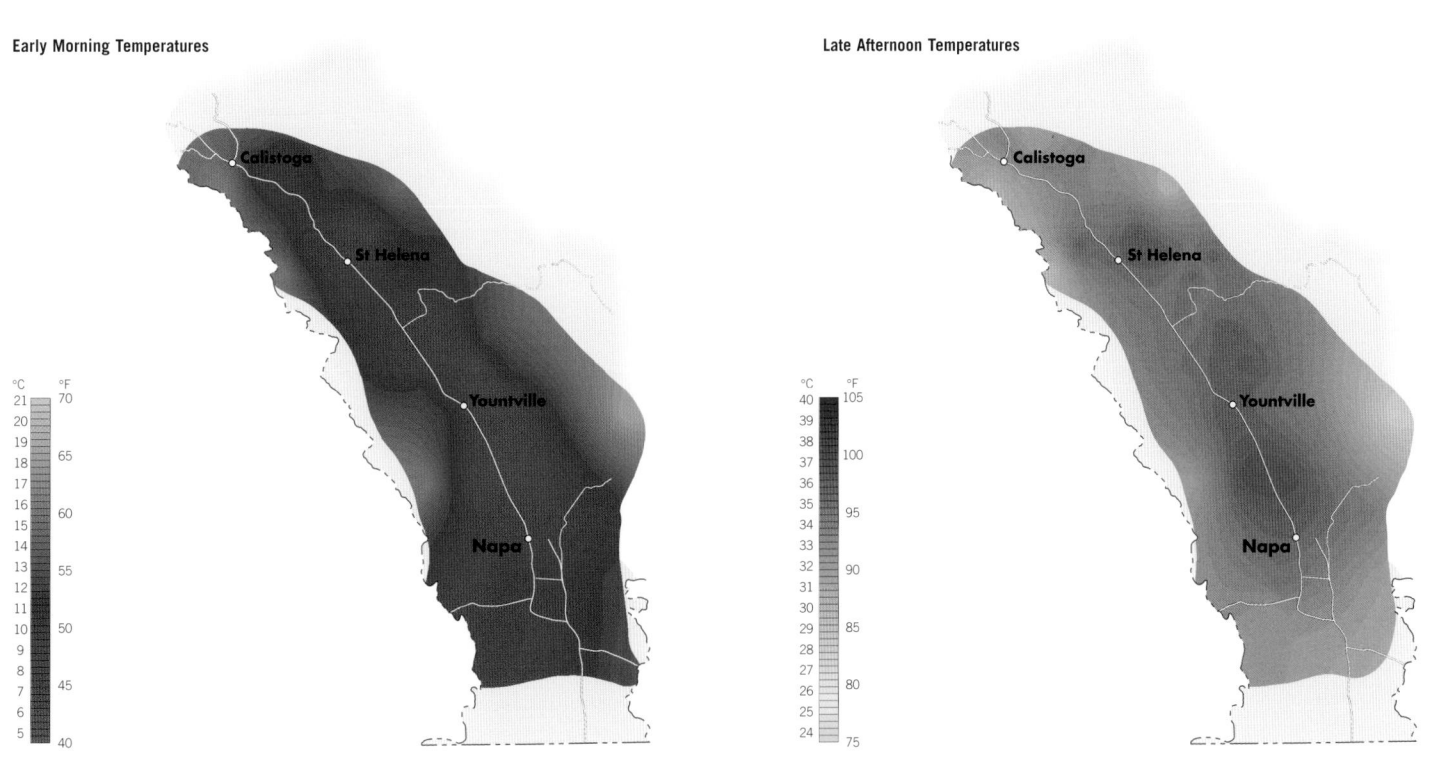

Syrah is being planted on some hillside sites and some fine Zinfandel is produced in various Napa Valley vineyards, particularly in the warm vineyards around Calistoga (whose climate is not unlike Alexander Valley's) and on Mount Veeder, but Napa does not have a cohesive answer to Sonoma's Dry Creek Valley.

That said, Napa County has one of the more highly developed and cogent sets of AVAs – certainly more logical than Sonoma's. Napa Valley is the general AVA and includes not just the world-famous main valley with its extraordinary concentration of modish restaurants, art galleries and gift shops as well as wineries, but also a considerable area of quite separate land such as hot Pope Valley and Chiles Valley, an AVA to the east which will surely be colonized by would-be vignerons, and American Canyon southeast of Napa town (not mapped opposite) which already has been. This southern territory towards the town of Vallejo has proved warm enough for extensive viticulture on land that has little in common with most of the Napa Valley but is entitled to the name.

Yountville is the southernmost AVA of the Napa Valley proper but, free of the extreme winds of Carneros, it can ripen later varieties than Chardonnay and Pinot Noir such as Cabernet Franc and, particularly, Merlot which thrives on some of the clay-rich alluvial fans to be found there. Luna has shown how well adapted Pinot Gris (or Grigio) and Sangiovese can be in this area too.

Stags Leap lies to its immediate east on generally higher ground and smack bang in the path of winds and fog generated by the coastal gap bridged by the Golden Gate. Stag's Leap Wine Cellars (as opposed to the nearby Stags' Leap Winery), famous for its 1973 Cabernet which trounced the best of France in the landmark Paris tasting of 1976, put the district's perfumed, non-blockbuster style of red wine on the map; Shafer has ensured it stayed there.

Oakville is where serious, meaty Cabernet country begins (even if it can also produce vote-catching Chardonnay and Sauvignon Blanc and some convincing Sangiovese). On well-drained soils on its western edge are some of the valley's most outstandingly successful sites for luscious but structured Cabernet Sauvignon such as the famous To-Kalon vineyard surrounding the recently extended Robert Mondavi winery and Martha's just below Harlan, another great if younger vineyard.

Rutherford is just north and is similarly glorious territory for lovers of sumptuous Cabernets, which often have the distinction of a slightly mineral note known as "Rutherford dust". This phenomenon is most common in great wines from the much-touted Rutherford Bench (perfectly well-drained, low-vigour bench-land along the west side of the valley), which have included in their heydays the best of Inglenook and Beaulieu (BV) and Heitz Bella Oaks. Current examples include Rubicon from Niebaum-Coppola (which now occupies the original Inglenook winery) and Livingston's Moffett vineyard. Caymus Special Selection Cabernet, made from an ancient plantation on the gravelly east side of the valley, is another Rutherford classic.

A little warmer than Rutherford, St Helena is not just the largest and busiest of the Napa Valley's wine towns (Oakville is little more than a crossroads and a fabulous grocery store). It is also the address of many of the valley's biggest wineries which ship in wine or grapes from well outside the area in some cases: the likes of Sutter Home, whose fortune was built on palest pink "White" Zinfandel bought in from the Central Valley; Beringer, a source of fine, geographically designated reds and whites and now owned by Australian brewers Foster's; tourist mecca V Sattui; and the once-great Louis Martini. St Helena can also boast the vineyards of the smallest, most cultish labels such as Grace Family, Vineyard 29, and Colgin Herb Lamb (even if the latter, like many of these cult Cabernets, is made at a custom crush facility elsewhere). The valley reaches its narrowest point just north of the town and some of the vineyards can be quite steep.

At the northern end of the valley Calistoga is all but surrounded by mountains, notably Mount St Helena to the north, which capture cold winter air at night and make spring frost, a perennial threat to all valley floor vineyards, a recurring danger here. Sprinkler systems and, particularly, wind machines and propellers are an eye-catching local feature of the vineyards on the volcanic soils around Calistoga. Equally arresting to the visitor are the extraordinary marzipan creation that is Clos Pegase winery and the white, modernistic Sterling winery, which looks down on them from the top of a short gondola lift. But many tourists are simply sated long before they reach this end of the valley.

This means that such a distinctive region as Diamond Mountain just southwest of the town, whose extremely mixed soil profile also includes volcanic elements, is not too overrun. Diamond Creek Vineyard was an early exponent of often impenetrable, vineyard-designated bottlings; sparkling wine pioneer Schramsberg an unlikely neighbour. The area is cooled by air from the Chalk Hill Gap.

A blend of the new, the cultish, and traditional favourites Stag's Leap and Caymus. It is practically impossible to acquire Screaming Eagle and Harlan unless you have been on their mailing list for many years. Dalla Valle's Maya is up there too but is much tougher than the regular bottling shown here.

County boundary

AVA boundaries are distinguished
by coloured lines

NAPA VALLEY AVA

■ CAYMUS   Leading producer

● Martha's Vineyard   Noted vineyard

Vineyards

Woods and chaparral

——1000—— Contour intervals:
below 100ft every 20ft
above 100ft every 200ft

▼ Weather station (WS)

Mountain vineyards are becoming increasingly important in Napa Valley. All along the western ridge are single-minded individuals perceived, not least by themselves, as very different creatures from those on the valley floor below. Spring Mountain, whose most supple wines are made by the brand Pride Mountain, benefits not just from altitude but from cool Pacific air too. Mount Veeder to the south produces altogether tougher wine from very thin, very acid soils with a strong volcanic element not dissimilar to those found over the ridge in the western Sonoma Valley (Monte Rosso, for example). York Creek makes fine Zinfandel as well as Cabernet.

On the gentler east side of the valley, vines are being planted and wineries constructed as fast as local planners will allow. Dunn, La Jota, and Chateau Woltner (a mountain hideout developed by exiles from Château La Mission Haut-Brion in Bordeaux) are some of the highest achievers on the cool, quiet, generally fog-free uplands of Howell Mountain. The sheltered Conn Valley benefits from bench-land soils and is clearly well suited to Cabernet. Atlas Peak to the south is even higher, and equally cool, with thin soils and a slew of Italian grape varieties planted by Antinori at Atlas Peak Vineyards. There are those who maintain that the Napa Valley may one day be just as well known for its Italian and Rhône grapes as for its Cabernet Sauvignon.

Napa Valley: St Helena

Latitude / Altitude of WS **38.3˚ / 197ft (60m)**
Mean July temp at WS **71˚F (21.7˚C)**
Annual rainfall at WS **35in (894mm)**
Harvest month rainfall at WS **September: 0.4in (10mm)**
Chief viticultural hazards **Over-winter drought, spring frost**
Principal grapes **Cabernet Sauvignon, Merlot, Chardonnay**

1:175,000

Km 0   2   4   6 Km

Miles 0   2   4 Miles

South of the Bay

The area mapped here, from south of San Francisco down to just north of Paso Robles (see overleaf), could hardly be more disparate in terms of both wine and social history.

The windswept, dry gravels of the Livermore Valley have been famous for white wine, especially Sauvignon Blanc with perhaps the most individual style in the state, ever since they were planted with cuttings from Château d'Yquem, no less, in 1869. The creative Wente family dominates the 1,600 acres (650ha) of vines under constant threat from urban development, and have carried an unappreciated torch for Livermore Semillon for well over a century.

The grey sprawl on the map has spread rapidly south of San Francisco Bay as Silicon Valley wallowed in a period of extraordinary growth. High above it on the Santa Cruz Mountains is quite incongruous wine country, older than the Napa Valley. Its isolated wineries are far fewer, and vineyards fewer still, but several of them are among California's most famous names.

In the 1950s Martin Ray of Mount Eden was the first winemaker to bring renown to this beautiful forested mountain area in the modern era. His eccentric, expensive wines, like those of his ex-cellarhand David Bruce, caused arguments and amusement in exactly the opposite proportion to those caused by their spiritual successor, Randall Grahm of Bonny Doon, whose ocean-cooled vineyards just northwest of the "alternative" town of Santa Cruz have succumbed to Pierce's disease. No matter. Grahm is an agent provocateur and an inspired improviser, scouring not just the state but the world

now for the raw ingredients for his highly original blends with names such as Le Cigare Volant and Il Fiasco.

The established leader in the region is Ridge Vineyards, high above the fog-line on a ridge overlooking the ocean one way and the Bay the other. Cabernet from the highest patch, Monte Bello, is often as fine and long-lived a red wine as any in California, thanks to old vine stock and the infertile soils on these steep slopes. (Ridge painstakingly trucks fruit, especially from ancient Zinfandel vines, from all over the state up to the winery at 2,600ft, or 790m.)

Just east of the Santa Cruz Mountains AVA is Santa Clara Valley, a wine region almost squeezed out of existence by the electronic revolution, yet just a little further south near the garlic capital of the world Gilroy, in the unofficial Hecker Pass district, ancient Rhône vines persist. The local wineries can sell everything they make at the cellar door and so the area's potential is considerably under-appreciated, and prejudiced by that grey sprawl.

The reason why Monterey County produces almost as much wine as the whole of Napa County lies on the valley floor, from Gonzales south beyond King City, a monument to corporate madness in the 1970s. The then large companies (several are now defunct) and private investors pursuing tax breaks were encouraged by the

Below Chalone's vineyards are high above the heavily milked flatlands of the valley floor in Monterey. The struggle at Chalone has been not to restrict yields but to find enough water to produce a commercial crop.

University of California at Davis and its preoccupation with degree days to plant in what promised to be a wonderfully cool-climate zone. The Salinas Valley, with its mouth open to the ocean on Monterey Bay, forms a highly efficient funnel for a regular afternoon visitation of cold sea air. The valley, with its short history of salad and vegetable growing and long history of exploitation (remember Steinbeck?), was enthusiastically turned over to vines in a planting spree that took in nearly 40,000 acres (16,200ha) – far more than Napa.

Unfortunately, the funnel proved all too efficient. On a hot day inland, clammy coastal air comes rushing up the valley with such force that it actually tears off vine shoots. The valley is extremely dry (with irrigation water aplenty from the underground Salinas River) but fiendishly cold, so grapes are regularly picked in December from vines which budded in February, giving Salinas Valley one of the longest growing seasons in the world of wine.

These huge vine farms, most notably the record 7,000-acre (2,800-ha) San Bernabe vineyard, which, like other monster vineyards Scheid and Lockwood, stretch for miles between the bottom of the map opposite and the top of the one overleaf. Planted with little regard for such niceties as varying local conditions, they initially yielded heavily irrigated, machine-picked grapes from horribly vigorous vines in various stages of maturity. The excessively herbaceous wines that resulted seriously sullied the name and reputation of Monterey. Even today, with viticultural practices much improved, most of the considerable produce of Salinas Valley is sold in bulk to the Central Valley giants to be blended with wine from warmer regions and sold under the basic California appellation.

The western section of Arroyo Seco is more sheltered from the winds, and Riesling and Gewürztraminer vines on its pebbly vineyards have been persuaded to rot nobly every year giving botrytized wines with particularly refreshing acidity.

Nowadays there are vines as far south as hot Hames Valley (see page 271) near the San Luis Obispo county line and up on the valley's western slopes in the Santa Lucia Highlands. In general this is vine-farming not winemaking country.

There are two more ambitious outposts, however. Chalone Vineyard, now with its own AVA, lies on a sun-scorched 2,000-ft (600-m) limestone hilltop on the road from Soledad to nowhere – except the Pinnacles National Monument. Chalone has, with varying degrees of success, made Chardonnay and Pinot Noir with the conviction that Burgundy's Corton has somehow migrated west. Burgundy, or more precisely limestone, was the inspiration for Josh Jensen's Calera, founded in equally splendid, equally arid isolation to grow Pinot Noir just 20 miles (32km) north in the same range (Mount Harlan AVA). The soil is right; the rainfall almost ruinously low. Calera estate wines are now subsidized by imports from the rapidly expanding Central Coast region to the south.

These labels are arranged *roughly north to south according to their provenance. They illustrate well that this area can offer more diversity of wine styles than most – and there isn't even room for Fogarty's Gewürztraminer or Concannon's Petite Sirah.*

- - - - - County boundary

AVA boundaries are distinguished by coloured lines

CHALONE   AVA

■ JEKEL   Leading producer

⬤ Pisoni   Noted vineyard
Vineyard

Vineyards

Woods and chaparral

—4000—   Contour interval 1000 feet

1:710,000

Km 0   10   20   30 Km

Miles 0   10   20 Miles

Southern Central Coast

The burgeoning Central Coast has known viticulture since the Mission era but came to the fore only in the early 1990s as a cheaper alternative for vineyard expansion to Napa and Sonoma. Technically it runs all the way from the vineyards south of San Francisco in the north (see previous page for a map of these and of Monterey County) to the subtropical climate of greater Los Angeles (whose wine country is discussed on page 286).

The two counties in between, San Luis Obispo and Santa Barbara, mapped here, are in full viticultural spate. The view from Highway 101, which winds through them, was transformed by the end of the 20th century from scrub oaks and cattle grazing to an undulating strip of vineyards that continues for miles on end.

This section of California is distinctive geologically: the San Andreas Fault runs down the eastern side of the region and so the vineyards are based on quite different, more marine-influenced, carbonate-infused soils, which, according to some authorities, is one of the reasons why wines made here have a certain voluptuousness. Certainly there is a parallel in textural differences and acidity levels between, say, Chianti Classico and the seaside Maremma on the one hand and the North and Central Coasts on the other.

The climate here is also primarily maritime, with very mild winters (vines may not always get the chance of a restorative sleep) and summers that are much cooler than the California norm (see factfile, which shows a mean July temperature roughly the same as that of the Mosel Valley in northern Germany).

San Luis Obispo County has at least three distinct zones, two of them in the crudely drawn Paso Robles appellation, which includes such a wide stretch of country. The rolling grassland east of Highway 101 is decidedly hot with no direct access for cooling ocean breezes. Its deep fertile soils are now home to a sizeable area of vineyard that supplies supple, fruity, though hardly demanding varietals, largely for North Coast wineries and contract bottlers. Mondavi, Beringer, J Lohr, and Australia's Southcorp are all big players in the district. Beringer's Meridian winery (formerly called Estrella River) stands out for its hilltop site, a vantage point dominating the increasingly viticultural landscape to the southeast.

The wooded hill terrain of the western section of Paso Robles on the other side of the highway has much more interesting soil and, being cooled by marine air (if rarely fog), has rather more in common with the Santa Clara Valley west of the San Andreas Fault. The historic fame of Paso Robles, such as it is, comes largely from potent Zinfandels, which are dry-farmed following Italian immigrant tradition. This was the area chosen by the Perrin family of Château de Beaucastel in Châteauneuf-du-Pape to plant with a wide range of French clones of Rhône grapes at Tablas Creek, and Larry Turley of Napa's Turley Wine Cellars has also shown faith by investing here.

Above Talley Vineyards in the Arroyo Grande grows some of California's finest Chardonnay. The Pacific in the distance has a cooling influence even this far inland.

Edna Valley, over the Cuesta Pass to the south, is different again. Sea air swirls in from Morro Bay, providing perfect conditions for the development of fungal diseases, and cools the valley to a Region I climate, which somehow manages to produce some quite luscious Chardonnays, albeit with a fine streak of lime to keep them lively. Edna Valley Vineyards (related to Chalone) is its prime local winemaking operation, although it has been joined by other wineries, most notably Alban, one of the Central Coast's most proficient exponents of red and white Rhône varieties.

To the immediate southeast, the more varied but generally even cooler Arroyo Grande is increasingly recognized as a source of particularly fine Pinot Noir and Chardonnay from the likes of Talley and Laetitia, once the champagne house Deutz's California venture.

Moving south again across the county line in Santa Barbara, the Santa Maria Valley, southern California's riposte to the Côte d'Or, provides conditions that are, if anything, cooler still. Its river runs out to sea in flat land that offers no opposition at all to the Pacific air. Some of its vineyard land is so low-lying that sea fog moves in at midday and overcropped fruit can easily be underripe and over-acid. This countryside is far from the stereotype of southern California, and indeed from balmy, palmy Santa Barbara itself,

which is south of the crucial mountains that run off the southeast corner of the map opposite, shielding it from the Arctic Ocean currents that produce fog in the Santa Maria and Santa Ynez Valleys. What is common to all of Santa Barbara County, however, in stark contrast to Sonoma's Pinot country, is remarkably low rainfall (as the factfile shows). This means that there is no hurry to pick before autumn rains, and, like grapes grown further north in Monterey and San Luis Obispo, Santa Barbara's grapes benefit from an extremely long growing season, building flavour over months and months.

Almost all the thousands of acres of grapes in Santa Maria Valley are owned by farmers rather than wineries, making vineyard names unusually prominent. Bien Nacido and Sierra Madre crop up on a range of different winery labels, while the still relatively limited roster of wineries in the region also buy grapes from up and down the Central Coast. Bien Nacido, Cambria (part of the Kendall-Jackson empire), and Byron (Mondavi's stake in the Central Coast) proceed in that order up the valley, in progressively warmer environments. Rancho Sisquoc is the most sheltered, except for the positively secluded Foxen in its canyon. The best grapes, Pinot Noir and Chardonnay in the main but Syrah too, are grown on slopes high enough – 600ft plus (180m) – above the valley floor to be on the fringe of the fog belt. Their naturally high acidity is offset by a fruity intensity which has something in common with the best of New Zealand. Much the most exciting winery in the

The Southern Central Coast *may be plundered heavily by wineries based miles to the north of San Francisco but these are some of the best wineries established in the region. The trend today is for more and more of them to grow at least some of their own grapes too.*

— — – – — County boundary

AVA boundaries are distinguished by coloured lines

YORK MTN AVA

■ **BYRON** Leading producer

⬤ **Dusi Vineyard** Noted vineyard

▨ Vineyards

▨ Woods and chaparral

═2500═ Contour interval 500 feet

▼ Weather station (WS)

Southern Central Coast: Santa Maria

Latitude / Altitude of WS **34.54° / 230ft (70m)**
Mean July temperature at WS **63.1°F (17.3°C)**
Average annual rainfall at WS **12in (314mm)**
Harvest month rainfall at WS **September: 0.4in (10mm)**
Principal viticultural hazard **Late ripening**
Principal grapes **Chardonnay, Pinot Noir**

area, with an air of frenetic experimentation matched only by Bonny Doon in Santa Cruz, is Au Bon Climat and its partner in the same unprepossessing premises, Qupé.

Just south of Santa Maria, in similarly cool, intensely rural conditions, is the unofficial Los Alamos region where several thousand acres of vineyard produce some particularly lively Chardonnay. Conditions are a bit warmer and more stable over the Solomon Hills to the south, particularly (as in Paso Robles) east of Highway 101. The promising Santa Ynez Valley, within easy reach of wine tourists and property developers from Los Angeles, is no obvious physical feature, but a sprawl of vineyards in rolling, oak-dotted hills around and to the north of Solvang, a town as peculiarly Danish as its name. East of the highway are some particularly well-favoured sites with warm days and cold nights that can yield impressive red wines, both the Bordeaux varieties and Syrah, as well as the Roussanne of Andrew Murray.

The true excitement of Santa Ynez, though, lies westward towards Lompoc and the ocean. Bryan Babcock has shown that the high acidities that are common here suit Sauvignon Blanc, Riesling, and Gewürztraminer well. The Sanford & Benedict vineyard meanwhile occupies a sheltered north-facing niche that perfectly suits Pinot Noir and produces some pretty smart Chardonnay too. The Sanford winery is only one of several wineries to hint at the potential of this vineyard – indeed of the Southern Central Coast as a whole.

1:725,000

Km 0 — 10 — 20 Km
Miles 0 — 5 — 10 Miles

Sierra Foothills and the Delta

The new map opposite shows two quite distinct wine regions: the historic but resurgent Sierra Foothills and the Sacramento Delta. The Delta, as Californians call it, lies between, and drains, both portions of the Central Valley: the Sacramento Valley in the north and the San Joaquin Valley in the south.

This map replaces one of the whole Central Valley south of Sacramento which adorned previous editions because, sad to say, the minutiae of this vast agricultural tract are of little interest to either wine-lover or geographer, with the exception of the fortified wine operations of Quady and Ficklin. The Central (or San Joaquin) Valley, marked on the map on page 271, is not essentially wine country at all, but a flat, extremely fertile, heavily irrigated tract of industrial farmland that stretches 400 miles (640km) long and up to 100 miles (160km) across and makes California one of the planet's most important growers of citrus, stone fruit, tomatoes, cotton, cattle, rice, nuts, and grapes.

It produces three-quarters of all the wine made in California (most wines carrying the simple California appellation will contain at least some wine from this undistinguished source) yet the number of wineries there accounts for only about 7% of the state's total – even if most of them are refinery-sized and one of them, E & J Gallo of Modesto, is the world's biggest winery by far and the size of a small town, with the biggest bottle factory west of the Mississippi supplying an army of bottling lines.

The climate is reliably, steadily, often stupefyingly, hot. No chance of a cooling marine influence this far inland. Vineyards take their place with orchards, cotton fields, and pasture and wine grapes with table and raisin grapes,

most notably Thompson Seedless or Sultana (which in its time was pressed into service during the long-distant white wine shortage). The vine varieties planted, or field-grafted, tend to be whatever is currently in demand (most notably Chardonnay, Zinfandel, and Merlot recently) although there is a heritage of older Chenin Blanc, (French) Colombard, Burger, Grenache, Barbera, and Carignan (which gains an e at the end in the US) vines. On these deep, nutritious, well-watered soils, vines are so productive and vigorous that red wines are often not that red. Hence the state's vast, and increasing, acreage of red-fleshed Rubired concentrated on the southern end of the Central Valley.

The northern portion of the Central Valley is more interesting and has been developed, with a vengeance, more recently. There are now considerable plantings in Yolo County west of Sacramento, with the best wines from western hillsides not far from the Napa county line within the Dunnigan Hills AVA. Local pioneer RH Phillips is owned by Canada's biggest wine company Vincor.

The midsection of this ingeniously plumbed agricultural wonderland draining the 14,000ft (4,270m) high Sierra Nevada, between the deep sea ports of Stockton and Sacramento, where the San Joaquin and Sacramento rivers curl west and flow sluggishly through dyked and drained marshland farms into the San Francisco Bay, has a very different character and style from the rest. This is the Delta, where the influence of the Bay is felt in much cooler nights than are found either south or north of here.

Lodi on the east of the Delta is situated on higher land. The area is farmed more by individuals than agribusinesses, and correspondingly

has a reputation for better table wines than the Central Valley average. The co-operatives that once absorbed so much of the local production are now fighting varietal wineries in the hands of such titans as Gallo, Sebastiani, Canandaigua, and Mondavi, whose Woodbridge range is produced here.

In the northwest portion of the Delta the Clarksburg AVA produces inexplicably fine, honeyed Chenin Blanc on a water table so high that the vineyards are almost afloat. The tradition here in Solano County and in Contra Costa County is for the best grapes to be plundered by perspicacious wineries outside the region, not least warehouse operations such as Rosenblum and Edmunds St John. Further south on sandy soils near Oakley surrounded by oil refineries and rail freight lines, Contra Costa harbours some of California's oldest vine stocks of Rhône varieties, as well as some ancient Zinfandel. Planted by Italian immigrants, these vines include Grenache of intensity unusual for California, Carignane, and Mourvèdre, which was ignored for years when called Mataro, but now underpins some of the more glamorous labels from California's so-called Rhône Rangers.

On the north side of Suisun Bay, which connects the Delta to San Francisco Bay, grapes grown in the Wild Horse Valley AVA tend to be sold under the magic name Napa Valley, to which they are also entitled.

Meanwhile, east of Sacramento and the Central Valley, in the foothills of the Sierra where the Gold Rush gave California its first notoriety, the wine industry that slaked the miners' thirst is quietly and determinedly being revived. In the late 19th century there were more than 100 wineries in these hills that

1:925,926

Km 0   10   20   30   40 Km
Miles 0   10   20 Miles

— · — · — County boundary

AVA boundaries are distinguished
by coloured lines

LODI   AVA

■ **LATCHAM**   Leading producer

◯ Eschen Vineyard   Noted vineyard

▨ Vineyards

▨ Woods and chaparral

〜2000〜 Contour interval 500 feet

▼ Weather station (WS)

Sacramento: Modesto

Latitude / Altitude of WS **37.39° / 66ft (20m)**
Mean July temp at WS **77°F (25°C)**
Annual rainfall at WS **12in (307mm)**
Harvest month rainfall at WS **September: 0.4in (10mm)**
Chief viticultural hazards **Rapid ripening, raisining**
Principal grapes **Chardonnay, Merlot, Cabernet Sauvignon**

At the top are two wines bottled *well outside the region which show respectively the exceptional quality of Delta Chenin Blanc and downstream Contra Costa's old vine stumps. Below are higher-altitude wines, the exceptional Renaissance community being north of the area mapped.*

promised so much. During Prohibition there was just one, and the vines, many of them Zinfandel, all but abandoned. But the land was (and is still) of such relatively low value that it was not worth pulling many of the vines out. California's treasure chest of Zinfandel plants with a long, long history is here together with, more recently, an unusually wide range of truly characterful wines at (so far) reasonable prices.

The first signs of a revival came in the late 1960s when Sacramento grocer and polymath Darrell Corti engineered a special, single vineyard bottling of some of this deep, dark, and intensely alcoholic fruit. Ever since, Amador County from which it came has been associated chiefly with Zinfandels that have more in common with port than table wine, even if other parts of the Sierra Foothills now being colonized by ambitious small-scale winemakers can demonstrate that the region has many other strings to its bow.

The Sierra Foothills begins in the north with North Yuba, 30 miles (48km) north of the northern limit of this map. North Yuba is an AVA for one winery only, but it is an astonishing one. Renaissance is the temple of the Fellowship of Friends, with gold labels and high ideals, among them clearly delineated Riesling and Cabernet Sauvignon grown on impoverished terraces at over 1,600ft (490m).

Next in line to the south, the wines of El Dorado County, its name a hopeful reference to the hills' most desirable natural resource, share a similar streak of natural acidity – not least because of the elevation of the rapidly expanding vineyards there, at above 2,400ft (730m) a record for California. Precipitation, rain or snow, is commonplace here, temperatures are lower and the wines from the thin soils tend to be relatively light (although of course anything is light relative to an Amador Zin). But a wide variety of fashionable Rhône and Italian varieties, and the great Riesling, have shown promise here and, provided consumers remember that quality is not proportional to alcohol, there seems little reason not to believe that El Dorado has a rosy if not golden future.

The vineyards of Amador County are at distinctly warmer, lower elevations of 1,000 to 1,600ft (300 to 490m) on a plateau where the altitude has little chance to temper the heat. This is especially true of Shenandoah Valley, west of the county's other AVA, Fiddletown. About three-quarters of plantings are Zinfandel vines of various ages, some of them pre-Prohibition. Old or young, dry or rich, almost chewable, Amador Zinfandel tends to taste as though it has come from a miner's bucket, and is none the worse for that. In a state whose wine producers can seem almost inanely obsessed by smoothly inoffensive Chardonnay and Merlot, it is refreshing to find a combination of grape and place with such a strong identity. Syrah also works well here, as does Sangiovese.

Calaveras County vineyards to the south have an elevation, and therefore climate, somewhere in between those of El Dorado and Amador, although soils in places are more fertile than in either. The leader of this rapidly expanding wine region (and there are developments in Mariposa County even further south too) is Ironstone Vineyards, the Kautz family of Lodi's extremely ambitious wine project and tourist attraction near Murphys. Fruit is currently blended between the two areas but the Calaveras Cabernet Franc merits solo attention.

Being coolish, fragmented, and distinctive, the Sierra Foothills is precisely the opposite of the Central Valley. At the end of the 20th century, this dynamic region crushed only half a per cent of the state's grape harvest but could boast almost as many wineries as the sprawling Central Valley below.

Southwest States

California's first Mission vines were planted between what is now downtown Los Angeles and the city of Pasadena to its north. The Mission San Gabriel still stands, but subdivision and smog have long since driven vineyards out of their original California home. Los Angeles' vines migrated west into what was then the desert area of Cucamonga. Early in the 20th century Cucamonga was a vast and prosperous vineyard, producing "common table wines and fine dessert wines". The road maps still credit it as the "Oldest winery in California".

Since 1650, long before even the Mission grape reached California, however, it was being fermented for the needs of Spanish missionaries in Arizona, New Mexico, and near El Paso in Texas. Texas has a special place in the history of the vine, if not of wine. It is the botanical heart of America – and can boast more native grapevine species than any other region on earth. Of 36 species of the genus *Vitis* scattered around the world, no fewer than 15 are Texas natives – a fact that was turned to important use during the phylloxera epidemic. Thomas V

Munson of Denison, Texas made hundreds of hybrids between *Vitis vinifera* and native grapes in the search for immune rootstock. Working with Professor Viala of the University of Montpellier he introduced many of the resistant rootstocks that saved not only France's, but the world's wine industry.

That of Texas itself was killed by Prohibition. In 1920 the state had a score of wineries. Revival after Repeal was slow and painful: a quarter of the state's 254 counties are still "dry" today. In the early 1970s a new start was made with experimental plantings of vinifera and hybrid vines in the High Plains region at nearly 4,000ft (1,200m) near Lubbock at what would become Llano Estacado and Pheasant Ridge wineries.

They chose well. Despite the infinite exposure and dismal flatness of the region, its soil is deep, calcareous, and fertile, its sunshine brilliant, its nights cool (and its winters very cold). Abundant water from the Ogalala aquifer feeds drip irrigation and helps offset extreme weather such as freeze, hail, and high temperatures. Constant wind keeps disease at bay and helps

cool the vineyards at night. Llano Estacado is now Texas's second largest winery making particularly competent, bright-flavoured reds that have something in common with Washington State's best.

Texas's biggest wine enterprise by far is 200 miles (320km) south near Fort Stockton, where the land-rich University of Texas planted an experimental vineyard in the late 1970s. In 1987 the 1,000-acre (400-ha) vineyard was leased to a consortium now in the hands of Domaines Cordier of Bordeaux. Their inexpensive varietals, which constitute more than half of all wine produced in the state, are labelled Ste Genevieve. Their Escondido Valley range is better.

More promising for quality is the Hill Country west of Austin in the heart of Texas, which has staked out three AVAs: Texas Hill Country, Fredericksburg, and Bell Mountain (the last for a single estate winery of the same name specializing in Cabernet). These three AVAs include a possible million acres (405,000ha), of which only about 500 (200ha) are planted, and a fluctuating roster of about 20 wineries operate.

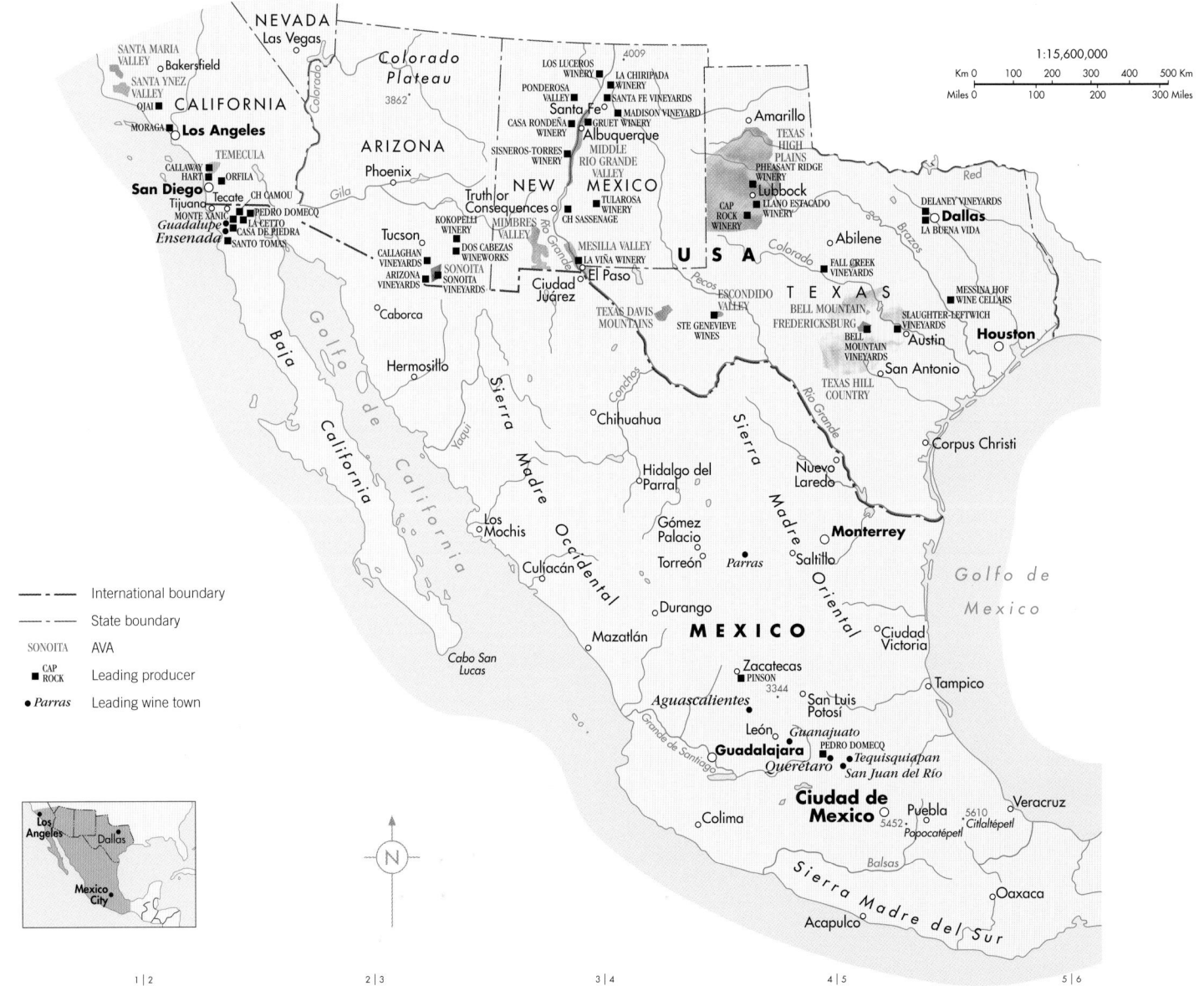

International boundary

State boundary

SONOITA AVA

■ CAP ROCK Leading producer

● *Parras* Leading wine town

Mexico

Thanks to the Spanish colonists, Mexico's is the oldest wine industry of the New World, founded in the 1520s when Governor Hernando Cortés decreed that all farmers plant ten grapevines a year for every Indian slave on their estate. But this precocious transformation of southern Mexico into vine country has been followed by centuries of stagnation. Today barely 10% of Mexico's 120,000 acres (48,600ha) of vines are suitable for table wine; the great majority produces table grapes, raisins, and, especially, brandy.

At these, almost tropical, latitudes, vines can flourish only in the far north or at high altitudes. The best and dominant area for table wine is at the northern end of the long finger of land, cooled by the Pacific, known as Baja California, especially in the Guadalupe Valley and to a lesser extent the San Vicente Valley. (On the much more humid Gulf of Mexico coast Muscadine and hybrid vines are a safer bet than vinifera, as in the southern United States.)

It was in the Guadalupe Valley near Ensenada that noble grape varieties first replaced the ignoble Mission (see page 268) in the late 19th century. Vinifera varieties were subsequently planted in Mexico's highland vineyards, specifically in Querétaro province north of Mexico City at altitudes of up to 6,500ft (2,000m). Here and in Zacatecas province to the immediate north, days are hot while nights are cool but wines can suffer as a result of heavy rains at vintage time. Oaked reds are best so far but Freixenet and others hope to make decent sparkling wine in these provinces. To the north is another historic highlands wine district in the Parras Valley.

The pioneers of modern Mexican table wine were Bodegas de Santo Tomás at Ensenada, then Bodegas Pinson with its Don Eugenio brand, and LA Cetto, which now owns some 3,000 acres (1,200ha) in Baja California, two-thirds of them in the Guadalupe Valley. Cetto makes remarkably successful wines from the Nebbiolo of his native Piemonte as well as Cabernet and very palatable Petite Sirah. White wines are fair, but so far scarcely interesting.

The Spanish firm Pedro Domecq invested heavily in the mid-20th century, like Martell, in brandy production in response to import controls. Today about half of the 6,500 acres (2,600ha) in the Guadalupe Valley are Domecq's, producing both the standard Los Reyes brand and the much more ambitious Cabernet blend, Château Domecq.

The Guadalupe Valley is also the home of Mexico's first "boutique winery" Monte Xanic, founded in 1988, a 150-acre (60-ha) estate intent on setting a new standard of quality. Château Camou, Valmar, and Casa de Piedra, which makes truly serious red, have followed.

The irony is that Mexican taste has so far lagged behind the increasingly exciting achievements of Mexico's modern vineyards and wineries. Most big bodegas lean heavily for their profits on low-quality sweet wines, and above all on brandy to mix with the national drink, Coca-Cola.

It is the Rockies that allow New Mexico to even think of growing wine: elevation cools the climate down to the point where, in the north of the state, only French hybrid vines will survive. The Rio Grande Valley provides almost the only agricultural land, falling from over 7,000ft (2,000m) at Santa Fe to 4,500ft (1,300m) at Truth or Consequences. Its three AVAs, from north to south, are Middle Rio Grande Valley, and Mimbres Valley and Mesilla Valley almost on the Mexican border. Insofar as New Mexico has any national reputation for wine it is, surprisingly, for sparkling wine made by the Gruet winery.

Southeast Arizona, with its one AVA, Sonoita, shares much of the character of southern New Mexico, although the unofficial Sulphur Springs Valley wine region about 50 miles (80km) east of Tucson is even warmer. The Callaghan winery has had some success with Cabernet and Merlot.

To the north wineries have been sprouting in Colorado, most of them in the shelter of the Grand Valley AVA of the Colorado River near Grand Junction at an elevation of 4,000ft (1,200m). Winter freeze and phylloxera threaten

Above Northern Baja, just two hours south of San Diego, produces about 90% of all wine made today in Mexico. Much of it is semi-desert but its east-west valleys draw in cooling breezes from the Pacific.

the mainly vinifera vines of which Chardonnay, Merlot, and Riesling are most common, although Viognier and Sangiovese are hardly surprising in a state as fashionable as this. Utah and even Nevada have their own wineries too.

Meanwhile in southern California the vine is under greater threat than ever before from Pierce's disease. The principal AVA Temecula rises in bumps and hillocks to elevations of up to 1,500ft (450m), a mere 20-odd miles (32km) from the ocean and linked to it by the vital corridor known as Rainbow Gap, which every afternoon cools this essentially subtropical area down to Region III (see page 270): no hotter than the upper Napa Valley. The region was planted with vines in the early 1970s to lure prospective investors in the Rancho California housing development between Los Angeles and San Diego. Callaway was the first famous wine name, Culbertson (now Thornton) the second, for fizz. White grapes have regularly responded better than red to the region's cool nights and early harvests and such red wines as are made tend to be light and fruity. Today, warding off Pierce's disease rather than stylistic niceties is the preoccupation.

This selection of labels is made up of six, *shown roughly west to east, from the southwest American states and two of Mexico's up-and-coming wine labels on the bottom right. Texas clearly has great potential for vine-growing, with the major disadvantage of endemic Pierce's disease.*

Pacific Northwest

The Pacific Northwest has several thriving, nay booming, wine industries in both the United States and Canada, although this is a decidedly recent phenomenon. For a long time such vines as were grown here produced jelly and juice, but Oregon, Washington, Idaho, and British Columbia are planting vinifera vines at an extraordinary pace, and producing some startlingly good wines from them.

Oregon's are perhaps the most distinctive. The Coast Range lines up as a sheltering sea wall as it does in the wine regions of northern California (though not in between). But here the ocean's warm North Pacific current brings rain instead of fog, modifying what might otherwise be more severe temperatures. The valleys of Oregon suffer the same sort of perplexing weather as Burgundy.

Eastern Washington (and eastern Oregon just across the wide Columbia River) is another world. In this semi-desert, irrigation is essential. The clear skies give long, hot days contrasting sharply with low temperatures at night. Even the grape varieties vary considerably, with eastern Washington (and southern Oregon) able to ripen the later, thicker-skinned vines associated with Bordeaux (and, increasingly, the Rhône, Italy, and Spain) rather than Burgundy and Alsace.

Just as distinct as their grapes are the scale and styles of the two industries. Both have been growing prodigiously, but at the turn of the century Oregon had less than 10,000 acres (4,000ha) of vinifera vines to Washington's total of 25,000 acres (10,000ha), even if for long Oregon had far more wineries. Oregon has always been the home of the craftsman winemaker vinifying grapes grown in small, personally managed, mainly estate vineyards. Eastern Washington originally operated on a quasi-industrial scale, with heavily irrigated grapes grown by farmers who might just as well have been growing cereals or apples, picked mechanically and shipped back to Seattle.

The roots of this difference lay in the terrain. The great concentration of Oregon's winegrowing is in the settled valleys west and south of Portland that have raised cattle, fruit, nuts, and a wide range of crops for a century. Vineyards have been slipped piecemeal into this busy, well-worked landscape. There is no monoculture here; you could drive through the Willamette Valley without seeing a vine. But when the grapevine came to Washington, it moved straight out onto the steppe-like wastes beyond the Cascade mountain range where monoculture under irrigation was the primary form of agriculture.

Washington has been changing fast, however, and several artisan operations are emerging, with as much emphasis on growing, or at least finding, great grapes as on making wine.

Oregon meanwhile is becoming less homespun, with the injection of capital and marketing skills from the big wide world outside. One of the biggest operations, King Estate, was built in a distinctly unOregonian French château style but with an associated nursery, Lorane Grapevines, that played its part, with others, in introducing much more suitable clones to the state's wine industry. King Estate's 350 acres (140ha) are insouciantly outside any of the state's six strictly regulated appellations.

The Willamette Valley AVA, the closest to Portland, is by far the most developed (see page 292 for more details). South of it the Umpqua Valley, with only about 600 acres (240ha) and fewer than ten wineries, benefits from more shelter, warmer summers, and drier autumns. Pinot Noir, Chardonnay, Cabernet Sauvignon, and Pinot Gris are the main varieties, although Riesling is the speciality of Hillcrest, which in the early 1960s was Oregon's first winery of the modern era. Here the dynamic Abacela winery has made toothsome Tempranillo, Cabernet Franc, and Syrah.

South again, near the California border, the slightly more densely planted Rogue Valley is even warmer, and its annual rainfall (about 12in, or 300mm) is almost as low as that of eastern Oregon. Cabernet Sauvignon and Merlot will usually ripen here (in contrast to the Willamette Valley) and are the favoured red grapes, with Pinot Gris, Chardonnay, and some Gewürztraminer and Riesling grown in the west of the region. Syrah and Viognier show promise.

Finally, Oregon has a share of two Washington AVAs (discussed overleaf), the Columbia Valley and a small but important extension of Walla Walla. This is also Cabernet Sauvignon and Merlot country and plantings continue apace, approaching 800 acres (320ha) of vineyard in Oregon alone at the turn of the century. A Columbia Gorge AVA is planned.

One of the more surprising wine regions in the US is in the Snake River Valley of Idaho, just over the Oregon state line (see map, far right). Idaho's wine country is on the same latitude as

Two of British Columbians' favourite *bottlings (however confusing the name of the Riesling producer) with one of the most exciting producers in southern Oregon and a faint but true Idaho Pinot Noir.*

Oregon's Umpqua Valley but 400 miles (640km) from the Pacific. As in eastern Washington the climate is continental, all the more extreme for being further south, and also considerably higher, at nearly 3,000ft (900m). Summer days can be very hot, the nights usefully cool, but winter arrives early. Winter freeze is the real problem and can devastate vineyards.

As throughout the Pacific Northwest, indeed throughout the United States, there is considerable cross-border traffic in grapes and wine. Idaho's dozen or so wineries most often buy in from Washington, but at the beginning of the century Ste Chapelle, the dominant producer since the 1970s, with new (Washington-based) owners, was fast increasing the state's acreage of 1,100 acres (2,700ha).

British Columbia, which now has more than 5,000 acres (2,000ha) of vinifera vines, arrived on the scene earlier but more tentatively, via a prolonged, though now virtually abandoned, dependence on French hybrid vines. The centre of Canada's expanding western wine industry is the Okanagan Valley, 200 miles (320km) east of Vancouver, where the long, narrow, deep Lake Okanagan wards off winter freeze. This is holiday country so land prices are higher but natural conditions are very similar to those of eastern Washington – in fact the south of the Okanagan Valley is so dry it qualifies as desert. Irrigation is essential, diurnal summer temperature variation is exceptional, early ripening grapes are favoured (for the same reasons as in Idaho) and acidities naturally high. The racy whites recall New Zealand in their refreshment value; Sauvignon Blanc may do as well here as the Alsace grape varieties that are much more widely planted.

With a vinifera acreage now about half that of Oregon's, it is likely that Canada's other major wine region will become much better known to the world's wine-lovers.

Left Mount Hood, Oregon's highest mountain, is clearly visible from eastern Washington vineyards such as Cascade Cliffs near Wishram. There is little to choose viticulturally between the Oregon and Washington banks of the Columbia River shown on the map, far right.

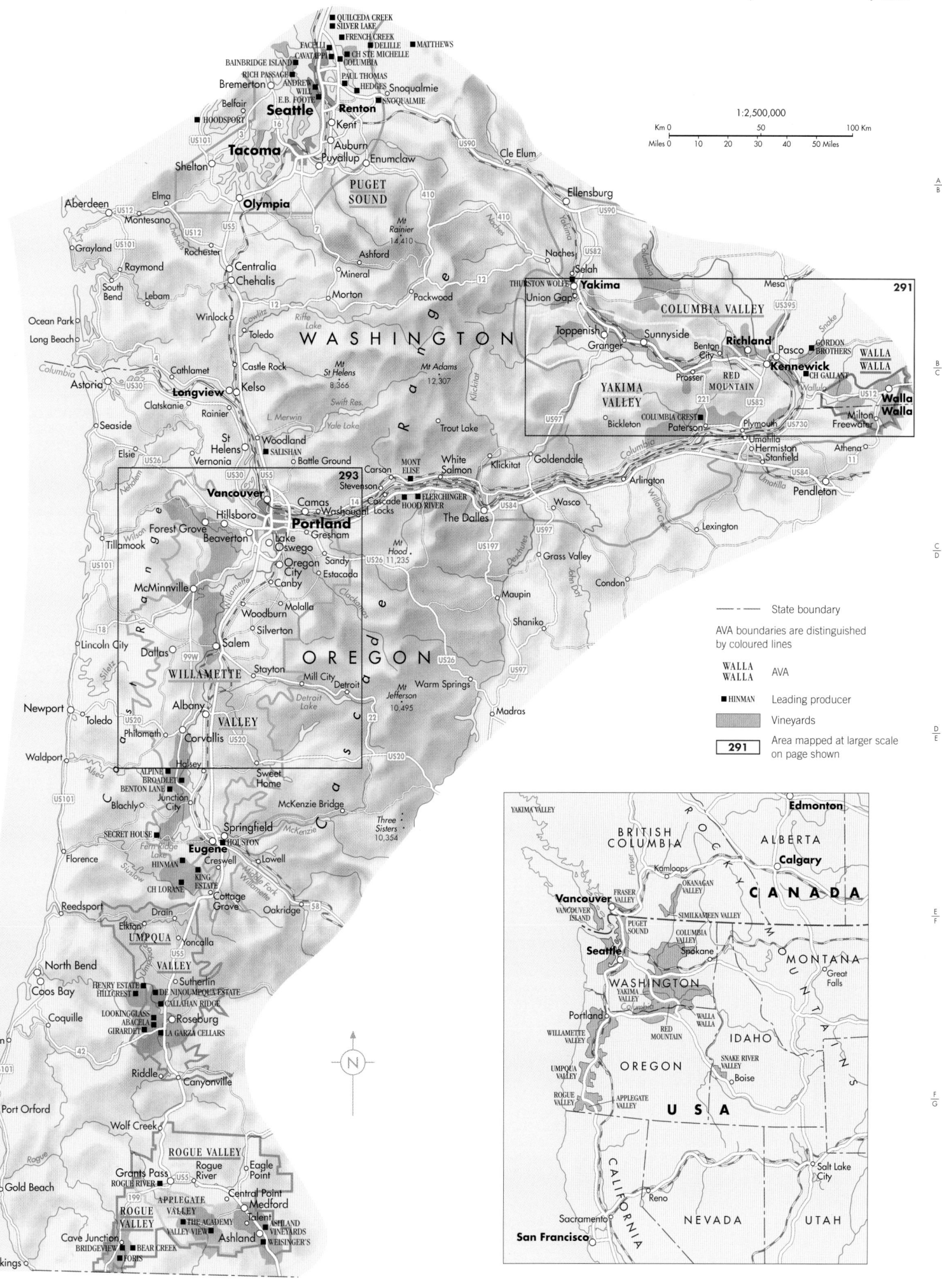

Washington

Eastern Washington, where all but 60 acres (24ha) of the state's vines are grown, does not look like wine country (see picture opposite). Most visitors reach it from the coffee and computer city of Seattle, round which so many of the state's wineries cluster. They drive through damp Douglas fir and ponderosa pine forests over the mighty Cascades and descend suddenly into semi-desert where in summer the sun shines reliably for up to 17 hours each day and where in winter an arctic chill settles for months on end.

During eastern Washington's relatively short growing season, the arid wheatfields that look as though they roll all the way to Kansas are punctuated by oases of green; growing apples, cherries, hops, and, increasingly, vines. This is low-cost farmland (far cheaper than California, for example) irrigated by water from the Columbia basin. The vines may be Concords for juice and jelly but the total area of vinifera vines has been expanding fast, surpassing 25,000 acres (10,000ha) at the turn of the century. Washington is definitively the US's second biggest vine-grower and producer of vinifera wine, albeit only a very small fraction of California's output.

The continental climate here has proved excellent for ripening fine wine grapes, on a latitude between those of Bordeaux and Burgundy, with the very important proviso that there is access to irrigation water – from rivers, reservoirs or from much more expensive wells. This, and the selling price of grapes relative to other crops, is the main brake on expansion. Rainless summers and autumns minimize disease problems while the hot days and cold nights of the desert induce good colour and singularly well-defined flavours in some (not all) varieties. Land prices may be low, but there is one big problem: one winter in every six or so, temperatures sink so low that a serious proportion of vines is damaged. In 1996, for example, only about half of an average crop was produced.

At least these icy winters help keep phylloxera at bay (virtually all vines are planted on their own roots), as do the fast-draining, relatively uniform sandy soils. (This part of the world was the arena for the giant Missoula floods which, during the Ice Age, thundered through the Columbia Gorge on their way to the Pacific, gouging out more ancient soils and carrying deposits from as far away as Montana.)

Vine-growing here has tended to be even more distinct from winemaking than in most American states. The dominant Stimson Lane group (Chateau Ste Michelle, Columbia Crest,

Snoqualmie) grows about a quarter of the grapes it needs. Most wineries buy in grapes, typically trucking them east over the Cascades, although the number of wineries – and estate vineyards – in eastern Washington has been increasing recently. They also tend to buy from a wide range of growers and blend heavily so that winery location is no clue to wine provenance. Partly so as to keep all blending options open, the giant Columbia Valley AVA (encompassing eastern Washington's more specific ones mapped here of Yakima Valley, Red Mountain, and Walla Walla) and the ultra-flexible term Washington State are widely used in preference to more specific appellations such as Yakima Valley.

This valley of scrub overlooked by snowy Mount Adams, carved by the Yakima River on its way east to join the Columbia, is Washington's coolest and oldest wine region. Chardonnay is the grape variety most popular with Yakima Valley farmers but the results can easily be insipid. (Washington's growers tend to rely on a single clone, which can emphasize this variety's natural monotone.) Red Willow vineyard was one of the first to show that Syrah, now being planted furiously, has considerable potential as a savoury but fruity addition to the state's more traditional roster of grapes.

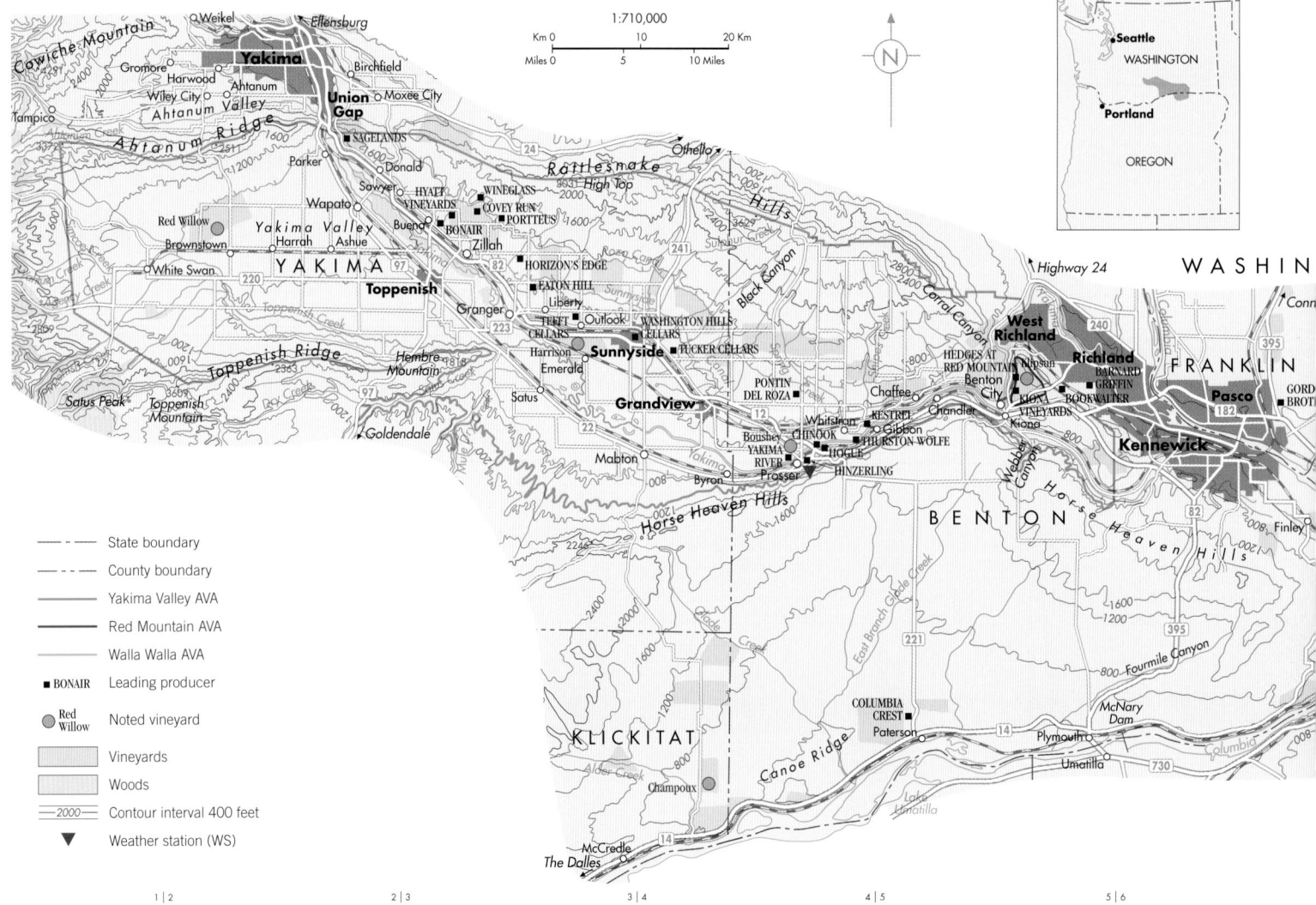

Legend

- - - - - State boundary
- · - · - County boundary
———— Yakima Valley AVA
———— Red Mountain AVA
———— Walla Walla AVA
■ BONAIR Leading producer
● Red Willow Noted vineyard
▨ Vineyards
▨ Woods
≈2000≈ Contour interval 400 feet
▼ Weather station (WS)

Between Yakima Valley and the Columbia River, the Horse Heaven Hills are particularly promising. The upper reaches such as those of Mercer, now Champoux, ranch are high enough for ancient, pre-Missoula clays to remain.

The lower, south-facing slope of Canoe Ridge is the source of fruit for the Chalone group's Canoe Ridge Vineyard winery in Walla Walla (a typical example of Washington's disregard for geographical precision) and many of Chateau Ste Michelle's better reds, including the joint venture with Antinori of Italy, Col Solare. It is also close enough to the broad Columbia River, in effect a series of lakes dammed for irrigation water and hydroelectricity, to be saved the worst extremes of weather, particularly winter freeze.

Between Yakima Valley and the smaller but more famous Walla Walla AVA are some of the state's warmest vineyards of all, including the famous Wahluke Slope that runs down from the Saddle Mountains to the Columbia River tilting vines southwards for maximum radiation in summer and encouraging cold winter air to drain away from them in winter. It was here, just north of the Tri-Cities of Richland, Pasco and Kennewick, that the original Sagemoor vineyard supplied grapes for some of the state's very first

Right Baby Sangiovese vines protected against winter freeze in Kiona Vineyards. Washington's growers are eager to widen their range from the Bordeaux grapes that so clearly thrive under these sunny skies. Syrah and Italian grape varieties are particularly popular.

wines. Merlot is the most widely planted variety here but the small, water-limited Red Mountain AVA has a reputation for Cabernet Sauvignon and the Kiona Vineyards winery has a long history of late-harvest whites complemented by Washington wines' naturally high acidity.

Summers as far inland as Walla Walla are also decidedly warm; winters dangerously cold, and rainfall high for eastern Washington. The genteel college town of Walla Walla is the source of many of the state's most sought-after reds and the fact that many of them have been based on grapes grown outside the AVA seems to have done nothing to harm its reputation. Total plantings here are still measured in hundreds rather than thousands of acres, although the slopes are increasingly invaded by would-be growers of the Bordeaux red varieties and, increasingly, Syrah which was the fourth most planted variety by the turn of the century. Such wines as are produced from grapes grown here tend to be powerfully fruity but with sturdy tannins too. The AVA, pioneered in the early 1980s by Leonetti and Woodward Canyon, spills over into Oregon to include the Seven Hills vineyard.

In 1999 a new Washington winery was bonded every 13 days. The total number, as in Oregon, had already swelled to well over 100. This rapid growth means that many vines are young. They are planted on young, light soils, often from single clones. Most vines are grown, and yields decided, by fruit farmers rather than winemakers. It is not surprising therefore that much of the state's wine output lacks subtlety. But the best wines, while sharing the deep colour, crisp acidity, and bright, frank flavours that typify Washington wine, have an extra intensity of rich, soft fruit that can last in bottle for up to eight years but tends to fade fast after that.

Chardonnay, Merlot, and Cabernet Sauvignon are in almost equal proportions the three most

planted grapes. Cabernet Sauvignon can be slightly grassy (which American palates dislike) unless grown somewhere warm enough to ripen it fully before temperatures start to fall. After a brief flirtation with Riesling (usually off-dry, although a dry version made by Wollersheim as far east as Wisconsin is one of the state's most impressive), Washington decided Merlot was its greatest gift to the world. Merlot certainly has a much clearer identity here than in California, but it is also inconveniently susceptible to winter freeze. Cabernet Franc has its followers, and not just because it is hardier. Lemberger (Austria's Blaufränkisch) has long been a local speciality because of its naturally low acidity and can produce delicious purple wines redolent of dusty blackberries, while Sangiovese has a small but growing following. From a wider range of white grape varieties, Sauvignon Blanc can be truly bracing, Viognier is increasingly popular, and Semillons such as L'Ecole 41's show it could really shine – if given the chance.

Grapes grown back west in the Puget Sound AVA are completely different – early ripeners such as Müller-Thurgau, Madeleine Angevine and Siegerrebe (increasingly supplemented by Pinot Noir and Pinot Gris) – a crew familiar to those who also live in a cool, rainy climate.

Cabernet and Merlot *are often most convincing when they are blended together. All but Walla Walla pioneers Leonetti and Woodward Canyon have their bases back east near Seattle (Sorella is made by Andrew Will). Ernie Loosen of the Mosel made Chateau Ste Michelle's superb botrytized Riesling.*

Washington: Prosser

Latitude / Altitude of WS **46.15˚ / 886ft (270m)**
Mean July temp at WS **69.8˚F (21˚C)**
Annual rainfall at WS **8in (199mm)**
Harvest month rainfall at WS **September: 0.4in (11mm)**
Chief viticultural hazard **Winter freeze**
Principal grapes **Chardonnay, Merlot, Cabernet Sauvignon, Riesling**

Oregon

Oregon prides itself on how unlike California it is. But most of the state is very unlike Washington to the north too. While summers in the Willamette Valley mapped opposite are much, much cooler and cloudier than those of the flashy state to the south (see factfiles), its winters are considerably milder than those of Washington's heavily continental wine country deep inland. Pacific influence washes in to Oregon's wine-land, especially the north of the Willamette Valley, through breaks in the Coast Range, so that cool summers and damp autumns rather than winter freeze are the perennial threats. (See page 288 for details of Oregon's other wine regions.)

The discovery (or invention) of the Willamette Valley as a modern wine region was made in the late 1960s at Dundee, near Lafayette in Yamhill County, by David Lett with his Eyrie Vineyards, and through the founding shortly thereafter of the Knudsen Erath (now Erath) winery nearby.

Had Lett planted Chardonnay and Cabernet, fame would have been slow to follow (especially since the latter would hardly ever have

Above Typically divided canopy for these leafy vines in the damp Willamette Valley of northern Oregon (see page 288 for details of Oregon wine made south or east of here). Note too the region's famous red soils. The current quest is to increase plantings of better quality Burgundian clones.

Just five of Oregon's many celebrated *Pinot Noir labels. Brick House is trying to grow organically – quite a struggle in this climate. Ponzi is an old hand at Oregon's treasured Pinot Gris. At the bottom are successful products of incomers from respectively Burgundy and Australia.*

ripened properly). But he hit on Pinot Noir. Since 1970 Oregon and Pinot Noir have been inextricably linked. The grey skies of this lush pastoral country can do what California had found next to impossible: conjure up the illusion of drinking fine red burgundy, even if Oregon Pinots are in general softer, rounder, and earlier-maturing than their European counterparts.

Almost as though this was the way Pinot Noir liked to be grown, the Willamette Valley has largely remained small-scale. The area attracted a different type of would-be winemaker from the high-rollers who head for Napa or Sonoma. Small means and big ideas produced a range of unpredictable wines, from the fascinating to the seriously flawed. Most of the early wines were fragrant but ethereal. But by the mid-1980s it was obvious that some of the Pinots had exciting staying power.

Whether or not this was what convinced them, high-profile foreigners moved in: from California, a succession of wine producers looking for a moodiness in Pinot that sunny skies could not give them; from Australia, Brian Croser of Petaluma, who set about making Argyle sparkling and still wines in an old hazelnut drying plant next to Dundee's fire station; and, most importantly for Oregonian pride, from Burgundy itself, Robert Drouhin and his daughter Véronique at Domaine Drouhin. Pinots made today vary from the suave, gently understated Drouhin style (which has well withstood comparison with Drouhin's wines back home) to the richly oaky wines of Beaux Frères, the winery part-owned by Oregon's other internationaly famous outside investor, wine guru Robert Parker.

Almost half the Willamette Valley's vineyards are given over to this capricious grape, even more than the state average of 40%. And Oregon's second most planted grape, Chardonnay, is rapidly being overtaken by the most Pinot Noir-like white grape of all, Pinot Gris. There is even a little surge of interest in Pinot Blanc, in this Pinotcentric state. Meanwhile Riesling and Gewürztraminer are being pulled out in response to the market's indifference.

This is a terrible shame, not least because they are far better suited than Pinot Noir's pale-skinned cousins to most sites, particularly those in the north of the valley. Broadly, the Willamette summer is coolest and dampest in Washington County's vineyards which are most open to Pacific incursion and particularly favour aromatic varieties, as Tualatin's output has shown. Pinot Noir, which is still the most planted single variety even this far north, tends to be fine rather than fat. The Ponzi family has shown that such wines can last, however.

Yamhill County to the south has very slightly more warmth but more frost problems, so vines are planted well above the frost-prone valley floor, ideally on east-facing slopes on the west side of the valley at between 200 and 700ft (60 and 210m). The famous Red Hills of Dundee – heavy, red-tinged Jory loams – provide the most established propitious combination of drainage and exposure to rainfall and the light that is so crucial in cloudy Oregon. The Chehalem Mountains to the north with their sedimentary WillaKenzie soils tend to ripen grapes earlier however, as do the promising Eola Hills to the south which are particularly rich in deposits from the famous Missoula floods (see page 290).

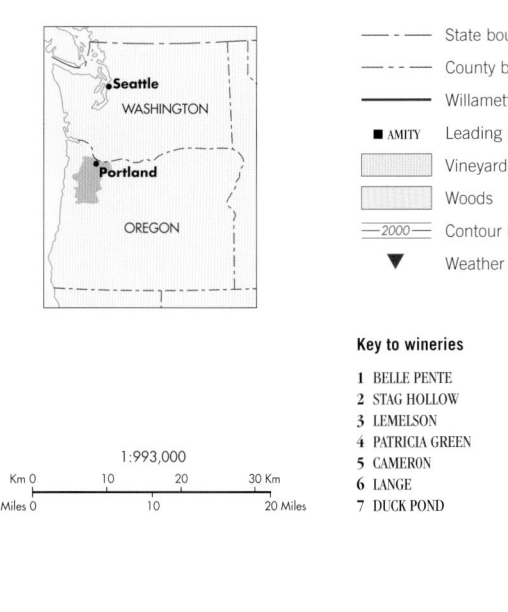

--- · --- State boundary
--- --- County boundary
———— Willamette Valley AVA
■ AMITY Leading producer
Vineyards
Woods
——2000—— Contour interval 1000 feet
▼ Weather station (WS)

Key to wineries

1 BELLE PENTE
2 STAG HOLLOW
3 LEMELSON
4 PATRICIA GREEN
5 CAMERON
6 LANGE
7 DUCK POND

1:993,000

Km 0   10   20   30 Km
Miles 0   10   20 Miles

Willamette Valley: McMinnville

Latitude / Altitude of WS **45.14˚ / 131ft (40m)**
Mean July temp at WS **65.85˚F (18.8˚C)**
Annual rainfall at WS **43in (1,097mm)**
Harvest month rainfall at WS **September: 1.6in (40mm)**
Chief viticultural hazards **Fungal diseases, underripeness**
Principal grapes **Pinot Noir, Chardonnay, Pinot Gris**

Successful grape growing in the Willamette Valley is about ripening grapes fully and early enough to pick them before the autumn rains arrive. Just when that happens, and how damaging the rains are, varies enormously each year. Many grape varieties such as Cabernet Sauvignon and Sauvignon Blanc are just too late ripening to be viable here. But even for early ripening varieties, Willamette Valley's vintage pattern is as wilful as any in France and arguably more wildly varied than in any other American wine region. Wine drinkers outside Oregon tend to fall in and out of love with the state's Pinot Noirs according to the success, or at least the obvious fruitiness, of the vintage on offer.

But there is another, superficially surprising problem: summer drought. The rains can arrive in September or October, but generally only after a cool, grey but often very dry summer. This means that many older vineyards can be starting to turn a nastily inconvenient yellow long before the photosynthesis needed for ripening is completed. Newer vineyards therefore tend to be designed with irrigation systems in place so that the vines are stressed not routinely but only when the grower deems it useful.

The early pioneers, often operating on extremely limited budgets, tended to establish vineyards as cheaply as possible, but higher-density planting is now reckoned to be a worthwhile luxury. Another relatively recent change to Oregon vineyard design is the use of rootstocks. Ever since phylloxera was first spotted here in 1990, sensible growers have planted vines grafted on to rootstocks that will both resist the fatal root-muncher and limit the amount of vegetation that distracts from the grape-ripening process.

Yields in these vineyards therefore tend to be more consistent and vines tend to ripen earlier, but the most important influence on the continually improving quality of Oregon Pinot Noir and Chardonnay has been the introduction of Burgundian clones of each variety.

For at least the first two decades most Oregon Pinot Noir was made from the Wädenswil clone originally from Switzerland and/or the clone so popular in California known as Pommard. They tended to yield wines that had fruit and charm (in a good year) but not necessarily structure and subtlety. The introduction of smaller-clustered clones such as (for fans of detail) 113, 114, 115, 667, 777, and 882, called Dijon clones in Oregon, has added new dimensions to Oregon Pinot, even if in most instances they are used as elements in a blend.

One of the reasons why Oregon Chardonnays have been relatively disappointing is probably the principal clone planted, Davis 108, whose main attribute in California was its late ripening and length of its growing season. Most years in Oregon this is a distinct disadvantage and many

Chardonnays have seemed rather thin and tart. This should improve as more suitable, and subtle, Dijon clones 76, 95, and 96 make more of an impact, but at the turn of the century at least, most white wine hopes were pinned on Pinot Gris – sometimes more for the name than any innate flavour. Oregon Pinot Gris is generally more like an aromatic Chardonnay than a rich Alsace Tokay Pinot Gris, although this will doubtless change as Oregon, regrettably, becomes less and less idiosyncratic.

One quirky institution that has done much to put the Willamette Valley on the international wine map and emphasize Oregon's distinction, however, will surely continue in its peculiarly relaxed yet informative style. The International Pinot Noir Celebration is a three-day Pinotfest involving fans and producers from all over the world. Every July they congregate in the college town of McMinnville to worship at the altar of Pinot and mutter about the iniquities of Cabernet- and Merlot-mania.

New York

New York is North America's third most important vine-growing state – although 20,000 (8,100) of its 31,000 acres (12,550ha) of vineyard are planted with labrusca grapes for grape juice and jelly. This is the *raison d'être* of the grape belt along the south shore of Lake Erie where fewer than ten of the state's 150 wineries can be found (making wine mainly from local French hybrids, described on page 268).

But like Ontario across the border, New York State is busy reinventing itself as a serious wine producer, with almost all new plantings being vinifera which now totals 4,500 acres (1,800ha).

More than two-thirds of all wineries are less than 15 years old, all of them small but ambitious operations, sprouting most noticeably in the Finger Lakes (now about 70 wineries) and Long Island (about 25), although the Hudson River region has about 25 as well.

Long Island, air-conditioned and occasionally battered by the Atlantic, is New York's answer to Bordeaux, both in terms of its maritime climate and the amiable and refreshing build of its wines. The pioneers were Alex and Louisa Hargrave who planted their first vines in 1973 in the silty-sandy potato fields of the North Fork, out at the eastern end of the island, almost surrounded by sea. The ocean influence blurs the seasons and maintains the mild weather for so long that the growing season here is much longer than inland.

Long Island now has 2,000 acres (800ha) of vines, all vinifera (Chardonnay, Cabernets, and Merlot mainly), and makes a substantial proportion of all New York State's premium wine. The island has two AVAs: the original North Fork and the cooler (and smaller) Hamptons, or South Fork. All the mapped wineries have good track records.

Vines have been grown commercially in upper New York State around the deep glacial trenches known as the Finger Lakes, just south of the great inland sea of Lake Ontario, since the 1850s. The Lakes moderate the climate, but it is still markedly continental: in many parts fewer than 200 days are frost-free and winters are long with temperatures down to -4°F (-20°C). American vines were the obvious choice initially and are still grown on about a third of the region's 7,500 acres (3,000ha), mainly for dessert wines. French hybrids such as Seyval Blanc and Vignoles were introduced in the 1950s and still represent a further third.

From the 1960s, however, Dr Konstantin Frank, a viticulturist from Ukraine and no stranger to cold winters, proved that relatively early ripening vinifera vines such as Riesling and Chardonnay could thrive in the Finger Lakes provided they were grafted on the right rootstocks. Today, some particularly fine, almost Saar-like dry, age-worthy Rieslings are made by the likes of Heron Hill, Hermann J Wiemer, and Vinifera Wine Cellars.

The research station at Geneva is known internationally for its work on vine-training and the Finger Lakes remains the commercial hub of the New York industry, not least thanks to the presence, since 1945, of the giant Canandaigua Wine Company. It is America's second biggest wine company after Gallo.

The Hudson River, where New York's first recorded commercial vintage took place in 1829 at what is now Brotherhood winery, is also a region of small wineries. Vinifera vines can be vulnerable here in a climate unmoderated by either ocean or lake and until recently most of the nearly 1,000 acres (400ha) have been French hybrids. Operations such as Millbrook, however, have demonstrated a vinifera future for this pretty, upstate region too.

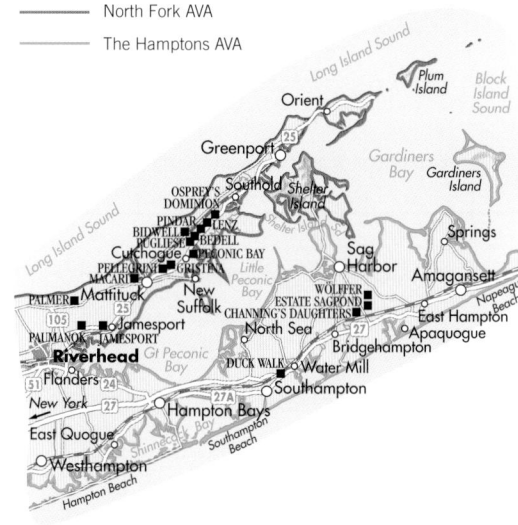

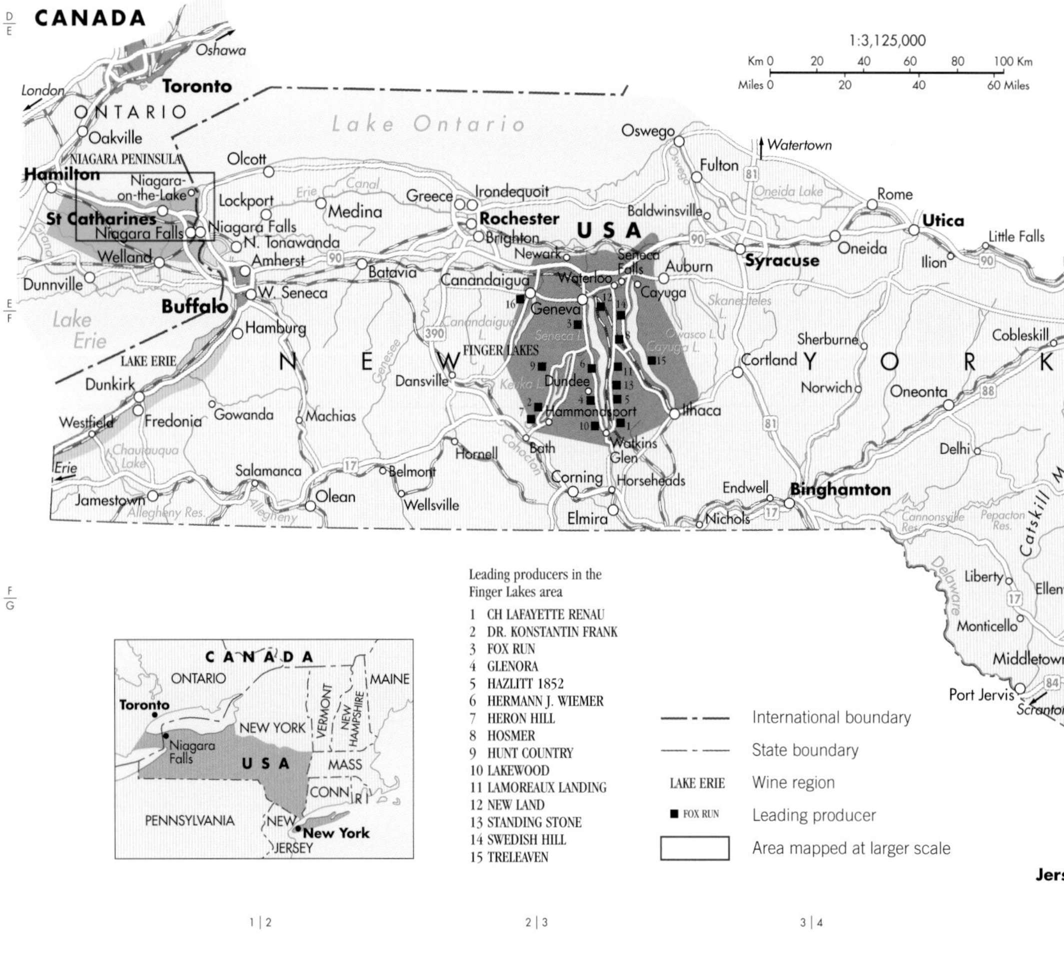

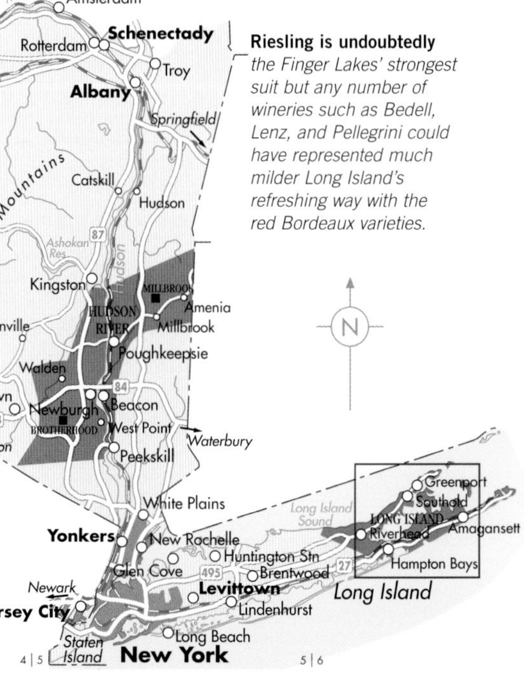

——— North Fork AVA

——— The Hamptons AVA

Riesling is undoubtedly *the Finger Lakes' strongest suit but any number of wineries such as Bedell, Lenz, and Pellegrini could have represented much milder Long Island's refreshing way with the red Bordeaux varieties.*

Leading producers in the Finger Lakes area
1   CH LAFAYETTE RENAU
2   DR. KONSTANTIN FRANK
3   FOX RUN
4   GLENORA
5   HAZLITT 1852
6   HERMANN J. WIEMER
7   HERON HILL
8   HOSMER
9   HUNT COUNTRY
10   LAKEWOOD
11   LAMOREAUX LANDING
12   NEW LAND
13   STANDING STONE
14   SWEDISH HILL
15   TRELEAVEN

——— International boundary

——— State boundary

LAKE ERIE   Wine region

■ FOX RUN   Leading producer

▭   Area mapped at larger scale

Est. 1979

Hermann J. Wiemer
Vineyards
Johannisberg Riesling
Dry
1999
FINGER LAKES   ALC. 11.5% BY VOL.

1998   1998
PALMER
Vineyards
North Fork of Long Island
CABERNET FRANC
PROPRIETOR'S RESERVE
ESTATE BOTTLED BY PALMER VINEYARDS
AQUEBOGUE, NEW YORK
ALC. 10.5% BY VOL.   750 ML

Canada

Canada, much of it frozen for much of the year, may on the face of it seem a decidedly chilly place to grow vines but wine is made, with increasing élan, in four different provinces. See page 288 for details of the rapidly growing British Columbia wine industry in the Pacific Northwest.

In the southeast corner of the country Nova Scotia has a few hundred acres of vines, mainly winter-hardy hybrids (some of them Soviet-bred from Mongolian stock) planted in particularly sheltered corners on the Atlantic seaboard. Quebec also has a small wine industry around the town of Dunham on the American border, whose mainly French hybrid vines need heavy protection each winter.

But the great majority of all Canadian wine is made in the province of Ontario, whose greatest concentration of vineyards, growing 80% of the country's grapes, is on the exceptionally favoured Niagara Peninsula mapped in detail below.

A combination of geographical quirks makes viticulture possible on the peninsula. This narrow strip of sandy loam is protected by vast lakes both north and south, these large bodies of water delaying budburst in spring thanks to the accumulated cold of winter, and prolonging ripening in autumn by storing summer sunshine in relatively warm water. The number of frost-free days is a crucial statistic in any wine district in this part of the world. The risk of frost is dramatically reduced on the Niagara Peninsula because of the Niagara Escarpment, whose eastern continuation is responsible for the famous Niagara Falls. This relic of an ancient sea runs like a rampart along the south of the peninsula bouncing cold winds off Lake Ontario back towards the lake and preventing pockets of dangerously cold air from forming.

Despite the ameliorating factors of its lakes and escarpment however, Niagara is still relatively cool, even if the Beamsville Bench in the middle of the peninsula seems particularly well favoured. The appellation's inherent strengths (as opposed to what the market favours) are much more likely to be nervy Rieslings than blowsy Chardonnays. Fully ripe Cabernet is a bonus rather than routine.

Ontario's two other appellations lie many miles to the west and south of the Niagara Peninsula and are therefore not mapped here. Lake Erie North Shore depends solely on Lake Erie to temper its climate, as does Pelee Island, completely surrounded by the lake and Canada's southernmost point. Because Lake Erie is the shallowest of the Great Lakes, it tends to freeze more easily and winters can be longer. Vintages can therefore vary considerably in these two appellations.

Canada's wine industry has only recently come of age. For long hampered by poor quality grapes and smothered by protective legislation, Ontario wine did not even aspire to compete on the world stage until the late 1980s. But now that labrusca vines are grown exclusively for juice and jelly and vinifera vines have overtaken hybrids, Ontario's best wines, all labelled VQA (Vintners Quality Alliance), can hold their own in comparisons with similar styles produced elsewhere, and triumphantly win any Icewine comparison hands down. Hundreds of thousands of cases of tinglingly sweet Icewine are made in Ontario every year, either from Riesling or, more commonly, from the luscious curranty French hybrid Vidal, whose wines can and should be appreciated almost as soon as they are bottled.

Above The chilly job of harvesting grapes for Icewine, Canada's pride and joy, made reliably, authentically, and in greater quantity than anywhere else in the world. These grapes, the popular Vidal variety, are being picked in January for Henry of Pelham.

Riesling, dry and sweet, is also highly successful in Ontario's cool climate, although producers such as Henry of Pelham and Lake Erie's Colio Estate Vineyards are determined to prove that in good years when summer is warm, Bordeaux red grapes can also be ripe enough to take barrel ageing.

— · — International boundary

■ CAVE SPRING — Leading producer

▦ — Woods

═500═ — Contour interval 100 feet

▼ — Weather station (WS)

For location map see opposite page

Niagara Peninsula, Ontario: St Catharines

Latitude / Altitude of WS **43.1° / 295ft (90m)**
Mean July temp at WS **71°F (21.7°C)**
Annual rainfall at WS **34in (860mm)**
Harvest month rainfall at WS **October: 2.6in (65mm)**
Chief viticultural hazards **Winter freeze, underripeness**
Principal grape **Chardonnay**

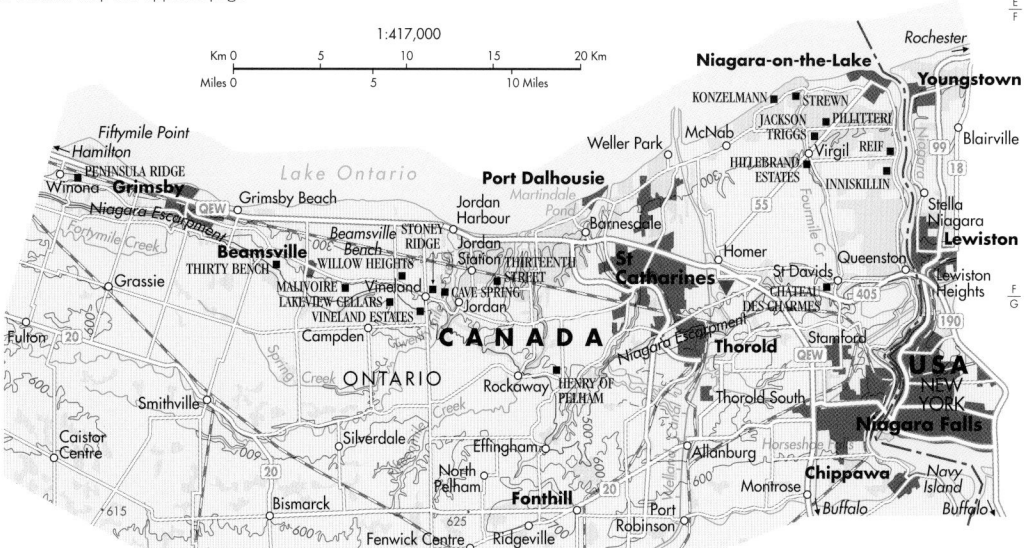

South America

After Europe, South America is the world's most important wine-producing continent. European vines were grown here, in Peru in 1531, long before they reached any other part of the New World apart from Mexico (see page 287). The continent's wine industries, just like its culture, continue to be heavily influenced by immigrants, welcome and less so – initially Spanish and Portuguese, more recently Italians, French, and Germans.

The most important South American wine producer is Argentina (see page 300) by quite a mile, even if Chile (see opposite) preceded it onto the international stage. Unknown to the rest of the world, Brazil is the continent's third most important producer in terms of quantity.

Brazil has yet to try its hand at wine exporting in any serious fashion. The local industry has concentrated on supplying light, sweetish, Italianate fizz to the domestic market. Vine-growing is divided between thousands of small-scale farmers, mainly in the humid Sierra Gaucha region in the Rio Grande do Sul, where hybrids, particularly Isabella, are a common choice for their resistance to rot and mildew. Grapes struggle to ripen fully but the Vale do Vinhedos (vineyard valley) subregion does best.

The most exciting new region is Campanha (once called Frontera) in the far south, where almost 2,500 acres (1,000ha) of vinifera vines are planted on sandy soils that offer good drainage – just like those over the border in Uruguay. The size of the domestic market has also attracted Chandon (as in Moët) to the Serra do Sudeste on higher ground to the northeast. There are also developments in the hot dry Vale do São Francisco in the northeast of the country, almost on the equator.

Unlike Brazilians, Uruguayans are some of South America's most dedicated wine drinkers, second only to the Argentines, making the unusual wine industry of Uruguay the continent's fourth largest. The modern era began in 1870 with Basque immigration and the import of superior European grape varieties such as Tannat, called Harriague after its original promulgator. In a direct parallel to Malbec's softening transformation under the sunny skies of Argentina, the Tannat produced in Uruguay is much plumper and more velvety than in its homeland in southwest France, and can be drunk when only a year or two old – most unlike the prototype Madiran.

Not that Uruguay's climate has much in common with that of Argentina's wine regions. It is sunny but much wetter, and nights in the southern, most important wine districts of Uruguay are cooled by the influence not of altitude but Antarctic currents in the south Atlantic. In years when the autumn rains arrive early, acidities can be uncomfortably high.

About 90% of Uruguay's wine is grown in the maritime climate of the southern coastal departments of Canelones, San José (in both of which there has been recent French investment), Florida, and Montevideo, whose low hills offer a wide variety of different terroirs on generally loamy soils. In Colonia and Carmelo in the far southwest of the country across the Rio de la Plata estuary from Buenos Aires, the alluvial soils can be so fertile that vines are too vigorous to ripen grapes fully. A significant proportion of new Uruguayan vineyards use the lyre trellis.

The original importations of Harriague succumbed to virus disease and have all but been replaced by vines more recently imported from France, called Tannat to distinguish them. There is also a little Petit Manseng from southwest France in addition to Viognier, Trebbiano, and Torrontés – as well as the usual "international" suspects, including Sauvignon Blanc, Cabernet, and Merlot which makes a juicy blending partner with the dominant Tannat.

In the Rivera department in the far northeast is a relatively new area that is viticulturally virtually indistinguishable from Brazil's promising new Campanha region. The vine has invaded sugar plantation country in the northwest and the centre of the country where poor soils and good diurnal temperature variation may yield interesting results. The Uruguayans are making a concerted effort to join the international wine party so obviously being enjoyed by Chile and Argentina.

But perhaps the greatest surprise in this roll call of regions is wine of remarkable quality from Peru, birthplace of pisco, the Chilean national spirit. The Tacama vineyards in Ica province benefit from the cold Pacific alongside in much the same way as those of the Central California Coast. Their Cabernet, Sauvignon Blanc, and a traditional method sparkling wine, first produced with the advice of Bordeaux's Professor Emile Peynaud, are another revelation of what the least expected quarters of the globe can learn to do.

We can expect to see many more *Uruguayan labels over the next few years as producers there follow Argentina and Chile into the limelight. Brazil and Peru are not far behind.*

 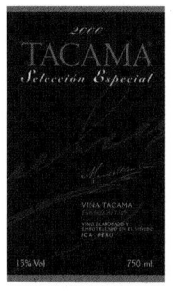  

— · — International boundary

COQUIMBO Wine region

▨ Wine-producing areas

▨ Land above 2000 metres

Chile

To the visiting European, Chile seems like the end of the world – a country whose culture and language may be comfortably familiar, but which feels like and is the very essence of isolation. It is this isolation, thanks to the inhospitable Andes to the east, the Pacific to the west, the sands of the Atacama Desert to the north, and the wastes of Antarctica to the south, that has given Chilean vineyards their most frequently touted distinction: freedom from the phylloxera louse. The vines can safely grow on their own roots, which means that a new vineyard is planted simply by sticking cuttings straight into the ground without the time and expense of grafting on to resistant rootstock.

But it is really the special qualities of Chile's grape-growing environment, together with some propitious vine importing in the 19th century, that make Chile today such a valuable source of inexpensive, fruity, reliably ripe, mainly red wine made from some of the world's most popular grape varieties.

The chief faults in the wines so energetically exported from Chile in the 1990s were the result of over-cropped vines and a certain monotonous predictability. In the early 21st century, however, some impressively concentrated, defiantly priced Superwines emerged (see labels overleaf for the best), and a whirl of plantings of superior clones and new varieties is rapidly widening the range of flavours available from these particularly dry, healthy vineyards. Rot and mildew are not unknown, but are much rarer than they are in most of Europe and even Argentina just across the Andes. The steady ripening process here, encouraged by day after day of uninterrupted sunlight, is thought to be a factor in Chilean wines' particularly high levels of flavonoids, believed, particularly by those who sell Chilean wine, to provide some protection against heart disease.

Chile's latitudes may seem rather low for good quality wine production (about the same as North Africa's, for example), but as a comparison of the factfiles of Meknès (see page 267) and Santiago (see overleaf) shows, the central slice of the country in which vines are grown is not excessively hot. The 870-mile (1,400-km) spine of vineyards is cooled by the chilly influence of the Humboldt Current, which steals inland from waters much colder than, say, California's at the same latitude, and the nightly descent of cool air from the Andes. Chile's day-night temperature variation is unusually wide, and this is almost certainly a factor in the clarity of the fruit flavours.

For decades vineyards were concentrated on a corridor of fertile flatland between the Andes and the much lower Coastal Range, but today Chile's restless wine entrepreneurs are much more experimental. The cool, near-coastal Casablanca Valley is being developed at a rapid rate (see map, right), as is the cool southerly subregion of Bío-Bío, while in the long Central Valley in between (see map overleaf), vines are creeping uphill, particularly on the sunnier, drier eastern slopes of the foothills of the Andes.

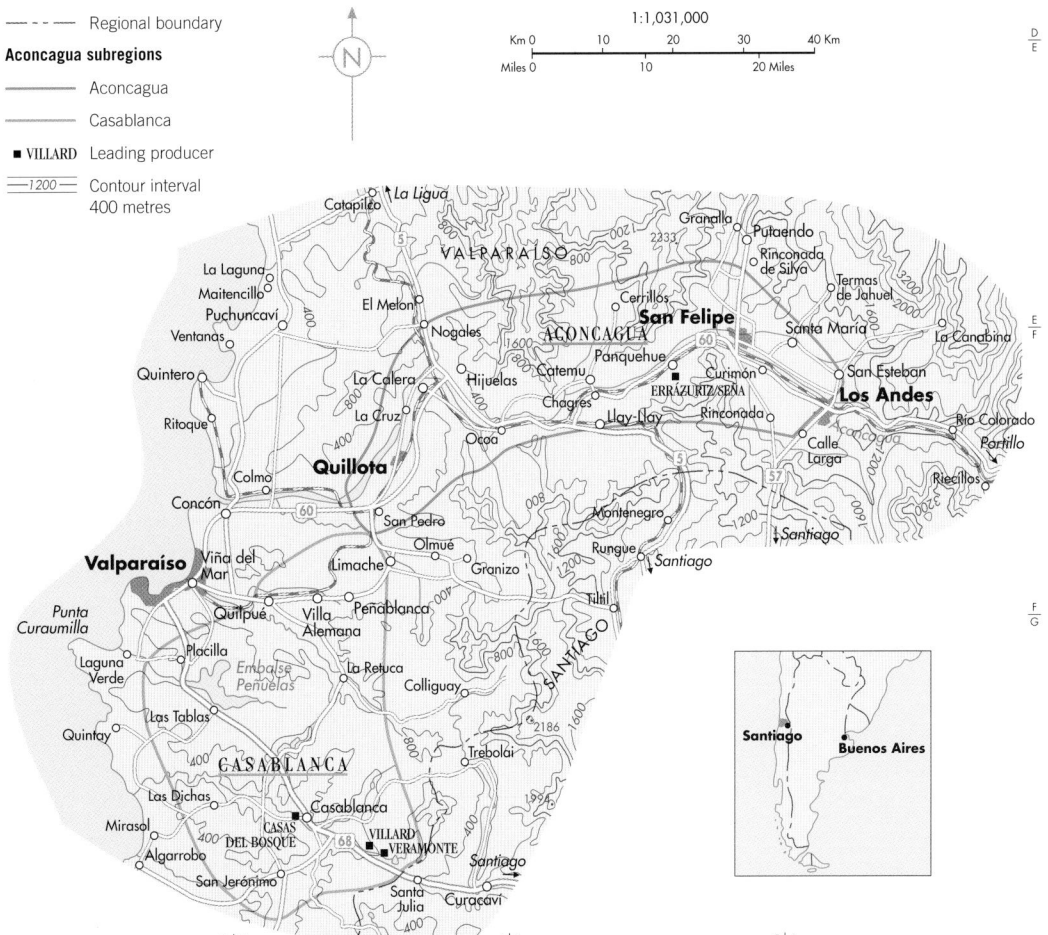

Right The choice of the Aconcagua Valley as the location for Viña Errázuriz in 1870 raised a few eyebrows among the wealthy Chilean winegrowers established in the regions south of Santiago, but Maximiano Errázuriz's gamble proved to be highly successful.

If Chile's wine country has any natural agricultural disadvantage it is that the summers are virtually rainless. Earlier farmers spotted this possible snag and dug an astonishing network of canals and gullies to flood the land with water from the snow that each year melts in the Andes. This admirable, if imprecise, sort of irrigation is being replaced in newer vineyards by drip irrigation which can both apply fertilizer (often necessary in Chilean soils) and respond more sensitively to each vine row's needs. With light but fertile soil and complete control of the water supply, grape growing is absurdly easy.

Irrigation is absolutely essential in most of the vineyards north of those mapped on these pages, in the Atacama and Coquimbo regions, whose main products are table grapes and pisco, Chile's curiously addictive Moscatel-based spirit. Viña Francisco de Aguirre, named after the conquistador supposed to have introduced grapevines to Chile, has shown that hillside vineyards even at these low latitudes can produce quite respectable table wine even from such exotic varieties as Syrah.

Between here and Santiago is the region of Aconcagua (mapped below), named after the highest peak of the Andes, at 23,000ft (7,000m). The region is made up of two extremely different subregions, the warm Aconcagua Valley itself and the particularly cool Casablanca Valley.

The warmth of the broad, open Aconcagua Valley, famous for Cabernet, is tempered by winds that regularly sweep cool mountain air coastward in the early afternoons and funnel

---

- - - - Regional boundary

Aconcagua subregions

——— Aconcagua

——— Casablanca

■ VILLARD   Leading producer

═══1200═══ Contour interval 400 metres

1:1,031,000

Km 0 ··· 10 ··· 20 ··· 30 ··· 40 Km
Miles 0 ··· 10 ··· 20 Miles

ocean air up from the river mouth most evenings to cool the west-facing foothills of the Andes. In the late 19th century the Errázuriz family's property at Panquehue was reputed to be the biggest single wine estate in the world. Today only a few hundred hectares of wine grapes are grown in the Aconcagua Valley, but under Errázuriz's auspices hillsides are being converted to vineyards, not least for Seña, the ambitious joint venture with Robert Mondavi of California.

The Casablanca Valley on the other hand, the very different valley between Santiago and the port of Valparaiso, has become almost synonymous with Chilean white wine. It was long thought to be too cold for viticulture, but in 1982 Pablo Morandé, then winemaker at Concha y Toro, converted his table grape vineyard with its traditional pergola to vertically trellised wine grapes and proved that Casablanca could produce white wines with a finesse quite unprecedented in Chile.

It took time for growers to take Casablanca seriously, but today dozens of bodegas and almost all of the big ones, buy or grow fruit here. The valley is too far from the Andes for cool mountain air in the evening, or even for access to meltwater for irrigation (so expensive bore-holes have to be sunk deep below the thin topsoils and access to water is the limiting factor in developing the valley for wine). It is so close to the sea, though, that cool breezes can be relied upon to lower afternoon temperatures by as much as 18°F (10°C) which, with the valley's mild winters, makes Casablanca's growing season up to a month longer than most other Chilean vineyards. Aromatic crisp whites are the usual result, from plantings that totalled about 7,400 acres (3,000ha) by the turn of the century. The valley is a natural home to increasingly fine Sauvignon Blanc, but Chardonnay was such a fashionable novelty for Chile in the 1990s that it still dominates Casablanca's vineyards – without necessarily having a particularly distinctive style.

Spring frost is a perennial and inconvenient threat, and it is not unknown for vineyards on the frost-prone open valley floor to suffer frost a week before harvest. The water shortage makes anti-frost sprinklers a luxury, however. The naturally low-vigour vines are also prey to worm-like nematodes so that vines have to be grafted on to resistant rootstocks. Growing costs are higher here than elsewhere, but Casablanca, Chile's answer to Carneros, has irrefutably widened the range of wines available from this ambitious wine exporter.

The map opposite shows the most important of Chile's five wine regions by far: the Central Valley, with its four subregions named after the Maipo, Rapel, Curicó, and Maule valleys that cross the central plain, like gradations on a thermometer, to pierce the low Coastal Range and find the sea. These are the geographical names most often found on wine labels.

Maipo has the hottest climate, an atmosphere occasionally polluted by the smogs of Santiago, and the smallest vineyard area of the Central Valley's subregions, but a high concentration of bodegas. Its proximity to the capital spawned a tradition of grand plantations and extensive homesteads belonging to Chile's 19th-century gentlemen-farmers, some of whom established such longstanding and important wine companies as Concha y Toro, Santa Rita (which controls Chile's bottle industry), and Santa Carolina.

It was here, just a convenient ride south of Santiago, that Chile's first generation of serious wine was made. Not from the common País grape (Criolla Chica in Argentina, Mission in California), which is still widely grown for the tetrapak wine sold within Chile, but from cuttings imported directly from Bordeaux in the mid-19th century before phylloxera ravaged the vineyards of Europe.

This is why Chile is such a rich repository of long-adapted Bordeaux grape varieties: Cabernet Sauvignon (which finally overtook País in total vineyard area in the late 1990s), "Sauvignon Blanc" (much of which is actually Sauvignon Vert or Sauvignonasse), and Merlot (an increasing proportion of which is now identified, and labelled, as the rather tougher old Bordeaux variety Carmenère). Maipo is essentially red wine country, and when yields are restricted can produce wines reminiscent of some of the Napa Valley's output.

The burgeoning and varied subregion of Rapel to the immediate south encompasses the valleys of Cachapoal in the north (including the Rancagua, Requínoa, and Rengo areas – all names found on wine labels), and fashionable Colchagua to the south (including San Fernando, Nancagua, and Chimbarongo). Colchagua has earned itself a reputation for Chile's most succulent and concentrated Merlot. Soils vary enormously in Chile even within small zones such as Colchagua, but there is some clay here, Merlot's classic partner, as well as the usual Chilean cocktail of loam, limestone, and sand with some volcanic areas. The rolling hills of Rapel with their very different mesoclimates suggest that this is somewhere with much to offer both wine producers and wine drinkers in the future.

Quite a way down the terrifying Pan-American Highway, with its ancient trucks and unpredictable fauna, are the vineyards of Curicó, including the zone of Lontué, which is also often specified on wine labels. Here the climate becomes slightly more temperate and irrigation is less likely to be a necessity. Miguel Torres of Catalonia famously invested in a winery here in 1979 (the same year that Baron Philippe de Rothschild struck another seminal transatlantic deal with Robert Mondavi of California), and this act of faith in wine country once thought of as being impossibly far south has been followed by many others. The San Pedro winery at Molina was dramatically upgraded and expanded in the 1990s, with the funds of Chile's dominant brewer and the expertise of Jacques Lurton of Bordeaux. It is surrounded by South America's largest block of vines (3,000 acres, or 1,200ha) and run, like much in the Chilean wine industry, with a technical precision far from any Latin American stereotype.

The southernmost subregion of the Central Valley, Maule, has three times the rainfall of Santiago (although the same dry summers) and Chile's greatest area of vines on substantially volcanic soils. Many of them are basic País, but there have been extensive plantings of Merlot, Chardonnay, and Sauvignon Blanc. There may be particular potential in Cauquenes 60 miles (100km) from Talca in the coastal hills, where sea mists usefully sweep in, just as they do in parts of California.

South of the area mapped opposite, with less protection from the Coastal Range and in even cooler, wetter conditions which favour such grapes as Riesling, Gewürztraminer, Sauvignon

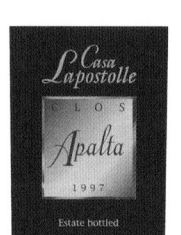

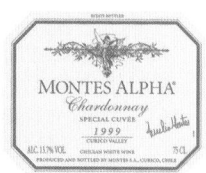

Four of Chile's most ambitious and *most successful wines – the Seña incorporating California expertise, Almaviva and Clos Apalta with very different influences from Bordeaux – above two of her finer white wines.*

Chile: Santiago

Latitude / Altitude of WS **33.23˚ / 1,542ft (470m)**

Mean January temp at WS **69.5˚F (20.8˚C)**

Annual rainfall at WS **13in (330mm)**

Harvest month rainfall at WS **March: 0.2in (5mm)**

Chief viticultural hazard **Nematodes**

Principal grapes **Cabernet Sauvignon, Chardonnay, Merlot, Carmenère**

Blanc, Chardonnay, and Pinot Noir, are the two subregions of the Sur (Spanish for South), Itata and Bío-Bío. They are still dominated by País and Moscatel, but serious pioneering work on the part of producers such as Viña Gracia, Concha y Toro at Mulchén, and Kendall-Jackson's Viña Calina suggests that they will warrant detailed mapping in the next edition of this book. Proponents of these southern areas like to point out that prevailing winds make the land, already much cheaper, less frost-prone than in Casablanca.

Since the early, well-publicized incursions of Torres and the Lafite-Rothschilds' investment in the Peralillo estate of Los Vascos, dozens of foreigners have invested in Chile's wine, and scores of flying winemakers have flown in and out. The most heartening aspect of all, however, is that Chile's own, often peripatetic, viticulturists and oenologists are such a well-qualified, well-travelled, and inspired lot, often backed by well-funded operators with experience in general fruit farming. There is currently an air of real confidence in the cellars that are mushrooming to cope with the produce of Chile's rapidly expanding vineyards (69,000 acres or 28,000ha of land were planted with vines in the last three years of the last century, increasing the national total by more than a third).

In the vineyards, the temptation is to overuse fertilizers and irrigation, although vines weighed down by Chile's naturally dense canopy and too many grapes have a nasty habit of failing to ripen properly. (Some growers are deliberately grafting onto special rootstocks now, both for resistance to problems such as nematodes, and just in case the recent influx of visitors from other wine regions – particularly during harvest when northern hemisphere wine producers have little to do at home – should bring phylloxera with it.)

In the cellars, since the emergence of an export-orientated economy, there has been extraordinary investment in hardware – resulting most particularly in the replacement of the unkempt old *rauli* (green beech) vats with stainless steel or new French oak. Yields are still relatively high in Chile. The fruit is usually, although not always, robust enough to take considerable oak influence, whether from expensive new barrels or much cheaper oak chips or inner staves. The model for Chile is California, not Burgundy. Technology is master here because nature needs so little taming.

- - - - - Regional boundary

Central Valley subregions

——— Maipo

——— Rapel

——— Curicó

——— Maule

■ CANEPA Leading producer

▨ Vineyards

——1200— Contour interval 400 metres

▼ Weather station (WS)

Argentina

The world's fifth biggest wine producer is this edition's most important newcomer to detailed mapping. It may seem incredible today that such a significant source of wine did not merit international attention back in 1994 but Argentina's climb into the spotlight has been exceptionally steep. Until the mid-1990s the country had little or no export aspirations, no sense of belonging to a wider world, and in wine terms at least, contented itself with producing vast quantities of mediocre wine, often oxidized and aged for years in vast old vats. Indeed, for many years its claim to vinous fame was that its largest producer, Peñaflor, owned the world's largest wine vat – hardly evidence of sophistication.

Much has changed, however. Economic stability has encouraged investment in new cellar equipment (particularly much-needed temperature control), in new vineyards at ever-higher altitudes, and in human expertise, much of it, initially at least, imported. Argentines themselves are drinking less but fruitier wine, and abroad Argentine wines have been seen as the next big thing by importers already familiar with what Chile has to offer.

The tree-lined city of Mendoza, Argentina's wine capital, is only 50 minutes by air from the Chilean capital Santiago – so close that shopping bags are a common sight on the crowded flights. Yet the plane has to clear the highest ridge of the Andes, a 20,000-ft (6,000-m) serrated blade of rock and ice. The centres of

Argentine and Chilean wine are cheek by jowl, yet poles apart in terms of natural conditions. Both lie in the low latitudes for winegrowing, but while Chile's wine regions owe their ideal growing conditions to their isolation as the meat in a sandwich between the cold Andes and the cold Pacific, Argentine vineyards, typically oases of green set in uncompromisingly arid semi-desert, exist because of altitude.

The altitudes at which Argentine vineyards flourish would be unthinkably high in Europe: from 2,300 up to 4,600ft (700 to 1,400m), and even 7,870ft (2,400m) in one case in the north. At this height overnight temperatures are regularly low enough to give well-flavoured, deeply coloured grapes. With little or no disease in the dry mountain air, usually on ungrafted roots and with abundant water, crops can reach yields virtually unknown elsewhere. The current challenge in Argentine viticulture, slowly moving to the sophistication of wires and shoot positioning, is to harness irrigation so as to deliver quality before quantity.

Phylloxera is not absent from Argentine vineyards (which is why Chilean growers are becoming uneasy now that Chilean wine companies are investing in Argentina's cheaper vineyard land) but it has so far posed no great threat. That flood irrigation has been common and soils are relatively sandy may be pertinent. Such plants as are affected seem to recover, growing new roots, in contrast to the experience of vine-growers elsewhere. An OIV study in 1990 confirmed Argentina's remarkably low incidence of vine disease; Argentine vines had developed hardly any tolerance to common vineyard chemicals.

But conditions in Argentine vineyards are not perfect and the weather is far from predictable. At these altitudes winters are cold (importantly, cold enough for vine dormancy) but spring frosts can present real danger. Summers in some of the lower-altitude, lower-latitude regions such as parts of San Juan and La Rioja provinces, and eastern San Rafael in the south of Mendoza (see map on page 296) can be just too hot for fine wine production. And as the factfile shows, Argentina's annual rainfall may be very low (even in El Niño years) but is concentrated in the growing season. In some areas, particularly in the province of Mendoza where three-quarters of Argentina's vines are planted, it has a nasty tendency to fall as hail, which can devastate an entire year's crop. One area particularly prone to hail is the east of San Rafael between the Diamante and Atuel rivers. The *zonda*, a fearsome hot, dry wind from the northeast is another liability, particularly at high altitudes, and particularly at flowering.

Soils tend to be relatively young and alluvial with quite a high proportion of sand in many areas. Such intensity as the wines have comes not from below but from above, from the intense sunlight, the dry air, and the diurnal temperature differences at these altitudes. Apart from in the most southerly vineyards of Patagonia, in Neuquén and Río Negro, full

Above This Catena Chardonnay vineyard at an altitude of almost 4,900ft (1,500m) near Tupungato in the Valle de Uco has broken new ground both for its irrigation channel and in terms of finesse for Argentine wine.

ripeness is easy to achieve. In fact, dedicated viticulturists may deliberately slow ripening by controlled drip irrigation, supplied reliably and plentifully as on the other side of the Andes by melted snow, in order to coax more flavour out of each vine. Argentina's high temperatures can be tasted in particularly soft tannins in the red wines, and often rather aggressive alcohol in the whites.

The country's most distinctive light-skinned grape (and most planted grape variety other than the coarse, pink-skinned Cereza, Criolla Grande, and Criolla Chica or Mission, which are grown strictly for local consumption) is Torrontés. The name is applied to three distinct varieties. Torrontés Riojana, named after La Rioja province, is the finest and reaches its apogee, albeit in a style of wine that is not especially fashionable at present, in the high vineyards of Salta province, notably around Cafayete. The origins of this florally perfumed but naturally crisp wine are still obscure but probably Spanish. Argentina's wine industry owes much of its current diversity of grapes and influences to mid-19th century immigration from Spain and Italy.

Deep-coloured Bonarda is Argentina's most planted red wine grape, and arguably the country's most underdeveloped wine resource (although Catena and La Agrícola pioneered serious versions). The country's wine reputation has so far been staked on its second most planted red wine grape Malbec, introduced to Mendoza in the mid-19th century, possibly via Chile's pre-phylloxera importations of vines from Bordeaux. (In the 18th century Malbec dominated in Bordeaux.) The opulent Malbec grown today in Argentina not only tastes very different from that which now dominates the vineyards of Cahors in Southwest France, it also looks different, with much smaller, tighter bunches and smaller berries. Early South American growers must have selected particular plants that seemed to perform well and these have since adapted perfectly to local conditions, although to keep its acidity and intensity of flavour Malbec is best grown at slightly higher altitudes than, say, Cabernet Sauvignon.

Four of Argentina's finest reds, all based on the local strain of Malbec, above a single-vineyard Cabernet made at Moët & Chandon's Terrazas winery in Perdriel and a promising Pinot Noir made at a Dutch-funded winery in the Valle de Uco itself.

In enviable contrast to that of Chile, Argentina's palette of grape varieties is varied and colourful. Other significant reds, in declining order of land claimed, are Tempranilla (sic), Cabernet Sauvignon, Sangiovese, Merlot, Syrah, and Barbera, all of them producing rich, savoury wines with powerful ripe flavours often far from those of the European archetypes but sometimes none the worse for that. Pinot Noir is so far limited, but may well have a future in new, cooler vineyards.

There has so far been little discipline in matching grapes to local conditions but the central heartland of Mendoza, that with the longest tradition for fine wine, has a reputation for especially fine Malbec from Luján de Cuyo, while Maipú (which is also developing its own controlled appellation system) may be better for Cabernet Sauvignon. Here the climate is temperate (almost cool in Agrelo) and soils unusually gravelly for Argentina (especially in Maipú). And there are none of the salinity problems that can cause difficulties in the lower districts which churn out oceans of table wine from Cereza, the Criollas, Pedro Giménez, Moscatel Alejandría, and high-yielding Bonarda.

Other widely grown grapes for "fine white wine", as Argentine authorities call anything pale and conceivably exportable, are Chenin Blanc, Ugni Blanc, an increasing acreage of Chardonnay, Sémillon, and Tocai Friulano.

Many of these light-skinned varieties are planted where it is difficult to see how they can ever attain both finesse and flavour, but at the beginning of the century some increasingly sophisticated Sémillon and Chardonnay began to emerge from Río Negro and the new higher, less fertile vineyards of Mendoza's Uco Valley, notably Tupungato.

Tupungato has been the focus of sophisticated modern vineyard development at altitudes of between 3,280 and 4,600ft (1,000 and 1,400m). Here the nights are sufficiently cool to produce delicate fruit flavours and acidity levels sufficiently high to encourage malolactic fermentation in the wineries (the older ones of which are some distance from these vineyards). The frost-free period lasts no longer than in New York's Finger Lakes region, however, and late frosts are a particular threat in the east of the Uco Valley on the slightly lower slopes of San Carlos.

Other likely areas for top-quality vineyard expansion in Argentina are Patagonia in the south and some of the higher valleys of San Juan such as Pedernal.

Peñaflor, with its associated Trapiche bodega, is the country's biggest producer, while Dr Nicolas Catena, whose interests include Catena Alta, Alamos, Gascon, and La Rural, is arguably Argentina's answer to Robert Mondavi of California.

There has been no shortage of outside investment recently to join that of champagne house Moët, which has operated Bodegas Chandon for decades, and the Swarovski family of Austria, which acquired Norton in 1989:

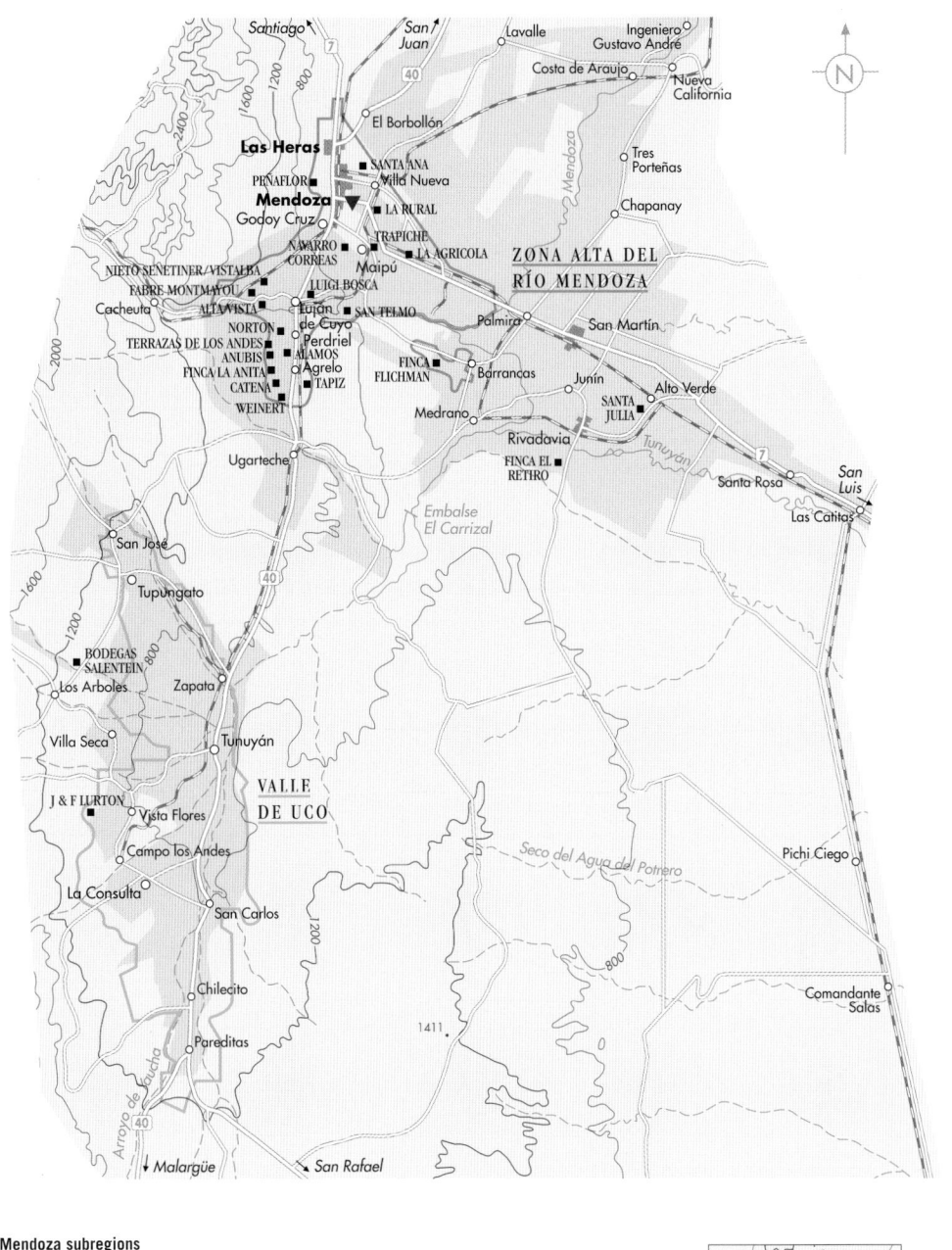

Kendall-Jackson from California; the Lurton brothers (near Tunuyan in high country); Jean-Michel Arcaute (Alta Vista) and Hervé Joyaux (Fabre Montmayou) from Bordeaux; Sogrape from Portugal (Finca Flichman); Pernod Ricard from France (Etchart); Seagram (Valentin Bianchi and San Telmo) and Allied Domecq (Balbi) from their corporate stratosphere; and, from over the Andes, a growing number of Chilean investors.

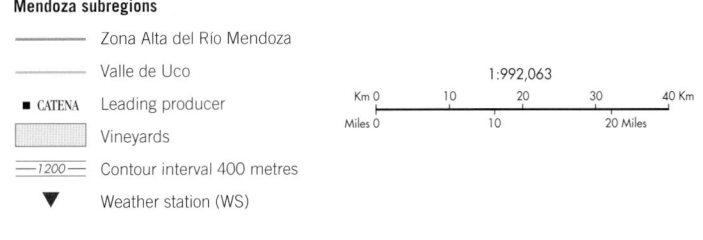

Mendoza subregions

——— Zona Alta del Río Mendoza

——— Valle de Uco

■ CATENA   Leading producer

     Vineyards

═1200═   Contour interval 400 metres

▼   Weather station (WS)

1:992,063

Km 0   10   20   30   40 Km

Miles 0   10   20 Miles

Argentina: Mendoza

Latitude / Altitude of WS **32.5° / 2,493ft (760m)**
Mean January temp at WS **75°F (23.9°C)**
Annual rainfall at WS **8in (200mm)**
Harvest month rainfall at WS **March: 1.2in (30mm)**
Chief viticultural hazards **Summer hail, _zonda_**
Principal grapes **Bonarda, Malbec, Criolla Grande, Cereza, Cabernet Sauvignon, Barbera, Sangiovese**

Australia

Of all the wine-producing nations included in this book, none exudes a level of vinous energy to rival Australia's. By the turn of the century, Australia had nearly 370,000 acres (150,000ha) of vineyard, a staggering 20% of it too young to be bearing fruit. Even as recently as 1996, the country had hardly 200,000 acres (80,000ha) of vines. In the short period from then until 2000 wine exports doubled.

Meanwhile, Australia's wine colleges continue to spew forth a new crop of technically adept winemakers each year, unleashing them on cellars throughout the northern hemisphere every September. There they spread the gospel of super-hygienic, ultra-efficient Australian vinification during the quiet season in southern hemisphere wineries, occasionally learning a little on their travels. Australian viticulturists roam the world's vineyards introducing canopy management techniques. The Commonwealth Scientific & Industrial Research Organization and the Australian Wine Research Institute have earned international respect. And mutually beneficial alliances continue to be forged between larger Australian and American or European firms.

One of the most notable aspects of Brand Australia, as the ever market-conscious Australians call it, is its consistency. Every single bottle of Australian wine reaches a certain minimum, perfectly acceptable level of quality, of exuberant if sometimes eventually tiring fruit, even if, as is statistically most likely, it comes from the heavily irrigated vineyards in the interior of the country. Almost two-thirds of every year's grape harvest is grown in one of the three big irrigated areas where canalized river-water turns bush into orchard and vineyard. They are shown on the map on the right as, in decreasing order of importance, Murray Darling (also known as Murray Valley), which straddles the Victoria-New South Wales border; Riverland and Swan Hill; and Riverina (Murrumbidgee).

The Australian wine industry and its breathtaking ambition (to achieve virtual wine world domination by the year 2025) is crucially dependent on irrigation water in general and the Murray River in particular. Current preoccupations include pollution of the river and the dangerously high level of salt in Australia's underground water that has resulted from wholesale clearance of the land by two centuries of settlers. Availability of good-quality irrigation water is the principal constraint to those who would convert this, the driest country on earth, into one big vineyard.

The large, inland irrigated areas, with their effortless mass-production of increasingly fresh, varietally distinct, and even some very good wines such as Griffith's botrytized Semillons, have become one of the major centres of power in the industry.

Australians believe in economies of scale – so much so in some cases that, despite almost feverish planting of vines at the end of the 20th and beginning of the 21st centuries, there is arguably a shortage of wineries. This is perfectly in line with the Australian tradition of shipping grapes or grape must long distances from vineyard to corporate cellar. There the produce of geographically quite distinct vineyards is often

State boundary
BASS PHILLIP ■ Leading producer
● Penola — Leading wine town
HUNTER — Wine region
Land 500-1000 metres
Land above 1000 metres
304 — Area mapped at larger scale on page shown

Western Australia map page 313

Tasmania map page 315

blended into a single wine, most typically one of the many brands so dear to the Australian international marketing plan.

That said, there is a creeping sense of geography among some sectors of the Australian wine business, and certainly among Australia's avid wine consumers – so much so that it has acquired its very own word: regionality. This is well-timed, for the Australian wine map has been changing fast (as a comparison of this one with its predecessor reveals) and Australia has been devising its own answer to the controlled appellation system. Geographic Indications, inevitably called GIs, do not of course attempt to dictate anything other than a, sometimes hotly contested, boundary.

The wine regions tend to hug the southern coast of Australia, which can offer a combination of lowish temperatures and rainfall, but Queensland has been quietly developing its own little wine industry, centred on the cooler, higher western slopes of the Great Dividing Range in the so-called Granite Belt.

Much of South Eastern Australia (a GI used liberally for that great quantity of wine made from

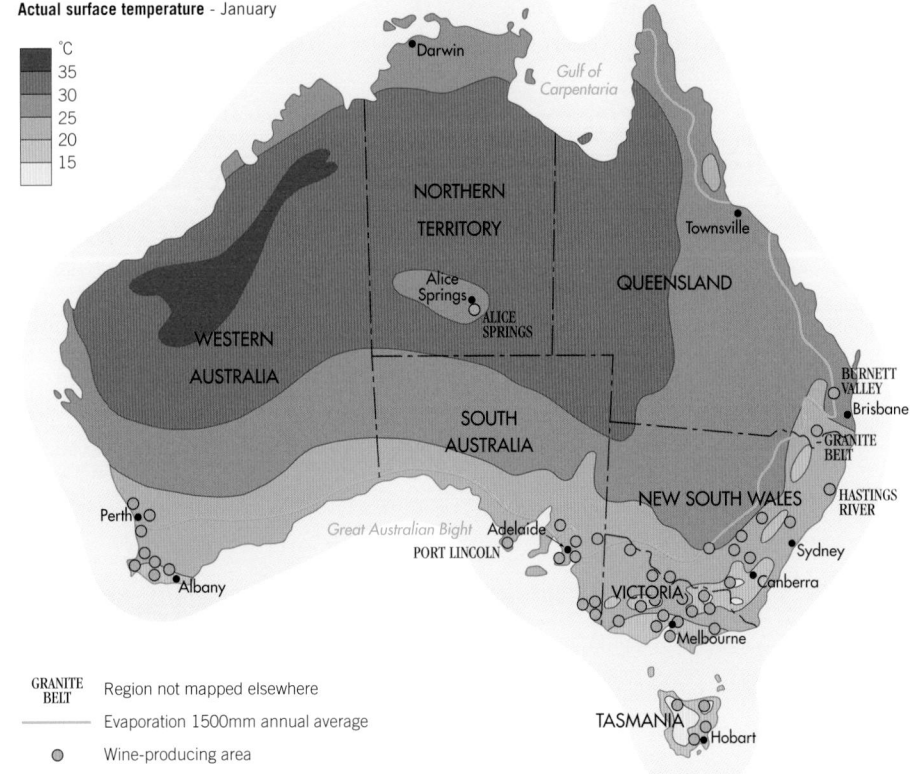

Actual surface temperature - January

°C
35
30
25
20
15

GRANITE BELT — Region not mapped elsewhere

——— Evaporation 1500mm annual average

● Wine-producing area

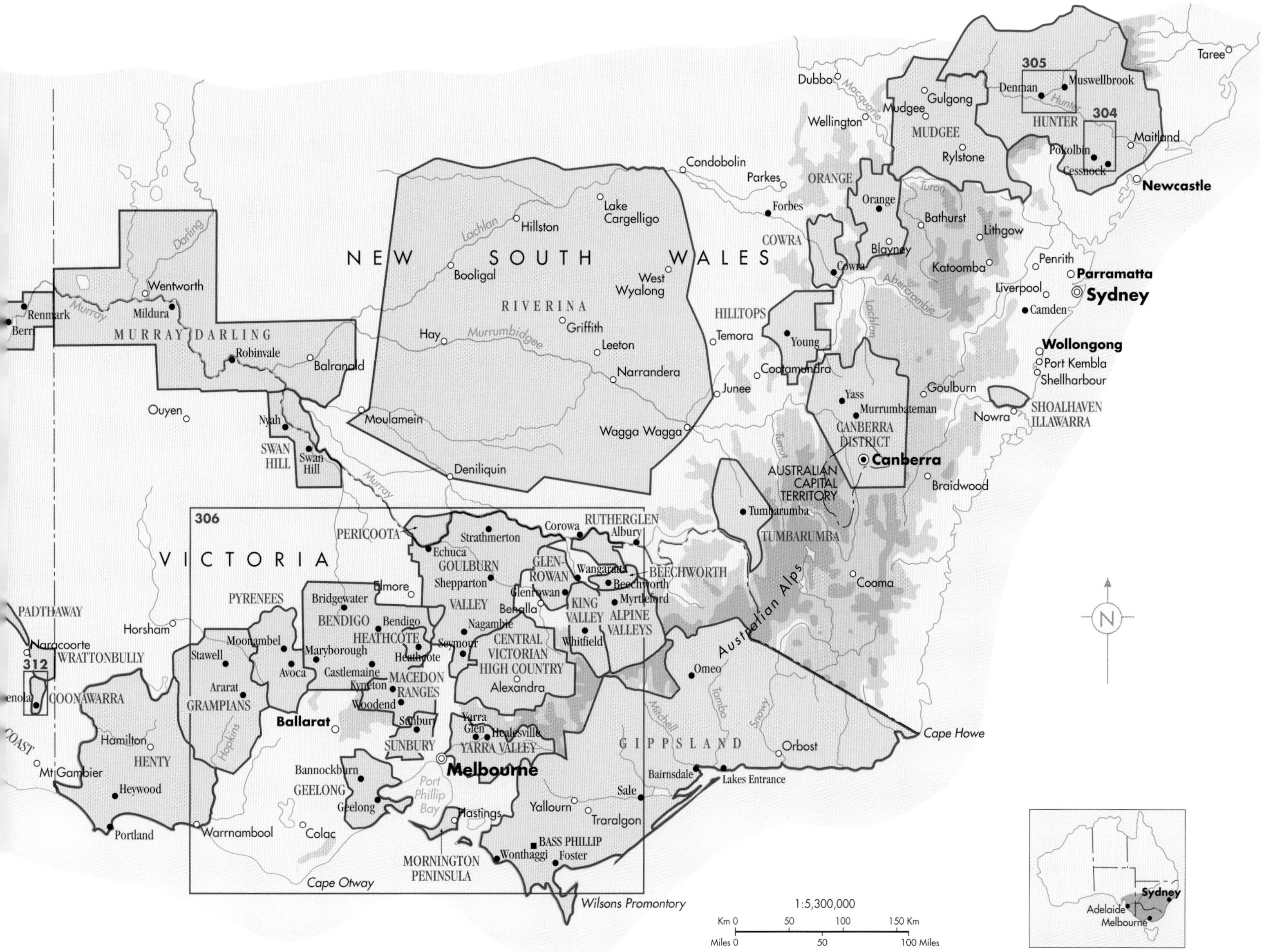

NEW SOUTH WALES

Taree
Dubbo
Gulgong
Denman
Muswellbrook
305
Mudgee
Wellington
MUDGEE
HUNTER
304
Rylstone
Pokolbin
Cessnock
Maitland
Newcastle
Condobolin
Parkes
Forbes
ORANGE
Orange
Bathurst
Lake Cargelligo
Hillston
Lithgow
COWRA
Blayney
Katoomba
Penrith
Cowra
Liverpool
Parramatta
Booligal
West Wyalong
Sydney
RIVERINA
Camden
Hay
Griffith
HILLTOPS
Wollongong
Leeton
Temora
Port Kembla
Shellharbour
Narrandera
Young
Junee
Cootamundra
Goulburn
Wentworth
Mildura
Renmark
Berri
Robinvale
Balranald
MURRAY DARLING
Moulamein
Yass
Murrumbateman
Nowra
SHOALHAVEN ILLAWARRA
CANBERRA DISTRICT
Ouyen
Nyah
Wagga Wagga
Deniliquin
AUSTRALIAN CAPITAL TERRITORY
Canberra
Braidwood
SWAN HILL
Swan Hill
Tumbarumba
306
PERICOOTA
Corowa
RUTHERGLEN
Albury
TUMBARUMBA
VICTORIA
Strathmerton
Echuca
GOULBURN
Shepparton
GLEN-ROWAN
Wangaratta
BEECHWORTH
Beechworth
Cooma
Elmore
VALLEY
Glenrowan
Bridgewater
Benalla
KING VALLEY
Myrtleford
ALPINE VALLEYS
PYRENEES
BENDIGO
Bendigo
Nagambie
Seymour
PADTHAWAY
Moonambel
HEATHCOTE
CENTRAL VICTORIAN HIGH COUNTRY
Whitfield
Omeo
Horsham
Maryborough
Heathcote
Naracoorte
WRATTONBULLY
Stawell
Avoca
Castlemaine
Kyneton
MACEDON RANGES
Alexandra
312
Ararat
GRAMPIANS
Woodend
Cape Howe
COONAWARRA
Ballarat
Sunbury
Yarra Glen
Healesville
GIPPSLAND
Orbost
HENTY
Hamilton
SUNBURY
YARRA VALLEY
Mitchell
Hopkins
Bannockburn
Bairnsdale
Lakes Entrance
Mt Gambier
Heywood
GEELONG
Melbourne
Sale
Portland
Geelong
Port Phillip Bay
Hastings
Yallourn
Traralgon
Colac
Warrnambool
Cape Otway
MORNINGTON PENINSULA
Wonthaggi
BASS PHILLIP
Foster
Wilsons Promontory

1:5,300,000
Km 0 50 100 150 Km
Miles 0 50 100 Miles

Adelaide
Melbourne
Sydney

the blended produce of virtually anywhere other than Western Australia) has the Mediterranean-type climate in which the vine luxuriates. Melbourne is on the same latitude as Córdoba in Spain. The Hunter Valley is on much the same latitude as Rabat, the capital of Morocco. Strong wines full of sugar but lacking acidity are what you would expect – and what Australia, for more than a century, was happy to produce, until strapping tonic wines fell out of favour and the country's wineries rapidly equipped themselves with refrigeration and switched to table wines. Nowadays the vine is increasingly colonizing new, cooler areas, including many that have never known viticulture before.

With the noble exception of some of the older vines in Barossa and McLaren Vale, the average vine age in Australia is notably young. Plantings have tended to swing from whim to whim of fashion. For example, not a Chardonnay vine was known in South Australia in 1970, but in the 1980s and early 1990s it sometimes seemed as though little else was planted. In the mid-1990s the pendulum swung again, the red wine craze was officially recognized, and so

much Shiraz and Cabernet Sauvignon was planted that there was a shortage of Chardonnay in 2001. Semillon, Riesling, and Verdelho were all established Australian favourites long before this French upstart invaded the country's vineyards.

Australia's most planted variety, Shiraz, benefited from a complete rehabilitation in the 1990s. Previously scorned for its ubiquity, even at times denatured for use as base wine for cheap white, sparkling, and fortified wine, it was finally recognized as what Australia does best, in red wine at least. Coonawarra and Margaret River (see page 314) may have a special way with Cabernet Sauvignon, but the nation collectively abandoned its belief in the necessary superiority of things imported and French. Nowadays, even wineries with considerable history are dropping Frenchified terms such as Château. Australia is now understandably proud of its own cultural identity, cuisine, and wine culture, complete with BYOs (bring your own), cardboard "casks" at the bottom end of the market, and the much-hyped show system with its medals and trophies for best of breed at or close to the top.

Above BRL Hardy's award-winning Banrock Station on the Lower Murray River in South Australia, a wetland preservation project designed to halt the rising water table and subsequent release of salt into the river.

New South Wales

New South Wales, the cradle of Australian winegrowing, has long since been overtaken by South Australia as the nucleus of the industry. But there remains one district 100 miles (160km) north of Sydney as famous as any in the country, even if in terms of vineyard acreage it is progressively being overtaken by the state's swelling roster of new wine regions.

The Lower Hunter Valley around Branxton and the mining town of Cessnock represents a triumph of proximity over suitability. The Hunter, as it is known, is a far from ideal place to grow grapes. The most northerly of Australia's traditional wine regions, it is subtropical: summers are invariably very hot and autumns can be vexingly wet. To counter the extreme heat, summer skies are admittedly often cloud-covered and the direct sun is diffused. But as one old hand puts it: "You can't manage the Hunter; the Hunter manages itself." More than two-thirds of the region's relatively high annual rainfall of 29in (750mm) falls in the crucial first four months of the year.

Vintage quality therefore varies considerably from year to year and the reason for the rash of wineries on the map on this page is not necessarily the Hunter's natural affinity with the vine, but the fact that it is just two hours' drive from Sydney and a mecca for wine tourists.

Surprisingly, being so far north, the Hunter was one of the first regions in Australia to concentrate entirely on table wines – perhaps because it for so long housed the movers and shakers in the nation's wine industry.

Key to wineries

1. CONSTABLE & HERSHON
2. HONEY TREE
3. TYRRELLS
4. LOWE FAMILY WINE CO.
5. BRIAN McGUIGAN
6. GLENGUIN
7. MEEREA PARK
8. VERONA
9. TAMBURLAINE
10. PEPPER TREE
11. TOWER
12. EVANS FAMILY

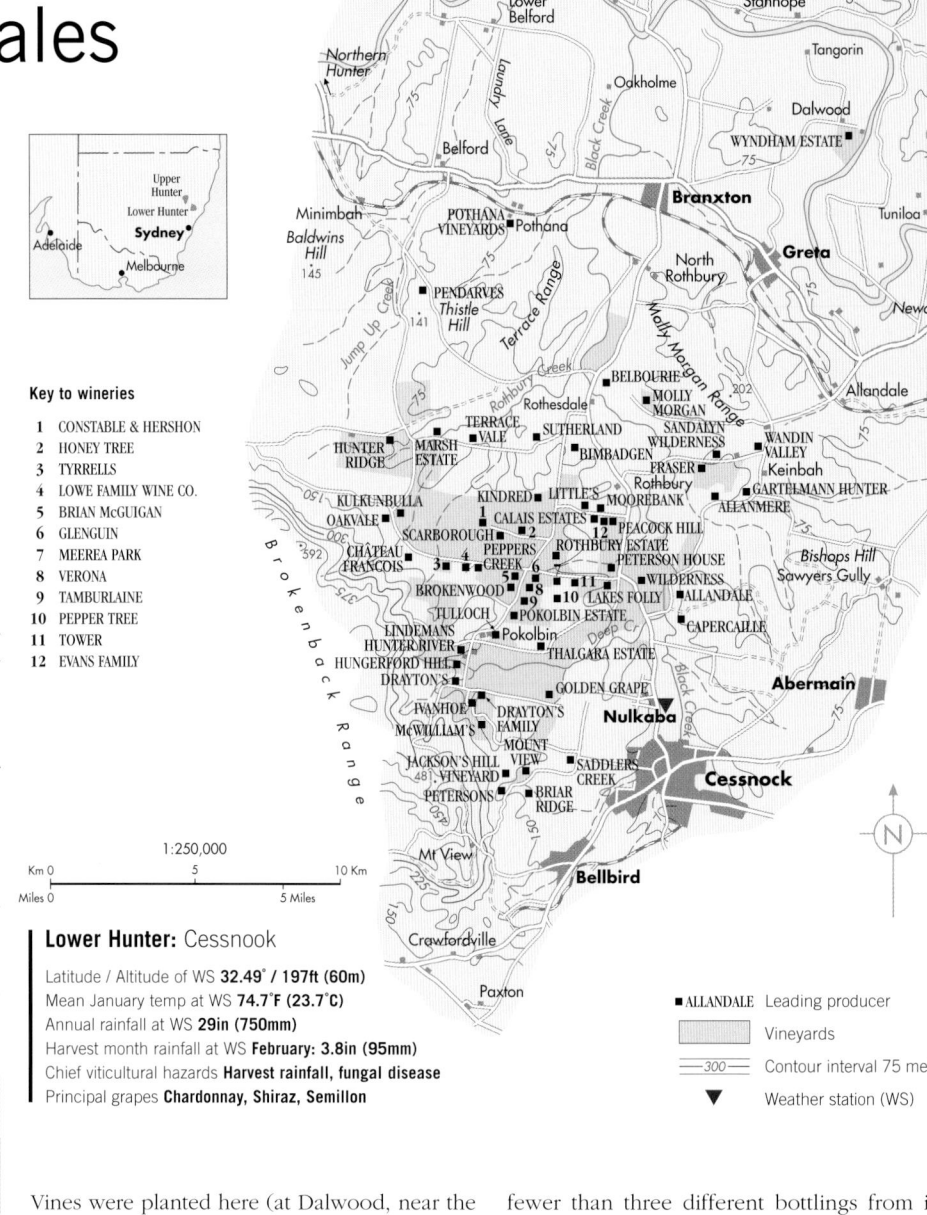

1:250,000

Km 0 .... 5 .... 10 Km
Miles 0 .... 5 Miles

Lower Hunter: Cessnook

Latitude / Altitude of WS **32.49° / 197ft (60m)**
Mean January temp at WS **74.7°F (23.7°C)**
Annual rainfall at WS **29in (750mm)**
Harvest month rainfall at WS **February: 3.8in (95mm)**
Chief viticultural hazards **Harvest rainfall, fungal disease**
Principal grapes **Chardonnay, Shiraz, Semillon**

■ ALLANDALE Leading producer
▢ Vineyards
〰300 Contour interval 75 metres
▼ Weather station (WS)

Vines were planted here (at Dalwood, near the river just east of Branxton) as early as 1828, but the soil that gave the Hunter Valley its reputation is found to the south in the foothills of the Brokenback Range. Around the east side of the hills there is a strip of weathered basalt, the sign of ancient volcanic activity, that restricts vine vigour and concentrates often distinctly mineral flavour into the grapes.

Shiraz, once known here as Hermitage, is the classic red grape based on some particularly old clones. Semillon is the traditional white, even if it has been overtaken quantitatively by Chardonnay. Rather soft and earthy but long and spicy, Hunter Shiraz from a successful vintage may ripen relatively early but lasts well and grows complex and leathery with time. Cabernet, no friend of wet autumns, is far less important here than in other areas.

Hunter Semillon is one of Australia's classic, if under-appreciated, wine styles. In the old days when Lindemans managed to squeeze no

fewer than three different bottlings from it – labelled variously Hunter River Riesling, Chablis, and White Burgundy – grapes would be picked at conveniently low ripeness levels, fermented in vat, and bottled fairly early without any softening (and accelerating) malolactic fermentation. The grassy young wines would age in bottle quite magnificently into green-gold, toasty, mineral-laden bombs packed with explosive layers of flavour. Today an increasing proportion of Hunter Semillon is picked riper and made just like a barrel-fermented Chardonnay, thereby ageing much faster and much less distinctively.

The Hunter was in the forefront of Australia's love affair with imported French grapes. In the early 1970s Murray Tyrrell did with Chardonnay what Max Lake had done in the 1960s with Cabernet: put down a marker no winemaker could ignore, his Vat 47. It launched a thousand – make that a million? – Australian Chardonnays.

Chardonnay is by far the principal, some might say only, grape variety in the Lower Hunter's younger, bigger sibling, the Upper Hunter, which lies 40 miles (60km) to the northwest on higher ground around Denman and Muswellbrook. Rainfall is lower here and irrigation freely practised. This is almost a one-winery

Left Looking over Tyrrells' vineyards and winery (which began life in a small wooden shack in 1864) towards the Brokenback Range. Compared to the Lower Hunter's scores of new wineries, Tyrrells is almost prehistoric.

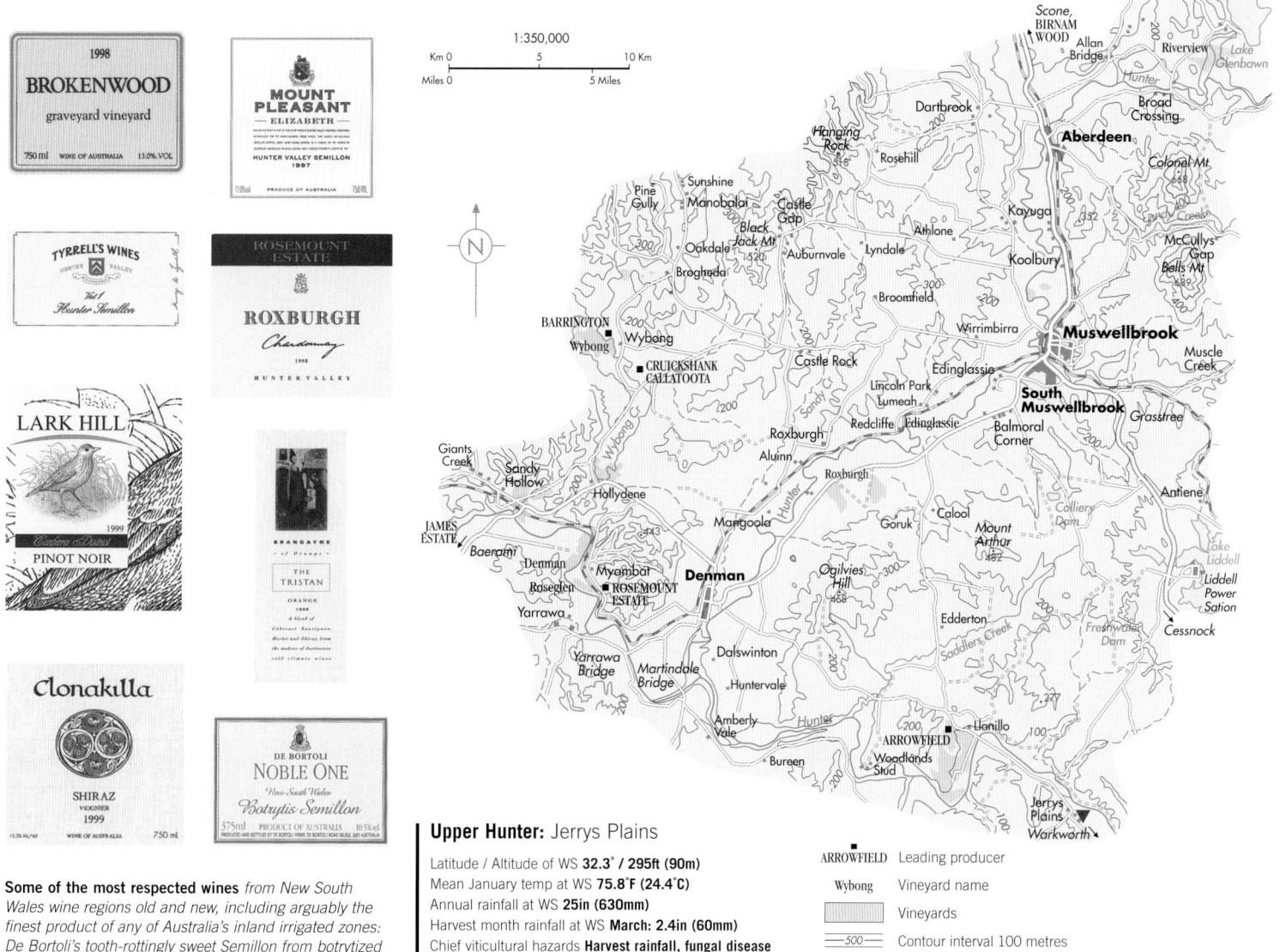

Some of the most respected wines *from New South Wales wine regions old and new, including arguably the finest product of any of Australia's inland irrigated zones: De Bortoli's tooth-rottingly sweet Semillon from botrytized grapes grown near Griffith.*

Upper Hunter: Jerrys Plains

Latitude / Altitude of WS **32.3˚ / 295ft (90m)**
Mean January temp at WS **75.8˚F (24.4˚C)**
Annual rainfall at WS **25in (630mm)**
Harvest month rainfall at WS **March: 2.4in (60mm)**
Chief viticultural hazards **Harvest rainfall, fungal disease**
Principal grapes **Shiraz, Chardonnay, Cabernet Sauvignon**

ARROWFIELD Leading producer
Wybong Vineyard name
Vineyards
500 Contour interval 100 metres
▼ Weather station (WS)

region, with Rosemount's expanding domain dominating all before it. The company grows and processes an increasing proportion of fruit grown far beyond the boundaries of the Upper Hunter, but its Roxburgh vineyard Chardonnay flies the most glorious flag for this historic but declining region.

To the west, about 1,500ft (450m) up on the western slopes of the Great Dividing Range, the little district of Mudgee (see page 303 for the location of all New South Wales wine regions, considered here from north to south) has also made its mark since the 1970s. Its origins are almost as old as those of the Hunter Valley, but Mudgee dwelt in obscurity until the hunt began for cooler districts to make wines of more pronounced grape flavours. Intense, long-established Chardonnay and Cabernet are its real successes. Montrose is the biggest cellar in the district, Craigmoor the oldest and now under the same ownership (Orlando), Huntington the best (though unknown outside Australia), and Botobolar admirably organic.

New South Wales has seen a quite remarkable quest for new wine regions, all of them in promising cooler, often higher, corners of the state. Orange, with its high altitude and volcanic soils on the slopes of Mount Canobolas (now extinct), was first planted in 1983 by wine-crazy librarian Stephen Doyle and his wife Rhonda. Bloodwood was the result, encouraged by interest in the area by Rosemount and more recently the ambitious Cabonne winery. Sauvignon Blanc as well as Riesling and Pinot Noir may have a future at higher altitudes here, while promising red wine vineyards planted with the usual suspects straddle the appellation's lower boundary at around 2,000ft (600m).

Cowra has a much longer history for lush, fulsome, exuberant Chardonnays grown at fairly high yields and much lower altitudes: only about 1,150ft (350m) on average. Hilltops, a little to the south, around Young, and higher than Cowra, is much more recent and, like most of these less famous New South Wales wine regions, tends to grow fruit – notably red grapes, Chardonnay, and Semillon – for others to vinify outside the region. There are half a dozen small enterprises of which by far the most important is Barwang vineyard, now owned by McWilliam's, one of the few substantial wine companies to keep its base in New South Wales.

The great surprise about Canberra District, the cluster of vineyards round the nation's capital, is firstly that there are so many of them, secondly that almost all are actually in New South Wales, and thirdly that they have been in existence for so long.

John Kirk planted the first vines at Clonakilla as long ago as 1971 and his son Tim can now boast a particularly Rhône-like Shiraz/Viognier blend and some fine varietal Viognier. This dark horse of a region may emerge from the limelight as a result of a governmental lure to BRL Hardy to establish a wine tourism centre within the Australian Capital Territory itself under the aboriginal name Kamberra. The highest vineyards such as Lark Hill's are not just cool but cold (frost can strike), and the result can be some of Australia's most delicate Pinot Noir. Madew is one of the country's most passionate exponents of Riesling.

Shoalhaven Illawarra on the coast is also being developed, although like Hastings River around Port Macquarie to the north it suffers from high humidity. Hybrids such as Chambourcin offer potential. Tumbarumba is another extremely cool high-altitude region of particular interest to bottlers of sparkling wine and Sauvignon Blanc, which may yet become one more of Australia's acknowledged accomplishments.

Victoria

Victoria is in many ways the most interesting, and certainly the most varied, of Australia's wine states; even if today it is nowhere near as quantitatively important as it was at the end of the 19th century, when it had as much vineyard as New South Wales and South Australia put together. Phylloxera, which has never reached South Australia, was fatally destructive.

The most important survivor of the pest was Victoria's northeast region. It continues to specialize in fortified dessert wines, including Australia's finest dark, sticky elixirs based on dark-skinned raisined Muscat and the more caramelised Tokay (the Muscadelle of Sauternes). After years of ageing in old wooden casks, often in baking hot conditions, they can achieve astonishingly silky richness, none more so than Rutherglen's Rare Muscats.

Brown Brothers of nearby Milawa looks outside the district for sites at up to more than 2,600ft (800m) in King Valley and the region now known as Alpine Valleys to provide cool growing conditions for fine table wines. These are made from an exotic array of adventurous grape varieties that were previously unheard of in inland Victoria. The likes of Pizzini (for surprisingly convincing Italianate grapes), Gapsted, and Symphonia are other labels associated with the wild and wonderful grown high up in the mountain air.

At rather lower altitudes around the historic gold-mining town of Beechworth some superlative Chardonnay is made by Giaconda, some ambitious Shiraz by Castagna, and some gloriously intense grapes are grown at Sorrenberg.

Like the northeast wine country, Great Western, the district made famous by Seppelt's

"champagne", never gave up either. Now called the Grampians, it lies 1,100ft (335m) up at the westernmost end of the Great Dividing Range, on lime-rich soil. Seppelt and Best's, a miniature by comparison, have a long record of producing good still and sparkling wines in deep, cool ancient caves here. Grapes for the oceans of fizz made at Seppelt Great Western come partly from Padthaway over the border in South Australia, partly from irrigated vineyards along the Murray, but those for its extraordinary and deservedly celebrated Sparkling Shiraz are grown locally. Mount Langi Ghiran's authoritatively peppery Shiraz eloquently explains why.

One other district that never disappeared, although it dwindled to one estate, Tahbilk (formerly Chateau Tahbilk), lies on the Goulburn River 80 miles (130km) north of Melbourne.

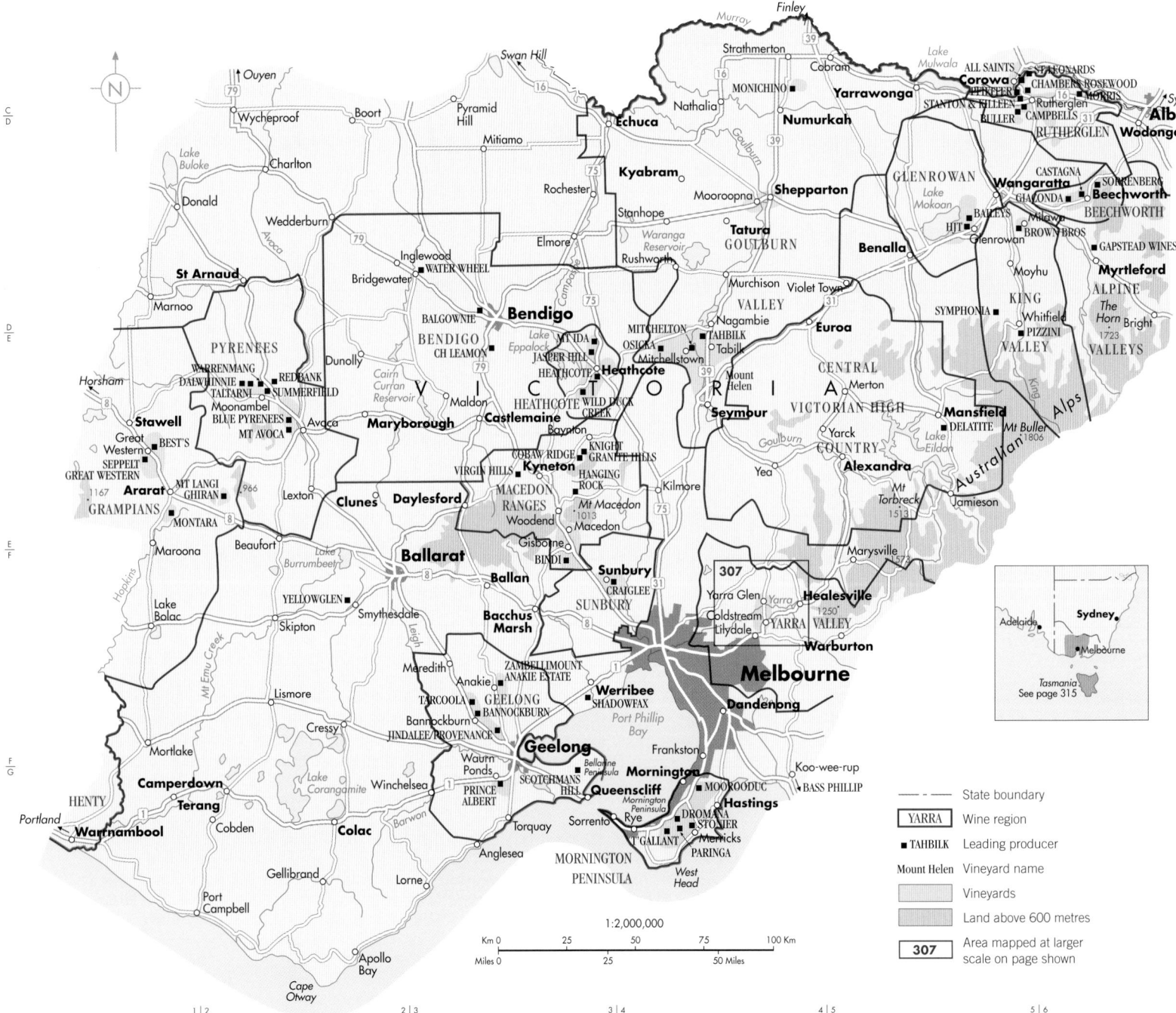

— · —	State boundary
YARRA	Wine region
■ TAHBILK	Leading producer
Mount Helen	Vineyard name
	Vineyards
	Land above 600 metres
307	Area mapped at larger scale on page shown

1:2,000,000

Km 0   25   50   75   100 Km
Miles 0   25   50 Miles

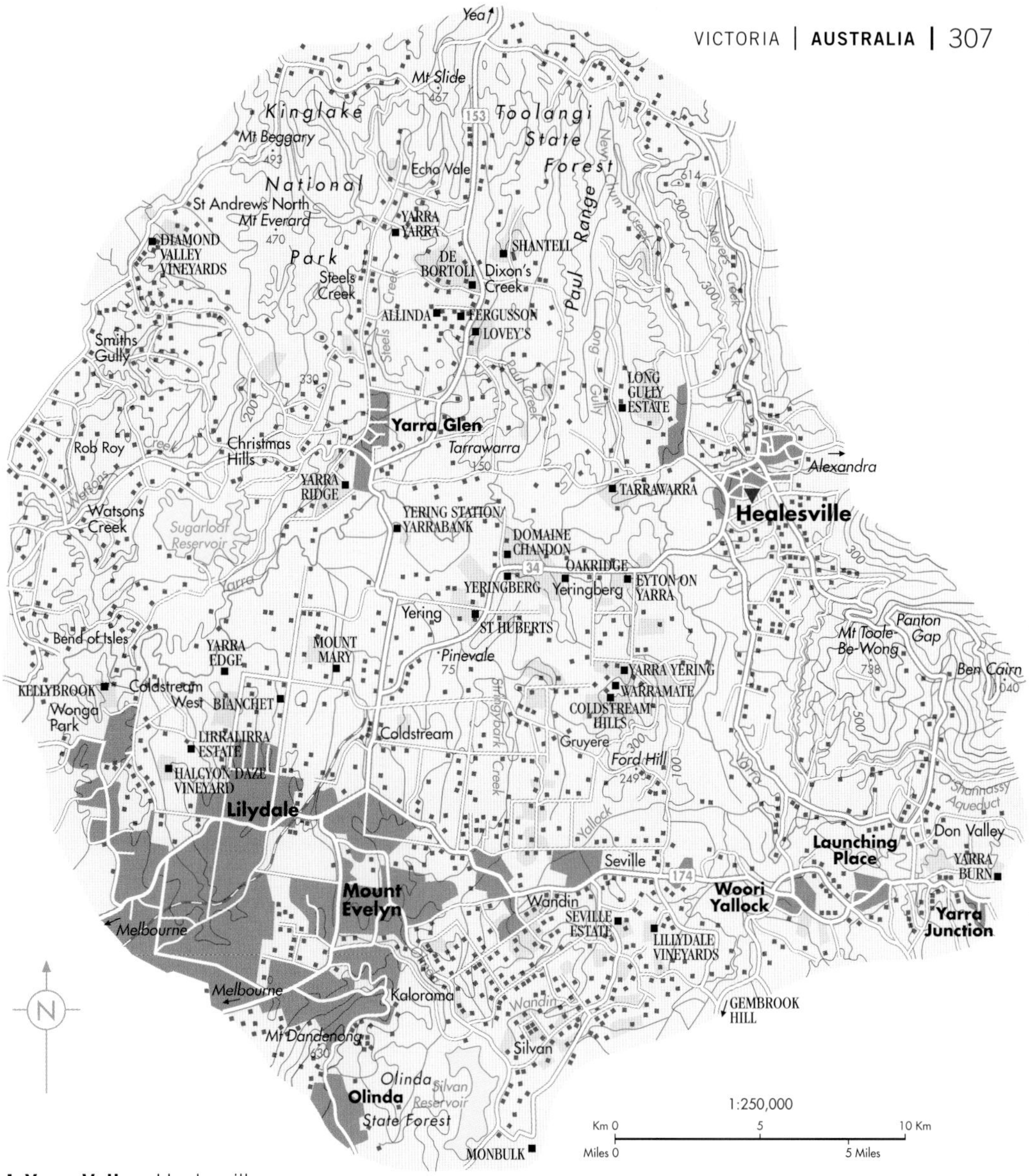

Pyrenees is the (ironic?) name of the rolling landscape east of the Grampians between Avoca and Moonambel. This region is not notably cool (except sometimes at night) and its showpiece wines are big reds from Redbank and Dalwhinnie, who has also made a fine Chardonnay.

Bendigo, east again, is if anything warmer still: its wines are epitomized (and were launched) by Balgownie's sumptuous reds. Then Jasper Hill and Mount Ida showed what could be done in slightly cooler country to the east and added lustre to Heathcote as a wine address. Ballarat is also old gold country although decidedly cooler, prompting Yellowglen to make sparkling wines in this relatively small wine region.

On the plains just north of Melbourne airport is another historic wine region. Sunbury has a fine standard-bearer in the shape of Craiglee whose Shiraz has remained admirably constant, savoury, and long-lived for decades.

But some of the most exciting recent developments in Victoria have resulted from the search for good vineyard land in cooler regions. The move has been either south towards the sea, or up into hilly areas. The Macedon Ranges between Kyneton and Sunbury can be almost too cold although Bindi's efforts suggest that Gisborne could be exciting Pinot Noir territory.

Pinot Noir is also the grape of choice for many growers in Victoria's new coastal wine regions. Both Bannockburn and Scotchman's Hill ripen bumptious Pinot on Geelong's barren windy wine country.

South of Melbourne the definitively maritime Mornington Peninsula may be better suited to

Yarra Valley: Healesville

Latitude / Altitude of WS **37.41˚ / 426ft (130m)**
Mean January temp at WS **65.5˚F (18.6˚C)**
Annual rainfall at WS **40in (1,010mm)**
Harvest month rainfall at WS **March: 2.5in (65mm)**
Chief viticultural hazards **Underripeness, fungal disease**
Principal grapes **Pinot Noir, Chardonnay, Shiraz, Cabernet Sauvignon**

■ MONBULK Leading producer
　　　　　　Vineyards
　━500━　　Contour interval 100 metres
　▼　　　　Weather station (WS)

For location map see opposite page

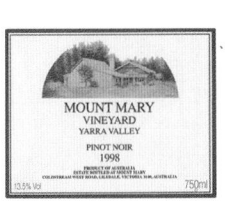

Victoria is a state *dotted with isolated specialists. Some of their produce is illustrated here: everything from the most luscious Chardonnay via admirably distinctive dry reds to one of the finest fortified wines in the world.*

Chardonnay, although the dozens of full- and part-time growers here try their hand at all sorts of grape varieties. Most successful perhaps has been T'Gallant with Pinot Gris (the drier version labelled Pinot Grigio), prompting a wave of enthusiasm for this grape.

In the greater Gippsland region off this map to the east is another vast array of different environments. The most convincing wine so far has been Bass Phillip.

But by far the best-known wine region within striking distance of the restaurants and concert halls of Melbourne is the Yarra Valley. The valley's topography is complex, with steep, shallow slopes at altitudes from 160 to 1,540ft (50 to 470m) and facing all points of the compass in this relatively cool, wet region (see factfile). Soils range from grey sandy or clay loam to vivid red volcanic earth so fertile that the great silver mountain ash trees along the creeks tower above the blue-leaved wattle.

The rebirth of the valley dates from the 1960s, when the once-powerful St Huberts

reopened its doors, rapidly followed by the customary clutch of doctors fanatical about wine. Three of them, Drs Carrodus at Yarra Yering, Middleton at Mount Mary, and McMahon at Seville Estate, all set impeccable standards on a tiny scale. Those who followed included Dr Lance at Diamond Valley and the wine writer James Halliday at Coldstream Hills, both fired with the desire to grow Australia's first great Pinot Noir.

Pinot Noir is clearly the Yarra Valley's strongest suit (Beaune in style rather than Nuits), although Chardonnay is more widely planted and there is no shortage of fine, harmonious examples as well as some clean-cut Cabernets from warmer sites.

The Yarra Valley has also laid the foundations for Australia's best-yet sparkling wine when, in 1988, Moët & Chandon opened Domaine Chandon in the region. Today virtually all of the big companies have bought their slice of Yarra and the standard of winemaking has never been higher.

S. Australia: Barossa, Clare, and Eden Valleys

South Australia is definitively to Australia what California is to the USA: *the* wine state. It crushes 46% of every vintage and houses all the most important wine and vine research organizations. Adelaide, the state capital, is fittingly hemmed with vineyards. A few still exist in the suburbs of the city. They stretch north on the arid Adelaide Plains, south through McLaren Vale, and southeast across the Mount Lofty Ranges to Langhorne Creek, source of much unattributed blending material. They stretch 80 miles (130km) north up into the hills from Watervale to Clare, but most of all northeast to fill the Barossa Valley, only 35 miles (55km) from the city, a settlement founded by German-speaking immigrants from Silesia in what is now Poland. Much, including a sense of community and an appetite for hard work and *Wurst*, is still Germanic to this day.

Barossa is Australia's biggest quality-wine district. It follows the North Para River for almost 20 closely planted miles (nearly 30km), and spreads eastwards into the next valley, Eden Valley, from the 750ft (230m) altitude of Lyndoch to 1,800ft (550m) in the east Barossa Ranges, where vineyards are scattered among rocky hills, dusty lanes, and eucalyptus.

Summer days are hot and generally dry. Unirrigated bushvines were traditionally the norm and, partly thanks to a malaise in the 1970s and early 1980s when the Australian wine industry neglected Barossa's old Shiraz vines for fashionable Cabernet planted in cooler climes, some of these are of a great old age.

Such vines can produce the most concentrated form of what has become one of the world's most distinctive wine styles, Barossa Shiraz. Rich and chocolaty, spicy and never shy, these wines can range from intriguing essences to unctuously alcoholic. Grapes ripen fast under the blistering sun, so fast that acidity often plummets before the grapes are picked. Some Barossa winemakers add tannin as well as acid. And instead of the long post-fermentation maceration that Bordeaux producers give their wines while extracting colour and tannins, Barossa reds are typically encouraged to finish their fermentation in American oak barrels, imbuing them with a heady sweetness and smoothness.

In sheer quantity Barossa is dominated by the likes of Penfolds (which blends its flagship Grange here from wines produced all over South Australia), Orlando (the original Jacob's Creek is a trickle near Rowland Flat), Beringer Blass, and Yalumba. But in the 1990s an army of solid, medium-sized enterprises such as Peter Lehmann and Grant Burge marched gloriously to the increasingly fashionable beat of what makes Barossa special, to be joined by newer,

Below The typically Australian Nuriootpa headquarters of the vast Southcorp wine group. Considering ambient temperatures, an amazing proportion of wine is stored out of doors. Refrigeration is vital.

Barossa subregions

———	Barossa Valley
———	Eden Valley
■ HERITAGE	Leading producer
Pewsey Vale	Vineyard name
▨	Vineyards
═300═	Contour interval 75 metres
▼	Weather station (WS)

For location see map on page 302

Barossa Valley: Nuriootpa

Latitude / Altitude of WS **34.29˚ / 899ft (274m)**
Mean January temp at WS **70˚F (21.1˚C)**
Annual rainfall at WS **20in (501mm)**
Harvest month rainfall at WS **March: 1in (25.4mm)**
Chief viticultural hazard **Drought**
Principal grapes **Shiraz, Riesling, Semillon, Grenache Noir, Chadonnay, Grenache Blanc**

1:217,500

Km 0 — 5 — 10 Km
Miles 0 — 5 Miles

Map labels: Mildura, Mapami, Highway, WOLF BLASS, Stockwell, Plush Corner, Moculta, Greenock, BAROSSA VALLEY ESTATES, THE WILLOWS, Nuriootpa, Sturt, Duck Ponds Creek, TORBRECK, GNADENFREI, SOUTHCORP/PENFOLDS, ELDERTON, GREENOCK CREEK, Marananga, KAESLER, Penrice, Parrot Hill, SEPPELT, VERITAS, HERITAGE, CHATEAU DORRIEN, SALTRAM, Hill of Grace, Seppeltsfield, PETER LEHMANN, OLD BARN, RICHMOND GROVE, Angaston, YALUMBA, BAROSSA, Tanunda, BASEDOW, Vine Vale, Lindsay Park, HENSCHKE, VALLEY, TURKEY FLAT, GLAETZER, Landhaus, Bethany, BETHANY, Mengler's Hill, Collingrove, Keyneton, Gomersal, ST HALLETT, Barren Hill, GRANT BURGE, Kabininge, ROCKFORD, 523, EDEN VALLEY, Rosedale, CHARLES MELTON, KRONDORF, Glen View, Mt McKenzie, CHATEAU YALDARA, CHARLES CIMICKY, JENKE, ORLANDO, MIRANDA, Three Rivers, Peggys Hill, Warpoo, Altona, Rowland Flat, Heggies, WARDS GATEWAY CELLAR, KIES, TREVOR JONES, Hill-Smith Estate, Adelaide, BURGE FAMILY, Lyndoch, ROSS ESTATE, BAROSSA SETTLERS, Steingarten, Pewsey Vale, Keynes Hill, TWIN VALLEY ESTATE, EDEN VALLEY WINES, MOUNTADAM, Eden Valley, Williamstown, Wynns High Eden, IRVINE, CRANEFORD, Springton, KARL SEPPELT GRAND CRU ESTATE

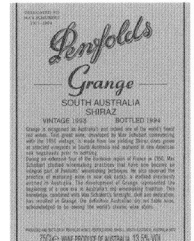

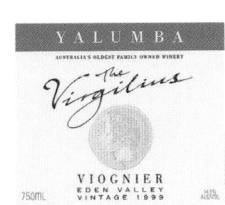

The Barossa's, arguably Australia's, *two most sought-after wines are at the top, followed by four massive Shirazes from Barossa and Clare, plus one classic white and Australia's finest Viognier, from the Eden Valley.*

smaller companies and individuals, often heavily dependent on mature bushvines.

There are old Grenache vines too (capable of even higher alcohols) and old Semillon, some of them Barossa's very own pink-skinned clone producing stunningly rich white wines. Barossa's Chardonnay is particularly rumbustious and on the most favoured dark grey-brown soils Cabernet Sauvignon can also shine in Barossa. But Shiraz is more dependable, summer in and summer out. Barossa summers are dry, and irrigated vines need enough water to compensate for a fierce evaporation rate – an increasingly difficult feat.

The Barossa industry was founded on some of Australia's best dessert wines. The stocks of mature, sometimes ancient, "ports" and "sherries" at such wineries as Seppelts' base at Seppeltsfield and Yalumba (which sold off its fortified wine business to what was then Mildara Blass in 1993) are extremely impressive. When modern times called for table wines, it was the Rhine Riesling, strangely enough, that Barossa did best (with the Silesian settlers came a fondness for the grape). Growers found that the higher they went into the hills to the east the

finer and more crisply fruity the wine became. In 1962 Gramp's, now subsumed into Orlando, planted a patch of schistous hilltop that a sheep would scarcely pause on, called it Steingarten, and gave Australian Riesling a new dimension.

Although Riesling is still widely planted in the Barossa Valley itself, it is now much more celebrated up in the eastern ranges within the Eden Valley, where it is the single most planted grape variety. Eden Valley Riesling at its best has a floral, sometimes mineral, top note to it when young, even if, like the Clare Valley Riesling with which it is inevitably compared, it becomes increasingly toasty after time in the bottle.

Eden Valley offers more than Riesling, however, particularly at lower altitudes. Henschke grows some of Australia's very best Shiraz at Keyneton, well up in the hills, and most notably from century-old vines in the (actually rather flat) Hill of Grace vineyard south of Moculta. Mountadam persists with ambitious Chardonnay in the south of the valley.

Riesling is even better entrenched in the prettily pastoral Clare Valley, well north of the Barossa's northernmost limit. Here, in the hands of a bevy of proponents as capable as Grosset, Knappstein, Mitchell, Mount Horrocks, Petaluma, and Pikes, it evinces perhaps Australia's most distinctive style of Riesling: firm and dry, sometimes almost austere in youth, but usually with a rich undertow of lime that can mature to toastiness after years in bottle. These are the wines for which Australia's fusion food has surely been designed.

The whole district of Clare, with the slightly cooler reaches of Watervale in the south, is a third the size of Barossa, but has a history almost as long and a singular quality of wine that attracts some of Australia's most skilful makers and blenders. Partly limestone soil and a climate more extreme than Barossa but heavily dependent on altitude make the Clare style sturdy yet structured. The red wines seem to have more definition and perhaps slightly more natural acidity and backbone, as evident in smooth-talking Cabernets and Shiraz from the likes of Jim Barry, Knappstein, Leasingham, and Skillogalee, and Wendouree's positively chewable reds.

Above Every November these South Australian valleys are streaked with purple, thanks to the Salvation Jane that heralds spring. This young vineyard supplies Tim Adams, a Clare veteran who was winemaker at Leasingham, now part of BRL Hardy.

1:250,000

Km 0 — 5 — 10 Km
Miles 0 — 5 Miles

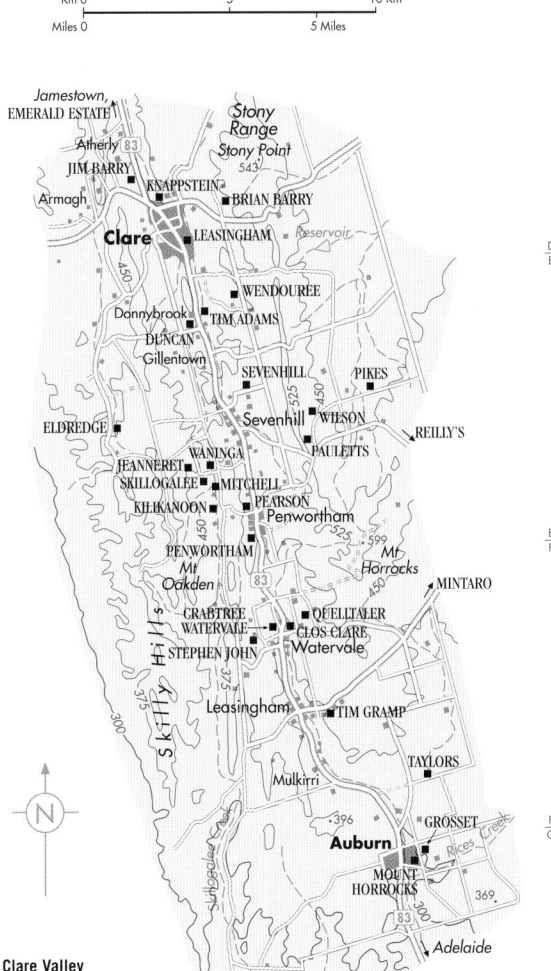

Clare Valley

■ GROSSET Leading producer

═══300═══ Contour interval 75 metres

For location see map on page 302

Left Petaluma's vineyards in Piccadilly Valley in the Adelaide Hills are the oldest of the modern era. More recently this pretty, relatively cool region has been substantially planted by private investors. Only favoured exposures and slopes have a sufficiently low risk of spring frost to be suitable for vines.

S. Australia: McLaren Vale and Adelaide Hills

The southern suburbs of Adelaide shade into the northern limits of McLaren Vale, once part of what was known as the Southern Vales but now a wine region with a proud sense of its own identity. It is the site of South Australia's oldest vineyard for a start: the John Reynell who gave his name to Chateau Reynella planted his vines in 1838. For much of the intervening decades Reynella claret and fortified wines were respected names, and the original underground cellar Reynell built is one of the historic spots of Australian wine. Today it is the headquarters of the almost equally ancient firm of Thomas Hardy & Sons, now part of one of Australia's largest wine companies BRL Hardy, along with the Tintara winery bought by the original Thomas Hardy in 1850.

Natural conditions for the vine could hardly be better than in this coastal zone, a narrow band between the heights of Mount Lofty Ranges and the temperate sea. There is usually adequate rainfall, a warm but not torrid summer, good air drainage to prevent frosts but a reasonably cool vintage season. Some vineyards even have a history of growing fine Sauvignon Blanc, thanks to a particularly low-yielding clone.

There is a confidence in McLaren Vale's glossily seductive reds with Shiraz, Cabernet Sauvignon, and more recently Merlot performing with brio here in such hands as Chapel Hill, d'Arenberg, Pirramimma, Tatachilla, Wirra Wirra, and Woodstock. Rosemount sources its Balmoral Shiraz here. Penfolds certainly soaks up a fair bit of the fruit for its many Bin numbered brands, while the old Seaview (now Edwards & Chaffey) is the sister winery within the Southcorp organization. Clarendon Hills, Fox Creek, and Noon have proved that McLaren Vale wines can achieve cult status (and perilously high alcohol levels). Coriole and Kangarilla Road have shown that the palette of varieties can be widened to include Sangiovese and Zinfandel respectively.

But it is increasingly in the cooler foothills of the Southern Mount Lofty Ranges to the north and east that winemakers are looking today. The vineyards spread north to link up with the eastern hills of the Eden Valley (see the map on page 303) in what is effectively a continuous, if spasmodic, region – apart from the hilly no-vine's-land between Clarendon and Stirling, which divides McLaren Vale from the much chillier Adelaide Hills.

The Piccadilly Valley on Mount Lofty was staked out in the 1970s by Brian Croser of Petaluma and Bridgewater Mill wineries as a defiantly cool area for Chardonnay vines, then a novelty in Australia. Today the cool, wooded hills to the east of Adelaide are being planted at a lick to supply the needs of many a corporate policy which demands cool-climate blending ingredients. But only a handful of individuals have been permitted to build wineries in what is effectively an eastern suburb of the city.

Only the southwestern corner of the Adelaide Hills is mapped in detail opposite. To the north,

Four of the most successful wines *produced in the Adelaide Hills (although Pinot Noir is still establishing its reputation there) above two of the most highly regarded McLaren Vale reds. This proud region will continue to provide "Eileen"'s backbone, even if a little flesh may come from the Clare Valley.*

vineyards around Gumeracha are warm enough to ripen Cabernet and Shiraz, but the dominant characteristic of Adelaide Hills wine, sleek acidity, is found in virtually all wines grown in the vineyards mapped here. The 1,300ft (400m) contour line provides all but the northern boundary of the appellation and at altitudes above this the weather can be very, very different from McLaren Vale or even Adelaide itself. Grey mist is common, as is spring frost, and chilly nights, even in summer.

The region is cool enough to provide sparkling wine producers with material and is one of Australia's few to have established a reputation for lively aromatic Sauvignon Blanc from the likes of Shaw & Smith, Geoff Weaver, and Nepenthe. Even the Chardonnays can be Sauvignon-like with their brisk nectarine flavours and lissom build. Pinot Noir is likely to shine here eventually, as Henschke acknowledges with its Giles bottling from Lenswood.

Meanwhile, just a few miles to the east, one of Australia's least sung but most historic and most rapidly expanding wine regions continues to produce its own salty idiosyncratic wines. Langhorne Creek (see map, page 302) is a bed of deep alluvium irrigated by (deliberate) late winter flooding from the diverted Bremer River. Bleasdale is the name of the best-known vineyard, planted by Frank Potts in the 1860s. Potts cut down the titanic red gums that thrived on the deep soil, sawing and working them with his own hands into a winepress, yachts, and a piano. Today the region is plundered by most of the big companies for its soft, gentle, mouthfilling Shiraz and, especially, Cabernet fruit.

Wine regions

⸺⸺⸺ McLaren Vale

⸺⸺⸺ Adelaide Hills

Adelaide Hills subregions

⸺⸺⸺ Piccadilly Valley

⸺⸺⸺ Lenswood

■ AMERY Leading producer

▓ Vineyards

≈300≈ Contour interval 75 metres

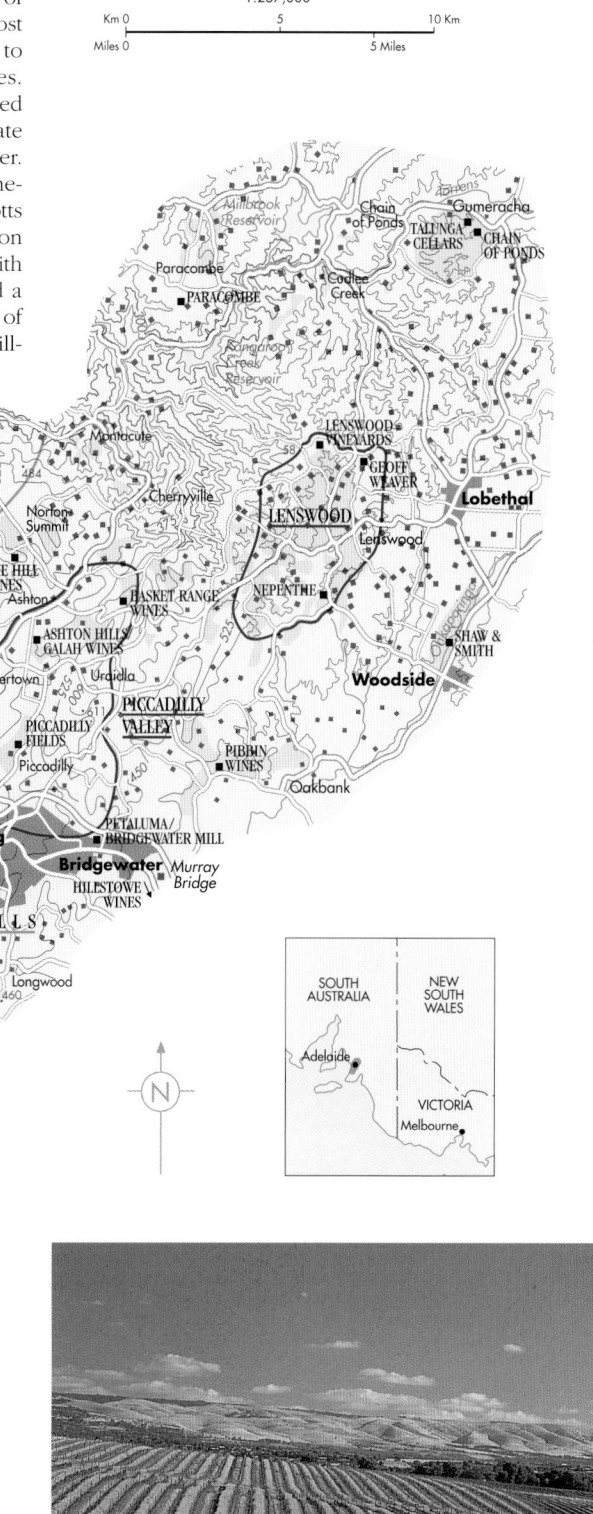

Right McLaren Vale's warmer, more open country can provide much larger plots for new vineyards such as this one. Total plantings in McLaren Vale, whose wineries number more than 40, are nearly ten times as extensive as those carved out of the Adelaide Hills.

S. Australia: the Far Southeast

The story of this, the coolest, most rapidly evolving corner of the wine state is to a large extent the story of terra rossa. As far back as the 1860s early settlers became aware of a very odd patch of ground 250 miles (400km) south of the Adelaide region and its essentially Mediterranean climate. Just north of the village of Penola a long, narrow rectangle, only nine miles by less than one (15 by 1.5km), of completely level soil is distinctively red in colour and crumbly to touch. A mere 18in (45cm) down, the red soil changes to pure free-draining limestone and, only 6ft (2m) below, there is a constant table of relatively pure water.

No land could be better designed for fruit growing. The entrepreneur John Riddoch started the Penola Fruit Colony and by 1900 the area, under the name of Coonawarra, was producing large quantities of a quite unfamiliar kind of wine, largely Shiraz, low in alcohol but brisk and fruity: in fact, not at all unlike Bordeaux.

This great resource, an Australian vineyard producing wines with a structure quite different from most, was for a long time appreciated by very few. Only with the table wine boom in the 1960s was its potential fully realized and the big names of the wine industry began to move in. Wynns, now owned by Southcorp, is by far the biggest winemaking landowner, but considerable amounts of Coonawarra fruit end up in wines blended and bottled many miles away. Producers such as Balnaves, Bowen, Leconfield, Majella, Parker, and Zema on the other hand offer something much closer to the estate model.

Shiraz was the original Coonawarra speciality but since Mildara demonstrated in the late 1960s that conditions were just as close to ideal for Cabernet Sauvignon, Coonawarra Cabernet has been one of Australia's remarkably few touchstone combinations of variety and place.

Coonawarra's soil was not the only reason. The area is considerably further south, hence cooler, than any other South Australian vineyard, and only 50 miles (80km) from an exposed coast, washed by the Antarctic currents and fanned by westerlies all summer. Frost is a problem in spring and rain at vintage time – enough to make a French grower quite nostalgic. Coonawarra has another problem: its isolation. The population is sparse to say the least. Penola is not much more than a hamlet. Labour is a scarce resource. This means that many vines are pruned and picked mechanically, and the region can all too easily seem cold and inhuman. (And when irrigation is used to overload vines with unripe fruit, the wines can lack warmth too.)

In any case, Coonawarra, limited by the hugely controversial extent of its eccentric soil, has not been able to satisfy the demand for its type of cool-climate wines. Diligent research in country further north known collectively as the Limestone Coast (all of it suffering a labour shortage but much of it with ridges of terra rossa where the receding ocean left ancient sand dunes) is producing ever more alternatives. Those areas established or proposed so far are mapped on page 302.

Padthaway was the first such, with not dissimilar soil and a rather warmer climate. Initially irrigated, it produced serviceable wine for blends in even more serviceable quantity but the trend today is towards more concentrated dry-farmed fruit that can be richer than the Coonawarra norm, often with a slightly minty note. BRL Hardy has even built a winery there – most unusual. But Wrattonbully just north of Coonawarra may yet prove even more interesting – provided the temptation to over-irrigate is resisted – although at the turn of the century it had not even half the vineyard area of Coonawarra or Padthaway. A few plantings around Mount Gambier have proved that this southern outpost is too cool to ripen Bordeaux grapes.

Vines have also been planted just west of Bordertown northeast of Padthaway and at Elgin on the coast due west of Coonawarra. But perhaps the most promising new wine regions are the remarkably similar Robe and Mount Benson further north up the coast. Fruit grown right on the coast here is much juicier than the sinewy ferments of Coonawarra, if less concentrated; while the average vine age is still decidedly in single digits. Soils are just the sort of gentle, infertile slopes beloved by the vine. Underground water is even better quality than in Coonawarra. Sea breezes cool the vineyards almost constantly and the prospects, give or take a frost or two, are good. Which is why, presumably, Southcorp is busy developing Robe and others are investing in Mount Benson.

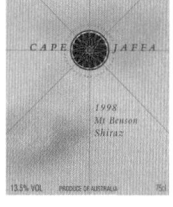

Four great reds from Coonawarra *(not all of them Cabernets). Merlot is showing real promise here too, both for blending and as a varietal. The bottom two labels represent early evidence of Mount Benson's potential.*

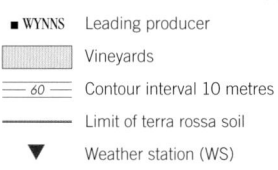

- ■ WYNNS   Leading producer
-    Vineyards
- ═ 60 ═   Contour interval 10 metres
- ────   Limit of terra rossa soil
- ▼   Weather station (WS)

For location see map on page 303

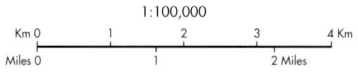

1:100,000

Km 0   1   2   3   4 Km
Miles 0   1   2 Miles

Coonawarra: Coonawarra

Latitude / Altitude of WS **37.17˚ / 164ft (50m)**
Mean January temp at WS **65.9˚F (18.9˚C)**
Annual rainfall at WS **22in (570mm)**
Harvest month rainfall at WS **April: 1.4in (35mm)**
Chief viticultural hazards **Underripeness, spring frost, harvest rainfall**
Principal grapes **Cabernet Sauvignon, Chardonnay, Shiraz, Riesling**

Western Australia

The most often cited wine statistic about "WA" is that it produces only 3% of the Australian crush. The people who most often cite this statistic are wine producers in other states exasperated by the amount of publicity given to the vineyards on the far southwestern tip of their vast country. But there is a good reason for it. These scattered vineyards produce far more than their fair share of Australia's most lauded wines, wines with a distinctive lightness of touch combined with ripeness of fruit – an unusual combination in Australia.

The first colonists of Western Australia were almost as quick to start winemaking as those of New South Wales. The Swan Valley, just upstream from the state capital, Perth, saw its first vintage in 1834. From the searing heat of the summer, with dry winds from the interior keeping temperatures close to 100°F (38°C) for weeks, the early vintners realized that their forte for many decades would be dessert wines.

It was however an experimental lot of dry white wine, made of Chenin Blanc in 1937, that put Western Australia on the nation's wine map. Houghton's White Burgundy (renamed HWB for export markets sensitive about the appropriation of European place names) became an Australian staple even in the east of the continent, being recognized as a consistent bargain. Originally it was a huge golden wine of intense flavour. It has since been tamed to be soft yet lively, dry yet faintly honeyed in character; a blend of Chenin Blanc with all manner of other grapes including Muscadelle, Semillon, Verdelho, and (recently) Chardonnay that has remained year after year Australia's best-selling dry white. The extraordinary bonus for such a keenly priced wine is that it is even more delicious after six to eight years in bottle.

It is hard to imagine primitive techniques producing a better white wine from so hot a region. Perhaps this is why it took Western Australia another 30 years to realize what potential lay in the cooler parts of this vast, almost empty state. When the move to cool-climate areas began in the late 1960s, Western Australia had plenty to offer. It still has.

Perth, around which is still clustered a small hot-climate wine industry, has blistering summers, but south down the coast the influence of Antarctic currents and onshore westerlies is felt in much more temperate conditions.

The large, underdeveloped Great Southern region, first staked out at Mount Barker in the 1960s and progressively extended westward, offers some of the coolest, wettest terrain in Australia. Plantagenet was the pre-eminent pioneer but has been decisively overtaken in size by Goundrey, which has been growing so fast that it buys in fruit from all over the state with the result that the name Mount Barker appears less and less on its labels. Mount Barker's most obvious strengths so far have been fine Riesling and some attractively peppery Shiraz.

Denmark on the coast is even wetter but often warmer. The cluster of small vineyards here grow early maturing varieties in the main;

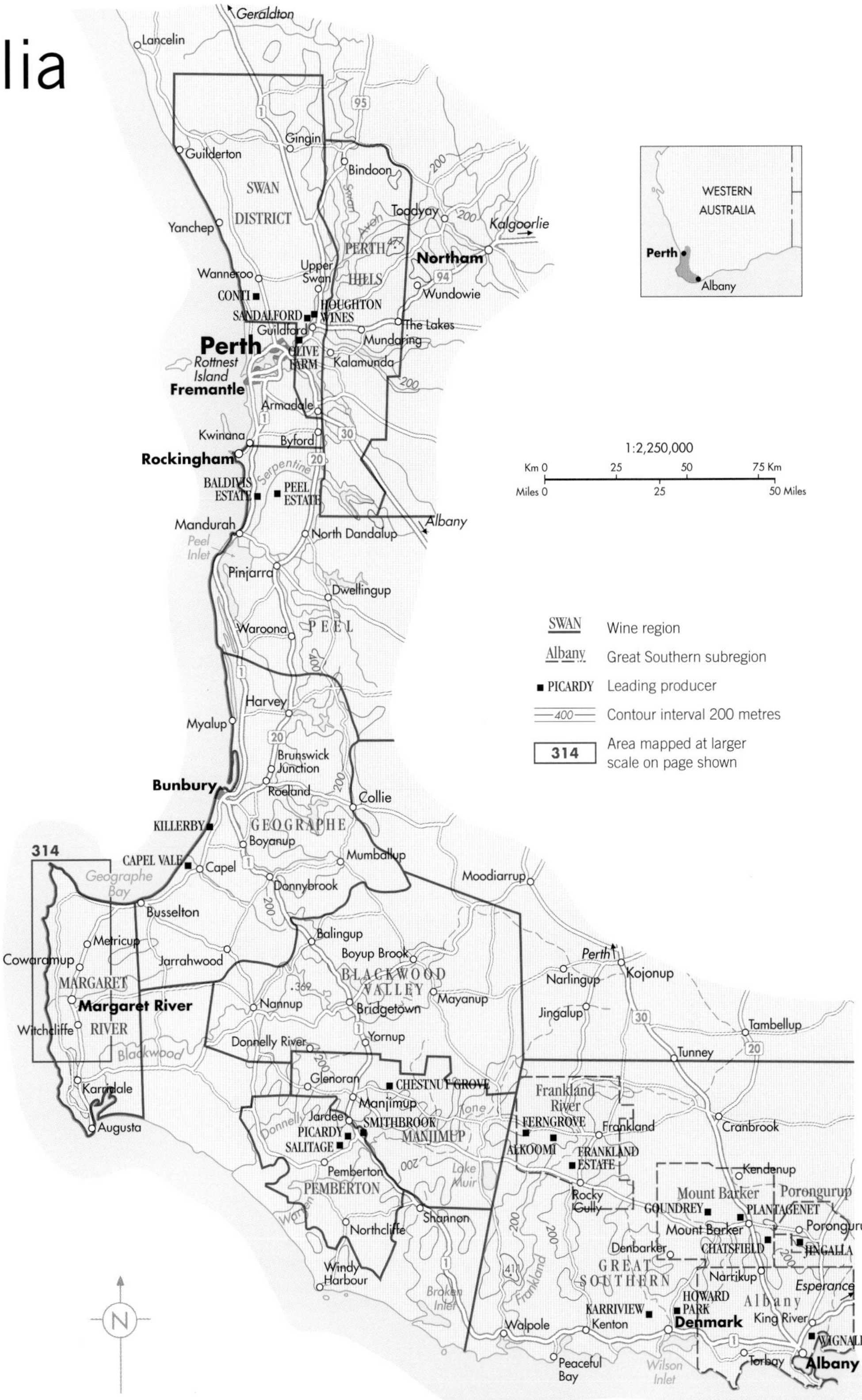

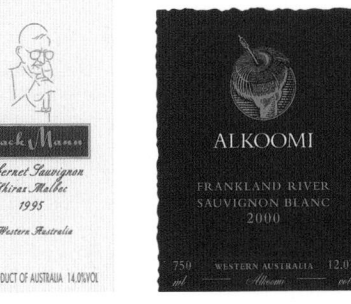

The varied styles of these, three of the most successful wines produced from fruit grown around Frankland in the expanding Great Southern region, illustrate how young this part of Australia is as a wine producer, and how embryonic the business of matching variety to area.

Map legend

SWAN	Wine region
Albany	Great Southern subregion
■ PICARDY	Leading producer
—400—	Contour interval 200 metres
314	Area mapped at larger scale on page shown

1:2,250,000

Left Wheeling out the netting to protect ripening grapes from foraging birds as harvest approaches is an annual chore in many Margaret River vineyards. Voyager is one of the most cosseted wine estates in this beautiful region.

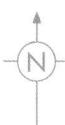

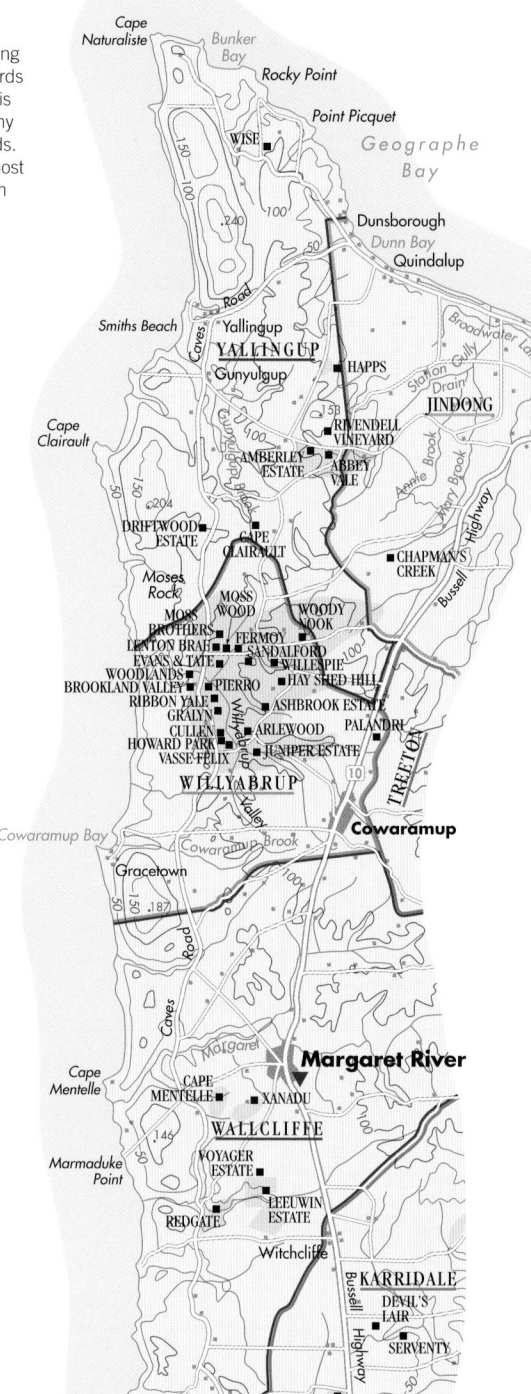

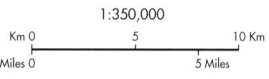

Margaret River subregions

— Yallingup
— Jindong
— Willyabrup
— Treeton
— Wallcliffe
— Karridale

■ CULLEN Leading producer

    Vineyards

─100─ Contour interval 50 metres

▼ Weather station (WS)

For location see map on page 313

1:350,000

Km 0   5   10 Km
Miles 0   5 Miles

Cullen and Moss Wood have kept *their reputations as great Cabernet producers intact since Margaret River's early days as a wine producer. Leeuwin Estate has managed to establish its Chardonnay as one of the country's finest, while Gralyn, for long a grower, is a relative newcomer as a wine producer.*

Margaret River: Margaret River

Latitude / Altitude of WS **33.57˚ / 295ft (90m)**
Mean January temp at WS **68.6˚F (20.4˚C)**
Annual rainfall at WS **45in (1,150mm)**
Harvest month rainfall at WS **March: 1in (25mm)**
Chief viticultural hazards **Wind, birds**
Principal grapes **Cabernet Sauvignon, Semillon, Chardonnay, Sauvignon Blanc**

most promising is Pinot Noir and Chardonnay although Merlot may work too. John Wade's own label may raise awareness of this region.

Thanks to an extraordinary influx of investment capital in the late 1990s, the inland Frankland region west of Mount Barker now has Great Southern's greatest concentration of vineyards, even though wineries are few and far between. Alkoomi has an established reputation for Sauvignon Blanc (and olive oil). Frankland Estate's strength is Riesling and a Bordeaux blend known as Olmo's Reward in recognition of the California professor who first suggested back in the 1950s that the area would be suitable for viticulture. The Westfield vineyard has long provided fruit for Houghton's superlative

red blend named after Jack Mann even if, as so often, Great Southern is not acknowledged on the label. Vintages here can vary considerably in quality and the vines' natural vigour needs vigilance in much of the region.

Vines are going into all manner of areas between here and Margaret River on the Indian Ocean coast. Most significant are the plantings at Manjimup and Pemberton which are finding it difficult to decide whether they wish to be considered as two separate wine regions. Manjimup is certainly warmer, further from the cooling influence of Antarctic currents on the coast, and can make some fine Verdelho at Chestnut Grove. Land even further inland around Perup is also being planted. In Pemberton the likes

of Picardy and Salitage are concentrating on Burgundy varieties, whereas Smithbrook has replaced its Pinot Noir with Merlot.

The emerging Great Southern region is 20 or 30 years behind Margaret River in vinous evolution and national recognition, as well as lagging well behind it in the vines' growth cycle. While some of Great Southern's coolest vineyards may not be picked until May, sparkling wine grapes are picked in February in Margaret River. For Margaret River, while being much cooler than Perth, is still quite warm. Summers are dry and warm, tempered by onshore winds known as the Freemantle Doctor. Winters are wet and not exactly cool – in fact vines can struggle to achieve dormancy. Spring can be so windy as to

Tasmania

affect flowering and reduce the crop, one of the reasons for the concentration of flavour in wines from the heartland of Margaret River.

Australia has few landscapes as green, or forests as splendid as the soaring karri and jarrah woods of this area, dotted with brilliantly coloured birds and lolloping kangaroos. Surf laps the rocky coastline and the introduction of vineyards surely tilted the whole slap-bang into paradise. The first wines emerged in the early 1970s, from Vasse Felix followed by Moss Wood and then Cullen – all of them, true to Australian wine history form, created by doctors. Critics immediately recognized a quite remarkable quality in the wines, particularly in the Cabernets. Sandalford, Houghton's neighbour and rival in the Swan Valley, rapidly moved in with a large plantation. Robert Mondavi of California became enthused and encouraged Denis Horgan to develop the enormously ambitious Leeuwin Estate, which rapidly became as famous for its creamily authoritative Chardonnay as for its annual, world-class outdoor concerts.

By the early 1990s there were 30 wineries in the area, a decade later twice as many and rising, although soils vary wildly and the infertile red loams are most prized. The classic Cabernet heartland of Willyabrup is particularly heavily planted and the vine now extends south through Wallcliffe and the cooler Karridale sub-region all the way to the south coast, where the dominant influence is Antarctica rather than the Indian Ocean. This is classic white wine country and Margaret River has established its very own vibrant, tropical fruit-flavoured blend of Semillon and Sauvignon Blanc. Cape Mentelle's is particularly fine.

Plantings are also increasing north of Willyabrup, in the milder Yallingup area and, more controversially, inland in Carbunup (more usually known as Jindong), where yields are high enough to satisfy as large an outfit as Evans & Tate.

The Margaret River region's obvious affinity with Cabernet has not acted as a brake on plantings of Shiraz (which typically reaches an appetizing halfway house of ripeness between Barossa heft and white pepper), Chardonnay, Merlot, even Zinfandel, and other classic Rhône grapes both white and red.

Those who take the three-hour drive between Perth and Margaret River can now see vineyards at virtually all points along the route. Just south of Australia's most isolated city a peculiar dusty grey soil formation known as Tuart Sands is adding yet another dimension – highly aromatic whites and vivid reds – from the likes of Capel Vale and Peel Estate, although labelling can be geographically vague. A shame, perhaps, in the case of the Geographe region.

Availability of water is, however, a brake on expansion in this corner of Australia. Western Australia's underground water is naturally high in salt (the land has been vigorously cleared) and a dam is a prerequisite for irrigation. Even so, this map is likely to change more than most over the next few years.

The relentless search for cooler climates in Australia logically leads to its southernmost, and sea-girt, state: Tasmania. In stark contrast to the mainland, this quaint island can boast grass that stays green all summer, as in northern Europe, and a ready market for woolly knitwear. For most of the late 1980s and 1990s when Tasmania emerged as a wine producer, it was reckoned primarily to be a useful source of base material for sparkling wine producers. But of all Australian wine regions, Tasmania has most to gain from global warming, and in the last vintages of the 20th century had the pleasure of seeing almost all of its grapes reach full ripeness.

The first modern wine producer was Moorilla Estate near Hobart on the south coast. The evidence from this and most other bottlings was that this is still an inconveniently cool place to grow red grapes such as Cabernet Sauvignon. But it has become increasingly clear that Riesling and Pinot Noir in particular can be exceptionally lively with a delicacy that can be lacking on the mainland. South Australian dry Rhine Riesling has little or nothing to do with Germany; Tasmanian Riesling could be grown on the Mosel – or New Zealand's South Island.

The number of Tasmanian wine producers is now approaching 100, most of them on a miniature scale. The most important by far is Pipers Brook, especially since it took over Heemskerk from Roederer, the two of them huddling together on one of many hills at the north tip of the island. The greatest threat to this vineyard carved out of Tasmania's rich and floriferous bush, and to many others, is the sea wind. Screens are necessary to preserve the vine leaves on the seaward slope. But ripening is as slow and sure as any vintner could hope for, and flavour correspondingly intense.

Other wine regions hug the east and southern coasts. There is clearly more pleasure in store from Tasmania's future vintages.

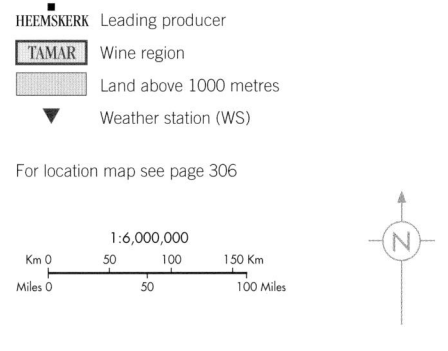

■
HEEMSKERK Leading producer

| TAMAR | Wine region

▓ Land above 1000 metres

▼ Weather station (WS)

For location map see page 306

1:6,000,000
Km 0   50   100   150 Km
Miles 0   50   100 Miles

Tasmania: Launceston

Latitude / Altitude of WS **41.32° / 558ft (170m)**
Mean January temp at WS **61.9°F (16.6°C)**
Annual rainfall at WS **27in (680mm)**
Harvest month rainfall at WS **April: 2.2in (55mm)**
Chief viticultural hazards **Underripeness, drought**
Principal grapes **Pinot Noir, Chardonnay**

Right Everything is green and small-scale in Tasmania, just two of many reasons why it feels so very different from the rest of Australia. These vines belong to the island's principal wine producer, Pipers Brook.

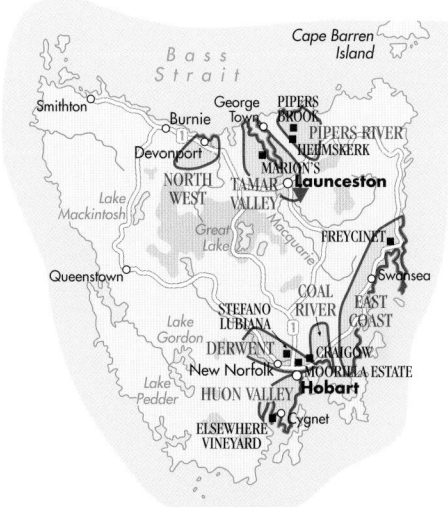

So far Tasmania has shown *the most obvious aptitude for Riesling, Pinot Noir grown in warmer sites such as Freycinet's, and base wines for sparkling wine producers. Most of these base wines are shipped to ambitious producers on the mainland but Pirie is Pipers Brook's ambitious Tasmanian-bottled fizz.*

New Zealand

Few wine-producing countries have quite so sharp an image as New Zealand. The word sharp is apt, for the wines are characterized by piercingly crystalline flavours and bracing acidity. But then a high proportion of the world's wine drinkers will never have experienced proof of this, for New Zealand is not just one of the most isolated countries on earth (more than three hours' flight from its nearest and domineering neighbour Australia), but is also small. It produces about the same amount of wine as Cyprus, less than a tenth as much as Australia. It has colonized four pages in this book simply because so many of those who try New Zealand wines fall madly in love with them.

This has happened only recently. In 1960 the country had less than 1,000 acres (400ha) of vines, mainly in Auckland and Hawkes Bay, and too many of them hybrids. By 1980 there were 14,000 acres (5,600ha), 2,000 of which were in the brand-new Marlborough region on the South Island (see page 318 for more detail). The 1980s saw stabilization and upgrading. In this first boom, poor varieties were planted in unsuitable places. Prices fell alarmingly. A government programme in the mid-1980s grubbed out over a third of the acreage. This was followed in the 1990s by the most amazing expansion – it almost seemed as though anyone with a few acres wanted to try their hand at vine-growing – so that by 2000 the total was more than 30,000 acres (12,000ha) and there were 358 wineries, double the numbers of just seven years before.

It was New Zealanders who coined the term and bought the concept of a "lifestyle winery": a bucolic way of life whereby, typically, a fine education is focused on producing, in the most pleasing environment, one of life's more delicious commodities from the earth.

New Zealand had some natural problems to contend with before this enthusiasm could be positively harnessed. Only 150 years ago much of this long, thin country was covered with rainforest. Soils here tend to be so rich in nutrients that vines, like everything else, grow too vigorously for their own good, a phenomenon exacerbated by the country's generous rainfall. Because of this, New Zealand wines in the 1970s and 1980s too often tasted of leaves rather than fruit, especially the reds. Grapes were often simply too heavily shaded to ripen properly.

The introduction of canopy management techniques, notably by state viticulturist Dr Richard Smart, changed all this, and allowed light to shine both literally and figuratively on New Zealand's unique style of wine. (Professor Hans Schultz of Geisenheim argues that increasing ultraviolet radiation due to ozone depletion in the southern hemisphere is also helping to build pronounced wine flavours even at New Zealand's high latitudes.)

Winegrowing New Zealand lies, in terms of the northern hemisphere, on latitudes between those of Morocco and Bordeaux (see factfiles overleaf). The effects of latitude are countered, though, by the Pacific, by strong prevailing westerlies, and by the effects of the mountains on their rain-clouds: factors that give the two islands a wide range of growing conditions – almost all cooler than the bare figures suggest. Enthused by the relative coolness (compared with Australia), most growers initially took Germany as their model. Far too much Müller-Thurgau was planted as a result.

Chardonnay finally overtook this dreary grape (admittedly less dreary in New Zealand than in Germany) in 1992 and it has been the country's most planted vine variety ever since, made in a relatively narrow range of crisp, often oaked styles (although see comments on Hawkes Bay on page 319).

It was not Chardonnay but Sauvignon Blanc, however, that made the world take notice of New Zealand. After all, decent Chardonnay is made virtually everywhere; a cool climate is needed if Sauvignon is to be lively, and the cool, bright, sunny, and windy northern tip of the South Island seems to have been designed to intensify the scarcely subtle twang of Sauvignon. Early examples in the 1980s opened a Pandora's box of flavour that no one could ignore and, most importantly, no other part of the world seems able to replicate.

The success of Marlborough Sauvignon, a wine you either love or hate, has made Sauvignon Blanc almost as widely planted in New Zealand as Chardonnay. But the third most important variety, by an increasingly large margin, is Pinot Noir, enjoying success for much the same reason as Sauvignon Blanc: New Zealand's cool climate. In a surprisingly wide range of wine

Three of the most sought-after Pinot Noir labels in a country besotted by this noble grape. Giesen also makes fine Pinot but its Riesling is just one of many exciting Kiwi examples. The greater Auckland region produces some admirable Bordeaux blends and one particularly ambitious Chardonnay, richer than Montana's top Gisborne bottling.

regions, this finicky grape offers another chance of succeeding where so many others (most importantly, much of Australia) have failed.

Among other red grapes, Merlot overtook the inconveniently late-ripening Cabernet Sauvignon in 2000. Bordeaux blends are in general more popular with Kiwis themselves than outside in the big, wide, Cabernet-saturated world. Other significant grapes include Riesling (which can be very fine here, either dry or sweet but too often in between) and other hopes are variously invested in Pinot Gris, Semillon, Gewürztraminer, and Cabernet Franc. Isolation has proved no defence against vine pests and diseases. Most of these new plantings are grafted onto phylloxera-resistant rootstocks.

New Zealand wine has come a long way since it was known locally as "Dally plonk", a reference to settlers from Dalmatia, lured from the kauri-gum forests of the far north to plant vineyards near Auckland in the early 20th century. They persisted despite a rainy subtropical climate; several of the families in what is now a surprisingly good red-wine area have Dalmatian names. As in Australia's Hunter Valley, cloud

Left Rippon pioneered Otago, now famous as a producer of dramatic Pinot Noir, in the early 1970s but its vineyard by Lake Wanaka still has to be netted against the predations of the local bird population as harvest time approaches.

cover moderates what could be overmuch sunshine and gives steady ripening conditions. Vintage-time rain and rot are problems. The most ingenious (and successful) answer has been to plant, as it were, out to sea – on an island east of the city that misses the mainland rain. Waiheke Island's Stonyridge and Goldwater Cabernets are evidence of a mesoclimate miraculously right for Bordeaux grapes.

Of the wineries using West Auckland grapes, Kumeu River is the most successful. Collards is another largely dedicated to local fruit. Most other Auckland wineries such as Nobilo's and Selaks (both owned by Hardys of Australia), Babich, Matua Valley, Delegat's, and Villa Maria draw on other wine regions for the majority of their grapes.

The wine giant Montana has over 60% of the New Zealand market following its purchase of Corbans (the second-largest company) in 2000. Both ferment in local sub-wineries in Gisborne, Hawkes Bay or Marlborough and finish their wines in Auckland. But many wine producers still transport white grapes long distances to their own crushers – a process that is not without some risk.

Gisborne on the east coast of the North Island (it has another name, Poverty Bay, like so many of New Zealand's wine regions) is a good example of a region plundered by the bottlers. It is the country's third most important wine region, after Marlborough and then New Zealand's answer to Bordeaux: Hawkes Bay (see page 319 for more detail), but has very few wineries. Gisborne, warmer but wetter than Hawkes Bay, especially in autumn, grows almost exclusively white grapes on relatively fertile soils and it has a particular reputation for Chardonnay.

The North Island's most exciting area for Pinot Noir is variously called Martinborough, Wairarapa, and Wellington; it is just an hour's drive west of the nation's capital over the mountains and into the country's eastern rain shadow. Temperatures may be lower but autumns are drier here than in other North Island wine regions, and its nearly 40 wineries, led by Ata Rangi, Martinborough Vineyards, and Dry River, have made some of New Zealand's most vividly varietal Pinot Noir so far. It has ranged from potently plummy to lean, dry, and earthy; but then so does burgundy. Here Chardonnay ripens well, keeping high acidity, while Riesling has demonstrated real potential.

Just across the windy straits on the South Island, the little Nelson region to the west of Marlborough has higher rainfall and richer soil than Martinborough but does well with similar grape varieties.

Meanwhile, well south of Marlborough, on the plains surrounding Christchurch and an hour's drive north in undulating terrain at Waipara, Canterbury's winemakers are producing crisp, flinty Rieslings and Chardonnays as well as Pinot Noir that ranges from disappointingly herbal to tantalizingly promising in extremely varied environments.

Canterbury's grapes struggle to ripen in some years. Even further south, testing the limits of cool-climate grape-growing, is Central Otago, the world's southernmost wine region. In this mountainous inland region the climate is not maritime, as in the rest of New Zealand, but continental, and vines have to be planted on hillsides to maximize radiation and escape frost

danger. In a good year, however, Central Otago can produce Pinot Noir, Pinot Gris, and Riesling to rank among New Zealand's finest, and many believe that this is where the Pinot grail is to be found. The old contention that New Zealand conditions are close to German is truer here than anywhere – and marginal vineyards can make wonderful wine.

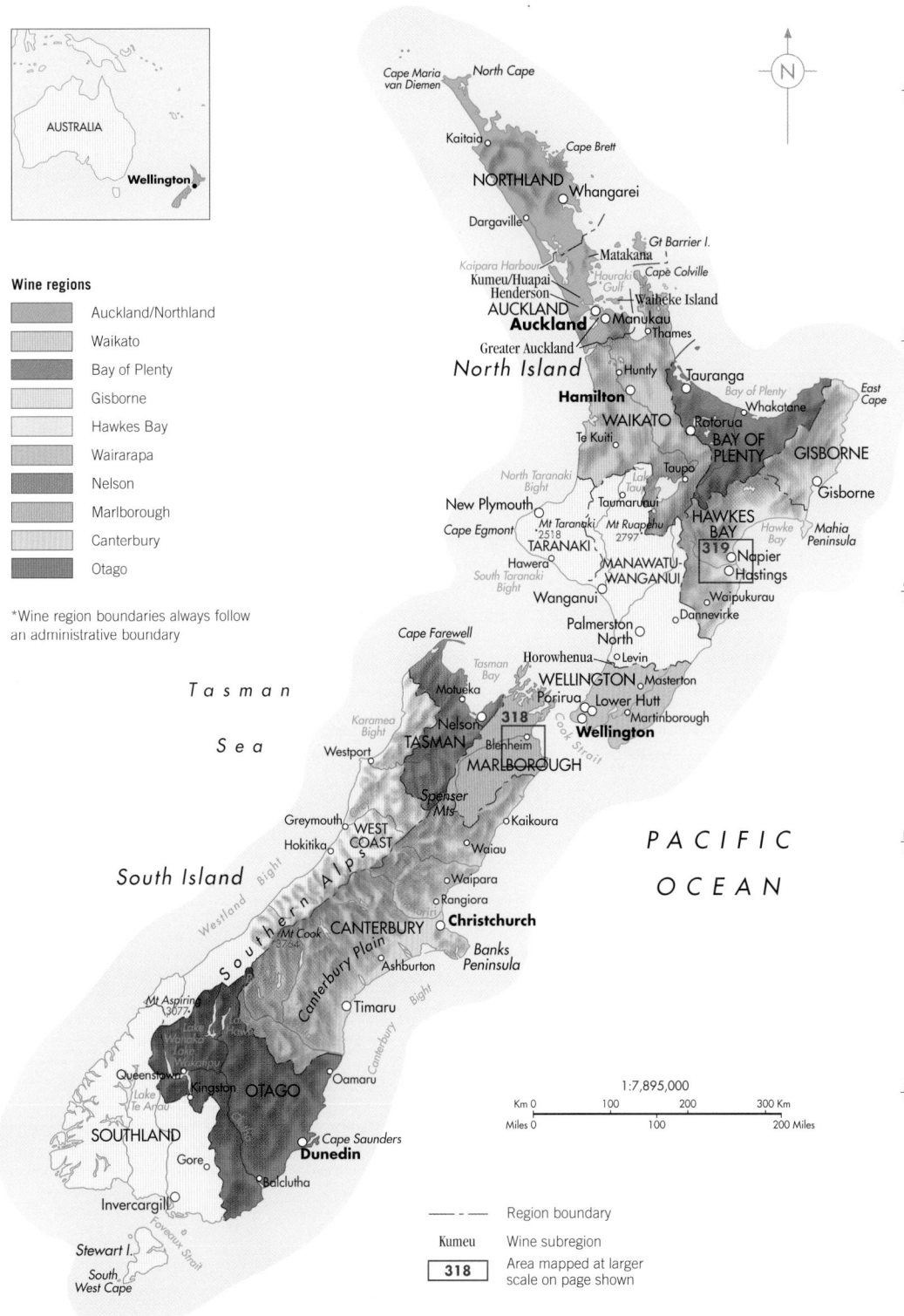

Wine regions

- Auckland/Northland
- Waikato
- Bay of Plenty
- Gisborne
- Hawkes Bay
- Wairarapa
- Nelson
- Marlborough
- Canterbury
- Otago

*Wine region boundaries always follow an administrative boundary

1:7,895,000

- — - — Region boundary
- Kumeu — Wine subregion
- 318 — Area mapped at larger scale on page shown

Marlborough

One settler planted vines at Meadowbank in Marlborough in 1867 but for most of the 20th century the South Island grew cereals, sheep, and nothing as exotic as vines until 1973 when Montana, the country's dominant wine producer, cautiously established a small commercial vineyard in Marlborough.

Lack of irrigation caused teething problems but by 1980 the first release had been bottled and the special intensity of Marlborough Sauvignon Blanc was too obvious to ignore. Such an exhilarating, easy-to-understand wine clearly had extraordinary potential, rapidly realized by, among others, David Hohnen of Cape Mentelle in Western Australia. In 1985 he launched Cloudy Bay, whose name, evocative label, and smoky, almost chokingly pungent flavour have since become legendary.

Montana's gamble was vindicated in 1990 when Marlborough overtook Hawkes Bay and Gisborne to become the country's most planted wine region (but with a mere nine wine producers). By the turn of the century it had more than 10,000 acres (4,000ha) under vine, almost half of them less than six years old. The number of wine producers had risen to 62 and the proportion of fruit leaving the region in bulk to be shipped across the Tasman Straits for processing in the North Island plummeted – much to the benefit of the resultant wine. Today an increasing proportion of the growers who once sold their grapes to one of the big companies have

their own label, which may well be applied at one of the region's busy contract wineries.

The wide, flat Wairau Valley has become a magnet for investors and those who simply like the idea of making wine their life – even if some of them have been planting so far inland that grapes may not necessarily ripen every year, and on land where the valley's precious water supply is scarce.

What makes Marlborough special as a wine region is its unusual combination of long days, cool nights, bright sunshine, and, in good years, dryish autumns. In such relatively low temperatures (see factfile) grapes might have difficulty ripening wherever autumn rains threatened, but here they can usually be left on the vine to benefit from a particularly long ripening period, building high sugars without, thanks to the cool nights, sacrificing the acidity that delineates New Zealand's wines.

This diurnal temperature variation is most marked just south of the area mapped below in the windy Awatere Valley, pioneered by Vavasour and now probably at saturation point because of a shortage of water. Both budbreak and harvest tend to be later in Awatere than on the Wairau Valley floor but summers can be long and hot enough to ripen Bordeaux varieties – in contrast to the main swathe of vineyards in the Wairau Valley. The much-photographed Brancott vineyards also tend to lag behind the valley floor because of their elevation.

But perhaps the most significant variation in Marlborough is that of soils. North of Highway 63, with a few exceptions round Woodbourne, soils are very much younger than those to the south. In places the water table can be dangerously high and the best vineyards on these young, stony soils are the best drained, on light loams over the shingle that was once the river bed. Mature vines develop deep root systems although young vines need irrigation to survive the dry summers.

South of the highway, the lowest-lying older soils are too poorly drained for fine wine production, but higher-altitude vineyards on the exposed, barren southern edge of the valley can produce interesting fruit from much drier soils.

Marlborough is also clearly capable of producing exceptional quality in Chardonnay, and in Riesling too with some inspiring late-harvest examples. But there is every sign that the region will be a source of serious, particularly fruity Pinot Noir as the region's growers pool knowledge of and enthusiasm for this new string to their bow.

The characteristically high acidity of grapes grown in Marlborough means that malolactic fermentation is crucial for still wines, and that the region can produce some fine base wines for sparkling wine. The champagne houses have been putting down roots here, and Cloudy Bay's Pelorus is just one sign of another of Marlborough's distinctions.

The Clifford Bay Sauvignon *is grown just south of the area mapped here in the Awatere Valley, while the Fromm wine shows that Marlborough has great potential as a producer of fully ripe Pinot Noir.*

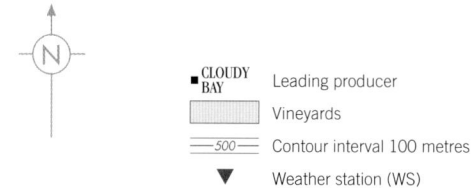

CLOUDY BAY — Leading producer

Vineyards

500 — Contour interval 100 metres

▼ — Weather station (WS)

Marlborough: Blenheim

Latitude / Altitude of WS **40.31° / 66ft (20m)**
Mean January temp at WS **63.9°F (17.7°C)**
Annual rainfall at WS **29in (730mm)**
Harvest month rainfall at WS **April: 2.3in (60mm)**
Chief viticultural hazard **Autumn rain**
Principal grapes **Sauvignon Blanc, Chardonnay**

Hawkes Bay

In New Zealand terms, Hawkes Bay is an historic wine region, having been planted by Marist missionaries in the mid-19th century. But it was Cabernets made here in the 1960s by the celebrated Tom McDonald for the Australian wine company McWilliam's (at a winery revived in 1990 by Montana for their Church Road label) that hinted at the long-term promise of the area. When serious planting began in the 1970s Hawkes Bay was a logical place to expand, especially with the Cabernet Sauvignon that was then *de rigueur*.

Hawkes Bay has been the Kiwi standard-bearer for claret-style reds ever since, but it was only in the late 1990s that the region began to make wines that demanded attention. The 1998 vintage, so hot and dry that Hawkes Bay's sheep had to be trucked west over the mountains to greener pastures, produced wines that not only had New Zealand's usual crisp definition, but they were obviously made from fully ripe grapes, and had the gentle but insistent tannins to suggest a serious future.

It was also in the late 1990s that growers began fully to understand and take advantage of the complexities of Hawkes Bay soils. It had long been obvious that the maritime climate of this wide bay on the east coast of the North Island, sheltered from the westerlies by the Ruahine and Kaweka ranges, could offer one of

The Hawkes Bay region is warm enough to ripen a wide range of red grapes. Bordeaux varieties have a long-standing reputation but both Syrah and Malbec show real class in examples such as the wines below.

the country's most favourable combinations of relatively low rainfall and high temperatures (albeit lower than Bordeaux's – see factfile below). What happened underground took longer to understand.

An aerial view of Hawkes Bay vividly shows the remarkable variety of deep glacial and alluvial soils and their distribution in a pattern flowing from mountain to sea. Silt, loams, and gravel have very different water-holding capacities; one vineyard can be at saturation point, shooting forth vegetation at an embarrassing rate, while another needs irrigation. It became clear that the ripest grapes were grown on the poorest soils which limited vine growth and on which irrigation could carefully control just how much water each vine received.

There are none poorer than the 1,500 acres (600ha) of deep, warm shingle that remain where the Gimblett Road now runs, northwest of Flaxmere, along what was the course of the Ngaruroro River until a dramatic flood in 1870. The late 1990s saw a viticultural land grab on these so-called Gimblett, or Twyford, gravels, a frenzy during which the last three-quarters of available land was bought and planted.

Other fine areas for ripening red Bordeaux grapes include Bridge Pa just south of and slightly cooler than here, selected sites on the limestone hills of Havelock North such as that colonized by Te Mata early on, and a cool, late-ripening strip of shingle along the coast between Haumona and Te Awanga.

New Zealand suffered excessive Cabernet Sauvignon worship like everywhere else in the

Above Looking across Te Awa Farm in the self-proclaimed Gimblett gravels area towards Hastings and the peak of Te Mata, also the name of one of Hawkes Bay's pioneer producers of fine reds from Bordeaux varieties.

1980s, but even in Hawkes Bay this variety cannot always be relied upon to ripen fully and plantings of the much more reliable, earlier-ripening Merlot have been increasing significantly. Malbec thrives here and ripens even earlier, although it is prone to poor fruit set. When Cabernet Franc is good it is very good. Like Bordeaux, this is a region of exaggerated annual variation, and for much the same reasons as in Bordeaux, most of Hawkes Bay's best-balanced reds are sensitively oaked blends.

Although the Chardonnay crown has been ceded to, or at least claimed by, Gisborne, Chardonnay is still Hawkes Bay's most planted grape variety, making some of New Zealand's most opulent white wines. And the Sauvignon Blancs produced here are big enough to take happily to oak ageing.

Hawkes Bay: Napier

Latitude / Altitude of WS **39.28° / 3ft (1m)**
Mean January temp at WS **66°F (18.9°C)**
Annual rainfall at WS **35in (890mm)**
Harvest month rainfall at WS **March: 3in (75mm)**
Chief viticultural hazards **Autumn rain, fungal disease**
Principal grapes **Chardonnay, Cabernet Sauvignon, Merlot**

- ■ UNISON Leading producer
-   Vineyards
- 200 Contour interval 100 metres
- ▼ Weather station (WS)

1:357,150

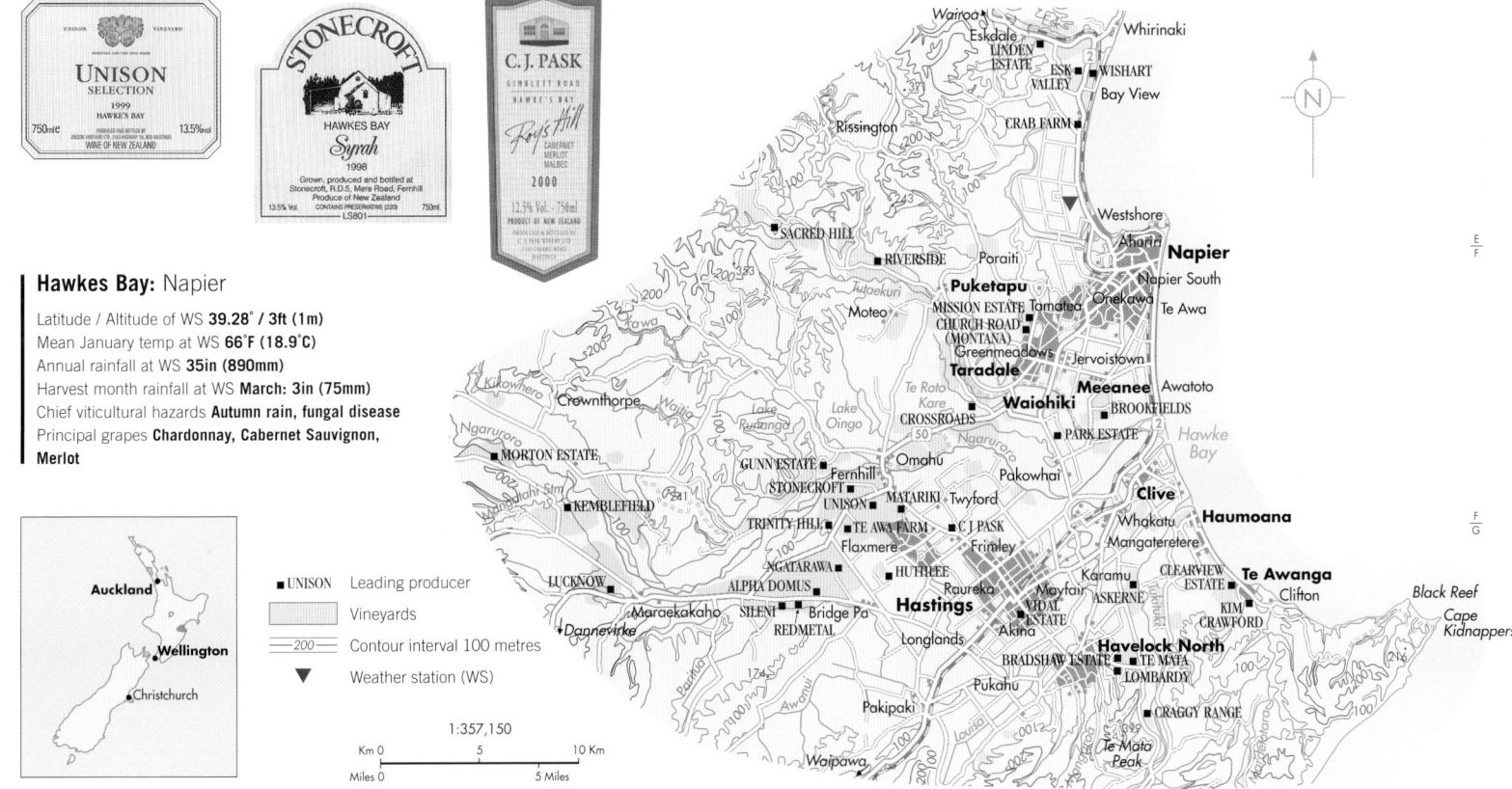

South Africa

The most dramatically beautiful wine country in the world is surely South Africa's. Blue-shadowed stacks of Table Mountain sandstone and decomposed granite rise from vivid green pastures dotted with the brilliant white façades of 200-year-old Cape Dutch homesteads. This may look like Eden but there are still too many problems for that enviable appellation. One day, however, the Cape will earn it.

Many of its vines thrive in an almost perfect Mediterranean climate, cooler than latitudes suggest thanks to the cold Benguela Current from Antarctica that washes the western Atlantic coast. Rain is usually concentrated in the winter months, but exactly how much falls varies considerably according to the Cape's diverse topography. Prevailing winter westerlies temper the climate; the further south and west – and nearer the sea – the cooler and better supplied with rain. Rainfall can be heavy on either side of mountain chains such as the Drakenstein, Hottentots Holland, and Langeberg ranges, yet dwindle to as little as 8in (200mm) a year within only a few miles.

The mountains also play a part in funnelling the famous Cape Doctor, a powerful southeaster that can ward off rot and mildew but can also batter young vines.

South Africa has rather more vineyard than Australia, which at the end of the 20th century was catching up fast. But only part of the South African grape harvest is sold as wine, the rest being low-grade stuff consigned either to distillation or grape-juice concentrate (South Africa is the world's largest producer of concentrate). The proportion sold as wine has been increasing but was still less than two-thirds in 1999.

This phenomenon is a hangover from the stifling regime that governed the South African wine industry for most of the 20th century. For much of the 19th, wine exports, and the Cape in general, flourished but phylloxera, the Anglo-Boer War and the collapse of the all-important British market for Cape wines brought intense hardship to wine farmers. This was eventually alleviated by the formation of the KWV in 1918, a giant co-operative organization designed to provide a market and control prices for everything produced on Cape vineyards, no matter what the quality.

The result has been that the pattern of winegrowing in South Africa, unlike any other New World country, is overwhelmingly co-operative-based. About 4,500 grape-farmers farm 250,000 acres (100,000ha) and most take their grapes to one of almost 70 co-ops. (The very size of some of the co-ops – and the weakness of the rand – gives them the means to make very passable wine at bargain prices, as northern European supermarkets are well aware.)

At the other end of the spectrum are the country's 90-odd wine estates, defined as producers who grow all their own grapes, rather than buy them in. A further 180 wine producers, some of them just as good, do not qualify for the estate designation. And a clutch of wholesalers, some of them significant in terms of quantity, also have their own bottlings.

Until 1992 the KWV also operated a quota system that stifled attempts to plant new vines in new places. The law-bending that resulted supplied the Cape with as many anecdotes as winemakers but it meant that it was well nigh impossible to explore new wine regions, even those offering the promise of cooler conditions and better-quality wines.

And the most crippling problem of all was that good vines were desperately scarce. Until recently an absurd quarantine system made their importation next to impossible. For long the vineyards were dominated by the remarkably well-adapted Chenin Blanc, supplemented by the sherry grape Palomino, red Cinsault (spelt Cinsaut in South Africa), and Sultana. Semillon was there, together with some Riesling, Cabernet Sauvignon, Pinot Noir, and Syrah (more often called Shiraz here) but Chardonnay, Sauvignon Blanc, and Merlot were practically unobtainable. Furthermore, what vines there were tended to be either poor clones or riddled with virus.

Today things are changing. Completely new wine areas are emerging and vineyards are being switched rapidly from white to fashionable red grapes – even if shortages and viruses still pose some problems. Chenin, traditionally called Steen in South Africa, is still the most planted variety but fell from 32% to just over 20% of the country's total vineyard between the mid-1980s and the turn of the century. During the same period the area planted with Cabernet Sauvignon grew from 5,700 to 16,500 acres (2,300 to 6,700ha), and the proportion of Cabernet that was healthy enough to reach full ripeness increased. Merlot and Shiraz (each of which can be sumptuous) were also being planted with gusto.

Pinotage is South Africa's own grape and second most planted red variety, the result of a 1920s crossing of Cinsaut (which was known then as Hermitage) with Pinot Noir. Like Shiraz in Australia, Zinfandel in California, and Malbec in Argentina, it was once spurned but is now valued as a local treasure. Once winemakers had learnt in the early 1990s to conserve its fruity aroma, it became extremely fashionable, whether as an answer to Beaujolais or as a more seriously oaked, if still fleshy, mouthful.

In 1973 the South African government, eager for international acceptance, introduced an elaborate system of control for Wines of Origin, which bears comparison with EU regulations. It designated, in decreasing order of geographical importance, regions, districts, and wards. Not all of these coincide with the geographical names most often found on labels, the most significant of which are marked on the map opposite. The pace of wine exploration is expected to yield many more new areas.

Historically the most famous wine name of South Africa is Constantia, a legendary dessert wine recognized by the late 18th century as one of the very greatest wines in the world. The original vineyard had been planted by the Cape's second Dutch governor Simon van der Stel (who also gave his name to Stellenbosch, the focus of fine wine production today in an area mapped in detail overleaf).

Above Like several other South African wineries, Buitenverwachting of Constantia has earned as worthy a reputation for its restaurant as its wines. Irrigation is not generally necessary in this relatively cool, wet zone.

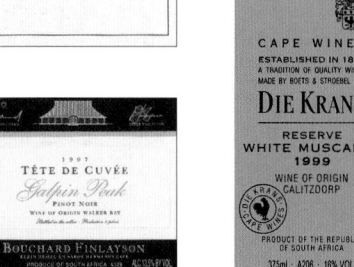

Klein Constantia's Vin de Constance is an attempt to replicate South Africa's historically most famous wine while Die Krans' Muscadel from Calitzdorp is typical of the wonderfully sweet, strong, concentrated dessert wines that South Africa's hottest vineyards can produce.

Constantia on the eastern slopes of Table Mountain has the advantage of a particularly mild climate with plenty of rain and cool breezes off nearby False Bay, but the disadvantage of being effectively a suburb of Cape Town. Such wineries as can afford to be there are mainly extremely good ones, making some particularly fine Sauvignon Blanc. New plantings extend even further south on the Cape peninsula.

Sea air from the Atlantic, on the other side of the Cape, also offers the producers (mainly co-ops) of Durbanville, Swartland, Piketberg, and right up in the north of Olifants River the chance to make fresh-flavoured table wines. Until recently the west coast was considered beyond the fine winemaking pale, but explorers, now

unfettered, are discovering such promising combinations of grape and place as Sauvignon Blanc in the heights of Groenekloof near Darling, and characterful Pinotage in some corners of Swartland's unirrigated farmland.

Further north the Vredendal co-operative has shown that decreased latitude need not mean decreased wine quality. Much of the crisp Chenin and Colombard that made South Africa seem the world's best source of bargain white wines comes from the Olifants River Valley region. The Orange River region, off the map to the north, is even hotter in summer and depends heavily on irrigation.

Summer temperatures in the great eastern sweep of arid inland scrub that is Little Karoo are so high that fortified wines, made possible only by irrigation, are the local speciality, along with some red table wines and ostriches (for their meat and feathers). Portugal's port producers are keeping a wary eye on developments.

A little closer to the gentle influence of the Atlantic, but still so warm and dry that irrigation is *de rigueur*, is Worcester. More wine is made here than in any other Cape region. Much of it ends up as brandy but this is the source of some well-made commercial red and white too.

If one region outside the immediate Cape area stands out for having established the quality of a

clutch of estates, and good co-op wine too, it is Robertson further down the Breede River Valley towards the Indian Ocean. Add to this sufficient limestone to support substantial stud farming and you have a useful white wine region, with a growing reputation for reds.

Perhaps the most exciting potential lies to the east, however. Overberg was not even classified as an official region back in the 1970s but today it can boast wines with an elegance uncharacteristic of the South African mainstream. Tim Hamilton Russell was the pioneer of Walker Bay near Hermanus. He showed that South Africa would one day produce serious Pinot Noir, but there are racy whites from Elgin's apple country, plantings in the hinterland of Cape Agulhas and at least as far east as Ruiterbosch, also known as Mossel Bay.

But without doubt the potentially greatest evolutionary step in South Africa is social. The KWV has been disbanded, or at least stripped of its governing powers. Black empowerment schemes and joint ventures are under way, albeit slowly in some cases. Labels such as Spice Route, Helderkruin, and, more emotively, Freedom Road, New Beginnings, Thandi (Xhosa for "cherish"), and Winds of Change bear witness to the start of a new era for South African wine. Impatience is understandable.

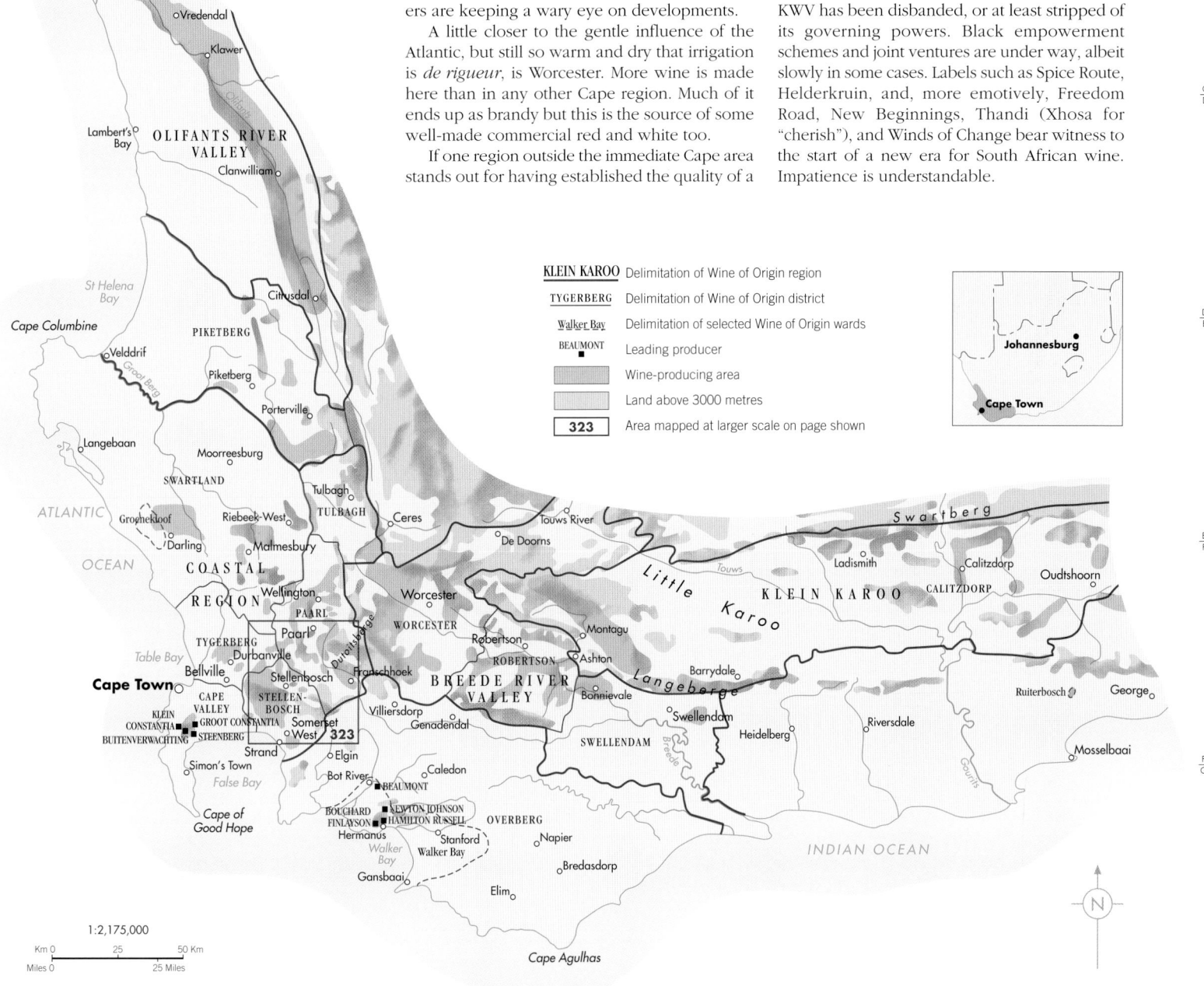

KLEIN KAROO — Delimitation of Wine of Origin region
TYGERBERG — Delimitation of Wine of Origin district
Walker Bay — Delimitation of selected Wine of Origin wards
BEAUMONT — Leading producer
Wine-producing area
Land above 3000 metres
323 — Area mapped at larger scale on page shown

1:2,175,000

Km 0   25   50 Km
Miles 0   25 Miles

Stellenbosch and Paarl

The area mapped opposite is the current hub of Cape wine activity. Those who compare it with the area mapped in previous editions will see that its centre has moved significantly towards the cooling influence of False Bay. Paarl, for long the centre of South Africa's once-vital fortified wine industry and site of the headquarters of the KWV and the annual Nederburg Wine Auction, is nowadays more marginal to the Cape wine scene than it once was (even though some extremely fine table wines are produced by the likes of Veenwouden, Fairview, Villiera, and Glen Carlou from vineyards that fall within the district of Paarl).

However exciting the results from some of South Africa's recent plantings in cooler areas elsewhere, the great concentration of South African winemaking is likely to remain centred on Stellenbosch, a leafy university town surrounded by Arcadian countryside whose curling white Cape Dutch gables have been captured in a thousand tourist photographs.

The soils of Stellenbosch vary from light and sandy on the western valley floor (traditionally Chenin Blanc country) to heavier soils on mountain slopes and decomposed granite at the foot of the Simonsberg, Stellenbosch, Drakenstein, and Franschhoek mountains in the east (the last two ranges in Paarl rather than Stellenbosch). The contour lines and distribution of blue on the map opposite are enough to hint at just how varied a range of terroirs can be found here.

North, further from the sea, temperatures tend to be higher but the climate is in general pretty perfect for growing (particularly red) wine grapes. Rainfall is just about right, and concentrated in the winter months; summers are just slightly warmer than Bordeaux. Like all South African wine producers, those of Stellenbosch used to feel the need to make a wide range of different varietals, red and white. Today, there is

a healthy trend towards identifying the variety a site grows best and concentrating on it. In the long term the majority of these vineyards are likely to be better at growing red than white wine, although Chardonnay seems to thrive virtually everywhere, and cooler corners in the far south and east of this map may produce some of the fine Sauvignon Blanc of which South Africa seems capable. Blends have long been important too, with the Cape being one of the few places where Sauvignon Blanc and Chardonnay are regularly found in the same bottle, and Cape Blend being a common, if elastically defined, style of red.

So established and varied are the vineyards of Stellenbosch that there has been time to subdivide what is, according to official South African wine nomenclature, a district in the Coastal Region. Five smaller wards have so far been recognized within the heart of the Stellenbosch district, but up to nine further geographically distinct entities have been identified in the area in between these five.

The first ward to gain official recognition was Simonsberg, including all the cooler, well-drained southern flanks of the imposing mountain of that name (although the heavy-hitting Thelema, not a wine farm when the boundaries were drawn up in 1980, is excluded). Jonkershoek Valley is a small but long-recognized area in the eponymous mountains east of Stellenbosch, while the equally minute Papegaaiberg sits on the opposite side of the town, buffering it from the thriving ward based on the sheltered Devon Valley. The much larger, flatter and more recent Bottelary ward to the north borrows its name from the hills in its far southwest corner. Stellenboschkloof (or Stellenbosch Valley) just west of the town has yet to be recognized as a ward, but it encompasses the many wineries on the main Cape

Above Wine country such as this between Wellington and Paarl is arguably the most beautiful in the world of wine. What is needed now are more healthy, top-quality vines to plant in it – there is no shortage of winemaking expertise.

Town road, as well as some of the higher-altitude sites such as Jordan, Uiterwyk, and Overgaauw.

The best wines on the whole come from estates around the town of Stellenbosch, which is open to southerly ocean breezes from False Bay, or high enough in the hills for altitude and cooling winds to be factors. The imposing Helderberg Mountains running northeast of Somerset West are an obvious factor in local wine geography, for example, and on their western flanks are many winemaking high-fliers.

The cooler areas include the detached and higher settlement of Franschhoek, originally farmed by Huguenots and still distinguished by its French place and family names. Under the laborious Wine of Origin nomenclature, Franschhoek is a ward within the Paarl district, along with Wellington off the map to the north.

Sites in Franschhoek, and at higher altitudes such as Anglo-American's spectacular Vergelegen winery high above Somerset West, are capable of making full-flavoured white wines stiffened by a spine of refreshing, life-saving acidity that is relatively rare outside Europe. South Africa is still forging its red wine identity – not least because until the late 1990s red winemaking premises and equipment were still relatively rare and heft was confused with quality. (The Afrikaans word for the traditional tough, thick reds of the Cape is *dikvoet*, meaning, literally, "thick foot".) Achieving full physiological ripeness in the vineyard, often hampered by virus-affected vines, is the current goal. To this end, the younger generation of Cape winemakers are now some of the world's best travelled and most benevolently curious.

Stellenbosch: Nietvoorbij

Latitude / Altitude of WS **33.54˚ / 479ft (146m)**
Mean January temp at WS **70.6˚F (21.5˚C)**
Annual rainfall at WS **29in (740mm)**
Harvest month rainfall at WS **March: 1.2in (30mm)**
Chief viticultural hazard **Vine viruses**
Principal grapes **Chenin Blanc, Colombard, Sauvignon Blanc, Chardonnay, Pinotage, Cabernet Sauvignon**

ELSENBURG Stellenbosch subdivision or ward

■ KANONKOP Leading producer

Vineyards

Woods

500 Contour interval 100 metres

▼ Weather station (WS)

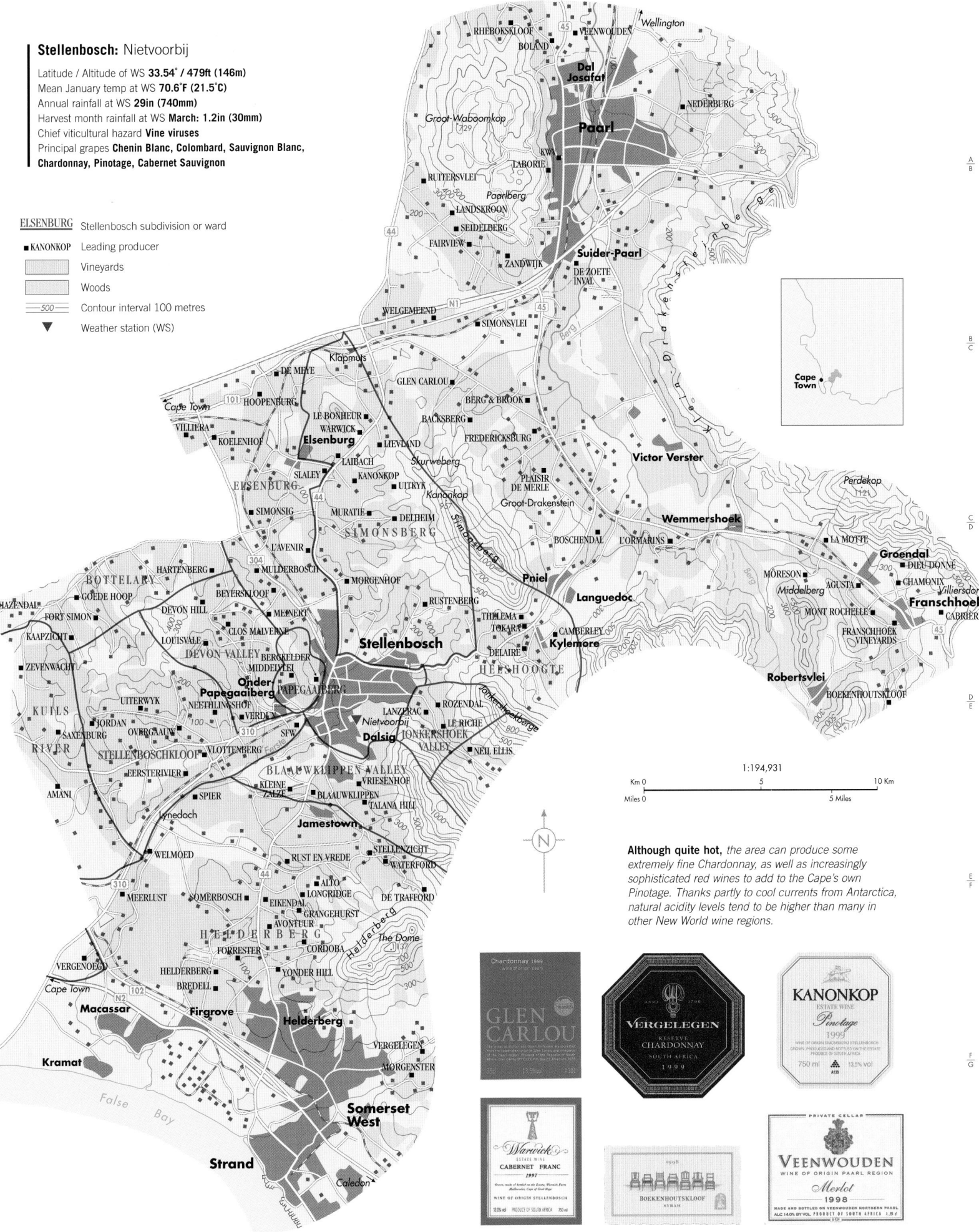

1:194,931

Km 0 — 5 — 10 Km
Miles 0 — 5 Miles

Although quite hot, the area can produce some extremely fine Chardonnay, as well as increasingly sophisticated red wines to add to the Cape's own Pinotage. Thanks partly to cool currents from Antarctica, natural acidity levels tend to be higher than many in other New World wine regions.

Asia

Above Picking Cabernet Sauvignon grapes at the Huadong winery, whose winemaking team has toured Bordeaux. The challenge now is to satisfy China's thirst for red wine.

Perhaps the most remarkable change in wine geography since the publication of the last edition of this Atlas has been the explosion of interest in both drinking and producing wine in so many parts of the world's largest continent, one which for so long seemed immune to its charms. Increasing exposure to Western ways and, in particular, Western cuisine, has undoubtedly played a part – as has the widely promulgated belief that red wine is not only lucky (because of its colour) but also healthy.

China's love affair with grape wine (*putao-jiu*), as opposed to mere *jiu*, meaning any alcoholic drink, was deliberately encouraged by the state in an effort to reduce cereal imports. China already makes far more wine than any other Asian country.

The vine was known to 2nd-century gardeners in China, who made wine with it as well as importing wine from near Tashkent in what is now the Central Asian republic of Uzbekistan, Asia's second biggest wine producer. European grape varieties were introduced at the end of the 19th century, but it was only in the late 20th century that grape-based wine insinuated itself into Chinese (urban) society.

China's vastness can offer a staggering range of soils and latitudes. Climate is more problematical. Inland it suffers typical continental extremes, while much of the coast, especially in southern China, is subject to monsoons. In Xinjiang province in the far northwest where about a quarter of all China's vines are planted, below sea level in the Turpan Depression, winters are so bitterly cold that vinifera vines have to be specially protected. Mainly table grapes and raisins are produced plus a little wine made by the state in retro oxidized fashion.

State wineries still operate all over China but it was only from the early 1980s when foreign expertise was invited to participate in joint ventures that wines of a sort recognizable to western palates (dryish, fruity, and entirely based on grapes) began to be made in China – some of them using imported must.

Rémy Martin was the first Western company to collaborate with the Chinese, just north of Tianjin in Hebei province, home to more than 15% of all Chinese vines. The success of Dynasty, a white wine of local Long Yan (Dragon's Eye) grapes flavoured with Muscat

(brought from Bulgaria in 1958) encouraged them to plant classic European varieties.

A second joint venture produced Great Wall, also in Hebei, now involving the Torres family of Spain. A third, Beijing Friendship, involving Pernod-Ricard, took the vine 75 miles (120km) northeast of Beijing, to the rainshadow of the Yan Mountains near the Great Wall itself.

On the face of it the Shandong Peninsula in the south of the mapped area looks the most likely place to grow European grapes. Shandong province already grows more than 10% of China's vines, with the only serious problem being the threat of fungal diseases in autumn. With a truly maritime climate, it offers well-drained, south-facing slopes. Allied Domecq now runs an operation that has resulted in Huadong Chardonnay and "Riesling". Changyu is an important domestic producer and other outside investors have included Seagram and Sella & Mosca of Sardinia.

Wine has invaded other parts of Asia. The Central Asian republics of Uzbekistan, Tajikistan, Kazakstan, Turkmenistan, and Kyrgyzstan have a long tradition of growing vines and making (usually rather syrupy) wines but vine-growing is quite new to such countries as Vietnam, Thailand, Taiwan, and Indonesia – each of which has a fledgling wine industry battling with the problems of tropical or near-tropical viticulture.

India has also been developing a wine industry, mainly at high altitudes in the tropics. We will clearly be hearing more of Asian wine.

Huadong involves Allied Domecq while India's Grover touts Michel Rolland of Pomerol as consultant. India is also capable of producing surprisingly fine fizz such as Chateau Indage's Omar Khayyám and Sula Brut.

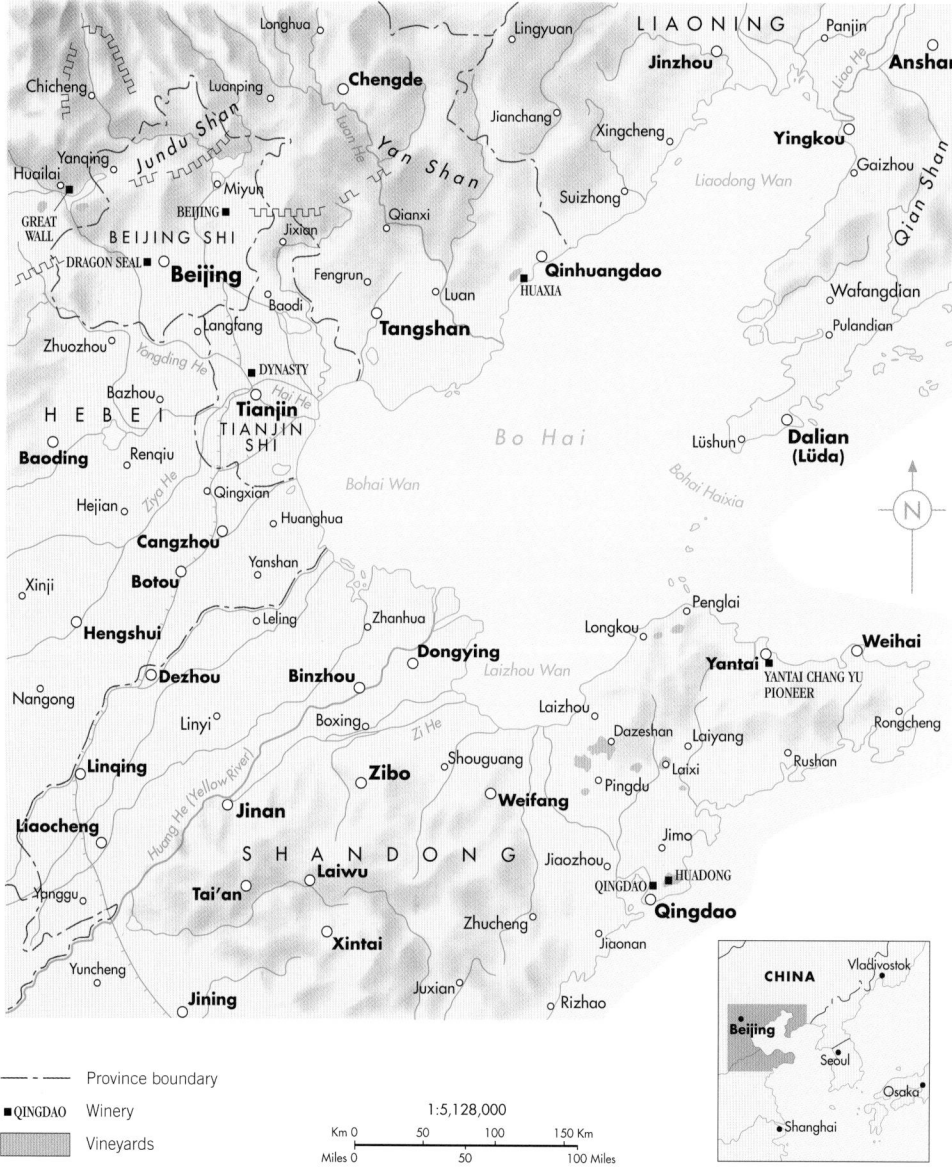

---- Province boundary

■ QINGDAO Winery

▨ Vineyards

1:5,128,000

Km 0   50   100   150 Km

Miles 0   50   100 Miles

Japan

Nature, in constructing Japan, seems to have had almost every form of pleasure and enterprise in view except wine. Although the latitude of Honshu, the main island of the Japanese archipelago, coincides with that of the Mediterranean, its climate does not. Like the eastern United States (lying in the same latitudes), it suffers from having a vast continent to the west. Caught between Asia and the Pacific, the greatest land and sea masses in the world, its predictably extreme climate is peculiar to itself. Winds from Siberia freeze its winters; monsoons from the Pacific and the Sea of Japan drench its springs and summers. At the precise moments when the vines most need sunshine they are lashed by typhoons.

The land the typhoons lash is hard-boned and mountainous, almost two-thirds of it so steep that only the forests prevent the acid soil from being washed into the short, turbulent rivers. The plains have alluvial paddy soils, washed from the hills, poor-draining and good for rice, not vines. The little gently sloping arable land there is is consequently extremely valuable and demands a high return.

It is not surprising, perhaps, that Japan has hesitated about wine; hesitated, that is, for about 1,200 years. History is exact. Grapes were grown in the 8th century AD at the court of Nara. Buddhist missionaries spread the grapevine around the country – although not necessarily with wine in mind. In 1186, near Mount Fuji, a seedling vinifera vine with thick-skinned grapes was selected and named Koshu. It remains the variety best suited to Japanese conditions: basically a table grape but also making crisp, quite delicate white wine.

By the 17th century Japan's characteristic pergola form of vine training had been invented, one that counteracts, as far as possible, the tendency to rot brought on by summer rain. The disadvantages of this system of vine-growing is that the spreading plant, its roots constantly watered, even in shallow soil, produces a huge crop of watery grapes. Sugar levels are so low that the law allows the addition of sugar up to an amazing 260g/l. Extract is also low: the wine tastes at best mild, at worst downright watery. Japan's best vinifera vines dedicated to wine production – albeit representing hardly more than 2,500 (1,000) of her vineyard total of 54,000 acres (22,000ha) – are now grown more conventionally.

A wine industry, in the modern sense, has nonetheless existed for 100 years. Japan's first outward-looking government sent researchers to Europe in the 1870s to study methods and to bring back vines. It soon became clear that American vines did better than French or German. Nor were the Japanese averse to the "foxy" flavour of eastern American grapes. Delaware has become the most planted variety, hybrids accounting for about 80% of Japan's vineyard. Neo Muscat, a crossing of Koshu Sanjaku and Muscat of Alexandria, is the only widely planted vinifera vine apart from Koshu.

The wine industry was based from the start in the hills around the Kōfu Basin in Yamanashi prefecture – within view of Mount Fuji and convenient for the capital. More than half of Japan's 130-odd genuine wineries (as opposed to blending and bottling plants or production centres for rice-based sake) are here. Japan is an enthusiastic importer of bulk wine and grape must, though imported content must now be specified on labels.

Up to the 1960s many small firms in Yamanashi made wine as sweet as possible for an unsophisticated market. Today the Japanese wine market is dominated by Mercian and Suntory (which has wine holdings elsewhere, notably the Bordeaux classed-growth Château Lagrange). Both now have supplies of the best European grape varieties, from some of the world's most manicured vines. In general Cabernet, Merlot, and Chardonnay are correct, if a trifle faint in comparison with the bumptious simplicity of local Koshu.

Nearby Nagano grows some of the finest Japanese wine but, like Fukushima prefecture to the east, source of Manns' admired Chardonnay, its total vineyard area is small. (Rainfall diminishes as you go east, while Yamanashi has the highest average temperatures and earliest budbreak, flowering, and vintage.)

Hokkaido, the northernmost island, is, on the other hand, an important grape grower in terms of quantity, while Hyogo around Kōbe and Yamagata in the northwest of Honshu may each grow fewer than 500 acres (200ha) of European varieties but some of their wines already show promise.

The two faces of Japanese wine: *the well-established Koshu grape made by Grace with grace, and a faithful copy of a European classic made from imported vines.*

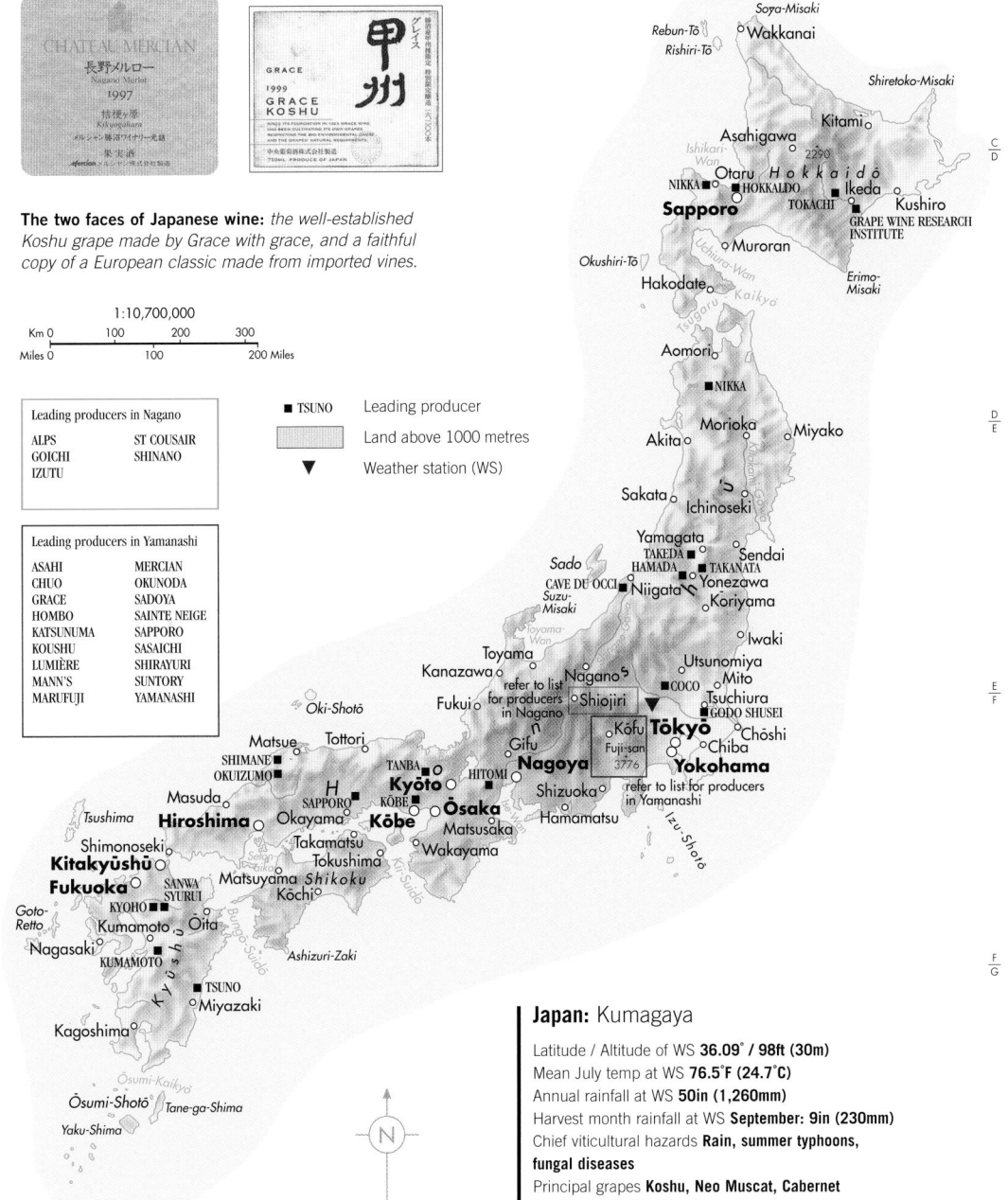

1:10,700,000

Km 0   100   200   300
Miles 0   100   200 Miles

Leading producers in Nagano

ALPS	ST COUSAIR
GOICHI	SHINANO
IZUTU	

Leading producers in Yamanashi

ASAHI	MERCIAN
CHUO	OKUNODA
GRACE	SADOYA
HOMBO	SAINTE NEIGE
KATSUNUMA	SAPPORO
KOUSHU	SASAICHI
LUMIÈRE	SHIRAYURI
MANN'S	SUNTORY
MARUFUJI	YAMANASHI

■ TSUNO   Leading producer

▦ Land above 1000 metres

▼ Weather station (WS)

Japan: Kumagaya

Latitude / Altitude of WS **36.09˚ / 98ft (30m)**
Mean July temp at WS **76.5˚F (24.7˚C)**
Annual rainfall at WS **50in (1,260mm)**
Harvest month rainfall at WS **September: 9in (230mm)**
Chief viticultural hazards **Rain, summer typhoons, fungal diseases**
Principal grapes **Koshu, Neo Muscat, Cabernet Sauvignon, Merlot, Chardonnay**

England and Wales

Above Denbies Estate on the North Downs near Dorking is a classic example of English wine's habit of combining wine production with a fully fledged tourist attraction.

English wine is not a joke. But it can be quite difficult to ripen a commercial quantity of grapes this far from the equator, as vignerons in Ireland, Belgium, Holland, and Denmark know too. For some time it was thought that England lies too far north for grapes to ripen – and besides, there is too much rain. The fact remains, however, that in the early Middle Ages the monastic vineyards of England were extensive and by all accounts successful. Had it not been for England's acquisition of Bordeaux (by the marriage of Henry II to Eleanor of Aquitaine in 1152), they would probably have continued without a break. But they faded away in the later Middle Ages, and after that only spasmodic attempts at winegrowing in England and Wales were made until the 1950s, when the renaissance began at Hambledon in Hampshire.

Now England and Wales have such confidence that some 2,150 acres (870ha) of vineyard are scattered widely over the southern half of the country, with the greatest concentration in the southeast – the counties of Kent, East and West Sussex, and Surrey – but also a large number of smaller vineyards (there are more than 370 in total) across the south to the West Country, along the Thames and Severn valleys, and in East Anglia, the driest part of England. The largest vineyard is Denbies, in Surrey, with 265 acres (107ha) – very much an exception in an industry where the average is just under 5.8 acres or 2.5ha. Well over 100 wineries now process the crop, which was as much as 3.5 million bottles in 1996 and averages around 2.5 million bottles per year. (Fruit set and summer temperatures are both extremely variable.)

The great majority of wine is white and, like the original model German wine, is becoming progressively drier. Müller-Thurgau, Seyval Blanc, and Reichensteiner are the three most popular vine varieties. German crossings, particularly Bacchus, Schönburger, and Huxelrebe, have also been widely planted. Madeleine x Angevine 7672 – a variety unique to the UK, bred by Georg Scheu in Germany in the 1930s – is also successful in blends, which most wines are. Early ripening red varieties such as Dornfelder and the more recently bred Rondo are increasingly planted, and the overall quality of red wines has improved markedly over the last few years. Bottle-fermented sparkling wines – some based on Chardonnay and Pinot Noir – are perhaps England's strongest suit and the best match champagne selling at the same price.

The wine normally needs chaptalization, as it does in Germany and often in Bordeaux and Burgundy. But overall quality has improved from a tentative start so that some experienced winemakers can make good white and red wines almost every year. Imports can (easily) be cheaper, but the wines being made in England and Wales today have their own uniquely crisp, aromatic, lively style – and can age better than many a fuller white.

English wine, a term loosely applied to Wales's fresh ferments too, is quite distinct from British wine, the name confusingly given to fermented, reconstituted grape concentrate imported into Britain, generally from wherever can supply the concentrate at the lowest price.

Nyetimber is made by Americans with French help but there are other fine sparkling wines which depend more thoroughly on British expertise. Hybrids such as the highly successful Seyval Blanc have to be labelled Regional rather than Quality Wine in Europe.

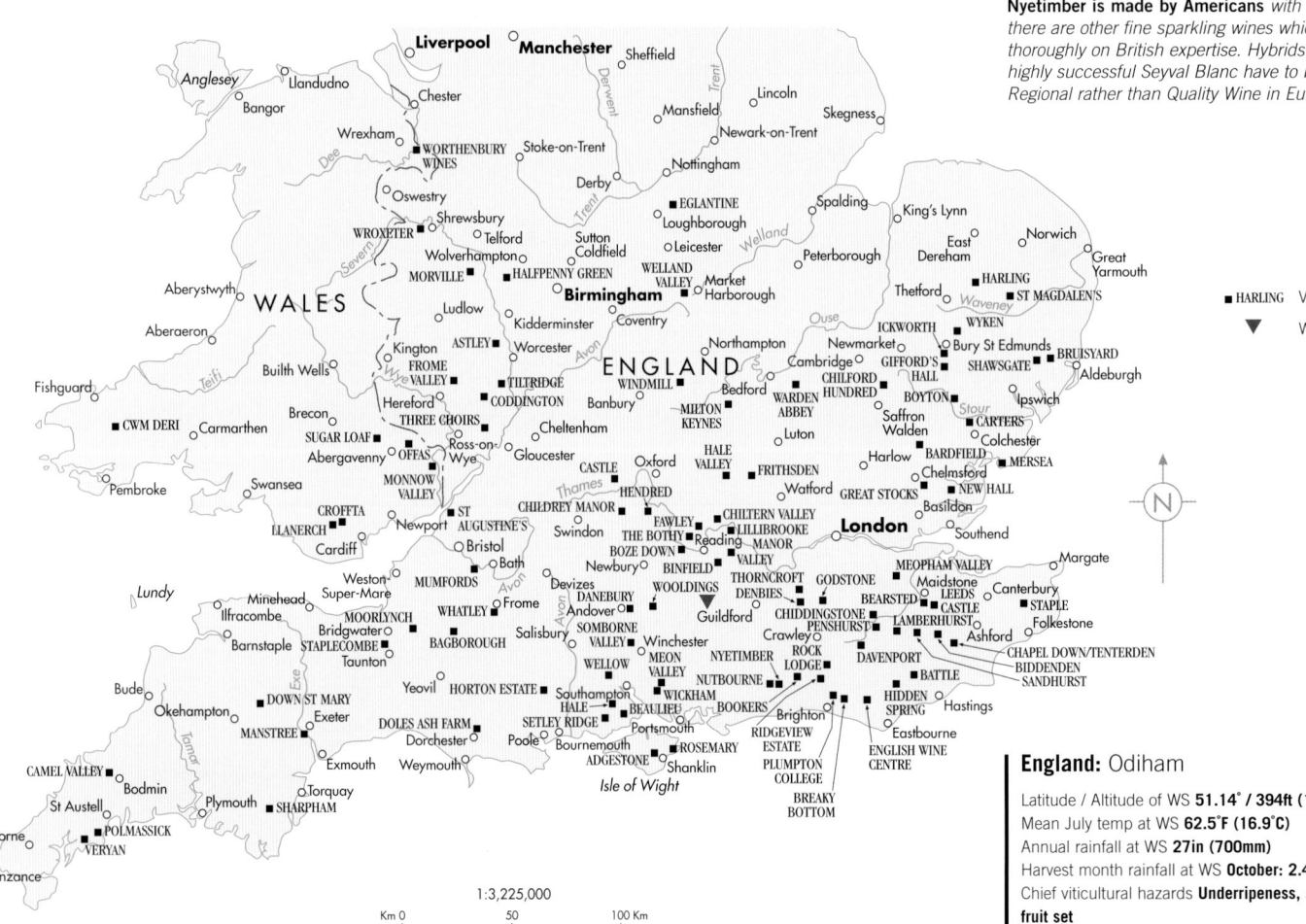

1:3,225,000

- ■ HARLING Vineyard
- ▼ Weather station (WS)

England: Odiham

Latitude / Altitude of WS **51.14° / 394ft (120m)**
Mean July temp at WS **62.5°F (16.9°C)**
Annual rainfall at WS **27in (700mm)**
Harvest month rainfall at WS **October: 2.4in (60mm)**
Chief viticultural hazards **Underripeness, autumn rain, uneven fruit set**
Principal grapes **Müller-Thurgau, Seyval Blanc, Reichensteiner**

Glossary

The aim of this list is to give you an insight into the most commonly used wine jargon. Terms used only in one region are explained in the relevant part of the Atlas. There are more French terms here than, say, Italian or Spanish, because they have been more widely adopted – and occasionally adapted. See also the Language of the Label boxes and the list of Common Tasting Terms that follows. Cross-references to other entries in the Glossary and Common Tasting Terms are denoted by italics.

acid vital component of wine and one that gives it zip and refreshment value. Most common wine acids are tartaric acid, malic acid, and to a lesser extent lactic acid.

acidify add *acid* to wine or *must* to improve its *balance*.

acidity total measure of *acids*.

Amarone style of wine made from dried grapes, originally from the Veneto.

appellation controlled, geographical wine name.

BA commonly used abbreviation for Beerenauslese, sweet German wine. See page 214.

bacterial diseases diseases (of the vine) spread by bacteria.

barrel any container for liquids made from wood although usually a *barrique* or *pièce*.

barrel ageing, barrel maturation process of maturing wine for months in *barrels* after *fermentation*.

barrel fermentation popular winemaking technique whereby the alcoholic *fermentation* takes place in *barrels*. Such wines (usually white) are said to be **barrel fermented**.

barrica, barrique standard Bordeaux *barrel* with a capacity of 225 litres.

base wines ingredients in a blend.

bâtonnage French for *lees stirring*, from *bâton*, French for stick.

blush wine very pale pink wine made from extremely short contact with red, black or purple grape skins.

bodega Spanish word for cellar or winemaking enterprise.

botrytis (Botrytis cinerea) generic term for *fungal diseases* of the vine known colloquially as rot. The benevolent form, noble rot, infects the grapes with a mould which concentrates the sugar and acidity in grapes, resulting in potentially magnificent, long-lived, very sweet **botrytized** wines. The malevolent form, grey rot, infects the grapes with mould which spoils flavour and, in dark-skinned grapes, destroys colour too.

bottle standard unit of wine volume containing 75cl.

bottle ageing, bottle maturation process of maturing wine in *bottle* (cf *barrel ageing*). Such a wine is said to have **bottle age**.

bottle deposit insoluble deposit that sticks to the inside of a bottle after *bottle ageing* (cf *sediment*).

bottling information generally mandatory on wine labels. See *château bottled, domaine bottled, estate bottled*.

calcareous one of the most used, and misused, descriptions of vineyard soils. Calcareous soils are based on limestone (prized in Burgundy) and occasionally include chalk (prized in Champagne).

canopy the green bits of a vine: shoots and, especially, leaves.

canopy management fashionable vine-growing technique whereby the position and density of the *canopy* is deliberately managed so as to maximize wine quality and optimize wine quantity.

capsule alternative word for *foil*.

carbonic maceration winemaking technique whereby grapes are fermented whole in a sealed container under the influence of carbon dioxide. See page 35 for more.

case standard container of 12 wine *bottles*, 24 halves, or 6 *magnums*. Smartest in wood, more often made of cardboard.

causses local term for southwest France's calcareous tableland.

CB common abbreviation for *château bottled*.

chai French, particularly Bordeaux, word for the building in which wine is stored, usually in *barrel*.

chaptalization winemaking process named after French agriculture minister Chaptal whereby the alcohol level of the resulting wine is boosted by sugar added before or during *fermentation*. Such a wine is said to have been **chaptalized**.

Château loose French (especially Bordeaux) term for a property on which wine is grown and, usually, made. Its vineyards are not necessarily a single, contiguous plot.

château bottled wine bottled at the same property where it was grown, or at least made.

classed-growth English for *cru classé*.

climat Burgundian word for an individual vineyard or *appellation*.

clone of a vine, plant specially selected for some particular attribute.

Clos French (particularly Burgundian) term for a specific, walled vineyard. Also used by pioneers in Priorat, Spain.

close spacing vine-growing technique dedicated to high *vine density*.

concentration winemaking process whereby some water is eliminated from the *must* before *fermentation*, thereby making more **concentrated** wine. To produce *balanced* wine, the must has to be balanced before concentration.

coulure vine-growing phenomenon whereby a significant proportion of the potential fruit fails to set when the vine flowers in early summer, usually due to unsettled weather. The effect is reduced *yield*.

cru French word meaning literally growth, but in wine terms generally a specific vineyard.

cru classé a generally Bordeaux term for a vineyard included in one of the region's important classifications, most often but not necessarily the 1855 Classification of the Médoc and Graves (see page 82) which divided the top properties into five divisions. Thus first-, second-, third-, fourth- and fifth-growths.

crush New World term for the annual grape harvest and business of winemaking.

custom crush facility winery making wines to order for a number of different vine-growers. Particularly common in California.

cuve French for vat or tank.

cuvée widely used, originally French term for a blend, used particularly for the final blend in sparkling winemaking.

cuvier French, particularly Bordeaux, term for the building where *fermentation* takes place where *cuves* are to be found.

deacidify winemaking process undertaken only in relatively cool climates whereby the *acidity* of a wine or *must* is deliberately reduced, usually by adding chalk or occasionally water.

diurnal temperature variation difference in average day and night temperatures. High variation is thought to result in deep colours and firm *acidity*.

Domaine French (particularly Burgundian) term for a wine-producing property.

domaine bottled wine bottled by the same person or enterprise as grew it.

dosage amount of sweetening added to a sparkling wine before bottling.

Eiswein sweet wine made from grapes frozen on the vine, a German and occasionally Austrian speciality.

élevage the winemaking process of "raising" a wine from *fermentation* to release.

enology US spelling of *oenology*

en primeur offer of a wine for sale before it is even bottled, most common in Bordeaux, generally in the spring following the *vintage*.

esca debilitating *fungal disease* that weakens vines.

estate bottled wine bottled at the estate on which it was grown.

fermentation generally synonymous with the alcoholic fermentation during which *yeast* act on the sugars in ripe grapes to transform sweet grape juice into much drier wine. See also *malolactic fermentation*.

field grafting vine-growing operation of *grafting* another, more desirable variety onto an existing root system in the vineyard.

filtration controversial winemaking operation designed to filter out any potentially harmful yeast or bacteria.

fining winemaking operation designed to clarify the wine by adding a **fining agent** such as albumen, casein or diatomaceous earth which attracts solids in suspension in the wine and precipitates them as sediment.

first-growth see *cru classé*.

flor *yeast* that forms a thick film on the surface of a wine. Vital to the production of lighter sherries and *vin jaune*.

foil the (largely superfluous) covering of the top of a *bottle* neck and cork. Useful for identification in bottle racks.

fortified wine wine made extra strong by spirit added at some point during the production process. Some of the best known are port, sherry, and madeira.

fungal diseases diseases spread by fungal infections, to which the vine is particularly prone.

futures wines sold *en primeur*.

garagiste see *microchâteau*.

generic wine named after a region or wine style (eg madeira, hock) rather than a *varietal*, or one which qualifies for an *appellation*.

grafting vine-growing technique whereby one plant, usually a *vinifera* cutting, is **grafted** on to another, usually a *phylloxera*-resistant *rootstock*.

Grand Cru widely used term which in Burgundy is designed to denote the very finest vineyards of the Côte d'Or and Chablis, as it is in Champagne and Alsace.

gris very pale *rosé*, same as *blush wine*.

hang time American expression for the (often additional) time grapes are allowed to stay on the vine in order to achieve full *physiological ripeness*.

hybrid vine variety bred by crossing one species (often *vinifera*) with another (often American). Hybrids are frowned on within Europe, sometimes unfairly.

jeroboam large bottle size containing 4.5 litres or the equivalent of six standard *bottles* in Bordeaux; 3 litres or four bottles in Champagne.

Keller German term for cellar.

lay down to deliberately give a wine *bottle ageing*, usually for some years.

late harvest style of wine, generally sweet, made from very ripe grapes.

lees the deposit left in the bottom of a vat, tank or *barrel*. The initial, considerable deposit after the first *fermentation* is known as the **gross lees**.

lees stirring winemaking operation of stirring up the *lees* to encourage aeration and interaction between them and the wine.

maceration carbonique French for *carbonic maceration*.

magnum large bottle size containing 1.5 litres or two standard *bottles*.

malolactic fermentation softening winemaking process which follows alcoholic *fermentation* in virtually all red wines and many whites whereby harsh malic (appley) *acid* is converted into softer lactic (milky) acid under the influence of lactic bacteria and heat. Often known simply as the **malolactic**, or just **malo**.

mesoclimate the climate of a small patch of land such as a vineyard (cf **microclimate** of a single vine, or **macroclimate** of a district or region).

méthode traditionnelle, méthode classique see *traditional method*.

microchâteau very small Bordeaux *château*, often without its own winemaking facilities; a garage is popularly imagined to suffice. In this book we have defined microchâteaux as producing no more than 1,000 cases, at least initially. See pages 106-110.

mildew downy mildew (peronospera) and powdery mildew (oidium) are two *fungal diseases* which persistently plague the vine and vinegrower. Spraying is the usual treatment.

millerandage uneven setting of fruit during flowering which can result in inconveniently uneven ripening.

mise the bottling process in French. **Mis(e) en**

bouteille au Château/Domaine means *château/domaine bottled*.

must the interim, pulpy stage between grape juice and wine during winemaking.

négociant French term for a merchant bottler (cf *domaine*).

noble rot see *botrytis*.

non-vintage used particularly for sparkling wines and champagne to denote a wine that is not vintage-dated but is a blend of the produce of different vintages. A common abbreviation is **NV**.

oaked used of wines subjected in some way to the influence of oak, whether full-scale *barrel maturation* or, much cheaper, some contact with oak chips, inner staves or the like. See page 36.

oenology see *vinification*.

old vines thought to imbue concentration and quality in a wine because *yields* are low.

owc common abbreviation in auction catalogues for original wooden *cases*.

pH important winemaking measure in juice and wine of the strength of *acidity* which can also affect colour and ageing potential. Water has a pH of 7, wine is usually about 3.5.

phenolics general term for the potentially astringent *tannins*, pigments, and flavour compounds in a grape or wine. In grapes they are concentrated in the skins.

physiological ripeness fashionable term for the stage reached by a grape when it is so ripe the skin starts to shrivel, the stem is brown rather than green and a grape can easily be pulled off the bunch.

phylloxera deadly vine pest of American origin, an aphid that feasts off vine roots. Its prevalence has made *grafting* on to resistant *rootstocks* essential in most wine regions. See pages 18-19.

pièce traditional Burgundy *barrel* holding 228 litres.

Pierce's disease fatal vine disease spread by insects, especially in the southern states of the USA and increasingly in California. See page 19.

Premier Cru widely used term which in Burgundy and Champagne denotes some of the best vineyards (though not as good as *Grand Cru*). In Bordeaux, a *first-growth* may be known as a **Premier Grand Cru (Classé)**.

punt indentation in the base of most bottles, useful for stacking

racking transferring wine off the *lees* from one container to another. See pages 31 and 37.

raisin dried grape, out of which a wide range of wines are made including *Amarone* and *Vin Santo*. Grapes may be said to be **raisined**, or to raisin on the vine.

remuage French for *riddling*.

Reserve much-used term which generally has very little meaning.

residual sugar one of wine's vital statistics, the amount of unfermented sugar remaining in the wine. A wine with an **RS** (common abbreviation) of 2g/l or less tastes dry.

reverse osmosis common *concentration* technique used in winemaking.

riddling sparkling winemaking operation whereby the *sediment* deposited by the second *fermentation* in *bottle* has to be shaken into the bottle neck for removal. It is increasingly mechanized today.

rootstock vine root specially chosen for some attribute, typically resistance to *phylloxera* although it may also offer aptitudes for particular soil types or may help to devigorate particularly *vigorous* vine varieties.

rosé common name for wine made pink by brief contact with red, black or purple grape skins.

rot see *botrytis* for details of this *fungal disease*.

saignée French term for bleeding, literally bleeding off some liquid from the fermentation vat to make the resultant wine more *concentrated*.

sediment the detritus of *bottle ageing*, particularly significant if the wine was not *filtered* or *fined* too heavily and the wine has been matured for some years.

settling allowing juice to stand (usually overnight) so that the bigger solids fall to the bottom of the **settling tank**.

sommelier wine waiter.

stirring see *lees stirring*.

sur lie French for a wine kept deliberately in contact with the *lees* in order to add flavour.

TA *total acidity*.

tannins cheek-drying *phenolics* from grape skins, stalks, and pips which preserve it and contribute to the ageing process.

TBA common abbreviation for Trockenbeerenauslese, German term for very sweet wine made from individually picked *botrytized* grapes.

terroir physical environment. See page 22.

tight spacing high *vine density*.

tirage process of leaving a bottle-fermented sparkling wine on the yeast *sediment* to mature it by encouraging yeast *autolysis*.

top grafting *grafting* over a mature vine from one variety to another in the vineyard.

total acidity the sum of all the many sorts of *acid* in a wine. One of wine's vital statistics.

traditional method sparkling winemaking operation whereby the bubbles are formed through the second *fermentation* taking place in *bottle*.

ullage head space between a liquid and its container, whether a *bottle* or *barrel*. As wines age, ullage tends to increase.

varietal wine sold under the name of the grape variety from which it was made (cf *generic*, for example). Not to be confused with the **variety** itself which is a plant.

vendange tardive French for *late harvest*.

vieilles vignes French for *old vines*.

vigneron French for vine-grower.

vigour vine's propensity to grow leaves or *canopy*. A **vigorous** vine may be too leafy to ripen grapes properly.

vin de cépage French for *varietal* wine.

vin de garde French for a wine to be aged.

vin de paille sweet dried grape wine traditionally made by drying grapes on straw mats.

Vin Doux Naturel sweet, strong wine made by adding spirit to grape juice before it has fully fermented. See page 142.

vine density measure of how closely vines are planted.

vine pull deliberate and often subsidized programme of pulling up vines, usually because of a national wine surplus.

vinifera European species of the grapevine genus *Vitis* responsible for well over 95% of all wine, wherever it is grown (cf *hybrid*).

vinification science and practice of making wine.

Vin Santo dried grape wine speciality of Tuscany.

vintage either the process of harvesting grapes or the year in which the grapes were harvested. All wine is therefore "vintage wine".

vintner originally someone who **vinted**, or made wine but now more usually someone who sells it.

viticulture science and practice of growing vines.

white how wines that are not red or pink are described, although in practice they vary from colourless to deep gold.

yield measure of how productive a vineyard is, usually in tonnes per acre or hectolitre per hectare. Multiply the former by about 17.5 to convert to the latter.

Common Tasting Terms

Some of the most helpful and measurable of the great many words used by tasters to describe a wine or tasting are listed below, in particular those which describe a wine's structure, components (acidity, sweetness, alcohol, tannin), and common faults. When describing a wine's flavour, on the other hand, words tend to be borrowed from other, similar-tasting or similar-smelling things because there is no objective wine tasting vocabulary for flavours. The smell of Muscat, for example, is often described as grapey (one of very few wines to smell thus). Cabernet Sauvignon flavour is conventionally described as blackcurrant if ripe, green pepper if unripe. But wine tasting is a thoroughly subjective experience and different tasters will experience different sensations. Many play the free-association game and jot down "rubber", "bubble gum", "wet wool", etc. Best to keep your mind and options open.

acetic wine that has gone irredeemably sour through contact with the air; smells of acetic acid, or vinegar.

aroma the primary grape-and-ferment smell of young wine.

astringent noticeably tannic, used generally for white wine.

autolysis enriching, bready flavour effect of ageing a sparkling wine in *bottle* on yeast *sediment*.

baked unappetizing flavour resulting from grapes or *bottle* getting too hot.

balance one of the key indicators of quality: all components in balance with each other.

blind tasting without knowing the identity of the wine(s).

body the "volume" of a wine, how unlike water it is; partly due to alcoholic strength. Body can range from light through medium to full.

bouquet the complex smell of a mature wine (cf *aroma*).

clean free from defects, fresh.

cloudy something is wrong; all wine should be bright.

complex scents-within-scents; suggestions of many different layers of minerals, fruits, flowers....

corked, corky wine that smells mouldy, usually but not always because the cork was tainted.

crisp attractively, refreshingly acidic.

dry the opposite of sweet, although an old wine in which the fruit is waning may be described as "drying out".

dumb not smelling of much (because too young or too cold).

finish aftertaste, like *balance*, a great indicator of quality; the more persistent the better.

firm attractively *tannic*.

flabby one of the tasting's more lampoonable terms meaning unappetizingly low in *acidity*.

flight series of related wines in a tasting.

foxy high-toned smell of native American grapes such as labrusca; think grape jelly.

full-bodied see *body*.

green common if imprecise term used for noticeable *acidity* or *tannins*.

hard uncomfortably *tannic*.

heady high in alcohol.

hot too high in alcohol.

horizontal tasting of different wines but the same *vintage*.

hydrogen sulphide see *mercaptan*.

lifted see *volatile*.

long what the *finish* should be.

maderized brown or going brown because of the effect of oxygen; on the way to *oxidized*.

mercaptan compound that smells of bad eggs or warm rubber, associated with *reduced* wines.

mouthfeel relatively new word for the (ideally flattering) tactile impact of a wine on the palate.

nose "smell", used as both verb and noun.

oaky excessive flavour derived from new *barrels*, inner staves or oak chips

oxidized wine that has gone flat-tasting and brown because of excessive exposure to oxygen.

pétillant very slightly sparkling.

rancio heady smell of fortified wine (or spirits) aged for years in wood or glass, often in high temperatures.

reduced starved of oxygen and smelling of *mercaptan*. Common in warm climate Syrah/Shiraz. Slight reduction can be rescued by aeration.

sappy translation of the French *sève*: the lively, forthright style of a fine young wine.

short what the *finish* should not be.

silky accurate word for a certain texture.

spittoon whatever is spat into; essential professional tasting equipment.

spritzig German for *pétillant*.

stalky green-wood flavour associated with an underripe vintage or too high a proportion of underripe stalks in the must.

sulphury the hot, throat-tickling smell associated with excessive use of the preservative sulphur dioxide. Used to be common in cheap young, slightly sweet whites.

tart too *acid* (cf *crisp*).

tannic uncomfortably high in *tannin* to be enjoyable now, but may be a good sign in a young wine designed for a long life.

vertical tasting of different *vintages* of the same wine.

volatile wine that is on the way to being *acetic*. Although technically a fault, a certain amount of volatile *acidity* can "lift" the *bouquet* of full-bodied reds quite excitingly. Such a bouquet is said to be "lifted".

Index

Châteaux, domaines, etc appear under their individual name. Main treatments are indicated in **bold**, page numbers in *italic* relate to illustration captions.

Gazetteer

This gazetteer includes place name references of vineyards, châteaux, general wine areas and other information appearing on the maps in the Atlas, with the exception of minor place names and geographical features which appear as background information in sans serif type. All châteaux are listed under C (eg château Yquem d') in the gazetteer. Domaines, wineries, etc appear under their individual name. The alphanumeric before the page number refers to the grid reference system on the map pages. Vineyards, etc are indexed under their main name (eg Perrières, les). Identical names are distinguished by either the country or region being indicated in italic type. Alternative names are shown in brackets: Praha (Prague), etc. Wine producers whose names appear on the maps are also listed.

Vale do São Francisco E5 296
Vale Dona Maria, Qta F6 208
Valea Calugăreăsca F4 258
Valea Lui Mihai D2 258
Valea Nucarilor F5 258
Valençay D2 53
Valence E4 130
Valencia F5 186
Valeriano E3 160
Valette E6 71
Valeyrac A3 87
Vall Llach C5 198
Valladolid D3 186, F1 191
Valle Central G3 296
Valle d'Aosta C2 157
Valle de Güímar B4 188
Valle de la Orotava B4 188
Valle de Uco D5 301
Valle Isarco A3 165
Vallée de la Marne C2 79
Vallée de Nouy, la E3 121
Vallée des Vaux C2 77
Vallée du Paradis, la D3 150
Vallejo B2 271, G6 275
Vallerots, les F5 64
Vallerots, les F5 64
Vallet C3 116, F3 117
Valletta E4 163
Valley of the Moon D2 275
Valley View G2 289
Vallone C4 183
Valls B2 197
Valmiñor D4 189
Valmur D4 77
Valozières, les F4 63
Valpaços B6 201
Valpantena D3 165
Valparaiso F3 297
Valpolicella D3 165, F3 169
Valpolicella Classico D2 165, F2 169
Valpolicella Valpantena F3 169
Valréas C3 135
Vals d'Agly D3, E2 150
Valtellina B6 157, B1 165
Valtellina F4 177
Valtellina Superiore B6 157, B1 165
Valtice G3 252
Valtravieso E3 191
Vancouver C3, E5 289, A5 293
Vancouver Island E4 289
Vár E2 251
Varades B3 116
Varese C4 157
Vargas, Marqués de B2 193
Vargellas, Qta de G4 209
Vár-hegy E2, E3 251
Varna B5, B6 257
Varogne, la F4 133
Varoilles, les D3 67
Varrains F3 119
Vasa G2 266
Vasse Felix C5 314
Vau de Vey D1 77
Vau Ragons D2 77
Vau, Qta do E1 209
Vauchrétien F5 118
Vaucoupin E6 77
Vaucrains, les F5 64
Vaud C2 239, E4 240
Vaudemanges C6 81
Vaudésir C4 77
Vaufegé E3 121
Vaugiraut E4 77
Vaulorent C4 77
Vaumuriens-Bas, les E5 61
Vaumuriens-Hauts, les E5 61
Vaunage, la B5 150
Vaupulent C3 77
Vaussier E1 146
Vaut, en E5 61
Vaux Dessus, les F2 59
Vaux, la E5 240
Vauxrenard B4 73
Vavasour G5 318
Vavatsinia F3 266
Vayres E4 83
Vayssette, Dom de B5 113
Veaugues C3 123
Vecchie Terre di Montefili D3 177
Veenwouden A4 323
Vega Sicilia F2 191
Vel'kŝ Krtiŝ G4 252
Velette, la E4 181
Velha, Qta G1 208
Veliko Turnovo B4 257
Vélines B4 115
Velké Pavlovice F3, G3 252
Velké Zernoseky E2 252
Vellé, au E4 67
Velle, sur la F3 61
Velvendos B2 263
Venâncio da Costa Lima E5 203
Vendôme A2 117
Vendrell, El C3 197
Venézia D4 165, G2 170
Venica B5 171
Venoge/Boizel, de 78
Ventana F4 281
Ventozelo, Qta de F6 208
Veracruz G5 286
Veramonte G4 297
Verano, el D2 275
Vérargues B3 139
Vercelli D3 157
Verchère, la B6 60
Verchers-sur-Layon, les C5 116
Vercots, les F3 63
Verdicchio dei Castelli di Jesi C5 173
Verdicchio di Matelica D5 173
Verdigny B3 123
Verdon G6 151
Verdots, Clos des B6 115
Verdun E2 323
Verduno B3 163
Verduno Pelaverga E3 157
Vérenay B5 131
Vergelegen F3 323
Vergelesses, les E2 63
Vergennes, les F5 63
Vergenoegd F1 323
Verger, Clos de F6 61, E1 62
Vergers, les F2 60
Vergisson F5 55, F3 70, A3 71
Vergne E3 163
Vérin D2 131
Veritas C2 308
Verlieux E2 131
Vermarain á l'Est, Bas de D3 60
Vermarain á l'Ouest, Bas de D3 60
Vermentino di Gallura A5 185
Vernaccia di Oristano C4 185
Vernaccia di San Gimignano B3 173
Vernonia C2 289
Vernou-sur-Brenne E5 121
Véroilles, les E5 66
Verona, *Italy* D3 165, G3 169
Verona, *New South Wales* C4 304
Vérottes, les G3 62
Verpelét B4 249
Verquiere, Dom de C5 137
Verroilles ou Richebourgs, les F4 65
Versailles, Dom de B3 113
Verseuil, en F4 61
Verthamon A2 101
Vertheuil G4 87, E2 89
Vertou C2 116, F2 117
Vertus G3 81
Veryan G1 326
Verzé E5 55, D4 70
Verzenay B5 81
Verzy B5 81
Vesúvio, Qta do G4 209
Vétroz F1 241
Vetrun C2 257
Veuve Clicquot Ponsardin 78
Vevey E5 240
Vezzano C2 166
VI.C.OR. E4 181
Viana A2 193
Viana do Alentejo F4 206
Viansa F3 275
Vibo Valéntia G4 182
Vicairies B4 123
Vicenza D3 165
Vicomté d'Aumelas, la C4 150
Victor Verster C5 323
Vidal Estate G5 319
Vide Bourse G3 60
Vidigueira F4 206
Vidin A1 257
Vie di Romans D4 171
Vieille Julienne, la E2 137
Vienne A4 130
Vierzon B3 117
Vieux Chêne, Dom du C4 143
Vieux Cussac D5 95
Vieux Donjon, le F2 137
Vieux-Thann G3 125
Vigna Rionda F6 163
Vignamaggio D4 177
Vignavecchia E4 177
Vigne au Saint, la E3 63
Vigne aux Loups A3 123
Vigne Blanche G5 59
Vigne Derrière F6 59
Vigne Derrière F1 60
Vigne di Zamò, le B4 171
Vigneau, Clos du D1 120
Vignerais, aux B4 71
Vignerondes, aux F3 65
Vignerons de Beaupuy, les A2 113
Vignerons de Buzet, les B2 113
Vignerons de Maury, les C3 143
Vignerons de Saumur, Caves des F3 119
Vignerons de Tursan, les D1 113
Vignes aux Gds, les E5 67
Vignes Belles F2 67
Vignes Blanches, les, Meursault G3 61
Vignes Blanches, les, Pouilly-Fuissé C4 71
Vignes Dessus, aux A3 71
Vignes Franches, les F2 62
Vignes Rondes, les E3 61
Vigness Moingeon D3 60
Vigneux F4 65
Vignobles du Rivesaltais, les C4 143
Vignois F5 67
Vignois, aux E5 67
Vignots, les D1 62
Vignottes, les F3 64
Vigo D4 189
Vihiers C4 116
Vila Nova de Gaia B4 201
Vila Real B5 201
Vila Velha, Qta da E1 209
Viladecans B5 197
Vilagarcía de Arousa B4 189
Vilariño-Cambados B4 189
Vila-rodona B2 197
Vilaseca de Solcina C1 197
Vilella Alta, la C4 198
Vilella Baixa, la C4 198
Villa, la F5 163
Villa Bel Air D2, D4 98
Villa Cafaggio D3 177
Villa Helena C3 279
Villa la Selva G6 177
Villa Maria F3 318
Villa Matilda D2 182
Villa Russiz C5 171
Villabuena de Álava A6 192, G5 193
Villafranca del Penedès D5 186, B3 197
Village, *Gevrey-Chambertin* F3 67
Village, *Meursault* G6 61, F1 62
Village, *Nuits-St-Georges* F4 65
Village, le, *Beaune* D4 63
Village, le, *Gevrey-Chambertin* F5 66
Village, le, *Meursault* D2 60
Village, le, *Nuits-St-Georges* F6 65
Village, le, *Santenay* F2 59
Village Bas, le A1 61
Village Haut, le A1 61
Villaine, A et P de A5 69
Villamediana de Iregua B2 193
Villanova i la Geltrú C4 197
Villány D3 249
Villard G4 297
Villatte, la D2 120
Ville-Dommange A2 81
Villefranche-sur-Saône G5 55, E5 73
Villemajou, Dom de D3 141
Villenave-d'Ornon F3 83, D5 101
Villeneuve, *Châteauneuf-du-Pape* E2 137
Villeneuve, *Switzerland* E5 240
Villeneuve-sur-Lot A3 113
Villero E5 163
Villers Allerand B3 81
Villers-Aux-Núuds A3 81
Villers-Marmery C6 81
Villette E4 240
Villié-Morgon C4 73, D4 74
Villiera C2 323
Villingen F3 235
Villy A2 77
Viña Tondonia F3 193
Viña Winery, la E3 286
Vinag D4 253
Viñas del Vero D4 195
Vincent Girardin A5 69
Vincent Pinard, Dom C3 123
Vin de Corse D4 147
Vin de Corse-Calvi C3 147
Vin de Corse-Coteaux du Cap Corse C4 147
Vin de Corse-Figari E3 147
Vin de Corse-Porto-Vecchio E4 147
Vine Cliff D5 279
Viñedos de Aldeabuena C4 193
Viñedos del Contino A1 193
Vineland Estates G4 295
Vinex Preslav B5 257
Vineyard 29 C3 279
Vinho Verde B5 201
Vinhos, JP E5 203, E4 206
Vini Sliven C4 257
Vinicola del Priorat C4 198
Vinifera Wine Cellars F2 294
Viniprom Rousse A4 257
Vinivel-Ivailovgrad D4 257
Vino Nobile di Montepulciano C3 173
Vinon C4 123
Vinos de Madrid E3 186
Vinos Piñol C4 196
Vin Santo B3, C3 173
Vins de Lavilledieu F2 53
Vins de l'Orléanais C3 53
Vins de Moselle B5 53
Vins d'Entraygues et du Fel F3 53
Vins d'Estaing F3 53
Vins du Bugey E5 53
Vins du Thouarsais D1 53
Vinsobres C4 135
Vinzel E2 240
Vinzelles F5 55, G4 70, D6 71
Violès D4 137
Violettes F5 65
Vionnaz F5 240
Vionne, la E5 67
Vipava A1 255
Viré E5 55, C5 70
Vireuils Dessous, les E1 61
Vireux, les E1 61
Virgin Hills E3 306
Virginia C5 269
Virginie, Dom B5 141
Viria, la B5 131
Virieu-le-Grand B4 149
Virondot, en F5 59
Visan C3 135
Visette F4 163
Viseu B4 205
Visp F4 241
Visperterminen F4 241
Vistalba B5 301
Vistrenque, la B6 150
Viterbo D3 173
Viticcio D3 177
Vitoria-Gasteiz D4 186
Vittorio Veneto D2 170
Vitusberg C5 229
Viu Manent D4 299
Vivier, le C5 74
Vlorë F4 255
Vlottenberg E2 323
Voegtlinshofen E4 125
Vogelleithen E4 244
Vogelsang, *Nahe* A5 225
Vogelsang, *Rheingau* C3 228
Vogelsang, *Saar* G4 219
Vogelsgärten F5 232
Vogtei Rötteln G2 235
Voillenot Dessous G2 60
Voillenots G2 60
Voipreux G4 81
Voitte G4 60
Vojvodina B5 255
Volano E2 166
Volkach E5 236
Volker Eisele C5 279
Volnay D5 55, F4 61
Von Strasser B2 279
Vongnes C4 149
Vorbourg C2 126
Vorderseiber C1 245
Vösendorf D5 246
Vosgros E4 77
Vöslauer Hauerberg F4 246
Vosne, de F3 65
Vosne, en E4 67
Vosne-Romanée C6 55, F4 65
Vougeot C6 55, F6 65, F3 66
Vougeot, Clos de F5 65, F3 66
Vouni G2 266
Vouvray B1 117, F3 121
Vouvry F5 240
Voyager Estate E5 314
Vráble G4 252
Vranje E5 255
Vranken Demoiselle 78
Vranken Monopole 78
Vratsa B2 257
Vriesenhof E3 323
Vrsac C6 255
Vulkanfelsen F2 235
Vully B2 239
Vŝchodoslovenská G6 252

Wachau C3 242, B1 245
Wachenheim E5 230
Wachenheim an der Weinstrasse D5 231
Wachtberg B5 245
Waiheke Island B5 317
Waiohiki F5 319
Wairau River F3 318
Waldäcker F4 247
Waldrach C4 216, G5 217
Waldulm E3 235
Walensee B5 239
Walkenberg C5 229
Walker Bay F3 321
Walla Walla C6 289, F3 291
Walla Walla Vintners F3 291
Wallcliffe E5 314
Wallhausen B5 224
Walluf C6 229
Walter Filiputti B4 171
Wandin Valley B5 304
Wanganui D5 317
Wangaratta C3 303, D5 306
Waninga E5 309
Warburton F5 306
Warden Abbey E4 326
Wards Gateway Cellar E1 308
Warramate C5 307
Warre 211
Warrenmang E2 306
Warrnambool G1 306
Wartbühl E5 235
Warwick C3 323
Washington A2 269
Washington Hills Cellars E4 290
Washougal C3 289
Wasseros A3, B3 229
Wasson Bros B6 293
Waterbrook F2 291
Waterford E3 323
Watervale F5 309
Water Wheel D3 306
Watzelsdorf B4 242
Wawern C3 219
Wehlen D1 223
Weibel B2 281
Weiden D6 242
Weilberg B4 231
Weinert C5 301
Weinheim C4 235
Weinsberg D5 235
Weinsteige E4 235
Weinviertel C5 242
Weinzierlberg B6 245
Weisenstein F1 223
Weisinger's G3 289
Weiss Erd E3 227
Weissenfels E3 237
Weissenkirchen C3 242, C1 245
Weisserstein D5 246
Weitenberg C1 245
Welgemeend B3 323
Welland E1 294
Welland Valley E3 326
Wellington, *California* C2 275
Wellington, *New Zealand* D5 317, E2 321
Wellow F3 326
Welmoed E2 323
Wemmershoek C5 323
Wendouree E5 309
Wente Bros A3 281
Wermuth B3 279
Westhalten F4 125, B3 126
Westhampton D5 294
Westhofen G5 232
West Linn B5 293
Westover A2 281
Westrey C4 293
West Richland E5 290
West Sacramento B3 285
West Seneca E1 294
West Slope B5 293
Weststeiermark G3 242
West Thracian Valley D3 257
West Virginia C5 269
Wettolsheim E4 125, C6 126
Whaler F3 272
Whangarei B5 317
Whatley F2 326
Whitehall Lane D3 279
Whitehaven F4 318
White Oak D5 273
White Plains G5 294
White Rock E5 279
White Salmon C4 289
Whitfield C3 303
Wickham G3 326
Wiebelsberg E5 128
Wien D5 242, B6 246
Wiener Neustadt E4 242
Wiesbaden D3 215, D5 226
Wiese & Krohn 211
Wiesloch C4 235
Wignalls F6 313
Wild Duck Creek E3 306
Wild Hog E4 273
Wild Horse C4 283
Wild Winds D4 293
Wildendürnbach B5 242
Wilderness C5 304
Wildsau B5 229
Willakenzie Estate B4 293
Willamette D2 289
Willamette Valley F4 289
Willamette Valley Vineyards D4 293
Willespie C5 314
William Fèvre B6 299
William Hill F6 279
Williams & Humbert 200
Williams Selyem E4 273
Williamstown F1 308
Willow Heights F4 295
Willows, The C3 308
Willunga G2 311
Willyabrup C5 314
Wilson E6 309
Wiltingen C4 219
Winden D5 242
Windesheim B5 224
Windmill E3 326
Windsor E5 273
Windwalker B5 285
Wineck-Schlossberg B2 127
Wineglass E3 290
Winery Lake Vineyard E4 275
Winkel D4 226, C3 228
Winterthur A4 239
Wintrich C5 221
Wintzenheim E4 125, C6 126
Winzenberg E4 128
Winzenheim B6 224, A5 225
Wirilda Creek G3 311
Wirra Wirra G2 311
Wisconsin B4 269
Wisdom & Warter 200
Wise A5 314
Wishart E5 319
Wisselbrunnen C1 229
Witchcliffe E5 314
Wither Hills F3 318
Witness Tree C4 293
Wittenheim G4 125
Wittlich B4 216
Wodonga D6 306
Wöhring B5 246
Wolf B3 223
Wolf Blass C3 308
Wolf Creek G2 289
Wölffer C6 294
Wolfieu Goldgrube B3 223
Wolfsmagen B4 235
Wolfsworth G3 247
Wolkersdorf C5 242
Wollongong B5 303
Wolxheim A5 125
Wonthaggi D3 303
Woodbourne F3 318
Woodburn D2 289, C5 293
Woodend D2 303
Woodland A3 285, C3 289
Woodlands C5 314
Woodside, *Adelaide Hills* D6 311
Woodside, *California* B1 281
Woodstock F3 311
Woodward Canyon F2 291
Woody Nook C5 314
Woodings F3 326
Woori Yallock C5 307
Worcester E3 321
Worms G5 232
Worthenbury Wines E2 326
Wösendorf D1 245
Wrattonbully C1 303
Wroxeter E2 326
Wuenheim F3 125
Wülfen B4 229
Wunnenstein D5 235
Württemberg E3 215
Württembergisch Unterland D4 235
Würzburg D3 215, F4 236
Würzgarten, *Bernkastel* B6 222, B3, C3 223
Würzgarten, *Rheingau* B5, A6 228
Wybong B3 305
Wyken E4 326
Wyndham Estate A6 304
Wynns C5 312
Wynns High Eden F3 308

Xanadu E5 314

Yakima B4 289, D2 290
Yakima River F4 290
Yakima Valley F5 289
Yallingup B5 314
Yalumba D3 308
Yamanashi F5 325
Yambol (lambol) C4 257
Yamhill Valley C4 293
Yannick Amirault, Dom C2 120
Yantai Chang Yu Pioneer F5 324
Yarrabank B4 307
Yarra Burn C6 307
Yarra Edge C3 307
Yarra Glen D3 303, B4 307
Yarra Junction D6 307
Yarra Ridge B4 307
Yarra Valley D3 303, F4 306
Yarrawonga C5 306
Yarra Yarra A4 307
Yarra Yering C5 307
Yass B5 303
Ycoden Daute-Isora B4 188
Yecla F4 186
Yellowglen F2 306
Yenne C4 149
Yerasa G3 266
Yerevan D5 261
Yeringberg B4 307
Yering Station B4 307
Yokohama F5 325
Yonder Hill F2 323
Yonkers G5 294
York Mountain C3 283
Yorkvillehighla F3 272
Young B4 303
Youngs B5 285
Youngstown F6 295
Yountville E4 279
Yves de Suremain, Dom C5 69
Yvigne, Clos d' B5 115
Yvorne F5 240

Zaca Mesa F5 283
Zacatecas F4 286
Zaer G2 267
Zagorje-Medimurje A3 255
Zagreb A3 255
Zakynthos (Zante) D1 263
Zalakaros C2 249
Žalhostice E2 252
Zambellimount Anakie Estate F3 306
Zambujal, Qta do F2 208
Zamora D2 186
Zandwijk B4 323
Zapadna Morava D5 255
Zaragoza D4 186
Zaum C5 245
Zayante C2 281
ZD D4 279
Zehnmorgen D5 233
Zeitz F4 237
Zeletin E4 258
Zell B5 216
Zellenberg D4 125
Zema Estate C5 312
Zemmer C4 216
Zemmour G2 267
Zenatta G2 267
Zeni A3 166, G4 167
Zerhoun G2 267
Zeutern C4 235
Zevenwacht D1 323
Zibo F4 324
Ziersdorf C4 242
Zimbro, Qta do E2 209
Zinfadel C3 279
ZinnkoepflÉ B3 126
Zistersdorf C5 242
Zitsa B2 263
Zlaté Moravce G4 252
Z-Moore F5 273
Znojmo F3 252
Zöbing C4 242
Zoete Inval, de B4 323
Zoopiyi F3 266
Zornberg E4 244
Zotzenberg F6 128
Zsadányi D4 251
Zuckerberg F5 233
Zürcher Weinland A4 239
Zürich A4 239
Zürichsee B4 239
Zwerithaler B2 245

Acknowledgements

Introduction *The Ancient World and Middle Ages* Hanneke Wilson; *Wine and Weather and In the Vineyard (& Factfiles)* Dr Richard Smart & John Gwalter; *How Wine is Made* Kym Milne; *Oak* Françoise Barbin-Lecrevisse; *Anatomy of a Winery* Christian & Cherise Moueix; Herzog & de Meuron.

France Jane Boyce; Annie Luchetta, Gérard Meyer, Elodie Pasty & Agnès Payan (INAO); Catharine Mana'ch, Marie Medeville & Chloe Wenban-Smith (Sopexa), Jean-Laurent Maillard (ANIVIT); *Burgundy* Jasper & Abigail Morris; BIVB; *Pouilly-Fuissé* Jean Rijckaert; *Chablis* Rosemary George; *Champagne* Dominique Foulon; Richard Geoffroy; *Bordeaux* James Lawther; Nellie Salvi; Florence Rafford (CIVB); *St-Emilion and Pomerol* Dominique Reynard; Fiona Morrison; Alan Sichel; *Loire Valley* Jacqueline Friedrich; *Rhône Valley* John Livingstone Learmonth; John Gauntley; Brigitte Clusel; *Bandol* John Gauntley; *Savoie* Wink Lorch; *Jura* Jean Rijckaert.

Italy Daniel Thomases; *Barolo* Simona Luparia (Slow Food).

Spain Victor de la Serna; *Priorat* René Barbier; *Jerez* Mauricio Gonzalez Gordon, Marqués de Bonanza; Godfrey Spence.

Portugal Luis Avides (ICEP Portuguese Trade & Tourism Office); Jorge Boehm; *Alto Douro/port*: Dirk Niepoort; Godfrey Spence; Tim Stanley-Clarke; *Madeira*: Patrick Grubb.

Germany Stuart Pigott; Kerry Brady.

Switzerland John C Sloan; Daniel Lehmann; Chandra Kurt.

Austria Thomas Klinger, Dorli Muhr, Caroline Lloyd, Bertold Salomon & Herta Wallner (Austrian Wine Marketing Board).

Hungary *Tokaj* Istvan Turoczi; Peter Vinding-Diers.

Czech Republic and Slovakia Sophia Coudenhove; Zdenek Reimann, Helena Baker.

Slovenia Aleš Kristančič; Erika Schuele-Grosso; Toni Gomiscek.

Croatia and the Balkans Mladen Vukmir; Stane Terlep; Paul Robert Blom.

Bulgaria Annie Kay.

Romania Dan & Roxana Muntean.

Greece Nico Manessis.

The Former Soviet Republics *Crimea* Gia Sulkhanishvili; Paul Robert Blom.

Moldova Alexei Musteasta.

Eastern Mediterranean Adam Montefiore; Mehmet Yalçın; Seyit Karagözoğlu; Janna Gur.

Cyprus Gareth Lawrence.

Tunisia Maurizio Micciche.

Algeria Abdelmadjid Merabet (ONCV).

Egypt David Pollock.

Morocco Noelle Arnault.

USA Thomas Pinney; *California* Bruce Cass; *Napa* Paul Skinner; *Southwest States and Mexico* Shirley Jones; Bruce Cass; *Oregon* Lisa Shara Hall; Rollin Soles; *Washington* Steve Burns (Washington Wine Institute); Lisa Shara Hall; Ron Irvine; *New York, Eastern States*: Richard Leahy; Richard Figiel; James Trezise.

Canada Linda Bramble.

Uruguay Daniel Pisano.

Chile Sue Pike; Jenny Ramage.

Argentina Cecilia Razquin; Dr Nicolas Catena; Jeff Mausbach; Ricardo Puebla.

Australia Hazel Murphy (Wines of Australia); Ernie Sullivan (Australian Wine & Brandy Corp); *Western Australia* Peter Forrestal; *Tasmania* Dr Andrew Pirie.

New Zealand Michael Cooper; *Hawkes Bay* John Hancock; *Marlborough* Allan Scott; Kevin Judd; John Stichbury.

South Africa Dave Johnson.

Asia Denis Gastin; Rupert Dean.

Japan Ronald Brown; Denis Gastin.

England and Wales Julia Trustram Eve.

We would also like to thank the following for their assistance:

Introduction *Wine and Weather and In the Vineyard* James Wolpert; Prof Alex McBratney; *The Winegrower's Year* James Herrick; *Oak* Jérôme François; James Taylor; *Storing Wine* Westbury Communications for Supreme Corqs; *Serving Wine 2* Victoria Morrall for Riedel Crystal.

France *Beaujolais* Bernard Georges; UIVB; Véronique Vallenot (BIVB, Chablis-Auxerrois); *Champagne* Christian Pol Roger; Isabelle Goldstein & Françoise Peretti (The Champagne Information Bureau);

Bordeaux Sue Glasgow (CIVB); Jean-Michel Cazes (Syndicat Agricole et Viticole de Pauillac); *St-Julien* Anthony Barton; *Margaux* Paul Pontallier; Séverine Pinte (Syndicat Viticole Pessac-Léognan); Syndicat Viticole de St-Emilion; Maria Monso (Syndicat Viticole Côtes de Bourg); *The Southwest* Douglas Wregg; *Pays Nantais* Nigel Wilkinson; Benoît Roumet (Bureau Interprofessional des Vins du Centre); *Rhône* Lance Gill; M-A Vinet (Inter Rhône); *Provence* Philippe Bieler; *Jura* Bill Baker; *Corsica* Jane Kay; Marc Robelin; Comité Intersyndical des Vins de Corse; Sylvie Ellul (Syndicat des Producteurs des Vin de Pays d'Oc).

Italy Alessandro Bottaro (Wines of Italy); David Gleave; *Barolo and Barbaresco* Pietro & Renato Ratti; *Tuscany* Maureen Ashley.

Spain John Radford; Carlos Read; Amy Battle, Lisa Grimley & Margarita Pérez (Wines from Spain); *Rioja* Jesus Angel; *Navarra* Mercedes Chivite.

Portugal Geoffrey Kelly; *Estremadura and Setúbal Peninsula* Peter Bright; *Bairrada and Dão* Amaral Bento; *Alto Douro/port* Miguel Potes.

Germany Prinz Michael zu Salm; *Pfalz* Christian von Guradze.

Switzerland Ben Lohrer.

Austria Philippe Blom.

Hungary Stephen Kirkland.

Czech Republic and Slovakia Vladimir Moskvar.

Albania Prof Vangjel Zigori.

Romania Daniel Thomases; David Broadbent; Gina Bullough.

Greece Yiannis Paraskevopoulos.

The Former Soviet Republics *Crimea* Charles Borden; Sophia Coudenhove.

Eastern Mediterranean Serge Hochar; Godfrey Spence.

Cyprus P Mestanas (Cyprus High Commission Trade Centre).

USA Gladys Horiuchi; *California* Bill Nelson; *Southwest States and Mexico* Louise Owens.

Canada Catherine MacMonagle (Wines of Canada).

South Australia Chris Ringland.

New Zealand *Hawkes Bay* Steve Smith MW; Gus Lawson; Gordon Russell; *Marlborough* Ivan Sutherland; Ollie Davidson; Mike Insley; Richard Bowling; Michelle Richardson.

South Africa Kate O'Connor (Wines of South Africa).

Asia Gabriel Tam.

Photographs

AKG, London/British Library 14; Berry Bros & Rudd 16 bottom; Anthony Blake Photo Library/John Sims 158, 162, 164, 174, 183; Art Archive/Egyptian Museum Cairo/Dagli Orti 12; Prof Denis Boubals 19 bottom left; John Brunton 167; Michael Busselle 52, 90, 148; Cephas Picture Library/Kevin Argue 295/Nigel Blythe 37 top left/Andy Christodolo 17, 22 top right, 145, 241, 300, 309/David Copeman 212/Chris Davis 324/Chinch Gryniewicz 188/Kevin Judd 4, 19 top right, 36 bottom right, 303, 316, 319/R & K Muschenetz 236, 282, 298/Alain Proust 2-3, 322/Mick Rock 8, 16 top, 21, 22 bottom left, 34, 35 bottom right, 36 top left, 37 top centre, 37 top right, 50, 68, 72, 75, 79, 80, 82, 88, 92, 96, 100, 102 bottom right, 108, 114, 122, 129, 132-133, 134, 136, 140, 178, 184, 187, 190-191, 192, 199, 202, 204, 206, 220, 229, 244, 248, 250, 259, 270, 274, 280, 284, 288, 291, 327/Martin Wells 326; Sue Cunningham 253; Roger Day 127; Patrick Eagar 35 top left, 54, 61, 64, 85, 99, 112, 161, 304, 314; EuroCave Importers/

Martin & Elizabeth Alpren 43 bottom left; Explorer/JP Bouchard 102 bottom left; Brian Jordan 153, 262, 265; Claes Lofgren 76, 123, 169, 176, 256; Jason Lowe 260; Marka/V Arcomano 180; Marco Polo/Heinz Hebeisen 196; Steven Morris 292, 315, 320; Occit' Media 20; Octopus Publishing Group/Russel Sadur 6, 7, 41 top right, 41 bottom left, 42 top right, 43 top right, 44 centre right, 44 bottom left, 44 bottom right, 46-47, 48 left, 48 centre, 48 right: Osterreich Werbung 243; Janet Price 58, 86, 106, 110 bottom, 119, 124, 142, 156, 207, 209, 216, 218, 222, 227, 232, 234, 310, 311; Prisma/Eurasia Press 172, 238/JD Dallet 194; Powerstock Zefa 155; Regents of University of California 19 bottom right; Retna Pictures/Carossio/Image du Sud 104; Robert Harding Picture Library/Michael Short 254: Root Stock/Hendrik Holler 51, 198, 200, 214, 224, 230-231, 237, 268, 276, 278, 297; Scope/Jean-Luc Barde 110 top, 152/Jacques Guillard 67, 147, 149/Michel Guillard 94; South American Pictures/Tony

Morrison 287; Southcorp Wines Europe 308; Margherita Spiluttini 39; Spiral Cellars 42 bottom left; University of Adelaide & DNRE, Rutherglen 19 top left; Werner Forman Archive 13: Jon Wyand 26, 49, 63, 71, 210, 266.

Illustrations

Lisa Alderson/Advocate: 24-27; Tim Loughhead/Precision Illustration: 23, 29, 32-33, 38-39, 57; Louise Morgan/The Art Market: 30-31.

Every effort has been made to trace the owners of copyright photographs. Anyone who may have been inadvertently omitted from this list is invited to write to the publishers who will be pleased to make any necessary amendments to future printings of this publication.